Other books by the same authors

Developmental Psychology (Second Edition)
Ann Birch

Individual Differences
Ann Birch and Sheila Hayward

Biopsychology
Sheila Hayward

Cognitive Processes
Tony Malim

Social Psychology (Second Edition)
Tony Malim

Research Methods and Statistics
Tony Malim and Ann Birch

Comparative Psychology
Tony Malim, Ann Birch and Sheila Hayward

Perspectives in Psychology (Second Edition)
Alison Wadeley, Ann Birch and Tony Malim

INTRODUCTORY
PSYCHOLOGY

Tony Malim and Ann Birch

with contributions from Sheila Hayward and Alison Wadeley

First published 1998 by
MACMILLAN PRESS LTD
Houndmills, Basingstoke, Hampshire RG21 6XS
and London
Companies and representatives
throughout the world

ISBN 0–333–66852–9 paperback

A catalogue record for this book is available
from the British Library.

This book is printed on paper suitable for recycling and
made from fully managed and sustained forest sources.

10   9   8   7   6   5   4   3   2   1
07   06   05   04   03   02   01   00   99   98

Printed in Spain

To Sheila and Derek

Thanks for your tolerance and support. We couldn't have done it without you.

Contents

Preface   xiii

Acknowledgements   xv

PART 1
An introduction to psychology   1

INTRODUCTION
Early beginnings   3

- What is psychology?   3
- Schools of psychology   5

CHAPTER 1
Theoretical approaches in psychology   14

- The physiological approach   15
- The psychodynamic approach   18
- The behaviourist (or learning theory) approach   21
- The cognitive approach   24
- The humanistic (or phenomenological) approach   28
- Which approach?   32
- What do psychologists do?   34

CHAPTER 2
Issues and debates in psychology   41

- Reductionism   41
- Free will and determinism   45
- The heredity–environment issue   51

CHAPTER 3
Controversies in psychological research   59

- Psychology and science   59
- Biases in psychological research   67

CHAPTER 4
Controversial applications of psychological research   79

- Advertising, propaganda and warfare   79
- Psychometric testing   91

CHAPTER 5
Ethics in psychology   101

- Ethics in psychological research with human participants   101
- The wider responsibilities of psychologists   105
- Psychological research and the use of animals   112

CHAPTER 6
Learning and behaviour   124

- Simple learning   125
- More complex learning   131
- Some applications of learning theory to humans   134
- Social learning theory   137

PART 2
Biological bases of behaviour   143

INTRODUCTION
Biopsychology   145

- Areas of study   145
- Why do we study biopsychology?   145
- Methods of study in physiological psychology   146

CHAPTER 7
Sensory systems   150

- The visual system   151

■ Hearing 155
■ Other sensory inputs 159

CHAPTER 8
The nervous system and behaviour 164

■ Cell structures and the communications
network 165
■ The central nervous system 169
■ Neurochemicals 174
■ The autonomic nervous system 178
■ The endocrine system 180

CHAPTER 9
Motivation and emotion 187

■ Homeostatic motivation 187
■ Nonhomeostatic motivation 193
■ What is emotion? 195
■ Theories and studies of emotion 198

CHAPTER 10
Consciousness and its altered states 203

■ Levels of consciousness 204
■ Body rhythms 208
■ The rhythms of sleep 210
■ Why do we sleep? 213

CHAPTER 11
Stress and anxiety 219

■ Anxiety 219
■ Stress and stressors 220
■ Models of stress 225
■ Individual differences involved in stress 228
■ Coping with stress 231

Epilogue to Part 2 236

PART 3
Cognition 237

INTRODUCTION
Cognition 239

■ What are cognitive processes? 239
■ Historical background 239
■ Some methods used by cognitive
psychologists 240
■ Cognitive science 241

■ Some concepts in cognitive psychology 241

CHAPTER 12
Attention 244

■ Selective attention 244
■ Is attention conscious or unconscious? 251
■ Vigilance or sustained attention 253
■ Psychophysics 257

CHAPTER 13
Perception 261

■ Sensation and perception 261
■ Theories, models and principles 269
■ Visual illusions 274
■ Do we have to learn to perceive? 278

CHAPTER 14
Memory 288

■ Early research 289
■ Models of memory 290
■ Real-life memory 303
■ You too can have a better memory 307

CHAPTER 15
Thinking and language 316

■ The nature of thinking 316
■ Concept formation 319
■ Problem solving 323
■ Language and thinking 331

PART 4
Animal behaviour 337

INTRODUCTION
Comparative psychology 339

■ Rationale for comparative psychology 339
■ Continuity or discontinuity 340
■ Fields of study 345
■ Methods of study of animal behaviour 348

CHAPTER 16
Instinct and learning 350

■ Adaptation to the environment 350
■ Development of behaviour within the
individual 355
■ A comparative study of learning and memory 363

CHAPTER 17
Animal communication 372

- ■ The bases of communication 372
- ■ Social communication 377
- ■ Teaching human language to animals 382

CHAPTER 18
Social behaviour of animals 395

- ■ Social organization 395
- ■ Territory and social organization 400
- ■ Social dominance 407
- ■ Parents and offspring 409

Epilogue to Part 4 418

PART 5
Human development 419

INTRODUCTION
The study of development 421

- ■ Influences on development 421
- ■ The ecology of development 422
- ■ Cultural influences on development 424
- ■ Research designs and methods 425
- ■ Ethical considerations 426
- ■ Theoretical approaches in the study of development 426

CHAPTER 19
Early socialization and attachment 428

- ■ Developing social relationships 429
- ■ The development of attachment 436
- ■ Attachment, separation and deprivation 445
- ■ Children's play 451

CHAPTER 20
Cognitive development 459

- ■ Piaget's theory of cognitive development 460
- ■ Cognitive development in a social context 468
- ■ Information-processing approaches to cognitive development 474
- ■ Language acquisition 478

CHAPTER 21
Intelligence – its origins and measurement 487

- ■ The measurement of intelligence 487

- ■ Alternative views of intelligence 492
- ■ Origins of difference in IQ 496

CHAPTER 22
Social behaviour 502

- ■ Cognitive-developmental theory and social cognition 502
- ■ Moral development 504
- ■ Development of gender 513
- ■ Understanding self and others 524

CHAPTER 23
Adolescence and adulthood 535

- ■ Adolescence 535
- ■ Lifespan development: the study of adulthood 543
- ■ Young adulthood 547
- ■ Middle adulthood 552
- ■ Late adulthood 557

PART 6
Social psychology 569

INTRODUCTION
Some perspectives on social psychology 571

- ■ Social role perspective 571
- ■ Learning perspective 571
- ■ Social cognition perspective 573

CHAPTER 24
Self and others 575

- ■ Social schemata 575
- ■ Attribution 581
- ■ The perception of self 587

CHAPTER 25
Relationships with others 594

- ■ Affiliation 594
- ■ Friendship, love and marriage 602

CHAPTER 26
Conflict and cooperation 614

- ■ Intergroup relations 614
- ■ Aggression 623
- ■ Prosocial behaviour 636

CHAPTER 27
Attitudes 648

■ The nature and function of attitudes 648
■ Measurement of attitudes 659
■ Prejudice and discrimination 662

CHAPTER 28
Social influence 677

■ Conformity and compliance 677
■ Leadership and followership 687
■ Group decision making 690
■ The influence of the crowd 696

PART 7
Personality and abnormal behaviour 703

INTRODUCTION
Definitions and issues in personality theory and abnormal behaviour 705

■ What do we mean by personality? 705
■ Assumptions made about personality 705
■ Atypical development and abnormal behaviour 707

CHAPTER 29
Type and trait approaches to personality 709

■ Personality types 709
■ Multitrait approaches 710
■ Is personality consistent? 718
■ Single-trait theories 722

CHAPTER 30
Psychodynamic and person-centred theories of personality 727

■ Freud's psychoanalytic theory 727
■ Person-centred approaches to personality 734

CHAPTER 31
Atypical development 744

■ Learning difficulties 745
■ Physical and sensory impairment 748
■ Emotional disturbances and behavioural difficulties 751

CHAPTER 32
The classification, diagnosis and causes of mental disorder 762

■ Normality and abnormality 762
■ Diagnosis and classification mental disorders 770
■ Categories and descriptions of mental disorders 776
■ Possible causes of mental disorders 783

CHAPTER 33
Treatments and therapies 790

■ Somatic treatments 791
■ Behavioural therapies 795
■ Cognitive-behavioural therapies 800
■ Psychoanalytic therapies 801
■ Humanistic-existential therapies 803
■ Treatment effectiveness and patient care 804

PART 8
Research methods and statistics 811

INTRODUCTION
Research methodology 813

■ Populations 813
■ Errors, systematic and random 815
■ Theories and hypotheses 816

CHAPTER 34
Some methods used in psychological research 820

■ Experiment 820
■ Experimental design and the control of variables 825
■ Nonexperimental methods 829
■ Correlational designs 837
■ Some further considerations in research 839

CHAPTER 35
Presenting the results 845

■ The use of statistics 845
■ Descriptive statistics 847
■ Statistical inference and significance 857
■ Correlation 864
■ Choosing an appropriate test 869

CHAPTER 36
Statistical tests 872

- Nonparametric tests 872
- Parametric tests 874

CHAPTER 37
Interpretation and presentation of research 890

- Interpretation and background to research 890
- Writing research reports 893

CHAPTER 38
Some projects 899

- Experimental projects 899
- Observational studies 901
- Correlational studies 904

APPENDIX 1
Some basic mathematical rules 907

APPENDIX 2
Do-it-yourself psychology equipment 909

APPENDIX 3
Statistical tables 911

Glossary G-1

Bibliography B-1

Index I-1

Preface

This book is aimed at a very wide cross-section of students who are encountering psychology for the first time. Readers may include those studying for GCE A-level in the United Kingdom or its equivalent elsewhere, or those beginning psychology as part of a university degree course. Additionally, there are many students studying for vocational courses, such as BTEC or GNVQ or their equivalent, those aiming for careers in education as teachers, or the health professions (as nurses, radiographers, midwives) and in social work – indeed, all those who will have to deal with people in their professional lives – for whom psychology is a component of their course. Beyond these, there are those who are interested in studying psychology for interest rather than to gain a qualification. We have attempted to take into account the needs of all these people.

Psychology is a very wide field, and one of our most difficult problems has been to decide what to include and what to omit. We have been guided to some extent by the syllabuses published by UK examination boards, but we have felt that there are areas of study essential to anyone beginning to study psychology that have been omitted by these syllabuses. These, such as the study of personality or attitudes, we have included. The content of the book, therefore, is dependent on what we have felt to be necessary for any new student of the subject.

- We have structured the book in eight parts, each of which represents a fairly discrete area of psychology and which has several chapters.
- Each chapter starts with objectives so that you can see what you can expect to know when you have completed it.
- There are self-assessment questions at intervals within each chapter. The aim of these is to encourage you to make your own assessment of how well you have mastered the material, without being tempted to look up the answer. Therefore, no 'set' answers are included, though of course you can always refer back to the text. Indeed, in some cases, you are asked to make a judgement, and there may be no clearly defined 'right' answer.
- Where it seems appropriate, we have included exercises designed to help you gain further insight into a particular aspect of the text. We hope you will find these helpful and interesting.
- At the end of each chapter we have included some further reading for those of you who wish to study particular areas in further depth. These have been annotated to give you an idea of what is contained in each reading and why we have recommended it.
- We believe the book is complete as an introductory text. The eight parts include an introduction and historical background together with issues and controversies in psychology, the biological bases of psychology, cognitive psychology, animal behaviour, human development, social psychology, personality, and atypical behaviour.
- Finally, research methods and statistical techniques are included that may enable you to conduct your own research. There are some research projects outlined, which could form the basis of your own practical research investigations.

Psychology is a subject in which many special terms are used. These have been highlighted in the text in bold blue type, and brief glossary definitions are included on each page where the term first appears. These definitions are collated as a single glossary at the end of the book. We have attempted to illustrate the book throughout with photographs, diagrams, drawings and even cartoons. 'A picture is worth a thousand words.' We have included a complete bibliography and a comprehensive index.

We, the authors, have had many years' experience teaching psychology at an introductory level, and feel we have first-hand knowledge of the difficulties that many new students face when tackling the subject for the first time. We have found the subject to be interesting, indeed fascinating, and very much hope that you will find it equally enjoyable.

Tony Malim *and* Ann Birch

Acknowledgements

The authors would like to thank Sheila Hayward and Alison Wadeley for their valuable contributions to the book. Sally Artz has been responsible for cartoons at intervals throughout the book, and our thanks are due to her.

Grateful acknowledgement is made to the following sources for permission to reproduce material in this book.

Photographs

Frances Arnold pp. 196, 233, 279, 434, 483, 525, 528, 558, 595, 603, 604, 624; Lionel Browne p. 435; Camera Press Ltd pp. 665, 707; David King Collection p. 126; Farworks Inc. p. 107; Format pp. 54, 245, 442, 511, 757; Daniel Fox p. 555; Freud Museum pp. 19, 728, 802; Sally & Richard Greenhill pp. 220 (right), 396, 508, 516, 713, 746, 803; Hulton Getty Images pp. 27, 616, 778, 781; J. Allan Cash pp. 71, 190, 402, 415, 491; Macmillan Archive p. 341; Richenda Milton-Thompson pp. 436, 453; MIT/Donna Coveney p. 482; Monkmeyer Press p. 213; Pepsi p. 82; Photofusion p. 610; Steve Redwood pp. 97, 160, 220 (left), 229, 472, 529, 538, 550, 560, 625, 682, 749, 806, 808, 821; Redferns p. 156; Rex Features pp. 206, 698; Natalie Rogers p. 28; Patrick Salvadori pp. 449, 473, 489, 542, 731; Science Photo Library p. 793; Solo Syndication p. 107; Topham Picturepoint pp. 224, 314, 317; University of Bristol p. 262; Weimar Archive p. 87.

Text and illustrations

Academic Press Limited, London, for figure on p. 131 from 'The role of directed Pavlovian reactions in simple instrumental learning in the pigeon' by B.R. Moore, in R.A. Hinde and J. Stevenson-Hinde (eds), *Constraints in Learning* (1973), pp. 159–188; and for figure on p. 494 from *Nadia: A Case of Extraordinary Drawing Ability in an Autistic Child*, by L. Selfe (1997). American Association for the Advancement of Science for material on p. 432 by Meltzoff and Moore (1977).

Blackwell Publishers, Oxford, for figure on p. 279 from *Child Development: A First Text*, by K. Sylva and I. Lunt (1982), p. 84.

Cordon Art, Baarn, Netherlands, for M.C. Escher's *Heaven and Hell* on p. 277.

HarperCollins Publishers Ltd and A.P. Watt Ltd for figure on p. 466 from *Children's Minds*, by Dr Margaret Donaldson (1978).

Harvard University Press for illustrations on p. 347 from *Promethean Fire*, by Charles J. Lumsden and Edward O. Wilson (1983).

IPC Magazines Ltd for material on p. 119 from 'When to experiment on animals' by P. Bateson, *New Scientist*, *109* (1496) (1986), pp. 30–32.

Macmillan Press Ltd for figure on p. 228, 'Transactional model of stress', from *Stress*, by T. Cox (1978).

Massachusetts Medical Society for Figure 10.2 on p. 211 from 'Medical progress sleep disorders: recent findings in the diagnosis and treatment of disturbed sleep' by A. Kales et al. in *The New England Journal of Medicine, 290* (1974), pp. 487–99.

Open University for figure on p. 267 from *Introduction to Psychology*, by I. Roth, vol. II (1992), p. 508.

Oxford University Press for figure on p. 212 from *Why We Sleep: The Functions of Sleep in Humans and Other Mammals*, by J. Horne (1988).

Phaidon Press for the illustration 'False Perspectives' on p. 277 by Hogarth (1754) in *Art and Illusion: A Study in the Psychology of Pictorial Representation*, by E.H. Gombrich (1960).

Plenum Press for figure on p. 369, 'A scheme for the three stages of memory storage', from *Perspectives in Ethology*, by R.J. Andrew (1985), 6:219–59.

Alex Scheffler for the figure on p. 755 from *Autism: Explaining the Enigma* by Uta Frith (1989).

Scientific American for illustrations on p. 285 by Illil Arbel in *Pictorial Perception and Culture*, by Jan B. Deregowski (November 1972), pp. 83, 85 and 86

Every effort has been made to trace all the copyright holders, but if any have been inadvertently overlooked the publishers will be pleased to make the necessary arrangements at the first opportunity.

PART I

An introduction to psychology

Part 1 provides you with an overview of the history of psychology, the main theoretical approaches and some of the more important debates, issues and controversies that concern psychologists in their work. It also looks at the use of the scientific method, and considers whether psychology should be thought of as a science. Because the topic of learning pervades so many areas of psychology, a chapter is included that examines theoretical approaches to the study of learning and some of their practical applications.

Many of the things discussed in this part of the book are examined further in other chapters. Therefore, you will almost certainly find it helpful to look again at aspects of Part 1 during and after your study of other areas of psychology.

Contents

INTRODUCTION
Early beginnings 3
▓ What is psychology? 3
▓ Schools of psychology 5

CHAPTER 1
Theoretical approaches in psychology 14
▓ The physiological approach 15
▓ The psychodynamic approach 18
▓ The behaviourist (or learning theory) approach 21
▓ The cognitive approach 24
▓ The humanistic (or phenomenological) approach 28
▓ Which approach? 32
▓ What do psychologists do? 34

CHAPTER 2
Issues and debates in psychology 41
▓ Reductionism 41
▓ Free will and determinism 45
▓ The heredity–environment issue 51

CHAPTER 3
Controversies in psychological research 59
▓ Psychology and science 59
▓ Biases in psychological research 67

CHAPTER 4
Controversial applications of psychological research 79
▓ Advertising, propaganda and warfare 79
▓ Psychometric testing 91

CHAPTER 5
Ethics in psychology 101
▓ Ethics in psychological research with human participants 101
▓ The wider responsibilities of psychologists 106
▓ Psychological research and the use of animals 112

CHAPTER 6
Learning and behaviour 124
▓ Simple learning 125
▓ More complex learning 131
▓ Some applications of learning theory to humans 134
▓ Social learning theory 137

Early beginnings

What is psychology?

Perhaps the most widely accepted definition of psychology is that it is the scientific study of behaviour and experience. That is to say that, through systematic research, psychologists aim to explore questions about the way human beings, and sometimes animals, behave and how they experience the world around them. This apparently simple and straightforward definition requires further explanation if the reader is to gain an adequate view of the nature of psychology. The aim of this introduction is to give a brief account of the early development of psychology and to examine significant events in the history of the subject up to about the middle of the twentieth century.

Psychology as a scientific discipline has a short history – only just over a hundred years. As a branch of philosophy it dates back to the time of Plato and Aristotle. Figure 1I.1 illustrates the philosophical origins of approaches to psychology.

The word 'psychology' is of Greek origin: *psyche* can be freely translated as 'mind' or 'soul' and *logos* indicates 'study' or 'line of teaching'; thus we have 'study of the mind'. This definition exemplifies what psychology was essentially about up to the end of the nineteenth century.

It was in 1879 that Wilhelm Wundt opened the first psychological laboratory in Leipzig, Germany. It is generally agreed that this event heralded the beginning of psychology as a scientific discipline in its own right. Prior to this, psychology had generally been regarded as a branch of philosophy. Before we consider the development of psychology as a scientific discipline, it will be of benefit to examine briefly the influence of some philosophical ideas.

Prescientific psychology

René Descartes (1596–1650), the French philosopher, had an important influence on the development of psychology as a discipline distinct from philosophy. Before Descartes, human beings tended to be viewed by philosophers as unique, mysterious products of God's will, whose mental life was beyond rational explanation. Influenced by scientific discoveries of the time in the field of medicine, most notably Harvey's discovery of the blood circulatory system, Descartes adopted a more analytical stance. He attempted to view the human being as a machine that could be studied and whose workings could be understood and explained. In his theory of **interactive dualism** he made a distinction between the mind (thinking, remembering, knowing) and the body (physiological processes). The interaction of mind and body, he believed, took place in the brain, and the seat of the mind was narrowed down to the pineal gland, a structure in the brain that serves to initiate hormonal activity.

The seventeenth century also saw the birth of the British Empiricist Movement, led by a group of philosophers, the most notable of whom were John Locke and Thomas Hobbes. **Empiricism** attempted to make sense of the human mind through the use of systematic and objective methods of study, rather than

---

GLOSSARY

Interactive dualism   A theory proposed by Descartes, in which human functioning is seen as an interaction between two independent substances: mind and body.

Empiricism   Study conducted through systematic observation and experiment.

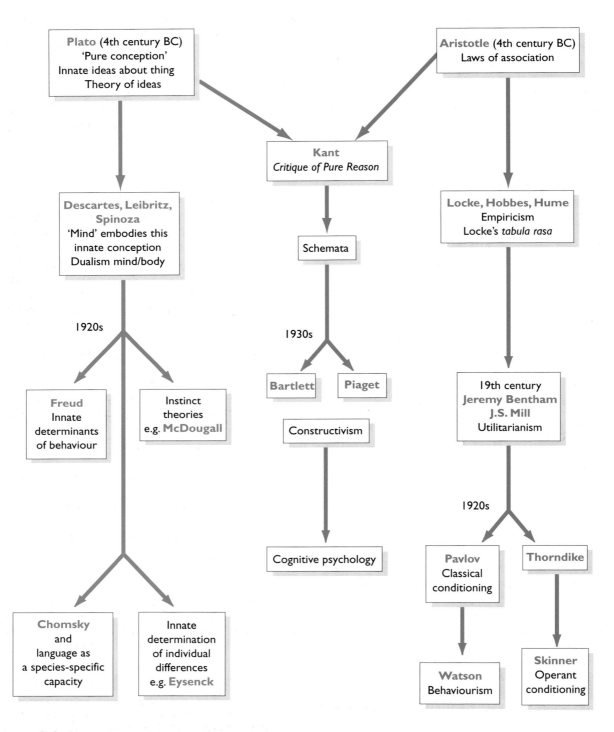

Figure 1I.1 Philosophical origins of psychological approaches

through reasoning or intuition. Mental life, the empiricists contended, was composed of 'ideas' that arose from sensory experience and entered the mind by means of perception. In contrast to Descartes, who believed that some ideas are present at birth, the empiricists saw the development of the mind as arising from experiences of, and interaction with, the environment. Thus the early seeds of the heredity–environment (nature–nurture) debate were sown (see Chapter 2).

In the early part of the nineteenth century there was a strong upsurge of philosophical opinion that contended that the study of human mental activity was worthy of attention in its own right outside the discipline of philosophy. This move was greatly advanced by the work of a group of German physiologists – Weber, who used weights to study muscle sense; Helmholz, who made an outstanding contribution to the study of vision and hearing; and Fechner, who investigated visual discrimination and perception. The findings of these early physiologists greatly influenced psychology as we know it today.

Scientific psychology

As previously indicated, the establishment of psychology as a scientific discipline in its own right is generally linked to the setting up in 1879 of the first psychological laboratory by Wilhelm Wundt. Before looking further at the work of Wundt and his contemporaries, it might be useful to examine the concept of schools of psychology.

Schools of psychology

As psychology developed as a discipline founded on the use of empirical methods (based on observation and the collection of data), there emerged a number of different schools of thought. Schools, in this context, can best be thought of as groups of psychologists who held common beliefs about both the subject matter of psychology – that is, what facets of mental functioning should be studied – and what methods of study should be used. Most schools developed as a revolt against traditional methods and beliefs at the time. However, they did not always replace earlier schools, but sometimes existed alongside them. Schools, as such, do not now exist, but each has provided ideas (some more influential than others) that have influenced

contemporary approaches to psychology (see Chapter 1). Therefore a knowledge of them can help us to make sense of the multitude of ideas and methods that currently characterize psychology.

The rest of this introduction contains a brief description of six major schools of psychology: structuralism, functionalism, associationism, behaviourism, Gestalt psychology and psychoanalysis (Figure 1I.2).

Structuralism

Inspired by the pioneering work of Fechner and other scientists, Wilhelm Wundt and his many collaborators founded the school of structuralism. Wundt believed that psychology should concern itself with the elementary processes of conscious experience. The structure of consciousness and immediate mental experience, he contended, could be broken down into basic elements and compounds in the same way that, in chemistry, one can describe the structure of water or air.

The elements of conscious experience were considered to be of two kinds:

▨ **sensations** – sights, sounds, tastes, smells and touch, which arise from stimulation of the sense organs; and
▨ **feelings** – love, fear, joy and so on.

The term 'image' was also used to describe experiences not actually present.

Three primary questions were addressed:

▨ What are the elements of experience?
▨ How are they combined?
▨ What causes the elements to combine?

An experience such as meeting and recognizing an old friend in the street was thought to be composed of many independent sensations, feelings and images, which were drawn together and synthesized by the mind.

GLOSSARY

Schools of psychology Groupings of psychologists who shared common beliefs about human functioning and subscribed to similar methods of study.

Structuralism A school of psychology, founded by Wundt, which focused on the scientific study of conscious experience.

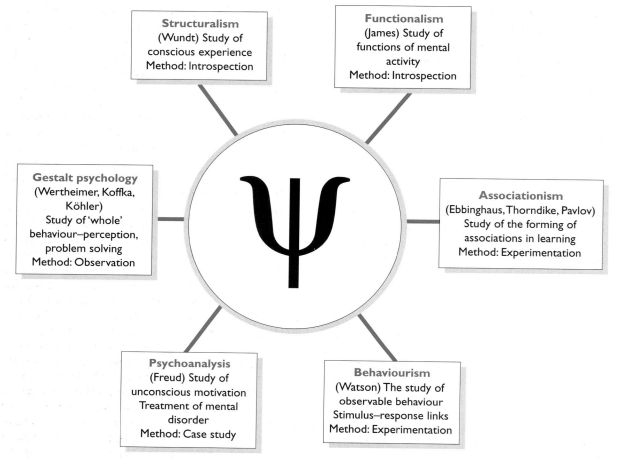

Figure 11.2 Early schools of psychology. The Greek letter Ψ (psi) is often used to stand for psychology

Introspection

In an effort to study the elements of consciousness in what they believed was an analytical and objective way, structuralists devised a technique known as **introspection**. This simply means that people were asked to consider and report on their own mental processes as they experienced a particular object or event. This was to be done in a prespecified and systematic way and required much training. For example, to be introspective about a flower, the reporter would be asked to describe the sensations of experiencing it in terms of its shape, size, colour, texture and so on.

The method of introspection proved difficult and inadequate, largely because of conflicting findings between introspectionists in different laboratories. Reaching agreement on the basic elements of a particular mental experience proved an impossible task and (predictably, perhaps) reporting on mental activity in humans was not quite so straightforward as observing what happens in a test-tube when two chemicals are combined.

Another prominent member of the structuralist school, Edward Titchener, developed and extended Wundt's ideas and later introduced them to the USA.

Structuralism declined in the early 1920s, partly through the failure of introspective methods to provide a coherent and generally accepted account of human mental activity and partly through the emergence of schools that offered alternative approaches to the study of psychology. These schools included functionalism, behaviourism and Gestalt psychology, each of which developed at least in part as a reaction against structuralism.

Functionalism

Whilst structuralism emphasized the structure of mental activity, **functionalism** was concerned with the purposes, or functions, of mental processes. Functionalism was strongly influenced by biology, and many of the concepts 'borrowed' from that discipline continue to influence psychology today.

Darwin and natural selection

The work and ideas of Charles Darwin had a monumental impact on the emergence of functional psychology. Darwin's revolutionary theory of evolution provided an account of the way living organisms change and develop over time through a process of **natural selection**. Living organisms have characteristics such as extreme strength, speed of movement and temperament, which are variable even within the same species. Organisms whose characteristics were best suited to their environment survived and reproduced, while organisms whose characteristics were less adaptable died out. Survivors would transmit to the next generation those characteristics that enabled them to survive. In this way a particular species might change quite extensively over several generations and, in some cases, an entirely new species could evolve. A more detailed account of Darwin's principle of natural selection appears in the introduction to Part 4 of this book.

The notion that humans had descended from animals was revolutionary – and shocking to many people. Among psychologists it led to a belief, which for many still persists, that by studying animals a greater understanding might be reached about the nature of human beings. (See Chapter 5 and the introduction to Part 4 for discussions of the use of animals in psychological research.) Darwin's work also drew attention to the importance of studying individual differences between members of a species. This idea was taken up and continues to provide an importance focus in psychology today, particularly in the field of psychometrics, the study of mental testing.

William James (1842–1910) was a leading figure in functional psychology, and his work has made a very significant impact on contemporary psychology. Influenced greatly by Darwin, James held that the function of consciousness was to enable humans to behave in ways that would aid survival through adaptation to the environment. Where these adaptive behaviours were repeated frequently they became habits. Habits, James believed, provided stability and predictability in society.

The range of topics studied by James was immense, and few psychologists would disagree that he was responsible for opening up the scope of psychology. In addition to a study of the functions of consciousness and the role of habits, he turned his attention to emotions and to the concept of self. As with the structuralists, his main method of study was introspection, though he encouraged the use of experimentation. His emphasis on the importance of observing similarities and differences between varying species greatly influenced the development of comparative psychology. The work of John Dewey (1859–1952) at the University of Chicago further established the ideas of functionalism. This work led to a new trend, that of attempting to apply research findings to practical problems. For example, the first intelligence tests for use with children were developed by the functionalists.

Associationism

The **associationism** movement was concerned with the idea that learning amounted to the forming of associations. The work of three scientists is important in this context: Hermann Ebbinghaus (1850–1909),

---

GLOSSARY

Functionalism A school of psychology that drew on Darwin's theory of evolution and which was concerned with the purposes of mental processes.

Natural selection The process, proposed by Darwin, through which those organisms best suited to their environment survived and reproduced – the 'survival of the fittest'.

Associationism A movement that emphasized the idea that learning results from the forming of associations between stimuli and events in the environment.

Edward Thorndike (1874–1949) and Ivan Pavlov (1849–1936). There follows a brief account of some of their main contributions.

The work of Ebbinghaus is often regarded as the basis of modern research into memory. Using himself as a subject and 'nonsense syllables' (such as TAF, ZUC, POV) as his experimental material, Ebbinghaus systematically studied factors that influence learning and forgetting. Nonsense syllables were used in preference to real words because Ebbinghaus believed they contained no meaning and thus offered a device that would enable him to study 'new' learning. New learning was regarded as the forming of associations within material that is not already associated with previous learning. His meticulous and painstaking methods of study, carried out over several years, produced much reliable quantified data. His work provided insights into remembering and forgetting that still hold good today. For example, he demonstrated that material is forgotten quite quickly in the first few hours after learning, but then the rate of forgetting becomes progressively slower.

Pavlov, a Russian physiologist, made a significant contribution to the study of learning through experiments with animals. During his investigations into the salivary reflex in dogs, Pavlov discovered that a stimulus, for example food (the unconditional stimulus), which is naturally linked with a particular reflex response, for example salivation (the unconditional response), can become associated with other stimuli that are present at the same time. In one series of experiments he showed that a dog, when offered food at the same time as a buzzer (the conditional stimulus) is sounded, will, after several presentations, begin to salivate when the buzzer alone is sounded. (Salivation now becomes the conditional response.) Thus an association is formed between the food and the buzzer and between the buzzer and the salivation response. This learning process became known as **classical** (or Pavlovian) **conditioning**. Its principles have since been applied to the study of human behaviour, for example as an explanation for the development of irrational fears or phobias.

Like Pavlov, Thorndike studied learning in animals. However, where Pavlov was interested in reflex, or involuntary, behaviour, Thorndike studied the associations formed between a stimulus and voluntary responses. His early experiments involved the use of a cat in a 'puzzle box' – a cage from which the animal could learn to escape by pulling a loop of string.

Thorndike measured the time taken by the cat to escape as an indicator of learning. His data showed that learning the correct 'escape' behaviour happened gradually. The 'reward' (freedom), he contended, was responsible for 'stamping in' the appropriate response. This insight formed the basis of Thorndike's **law of effect**, which has been developed further by Skinner in his study of operant conditioning (see Chapter 1).

Behaviourism

While functionalism was at its height in the USA, a young student, John Watson (1878–1958) graduated in psychology at the University of Chicago. He went on to revolutionize psychology by changing it from the study of conscious experience to the study of behaviour. In an influential paper, 'Psychology as a behaviourist views it', in 1913, Watson attacked the structuralist emphasis on consciousness and mental experience and also condemned the use of introspection as a method that claimed to be reliable and objective. Psychology, he believed, should be about the study of observable behaviour that all could agree upon, and the aim of psychology should be to describe, predict, understand and control behaviour. He contended that psychologists should '...never use the terms consciousness, mental states, introspectively verify, imagery and the like' (1913, p. 166).

Advocates of **behaviourism** did not reject the existence of mind and consciousness as critics have sometimes suggested. Rather they viewed these concepts as impossible to observe and contributing little to a scientific approach in psychology.

Watson and his colleagues believed that behaviour is moulded by experience. He therefore had a natural interest in learning, and his view of learning relied to a great extent on Pavlov's account of classical condition-

---

> **GLOSSARY**
>
> **Classical conditioning** The process through which a reflex response becomes associated with a stimulus that would not naturally activate that behaviour.
>
> **Law of effect** Thorndike's proposal that behaviour that has positive effects, for example, reward, is likely to be repeated, whereas that which has negative or no effects is not.
>
> **Behaviourism** A revolutionary school of psychology, founded by John Watson, where the focus was the study of observable behaviour to the exclusion of internal mental processes.

ing described earlier. However complex a piece of behaviour might be, it was possible, behaviourists believed, to break it down and analyse it in basic stimulus–response units. Much of the behaviourists' research into learning was carried out on animals, rather than humans, partly because animals were easy to obtain and greater control could be exercised over their environments, and partly because they accepted the idea that humans and animals are related both physiologically and behaviourally.

Though Watson's view of the nature of human beings was considered by critics to be mechanistic and oversimplified, his focus on the study of observable behaviour allowed him to formulate clear hypotheses, which could be tested by experimentation. This shift in emphasis towards the use of more objective and systematic methods was one of his greatest contributions to psychology.

Following the work of Watson and his followers, behaviourism gathered strength, and its principles and methods of study became an integral part of psychology. By the middle of the twentieth century it was widely accepted that psychology was about the study of behaviour rather than conscious experience. This momentum has been sustained to a large extent in contemporary psychology by the efforts of the behaviourist B. F. Skinner (see Chapter 1). Skinner extended principles derived from his work with animals to a consideration of human behaviour. However, as will become clear in Chapter 1, although behaviourism has left an indelible mark on contemporary psychology, alternative perspectives have been offered, largely through the emergence of cognitive psychology and humanistic psychology, which have modified its influence and endorsed the value of also studying mental processes and conscious experience.

Gestalt psychology

Functionalism and behaviourism came into being in the USA partly as a protest against structuralism. Around the same time, another movement against structuralism developed in Germany – the Gestalt School. The leading proponents of the Gestalt view were Max Wertheimer (1880–1943), Kurt Koffka (1876–1941) and Wolfgang Köhler (1887–1967).

Gestalt psychology opposed the atomist approach of the structuralists and later the behaviourists. Atomism is a belief that, to understand a phenomenon, it is best to break it down and investigate its constituent parts.

(See Chapter 2 for a discussion of the related concept of reductionism.) In contrast, Gestalt psychologists argued that people perceive the world in 'wholes'. 'The whole is greater than the sum of its parts' exemplifies this view. *Gestalt*, roughly translated, means 'whole', 'shape' or 'configuration'.

Wertheimer produced an early demonstration of this holistic approach through his experiments on apparent movement. He showed that, when two lights were presented a small distance apart and then switched on and off alternately, at certain time intervals a person reported seeing not two lights being lit, but one light which appeared to move from one location to the other. Wertheimer called this effect the **phi phenomenon**. He claimed that it contradicted the structuralist view that perception could be understood by analysing the basic elements of the perceiver's experience. The phi phenomenon is more familiar to us in the form of apparent movement in illuminated advertisements and the like. Further research by the Gestaltists led to the development of a set of principles of perceptual organization. Such organization, they believed, arose through the brain's innate ability to structure and organize the perceptual field into meaningful 'patterns' rather than perceiving the separate elements. Figure 1I.3 illustrates some of the main Gestalt principles of organization: figure–ground, proximity, similarity, closure.

In the figure–ground situation, focusing attention on an object causes it to 'stand out' sharply from its context, while the context or 'ground' is less clear. The ambiguous figure illustrates a situation where the figure and ground reverse as the brain switches attention from one to the other. In the proximity figure, the dots are perceived in groups of two rather than as eight separate items, while with the similarity figure, the equally spaced dots are perceived as groups of two. In closure, the figure is perceived as a circle rather than as four curved lines.

GLOSSARY

Gestalt psychology School of psychology that opposed behaviourism and proposed that behaviour should be studied as a whole.

Atomism A belief that to understand a phenomenon, it is best to break it down and study its constituent parts.

Phi phenomenon The perception of movement which results from presenting two separate objects (or lights) in quick succession.

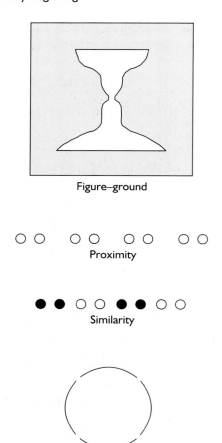

Figure–ground

Proximity

Similarity

Closure

Figure 1I.3 Gestalt principles of perceptual organization

The Gestalt principles of organization can be subsumed under the overall guiding principle of **Prägnanz**. This refers to the principle governing the brain's attempt to perceive objects in the 'best' and most meaningful way. Critics have pointed out that these principles are purely descriptive, and offer no explanations as to how or why the brain operates in this way.

Learning and problem solving also received much attention from the Gestaltists. Köhler investigated problem solving in apes. One study involved an animal in a cage with food out of reach beyond the cage. Inside the cage were a number of sticks that, if slotted together, were long enough to reach the food. After a period of inactivity, the animal quite suddenly solved the problem by slotting the sticks together and reaching for the food. Köhler claimed that, because all the

elements for the solutions were available, the animal perceived the problem situation, as a whole, formed a hypothesis about its solution and responded appropriately. He called this process 'insightful learning'. (See also Chapter 6.)

The tendency of the Gestalt psychologists to rely for their data on subjective observations and reports of conscious experience, rather than on carefully controlled behavioural methods, attracted criticism from the behaviourists. Gestaltists have also been accused of posing more problems than they actually solved. Nonetheless the influence of Gestalt psychology is great in some areas of contemporary psychology, for example in the study of perception and problem solving (see Chapter 13). Also the concept of 'wholeness' has been adopted in Gestalt approaches to therapy (see Chapter 33). Gestalt views can also be detected in some contemporary approaches to learning in the field of education. For example, work on discovery learning is rooted in early Gestalt ideas.

Psychoanalysis

The school of **psychoanalysis** stands apart from the other schools in that the focus of attention is neither the nature or functions of consciousness, nor the stimulus–response links that influence behaviour. Psychoanalysis, which developed from the work and theories of Sigmund Freud (1856–1939), proposed an account of human mental activity that relied heavily on the notion of an **unconscious mind**.

Towards the end of the nineteenth century, science had been making huge advances, and psychologists believed that the time was near when a full understanding of human mental life and behaviour would be reached. This view was shared by Freud, a young physician working as a neurologist in Vienna.

However, in the course of treating psychiatric patients over many years, Freud became convinced that many of the nervous symptoms displayed by

---

GLOSSARY

Prägnanz Gestalt principle that the brain attempts to perceive objects in the 'best', most meaningful, way.

Psychoanalysis Sigmund Freud's theory of personality, which relied on the study of the unconscious mind.

Unconscious mind A 'hidden' part of the mind harbouring repressed memories that may influence the conscious mind.

patients could not be explained purely from a physiological point of view. Nor could the rational and systematic laws of science be applied to irrational and self-defeating behaviours such as phobias (excessive fears) and conversion hysterias (physical complaints that have no apparent physiological cause). It was against this background that Freud developed his now famous psychoanalytic treatment of neurotic disorders. His therapeutic work led to the development of a comprehensive theory of personality and child development that focused largely on the emotional aspects of human functioning. Thus the term 'psychoanalysis' can relate both to the treatment and to the theory. Freud's starting point was a thorough analysis of his own personal experiences and the development of case studies of his patients.

Psychoanalytic theory

- The human personality contains, and is greatly influenced by, an unconscious mind harbouring repressed ('forgotten') memories, which determine conscious thoughts and behaviour. A third level of consciousness, the preconscious, contains thoughts that may not be conscious at a given time, but which are accessible to us.
- Human beings are born with a number of instinctual drives that regulate and motivate behaviour, even in childhood. The source of these drives is psychic energy and the most powerful, the libido, is sexual in nature.
- The personality consists of three major structures: the id, which is biologically determined and represents all the instinctual drives that are inherited; the ego, which develops in order to help satisfy the id's needs in a socially acceptable way; the superego, representing the individual's internal framework (conscience and ego ideal) of the moral values which exist in the surrounding culture.
- Experiences gained in early childhood have a crucially important influence on emotional and personality development. Development of the personality is seen as proceeding through a number of psychosexual stages. During each stage, satisfaction is gained as the libido is directed towards a different part of the body. Failure to negotiate satisfactorily a particular stage results in fixation, or halting of development at that stage. Fixation causes the individual to retain

some of the characteristics of that stage in later life and in severe cases may result in neuroses in adult life.

Freud's work attracted many followers, but his theory also generated much debate and controversy. His notion of 'infantile sexuality' outraged Victorian society. Many psychologists believed his methods of study to be unscientific and the concepts he employed vague and difficult to verify (see Chapter 1 for a more detailed critique of psychoanalytic theory). Even among his original followers there were dissenters, such as Carl Jung and Alfred Adler, who eventually broke away from Freud to develop their own modified versions of his theory.

Jung's version of psychoanalytic theory differed from Freud's in two main respects:

- Freud's conceptualization of the unconscious mind was extended by Jung, who proposed that there existed also a collective unconscious. Jung reasoned that the human mind should contain a record of human experience in the same way as the body reveals the past structures of our ancestors. The collective unconscious, Jung believed, is not directly available to us but is revealed in the myths and artistic symbols that different cultures create. The collective unconscious contains archetypes, universal symbols that occur again and again in art, literature and religion.

GLOSSARY

Libido A form of psychic energy that Freud regarded as sexual in nature, compelling people to act in ways likely to reproduce the species.

Id Freud's term for that part of the personality that is biologically determined. It operates on the 'pleasure principle': that is, seeking pleasure and avoiding pain.

Ego In Freud's theory, that part of the personality that operates on the 'reality principle': that is, controlling the id's demands until an appropriate time or place. It aims to strike a balance between the demands of the id and of the superego.

Superego In Freud's theory, the moral aspect of the personality made up of the ego-ideal (a sense of what is right and proper) and the conscience (a sense of what is wrong and unacceptable).

Archetypes Universal symbols, described by Jung, which repeatedly occur in the religions, art, fables and legends of many different cultures: for example, 'God', 'the wise old man', 'the fairy godmother'.

Box 1I.1 Some significant dates in psychology

400 BC Hippocrates proposed a relationship between personality characteristics and body types.

350 BC Aristotle formulated a series of questions about the nature of the soul and its relationship to the body.

1650 René Descartes proposed an interaction between the mind and the body.

1651 Thomas Hobbes contended that mental life was composed of 'ideas' that arose from sensory experience.

1690 John Locke extended Hobbes' ideas further by proposing that the mind of a newborn is a *tabula rasa* (blank slate).

1838 Johannes Müller declared that a connection between the brain and the sense organs must be responsible for the nature of our experience.

1859 Charles Darwin published *The Origin of Species*, which proposed the theory of evolution through natural selection.

1850 Gustav Fechner developed a series of experimental and statistical procedures in order to measure the relationship between physical stimuli and sensations.

1861 Paul Broca demonstrated by postmortem autopsy that a patient's inability to speak arose from damage in a specific area of the brain.

1879 Wilhelm Wundt founded the first laboratory for experimental psychology at the University of Leipzig.

1885 Hermann Ebbinghaus reported a series of experiments that are regarded as the basis of modern research into memory.

1890 William James published his influential *Principles of Psychology* in the USA.

1896 Edward Thorndike reported the findings from his experiments on animal learning.

1900 Sigmund Freud published *The Interpretation of Dreams*, which set out many aspects of his psychoanalytical theory.

1906 Ivan Pavlov published the findings from his experiments on classical conditioning.

O.K. — SO WE'LL LEAVE THE FREE ASSOCIATION AND GO INTO DREAM ANALYSIS.

■ The libido was seen by Jung as primarily spiritual in nature rather than essentially sexual, as had been posited by Freud.

Jung was also concerned with personality 'types'. He was responsible for proposing that humans are born with a temperament that is either introverted (primarily concerned with oneself) or extraverted (primarily concerned with the outside world). Introversion and extraversion have subsequently become important concepts in contemporary theories of personality.

Adler regarded the need for power and superiority as the most important human drive. Whilst not denying the existence of unconscious motives, he saw human motivation as being largely conscious. He had considerable success in treating mental disorders, particularly with young people suffering from minor maladjustments. His methods were quicker and simpler than those of Freud and therefore were less likely to become a dominating force in the life of a patient. Birth order – the order in which children are born within a family – was viewed by Adler as an important influence on the development of personality.

1912 Max Wertheimer published the earliest account of Gestalt psychology.

1913 John Watson revolutionised the course of psychology with his paper 'Psychology as the behaviourist views it'.

1917 Wolfgang Köhler published his findings from studies of problem solving in apes.

1929 Karl Lashley formulated his Law of Mass Action, following experiments in which he removed areas of the brains of rats.

1938 B.F. Skinner summarized his early work on operant conditioning in his book *The Behaviour of Organisms*.

1951 Carl Rogers published *Client-Centred Therapy*, a precursor to the formation of the Association of Humanistic Psychology in 1962.

1952 Jean Piaget's *The Origin of Intelligence in the Child* was translated from French into English; it should be noted that Piaget had been studying children and publishing his findings in Switzerland since the 1920s.

1954 J. Olds and P. Milner identified 'pleasure centres' in the brains of rats.

1958 A. Newell, J.C. Shaw and H.A. Simon devised the General Problem Solver, a computer program designed to simulate human thinking.

1962 D. Hubel and T. Wiesel demonstrated a relationship between particular features of a visual stimulus and the activity of specific neurons in the visual cortex.

1979 A society known as *Cognitive Science* was founded to further the study of the use of computers in the simulation of human thinking.

Events occurring in the 1980s and 1990s may subsequently prove also to be of lasting significance to the course of psychology

Psychoanalysis as a therapy

Psychoanalysis as a therapy is very widely used in the treatment of neuroses and sometimes in the treatment of nonneurotic disorders. There is an assumption by psychoanalysts that it is in the unconscious part of the personality that conflict occurs. Therefore the aim of psychoanalysis is to explore the individual's unconscious mind in order to understand the dynamic of abnormal behaviour.

During treatment the individual is encouraged to re-experience traumatic events and feelings encountered in childhood, express them in a safe context and then return them, devoid of anxiety, to the unconscious.

In classical psychoanalysis, therapy involves **transference**, the client's projection and displacement of thoughts and feelings onto the analyst; **free association**, where the client says whatever comes into his or her mind, no matter how trivial or irrelevant it may seem; and dream analysis, which involves the analyst interpreting the content of the client's dreams.

Though the psychoanalytic process may sound quite straightforward, it is usually difficult and time-consuming. Psychoanalytic theory and methods of treating mental disorders are still a significant force in contemporary psychology. Many of Freud's original ideas have been adopted and in some cases modified by subsequent psychoanalytic theorists, known as post-Freudians (see Chapter 1).

Note that psychoanalytic therapies are considered more fully in Chapter 33.

Exercise 11.1

Box 11.1 contains a list of important events in psychology. As you work through this book, refer to the list of dates in Box 11.1 and see if you can trace the influence of some of these events in modern psychology.

GLOSSARY

Psychoanalysis as a therapy A treatment, originally used by Freud, which uses techniques designed to explore the unconscious mind.

Free association A psychoanalytic technique where the patient is encouraged to talk about whatever comes to mind, no matter how inappropriate it may seem.

Transference A process in psychoanalytic therapy where thoughts and feelings are transferred on to the therapist.

CHAPTER I

Theoretical approaches in psychology

The physiological approach   15
- Some research findings from physiological psychology   16
- Evaluation of the physiological approach   18

The psychodynamic approach   18
- Post-Freudians   18
- Evaluation of the psychodynamic approach   20

The behaviourist (or learning theory) approach   21
- Some practical applications of the behaviourist approach   22
- Evaluation of the behaviourist approach   24

The cognitive approach   24
- Methods of study   25

Models in cognitive psychology   25
- Cognitive development   26
- Evaluation of the cognitive approach   27

The humanistic (or phenomenological) approach   28
- Carl Rogers   28
- Abraham Maslow   29
- Victor Frankl   29
- Recovery Movement   30
- Evaluation of the humanistic approach   31

Which approach?   32
- Levels of explanation   32

What do psychologists do?   34
- Areas of psychological research   35
- Some fields of study   36
- Some professional activities   37
- Psychologists' qualifications   37

Objectives

By the end of this chapter you should be able to:

- Describe and evaluate five major theoretical approaches to psychology: physiological, psychodynamic, behaviourist, cognitive and humanistic;

- Discuss different levels of explanation of psychological functioning;

- Have an appreciation of the main areas of research interest and professional activity in psychology

As outlined in the introduction, for the first 50 years or so of its existence as a separate discipline, psychology was organized around separate schools, each with its own distinct ideas of what psychology should be about and how it should be studied. Psychologists tended to identify themselves as structuralists, functionalists, behaviourists, psychoanalysts or Gestaltists. Today, with the realization that the problems psychologists have set themselves will not be solved by one particular set of ideas and methods, it is accepted that many different routes must be taken if a full understanding is to be reached about psychological functioning. Psychologists are now often classified according to their professional commitments – clinical psychologist or educational psychologist, for example – or to their specific fields of study, such as social, developmental or cognitive psychology. (The section headed 'What do psychologists do?' at the end of this chapter gives a brief overview of some of the main fields of study in psychology and some of the practical situations in which psychologists work).

Though schools of psychology as such no longer exist, within each field of psychology can be seen many different approaches to the study of psychological phenomena, and some of the ideas of the early schools continue to influence many of the modern-day approaches. **Approach** in this context is not easy to define exactly, but it is to do with basic assumptions that are made about what human beings are like, theories used in order to help explain human and animal behaviour, and the kinds of research methods used to study them. For example, the learning theory approach, influenced heavily by the behaviourist school, still strongly emphasizes the effects of the environment on psychological functioning, and continues to use the concept of reinforcement in attempts to explain and change human behaviour. Also, the experimental method is still the major technique used in research, in preference to more subjective methods.

Five major approaches in psychology are physiological, psychodynamic, behaviourist (or learning theory), cognitive and humanistic (see Figure 1.1). Each will be discussed below. There is some overlap between these approaches, and they should not be seen as separate, competing bodies of knowledge and theory. Rather they represent different but complementary views and methods of understanding psychological functioning.

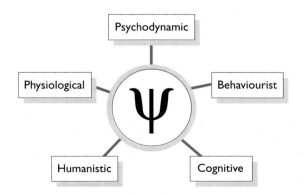

Figure 1.1   Five major theoretical approaches in psychology

The physiological approach

Psychologists who take a physiological approach, as the name implies, look to biology as a means of describing and explaining psychological functioning. Our behaviour, even what we think and feel, is assumed to be linked to our physiological make-up. For example, schizophrenia may be seen as arising almost entirely from malfunctions in biochemical processes in the brain. Some of the labels attached to researchers who take this approach, albeit in rather different ways, are biopsychologist, neuropsychologist, psychobiologist and **physiological psychologist**.

Physiological psychologists are interested in a wide range of phenomena and issues. Research has developed rapidly over recent years into the functions of the nervous system (particularly the brain) and the hormonal system, and into how these two systems interact and influence behaviour and mental activity. Some of the questions that have been asked by scientists in the course of this research are:

■ What activities occur in the nerve cells (neurons) of the brain and senses when we perceive patterns or colour?
■ To what extent does the brain function as a single unit and to what extent as a collection of 'parts', each with its own particular function (localization of brain functions)?
■ What activities occur in the brain during different states of consciousness, such as wakefulness, sleep and coma?
■ What are the links between the hormonal system and emotion, aggression and sex differences in behaviour?
■ What physiological mechanisms underlie needs and motivations?
■ What changes take place in the nervous system when a memory has been established or something has been learned?
■ How might a person's mental state affect his or her health?

Box 1.1   Reductionism and the mind–body problem

There are some scientists who believe that all psycho-logical phenomena can be explained by reference to (can be 'reduced to') physiological activity, particularly brain processes. This philosophical viewpoint has been termed **reductionism**. The term may be used also in relation to views held by behavioural and other psychologists.

Reductionism in relation to physiological psychology implies that, if we are to understand psychological functioning, we must analyse these functions in terms of ever smaller units of analysis, such as nerve activity, muscle movements or chemical processes. This view, taken to its logical conclusions, could lead to psycho-logical explanations of behaviour becoming redundant. (A more detailed discussion of reductionism will appear in Chapter 2.)

The reductionist issue is closely linked to a continuing and extremely controversial issue, that of the mind–body problem. This issue is concerned with the relationship between the mind (or awareness) and the neurophysio-logical processes within the body, how the two interact and the influence of one on the other. The debate began in the seventeenth century, with the work of the philosopher, René Descartes (see the introduction). Descartes' theory, known as interactive dualism, put forward the view that the human body, like that of animals, was basically a machine. However, what distinguished humans from animals was the existence in the former of a soul, which was intangible but which interacted with the physical body through the pineal gland located in the brain.

In modern times most people would equate the term 'mind' with 'brain'. But the word 'mind' was originally created to identify a psychological rather than a physiological concept. The mind is usually regarded as the root of awareness, or consciousness, rather than as a physiological mechanism. Many examples exist of the effect of body on mind (a cup of coffee may act as a stimulant) and also of mind on body (for some the prospect of flying or even a visit to the dentist can produce trembling and sweating). Also, research has confirmed that the brain is involved in the experience of consciousness, though it is not certain how and to what extent. Therefore the question remains: if it is impossible to link the intangible mind to a particular part of the body, how can we study the interaction between the two? There is currently no adequate answer. However, knowledge is constantly expanding and, as our understanding of physiological mechanisms increases, it becomes clear that mind and body are closely integrated.

Another aspect of the biological approach is interest in the role of heredity in behaviour. In the relatively short time since Darwin suggested that variations among individuals of a species could be passed on to future generations, much knowledge has accumulated regarding genetic transmission. For example, it is known that inheritance occurs through a chemical code carried in the genes. However, while the transmission of physical characteristics is well under-stood, the role of heredity in behavioural character-istics such as intelligence and personality is less clear cut. Linked to this has been interest in the relative importance of heredity and environment in the development of psychological characteristics (the nature–nurture debate), a long-standing controversy in psychology. It is now generally accepted that the key question that needs to be addressed is not which of the two, heredity or environment, is the more important, but how do the two *interact* to influence the development of behaviour? This question will be addressed later in the chapter, and is considered again in the introduction to Part 4.

Some research findings from physiological psychology

There follows a brief outline of some research that has focused on the physiological mechanisms underlying behaviour. The aim here is to provide the reader with a 'feel' for the kinds of investigations carried out and some of the techniques used.

Localization of brain function

In 1861, Paul Broca, a doctor, demonstrated by postmortem autopsy that a patient's inability to speak arose from a defect in a specific area of the brain. This evidence of localization of brain function contributes to the gradually emerging view that behaviour had a physical base.

Lashley's findings

In the 1920s, Karl Lashley carried out a series of classic experiments in which he demonstrated that learning and memory in rats is impaired if part of the cortex of the brain is removed. Lashley used a technique known as ablation, the removal of parts of the brain by surgery or by burning out with electrodes. Many of his experiments demonstrated that the amount of brain tissue destroyed appeared to be more important to the animal's behaviour than the specific part of the brain involved (Lashley, 1929). He believed that all parts of the brain were probably involved in every action (the Law of Mass Action).

ESB

Much research has been carried out into electrical stimulation of the brain (ESB). ESB involves the stimulation of neurons by means of a mild electrical current passed through an implanted electrode. Typically the main aim of this research is to investigate the effects of such stimulation on behaviour, particularly emotions. In the 1950s, using ESB, Olds and Milner identified pleasure centres in the brains of rats – areas that, when stimulated, led the rat to return to the area of the cage where it had been stimulated.

GAS

Much well-established research has highlighted the close interaction between mental processes and physiological changes within the body. Hans Selye (1956, 1974) has pioneered research into the physiological changes associated with stress in both animals and humans. Selye's work led him to propose the General Adaptation Syndrome (GAS), which describes the hormonal, biochemical and other bodily changes that occur and which interact with psychological factors within the individual during the experience of stress.

Psychoimmunology

The notion that people can influence their own health by their thoughts or feelings used to be treated with scepticism. However, the work of Cousins in the 1970s led to the development of research into psychoimmunology – the study of mental states and their effect on health (see Cousins, 1989, for a review). Cousins, a newspaper editor, was diagnosed with Hodgkins disease, a form of cancer that affects the immune system; doctors did not expect him to live long. However, he recovered, claiming that this was due at least in part to his determination to think positively and find ways of lifting his spirits.

At first, Cousins' beliefs were dismissed as untenable, but as fresh information became available about the functioning of the immune system, his ideas were treated more seriously. Today, scientists, using advanced biochemical techniques, are attempting to identify some of the body's chemicals and hormones that are influenced by different mental states, and which may affect the responses of the immune system (Maier and Laudenslager, 1985; Pert, 1990).

Schizophrenia

A great deal of research has been carried out in an attempt to understand the nature and causes of schizophrenia. Some of this work has indicated the influence of social, cultural and family factors on the development of the condition. A major line of enquiry has focused on possible biological differences between schizophrenic individuals and other people. For example, evidence is accumulating that schizophrenia, or some variants of it, may have a genetic base. Using advanced techniques of molecular biology, Sherrington et al. (1988) have located a genetic abnormality in members of a family having an unusually high incidence of schizophrenia. Research such as this

GLOSSARY

Localization of brain function An assumption that specific areas of the brain control particular psychological functions, such as language.

Ablation Removal of parts of the brain by surgery or by burning out with electrodes in order to observe modifications in an animal's behaviour.

Electrical stimulation of the brain (ESB) Placing an electrode in certain parts of the brain in order to stimulate neurons by means of a mild electrical shock. In this way, it is possible to observe the effects of such stimulation on behaviour.

General Adaptation Syndrome (GAS) Selye's three-stage model, which describes the body's physiological responses to stress.

Psychoimmunology The study of mental states and their effect on health.

does not, however, rule out other possible causes of schizophrenia.

Evaluation of the physiological approach

The physiological approach endeavours to work towards an understanding and explanation of the biological basis of behaviour. It is unique as an approach within psychology in the range of factors it considers and in the level at which it seeks to explain them. The physiological approach is the only one that attempts to relate behaviour to the workings and genetic make-up of the body. Other approaches, for example psychoanalysis, may subscribe to the view that behaviour is biologically based, but the concepts used and the phenomena studied are largely psychological rather than physiological.

As already noted, much valuable evidence has accumulated about the biological basis of behaviour. However, physiological psychology is not yet sufficiently advanced to offer total explanations for memory, stress, learning, emotions and so on. Moreover the complexity of the physiological system and the countless environmental influences that may affect it make it difficult to predict behaviour and explain it in purely physiological terms. This complexity and the way in which factors interact make it difficult also to draw specific conclusions about one factor, for example genetic links with schizophrenia, without taking into account other factors, such as cultural or family influences. However, our knowledge is increasing and the insights gained are being applied – in medicine, in business and in everyday life. For example, the concept of stress has been widely studied, as have the methods for coping with it. The use of psychoactive drugs has profoundly changed the treatment of mental disorders. Developments in areas such as psychoimmunology may have even greater impact in the future.

Some psychologists are afraid that overemphasizing physiological links with behaviour may lead to reductionist explanations which override the value of psychological explanations. A more positive view would be to accept that physiological mechanisms underlie behaviour and should be studied. Insights from this research may be used to complement purely psychological observations and measurements, resulting in a more complete description and explanation of behaviour. (A more detailed examination of physiological psychology can be found in Part 2.)

? SELF-ASSESSMENT QUESTIONS

1. Briefly outline some of the issues that concern physiological psychologists.
2. What do you understand by the mind–body problem?
3. Briefly describe three pieces of research carried out by physiological psychologists.
4. What are the strengths and limitations of the physiological approach?

The psychodynamic approach

The **psychodynamic approach** focuses largely on the role of motivation and past experiences in the development of personality and hence, behaviour. It has arisen from Freud's psychoanalytic theory, a brief outline of which has already been given in the introduction. Freud's pioneering approach was the impetus for many similar theories, which share many of the same assumptions about human beings but which differ in conceptual detail. Therefore, it is appropriate to examine the wider context of psychodynamic theories rather than just Freud's theory.

Post-Freudians

As has already been noted, many of Freud's original ideas have been adapted and modified by subsequent psychodynamic theorists, known as **post-Freudians**. Some of the ideas of Jung and Adler have already been outlined in the introduction to Part 1. The work of three others, Anna Freud, Klein and Erikson, is briefly considered below. As was the case with Freud, much of the work of post-Freudians was centrally concerned with clinical problems and the treatment of mental disorders.

Anna Freud, Sigmund Freud's daughter, was part of the Continental school of psychoanalysis, though she

---

GLOSSARY

Psychodynamic approach An approach that draws on Freud's psychoanalytic theory and which focuses on the role of motivation and past experiences in the development of personality.

Post-Freudians Psychodynamic theorists who subscribe to many of Freud's original ideas, but who have modified aspects of psychoanalytic theory and practice.

Anna Freud, shown here with her father, Sigmund, adapted and modified his ideas. She worked largely with older children and adolescents

came to Britain shortly before the Second World War, at the same time as her father. As part of the movement, starting in the 1930s, to apply a full psychoanalytic approach to problems of childhood, Anna Freud worked largely with older children and adolescents.

The publication of *The Ego and the Mechanisms of Defence* (1936) encouraged a new tendency in psychoanalysis to attach more importance to the conscious mind, or ego, than had previously been the case. Anna Freud believed that the term 'psychoanalysis' could not be applied to any technique that focused attention on the unconscious mind to the exclusion of everything else. She also expressed the belief that her father had overstressed the influence of sexuality in early childhood and had neglected its importance in adolescence. She saw adolescence as a time when there is an upsurge in the activity of the **libido** (sexual energy) and young people experience renewed sexual feelings and strivings. The intensity of these inner drives, she contended, results in excessive emotional upset as the adolescent tries to cope with the resulting impulses and desires.

Melanie Klein was one of the leading figures in European psychoanalysis but, like Anna Freud, established herself in Britain in the 1930s. From her background as a nursery teacher she related much of Freud's psychoanalytic theory to the development of very young children. She developed a therapeutic technique for analysing children's play that made it possible for psychoanalytic principles to be applied to children as young as two to six years old. **Play therapy** is the term used to describe a means through which a psychoanalyst can use play to get in touch with a child's unconscious in order to help the child deal with emotional difficulties.

In Klein's version of play therapy, simple play materials were used, for example male and female dolls, small models of familiar objects, such as cars, wheelbarrows or swings, and materials such as paper, string, clay and water. The child was allowed free access to play with all these objects and materials while the analyst knelt and attended to the content of the play.

Occasionally she would offer an interpretation of the play to the child, and would encourage **transference**: that is, she encouraged the child to transfer feelings towards the parents onto herself. Interpretations of the fantasy life of the child as revealed in play were given. Klein's methods offered new insights into development during the earliest years of childhood. Her views and methods dominated the mainstream of orthodox psychoanalysis in Britain. Prominent analysts such as D.W. Winnicott and John Bowlby, who were closely associated with the Tavistock Clinic where Klein worked, supported and were influenced by her views.

Erik Erikson began his psychoanalytic training with Anna Freud, whose interest in child analysis greatly influenced his work. In 1933, Erikson left Europe and began to practise as a child analyst in the USA. Though subscribing to much orthodox psychoanalytic theory, Erikson believed that Freud overemphasized the role of sexuality in the personality and neglected the importance of the social forces that influence development. He therefore proposed a series of psychosocial stages (rather than psychosexual stages, as proposed by Freud) through which individuals pass during their lifetime. In contrast to Freud, who particularly emphasized the importance of the childhood years for later personality, Erikson viewed the stages of development as covering the whole lifespan. Each stage was marked by a central crisis, the successful management of which would lead to the development and maintenance of a well-balanced personality.

Much of Erikson's clinical practice was carried out with troubled adolescents. His view that the conflict of 'identity versus role confusion' encountered during adolescence is the central crisis of all development has received wide support amongst psychologists. Erikson has made a substantial contribution to the field of developmental psychology, and in particular to the area of lifespan development, where his theory is the single most important influence. A more complete account of Erikson's theory can be found Chapter 23.

Evaluation of the psychodynamic approach

The psychodynamic approach attracts both wide acclaim and vigorous criticism. Freud's theory has made a monumental contribution to our understanding of the human personality. His emphasis on the importance of early childhood for later personality development and his attempt to account for individual differences in development have stimulated a great deal of research. His theory has also offered insights that have greatly influenced disciplines such as art, English literature and history. As already noted, psychoanalytic methods of treating mental disorders are widely used by many psychologists. Criticisms of the psychodynamic approach, starting with those levelled at Freud's original theory, can be summarized as follows:

- Though there is an abundance of research that claims to offer supporting evidence for psychoanalytic theory (for reviews see Kline, 1981a and Fisher and Greenberg, 1977), alternative explanations are often available to account for the findings. Not only can the theory not be reliably supported, it lacks **falsifiability**. In other words, it cannot be refuted – a serious violation of the scientific method, according to Popper (1959) (see Chapter 3).
- Eysenck and Wilson (1973) made a spirited attack on Freud's theory, which centred mainly on shortcomings in the way his data were collected. Freud's use of case studies of a limited sample of disturbed adults, interpreted without the benefit of quantitative data or statistical analyses, was considered to be 'unscientific'. (A more detailed account of Eysenck and Wilson's criticisms appears in Chapter 30.)
- Criticisms have been made of Freud's overemphasis on the role of biological factors in personality development. His insistence that the goal of all behaviour is to satisfy biological needs was not shared by other psychodynamic theorists such as Jung, Adler and Erikson. Whilst recognizing the importance of biological factors, these theorists subscribed also to the *social* nature of human beings.
- Attention has been drawn to the problems encountered in trying to assess the effectiveness of psychoanalysis as a therapy, largely arising from the controversy over what constitutes a 'cure'. Eysenck (1952) reviewed five studies of the

---

GLOSSARY

Transference A process in psychoanalytic therapy where thoughts and feelings are transferred on to the therapist.

Falsifiability The ability to show, when using the scientific method, that a theory may be false, rather than simply producing data to support it.

effectiveness of psychoanalysis and concluded that it achieved little that would not have occurred without therapy. However, using different criteria of the notion of 'cure', Bergin (1971) put the success rate of psychoanalysis at 83 per cent.

As we have seen, Freud's approach spawned many other psychodynamic theories of human personality. There are many similarities, but also many differences. One key similarity lies in the view that early childhood experiences crucially affect an individual's later personality. This 'similar-but-different' nature of psychodynamic models makes it difficult to determine which is the most accurate.

Because of the subjective nature of psychodynamic theories and their complexity, it is difficult to find effective ways of evaluating differences between them. Also, like Freud's theory, other psychodynamic models lack falsifiability, and in general can describe but not predict human behaviour.

(Note that a more detailed account of psychoanalytic theory appears in Part 7.)

❓ SELF-ASSESSMENT QUESTIONS

1. Briefly explain what is meant by the psychodynamic approach.
2. Give an outline of the views or work of one of the post-Freudians.
3. Explain the main strengths and shortcomings of the psychodynamic approach.

The behaviourist (or learning theory) approach

Where physiological psychologists focus on genetics and an individual's biological make-up, behaviourists or learning theorists focus on the influence of the environment. They choose not to be concerned with the internal mechanisms that occur inside the organism. Questions likely to be explored are:

- Under what conditions might certain behaviour occur?
- What might be the effects of various stimuli on behaviour?
- How do the *consequences* of behaviour affect that behaviour?

Questions such as these are relevant to the behaviourist view that human beings are shaped through constant interactions with the environment. Put more simply, learning and experience determine the kind of person you become.

The behaviourist approach to psychological functioning is rooted in the work of associationists, Pavlov and Thorndike, and the early behaviourists, Watson and Hull, all of whom studied learning in the form of conditioning (see the introduction to Part 1). Pavlov studied the conditioning of reflex responses, or **classical conditioning**, whilst Thorndike's work focused on the conditioning of voluntary behaviour, now referred to as **operant conditioning**, and later researched further by B. F. Skinner.

Behaviourism had a profound influence on the course of psychology during the first half of the twentieth century. Its offshoot, stimulus–response psychology, is still influential today. **Stimulus–response psychology** studies the stimuli that elicit behavioural responses, the rewards and punishments that influence these responses, and the changes in behaviour brought about by manipulating patterns of rewards and punishments (see Box 1.2). This approach does not concern itself with the mental processes that occur between the **stimulus** and the **response**. The work of B.F. Skinner on operant conditioning is central here; however, Skinner preferred to concentrate on the relationship between responses and their consequences because it was not always possible to determine which stimuli brought about which responses.

Skinner, in his *Behaviour of Organisms* (1938), described experiments he conducted with rats and later with pigeons. For instance, he conditioned rats to

GLOSSARY

Classical conditioning The process through which a reflex response becomes associated with a stimulus that does not naturally activate that behaviour.

Operant (or instrumental) conditioning The conditioning of voluntary behaviour through the use of reinforcement and punishment.

Stimulus–response psychology An approach concerned with studying the stimuli that elicit behavioural responses and the rewards and punishments that may influence these responses.

Stimulus (S) A situation, event, object or other factor which may influence behaviour.

Response (R) Behaviour that occurs as a reaction to a stimulus and which can be measured.

Box 1.2 Stimulus–response psychology

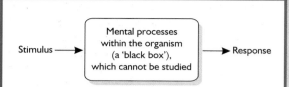

Stimulus ⟶ [Mental processes within the organism (a 'black box'), which cannot be studied] ⟶ Response

Early behaviourists such as Watson believed that behaviour could be analysed into basic S–R units, referred to as 'reflexes'. Their task was (a) to identify those responses that were instinctive and those that were learned and (b) to investigate the laws that governed learning. The brain was seen as a complex 'telephone exchange', which was unobservable and therefore should not be studied.

The main goal of psychology should be to predict how the organism will respond to a particular stimulus and, from a given response, be able to determine which stimuli were present.

press a bar in a 'Skinner box' in return for a reward of food (Figure 1.2). He was able to measure learning accurately under closely controlled conditions, varying the frequency of reward, or reinforcement, and sometimes applying irrelevant stimuli. Though he started his research with animals, Skinner worked towards a theory of conditioning that could include

Light
Screen

Lever
Water
Food tray

Figure 1.2 Skinner conditioned rats to press a lever in return for a reward of food

humans. This work is described in *Science and Human Behaviour* (1953). Note that a more detailed discussion of Skinner's theory of operant conditioning can be found in Chapter 6.

Some practical applications of the behaviourist approach

The influence of the behaviourist approach, with its emphasis on the manipulation of behaviour through patterns of reinforcement and punishment, can be seen in many practical situations, both in education and in psychotherapy. Below is a brief account of some of these practical applications.

Programmed learning

Skinner applied the principles of operant conditioning to the formal learning situation. He developed a system known as 'programmed learning', in which teaching machines are sometimes used, although it can take the form of written self-teaching units. The material to be learned is broken down into a large number of small segments, or frames. The student works through the frames sequentially and is required to respond at the end of each one. Correct responses receive reinforcement in the form of immediate feedback and, if correct, the learner proceeds to the next frame. In this way behaviour is shaped. The sequence described above is known as a linear programme. A more complex sequence, known as a branching programme, can also be used. (See Chapter 6 for a more detailed discussion of programmed learning.)

Programmed learning was not adopted as widely as had been envisaged by Skinner. Reports of its effectiveness relative to conventional learning methods are variable.

Behavioural therapies

Therapeutic techniques based on conditioning processes are generally referred to as **behavioural therapies**. Walker (1984) has proposed that techniques based on operant conditioning should be referred to as

GLOSSARY

Behavioural therapies Therapeutic techniques that are based on the principles of either classical or operant conditioning.

behaviour modification and that techniques that rely upon the principles of classical conditioning should be known as behaviour therapy. This distinction is used in the descriptions that follow.

Behaviour modification   This is a technique that is used to change or remove unwanted behaviour. Its central principle, taken from operant conditioning, is that behaviour that has favourable consequences – that is, which is positively reinforced – is likely to be repeated, and behaviour that is ignored is likely to die out. The desired behaviour is broken down into a sequence of small steps. Each step achieved is immediately rewarded, but gradually more and more of the required behaviour is demanded before the reward is given. This process is known as **behaviour shaping** through successive approximations.

Behaviour modification has been widely used in clinical settings with mentally handicapped children and adults and especially with autistic children. Typically a shaping technique is used. For instance, Lovaas (1973) developed a programme to modify the behaviour of autistic children from withdrawal to talking and social interaction. Appropriate responses were initially rewarded with sweets. Later, when the children became more responsive, cuddling was used as a reinforcement for 'good' behaviour.

Token economy systems are based on the principle of secondary reinforcement. Tokens are given in exchange for desirable or acceptable behaviours. These can then be exchanged for primary (or direct) reinforcements, such as sweets or extra outings.

There is evidence that well-organized token economy systems do promote desirable behaviour, particularly in an institutional setting. However, doubts have been raised about whether the effects are due to reinforcement or to other variables, and also about the long-term effectiveness of such programmes in the 'real world'. Also, in some situations involving token economies, ethical concerns have been expressed (see Chapters 5 and 33).

Behaviour therapy   This is a term usually applied to techniques based on classical conditioning which deal with involuntary or reflex behaviour. It aims to remove maladaptive behaviours and substitute desirable ones. One example of such a technique is **systematic desensitization**, which is mainly used to remove phobias. For example, a patient who had an irrational fear would first be taught to relax. Gradually the feared object would be introduced to the patient in a step-by-step process until the patient could tolerate actual contact with the object without anxiety. A second example is aversion therapy, which is used mainly to treat addictions or other unwanted behaviour. (See Chapter 5 for a consideration of some of the ethical issues surrounding the use of behavioural therapies.)

A more detailed examination of the principles and applications of classical and operant conditioning can be found in Chapter 6.

Biofeedback

Biofeedback is a technique that draws mainly on the principles of operant conditioning. Individuals are trained to control bodily processes such as heart rate and blood pressure, which are autonomic responses and not normally under voluntary control. Typically, patients are connected to a machine that gives a continuous reading of heart rate and blood pressure. They are trained to relax, and are asked to try consciously to reduce either one or both of these bodily processes. When the readout falls to a given target level, a bell or tone sounds. The patient aims to maintain that level. The reinforcement for hypertensive patients in doing this is the knowledge that they are helping to improve their own health (see Mercer, 1986).

From a theoretical point of view, biofeedback demonstrates that the processes of classical and operant conditioning are more closely interleaved than was once thought, since it works on autonomic responses, thought to be the province only of classical conditioning.

GLOSSARY

Behaviour shaping In operant conditioning, the process involved in the learning of new behaviour by reinforcing successive approximations to the desired response.

Token economy A version of behaviour modification where reinforcements are given not in the form of an immediate reward but in the form of tokens, which can be exchanged later for a reward of the individual's choice.

Systematic desensitization A technique used in behaviour therapy to eliminate phobias by gradually introducing the object of the phobia whilst pairing it with something pleasant.

Biofeedback The use of techniques that draw on the theoretical bases of both classical and operant conditioning. Patients are trained to control bodily processes such as heart rate and blood pressure, which are under autonomic control.

The technique of biofeedback is also discussed in Chapter 33.

Evaluation of the behaviourist approach

The behaviourist approach has been a dominant influence in psychology. It represents one of the 'hardcore' approaches, which has contributed a great deal to our understanding of psychological functioning and has provided a number of techniques for changing unwanted behaviour. Its use of rigorous empirical methods has enhanced the credibility of psychology as a science. (See Chapter 3 for a discussion of behaviourism in relation to the scientific method.) Criticisms of the approach include the following:

- Its mechanistic views tend to overlook the realm of consciousness and subjective experience, and it does not address the possible role of biological factors in human behaviour.
- Individuals are seen as passive beings who are at the mercy of their environments. This emphasis on environmental determinism leaves no room for the notion of free will in an individual. (A more complete discussion of the issue of free will and determinism appears in Chapter 2.)
- Its theories of classical and operant conditioning cannot account for the production of spontaneous, novel or creative behaviour.
- Its basis in animal research has been questioned (see Chapter 5 on the use of animals in psychological research).
- One of the assumptions commonly made by behaviourists is that the principles of classical and operant conditioning apply to any response in any species. Laboratory studies using a wide range of species seemed to confirm this idea. However, researchers coming from **ethology** (the study of the natural behaviour of animals) have drawn attention to some of the biological limits of conditioning. This is concerned with the study of species-specific behaviours (behaviour characteristic of all members of a particular species), which are likely to be influenced by the genetic make-up of a species as well as by learning. (See Chapter 6 for a discussion of the biological limits of conditioning.)
- Clinical psychologists who adopt behaviourally oriented therapies have been criticized for treating the probable symptoms of mental disorders whilst often ignoring possible underlying causes. (See Chapter 33 for an evaluation of the behavioural approach to therapy.)

? SELF-ASSESSMENT QUESTIONS

1. What, according to the behaviourists, is the most important influence on the development of behaviour?
2. Briefly explain how Skinner applied the principles of operant conditioning to programmed learning.
3. Describe one behavioural therapy based on the principles of classical conditioning and one based on the principles of operant conditioning.
4. Briefly evaluate the behaviourist approach.

The cognitive approach

The **cognitive approach** contrasts sharply with that of both the psychoanalysts, with their emphasis upon the importance of the unconscious mind, and the behaviourists, who focus largely upon the links between external events and behaviours. Cognitive psychologists believe that the events occurring within a person must be studied if behaviour is to be fully understood. These internal events, often referred to as **mediators**, since they occur between the stimulus and the behaviour, include perception, thinking processes such as problem solving, memory and language. Unlike psychoanalysis and behaviourism, the cognitive approach does not espouse a single body of theory, and no single theorist has predominated in the way that Freud influenced psychoanalysis and Skinner behaviourism. What cognitive psychologists have in common is an approach that stresses the importance of studying the mental processes that affect our

---

GLOSSARY

Ethology The study of the natural behaviour of animals.

Cognitive approach An approach that is concerned with thinking and related mental processes, such as perception, memory, problem solving and language.

Mediators In cognitive psychology, the internal, mental events that occur between a stimulus and the behaviour that results.

behaviour and enable us to make sense of the world around us. Thus cognitive psychologists may ask questions such as:

- How do we remember?
- Why do we forget?
- What strategies do we use to solve problems?
- What is the relationship between language and thought?
- How do we form concepts?

There is a general belief that cognitive processes operate not randomly but in an organized and systematic way. The human mind is therefore often compared to a computer, and human beings are seen as information processors who absorb information from the outside world, code and interpret it, store and retrieve it.

The influence of the cognitive approach can be seen also in many other areas of psychology, the assumption being that some kind of mediational processes underlie behaviour. Thus one might talk about a cognitive approach to moral development or a cognitive theory of emotion. Within social psychology, a primary interest is in social cognition, the mental processes implicated in the way individuals perceive and react to social situations, and, conversely, the way in which social situations may influence our thought processes.

Methods of study

Clearly the processes that cognitive psychologists study are not directly observable: one cannot lift off the top of an individual's head and observe memory at work! However, it is recognized that insights into mental processes may be inferred from an individual's behaviour, provided that such inferences are supported by objective, empirical data. Therefore the experimental method, with its emphasis on objectivity, control and replicability, is often used. Some examples of experiments that may be encountered in the area of cognitive psychology are outlined in Box 1.3.

Models in cognitive psychology

As already noted, one of the difficulties facing cognitive psychologists is that of attempting to study processes that are not directly observable. Hebb (1949) proposed some clear guidelines as to how this problem might be partially dealt with. He suggested that, in order to study ;information processing by the nervous system, it was not necessary to have a precise knowledge of the brain and its functions. Until firm physiological evidence was available one could propose hypothetical (or possible) models of the way some aspects of the nervous system – for example, that relating to memory – might operate. A model could then be tested by experimental or other means and, in the light of research findings, might be adapted or replaced by a new model.

The use of models in cognitive psychology has proved a valuable and fruitful means of gaining information. There follows a brief account of some models that have been developed and tested in cognitive psychology.

The Broadbent filter model of selective attention

This model represented an attempt by Broadbent (1958) to explain how the nervous system selects some stimuli to pay attention to, while ignoring others. The model, which focused on the processing of auditory information, proposed that a filter exists, very early in processing, which is attuned to the physical features of the incoming stimuli. These are passed through for higher processing in the brain whilst other unattended information is filtered out and lost.

Later models of selective attention were proposed by Treisman (1964a) and Deutsch and Deutsch (1963). The latter model was revised by Norman (1976). These models are discussed further in Chapter 12.

Atkinson–Shiffrin two-process model of memory

Atkinson and Shiffrin (1971) proposed a model that illustrated the relationship between short-term memory (STM) and long-term memory (LTM) (see Chapter 14). A central feature of this model was its emphasis on the role of rehearsal, which has two main functions: to maintain incoming information in STM, and to transfer

---

GLOSSARY

Social cognition The mental processes implicated in the way people perceive and react to a social situation, and also the way social situations may influence our thinking.

Information processing A term used to describe the mental operations that come between a stimulus and response.

Model A hypothetical, testable proposition about the way some aspect of psychological functioning operates.

Box 1.3   Some experiments carried out in cognitive psychology

Gregory (1972b), in his study of perceptual illusions, investigated participants' perception of the Müller-Lyer figure and the Necker Cube (see Chapter 13). His findings indicated that, when the figures are removed from their flat paper background and represented as luminous figures suspended in the dark, they are perceived as three-dimensional. This finding contributed to Gregory's theory as to why people are 'taken in' by such illusions.

Neisser investigated feature detection theory (FDT) in his research into pattern recognition. FDT maintains that patterns such as letters of the alphabet are made up of a number of basic features such as vertical lines, curves and diagonal lines. For example, the letter T may be analysed as one horizontal feature and one vertical feature. Recognition of letters involves the brain in detection of these basic features.

In a series of well-known experiments, Neisser (1964) presented participants with tasks requiring them to search through lists of letters in order to locate a prespecified letter placed in various different positions in the lists. He found that participants located the letter A much more quickly in lists made up of rounded letters such as O, Q and G than in lists containing angular letters

such as N, E and W. This confirmed the hypothesis derived from FDT that, the fewer the common features between the target and nontarget letters, the more quickly the patterns are analysed by the brain.

Loftus has studied some of the effects of memory on eyewitness testimony (Loftus, 1980; Loftus and Hoffman, 1989). She has tested the hypothesis that memory is reconstructive in nature: that is, our memory for events is often unreliable in that we sometimes reconstruct the past in line with what we believe could or should have happened. This process, Lotus believes, can be greatly influenced in a court setting by the kinds of questions witnesses are asked.

In one of her experiments Loftus (1979) showed three groups of participants a film of a car accident. One group were asked to estimate the speed of the cars when they hit each other. A second group were asked an identical question but with the words 'smashed into' substituted for 'hit'. The remaining participants were used as a control group and were not asked to estimate speed. Findings showed that the 'smashed into' group estimated speed as significantly higher than that estimated by the 'hit' group. (See also Chapter 14.)

---

information from STM to LTM. The notion of two memory processes has received much research support. However, other models have also been proposed, the most significant being that of the levels or depths of processing model (Craik and Lockhart, 1972).

Computer simulation of human thinking

With the advent of the computer, many computer programs have been developed that have attempted to model human thinking. This approach is known as computer simulation (see Chapter 15).

Perhaps the most famous of these programmes is the General Problem Solver, devised by Newell, Shaw and Simon (1958) and Newell and Simon (1972). This program attempted to simulate the strategies used in human problem solving. It proposed that much human problem solving is heuristic: that is, it is based on the testing of intelligent 'hunches'. Newell et al. support this heuristic model with evidence derived from

participants thinking aloud about the strategies used as they worked on problems.

As more sophisticated programs have been devised in order to simulate human thinking, a controversial debate has developed. Some critics question the whole premise of likening people to machines. Others argue that computers can do only what they are programmed to do, and that we do not yet know enough about the way the human brain works to be able to reflect its activity in computers.

Cognitive development

A brief word should be said finally about the work of psychologists who have studied cognitive development. The most significant of these is Jean Piaget, who has made a monumental contribution to our understanding of the development of logic and concept attainment from childhood to maturity. Jerome Bruner and the Russian psychologist L.S. Vygotsky have also made an outstanding contribution to an understanding

Jean Piaget, the most significant figure in the study of cognitive development

of cognitive development in children. An account of these two theories and some of their practical applications can be found in Chapter 20.

Evaluation of the cognitive approach

The cognitive approach emphasizes the importance of mediational processes, such as perception and thinking, which occur between a stimulus and a response. Research carried out by cognitive psychologists has aided our understanding of these processes. Practical insights have also been offered into such issues as how memory may be made more effective, how to improve problem-solving skills, and the merits and limitations of eyewitness testimony in court. Criticisms of the cognitive approach include the following:

■ A problem with the cognitive approach lies in its lack of integration. Though 'cognitive theories' exist in many different areas of psychology, no single, coherent theory links these areas into an identifiable framework. For example, in addition to theories of perception, memory and thinking, we refer to cognitive theories of emotion (though as yet an emotional theory of cognition has been largely ignored), cognitive dissonance and social cognition, but the descriptions and terminology used tend to vary in each area. This lack of integration may exist in part because of the lack of a single important theorist, as noted earlier.

■ The information-processing metaphor drawn from computing and emphasizing 'the human being as a machine' has offended some psychologists. They point out that the computer analogy fails to recognize the most fundamental differences between humans and machines: for example, people forget, computers do not; people are emotional and irrational whilst computers are logical and unable to feel emotion. It must be remembered that the information-processing model is a metaphor, and as such it has limitations in explaining human behaviour.

■ The wide use of laboratory experiments in cognitive psychology has been criticized, largely because findings are said to be 'artificial' and not in keeping with behaviour and events occurring in the 'real world'. It is suggested that people's behaviour may be influenced by the setting and by characteristics associated with the experimenter. (See Part 8 for a more complete evaluation of the experimental method.) Currently, however, there is a trend towards using more ecologically valid methods of study, particularly in the field of memory.

The cognitive approach is expanding rapidly within psychology. The trend towards **cognitive science** is encouraging increasing dialogues among disciplines, including psychology, computer science, physiology and linguistics. It is possible that some exciting developments lie ahead. (A more detailed examination of cognitive psychology can be found in Part 3.)

SELF-ASSESSMENT QUESTIONS

1. Explain why the cognitive approach is often referred to as an 'information-processing' approach.
2. Outline some of the questions explored by cognitive psychologists about human mental activity.
3. What do you understand by the term 'model' in cognitive psychology? Give an example.
4. Consider the main strengths and limitations of the cognitive approach.

The humanistic (or phenomenological) approach

For many years psychology was dominated by two great schools: the psychoanalysts, with their emphasis on instinctive, irrational human beings influenced by the contents of an unconscious mind, and the behaviourists, who viewed humans as mechanistic beings controlled by the effects of the environment. Towards the middle of the twentieth century, a third great force appeared, which offered a view of the human being as a free and generous individual with the potential for growth and fulfilment. This third force gave rise to the **humanistic approach**, some of the main tenets of which appear below:

- Humanistic psychologists believe that psychology should be concerned with the subjective, conscious experience of the individual; this is often referred to as a phenomenological viewpoint.
- They emphasize the uniqueness of human beings and their freedom to choose their own destiny.
- They regard the use of scientific methods as inappropriate for the study of human beings.
- A major aim of psychology, they believe, should be to help people maximize their potential for psychological growth.
- The humanistic view is optimistic. Humans are seen as striving to achieve their potential – to achieve the maximum personal growth within individual limitations

Two leading exponents of the humanistic approach are Carl Rogers (1902–87) and Abraham Maslow (1908–70).

Carl Rogers

Carl Rogers was a clinical psychologist and, like Freud, developed many of his views through his work with emotionally troubled people. During this work he observed that many psychological problems arise from what he called the would/should dilemma. This refers to the conflict between what people believe they ought to do (shoulds) and what they feel is best for them (woulds). For example, an individual may feel that he or she would like to get on with some important work at the office, but should spend more time with the family. The discomfort caused by the would/should dilemma results in anxiety.

Carl Rogers was a leading exponent of the humanistic approach

Philsophical basis of Rogers's work

Rogers's theory of the human personality started from the premise that people are basically good. Each individual is unique and has a basic need for positive egard: that is, to have respect and admiration from others. All people, Rogers believed, are born with the **actualizing tendency**, a motive that drives us to grow and develop into mature and healthy human beings. Central to the theory is the concept of the self, the person's view, acquired through life experiences, of all

---

GLOSSARY

Cognitive science An interdisciplinary area of research, which studies the use of computers to simulate human thought processes and related phenomena.

Humanistic approach Concerned with an individual's own subjective perceptions and feelings about their experiences.

the perceptions, values and attitudes that constitute 'I' or 'me'. This **perceived self** influences the individual's perception both of the world and of his or her own behaviour. The other aspect of self, according to Rogers's theory, is the **ideal self**, one's perception of how one should or would like to be. Thus a woman might perceive herself as successful and respected in her career but with certain shortcomings as a wife or mother (which might or might not be true). Her ideal self might demand that she be equally successful in both these spheres of her life. Good psychological health exists where the perceived self and the ideal self are relatively compatible. It is when there is a serious mismatch between the two or between the self and experiences of the real world that psychological problems arise.

Client-centred therapy

Rogers developed a form of **client-centred therapy** in which the clients (not 'patients') have the power and motivation to help themselves, given the right circumstances. The facilitator (not 'therapist') attempts to create a warm, accepting atmosphere in which this can happen. Unlike the situation in other kinds of therapy, the facilitator is not an expert, authority figure, and the therapy is nondirective. The aim is to help clients clarify their thoughts on problems to gain greater insight into them. This greater understanding helps clients to recognize their own strengths and limitations, and is very often accompanied by an increase in self-esteem. Along with this, a clearer understanding of constraints that are real, as opposed to imagined or self-imposed, can eventually help the client to decide how to act. The key factor in Rogerian therapy is that clients become more in control of their fate and find satisfactory solutions to problems. The facilitator does not offer a judgment on the appropriateness of the client's solutions.

Rogers and other humanistic psychologists often use a group setting for therapy. Group therapy, they believe, allows individuals to express their problems openly to others, and the feedback they receive also provides valuable insights about how they are perceived by others.

Abraham Maslow

Both Rogers and Maslow believed that self-awareness and the ability to come to terms with oneself are necessary ingredients for psychological well-being.

Both also saw human beings as striving to achieve their potential – to achieve the maximum amount of personal growth possible within their individual limitations. However, where Rogers emphasized the importance of the self-concept, Maslow was greatly concerned with the motives that drive people. Maslow believed that there are two kinds of motivation:

- deficiency motivation, the need to reduce physiological tensions such as hunger and thirst, which may be seen as correcting inadequacies; and
- growth motivation, which has to do with the satisfaction of needs such as the need to be loved and esteemed; growth motives operate on the principle that, when no deficiencies remain, people have the need to develop beyond their present condition.

As Maslow studied motives in a wide variety of situations he noticed that they tended to fall into a specific pattern, which could be arranged into a hierarchy (see Figure 1.3). Maslow's **hierarchy of needs** has become almost synonymous with his name. He believed the needs in the hierarchy to be inborn and present, at least initially, in all people. Lower needs, such as those for satisfaction of hunger and thirst, must be at least partially satisfied before needs further up the hierarchy become important. Maslow viewed the motive towards **self-actualization** – the need to find self-fulfilment and realize one's full potential – as the pinnacle of achievement in the satisfaction of needs.

Victor Frankl

Rogers and Maslow are the best-known exponents of the humanistic approach. However, another theorist

---

GLOSSARY

Actualizing tendency Rogers's term for a motive that exists in everyone to develop into mature, fulfilled human beings. Similar to Maslow's notion of self-actualization.

Perceived self Rogers's term for the individual's own view of what he or she is like, arrived at through life experiences and through feedback from other people.

Ideal self Rogers's term for how one should, or would like, to be.

Client-centred therapy Rogers's approach in which the clients (not 'patients') are encouraged to take control over the process of therapy.

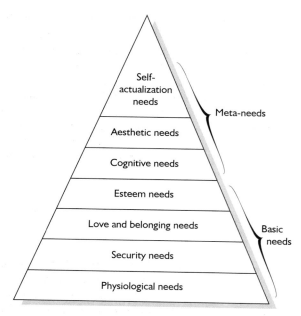

Figure 1.3 A representation of Maslow's hierarchy of needs (after Maslow, 1959)

whose basic assumptions fit within this approach is Victor Frankl. Born in Vienna in 1905, Frankl was initially greatly influenced by Freud's ideas about mental illness. Like Freud, he was exposed to the threat of the Nazis during the Second World War. Frankl spent three years trying to survive in a concentration camp, an experience that had a profound effect on his later theory. His best-known work, a book entitled *Man's Search for Meaning* (1992), prompted the development of a theoretical framework that he called **logotherapy**.

Logotherapy

Logotherapy espouses a number of basic assumptions, which are similar to those of other humanistic theorists:

■ Like Rogers, Frankl believed in the freedom of individuals to control their own destiny, though he admitted that there are some circumstances that may limit this freedom. However, he believed that the real issue 'is not freedom from conditions, but it is freedom to take a stand towards these conditions' (1992, p. 132) Even within a concentration camp, individuals, he believed, had choice over their attitudes towards their experiences.

■ Frankl believed that the meaning of a given set of experiences could only be truly determined by the person having the experiences. In order to understand an individual's behaviour, it is necessary to understand the meaning attributed by that individual. Thus Frankl's beliefs can be said to be phenomenological.

Frankl placed issues of meaning at the centre of his theory. He believed that a fundamental purpose in life is to find meaning in a world that seems meaningless. By meaning he meant a person's understanding of immediate experiences and the attitude he or she takes towards those experiences. He emphasized the need to focus on the here and now of experiences (unlike psychoanalysts, who emphasize the individual's past).

In a therapeutic context, Frankl explained that the aim of logotherapy is to help patients to become fully aware of their own responsibleness. The therapist's role does not involve imposing value judgments on patients, but should help them to discover their own values. This seems very like Rogers' client-centred therapy, though a key difference lies in Rogers' belief that certain kinds of values – for example, that all people are basically good – are necessary in healthy human beings.

Frankl suggested three ways in which meaning in life can be discovered:

■ through achievement;
■ through a transcendent experience (for example, love or an appreciation of art);
■ by the attitude an individual takes when faced with unavoidable suffering (for example, a terminal illness or experiences in a concentration camp).

The idea of finding meaning through suffering is a key theme in Frankl's theory.

Recovery Movement

This is a term that encompasses a number of approaches that share similar themes and assumptions. Its origins lie in the formation in 1935 of

---

GLOSSARY

Logotherapy A theoretical framework and therapy developed by Frankl, which emphasizes the need for individuals to discover their own meaning in life in order to grow and develop psychologically.

Alcoholics Anonymous (AA), a programme for the treatment of alcoholism. AA's philosophy of emphasizing the possibility of a person's recovery with help from social and spiritual sources has been adapted by many other groups, including Gamblers Anonymous and Overeaters Anonymous.

Philosophy of the Recovery Movement

Some of the basic ideas that are central to the **Recovery Movement** include the following:

- There is a belief that no matter how traumatized an individual is, there is a hidden core within, which will allow that person to grow and develop. This hidden core is sometimes referred to as the inner child. Through the inner child, an individual can reexperience the feelings and desires of childhood.
- The most serious problems that people experience arise from traumas that lead to feelings of shame. For example, a child growing up with an alcoholic parent will suffer a number of traumas. The most damaging of these is a sense of self-blame for the parent's problems, which often destroys the individual's sense of self-worth.
- Feelings of shame are closely connected to guilt, which may develop from the age of about four, as a child develops moral concepts (Bradshaw, 1988).

Recovery Movement therapy

The approach taken by AA to help sufferers of alcoholism illustrates the approach of the Recovery Movement. It combines self-help with social support. Sufferers are encouraged to view alcoholism as both a disease and a social problem. The solutions, it is believed, lie in the 12 steps to recovery. This begins with the individual acknowledging that at that point he or she is powerless over the problem (Step 1), seeking help from a Higher Power (Step 2), and ends with the individual resolving to practise the 12 steps and to share the message with others (Step 12).

Evaluation of the Recovery Movement

The Recovery Movement has become very popular over the past few years. Glassman (1995) argues that one must allow for the possibility that some practitioners within the movement have questionable credentials. However, he stresses that this should not detract from the usefulness of its theories. As in most other theories, for example those of Freud and Skinner, there is a belief that individual development is strongly influenced by the family. In suggesting that cultural pressures may work against feelings of self-worth and that most individuals are unable to resist those pressures, the Recovery Movement addresses the relationship of the individual to society in a way that most psychological theories do not.

Evaluation of the humanistic approach

The humanistic approach has served the valuable purpose of forcing psychologists to take account of the subjective experience of the individual and the importance of self-esteem and meaning in psychological functioning. Its insistence that the scientific method, as presently conceived in psychology, is an unsatisfactory vehicle for studying subjective experience has encouraged psychologists to look for more appropriate methods. In summary, humanistic psychology represents an important counterbalance to the more deterministic approaches that have dominated psychology for most of the twentieth century.

In a practical sense, humanistic psychologists have done much to advance methods of assessing self-concept and of developing therapeutic techniques that encourage self-respect and autonomy in individuals. The main criticisms of humanistic psychology centre on the following:

- As with psychoanalysis, its terminology is not clearly defined and is therefore not easily testable. Data used to support the theories have tended to come from case studies and interviews, which, unlike experiments, do not use falsifiable predictions. However, Rogers himself has called upon psychologists to investigate some of his ideas. Also, he and his colleagues have

---

GLOSSARY

Recovery Movement A term used to describe a number of approaches and therapies that share similar, humanistically oriented, assumptions. It is illustrated by the '12 steps' approach of Alcoholics Anonymous.

contributed to psychotherapy research by tape-recording therapy sessions and making them available for analysis by researchers. Some empirical studies have been carried out using the **Personal Orientation Inventory** (Shostrum et al., 1976), which claims to be a measure of self-actualization. Also, the **Q-sort Technique** (Stephenson, 1953) has been used by Rogers and others to examine the self-concept and as an assessment instrument to study changes in a client's perceptions of self during the course of therapy.

■ Differences in concepts and emphasis between humanistic theories are not easy to assess. For example, both Rogers and Maslow believed that there is a common set of values for healthy individuals, while Frankl rejected this view. Who is correct? The concept of shame plays a prominent part in the theoretical framework of the Recovery Movement. How important is this concept?

■ The client-centred therapy advocated by Rogers has some limitations. For example, it seems to be most successful with people who are more articulate and who are motivated to seek help. Clients who are withdrawn or seriously disturbed may need more direct help in changing their behaviour.

■ Some have criticized the values espoused by humanistic psychologists. The view has been expressed that the theories of Rogers and Maslow place too much emphasis on the well-being of the individual at the expense of concern for the welfare of others (Wallach and Wallach, 1983). The same could be said of Frankl's logotherapy.

? SELF-ASSESSMENT QUESTIONS

1. Outline the most important ways in which the humanistic approach differs from other approaches.
2. Briefly describe the main aspects of Rogers's theory of human personality.
3. Give a brief account of Maslow's 'hierarchy of needs'.
4. Explain what Frankl meant by 'logotherapy'.
5. Outline some of the principles that are central to the Recovery Movement.
6. Evaluate the humanistic approach.

Which approach?

The details of the five approaches outlined in Box 1.4 will become clearer as you encounter them in greater depth in your wider study of psychology. The conflict of ideas and beliefs between these different approaches may seem confusing, and you would be forgiven for asking 'Which is the right approach?' However, it is important to realize that no one approach contains the whole truth about psychological functioning. Each focuses on different aspects of human behaviour or experience and, as such, may be seen as complementary rather than competing. Indeed many psychologists, whether carrying out research or working in practical situations, feel free to select from different approaches those ideas that seem most helpful to the particular situation in which they are operating. A summary of the main areas of research interest and professional activity is contained below in the section 'What do psychologists do?'.

Psychology is a young discipline relative to other sciences. As such, it has no global **paradigm**, or single accepted theory, about the nature of human beings in the way that biology has been influenced by Darwin's theory. Until this is possible in psychology, the scope and variety of the many different approaches allow us to adopt different levels of explanation in order to explain human functioning.

Levels of explanation

It is possible to describe and explain an aspect of human functioning in many different ways. The following example should help to illustrate this fact: the simple act of shaking hands when you meet an old friend could be described and explained from many different perspectives (see Figure 1.4).

■ It could be reduced to an account of the neural and muscular activities that occur (physiological approach).

■ It might be seen as an activity that is the result of previous conditioning processes: that is, it has been associated with rewards or reinforcement and is triggered by an appropriate stimulus, in

GLOSSARY

Paradigm As used in psychology, a global theory or generally accepted perspective on the nature of human behaviour.

Box 1.4 Five major approaches to psychology

	Physiological	Psychoanalytic	Behaviourist	Cognitive	Humanistic
Basic assumptions about human beings	Behaviour is linked to physiological processes – genetic, hormonal, biochemical. The study of the nervous system (especially the brain) is of prime importance.	Based on Freud's theory. Human personality is influenced by an unconscious mind harbouring repressed memories, which determine conscious thoughts and behaviour.	Human personality is determined by learning and experience of the environment. The main learning processes are classical and operant conditioning (reinforcement).	The human mind is likened to a computer, which selects, codes, stores and retrieves information. Studies mainly perception, memory, problem solving and language.	Human beings are seen as unique and essentially good, with freedom of choice over their own destinies. They have an inborn motive to self-actualize.
Assumptions about development	A sequence of behavioural change determined by the maturation of the nervous system and endocrine (hormonal) system.	A number of psychosexual stages. Failure to negotiate a stage satisfactorily results in fixation (halting of development) at that stage. Early childhood experiences determine future personality.	No fixed stages of development. A child's repertoire of behaviours increases as further adaptive responses are acquired.	Cognitive development proceeds through stages (Piaget). Information-processing approach: study of development of perception, memory, strategies in problem solving, etc.	Development of self-esteem through unconditional positive regard from others is central (Rogers). Lower levels in a hierarchy of needs must precede the attainment of higher needs (Maslow).
Preferred method of study	Experimentation (humans and animals).	Clinical case studies.	Experimentation (humans and animals).	Experimentation; computer simulation; Piaget – clinical interview	Case study.
Recent advances in research and/ or practice	Physiological basis of stress and their effects. Use of psychoactive drugs to treat mental disorders. Psychoimmunolgy – study of mental states and effects on health.	None, though psychodynamic therapies are still widely used.	None as such though behavioural therapies are still widely used.	Cognitive science; multidisciplinary approach, which studies computer simulation of thinking. More ecologically valid approaches to studying cognitive processes, e.g. memory in 'real life'.	Popularity of the Recovery Movement (treatment of disorders such as alcoholism and drug addiction). Use of ideas drawn from Rogers's client-centred therapy in the field of counselling.
Main criticisms	Overemphasis of physiological links with behaviour may lead to reductionist explanations that detract from the value of psychological explanations.	'Unscientific' methods of study; difficult either to support or refute Freud's theory; difficulty of evaluating different theories and the effectiveness of therapies.	View of humans as passive beings at the mercy of the environment; failure to consider the role of biological factors in the development of behaviour.	Heavy emphasis on experimentation; 'human-as-computer' analogy is unacceptable to many.	Concepts and terminology not clearly defined or easily testable. Overemphasis on subjective data from case studies.

this case meeting an old friend (behaviourist approach).

- It could be argued that thought processes are important. Your purpose in shaking hands is to demonstrate to your friend that you remember him well and still hold him in high esteem (cognitive approach).
- Psychodynamic explanations could be introduced. Physical contact with someone you previously found attractive may affect your emotional state (psychoanalytic approach).
- Each person's subjective experience of the situation might be considered. The need for acceptance and approval by others may be seen as an important variable (humanistic approach).

Many other perspectives or levels of explanation might also be employed. For example, social and cultural factors most certainly play a part in the act of shaking hands. Whilst some psychologists concentrate their efforts on one particular approach, many others are happy to draw upon a number of different levels in their attempts to describe and explain human behaviour and experience.

Exercise 1.1

Think of your own example which may illustrate the use of different levels of explanation. Represent your example as a diagram as in Figure 1.4.

What do psychologists do?

There is no simple way of answering this question; there are many different fields of study in psychology and many different kinds of work that psychologists do. It is intended that this section will give the reader a

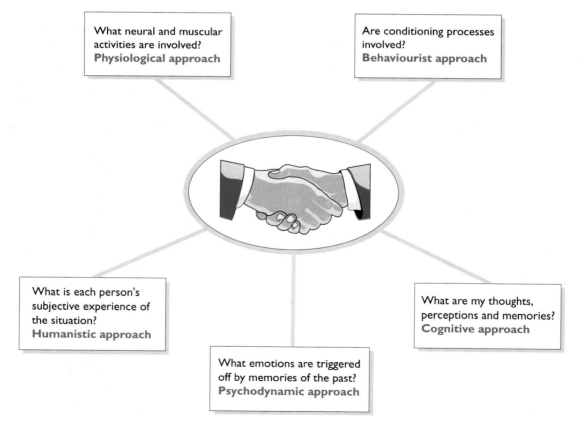

What neural and muscular activities are involved?
Physiological approach

Are conditioning processes involved?
Behaviourist approach

What is each person's subjective experience of the situation?
Humanistic approach

What are my thoughts, perceptions and memories?
Cognitive approach

What emotions are triggered off by memories of the past?
Psychodynamic approach

Figure 1.4 Levels of explanation: different ways in which you might explain the act of shaking hands with an old friend

feel for some of the main areas of research interest and professional activity (see Figure 1.5). It is important to note that there is often overlap between the categories given below.

Areas of psychological research

Research in psychology is carried out mainly in academic settings such as universities, and reflects the interests of the staff engaged on it. It can be divided broadly into two categories: **pure research** and **applied research**.

Pure research

This is research that is carried out primarily for its own sake to increase our knowledge and understanding of how organisms (this can include both humans and animals) behave. The major fields of study are outlined below.

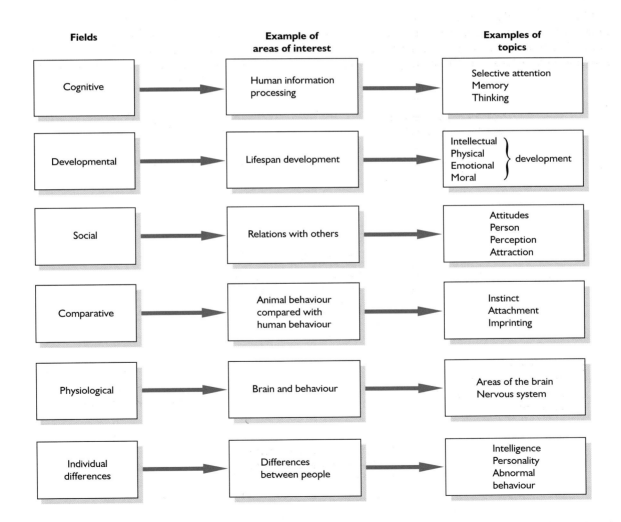

Figure 1.5 Areas of research in psychology

Applied research

Typically, though it may also take place within one of the fields of study outlined below, the problem investigated in applied research will be a practical one such as understanding drug addiction or the causes of bullying in schools. Applied research may be carried out either in an academic environment or in a work or other social setting.

Though a distinction has been made between pure and applied research, in reality there is often a great deal of overlap between the two. The work of the Applied Psychology Unit (APU) at Cambridge University is a good example. The APU was started by Craik and Bartlett, and carried on by Broadbent and Baddeley. It produced not only practical solutions to problems, for example the effective design of decimal coinage and postal codes, but also theoretical contributions to areas of knowledge such as attention, vigilance and memory.

Some fields of study

Research is carried out in many different branches of psychology. Below is a brief outline of the main fields that are dealt with in this book.

Physiological psychology (covered in Part 2)

Physiological psychologists look for explanations of behaviour in the physiological structures of humans and animals. For instance, Faraday (1973) investigated the physiological changes that occur in people during sleep and dreaming; Horne (1992) studied the incidence of motorway accidents, and showed that they correlate closely with circadian rhythms, changes in the physiological functions of the body at different times of the day. The data suggested that there were three 'high risk' periods – midnight to 2 am, 4 am to 6 am and between 2 and 4 pm in the afternoon.

Cognitive psychology (covered in Part 3)

This is a central discipline within psychology, and is concerned with the way in which the nervous system processes information. Typical areas of research include that carried out into perception, memory and problem solving. Within memory research, for example, researchers may be concerned, as Baddeley and Hitch (1974) have been, with working memory, or memory for material we are currently attending to. We need, for example, to store an address that we have looked up in an address book long enough to be able to write it on an envelope.

An area of cognitive psychology that has come to the fore relatively recently is cognitive science. This involves the use of computers to simulate the workings of the human brain.

Comparative psychology (covered in Part 4)

Comparative psychologists specialize in the study of animal behaviour both in natural environments and laboratory conditions, often making comparisons with the behaviour of humans. You could cite as an example the research of Krebs et al. (1978) into optimal foraging theory, the way in which animals learn how to obtain the best food supply with the least risk of predation.

Developmental psychology (covered in Part 5)

This is concerned with the way in which humans develop and change throughout their lifespan. Research is carried out into social, emotional and intellectual behaviour in humans. For example, in Switzerland, Piaget carried out research with children of different ages to investigate the way a child's intellect develops; in Holland, van Ijzendoorn and Kroonenberg (1988) investigated cross-cultural differences in babies' attachment to their mothers; Levinson (1978a) carried out interviews with 40 American males in order to study adult development.

Social psychology (covered in Part 6)

This is concerned with the effects upon behaviour of humans' interactions with each other. For example, Joy et al. (1977) studied the impact of the advent of television in a small Canadian community on the incidence of aggressive behaviour in that community; Silva (1990) investigated the personal characteristics that are important when we choose a marriage partner.

Individual differences (personality and abnormal psychology are covered in Part 7; intelligence is covered in Part 5, Chapter 21)

This field of study is concerned with ways in which people may differ from each other on such dimensions as personality, intelligence or abnormal behaviour. It is

HIM ? HE'S THE EDUCATIONAL PSYCHOLOGIST.

closely related to psychometrics, the measurement of psychological functioning. As an example, Eysenck devised an inventory, known as the Eysenck Personality Inventory, to measure two dimensions of personality: introversion and extraversion.

Some professional activities

If you thought you would like to work in psychology, what might you find yourself doing? In addition to the work done by research psychologists, as described above, there are many other areas of professional activity, some of which are briefly outlined below:

Clinical psychology

Clinical psychologists, who are the largest single group of psychologists, are concerned with problems of mental disorder. They may work with psychiatrists (doctors who specialize in the study and treatment of mental disorder) in a hospital context or with other health professionals in the community.

Educational psychology

Educational psychologists work with children and adolescents in schools, colleges, nurseries, special units or in the home; they collaborate closely with parents and teachers. Their work will include assessing a child's progress at school, considering children's emotional and academic needs, and providing help and advice.

Occupational (industrial) psychology

Occupational psychologists will probably be employed in industry or the public services. Some of their responsibilities are likely to include selecting and training individuals for employment, and advising on working conditions and health matters in the workplace. They may carry out applied research into the way people 'fit' with machines of many kinds, from cars to computers (ergonomics).

Counselling psychology

Counselling psychologists work with individuals, families, couples or groups, either privately or in primary health care in the health service. Their main aim is to improve people's well-being, alleviate distress, and help people to solve their own problems and take their own decisions.

Forensic psychology (criminological or legal psychology)

Forensic psychologists may be involved in therapeutic work with individuals or with groups who have come into conflict with the law. They may carry out research into the psychological processes that underlie certain offences, such as rape or other violent crimes. Some work with police and are involved in producing profiles of criminals.

Health/sports/community psychology

These are emerging fields of applied psychology in which clinical or social psychologists may work in a variety of different settings such as universities, hospitals or within the community.

Psychologists' qualifications

It should be emphasized that psychology is a graduate profession, and all the occupations described above assume at the least possession of a first degree in psychology. Many of them require also a postgraduate qualification.

In the United Kingdom, psychology is under the control of a professional body, the British Psychological Society (BPS), which offers graduate membership to those with a degree that has sufficient psychological content. The BPS (1996) has produced a careers pack that fully sets out the scope of the careers described above and the routes one may take to enter them. In countries other than the United Kingdom, the qualifications required for careers in psychology will vary.

Chapter summary

- A variety of approaches exist in psychology, which have been influenced by the former schools of psychology. Approaches vary in their assumptions about the nature of human beings and the kinds of theories and research methods used to study them. Five major approaches are the physiological, the psychodynamic, the behaviourist (or learning theory), the cognitive and the humanistic.

- Physiological psychologists look to biology as a means of describing and explaining psychological functioning. Their research interests include the study of the nervous system, particularly the brain; different states of consciousness, such as wakefulness and sleep; the effects of the hormonal system on behaviour; the physiological mechanisms that underlie motivation, emotion and cognitive processes; and the role of heredity in the development of behaviour.

- A relatively new area of research is known as psychoimmunology: the study of mental states and their effect on health. Much work has centred on links between stress and the functioning of the immune system.

- A philosophical issue that exists in physiological psychology is the question of the relationship between the mind and the neurophysiological processes in the body (the mind–body problem). Some scientists take a reductionist approach, believing that all psychological functioning can be explained by reference to physiological activity.

- The physiological approach has made great strides in understanding and explaining the biological basis of behaviour, though it is not yet sufficiently advanced to offer total explanations. The use of psychoactive drugs has transformed the treatment of mental disorder.

- Some psychologists believe that overemphasizing physiological links with behaviour may lead to reductionist explanations, which override the value of psychological explanations.

- The psychodynamic approach has arisen from Freud's psychoanalytic theory. It focuses largely on the role of motivation and past experiences in the development of personality and behaviour.

- Many of Freud's original ideas have been modified and adapted by subsequent psychodynamic theorists (post-Freudians), for example Anna Freud, Melanie Klein, Erik Erikson.

- Freud's theory and those of the post-Freudians have made a very significant contribution to our understanding of the human personality. The emphasis on the importance of early childhood for later personality development has stimulated a great deal of research, the influence of which can be seen in many present-day approaches.

- Criticisms of the psychodynamic approach include those levelled at Freud's original theory. For example, phenomena described by Freud, such as instinctual drives, are not directly observable; alternative explanations for research findings make it difficult to support much of the theory and also render it unfalsifiable; there are methodological problems arising from the use of biased samples and the clinical case study method. The subjectiveness and the 'similar but different' nature of other psychodynamic theories make it difficult to determine which is the most effective.

- The behaviourist approach is rooted in the work of associationists, Pavlov and Thorndike, and early behaviourists such as Watson. Behaviourism had a profound influence on the course of psychology during the first half of the twentieth century.

- Behaviourists view human personality and behaviour as being shaped through learning and experience within the environment. They choose not to concern themselves with the possible influences of physiological processes within the person.

- A key figure in behaviourism was Skinner. His work on operant conditioning, using animals, focused on the stimuli that may produce particular responses and the rewards (reinforcement) and punishments that may influence and change behaviour. Skinner produced a theory of operant conditioning that could apply to humans as well as animals.

- Practical applications of the behaviourist approach include Skinner's development of programmed learning systems, which have been influential in the field of education; behavioural therapies, which have been widely used in clinical settings in order to help people to change unwanted behaviour; and biofeedback techniques, which have been used in medical contexts to help people control problems such as high blood pressure and heart rate.

- The behaviourist approach has contributed much to our understanding of human behaviour and ways in which it might be changed. Its use of rigorous empirical methods has enhanced the credibility of psychology as a science.

- Criticisms of the behaviourist approach centre upon its failure to address the role of consciousness and subjective experience and the probable role of biological factors in influencing behaviour. The validity of using animals in research has been questioned. Its theories cannot account for novel and creative behaviour, and the emphasis on environmental determinism leaves no room for the notion of free will in an individual.

- In contrast to the behaviourists, cognitive psychologists believe that the events occurring within a person (mediators) must be studied if behaviour is to be fully understood. Consequently they have addressed themselves to the study of processes such as perception, thinking, memory and language.

- The human mind is often compared to a computer, and this approach has become known as an information-processing approach.

- Because the processes studied by cognitive psychologists are not directly observable, methods of study have been developed based on the use of models. A model is a hypothetical example of how some aspect of the nervous system may work, which can then be rigorously tested through experimentation and sub-

sequently adapted or replaced by a new model. Examples of models that have been developed and tested are the Broadbent filter model of selective attention and the Atkinson–Shiffrin model of memory.

- Computer programs have been developed that have attempted to model human thought processes. This approach is known as computer simulation. An early and very significant computer simulation model was the General Problem Solver devised by Newell, Shaw and Simon.

- An area of cognitive psychology involves the study of intellectual development. The most significant theorist here was Jean Piaget.

- The cognitive approach has enhanced our understanding of processes such as perception, memory and thinking. There have been many practical applications of this work: for example, how to improve memory and problem-solving skills and the limitations of eyewitness testimony in court cases. The relatively new discipline of cognitive science is encouraging increasing collaboration between disciplines such as psychology, computer science, physiology and linguistics.

- The cognitive approach has been criticized for its lack of cohesion – no single theory links cognitive approaches into an identifiable framework. The limitations of computer simulation to explain human thinking have been stressed by some psychologists. The use of laboratory experiments, particularly in the study of memory, is said to be 'artificial' and not ecologically valid.

- Humanistic psychologists believe that psychology should be concerned with the subjective, conscious experience of the individual (phenomenology). They emphasize the uniqueness of human beings and their freedom to choose their own destiny. The use of the scientific method is seen as inappropriate for the study of human beings. A major aim should be to help people to achieve self-actualization.

- Two leading exponents of the humanistic approach are Carl Rogers and Abraham Maslow. Central to Rogers's theory is his belief in the importance of the self-concept. Each individual is seen as unique and having a basic need for unconditional positive regard. Rogers' client-centred therapy is used to help clients to gain insight into themselves and to solve their own problems with the help of a facilitator.

- Maslow was greatly concerned with the motives that drive people. He noted that motives tend to form a hierarchy; this became known as his hierarchy of needs. At the pinnacle of the hierarchy is the need for self-actualization.

- Another theorist whose basic assumptions fit within the humanistic approach is Victor Frankl, who developed a theoretical framework and therapy that he called logotherapy.

- The Recovery Movement, which originated with the formation of Alcoholics Anonymous in 1935, encompasses a number of approaches that share similar themes and assumptions as those to be found in humanistic psychology.

- The main value of the humanistic approach within psychology has been its focus on the subjective experience of the individual and the importance of self-esteem and meaning in psychological functioning. It has provided a valuable counterbalance to behaviourism and psychodynamic approaches.

- Criticisms centre on the use of loose terminology, which is not easily testable, and on its subjective methods of study, such as the use of the case study. Also, differences in concepts and emphasis between humanistic theories are not easy to assess.

- It is important to note that none of the five major approaches described contains the whole truth about psychological functioning. Therefore they should be seen as complementary to each other. Different levels of explanation should be adopted in order to understand human behaviour and experience.

- Psychologists work in a wide range of different fields. Some are concerned with pure research designed to help our understanding. Others work on applied research, which addresses itself to solving practical problems. There is much overlap between pure and applied research. Fields of study include cognitive, developmental, social, comparative and physiological psychology and the study of individual differences. Areas of professional activity within psychology include clinical, educational, occupational, counselling, forensic and health psychology.

Further reading

Schulz, D. (1987). *A History of Modern Psychology*, 4th edn. New York: Academic Press. This book gives a good, general survey of the history of psychology.

Richards, G. (1996). *Putting Psychology in its Place: An Introduction from a Critical Historical Perspective*. London: Routledge. This book explores the development of psychology with particular emphasis on how it has been affected by the historical contexts. It also includes useful sections on how changes in the discipline have shaped its approach to issues such as gender, 'race', war and the use of animals in psychology.

Glassman, W.E. (1995). *Approaches to Psychology*, 2nd edn. Buckingham: OU Press. A highly readable book, which offers the reader an understanding of what psychology is, how it works, and how it came to be that way. It covers the five major approaches, methods of study and perspectives on development, social behaviour and abnormal behaviour.

CHAPTER 2

Issues and debates in psychology

Reductionism   41

- Physiological reductionism   42
- Biological reductionism   43
- Experimental reductionism   43
- Machine reductionism   43
- Evaluation of reductionism   44
- Alternatives to reductionism   45

Free will and determinism   45

- Free will   46
- Determinism   47
- Soft determinism   48
- Free will and determinism in theory and practice   48
- Final thoughts on free will and determinism   50

The heredity–environment issue   51

- Empiricist view   51
- Nativist view   51
- Changes in the emphasis of the heredity–environment question   51
- What is meant by heredity and environment?   52
- Do we construct our own environment?   53
- The heredity–environment issue in perspective   55
- How do heredity and environment interact?   55
- Conclusions about heredity and environment   55

Objectives

By the end of this chapter, you should be able to:

- Define, describe and evaluate 'reductionism';

- Define 'determinism' and 'free will';

- Make an evaluation of free will and determinism and explain where psychoanalysis, behaviourism and humanistic psychology stand on this issue;

- Trace the development and make some evaluation of the questions of 'heredity' and 'environment' in psychology.

One of the reasons why modern psychology seems such a fragmented discipline is that the different approaches take up different positions on a number of key philosophical issues. This not only affects the basic view of the nature of human behaviour, but also dictates how research should be conducted and how the findings should be applied.

In this chapter, three of these issues will be addressed: reductionism, determinism and free will, and the heredity–environment issue. Among other issues, the mind–body problem has already been briefly considered in the last chapter, and a comparison of idiographic and nomothetic approaches to the study of human behaviour is addressed briefly in Chapter 4.

Reductionism

The basic idea of **reductionism** is that some complex phenomena can be explained by breaking them down

REDUCED TO MANAGEABLE PROPORTIONS, HE'S MUCH EASIER TO STUDY !

into separate, simpler parts. Reductionism claims that the chosen level of explanation is the only one needed to give a full account of behaviour. In psychology this has been done in four different ways (see Figure 2.1).

Physiological reductionism

Garnham (1991) proposes that one definition of reductionism is that it refers to the notion that psychological explanations can be replaced by explanations in terms of brain functioning or in terms of physics and chemistry.

Because human beings are biological organisms, **physiological reductionism** means that all actions, perceptions, thoughts, feelings, memories and disorders can be explained using neurophysiological concepts. The advantage is that all kinds of behaviour can be described in concrete and concise terms and so are susceptible to scientific methods of research. Thus it becomes possible to predict, understand and control

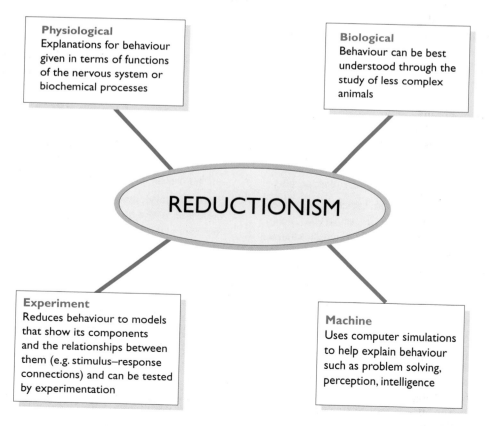

Physiological
Explanations for behaviour given in terms of functions of the nervous system or biochemical processes

Biological
Behaviour can be best understood through the study of less complex animals

REDUCTIONISM

Experiment
Reduces behaviour to models that show its components and the relationships between them (e.g. stimulus–response connections) and can be tested by experimentation

Machine
Uses computer simulations to help explain behaviour such as problem solving, perception, intelligence

Figure 2.1   Four different examples of reductionist explanations of behaviour

behaviour and therefore to fulfil the aims of psychological science.

Examples of physiological reductionism

Recent discoveries have shown a physiological basis for some mental disorders, such as depression and schizophrenia. This has increased the hope that such disorders may be eradicated by physiological or chemical treatments.

Memory loss, pain, addiction, delinquency and even the extent of sex-stereotyped behaviour in humans (Peele, 1981) have been claimed to have physical explanations. Thus there is a kind of 'hoped for' reductionism – that physical explanations will eventually be found for all behaviour. Few psychologists would subscribe to the view that this exclusively physiological reductionist approach is desirable.

Biological reductionism

Hebb (1974) advocated **biological reductionism**: human behaviour can best be understood through the study of less complex animals.

Examples of biological reductionism

Ethologists, such as Lorenz (1966), who put forward a theory of human aggression from his observations of different animal species, and sociobiologists subscribed to this kind of reductionism. Other examples include comparative studies of animals, which throw light on such diverse human behaviours as attachment, communication, territoriality, dominance, sexual behaviour, monogamy, learning and parenting.

A problem with biological reductionism is that it assumes an evolutionary continuity of behaviour between humans and animals. Not all psychologists accept this. This is further discussed in Chapter 5 and in the introductory section to Part 4 (animal behaviour).

Experimental reductionism

Experimental reductionism attempts to reduce behaviour to models showing its components and the relationships between them. For example, radical behaviourist reductionism explains all behaviour in terms of 'stimulus–response' connections.

Examples of experimental reductionism

Westland (1978) suggests that any research that looks at one aspect of behaviour rather than the whole person is reductionist. For example, measurement of personality or intelligence without reference to people's emotional or motivational states, their social or cultural background, or the test conditions, will not provide a complete explanation of behaviour.

Another example is provided by laboratory investigations into social phenomena such as conformity or obedience (see Chapter 28), which may not tell us much about the whole person's behaviour outside the experimental situation.

Experimental reductionism may make psychologists vulnerable to criticisms that all they do is pull habits out of rats, or that psychology is no more than the science of the young US white male undergraduate. Perhaps this is the price psychologists must pay for greater precision and scientific status of precisely defined terms and carefully controlled research strategies.

Machine reductionism

Machine reductionism uses computer simulations to help explain such phenomena as problem solving, perception and intelligence.

Example of machine reductionism

The computer is analogous to the brain, the program to the workings of the mind. There have been impressive simulations created, particularly in problem solving.

GLOSSARY

Reductionism A belief that all psychological phenomena can be explained by investigating them at a simpler, more basic, level.

Physiological reductionism Explanations of behaviour are given in terms of the functions of the nervous system or biochemical processes.

Biological reductionism Proposes that behaviour can be best understood through the study of less complex animals.

Experimental reductionism Reduces behaviour to models that show its components and the relationships between them (for example, stimulus–response connections) and can be tested by experimentation.

Machine reductionism Uses computer simulations to help explain behaviour such as problem solving, perception, intelligence.

Although machine reductionism can provide useful models of human cognitive functioning, there are limitations. For example, just because machines and humans produce similar outputs, this does not mean that they were arrived at in the same way.

The most difficult problem for machine reductionism is to reproduce the unique qualities that make human behaviour so unpredictable. Computer memories do not fade with time, computers do not become bored or tired, they do not think, they are not conscious and they do not exercise free will. In many ways machine analogies are probably better at telling us what humans are not like.

Evaluation of reductionism

Reductionism is more compatible with the idea of psychology as a science than other, higher-level explanations. This can mean higher status and greater respectability. Scientific method seeks explanations that are as economical as possible, and reductionism contributes to this. If scientific status is desirable, then psychologists must look for the simplest level of explanation that gives a full account of human behaviour without losing vital material.

However, Putnam (1973) said, 'psychology is as undetermined by biology as it is by elementary particle physics . . . people's psychology is partly a reflection of deeply entrenched societal beliefs' (p. 141). This reflects the view held by many other psychologists.

Legge (1975) explained reductionism by using the example of signing one's name. The psychological description of this would be 'He signed his name'. However, the activity could be described at a lower level in terms of the muscular contractions involved. An even more specific description could be that of the brain activity that initiated the muscular contractions. An even smaller 'unit of analysis' might be that of the chemical changes involved in the brain. Legge argued that such a reductionist approach may not, by itself, be helpful or meaningful, for two reasons:

■ As the units analysed become smaller and more specific the resulting descriptions become more lengthy, complex and difficult to handle meaningfully.
■ A name may be signed with many different writing instruments and materials, from the use of a marker pen on a whiteboard to that of a ballpoint pen on a cheque. Whilst an individual's signature would retain many of its distinctive characteristics in each case, the pattern of muscle movements involved would vary and the resulting descriptions of the physiological mechanisms involved would be different.

Legge concluded that the distinguishing features of a signature arise from a pattern that is independent of the physiological mechanisms involved. Therefore a psychological account of the activity may be preferable to a longer, more complex physiological one.

Cohen (1977) argued that to seek single causal explanations for human behaviour is hopeless. Behaviour is too variable and determined by too many factors. Sometimes lower-level explanations are helpful; sometimes more than one level will be necessary. Using the example of memory she says that, when people make errors of recall, it is not very helpful to explain this by saying 'they did it because they forgot'. It is more useful to talk in reductionist terms about decay of memory traces. On the subject of mental disorders, however, physiological explanations alone may be insufficient, and it may be necessary to draw on social and cultural factors as well.

Peele (1981) also questioned the wisdom of moving away from psychoanalytic, humanistic and non-physiological explanations towards physiological reductionism, even though it offers 'compact causal explanations' and 'holds out the promise of clear-cut remedies that would otherwise seem painfully beyond solution'. He illustrated this by using examples of addiction and mental illness:

■ Addiction has been explained in physiological terms such as a genetic predisposition or lack of naturally occurring pain-relieving chemicals called 'endorphins'. In an experiment on morphine dependency in rats, Alexander et al. (1978) kept one group of rats in isolated and cramped conditions, and another in pleasant, roomy conditions in the company of other rats. In both groups the only liquid available for drinking was morphine solution. This continued until the rats were habituated to the morphine; then, in a series of test trials, they were given a choice between water and the original solution. Isolated rats drank significantly more morphine solution than the social rats. This demonstrated that the process of dependency is strongly influenced by social and environmental factors, not just physiological ones.

■ Another example is what is called learned helplessness (Seligman, 1974). It is based upon animal experiments which showed that, when rats are faced with inescapable, uncontrollable, noxious stimuli, such as electric shocks, they learn to be passive in the face of them and react by withdrawing. Similarly people who learn that they can do nothing to influence what happens to them develop helplessness and apathy and eventually become depressed. Although this can happen to both men and women, women are more at risk because of their status in society and their lack of power relative to men. Women come to depend on others for their feelings of self-worth so that they tend to blame themselves when things go wrong or when the social reinforcement they need is not forthcoming. They thus become more vulnerable to loneliness and depression.

■ This social psychological explanation of depression does not point to treatment by physiological means, yet drug therapy persists, as does the search for physiological explanations.

Alternatives to reductionism

Autonomism

Autonomism is reflected in the work of Freud and of humanistic psychologists. It suggests that same-level explanations of behaviour are desirable and lower-level ones are not. Humanistic therapy, for example, focuses on experience, emotion and choice and an understanding of the world as the client sees it. Unfortunately this overlooks biological and physiological aspects of the person and so is, possibly, incomplete.

The 'slice of life' school

In the 'slice of life' school the idea is to study behaviour in large, complete segments to obtain as complete a picture as possible. This means a move away from experiment towards descriptive and observational methods. There is a loss of control, but a gain in realism. The problems are: what slice of life do you select? How complete can the records of behaviour be? Should you include a person's personal and cultural history? This approach is rich but very complex. It is hard to decide which of the variables observed determine behaviour and which do not.

Interactionism

The interactionism approach could incorporate biological, mechanical and social aspects of behaviour. It could include observation as well as experiment and also computer simulation. In short, all the approaches so far described would be drawn together to complement each other. There is the possibility that by this means a complete account of human behaviour could one day be produced.

In contrast with this, Rose (1976) proposed a hierarchical model of explanations of behaviour ranging from holistic assumptions of people such as sociologists to the physical explanations of physics. Psychology is placed between these extremes. Rose argued that the debate about holistic versus reductionist explanations is unimportant as each level on the hierarchy uses terminology and methods suited to itself. To use one level to help explain another is, he suggested, a fruitless exercise.

? SELF-ASSESSMENT QUESTIONS

1. Give a general definition of the term 'reductionism'.
2. Name four kinds of reductionism and provide examples of each.
3. What objections have psychologists raised to reductionism?
4. Describe three alternatives to reductionism.

Free will and determinism

The determinism–free will issue is one of the oldest philosophical issues in the study of human behaviour,

---

GLOSSARY

Autonomism A notion that same-level explanations are preferable to lower-level ones. For example, humanistic psychologists tend to focus on a person's perceptions but ignore possible biological and physiological influences.

'Slice of life' school An approach that encourages the study of large sections of behaviour in order to obtain a more complete understanding.

Interactionism As an alternative to reductionism, the study of behaviour by considering a range of different perspectives and methods of study.

and one of the most pervasive. It is an important consideration in other areas such as the mind–body issue, the nature–nurture and the idiographic–nomothetic debates, and the question of the suitability of the scientific method in psychology.

The core of the determinism–free will issue is whether human behaviour results from forces over which an individual has no control or whether it is the result of free choice. This section will examine in more detail what is meant by determinism and free will and then relate them to three major forces in psychology: psychoanalysis, behaviourism and humanistic psychology. In each case, both theoretical and practical implications will be discussed.

Free will

A major difficulty lies in defining exactly what we mean by **free will**. The term has been associated with the writings of Plato, Kant and Descartes. Descartes in particular has argued that humans are unique among living things because they have a soul. This allows them to plan and make free choices. Psychological approaches that lean most towards free will are existentialism and the more familiar branch of humanistic psychology.

Valentine (1992) discusses a number of different interpretations of the concept of free will. Some of these interpretations are outlined below:

- **Choice**. A lay person may suppose that free will exists if the actor in a particular situation had a real choice and could have acted differently. However, Valentine argues that this proposition is untestable and could never be shown to be true even if the same circumstances could be repeated.
- **Behaviour that is uncaused**. Free will might logically be defined as the opposite of determinism, but this is not what psychologists mean by the term. It would mean that behaviour is uncaused, capricious and random. Experience does not support the view that behaviour is unpredictable. It is possible to discern behaviour patterns that, to some extent, do seem predictable. This position is in line with the idea of **soft determinism** – a term coined by William James (1890).
- **Voluntary behaviour**. A distinction has been made between voluntary and involuntary behaviour. The former suggests that we have some control,

the latter the opposite. For example, coughing to attract someone's attention is not the same as that which results from a tickle in the throat.

Perceptions and feelings of freedom

Westcott (1982) attempted to subject interpretations of freedom to empirical investigation. He asked Canadian undergraduates to rate how free they *thought* they were and how free they *felt* in different situations. Some of their key findings were as follows:

- Absence of responsibilities, existence of alternatives and opportunities for active decision making were rated significantly more highly on being free than on feeling free.
- Release from noxious stimulation (for example, awareness that a persistent headache had gone) and the performance of a physical skill were rated significantly higher on feeling free than on being free.
- Feeling free seemed to be related to situations where individuals perceived themselves as free and *liked* the situation.
- The most frequent examples of situations where individuals did not feel free were those involving outside constraints, unpleasant feelings and conflict and indecision.

Arguments for free will

- Valentine suggests that the main argument for the existence of free will lies in the idea of moral responsibility. If we accept that people are responsible, at least some of the time, for their own moral actions, we cannot deny the existence of free will. Koestler (1970) said that whatever one's philosophical stance on the issue of free will and determinism, in everyday life it is impossible not to accept the notion of personal responsibility – and responsibility implies freedom of choice.

GLOSSARY

Free will An ability to exercise control over one's behaviour and to make choices.

Soft determinism A term used by William James to describe a compromise between free will and determinism. Behaviour is determined by the environment, but there is an element of freedom where people's actions are in line with their wishes.

■ An important factor that cannot be dismissed when considering free will is based in subjective impressions – people *feel* they have freedom of choice over their lives. However, Valentine (1992) argues that subjective impressions are notoriously unreliable and do not guarantee truth, however firmly they may be held.

Arguments against free will

■ A major problem faced when trying to justify the existence of free will lies in the difficulty of formulating an adequate definition of what we mean by it. As we have seen above, there are a number of different definitions, and this makes it difficult to give a coherent account of the concept.

■ A second drawback is that if we take an extreme stance on the notion of free will, it is difficult to justify the scientific approach to the study of behaviour. The scientific approach makes the assumption that events in the world are not random but ordered and thus determined (see Chapter 3). Also, the more that is learned about factors that determine behaviour, the less likely it is that humans have total freedom over their actions.

Determinism

Determinism follows loosely from the work of the philosophers Locke, Berkeley and Hume, who believed that human behaviour is the result of forces over which one has no control. This applies to factors both within and outside the person.

Internal causes (biological determinism) include a biological need state (for example, hunger or thirst), instinctive energy or genetic endowment. Classical psychoanalysis is an example of biological determinism. **Sociobiology**, which explains all individual and social behaviour in terms of the selection of genes in evolution, represents an extreme form of biological determinism. (For a discussion of sociobiology, see the introduction to Part 4.) External causes (environmental determinism) may include learning experiences or stimuli in the environment. An example might be radical behaviourism. All behaviour thus has a cause and cannot have happened any other way.

Points arising from this approach include the following:

■ The approach is compatible with scientific method, and is one of the central assumptions of this method. Determinists assume that human behaviour is orderly and obeys laws, and so is explainable and predictable. A person's current behaviour is the result of what went before and the cause of what is to come. When you know a person's history and current situation you can predict what that individual will do next.

■ If you can predict behaviour you can also control it. Knowing a person's history and current state, it is necessary only to arrange circumstances to obtain the desired reaction. (Skinner described a Utopian society created along these lines in *Walden Two*, 1948.)

■ If behaviour is determined by events outside one's control then the idea of responsibility vanishes. Neither criminal nor benevolent acts are the result of free choice, so that notions of praise and blame are worthless. To punish or reward people for certain behaviour may therefore be a pointless exercise. This has important implications for the penal system. An environmental determinist might see criminals as victims of circumstances beyond their control: it is not the criminal that needs changing but the environment. Imprisonment and various other forms of punishment might be seen to be appropriate as providing new learning experiences aimed at producing more socially desirable behaviour. If one believes in free will, punishment becomes retribution, because the criminal act is the result of free choice.

Arguments for determinism

■ The scientific approach is based upon determinism (see Chapter 3).

■ Science is a successful route to knowledge.

■ Therefore determinism seems to make sense – it has face validity.

GLOSSARY

Determinism A belief that human behaviour is caused by forces, internal or external, over which one has no control.

Sociobiology A term coined by Edward Wilson to refer to attempts to explain social behaviour in terms of evolutionary factors.

Arguments against determinism

- The assumption that one can ever arrive at a complete description of the current state of a person is probably not justified. To do this takes time, during which the individual has moved on.
- It is a false assumption that accurate predictions are possible. Even physicists have to build 'uncertainty factors' into their laws. If physicists have this problem, where does that leave psychologists with their notoriously unpredictable subject matter of human behaviour? They may argue in their defence that it is not the inherent nature of the subject matter but their own lack of skill in making precise measurements that makes it difficult for them to make accurate predictions.
- Determinism is unfalsifiable. If determinists cannot find a cause for human behaviour they assume, not that a cause does not exist, but that they have not been able to discover one yet. For example, an advocate of free will (FW) might challenge a determinist (D) to predict what FW will do next. FW can prove D wrong by choosing not to do as D predicts. But this does not invalidate D's position because D's prediction has added another variable. FW has behaved in a different way from the way he or she would have done had he or she been ignorant of D's prediction.

Soft determinism

This view holds that behaviour is determined by the environment, but only to a certain extent. While a person can choose between a number of courses of action, there is only free will if there is no coercion or compulsion. Where there is consistency between a person's wishes and actions, there is an element of free will. A hard-line determinist would argue that there is no element of choice: all behaviour is caused by events outside one's personal control.

A soft determinist approach sees the problem as one of freedom versus coercion; a hard determinist approach sees the problem as one of freedom versus causation.

Free will and determinism in theory and practice

Psychoanalysis

In classical psychoanalysis the cause of behaviour is located within the individual. Behaviour is driven by powerful instinctual forces of which the individual is largely unaware. These forces are largely sexual and aggressive. The behaviour that results may be either constructive and self-preserving or destructive or even self-destructive. Behaviour originates from within, but the individual has little free choice about how to

---

Box 2.1   The free will versus determinism issue

Does human behaviour result from forces over which one has no control (determinism)?

Or do people have freedom of choice over their actions (free will)?

A solution might involve considering the stance of 'soft determinism': behaviour is determined by events in the environment, but where a person's actions are consistent with their wishes, some degree of free will exists.

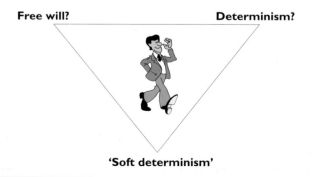

Free will?   **Determinism?**

'Soft determinism'

behave. Determinism holds that no behaviour is without a cause; psychoanalytic explanations therefore score highly.

One of the attractions of Freudian theory is that it can deal with aspects of behaviour and experience that other approaches find it hard to explain – dreams, slips of the tongue, sense of humour and the wide appeal of great works of art are examples. Accidents also may sometimes be explained by arguing that they are unconsciously motivated. If you fall off your bicycle on your way to take your psychology exam and sprain your wrists there may be said to be an unconscious connection! Freudian theory can explain the development of personality, sex role, morality and various mental disorders.

The determinist approach also has implications for psychoanalytic therapy. Every detail that the analysand is urged to divulge (thoughts, dreams, wishes: seemingly disconnected, meaningless trivial or inoffensive details) is seen as a possible window on the unconscious mind, which determines behaviour. The impression of freedom in the psychoanalytic situation is an illusion.

More recently ego psychologists, such as Karen Horney, Anna Freud and Erik Erikson, have challenged this extreme determinist view. They see the goal of analysis as 'ego strengthening'. This puts individuals more in command of their fate by making them more able to deal with the demands of reality. Horney even suggested self-analysis.

(See the introduction to Part 1 for an account of the psychoanalytic approach.)

Behaviourism

Radical behaviourism is an example of environmental determinism. It is theoretically possible to predict and control behaviour by means of a full knowledge of a person's genetic limitations, past experiences and current situation. All behaviour is rational (it obeys laws) and people are therefore fundamentally alike.

Skinner (1971) rejects free will as an illusion. Only by recognizing that behaviour is environmentally determined is it possible to harness the environment to create and maintain socially acceptable behaviour. In our society poorly defined, inconsistent and uncontrolled reinforcement contingencies give an illusion of freedom. We need to recognize that behaviour is already controlled; the control needs to become more systematic if Western societies are not to head for self-destruction. Freedom does not mean self-determination but freedom from aversive control. Skinner believed this can be achieved through the careful use of positive reinforcement, with minimal use of negative reinforcement and punishment.

Some critics of the behaviourist view argue that determinism and free will can be seen in the processes of learning known as classical and operant conditioning. In the former the organism is passive. The conditional stimulus produces an automatic conditional response in a machine-like manner. Clearly such behaviour is determined. In operant conditioning the organism could be seen as having free choice over which response to make. (Pavlov's dogs had no choice but to salivate to the sound of a bell but a rat in a Skinner box can choose whether or not to press a lever.) Skinner rejects this distinction, arguing that operant behaviour is determined by a history of reinforcement which affects the probability with which responses will occur. Some responses to a stimulus will have been reinforced more often than others and so are more likely to recur.

Behaviourism can also explain seemingly altruistic behaviour in animals (see Chapter 18). If conditioning determined behaviour, organisms would act only in their own interests and not be altruistic. Wertheimer (1972) gives the example of pigeons playing ping pong. A hungry pigeon can be trained by behaviour-shaping techniques to peck a ping pong ball off the opposite side of a miniature ping pong table for the reinforcement of a few seconds' access to some seed. The bird, once trained, can be placed opposite an equally well-trained partner. The pigeons peck the ball to and fro until one fails to return it. Then a few seconds elapse in which the winner can feed. Then the game begins afresh. The birds become more skilled, the rallies lengthen and the opportunities for feeding diminish. At this point the birds are likely to allow the ball to fall off the table, thus allowing the other to feed. This seems to be cooperative, insightful, unselfish and therefore free behaviour. Skinner, however, argues that this is not the case. Relatively more frequent reinforcement results from allowing one's partner to win. Sharing pays better than selfishness.

Environmental determinism and behavioural therapies Therapies influenced by the environmental determinism of radical behaviourism include:

■ Systematic desensitization for the treatment of phobias;

- Modification of problem behaviour in children;
- Treatment of self-injurious behaviour through aversion therapy;
- Development of self-care in the mentally ill by the use of token economies;
- Cognitive behaviour therapy, such as Ellis's rational emotive therapy.

The stereotyped picture of the behaviour therapist is of one who controls a passive client, but many modern behaviour therapies encourage the active participation of the client, aiming to teach self-control and coping. One example is systematic desensitization for phobic behaviour. Clients develop their own hierarchy of feared situations and learn to face these with the support (not the control) of the therapist. They might also arrange their own reinforcements for positive behaviour.

Biofeedback is another example of therapy where the client is in control. A physiological measure such as pulse rate or galvanic skin response (GSR) is taken, amplified and continuously fed back to the person visually or audibly. Clients learn to control their own physiological responses. Reinforcement is the knowledge of progress made. This is useful in the treatment of headaches and nervous tension, for example. (See Chapter 1 for an account of the behaviourist approach.)

Humanistic psychology

This is often said to be the nearest one can get to free will in psychology. Humanistic psychologists have a problem with scientific method because it is based on the assumption of determinism and reductionism. Humanistic psychologists advocate study of the whole person and are especially critical of experimental method in psychology and of the behaviourist tradition of studying animal behaviour and then extrapolating this to humans. They view humans as unique, and reject a method that removes freedom and dignity from experimental participants: if we can view animals in experiments as objects, how long will it be before we start to see humans in the same way?

Rogers's client-centred therapy reflects the view that we are in charge of our own lives and responsible for our own personal growth. Both client and facilitator are free agents. If clients choose to allow their lives to be determined by forces outside themselves they are still,

paradoxically, acting freely. (See Chapter 1 for an account of the ideas of humanistic psychologists.)

Final thoughts on free will and determinism

The free will side of the argument needs to see a person as actively responding to forces rather than being passive in the face of them. The cause of behaviour is likely to be located within the individual. Concepts such as cognition, reason and judgment would be used when a person decides how to deal with an environmental or physiological demand.

Soft determinism seems to have more face validity than either hard-line determinism or pure free will. In a society that advocates personal responsibility, hard-line determinism is unacceptable and free will is difficult to define satisfactorily. If there is inconsistency between a person's desires and actions, a sense of freedom can still be achieved by changing one's desires or one's actions so that they are in line with each other.

The argument in psychology is likely to be between soft and hard determinism rather than between free will and determinism. Unless some aspects of behaviour are determined, the scientific approach cannot be justified:

> The scientist can ignore the free will/determinism question if he wishes, with the proviso that there is one extreme position – that of complete indeterminacy – which he cannot hold since it is inconsistent with his activities. No regularities, no science. The scientific view of man must therefore hold that man's behaviour is, at least to some extent, lawful and predictable. (Wertheimer, 1972, p. 31)

Free will and determinism are not mutually exclusive. While humanistic psychologists lean towards free will, but still accept that there are constraints on behaviour, determinists accept the existence of 'uncertainty' factors. It is possible to take an entirely environmental approach and see behaviour as externally controlled or else to argue that control comes from within the individual, exercised by internal biological forces (hence nature–nurture debates). If we see free will and determinism as extremes on a continuum, then the question to be asked is not whether behaviour is free or determined, but where on the continuum it lies.

❓ SELF-ASSESSMENT QUESTIONS

1. Distinguish between free will, determinism and soft determinism.
2. Explain where psychoanalysis, behaviourism and humanistic psychology stand on the free will–determinism issue and show how this is reflected in their therapeutic approaches.

The heredity–environment issue

The heredity–environment issue (often referred to as the nature-nurture debate) in psychology concerns the role of **genes** and environment in determining behaviour. Historically, the heredity or nature side of the controversy is associated with the nativists, who argued that behaviour is (for the most part) determined by innate or inherited factors. Environmentalists, or empiricists, were associated with the environment or nurture side. They argued that behaviour is mainly determined by experience.

Empiricist view

The empiricist position was that the baby's mind at birth is like a blank state (*tabula rasa*) on which experience will write. Behaviour that is acquired as the baby grows is the result of experiences, especially learning. Therefore changes in the environment produce changes in the individual. Within their physical limitations, anyone can become anything, provided the environment is right.

Nativist view

The nativist position was that individuals are born with an inherited 'blueprint'. Behaviours that are not already present at birth will develop as though they were on a genetic time-switch: that is, through the process of maturation. The environment has little to do with individual development, and there is little anyone can do to change what nature has provided.

It follows from these two views that learned behaviours are within our control; innate ones are not, unless they are modified through genetic engineering. The question of what psychologists might be able to control and what is beyond their control occurs in many areas of research. Examples include the origin of language, personality, mental illness, aggression, gender differences and intelligence. However, it is the purpose of this section to deal with the general problem of heredity and environment rather than with specific issues. The reader may be familiar with research in some of these areas and should consider its validity in the light of what is to come.

Changes in the emphasis of the heredity–environment question

The heredity–environment debate is older than psychology itself and is still as vigorous as ever. Its emphasis has altered over the years. These changes were discussed in a classic paper by Anne Anastasi (1958) and can be summarized as follows.

Which one?

At its most extreme, the nature–nurture debate asked which of the two, heredity or environment, was responsible for behaviour. Anastasi argued that to ask the question in an 'either/or' form was illogical. One could not exist without the other. Both heredity and environment are absolutely necessary for the person to exist; therefore both must exert an influence on the person.

How much?

If it is accepted that both nature and nurture play a part in determining behaviour, how much is contributed by each? Thus the either/or question is replaced by an assumption that the two forces operate in an additive, but still separate, way: $X + Y =$ behaviour. In Anastasi's opinion, such an attitude is as illogical as its predecessor. Even if we consider that, say, 80 per cent of intelligence is due to nature and 20 per cent to nurture, that 80 per cent still has to exert its influence in an environment and the 20 per cent can only be expressed through the organism. To ask 'how much?' is simply to ask 'which one?' in a slightly more complicated way. It is still illogical.

GLOSSARY

Gene The carrier of heredity factors, situated on the chromosomes and represented as a DNA sequence.

In what way?

If neither of the previous two questions is useful, the obvious answer is to consider that genetics and environment interact. The argument is as follows:

■ Genetics and environment exert an influence on each other such that X × Y = behaviour. A useful analogy is the area of a rectangle. The rectangle cannot exist unless both length and width are present, yet its area is altered by changes in either of them. Similarly behaviour is determined by both heredity and environment.

■ Different environments acting on the same genetic pattern would result in different behaviours. Similarly the same environment would produce different behaviours from individuals who were genetically different.

■ Genes never determine behaviour directly; they do so only via the environment. Likewise the environment does not affect behaviour directly but only via the genetic make-up of the individual.

■ It is thus much more logical to accept that nature and nurture interact. This raises the inevitable question, 'In what way do they interact?' How do changes in one affect the influence of the other? This is the question that now occupies psychologists.

What is meant by heredity and environment?

Defining heredity and environment is not as simple as it appears. Lerner (1986) offers a solution by suggesting that we should think of environment as having different levels (these ideas he borrowed from Riegel, 1976). Anastasi elaborated her ideas further by suggesting that the influence of heredity and environment can vary from very powerful to relatively weak. The ideas of Lerner and Anastasi are summarized in Figure 2.2 and Box 2.2, respectively.

Figure 2.2 Levels of the environment: pressures from the environment exerted on the developing child prenatally and postnatally (Lerner, 1986)

Box 2.2 Heredity and environment: the views of Anastasi (1958)

The continuum of heredity

Heredity's influence on the individual operates via the environment along a continuum of 'indirectness'. At one extreme of the continuum influences are 'least indirect' while at the other end they are 'most indirect'.

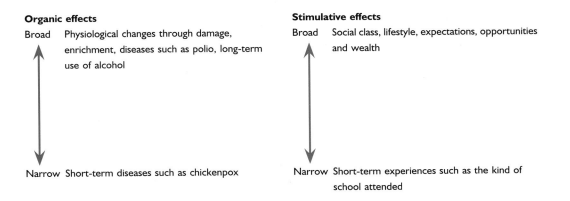

Least indirect			Most indirect
1 Resistant to change E.g. Genetic conditions that cannot be treated such as Down's Syndrome	2 Can be modified by the environment E.g. Hereditary defects such as deafness, which can be modified by training	3 Inherited susceptibility E.g. Predispositions to develop conditions such as schizophrenia or heart disease will appear only if environmental conditions are suitable	4 Social influence E.g. Social stereotypes may lead to the child's meeting particular expectations. For instance, females may not develop mathematical or technical skills

The continuum of the environment

The environment can exert different degrees of influence on the behaviour of individuals. The effects are of two different types: organic effects and stimulative effects. Each of these lies on a continuum between broad, general effects and narrow effects.

Organic effects

Broad   Physiological changes through damage, enrichment, diseases such as polio, long-term use of alcohol

Narrow   Short-term diseases such as chickenpox

Stimulative effects

Broad   Social class, lifestyle, expectations, opportunities and wealth

Narrow   Short-term experiences such as the kind of school attended

Do we construct our own environment?

An alternative view of the nature of the environment is **constructionism**, which goes against what is proposed in mainstream developmental psychology, and suggests that people may construct or contribute to their own environments (Scarr, 1992). Scarr proposes that children construct reality from the opportunities that exist in their environment, and this constructed reality has a considerable influence on variations among children and individual differences between adults.

One way of considering how individuals may influence their own environments is to think about how certain behavioural or psychological character- istics may elicit particular responses from other people.

Eliciting responses

An individual's behaviour or biological characteristics may call forth particular responses from other people. This can be illustrated in a number of ways:

■ **Temperament**. Babies vary in a number of temperamental characteristics: for example how active they are, how responsive to others, how easily upset. Some theorists have proposed that it is these characteristics in infants that influence the nature of their relationships with parents and other people. For instance, Belsky and Rovine (1987) have suggested that children with different temperamental characteristics present differing challenges to their caregivers and these in part determine those caregivers' responses to them. Happy, easy-going babies are more likely to elicit positive responses than are more 'difficult', discontented children.

■ **Gender**. It is well documented that people tend to react differently to boys and girls on the basis of their, often stereotyped, expectations of masculine and feminine characteristics. To quote just one example, in a study by Rubin et al. (1974) parents were asked to describe their new-born babies. Even though boys and girls were very similar in health and in size and weight, boys were generally depicted as more alert, stronger and better

An agressive child may provoke hostile responses in others

coordinated than girls. Girls were described as smaller, softer and less attentive than boys.

■ **Aggression**. Rutter and Rutter (1993) describe how aggressive children think and behave in ways that lead other children to respond to them in a hostile manner. This in turn reinforces the antisocial child's view of the world as negative and hostile, and a self-perpetuating spiral of antisocial behaviour follows. Thus, aggressive children tend to experience aggressive environments partly because they elicit aggressive responses in others.

(See Gross, 1995, for a discussion of other ways in which individuals may influence their own environments.)

The heredity–environment issue in perspective

The writings of Lerner and Anastasi cited above show just how complex the heredity–environment issue has become. To add to this complexity, Lerner points out that, potentially, there are an infinite number of different environments. In addition it is estimated that there are over 70 trillion potential **genotypes** (genetic types). (Even identical twins who share the same genotype have different environments from the start, since they occupy different points on the placenta.) Further to this, recent genetic research seems to suggest that genetic endowment does not place fixed limits on an individual and that even some genetic characteristics are flexible. Given that this infinite number of environments will interact with the enormous number of potential (and possibly flexible) genotypes to produce behaviour, it might be tempting to give up research into such a vast problem at this point. However, it is still possible to go on to consider the second question in the nature–nurture debate: 'How do heredity and environment interact?'

How do heredity and environment interact?

In trying to answer this question, Anastasi and others have used the concept of **norm of reaction**. Rather than seeing the genotype as a kind of blueprint for development, Anastasi prefers to think of it as something that sets upper and lower limits. There are a number of potential outcomes for individuals

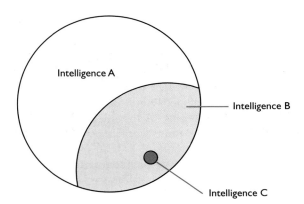

Figure 2.3 The Hebb/Vernon model of intelligence

within the range of their genetic limitations, and this is the 'norm of reaction'. Which one eventually develops will depend on the interaction of their genes with a particular environment.

A famous example provided by Hebb (1949) on intelligence illustrates the norm of reaction idea. The genetic upper and lower limit to intelligence makes up Intelligence A. Intelligence A interacts with the environment so that some or all of it is realized. This is known as Intelligence B. However, the usefulness of 'norm of reaction' is limited. For example, there is no way of measuring Intelligence A or B. Intelligence tests are not the answer as they can assess only a portion of Intelligence B. This portion is known as Intelligence C – see Figure 2.3 (Vernon, 1969). Also, they may attempt to draw on parts of Intelligence A that have not yet developed. However, in many aspects of behaviour, including intelligence, there is often no way of assessing what potential could be expected even when the genotype (which could be flexible) is known. It has to be accepted, therefore, that in most cases the norm of reaction, as an explanation of heredity–environment interaction, is limited.

Conclusions about heredity and environment

In conclusion a number of points may be made:

GLOSSARY

Genotype All the inherited characteristics present in an individual's chromosomes.

'Norm of reaction' The upper and lower limits of genetic potential within which an individual will develop.

1. Given the potential variability in genotypes, coupled with the infinite variations in environment, the inevitable conclusion is that no two individuals (even identical twins) are alike.

2. It follows from (1) that it is nonsense to look for general laws of behaviour that are couched in environmental terms (as in radical behaviourism, for example). Instead it would make more sense to look for individual laws that can explain a person's unique developmental pattern. Nativists must at least accept the influence of the 'norm of reaction' and even, perhaps, the idea of flexible genotypes. An added dimension comes from the constructionist view that individuals do not simply respond passively to their environments. They actively play a part in creating and shaping their own experiences.

3. An item of animal research will serve to illustrate the complexity of the current state of affairs. Various strains of pregnant mice were subjected to a variety of environmental stressors, such as swim tanks, noise and so on. Their offspring were then compared with the offspring of controls. The experiences of the mother while pregnant had different effects on the behaviour of the offspring but these effects varied according to both the genotype of the mother and that of the offspring. Here the mother's genotype interacted with her environment and that influenced the prenatal environment of the offspring, which interacted with its genotype to produce the final behaviour (De Fries, 1964).

4. If the insights from De Fries's study were thought of in human terms, individuals' behaviour is also likely to be influenced prenatally. They will also experience different social, cultural, domestic and scholastic environments. How does this affect something like educational policy? According to the norm of reaction argument, each person needs individual attention in a uniquely tailored environment. However, in practice, it is more usual to adopt the view that everyone deserves the best, no one should have more advantage than another, and what is best for one is best for all. Passionate arguments develop about selection and streaming in education and about which school a child should attend. It should be borne in mind that a so-called 'better' environment is not ideal for everyone. This is, of course, just one narrow application of the nature–nurture question. The reader will doubtless think of many others.

5. Recent developments in genetics now suggest that the idea of a 'norm of reaction' must be modified and that genetic endowment is more flexible than was previously thought. Rigid upper and lower limits to development may not exist.

❓ SELF-ASSESSMENT QUESTIONS

1. Identify three stages in the development of the heredity–environment debate.

2. Summarize the ideas of Lerner (1986) and Anastasi (1958) in relation to the meaning of heredity and environment.

3. Explain some ways in which people might construct or contribute to their own environments.

4. How do heredity and environment interact?

Chapter summary

■ Key philosophical issues, such as the problem of reductionism, free will versus determinism and heredity versus environment, promote much debate in psychology.

■ A reductionist approach is one that suggests that complex phenomena can be explained by breaking them down and studying their separate simpler parts.

■ Physiological reductionism implies that psychological phenomena such as memory loss, pain, addiction, deliquency and mental disorder can be explained in terms of brain functioning or other neurophysiological functions. Biological reductionism suggests that human behaviour can best be understood through the study of less complex animals. Experimental reductionism, typified by the behaviourist approach, attempts to study the component parts of behaviour through experimentation. Machine reductionism uses computer simulations to help explain phenomena such as problem solving and intelligence.

■ Reductionism ties in well with the idea of psychology as a science and is compatible with the scientific method. Critics argue that reducing psychological phenomena to smaller units of analysis may cause psychologists to lose sight of the 'whole person' and fail to discover distinguishing features that are independent of the separate mechanisms involved.

■ An alternative approach to that of reductionism is autonomism, which is reflected in the work of Freud and of humanistic psychologists. It suggests that same-level explanations of behaviour, such as the study of a person's unique experience, are desirable, whereas lower-level explanations are not.

■ The 'slice of life' school suggests that behaviour should be studied in large, complete segments to obtain as complete a picture as possible, using descriptive and observational methods.

■ An interactionist approach would incorporate the study of biological, mechanical and social aspects of behaviour, and would combine methods such as experimentation, observation and computer simulation. This could lead to a more complete account of human behaviour.

■ In contrast, Rose (1976) has proposed a hierarchical model of explanations of behaviour ranging from holistic assumptions to physiological explanations. To use one level to explain another, he suggests, is a fruitless exercise.

■ The core of the determinism–free will issue is whether human behaviour results from forces over which an individual has no control or whether it is the result of free choice.

■ There is a difficulty in defining exactly what we mean by free will. Some may see free will as existing if an individual has real choice in a situation and could have acted differently. Others may define free will as the opposite of determinism, implying that behaviour is random and uncaused.

■ Valentine (1992) argues that free will exists where people are responsible for their own moral actions and where they feel they have freedom of choice over their lives.

■ Within psychology, the humanistic approach is said to be the nearest one can get to free will since humanistic psychologists view human beings as unique and in control of their own destiny.

■ A distinction can be made between biological

determinism, which is exemplified in psychoanalytic theory and sociobiology, and environmental determinism as was upheld in radical behaviourism.

■ Arguments in favour of determinism emphasize that the scientific approach, a successful route to knowledge, is based on determinism. Arguments against stress that there are too many 'uncertainty factors' for us to be able accurately to predict human behaviour.

■ Soft determinismm provides a compromise view in that it holds that behaviour is determined by the environment but only to a certain extent, since freedom of choice exists only where there is no coercion or compulsion. The argument in psychology is likely to be between soft and hard determinisms rather than between free will and determinism.

■ Free will and determinism are not mutually exclusive. They should be seen as extremes on a continuum. The question then to be asked is not whether behaviour is free or determined, but where on the continuum it lies.

■ The heredity–environment issue concerns the role of genes and environment in determining behaviour. Nativists argue that behaviour is mainly determined by inherited factors, while empiricists argue that behaviour is largely determined by experience.

■ Anastasi (1958) argued that it was fruitless to pose the question of which of the two, heredity or environment, is responsible for behaviour since one could not exist without the other, therefore both must exert an influence on the person. Nor is it logical to consider the relative contributions of each.

■ A logical proposition is to consider that genetics and environment interact with each other. This raises the question 'In what way?'. This is the question that now occupies psychologists.

■ The complexity of the debate is emphasized by Lerner (1986), who believes that a solution lies in thinking of environment as having different levels. Anastasi proposed that the influence of both heredity and environment can vary from very powerful to relatively weak.

■ One view is that people may construct or contribute to their own environments. For example, an individual's characteristics (which may be innate) such as temperament, gender or level of aggression, may elicit particular responses from other people, which may in turn influence the individual's behaviour.

■ Anastasi and others have proposed the concept of 'norm of reaction' to explain how heredity and environment may interact. An individual's genes are seen as imposing upper and lower limits for their potential behaviour. Where, within these limits, an individual's behaviour falls may be determined by the environment. However, recent developments in genetics now suggest that genetic endowment is more flexible than was previously thought. Rigid upper and lower limits to development may not exist.

Further reading

Gross, R. (1995). *Themes, Issues and Debates in Psychology*. London: Hodder and Stoughton.

Chapter 23 gives an interesting and readable account of idiographic and nomothetic approaches; Chapter 5 considers heredity and environment and Chapter 12 the issue of free will and determinism.

Valentine, E.R. (1992). *Conceptual Issues in Psychology*, 2nd edn. London: Routledge.

Chapters 2 and 3 cover determinism and free will and the mind–body problem in some depth; chapter 11 looks at reductionism in relation to physiological psychology and Chapter 14 examines idiographic psychology and considers whether a science of the individual is possible.

CHAPTER 3

Controversies in psychological research

Psychology and science 59
- Routes to knowledge 59
- What is science? 60
- Applying scientific method in psychology 62
- The standing of psychology as a science 65

- New developments in psychological research methods 66

Biases in psychological research 67
- Eurocentric bias in psychology 67
- Culture and psychology 68
- Race and gender bias in psychology 71

Objectives

By the end of this chapter you should be able to
- Explain what is meant by the terms 'science' and 'scientific method';
- Discuss the use of scientific method in psychology and consider alternatives to the scientific approach to psychology;

- Explain what is meant by cultural bias in psychological theory and research studies;
- Identify ways in which racial or gender bias may affect psychological theory and research studies and suggest ways in which cultural bias may be overcome.

The sections in this chapter cover two major controversies in psychological research. The first concerns whether it is appropriate to think of psychology as science. The second is to do with forms of cultural bias in psychological research and how they may be overcome.

Psychology and science

To many people the term 'science' is something that can be applied only to the life or physical sciences such as biology, chemistry or physics. They are unlikely to place psychology with such subjects. If asked to justify reasons for excluding it, they may argue that psychological subject matter is not scientific, that psychologists do not collect information in a scientific way and that they do not have scientific theories. As a result, it can come as a surprise to learn that psychology shares many characteristics with the natural sciences. In fact, psychologists often do adopt a scientific approach and feel that they are well justified in defining psychology as the scientific study of behaviour.

The purpose of the first part of this section is to explain what science is. We shall then explore some of the problems psychologists encounter when they adopt a scientific approach. We can then go on to consider whether science and scientific method are appropriate in psychology. The section closes with a brief account of some of the new developments in this area.

Routes to knowledge

The scientific approach is just one way of acquiring knowledge about the world. Peirce (1951) describes three others: the method of tenacity, the method of authority and the method of intuition

The method of tenacity

Tenacious believers convince themselves of 'truths' by frequent repetition of them. They are adept at dealing with information that contradicts their beliefs, perhaps reinterpreting it to suit themselves. Festinger et al. (1956) encountered this when they infiltrated a quasi-religious group who believed themselves to be in touch with extraterrestrials from the planet Clarion. The group had been warned of the day on which the world was to end, and they were expecting to be rescued by means of flying saucers. When disaster did not strike, some members of the group were disillusioned and left. Others convinced themselves that their faith had saved the world so that the incident simply served to strengthen their commitment. Such a route to knowledge is obviously error prone!

The method of authority

In this case, something is true if it comes from a credible authority. The authority may be the Bible, the leader of government, parents, television or 'an expert'. Belief in authority as a source of knowledge is based on trust. The authority is not necessarily wrong but it could be unreliable since its own source of information could be at fault or it could be swayed by its own interests and values.

The method of intuition (the a priori method)

This is the 'stands to reason' or 'common sense' method. If enough people agree that something is true then it must be so. (For example, in the Dark Ages it stood to reason that the Earth was flat since everyone agreed that if it were not they would have fallen off!). Critics of psychology sometimes say that much of psychological knowledge is common sense. At times, common sense does prove to be accurate but psychologists have shown that it is not always to be trusted. For example, we would expect group decisions to be relatively sensible ones but research has shown that group decisions in some circumstances can often be more risky than those made by individuals – a phenomenon known as the 'risky shift' (Stoner, 1961). Common sense can be extremely misleading. (The phenomenon of Stoner's 'risky shift' and some later research findings are discussed in Part 6.)

So how does science differ from these routes to knowledge? To answer this question it is necessary to look in detail at the characteristics of the scientific approach.

What is science?

The word 'science' is derived from the Latin *scire* meaning 'to know'. Science is just another way of gathering knowledge, and it has its own way of answering questions and solving conflicts between different explanations. It coexists with the other three routes to knowledge and, at the moment, is favoured by many psychologists. However, if psychology is to be regarded as a science, it must share with other sciences certain:

■ aims,
■ assumptions,
■ ways of carrying out research,
■ ways of building and modifying theories.

The aims of science

The four main aims of science are description, prediction, understanding and control.

Description The most basic scientific aim is to achieve objective description of events. This differs from everyday description in the precision of the methods used. Scientific description should be as free as possible from biases arising from personal values and interests, but this is an ideal as human observers can never achieve complete objectivity.

Prediction This arises from good, objective description, which reveals patterns and thus makes prediction possible. If scientists can make accurate predictions, the status and credibility of their knowledge is enhanced. For example, psychologists may regularly observe that children who enjoy watching a lot of violent programmes on television also tend to be highly aggressive in their own behaviour. The prediction could then be made that the more exposure a child has to violent TV programmes, the more aggressive that child will be. Research may then verify or refute this prediction.

Understanding If prediction turns out to be reliable, the scientist can go on to study the relationship between cause and effect. It may be that exposure to TV violence and aggressive behaviour go together but why is this so? It could be that children are imitating what they see. Alternatively it may be that naturally aggressive children choose to watch more violence on TV. These two explanations could be tested out to see which receives more support, thus leading us to a much sounder understanding of the processes involved.

Control Accurate prediction and thorough understanding put the scientist in the position of being able to arrange for an event to happen and thus control it. For example, if we can show that aggressive behaviour is the result of imitation then it should be possible (but not necessarily ethical) to control it by changing children's TV diet.

The assumptions of science

Scientists make four key assumptions about the natural world: these are to do with order, determinism, empiricism and parsimony.

Order Scientists share the belief that events in the world are not random and haphazard. The implication of this is that it is possible to discover regularities and patterns (order), which will eventually lead to the formulation of laws. Thus some psychologists assume that it is possible to discover laws of behaviour.

Determinism If there is order in events then it makes sense to assume that they are causally related. Psychologists who accept this view usually talk about behaviour being determined either environmentally or biologically or through an interaction of both. The ultimate implication of **determinism** is that no psychological event is irrational. It will always have an underlying cause, which will eventually be detected.

Empiricism **Empiricism** is derived from a Greek word meaning 'experience'. Scientists prefer empirical data: that is to say, information gathered through direct sensory experience rather than by introspection, faith or hearsay. Empirical data are publicly observable so they can be used to settle disputes about the superiority of one belief over another. Thus, inconsistent observations should eventually be discarded and consistent ones retained.

Parsimony In scientific theory, **parsimony** refers to economy of explanation. A good parsimonious explanation does not go beyond the available empirical evidence. It applies to a wide variety of participants and contains very few contradictions. Behaviourism is often held up as a good example of a parsimonious theory whereas psychoanalytic theory is not.

Characteristics of scientific method

Scientific method is not just concerned with how data are collected. Of equal importance is the manner in which theories are constructed and modified. Most importantly, the methods of data collection should be objective and the theories should be systematically tested and refined.

A feature of scientific method is that data are collected in an unbiased, objective way. The laboratory experiment features as the clearest example of the scientific approach in this respect but it is not the only scientific method. Other methods can be scientific if they take an objective approach. There are three main ways in which objectivity can be maximized: this can be through **control**, **operational definition** and **replicability**.

Control This is best illustrated if we take the example of the laboratory **experiment** in which the

---

GLOSSARY

Determinism A belief that all human behaviour is caused by internal and/or external forces over which one has no control.

Empiricism An approach that advocates the collection of information through the senses rather than by faith or hearsay.

Parsimony When applied to research, an economical explanation that does not go beyond the available data.

Control The rigorous design of an investigation to eliminate as far as possible all sources of bias.

Operational definition A definition that sets out exactly what a particular term means so that it can be measured and quantified.

Replicability The possibility of something being repeated in exactly the same way.

Experiment A method of investigation in which one or more variables (the independent variable) are manipulated in order to examine their effect on behaviour (the dependent variable), All other variables are controlled.

experimenter manipulates an independent variable (IV), observes and measures the effects of that manipulation on a dependent variable (DV), and holds all other variables constant. A rigorously designed experiment 'purifies' the effect of the IV on the DV and makes the intervention of unwanted influences less likely. For example, a test of the effect of alcohol (IV) on driving ability (DV) would need to include many controls to ensure that the only variable that was affecting driving ability was alcohol rather than, say, previous driving experience or drinking history.

Operational definition This means that the scientist must define exactly what particular terms mean so that they can be measured and quantified. Psychologists may find themselves devising measures of aggression or anxiety or attachment strength in order to avoid ambiguity and satisfy this aspect of objectivity.

Replicability One way to check the objectivity of findings is to see if they can be repeated. Scientific research is painstakingly reported so that scientists can check each other's findings. If similar results are yielded with the same or different participants and in different contexts then they are more convincing and can be used to construct a body of knowledge, or theory.

The use of theory

A psychological theory is a general system for explaining the underlying principles of behaviour. The process of gathering knowledge leads ultimately to the construction of theories. How this is done is the second hallmark of scientific method.

Research and theory stimulate each other through the processes of induction and deduction. The first step in building knowledge is induction, which involves creating theories from observing regularities in empirical data. Information is summarized and integrated into a coherent whole. Deduction, on the other hand, involves deriving testable statements from theory. Such a statement is known as a hypothesis (hence the term **hypothetico-deductive method**). The induction/deduction process is cyclical and self-perpetuating. The scientist uses the theory as a guiding framework for research so that the investigations are done in an systematic way. A theory is never static. It is

refined and changed all the time on the basis of empirical evidence. A scientist would never talk of proving a theory – only of supporting it. Evidence may eventually cause it to be substantially modified, or even abandoned. Theories are not truths, only probabilities. (The induction/deduction process is illustrated in Figure 3.1.)

The implication of this is that psychology can be scientific only if its theories qualify through being testable (and so refutable), parsimonious, and a fertile source of new hypotheses. Refutability, in Popper's (1972) view, is a hallmark of a scientific theory. He argues that we should adopt a critical attitude to theories and attempt to refute them as it is all too easy to interpret data in ways that support our predictions. Good scientific theories emerge from the testing process as valid and reliable. This in turn improves their powers of prediction and therefore their practical value. As we shall see, psychological theories do not always meet these stringent criteria.

Applying scientific method in psychology

If it can be argued that psychology is a science, then psychologists can apply scientific method as a means of gathering information, but this is not a problem-free approach.

The overwhelming difficulty for psychologists in using scientific method lies in their subject matter – other human beings. Both participants and researchers are known to introduce various forms of bias into the research situation, for example biases arising from the characteristics, perceptions and expectations both bring to the experimental situation. So well known is this source of bias that it has become a research area in its own right, known as 'the social psychology of the experiment'. The special nature of psychological research makes the aims of scientific method (control, operational definition and replicability) so much more difficult to realize.

GLOSSARY

Theory A general system for explaining the underlying principles of a phenomenon.

Hypothesis A testable statement, drawn from a theory, and usually written in the form of a prediction of an expected relationship between two variables.

Refutability The possibility of being able to show that something is unlikely to be true.

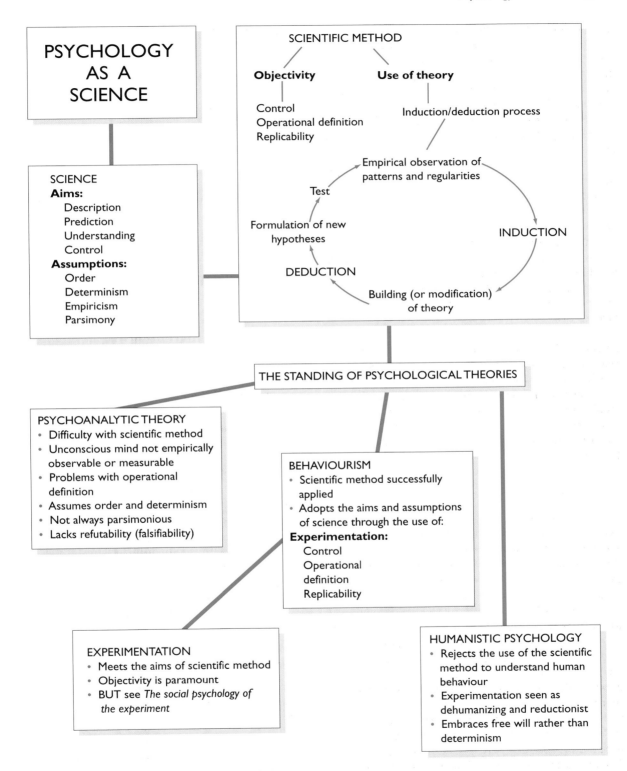

Figure 3.1 Psychology as a science

This, in turn, creates problems in the formulation and testing of theories.

The social psychology of the experiment

Research in this area has tended to focus on the experimental method. This is not to say that the pitfalls described do not apply to other methods. All research is affected to a greater or lesser extent by the situation in which it takes place, the participants involved, and the experimenters.

The influence of the situation   Human participants are often affected by the knowledge that they are being observed. Orne (1962) said that they are influenced by demand characteristics, by which he meant cues in the experimental situation that might alert the participants to the hypothesis being tested: for example, the physical set up of the experiment or the experimenter's behaviour. Orne and Evans (1965) found that out of 18 participants, 15 were prepared to pick up a snake that they were told was poisonous, plunge a hand into a container of fuming 'nitric acid' to retrieve a coin and then throw the 'acid' in the face of an experimenter – actions that would be extremely unlikely outside the experimental situation. What is more, participants may maintain that they suspected no deception. Tedeschi et al. (1985) called this 'a pact of ignorance' – participants who think they have 'caught on' to the experimenter's hypothesis do not let the experimenter know, either in order to save face, or so as not to 'spoil' the experiment. The experimental situation can alter participants' behaviour in so many ways that the goal of objectivity is not achieved; neither is the participants' behaviour a good indication of how they would behave normally (that is, there may be a lack of ecological validity).

The influence of the participant   Participants can affect the objectivity of research in two ways according to who they are and how they behave.

A recurrent criticism of psychology is that it is the science of the white, male, American undergraduate (or failing that, of the laboratory rat). Tedeschi et al. (1985) cite a number of surveys covering the years 1969 to 1979; they found that, in each year, a minimum of 70 per cent of social psychology research projects used college students. This severely limits the generalizability of the findings. Also important is the idea that many participants were volunteers. Ora (1965) found

that volunteers are more easily influenced, moody, in need of approval, aggressive and neurotic than were nonvolunteers. Again, the generalizability of research data obtained from such people would be limited.

The second factor that reduces the suitability of scientific method in psychology concerns participants' behaviour. Weber and Cook (1972) identified four roles that participants being studied might adopt:

■ The faithful participant tries to react to the situation as naturally as possible. This may be deliberate, or just borne out of disinterest.
■ The cooperative participant tries to discover the hypothesis being tested so that they can do their best to help prove it.
■ The negativistic participant tries to discover the hypothesis in order to disprove it.
■ The evaluatively apprehensive participant believes that the experimenter is capable of uncovering some hidden truth about them and does what they can to avoid being evaluated negatively.

Of these four roles, the faithful participant is clearly the most desirable, but it is not always possible to know which stance is being adopted. As a result, the objectivity of research is threatened once again, and with it, the suitability of scientific method for collecting knowledge about humans.

The influence of the experimenter   Rosenthal (1969) has conducted a number of classic pieces of research into the influence of the experimenter on research results and has discovered three problems:

■ **Biosocial or physical characteristics** of the experimenter such as age, sex, race and appearance. Participants' prejudices and stereotypes may well affect the way they respond to different experimenters.
■ **Psychosocial factors**, which have to do with the experimenter's social skills in dealing with

---

participants. The experimenter may be friendly and supportive so that participants are at ease and feel cooperative. On the other hand, they may find the experimenter off-putting.

■ **Experimenter expectancy effects**. Experimenters who have a hypothesis in mind may end up validating it simply because of their belief about how the results will turn out. The hypothesis then becomes a self-fulfilling prophecy. It is assumed that the experimenter unwittingly influences the results, not that it is a deliberate action.

The standing of psychological theories and approaches

As stated earlier, part of the scientific approach has to do with theory building and modification. Psychology is unusual among sciences in that it can often explain the same thing from a number of theoretical viewpoints. These differ in terms of how closely they fit the scientific standard. Four approaches are outlined below (see Chapter 1 for more detail on some of these): introspection, psychoanalytic theory, behaviourism and humanistic psychology.

Introspection In the early days of psychology, data were gathered in the form of introspections made in carefully controlled conditions – an approach advocated by Wundt (1879). In spite of attempts to control things such as stimuli and instructions to participants, it proved very difficult to achieve the aims of operational definition and replicability. Introspection also failed because the data were not empirical.

Psychoanalytic theory The psychoanalytic approach of Sigmund Freud (1856–1939) has had similar problems in adopting scientific method. The subject matter – the workings of the unconscious mind – is neither empirically observable nor easily defined. Psychoanalytic theory also runs into difficulties with control and replicability. It assumes order and determinism, but the assumptions of parsimony and empiricism are less easily met. Although it has been claimed that psychoanalytic theory can be tested experimentally (and many attempts have been made to do so), opponents of psychoanalytic theory argue that it is not suitable for scientific testing as it is often irrefutable – the theory can account for apparently contradictory research evidence.

Behaviourism Possibly the most successful application of scientific method to psychology has been achieved by the behaviourist school (Watson, 1919). Behaviourists rejected earlier approaches, advocating instead publicly observable behaviour as the proper subject matter for psychology. Behaviourist research was, and still is, characterized by rigorous control, operational definition and replicability. The four assumptions of science – order, determinism, empiricism and parsimony – are accepted as central. Behaviourist theories are a source of readily testable hypotheses because the subject matter lends itself to testing. For all its shortcomings, as a source of scientifically researched data, the behaviourist approach has few equals in psychology.

Humanistic psychology The humanistic approach takes conscious experience as its focus of attention and so shares similar problems to those of introspection and psychoanalysis. Scientific testing is not easy, at least in part because there is no coherent humanistic theory to work from. Nevertheless, Carl Rogers, a founder of the humanistic school, made great strides towards more systematic testing of humanistic ideas. In particular, he developed Q-sort techniques (devised by Stephenson in 1953) as a way of assessing the effectiveness of the his own 'client-centred therapy'. However, one of the central tenets of the approach is that scientific method is not the best route to knowledge about humans and that the only meaningful way to understand them is to see the world from each person's unique perspective. Since one person's inner world is not open to public scrutiny, observations could never be empirical. Humanistic psychologists also reject the idea of determinism in favour of free will, preferring to see humans as exercising choice over their actions, in which case assumptions of order and parsimony are untenable. Finally, humanistic psychologists reject experimentation as a means of finding out about humans, seeing it as dehumanizing and reductionist.

The standing of psychology as a science

So is psychology a science? The answer to this question is not straightforward, and is closely linked to how we define science. If it is defined by its aims then, on the whole, psychology is scientific. If it is defined by its assumptions, then some schools of psychology fit the mould more comfortably than others.

Even if it is assumed that the aims and assumptions of science are appropriate in psychology, then there are still difficulties in conducting research objectively because of the special nature of the subject matter. However, it is important to remember that psychologists are not alone in the problem of achieving objectivity. All scientists are human beings, and it is in their nature to select and interpret information. Consequently, their personal values and biases will always intervene regardless of their subject matter. If psychology fails the science test on the grounds of insufficient objectivity then so do other sciences.

Turning finally to the way in which theories are built and tested, it can be said that some psychologists do take a scientific approach but this is not equally true for all schools of psychology. Different schools focus on different types of subject matter, some of which are more easily operationally defined and tested than others. Schools also differ in their approach to research methods. The humanistic school, for example, regards tightly controlled experimentation as unsuitable for understanding human experience. Others, such as the behaviourists, regard it as essential.

The philosopher Kuhn (1962) says that an essential characteristic of a mature science is that it has a uniting **paradigm** – something that psychology lacks. (A paradigm is a set of assumptions about what should be studied and how – it is a common global theory or perspective such as Darwinism in biology.) In fact, Kuhn says that until psychology has a paradigm, it is not science but pre-science. If this is the case, then it is too soon to ask questions about the applicability of the scientific approach to psychology. There can be no clear answers as long as it incorporates so many differing schools of thought. Behaviourism is, perhaps, the closest psychology has ever been to having a uniting paradigm (Valentine, 1982).

New developments in psychological research methods

Some psychologists do seem to value the traditional scientific approach more than others. It is interesting to note that, when Sigmund Freud was a young man in the latter part of the nineteenth century, the scientific route to knowledge was relatively new and caused great excitement. Freud's theory, amongst others, was eventually criticized for not being amenable to scientific testing. Ironically, we are gradually moving towards a situation where the suitability of the

scientific route to understanding human behaviour is being questioned – a change Freud might well have welcomed.

Some psychologists have long argued for a shift away from hard-line **quantitative research**, such as experimentation, to approaches that are more **qualitative**, and these fit less comfortably with traditional scientific aims and assumptions. Quantitative research tends to emphasize the empiricist paradigm (which involves measurement and statistical analysis) and takes the view that it is possible to understand the world in an objective and dispassionate way. Those who favour more qualitative approaches are critical of empiricism for many reasons. They say:

- It produces findings that lack ecological validity (for example, as in some laboratory studies of memory);
- It values objectivity and distance from the participant (which, in fact, is impossible to achieve as every research situation is a social situation);
- It takes people out of their social context (and so gives a narrow and artificial view of people's experiences from the rather patronizing perspective of the 'experimenter' controlling 'subjects');
- It operationalizes terms to reduce them to something measurable (thus losing their full meaning for the participant on whom the researcher's meanings are imposed).

New paradigm research

An emphasis on qualitative methods is characteristic of **new paradigm research**, which offers a number of alternatives to the traditional empirical approach. New paradigm researchers generally:

GLOSSARY

Paradigm A common, global theory that carries a set of assumptions about what should be studied and how.

Quantitative research An approach that involves measurement and analyses in a numerical form.

Qualitative research Research that involves collecting nonnumerical data.

'New paradigm' research A style of research that uses qualitative methods in the collection and analysis of data: for example, case study or role play.

- See the researcher and participant as collaborators in research rather than as 'controlling experimenter' and 'responding subject';
- Prefer more open-ended, detailed analysis of what people say, write or do, arguing that, in order to understand them, we have to appreciate that they construct their own view of the world in a way that has meaning for them based on their social, cultural and historical background;
- Utilize the more familiar techniques of the case study, certain kinds of observation, role play or interview but also use other techniques of gathering information, such as 'action research' and discourse analysis.

The issues raised by new paradigm researchers have important implications for the question about the suitability of scientific method in psychology because, as we have seen, science is more allied to traditional empiricism. Nevertheless, quantitative and qualitative methods have coexisted for a long time in psychology and both have a great deal to offer. Perhaps a more positive and productive solution to the question of the scientific status of psychology would be to acknowledge the value of mixing the best of the different paradigms together and taking a pluralist or eclectic approach to understanding human behaviour. This would surely be preferable to adopting an adversarial stance and trying to argue that one approach is better than the other.

SELF-ASSESSMENT QUESTIONS

1. What routes to knowledge are there apart from the scientific one?
2. What are the aims and assumptions of science?
3. What are the characteristics of scientific method?
4. How are scientific theories built and modified?
5. What is meant by 'the social psychology of the experiment'?
6. Compare two psychological theories in terms of their scientific status.
7. Explain why Kuhn thought psychology was still pre-science.
8. Briefly explain what is meant by 'new paradigm' research.

Biases in psychological research

Eurocentric bias in psychology

Critics of psychology say that, far from being an unbiased, value-free and objective science, it is profoundly Eurocentric (Howitt and Owusu-Bempah, 1994). By this they mean that it is steeped in cultural values that are part of American and European life, and that these values shape psychological theories and research studies. There is also the view that psychologists, unwittingly or otherwise, hide their cultural bias behind science. In other words, although they appear to take a cool and objective view of human behaviour, the so-called 'universal' theories that result are, in fact, invented in their own culture. Furthermore, the Eurocentric standards in these theories tend to be seen as 'normal' and 'natural' so that cultures that do not share them are viewed as somehow failing to measure up. Because biases like these can arise, it is important to remind ourselves that science cannot give us absolute truths. Scientific knowledge is a social creation, which could be seen as serving the needs of the dominant groups in society. In psychology, those groups are North American and European.

'Culture boundedness'

There is a growing awareness of 'culture boundedness' in psychology and, with it, a clearer realization of some of the serious shortcomings of the discipline. Berry (1983) commented that some American psychology was so culture bound that it should not be employed in cultures outside the United States, not even in Canada. Howitt and Owusu-Bempah go further. They say 'Psychology has not simply colluded in the denial of the needs of culturally and racially diverse groups, it has trained psychologists unfit or incompetent for work in a multi-cultural society' (p. 140).

Clearly, this is a situation that psychologists must address, since the consequences of bias are too important to ignore. But where do they start? A good

---

GLOSSARY

Eurocentric Heavily influenced by cultural values that are part of American and European life.

Culture bound Implies that the content of, for example, an IQ test contains material that is suitable only for members of a particular culture.

place to begin would be to examine what is meant by 'culture'. The next step would be to identify some of the biases resulting from a culture-bound view. Only when psychologists begin to understand what they are dealing with will they be in a position to act constructively to counteract bias. In this chapter we shall follow this route, ending with the issues of race and gender as specific examples of culture bias in psychology. As we go along, a useful general point to bear in mind is that overarching much of psychology is the Eurocentric view that science should be favoured as the main route to knowledge, and this in itself is a form of bias.

Culture and psychology

One reason why psychologists compare cultures is that they see it as a way of addressing the 'nature–nurture' debate. The reasoning behind this is that if they can find that certain behaviour patterns are 'universal' regardless of environment, then that behaviour is more likely to be 'human nature'. Behaviour patterns that differ between cultures are seen as 'culturally relative' and more open to the effects of environment. In practice, this is an issue that is very hard to resolve since research across cultures is fraught with theoretical and technical difficulties.

What do we mean by culture?

First, psychologists must be clear about what is meant by culture. Moghaddam et al. (1993) take a wide view. They say it is the 'human-made part of the environment' and that it can be both objective and physical (for example, everyday objects and structures, works of art) and subjective and psychological (for example, beliefs, identities and values). They make the important point that humans both shape their culture and are shaped by it. Another useful approach is taken by Triandis (1990), who talks of 'cultural syndromes'. By this he means that a culture consists of a particular combination of beliefs, values, attitudes, norms and behaviours, and that these distinguish it from other cultures. Brislin (1993) adds that such syndromes are:

■ Passed down the generations,
■ Taken for granted and not generally discussed,
■ Apt to arouse strong feelings within the culture if cultural values are violated,

■ Apt to lead to clashes with people who have sharply contrasting cultural syndromes.

Triandis (1990) and Hofstede (1980) have, between them, suggested a number of general ways in which cultural syndromes might vary, and these appear in Figure 3.2. In addition, there are many ways in which members of different cultures may express the elements of the syndrome even when they 'score' similarly on them, so it is important that psychologists take this into account. Furthermore, as Brislin reminds us, culture is not static. Individuals within a culture may vary in how committed they are to its values at different times in their lives, and cultural values can be flexible or even change significantly over time. It is also important to remember that the similarities between what we would casually call 'different' cultures often outweigh the differences. All of these things make the effects of culture particularly difficult to research simply because of the problems they present to psychologists attempting to obtain truly comparable samples from different cultures.

'Cultural psychology'

We can see that studying different cultures does not necessarily mean travelling the world and seeking out remote groups of people untouched by Western ways. In explaining this, Much (1995) draws a distinction between traditional cross-cultural psychology and the newer 'cultural psychology'. The traditional approach involved devising theories and measuring instruments in the home culture and then imposing them on other cultures in the hope that cultural universals would eventually be discovered. Cultural psychology, on the other hand, does not assume that there is an 'intrinsic psychic unity' about humankind that is seeking to be discovered. Instead it lays emphasis on different social systems as the source of variation between people. Thus, modern cultural psychologists may find similar cultures to their own in other parts of the world and very different cultures on their doorstep.

GLOSSARY

Culture relating to a group of people where common beliefs, values, attitudes, behaviour, valued objects and works of art are distinct when compared with other groups.

Figure 3.2 Some dimensions of cultural differences (based on Triandis, 1990 and Hofstede, 1980)

Dimension	Notes
Individualism – collectivism	Individualism is more common in Western cultures and collectivism in Eastern cultures. The first is characterized by individual responsibility and achievement, the second by group responsibility and support.
Power distance	Cultures differ in the prevalence and nature of power relationships where some individuals or groups may be deferential to others.
Masculinity – femininity	Masculine cultures (e.g. Japan) emphasize work, achievement, strength and effectiveness. Feminine cultures (e.g. Sweden) emphasize quality of life, interpersonal relationships, nurturing and care.
Tight – loose	A tight culture is one in which norms are strictly defined. In a loose culture a great deal of freedom would be acceptable.
Uncertainty avoidance	This refers to the degree to which a culture tries to plan for the future and maintain stability.
Cultural complexity	This can be defined by the number and diversity of roles occupied by people in the culture. (Certain individuals may have very clearly defined roles, e.g. the Pope). Complex cultures also seem to lay great emphasis on time.
Emotional control – expressiveness	This refers to whether it is more usual to express emotions openly or to exercise restraint.
Contact – no contact	This is to do with the culture's rules of proximity (physical distance) between individuals: e.g. how close individuals permit others to get and how status and relationships affect this.

Sources of cultural bias in psychological theory and research

A brief consideration of the dimensions of culture shown in Figure 3.2 will give an idea of the kinds of values that shape Eurocentric psychology. It has grown up against a complex cultural background which tends to emphasize individualism, power-distance, masculinity and uncertainty avoidance and which is relatively tight, distant and emotionally inexpressive. This affects how research questions are framed, how research findings are interpreted and how theories are constructed and modified, but, most importantly, it seems to set the standard against which all other cultures are compared. The widely influential theories of Freud, Piaget and Skinner can all be considered Eurocentric by these criteria even though there has been some success in applying them across cultures.

There are many ways in which cultural bias can be perpetuated in psychology, but here we shall consider just three. They concern choice of research participants, choice of methods and how findings are communicated to a wider audience.

Choice of research participants It is generally well known that much American psychology is based on studies using readily available, white, undergraduate students who can be invited, induced or expected to act as research participants. Undergraduates could hardly be thought of as widely representative of other Americans, let alone other cultures; nevertheless participants of other types rarely appear in the research literature. In fact, in a content analysis of 20 years of publications in six of the American Psychological Association's journals, Graham (1992) found that less than 4 per cent of the 15 000 published articles were about African Americans. In addition, there had been a drop to 2 per cent on the final five years covered by the study. This selectivity may happen simply because participants other than undergraduates take more time, effort and money to recruit. Alternatively, it could be that cultural research is often very 'socially sensitive' and so tends to be avoided. On the other hand, it could signify lack of interest by the researcher based on the view that different cultures are not important.

Choice of methods The distinction drawn by Pike (1967) between 'emics' and 'etics' helps to explain why the methods, derived from particular theories and used to study different cultures, are likely to be a source of bias.

■ **Etics**. To take an etic view is to study a culture from the outside using criteria common to the 'home' and the studied culture.
■ **Emics**. The emic view studies a culture from the inside, perhaps using participant observation or by devising measures within the culture, often in collaboration with one or more of its members.

Problems arise when measures devised on the basis of Eurocentric psychological theory (for example, certain IQ tests) are 'exported' to other cultures and treated as though they are etics when they are, in fact, emics. Their use outside the home culture then becomes an 'imposed etic', which could render the measure, and any theoretical conclusions drawn from the resulting data, largely or completely invalid. The etic/emic distinction can thus explain why certain findings cannot always be replicated outside the home culture. (Examples in psychology include Milgram's *Obedience to Authority* research (1974) and Sherif et al.'s (1961) Robber's Cave studies into intergroup conflict, discussed in Part 6.)

One danger in researchers' failing to recognize that they are using an imposed etic is that they may simply bend their findings to fit their theoretical, and hence cultural, view (for example, explaining IQ differences in terms of genetics). A possible solution would be to take the emics of the two cultures to be studied and use what they have in common to arrive at a 'derived ethic' which is equally valid in both cultures (for example, a culture-fair IQ test). This, of course, is easier said than done.

Communicating findings to a wider audience One important way in which bias can be perpetuated is in psychological publications. Eurocentric psychology has a 'written tradition' – it likes to communicate its findings in writing. However, before publication, books and research papers are 'filtered' by the dominant culture so that anything that is not mainstream or does not fit the prevailing view may be selected out. The content of what remains is highly Eurocentric. Smith and Bond (1993), for example, analysed two widely available social psychology textbooks, the first by Baron and Byrne (1991) and the second by Hewstone et al. (1988). They found that the books contained 94 per cent and 68 per cent American studies respectively, even though the second one is a British textbook written by a team of European authors. Overall, Smith and Bond estimate that 64 per cent of psychological research worldwide is American, and much of this will predominate in published material. A related source of bias in written matter, as we shall see, is that particular views of others can be perpetuated in the choice of words. This is important simply because Eurocentric psychology markets its literature so successfully all over the world.

History of cultural bias

Cultural bias in psychology has a long history. So long, in fact, that Bulhan (1985) likens the actions of psychological researchers to the political colonialists of the past. Just as, throughout history, members of dominant cultures have seen it as their right to invade other cultures and help themselves to valuable raw materials, so psychologists have practised 'scientific colonialism'. By this he means that they too have invaded any other culture that interests them and helped themselves to valuable raw data to use for their own gain. At its worst, this can grow into a kind of autocolonialism where the colonized culture 'actively participates in (its) own victimization' (p. 44) and hands its power over to the invader. If this does not happen, the invading culture will eventually seek to

---

> **GLOSSARY**
>
> **Emics** The study of a culture from the inside, often with the collaboration of members of the studied culture.
>
> **Etics** The study of a culture from the outside using criteria common to the 'home' and the studied culture.

impose its own values on the colonized culture. Political colonialists do this by 'Westernising' other cultures while Eurocentric psychologists either ignore, marginalize or 'Europeanize' them.

Race and gender bias in psychology

So far, we have seen a number of general biases that arise in Eurocentric psychology and how these can affect the nature of psychological knowledge. A further important consequence of adopting a particular cultural view is that certain ways of grouping or categorizing people will be seen as appropriate. The dominant view in Eurocentric psychology is that it is meaningful and useful to separate people in terms of race and gender. The unfortunate result of this is that it encourages psychologists to emphasize differences between races and sexes, compare them to each other and make value judgments about them. Black people

and women in particular have not done well out of such comparisons. Indeed it has been argued that they have been rendered virtually invisible through being ignored, marginalized or Europeanized. In the following sections we shall see some of the results of these biases and consider how the situation can be resolved.

Racial bias in psychology

The culture out of which Eurocentric psychology has arisen tends to make three main classifications of race based on superficial appearance. These are African, Mongoloid, Caucasoid (or black, yellow and white, to which some add a fourth category of American Indian or red). There is a persistent myth that these 'races' are biologically very different. This view persists in spite of clear evidence that genetic differences between them are minuscule. In addition, to apply simple categories like these to people is both to take them out of their

A farming family in Nigeria. How relevant is Eurocentric psychology to their situation?

cultural context and to ignore individual differences. They come to be seen as 'all the same', as 'different from the (white) norm' and ultimately 'less worthy'. Since it is most likely that it is the predominant white standard against which people are judged, 'nonwhite' groups will almost invariably be found wanting. The discrimination that often results has led Howitt and Owusu-Bempah, amongst others, to accuse psychology of being not only culturally biased but also racist.

Old racism The racism of psychology has a long history. Howitt and Owusu-Bempah give many examples of what they call 'old racism'. This is based largely on assumptions about the importance of alleged biological differences between races, particularly genetic ones. Such a view was fuelled by 'bad gene' theorists, who were opposed to racial mixing on the grounds that so-called inferior genes in certain races would dilute the quality of the gene pool in other races and destroy their culture. Some of the results of this idea are plain to see. Hiding behind 'science', and using IQ testing (an imposed etic) to provide 'objective' evidence, psychologists have colluded in discriminatory immigration and education policies and even in **eugenics** and '**ethnic cleansing**' such as that carried out by Adolf Hitler and, more recently, in former Yugoslavia. Sadly, in spite of its name, 'old racism' is not a thing of the past, but is alive and well. (For more about the controversial uses of IQ tests, see Chapter 4.)

New racism Howitt and Owusu-Bempah say that, although some of the more outrageous, overt expressions of 'old racism' may have disappeared from psychology, racism is still there but in a subtler form. This 'new racism' is expressed in a number of ways, for example:

- Thinking of racism as characteristic only of extreme groups;
- Denying that racism is a problem;
- Being 'colour blind' (that is, thinking that to acknowledge that racism exists simply perpetuates it);
- Seeing people who are the victims of racism as responsible for their own misfortune.

It is also practised in a number of ways:

- By formulating theories and asking research questions that perpetuate boundaries between

races, for example, hereditarian views of intelligence, intergroup conflict theories of prejudice;
- By 'filtering' the content of research journals and textbooks to reflect the views of the dominant culture;
- By choice of words in written material that suggest that other races are not only 'different' but also 'deficient': for example, primitive, tribal, savage (that is, like animals) or non-Western (that is, an undifferentiated mass) or 'culturally deprived' (not as good);
- By failing to support research interests that might further an understanding of other cultures;
- By failing to appoint psychologists from outside the dominant cultural group;
- By exercising 'tokenism': for example, appointing a few black psychologists but relegating them to marginal research areas.

So Howitt and Owusu-Bempah show that racism still features in modern psychology and has yet to be actively and effectively confronted and eradicated. Even replacing racism with racial tolerance does not go far enough since it only amounts to 'the best that bigots can achieve' (p. 17) and is about as constructive as replacing a headache with a toothache. The authors are in no doubt about the seriousness of the problem. They warn that racism is, possibly, 'psychology's most versatile and persistent theory. . . From the perspective of its victims, racism inhibits human growth, limits productive living and causes death' (p. 37).

Gender bias in psychology

In relation to race, we saw how applying a Eurocentric standard can lead to discrimination against certain groups. Just as the culture of psychology is dominated by white standards, so it is dominated by male standards. The problem with this is that women, like certain racial groups, are in danger of suffering discrimination as a result of being viewed as 'all the same', 'different from the (male) norm' and 'less

---

GLOSSARY

Eugenics An attempt to improve the human race by improving inherited qualities.

Ethnic cleansing The removal of a particular cultural group from a geographical area.

worthy'. Race, as we saw, is a convenient label and more of a social invention than a biological reality. The same applies to gender. Male and female may be physiologically distinguishable but, psychologically, similarities between the sexes far outweigh the differences. Nevertheless, clearly differentiated social categories prevail. To help emphasize that anatomy is not necessarily destiny, psychologists like to draw a distinction between biological sex (male and female) and psychological gender (masculine and feminine).

Themes in gender bias Many of the themes raised in connection with racial bias reappear when we consider gender bias. In both cases, the use of white, masculine theories and methods amounts to an imposed Eurocentric etic. In the case of females, Matlin (1993) suggests this renders invisible many things that are important in their lives such as:

■ Exclusively female experiences such as pregnancy and menopause;
■ Almost exclusively female experiences such as rape and sexual harassment;
■ How females fare in male-dominated domains: for example, certain workplace settings.

Much of the literature in this area focuses on the damage gender bias can do to women, but it is important to remember that it can work both ways and be disadvantageous to both men and women.

'Old' and 'new' sexism In considering the effects of gender bias we can borrow from Howitt and Owusu-Bempah's ideas about racism and talk of 'old sexism' and 'new sexism'. We are, hopefully, seeing a decline in blatant examples of old sexism, which sees women as biologically predisposed to be witches, mothers or sex objects. However, we must guard against more subtle forms of 'new sexism', which is simply old sexism in disguise, and be active in eliminating it. As with racism, it is not enough to think of sexism as:

■ Characteristic only of extreme groups;
■ Not a problem;
■ Something to be ignored (because to raise it as an issue only perpetuates it);
■ Women's fault.

Like racism, sexism can be practised in a number of ways:

■ By formulating theories and asking research questions that perpetuate boundaries between the sexes: for example, by using Freudian theory as a basis from which to test the detrimental effect of working mothers but not of working fathers; by starting from the assumption that it is legitimate to look for sex differences (as opposed to comparisons);
■ By filtering what is published in research journals and textbooks to reflect the stereotyped view of male and female and to emphasize differences: for example, failing to publish research that shows similarities rather than differences or which identifies variables other than gender as a source of females' disadvantage (the 'file-drawer phenomenon');
■ By choice of words when describing women and what they do: for example, use of the generic masculine (he) to denote both sexes; in embedded figure tests where women typically take longer than men to locate a hidden shape, they are called 'field dependent' (the label for males is 'field independent'), rather than calling women 'context aware' and men 'context blind';
■ By failing to support research interests that concern women: for example, experiences of menstruation or childbirth;
■ By failing to appoint or promote women academics;
■ By exercising '**tokenism**': for example, appointing a few women but then marginalizing them and/or their research interests.

In relation to gender bias in the psychological theories (which of course underpin research) Hare-Mustin and Maracek (1990) distinguish between alpha bias and beta bias:

■ Theories with alpha bias exaggerate differences between men and women;
■ Theories with beta bias minimize the differences.

Neither approach is particularly helpful because the first tends to perpetuate sex stereotypes and the second tends to make women invisible by applying male standards to all. To overcome this, Hare-Mustin and Maracek suggest we adopt a **constructivist standpoint**. By this they mean we should recognize that men and women seem different only because that is the social reality we have created about them. This 'reality' is based on the pervasive myths and folklore of our alpha-

Figure 3.3 Types of bias in psychological theories (Worell and Remer, 1992)

Type of bias	Explanation
Androcentric	The male view is seen as legitimate for explaining experiences of both sexes.
Gendercentric	Males and females are seen as developing along different paths.
Ethnocentric	American–European or 'Eurocentric' bias manifested in, for example, viewing the nuclear family, or specific roles for men and women, as normal.
Heterosexist	Seeing heterosexism as the normal and desirable state and other sexual orientations as deficient.
Intrapsychic	Attributing behaviour to internal factors. In effect, this blames people for their behaviour: e.g. women's subjugation is due to their own inherent weaknesses.
Deterministic	Emphasizing the importance of early experience for 'fixing' behaviour patterns at a young age.

biased culture, and its falsity can be demonstrated many times in research.

A classification of psychological theories Worell and Remer (1992) also provide a useful classification of psychological theories to show how they might lead to gender bias in research. These are shown in Figure 3.3. Freudian psychoanalytic theory stands out as an excellent example of all of these kinds of bias, yet its influence is still great:

■ It is **androcentric** because it explains the experiences of both males and females from a male viewpoint;
■ It is **gendercentric** because it sees development of males and females as taking different routes (e.g. the Oedipal and Electra conflicts in the phallic stage of development);
■ It is **ethnocentric** because of its Eurocentric background;
■ It is **heterosexist** because it sees heterosexism as normal and homosexuality or lesbianism as abnormal;
■ It is both **intrapsychic** and **deterministic**, seeing behaviour as determined by the operation of instincts.

Erikson's (1963, 1968) theory of psychosocial development and Kohlberg's (1975) theory of moral development can be seen as androcentric, ethnocentric and intrapsychic. However, neither of them is deterministic as both are lifespan approaches. Erikson's theory could be seen as somewhat gendercentric and heterosexist because of the differences it sees in the developmental paths of males and females. Kohlberg's theory tends not to address the heterosexism issue being more concerned with cognitive development. Neither is it gendercentric – men and women follow the same route except that females allegedly do not progress as far as males.

GLOSSARY

'Constructivist standpoint' Hare-Mustin and Maracek's term to describe the view that men and women are different only because of the social reality we have created about them.

Androcentric Explaining gender differences from a male standpoint.

Gendercentric Viewing the development of males and females as taking different routes.

Ethnocentric Viewing cultural, racial or gender differences from a particular ethnic standpoint.

Heterosexism Viewing heterosexism as normal and homosexuality as deviant.

Intrapsychic Attributing behaviour to internal factors.

Deterministic Emphasizing early experience as determining behaviour patterns.

Solutions to gender bias   Worell and Remer's solution is to suggest that we examine all psychological theories for evidence of the six types of bias and transform them into a feminist theory format that is beneficial for both males and females. Characteristics of the feminist approach and some ways of transforming biased theories are as follows:

- **Gender free**. Dispose of androcentric and gendercentric theories by concentrating on the similarities between males and females, avoid stereotypes and sexist language and emphasize the role of socialization, rather than biological processes, in affecting behaviour.
- **Flexible**. Dispose of ethnocentrism and heterosexism by using concepts that apply to everyone regardless of age, culture, race, sexual orientation or gender.
- **Interactionist**. Drop the intrapsychic emphasis and devise an approach that sees behaviour as having multiple causes, both individual and environmental.
- **Lifespan**. Dispose of deterministic ideas and see development as a lifelong process with options for growth and change at any age.

Many feminist theorists are optimistic about the progress that is being made to eradicate gender bias. The psychology of women, for example, has now become institutionalized and is an option in many degree courses. Crawford and Unger (1995) write 'The new psychology of women and gender is rich and varied. Virtually every intellectual framework from Freudian theory to cognitive psychology (and) . . . virtually every area of psychology, from developmental to social, has been affected' (p. 39). But there is still much to do.

What can be done about racial and gender bias?

Howitt and Owusu-Bempah warn that racial bias and the resulting racism must be rooted out completely. It is wholly unsatisfactory, they say, simply to replace it with 'tolerance'. The same reasoning can be applied to gender bias. It might seem sensible, therefore, to establish alternatives, such as Black Psychology or Psychology of Women but, unless handled with care, these may simply create new and different divisions. Howitt and Owusu-Bempah also comment that, apart from in its extreme forms, racism appears to be harder to identify than sexism, and that this may be one reason

why women have had relatively greater success in challenging sexism. So what can be done? Since bias seems to operate on at least three levels – individual, institutional and cultural – any attempt to bring about change would need to address all of these.

The individual level   On an individual level psychologists should strive to:

- Become sensitive to their own and others' biases;
- Empathise with the victims of bias;
- Decide actively to resist bias rather than ignoring it.

The institutional level   On an institutional level bias can be tackled in many ways. Howitt and Owusu-Bempah (1994) suggest ten ways to combat racial bias in particular. These have been adapted to show how they can be applied equally well to tackling gender bias in psychological institutions:

1. Examine the policies and practices of the institution, paying special attention to racism and sexism. Publish anti-racist and anti-sexist materials.
2. Adopt and implement equal opportunities policies: for example, the BPS ethical guidelines for research with human participants (1993) contains notes on avoidance of sexist language (but not, as yet, of racist language).
3. Scrutinize the curriculum in psychological education and training to make it more relevant to a multicultural society.
4. Evaluate and monitor the professional practice of members of the institution.
5. Commit the institution to equality, perhaps through a formal ethical requirement.
6. Join with other organizations (for example, medical, educational) to combat bias.
7. Prepare and equip students and practitioners to provide an unbiased service in a multicultural/multiracial society.
8. Provide anti-racist/sexist resource materials for teachers and practitioners to help raise self-awareness.
9. Provide journal editors and committees with guidelines to help them monitor research papers for unacceptably biased content. Among other things, such committees should be alert to the use of 'imposed etics' and insist that researchers either adopt an emic approach or strive to employ

derived etics which have 'equivalence' of meaning in the home and studied culture.
10. Take steps to recruit disadvantaged groups to the profession: for example, through publicity and educational materials and the provision of grants.

The cultural level On a cultural level, bias is infinitely harder to tackle because of the sheer scale of the problem. The Eurocentrism of psychology is pervasive and deep-rooted, and it can be politically very sensitive to attack the status quo, but this should be no excuse for inactivity. As we have seen, it is possible to work away at the problem on a number of other levels and to create clear standards to aspire to. It is also important to realize that significant change is likely to come about both slowly and painfully.

Nevertheless, as Howitt and Owusu-Bempah remind us, we have a moral obligation to work to reduce all kinds of bias in psychology, since not to do so is tantamount to complicity.

❓ SELF-ASSESSMENT QUESTIONS

1. What do psychologists mean by 'culture'?
2. What is meant by 'Eurocentric bias' in psychology?
3. Outline three ways in which Eurocentric bias might be perpetuated.
4. Give examples of racial and gender bias in psychology.
5. Suggest at least six ways of combating racial or gender bias in psychology.

Chapter summary

- The scientific approach is one method for acquiring knowledge about the world. Three other ways are through the method of tenacity (frequent repetition of 'truths'), the method of authority (deriving 'truths' from a credible authority) and the method of intuition (a priori, or 'common sense').

- If psychology is to be regarded as a science, it must, like other sciences, share certain aims, assumptions, ways of carrying out research, ways of building and modifying theories.

- The four main aims of science are objective description of events, accurate prediction, reliable understanding, control of events.

- Scientists make four key assumptions about the natural world. These are order: a belief that events do not occur randomly; determinism: an assumption that events have an underlying cause; empiricism: data should be collected through direct experience that is observable; parsimony: data does not go beyond the empirical evidence.

- Characteristics of the scientific method are: objectivity, which can be achieved through rigorous control of variables, use of operational definitions and replicability; and use of testable theory, which is derived from observing regularities in the data. Popper argues that good theories should also be refutable.

- The main difficulty experienced by psychologists arises from their subject matter – human beings. Both participants and researchers may introduce bias into the research situation, particularly in experiments. This source of bias is known as 'the social psychology of the experiment' and it has been widely researched.

- Research has focused mainly on the influence of the situation, the influence of the participant, and the influence of the experimenter.

- In psychology, the psychoanalytic approach has problems in meeting the demands of the scientific method, since the subject matter is not easily observable or definable; control and replicability are difficult. It assumes order and determinism, but parsimony and empiricism are less easily met.

- The behaviourist approach comes the closest to meeting the criteria of the scientific method. Behaviourist research is characterized by rigorous control, operational definition and replicability; order, empiricism and determinism are assumed; theories are testable.

- Humanistic psychologists generally reject the use of the scientific method and believe that the world should be understood through each person's unique perspective. The idea of determinism is rejected, and human beings are seen as having free will over their actions. Experimentation is seen as dehumanizing and reductionist.

■ The question of whether psychology is a science is not easy to answer. If science is defined by its aims, then psychology is a science. If it is defined by its assumptions, then some areas of psychology are more scientific than others. However, if psychology does not meet the full requirements of a science, then nor do other sciences; all scientists in whatever subject area are human beings and may fail the test of objectivity.

■ The philosopher Kuhn argues that an essential characteristic of a mature science is that it has a uniting 'paradigm'. He argues that as psychology does not yet have such a common global theory, it should, for the time being, be regarded as pre-science.

■ Some psychologists are questioning the suitability of the traditional scientific route to understanding human behaviour and have argued for a move away from quantitative research such as experimentation to approaches that are more qualitative.

■ Qualitative approaches to research are more likely than empiricist approaches to be ecologically valid and to preserve the essential social nature of human beings.

■ New paradigm research epitomizes the qualitative approach to research. It emphasizes the researcher and participants as equal partners in research, a more open-ended and detailed analysis of what people say, write or do in order better to understand their unique perspectives on the world, and the utilization not only of methods such as case study and observation, but techniques such as 'action research' and discourse analysis.

■ New paradigm research raises important questions about the suitability of scientific method in psychology. However, a positive and productive solution might be to attempt to use the best of both approaches in order to understand human behaviour.

■ Critics of psychology argue that psychology is profoundly Eurocentric. By this is meant that it is steeped in cultural values that relate to American and European life and which shape psychological theories and research studies.

■ There is a growing awareness in psychology of the biases arising from 'culture boundedness'. Howitt and Owusu-Bempah go as far as to argue that training in psychology produces psychologists who are unfit for work in a multicultural society.

■ An important point to bear in mind is the Eurocentric view that science is the most appropriate route to knowledge and that this, in itself, is a form of bias.

■ Cross-cultural research in psychology suffers many theoretical and technical difficulties. For example, psychologists do not agree on a clear definition of 'culture' or the most effective ways of comparing cultures.

■ The traditional approach to cross-cultural research involved devising theories and tests in the home culture and then applying them in another culture in the hope of finding cultural universals. The newer 'cultural psychology' makes no assumptions that such universals exist but emphasizes instead different social systems as the source of variations between people.

■ A Eurocentric approach to psychology fails to recognize the many dimensions of cultural difference, and tends to emphasize individualism, power-distance, masculinity and uncertainty avoidance. This appears to set biased standards against which all other cultures are compared.

■ Among the many ways that cultural bias may be perpetuated in psychology are the choice of research participants, the choice of methods, and ways in which findings are communicated to a wider audience.

■ American psychology tends to utilize as research participants white, undergraduate students who are representative neither of other Americans nor of other cultures.

■ Using a distinction made by Pike (1967), methods of studying other cultures may take either an 'etic' approach (studying a culture from the outside using criteria common to the 'home' and the studied culture) or an 'emic' view (studying a culture from the inside, often collaborating with its members in devising suitable criteria).

■ Confusion arises when Eurocentric theories and methods are used in other cultures and become 'imposed etics', which may result in the findings' becoming invalid. A solution may be to take the 'emics' of the two cultures to be studied and use their common ground to arrive at a 'derived etic' that is equally valid in both cultures.

■ Eurocentric psychology has traditionally communicated its findings in writing through books and research papers in which anything that does not fit the prevailing view may be 'filtered' by the dominant culture

■ Bulhan (1985) argues that Eurocentric psychologists attempt to ignore, marginalize or 'Europeanize' other cultures.

■ The dominant view in Eurocentric psychology is that it is meaningful to separate people in terms of race and gender. This leads to value judgments, which may be racist and sexist.

■ 'Old racism' is based on assumptions about the importance of alleged biological differences between races, particularly genetic ones What were seen as inferior genes of some races led to discriminatory immigration and education policies. Psychologists have colluded in this view by using so-called 'objective' IQ testing (an 'imposed etic').

■ Howitt and Owusu-Bempah argue that racism still exists in psychology, though in a more subtle form. It is perpetuated mainly by biased ways of thinking, by practices that marginalize and 'tokenize' black psychologists, and by filtering the content of research journals and textbooks to reflect the views of the dominant culture.

■ Many of the themes raised in relation to racial bias apply also to gender bias in psychology. Women are often viewed as 'all the same', different from the 'male norm' and 'less worthy'. Matlin (1993) argues that the use of white, masculine theories and methods reduces the importance of many things that are important in the lives of women: for example, pregnancy, menopause, rape and sexual harassment. 'New sexism' is practised in many of the same ways as 'new racism'.

■ A number of different kinds of gender bias exist in many psychological theories. Examples include Freud's psychoanalytic theory, Erikson's theory of psychosocial development and Kohlberg's theory of moral development.

■ A feminist approach and some ways of transforming biased theories include concentrating on the similarities between males and females, avoiding stereotypes and sexist language, emphasizing the role of socialization rather than biological processes and using concepts that apply to all, regardless of age, culture, race, sexual orientation or gender.

■ Many feminist theorists believe that progress is being made to eradicate gender bias. For example, the psychology of women is an option in many degree courses.

■ A solution to racial and gender bias in psychology should do more than simply replace it with 'tolerance'. Strenuous attempts should be made to bring about change at the individual level, the institutional level and the cultural level.

Further reading

Gross, R.D. (1995). *Themes, Issues and Debates in Psychology*. London: Hodder & Stoughton.
Chapters 6, 8 and 11 cover issues of feminism in psychology, cross-cultural psychology and psychology as a science in some depth.

Howitt, D. and Owusu-Bempah, J. (1994). *The Racism of Psychology: Time for Change*. Hemel Hempstead: Harvester Wheatsheaf. A subtle account of how psychology has supported racism throughout its history, and how antiracist psychology can be followed in the future.

Matlin, M. (1992). *Feminist Perspectives in Therapy*. New York: Wiley. The early chapters in particular are useful for general information about how women have been, and are, regarded in psychology.

CHAPTER 4

Controversial applications of psychological research

Advertising, propaganda and warfare   79

▥ Advertising and propaganda   79
▥ Techniques of persuasion   80
▥ Recent models of persuasion   83
▥ Putting theory into practice   83
▥ Understanding and resisting persuasion   87
▥ Persuasion and ethics   89

▥ Concluding note on psychology and warfare   90
Psychometric testing   91
▥ Intelligence testing   92
▥ Personality testing   93
▥ Controversies surrounding psychometric testing   94
▥ Conclusion   98

Objectives

By the end of this chapter you should be able to:

▥ Explain what is meant by the terms 'advertising' and 'propaganda';

▥ Outline some of the findings from the Yale studies of persuasion and describe two more recent models of persuasion;

▥ Describe some of the persuasion techniques used by advertisers and propagandists and consider some ways in which people can resist persuasion;

▥ Consider the ethics of persuasion;

▥ Provide examples of 'psywar' research and explain why 'psywar' research is such a contentious area;

▥ Explain the term 'psychometric testing' and say what it is used for;

▥ Describe some examples of psychometric tests and consider some of the controversies surrounding the uses of psychometric testing.

There is an increasing awareness within the psychological community and amongst the general public of the power of psychological knowledge to affect people's lives and bring about change. As we shall see in connection with clinical applications of research and with animal research (see Chapter 5) this knowledge can be of great benefit to people. This chapter considers two further areas of psychology where the application of psychological knowledge is particularly controversial. The first section examines the application of psychological research to advertising, propaganda and warfare, and the second section considers controversies surrounding the use of psychometric tests (such as those used to measure intelligence or personality). In each case, there is great potential for good but also for harm. Psychologists are in a strong position to let people know about these influences so that they can understand what is happening and make informed decisions for themselves about how to act.

Advertising, propaganda and warfare

Advertising and propaganda

Advertisers and propagandists are both in the business of **persuasion**. They have a great deal in common in terms of the techniques they use to persuade, although their underlying motives may be different. In addition, they are both phenomena of the twentieth century, cashing in on the growth of mass communication. 'Advertising' is a term usually applied to attempts at 'mass selling' of products, services, information or ideas via the mass media. The term 'propaganda' became widespread during World War I and, in most people's minds, it conjures up images of being fed biased ideas through the use of lies, manipulation and deception. Pratkanis and Aronson (1991) give a wider definition. They say it is:

> mass suggestion or influence, through the manip-
> ulation of symbols and the psychology of the
> individual. Propaganda is the communication of a
> point of view with the ultimate goal of having the
> recipient of the appeal come to 'voluntarily'
> accept this position as if it were his or her own.
> (Pratkanis and Aronson, 1991, p. 9)

Not all propagandists are necessarily dishonest or malevolent. Some of them firmly believe in the worth of their message and look on their attempts to persuade as helpful to others. For example, there is the view that education is a form of propaganda. Through the education system, we are, after all, giving school-children a particular body of knowledge that has been deemed worthwhile. Certain religious groups who try to persuade others to join them might also consider their actions to be in people's best interest. However, in both these cases, the message is one-sided. Pratkanis and Aronson urge us to remember that not all persuasion qualifies as propaganda. Some persuasion comes about through open, balanced and honest debate from two or more different viewpoints, in which case it is educational in the true sense.

We are bombarded daily with attempts to persuade us to buy a product, vote a certain way, adopt a particular health behaviour or make donations to charity. Persuasion, in all its forms, is a part of modern life, and the explosion in communications means that we now live in a world that is so 'message dense' that our limited capacity, information-processing, cognitive systems are overloaded. At the same time, people are growing more knowledgeable and cynical about others' attempts to persuade. We can all think of examples of misleading advertisements, dishonest politicians, unnecessary health scares or cases where charity funds have disappeared. Knowing this, advertisers and propagandists are faced with having

WHAT HAVE YOU GOT ?

to develop ever more ingenious ways of attracting our attention and changing our behaviour. The existence of campaign managers, image consultants, PR companies and market research organizations is testimony to how seriously persuasion is taken these days. It is big business and it pays.

Techniques of persuasion

Immediately after World War II, prompted by an interest in wartime propaganda and persuasion, the US Government gave its support to an extensive pro-gramme of research at Yale University. Amongst the questions the government wanted to answer were 'Are some messages more persuasive than others?' and 'Are some people more persuasible than others?' The psychologists at Yale accordingly developed the 'communication model of persuasion' (see Figure 4.1). This model views persuasive communications as depending on the action of four main variables at

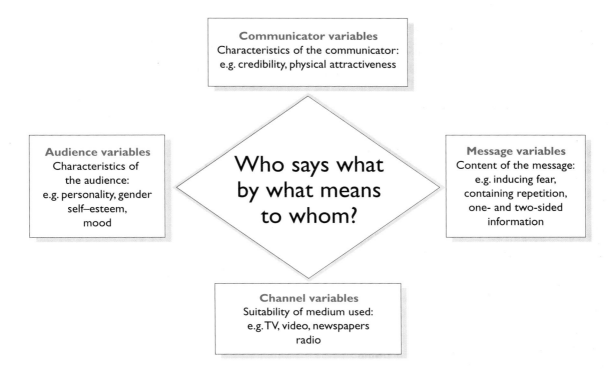

Figure 4.1 The Yale communication model of persuasion

different stages in the communication process. The model can be summed up as asking 'Who says what by what means to whom?' The variables are:

- Communicator variables;
- Message variables;
- Channel variables;
- Audience variables.

In any persuasive communication, these variables exert differing amounts of influence on the persuasion process. Persuasion can succeed or break down because of any one of these or through the combined action of more than one. It is worth looking briefly at some of the early research into this model because of its important influence on later work.

Communicator variables

These are often relatively superficial characteristics of the communicator, for example:

Communicator credibility   In a simple test of this. Hovland and Weiss (1951) asked participants to read

an article advocating the building of nuclear powered submarines. (This was before they actually existed.) Some participants were told that the message they were reading was by the respected physicist J. R. Oppenheimer, while others were told the message was from the Russian newspaper *Pravda*. Oppenheimer was seen as a more credible source to these participants, who were consequently more persuaded to his view.

Communicator personal characteristics   Physical attractiveness, expertise, trustworthiness and prestige also seem to be important communicator variables and, at times, these can override the credibility of the message. Advertisers know this when they employ celebrities to help sell their products, even if the connection is tenuous.

Message variables

The content of persuasive messages has been varied in a number of ways: for example, to induce fear, to include one- or two-sided arguments and to contain repetition:

Advertisers often use celebrities to help sell their products; here tennis star André Agassi helps promote Pepsi Max

Fear arousal Leventhal (1970) found that fear arousal could aid persuasion but only if it was handled carefully. Too much fear can cause people to 'switch off'. A recent example in the UK, which follows Leventhal's recommendations, concerns the campaign to promote 'safe sex' as a protection against AIDS. The message must arouse some fear by making people feel they really are at risk. It must also make it clear that failure to follow the given advice could result in dire consequences. Having thus gained people's attention and worried them sufficiently, it is then vital to offer them a 'do-able' response (in this case, always use a condom), which will reduce the fear. Persuasion is then more likely.

One- and two-sided messages Hovland et al. (1949) published a study reporting the effects of one- or two-sided messages on American soldiers who were still involved in World War II. Germany had been defeated but the Pacific war against Japan looked set to continue for some time. In these circumstances it was necessary to convince the soldiers of the struggle ahead. Some were given a one-sided message stressing Japan's strength. Others heard a two-sided message, which was the same as the one-sided message but included arguments about Japan's weaknesses. Research such as this tends to show that, if people are already broadly in agreement with a message, a one-sided argument is more persuasive. If the recipients of the message disagree, a two-sided message is more effective in persuading them towards the opposite view. Overall, though, group averages show no differences.

Repetition In *Mein Kampf* ('My Struggle' 1925), Adolf Hitler combined the power of the one-sided message and repetition when he wrote of the importance of repeating slogans and never allowing contradictory messages to intervene. Indeed, more recent psychological research by Zajonc (1968) has shown how repetition can lead to liking. He calls this the 'mere exposure effect' and there are many examples of this in advertising. Repetition of brand names during commercials is shown to be effective in people's purchasing patterns when they choose familiar products over equally good but less familiar ones. During election campaigns, political candidates make sure they are in the public eye as much as possible. However, it is important to guard against over-exposure and causing people to become irritated. Repetition works best if people are not paying too much attention to the message. If they are likely to pay closer attention, repetition with variation works well and guards against boredom. The Gold Blend coffee adverts, which weave a mini soap opera around coffee drinking, are a good example of this.

Channel variables

These concern which medium is used to convey a message, for example, TV, video, newspapers, magazines, radio, or mail shots:

Audio and visual messages These depend more on making an immediate, if superficial, impact. In practice, this means that the characteristics of the communicator (credibility, attractiveness etc.) come to the fore. They can distract the recipient away from the message, making its content less important.

Written messages If the message is written, it allows for more careful thought and checking, so the quality of the arguments is more important. When

Kennedy and Nixon were battling for election to the US presidency in the 1960s, Kennedy appeared many times on TV looking tanned and relaxed. Nixon, on the other hand, looked pale and troubled. Although it was generally felt that, on paper, Nixon's arguments were sounder and more compelling, Kennedy still won by a narrow margin.

Audience variables

These include individual differences such as intelligence, personality, self-esteem and gender, and studies of their effects give very mixed findings. Clearly they do not operate in isolation from each other, and they can affect all or some of the stages in the persuasion process differently. Here is a selection of the findings:

Intelligence   Greater verbal intelligence seems to be linked to greater persuasion if the message is complex and sound and less persuasion if the message is simple and flawed.

Self-esteem   Some studies have shown a negative relationship between persuasibility and self-esteem but others (such as Rhodes and Wood, 1992) think people with moderate self-esteem are more persuasible. They are not so distracted by the wish to make a good impression that they will not listen, neither are they so sure of themselves that they are immovable.

Mood   Bless et al. (1990) discovered that people in a good mood were more likely than people in a bad mood to be swayed by superficial persuasive messages. People in a bad mood, however, could still be persuaded but only by good quality arguments.

Understanding   Cacioppo and Petty (1982) think that people differ in their 'need for cognition' (understanding). They developed a scale to measure this and used it to distinguish high scorers, who tend to work hard to comprehend messages, from low scorers, who do not. To persuade the former group it proved important that persuasive messages were of high quality as they are more likely to spot the flaws in weak arguments.

Recent models of persuasion

Studies in the Yale tradition have done much to study the effects of 'Who says what by what means to whom?'

but they have tended to skirt the issue of why certain communications work better than others. Recent models have focused much more on the cognitive (thought) processes people employ when faced with a persuasive message.

We are bombarded by messages from many sources and cannot possibly process them all. Some psychologists describe people as 'cognitive misers' who like to take 'mental shortcuts' and are lazy about how much information they will process. At other times, they give information their full attention. Would-be persuaders know that both lazy and thoughtful processing can lead to persuasion under different circumstances. Two models of persuasion have emerged that use these ideas. These are the **elaboration likelihood** model, or ELM (Petty and Cacioppo, 1981), and the **heuristic** model of persuasion (Chaiken, 1987) (see Box 4.1).

In both these models, it is agreed that central (or systematic) processing leads to more lasting retention of the message than does peripheral (or heuristic) processing. It should, therefore, be easier to predict people's behaviour after they have carried out central processing of a message than after they have carried out peripheral processing. Nevertheless, many advertisers are successful in encouraging peripheral processing of messages that lasts long enough for us to buy their products.

Putting theory into practice

Many of the early recommendations from the Yale studies can be reinterpreted in the light of newer models of persuasion and used by advertisers and propagandists to increase the chances of persuasion. Careful manipulation of communicator, message, channel and audience variables in combination with an understanding of central and peripheral processing should enable them to develop effective persuasive communications, which will then, they hope, translate into attitude and behaviour change.

There are many other tactics that potential persuaders might use, all of them derived from psychological research. Box 4.2 lists some of these (see also Chapter 28). Refer to this before reading on.

In the real world, persuaders know that they can never be 100 per cent successful, but they can make some impact by combining everything they know about persuasion. Three examples that illustrate this are given by Pratkanis and Aronson (1991). The first of these (the Greenpeace appeal) leans more towards

---

Box 4.1   More recent models of persuasion

The elaboration likelihood model, or ELM (Petty and Cacioppo, 1981). In this model there are two routes to persuasion:

- The **central route** involves active (thoughtful) processing of a message and careful scrutiny of its content, merit and logic. We are more likely to process actively (elaborate) if a message has personal relevance and we feel involved with it. The success of this route tends to depend on the quality of the arguments presented.
- The **peripheral route** involves relatively shallow (lazy) processing. There is little attention to the message's content, merit or logic. We are less likely to elaborate a message that is not particularly personally relevant or involving. Its success in persuading us depends more on superficial cues, such as communicator variables, than on the content of the message itself.

The heuristic model of persuasion (Chaiken, 1987).

This model broadly agrees with the distinction between central and peripheral processing made by the ELM but substitutes the terms 'systematic' and 'heuristic' processing. It goes on to add that, when we are disinclined to give a message our full attention for whatever reason, we apply 'heuristics' or 'rules of thumb'. These enable us to process a message with minimum effort. For example, a heuristic we often use is that people who have personal experience of something are generally right about it. Another heuristic is that people will express opinions more honestly and openly if they believe they are having a private conversation. Both of these heuristics are used in certain 'hidden camera' washing powder advertisements in which a celebrity approaches a woman buying the advertiser's powder. She clearly has plenty of experience of washing the family's clothing and expresses a favourable opinion to him about the product. Only then is it revealed to her that she is being filmed.

---

advertising. The second example (how cults create converts) leans more towards propaganda. The third example directly concerns how propaganda has been used in warfare. All of them borrow from the same stock of persuasion techniques.

The Greenpeace appeal

Greenpeace's appeal for donations, which began in the USA, involved the following techniques, which encourage a mixture of central and peripheral processing:

- They targeted those most likely to be able to contribute, for example home-owners.
- They used a mailshot, knowing that written material could be carefully scrutinized.
- The envelopes they used stood out through being larger than usual and by having an eye-catching message on the outside.
- The envelopes were an official-looking colour, thus creating an impression of credibility.
- Inside there were free stickers, thus inducing the norm of reciprocity. In addition, use of the stickers would mean adopting the Greenpeace group identity. The appealing animals on the stickers would also serve as a distracter from central processing.

- The enclosed letter was addressed 'Dear Friend' (a **granfalloon** technique).
- A questionnaire about toxic waste was included. Completion of this would encourage the individual to think about the issues involved and thus engage in a kind of self-persuasion.
- Information in the letter raised fears about toxic waste and offered a 'do-able' solution, namely to contribute to a group who were actively and, allegedly, successfully engaged in reducing the risks of such waste (and who were prepared to take the real risks for you).
- A choice of contributions was offered ranging from $15 to $100. The contrast effect thus induced would, hopefully, result in the choice of more than the minimum amount.

GLOSSARY

Granfalloon A loosely connected social group that forms solely because its members believe they have something special in common.

Cult A group of people who are devoted to a particular system of worship or who pay homage to a particular person or thing.

Brainwashing Techniques of persuasion which involve the total recasting of an individual's mind-set.

Box 4.2 Some techniques used in persuasive communications

Techniques based in social influence

■ Creating **granfalloons** ('proud and meaningless associations of human beings'). This is based on Tajfel's (1982) idea of minimal groups where people can be given a feeling of group identity sometimes on the flimsiest of pretexts. Persuaders encourage this by giving their product a 'personality' so that buying it gives the consumer a sense of belonging to a special group.

■ Using nonverbal aspects of communication well: for example, using open gestures and a direct, but not overbearing, gaze. This avoids intimidating the audience and makes the persuader seem honest.

■ Creating a norm of reciprocity. If someone gives you something, it is usual to give in return. A small free gift or sample given before making a serious attempt to persuade can induce this in people and encourage them to return the favour by buying from the giver.

■ Using a number of persuaders and/or using 'converts' as models. Seeing that a number of people are already persuaded can help to increase pressure to conform.

Techniques that encourage peripheral processing or use of heuristics

■ Choose wording of the message carefully (for example, 'There is no cheaper insurance') or use 'purr words' such as 'best ever'. There may be plenty of others that are equally cheap and the advertiser's 'best ever' may still be inferior to a competitor's product! Words can deceive and create misperceptions.

■ Use 'decoys': that is, compare the product with an inferior one. This produces a 'context effect' and makes the advertiser's product look better than it really is. (But it is not often used by well-known brands. Why give the competitor free publicity?)

■ Appear to argue against self-interest or for no personal gain. If the communicator finds the message that compelling there must be something in it.

■ Package the product carefully to encourage heuristics such as 'Brown paper packages contain wholesome products', 'Soberly dressed politicians are more trustworthy'.

■ Use vivid images; distract attention from weak messages with humour, music or plenty of action. This makes the message more memorable and attention-grabbing and discourages central processing.

Techniques that play on cognitions and emotions

■ Allowing the audience to draw its own conclusions. This 'self-persuasion' technique works well with interesting and fairly simple messages but care must be taken not to patronize the audience.

■ Creating a feeling of 'cognitive dissonance' in people then offering them a way to reduce it: for example, uncomfortable feelings raised by charity appeals can be reduced by giving to the charity.

■ Creating **factoids** (Mailer, 1973): that is, facts that did not exist before the media created them. Once created, these are difficult to undo. Hitler and Goebbels created factoids about Germans as the 'master race' and the Jewish people as 'conspirators' against it.

■ Encouraging people to role-play mentally. 'Slice of life' adverts do this by showing families not too unlike the viewer's own. This makes it easy for viewers to imagine themselves enjoying the benefits of a product.

■ Creating a sense of scarcity: for example, 'Buy now while stocks last!' The promise of possessing something allegedly rare and desirable can discourage us from considering alternatives.

Well-known sales techniques (discussed more fully in Chapter 28)

■ **Foot in the door**. Make a small request first, followed by a larger one. Some advertisers offer a short-term trial subscription to a magazine and then ask for a longer commitment.

■ **Door in the face**. Ask for too much, wait for the refusal and then ask for something less. Unscrupulous salespeople may initially offer something at too high a price and then appear to 'do you a favour' by grudgingly dropping the amount.

■ **Low-ball**: that is, obtain agreement and only then let the person know there are strings attached. Some garages offer free roadside assistance if you buy your car from them (but only if your car is regularly, and expensively, serviced by them).

How cults create converts

When we hear of the power of **cults** to persuade, it is tempting to think there is some sort of '**brainwashing**' involved (as used by the Communist Chinese on American POWs during the Korean War). Pratkanis and Aronson explain that brainwashing entails nothing more exotic or irresistible than the persuasion techniques already outlined, and that many groups, not just the more unusual cults, can be seen to use them. They list seven ways in which cults can be persuasive once a suitably impressionable person has been found:

- A new social reality is presented. To do this, the cult 'filters' information to the potential convert about what is and is not acceptable. This message is driven home through frequent repetition and reward. The convert may be cut off from others (such as family) who may challenge the message.
- A 'granfalloon', or feeling of identity, is created, perhaps through giving up possessions and adopting particular habits, foods and ways of dressing that make it difficult to integrate with others outside the group.
- Commitment is encouraged through creating **cognitive dissonance**, then offering a way to reduce it. The 'foot in the door' technique works well here. Once an initial commitment has been made, it is harder to go back on it than to go along with it. The creation of opportunities to reduce guilt is also effective.
- The credibility and attractiveness of the leader is established, perhaps by creating myths about their connection to God or Jesus.
- The potential convert can be sent to give the message to nonconverts. This acts as a form of self-persuasion.
- The potential convert can be distracted from questioning the group's doctrine: for example, through rituals and self-deprivation (usually of food or sleep). Anticult thoughts are dismissed as being 'from Satan'.
- A vision of the 'promised land' can be created, towards which the potential convert will need to work. (This is similar to creating a 'factoid'.)

Propaganda and warfare

During World War I the use of propaganda by the USA and Britain proved to be one of the vital ingredients in ensuring the defeat of Germany. Adolf Hitler learned a great deal from studying the tactics that had been used, and this undoubtedly helped him to establish and maintain a German state controlled by the Nazi party. To assist him in this, he created the Ministry of Popular Enlightenment and Propaganda and appointed Joseph Goebbels to oversee it. Hitler and Goebbels favoured what we now call the peripheral route to persuasion

and often used appeals to the emotions. They were scathing about the intellects of most people, and limited most of their propaganda to a few key points and frequently repeated slogans. Hitler concerned himself very little with the ethics of his propaganda ministry's actions, arguing that the ends (swift victory) justified the means. Some of the techniques employed were as follows.

Selective filtering of material Once in power, the Nazi party gained control of the mass media to ensure that the information reaching the people was selectively filtered. Journalists were carefully chosen and systematically rewarded and punished for their efforts (in some cases, by being allowed privileged access to certain stories). A bold Nazi image was created through the use of attention-getting posters and slogans. Pro-Nazi messages were mixed into popular entertainment programmes and linked to Aryan prowess at the 1936 Olympic Games.

Encouragement of factoids Goebbels suggested phrases and images to people to encourage 'factoids': for example, he coined the term *Schleichende Krise* (creeping crisis) to help persuade the German people that England was in an increasingly weak state of economic and political unrest.

Impression of consensus Films of mass rallies helped to give the impression of consensus with Hitler and approval of him.

Creation of grandeur Massive stadiums were built as meeting places. These allied the Nazis in people's minds to great and powerful cultures of the past and left them feeling dwarfed by the scale of Nazi power.

Creation of band of supporters Initially a band of loyal supporters (Hitler Youth) was created, easily identified by their brown shirts. The ridicule that this sometimes provoked would have created unpleasant feelings of dissonance which could then be dispelled by becoming even more dedicated to the cause.

> **GLOSSARY**
>
> **Cognitive dissonance** A sense of tension brought about by holding beliefs that conflict with one another.
>
> **Factoid** A fact that did not exist until it was created by the media.

A German wartime propaganda poster aimed at the Russian population, blaming atrocities on Jewish Communist commissars

Creation of 'granfalloons' One of the most powerful techniques used was to combine the 'granfalloon' with existing fear and frustration. World War I had left Germany in serious and demoralizing economic difficulties, and many people felt insecure about the future. Hitler and Goebbels began to create the idea that the Jews were responsible for draining the nation's resources. This had the effect of turning Jews into an out-group and Aryans and Nazis into an in-group with a strong identity. It also created a scapegoat for the in-group's feelings and legitimized persecution of the Jews for the purposes of restoring Germany's status.

Use of radio During World War II, radio was used by all sides in attempts to weaken the enemy's resolve. The Nazis used the British traitor William Joyce, who broadcast German propaganda to the British under the name 'Lord Haw-Haw'. Iva Ikuko Toguri D'Aquino broadcast to the Allies from Japan under the name of 'Tokyo Rose'. These broadcasts were in addition to frequent leaflet drops from the air.

Promoting a 'war of nerves' Before each new aggressive move in Europe, the German ministry of propaganda started a 'war of nerves' against their target by, for example, alleging that German minorities were being persecuted in the target country and that the German forces were invincible. This had the effect of weakening and dividing the target country and causing its allies to hesitate.

Promoting the leader/father figure The answer to the nation's problems was firmly located with one man – Adolf Hitler – who was portrayed both as a benevolent and modest father figure and as a steadfast military man supported by the mass approval of the people.

Naturally, the Allies had their own propaganda agencies, which worked hard to counter the enemy's messages and demoralize its military forces and civilians while, at the same time, keeping up morale and strengthening resolve at home. Propaganda is a prominent feature of any modern war and there are many examples of its use in Vietnam, Korea, the Falklands and, more recently, in the Gulf and former Yugoslavia. Many of the tragic consequences of war are clear for all to see but it is always technically very difficult to assess whether propaganda played a part in the loss or protection of people's lives. Furthermore, once a war is over, propaganda which could be wildly inaccurate is seldom corrected and it is not known how persistent its effects, if any, are. For the survivors, the messages they were exposed to may well be retained, helping to keep low-level hostility and prejudice ready to resurface during the next conflict.

Understanding and resisting persuasion

Pratkanis and Aronson express concern that people have seen so many examples of the use of persuasion to coerce and manipulate that they have grown weary even to the point of inactivity: for example, no longer bothering to vote in elections or make donations to charity. They suggest that inaction is not the most constructive solution and that there must be a middle route between 'naïve acceptance on the one hand and total cynicism on the other' (p. xii) about the content of messages received from others and their intentions in

Box 4.3 Some persuasion techniques and how to resist them (see Box 4.2)

Persuasion technique	Ways of resisting persuasion
Techniques based on social influence	
■ Granfalloons	■ Come to terms with the disappointment of not being a member of a 'special' group (for example, ask 'Is it really worth it?'). Look for common ground between the desired goal and alternatives. Think of the out-group as individuals like yourself. Don't get all your self-esteem from this one source.
■ Nonverbal aspects of communication	■ Observe these carefully. What does the communicator have to gain?
■ Creating a norm of reciprocity	■ You are not obliged to give in return.
■ Using a number of persuaders and/or converts	■ Recognize that you can act independently and that the image of consensus is probably superficial.
Techniques that encourage peripheral processing or use of heuristics	
■ Carefully chosen wording	■ Try rephrasing the message.
■ Decoys	■ Focus on the actual merits of what is being advertised.
■ Arguments against self-interest	■ Question the motives of the persuader
■ Packaging	■ Beware of your own heuristics!
■ Distracters	■ Ask why it is necessary for the persuader to distract you.
Techniques that play on cognitions and emotions	
■ Self-persuasion	■ Play 'devil's advocate' and try to counter-argue.
■ Cognitive dissonance	■ Consider alternative ways of reducing dissonance.
■ Factoids	■ Question the motives of the persuader and consider the consequences of being persuaded.
■ Mental images	■ Recognize that you are being sold a (probably unobtainable) dream.
■ Sense of scarcity	■ Be prepared to walk away if you cannot get what you want. Recognize that frustration is a natural response to being thwarted so give yourself time to 'cool off'.
Well-known sales techniques	■ Realize that you can say 'no' at any time and consider
■ (foot in the door, door in the face and low-ball)	how you got into the situation in the first place.

trying to persuade us. Their book, *Age of Propaganda*, aims to inform people about persuasion techniques so that they can:

■ understand what is happening,
■ tell a 'con job' (p. xiii) from an honest message,
■ protect themselves if they so wish,
■ ultimately come to use persuasion wisely.

Many attempts to persuade, as we have seen, exploit the idea that people are 'cognitive misers' who can be reached through the peripheral route to persuasion and are more open to mindless propaganda than to thoughtful persuasion. This is of particular concern since Gerbner et al. (1986) showed that the mass media give us a grossly misleading picture of the world. Heavy viewing of television, in particular, tends to correlate with holding certain views: for example, seeing women as less capable than men and society as more violent than it really is. After research by Iyengar and Kinder (1987) had shown that the effect of heavy viewing on people's views is causal, Pratkanis and Aronson concluded that 'the content of the mass media sets the public's social and political agenda' (p. 54). Thus the burden is on the recipients of the message to scrutinize it carefully and to realize that they do have a choice about whether to accept it or, indeed, whether to think about the message at all. There are at least four things that can be done:

1. Understand persuasive tactics and how to resist them (see Boxes 4.2 and 4.3).
2. Induce **reactance**. This is brought about by letting people know that attempts are being made to persuade them. The resulting 'reactance' causes them actively to resist the message because they feel their personal freedom is being threatened.
3. Use **inoculation**. McGuire (1964) exposed people to a weakened form of a persuasive message before giving them the full message. This prior warning 'inoculated' them in that it allowed them time to formulate counter-arguments and made them more resistant to persuasion. Inoculation works particularly well with issues that have personal relevance.
4. Establish regulatory bodies. The role of these is to monitor messages and ensure that they are fairer and more honest. This raises a particular dilemma in democracies that advocate free speech since regulation could be seen as a from of censorship or 'gagging'. Yet regulatory bodies do exist and persuaders respond by arranging their messages very carefully to stay within the limits of the law. That this is not always successful can be seen in the number of prosecutions brought against advertisers and in the number of official apologies made on TV and in other mass media.

Persuasion and ethics

The scale of influence exercised by persuaders is enormous, ranging from charity advertising to attempts by fanatics to recruit followers. In addition, many professions, such as law, politics, teaching and medicine, depend on successful persuasion. Persuasion can be used for both good and evil ends, and this raises important ethical questions about what its role should be and what the values of the persuaders themselves are. Pratkanis and Aronson say that ethical issues can be approached in three ways:

■ Consider whether the ends justify the means. If we need to persuade in order to save lives then the answer is probably yes. If we are car salespeople on commission trying to persuade customers to buy then the answer is less clear.
■ Consider the means rather than the ends. It is generally agreed that we should avoid misleading, false, filtered information that arouses unpleasant emotions, but there are always fuzzy areas here, such as when we tell 'white lies'.
■ Consider both the means and the ends. Try to balance the importance of persuading people with the means of persuasion.

This is obviously a very complex problem with no easy answers. Pratkanis and Aronson comment that very often the means determine the ends. If we feel honestly dealt with we may accept a message but if we suspect foul play we shall reject it. The experience of British and American propagandists acts as a warning here. During World War I, they created long-term problems by failing to consider both the means and the ends of their successful anti-German campaign and concentrating instead on short-term gain. Once it became known that their propaganda had, at times, been less than honest it was harder to persuade the sceptical World War II Allies about the reality of Nazi atrocities against the Jews.

Exercise 4.1   Techniques of persuasion and how to resist them

Over the next week or so, pay particular attention to forms of advertising in the media: on TV and radio, in newspapers and magazines, on bill boards, and so on. See if you can recognize some of the techniques of persuasion that have been discussed in this section. Think of some ways in which people might resist them.

GLOSSARY

Reactance In relation to persuasion, the technique of letting people know that they are being persuaded so that they can react against it.

Inoculation In relation to persuasion, the technique of presenting a weakened form of the message to allow people to form counter-arguments.

Pratkanis and Aronson say that we should ask 'What forms of education and persuasion will serve society and ourselves best?' (p. 218). Sadly, open and honest debate about the techniques of persuasion and wise evaluation of them does not seem to be commonplace. In addition we seem to be reluctant to engage in honest and reasoned argument about important issues, preferring instead to lazily process other people's messages about them while growing ever more cynical about the motives of the persuader. The danger in this is that we could become so ill-informed about both techniques of persuasion and important issues that we are unable to act appropriately when it matters. If that were to happen, Hitler's view that the masses are ignorant could, eventually, become a reality.

Concluding note on psychology and warfare

In his book *War on the Mind*, Peter Watson (1978) debated the important question of whether war is an inevitable part of human life and, reluctantly, concluded that it is. Other important writers, such as Sigmund Freud and Konrad Lorenz, have expressed similar views, but not all psychologists would agree. In particular, learning theorists stress environmental determinants of behaviour and argue that, theoretically, it should be possible to avoid conflict. The truth probably lies somewhere in between. Humans may have a biological predisposition to fight with other humans but they can also bring higher cognitive abilities to bear on the situation. For psychologists, studying the role of heredity, environment and cognition in human conflict is more than an interesting academic exercise. The fact that humans can now conduct wars using technology that could destroy the planet is too important to ignore and makes an understanding of **psywar** ever more pressing.

The use of persuasion techniques in spreading wartime propaganda is only one way in which psychology can be applied to war. Watson documents many other applications, some of which are listed in Figure 4.2. All of them raise important ethical questions. In discussing these, Watson says 'the military use of science is justifiable but only when it is used to conserve life or if it is in response, direct or anticipated, to some new threat. The deliberate development of weapons of unnecessary suffering, on the other hand, is out' (p. 18). However, few applications of 'psywar' research are ethically quite so clear cut as in the two examples given

Figure 4.2 A selection of 'psywar' research areas (based on Watson, 1978)

■ Why wars occur
■ How wars can be prevented or halted
■ Peace maintenance
■ Recruitment to the military
■ Military leadership and followership
■ Military group dynamics
■ Loyalty and treason
■ Selection of military personnel to work behind enemy lines
■ How soldiers can be trained to spot booby traps
■ Identification of people who are good at code-breaking, sensing danger or keeping secrets
■ Assessment of the effects of different attitudes to risk-taking in military personnel
■ Design of weapons, war vehicles, radar screens, control panels and so on
■ Improving perception under less than ideal conditions, for example in the dark
■ Why atrocities occur and what can be done to prevent them
■ How to stop people 'chickening out' of combat
■ Training people to kill
■ Preparing prisoners to withstand the effects of captivity
■ Helping military personnel to cope with stress before, during and after combat
■ How survivors survive

by Watson, so in this area, as in others, psychologists find themselves facing ethical dilemmas.

No psychological research is ever entirely objective. It always takes place against a background of social, cultural and political values. Psychologists are not immune from these; consequently it would be naïve to think that all psywar research is for the noble purpose of self-defence or to make conflict less likely. Psychologists know that the same findings can be turned to both defensive or offensive ends. As Watson, says 'Psychology can be a worrying science in the hands of the military' (p. 18). However, psywar research is not something that psychologists can ignore simply because it is distasteful or can be abused. It has the potential to affect the fates of vast numbers of people for better or worse, which makes it, perhaps, one of the most socially sensitive research areas of all.

GLOSSARY

Psywar The psychology of war.

❓ SELF-ASSESSMENT QUESTIONS

1. Explain what is meant by advertising and propaganda.
2. Give one example each of source, message, channel and audience variables as identified in the Yale studies.
3. Outline the ELM and heuristic models of persuasion.
4. Explain some of the persuasion techniques that might be used in charity appeals or to convert people to cults.
5. Describe some of the propaganda techniques used by Adolf Hitler and Joseph Goebbels during World War II.
6. Explain four ways in which people might resist persuasion.
7. Comment on the ethics of psychological research into advertising, propaganda and warfare.

Psychometric testing

The term 'psychometric test' refers to any technique that has been devised for quantifying (measuring) an aspect of psychological functioning. Such tests are derived from the 'psychometric model' of human behaviour. According to Kline (1992), this model 'claims that all behaviour is explicable in terms of factors of ability, personality, motivation and state or mood together with the situation in which individuals find themselves' (p. 101).

The most widely known tests are those that measure intellectual abilities or personality, although psychometric techniques can be applied more widely than this. People are most likely to come into contact with testing in educational, occupational and clinical settings:

- **Educational** – used to assess accomplishments, to select and sort children according to ability, to diagnose problems, to predict future performance and to check the effectiveness of teaching techniques;
- **Occupational** – for purposes of selection, careers guidance and assessment of training needs;
- **Clinical** – used for diagnosis and to assess treatment needs and progress.

Kline (1992) explains that psychological tests fall into five categories (there is some overlap between the first two). Only some of these can be considered truly psychometric in that they are based on established population norms (average scores) against which individual scores can be compared. **Projective techniques** and motivational tests, for example, are generally known as **ipsative tests** (see also Chapter 30). They are not based on preestablished norms, and comparisons between individuals on the basis of test results cannot be made.

- **Ability tests**. Intelligence tests are included here and typically measure general reasoning ability along with verbal, numerical and spatial ability.
- **Aptitude tests**. These usually measure a collection of traits that might come in useful in a specific situation: for example, high scores on hand–eye coordination could form part of a test for selecting trainee pilots to fly high-performance aircraft.
- **Personality tests**. These usually take the form of questionnaires but also include projective techniques.
- **Motivational tests**. These can measure present state, mood or interests.
- **Other tests**. Clinical and neuropsychological tests are included here.

In all of these cases, tests should be carried out only by properly trained professionals. The consequences for individuals of the way in which test results are used can be far-reaching. For this reason it is vital that the tester knows the limitations of a given test and how to interpret the results. Test results should not be used in isolation but as a supplement to other techniques as part of an overall assessment. They should be thought of only as an aid to reaching decisions.

> ### GLOSSARY
>
> **Projective techniques** Tests that contain ambiguous stimuli to which individuals will respond by 'projecting' their own meaning. Responses are interpeted and can lead to an assessment of an individual's personality.
>
> **Ipsative tests** Tests (for example, projective tests) that are not based on preestablished norms, but which require an individual to reveal his or her personality by responding to ambiguous stimuli or through self-assessment.

Box 4.4 Stanford–Binet Intelligence Scale for six to eight-year-olds (1986)

The Stanford–Binet scale groups its tests into four broad kinds of intellectual abilities: verbal reasoning, quantitative reasoning, abstract/visual reasoning and short-term memory (Sattler, 1988). A separate score is yielded for each area. Below are some examples of items similar to those found in the Verbal and Quantitative Reasoning sections of the test for six to eight-year-olds. Scores are interpreted by comparing them with average scores for the age group, which have been arrived at during the standardization process.

Verbal reasoning

Vocabulary
Defines words such as 'letter' and 'penny'

Comprehension
Answers questions such as 'Why do people clean their teeth?' and 'Where do people buy clothes?'

Absurdities
Points out the amusing aspects of a picture, such as a man driving a tractor in the sea or a toothless woman cleaning her teeth.

Quantitative reasoning

Quantitative
Performs simple arithmetic tasks, such as choosing a die with four spots because the number of spots is equal to the combination of a three-spot and a one-spot die.

Number series
Gives the next number in a series such as

| 23 | 20 | 17 | 14 | 11 | ___ |

Equation building
Builds an equation from the following display:

3 6 9 + =

An acceptable response would be $3 + 6 = 9$

Intelligence testing

Assessment methods

The form that intelligence tests take will be determined by the underlying theory of how intelligence is structured. Kline (1992) says that modern tests tap into two kinds of ability: '**fluid intelligence**', comprising basic reasoning skills, which are not much affected by environmental experience; and '**crysallized intelligence**', which is the social manifestation of fluid intelligence, differs between cultures and is, therefore, affected by experience. Both of these can be measured in intelligence tests. British and American tests often contain verbal, numerical, and spatial items as well as testing general knowledge. They generally reveal one or more IQ (intelligence quotient) scores. Examples include:

■ **The Stanford–Binet Intelligence Scales** cover a wide age range from childhood onwards and test verbal, numerical, abstract/visual reasoning and short-term memory (see Box 4.4).
■ **The Wechsler Scales** cover ages ranging from preschool to adulthood. They give verbal (word and number items) and performance (visual and spatial reasoning) IQ scores as well as a general IQ.

■ **The British Ability Scales (BAS)** can be used with children and adolescents, and comprise 23 tests which give visual, verbal and general IQ scores.
■ **Raven's Progressive Matrices** have no verbal items at all. Test items include shapes and patterns and can be used with virtually any age, educational level or cultural background. This test is more 'culture-fair' than others which have a strong verbal element.
■ **The Mill Hill Vocabulary Scale** is the verbal companion to the Raven's Matrices. It comprises two sets of 44 words of increasing difficulty which the test-taker has to define. Again, the test can be used from childhood to adulthood.
■ **AH series tests** can be given to groups of people simultaneously. They contain numerical and verbal items and are used for selection to

---

GLOSSARY

Fluid intelligence. Basic reasoning ability, which is not much influenced by environmental experience.

Crystallized intelligence The social manifestation of 'fluid intelligence', which develops in response to experience of the environment.

apprenticeships, various occupations or higher education.

Clearly, most of these tests draw heavily on the culture in which they were designed, and this lays them open to accusations of cultural bias, especially if they are used with people from different cultural backgrounds. (This is an issue we shall discuss later in this section.) A solution offered by some psychologists is to use measures of brain activity that have been shown to correlate with intelligence test scores but, as Kline says, these are physiological, not psychometric, tests.

Personality testing

Assessment methods

In personality testing, as with intelligence testing, the underlying theory determines the assessment method. Theories differ according to whether they are nomothetic or idiographic. **Nomothetic theories** are based on the idea that there are universal principles that can be applied to everyone and used to compare them with each other. These approaches give rise to **normative tests** ('questionnaires' and 'inventories'), which depend largely on self-report (for example, the

Eysenck Personality Inventory or EPI, Cattell's 16 PF, both of which are fully described in Chapter 29, and the Minnesota Multiphasic Personality Inventory or MMPI). Some of these tests measure characteristics that are assumed to be normally distributed such that most people will score within a given range around the mean (see Chapter 35). A score at one of the extremes would, statistically speaking, be very unusual.

Idiographic theories start by identifying characteristics that all people may have to some extent, but see the individual's combination of these characteristics as unique. These approaches give rise to ipsative tests, which encourage individuals to reveal their own personality structure through self-assessment (for example, Kelly's Repertory Grid and the Q sort, both

---

GLOSSARY

Nomothetic theories Based on the idea that there are laws of behaviour that are applied to everyone and can be used to compare people with each other.

Idiographic theories A belief that human beings are unique and can be understood only through the use of techniques, such as ipsative tests or case studies, that are designed to reflect that uniqueness.

Box 4.5 The Rorschach test (Rorschach, 1921) – a projective test

The Rorschach is an example of a projective test. Projective tests have been loosely defined as ambiguous stimuli to which participants are asked to respond by projecting their own meaning onto them. It is assumed that the individual's responses will reveal aspects of his or her personality along with their conflicts and motivations. Participants are not aware of the purposes of the test, so may disclose things about themselves that they would normally be unwilling to reveal.

The test consists of ten symmetrical shapes that resemble ink blots, such as the one above. Participants are asked to describe what they see in the shapes. The tester notes down what the participant says, how long before the response is made, whether the whole shape is used or just parts of it, any recurring themes emerging, and the participant's general reaction to the test.

Characteristic responses are 'a flower' or 'a bearskin rug', which do not suggest any significant anxiety or conflict. Responses that reveal themes relating to sexual matters or death are often seen as indicating serious underlying conflicts.

Interpretation and scoring are complex tasks, which require substantial training. Critics argue that scoring is a highly subjective and unreliable process, which has limited predictive value. However, a new scoring system is currently available, which is supplemented by a computer scoring service and software for microcomputers (Exner, 1986), though not enough studies have been carried out to assess its validity with confidence.

of which are described in Chapter 30). Psychodynamic assessment techniques can also be fitted in here: for example, projective techniques such as the Thematic Apperception Test (TAT) or the Rorschach inkblot test (see Box 4.5). The material in these is relatively unstructured. The client 'projects' meaning onto it and can then work on interpreting responses with the help of the analyst.

As Kline (1992) reminds us, only normative tests are truly psychometric. Ipsative tests do not yield scores that can be compared with norms. Problems arise if different people are compared on their ipsative test scores or when comparisons are made between normative and ipsative measures of a similar characteristic. Meaningful comparisons are possible only when comparing scores from the same normative test.

Controversies surrounding psychometic testing

Technical, practical and theoretical considerations place limits on how much we can trust test results to give a true measure of psychological functioning. In addition to this, ethical considerations arise when we consider the testing situation itself and the uses to which test results are put. Here we shall consider some of the many issues that make the use of psychometric tests so contentious. The following points apply to all kinds of testing although some of the ethical issues are more pertinent than others to specific types of tests.

Technical and practical considerations

Psychologists strive to devise technically precise tests, which have a number of important qualities (see also Chapter 34):

■ **Reliability**. The test should give consistent results over time (test–retest reliability). The items in it should also be measuring the same thing. (This can be assessed through 'split-half' or 'part–whole' reliability testing.)

■ **Validity**. The test should be relevant: that is, it should test what it claims to test. It should look as if it is relevant (face validity), it should contain items that are meaningful to the test-taker (content validity), results from it should correlate positively with other tests of the same thing (concurrent validity), it should forecast future performance in particular areas (predictive

validity), and it should measure a concept that is meaningful (construct validity).

■ **Standardization**. This involves 'trying out' test items on a representative sample of the population for whom it is intended and making appropriate adjustments. This results in the establishment of 'norms' against which individuals can then be compared.

■ **Discriminatory power**. A test should be sensitive enough to enable us to tell people apart.

Testers also have to take into account a number of practical matters:

■ **Standardization of testing conditions**. The conditions under which people take the test should be the same for everyone in terms of instructions, treatment by the tester, and so on, in order to guard against the possible effects of tester bias. Even the best-designed test can be abused in unskilled hands. This is why educational, occupational and clinical psychologists must be trained to use tests. People outside these professions can obtain BPS training.

■ **Mood and motivational state of test-takers**. These can influence test performance. Some testing procedures take their influence into account, but others do not.

■ **Social desirability bias**. Test-takers may alter their answers, or even lie, if they want to project a certain image. Some tests try to guard against this by building in 'lie scales'.

■ **Test wisdom**. Through familiarity with tests or coaching, people can become test-wise and affect their results considerably, for example raise their

---

> GLOSSARY
>
> **Reliability** In relation to psychometric tests, that the items within them should be consistent with each other and that the test should give consistent results over time.
>
> **Validity** In relation to psychometric tests, that they are testing what they claim to be testing: for example, 'intelligence' or 'personality'.
>
> **Standardization** In relation to psychometric tests, the process of 'trying out' the test on a representative sample of the population for whom it is intended, and establishing norms (average scores).
>
> **Discriminatory power** The ability of a psychological test to separate individuals' performance from one another.

IQ score. This makes a nonsense of comparing the score against norms or other individuals' scores (unless of course they are all similarly test-wise!).

No psychometrician has yet come up with a perfect testing technique that overcomes all these problems. Experienced and properly trained testers are fully aware of the limitations they impose on the veracity of test results. Unfortunately, less well-informed people may overvalue test results.

Theoretical considerations

There are a number of general issues concerning testing that we should always be aware of when interpreting and applying results, for example:

- Theoretical assumptions underlie all tests and tend to be determined by the dominant cultural group (see 'cultural bias' in Chapter 3). The test items, norms and interpretations are thus based on the dominant group's values. This could introduce bias, which might prove disadvantageous to people in other cultural groups: for example, denying them access to certain jobs or educational opportunities.
- There is a risk of **reification** (the process by which theoretical concepts assume reality in people's minds). Concepts such as intelligence and personality became real to us once their existence was suggested and extensively researched, but we should remember that they are not absolute truths but inventions that have proved convenient and useful.
- Psychometricians assume that certain characteristics (such as intelligence and personality) are stable, and that their tests tap into this relatively stable 'core'. Variations in scores over time simply indicate that the individual is superficially adapting to change. However, it is debatable whether we do have stable characteristics that operate independently of our circumstances and which can, therefore, be reliably measured.
- Psychometricians assume that test results are reliably linked to behaviour. If they were not there would be little point in them. However, there is some evidence (for example, Hartshorne and May, 1928) that this is not always the case. The strongest critics of testing say that test results vary so much over time that they are no more to be trusted in predicting behaviour than astrology or graphology.

Ethical considerations

There are many examples of undue reliance on test scores that are then used to inform decisions that affect people's lives, perhaps through unfair discrimination in education or at work or through misdiagnosis of a clinical condition. The development of the 11+ test, used for educational selection in Britain, is one example. Doubts about its theoretical and statistical basis ensured that it had all but disappeared by the 1970s, but it had already had an enormous impact on the educational careers of many schoolchildren. More recently, Palmer (1995) described a case, which eventually went to court, in which a suspect personality test was used to select 20 nurses for ten posts. The ten successful candidates were white and the ten unsuccessful candidates were black. In clinical settings, the possible overdiagnosis of schizophrenia in black compared with white patients is well documented (Fernando, 1991). Understanding technical, practical and theoretical shortcomings of tests is clearly a vital part of test-users' training, but they must go further than this to take account of the wider, ethical implications of their work. Here we shall consider some of the ethical issues faced by tester users and their clients.

Test bias Tests often show differences in scores between certain groups. Kaplan and Saccuzzo (1989) quote evidence that black Americans typically score up to 15 IQ points below white Americans. This unpopular finding is not in dispute but the reason for it is. There are at least two possibilities:

- The test is biased – it is culturally loaded in favour of certain groups, therefore the content is not valid for other groups;
- The test is not biased and shows up real differences.

Regarding test bias, Kaplan and Saccuzzo say that content validity is no longer a central issue. For

---

GLOSSARY

Reification The process whereby theoretical concepts may be perceived by people as real entities.

example, the widely used Stanford–Binet test, which was standardized on white children and adults, has been widely validated on other groups. Furthermore, during the 1970s, psychologists working on the educational enrichment programme Headstart found that differences in black and white children's performance remained on both black and white dialect versions of this test. Excluding items that were potentially biased also produced no change. To complicate the issue, other studies in the United States and Britain have shown that groups such as Jewish and Oriental people score higher than the white Gentile population that provided the test norms (Colman, 1991). Clearly, there are factors other than test bias at work.

Blaming the test avoids the more difficult politically and socially sensitive possibility that there are real differences. Some psychologists have argued that these differences are largely due to innate, unchangeable racial differences in intelligence (for example, Jensen, 1969). Others claim that this is racism under the cover of science and that it has been used in a political conspiracy to justify discriminatory practices. Indeed, in some American states, concerns about bias in testing have led to outlawing certain kinds of tests or severely restricting their use.

An alternative and much more plausible view is that test results reflect environmental factors such as social disadvantage. In this case social inequalities must be addressed, which is an eminently more challenging and lengthy process. Colman (1991) concludes that differences in test scores are due to real differences, rather than to test bias, and that the evidence for this is strongly in favour of environmental influences. Nevertheless, psychologists are still not sure how these influences operate and to what extent they affect measures of intelligence.

Labelling Some critics complain that tests are reductionist (see Chapter 2). They oversimplify a complex person by applying a convenient label. The problem with this is that labels may become self-fulfilling, meaning that people begin to behave in ways that fit their labels. In clinical settings (for example, Rosenhan, 1973) mental disorder labels carry stigma with them and seem to be particularly 'sticky' in that they are very difficult to shake off. In schools, labelling a pupil as a 'spurter' as a consequence of testing (for example, Rosenthal and Jacobson, 1968) was thought to enhance the child's

ability. In the workplace, labelling employees as lacking potential could be extremely damaging to their self-esteem and job performance.

Studies such as these appeal to folk wisdom. We are inclined to believe that labelling works. However, close examination of research findings reveals very little evidence that it does, at least in the direct way the studies have claimed. Defenders of testing also reply that a test score gives only a general indication of functioning and is part of a more general assessment. In professional hands tests have many uses when combined with other techniques: for example, they can provide a vehicle for interaction and allow the tester time to make other less formal assessments. Just in case there is a danger that labelling could work to the test-taker's disadvantage, testers prefer to describe results in general terms rather than to use a rigid label or test score.

The test-taker's rights and the tester's responsibilities There are a number of issues to consider under this heading. All of these highlight the importance of proper training of the tester, whose responsibility it is to safeguard test-takers by explaining to them the following rights before testing takes place:

■ to refuse to be tested;
■ to know test results (but see 'Communicating results');
■ to know who will have access to the results and why;
■ to expect confidentiality of results;
■ to expect that test results will be secure.

Divided loyalties Testers may sometimes find themselves with a conflict of interests between the test-taker and the institution that pays the psychologist to carry out the testing. For example, if a test could show which employees are most likely to crack under stress, would the employees or the institution benefit most from knowing the results? Information given to the employee could allow the purpose of the

---

GLOSSARY

Headstart An educational enrichment programme designed in the USA to provide enhanced learning experiences for deprived preschool children.

themselves and render further testing useless. Information given to the institution could be used to justify staff changes or redundancies. Testers must decide where their loyalties lie and let all parties know this in advance so that ownership of data is clarified. (See also 'Communicating results'.)

Communicating results   Understanding all the limitations of testing and their likely abuses has an important bearing on how test results are communicated. Trained testers follow strict procedures when doing this, taking into account, among many other things, the likely impact on the person or organization receiving the information. Generally, results are communicated in broad terms rather than in the form of precise scores or specific labels. For example, an employer might be told a particular employee has a 'low probability' of cracking under pressure and that this prediction is accurate 68 times out of 100. It is important that test results on their own are not overvalued and misunderstood. It is for this reason that counselling to discuss the interpretation of results should be available.

Privacy   In personality testing in particular, it is sometimes necessary to disguise the purpose of a test to prevent the test-taker from manipulating the situation and distorting the result. However, in disguised tests, test-takers might believe that they could unwittingly give something away that they would rather have kept to themselves. Clearly, a delicate balance must be struck between the costs and benefits to test-takers of intrusions into their

A psychometric test should be administered only by a trained professional, who is aware of its limitations

privacy. In defence of such tests, Kaplan and Saccuzzo (1989) say that they are not as revealing as people imagine, and that privacy is invaded only if intrusion is unwelcome or detrimental. In addition, the trained tester is bound by the procedures outlined above. The only circumstances where confidentiality can be breached is when test results indicate a danger to the test-taker or others or when results can be subpoenaed by the courts. If people know all these things in advance and still consent to being tested it is highly unlikely that they are unwilling test-takers.

Use of test results   Test results are worth nothing unless they can be used, but how this is done is an important ethical issue. In connection with selection for work or education, Hunter and Schmidt (1976) say that what selectors do depends on whether they believe tests are biased. There are four possible courses of action:

Unqualified individualism. Take the highest scorers on the grounds that they will do the best job. Use other factors, such as age, race or sex, if they help to improve prediction of performance.

Qualified individualism. Take the highest scorers as above but ignore other factors on the grounds that this helps to counteract discrimination – the best will come through regardless.

Quotas. This is a kind of proportional representation. Test-takers are divided into subgroups, and the highest scorers are selected from each group in the same proportions that occur in the target population.

Compromise. This strikes a balance between individualism and quotas. Test results from disadvantaged groups are adjusted to take account of possible bias. All scores are then pooled and the highest scorers selected.

Kline warns that test results should not be used on their own in this way but should be put to 'humane use' (p. 4). The mechanical and inhumane use of testing results from:

overvaluing test scores;
failing to use other relevant information to supplement them;
failing fully to discuss test scores.

The introduction of Standard Assessment Tests (SATs) in state schools in England and Wales is a case in point. The tests, in English, Maths and Science, were

point. The tests, in English, Maths and Science, were fully introduced in 1995 for 11-year-olds at Key Stage 2 of the National Curriculum. Many teachers agree that test results are a useful measure of achievement and that they can be used diagnostically to identify areas of weaknesses. It is the issue of using test results to produce schools league tables which is hotly disputed. At the time of writing opponents of the publication of tables argue that:

- The SATs are still in the experimental stage;
- Undue weight will be placed on test performance, leading to a narrowing of the curriculum;
- They fail to take into account the many factors that influence children's performance. In particular they ignore the 'value-added' factor: that is, the amount children have actually gained taking into account their different starting points;
- It will be divisive. Failure to discuss the full meaning of results will result in parents moving children to the 'better' schools. Government funding will follow, leading eventually to the closure of schools that are successful in ways not shown by their position on the league table.

In this case, the use of test results to produce league tables, rather than to inform parents and teachers about children's educational needs, has become an important and unresolved political issue, which could have far-reaching effects on the education of many English and Welsh children.

Conclusion

In this section, we have concentrated on the many shortcomings of psychometric testing at the expense of their strengths. Kline (1992) says that, properly used, psychometric tests can save time and money that would otherwise be used in lengthy assessment procedures. They are easy to administer, sometimes to many people at once. Some of them can even be given and efficiently scored by computer, thus giving immediate results as a basis for further assessment. Well-constructed tests, he claims, are far more objective than some other forms of assessment. Teacher assessments, for example, may be influenced more by a child's effort than by actual ability. Tests can never be totally free of inaccuracies but they are, in theory at least, good for promoting equal opportunities.

A cynical way of viewing tests is that they are a major and profitable commercial interest and that this is one reason for their proliferation, particularly in the workplace. In the real world of applied psychology, Imich (1991) writes that, when working with individual children, increasing numbers of educational psychologists believe that psychometric tests have no positive value. They prefer instead to concentrate on helping children to achieve skills that will give them access to the National Curriculum. In the field of clinical neuropsychology, Hall (1991) comments on a decrease in the use of personality tests in favour of sophisticated tests of cognitive functioning. If trends like these continue, the fear that psychometric techniques may, one day, become so sophisticated that they will be administered, scored and interpreted by computer will soon be a groundless one.

SELF-ASSESSMENT QUESTIONS

1. What is meant by the term 'psychometric test'?
2. Give examples of the use of psychometric tests in educational, occupational and clinical settings.
3. In what ways do theories of intelligence and personality affect the form of the tests that arise from them?
4. Outline the technical, practical, and theoretical limitations of psychometric tests.
5. What ethical considerations are there in the field of psychometric testing and how have psychologists attempted to resolve them?
6. According to Kline (1992) what strengths do psychometric tests have?

Chapter summary

- There is increasing awareness of the power of psychological knowledge to affect people's lives and bring about change. Areas of psychology where the application of psychological knowledge is particularly controversial are in advertising, propaganda and warfare, which involve persuasion, and in the use of psychometric tests, which are used to measure psychological functioning.

- The communication model of persuasion, developed at Yale University immediately after World War II, views persuasive communications as depending upon communicator variables, message variables, channel variables and audience variables.

- Communicator variables are often relatively superficial characteristics of the communicator, for example communicator credibility and physical attractiveness, expertise, trustworthiness and prestige, all of which may influence the power of the message. For example, the use of a top celebrity in an advertising campaign can be more effective than using an unknown person.

- Messages designed to induce fear must be carefully handled so that people feel they know what response will be effective. Messages that promote a one-sided argument (stressing the value of something) are more effective if people are already in broad agreement with the message; two-sided arguments (giving a balanced view of both strengths and weaknesses) are more effective if people initially disagree; repetition of a message is effective in persuading people, provided over-exposure does not occur.

- Audio and visual messages, as in radio and TV, depend on making an immediate impact. A written message allows for more careful thought and checking, so the quality of the arguments is more important.

- Audience variables may influence the effectiveness of the message. For example, highly intelligent people are more easily persuaded if the message is complex and reasoned rather than simple and flawed.

- More recent models of persuasion have focused more on the thought processes people employ when faced with a persuasive message. For example, the elaboration likelihood model (ELM) suggests that the central route to persuasion involves active (thoughtful) processing of a message whereas the peripheral route involves relatively shallow (lazy) processing.

- People are more likely to process a message actively if it has personal relevance than if it does not involve them.

- The heuristic model suggests that when we are disinclined to give a message our attention, we apply 'heuristics' (rules of thumb). These enable us to process a message with minimal effort. In both the heuristic and ELM models, it is agreed that central (or systematic) processing leads to more lasting retention of the message than does peripheral (heuristic) processing.

- Advertisers use recommendations both from the Yale studies and from the newer models to increase the chances of persuasion. Many other tactics are used, for example the 'foot in the door' technique (making a small request first followed by a larger one). Examples of the use of persuasion techniques can be seen in the Greenpeace appeal for donations and in the way in which cults create converts.

- Propaganda involves the use of persuasion techniques to promote a point of view that people will accept as their own. It is a prominent feature in any war. Propaganda was widely used by both the Allies and the Germans during the two world wars.

- Techniques used by the Nazis included controlling the mass media and 'filtering' messages, promoting a strong image of German power, creating the idea that the Jews were responsible for draining the nation's resources, and so on.

- Ways of resisting persuasion include understanding the techniques used and how to resist them, inducing 'reactance' (letting people know they are being persuaded), using 'inoculation' (exposing people to a weakened form of the message before they receive the full message), and the use of regulatory bodies to monitor messages in the mass media.

- The use of persuasion techniques in spreading wartime propaganda is just one way that psychology can be applied to war. Watson (1978) describes other 'psywar' research areas, including 'why wars occur and how they can be prevented', 'military leadership and followership', 'military group dynamics'. These areas all raise ethical dilemmas for psychologists.

- The most widely used psychometric tests are those that measure intellectual abilities or personality, usually in educational, occupational and clinical settings. Kline (1992) suggests that psychometric tests fall into five categories: ability tests, aptitude tests, personality tests, motivational tests and others such as clinical and neuropsychological test. Testing should be carried out by trained professionals.

■ Tests of intelligence, such as the Stanford–Binet and the British Ability Scales, usually yield one or more IQ scores. The form the test takes will be determined by the underlying theory of how intelligence is structured. Most tests draw heavily on the culture in which they were designed.

■ The form taken by tests of personality will vary depending upon whether the underlying theory takes a nomothetic view (that there are universal laws of behaviour, which can be used to compare people with each other) or an idiographic view (a belief that humans are unique and can be understood only through techniques such as ipsative tests).

■ Controversies surrounding the use of psychometric testing include the extent of reliability, validity, standardization and discriminatory power, the conditions under which people take the tests, the mood and motivational state of test-takers, the extent to which test-takers may produce 'socially desirable' answers, and the effects of coaching.

■ When interpreting tests and applying the results, testers should be aware of theoretical assumptions that underlie them and which may cause bias, and that scores on tests may not be stable over time or be consistently linked to behaviour.

■ Ethical considerations centre on a number of issues: tests may be 'culture bound' and discriminate against those from other cultures; labelling people may result in a self-fulfilling prophecy (living up to expectations); the test-taker's rights and the tester's responsibilities; the way results are communicated; the possible invasion of privacy if test-takers are not given the true reason for the testing; the use to which test results are put.

■ Kline argues, that properly used, psychometric tests can save time and money that would otherwise be used in lengthy assessment procedures. Critics say that psychometric tests provide a profitable and commercial activity and have no positive value.

Further reading

Pratkanis, A. and Aronson, E. (1991). *The Age of Propaganda: Everyday Uses and Abuses of Persuasion*. New York: Freeman. A very readable text, which highlights the theory and practice of persuasion and propaganda with lavish use of illustrative examples.

Watson, P. (1978). *War on the Mind*. New York: Basic Books. One of the few textbooks written in this area. The material is rather dated, but it does give an impression of the many ways in which psychology can be applied to aspects of war.

Kaplan, R.M. and Saccuzzo, D.P. (1989). *Psychological Testing: Principles, Applications and Issues*, 2nd edn. California: Brooks Cole. Contains very useful chapters on the controversies surrounding psychometric testing.

Kline, P. (1992). *Psychometric Testing in Personnel Selection and Appraisal*. London: Croner. A small specialist book, which provides good background on the nature and uses of psychometric tests.

CHAPTER 5

Ethics in psychology

Ethics in psychological research with human participants   101
- BPS ethical guidelines   102
- Examples of ethically questionable research   105
- Ethical guidelines in use   105

The wider responsibilities of psychologists   105
- Applications of research in clinical settings   106
- Ethical issues in socially sensitive research   108

Psychological research and the use of animals   112
- The type and incidence of animal research in psychology   113
- Practical issues in animal research   113
- Practical applications of animal research in psychology   115
- Ethical aspects of animal experimentation   116
- Towards a resolution of the debate   117
- Closing the gap between animals and humans   120
- Conclusion   120

Objectives

By the end of this chapter you should be able to:

- Identify ten areas of concern in the BPS ethical guidelines for research with human participants and comment on each one;

- Consider some ethical issues which apply in particular to students doing investigations as part of an introductory psychology course;

- Appreciate particular psychological investigations which have raised ethical issues;

- Comment on psychologists' everyday experience of applying ethical guidelines;

- Identify some ethical issues raised by psychotherapy in general and behavioural treatments in particular;

- Explain what is meant by, and give examples of, 'socially sensitive research';

- Consider some of the dilemmas psychologists face when conducting socially sensitive research;

- Describe the kinds of research psychologists conduct with animals and comment on its incidence;

- Analyse practical and ethical issues raised by animal research in psychology.

Ethics in psychological research with human participants

One of the primary aims of psychology is to improve the quality of human life and to do this it is necessary to carry out research with human participants. They are a vital resource. Without them there would be no psychology and no advances in knowledge. If psychologists are to enjoy the freedom they need to conduct research, they must take great care that they do not create an atmosphere where people are unwilling to take part in psychological research. Above all else, however, psychologists have a duty to respect the rights and dignity of research participants. Consequently they must maintain high ethical standards whatever their field of research or practice. This means that they must abide by certain moral principles and rules of conduct and these serve to protect research partici- pants, the reputation of psychology and the psychol- ogists themselves.

BPS ethical guidelines

The British Psychological Society regularly publishes and revises general ethical guidelines concerning the use of human participants in research, the most recent in 1993. The Society also publishes guidelines about the use of animals in research and about professional and ethical conduct in various areas of psychological practice. However, as with all guidelines, there is room for interpretation and there will always be a point at which the psychologist has to exercise judgment, since no code of ethics can take care of all possible situations. Box 5.1 summarizes the main points of the BPS guidelines concerning research with humans and offers some extra information about how psychologists might deal with any problems that may arise. These issues can be more conveniently arranged under two headings: 'Risks' and 'Informed consent'.

Risks

■ **Psychological stress**. The most obvious form of risk a participant is likely to encounter is some form of psychological stress such as fear, anxiety, embarrassment, guilt or loss of self-esteem. Psychologists have an ethical obligation to avoid causing these as far as possible and to protect participants from unforeseen risk. This may mean abandoning or redesigning the research.

■ **Coercion**. A less obvious form of risk arises from coercion of participants to take part in research. This is especially important when participants are not self-selected volunteers and are offered payment or other perks for their cooperation. Participants may feel obliged to take part in the research because of these.

■ **Deception**. Deception is another form of risk. It may be necessary to withhold information from participants for a variety of reasons: for example, it could make a nonsense of the experiment if participants knew the hypothesis being tested. If there is no alternative to deception, and the research is important enough to warrant it, then the researcher should be careful to debrief the participants afterwards in order to ensure that there has been no lasting harm.

■ **Privacy**. Finally, if breaches of confidentiality or privacy have occurred, measures must be taken to ensure the anonymity of participants and, if it is possible, give them the option to withhold their data. Sometimes, the latter would not be possible. For example, Humphreys (1970) was able to conduct research into homosexual acts in public toilets by acting as a lookout for the participants. While the breach of privacy is obvious, it could be argued that the participants had, in a sense, granted the researcher permission to observe them.

Informed consent

Informed consent is a second key issue in research because it is not always desirable to inform partici- pants fully, nor is the researcher always in a position to do so: for example, if the research is into new areas. Even with the best of intentions, the researcher may fail to inform participants fully because they are told too little or they fail to understand. In some research (for example, Zimbardo's (1973) prison simulation study) it is not possible to inform potential participants in full because the researcher cannot know in advance how things will progress.

GLOSSARY

Debriefing After an investigation, the investigators discuss with the participants the nature of the research, the findings, and any other matters that are needed to ensure the participants' well-being.

Informed consent In relation to research studies, ensuring that the participants are informed as fully as possible by the investigator about the purpose and design of the research, before the research proceeds.

Box 5.1 A summary of the 1993 BPS ethical guidelines for research with human participants and some comments on their use

Guideline	Explanation	Comments
1. General	In all cases, investigators must consider the ethical implications and psychological consequences for the participants in their research. This should be done for all participants taking into account ethnic, cultural, social, age and sex differences.	The best informed judges of whether a piece of research is ethically acceptable will probably be members of the population from which the participants are to be selected. It is not always possible to do this if, for example, the participants are children or intellectually impaired, in which case people acting for them would be consulted.
2. Consent	Whenever possible, investigators should obtain the consent of possible participants in a research project. This usually means 'informed consent', that is, the investigator should explain, as fully as possible, the purpose and design of the research before proceeding.	In some cases this will mean advising participants that the research procedures involve discomfort or other risks which they would not normally encounter. In such cases, the researcher must seek the guidance of colleagues before asking for consent.
3. Deception	Psychologists must avoid deceiving participants about the nature of the research wherever possible. However, there will occasions when to reveal the research hypothesis to participants would make the research pointless and so deception would be considered.	Deception should not be used if there is an alternative procedure to the one proposed. If deception is being considered, safeguards include consultation with others about its acceptability, e.g. individuals similar to the proposed participants, colleagues and various ethical committees (for example, those set up by the BPS). Sometimes, it is possible to ask participants if they would accept deception until after the research is completed. At all times, it should be considered how participants are likely to be affected by finding out later that they have been deceived.
4. Debriefing	This is more than just informing the participants of the nature of the research and the findings after the study is over. It must take the form of 'active intervention', i.e. the psychologist must be prepared to discuss the procedures and findings with participants and endeavour to ensure that they leave the research situation, as far as possible, in the state in which they entered it.	Intention to debrief participants later is no excuse for exposing them to unacceptable levels of risk, neither is the inability to debrief them (e.g. as in some observational research).
5. Withdrawal from the investigation	Investigators must inform participants of their right to withdraw, without penalty, at any stage of the research. They should be prepared to remind participants of this right and to stop any procedure which appears to be causing discomfort.	This may be difficult to achieve (e.g. with children or in observational research) but it should still be attempted. After debriefing, participants have the right to withdraw their data and see it destroyed in their presence.

continued

6. Confidentiality and privacy	Participants are protected by law (The Data Protection Act 1984) in that they have the right to expect that any information provided by them will be treated confidentially and that their identities will not be revealed.	Failure to observe confidentiality would quickly ruin the reputation of research psychologists; nevertheless, they have a duty to break this guideline if they discover a situation where human life is in danger, e.g. if a suicide threat had been made. This guideline may also be broken if participants give full and knowing consent to their identity being revealed (preferably after seeing a written account of the research report.)
7. Protection of participants	This refers to protection of participants from mental or physical harm during psychological investigations. Risks greater than those likely to be encountered in everyday life should be avoided. Participants should also be asked to reveal any medical conditions, or other problems, which might put them at special risk. If encroachments of privacy are likely, the participants must understand that they do not have to reveal anything private or personal.	Discussion of results with participants must be done with the utmost care and sensitivity. Test results, for example, may be poorly understood by the layperson and this could cause undue anxiety. Participants should also be informed about how to contact the investigator should some unforeseen consequence of the research arise either immediately after the investigation or later on. The researcher is then obliged to correct or remove the problem.
8. Observational research	In observational research individuals cannot always give informed consent, nevertheless it is still important to respect people's privacy and well-being especially as, in some cases, it will not be possible to obtain informed consent or provide a debriefing.	Observations should be made only in those situations where people would normally expect to be in public view and not where they expect to be unobserved. Covert participant observations present a particular problem here especially as they raise further issues of deception and confidentiality.
9. Giving advice to participants	If, during an investigation, a researcher becomes aware that a participant has a significant psychological or physical problem, there is an obligation to reveal this to the participant and to attempt to help them obtain professional advice should they wish it.	This is a sensitive issue. Few research psychologists are expert enough to make on-the-spot diagnoses. On the other hand, if a participant does seek advice from the researcher, it is only acceptable to give it if it were agreed beforehand as part of the research design and the psychologist is appropriately qualified.
10. Monitoring colleagues	Investigators share a moral responsibility to maintain high ethical standards and should monitor their own work and that of colleagues.	This applies at any level of research including student investigations. All research projects need to be carefully assessed on ethical grounds before proceeding.

If the researcher feels that it is necessary to proceed without obtaining informed consent there are two further possible courses of action. One is to run a pilot study and interview participants afterwards about how acceptable they found the procedure. Alternatively role-play could be used where fully informed participants act out the procedures. The latter was used by Zimbardo (1973) in his famous prison simulation exercise.

Examples of ethically questionable research

The reader will probably be familiar with some examples of psychology research which have been attacked on ethical grounds and which have been defended on the basis of their contribution to knowledge. Social psychology is particularly rich in examples, although there are many others: for example, in developmental psychology (see Box 5I.3 in Part 5), bio-psychology (see Box 2I.2, in Part 2) and psychometrics (see Chapter 4). Solomon Asch's (1956) classic conformity experiments are well known, as is Milgram's research on obedience and Zimbardo's 'prison' experiment (see Chapter 28, for a detailed discussion of the ethical issues raised by these two studies) and there are a number of 'bystander apathy' experiments. These all involved some deception of the participants and, in some cases, considerable stress, but could be justified on the basis of what was learned about group influence.

Ethical guidelines in use

So what is the experience of psychologists in the real world of psychological research and practice? The BPS has guidelines and disciplinary procedures which can be used to consider complaints against its members and these may result in a charge being dismissed or a psychologist being reprimanded, expelled from the Society or encouraged to retrain. This applies only in extreme cases, so how do psychologists handle the less extreme day-to-day problems? In 1995, Lindsay and Colley surveyed 1000 randomly selected members of the BPS and asked them to describe an incident that they, or a colleague, had experienced in the last year or two that was ethically troubling. Of those surveyed, 172 respondents produced usable returns and these gave 263 incidents. Seventeen per cent described issues of confidentiality especially where nondisclosure of information could put another person at risk; 10 per cent of incidents were connected with research and were mainly to do with the issue of informed consent. A number of issues arose from Lindsay and Colley's survey.

Lindsay and Colley thought that applying the ethical guidelines raised one set of dilemmas but they also identified an unforeseen dilemma concerning psychologists' worries about whether they could do an adequate professional job in the face of financial cuts and lack of teaching resources. This, of course, is not covered by any code of ethics. Lindsay and Colley also noted that 37 per cent of the respondents said that they had no ethical dilemmas in their work and query whether this reflects the truth or simply a lack of awareness of ethical issues.

Approaching the real world situation from another angle, Lindsay (1995) examined the nature of the first 58 complaints reported to BPS investigatory panels in 1993–4 and found that most concerned client-related professional psychology (only eight were research related). This may seem like a small number but it is increasing and the fact that there were any complaints at all underlines the point that guidelines are only recommendations. Applying them is not always straightforward nor is it any guarantee that psychologists, their clients or research participants will be completely protected.

Finally, not all the complaints made against psychologists can be dealt with by the BPS since not all psychologists are members. At the very least, perhaps, potential clients could check that any practising psychologist they may encounter is registered with the BPS as a chartered psychologist (C. Psychol). This will confirm that the psychologist is genuine and properly qualified, and it will allow a client to refer any complaints they may have against the psychologist to the BPS, who will investigate and take the necessary action.

The wider responsibilities of psychologists

In this section, we will consider two of the ways in which psychological research may have wider implications:

■ when it is applied in **clinical settings**;
■ when it is into socially sensitive subject areas.

⁇ SELF-ASSESSMENT QUESTIONS

1. Summarize the main points of the BPS guidelines for research with human participants and comment on each one.
2. Assess the ethical standing of two pieces of psychological research.
3. Comment on psychologists' everyday experience of ethical issues.

If one of the main purposes of psychological research is to gain greater understanding of behaviour in order to improve the quality of human life, psychologists must, at some point, put their ideas into practice. The main settings in which they do this are educational, occupational and clinical. Ethical issues raised in psychometric testing are especially relevant in the first two and these were discussed in Chapter 4 along with other controversies surrounding its use. Here we will concentrate on applications of psychological research in clinical settings, using behaviourist techniques as a specific example, before going on to discuss the possible consequences of carrying out socially sensitive research.

Applications of research in clinical settings

People seeking help with psychological problems are often especially vulnerable. They may be emotionally upset. Their relationships with others may be under strain and they may be concerned about what seeking help says about their ability to cope. There is also the double handicap of both having a psychological problem and having to deal with other people's attitudes towards it which are not always well-informed, positive or helpful. Furthermore, this vulnerability should lead us to question whether the troubled person would really be able to give informed consent to a therapist.

In an attack on **psychotherapy** in general, Masson (1992) expressed doubts about whether psychotherapies were effective and concern about the financial, emotional and sexual power therapists could be seen as having over their clients. In defence of psychotherapy, Holmes (1994) argued that psychologists were no better or worse in these respects than other professionals such as medical doctors or lawyers. Nevertheless he recommends that all types of psychotherapy need regulatory bodies, standards and codes of practice and procedures for expulsion of the minority who do abuse their power. Currently, many different kinds of treatment are available. Clients may be confused about:

■ The qualifications of who is treating them;
■ Why certain procedures are being carried out;
■ What to do if they have a complaint about any aspect of treatment.

Behavioural techniques

One group of therapeutic techniques that people may be offered arises from the behaviourist approach to psychology. Behaviourist approaches (often distinguished from nonbehavioural psychotherapies) are based on principles of learning gained from research with animals (see Chapters 1 and 6). One of the main assumptions of behaviourists is that many problems are the result of learning maladaptive habits. These are learned in the same way as **adaptive behaviour** and can be unlearned given the appropriate treatment. In spite of the demonstrable success of this approach, some critics accuse behaviourists of being manipulative, coercive and controlling, conditioning people against their will into behaviour patterns which they would not necessarily choose. How far is this image of the behaviourist psychologist justified?

Some writers find it useful to distinguish between behaviour therapy (based on Pavlovian or classical conditioning) and behaviour modification (based on Skinnerian or operant conditioning principles). Behaviour therapy includes relatively uncontentious techniques such as systematic desensitization for phobias and the use of electric alarm blankets for the treatment of persistent nocturnal enuresis (bedwetting). Ethical questions are more likely to be raised where pain or sickness is involved as in aversion therapy.

Aversion therapy A well-known example of the power of aversion therapy is provided by Lang and Melamed (1969). (This study is described in connection with applications of animal research later in this chapter and in Chapter 33.) In this case there is little doubt that aversion therapy saved the child's life. It is the means by which it was done that is in question. A more contentious use of aversion therapy is its

---

GLOSSARY

Clinical settings Settings (such as hospitals or private practices) where people are receiving treatment for a physical or psychological condition.

Psychotherapy Treatments for mental disorder which use psychological methods, such as behavioural therapies or psychoanalysis, rather than medical methods, such as the prescribing of drugs.

Adaptive behaviour Behaviour which is well-adjusted to the individual's environment and therefore is likely to aid survival.

potential to treat other conditions such as homosexuality, and this takes us into the realms of socially sensitive research (see later).

Token economies Stated simply, behaviour modification uses the idea that behaviour can be shaped and changed by the controlled use of reinforcement and punishment. One of the best known applications of behaviour modification is the 'token economy' (see Chapter 33).

In 1968, Ayllon and Azrin introduced an economic system into a ward of schizophrenics whereby tokens could be earned for desirable behaviours such as general hygiene, self-care and work on the ward. Tokens could be saved and exchanged for such things as TV viewing time, cigarettes and sweets, clothes or cosmetics. The principle behind this was that desirable behaviours would increase because they were rewarded. While it was no cure for schizophrenia, the frequency of social and self-care skills in long-stay patients did improve considerably. Not only does the behaviour of participants change, but often, the morale and enthusiasm of staff improves when they begin to see the beneficial effects of their efforts in implementing a programme.

What is ethically problematic about techniques that are so obviously beneficial? Objections centre on four concerns:

- The use of punishment or pain;
- Deprivation;
- Free will;
- Cure.

The use of punishment or pain It has been argued that punishment only has a temporary suppressive effect, and as it produces negative reactions in the learner, it is important to have controls against its use. To guard against the free use of electric shock (such as in aversion therapy), Miron (1968) suggests psychologists should first try the shock on themselves! This is a form of **countercontrol** (Skinner, 1971). (However, punishment is part of everyday life and to treat problem behaviour without it would not teach the patient much about how to cope in the real world.)

Deprivation In some behaviour modification procedures, it is necessary to deprive the experimental

THE FAR SIDE

Professor Gallagher and his controversial technique of simultaneously confronting the fear of heights, snakes, and the dark.

participant of reinforcers in order to encourage them to respond. Reinforcement becomes dependent on the appearance of certain behaviours as in token economies. Token economies fell foul of the critics when some of them appeared to infringe basic human rights: for example, when attendance at church, food or privacy were made contingent upon the performance of desirable behaviours. While such extreme measures may not be used today, the behaviourists argue that the level of reinforcement on a programme may be higher than that normally experienced by a patient and that not to use such techniques may deprive that person of the chance of rehabilitation.

Free will The criticism that behavioural techniques remove people's freedom to act as they wish is a problem for all deterministic approaches. Radical behaviourists would answer that it is not a question of imposing restrictions where none existed before. Their theoretical position is that all behaviour is controlled. The ethical problem is not whether behaviour should be controlled but who should presume to take control of another and for what ends. In their eyes, behavioural techniques simply make systematic use of the processes already at work in everyday life and people's alarm at their methods results from recognition of how powerful this can be.

This does not mean that behaviourists are not concerned about the possibility that their methods could be used to exploit others. Accordingly, many behavioural therapists now turn much of the power to the client. For example, in systematic desensitization clients construct their own hierarchy of feared situations with the therapist's help and then have considerable control in the pacing of exposure to them. There are also strict codes of conduct for therapists. All these things help towards 'countercontrol'.

If the wider ethical implications of behavioural therapies are considered, then in terms of costs and benefits, they fare well. In certain areas of disorder such as sexual dysfunction, enuresis, nervous tics and habit disorders, treatment is very effective. It can alleviate suffering, improve the quality of life and even save lives.

Cure Behavioural therapies are often attacked as ethically unsound because they define 'cure' as disappearance of the problem behaviour. (To psychologists who see problem behaviour as a symptom of something more deep-rooted, all the behaviourist has done is to cover the real problem up.) Radical behaviourists can answer this in three ways:

- If it is accepted that the problem is the product of faulty learning, new learning does eradicate the whole problem.
- If the whole problem has not been cured, it should reappear in the form of a new symptom but symptom substitution seems to be comparatively rare.
- If behaviour is determined by experiences in the environment, then problem behaviour is the result of a faulty environment. It is society, not the individual, which needs to change. This is ultimately a political issue raising new ethical concerns about whether people are simply being treated so that they fit in better with an oppressive social system.

Of course, behaviourist techniques are not the only ones available and they are often mixed, to good effect, with other approaches (for example, as in cognitive behavioural therapy) to suit the client. In all cases, however, the consequences of cure can be far-reaching and the change in the client may have implications that affect their spouse, family and others.

(Note that behavioural therapies are discussed further in Part 7.)

Clinical settings – concluding remarks

There are many other types of treatment, not fully discussed here, where still more ethical concerns are important. For example, consider the problems involved in various kinds of biomedical intervention such as electroconvulsive therapy (ECT), the use of psychoactive drugs and psychosurgery (discussed in Chapter 33). Some would argue that these are strictly in the realm of **psychiatry** but the boundaries between psychology and psychiatry can be fuzzy, especially as the conditions treated manifest themselves psychologically.

Psychological knowledge could not advance without a certain amount of risk both to the researchers and their participants or to clinical psychologists and their patients. If in the end, as Hawks (1981) asserts, psychologists are working towards the ultimate goal of prevention of psychological problems, rather than cure, ethical risks are a relatively small price to pay along the way.

Ethical issues in socially sensitive research

Writing for the *American Psychologist* in 1988, Sieber and Stanley used the term **socially sensitive research** to describe:

studies in which there are potential social consequences or implications, either directly for the participants in research or the class of individuals represented by the research. For example, a study that examines the relative merits of day-care for infants versus full-time care by the mother can have broad social implications and thus can be considered socially sensitive. Similarly, studies aimed at examining the relationship between gender and mathematical ability also have significant social implications.

(Sieber and Stanley, 1988, p. 49)

As Gross (1992) reminds us, 'we should regard every psychology experiment as an ethical situation' (p. 51), but some areas of research, such as those mentioned in the quote above, pose particular problems. Socially sensitive research is more likely than most to attract a great deal of interest from psychologists, the media, and hence the general public. There are plenty of examples where psychologists and their families have been threatened (as in the case of some animal researchers) or ostracized (as in the case of researchers into race and intelligence) as a result of their work. Howitt adds:

Psychological research touching on important social issues will rarely have a calm passage. Tackling questions which are not simply difficult, but controversial, involving moral as well as other questions, will hardly enamour psychologists to each other, let alone the rest of the community.

(Howitt, 1991, p. 149)

It is understandable, then, if psychologists choose to sidestep the issue altogether by refusing to carry out research of a socially sensitive nature. However, to avoid such research completely would leave them simply studying 'safe' areas and ignoring the thornier issues where their work could, perhaps, have an important and beneficial effect. Sieber and Stanley say:

Sensitive research addresses some of society's most pressing issues and policy questions. Although ignoring the ethical issues in sensitive research is not a responsible approach to science, shying away from controversial topics, simply because they are controversial, is also an avoidance of responsibility.

(Sieber and Stanley, 1988, p. 55)

Examples of socially sensitive research

Psychology is rich in examples of socially sensitive research. Studies of racial or gender differences, child-rearing practices, the impact of ageing or health-related issues such as drug abuse or sexual behaviour are just a few examples from many. Milgram and Zimbardo's

research, referred to earlier, are also relevant here. Concerning negative social consequences for the individual participants, both researchers felt confident that there had been no long-term negative effects. Indeed, in some cases, change for the better had occurred. However, the studies could be considered to be socially sensitive in the wider effect they had on people who were more generally anxious about the implications of the findings. If ordinary people would do such extraordinarily unpleasant things in research situations, what hope was there that any of us would behave humanely in the real world?

Other examples of well-known socially sensitive research are discussed below.

Bowlby's research into attachment Bowlby's (1951) view that 'Mother love in infancy and childhood is as important for mental health as are vitamins and proteins for physical health' had a profound effect on social policy concerning childcare. He argued that, ideally, a child up to the age of five years should have the unbroken, loving care of its mother or permanent mother substitute. During World War II, the role of women had changed considerably as they joined the workforce in large numbers to help the war effort. State nursery care helped many of them to cope with the practicalities of single parenthood while their partners were in the forces or with widowhood if their partners were killed. After the war, many men were unemployed and it could be argued that women were under pressure to hand their jobs over.

Bowlby's findings were timely in this respect. Although they undoubtedly did a great deal of good in improving aspects of childcare, they also encouraged the belief that a woman's place was at home with her children. Sadly, the guilt and pressure this has caused both working mothers and fathers continues to this day and childcare facilities in the UK remain inadequate. However successful a mother is at mixing career and home life the confusion that persists will probably lead her to feel that wherever a woman's place is, it is probably in the wrong. (See also Chapter 19 in Part 5 for a further discussion of Bowlby's ideas.)

Psychoanalytic studies Freud's influence on Western thinking has been profound and many of his ideas have crept into our everyday language. He was one of a number of influential psychologists who emphasized the importance of early experience, especially the role parents played in helping or hindering the infant or child as it moved through various stages of psychosexual development. These ideas placed a huge responsibility on parents, who would find themselves wondering what they had done wrong if the child subsequently developed problems. Another influence from Freud's theory has been the perpetuation of the idea that women suffer from 'penis envy'. This resulted in women being seen as incomplete and inferior compared to men and driven to recover their lost penis, preferably through giving birth to a male child. Finally there is the possible damage done by emphasizing infantile and childhood sexuality, which could have us believing that the accounts of some sexually abused children are based on fantasy. (A more detailed discussion of Freud's theory appears in Chapter 30.)

Intelligence   Any research which links intelligence with genetic factors can have far-reaching consequences for different social classes or races. Burt used studies of identical twins who had been separated early in life and reared apart to support his ideas that measured intelligence was largely affected by genetics rather than experience. His thinking greatly influenced recommendations made in the Hadow Report (1926) for selection at 11 years old for different types of education: that is, in grammar, secondary modern or technical schools. Generations of children have been affected by the 11+ examination even though a controversy has long raged about whether Burt invented some of his data and manipulated it to achieve the desired results. Other psychologists, such as Eysenck (1973) and Jensen (1969), who have argued for a biological basis to differences in IQ test performance, are treading in similarly socially sensitive areas. (Controversies surrounding the use of IQ tests are discussed further in Chapter 21.)

Cautionary notes about socially sensitive research

The influence of prevailing views   One alarming aspect of socially sensitive research findings is that their influence can be difficult to dislodge, even when there is little evidence for them or a wealth of evidence against them. One possible reason for people's immovability in this respect is that research can sometimes fit well with the prevailing zeitgeist (intellectual mood of the times) and so it can tell people, including psychologists, what they are ready to hear. Their subsequent actions, for example, in changing social policy, are then somehow legitimized by scientific research even though the reliability of that research may be less than perfect.

On the other side of the coin, psychologists can sometimes interpret socially sensitive research findings in ways that are not readily accepted. This is particularly likely to happen if the psychologists' (ideally) academic, objective view is not in tune with the institution for which research is being carried out. Levy-Leboyer (1988) illustrates this with an example of a psychological study carried out for the French telephone department into vandalism of public telephones. The telephone company believed most vandalism was caused by young criminals intent on stealing from those payphones that were likely to contain the most money. The psychologists' research gave a different picture. Instead, they suggested that the busiest phones were most likely to break down, often due to being full, and not return money. These were consequently most often damaged because it was the only way people (of all kinds) could express their frustration. The psychologists suggested phone booths should contain maps showing the nearest alternative phone and instructions about where to go for reimbursement. However, the telephone department disagreed with these findings (perhaps because they did not fit with their prevailing views about young vandals). They subsequently invested in strengthening the payphones and introducing a phone-card system.

Lack of preparedness for consequences   Sieber and Stanley (1988) say that although existing ethical principles warn psychologists to be cautious when conducting socially sensitive research, there is no code of conduct explaining exactly how to be cautious or deal with the consequences. For example, although Milgram and Zimbardo would have realized they were researching into sensitive issues and were ready for some of the consequences, it is debatable whether they were fully prepared for the strength of reaction their findings caused. Mindful of the risks psychologists run in conducting such research, Sieber and Stanley identified ten ethical issues which are especially pertinent in socially sensitive research. In an attempt to help psychologists remain vigilant they also suggested ways in which the issues could cause problems. These are presented in Box 5.2.

Box 5.2 Ethical issues in socially sensitive research and reasons to be cautious (adapted from Sieber and Stanley, 1988)

Ethical issue	Reasons to be cautious
■ Privacy	The risk here is that some research may be used to shape public policy: e.g. AIDS research could, perhaps, lead to later breaches of privacy through requiring by law that certain people be tested for HIV.
■ Confidentiality of data	Breaches of confidentiality about, for example, being found to be HIV positive could have serious social and economic consequences for the individual due to general lack of understanding about how HIV is transmitted between people. Consider, for example, the consequences of breaching confidentiality of a participant who confesses to having AIDS but not telling their partner.
■ Sound and valid methodology	Findings based on unsound or invalid methodology may find their way into the public domain where the flaws and carefully qualified conclusions drawn from them may not be as fully appreciated as they might be between researchers. Such findings may be unwittingly or cynically used to influence public policy (possibly as in the Hadow Report – see text).
■ Deception	This really refers to self-deception in which research may lead people to believe in a stereotype formed from hearing about certain findings, e.g. hearing that boys are more able at maths than girls could lead girls into deceiving themselves that this is generally true of all girls including themselves.
■ Informed consent	It is always important for the researcher to obtain fully informed consent from participants but this is especially important in socially sensitive research.
■ Justice and equitable treatment	Research interests, techniques or findings should not result in some people being treated unfairly, e.g. through creating unfavourable prejudices about them or withholding something potentially beneficial, such as a particular experimental drug or educational technique from some but not others.
■ Scientific freedom	This must be weighed against the interests of wider society. Many scientists agree that science advances through open discussion and competition of ideas. Censorship of scientific activity is usually thought to be unacceptable but there are some kinds of research which should be, and are, carefully monitored.
■ 'Ownership' of data	This is a complex and largely unresolved issue which involves trying to decide who can have access to scientific data. Scientists generally welcome openness but in the wrong hands or poorly understood, certain findings, especially socially sensitive ones, could be potentially explosive and used to manipulate, coerce or subjugate people.
■ Values and epistemology of social scientists	This refers to scientists' theoretical beliefs (and personal beliefs) about human nature and how best to understand it. Psychologists must recognize that their research is not value-free and that this may be reflected in the kinds of research question they ask, how they conduct research and how they interpret findings. To even ask the question 'What is the effect of race on IQ?' is to assume that race, IQ and any connection between them are of importance. The research by Levy-Leboyer, described in the text, illustrates how different values can cause people from an academic or business background to carry out and/or interpret research differently.
■ Risk/benefit ratio	While most people would agree that it is unacceptable to carry out research where the costs outweigh the benefits, risks and benefits may be that much harder to assess accurately in socially sensitive research so it is more than usually important that they are carefully considered.

Socially sensitive research – concluding remarks

Sieber and Stanley advise that, in general, research psychologists must always be acutely aware of their role in society and work hard to make explicit such things as their theoretical background and limits to the generalizability of their research when they publish it. They should also attempt to keep open clear lines of communication with the media and policy makers in order to minimize distortion or abuse of research findings, however difficult this may be.

Scarr (1988) concludes on a similar note. She argues that psychologists cannot afford to avoid socially sensitive research, even if they discover socially uncomfortable things. There is a desperate need, she says, for good studies that highlight, for example, race and gender variables. Her point is that, if we hide from such findings, we will never be in a strong position to tackle any of the inequalities that can be so damaging to certain groups of people. In his well-known book *The Social Animal*, Aronson (1992) ends a brief discussion of 'the morality of discovering unpleasant things' (p. 422) by agreeing that such research should not stop or be conducted secretly. Instead, he recommends that the public are carefully educated about socially sensitive research findings so that they are empowered to be vigilant about their abuse.

Howitt (1991) is, perhaps, less optimistic and more cautious. He agrees that it is important for psychologists to be well-intentioned and careful but thinks that they should recognize their limitations. He argues that psychologists can only give us a particular view of human nature and that such a view is affected by historical times and prevailing social values. For these reasons, it is impossible for psychological research to be objective, value-free and somehow capable of revealing the absolute truth. Its basis in research may give the illusion of objectivity but, ultimately, it may be no more valid than any other way of interpreting events. Psychologists should not, therefore, seek to impose a collective professional view on others about socially sensitive issues from a supposed scientific 'high ground'. He argues that psychologists are not yet in a position to influence social policy, which is probably why there is no recognized set of principles to guide socially sensitive research. Nevertheless he senses positive change ahead as psychologists become more aware of their wider social responsibilities and concludes by saying that:

With the changes in the priorities of psychology, pressure may increase for a new sort of ethic – a social ethic, rather than an individual one orientated towards the individual research participant.   (Howitt, 1991, p. 161)

❓ SELF-ASSESSMENT QUESTIONS

1. What is meant by the term 'socially sensitive research'?
2. Identify two research areas which could be thought of as socially sensitive and explain your choice.
3. Outline three cautions that psychologists conducting socially sensitive research should observe.
4. What are the views of Scarr, Aronson and Howitt on socially sensitive research in psychology?

Psychological research and the use of animals

It is recommended that you read the introduction to Part 4 in conjunction with this section.

If we consider the strength of feeling that surrounds the use of animals in research, it can come as a surprise to learn that the existing legislation (Animals: Scientific Procedures Act 1986), which protects living vertebrates, is the first since 1876. During the 1980s, the promise of this new legislation gave a fresh impetus to debates about the use of animals in research and the arguments rage on to this day in psychology as well as in other disciplines.

It is important to be aware that most psychologists do not carry out research with animals, neither are they involved in using animals for product testing, farming or exhibition in zoos. In addition, not all animal research in psychology involves intrusive experimental methods. These points are not meant to imply that psychologists can dodge their responsibilities to animals and, as we will see, they have not tried to do so. Nevertheless, psychological research with animals has received its share of adverse publicity and the reader is encouraged to examine some of the readily available literature from the **antivivisectionist** and animal liberation movements and to consider their claims in the light of what is presented here.

The following questions will be addressed:

■ What kinds of research do psychologists conduct with animals and what is its incidence?
■ What practical issues are raised by animal research in psychology?
■ What ethical issues are involved?
■ How are psychologists attempting to resolve these ethical issues?

The type and incidence of animal research in psychology

One way to test the type and incidence of animal research is to survey psychological research publications. Accordingly, in the USA, Coile and Miller (1984) reviewed all the articles published in the American Psychological Society's journals in the preceding five years. They found that of the 608 articles examined, only 7 per cent reported research primarily on animals and no instances of the kind of research condemned by animal rights campaigners were found. Of course, published research does not cover all research but the authors still maintained that there is far more abuse of animals on farms and in zoos than in any research facility.

In the UK, Thomas and Blackman (1991) used a different method. They surveyed all the 67 higher education departments known to offer first degree courses in psychology and compared their findings with similar data collected by the British Psychological Society in 1977. Sixty-two of the departments responded to their questionnaire. It emerged that between 1977 and 1989 the numbers of vertebrates used in these departments dropped from 8536 to 3708 – a decline of 43 per cent – and the number of departments using animals dropped from 39 to 29. There was also a sharp decrease in experimental work on animals and a corresponding increase in observational studies. (As a matter of interest, in 1989, 92 per cent of the animals used were rats or mice, 6 per cent were pigeons or other birds and 1 per cent were monkeys.)

Thomas and Blackman call this decline in animal research disconcerting since animal models have proved so useful in psychology. They add that it is causing 'a fundamental shift in psychology's subject base' (p. 208). They doubt whether this is due to new legislation or the actions of pressure groups. Instead they suggest it is due to a shift in research interests.

Indeed, Furnham and Pinder (1990) reported that although young people's attitudes to animal experimentation were generally positive, they were unwilling to do such research themselves. Thomas and Blackman conclude that undergraduates should be exposed to a positive and reasoned case in favour of animal research.

If you look through the rest of this book, you will find a wealth of examples of the kinds of animal research that interest psychologists. See, for example, work by Riesen (1950), Hubel and Wiesel (1962) Blakemore and Cooper (1970) in Part 3; Lorenz (1937), Savage-Rumbaugh (1990) and Goodall (1978) in Part 4; Harlow (1959) in Part 5. These examples cover a wide variety of methods and research interests, ranging from experimental analysis of brain function through to social behaviour in the natural environment, and all have made important contributions to psychology.

Practical issues in animal research

On what practical grounds do psychologists justify their use of animals?

Broadbent (1961) justifies the use of animals in psychological research in three main ways:

■ **Continuity through evolution**. If it is assumed, as in Darwin's view, that all species are biologically related to each other through evolution, then it can be argued that their behaviour patterns are also related. Just as human anatomy (for example, the nervous system) can be understood by reference to other species, so can human behaviour. In many respects, humans differ from other animals in complexity only, so much can be learned about them by reference to other species.
■ **Ethical restrictions on research with humans**. Many laboratory experiments that are carried out on animals would not be permitted with humans for ethical reasons. Examples are controlled interbreeding experiments (for research into genetic correlates of behaviour), various kinds of deprivation (social, maternal, perceptual, sensory), and brain and tissue research.

GLOSSARY

Antivivisectionist movement A movement that is opposed to the use of live animals in experiments.

I SAY, TREATED HUMANELY, IT'S PERFECTLY ETHICAL TO STUDY THEM.

■ **Studying simpler systems**. One of the standard techniques of science is to study simpler systems in order to understand more complex ones. If we accept the notion of continuity between animal species (as in 1) then studies of the behaviour and nervous systems of animals could reveal a great deal about humans.

To these three points, two more can be added:

■ **Convenience**. Animals make convenient subjects for several reasons. They reproduce rapidly so the effects of early experience and selective breeding can quickly be assessed, heredity and environment can be precisely controlled in nature-nurture research, and emotional involvement with animal subjects is less likely than with humans so the experimenter's objectivity is improved.

■ **Generating hypotheses for human studies**. Animal experiments can be useful in the early stages of research as a means of generating hypotheses for subsequent testing on humans. Alternatively, research findings which are only suggestive or correlational in nature with humans

could be tested experimentally on animals in order to isolate cause and effect.

Note that the above points are also discussed in the introduction to Part 4.

On what practical grounds can animal research be opposed?

Practical objections have two main themes. The first concerns whether it is reasonable to transfer (extrapolate) findings from animals to humans and the second concerns objections about the nature of the research methods used.

Antiextrapolationists emerge from a number of camps.

■ **Uniqueness of humans**. Some argue that the human condition is unique: that is, that humans are qualitatively different from animals as well as quantitatively different. Humanistic psychologists subscribe to this view as do those who disagree with Darwin's theory of evolution or who object on religious grounds. Koestler (1970) wrote that to transfer findings from rats to humans was to commit the sin of 'ratomorphism', that is, to see humans and rats as being very alike when in fact they are very different. Another argument is that unique human attributes such as language and the relatively greater openness to learning and flexibility of human behaviour make comparisons between humans and animals less valid.

■ **Anthropomorphism**. Others argue that there is a danger that researchers may be unable to adopt an objective view of their animal subjects so that they attribute them with human qualities for which there is no real evidence – this is known as anthropomorphism.

■ **Animal rights**. Animal rights campaigners may well draw on cases where extrapolation of findings about drugs from one species to another has been inappropriate. The implication of this is

---

GLOSSARY

Antiextrapolationists In relation to animal research, a group who believe that it is not reasonable or desirable to apply the findings from animal studies to humans.

that, if physiological reactions to the same chemical differ so much between species, how can we be confident in transferring findings about behaviour from one to another?

■ **Use of alternative opportunities**. Finally, it could be argued that the need to extrapolate could be avoided altogether if psychologists made full use of all the opportunities open to them. For example, there are plenty of cases of naturally occurring deprivation in infants and children so why subject laboratory animals to deprivation (as in Harlow's (1959) research with monkeys)?

Research methods

Regarding research methods, there is a pay-off to be considered between laboratory-based research and field research. One objection to laboratory experimentation concerns the degree of control exerted over events. There is no doubt that the precision thus achieved is a strength of the method, but it is also its greatest weakness because it leads us to doubt whether laboratory experiments have **ecological validity**. In other words, we should question whether the results would be meaningful in the real world. Field experiments might have greater ecological validity but, although realism is gained, control is lost. It is also tempting to think that studying animals in their natural environment is more acceptable than laboratory – based research, but Cuthill (1991) expressed concern that some techniques of field research could, if not properly controlled, seriously threaten the survival of a species: for example, where animals are captured and recaptured for tagging, or when decoy or dummy animals are used to test the animals' responses, or when the mere presence of observers is disturbing. Even relatively unintrusive naturalistic observation could affect certain species, so it needs to be carried out with the utmost sensitivity.

Practical applications of animal research in psychology

In 1985, Neal Miller published a detailed article describing research on animals which he considers to be valuable. This was, at least in part, a response to various animal rights groups who, he said, could mislead people with 'grossly false statements' about animal research. Rather than help animals, he says their actions impede research which is beneficial to both animals and humans. He suggests that their energies could be more usefully directed towards fighting for the conservation of endangered species or towards raising funds for refuges for abandoned or mistreated animals.

Benefits to animals

Miller notes the many ways in which animal research has benefited animals. For example, a better understanding of the behaviour of animals which damage crops or carry disease has led to the development of deterrents (such as specially designed 'scarecrows', Conover, 1982) thus doing away with the need for lethal control. Animal research has also helped in the preservation of endangered species and has done much to promote the health of domestic pets. It has also led to improvements in animal husbandry, animal welfare in zoos and on farms and in conservation of animal species and their habitats.

Benefits to humans

From a psychological point of view, research into animal learning stands out as being of great practical use to humans. Some examples will serve to illustrate this contribution.

Treatment of nocturnal enuresis In 1938, Mowrer and Mowrer used principles derived from Pavlov's experiments on classical conditioning in dogs to develop an alarm blanket for the treatment of persistent night-time bedwetting (nocturnal enuresis) in children. Apart from the obvious benefits to be had from the disappearance of the enuresis, Mowrer and Mowrer found that the children improve in other ways too. Teachers, for example, noted improvements in various aspects of such children's personality and behaviour even though they were unaware that the children had been enuretic.

Life saving Pigeons have been trained to detect coloured life rafts against the background of the sea

---

GLOSSARY
Ecological validity A situation where findings (from research) are meaningful in the real world.

using operant conditioning techniques derived from Skinner's work (Simmons, 1981). Pigeons can be trained to peck discs of different colours to earn food rewards and they will generalize this training to similar situations. In tests, their keen vision enabled them to detect 85 per cent of life raft targets compared to the 50 per cent detected by helicopter crews.

Behaviour change in educational settings Teaching machines, programmed learning and token economies, all derived from operant conditioning principles, have been successfully used in educational settings (see Chapter 6).

Behaviour change in clinical settings (see preceding section and also Chapter 33) Walker (1984) draws a distinction between behaviour therapy (based on classical conditioning) and behaviour modification (based on operant conditioning). Both are derived from experiments using animals and have been used to explain and treat some kinds of mental disorder.

The classic case of Little Albert (Watson and Rayner, 1920) who was conditioned to fear a white rat, spawned a variety of behaviour therapy techniques for the treatment of phobias, including systematic desensitization and flooding (implosion). Another technique derived from classical conditioning is aversion therapy. Lang and Melamed (1969) described how this had been used to save the life of a nine-month-old baby who was malnourished and dehydrated through persistent ruminative vomiting (regurgitation and rechewing of food). After all other treatments had failed, the therapists trained the infant to develop a conditioned aversion to vomiting by applying a series of one second long electric shocks to his calf whenever he showed signs of regurgitation. The infant learned not to vomit in order to avoid the shock, and subsequently, he made a complete recovery.

Behaviour modification also has many applications in clinical settings. In one case described by Isaacs et al. (1960), a schizophrenic man, who had been mute for years, was gradually trained to speak again by using behaviour-shaping procedures with chewing gum as a reinforcer. Token economies used in clinical settings are another good example of operant conditioning principles in practice.

Animal helpers Pfaffenberger (1963) was able to improve on the efficiency of guide dogs for the blind by selective breeding and by applying research findings concerning the most sensitive periods for learning in a puppy's life. Willard (1985) has trained Capuchin monkeys to be home helps for disabled and paralysed people. Monkeys can learn to serve drinks with a straw, place a magazine on a reading stand, open and close doors, operate lifts and carry out a variety of other tasks for the reward of food or fruit juice dispensed by the disabled person.

Miller (1985) concludes that there is a strong financial and moral case for continuing to back animal research and others would agree. He argues that the work of Lorenz (1937) on imprinting, for example, is linked to the well-known work by Harlow (1959) on deprivation of maternal contact in infant monkeys. More recent developments from this have led to improvements in the care of premature babies for whom contact comfort is now known to be an important factor in improving their survival rate.

Green (1994) uses the examples of diseases that are on the increase and whose nature and progress could be better understood through animal research. Alzheimer's disease is one such condition, which is increasing in incidence due to growing numbers of elderly people. It leads to long-term degeneration and affects not only the sufferer but the sufferer's family and carers. AIDS is another example where the effects are not confined to the affected individual. Although these are, strictly speaking, physical rather than psychological conditions, their impact reaches beyond the physical to psychological and social aspects of a person's life.

Ethical aspects of animal experimentation

Moral absolutism

The view that all animal research should be banned is an example of what Michael Eysenck (1994) calls 'moral absolutism'. Another moral absolutist view would be that there should be no restrictions whatsoever on animal research. Both of these extremes would be difficult to live with and both seem to close the door to further debate. This is why psychologists often find themselves preferring 'moral relativism':

that is, the view that, after weighing up various arguments, some research is permissible and some is not.

Moral relativism

Adopting a position of moral relativism, in 1985, the British Psychological Society and Experimental Psychology Society jointly issued some guidelines (most recent edition 1993) to assist in the planning of experiments on animals. In general, they say researchers have an 'obligation to avoid, or at least minimise, discomfort to all living animals'. The guidelines are summarized in Box 5.3. As we saw in the earlier discussion of ethical issues in research with humans, these are only guidelines and they can take us only so far. There will often come a point where professional judgment has to be made, especially where there are 'fuzzy' areas (for example, whether in some research the 'ends justify the means'). Some of the main contenders in recent debates are Gray, Ryder and Singer.

Arguing for animal research:

▨ Gray (1991) makes the case that to inflict suffering unnecessarily is wrong, nevertheless we sometimes have a special duty to protect our own species. This duty starts with our closest kin and then spreads to other humans and then to other species. He argues that the resulting behaviour is at least partly biologically based.

▨ This obligation to our own species creates a perplexing imbalance of interests. For example, it is possible to think of a number of cases where great pain and suffering in humans could be avoided if experiments (even painful ones) were carried out on animals.

▨ Although Gray accepts that some procedures could cause such immense suffering to animals that they should never be done, he still maintains that we have a moral justification to do other research where the ends justify the means. The dilemma comes in deciding at which point this is true.

Arguing against animal research:

▨ Ryder (1990) attacked Gray's views as **speciesist** (discrimination and exploitation based upon a

difference between species) and aligns it with racism and sexism.

▨ Singer (1991) supported Ryder and added that, although there could be a biological basis to speciesism, as Gray had suggested, this did not excuse us from our moral obligations to other species as we are not bound to behave according to our biological make-up.

Towards a resolution of the debate

A number of issues have been raised in an attempt to contribute to a resolution of this debate.

Costs and benefits

Bateson (1986) says that costs and benefits of animal research should be considered by people on both sides of the debate. He suggests that a committee made up of research scientists, animal welfare representatives and neutral parties should consider three important issues in deciding whether a research proposal should be accepted. (Although these proposals relate to medical research they can easily be related to psychology.) The issues are:

▨ Certainty of medical benefit;
▨ The quality of the research;
▨ The degree of animal suffering involved.

If the first two are high and the third low, then the research would probably be permitted. See Figure 5.1. The committee's most important function would be in deciding how to proceed in different circumstances: for example, when animal suffering was likely to be high but the quality of research and the certainty of medical benefit were also high.

GLOSSARY

'Moral absolutism' The holding of an extreme view. For example, in relation to animal research, either that all animal research should be banned or that there should be no restrictions at all.

'Moral relativism' A compromise view. For example, in relation to animal research, that after weighing up various arguments, some research is permissible and some is not.

'Speciesism' Discrimination and exploitation based upon differences between species.

Box 5.3   A summary of guidelines for the use of animals in research jointly proposed by the British Psychological Society and the Experimental Psychology Society 1985 (most recent edition 1993)

1. **Regard for the law.** New legislation following the Government bill 'Animals (Scientific Procedures)' was passed in 1986. Its purpose is to control the use of animals in all kinds of scientific research including psychology, and it is the first review of such legislation since 1876. In the UK, *The Universities Federation for Animal Welfare Handbook* was, until now, the only set of guidelines in general use. It is the duty of all animal researchers to be familiar with the most recent legislation and abide by it.

2. **Ethical considerations.** If the research necessitates that animals should be confined, constrained or stressed in any way, the experimenter must be sure that the means justify the ends. If the knowledge to be gained is trivial, alternatives should be favoured.

3. **Knowing the species.** In order to avoid distressing animals unduly, the experimenter should have a sound understanding of how the species being studied responds to different situations. Some species may suffer more from a particular research situation than others, in which case the one least likely to suffer should be preferred. In any case, distressed animals do not make good subjects so it is in the experimenter's best interests to care for them properly.

4. **Numbers of animals.** Experimenters should have a sound knowledge of experimental design such that the minimum number of animals can be used to maximum effect. Statisticians may be able to advise on techniques of analysis which can give meaningful results from the fewest number of subjects.

5. **Endangered species.** For obvious reasons, endangered species should not be used unless the research is a serious attempt at conservation.

6. **Animal suppliers.** Experimenters should take care to use reputable suppliers so that breeding, housing and transport of animals is handled competently. If animals have to be trapped in the wild then it should be done as humanely and as painlessly as possible.

7. **Caging and social environment.** This should take into account the social habits of the species. Some are distressed by being isolated, others will be distressed by being caged together.

8. **Fieldwork.** Researchers observing animals in the wild must disturb them as little as possible otherwise their breeding patterns may be upset and their survival threatened. If capture is necessary, for marking or attaching transmitters, then a good knowledge of what the species can tolerate is necessary. Capture and recapture may be too stressful for the animal and certain kinds of marking intolerable.

9. **Studies of aggression and predation including infanticide.** Even though pain and injury may occur to animals in the wild, this is little excuse for staging it in the lab so any research into aggression and predation should be done through field studies. If staging of encounters is absolutely necessary, then the use of models or animals behind glass screens should be considered. In any case numbers should be kept to a minimum.

10. **Motivation.** In some experiments, animals may be motivated to behave by being deprived of food. Again, the needs of individual species should be understood. What amounts to a short period of deprivation for one could be intolerable to another. In addition, unchecked food intake is harmful to some animals.

11. **Aversive stimuli and stressful procedures.** These procedures are illegal unless the researcher has a Home Office licence and other relevant certificates. To get these the researcher has to justify the method, show that other techniques are unsuitable and show that suffering is kept to a minimum. It must be demonstrated that the animals' suffering is justifiable in terms of the scientific contribution of the research.

12. **Surgical and pharmacological procedures.** Again a Home Office licence and the necessary certification is required. The researcher must be experienced in this field and be able to train others appropriately. The researcher must know how to use anaesthesia techniques and how to prevent postoperative infection in vertebrates. If drugs are to be used, the researcher must be aware of their behavioural effects and toxicity levels and should conduct pilot studies where these are unknown.

13. **Anaesthesia, analgesia and euthanasia.** A Home Office licence and certification is also necessary here. The researcher must know how to use anaesthesia techniques and analgesics (postoperatively). If a subject suffers severe and enduring pain, euthanasia, as set out in the UFAW handbook, should be used.

14. **Independent advice.** If the researcher is in any doubt about an animal's condition during the research, the advice of an expert should be sought. Ideally this would be a qualified vet with no vested interest in the research.

15. In general, researchers have an 'obligation to avoid, or at least minimize, discomfort to all living animals'.

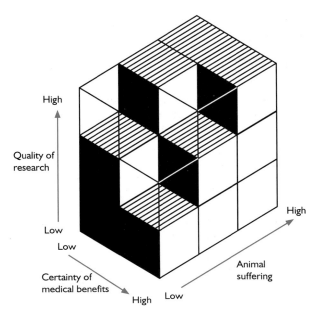

High

Quality of
research

Low

Low

High

Low

High

High

Animal
suffering

Certainty of
medical benefits

Figure 5.1 The Bateson model (Bateson, 1986)

Exercise 5.1

Look at the account of Harlow's research into deprivation in infant monkeys in Box 19.3, Chapter 19. Where would you locate this research on the Bateson model?

Do you believe that the psychological benefits of this research justified its being carried out? Justify your decision.

Animal suffering

At this point in the debate we are still skirting issues such as how we assess the degree to which an animal suffers in a research. Bateson (1991, 1992) again attempted to resolve this. He used findings from the Institute of Medical Ethics working party's investigations into animal suffering to develop several criteria to help researchers to judge whether the species they intended to study could feel pain. In summary, these are:

■ Does the animal have anatomical, biochemical and physiological mechanisms similar to those in a human that are known to be related to the experience of pain?

■ When stimulated in particular ways, does the animal behave in a similar way to humans who are thought to be in pain?

■ Do analgesics (painkillers) alter this behaviour?

By comparing various species on these criteria, Bateson arrived at the conclusion that insects probably do not feel pain but that animals on the same evolutionary level as fish and octopuses and above probably do. If this is the case, we are then left with the problem of pitting animal and human suffering against each other.

Sentiency

Offering an alternative criterion to 'suffering', Ryder (1991) suggests that **sentiency** should be the basis of our decisions (by sentiency he means that a creature is capable of 'sensing', feeling and having consciousness.). Unlike Bateson, however, Ryder is not prepared to compromise and thinks that sentient animals should not be used in research at all.

Deservingness

Green (1994) offers a further consideration: that is, how 'deserving' humans might be in benefiting from animal research. He gives a range of examples to illustrate different grades of deservingness (note that, in all these cases, animal research could help us to understand and alleviate human suffering but in none of them are animals responsible for the human's plight):

■ Problems that seem to be self-inflicted such as in smoking and lung-disease.

■ Problems arising from how human society is organized: for example, in ways that encourage problems such as stress-related disorders or depression. Such problems are self-inflicted in a wider sense.

■ Disorders that are not self-inflicted: for example, Alzheimer's disease.

Unfortunately, all of the four considerations described raise further problems. In Bateson's model, for

---

GLOSSARY

Sentiency Capability of 'sensing', feeling and having consciousness.

example, quality of research design may be relatively easy to judge but assessment of animal suffering and certainty of medical benefit is much more difficult. Similarly, there are problems in deciding how to judge suffering, sentiency and deservingness and we are not yet able to do so with real certainty. However, if animal research is halted until we can decide, the consequences could be catastrophic and we would find ourselves back in a position of moral absolutism. Morton (1992) suggests a compromise in that reports of research using animals always include accounts of any anticipated or unforeseen adverse effects so that they can be avoided or minimized in future research. Morton realizes that this leaves researchers vulnerable to attack but thinks that openness allows for broader consent from people who are not engaged in research.

Closing the gap between animals and humans

The arguments outlined so far focus on seeking dividing lines between species so that we can continue with research. Dawkins (1993) is critical of such approaches and calls them 'regrettable'. He says they support the idea of the 'discontinuous mind' which promotes the view that there is a yawning gulf between humans and other species, even closely related ones such as gorillas. Dawkins and others prefer to work towards closing the perceived gaps between species, thus making animal research less acceptable. Vines (1993, 1994) agrees with Dawkins and adds that some sort of consciousness in both birds and mammals is discernible through their behaviour but its role and nature remain a 'profound mystery' (p. 31). This mystery needs to be unravelled so that we can reexamine our conventional exploitative relationship with other animals.

One consequence of such approaches is the **Great Ape Project** – the brainchild of Professor Singer (see Singer, 1993; Singer and Cavalieri, 1993). Singer is supported by a group of 34 biologists, philosophers and writers whose purpose is to bring the great apes (gorillas, chimpanzees and orang-utans) into the human fold and give them the same moral rights including protection under the law. Three principles have been derived and these make up the Declaration of Great Apes:

■ the right to life,

■ protection of individual liberty,
■ prohibition of torture.

Naturally, not all human rights extend to the great apes because of their different interests, but even to acknowledge those listed above would mean an end to the use of great apes in experimentation and as exhibits in zoos. In support of this, Singer quotes research into chimpanzee behaviour by Goodall (1978) and into chimpanzee language by Savage-Rumbaugh (1990) both of which help to close the gap. (Indeed, humans share 98.4 per cent of their DNA with both the common and pygmy chimp, a little more than with the gorilla.) Ironically, it is research with great apes that is likely to help the Great Ape Project along and, if we ever arrive at a solution, we then have the problem of what to do with the research animals. As BBC's Horizon programme 'Chimp Talk' (1993) showed, the ageing Washoe will need sensitive care for the rest of her life. The best that can now happen is that research with great apes is phased out and that the reasoning behind this leads to the phasing out of other animal research as well.

See Chapter 17 for a more detailed discussion of attempts to teach human language to animals.

Conclusion

We have seen that any kind of animal research, whether it is experimental or naturalistic, can affect animals in undesirable ways, yet to stop all animal research could be detrimental to both humans and animals. There are some alternatives to the use of animals in medical research, such as tissue research and in vitro techniques, but much of the content does not apply to psychological research which tends to focus on the intact, living individual. There is some scope for computer simulations of behaviour, particularly in the field of cognition but again, these do not suit all areas of enquiry.

Finally, it is worth considering the implications of the rationale that ultimately underlies all animal

---

GLOSSARY

Great Ape Project A project supported by biologists, philosophers and writers, the aim of which is to give the great apes (gorillas, chimpanzees and orang-utans) the same moral rights (including protection under the law) as humans.

research: that human life is more valuable than animal life. A dangerous extension of this rationale is to argue that some human lives, such as those of the terminally ill, the intellectually impaired and life prisoners, are less valuable than others. During World War II unscrupulous scientists used the 'value of life' argument to justify research on prisoners, and sometimes their own military forces, into surgical procedures, germ warfare and human endurance. Ironically, some of the findings from this research could prove immensely useful to humankind but the means by which it was gained are so repugnant that it is unlikely that they will ever be released. The dilemma about animal research remains and as, at present, there are few viable alternatives, it is likely to be with us for some time.

? SELF-ASSESSMENT QUESTIONS

1. Outline practical arguments for and against the use of animals in psychological research.
2. Give three examples of animal research which has been of benefit to humans.
3. List 10 of the 15 ethical guidelines on animal research issued by the BPS.
4. Outline the views of Gray, Ryder and Singer on animal research.
5. Comment on the worth of 'cost–benefit analysis', suffering, sentiency and deservingness in helping to resolve ethical questions about animal research.
6. Describe some of the ways in which psychologists have tried to close the gap between animals and humans.
7. What alternatives are there to animal research?

Chapter summary

- The British Psychological Society (BPS) regularly publishes and revises general ethical guidelines and codes of practice regarding the use of human participants in research. Guidelines can be summarized under the headings of 'risks' and 'informed consent'.

- The risks that psychologists may encounter in their research include: psychological stress caused to the participant which psychologists have an obligation to avoid; a participant's feeling of coercion when offered payment for their cooperation; deception should be avoided and, if it is inevitable, participants should be debriefed; breaches of confidentiality should be avoided and participant's privacy preserved.

- Informed consent should be sought from participants, or if this is not possible, a pilot study or preliminary role-play should be carried out, interviewing participants afterwards to elicit their feelings about the experience.

- Examples of psychological research that has been ethically questionable include Asch's conformity experiments, Milgram's 'obedience' research and Zimbardo's prison simulation. Both Milgram and Zimbardo presented a spirited defence of their procedures, arguing that all precautions had been taken to avoid psychological harm to participants and

showing an awareness of their responsibilities for the consequences of their findings.

- In 1995, Lindsay and Colley interviewed members of the BPS asking them to describe an incident they had experienced over the last year which was ethically troubling. Experiences described included those relating to issues of confidentiality and those to do with obtaining informed consent. It was noted that 37 per cent of respondents said they had no ethical dilemmas in their work and this raises the question of whether or not psychologists are fully aware of ethical issues.

- Complaints about psychologists to the BPS, though small in number, raises issues about how ethical guidelines can be implemented, particularly since not all psychologists are members of the BPS.

- Ethical concerns in relation to the use of psychotherapy in clinical settings have been expressed. These include doubts about whether psychotherapies are effective and about the financial, emotional and sexual power therapists could be seen as having over their clients. Many different kinds of treatments exist and clients may be confused about the qualifications of the psychotherapist and what to do if they have a complaint.

Examples of behavioural therapies (based on Pavlovian or Skinnerian conditioning) are aversion therapy and behaviour modification. Behavioural therapies have been criticized for being manipulative, coercive and controlling, conditioning people against their will. Objections centre on the use of punishment or pain, deprivation, free will and their notion of 'cure'.

However, many behavioural therapists now devolve much more power to the clients and in certain disorders, for example sexual dysfunction, enuresis and habit disorders, treatment is very effective.

Other types of treatment that raise ethical concerns include electroconvulsive therapy, the use of psychoactive drugs and psychosurgery.

It has been said that psychological knowledge could not advance without a certain amount of risk to researchers and their participants or to clinical psychologists and their patients.

Socially sensitive research involves studies in which there are potential social consequences or implications for the participants or the class of individuals represented by the research: for example, studies of racial or gender differences, child-rearing practices, health-related issues such as drug abuse or sexual behaviour.

Specific examples of socially sensitive research include Bowlby's studies in support of his 'maternal deprivation' hypothesis, Freud's work which stressed the importance of early experiences and the role played by child-rearing practices and Burt's twin studies in support of his view that intelligence was largely inherited, which influenced the policy on selection at 11 for different types of education.

Dangers of socially sensitive research findings lie in the difficulty with which they may be dislodged even when there is little supporting evidence and also in situations where research findings are not in tune with the institution for which the research is being carried out.

Scarr (1988) argues that psychologists should not avoid socially sensitive research, since there is a need for good studies that highlight, for example, race and gender issues in the quest for equality of opportunity. Howitt (1991) argues that psychologists are not yet in a position to influence social policy and should be aware of their limitations.

The use of animals in psychological research raises ethical issues. Examples include work by Blakemore and Cooper (1970), Harlow (1959), Savage-Rumbaugh (1990). Animals: The Scientific Procedures Act 1986 is designed to protect living vertebrates.

Justifications for the use of animals in research include the notion that if Darwin's evolutionary theory is correct, much can be learned about humans by studying less complex organisms; also, it has been argued that many laboratories' experiments carried out on animals would not be ethically acceptable with humans and because animals reproduce quickly, it is possible to assess the effects of early experience on later behaviour more easily than with humans.

Arguments against animal research centre on the problem of anthropomorphism and also on the uniqueness of humans and the different physiological make-up of animals, which make it impossible to generalize from animal to human behaviour. Concern has been expressed that some kinds of field research might have an adverse effect on some animals and threaten the survival of a species.

Miller (1985) argued that much animal research has been valuable not only in benefiting humans but also animals themselves. For example, animal research has done much to preserve endangered species and to promote the health of domestic pets. Miller concludes that there is a strong financial and moral case for continuing to back animal research.

Animal research that has been of use to humans includes the application of Pavlov's classical conditioning experiments with dogs to the development of a treatment for nocturnal enuresis in children. Also, in line with Skinner's operant conditioning techniques, pigeons have been trained to detect coloured life rafts against the background of the sea much more effectively than helicopter crews.

The BPS and Experimental Psychology Society jointly issued guidelines to assist in the planning of research with animals. An overarching principle is the researchers' obligation to avoid or minimize discomfort to all living animals.

Gray (1991) argues that we have a moral justification to do research with animals, where the end in terms of the benefit to humans justifies the means. Ryder (1990) attacked Gray's views as 'speciesist' and aligned it with racism and sexism.

■ Bateson (1986) suggests that a committee of research scientists, animal welfare representatives and disinterested parties should be formed to consider the costs and benefits of animal research in relation to three issues: certainty of medical benefit, the quality of the research and the degree of animal suffering involved. If the first two are high and the third low, the research would probably be permitted.

■ Other issues to be considered in order to resolve the debate are ways in which the degree of animal suffering can be assessed in research; whether the creature is capable of 'sensing', feeling and having consciousness; how 'deserving' humans might be in benefiting from animal research.

■ The dilemma about animal research remains and as at present there are few viable alternatives, it is likely to continue for some time.

Further reading

Gross, R.D. (1995). *Themes, Issues and Debates in Psychology*. London: Hodder and Stoughton. Chapter 10 gives a clear and detailed account of ethical issues in psychological research with humans and animals. It goes on to examine ethics in behaviour change, especially in clinical settings.

Fairbairn, S. and Fairbairn, G. (eds) (1987) *Psychology, Ethics and Change*. London: Routledge & Kegan Paul. This book concentrates on the moral dimensions of psychological practice in clinical settings. It is a multiauthor text with contributions from practitioners in a variety of fields.

CHAPTER 6

Learning and behaviour

Simple learning   125
- Habituation   125
- Associative learning   126
- Classical conditioning   126
- Operant conditioning   128
- Biological limits of conditioning   130

More complex learning   131
- Cognitive maps   131
- Insight learning   132
- Learning sets   134

Some applications of learning theory to humans   134
- Programmed learning   135
- Evaluation of programmed learning   137

Social learning theory   137
- Observational learning   138
- The importance of cognitive factors   138
- Identification   139
- Evaluation of social learning theory   139

Objectives

At the end of this chapter you should be able to:

- Understand what is meant by learning and appreciate some of the questions that have been explored by learning theorists;

- Discuss several different forms of simple learning including habituation, classical conditioning and operant conditioning and be aware of some of the biological limits of conditioning in animals;

- Appreciate some more complex forms of learning observed in animals, particularly cognitive learning, including the formation of cognitive maps, insight learning and learning sets;

- Consider and evaluate some of the basic principles of social learning theory;

- Describe and assess some of the clinical and educational applications of learning theory to humans.

Learning is involved in all aspects of our development. Almost any activity you can imagine – from getting dressed in the morning to forming political beliefs and opinions, from reading this book to making friends – is affected in some way by learning. Whether it be playing a sport such as cricket or tennis, memorizing a set of formulas for an exam or developing the skills of social interaction in infancy, our early efforts are generally crude and rudimentary, but become more skilled with practice or experience.

This leads us to consider what exactly we mean by learning. Many different definitions have been proposed. One that would probably be acceptable to most psychologists is 'Learning is any relatively permanent change in behaviour (or behavioural

> **GLOSSARY**
>
> **Learning** Relatively permanent changes in behaviour that occur as a result of experience.

potential) produced by experience' (Tarpy and Mayer, 1978). Key words here are:

- **relatively permanent** – temporary changes resulting from illness or the use of drugs are not included;
- **produced by experience** – changes resulting from physical growth or brain damage would not be classed as learning.

Psychologists have traditionally been interested in learning. During the first half of this century, a great deal of effort was directed towards the study of animal learning and two convenient species were generally used in laboratory studies, the rat and the pigeon. Much of this early work on learning was done from a behaviourist perspective (see Chapter 2) and was concerned with the formation of associations, learning to link certain things together. By investigating a wide range of different learning situations, it was hoped to arrive at general 'laws of learning' that might apply to most species, including humans. Many different models and theories of **associative learning** were produced, and some of them will be considered in this chapter along with more sophisticated models that took account of processes such as forming 'cognitive maps', understanding rules and principles or drawing on insight to solve problems.

Some of the questions to be explored are:

- How does learning take place – what are the processes involved?
- What are the biological constraints on learning in animals?
- Are there learning processes which are applicable to both animals and humans?

Simple learning

Habituation

Habituation is thought to be the very simplest form of learning necessary for survival. It involves learning not to respond to a particular stimulus. Learning what not to do is as important to an animal or human as learning to respond to particular signals. By learning to ignore innocuous stimulation, the animal's energy can be conserved for other, more important activities (Thorpe, 1963) For example, birds will learn to ignore the scarecrow that previously caused them to flee, they habituate; humans may habituate to the ticking of a clock or the sound of traffic noise.

Clark (1960) demonstrated habituation in marine rag worms, *Nereis*, which live in tubes they have constructed in the sandy floor of the sea. In the laboratory, Clark was able to get the worms to live in glass tubes in shallow basins of water. He found that touching the protruding head of the worm, jarring the basin, a sudden shadow passing over and various other stimuli caused the worms to retract into the tube. The majority of worms reemerged within a minute. If the stimuli were repeated every minute, the number of worms responding gradually diminished until none were retracting; they had habituated. The phenomenon of habituation shows that animals and humans can learn to ignore a stimulus that continues to be experienced, so conserving energy for other more necessary functions.

Habituation also forms the basis of a technique used in research when it is unclear whether or not an animal can recognize a particular stimulus. For example, Ryan (1982) investigated whether a pigeon could recognize others of the same species by first placing an object pigeon next to it and recording the frequency of the bowing movements which occurred. After about five five-minute trials, the subject pigeon ceased to bow – it had habituated. When a second object pigeon, identical to the first one to the human eye, was presented, the subject's bowing promptly recommenced.

The method of habituation is also commonly used with human babies to study the perception of form, movement and colour. A stimulus is repeatedly presented until the baby stops attending to it (habituation). Then a different stimulus is presented. If the baby still ignores the stimulus, despite the change, it can be assumed that the baby has not perceived a difference between the two stimuli. If, however, the baby's attention is renewed in response to the second stimulus, the investigator assumes that the baby did perceive a change in the stimulus. Maurer and Barrera (1981) used the habituation technique to

---

GLOSSARY

Associative learning Learning to associate one stimulus with another or with particular consequences.

Habituation Learning to ignore a stimulus which is presented continuously, for example the ticking of a clock or the sound of traffic noise.

investigate infants' perceptions of face-like stimuli. This experiment is described in Chapter 13.

Associative learning

This relates to the kind of learning that takes place when a stimulus becomes associated with another stimulus or with particular consequences. For example, a baby learns to associate the sight of a feeding bottle with milk; a dog learns to 'sit' because a reward is given; in an experiment, a honey bee picks out the blue dish from a selection of dishes because it has previously found sugar solution there: it has associated sugar with the colour blue. The best known types of associative learning are classical and operant (or instrumental) conditioning.

Classical conditioning

Reflex behaviour is involuntary; it arises automatically in response to an appropriate stimulus; examples are salivating at the smell of food, feeling fear when faced with something frightening. The theory of **classical conditioning** aims to account for the way in which reflex behaviour may become associated with a new stimulus that does not naturally activate that behaviour. Put simply, an individual may learn to respond in a particular way to a given stimulus because of its association with something else. Pavlov (1927), a physiologist, was studying the salivary reflex in dogs when he observed that the dogs salivated not only at the sight and smell of food, a 'natural' response, but also at the sight of the food container alone. Through a series of experiments, he demonstrated that dogs could be conditioned to salivate to other 'unnatural' stimuli, such as a buzzer being sounded, provided the stimulus was repeatedly presented at, or slightly before, the presentation of food. Such a pairing caused an association to be formed between the buzzer and the food and subsequently between the buzzer and the salivation response. A conditioned reflex had been formed. Figure 6.1 illustrates the process of classical conditioning and the terminology associated with it.

Pavlov further demonstrated that the following processes could occur after conditioning:

■ If the **conditioned stimulus** continued to be present but without the food, the salivating response would cease or become extinguished.

■ After **extinction**, the **conditioned response**, salivation, may reappear when the relevant stimulus is presented, though it is much weaker. This reappearance is known as **spontaneous recovery**.

■ The dog would generalize its response by salivating to sounds similar to the buzzer.

■ The opposite process to **generalization** is **discrimination**: if two different tones were sounded but food was presented with only one of them, the dog would learn to discriminate

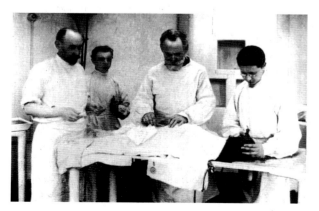

Ivan Pavlov's work with dogs was central in developing his theory of conditional reflexes

> **GLOSSARY**
>
> **Classical conditioning** The process through which a reflex response becomes associated with a stimulus which would not naturally activate that behaviour.
>
> **Conditioned stimulus (CS)** In classical conditioning, a stimulus which, when repeatedly paired with an unconditioned stimulus, produces a conditioned response.
>
> **Extinction** In classical conditioning, the halting of the CR when the CS is repeatedly presented but is not paired with the UCS.
>
> **Conditioned response (CR)** In classical conditioning, a response to a formerly neutral stimulus which because of repeated pairing with a conditioned stimulus produces a conditioned response.
>
> **Spontaneous recovery** In classical conditioning, the reappearance of the CR when the CS is presented some time after extinction has occurred.
>
> **Generalization** In classical conditioning, the process whereby a CR is produced to a stimulus similar to the conditioned stimulus.
>
> **Discrimination** In classical conditioning, selectively responding to the CS but not to stimuli which are similar to the CS.

Figure 6.1 The process of classical conditioning.

Procedure	Response
Before conditioning	
Food (UCS) ——————→	Salivation (UCR)
Buzzer (CS) ——————→	No response or irrelevant response
During conditioning	
Food plus buzzer ——————→ (UCS) (CS)	Salivation (CR)
Repeated pairing of the UCS and CS	
After conditioning	
Buzzer (CS) ——————→	Salivation (CR)

UCS = unconditioned stimulus; CS = conditioned stimulus;
UCR = unconditioned response; CR = conditioned response

between them and salivate only to the tone associated with food.

The last process, conditioned discrimination, has been of great value for measuring the perceptual abilities of animals. After the animal has been trained to respond to one particular stimulus, for example a certain shape, colour or sound, it can then be tested to see how far it can discriminate this stimulus from others of increasing similarity. To give two examples from many hundreds, von Frisch (1967) used this method in his classic studies of the colour vision of bees; Wells (1962) used it to investigate the sensitivity of touch in the octopus (these studies are discussed in Part 4).

Conditioned reflexes of the kind investigated by Pavlov have been observed in many different animals. For example, birds learn to avoid the black and orange caterpillars of the cinnabar moth after finding that the taste of them is offensive; then they generalize this avoidance response to wasps and other black and orange patterned insects (Manning and Dawkins, 1992).

In natural settings, a 'pure' conditioned reflex is not so apparent as in a laboratory experiment. For example, foraging bees do not simply learn to associate a colour with the nectar reward, they also learn at what time

Box 6.1 Classical conditioning in humans

Pavlov's procedures and terminology were soon applied to experimentation with young children. Watson and Rayner (1920) demonstrated that fear could be developed through classical conditioning and could be eliminated in the same way. Watson proposed that the emotion of fear (UCR) in infants is a natural response to a loud noise (UCS). He produced a fear of rats (and indeed of all white furry things) (CR) in a nine-month-old baby by repeatedly associating the appearance of a rat (CS) with the sound of a loud gong (UCS). This is the, now notorious, 'Little Albert' study which has been heavily criticized for its unethical procedures.

Learning theorists propose that classical conditioning may be responsible for the development of many phobias (irrational fears). For example, the child who undergoes a frightening experience associated with the presence of a dog may develop a long-lasting fear of dogs.

Marquis (1931) demonstrated the process of classical conditioning in ten new-born babies by sounding a buzzer shortly before or at the same time as they received their bottle. After this treatment had continued for eight days, it was noted that the infants made sucking movements and generally increased their activity when the buzzer was presented without the food. Marquis concluded that 'systematic training of the human infant ... can be started at birth'.

Studies of classical conditioning have demonstrated the existence of a powerful process capable of influencing reflex behaviour in both animals and human beings. This is of special interest in relation to humans because of the role classical conditioning plays in the development of emotional responses. For example, at a very early age, things or people that are present when a child feels happy and content become a conditioned stimulus for these same contented feelings in later life. Similarly, those associated with unpleasant or stressful feelings may become conditioned stimuli for feelings of anger and anxiety later on.

during the day the nectar secretion is highest and also the location of the flowers relative to their hive.

Operant conditioning

Unlike classical conditioning, **operant (or instrumental) conditioning** is concerned with voluntary rather than reflex behaviour. The theory is based on Thorndike's (1913) 'Law of Effect', which states that behaviour resulting in pleasant consequences is likely to be repeated in the same circumstances, whereas that which has no such pleasant consequences dies away.

Thorndike investigated this type of learning with cats using a 'puzzle box' – a cage with a door that could only be opened from inside by pulling a loop of string. Typically a cat was placed in the box and tried hard to escape. In the course of its efforts – by chance – it pulled the string and escaped through the open door. Several more trials were carried out and eventually the cat pulled the string immediately it was placed in the box. Thorndike measured the time taken by the cat to escape as an indicator of learning. His data showed that learning the correct 'escape' behaviour happened gradually – a situation he named **trial and error learning**. The reward (freedom) he contended was responsible for 'stamping in' the appropriate response.

Operant conditioning is similar in principle to Thorndike's trial and error learning. In his book *Behaviour of Organisms* (1938), Skinner described a series of laboratory experiments he conducted with rats. He constructed a small box containing a lever, a food dispenser and (sometimes) a panel to display lighted stimuli. A rat placed in the box spontaneously explores its surroundings and eventually, by accident, presses the lever. This activates the food dispenser and a pellet of food is presented to the rat. Subsequently, each time the animal's behaviour approximates to what is required, food is presented until eventually the 'reward' – known as **reinforcement** – is produced only when the animal presses the lever. This procedure is known as **behaviour shaping**; the desired behaviour is shaped by rewarding a series of responses that are successive approximations – that is, they approximate more and more closely to the desirable behaviour. The desirable behaviour, in this case, lever pressing, was named an operant. The reward, which increases the likelihood of the behaviour (or operant) being repeated, is the **reinforcer**. The process whereby the food is presented in response to the lever-pressing behaviour is known as **positive reinforcement**.

Skinner and others have repeatedly demonstrated that the techniques of operant conditioning can be used to produce quite complex behaviour in animals. By carefully shaping the component behaviours, he trained pigeons to act as pilots in rockets and to play table tennis.

As with classical conditioning, generalization, discrimination and extinction can be demonstrated:

- An animal may generalize its response to situations which are similar but not identical to the one in which it was originally conditioned. Therefore, if a rat is conditioned to respond when a one-inch plastic square is presented, it will also press the lever in response to a circle of a similar size.
- A rat may be conditioned to discriminate between the circle and the square if it is reinforced only when it presses the bar in response to one of them, but not the other.
- If reinforcement is discontinued, extinction of the operant response will occur. For reasons which are not clear, this takes longer than with classical conditioning.

Schedules of reinforcement

Skinner also demonstrated that the kind of patterns, or **schedules**, of reinforcement given would differentially

---

GLOSSARY

Operant (or instrumental) conditioning The conditioning of voluntary behaviour through the processes of reinforcement and punishment.

Reinforcement The process whereby a reinforcer increases the likelihood of a response.

Behaviour shaping In operant conditioning, the process involved in the learning of new behaviour by successively reinforcing behaviour which approximates to the desired reponse.

Reinforcer In operant conditioning, a stimulus following a response, which makes that response more likely to recur.

Positive reinforcement In operant conditioning, the process whereby a response is made more likely by being following by a desirable stimulus (a positive reinforcer).

Schedules of reinforcement In operant conditioning, the varying conditions that determine when a response will be followed by a reinforcer.

affect the kind of learning which occurred. The two main schedules are:

■ **Continuous reinforcement** – where a reward is given to every instance of the desired behaviour;
■ **Partial reinforcement** – where an animal is reinforced only some of the time.

The four partial reinforcement schedules that are most commonly used are:

■ Fixed interval: the animal is reinforced after regular time intervals, say every 50 seconds, provided at least one lever pressing response is made during that time.
■ Variable interval: reinforcement is given on average every, say, 50 seconds, though not precisely at the same time intervals.
■ Fixed ratio: the animal is reinforced after a regular number of lever-pressing responses, say after every four responses.
■ Variable ratio: reinforcement is given on average every, say, four responses, though not exactly after each fourth response.

Each schedule has a different effect on learning. In general, continuous reinforcement produces the quickest learning, while partial reinforcement produces learning which lasts longer in the absence of reinforcement.

The consequences of behaviour

Skinner believed that behaviour is shaped by its consequences. We have already noted that one such consequence is positive reinforcement, something which is pleasant. Other consequences might be negative reinforcement and punishment.

Negative reinforcement refers to the removal or avoidance of something unpleasant. For example, an electric shock is switched off when the rat presses the lever. This is known as escape learning. Skinner showed also that if a light is flashed just before an electric shock is given, the rat would learn to press the lever in response to the light, thus avoiding the shock – an example of avoidance learning. Like positive reinforcement, negative reinforcement results in the desired behaviour being strengthened.

Punishment refers to the delivery of an undesirable stimulus following a response, for example, when an electric shock is given in response to the lever-pressing behaviour. Skinner believed that just as reinforcement (positive and negative) can be used to strengthen a response, making it more likely to be repeated, so punishment weakens the response and makes it less likely to recur. However, he argued that punishment is not a suitable technique for controlling behaviour, since it simply suppresses unwanted behaviour without strengthening desirable behaviour. Studies with rats carried out by Estes (1944, 1970) showed that punishment appeared only to diminish lever-pressing behaviour for a short time, but did not weaken it in the long term.

Whether or not punishment is effective with children is a vexed question. Studies have shown that in the short term it appears to suppress undesirable behaviour. It can, however, have unintended emotional effects such as anger and frustration and, in some circumstances, it may actually become reinforcing, as in the case of the child whose tantrums are designed to gain attention. In these circumstances, it may increase, rather than reduce, the unwanted behaviour.

Secondary reinforcement

Some stimuli, known as **secondary reinforcers**, become reinforcing because they are associated with primary reinforcers such as food or water. Thus, Skinner found that a rat would press the lever in response to the clicking noise heard when a food pellet was delivered, even on occasions when no food was in fact produced.

The conventional view of operant conditioning was that reinforcement is only effective if it is given quickly

---

GLOSSARY

Continuous reinforcement In operant conditioning, a schedule in which a reinforcer is given to every instance of the desired behaviour.

Partial reinforcement In operant conditioning, a schedule in which a reinforcer is given only after some responses.

Negative reinforcement In operant conditioning, the process whereby a response is made more likely because of the removal or avoidance of something unpleasant (a negative reinforcer). This is *not* the same as punishment.

Punishment The delivery of an undesirable stimulus following a response. Punishment weakens the response and makes it less likely to recur.

Secondary reinforcer In operant conditioning, a stimulus which becomes reinforcing because of its association with primary reinforcers such as food or water, which have direct biological significance.

Box 6.2 Operant conditioning with humans

As with classical conditioning, research has shown that infant behaviour may be shaped through the techniques of operant conditioning. For example, in a study of language acquisition, Rheingold et al. (1959) and Bloom (1979) showed that the number of sounds made by three-month-old babies could be increased if an adult reinforced the infant's utterances with verbal responses.

Operant methods have also been systematically used in order to change undesirable behaviour in humans. This is known as the technique of behaviour modification (discussed in greater detail in Chapter 33). The use of reinforcement to improve the classroom behaviour of disruptive children, to teach basic hygiene routines to the mentally handicapped, to encourage autistic children to communicate, has received a large measure of success. In all cases, the techniques used operate on the basis of ignoring undesirable behaviour, resulting in its extinction, and reinforcing desirable behaviour, which should then be repeated.

Within the home environment, parents use many of the techniques of operant conditioning, albeit unconsciously. Consider how a young child is potty trained or learns table manners. Reinforcers in the form of praise and hugs are freely given as the child proceeds. And as Skinner indicated, partial, rather than continuous reinforcement is usually more effective, particularly with an older child. The child who is praised for being helpful around the home is more likely to repeat the behaviour if the praise is given only some of the time.

---

following a response such as bar pressing – a principle known as **contiguity**. The principle of secondary reinforcement has proved useful in overcoming the adverse effects of delayed reward. For example, secondary reinforcers such as clicking noises are useful for training animals, as in a circus when it would be difficult to give a reward immediately after the animal's response.

Exercise 6.1 Operant conditioning in action

See if you can work out a procedure, based on the principles of operant conditioning, that a teacher could use to encourage children to improve their handwriting.

What reinforcers might be used?

How might the 'undesirable behaviour' (poor handwriting) be extinguished?

Which would be the more effective, continuous or partial reinforcement?

Biological limits of conditioning

The descriptions of classical and operant conditioning above suggest that the two learning processes are quite straightforward – animals or humans learn to associate a stimulus with a reinforcement (classical conditioning) or a response with a reinforcement (operant conditioning). However, in practice, if one brings an ethological approach into laboratory situations, it is clear that animals often bring their own natural species-specific behaviours to a learning situation and these may affect the way they respond. (**Ethology** is the study of animal behaviour in the natural environment.) An interesting example comes from pigeons used in operant conditioning studies because they will readily learn to peck at a key on the wall of the Skinner box to obtain a reward of either food or water. Close examination of the pigeon's pecking behaviour shows that when hungry and pecking for a food reward, the pigeon's bill is open and its eyes are partially closed. However, when pecking for water the bill is almost closed and the eyes are fully open. See Figure 6.2. In (a) the reward is food; the eyes are almost closed and the bill is opened as if to seize a food item. In (b) the bird is pecking for a water reward and the bill is almost closed whilst the eyes remain fully open.

These two 'styles' of pecking mirror exactly the contrasting styles used in a natural setting by a pigeon pecking to pick up food grains compared to that of a pigeon which dips its bill into water to drink. In other words, the pigeon pecking in a Skinner box is treating

---

GLOSSARY

Contiguity The need to give reinforcement at or very soon after the presentation of a stimulus or response.

Ethology The study of animals in their natural environments.

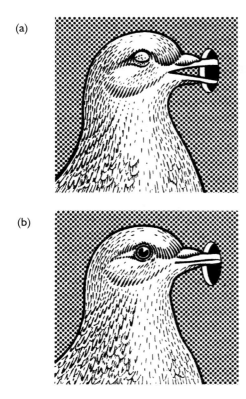

Figure 6.2 Trained pigeon in a Skinner box pecking a key to obtain a reward (from Moore, 1973)

the same key as if it were food in one situation and as water in the other.

Many other studies have shown that animals appear to learn most easily those responses which are closest to their natural behaviour and these responses may not necessarily fit with the 'general laws of learning' proposed by traditional learning theorists. Some examples are contained in Box 6.3.

SELF-ASSESSMENT QUESTIONS

1. What do you understand by 'learning'?
2. Explain with an example the process of habituation.
3. Briefly outline the chief features of (a) classical conditioning and (b) operant conditioning.
4. Referring to appropriate studies, discuss some of the biological limits of conditioning in different species.

More complex learning

As we have seen, classical and operant conditioning arise from an animal making associations between stimuli or events; much animal learning can be explained by reference to these two processes. However, since the early part of this century, psychologists have studied more complex forms of learning which often involve some kind of cognitive activity (thinking, interpreting, understanding) rather than merely making simple associations. Three examples of cognitive learning in animals will be examined: the formation of **cognitive maps**, insight learning and the phenomenon of learning sets.

Cognitive maps

Much research has been concerned with how rats learn to negotiate their way through a complex maze. Hull (1943) envisaged the rat building up a chain of stimulus–response (S–R) associations as it moved through the maze. The rat associates a corner or turn with the goal. As it proceeds further, it learns that a previous turn leads to the first S–R association.

GLOSSARY

Cognitive map A hypothetical structure which represents a mental 'picture' of a location or learning situation.

Box 6.3   Conditioning and the natural behaviour of animals

'Misbehaviour' in animals Breland and Breland (1961), pupils of Skinner, used techniques of operant conditioning to train animals to perform eyecatching tricks for TV commercials. They reported, however, that sometimes, instead of performing the desired behaviour, the animal would 'misbehave' and do something that was closer to its natural behaviour. So, a pig trained to drop money into a piggy bank would root with its snout on the way to the bank and chickens required to ring bells would scratch and peck at the ground instead. The Brelands came to accept that an animal does not always simply associate stimulus and response – its instinctual behaviour may set limits on what can be learned.

An ethological example An example taken from an ethological perspective investigates contiguity (the need to give reinforcement at or very soon after the presentation of a stimulus or response) Barnett (1963) showed that contiguity, as demonstrated in traditional learning theory experiments, is not always necessary to ensure that learning in the form of classical conditioning takes place. He described how rats only nibble at very small amounts of any new foods that are found in their territory. If the food is subsequently found to be 'safe', they gradually eat more on successive occasions until they are eating normal amounts. If it is poisonous and they survive, they avoid it completely in future – a conditioned response. This behaviour explains why poisoning rats is no easy task. The interesting point to note from a learning theory view is that a delay of hours usually occurs between a rat tasting the poisonous bait – the conditioned stimulus (always disguised with sweet substances) – and the resulting feelings of sickness – the unconditioned stimulus. These findings have been confirmed also in laboratory experiments.

Further, it has been shown that while rats can learn to associate taste with sickness after one tasting and a long delay, birds are more likely to associate the *appearance* of food with the effects of sickness (Martin and Lett, 1985). Unlike rats and some other mammals, birds are visual hunters. In this way they can learn to avoid harmful foods such as poisonous caterpillars in the wild. These are very good examples of two different species learning the same thing – which foods cause sickness – by different means which fit with their natural way of selecting food.

Gradually, the maze is learned through a set of simple associations, one leading automatically to the next. Tolman (1932), however, believed that during the exploration phase, rats do not simply learn a number of right and left turning responses, but form some kind of mental picture of the whole maze – a cognitive map. They can then use this to find their way through, avoiding turns which may lead to a blind alley and choosing routes which lead most quickly to the goal box. A typical experiment carried out by Tolman is described in Box 6.4, along with a later study by Olton (1979).

It is clear from the studies described that some animal learning involves quite complex cognitive activity, rather than merely the forming of stimulus–response associations.

Insight learning

Everyone has experienced the situation where, after pondering a problem for several minutes, the answer has 'come in a flash'. Animal researchers have argued that there are many instances of the same phenomenon in animals. They have used the term **insight learning** when they have observed animals solving problems very quickly without any obvious trial and error activities.

In an important series of experiments carried out in the 1920s, Köhler demonstrated insight learning in chimpanzees. The animals were set a series of problems to solve. In one famous example, Sultan, Köhler's most intelligent chimpanzee, was placed in a cage with a piece of fruit just out of reach (see Figure 6.3). Outside the cage were a number of sticks which, if slotted together, were long enough to reach the fruit. After a period of inactivity, the animal quite suddenly solved the problem by slotting the sticks together and

> GLOSSARY
>
> **Insight learning** Learning in which the learner perceives relationships in a problem suddenly without any obvious trial and error activities.

Box 6.4 Cognitive maps in rats

Tolman used two groups of rats, an experimental group, which were allowed to explore a maze like the one shown, and a control group which had no opportunity to explore the maze. Neither group was given any reinforcers such as food. Then both the experimental and control rats were placed in the maze and food was introduced as a reinforcer. Tolman found that the experimental group learned to run the maze much more quickly than the control group. He believed that this was because they had learned the layout of the maze and formed a cognitive map during their earlier, unreinforced explorations. Learning such as this, which occurs without reinforcement and which can be inferred from the animal's behaviour, is known as latent learning. The cognitive map thus enabled the rat to learn a specific route more easily once reinforcement was given.

More recent research provides evidence of cognitive maps in animals. Olton (1979) carried out a study in which rats learned a maze which consisted of a centre platform with eight identical passageways radiating from it, each with food placed at the far end. The rat had to learn to visit each passageway, retrieving the food there, without visiting any one twice. The rats succeeded in this task very well. After around 20 trials, they rarely returned to a passageway they had already visited. Interestingly, the rats visited the passageways randomly rather than in an obvious order such as clockwise, suggesting that they had not learned a rigid sequence of responses. The researchers concluded that a rat developed a cognitive map of the maze which allowed it to note and recall the passageways it had already visited.

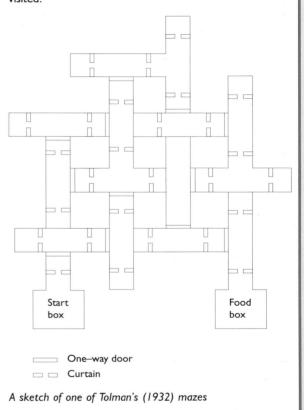

A sketch of one of Tolman's (1932) mazes

⬜ One–way door

⬜ ⬜ Curtain

Figure 6.3 A problem situation used by Köhler (1925) with chimpanzees

reaching for the food. Köhler called this process 'insightful learning'. He believed that during the initial period of inactivity, the animal was thinking – he called this cognitive restructuring. This resulted in a sudden insight into the problem followed by the animal performing a solution.

There are important differences in the behaviour of Köhler's chimpanzees compared to Thorndike's cats or Skinner's rats and pigeons described in the last section:

■ In the former, the solution came *suddenly* rather than after a period of trial and error (though it is possible that the chimpanzees engaged in mental trial and error).

■ Also, once the problem had been solved, the chimpanzee would make few irrelevant movements, unlike the Skinnerian rat which would continue to make irrelevant moves for many trials.

■ Köhler's chimpanzees demonstrated that they could transfer what they had learned to a new and different situation; for example, in one situation, Sultan would pile up boxes in order to reach a bunch of bananas which were otherwise out of reach, or would fit two sticks together to pull down the bananas.

Critics have pointed out that there were methodological flaws in Köhler's work. For example, he did not always record what relevant experiences the chimpanzees had prior to the study. Also, because of a lack of strict control, his results were sometimes open to alternative interpretations. Nonetheless, his research findings have generally been accepted as valid by many psychologists and animal researchers.

Learning sets

Harlow (1949) argued that insight learning as investigated by Köhler may not be a different process from operant conditioning, but merely arises from prior experience with trial and error learning. He proposed that insight learning could appear to occur if the animal formed a **learning set**. If an animal can form a learning set, it means that it has learned not just a problem, but something of the principle behind the problem.

In typical experiments, Harlow gave rhesus monkeys a range of discrimination tasks. For example, the monkey is presented with two dissimilar objects, say a tennis ball and a matchbox. The matchbox always covers a small item of food; the tennis ball never has a reward. After several trials, the monkey chooses the matchbox immediately. The trials are continued in the same way but using different objects. The objects are repeatedly changed after each correct discrimination. As the number of discriminations increases, the monkey learns each new task more quickly, eventually after only one trial; this is despite the fact that viewed as an individual problem, it is just as difficult as the first one. It has learned the principle behind the problem, or in Harlow's terms, has formed a learning set.

In more complex tasks, Harlow demonstrated that monkeys could learn principles such as 'odd one out' of three objects and choosing the 'left-hand object' or 'plastic shape with corners' such as a square or triangle.

Harlow argued that his research showed that what Köhler called 'insight learning' arose from operant conditioning which involves trial and error learning. However, it is clear that the formation of learning sets involves more than simple stimulus–response learning. In the learning set experiments, the fact that the animals were able to learn principles such as 'odd one out' meant that, at the very least, they were recalling what happened in earlier trials and then applying it in later ones. This strongly suggests that some cognitive activity occurred, since memory was involved.

Another way in which monkeys showed themselves capable of forming learning sets was in 'repeated reversal' problems. Here, the animal is trained to choose object A in preference to object B. Once learned, object B is now rewarded and object A is not; when this reversal is learned, the reward is then switched back to object A and so on. The monkeys became increasingly faster at learning each reversal, again implying that they had learned a principle.

? SELF-ASSESSMENT QUESTIONS

1. What do you understand by 'cognitive activity' in relation to learning?
2. Referring to an appropriate study, explain what Tolman meant by a 'cognitive map'.
3. Briefly describe Köhler's studies of insight learning in a chimpanzee. Explain how the chimpanzee's behaviour differed from that of Skinner's rats and pigeons.
4. What did Harlow mean by a 'learning set'. Describe the typical procedure in a 'repeated reversal' problem.

Some applications of learning theory to humans

So far, the main thrust of this chapter has been towards learning processes as they have been observed in animals, though some comparisons have been made

---

GLOSSARY

Learning set A hypothetical structure involving memory, representing the learning of a principle which underlies a problem.

with human learning. The current section aims to draw attention to some ways in which particular theories of learning, developed using animals, have been deliberately applied to practical situations involving humans (see also Chapter 1). There are three important applications of conditioning theory: behavioural therapies, biofeedback techniques and programmed learning. Behavioural therapies and biofeedback techniques are fully discussed in Part 7, so they will be described only briefly here.

■ **Behavioural therapies**, which aim to remove maladaptive (inappropriate) behaviours and substitute desirable ones, drawing on the theories of classical and operant conditioning. Therapeutic techniques based on conditioning processes are usually referred to as either behaviour modification or behaviour therapy. Walker (1984) proposed that techniques based on operant conditioning should be referred to as behaviour modification and techniques which rely upon the principles of classical conditioning should be known as behaviour therapy. Behaviour modification and behaviour therapy are described and evaluated in Chapter 33. Ethical issues relating to behavioural therapies were discussed in Chapter 5.
■ **Biofeedback techniques**, which employ the theoretical bases of both classical and operant conditioning in clinical settings. Through the use of this technique, individuals are trained to control bodily processes such as heart rate and blood pressure which are autonomic processes and not normally under voluntary control. Biofeedback techniques are described and evaluated in Chapter 33.
■ **Programmed learning**, a method of instruction that applies the principles of operant conditioning to formal learning situations in educational fields.

Programmed learning

Programmed learning is a method of instruction based on the principles of operant conditioning. It has been used in formal educational settings such as schools, colleges and universities, in the armed forces (where it has been widely used) and in industrial training settings. Its main advantage is that it allows individual learners to work through organized learning material at their own pace and to receive feedback on their achievements at regular intervals.

Early programmes were presented on teaching machines; more recently computers have been used as a medium and many textbooks and self-study materials have employed the techniques of programmed instruction.

Theoretical background

Pressey (1926) produced the first recognizable teaching machine, which involved the presentation of small items of information followed by multiple choice answers (a number of answers, only one of which is correct). These were presented through a small window in a drum and students were required to press a key corresponding to the correct answer before a new question became available.

In 1954, Skinner applied his findings from animal conditioning to the production of the first linear teaching programme (see below). Traditional classroom teaching, he argued, was inefficient because it failed to take account of the different abilities and previous knowledge of a group of students; lessons could not move according to the needs and pace of individual learners.

The theoretical base of programmed learning drew on the following principles of operant conditioning:

■ A motivated learner's actions which are followed by rewards (that is, are reinforced) are likely to be repeated and learned. The reward should follow as swiftly as possible after the response.
■ Actions which are not reinforced are likely to disappear (become extinguished).
■ Behavioural patterns may therefore be shaped by the use of controlled stimuli. In other words,

---

GLOSSARY

Behavioural therapies Treatments for mental disorder which draw on the principles of classical and operant conditioning.

Biofeedback techniques Techniques which draw on the theoretical bases of both classical and operant conditioning. Patients are trained to control bodily processes such as heart rate and blood pressure, which are under autonomic control.

Programmed learning A method of instruction based on the principles of operant conditioning. Individuals work through organized learning material at their own pace and receive feedback on their progress at regular intervals.

learning can take place as a result of a series of small steps leading to a desired outcome.

Skinner's linear programmes

Skinner's remedy to the shortcomings of traditional teaching was the **linear programme**, the main characteristics of which are:

- Subject matter is arranged in very small steps, known as frames, which are presented to the learner in a logical sequence.
- The learner is required to make a 'constructed response' usually by writing a word or phrase in response to a question (each step is so small that there is almost no likelihood that the response will be incorrect).
- For each correct response, the learner is given reinforcement in the form of immediate feedback on the accuracy of the response. In the case of an incorrect response (which should occur only rarely), the learner moves back to the item for another attempt before moving on.

The linear programme, therefore, is made up of a series of frames, each containing a small amount of information to which a learner must respond. Frames also contain the answer to the problem set in the preceding frame. Figure 6.4 illustrates a small extract from a possible linear programme on operant conditioning.

A key principle of programmed learning is that individual learners work at their own pace by actively participating in the process. Their learning is shaped through a schedule of continuous reinforcement. Motivation is ensured through the satisfaction felt when correct responses are given.

Frame 1	Associative learning is one of the most basic forms of learning. It involves making a new connection or as_____ between events or stimuli in the environment.
	ASSOCIATION
Frame 2	Associative _____ means to make a new association between events or stimuli in the environment. Psychologists distinguish between two forms of associative learning: classical and operant conditioning.
	LEARNING
Frame 3	A dog buries a bone or chases a ball. Since these responses are voluntary and spontaneous, they are considered to be operant _____
	RESPONSES
Frame 4	In operant conditioning we can increase the probability of a response being repeated if we can reinforce it. A reinforcer can be anything which is likely to cause the behaviour to be_____
	REPEATED
Frame 5	For example, if we want to teach a dog to 'shake hands' when we say 'Shake', we might lift its paw several times and on each occasion, give it a treat. If the treat causes the dog to repeat the 'shake hands' response, it can be called a _____
	REINFORCER

Figure 6.4 An extract from a linear programme on operant conditioning

Branching programmes

In contrast to linear programmes, **branching programmes** begin with a frame that usually contains much more information than is presented in a linear programme. The information is followed by a multiple-choice question. A learner who chooses the right answer will be passed on to the next frame. Wrong answers lead to a detour to a remedial programme designed to show learners where they went wrong and why. The learner is then returned to the original frame to make another response.

Branching programmes offer greater flexibility than linear programmes in that they provide a variety of different routes through the material, depending on the student's ability and level of understanding.

GLOSSARY

Linear programme A form of programmed learning where subject matter is arranged in very small steps, known as frames, which are presented in a logical sequence and require the learner to make a response. The response is reinforced through immediate feedback.

Branching programme A form of programmed learning which provides a variety of routes through the material, depending on the learner's ability, interest and level of understanding.

Evaluation of programmed learning

Strengths

Though programmed learning did not result in the revolutionary changes in teaching and learning envisaged by Skinner, it has been extremely effective in specific situations. Curzon (1980) claimed that programmed learning seems to have been particularly useful in the following situations:

- The learning of physical skills which lend themselves to being broken down into small steps, for example some engineering processes.
- The study of a subject for which there is a hierarchy of facts, for example, in mathematics or logic.

With the advent of computer-aided instruction, many effective programmes have been developed for use in a wide range of subjects in many different settings, from the primary school classroom to the business world.

In addition, the principles of programmed learning have been applied and are currently used in many textbooks and self-study materials. These have provided a useful method of study for individuals who are unable or who do not wish to attend conventional classes.

A study by Cavanagh (1963) compared programmed learning with conventional teaching in the training of technicians in the services. The main findings were:

- Achievement in both groups was similar;
- Students trained by programmed learning mastered the material more quickly than those taught by conventional methods;
- Retention and recall of learnt material was significantly better in the programmed learning group than in the conventionally taught group.

The findings from this study seem to suggest that programmed learning is a teaching and learning approach which has much to recommend it.

Criticisms

Critics have objected to Skinner's application to humans of principles drawn from animal conditioning. Human behaviour, it is argued, is too complex to be compared to the conditioning of rats and pigeons.

Perhaps the fundamental flaw in programmed learning which has prevented it from becoming the panacea expected by Skinner is its solitary nature, which can lead to boredom and lack of motivation. Programmed learning does not provide opportunities for the stimulation and social support from fellow learners that can be found in the traditional classroom setting.

 SELF-ASSESSMENT QUESTIONS

1. List and briefly describe three practical applications of conditioning theory.
2. Describe the main principles on which pro-grammed learning is based.
3. Briefly explain how a linear programme operates.
4. What is a branching programme?
5. State some of the strengths and limitations of programmed learning.

Social learning theory

Theorists who attempted to use the insights derived from classical and operant conditioning to account for the development of complex human social behaviours experienced some difficulties. Critics questioned the validity of extrapolating the findings of animal experiments to human behaviour and also raised doubts as to the likelihood of all complex human behaviour being derived from reinforcement of the spontaneous responses of the young child. The concept of **observational learning (or modelling)** had been proposed to explain language acquisition during early childhood and seemed appropriate also to the acquisition of social behaviour. Therefore, the scope of learning theory was enlarged during the 1940s and 1950s to include **social learning theory** to explain how children may learn new behaviour by imitating another person.

GLOSSARY

Observational learning (modelling) Learning by imitating the behaviour of a model.

Social learning theory A theory derived from traditional learning theory. It emphasizes the role of observational learning in development and that behaviour is mediated by cognitive variables.

Obervational learning

Observational learning has been extensively studied by Bandura and his colleagues (1963, 1977). A long series of experiments was carried out, mainly using nursery school children as participants.

In his most famous studies, Bandura exposed groups of children to either a real-life situation or to a film in which a model knocked down and beat a rubber 'Bobo' doll. The children were then given the opportunity to reproduce the behaviour observed and their responses were compared to those of a control group who had not seen the model. Findings indicated that the children who had watched the model behaved more aggressively than did the control group, often reproducing many of the specific acts of the model. Bandura concluded that children can learn through imitation quite spontaneously without any deliberate effort on the part of either the model or the learner. Box 6.5 describes a later study carried out by Bandura.

Bandura and others went on to investigate what characteristics of a model were most likely to encourage imitation in children. Studies showed that children are more likely to perform behaviour that is imitated from models who are:

■ similar in some respects to themselves,
■ exhibit power and control over some desirable commodity,
■ are warm and nurturant.

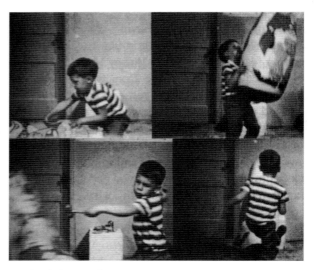

Bandura's famous 'Bobo doll' studies showed that children can learn through imitation quite spontaneously

The importance of cognitive factors

Unlike traditional learning theorists, social learning theorists emphasize the important cognitive, or mediating, variables, which intervene between a stimulus and response. Bandura proposed that the ability to observe and then reproduce behaviour involves at least four mediating skills:

Box 6.5   Learning and performance

In a later study, Bandura showed that children may learn the behaviour of a model without necessarily reproducing that behaviour. Three groups of children were shown a film of a model behaving aggressively. One group saw the model punished for the behaviour, one saw the model rewarded and in the third group, the model was neither rewarded nor punished. Subsequent observation of the children's behaviour revealed different levels of imitation. The 'model punished' group reproduced less aggressive behaviour than did the other two groups.

Bandura concluded that **vicarious** punishment (experiencing the model's punishment as though it had been administered to oneself) had influenced the child's learning of the aggressive behaviour. However, when the children were then offered rewards for imitating the model's behaviour, all three groups produced equally aggressive behaviour.

These findings suggest that it is necessary to distinguish between acquisition (learning) of behaviour, and the performance of that behaviour. This is an important insight which has alerted many developmental psychologists to the need to ensure that research procedures allow children fully to express what they know, feel and can do.

- Paying attention to appropriate and distinctive features of the behaviour whilst ignoring irrelevant and distracting aspects of the model;
- Retaining the critical features of the performance in memory;
- Accurate duplication of the model's behaviour;
- Being motivated to reproduce the behaviour observed. The key motivating factors are seen by Bandura as reinforcements in the form of internal, external or vicarious rewards.

These processes, Bandura contended, are evident in all kinds of modelling, from the imitation of single acts to the reproduction of complex social behaviour.

Identification

Identification is a concept derived originally from psychoanalysis and introduced by Freud. It is said to be the process through which a child adopts the feelings, attitudes and behaviour of other people, initially the parents. It is similar to imitation in that it involves the child copying the behaviour of others, but where imitation involves copying very specific acts, identification is more concerned with copying general styles of behaviour and becoming like other important people in our lives. Most psychologists view identification as a fundamental process in the socialization of the child. For example, a very young child may identify with his father and act in ways he believes his father would act. Later, he may identify with whole social groups and act according to the group identity involved.

Evaluation of social learning theory

Social learning theory has highlighted imitation as a powerful mechanism of social learning for children. Observational learning is clearly implicated in the development of a whole range of behaviours, from the phenomenon of a small boy pretending to shave like his father to the development of moral behaviour and gender role identity (see Chapter 22).

Studies of learning by observation, with their emphasis on modelling in children of different ages and in a variety of situations, appear to provide a more coherent view of the role of learning in development than do traditional conditioning studies with their emphasis on animal learning.

However, social learning theorists have been criticized for their overuse of experimentation as a method of study. Development is a complex, long-term process. Critics draw attention to the limitations inherent in attempting to telescope the whole socialization process into a single, usually laboratory-based, situation.

Another objection to social learning theory arises from the notions of reward, reinforcement and punishment, which although central are not very clearly defined. Also, Scarr (1992) complains that Bandura's acknowledgment of the role of biological factors in development is very limited.

Finally, critics have drawn attention to the ethical issues involved in Bandura's early experiments in which children were forced to witness adult violence. Today, this might be viewed as abuse.

? SELF-ASSESSMENT QUESTIONS

1. Why was the scope of traditional conditioning theory extended to include social learning theory?
2. Briefly describe an early study which illustrates Bandura's approach to the study of observational learning in children.
3. Discuss the implications of a study which distinguished between the acquisition (or learning) of behaviour and the manifestation (or performance) of that behaviour.
4. What, according to Bandura, are the cognitive processes involved in observational learning?
5. What do you understand by 'identification'? What is its role in the socialization process?
6. What are the strengths and limitations of the social learning theory approach?

GLOSSARY

Vicarious Experiencing something as though it were happening to oneself.

Identification The process through which someone adopts the feelings, attitudes and behaviour of another person (or group) and becomes like them.

Chapter summary

- Learning can be defined as any relatively permanent change in behaviour (or behavioural potential) which is produced by experience. Early work on learning in animals was carried out by the behaviourists, who aimed to arrive at general 'laws of learning' which would apply also to humans.

- Habituation is thought to be the simplest form of learning necessary for survival. It involves learning to ignore a stimulus which is repeated continuously, so conserving energy for other, more necessary functions.

- Associative learning relates to the kind of learning that occurs when a stimulus becomes associated with another stimulus or with particular consequences. Classical and operant conditioning are examples of associative learning.

- Pavlov, in his work with dogs, showed that if an unconditioned stimulus (UCS) such as food was presented at the same time as a conditional stimulus (CS), such as a buzzer being sounded, the dog would produce a conditioned response (CR) (salivating) in the same way as it would to the food alone (an unconditioned response, UCR). This process has become known as classical conditioning. Pavlov also demonstrated that generalization (salivating to stimuli that are similar to the UCS) could occur and that the dog could be trained to discriminate between stimuli.

- The process of classical conditioning has been found to occur in many different animals and in humans. Of particular interest to psychologists is the role classical conditioning plays in the development of emotional responses, such as happiness or fear.

- Operant conditioning relates to voluntary, rather than reflex behaviour. It was based on early work carried out by Thorndike whose Law of Effect stated that behaviour which has pleasant consequences (reinforcement) will be strengthened.

- In Skinner's experiments, typically a rat or pigeon was conditioned to make a simple response, such as pressing a lever, to obtain reinforcement, such as food. Behaviour shaping relates to the reinforcement of responses which approximate to what is required until a complex response is produced. An animal may generalize its response in similar situations and can be conditioned to discriminate between two stimuli. Varying schedules of reinforcement demonstrated that learning could be maintained when the reinforcement is given only part of the time. Schedules included fixed interval, variable interval, fixed ratio, variable ratio.

- Reinforcement in operant conditioning can be either positive (something desirable) or negative (the removal of something unpleasant). Punishment refers to the delivery of an unpleasant stimulus, in order to suppress the response.

- Operant conditioning forms the basis of a technique known as behaviour modification, which is used to change undesirable behaviour in humans. Other examples of operant conditioning in humans include the early training of young children in such things as table manners or road safety. Reinforcement is often given in the form of praise or hugs.

- Ethologists have drawn attention to some of the biological limits of conditioning in animals. Animals bring their own species-specific behaviour to a learning situation, which often affects the way they respond. For example, pigeons pecking at a key to obtain food do so with the eyes almost closed and the bill open; a pigeon pecking to obtain water does so with the bill almost closed whilst the eyes remain open.

- In contrast to simple associative learning, more complex learning often involves some kind of cognitive activity. For example, Tolman studied the way rats learn to negotiate a maze and concluded that they were able to form a 'cognitive map' of the maze which enabled them to learn a specific route more easily. Köhler, studying learning in chimpanzees, suggested that they were able to solve a problem suddenly without any obvious trial and error learning, provided all the elements for the solution were within their field of view. He called this process 'insightful learning'. Harlow demonstrated that monkeys could learn principles such as 'odd one out' of three objects by forming a 'learning set'.

- Applications of conditioning theory include the use of behavioural therapies which are used with humans to remove inappropriate behaviour. Techniques based on operant conditioning are usually known as behaviour modification, and those using the principles of classical conditioning as behaviour therapy.

■ Programmed learning is a method of instruction based on the principles of operant conditioning. A linear programme involves subject matter being presented to a learner in small steps known as frames. The learner is required to make a response and for each correct response receives reinforcement in the form of immediate feedback on the accuracy of the response. A branching programme works on the same principles, but is more flexible and comprehensive. For example, it is possible for a learner who is experiencing difficulty to digress to a remedial programme before continuing with the original programme.

■ Programmed learning is particularly useful for learning a subject in which there is a hierarchy of facts, as in mathematics. It enables learners to work at their own pace and in flexible locations. Some computer-aided learning programmes and textbooks use the principles of programmed learning. However, critics have drawn attention to the solitary nature of programmed learning, which can lead to boredom, and the lack of opportunity for social support from peers.

■ Social learning theory aims to explain how children develop social behaviour through the process of observational learning (modelling). Children may learn new behaviour by imitating another person.

■ Identification is similar to imitation but is concerned with children copying general rules of behaviour and becoming like other people. This is an important process in the socialization of children.

■ Bandura's experiments showed that young children who had been exposed to a model behaving aggressively would imitate the model's behaviour and themselves behave aggressively. He made a distinction between acquisition (learning) of behaviour and whether the learned behaviour was actually performed. Characteristics of a model that may encourage children to imitate them include similarity, nurturance, having power and control over something desirable. Social learning theorists emphasize the importance of cognitive, or mediating, variables in observational learning, for example attention, memory and motivation.

■ Social learning theory, using humans rather than animals as participants in research, has highlighted imitation as a powerful mechanism of social learning for children. Critics have drawn attention to the limitations of laboratory experiments as a means of studying long-term socialization processes. Central concepts such as reward and punishment are not clearly defined and the role of biological factors receives only limited attention.

Further reading

Manning, A. and Dawkins, M.S. (1991). *Animal Behaviour.* Cambridge: Cambridge University Press. Chapter 6 gives an interesting view of learning processes from the perspective of the study of animal behaviour.

Schwartz, B. (1989). *Psychology of Learning and Behaviour,* 3rd edn. New York: Norton. This book offers a comprehensive review of conditioning processes and includes a discussion of ethology and cognition.

Walker, S. (1984). *Learning Theory and Behaviour Modification.* London: Methuen. Examines how the work of figures such as Thorndike, Watson, Pavlov and Skinner have influenced theories in educational and clinical practice, and formed the basis of behavioural therapies.

PART 2

Biological bases of behaviour

The aim of this part of the book is to examine the physiological mechanisms of the body such as the sensory system, the nervous system and the endocrine system and to see how these relate to mental processes such as those involved with perception, emotions, stress and biorhythms. It begins by discussing the reasons for studying physiology in conjunction with psychology, together with the methods of study used and the ethical basis for their usage. Information must first enter an organism before assimilation, learning or reactive behaviour can occur. This occurs through one of the five senses: seeing, hearing, touch, taste and smell; therefore the human sensory system is discussed, followed by a consideration of the nervous system and endocrine system. The rest of Part 2 looks at interactions between physiology, mental processes and behaviour in such areas as emotion, motivation, stress and different states of consciousness.

Contents

INTRODUCTION
Biopsychology   145
- Areas of study   145
- Why do we study biopsychology?   145
- Methods of study in physiological psychology   146

CHAPTER 7
Sensory systems   150
- The visual system   151
- Hearing   155
- Other sensory inputs   159

CHAPTER 8
The nervous system and behaviour   164
- Cell structures and the communications network   165
- The central nervous system   169
- Neurochemicals   174
- The autonomic nervous system   178
- The endocrine system   180

CHAPTER 9
Motivation and emotion   187
- Homeostatic motivation   187
- Nonhomeostatic motivation   193
- What is emotion?   195
- Theories and studies of emotion   198

CHAPTER 10
Consciousness and its altered states   203
- Levels of consciousness   204
- Body rhythms   208
- The rhythms of sleep   210
- Why do we sleep?   214

CHAPTER 11
Stress and anxiety   219
- Anxiety   219
- Stress and stressors   220
- Models of stress   225
- Individual differences involved in stress   228
- Coping with stress   231

Epilogue   236

Biopsychology

Referred to as **biopsychology, physiological psychology**, or occasionally psychobiology, this area of psychology explores the relationship between the mind and the body, and the interactive influence of one upon the other (see the discussion of the mind/body problem in the introduction to Part 1). As a simple example, if you have a cold (a physical virus infection), you may also feel that you have difficulty 'thinking straight', writing your psychology essays becomes exceedingly difficult! On the other hand, if you have a number of mental problems (exams looming, a quarrel with your mother or friend and your dog bit the postman), you may not undertake your work or physical activities with your usual gusto. This part aims to explore the mechanisms underlying these associations.

Areas of study

Two main areas of study include response mechanisms of the body, the internal environment of the body, and the interaction of these with the mind, the thought processes, memory and other higher functions.

Response mechanisms

The process of responding to incoming stimuli forms a chain of events along the following lines:

sense organs
↓
nerves (or nerve fibres)
↓
nervous systems
↓
muscles and glands
used in making the appropriate responses

These response systems are based in anatomy and physiology, the physical structure and functioning of the human body.

Internal environment

The internal environment includes a complex of substances within the individual's body:

- Food materials;
- Secretions of glands;
- Metabolic products;
- Blood and lymph constituents; and
- Chemicals manufactured in the body and the brain.

The internal environment of the body involves biochemistry (the chemical substances involved in the body's structure and functioning) and endocrinology (the glands and hormones that influence these functions).

Why do we study biopsychology?

Human beings have always been curious to know how things work, and this extends to the workings of the human body. From this biological basis, it is a short step to enquire into the 'workings' of the brain, which does

> **GLOSSARY**
>
> **Biopsychology (physiological psychology)** An area of psychology which studies relationships between physiological and psychological make-up and the interactive influence of one on the other.

not function on a 'rods and pulleys' basis, but electrically and chemically. The question then arises as to whether the brain is synonymous with the mind and whether the mind controls the body. This has been called the mind/body question and it has been discussed in the introduction to Part 1.

Methods of study in physiological psychology

In order to try to understand the relationship between the nervous system, the human body, thought processes and behaviour, psychologists have had to find methods of study that are not harmful to the individuals they are studying. So many of the processes involved are complex; they do not always seem to provide consistent results, because not all the variables can be controlled in a living human being. Currently, there are three main methods of study used in physiological psychology: the clinical method, the experimental method and scientific inference.

The clinical method

It would obviously be unethical to damage a person in order to examine the resultant loss of function, but people tend to suffer accidental damage or illness from time to time. By careful examination of these individuals, it is possible to understand what physical damage has produced loss of which function. For example, stroke victims have provided a great deal of information for clinicians. A stroke results where a haemorrhage or a blockage of blood vessels has occurred in the brain. The result can be a blood clot that presses on the brain, preventing normal functioning of that area, or a deficit of blood to an area, which again prevents normal functioning. Early information from stroke patients showed that the left side of the brain controls the right side of the body and vice versa, for when the brain damage was on the left, paralysis occurred on the right side of the body. In addition, right-sided paralysis was usually accompanied by loss of speech, which almost never occurred with left-sided paralysis. From this, we may deduce that speech is a function of the left side of the brain.

Accident victims from occupational, home or motor accidents often demonstrate loss of functioning that can be related to the degree or site of the head injury they have sustained. Before the compulsory introduc-

tion of motorbike helmets, thousands of people contributed to this type of information; motorbike accidents inevitably caused head injuries, which could then be related to loss of function such as speech defects, paralysis and personality changes. Fortunately, this source of information is now much reduced.

Physiological damage is nowadays assessed by X-rays, electroencephlalograms (EEGs) and computerized scans (see Box 2I.1), which are informative and provide cross-sectional pictures of brain areas.

X-rays

X-rays show damage to solid structures, such as the cranium or skull, the bony casing of the brain.

The black and white image produced will show abnormalities in the brain, such as increased or reduced blood flow. PET and MRI scans produce coloured images, which give more information (see Box 2I.1).

EEG

An electroencephalogram (EEG) is a recording of the electrical activity of the cortex, or surface, of the brain. Electrodes are placed at specific points on the outer surface of the patient's skull; these pick up electrical impulses from the brain's surface. Recordings from accident victims can be compared with normal tracings, and problems detected in this way (see Figure 2I.1). EEGs are also frequently used in the diagnosis of epilepsy and brain tumours.

Computerized scans

Computerized scanning (see descriptions in Box 2I.1) gives 'pictures' of the brain based on information of the

---

> **GLOSSARY**
>
> **Clinical method of study** in physiological psychology, examination of individuals who have suffered accidental damage to the brain in order to understand the effects on physical and psychological functioning.
>
> **Electroencephalogram (EEG)** A method of recording the electrical activity of the brain by placing electrodes on the scalp.
>
> **Computerized scanning** Techniques which use computers to obtain 'pictures' of the brain in order to study its functioning.

Box 21.1   Scanning techniques used in diagnosis

CAT (or CT) scan

In computerized axial tomography (CAT), a moving beam of X-rays is passed across the patient's brain, in horizontal cross-section. The moving X-ray detector on the other side measures the amount of radioactivity that gets through, thereby detecting any difference in tissue density. The computer takes up this information and constructs a two-dimensional black and white image of the cross-section. Cross-sectional images of all areas of the patient's brain can be produced. This is known as a noninvasive technique, since it does not require surgery or the introduction of foreign substances into the patient's body.

PET scan

In positron emission tomography (PET), a substance used by the brain, for example glucose or oxygen, is tagged with a short-lived radioactive isotope and injected into the bloodstream. The radioactive molecules emit positrons, which are detected by the scanner. The computer analyses millions of these detections and converts them into a moving picture of the functioning brain, in horizontal cross-sections. These can be

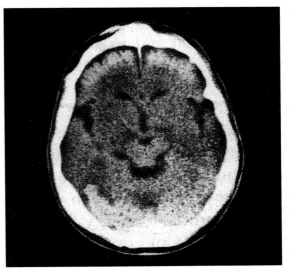

An image from a CT scan

projected onto a colour screen; the metabolic rates of specific areas (where the tagged substance is being used more quickly) is indicated by a variety of specified colours on the screen. Moving pictures can indicate not only the sites of injury, tumours and nonactivity, but also the distribution in the brain of psychoactive drugs, and may indicate possible abnormal physiological processes in the brain. This is an invasive technique, because it involves introducing substances into the body.

MRI scan (sometimes called NMR scan)

Magnetic resonance imaging (or nuclear magnetic resonance imaging) is superior to CAT scans because it produces higher quality pictures and therefore more information, yet does not require the invasive techniques of the PET scan. In MRI, the patient is placed inside a large circular magnet that causes the hydrogen atoms in the body to move. When the magnet is turned off, these revert to their original positions, producing an electromagnetic signal that is translated by the computer into pictures of brain tissue.

CT scanner

Relaxed

(a)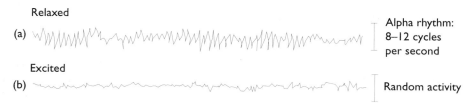

Alpha rhythm:
8–12 cycles
per second

Excited

(b)

Random activity

Figure 21.1 Electroencephalogram (EEG) recordings
These are obtained by placing electrodes on the scalp, which then record the electrical activity of the cortex on a trace. Above is (a) a typical alpha rhythm, which is the wakeful, resting state. This is 'blocked' by either (b) arousal, a higher level of cortical activity, or sleep patterns (which are illustrated in Figure 10.3).

metabolic functioning of certain areas (metabolic means the way in which the brain and the body use up fuel to produce energy for action).

Psychological tests

Loss of cognitive functioning is assessed by psychological tests, such as IQ tests, naming and memory tasks and problem solving, which can be repeated from time to time in order to measure changes. The difficulty here is that there is no baseline measure of how well the individual functioned in any particular way before the accident. Comparisons can only be made to norms established on a healthy population.

He's never met her, but he says she has the most beautiful brain scan and EEGs he's ever seen.

The experimental approach

The experimental approach to studying the nervous system is subject to keen ethical scrutiny (see Box 21.2). There are no problems with establishing test norms, for use as comparison data, as mentioned previously, but at the same time no risks of permanently damaging people can be taken; even seemingly simple experiments can prove disastrous. For example, in the 1960s some experiments were carried out to establish the location of the speech areas in the brain. Sodium amytal was introduced into the carotid artery, with the intention of temporarily inactivating the speech centre. Unfortunately, some participants did not recover their speech as expected. Nowadays, more stringent controls would ensure that any potentially dangerous experiment would be modified.

Scans or EEGs can be performed with intact, normal people, where input stimuli can be varied and the resultant changes in the responses on the traces or the screen can be noted. These can be used for comparison with clinical patients.

Scientific inference

While it would not be scientifically acceptable to generalize from a clinical or experimental sample of one individual to the whole population, it is possible to make inferences from a number of patients suffering similar damage and functional deficits, or from batches of experimental data providing similar findings. Information that points the way to a hypothesis can be substantiated by further clinical trials or controlled experiments, and sound conclusions drawn. Scientific inference is based on known occurrences but looks forward to an overall picture

Box 21.2   Ethics in physiological psychology

The British Psychological Society has a strict code of ethics, which must be applied in all areas of psychology: investigations, experimentation and treatment (see Chapter 5). Some areas of physiological psychology would also be subject to General Medical Council guidelines. One important area covered is risk.

The most obvious form of risk is that a participant might experience some form of distress, such as fear, anxiety, stress, guilt or loss of self-esteem. Psychologists have an ethical obligation to avoid causing these, even if it means abandoning a research project. Participants must not be asked to run physical risks, by either performing dangerous tasks or ingesting potentially harmful sub-stances. Some of the studies and experiments that were carried out in the past would not now be allowed by an ethics committee.

Research with animals

This is a highly emotive issue and one which is argued strongly on both sides by those for and those against the use of animals in research. Drugs and experimental surgery are always piloted on animals first. Ethical objections include the use of animals as experimental subjects at all, although in fact the animal species may also benefit from the findings.

Animal experiments are now subject to a stringent code of ethics and must avoid any unecessary pain and suffering to the animal. Research is governed by the Animals (Scientific Procedures) Act, 1986, which protects living vertebrates.

For a more complete discussion of ethical issues in relation to both humans and animals, please see Chapter 5.

CHAPTER 7

Sensory systems

The visual system 151
- The pupil 151
- The retina 152
- Colour vision 153
- Influences on perception at eye level 154
- Visual pathways and perception 154

Hearing 155
- Properties of sound 155

- The anatomy of the ear 156
- Auditory pathways in the brain 157
- Analysis and perception of sound 158

Other sensory inputs 159
- Olfaction (smell) 159
- Taste 160
- Somatosenses 160

Objectives

By the end of this chapter you should be able to:

- Understand the basis of how humans receive input through the five senses;

- Be familiar with the human visual system, from eye to brain;

- Understand the relationship between the visual system and perception;

- Have a working knowledge of the auditory system;

- Understand basic concepts relating to smell, taste, touch and kinaesthetic feedback.

Perception is the process whereby the brain makes sense of the information received from the senses. Gregory (1966) suggests: 'Perception is not simply determined by stimulus patterns; rather it is a dynamic searching for the best interpretation of the available data'. (See Chapter 13 for a more complete discussion of the process of perception.)

Sensation, therefore, is the primary process of data collection from the environment. Perception is the secondary process of interpreting these data; the brain may add to the sensory input from memory or try to rationalize what it believes it should be seeing. Where information is ambiguous, the brain comes to the best solution it can (see Figure 13.17 on p. 276 for an example of an ambiguous figure).

The physiological basis of sensation is specific to each of the senses, or modalities. Each sense has receptors designed for its own specific job. If your eyes are injured and can no longer be used for seeing, your hearing may become more acute to compensate, but you cannot use your ears for 'seeing' because the mechanisms of action are totally different. The phenomenon

---

GLOSSARY

Perception The psychological process whereby the brain makes sense of information coming through the senses.

Sensation The stimulation of a sense organ such as the eye or the ear which is necessary for perception to occur.

Box 7.1 Blindsight

Damage to one side of the visual cortex produces a loss of vision in the visual field on the opposite side, or total loss of vision if damage involves all of the visual cortex. Weiskrantz (1987) and Weiskrantz et al. (1974) found that if an object is placed in a patient's blind field and the person is asked to reach for it, he or she will be able to do so accurately. Patients even open their hand wider when a larger object is presented. Patients are surprised when their hand contacts the object.

This phenomenon shows that visual information can control resultant movements, without conscious awareness of visual sensation. The physiological mechanisms that make this possible are not wholly understood, but an essential link seems to be intact connections between two adjacent subcortical areas, the superior colliculi and the lateral geniculate bodies (the latter is described later in this chapter).

---

known as blindsight (see Box 7.1) appears to be related to consciousness rather than vision.

Humans are highly visually oriented beings; at least 80 per cent of our input comes through our visual system, and the next largest percentage through our auditory system, with the other three modalities sharing the remaining few per cent. The priorities in this chapter are therefore similar.

The visual system

The eye is the first-line recipient of incoming visual stimuli; therefore, it is necessary to know a little about its structure and functioning (Figure 7.1).

Some visual system! Only two eyes, and those both facing the _SAME WAY_ !

Light rays from objects in the visual field enter the eye through the lens, which changes shape in order to focus these light rays onto the **retina**, at the back of the eye, to provide a sharp image. If we say that people are short-sighted or long-sighted, what we usually mean is that the lens cannot accommodate enough (shorten or stretch) to provide a clear image. This is why sight usually gets worse as people get older: the lens and its controlling muscles are not working as well as they did when they were younger.

The pupil

The pupil of the eye (effectively, the opening in the coloured iris) controls the amount of light entering the eye; in bright sunlight it contracts, and in dim lighting it

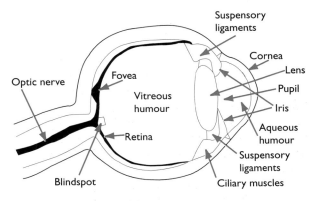

Figure 7.1 Diagram of the eye

GLOSSARY

Retina A layer of light-sensitive cells at the back of the eye which receives light waves and converts them to electrical pulses for transmission to the brain.

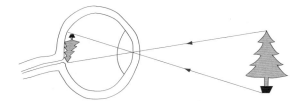

Figure 7.2 Visual stimulus and retinal image

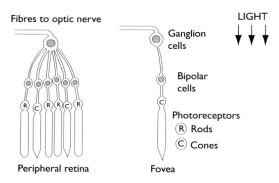

Figure 7.3 Diagram of the retina

dilates, or opens, to let in the maximum light possible. There are other reasons for pupils dilating: if we are very interested in something, or if we are afraid or disturbed, or under the influence of certain drugs, our pupils will dilate even in bright light. The pupils are not under conscious control but are controlled by the autonomic nervous system, which is described in Chapter 8.

The retina is the inner surface at the back of the eyeball. The image on the retina is upside down (see Figure 7.2) due to the crossover of light rays through the lens, as with a camera, focusing light onto a film.

You do not perceive objects as being upside down because the brain 'turns' them the right way again; this is one of the differences between seeing and perceiving. Seeing is the physical process involved in vision, whereas perceiving is what the brain does with the incoming visual information. This is discussed more fully in Chapter 13.

The retina

The retina consists of a layer of light-sensitive cells called **photoreceptors**. There are two main types of these: rods and cones. **Rods** function best in dim light, are sensitive to movement but are not sensitive to colour; there are approximately 120 million rods in each human retina. Although there are fewer cones (about six million), they provide most of our visual information. **Cones** are colour sensitive, function mainly in bright light and are concentrated mainly in the centre of the retina, to provide high **visual acuity**. This is the ability to see details sharply; the visual acuity of a hawk, for example, is far greater than that of a human. The hawk can spot a mouse at 500 metres, whereas a human cannot; each is specialized to what is important to it. The area of highest visual acuity on the retina is called the fovea, which consists almost entirely of cones. Figure 7.3 shows the difference between connections in the periphery, where a number of photoreceptors share one nerve fibre, and the fovea, where one cone transmits to one nerve fibre.

The retina appears to have been put on 'inside out'. The nerve fibres (or **axons**) leaving the rods and cones transmit visual information to the brain, actually travelling across the surface of the retina. These link into **bipolar cells** and **ganglion cells** (see Figure 7.3), which are also on the surface of the retina, in addition to the blood vessels that serve the area. However, this does not seem to interfere with the quality of information picked up and transmitted by the retina. The only place where information is not registered is the blindspot. This is where the nerve fibres from the photoreceptors collect together and form the commencement of the optic nerve. We are not usually aware of a 'gap' in our vision caused by the blindspot, for two reasons:

■ the brain compensates and fills the gap for us, and
■ we have two eyes; it is unlikely that the same 'bit' of visual input would hit the blindspot of both eyes.

Exercise 7.1

Find your blindspot.
Copy this square and circle onto a blank sheet, keeping them 75 mm apart.

■   ●

Cover one eye. Focus on the square. Move the sheet slowly towards or away from you, still focusing on the square. Suddenly the circle will 'disappear'.

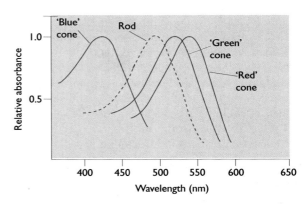

Figure 7.4 Rods, cones and wavelengths of light in nanometres ($1\,\text{nm} = 1 \times 10^{-9}$ metres)

Functions of the retinal cells

Rods Rods are situated mainly at the periphery of the human retina. As they are sensitive to movement, this assists you to see a potential predator creeping up from the side. How often have you said, 'I saw something move out of the corner of my eye'? You are aware of the movement before you have identified what the moving object is.

Another function the rods perform is to enable you to see in dim light. When you go into a dark room, away from bright light, you initially feel that you cannot see a thing! After a few seconds, vague shapes are discernible, and after approximately seven seconds, you are coping reasonably well. This is called **dark adaptation** and represents the length of time it takes for the rods to take over vision from the cones. Colours are not recognized by the rods, hence the saying 'all cats are grey in the dark'!

Cones As mentioned earlier, cones are responsible for vision in bright light and provide for high visual acuity. Both rods and cones have nerve fibres that connect into a reduction system of bipolar cells and then to ganglion cells. As Figure 7.3 above shows, many receptors ultimately share one axon, except in the fovea, where there is a one-to-one relationship between photoreceptor cells and axons. Messages from this area obviously take priority.

Colour vision

Cones are also thought to be responsible for colour vision. There are a number of different theories of how we see in colour.

Trichromatic theory

First proposed in the nineteenth century by von Helmholtz (1885), **trichromatic theory** suggests that there are three types of cone, each being sensitive to light of a particular wavelength: red, green or blue. Figure 7.4 shows the wavelengths that transmit these colours. Where these 'overlap', we see 'mixed' colours: yellow, orange, and so on. Rods transmit their information as black/white/shades of grey, as they function in dim lighting. The perception of colour is due to the integration of information by the brain, from information provided by these receptors. This theory is supported by findings from studies of colour blindness, in which deficits in one or more colour receptors show a lack of perception of the related colours. This cannot be the whole story, of course, as the theory does not satisfactorily explain how we see bronze, for example. This may well be due to an interaction of innate colour-recognition processes and learned concepts, such as 'shiny' or 'metallic'.

Opponent process theory

Colour perception is very much a subjective experience. Hering (1878) observed that people never

---

GLOSSARY

Dark adaptation The process whereby the eyes adjust from bright to dim lighting.

Trichromatic theory In relation to the visual system, the proposal by Helmholtz (1885) that there are three types of cone, each being sensitive to light of a particular wavelength, red, green or blue.

reported seeing 'yellowish-blue' or 'reddish-green'. This led him to propose that red–green and yellow–blue perceptions were separate and opponent processes. This has been supported by later physiological findings that demonstrate colour-opponent cells in the retina (Svaetichin, 1956) and in the lateral geniculate bodies (DeValois and Jacobs, 1984; DeValois and DeValois, 1988). A third factor, the perception of luminance, is also necessary for a complete description of colour coding. This, it has been suggested, can be regarded as the proportion of red, green and blue recognized in the perception of any one colour.

These two theories, trichromatic theory and **opponent process theory**, are not necessarily irreconcilable. Hurvich (1981) suggests a two-stage colour theory that combines both theories. The three types of colour receptor of trichromatic theory may stimulate the appropriate colour-opponent cells for their wavelength, while inhibiting the inappropriate colour-opponent cells. The output from these would determine the resultant colour perceived.

Influences on perception at eye level

At the retina

When light rays strike the retina, a chemical change occurs in the photoreceptors. Human photoreceptors consist of rods and cones. Rods contain a visual pigment, rhodopsin. There are three types of cone, each containing a different visual pigment, which is sensitive to different wavelengths of light. These photopigments liberate electrical energy that produces the electrical potential, or impulse, which is transmitted along an axon. From now onwards, all visual information is transmitted electrochemically; there are no 'pictures' in the brain.

It is possible that some form of visual selection takes place in the retina, selecting information that is important or filtering out information that is less important. Hartline (1938) demonstrated that this happens with frogs; there are specific cells in the frog retina (crucial to survival) that act as 'bug detectors', and others which fire when the creature's horizon darkens, warning of the possible approach of a predator. Human equivalents of these have not been found because of the problems of experimenting with human eyes; however, we have recognized that rods respond to movement and cones differentially to colours.

Monocular influences

In order to focus on objects, the lens changes shape, pulled by the **ciliary muscles**. Information from **kinaesthetic receptors** in these muscles is fed back into the brain, giving primary spatial information about the object (where it is located in space) and information about the **accommodation** of the eye: that is to say, the amount it has had to change in order to focus on the object it is looking at.

Binocular influences

We normally use both eyes for focusing on objects, and the eyes are turned or converged to focus on the object. Feedback from kinaesthetic receptors in these muscles is integrated with the information on accommodation to confirm the spatial arrangement of objects in the visual field.

Visual pathways and perception

From the retina, visual information is electrically coded and passed along individual axons to bipolar cells (see Figure 7.3 above), then on to ganglion cells, where information may be combined (except for cells in the fovea, as we have already mentioned, where each has one-to-one cell-to-axon representation). Axons then ascend towards the brain via the optic nerve.

Information from each eye crosses over at the **optic chiasma**, so that there is an overlap of information from each eye transmitted onwards to the brain (see Figure 7.5). Both optic tracts then continue to the lateral geniculate bodies, situated in the thalamus, one of the subcortical structures of the brain. Each optic tract then

---

GLOSSARY

Opponent process theory The proposal that perception of red–green stimuli is a separate and opposing process to the perception of yellow–blue stimuli.

Ciliary muscles Muscles in the eye which operate to change the shape of the lens.

Kinaesthetic receptors Receptors which provide information about our bodily movements. They are located in the muscles and in the inner ear.

Accommodation In relation to the visual system, the alteration that occurs in the shape of the lens of the eye in order to provide sharp focus on the retina.

Optic chiasma The point at which the optic nerve from each eye meets.

relays information onwards to the visual cortex, the part of the brain that recognizes and deals with visual information. It also sends information to other areas of the brain that incorporate visual information into their main activities.

The visual cortex is situated at the back of the brain. As you can imagine, dealing with such complex and voluminous information as visual input, scientists are still unravelling many of its complexities. We shall mention only a few of their findings to date.

■ Hubel and Wiesel (1979) and Hubel (1977) discovered that neurons (brain cells) in the visual cortex responded selectively to specific features of the visual world. They initially identified two kinds of cells: simple cells, which responded to only one stimulus, and complex cells, which would respond to a specific range of stimuli and movement of those stimuli. Other neurons were not sensitive to features such as the slope of lines, but were sensitive to, for example, colour (Livingstone and Hubel, 1987).

■ Blakemore and Cooper (1977) found that kittens who had been deprived of specific visual stimuli from birth were later unable to respond to those stimuli; their neurons had either atrophied or possibly been commandeered for other purposes by the brain.

These experiments, and many others, demonstrate that even before birth brain cells are already specialized for a specific purpose, not only as 'visual' cells but also for a particular role within that system.

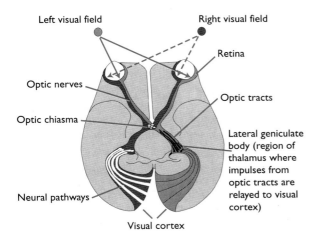

Figure 7.5 Visual pathways in the brain

? SELF-ASSESSMENT QUESTIONS

1. Describe how rods, cones and axons transmit visual information.
2. How do we see colour? (Compare opponent process and trichromatic theories.)
3. What are the effects on visual perception of:
   monocular influences?
   binocular influences?
4. Draw a diagram of the visual pathways from the eye to the visual cortex.
5. What occurs at the optic chiasma? What is the result of this?
6. How is visual information represented in the cortex? (A description and discussion of the work of Hubel and Wiesel, Livingstone and Hubel, and Blakemore and Cooper is relevant here.)

Hearing

For most people, hearing is the second most important sense, after vision. Sounds are transmitted by sound waves; molecules of air are displaced and re-form, temporarily changing air pressure. This is recognized by the receptors in the ear, starting with the eardrum; these receptors are mechanoreceptors, responding to pressure, a process different from that of the photoreceptors of the visual system.

The human auditory system is stimulated by **sound waves** of between approximately 30 and 20 000 cycles (or vibrations) per second. This sounds impressive but is nowhere near the range of a dog, and far from the upper limits of a bat's auditory perception.

Four aspects of the auditory system will be considered: the properties of sound, the anatomy of the ear, the auditory pathways in the brain and the perception of sound.

Properties of sound

Three properties of sound are loudness, pitch and timbre (see Figure 7.6).

GLOSSARY

Sound waves Molecules of air which temporarily change air pressure in the ear and which are recognized by the auditory system as sound.

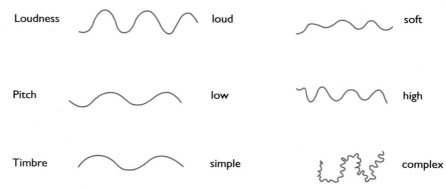

Figure 7.6 The perceptual properties of sound

Sound levels at rock concerts average between 110 and 120 dB. In front of modern guitar amplifiers like these levels can reach 140 dB – the same as a jet plane. This can cause pain, and may permanently damage the listeners' ears

Loudness

More vigorous vibrations produce greater air displacement and pressure, and this is recognized by the auditory system as **loudness**. Because the receptors within the ear (which we will look at in a moment) have to move to respond to loudness, a very high volume causes the perception of physical pain. Sustained loudness can damage the receptors.

Pitch

Pitch has already been mentioned in the introduction. It is the frequency of vibration of the sound waves. It is measured in cycles per second or hertz, after the nineteenth-century scientist who discovered this property of sound.

Timbre

Timbre is the nature of a sound, whether it is the sound of a car engine or a person talking. Sounds that occur naturally are complex, containing more than one frequency of vibration; the resultant mixture determines the sound's timbre.

The anatomy of the ear

Figure 7.7 gives a diagrammatic representation of the outer, middle and inner ear. Sound is channelled by the

> **GLOSSARY**
>
> **Loudness** The amplitude of sound waves.
>
> **Pitch** The frequency of sound waves.
>
> **Timbre** The nature of sound: that is, the degree of mixing of pure sound frequencies.

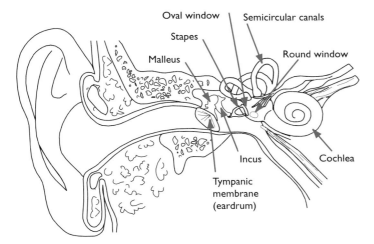

Oval window | Semicircular canals
Stapes
Malleus | Round window
Incus | Cochlea
Tympanic membrane (eardrum)

Figure 7.7 The outer, middle and inner ear (not to scale)

pinna (outer ear) into the external auditory canal, to the eardrum (**tympanic membrane**).

The tympanic membrane marks the commencement of the middle ear. It vibrates with the sound waves, activating the small bones (ossicles) behind it. The bone nearest the tympanic membrane is called the malleus or hammer; this strikes the next bone, appropriately called the anvil or **incus**. This transmits the vibrations to the third bone, the stirrup or **stapes**, so called because it is stirrup-shaped and also associates with the names of the other bones. The flat side of the stapes connects with a membrane called the oval window.

The oval window marks the commencement of the inner ear and covers the aperture in the bone that encases the cochlea. This is a complex structure, which resembles a snail shell in appearance (hence its name, from the Greek word for snail). The cochlea is filled with fluid, which can be compressed to allow movement caused by another membrane, called the round window.

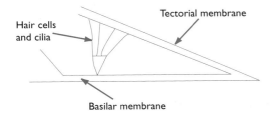

Hair cells and cilia
Tectorial membrane
Basilar membrane

Figure 7.8 Structures in the organ of Corti

Inside the cochlea is a receptor called the organ of Corti, which consists primarily of three important parts. The basilar membrane, which vibrates with the sound waves, in turn vibrates the hair cells that are attached to it. The other ends of the hair cells are attached to a rigid, overhead membrane, the tectorial membrane (see Figure 7.8). Because this membrane does not move freely, the hair cells and the cilia (fine hairs on them) are bent; this produces electrical impulses that are passed along the nerve fibres leaving the cochlea (cochlear nerve), to the auditory nerve.

Auditory pathways in the brain

Information about auditory stimuli leaving the cochlea, via the cochlear nerve, travels first to the cochlear nucleus in the medulla, a subcortical structure of the brain. From here, it passes to the midbrain, then on to the medial geniculate nucleus in the thalamus, another subcortical structure. By now, information from each ear is being sent to both sides of the brain; this helps with the **localization of sound** (see below). Information is now passed to the primary auditory cortex for conscious recognition of the sound. Information from each ear is passed to both sides of the cortex. Figure 7.9 shows a diagrammatic representation of the route taken by auditory information from the right ear. As can be seen, it arrives not only at the ipsilateral (same side) cortex, but also at the contralateral one (opposite side). Information would be

---

GLOSSARY

Pinna External part of the ear.

Tympanic membrane Known as the ear drum, a structure in the ear which vibrates with sound waves and transmits them to ossicles behind it.

Malleus A bony structure (ossicle) in the ear which strikes the incus as the tympanic membrane vibrates.

Incus A bony structure (ossicle) in the ear which is struck by the malleus as the tympanic membrane vibrates.

Stapes A bony structure (ossicle) in the ear which transmits vibrations from the incus to the oval window.

Cochlea A snail-shaped structure within the ear that contains auditory sense receptors.

Localization of sound The ability of the auditory system to detect the location of particular sounds.

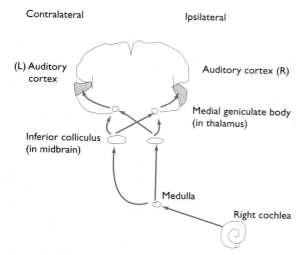

Contralateral   Ipsilateral

(L) Auditory cortex

Auditory cortex (R)

Medial geniculate body (in thalamus)

Inferior colliculus (in midbrain)

Medulla

Right cochlea

Figure 7.9 Central pathways of the auditory system (right ear only shown here)

transmitted from both ears, and any discrepancy between the arrival times at the cortex and subcortical areas contributes information on where the sound is coming from.

Analysis and perception of sound

Detection and perception of pitch

The basilar membrane has differing physical properties along its length and interacts differentially with its surrounding fluids, with the result that high frequencies are mediated nearest the oval window, ranging to low frequencies at the farther end (von Bekesy, 1960). Perception of pitch is liable to damage through physical illness or deterioration due to age; the highest and lowest registers are lost first. The least damage occurs in the middle registers, which is why people with a degree of deafness can hear some sounds and not others; sound perception is not wholly dependent upon loudness.

Detection and perception of loudness

Information regarding the loudness of a stimulus is thought to be dependent on the amount of movement of the hair cells of the cochlea. More intense vibrations produce a more intense force on the cilia, which is encoded by the cochlear nerve as an increased rate of firing. Investigators believe that the loudness of low-frequency sounds is encoded by the number of axons that are active at that time.

Studies using modern equipment have demonstrated that the softest sound that can be detected by the hair cells is that which will move the tip by between 1 and 100 picometres (trillionths of a metre). No wonder we say we can hear a pin drop! This sensitive mechanism can be damaged by loud noise, especially if it is constant, which is why Health and Safety experts insist on ear protectors for workers in noisy industries. Loudness is measured in decibels (dB); above 85 dB, prolonged exposure leads to nerve deafness. It is possible to become habituated to loud noise, but that does not prevent the physical damage, only the psychological damage. Figure 7.10 outlines some commonly encountered noise levels.

Detection and perception of timbre

Detection of timbre, or complex sounds, is dependent on the auditory system's ability to 'undo' sounds. This detection is due to the ability of the system to recognize which areas of the basilar membrane are being stimulated at any given time.

When you consider that we can listen to an orchestra playing and recognize the independent sounds of several different instruments, the complexity of the analysis being carried out is amazing. Of course, a degree of learning and training is inherent here, but the potential to perform the task is already present.

Localization of sound

Having two ears, one on each side of the head, is our first aid to locating the source of a sound (binaural localization). There are two main cues for locating sounds: phase differences and intensity differences.

Phase differences Low-pitched sounds may be detected by means of phase differences. Sound waves are likely to arrive at each ear at a slightly different phase of their cycles. These minute differences are detected by the basilar membrane and recognized in the auditory neurons in the medulla.

Differences in high-frequency sounds would be difficult to detect by this method because of the small amplitude of high-frequency waves.

Intensity differences This cue is useful for detecting the source of high-frequency sounds. High-

Figure 7.10 Some commonly encountered noise levels

dBa	Noise
140	
130	Pain threshold
120	Pneumatic drill/loud car horn
110	
100	
90	Inside subway train
80	(Permanent damage from long-term noise)
70	Average street-corner traffic
60	Conversational speech
	Typical office noise levels
50	
40	Living room
30	Library
20	Bedroom at night
10	Broadcasting studio
1	Threshold of hearing

frequency sound waves are absorbed by the head, producing sonic shadowing of any sound that arrives slightly 'off centre' of the two ears. This is why, if a sound is dead centre, it is difficult to say whether it is in front of or behind the head. Information from the organs of Corti, as to which is receiving stimulation first, is recognized in an adjacent area of the medulla.

SELF-ASSESSMENT QUESTIONS

1. Draw a rough diagram of the middle and inner ear, labelling structures important for the perception of sound.
2. How do humans detect (a) loudness, (b) pitch, and (c) timbre?
3. Describe two ways in which we can localize sound.

Other sensory inputs

In classical terms, there remain only three more senses to describe: **olfaction** (smell), taste and touch. However, other important sensory perceptions need to be mentioned, such as the perception of pain, and kinaesthesia, in order to give a more rounded picture of human perceptions.

Olfaction (smell)

The sense of smell is a chemical sense, recognizing chemical molecules of substances that are passing through the olfactory system, which involves areas of the nose and the brain. In vertebrates other than humans, a much larger area of the brain is involved in olfaction, because smell is a much more important cue for many species other than for humans.

Olfactory receptors (see Figure 7.11) are contained within two small areas, each about 2.5 cm square, at the top of the nasal cavity. A sniff draws air upwards to pass these sensitive areas. Aromatic molecules that have dissolved in the air are drawn across the mucous membranes, which contain the receptors, and their chemical components are detected here.

The neurons of the olfactory receptors send information to the olfactory bulbs at the base of the frontal lobes of the brain. From here, the olfactory tracts (nerve pathways) project directly to the primary

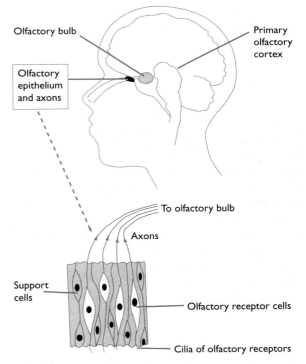

Figure 7.11 The olfactory system

GLOSSARY

Olfaction The sense of smell.

olfactory cortex, as well as sending information to the hypothalamus, which probably integrates information about whether food should be accepted or rejected on the basis of its odour.

Tanabe et al. (1974) found that neurons in the olfactory cortex respond selectively to different odours, but as yet scientists have not discovered how we recognize different types of smell. Smell seems to be a highly evocative sense; it can be strongly linked with memories, yet we seem to lack the words to describe it. For example, we would all instantly recognize the smell of freshly baked bread, but can you describe it? It would seem that olfaction is a sense we use for recognition and discrimination, rather than for discussion. The smell of food also helps us decide whether or not it is palatable before we taste it.

Taste

This sense helps us decide which things we eat and which we spit out! Taste, or gustation, is another chemical sense. Molecules of the substance tasted are dissolved in the saliva and stimulate the taste

Particular smells can conjure up vivid memories

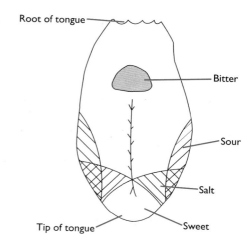

Figure 7.12 Regions of the tongue involved in taste

receptors. These are situated mainly on the tongue; different regions of the tongue contain different types of receptor, for sweetness, saltiness, bitterness and sourness (see Figure 7.12). Generally speaking, sweetness and saltiness are attractive flavours, while bitterness and sourness may indicate foods that have 'gone off' and are therefore repugnant.

Taste receptors are quickly worn out; they have an approximate life of ten days before they are replaced. The new cells take over the axonal connections of the degenerated cells. These axons pass via the cranial nerves to the subcortical regions of the medulla and the thalamus. From here information is sent to the primary gustatory cortex. Taste is the only sense that projects solely ipsilaterally (that is, from the left of the tongue to the left side of the brain, and from the right side of the tongue to the right of the brain). Presumably, as we have only one mouth and one tongue, there is no need for cross-referencing as a failsafe system.

Not only are tastes discriminated at the receptors in the tongue, but responses are also differentiated by different neurons in the cortex (Yamamoto et al., 1981). Complex tastes, involving more than one of the four primary tastes, are analysed at cortical level. The principle common to all the senses holds true here, in that sensation is processed at sensory receptor level, while perception is analysed within the brain.

Somatosenses

These include (a) **cutaneous senses**, such as touch, temperature and pain responses, and (b) **kinaesthesia**, which provides information about body positions and movement.

Cutaneous senses

There are a number of different types of receptor contained in the skin, each with a different job of detection. Skin consists of the epidermis (outer layer), dermis (a much thicker inner layer) and subcutaneous tissue, a deeper layer containing the main nerves, veins and arteries. Cutaneous receptors occur mainly within the dermis. On our bodies, we have glabrous skin (hairless), such as on our palms and fingers, and hairy skin, as on the rest of the body – although some people are demonstrably more hairy than others.

Pacinian corpuscles These are the largest sensory end-organs in the body. They are found in the dermis of glabrous skin, the external genitalia, the mammary glands and various internal organs. Each consists of up to 70 layers, wrapped around a single nerve fibre. The corpuscle is filled with viscous fluid. It is sensitive to vibration, and each movement produces a response in the corpuscle's axon.

Ruffini corpuscles These are found mainly in hairy skin. Smaller than Pacinian corpuscles, they respond to fluttering movements or low-frequency vibration.

Meissner's corpuscles These are found in papillae, small projections of dermis that have risen upward into the epidermis. These respond to mechanical stimuli, such as touch or pressure.

Merkel's discs Usually found adjacent to sweat ducts and close to Meissner's corpuscles, they also respond to mechanical stimuli.

Krause end-bulbs These are found in mucocutaneous zones, the junctions between mucous membranes and dry skin, for example the eyelids, edges of lips, penis and clitoris. They consist of loops of axons, forming bulbs, each bulb containing between two and six axons. They respond to mechanical stimuli.

Free nerve endings Free nerve endings are the simplest type of sensory receptor; they are literally a branching nerve that terminates in the dermis and deeper layers of the epidermis. Some respond to mechanical stimuli, some to warmth or cooling, and some to noxious (unpleasant) stimuli; some respond to two or three of these and are called polymodal.

Threshold of sensation

Threshold of sensation varies with the sensitivity of bodily areas. In the bodily areas of high sensitivity, such as the fingers, a single impulse elicited by a stimulus (for example, a momentary touch with the tip of a pencil) is also recognized consciously by the individual. In less sensitive areas, several impulses need to occur before conscious recognition is made. This is why, if a fly alights on the tip of your finger, you are instantly aware of it, but if it alights on your arm or shoulder, you may not be aware until it moves over your skin. (A further discussion of sensory thresholds is contained in Part 3, Chapter 12.)

Spatial resolution

Whether a stimulus is coming from a single point or two points on the body is recognized differentially by different body areas, owing to the density of receptors in the skin of that area. Demonstrate this to yourself by the spatial resolution exercise (see Exercise 7.2).

Exercise 7.2

Cutaneous sensations. Place the fingers of one hand into icy cold water and the other hand into hot water (but not hot enough to burn yourself, this is not a pain experiment!). After 30 seconds put both hands in tepid water. Note the different sensation experienced by both hands.

Spatial resolution. If you take a pair of dividers and lightly touch a fingertip, two points can be felt at a distance of only 2 mm apart, whereas on the arm you may find a distance of up to 30 mm is necessary. Of

GLOSSARY

Cutaneous senses Receptors located mainly in the skin which give information about touch, temperature and pain.

Kinaesthesia The process which describes the feedback from sensations in the muscles and joints which provides information about body positions and movement.

Threshold of sensation The minimum stimulation of a sense organ that can be detected by the individual.

course, this experiment works best if you can find a friend to act as blindfolded participant while you carry out these investigations!

Pain

Considering the trouble it gives us, we still know comparatively little about pain. Free nerve endings appear to respond to painful stimuli, but this is not the only source of information. Intense mechanical stimulation causes a strong reaction in other appropriate receptors, which may be recognized as pain. In addition, most painful stimuli cause tissue damage, which promotes a chemical reaction in the surrounding area, thereby sending chemical messages through the body (Besson et al., 1982). Pain is also the result of tissue damage, for example in burns. Damaged cells release prostaglandin, which sensitizes free nerve endings to histamine, another chemical released by damaged cells. (Aspirin blocks the synthesis of prostaglandin, thereby reducing pain.) An investigation into the numerous theories of pain is outside the scope of this book.

Kinaesthesia

Even with your eyes closed, or in the dark, you know what position your limbs are in. You can put your finger on the end of your nose with your eyes shut. These feats are due to receptors (primarily Pacinian corpuscles and free nerve endings) in the muscles and where muscles and tendons join, which send information to the brain on muscle stretch, pressure and blood supply. Pacinian corpuscles and free nerve endings are also found in the outer layers of many internal organs. These send information on organic sensations such as pain, pressure and stretch. Kinaesthetic receptors in the muscles of the eye send back information on eye movements and lens accommodation. This helps to determine the movement and location of objects in the visual field.

Ascending pathways and the somatosensory cortex

Axons from somatosensory receptors link into the nerves that ascend the spinal column to subcortical areas of the brain, and thence to the somatosensory cortex. This is an area on each side of the cortex that gives conscious recognition to the information from all the sensory receptors, from all parts of the body.

In the same way that density of receptors in the skin is not equally distributed, there is also differential representation in the cortex for different areas of the body. If the somatosensory cortex is represented as a pie-chart, the head and face get almost half of the pie! The hands then take a quarter, and the remainder of the body shares the other quarter.

? SELF-ASSESSMENT QUESTIONS

1. How do we become conscious of smells?
2. What are the processes that enable us to recognize taste?
3. Describe some sensory receptors located in the skin, and their specific purpose.

Chapter summary

▓ It is important to distinguish between sensation – a physiological process, which involves the stimulation of a sense organ – and perception – the psychological process whereby the brain interprets the sensations received.

▓ Each of the senses has specific receptors, which are responsive to a different kind of physical energy. For example, the eyes are responsive to light rays.

▓ In humans, about 80 per cent of all information from the outside world comes to us through the visual system.

▓ Light rays from objects in the visual field enter the eye through the lens, which changes shape and focuses the light rays onto the retina, as an inverted image, at the back of the eye. The pupil of the eye (the opening in the coloured iris) controls the amount of light entering the eye.

■ The retina consists of a layer of light-sensitive cells called photoreceptors, of which there are two main types: rods and cones. Rods function best in dim light, and are not sensitive to colour. Cones are colour-sensitive, and function mainly in bright light. The retina also contains biopolar and ganglion cells.

■ The blindspot is an area of the retina where the nerve fibres from the photoreceptors form the commencement of the optic nerve. Though no information is registered here, we are not usually aware of a 'gap' in vision.

■ Two theories of how we see in colour are: trichromatic theory, which stresses integration by the brain of information from three types of cone, each sensitive to a particular wavelength of light (red, green and blue); and opponent process theory, which suggests that red–green and yellow–blue perceptions are separate processes.

■ Hurvich (1981) proposed a two-stage colour theory, which combines trichromatic and opponent process theories and sees them as complementary.

■ The visual pathways from the half of each retina nearest to the nose cross over at the optic chiasma and continue to the lateral geniculate bodies and then on to the visual cortex of the brain.

■ The human auditory system is able to detect and discriminate three main properties of sound: loudness, pitch and timbre.

■ The human ear is a specialized mechanoreceptor. It transforms sound waves into nerve impulses, undoing complex sound input so that we can recognize individual components.

■ We can localize sounds by detecting phase and intensity differences, aided by the fact that both ears are placed on opposite sides of the head.

■ Specialized receptors in the skin provide sensory information on pressure, temperature, vibration and other variable forms of 'touch'.

■ Pain is a complex phenomenon not yet fully understood. Free nerve endings are certainly involved, but we are also aware of pain in other ways.

■ Sensory receptors located where muscles and tendons join send kinaesthetic feedback to give information on the body's movements and position.

Further reading

Atkinson, R.L., Atkinson, R.C., Smith, E.E. and Bem, D.J. (1993). *Introduction to Psychology*, 11th edn. Orlando, FL: Harcourt, Brace Jovanovich. Chapter 4 covers the visual sense in some detail and examines more briefly the auditory and other senses. Some excellent illustrations.

Wade, N.J. and Swanston, M. (1991). *Visual Perception*. London: Routledge. An interesting account of visual perception, in particular Chapter 3 which covers visual optics and neurophysiology.

CHAPTER 8

The nervous system and behaviour

Cell structures and the communications network   165
- How do neurons and axons work?   166
- The electrochemical process of nervous transmission   166
- The synapse   167

The central nervous system   169
- The brain   169
- The spinal cord   173

Neurochemicals   174
- Neurotransmitters   174
- Neuromodulators   176
- Pheromones   177

- Drugs – their effects on mood and behaviour   177

The autonomic nervous system   178
- The sympathetic division   179
- The parasympathetic division   180

The endocrine system   180
- The pituitary gland   180
- Other glands in the human endocrine system   181
- Endocrine links with the nervous system   183
- Interactional effects with behaviour   183

Objectives

By the end of this chapter, you should be able to:

- Outline the functional divisions of the nervous system;

- Describe some of the structures of the central nervous system, and their functions;

- Appreciate the role played by neurotransmitters in the nervous system;

- Understand the functions of the autonomic nervous system;

- Understand the structure and functioning of the endocrine system.

The nervous system of the human body is highly complex, more complex than that of any other earthly creature, alive or extinct. This chapter looks at the structure and functions of the nervous system. Structures such as neurons, axons and synapses are described, and their functions outlined. Although the nervous system is a 'whole', it can for ease of examination be theoretically divided according to types of function.

As can be seen from Figure 8.1, the nervous system can be functionally divided in two: the **central nervous** system, which is the centre of human operations, and the **peripheral nervous system**, which, as the name

> **GLOSSARY**
>
> **Central nervous system (CNS)** The brain and the spinal cord.
>
> **Peripheral nervous system (PNS)** The spinal and cranial nerves radiating from the CNS to the rest of the body. The PNS is subdivided into the somatic nervous system (SNS) and the autonomic nervous system (ANS).

NERVOUS SYSTEM

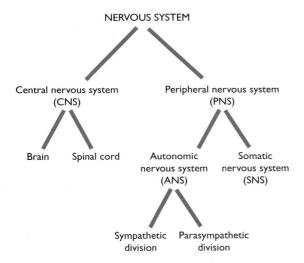

Figure 8.1 Organization of the nervous system

implies, is the remainder, around the 'edges'. The central nervous system (CNS) comprises the brain and spinal cord. The brain deals with so-called higher functions, integrating messages from the senses, instructing activities, memorizing and thinking. The spinal cord carries the major nerve fibres between the brain and other areas such as the limbs and trunk; it also integrates reflex actions. The CNS will be examined in greater detail later in this chapter, as its functions are of particular interest to psychologists.

The peripheral nervous system (PNS) includes the **somatic nervous system (SNS)** and the **autonomic nervous system (ANS)**, which both interact with the CNS. The somatic nervous system carries messages to and from the muscles controlling the skeleton, while the autonomic nervous system carries messages to and from the body's internal organs. The ANS is looked at in more detail later in this chapter; it is involved with emotional experiences that are of interest to psychologists studying behaviour.

Cell structures and the communications network

The major cells in the nervous system are **neurons**. From the electrical activity of a neuron, messages are passed along its axon (nerve fibre) towards the next neuron. There are other cells in the nervous system, which provide support for neurons, but these are not described here, as they are of less interest to psychologists in the study of behaviour.

There are three main types of neuron:

■ **Sensory neurons**, which pick up information from the sensory receptors described in Chapter 7; they send this information onward to the central nervous system (the brain and spinal cord).

■ **Connector neurons**, which are mainly located in the central nervous system, 85 per cent of them being located in the brain. These receive incoming information from the senses or the body's internal environment, 'compute' this information and pass the information on for action to be taken by the individual. This information may be passed to:

■ **Motor neurons**, which send messages from the central nervous system to the muscles and those parts of the body involved in activity. Figure 8.2 illustrates how these three types of neuron function if you see a friend and wave.

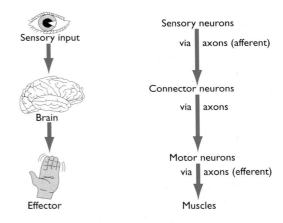

Figure 8.2 Chain of events occurring in the nervous system when you 'see a friend and wave'

How do neurons and axons work?

Read this explanation in conjunction with consulting Figure 8.3. Information from sensory receptors or from other neurons is picked up by the receiving dendrites of a neuron and passed into the soma, or cell body. If sufficient dendrites receive information, or if the stimulus is sufficiently strong, the cell body will be stimulated to produce an electrical impulse; this is called firing. This impulse will pass along the axon by an electrochemical process (shown in Figure 8.4) until the axon branches out into sending dendrites and terminal buttons, which transmit to the next neuron. In the case of motor neurons, the axons end in motor end plates, which connect directly with the muscle fibres.

The electrochemical process of nervous transmission

Sending nerve impulses around the body is often referred to in terms of electrical activity. The actual basis of this electrical activity is a chemical action.

All molecules in the body carry either a positive or a negative charge, depending on their particular constituents. For example, potassium (K^+) and sodium (Na^+) are both positive, whereas chlorine (Cl^-) is negative.

Inside the axons (nerve fibres), there are primarily potassium (K^+) ions and large, negatively charged protein molecules. Outside the axon are sodium (Na^+) and chloride (Cl^-) ions. The wall of the axon is normally impermeable (permits no entry or exit) to molecules, and an active transport system, called the sodium pump, transports Na^+ molecules to the outside of the membrane. This is in order to maintain the resting potential of the axon as negative compared with the outside environment.

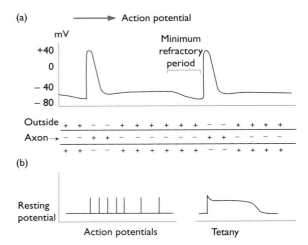

(a) → Action potential

(b)

Figure 8.4 The electrochemical process of nervous transmission
(a) Action potential caused by changes of polarity in the axon
(b) The pattern of firing produced by stimulation of an axon

When a neuron is stimulated by neurotransmitters to 'fire' an impulse along its axon, this resting potential is disturbed and chemical changes take place. The membrane is depolarized and positively charged Na^+ ions rush in from outside. These are quickly retransported by the sodium pump. During this change of electrical activity, an action potential occurs (see Figure 8.4(a)). This represents the electrical activity in that section of the axon. In reconstituting this section of the membrane, the next section of membrane is depolarized, and the chemical and electrical activity is repeated over again.

In this way, firing proceeds along the axon, producing a series of action potentials (often called spikes, for obvious reasons!). The spikes are always the same size, although the spacing between them may vary, according to the rate or intensity of neuronal activity.

The constant size of the action potential is due to what is called the all-or-none law. A neuron never half-fires; it either fires or it does not, thereby producing a consistent size action potential. If the neuronal stimulation is weak, impulses will not be passed along the axon. Firing will not occur until sufficient stimulation is present to be above the **threshold of response**, the

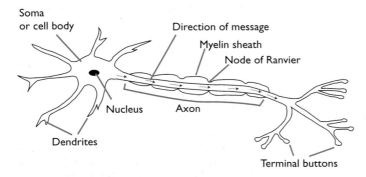

Figure 8.3 A neuron, including axon and dendrites

level at which depolarization will occur. If weak impulses have to be summated (added together) before firing can occur, this will be shown as a slow response rate of firing (wide spaces between the spikes). After each spike comes a period (milliseconds only) during which the axon cannot fire again (the **absolute refractory period**), when the sodium ions are transported out and the membrane reconstitutes. As this period progresses, the stimulation required for firing gradually becomes less (the **relative refractory period**). However, if the stimulation is abnormally intense, firing may be maintained without any refractory period. This is called tetany (see Figure 8.4(b)). This is what happens to the nervous system if the tetanus virus is introduced into the body.

Information can only be transmitted one way along an axon: there is no two-way traffic, which would cause chaos.

All but the smallest axons in the human body are covered by a myelin sheath, which is punctuated at intervals by the nodes of Ranvier. Any decrease in the electrochemical activity in the axon is regenerated at the next node of Ranvier, which provides a burst of activity to send the message onward. This is why the axon's conduction process is called saltatory conduction (from the Latin *saltare*, to dance). it proceeds in leaps and bounds!

The synapse

The area where an axon connects with the dendrite of another neuron is called the **synapse** (see Figure 8.5). Axons do not join directly onto the dendrites or the cell body of the next neuron; there is a gap, called the synaptic cleft. The electrical activity of the axon cannot proceed across the synaptic cleft, so a different process bridges the gap.

Chemicals called **neurotransmitters** (transmitter substances) are contained in the terminal buttons of the sending dendrites. When these are electrically stimulated by the axon, they are released across the synaptic cleft, onto specialized receptor sites in the receiving dendrites of the next neuron in the chain.

If sufficient transmitters are received by sufficient dendrites, this will prompt the next neuron to fire, and the message is passed on. If insufficient transmitter is received, the message will lapse. This system also prevents random firings (generated by the brain itself, which hates inactivity) from being passed on as genuine messages.

In addition, certain transmitters have an inhibitory action, that is to say they discourage firing. A balance of activating and inhibitory transmitters ensures the passage of genuine messages. However, psychoactive drugs, such as amphetamines, often mimic the action of certain neurotransmitters, which is why people under the influence of drugs 'see' and 'hear' things that are not really there.

Once the transmitters have caused the neuron to fire, they have completed their task and need to be deactivated, or they will continue to instruct firing. They are deactivated by reuptake, or reabsorption into the membrane of the dendrites from which they came. A few, notably acetylcholine (a neurotransmitter active in, for example, the 'memory' areas of the brain) are

Figure 8.5 The synapse

> ### GLOSSARY
>
> **Threshold of response** The minimum level of a stimulus needed to activate a response.
>
> **Absolute refractory period** The one or two milliseconds following the firing of a neuron during which the axon cannot fire again.
>
> **Relative refractory period** A very short period after a neuron has fired during which the threshold of response is increased.
>
> **Synapse** The small gap (referred to as the synaptic cleft) which exists between the axon of one neuron and the dendrite of the next.
>
> **Neurotransmitter** A chemical 'messenger' stored in the terminal buttons of the transmitting dendrite. When electrically stimulated by the axon, they are released across the synaptic cleft to the dendrites of the next neuron.

Box 8.1 Neural networks

Of course, neurons do not work in isolation or even simply in long 'strings', as Figure 8.3 may have implied. There are millions of interconnections between neurons, and this facilitates the flow of information to other areas. Are these simply random connections or is there some meaningful pattern?

As early as 1949, Donald Hebb suggested that learning is consolidated in the brain by activation of cell assemblies, groups of neurons that fire systematically to respond to a specific stimulus. This causes structural changes to the cells, possibly even the growth of new synapses. As this reoccurs, the cell assembly 'learns' and responds each time, forming the neural basis of memory.

This idea is similar to a recent approach to modelling the function of neural circuits, called neural networks. Connectionist models (see diagram) are computer models that simulate the activity of neurons; connections may be either excitatory or inhibitory. Neural networks can be taught to recognize a particular stimulus, and connections can be strengthened by reinforcement, or an inhibitory system can be inbuilt to refine responses to one particular stimulus. A network can be 'shown' a particular stimulus and its output monitored. After several presentations of the same stimulus, the output shows a strong and reliable response pattern.

The effects upon responses can include:

■ **Generalization.** When a network has learned to recognize a specific stimulus and is then shown a similar stimulus, its output pattern will resemble the one it gives to the known stimulus.

■ **Discrimination.** If a network learns several similar stimuli, it will learn to distinguish between them and produce different output patterns for each.

■ **Degradation.** If a network or its connections (synapses) are damaged, the network does not cease functioning but produces a deterioration of performance, usually relevant to the level of damage.

As more is learned about neural networks, more realistic models are being constructed. The brain almost certainly contains many thousands of networks, each involved

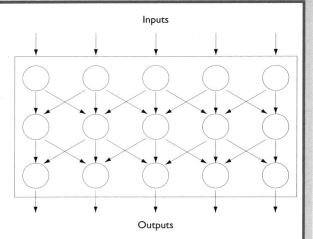

Inputs

Outputs

Connectionist models of the brain suggest a neural network of connections (depicted by arrows) linking neurons that are involved in joint activities, such as responding to a specific stimulus. A simple neural network model

with individual functions and exchanging information with other networks. How closely network models represent the activity of the brain is a question still being refined. Connectionist scientists are constantly refining techniques modelling neural networks. These are areas of research that show the greatest promise of explaining, in the not-too-distant future, how the human central nervous system works. For example, a simulation experiment used present-generation supercomputers to identify photographs of outdoor scenes. A neural network was 'trained' to classify regions in terms of segmented images from an image database. Eleven classifications were set up, including trees, houses, pavement, sky, road and car.

On presentation of the test photographs of outdoor scenes, between 70 and 81 per cent of images and areas of the photographs were correctly identified by the computer. This demonstrated that features can be extracted in parallel and labelled in parallel (Campbell et al., 1995).

deactivated by enzymes, which lock on, rendering them inactive, and break them down to their constituent chemicals for recirculation and later reassembly. Acetylcholinesterase, the enzyme which deactivates acetylcholine, is extremely energetic: one molecule can deactivate 5000 molecules of transmitter.

1. What are the similarities and differences between sensory, connector and motor neurons?
2. Draw a diagram of a synapse and explain briefly how it 'works'.
3. Reread the section 'The electrochemical process of nervous transmission'. Now explain briefly, in your own words, how transmission of impulses takes place.
4. What is the all-or-none law?
5. What are connectionist models?

The central nervous system

The CNS is the centre of neural activity; integrating incoming information, organizing thought processes, making decisions and issuing instructions to the body. It comprises the brain and spinal cord; these are described below. Damage to the CNS is not regenerated (repaired) as occurs with other areas of the body.

The brain

The brain is soft and floats in its own waterbed for protection. It cannot feel pain if damaged directly, as it has no pain receptors. An adult brain weighs about 1.361 kg and contains around 100 billion neurons, which die in vast numbers and are not regenerated. The brain receives about one-fifth of the blood pumped out by the heart; it needs the glucose and oxygen in the blood in order to function efficiently. If deprived of oxygen for more than three or four minutes, irreparable damage is likely to occur.

Structure of the brain

The brain is divided into two halves, called hemispheres. The outer covering of the brain is called the neocortex ('neo' meaning 'new', as this only occurs in animals which have evolved comparatively recently; 'neocortex' is usually simply abbreviated to cortex). Owing to the quantity of neurons in the cortex, it appears grey in colour, giving rise to the common reference to 'grey matter'. Other structures contained within the brain are referred to as subcortical structures, often called 'white matter'.

The blood-brain barrier is a filter system that prevents some substances from reaching the brain even when carried in the bloodstream. This barrier works both ways, and some substances produced by the brain do not enter the body and would be regarded by the body as 'foreign'. Some investigators believe that multiple sclerosis is due to virus damage of the blood-brain barrier, which then permits CNS myelin protein to enter the bloodstream and be transported round the body. This mobilizes the immune system against the 'foreign invader', which then destroys the myelination in the CNS. With its insulation gone, axons cannot keep their messages separate and they become scrambled, so activities cannot be instructed clearly.

Areas of the brain

The cortex   This is approximately only 4 mm thick, and covers the entire surface of the brain. Its many convolutions and folds means that a greater surface area is contained within the small space inside the skull. In fact, if you unfolded and ironed out the cortex, it would cover approximately 0.232 m^2.

For ease of reference, each hemisphere is divided into four lobes: frontal, parietal, occipital and temporal (named after the bones of the skull that cover them, see Figure 8.6). For decades now, physiologists and psychologists have been 'mapping' areas of the cortex according to their functions.

Conscious processes such as thinking and decision making are thought to be controlled by the frontal lobes of the cortex. It is also thought that memories are stored by the cortex, but the exact method of storage has not yet been determined.

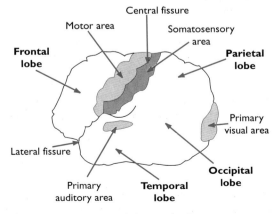

Figure 8.6   Some areas of the cerebral cortex

Box 8.2 Localization of speech (an example of lateralization)

In most people, speech is localized in the left hemisphere of the cortex. Investigation has identified several specific areas associated with the comprehension and production of speech.

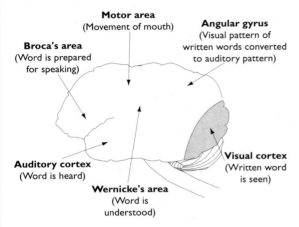

Language areas of the brain

Broca's area

During the nineteenth century, Broca was investigating speech loss in a patient and identified an area of damage to the cerebral cortex, in the left frontal lobe. Similar damage to the right frontal lobe did not usually produce loss of speech. It appeared that in this area, words were formulated or prepared for speech. (The actual production of speech also involves the motor cortex, which controls the tongue, mouth and larynx.)

Incomplete damage to Broca's area means that individuals have difficulty formulating words. Nouns are often produced in the singular, and less important words are often omitted. There is no difficulty understanding spoken or written language, which suggests to investigators that areas other than this are responsible for the comprehension of speech.

Wernicke's area

Wernicke in 1874 identified an area in the temporal cortex of the left lobe that was involved with the comprehension of words. Individuals with damage to this area had difficulty understanding words. They could hear and articulate words, but their speech tended to be meaningless and their comprehension very limited.

Angular gyrus

This is an area of the brain involved in reading. It matches a written word to its auditory code. The flow diagram below shows a representation of all the areas of the brain involved in the process of reading aloud. It is no wonder that so many people have difficulty with this, apart from the embarrassment of being 'on stage'.

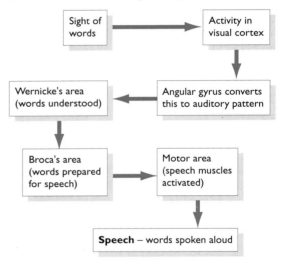

Reading aloud: the probable sequence of events in the cortex

Some motor and somatosensory areas are delineated in Figure 8.6, such as the visual and auditory cortex, as discussed in Chapter 7. Along the central sulcus (or fold) is the primary motor cortex and its associated area next to it, which contain neurons involved in movement. The other side of the central sulcus is the somatosensory cortex, which integrates information from the body senses, such as touch, pressure and pain.

This mapping of areas of the cortex seems directly opposed to Lashley's **law of mass action**, which suggested that the cortex functioned as a whole rather than as discrete areas. However, Lashley was looking at the cortex with the intention of identifying where learning and memory occurred. These functions, as mentioned previously, do not seem to be specifically located in one area of the cortex but are spread throughout it.

The cortex of the two hemispheres may appear identical to look at, but in humans one hemisphere is usually dominant. In most people, this is the left hemisphere, which controls the right side of the body. Some functions are contained in only one hemisphere, for example speech, which is usually in the left hemisphere. In some left-handed people, speech is on the right, where the two hemispheres have been 'switched'; in other cases, left-handedness may have occurred for other reasons (Beaumont, 1988).

The nondominant hemisphere, usually the right, appears to be responsible for functions such as spatial localization (being aware of the relationships of objects in the spatial field). This may be of use to humans in many ways: for example, for architects, artists and tennis and squash players, spatial localization is well developed. It is interesting to note how many top-class tennis players and artists are also left-handed. These people presumably have their spatial representation in their dominant hemisphere; does this therefore mean that their speech centres are located in their nondominant hemisphere? If so, with what effect? Further studies would be necessary to answer these questions in relation to specific individuals.

Scientists are still not sure whether functions other than speech are localized in a specific hemisphere; it is not permissible to carry out true experiments on people's brains, purely out of scientific interest, as we discussed in the Introduction. Instead, psychologists often take the opportunity to examine the functioning of patients who have had brain surgery. This was the basis for Sperry's work on **'split brain' patients**; his patients had received brain surgery to prevent the spread of epileptic seizures that were becoming life-threatening. Once recovered from the operation, his patients were asked to carry out a variety of perceptual tasks, the results of which give us some insight into the functioning of the two hemispheres (see Box 8.3).

Subcortical structures Figure 8.7 shows some of the subcortical structures of the brain; the functions of some of these are described briefly below, and these structures will be mentioned again during the course of this book. The pituitary gland is described in a later section, as it is part of the endocrine system, but is included in this diagram in order to demonstrate its location.

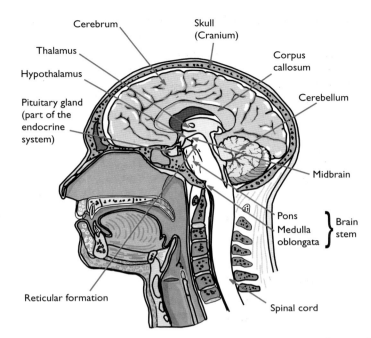

Figure 8.7 Cross-section of the brain, showing some subcortical structures

The **brainstem** is an extension of the spinal cord and contains structures such as the pons, the medulla oblongata and the reticular activating system or reticular formation. Parts of the brainstem control our most basic and vital functions, such as breathing, waking, sleeping and maintaining our heartbeat.

The **reticular formation** consists of clusters of neurons situated at the top of the brainstem. It is important in arousal and wakefulness. The reticular formation monitors arousal through the network of neurons by which stimulation passes from exterior and interior sources. If the reticular formation is extensively damaged, it may not be possible to arouse a patient. (See also Chapter 12 for a discussion of arousal.)

The **thalamus** consists of an egg-shaped cluster of neurons situated just above the brainstem. There is a

---

GLOSSARY

Law of mass action The proposal by Lashley that the cortex functions as a whole rather than as separate areas and the effects of damage would depend upon the amount damaged.

'Split brain' patients People who have undergone commisurotomy, an operation that severs the corpus collusum, so that the two hemispheres of the brain are no longer connected.

Box 8.3   In two minds?

Sperry (1968) reported the behavioural, cognitive and perceptual outcomes of commisurotomy, the so-called 'split brain' operation. This is an operation that severs the corpus callosum and the fibres that connect the two hemispheres across this structure. The operation is performed rarely, in specifically identified patients with severe epilepsy, to prevent the electrical disturbances spreading from one hemisphere to the other.

Careful investigations prior to the operation assured Sperry that patients' brain functioning would not be significantly impaired, but there would be postoperative differences. These were to be the subject of his further studies.

After the operations, all patients were either seizure-free or experienced only minor seizures. None appeared to have changes of personality or loss of intelligence. Perceptual responses were, however, affected; Sperry suggested that the two hemispheres appeared to be functioning independently, almost as two separate brains. For example:

- If a visual stimulus was presented to a patient's right visual field (by use of a central screen), and an appropriate response made, when the same stimulus was then presented to the left visual field, the patient responded as though it had not been seen before.
- In reading and writing (bearing in mind that in most right-handed people the left hemisphere mediates speech and reading responses): if visual material was presented to the right visual field, it could be described in speech and writing in the normal way, being mediated by the left visual hemisphere.

However, if an object was presented to the left visual field, patients were unable to name it, but could select a similar object from a choice of objects available. In both cases, information appeared not to be passed from one hemisphere to the other; each hemisphere was 'doing what it does best', but independently.

The right side of the brain is capable of recognizing and producing some language, but this is limited, although some people have language represented bilaterally (Beaumont, 1988). Ornstein (1986) suggests that the left hemisphere is specialized for analytical verbal and mathematical functions, processing information sequentially (one item at a time, in straight lines), while the right hemisphere is impressionistic, holistic and processes several items at the same time. Sperry's work would seem to substantiate claims for lateralization of functions (different functions being mediated by separate hemispheres), although some are undoubtedly represented bilaterally.

Cohen (1975) suggests that it may be invalid to generalize from these patients, who have experienced abnormal brain functioning for some time, to normal people. She suggests that the hemispheres normally function together, using a mixture of 'left' and 'right' skills. Mackay (1987) investigated whether split-brain patients demonstrated two separate forms of consciousness or free will, but decided that there was insufficient evidence to assume this, although they occasionally appeared to be unaware of decisions made by one hemisphere or the other.

---

thalamus in each hemisphere, both acting in unison. Most subcortical structures are represented bilaterally (in both hemispheres). Some of the neurons in the thalamus receive incoming information from the senses and direct it onward through the brain. In this way, they act as a relay station; for example, the lateral geniculate bodies of the visual system (mentioned in Chapter 7) are situated in the thalamus.

Other thalamic neurons play an important part in the control of sleep and wakefulness; we shall mention these again in Chapter 8.

The **hypothalamus** is situated just below the thalamus and is a much smaller structure. Again, it is represented bilaterally. It regulates the body through the endocrine system, as described later, and ensures that the body maintains homeostasis. This is the balanced state of the body in which breathing, heart rate, blood pressure and temperature are all normal and comfortable for the individual concerned. The hypothalamus instructs changes to ensure that this balance is maintained without conscious thought and instructions on the part of the individual concerned. These activities are carried out through the ANS described later in this chapter.

The hypothalamus also plays a role in emotional states and responds to stress. The so-called 'pleasure centre' and 'pain centre' are also located in the hypothalamus. These are areas which, when stimulated electrically, produce sensations of either pleasure or pain (Olds and Milner, 1954).

The **limbic system** is a group of brain structures sometimes called the 'old brain' because they are present in animals further down the phylogenetic scale. The limbic system has close links with the hypothalamus and appears to impose extra control over some of the instinctive and emotional responses mediated by the hypothalamus, by inhibiting them.

The **hippocampus**, an area of the limbic system, is involved with the laying down of new memories. If the hippocampus is damaged by a virus infection or surgically removed, the patient will not remember new people met after that time nor fresh events (anterograde amnesia). Old, long-standing memories and old friends will be recalled with no problem, however, as these are already 'set' (Squire, 1986). It is possible that emotions are important in selecting what we must learn; great fear will teach us never to cross the motorway on foot again!

The **amygdala** is another area in the limbic system. It is also involved with the control of emotional responses. Lesions in the amygdala often result in undirected aggressive responses, as though the emotional response cannot be coordinated properly.

The **corpus callosum** is a physical rather than a functional structure. It is the bridge where nerve fibres cross over from left to right, and vice versa. If this structure is severed (as in commisurotomy), information is no longer passed to the other side of the brain, with some strange behavioural results (see Box 8.3).

The **cerebellum** is situated at the back of the brain, and is associated with coordinating movement to make it smooth rather than jerky. It also stores memory of movement patterns, so that you do not have to concentrate on how to walk or run, and ensures that once you have learned to ride a bike, you will never forget.

Although each brain area may have its own specific role, activities are interrelated and therefore areas of the brain must be interrelated. Damage to one area of the brain may well affect the functioning of other areas. Once damaged, the brain, unlike other areas of the body, does not regenerate. There are claims from individuals that they regain functions, but this is unusual except in the case of young children, in whom **plasticity** occurs. This is the ability of the young brain to take over the roles of damaged areas, presumably because functions are still being delineated (Rose, 1976).

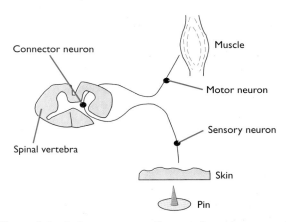

Figure 8.8 A three-neuron reflex arc. Sensations pass via the sensory neuron to the connector neuron, which instructs the motor neuron to contract the muscle, thereby withdrawing from the 'sharp' stimulus

The spinal cord

Running the length of the body, from brain to 'tail', the spinal cord is housed within the vertebrae of the spinal column. It consists of collections of axons running to or from the brain to various parts of the body. Pairs of major nerves emerge at specific points along the spine, to activate the nerves of the arms, the legs and areas of the trunk.

The spinal cord does not always send information to the brain and wait for a reply; it has its own quick system for simple tasks, known as the reflex arc (see Figure 8.8). If you step on something sharp when barefoot, the information travels via the sensory input to a sensory neuron, and then to connector neurons housed in the spinal column. These immediately instruct the motor neurons of the leg to contract, pulling the leg away from the point of contact.

Simple reflexes may only involve sensory and motor neurons: for example, where the bent knee is tapped and jerks upwards. This is the kind of test you may have seen carried out by doctors to see whether the reflex arc is functioning effectively.

GLOSSARY

Plasticity The ability of the brain when damage occurs (usually only in young children) to take over the functions of damaged areas.

1. Trace or copy Figures 8.6 and 8.7, including the arrows but not the labels. Now close the book and fill in the labels on your diagrams. Check your answers and correct if necessary.
2. Briefly describe the functions of three subcortical areas.
3. What is 'plasticity'?
4. What happens during a reflex action?
5. Describe the problems that may be experienced after a 'split-brain' operation.

Neurochemicals

Among the chemicals circulating in the brain are some which have direct bearing on the behaviour of the individual. These include **neurotransmitters**, which we have mentioned and will now examine in more detail, together with neuromodulators. In addition, pheromones are briefly described here, while hormones are discussed fully in the section on the endocrine systems. Finally, we will look at the way in which psychoactive drugs act on the brain, in the light of our understanding of brain chemicals. It is outside the scope of this book to examine the processes of addiction, although this will be mentioned from time to time.

Neurotransmitters

Neurotransmitters are the chemicals released at the synapse. They are involved in the transmission of messages, as previously described. Their action can be either excitatory (promoting action) or inhibitory (lessening activity), depending on the site where they are acting. To date, at least 40 neurotransmitters have been identified, but we will confine ourselves to discussing only a few, those identified as being of prime importance and of greatest interest to psychologists.

Acetylcholine

This is the transmitter substance that is found in the hippocampus, as we mentioned earlier, and surrounding areas of the brain. This location suggests that it is involved with memory and learning. The same transmitter is also found at the neuromuscular junction

(that is, where axons from motor neurons connect with muscles) and is involved with movement of the skeletal system.

The main difference between these two systems lies in the receptor sites: the skeletal receptors are nicotinic receptors, because they are stimulated by nicotine, a poison found in tobacco leaves, whereas the receptors in the CNS are primarily muscarinic receptors, stimulated by muscarine, a poison found in mushrooms. These different receptors, while both detecting acetylcholine, are linked to different physiological systems, which then respond differently.

The monoamines

These are a chemically similar group of neurotransmitters, all of which have specific actions, so will be described individually. Three (dopamine, norepinephrine and epinephrine) form a related subgroup, called the catecholamines, dopamine being the precursor (or previous chemical step) of the other two.

Dopamine Dopamine has been identified as a transmitter involved in movement, especially the initiation of movements, attention and learning. It is synthesized in the CNS in the neurons of the substantia nigra (see Figure 8.9) and circulates through the dopamine circuit.

Degeneration of these neurons can occur with age, meaning that not enough dopamine is produced; this causes Parkinson's disease. This is characterized by delay in initiating movement, a shuffling walk, tremors of the limbs while inactive, and an inability to regain balance. Treatment to date involves the administration of L-dopa, a synthetic form of the precursor of dopamine, which alleviates the distressing symptoms, at least for a while.

Recent research has suggested that a cause of some cases of Parkinson's disease may be the chemical MPTP, which attacks the dopaminergic neurons. Several years ago, a number of young people took illicit drugs that contained MPTP. This had the effect of destroying their dopaminergic neurons, effectively making them pre-

---

GLOSSARY

Neurotransmitter A chemical that is released by one neuron and then crosses the synaptic gap to be received by special receptor sites on the dendrites of the next neuron in the chain.

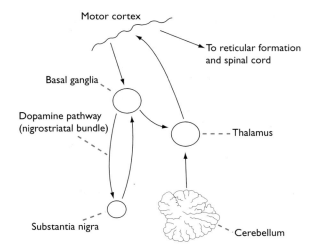

Figure 8.9 The influence of dopamine pathways on movement

mature sufferers of Parkinson's disease (Langston et al., 1983). Currently, new operations are being pioneered, involving brain surgery, to alleviate Parkinsonian symptoms. The transplant of dopaminergic neurons from a human foetus is not being carried out in Great Britain, owing to the ethical constraints of using foetal material.

If sufferers of Parkinson's disease are given too high a dose of L-dopa, they exhibit symptoms similar to those of people who suffer from schizophrenia. Excess dopamine, or an excessive number of dopamine receptor sites, which would enhance the action of circulating dopamine, has been implicated in schizophrenia. It would be too simplistic, however, to state that excess dopamine causes schizophrenia; this may be the effect, rather than the primary cause of the problem. Sufferers from schizophrenia may experience hallucinations (auditory and/or visual), and sometimes exhibit strange motor movements, excessive movements or no movement at all (called catatonia). (For a fuller description of schizophrenia, see Chapter 32.) The dopamine circuit also projects to the limbic system, which is involved with emotion; this could account for the mood changes and aggressive outbursts sometimes suffered by schizophrenics.

Excess dopamine in the CNS is destroyed by the enzyme monoamine oxidase (MAO for short). This enzyme also circulates in the blood, where it deactivates certain amines that are present in some foods, such as cheese, chocolate and broad beans.

Unless deactivated, these amines could cause a high rise in blood pressure.

Serotonin Serotonin (also called 5HT) has been shown to be involved in the regulation of mood. Its action is inhibitory, which means that it tends to depress CNS activity. It is also involved in the regulation of pain, in the control of eating, sleeping and arousal, and also in the control of dreaming. At most synapses, its effects are inhibitory rather than excitatory, and its behavioural effects are largely inhibitory.

Serotonin is present in the midbrain, in a cluster of cells called the raphe nuclei, and in the medulla. These structures send nerve fibres to the forebrain, the cerebellum and the spinal cord, which suggests a widespread method of influencing arousal, sensory perception, emotion and thought processes.

Norepinephrine/noradrenaline Norepinephrine is chemically exactly the same as noradrenaline, and epinephrine is identical to adrenaline. Many books interchange these terms, but I have decided to use the terms 'norepinephrine' and 'epinephrine' for the neurotransmitters and 'adrenaline' and 'noradrenaline' when referring to the hormones. All are produced by the core of the adrenal glands (see the section on the endocrine system).

Noradrenergic neurons in the brain are situated in the lower brainstem and are mainly involved in arousal and wakefulness. In the CNS, norepinephrine plays an excitatory role and is more widespread than epinephrine, which has an inhibitory effect. Both transmitters are present in the axons of the autonomic nervous system, which is described in the next section. Noradrenergic axons release their neurotransmitter through swellings on the axon (called varicosities, see Figure 8.10), rather than from terminal buttons, as do other neurotransmitters.

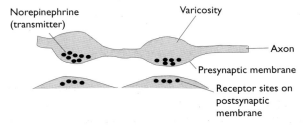

Figure 8.10 Norepinephrine is released from varicosities (swellings) in the axons, rather than from terminal buttons

Like dopamine, excess norepinephrine and epinephrine are destroyed by the enzyme MAO.

Amino acid transmitters

This group of transmitters differs from the others as amino acids are used for protein synthesis by all cells in the brain. However, three of them play a particularly important role as neurotransmitters; these are glutamic acid, GABA (gamma-aminobutyric acid) and glycine.

Glutamic acid Often called glutamate, glutamic acid is found throughout the brain and appears to be the principal excitatory neurotransmitter. It is produced liberally by the cells' metabolic processes. Monosodium glutamate, found in a number of manufactured foods, also contains glutamic acid, and people who are hypersensitive to glutamate may experience neurological symptoms, such as dizziness or hyperactivity, when they eat foods containing too much glutamate.

GABA GABA is produced from glutamic acid (its precursor) by the action of an enzyme that modifies its chemical structure. GABA has a widespread distribution throughout the brain and spinal cord, and exerts an inhibitory influence. This is essential in the CNS to control the number of neurons that are excited through the interconnections of the brain. Without GABA, the brain would be firing uncontrollably.

Glycine Glycine also appears to be an inhibitory neurotransmitter, mainly in the spinal cord and lower brain. Not a great deal is known as yet about glycine. The bacteria that produce tetanus (lockjaw) release a chemical that blocks the receptor sites of glycine. Because the inhibitory effect of glycine can no longer work, muscles contract continuously, which is the behavioural effect of tetanus.

Peptides

Peptides are amino acids linked by peptide bonds; many are released by neurons. Some serve as neurotransmitters, others appear to act as neuromodulators. Psychologists are particularly interested in the opiate-like peptides classed as endorphins, because of the effect they have on behaviour.

Early work by Pert et al. (1974) identified opiate receptors in the brain and endorphin-containing neurons in the hypothalamus. Projections reach the amygdala and the higher brainstem. Endorphins act as pain-reducing agents – the brain's own anaesthetic.

Enkephalins are chemically similar to endorphins but occupy different areas of the brain. Identified by Hughes et al. (1975), enkephalins are widespread throughout the nervous system and, like endorphins, appear to have the function of pain modulation. In the peripheral nervous system, enkephalins are found in the adrenal medulla (in the endocrine system, described later) and in the nerve fibres of the intestinal system.

Functionally, it has been suggested that it is the endorphins and enkephalins that are mobilized during activity such as fighting. They will then modify any pain suffered until the fight is over and the individual can retire to care for the wounds sustained.

The enkephalins have been suggested as being instrumental in many previously unexplained phenomena, such as acupuncture. It is suggested that the needles may be stimulating the localized production of enkephalins. The production of endorphins and enkephalins may also help to explain why a rugby player might complete the game and find afterwards that he has a broken collar bone. Perhaps it may explain a phenomenon you yourself may have observed. For the past few hundred years at least, vets and blacksmiths have been applying a twitch to horses who are difficult to handle. (A twitch is a piece of rope, wound around the horse's upper lip, and tightened.) It sounds cruel, and many people have thought that the pain of the lip was taking all the horse's attention and letting the vet get on with the job in hand. But if you watch a horse with a twitch, the eyes droop and the animal appears calm, almost sleepy, not at all like an animal in pain. Perhaps this area stimulates the production of enkephalins, which induces a calming effect. Perhaps we humans are not so different either. Next time you feel very upset, try pinching your top lip between thumb and finger for a while – does it work for you?

Neuromodulators

Neuromodulators are chemicals that are diffused widely throughout the brain, only not occurring at the synapse, as do neurotransmitters, or within specific pathways. They act in conjunction with neurotransmitters, as their name implies, modulating the activity of surrounding chemicals. Some receptor sites are organized to receive both neurotransmitters and neuromodulators.

Pheromones

Pheromones are chemicals that are released by the body through sweat, urine or the excretions of specialized glands. These chemicals are detected by the recipient's sense of smell. In animals other than humans, they are primary signals for attracting mates and initiating sexual behaviour, by acting upon the hormonal systems of potential mates. In addition, these chemicals are used as 'markers' for delineating territories and repelling would-be adversaries.

Humans produce pheromones, and recent research has attempted to identify how important these are in their original attraction/repellant roles. As proportionally less of the human brain is used for identifying and integrating smell-patterns (we do not go sniffing at each other for identification, as dogs and cats do), it is probable that these chemicals are less important to us than to animals farther down the phylogenetic scale.

Drugs – their effects on mood and behaviour

Drugs affect behaviour because of their effect on neurotransmitters. They generally exert their influence at the synapse by either imitating or blocking the action of a specific neurotransmitter. Psychologists are especially interested in the effects of **psychoactive drugs** – drugs that alter mood or thought processes.

There are five broad categories of drugs:

- minor tranquillizers,
- neuroleptics (major tranquillizers),
- stimulants,
- antidepressants,
- opiates.

Figure 8.11 gives a brief general summary of the effects of these categories of drugs on mood and behaviour, along with the effects on neurotransmitters.

The first four of these categories – major and minor tranquillizers, stimulants and antidepressants – are

---

GLOSSARY

Neuromodulators Chemicals that act in conjunction with neurotransmitters, moderating their activity.

Pheromones Chemicals released through sweat, urine or the excretions of specialized glands. In animals they are primary signals for attracting mates. Their importance in humans is uncertain.

Psychoactive drugs Drugs which may alter mood or thought processes.

Figure 8.11 Summary table of the action of some psychoactive drugs

Effect group	Chemical group and examples	Neurochemical affect	Effect on mood or behaviour
Minor tranquillizers	Benzodiazepines (e.g. Librium, Valium)	Enhance release of GABA (inhibitory)	Calming effect, reduce anxiety
Neuroleptics (antipsychotics)	Phenothiazines (e.g. chlorpromazine) butyrophenones (haloperidol)	Dopamine – drug occupies receptors	Reduce psychotic experiences and strange motor movements
Stimulants	Amphetamines (Dexadrine)	Block reuptake of dopamine and norepinephrine	Increase alertness and feelings of confidence
Antidepressants	(1) Tricyclics	(1) Block breakdown of norepinephrine and serotonin	Produce lifted mood, feelings of euphoria, block REM sleep
	(2) Monoamine oxidase inhibitors	(2) Block action of enzyme MAO, thus enhancing action of norepinephrine and serotonin	
	(3) Axiolytics (SSRI, e.g. Prozac)	(3) Prolong the action of serotonin	Reduce anxiety
Opiates	Morphine	Mimic action of endorphins	Soothing, calming, pain-reducing

Box 8.4   Opiates and other psychoactive drugs

Opiates

Opiates are drugs that may be prescribed for the control of strong pain. They include the medical version of opium, which is morphine, chemically the same as heroin. These drugs are highly addictive. They act on the opiate receptor sites normally used by the endorphins and enkephalins. If used regularly, they depress the individual's own production of endorphins. If the drug is withdrawn, the individual not only suffers the withdrawal symptoms that accompany the loss of any drug, such as nicotine, but also has reduced pain-modulating capacity, due to the low level of natural endorphins. Naturally, the clinical administration of opiate drugs is carefully controlled and monitored.

Other psychoactive drugs

We hear a great deal nowadays about nonprescribed psychoactive drugs and 'designer' drugs, which are mixes of known psychoactive substances, all of which are active in the brain, usually at neurotransmitter level. Undoubtedly, altering the chemical balance of the brain always has its dangers, whether done clinically or experimentally, as the young sufferers of Parkinson's disease (previously mentioned) would doubtless testify. Impurities and injudicious 'mixes' are probably the most harmful, but the problems of addiction and how to break the cycle, and how not to pass the addiction to one's children, given there may be a genetic component, are all problems as yet insoluble.

LSD (lysergic acid diethylamide) is a hallucinogenic drug which appears to stimulate certain of the serotonin receptors; the hallucinations that occur have been likened to 'dreaming while you are awake'. Of course, dreams can be pleasant or frightening, and as yet no one has satisfactorily explained the mechanism whereby the hallucinations recur even when the individual is not on the drug. LSD does not seem as addictive as was originally thought, but this is probably situation dependent.

We hear about 'exercise addicts' who are apparently 'high' on the catecholamines produced during exercise and who suffer withdrawal symptoms if their exercise is curtailed. How well researched the syndrome is remains to be seen, but the body does adapt upwards – or downwards – to changed chemical levels.

Curare is a drug that was synthesized from plants by the South American Indians as a poison with which to tip their arrows. Curare occupies the nicotinic receptor sites used by the neurotransmitter acetylcholine, which effectively blocks the neuromuscular junction, causing paralysis. Consciousness is not affected. In modern times, a form of curare was used during operations as a muscle relaxant, so that muscles would not contract during surgery. In addition, an anaesthetic needs to be used (so that the patient is not conscious and does not feel the pain of the scalpel), together with a respirator to compensate for lack of tone in the respiratory muscles.

---

used to treat mental disorders and are discussed more fully in Chapter 33. Box 8.4 briefly considers the effects on behaviour of opiates and other psychoactive drugs.

? SELF-ASSESSMENT QUESTIONS

1. What are neurotransmitters?
2. Write a paragraph on each of the following: (a) acetylcholine, (b) dopamine, (c) norepinephrine, (d) serotonin, (e) endorphins/enkephalins and (f) GABA.
3. Briefly describe: (a) neuromodulators and (b) pheromones.
4. What are psychoactive drugs? Describe the action and consequences of one psychoactive drug.

The autonomic nervous system

The ANS is the part of the peripheral nervous system that is concerned with the regulation of internal structures: smooth muscle, heart muscle and glands. Smooth muscle is found in the intestines, bowel, bladder, blood vessels, skin (around hair follicles) and eyes (controlling pupil size and accommodation of the lens).

'Autonomic' means self-controlling or self-regulating; as you can see from the above description, most of the structures mentioned are controlled without our conscious intervention, with the exception of bladder and bowel, which we learn to control at an early age. This should imply that we could learn to control our heart rate and blood pressure, but few of us do. A technique called biofeedback has been taught to some patients suffering from high blood pressure (see Chapter 6). They were connected to apparatus that constantly monitored blood pressure and were asked to concentrate on lowering their blood pressure to an acceptable level. When this was reached, a tone sounded. This was the only reinforcement they needed, plus of course the knowledge that they were improving their health. Unfortunately, the improvement was not maintained once they were disconnected from the apparatus.

The ANS consists of two separate systems, the **sympathetic division** and the **parasympathetic division**, both of which have nerve connections to most internal organs. The two divisions act like two ends of a see-saw: when one end is 'up', the other is 'down'. Both cannot be active and in control of the body at the same time, as they often have opposing effects on the same organ (see Figure 8.12).

In Figure 8.12 the action of the sympathetic division on the gut may here seem the opposite to your own observation; when experiencing a strong emotion such as fear, you may have noticed a churning feeling in the stomach ('butterflies'). This is due to a parasympathetic surge, before the sympathetic takes over. Sometimes you go as far as emptying the bladder or bowel. Once you become embroiled in your fight, or other activity, 'butterflies' cease as the sympathetic is in control.

GSR stands for galvanic skin response. It is a measure of the electrical resistance of the skin. This is decreased by sweating, when the skin gets wet; it is associated with anxiety-provoking situations, such as fear or anger, and other strong emotions such as love, hate and passion. This is the process used by lie-detector machines – notoriously unreliable, as good spies are trained to control their autonomic responses.

The ANS works in close conjunction with the endocrine system, another of the body's systems that is not under conscious control (see the next section). Activities of the ANS are coordinated by the hypothalamus and the limbic system. These links can be seen to be important as the hypothalamus also effectively controls the endocrine system, because of its close links to the pituitary gland. The limbic system is involved in emotional responses, which also need the involvement of the ANS.

Figure 8.12 Actions of the ANS on organs of the body

Structure	Sympathetic action	Parasymphetic action
Heart	Increases rate	Resting rate
Blood vessels	Dilates	Contracts
Pupils	Dilates	Contracts
Gut	Slows movement	Speeds movement
Salivary glands	Decreases production	Maintains production
Bronchi (lungs)	Dilates (aids breathing)	Resting state
Adrenal glands	Stimulates	Resting state
Liver	Releases glucose	Stores glucose
GSR	Decreases	Increases
Bladder, bowel	Relaxed	Toned
Skin		
Hair follicle	Erected	Relaxed
Capillaries	Dilated (blushing)	Contracted

The sympathetic division

This division becomes more active when the individual becomes active. Imagine this situation: you are walking down the high street when you see a lion. You have the choice of running away or staying to fight (the 'fight or flight' syndrome). Your CNS will make the conscious decision for you, but your ANS has already become mobilized, without needing conscious instruction. Whichever alternative is chosen, activity is the order of the day; therefore the sympathetic division speeds up the heart rate (remember that nerve impulses take only split seconds to travel), dilates the walls of the blood vessels to speed blood to the limbs, dilates the pupils so that you can see your adversary more clearly, releases glucose into the bloodstream for energy, and brings other changes into play that are advantageous for an active state (see Figure 8.12). The actions of the ANS are reinforced by the activity of the endocrine system; sympathetic nerves also directly stimulate the adrenal glands to release adrenaline.

When all danger is past, the parasympathetic division takes over to restore the body's balance.

> **GLOSSARY**
>
> **Sympathetic division of the ANS** Mobilizes the body's resources when there is a need to be active, for example in threatening situations.
>
> **Parasympathetic division of the ANS** Restores and conserves the body's resources: for example, after a period of activity or threat.

The parasympathetic division

This is the division of the ANS which seeks to conserve the body's resources. It prompts salivation and gastric movements, including peristalsis (the movement of food through the small intestine), and encourages blood flow to the gastrointestinal system and storage of glucose by the liver.

? SELF-ASSESSMENT QUESTIONS

1. What effects do the sympathetic division of the ANS have on major organs or structures of the body?
2. What are the advantages to the individual of sympathetic changes in heart rate, blood pressure and other specific effects?
3. Why is the parasympathetic division of the ANS necessary?

The endocrine system

The **endocrine system** is a system of glands and their secretions which act within the body. The human body is under the control not only of the nervous system, but also of a complementary system of hormones (chemicals), which are released by specialized neurons or glands into the bloodstream or other areas of the body. These are released in response to situations or impulses or the normal cycles of the body, and are not usually a product of conscious control, but are regulated automatically by the body itself. Their action is effectively much slower than that of the nervous system, but their effect is longer lasting, as the chemicals will continue circulating until they are broken down by the body. The pituitary gland is often called the 'master gland' as it directs the activities of many other glands in the body.

The pituitary gland

Although the **pituitary gland** is situated within the cranium, it is part of the endocrine system rather than the nervous system. However, as you would expect from its siting, it has very close links with the nervous system. The hypothalamus, the brain structure next to

the pituitary, exerts a great deal of control over the endocrine system. It has some neurosecretory cells that manufacture hormones to be released directly into the bloodstream serving the anterior pituitary (see Figure 8.13). This prompts the anterior pituitary to secrete its hormones and release them at the appropriate time. Some of these hormones are briefly described below.

Anterior pituitary hormones

- **Growth hormone** is released steadily throughout childhood, with an extra 'spurt' during adolescence (prompting the concurrent growth spurt). This is terminated in girls by the onset of menstruation, and in boys by the increased production of testosterone.
- **Gonadotrophic hormone** controls the production of the male and female sex hormones by

GLOSSARY

Endocrine system A system of glands which produce hormones and release them into the bloodstream. The system interacts with the nervous system in influencing many kinds of behaviour, for example 'fight or flight'.

Pituitary gland The 'master gland', so called because it releases hormones which direct the activity of many other glands.

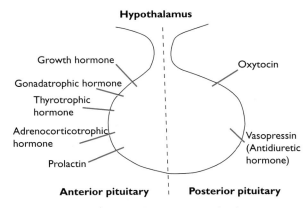

Figure 8.13 Hormones of the pituitary gland

prompting the appropriate sex glands (testes in males and ovaries in females) to produce their hormones.

■ **Thyrotrophic hormone** prompts the thyroid gland to secrete thyroxin, which controls the body's metabolic rate (the rate at which the body uses up food for fuel, in order to produce activity).

■ **Prolactin** prompts the production of milk in pregnant and nursing mothers.

■ **Adrenocorticotrophic hormone** (ACTH for short) signals to the adrenal glands to produce their secretions; this is sometimes referred to as the 'stress' or 'activity' response.

Posterior pituitary hormones

The hormones of the posterior pituitary are actually manufactured in the hypothalamus but stored in the posterior pituitary. The instruction to release them into the bloodstream also comes from the hypothalamus. These hormones are:

■ **oxytocin**, the hormone that controls the release of milk and the contraction of the uterus during childbirth; and

■ **vasopressin**, or antidiuretic hormone, which regulates the output of urine by the kidneys.

Other glands in the human endocrine system

Glands are situated throughout the body (see Figure 8.14); each has a specific role or activity and produces its own specific secretions.

Having briefly outlined the actions of the pituitary gland, it is now possible to look at the activity of some of the other glands that are relevant to the purpose of this book. Of course, all glands have bearing not only on the body but also on the mental state of the individual, but it is outside the scope of this book to discuss them all. However, certain are of paramount importance to the understanding of overt behaviour and will be mentioned here.

The adrenal glands

These sit like three-cornered hats on top of the kidneys (see Figure 8.14). Their secretions are prompted by ACTH from the anterior pituitary gland. There are two active parts to the adrenal gland: the adrenal medulla and the adrenal cortex.

The adrenal medulla (the central area of the gland) secretes adrenaline and noradrenaline, needed by the body to assist physical activities. Both of these hormones are involved in the 'fight or flight' syndrome (discussed earlier), which is mediated by the ANS. They also have a role to play in the physiological processes of the emotions, which we shall look at in Chapter 9. Adrenaline acts on the heart muscle,

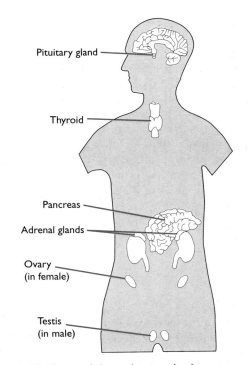

Figure 8.14 Some of the endocrine glands

prompting the heart to beat faster; this is one reason why athletes 'psych themselves up': they promote a flow of adrenaline by psychological means which is then used by the body for physical purposes.

The adrenal cortex, the outer layers of the gland, produces the corticosteroids, for example cortisol and hydrocortisone, utilized by the body for a number of physiological purposes, including the regulation of blood pressure. This is called into play during the 'fight or flight' syndrome, and also when the individual is under stress. Excess production of corticosteroids, for example when an individual is under constant stress, is detrimental to the body, because of the hypertension (raised blood pressure) and other physical changes they promote, which undermine the immune system.

The pancreas

Cells in the pancreas produce insulin, which prompts the cells in the liver to break down glucose (simple sugar) for use by the body, or for storage as glycogen by the liver. The pancreas releases its insulin according to how much sugar has been ingested and how much exercise the person has taken to burn up the sugar. Diabetics (with diabetes mellitus) do not produce enough insulin for this process and have to inject themselves with insulin to 'top up' their own supply. They become adept at gauging how much insulin they need, bearing in mind their exercise/food balance (because all carbohydrates consumed are converted to sugar by the body).

However, injected insulin is released into the body on a regular timescale, rather than according to need, as is naturally occurring insulin, and diabetics who miss meals, or who are subject to physical or mental stress, may lapse into an insulin coma. Warning behaviours for this may include unprovoked anger, irritation or aggressiveness, because the brain is the first organ to respond behaviourally to a lack of sugar. You yourself may have noticed you feel bad-tempered if you have not eaten for some time. An injection of a glucose solution quickly resolves an insulin coma.

The gonads

This is the term used for both male and female sex glands: the testes in males and the ovaries in females. The hormones they produce govern – and differentiate – male and female sexual and reproductive behaviour.

However, in humans especially, a great deal of the behaviour is controlled by the CNS; we are not entirely at the mercy of our hormonal state. Most of the experimental work on neural–hormonal connections has been carried out on animals, so we must be careful not to extrapolate directly to humans.

In both sexes, there is an increase in the production of the sex hormones during adolescence, ready for the reproductive period of life. In males, androgens are produced, which prompt physical changes such as the growth of body hair, deepening of the voice and an increase in sexually oriented behaviour, which is often culturally defined and limited. Increased aggression has also been linked with androgen production and demonstrated experimentally in many species other than humans. In men, there are likely to be neural and cultural influences as well.

A growth spurt in males occurs around the same time, owing to extra production of growth hormone, whereas in females, the growth pattern in adolescence is much less marked and the onset of menstruation signals the decline of growth hormone secretion. A description of the female sex hormones is given in Box 8.5.

The thyroid

The thyroid gland produces thyroxin, which influences the body's metabolic rate (the rate at which the body uses up food to produce energy). This influences behaviour in that an overproduction of thyroxin accelerates metabolic rate, causing the individual to become highly active, jumpy and 'nervy', which is coupled with weight loss. Underproduction of thyroxin leads to lethargy and weight gain.

The pineal gland

In lower vertebrates such as sharks, frogs and lizards, the pineal gland detects changes in levels of illumination; hence it is often referred to as the 'third eye'. In humans, it secretes a hormone called melatonin which is synthesized from serotonin. Melatonin is influential in the body's circadian rhythms, the daily cycle of sleeping and waking activities (more of this in Chapter 10). Sugden et al. (1985) suggest that there is complex biochemical control of circadian rhythms, involving chemicals manufactured by the pineal gland.

Other glands in the human body

There are other glands in the human body that produce secretions rather than hormones, for example the salivary glands, which are the first step in the chemical digestive chain of events. As mentioned in the previous chapter, the salivary glands are linked to the ANS, and the production of saliva is suspended in strong emotional states such as fear. Another gland that produces secretions rather than hormones, but is linked to the reproductive cycle, is the prostate in males. This is a gland very rarely mentioned, yet it has an important function; it manufactures the seminal fluid that surrounds the sperm. Probably because so few men realize they have a prostate gland, cancers of the prostate are often ignored until too late. By and large, glands that produce secretions, rather than hormones, do not have such a direct influence on behaviour as do the hormone-producing glands.

Endocrine links with the nervous system

Links with the CNS

The most obvious link between the endocrine system and the CNS is that the hypothalamus controls the pituitary gland; as this in turn orchestrates most of the other glands, endocrine control can be traced back to the hypothalamus. There is feedback from hormonal levels to the CNS which determines whether glands are then prompted to release or cease production of further hormones. This link is often called the HPA (hypothalamus–pituitary–adrenal axis).

Links with the ANS

The ANS prompts the release of adrenaline from the adrenal glands in strong emotional states and when there is a need for increased physical activity. The ANS also influences metabolic rate, through the thyroid gland.

Links with the PNS

The skeletal system is linked directly to the CNS to perform voluntary movements, through the PNS, which sends out impulses along axons to the limbs. However, there are hormonal influences involved, through both the production of adrenaline and, to a lesser extent, the activity of the thyroid and pancreas.

When overt activity is inappropriate or impossible, the restless pacing up and down of a frustrated or disturbed individual characterizes the PNS/endocrine link.

Interactional effects with behaviour

The endocrine and nervous systems, it can be seen, do not function in isolation but as an intergrated whole. External stimuli are recognized and sorted by the CNS, which activates the ANS and endocrine systems to change the internal environment, and the PNS is then brought in as the effector, to carry out whatever needs to be done. Alternatively, if the internal state of the body changes through anxiety or hormonal imbalance rather than the perception of external stimuli, feedback from the hormonal levels activates the CNS and ANS, and frequently the PNS as well, in either effective or ineffective actions.

In effect, we have three systems that interact:

- **Mechanical.** Skeletal and muscular processes are necessary for the expression of overt behaviour – remember that even speech is overt behaviour and requires muscle and bone movement.
- **Chemical.** The endocrine function controls hormonal chemical messengers, which are circulated in the bloodstream.
- **Neural.** The mechanisms of the nervous system are capable of complex and modifiable action. They can learn by experience and adapt to changes in the environment.

Reactions to environmental stimuli

Changes in the environment that are perceived by the individual to be relevant or important set off a chain of activity, which needs to be completed in order to restore the individual's equilibrium (see Figure 8.15).

External stimuli are recognized by the CNS, and the ANS is alerted. This prompts appropriate hormonal change to occur, which assists the nervous system in sustaining the behaviour already instigated (hormonal changes are slower to start, but as a rule, of sustained duration). If you were crossing the road and a car blew its horn at you (external stimulus), you would recognize the sound (CNS activity) and skip promptly onto the pavement (PNS activity, instructed by CNS). At the same time, your ANS has been alerted to deal with this emergency, which has brought in the

Box 8.5 The menstrual cycle and its effect on behaviour

The menstrual cycle, of approximately 28 days in the human female, encompasses a number of hormonal changes, often paralleled by behavioural changes. In some cases, the physical and behavioural effects of these changes are unpleasant, to say the least; this has been termed premenstrual syndrome (PMS). There has been some debate as to whether the syndrome exists as a physical entity or whether it is 'all in the mind', as some suggest. Who is to judge?

Menstruation is marked by the uterus shedding its lining and associated blood vessels. As mentioned above, the reproductive cycle involves a sequence of hormonal events, controlled by the pituitary. Gonadotrophic hormones, especially follicle-stimulating hormone (FSH) from the anterior pituitary, stimulate the growth of ovarian follicles, cells surrounding each ovum. The ovum or egg cells are present in every female from birth, but need to be developed before being passed into the uterus for fertilization. Usually, one is released each month; if two are released and fertilized, they will grow into dizygotic (non-identical) twins.

The maturing follicle secretes oestradiol, one of the female cycle hormones. As the level of this hormone rises to a peak, there is a rise in the secretion of luteinizing hormone (LH). This causes ovulation to occur, the ovum is released into the uterus and the follicle ruptures, becoming a corpus luteum, producing oestradiol and progesterone, both hormones which prepare the uterus for pregnancy by maintaining the lining and also prevent the ovaries producing another follicle. If the ovum is not fertilized, the production of oestradiol and progesterone ceases and the lining of the uterus is shed. The diagram shows the relative timespan of these hormonal activities.

Behavioural changes associated with these changes in hormonal levels are often a point for argument, but it is usually agreed that increased sexual activity corresponds with the 'peaks' associated with oestradiol and LH, while high progesterone levels, which would normally be maintained throughout pregnancy, indicate a slowing of generally active behaviour.

In addition to these fluctuating behaviour patterns, a number of women complain of increased fluid retention in PMS, giving a 'bloated' feeling at the progesterone peak and for some days into menstruation. It has been suggested by some studies (reviewed by Floody, 1983) that aggressive behaviours are more likely to occur shortly before the onset of menstruation. Others suggest that imbalance of progesterone/oestradiol is marked by aggressive or antisocial behaviours, such as shoplifting. Restoration of the hormonal balance by the administration of one or other of the hormones, usually progesterone, has had excellent results in changing behaviour. If hormonal imbalance is at the basis of PMS, it is understandable why only some, and not all, women suffer from it, and some for only part of their reproductive lives. As a syndrome, it should not be rejected out of hand, especially by those who have never experienced it. It can be as real, as complex and as distressing as male impotence.

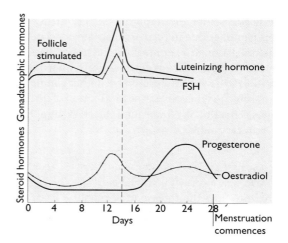

Relative amounts of sex hormones in the bloodstream throughout a 28-day menstrual cycle

endocrine system; adrenaline is released into your bloodstream, which takes a little while to circulate. This explains why, after you are safely on the pavement, your heart starts thumping and your knees feel like jelly (hormonal change)!

Reactions to internal changes

Changes in the internal environment of the body may be brought about for a variety of reasons: changes in emotional state, malfunction due to illness or cyclical

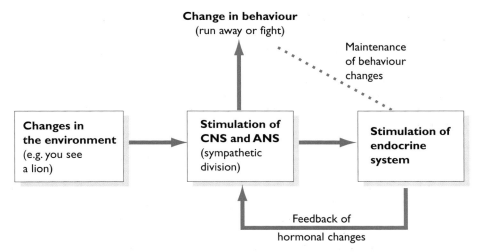

Figure 8.15 Reactions of the nervous and endocrine systems to enviromental stimuli

changes. An example of a cyclical occurrence is menstruation (see Box 8.5).

1. (a) List the hormones produced by the anterior pituitary.
   (b) Which further hormones are prompted by each of these?

2. What behaviour changes are attributable to these hormones?
3. How does the activity of the endocrine system integrate with that of the nervous system?

Chapter summary

- The basic unit of the nervous system is a neuron, which sends impulses along axons, through terminal buttons at the synapse, to the dendrites of other axons.

- Messages are conveyed along axons by an electro-chemical process. The rate of firing conveys further information.

- Sensory neurons convey information to and from the senses, motor neurons to and from the skeletal system.

- Connector neurons are located mainly in the brain, with some in the spinal cord. Connectionist models attempt to explain how the neurons in the brain are interconnected in activity-related groups, which may represent human learning patterns.

- The brain is the organ that controls the human organism. It integrates and makes sense of input, makes decisions, remembers what is important and instructs the body to carry out response behaviours.

- The spinal cord carries the major nerve fibres between the body and the brain, and can implement reflex activity without conscious intervention.

- Together, the brain and spinal cord constitute the CNS. If damaged, it does not regenerate. Neurons that die are not replaced, but we start out with so many that we never run out of them.

- Neurotransmitters act at the synapse and are the CNS 'failsafe' system, to ensure that only genuine messages are passed onwards. Not all neurotransmitters are diffused throughout the brain, but each of them is usually specific to an area or circuit.

- Mood is influenced by the activity of specific neurotransmitters, through the areas of the brain where they are generated, to the areas of the brain to which they send projections.

- Neuromodulators are chemicals which circulate more widely through the nervous system, moderating the activity of neurotransmitters, usually through adjacent receptor sites.

- Pheromones are chemicals which are exuded by the body to give out signals. In humans, these may convey information about the sex and identity of the individual, but do not seem to have such an important role as in other animals.

- Psychoactive drugs generally exert their influence at the synapse, by either imitating or blocking the action of a specific neurotransmitter (see Figure 8.11). Mood changes may be brought about in this way. Many psychoactive drugs are addictive, and some also depress the body's own natural production of chemicals.

- The ANS mobilizes and integrates the body's physiological responses to changes of situation and mood, without the individual's conscious intervention.

- There are strong links with the CNS and the endocrine system.

- The two divisions of the ANS both exert an influence on the same areas of the body, but these two systems do not take action at the same time. The sympathetic division mobilizes the body's energetic responses, while the parasympathetic division controls the conserving mode of the body.

- The activity of most endocrine glands is prompted by hormones from the pituitary gland, which is itself under the control of the hypothalamus, a subcortical brain structure.

- Hormones secreted by the endocrine glands are as essential as the nervous system in integrating human activity; harmonious interaction of neural, chemical and skeletal systems is important for coherent, balanced activity.

- While nerve impulses can travel through the body in a fraction of a second, hormones are much slower to reach their target site, requiring seconds if not minutes. However, the action of hormones is sustained for as long as the chemicals continue to circulate in the body.

Further reading

Shepherd, G.M. (1988). *Neurobiology.* Oxford: Oxford University Press. An in-depth account of the biology of the brain and the nervous system.

Carlson, N.R. (1991). *Physiology of Behaviour.* Boston, Mass.: Allyn & Bacon. A detailed textbook on all aspects of human physiology and its relationship to behaviour.

CHAPTER 9

Motivation and emotion

Homeostatic motivation   187
- Motivation for eating   188
- Eating disorders   190
- Other views of homeostasis   192

Nonhomeostatic motivation   193
- Arousal theory   193
- Sexual behaviour   193
- Self-stimulation of the brain   194

What is emotion?   195
- Recognizing emotions   196

Physiological aspects of emotion   197
Theories and studies of emotion   198
- James–Lange theory   198
- Cannon–Bard theory   199
- Schachter and Singer's two-factor theory   199
- Lazarus's cognitive theory   199
- Arousal theory and emotion   201
- Social theories of emotion   201

Objectives

By the end of this chapter, you should be able to:

- Distinguish between examples of homeostatic and nonhomeostatic motivation;

- Understand the physiological basis of emotion, and the psychological recognition of emotions in the self and others;

- Compare and contrast a number of theories of emotion.

Motivation is an issue at the heart of psychology: why do people behave as they do? Why does behaviour take one form and not another? And what makes people behave differently from – or similarly to – each other?

In this chapter, we have linked motivation and emotion, as these two phenomena are often linked in real life. If you feel great fear (emotion), you are motivated to run away – although you may stay and fight instead; the resulting behaviours are not always what would be predicted from either the extent of the emotion or the situation. This is what makes the study of motivation and emotion so complex and interesting.

Atkinson et al. (1993) suggest that, while motives are internally caused, emotion is a response to an external stimulus. In this chapter, we will examine both motivation and emotion; see if you agree with their assertion at the end.

Homeostatic motivation

Homeostasis is a term that was first used by the physiologist Cannon in the 1920s, to describe the process through which the body's balanced state is maintained (see Figure 9.1). Homeostasis has been recognized as one factor in the motivation of human behaviour.

Most homeostatic mechanisms are controlled automatically, by the ANS and the endocrine system

> **GLOSSARY**
>
> **Homeostasis** The process by which the body maintains a balanced state through the regulation of, for example, blood pressure, temperature, heart rate, chemical balance, digestion, respiration.

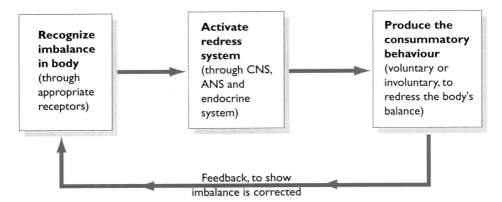

Figure 9.1 Diagrammatic representation of homeostasis

(described in the previous chapter), and the hypothalamus, which is the structure in the CNS linking the autonomic and endocrine systems. Blood pressure, heart rate, temperature, chemical balance inside and outside the body's cells, levels of oxygen and carbon dioxide in the blood, digestion, respiration and hormonal balance – all these are regulated without conscious effort on the part of the individual. Sensations of hunger or thirst are produced autonomically and raised to our conscious awareness; the final act of eating or drinking is due to a conscious decision; that is to say, the motivation arises homeostatically (involuntarily) but the resulting consumatory behaviour is voluntary. The motivation of eating behaviour is a complex and interesting area of study, and one which also demonstrates that homeostatic mechanisms are not the whole answer to why people behave as they do.

Motivation for eating

How do you know that you are hungry? What is your subjective experience that motivates you to seek out food? You may have an 'empty' feeling in the upper abdomen, stomach rumbling noises, feelings of weakness or even a headache, or a combination of factors. Physiologists have found that there are several factors that signal and cause an animal to find food.

The immediate signal

The first signal may be the absence of food in the stomach. Cannon and Washburn (1912) investigated this probability; Washburn swallowed a balloon that could be inflated within his stomach, and the

researchers found that the contractions of the stomach coincided with reported feelings of hunger. When the balloon was inflated, the contractions no longer took place.

Neural factors

Since many ANS functions are controlled from the hypothalamus in the brain, it seemed reasonable to search for some type of 'control centre' there. Hetherington and Ransom (1942) and Anand and Brobeck (1951) claimed to have identified areas of the hypothalamus that promoted feeding behaviour (in the lateral hypothalamus area, LHA) and an adjacent satiation centre (in the ventromedial hypothalamus, VMH), which cuts off feeding behaviour when the individual is sated. Certainly, the hypothalamus is involved in feeding behaviour, but it is not the sole area of control.

Set point theory

Identification of the influence of these two areas of the hypothalamus brought forward the suggestion that a balance obtained between the two would result in an individual's body weight set point. **Set point theory** suggests that individuals will eat to maintain their own body weight. This seemed like a useful explanation for why slimmers succeed for only a while and then go

Box 9.1   Glucose receptors

How does the body monitor its glucose levels? In the blood vessels, the brain (hypothalamus) and other organs of the body are glucose receptors, neurons that detect the amount of glucose present in the body. If the level drops and no food is available, more glucose is released from the liver, which is the body's storehouse for glycogen (the storable form of glucose).

Investigations have shown that glucose receptors in the hypothalamus are not the primary and most important signal for low glucose levels and initiating feeding. Even when the hypothalamus is damaged, feeding behaviour follows a regular pattern.

Russek (1971) demonstrated the importance of the glucose receptors in the liver. He injected glucose into the hepatic portal vein of a dog (a vein that carries blood from the intestines to the liver). This injection caused the dog to stop eating and induced long-term satiety, whereas a similar injection into the jugular vein, in the neck, carrying glucose around the body, had little effect on eating behaviour.

There appears to be an interactional effect between hepatic and hypothalamic receptors. Shimizu et al. (1983) found that the response firing rate of detectors in the hypothalamus was reduced when glucose was injected close to the liver. This would seem to suggest a linkage between the two systems; in the absence of one, hunger can be evoked by the other.

---

back to their previous weight. Set point theory has been demonstrated experimentally with rats (for example, Keesey and Powley, 1975), but other factors may also intervene with humans. In addition, set point theory does not explain why people should, for example, gain weight in middle age. According to the theory, they would be modifying their calorie intake to allow for a more sedentary lifestyle. Eating behaviour is not wholly physiological in humans; abnormal eating patterns such as are found in obesity and anorexia will be discussed later.

The glucostatic hypothesis

The **glucostatic theory** is based on the hypothesis that as glucose is the body's fuel, carried in the bloodstream, it is likely that levels of glucose relate to feelings of hunger. Louis-Sylvestre and Le Magnen (1980) monitored a rat's blood glucose levels and found that six minutes before the start of a meal, the glucose levels fell by 6–8 per cent. A few minutes into the meal the blood glucose levels rose. Another meal was not taken until levels dropped again. Campfield et al. (1985) found that if they injected a small amount of glucose into the rat, the meal was postponed by the animal, as if the hunger signal was removed. We can relate this to human behaviour: if you feel hungry and eat a chocolate bar (containing sugar, which needs little transformation to glucose), you may find that you no longer feel hungry, and may then choose to delay or miss a meal. Bellisle et al. (1984) found that people who

skip breakfast have lower blood glucose levels at lunchtime, and consequently tend to eat more lunch. (See Box 9.1 for a consideration of how the body may monitor its glucose levels.)

Social and environmental factors

Certainly for humans, meals, from grand banquets to having a sandwich at lunchtime with a friend, are often social occasions. We also tend to eat more at a meal when in company. De Castro and de Castro (1989) asked subjects to keep a food diary for seven days, not only of what they ate, but also of with whom they ate it. Subsequent analysis showed that when in company, subjects ate more. In addition, they also found that, although people stated that they would usually eat one large meal and one small meal per day, this rule no longer held; meal sizes related only to company rather than to the size of the previous meal.

Incentives to eat

The sight or smell of attractive food is also an incentive for humans to eat. Salivary glands are stimulated by the sight – or even the thought – of attractive food. A dish of strawberries or an attractive cake might encourage many people to eat, although they had not previously felt hungry.

Routine

Humans are also 'trained' to expect to eat meals at regular times. If you are absorbed in a task, you may not feel hungry. On catching sight of the clock, you may realize it is past your regular mealtime and hurry to get something to eat. Expectancy plays a role in human feeding behaviour.

Flavours

Sweet flavours, as shown in Chapter 7, are recognized by the tongue as pleasant and palatable. Brala and Hagen (1983) demonstrated that sweet flavours actually make subjects feel hungrier and can encourage further intake of food.

Humans thrive on a varied and wide-ranging diet, unlike some animals, for example koalas, who eat only eucalyptus leaves. If we ate only one food constantly, we would certainly become tired of it. Rolls et al. (1981) found that people would eat a larger meal if they were offered four different types of sandwich filling.

Eating disorders

These include obesity, anorexia nervosa and bulimia. The causes and treatments of these problems are still being investigated.

Koala bears eat only eucalyptus leaves, unlike humans, who thrive on a varied and wide-ranging diet

Obesity

There are certainly many different causes of obesity. Genetic or acquired physiological problems, faulty learning about eating behaviour, and psychological problems such as stress are all blamed.

Physiological problems The hereditary basis to obesity was investigated by Stunkard et al. (1986), who found that the bodyweight of people who had been adopted was correlated with that of their biological parents but not of their adoptive parents. Other similar studies support the probability of a genetic factor in obesity.

Individuals vary in the efficiency of their **metabolism**. People with an efficient metabolism will gain weight on the same dietary intake as others with a less efficient metabolism, who may lose weight (Rodin et al., 1989).

Dieting may in fact be detrimental to weight control in obese people. During the diet, weight is lost and the metabolism becomes more efficient, as a reaction to 'lean times'. Once the diet is stopped, the increased efficiency of the metabolism will produce an increase in weight, rather than a maintenance of the newer, slimmer person. No one has yet identified why some people have a more efficient metabolism than others.

Psychological problems A range of psychological variables has been suggested as causing obesity:

- Lack of oral gratification;
- Food as a substitute for affection;
- Lack of impulse control;
- Stress and/or depression.

Lack of oral gratification in infancy refers to Freudian theory, in which Freud suggested that lack of sucking time at the breast or bottle during the first stage of development led to a need in adulthood to seek oral gratification (see Chapter 30). Overeating could be regarded as an excessive psychological drive to put food in the mouth; however, some obese people consume no more food than others of normal body weight. In the same way, eating too fast is regarded as another possible indicator of lack of oral gratification in infancy. However, it is only a minority of obese people who eat too fast, as do some normal-weight people, so this can hardly be regarded as a major cause of obesity.

Food as a substitute for affection is again a very intangible suggestion and one that is difficult to research. This idea may be approached in two ways:

- A parent feels unable to give a child affection, for whatever reason, and gives gifts of food (sweets, biscuits, cakes) whenever the child appears to crave affection. Consequently, the child learns to respond to internal feelings of affection (motivation towards love) by eating.
- A child or adult feels unable to give or receive love from others, and feels that he or she must love him or herself; food is the expression of affection.

Both of these eventualities may have a circular effect, in that once people have put on weight, they see themselves as unlovable by others and food as the self-consolation. Overweight adults were often overweight as children.

Both of these positions have proved difficult to research, as they would necessarily involve introspection. This is a technique regarded as open to bias by the individual who is examining innermost thoughts and needs. Lack of appropriate methods are available for the measurement of intangible elements, such as the need for affection. How do you measure 'enough affection'?

Lack of impulse control refers to a person's inability to control the desire to eat. It suggests that personality characteristics may be responsible for obesity. Lack of impulse control may be a general characteristic, applied to any behaviour, or specifically with regard to food consumption. This may be the case in overweight people, who see something they would like and eat it, with no regard for consequential weight gain.

This suggestion would seem to concur with physiological studies which suggest that people will eat more when attractive food is available. If this coincides with a personality deficiency of lack of control, the result may be obesity. However, this does not explain why the 'lack of control' is a characteristic present in some but not others, and why it should be specifically directed at food in some people.

People suffering from stress and/or depression may react by eating more than usual, especially sweet foods

(comfort foods, as they have been called). This may have the effect of making the individual put on weight. It has also been suggested that, while depressed, people may cease to care about their appearance, and therefore do not aim to maintain a pleasing body outline – whether this is a conscious decision or not has yet to be demonstrated.

Conversely, many stressed or depressed people in fact lose weight, having little interest in food as a substitute or even as a means of self-maintenance. Others may not find their appetite or body weight affected at all.

Rodin and her colleagues (1989) reviewed the literature on some of the causes of obesity suggested above and found very little empirical support for any of them. In fact, unhappiness and depression seemed more likely to be the effects rather than the causes of obesity.

Obesity, like the motivation for eating, appears to be multifactorial. A number of physiological or psychological factors may be involved, in any combination, for any one individual. The process of identifying these could be extremely time-consuming and probably tedious for the individual concerned. This is why obesity is very difficult to treat successfully.

Anorexia nervosa

Anorexia nervosa is a life-threatening problem, predominantly Western-world based and mainly affecting adolescents; it is 20 times more common in girls than boys. The individual refuses to eat or eats only minimal amounts, resulting in extreme weight loss. Possible causes put forward include those that are:

- social,
- cultural,
- emotional, and
- physiological.

Box 9.2 discusses some possible causes of anorexia nervosa.

Treatments for anorexia Current treatments for anorexia include social, emotional and physiological

> **GLOSSARY**
>
> **Anorexia nervosa** An eating disorder mainly affecting adolescents. The individual, fearing obesity, refuses to eat or eats only small amounts, resulting in extreme weight loss.

Box 9.2 Anorexia nervosa – some possible causes

Social causes

Learning theorists suggest the sufferers are trying to emulate the slim models so valued by Western society. In order to look like a model, the young girl refuses to eat in order to lose weight, but fails to recognize when her body outline has gone beyond slim, to gaunt.

Family conflict has also been suggested as a cause. Adolescence, it has been suggested, is often a time of rebellion against parental values or control. The anorexic adolescent may feel unable to rebel openly, but the refusal of food takes the place of rebellion. Alternatively, other members of the family may be in conflict, parents with each other or other siblings. If this conflict cannot be brought out into the open and resolved, the conflict is deflected on to the sufferer's 'disease'. The family is often a family of 'achievers', and it has been suggested that the anorexic individual may feel inadequate.

Cultural causes

Certainly most anorexics have a distorted body image; they see themselves as 'fat', while seeing others of the same dimensions as 'thin'. Body image is culturally defined. Some cultures expect women to be fatter than other cultures' expectations. Even within Europe, there are cultural variations.

Emotional causes

Psychoanalytic theorists suggest that the sufferer equates food with sexual love, and refusal of food is a rejection of sexuality. The desire to retain a small body may be the expression of the wish to remain a child. In severe cases of anorexia, menstruation ceases, which supports the wish to revert to childhood and deny sexuality.

Anorexics are not uninterested in food. Some spend a great deal of time collecting recipes and cooking meals for others but will then not partake, saying they are 'not hungry'.

Physiological correlates

As a result of severe weight loss in females, menstruation ceases, and the stored ova may be damaged, depleted or reabsorbed. Osteoporosis (a condition in which the bones become brittle) and subsequent bone fractures are common.

Artmann et al. (1985) reported that CT scans of anorexic patients revealed changes in the brain: widened sulci and enlarged ventricles. Suggestions that anorexia may be caused by structural or biochemical abnormalities in the brain mechanisms controlling metabolism or eating behaviour have been investigated by researchers. A literature review by Fava et al. (1989) evidenced changes in levels of norepinephrine, serotonin and opioids, but whether these are the cause or the result of anorexia has not been demonstrated.

A study by Broberg and Bernstein (1989) showed that, when presented with warm, appetizing food (visual and olfactory stimulation), anorexic subjects produced more insulin in their bloodstream than did thin, nonanorexic subjects (the control group). Even so, the control group ate the food, while the anorexics did not, saying that they were not hungry. Learning theorists would suggest they find the symptoms of hunger reinforcing.

---

treatments, but reports of success are not much more than 50 per cent (for example, Patton, 1989). Some anorexics have to be hospitalized and fed intravenously. Even with treatment, approximately one in 30 dies.

Bulimia nervosa

Bulimia nervosa involves the rejection of food followed by 'binges', during which the individual gorges, frequently on a particular type of food. This is usually followed by feelings of guilt, self-induced vomiting and the use of laxatives.

Sufferers from bulimia seldom lose as much weight, and rarely to such life-threatening proportions, as do anorexics. However, they often have an equal fear of obesity. The continual vomiting may have physiological consequences such as intestinal damage and nutritional deficiencies.

Other views of homeostasis

Many variations on the basic model of homeostasis have been produced; these attempt to explain not only

---

GLOSSARY

Bulimia nervosa An eating disorder where the individual fears obesity and consequently 'binges' on certain foods and then induces vomiting or uses laxatives.

the mechanisms instigating behaviour, but also why the behaviour ceases. For example, a hungry animal will stop eating before the ingested food has been digested, raising blood glucose levels to 'full'. The basic model of homeostasis failed to explain why this occurs. In addition, the homeostatic model fails to explain the phenomenon of feedforward, observed by McFarland (1971). An animal will drink extra in anticipation of thirst, or eat more than usual in anticipation of a 'hungry' period. Simple cause-and-effect mechanisms are inadequate explanations for such motivated behaviour.

? SELF-ASSESSMENT QUESTIONS

1. (a) What is meant by the term 'homeostasic motivation'? (b) Explain briefly how the body's internal systems are involved.
2. Describe the processes involved in one type of homeostatic behaviour.
3. Describe what happens when the system fails to operate (a) in motivating eating behaviour, and (b) in cutting off the eating behaviour.

Okay, okay — I say "Lack of non-homeostatic motivation"— you say "Lazy" ...

Nonhomeostatic motivation

Homeostatic motivation can provide some explanation for life-sustaining behaviour. The same explanation does not hold for other motivated behaviours. These include:

■ play,
■ sexual behaviour,
■ curiosity (see Box 9.3),
■ gambling,
■ addiction, and
■ risk-taking.

Some of these can be seen as life-threatening rather than life-maintaining. Neural factors, hormonal factors and physiological mechanisms that feature in homeostatic motivation may contribute to these other forms of motivation, but not in the same way.

Arousal theory

Arousal has been defined as a 'state of mental readiness for activity'. Arousal is mediated in the CNS through the reticular formation (see Chapters 8 and 12). Low arousal may be manifest by a drowsy or bored state, indicating a low level of activity in the reticular formation and the areas of the cortex to which it projects. High arousal states, excitement, panic or hysteria, are the behavioural equivalents of high neural arousal. Arousal is nonspecific and can be assumed to apply to many forms of motivation.

Arousal theory suggests that animals, including humans, are constantly seeking an optimum level of arousal. An animal that is constantly seeking food is unlikely to exhibit curiosity, because its arousal level is already fulfilled. Given that there is no homeostatic value in curiosity, is it simply a behaviour that occurs in a vacuum, to fill time? In humans, this is not always so; people sometimes become so involved in an activity that they forget to eat. This would seem to contradict a well-known theory of motivation proposed by Maslow (1970), that needs occur in a hierachy; basic needs have to be satisfied first before higher, less tangible needs can be fulfilled (see Figure 1.3 in Chapter 1). This is not borne out by the fact that people will go on hunger strike, or even die, to support a principle.

Sexual behaviour

Whether sexual behaviour should be regarded as homeostatic or nonhomeostatic in humans is debatable. Some people lead entirely celibate lives, so

> ### Box 9.3 Motivation, curiosity and exploration
>
> Many animals exhibit the motivation to explore their surroundings even when they are not pursuing specific goals such as food, drink or escape. Some also exhibit what can only be described as curiosity, for example watching others of the same or different species, or investigating objects which have no relevance to them (for example, having no odours that might indicate food). People, too, demonstrate curiosity, in varying degrees.
>
> Blanchard et al. (1976) demonstrated that rats who were placed in a strange maze would explore it thoroughly, even if there were no rewards offered. This could be regarded as potentially life-preserving behaviour, since if a threat was presented, the rats would know which way to run for escape.
>
> Less obvious is the motivation of the monkeys observed by Harlow et al. (1950). They would solve puzzles and perform difficult tasks solely for the reward of watching other monkeys through a window. As far as one can tell, there was no intrinsic benefit to the watchers; they did not learn life-saving behaviours from those whom they watched. The reason may have been to provide neural stimulation. As suggested earlier, a state of inactivity is not the brain's ideal state; monkeys in captivity may lack neural stimulation, and this may have been the motivation for their actions.
>
> People, too, like to explore their environment, even when to do so is potentially life-threatening, as in the case of mountain-climbing or space exploration. It does not appeal to all people equally, however. According to homeostatically derived theories, if you have never climbed Everest, you should be desperate to rush off and do so! Clearly, neural stimulation is not the only motivation here. Suggestions are that certain personality traits, such as sensation seeking or a need for achievement, may influence motivation, but these do not explain why one specific activity rather than another is chosen. Curiosity and exploration have no simple explanation.

sexual activity can be viewed as not essential to the maintenance of the individual, although necessary for the species. Sociobiologists would argue that the individual should be motivated to pass on his or her genes, but obviously this motivation does not apply to all people.

Hormonal factors are of obvious importance in motivating sexual behaviours. A rise in the levels of the sex hormones, **androgens** in males and **oestrogen** and **progesterone** in females, occurs during adolescence, and is matched by an increase in sexually oriented behaviour.

Neural factors also play a role in mediating sexual behaviour. In males, the **medial preoptic area** of the brain, just below the hypothalamus, has been shown to be important (Sachs and Meisel, 1988). This region has a high number of androgen receptors. In females, this area has a high level of oestrogen receptors, but this is linked far more to the motivation of maternal behaviour than to sexual behaviour (Numan, 1974). After giving birth, oestrogen levels rise and progesterone levels fall. The critical area for female sexual behaviour is the **ventromedial hypothalamus**, which contains receptors for both oestrogen and progesterone. Both males and females circulate some hormones of the opposite sex, but have fewer receptor sites available for them, so their effect is less marked.

Self-stimulation of the brain

Olds and Milner (1954) implanted an electrode into a rat's brain in the medial forebrain bundle area of the hypothalamus. By pressing a lever, the animal could send a mildly stimulating electric current through this area. The animals seemed to enjoy doing this, to the extent that food and sexually receptive females were ignored. Their motivation for performing this activity was not identifiable, except to say that it seemed to give

> ### GLOSSARY
>
> **Androgens** Male sex hormones.
>
> **Oestrogen** A female sex hormone.
>
> **Progesterone** A female sex hormone.
>
> **Medial preoptic area** An area of the brain just below the hypothalamus, which has been shown to be implicated in male sexual behaviour.
>
> **Ventromedial hypothalamus** An area of the brain which contains receptors for female hormones and which is implicated in female sexual behaviour.

Box 9.4   Addiction

Administration of amphetamines and cocaine enhances the action of the neurotransmitter dopamine, producing an excitatory effect. The effects of opiates and alcohol are both excitatory and inhibitory. It is thought by most researchers that the excitatory effects are those which give rise to addiction, through reinforcement by the chemical processes.

For addicts, the long-term dangers of addiction are ignored in favour of the short-term pleasure. However, in addition to the physical addiction, there is the process of psychological dependence, which is prompted by the wish to be removed from a painful situation. (A full discussion of addiction is outside the scope of this book.)

There does not seem to be a direct biochemical cause for an addiction to gambling, but it is probable that its devotees achieve a neurochemical 'high' through previous experience of winning. The irresponsible activities of some share dealers have been likened to gambling addiction, the only difference being that they are using other people's money.

Researchers have shown that genetic processes are also involved in addiction; not everyone stands an equal chance of becoming addicted to everything (Cloninger, 1987).

Consequences of addiction

Drug addiction causes a high rate of damage to the human species. Alcohol produces liver damage and cirrhosis, cerebral haemorrhage and brain damage (Korsakoff's syndrome), foetal alcohol syndrome in the babies of alcoholic mothers, and damage to innocent victims of car accidents caused through drunkenness. Cocaine and other 'illegal' drugs often cause psychosis, brain damage (especially when contaminated as 'designer drugs') and death from overdose; addicts who inject and share needles run the risk of HIV; babies may be born with brain damage and subsequent physiological and psychological problems; and a great deal of crime has been identified as emanating from the provision and acquisition of these types of drug. Smoking greatly increases the chances of lung cancer, heart disease and stroke; women who smoke often give birth to smaller babies. Those addicted to gambling run the risk of financial ruin and its associated loss of status, friends and family. The results of addiction can be far-reaching.

them pleasure; consequently this area was termed the 'pleasure centre'. However, its exact purpose is undefined, but coming as it does within the dopamine circuit, it is thought to be involved with the reinforcement of activities (see Addiction in Box 9.4).

? SELF-ASSESSMENT QUESTIONS

1. What is meant by nonhomeostatic motivation?
2. Describe and discuss an example of this type of motivation.
3. What does arousal theory contribute to our understanding of nonhomeostatic motivation?

What is emotion?

Tell me, where is fancy bred? Or in the heart or in the head? How begot, how nourished?
(Shakespeare, *The Merchant of Venice*, Act III, Scene 2)

By the sixteenth century, one of our greatest playwrights and a keen student of human behaviour was asking about the development, manifestation and expression of human emotions. Early philosophers who tried to represent people as rational beings came across the phenomenon of emotion, in which rationality tends to fly out of the window.

According to Darwin (1872), we should not consider ourselves the only species that has emotions. Animals, too, present fear, rage, and possibly something even akin to love: consider swans who mate for life and mourn despondently at the loss of a mate. Darwin in fact suggested that there are specific, fundamental emotions that find expression in each individual. The exploration of the mechanisms of these emotions and their expression has kept psychologists occupied for many years.

There are a number of components in emotion:

1. The perception of the emotion-arousing stimulus (*For example, an armed robber enters the bank where you are waiting to be served*).

2. Subjective feeling or experience of emotion (pleasant/unpleasant) (*In most people, fear*).
3. Involuntary physiological changes of the body's internal balance (arousal/depression) (*Arousal*).
4. External bodily changes (facial/posture) (*Face shows fear, body freezes or steps back*).
5. Cognitive factors; awareness of situation, previous experience, memory (*Have seen this on television; people may get killed*).
6. Voluntary behavioural consequences; a response to the stimulus (*Do as the robber says, he has the gun!*).

While it is usually agreed that 1 comes first and 6 comes last of the above components, the order of 2 to 5, or their relative importance, is still a matter for discussion and theory, as we shall see in the next section.

Smiling may actually make us feel happier

Recognizing emotions

It has been suggested that we first 'name' emotions to ourselves by observing them in others. But how accurate are we in observing emotions in others? Certainly, there seem to be emotional experiences that have universally recognizable facial expressions, as cross-cultural studies have shown (Morris, 1982).

Ekman (1982) suggested there are six primary emotions: sadness, happiness, fear, disgust, anger and surprise. To this list, another researcher (Plutchik, 1980) added acceptance and expectancy. Other researchers have identified 11 or more, which raises the question 'What do we mean by primary emotions?' Can we determine this by finding out how good we are at recognizing emotions in others?

An interesting experiment was carried out by Laird (1974), which demonstrated that observers had some difficulty identifying the emotion portrayed on still photographs, although they were more accurate in identifying the posed emotion portrayed in photographs of actors. Presumably, we all have expectations of how emotions will be portrayed (which is why actors are successful here), but as humans we do not always show exactly the facial expression others would expect of us.

Feedback from facial muscles (facial feedback hypothesis)

Not only do the facial muscles expressing emotion provide feedback to the brain indicating what they are

doing ('I am smiling'), but this also enhances the mood that is being experienced. This **facial feedback hypothesis** was demonstrated experimentally by Ekman et al. (1983), who told participants he was measuring facial muscle movement and asked them to arrange their facial muscles in particular ways and hold these for ten seconds. The resulting expressions corresponded to basic emotions such as anger, disgust, happiness and fear, although the subjects were not expressly told that they were portraying emotional states.

It was found that when participants were portraying happiness and disgust, their heart rates slowed; for anger and fear, heart rates were accelerated. This would seem to suggest that feedback from facial muscles can affect autonomic arousal. In fact, these effects were stronger than when the same participants were overtly asked to 'feel' these emotions.

Neural mechanisms for the recognition of facial expressions

Facial expressions are very important to humans as a species (and other primates, too). Not only is it important for us to recognize the faces of people we

---

GLOSSARY

Facial feedback hypothesis A proposal that we recognize emotions through feedback from the facial muscles: for example, smiling will promote feelings of happiness.

know, but also their facial expressions tell us what sort of mood they are in.

Face-sensitive neurons have been identified in the inferior cortex of the temporal lobe (see Figure 9.2), in the visual association area, which is next to the visual cortex (described in Chapter 8). Baylis et al. (1985) found that most of these neurons are sensitive to recognizing differences between faces. This sensitivity would suggest why you may well recognize someone's face but cannot remember their name.

Rolls et al. (1989) suggested that while this area has neurons predisposed to respond to faces, they learn to respond to a specific face and then respond differently if a new face is presented. This learning process may well be similar to that modelled by the neural networks that were described in Chapter 8.

However, the ability to recognize emotions in other people's faces may be mediated by a different area of the brain. Bruyer et al. (1983) found that a person with **prosopagnosis**, who cannot recognize faces, can still recognize and name emotions in faces. Evidence from patients with stroke or accidental brain damage suggests that the right hemisphere seems to recognize emotions more easily (Etcoff, 1985). Fried et al. (1982) found that stimulation of the middle temporal gyrus disrupted the recognition of emotions.

Recognition of emotions in others is also mediated by voice patterns, especially pitch, timing and accentuation. A rise in pitch, for example, indicates fear or alarm; this seems to be a universal signal, whereas others may be culturally based. Evidence from damaged individuals again implicated the right hemisphere as being more involved than the left (Ley and Bryden, 1982).

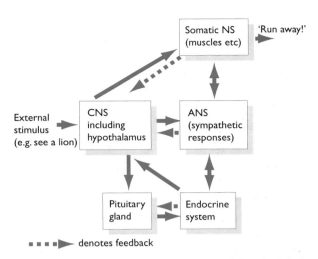

Figure 9.3 Diagrammatic representation of the physiological processes of emotion

Physiological aspects of emotion

When we are experiencing emotion, a number of internal changes take place, which are mainly involuntary. Observation of the emotion-arousing stimulus produces activity in the cortex; subcortical structures, in particular the hypothalamus, are also 'notified'. This prompts the sympathetic section of the ANS (the activity division) into action, accelerating heart rate, increasing blood pressure, dilating pupils and all the other involuntary responses necessary for increased activity (you may wish to refresh your memory by referring to Figure 8.12, Actions of the ANS on organs of the body). The decision-making processes of the cortex decide on a suitable course of action, which is implemented by the body. Feedback from the results of this restore the body's processes to baseline (see Figure 9.3). In addition, the hypothalamus sends nervous impulses to the pituitary gland, which brings the endocrine system into play. The adrenal glands release adrenaline, which maintains the increased heart rate, thereby assisting the body's activity. Saliva production is not needed during strong emotion, as eating and digestion will not be taking place at the same time, and insulin production and release will be slowed.

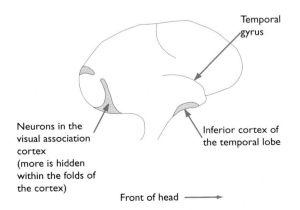

Figure 9.2 Neural mechanisms for facial recognition

GLOSSARY

Prosopagnosis A state in which an individual cannot recognize faces, usually because of brain damage.

Strong emotions, such as fear, anger or extreme grief, arouse sympathetic responses in the ANS. Quieter emotions, such as contentment and sadness, are thought to activate the parasympathetic division of the ANS.

1. How do we recognize emotions in ourselves or others?
2. How is recognition aided by neural mechanisms?
3. What are the physiological responses associated with strong emotions?

Theories and studies of emotion

At the outset of this chapter, a number of events were identified which occur during emotion. Experimental work by psychologists and physiologists has tried to identify the order of these events and what changes are associated with each event. In turn, this has given rise to a number of different theories of emotion, none of which yet seems to answer all the questions posed.

One question asks whether the feeling of emotion precedes or follows the expression of emotion. Another question is, exactly how do bodily responses vary between different emotions, or is there simply a continuum of arousal? We will look at a number of theories to see how these questions can be addressed.

James–Lange theory

At the end of the nineteenth century, the American psychologist William James and the Danish physiologist Carol Lange were both investigating the processes involved in emotion, although working separately. Both came to the same conclusion, which is why the theory became known as the James–Lange theory. They suggested that bodily changes produce the feelings of emotion (see Figure 9.4); you run away from the lion, which then promotes the feelings and recognition of fear. This seems the opposite to the common-sense point of view.

This theory, it must be remembered, was proposed while investigations into the transmission of nerve impulses was in its infancy. James and Lange were looking at subjective experiences and trying to reconcile them with the known physiology of the time. For example, if you are crossing the road, and a car comes along unexpectedly, blowing its horn at you, you skip quickly on to the pavement. A second or so later, you realize that your heart is pounding and your knees feel shaky, yet you are now out of danger.

James and Lange were interpreting this type of phenomenon by saying that the physical action (of running out of the way) had promoted the feeling of fear (we all recognize a pounding heart and wobbly knees as the concomitants of strong emotion). With the knowledge that you now have, you will realize that the heart goes on pounding for some seconds longer because of the adrenaline released by the endocrine system, our slower-acting back-up system.

By the 1920s, physiologists such as Walter Cannon were pointing out weaknesses in the theory:

■ People who have paralysis of the limbs and cannot take physical action still feel emotion, so the actions cannot be the cause of the feelings of emotion.
■ Sympathetic changes in the ANS are relatively slow to occur, while emotional experience is not, so physiological changes cannot be causing the feelings of an emotion.
■ Many of the same physiological changes occur in a number of different emotional states. This cannot be the only means of telling the individual which emotion is being experienced.

An interesting investigation was carried out by Hohmann (1962). Twenty-five adult males who had suffered spinal cord damage and were at least paraplegic as a result were asked about changes in emotional feelings and experiences. They reported significantly reduced emotional experiences, especially with regard to anger, fear and sexual feelings. This would seem to demonstrate that feedback from the peripheral nervous system may be necessary for the

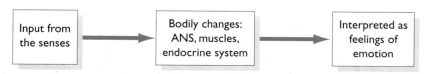

Figure 9.4 The James–Lange theory of emotion

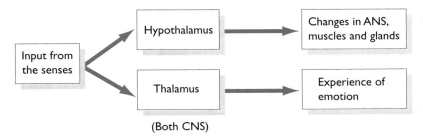

Figure 9.5 The Cannon–Bard theory of emotion

full experience of an emotion, although not, as James and Lange suggested, being the primary root-cause.

Cannon–Bard theory

Cannon (1927) and a colleague, Bard, suggested a 'central' theory of emotion, called 'central' because emphasis was laid on the involvement of the central nervous system. Cannon suggested that the feeling of emotion and preparing the body for action occurred at the same time, but independently (see Figure 9.5). In addition, he proposed that the thalamus was responsible for emotional experience and the hypothalamus for the expression of emotion.

Subsequent investigations have confirmed the involvement of the hypothalamus in emotion. It sends instructions to the ANS and also the pituitary gland, which controls the endocrine system, both of which are fundamental to physiological changes during emotion. However:

- little physiological evidence has been found for the involvement of the thalamus; and
- other investigators (for example, Schachter, 1964) have also questioned the likelihood of two such processes occurring at the same time but without any linkage between the two.

Schachter and Singer's two-factor theory

The theories we have looked at so far imply that either physiological processes determine emotional feelings or that the two occur together, but independently of each other. In 1953, Albert Ax tried to demonstrate a way in which the physiological processes varied for two different emotions: fear and anger. He took baseline blood levels of both adrenaline and noradrenaline, and then had his assistant play out two roles with different subjects. In the first condition, the assistant behaved in a clumsy and incompetent way,

designed to produce anger in the subject, and in the second condition he set fire to the apparatus to which the subject was strapped, thereby inducing fear. (It is unlikely that this experiment would now be passed by an ethics committee!) Blood levels of adrenaline and noradrenaline were measured immediately after these two conditions, and Ax stated that fear produced higher adrenaline levels, while anger produced higher noradrenaline levels. However, subsequent researchers have been unable to replicate these results. It is unlikely that emotional differentiation could be tied to the levels of just one hormone.

Researchers realized that more than physiological factors must be involved. Schachter and Singer (1962) suggested a second factor, cognition, recognizing that the observed stimulus and circumstances play an important part in determining the emotion experienced. Figure 9.6 gives a diagrammatic representation of Schachter and Singer's **two-factor** (or cognitive labelling) **theory of emotion**. Their classic experiment which demonstrates this cognitive theory of emotion is described in Box 9.5.

Lazarus's cognitive theory

The importance of cognitive interpretation of circumstances in determining arousal levels is central to Lazarus's theory. He suggests that some degree of cognitive processing is essential before an emotional reaction, either overt or internal, can occur. An illustration of Lazarus's **cognitive appraisal** theory can be seen in Speisman et al.'s (1964) study, described in Box 9.6.

GLOSSARY

Two-factor theory of emotion Schachter's theory which proposes that both physiological processes and cognitive appraisal are implicated in the experience of emotions.

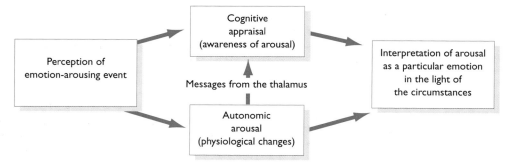

Figure 9.6 Schachter and Singer's two-factor (or cognitive labelling) theory

Lazarus et al. (1980) proposed a theory suggesting that emotion is a cognitive function, arising as a result of appraisal of a situation:

- A stimulus may be appraised as nonthreatening, leading to positive emotional states. The actual emotion experienced depends upon other characteristics or circumstances.
- A stimulus appraised as threatening leads to direct action, such as attack, retreat or freezing, together with physiological responses such as

those which accompany negative states, including fear, anger or depression.

- If direct action is impossible, coping strategies may be employed to reappraise the situation

---

GLOSSARY

Cognitive appraisal A process through which we assess the possible effect of a situation on our state of well-being, before responding to it.

Box 9.5   Schachter and Singer's (1962) adrenaline experiment

Schachter and Singer (1962) carried out an experiment whereby participants were injected with either adrenaline (experimental group) or a placebo (control group). (A placebo is a substance that has no demonstrable physiological effect.)

Some of the participants in the experimental group were told that they would experience autonomic arousal – increased heart and respiration rate – while the others were told that they might experience some numbness. All the participants were then placed in a room with a confederate of the experimenters, one at a time. This 'stooge' either behaved in a happy or an angry manner, to see whether the aroused participants would follow his behaviour. The participants who already had an explanation for their feelings of autonomic arousal did not follow suit; they had no need to add further cognitions to their explanation for feeling aroused. The others who had received adrenaline but no explanation, took on the happy or angry manner of the stooge. There was no change in the behaviour of the control group.

Schachter and Singer concluded from these results

that, while physiological arousal is necessary in emotion, cognitive appraisal of the situation is necessary to determine the emotion associated with that arousal. Students of methodology will be interested to notice that Schachter and Singer used adrenaline as the independent variable, measuring reported emotional behaviour as the dependent variable, whereas Ax (1953) used induced emotion as the independent variable and measured resultant hormonal levels as the dependent variable.

Follow-up experiments (for example, Maslach, 1979) have had some difficulty in reproducing these results and have also suggested that induced autonomic arousal produces more negative ratings than would be expected. In other words, participants stated that they were more angry than would have been expected in the 'angry stooge' situation, or less happy than would be expected in the 'happy stooge' situation. In a real-life situation, the same stimulus would elicit physiological and cognitive responses, leading the subject to perceived arousal and emotional feeling, which are interpreted together as the appropriate emotion.

Box 9.6   Speisman's 'circumcision' experiment

In an experiment (Speisman et al., 1964), participants were shown a film of African tribal male circumcisions. The film would normally cause stress in viewers. Four different commentaries accompanied the film:

■ Group 1 received a commentary that emphasized the pain suffered by the young boys in the film;
■ Group 2 saw the film without any commentary;
■ Group 3 heard a commentary that denied that much pain and suffering was involved;

■ Group 4 received an 'intellectual' commentary, emphasizing tribal procedures and the prized entry into manhood.

Emotional responses from those watching the film were highest in Group 1, followed consecutively by 2, 3 then 4. From these results, it was concluded that emotional reactions are strongly influenced by people's interpretations of an event.

benignly, in order to live with the threat. These coping strategies may be simply to redefine the threat as 'not as bad as it was first perceived'.

This theory has been used to explain some forms of human behaviour, for example why a woman continues to live with a man who is violent towards her. The stimulus (the man) is appraised as threatening, but for various reasons the woman cannot take direct action. She cannot fight back, he is stronger; she cannot run away, she has nowhere to go. The solution is to reappraise the situation. Perhaps he won't hit me again, he is very contrite next day, and so on. Living with this reappraised threat is less problematic than fear of the unknown life outside of that situation.

This theory is primarily descriptive, but the underlying mechanisms involved in emotion, the relationship between cognitions, feelings and expressions of emotion, are largely undefined.

Arousal theory and emotion

A number of researchers have suggested that arousal theory could form the basis of a theory of emotion, given that arousal is a nonspecific physiological response, heightening a person's awareness. Mandler (1982), for example, suggested that the interruption of ongoing thought processes or behaviour sequences is sufficient to activate the ANS. This creates a state of general physiological arousal, which is then given an emotional label, based on a cognitive interpretation of the situation or stimulus. This would seem to suggest that all emotional physiological responses are the same and that differentiation arises solely at cognitive level. However, sadness and depression are seen as parasympathetic responses and not simply a lack of arousal.

Social theories of emotion

There are a number of theories of emotion which concentrate either wholly or primarily on the social aspect of emotion. As this chapter is mainly concerned with the relationship between psychological and physiological phenomena, these will be mentioned only briefly.

Averill's social theory

Averill (1983) sees emotions as transitory social roles: a person adopts the role defined by his or her culture for the emotion being experienced.

Weiner's attributional theory

Attribution theory (see Chapter 24) suggests that we attribute causes to all events that happen, whether or not we have adequate information to do so. Weiner (1985) sees emotions as coming from these attributions. These may initially be just 'good' or 'bad' reactions, which are then refined into recognizable emotions once a cause has been attributed to the situation.

SELF-ASSESSMENT QUESTIONS

1. Which physiological mechanisms are involved in emotions?
2. Referring to experimental evidence, explain why cognitive factors need to be involved in any explanation of emotion.
3. Describe one theory of emotion that is supported by experimental evidence, including a brief description of this evidence.

Chapter summary

- Homeostasis, the process through which the body's balanced state is maintained, has been recognized as a factor in human motivation.

- The body's homeostatic responses are largely involuntary, automatically controlled through the action of the ANS. You do not have to think, 'I am cold; I will produce goosepimples.'

- Many of the behavioural responses to homeostatic motivations are voluntary, for example eating and drinking. Negative feedback cuts off the consummatory behaviour, but the precise mechanisms for this are not clearly understood.

- Physiological factors involved in the motivation of eating behaviour include the detection of reduced glucose levels in the body by receptors in the liver, the hypothalamus and the circulatory system. Satiety is signalled by the hypothalamus before the ingested meal is digested, or overeating would result.

- Psychological factors that prompt eating include the sight or smell of attractive food, the availability of a variety of foods, company for a meal and the prompting of the time of day.

- Eating disorders such as obesity, anorexia nervosa and bulimia have been studied by psychologists and their causes are thought to be multifactorial.

- A wide range of motivated behaviours are not essential to the survival of the individual. The behaviour may, in some cases, be life-threatening, as in the case of many addictive behaviours.

- Specific neurochemical circuits have been identified as being involved in many of these motivated behaviours. While these are involved in the motivation of addiction, they do not offer a complete explanation. It is clear that psychological dependence is also involved.

- Nonspecific theories of motivation, such as arousal theory, attempt to explain 'why' humans should involve themselves in these activities, but no wholly satisfactory explanation has yet been offered. When this is found, society may have the answer to addiction.

- The perception of an emotion-arousing stimulus brings about physiological changes, involving the ANS and the endocrine system.

- Facial expressions that accompany these emotions send feedback information from the facial muscles via nerves to the cortex. Some of these facial expressions are almost certainly innate and have been demonstrated across cultures. Others may have been learned through early social interactions.

- The recognition of faces and facial expressions is important to us as a species in that it conveys important social information.

- A wide range of theories has been offered concerning emotional states, none of which has wholly explained the relationship between our physiological responses, our cognitions and our feelings of emotion.

Further reading

Goleman, D. (1995). *Emotional Intelligence*. London: Bloomsbury. An informative book which suggests that those who are aware of their own and other people's emotions are more likely to be successful in interpersonal interactions and, therefore, throughout life; not a textbook, but a great deal of research is cited.

Plutchik, R. (1994). *The Psychology and Biology of Emotion*. London: Harper Collins. A review of 30 years of research into this field. The author suggests that the study of emotion is an area in its own right, not merely a 'branch' of other areas of psychology.

CHAPTER 10

Consciousness and its altered states

Levels of consciousness   204

▨ Consciousness   204

▨ Unconscious, subconscious and preconscious   204

▨ Hypnosis   205

▨ Drug-induced states   208

▨ Epilepsy   208

Body rhythms   208

▨ Biorhythms   208

▨ Circadian rhythms   209

The rhythms of sleep   210

▨ Physiology of sleep   210

▨ Stages of sleep   211

▨ REM sleep and dreaming   212

Why do we sleep?   214

▨ Theories of sleep   214

▨ Theories of dreaming   215

Objectives

By the end of this chapter you should be able to:

▨ Discuss different approaches to the concept of consciousness;

▨ Describe altered states of consciousness and their implications;

▨ Understand the relationship of biorhythms to psychological states;

▨ Describe the physiological processes involved in sleep;

▨ Outline theories which attempt to explain why humans sleep;

▨ Consider some theories of dreaming.

In 1890, William James wrote 'The explanation of consciousness is the ultimate question for psychology.' His words remain true to this day and psychologists are still perplexed by a number of related questions. What is **consciousness**? Where is it to be found? What are its functions? Do we have an unconscious mind? Is consciousness just one thing or several? What happens to it when we die?

No other experience is so obvious to oneself as one's own consciousness and yet it is impossible to prove the existence of consciousness in others. It is not publicly observable and therefore not scientifically testable. We can convince ourselves of our own consciousness through introspection, but we can only infer its existence in others since they can only be observed from the outside. However, consciousness is not entirely alone in this way. Many cognitive functions

---

GLOSSARY

Consciousness In general, this refers to a state of awareness of external and internal events experienced by an individual, though a range of more specific definitions have been proposed by different theorists.

such as memory, attention and perception are inferred from observing people's behaviour.

Consciousness implies a state of awareness. The term 'altered states of consciousness' is meant to apply to any state of awareness which differs from that normally experienced. Altered states can vary from highly focused attention to the sleep state of dreaming. Although the sleep state may sound like a lack of consciousness, there are neural activities continuing and the sleeper can be roused, whereas in states of coma and persistent vegetative state (PVS) (see Box 10.1) the individual cannot be roused. And the state of awareness under which an individual is functioning can be changed artificially through, for example, drugs, hypnosis and meditation.

Levels of consciousness

Consciousness

It does not seem possible to regard consciousness as a simple continuum, from high arousal at one end to deep sleep at the other. Where, along this continuum, would you place trance states or drug-induced states? Where does sleepwalking fit into our accepted idea of sleep as 'resting the body'? Certainly, consciousness must involve thought processes, memories and sensory inputs, but levels of all of these vary during different states of consciousness.

James (1890) spoke of the 'stream of consciousness' – a kind of internal monologue which is always present. We are aware of external events through the combined information from all our senses, yet we can switch and channel attention to heighten awareness of certain aspects of the external environment.

Kihlstrom (1984) suggests that the functions for which we use consciousness are:

- ▨ monitoring ourselves and our environment, in order to make accurate cognitive representations; and
- ▨ controlling our behaviour – when to begin and when to end specific behaviours and cognitive activities.

Awareness

A term most often used as synonymous with consciousness is 'awareness'. It can be argued that awareness commences before a child is born. There is strong evidence that the foetus reacts to loud noise from outside the mother's body, and that external sound stimuli may affect later cognitive development. During childhood and adulthood, selective attention allows our awareness to be focused on specific stimuli (**focal attention**), while filtering out other events. You may be so engrossed in a book that you fail to hear or see what is going on around you. If someone says your name, however, you will hear it, because your threshold of attention is lower for this than for almost anything else. Other things around you, of which you are only vaguely aware, are within your **peripheral attention**. These can be brought into your focal attention at will, similar to the way in which Freud suggested that the preconscious can become conscious. See Chapter 12 for a fuller discussion of attention.

Habituation

Habituation occurs when a stimulus is so constant that it is no longer given conscious attention. Humans in urban societies become habituated to the constant noise of traffic. It would be detrimental to well-being to be constantly aware of and attending to that level of noise. Any change in the background noise immediately raises conscious awareness. Habituation, therefore, has survival value. EEG patterns can reflect the neural state of habituation. If a stimulus is introduced, the EEG pattern is disrupted to reflect the introduction of the stimulus.

There are so many stimuli around us that do not gain our conscious (focal) attention, to which we may say we are habituated. We are not unconscious of them; perhaps it would be more correct to say they are in our preconscious or subconscious, our peripheral attention. See also Chapter 6 for a discussion of habituation.

Unconscious, subconscious and preconscious

We sometimes say we have done a well-rehearsed action 'unconsciously'. Driving a car on a clear country road, or ironing, for example, does not occupy our full

---

GLOSSARY

Focal attention The process of attending to particular aspects of the environment while other aspects are ignored.

Peripheral attention Other aspects of the environment that are not currently the object of focal attention

attention, but the action is not truly unconscious; it would be more correct to call it subconscious or preconscious, just below the level of conscious awareness. 'Unconscious' implies a total lack of awareness. If you are knocked out in the boxing ring or through an accident, you are unconscious.

Other psychologists may not agree with this definition of 'unconscious'. Freud, for example, viewed the unconscious mind as the repository for repressed memories. He suggested that the preconscious could become conscious if we switched our awareness to it.

These distinctions are not agreed by cognitive psychologists, who draw their conclusions from the level of mental processes during altered states of consciousness. Norman (1993) makes no distinction between preconscious and subconscious when discussing processes which are not wholly conscious. Hilgard (1977) suggests that we may use problem-solving abilities that are not always available to our conscious minds. You may have found that an answer sometimes pops into your head, yet you have no idea how you 'computed' it. The processing may have been subconscious, but the answer becomes conscious. Both may well have involved the cortex, which would suggest that not all cortical activities are necessarily conscious.

Neuropsychologists make distinctions between consciousness and unconsciousness on the basis of demonstrable activity within the nervous system through clinical observation. EEG, PET, CT and MRI scans (see the Introduction to Part 2) contribute to this information. Objective information such as this has assisted in defining the difference between, for example, **persistent vegetative state (PVS)** and coma, but even this is limited and cannot always predict outcomes (prognosis).

Hypnosis

Kihlstrom (1985, p. 385) defines **hypnosis** as: '. . . a social interaction in which one participant (designated the subject) responds to suggestions offered by another person (designated the hypnotist) for experiences

---

GLOSSARY

Persistent vegetative state (PVS) A term used to describe an individual who, following a head injury, anoxia or other trauma, exists in a coma-like state, showing no visible signs of consciousness.

Box 10.1   Persistent vegetative state and coma

Persistent vegetative state (PVS) was brought to the public eye following the battle to allow Tony Bland to die. He had been a PVS patient for three and a half years, due to anoxia (lack of oxygen to the brain) suffered during the Hillsborough football stadium disaster in 1989. The term PVS was coined by Jennett and Plum (1972) to describe patients who appeared to recover from coma, showed periods of waking and sleeping, but never regained full cognitive functions. This state can appear after severe head injury or anoxia caused by asphyxia, anaesthetic accidents, cardiac arrest, near drowning or hypoglycaemia (unconsciousness caused by injecting too much insulin, which sometimes happens in diabetes) (Jennett, 1993).

To the ordinary observer, there is no ostensible difference between PVS and coma; the patients seem to be permanently unconscious, for months or years. Neurological investigations and clinical observations suggest that in PVS there is brainstem activity, which supports lower functions, such as breathing and the sleep/wake cycle, but little or no activity in the cortex,

which is the region for higher processes such as information processing, problem solving and memory. If recovery from a vegetative state is to occur, it is most likely within the first year. After that time, it may be considered permanent (British Medical Association). However, recent cases identified in 1996, where consciousness has been regained after two years or more, raises the questions of (a) whether the state was misdiagnosed originally, or (b) whether recovery is possible after a period of one year. At one time, very little treatment could be offered to PVS patients, but this is gradually changing (see Epilogue to Part 2).

Coma usually follows severe head injury. Major neurological functions are disrupted. Usually within between two weeks and four months, functioning starts again spontaneously. Cortical functions such as visual tracking (following a moving object with the eyes), limb movement and vocalizations begin, together with reinstatement of the sleep/wake cycle. If these are not evident, vegetative state is suspected.

Paul McKenna, the hypnotist, makes suggestions to a participant

him or her. The participant may be asked to concentrate all thoughts on a small object such as a pendant and may be encouraged to feel sleepy, though is told he or she will not really be asleep but will listen to the hypnotist.

■ Once a sleeplike state is induced, the hypnotist will suggest that the participant performs various tasks. These can include physical actions such as raising the arms or may include the participant regressing to childhood or experiencing a hallucination such as imagining a monster frog hopping about the room. After being 'awakened', participants may perform a task (suggested during the hypnotic state) in response to a signal from the hypnotist, for example, standing on a chair when the hypnotist taps the table.

In a highly aware state, cognitive processes may be very active, examining and analysing incoming stimuli. In a more relaxed state, these processes are less focused and therefore more open to suggestibility or receptive to suggestions from others. It is with this state that hypnotists work, placing suggestions into receptive minds. The voice of the hypnotist becomes the focus of attention and other stimuli are filtered out.

Hypnotized subjects are not 'asleep', as is the common concept. The hypnotic state is nothing like sleepwalking. In many therapies that use hypnosis (for enabling people to give up smoking, for example), the client is conscious but relaxed, listening only to the hypnotist. An association is formed between the pleasant feeling of the relaxed state, the soothing voice of the hypnotist and the suggestion that the client no longer desires or needs to smoke in order to feel relaxed.

Hypnosis can be used to encourage people to recall memories openly that they have repressed as being painful. Recalling incidents of abuse as a child is an example that has received much publicity; in some cases, doubt has been cast on whether the incident was recalled by the client or suggested by the hypnotist, as the client is obviously so open to suggestion.

involving alterations in perception, memory and voluntary action.'

In hypnosis, a willing participant allows a hypnotist to influence his or her behaviour through relaxation and suggestion. Typically, the induction procedure is as follows:

■ For about ten minutes, the hypnotist talks to the participant, making suggestions designed to relax

GLOSSARY

Hypnosis Either the inducing of an altered state of consciousness where an individual can be induced by another person to perform involuntary actions (state theory) or a situation where a participant voluntarily complies with suggestions from a hypnotist (nonstate theory).

Deeper states of hypnosis are sometimes achieved, as in stage hypnosis, in which people act in ways that seem out of character and report later that they cannot remember what they did while hypnotized. The ethics of inducing these states simply for the entertainment of others is questionable, and whether there are long-term repercussions for the individual concerned is an area that has not been researched. It is highly unlikely that an individual could be hypnotized to commit any action to which he or she was completely opposed (for example, assault or murder), even under deep hypnosis.

In other instances, hypnosis has been used instead of anaesthetic during operations. Patients reported no experience of pain, and bleeding was reduced (Hilgard, 1977).

There are two main theories offered as to what actually happens to an individual during hypnosis: 'state' theory and 'nonstate' theory.

State theory

State theory views hypnosis as an altered state of consciousness. Hilgard (1977) describes it as a dissociative state, in which there exists various systems of control which are not all conscious at the same time. This can be compared to the way that an individual with multiple personalities would slip into a different personality and have no thought or feeling or even knowledge of the 'other self'. Hilgard's concept of the **'hidden observer'** illustrates this. He suggests that in many hypnotized participants, a part of the mind that is not within immediate awareness seems to be monitoring what is happening to the participant.

Nonstate theory

Nonstate theory suggests that participants are merely being compliant; they are 'going along' with the hypnotist. Hypnosis, these theorists believe, can be explained in terms of processes such as relaxation, motivation, imagination and compliance. Wagstaff (1981) proposed that there may be three different stages to hypnosis:

- Through the hypnotist's suggestions and through his or her own past experiences, the participant assesses what is expected.
- The participant uses imagination and develops strategies to achieve the expected behaviour.

Box 10.2 Meditation and trance states

Meditation has been practised by humans for thousands of years and is strongly associated with many Eastern religions and traditions. During meditation, the attention is strongly focused on a stimulus, either external, such as the tip of a candle flame, or internal, such as the repetition of a mantra, words or phrases that have a rhythm and are designed to bring the individual to a higher level of consciousness. In the religious context, the aim is to bring the person nearer to high levels of selflessness, transcending the bodily state.

During meditation, all extraneous stimuli are excluded, the heart rate and breathing rate slow, and blood pressure and basal metabolic rate drop. The body is immobilized and therefore its physical demands are reduced to the lowest levels, enabling fasting to be carried out for long periods of time. The physical processes of the body are all rested by the process of meditation; relaxation also achieves this but not so deeply and completely. Devotees of meditation say that they feel more refreshed after half an hour's meditation than after a night's sleep; this is obviously achieved only by practice. This assertion would seem reasonable, in that during sleep the body is not always immobilized, and the brain may be more active than when simply repeating a mantra.

Trance states have been observed in individuals from a number of different cultures. During trance, it is suggested, the individual's 'mind' is no longer within the body. This is a much more difficult state to define or prove objectively. In many cultures, those who exhibit trance states are revered, and their pronouncements while in a trance are accepted as messages from gods or people who have died. Again, very little scientific investigation has been conducted on trance states, although no one denies that they happen. It may be that the 'messages' are a product of the individuals' own thought processes of which they are not consciously aware.

GLOSSARY

'Hidden observer' In hypnosis, Hilgard's term for a part of the participant's mind which becomes dissociated from the hypnotized part, and is able to observe what is happening.

■ If this does not work, participants either withdraw from the activity or fake their responses.

Clinical and experimental evidence has so far produced conflicting results on which of these theories may be correct and there is still no conclusive answer about whether hypnosis is truly an altered state of consciousness. However, the debate continues and has become a lively area of research within psychology.

Drug-induced states

Having read Chapter 8, where the action of drugs is briefly explained, the reader will not be expecting transcendental explanations for drug states. The explanation for changes in perception, feelings and experiences is wholly chemical, mainly due to chemical changes at the synapse, thereby sending false messages to the cognitive parts of the brain. These false messages are responsible for people's out-of-character actions while under the influence of drugs.

Epilepsy

Epileptic attacks can range from brief apparent lapses of attention to intense electrical activity in the brain, causing unconsciousness and severe muscular contractions. Anyone might have an attack, if sufficiently provoked; some years ago, stroboscopes were implicated as causing changes in the electrical activity of the brain, because of the rhythmical changes in their light patterns. Experiencing one seizure does not therefore necessarily denote epilepsy; people with epilepsy have a low seizure threshold. Partial seizures, as the name implies, involve only part of the brain and are usually confined to one hemisphere. Generalized seizures involve both hemispheres. Seizures usually emanate from a focal point, which is often difficult to locate, whether by EEG or scans; 30–40 per cent occur in the temporal lobe.

Causes of epilepsy may be symptomatic – related to some definable brain injury or deformity, or infection such as meningitis. The majority of cases of epilepsy are idiopathic – there appears to be no specific cause, although some genetic factors have been demonstrated. Some cases of epilepsy have been linked to drug abuse, emotional disturbances and hormonal changes, such as those occurring during adolescence. Epilepsy is usually controllable by such drugs as phenytoin or nitrazepam.

SELF-ASSESSMENT QUESTIONS

1. What is meant by 'altered states of consciousness'?
2. How do we define awareness?
3. Briefly describe and contrast two altered states of consciousness from those discussed so far.

Body rhythms

Biorhythms

The human body exhibits a number of regular, recognizable rhythms, the most noticeable of which are the **circadian rhythms**. This term comes from the Latin *cirra*, meaning 'about' and *dies*, meaning 'a day'. Circadian rhythms are those which we exhibit

Box 10.3   Sensory deprivation

The brain normally has a continuous input of stimuli, which is attended or rejected, responded to or 'filed'. If all stimuli cease, the brain is then in an abnormal state and may attempt to fill this vacuum with stimuli of its own making - hallucinations. Even if external stimuli are cut off, the chemical activity of the brain cannot be switched off like a light bulb.

Sensory deprivation experiments (for example, Lilley, 1977) involve people wearing headgear that cuts off sound and vision, and floating in a tank of body-heat water, which deprives the remaining senses. Subjects soon begin to hallucinate, accusing their researchers of 'talking about them', or other imaginary experiences; when they become distressed, usually within a few hours, the experiment is halted.

Partial sensory deprivation for a short period of time has been used therapeutically for those who lead high-stress lifestyles. However the deprivation is not total, as soothing music is played to them. The aim is to reduce their sensory input for a time, rather than have them experience total deprivation.

GLOSSARY

Circadian rhythms The body's 24-hour cycle of various biological functions, such as sleeping–waking, blood pressure, temperature, breathing rate.

throughout the day, sleep being the most obvious because it takes up approximately one third of our 24-hour day. Mose animals also exhibit a circadian rhythm, even when they are **nocturnal** (active by night rather than day). (See Project 7 in chapter 35 for an investigation which aims to examine the relationship between circadian rhythms and performance on a vigilance task.)

Other body rhythms may take more than a day to be repeated, for example the menstrual cycle (approximately 28 days). These are called **infradian rhythms**, from the Latin *infra*, meaning below; these cycles occur less often than once a day. Hibernation in some animals is another example of an infradian rhythm; it takes months to recur.

Some body rhythms occur more than once a day. These are called **ultradian rhythms**, from the Latin word *ultra*, meaning above or over. Rhythms that occur more than once a day include the hunger 'cycle', usually about every four hours in Western society. Sleep, while being part of the circadian rhythm, also itself contains these less-than-a-day rhythms – stages within the pattern of sleep.

Circadian rhythms

Does our body have a natural 24-hour rhythm, or is this due only to the light/dark cycle of our planet? If we

. . . And, for a perfect example of the way non-stop partying affects the Circadian rhythms . . .

Box 10.4   Shift work

Bearing in mind what we know about circadian rhythms and the consequences if they are disrupted, what happens to the body when an individual has to do shift work? A study with nurses, moving from day shift to night shift, found that for some nurses, it took almost a full week for body mechanisms to readjust and function as if it were daytime (Hawkins and Armstrong-Esther, 1978).

The implications of these and other findings would seem to recommend that shift changes should be for longer than a week (perhaps three to four weeks) and that shifts should be rotated clockwise. Workers who rotate shifts weekly have more accidents at work, show lower productivity, and experience insomnia, digestive problems, fatigue and psychosomatic illnesses such as depression, owing to the individual's body being under stress. In spite of this evidence, there are still major companies today who are running weekly shifts that rotate anticlockwise!

---

lived in 24-hour 'light', would our bodies still produce the same rhythm? These were some of the questions scientists aimed to answer when, in 1972, a French caver called Siffre volunteered to spend seven months underground. He had adequate food, water and books, and a telephone link to the outside world. He was monitored by video camera and computer. He established a pattern of existence without cues as to time or the light/dark cycle.

The cycle that he established was approximately 25 hours, one hour longer than the circadian rhythm which has access to light/dark cues. This demonstrated that people have an innate mechanism for the circadian rhythm that will continue to function in the absence of daylight.

This raises the question of whether blind people are experiencing a longer cycle circadian rhythm than

---

GLOSSARY

Nocturnal Active by night rather than by day.

Infradian rhythms Body rhythms which promote functions that occur less often than once a day, for example the menstrual cycle in females, or hibernation in some animals.

Ultradian rhythms Body rhythms which promote functions which occur more than once a day: for example, the hunger cycle.

sighted people. Miles et al. (1977) report the case of a young, professional man who had been blind from birth. He had a circadian rhythm of 24.9 hours. In order to stay in phase with the rest of society, he had to take doses of stimulants and sedatives at appropriate times. Attempts to shift his sleep/wake cycle by controlling his sleep pattern in a laboratory were unsuccessful.

Disruption of the circadian rhythm

If the circadian rhythm is disrupted, for example by flying to another part of the world, so that we land in a different time zone from that of where we took off, the body has to readjust. Sleep has to be reinstated at a different time, as do eating patterns.

What is not so obvious is that our other patterns have been disrupted. For example, during the night not only does a person sleep, but also the breathing rate and heart rate slow considerably, and body temperature and blood pressure both drop. All these have to be changed. If you are staying for a fortnight's holiday, it may take you a few days to 'feel right' after your experience of jet-lag. Pilots, who are constantly flying across time zones, tend to ignore local times and keep to their own body clocks. The circadian rhythm seems to adapt more easily when travelling from east to west, rather than from west to east, possibly because our innate rhythm may be 25-hour, and we can make the adaptation more easily.

Hormonal causes governing the menstrual cycle were described in Chapter 8. Other biological mechanisms involved in running the body's biorhythms will be discussed in the next section.

? SELF-ASSESSMENT QUESTIONS

1. What are biorhythms?
2. What are the physiological consequences of disrupting the circadian rhythms?
3. What are some possible behavioural consequences of disrupting the circadian rhythms?

The rhythms of sleep

Sleep is an altered state of consciousness; it is by no means a total lack of consciousness, as external stimuli (such as loud noises) filter through and may be

incorporated into any ongoing neural activity, for example dreams. Additionally, it is possible to rouse a person from sleep, whereas it is not possible to rouse someone who is unconscious.

Sleep is part of the circadian rhythm; it happens once in 24 hours (excluding catnaps). During sleep, ultradian rhythms emerge as different stages of sleep succeed each other. These are identifiable and definable by **electroencephalogram (EEG)** patterns and, in the instance of dream sleep, by observation. In this section, we shall be looking at the physiological processes of sleep, and stages of sleep.

Physiology of sleep

In birds and reptiles, the pineal organ, situated in the brain, has receptors that are directly stimulated by light, which can penetrate the thin layer of skull above the pineal. This gives the first clue as to whether it is time to sleep or to wake. In humans, the pineal gland is situated deeper in the brain, at the top of the brainstem. Projections carrying nervous impulses from the retina bring light/dark information to the pineal. The pineal secretes melatonin; more seems to be produced in response to fading light.

The melatonin produced by the pineal gland acts upon the raphe nuclei (a group of cells situated in the pons, see Figure 10.1), which produce serotonin, a neurotransmitter with an inhibitory, or slowing down, effect on the CNS, particularly in the region of the reticular formation, which is known as one of the body's arousal systems.

However, the key pacemaker of the circadian rhythm seems to be the supra-chiasmatic nucleus (SCN), in the hypothalamus. This contains around 10 000 small neurons (Meijer and Reitveld, 1989), which synapse onto each other and are thought to be neurosecretory cells that may send neuromodulators to influence many areas of the brain. The projections from the retina to the pineal gland come via the SCN, but this is not the main method of maintaining the circadian rhythm. As Siffre had shown, it can be maintained in the absence of a light/dark cycle. The neurons of the SCN display an

---

GLOSSARY

Electroencephalogram (EEG) A method of recording visually the electrical activity of the brain by placing electrodes on the scalp.

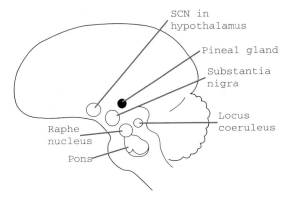

Figure 10.1 Regions of the brain that have been reported to be involved in controlling arousal or sleep

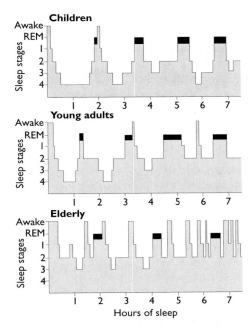

Figure 10.2 Normal sleep cycles of humans at different ages. Source: Kales and Kales (1974)

endogenous (inbuilt) circadian rhythm. If the nucleus is damaged, the circadian rhythm becomes disorganized. The SCN also sends projections to the raphe nuclei, which, we have already shown, is involved in the circadian cycle.

Also involved in the sleep/wake cycle are a group of neurons known as the locus coerulus, situated in the reticular formation. The rate of firing of these neurons declines just before sleep and increases abruptly just before waking (Aston-Jones and Bloom, 1981), indicating that they may be involved in vigilance rather than the sleep/wake cycle. It is thought that these neurons also play a role in **REM sleep** (rapid eye movement sleep, usually indicative of dreaming), as their rate of firing drops to zero during REM.

Stages of sleep

An individual's night's sleep consists of a number of sleep cycles, each about 90 minutes' duration, which combine different levels of sleep. Our sleep pattern is not a smooth curve in which we fall more and more deeply asleep until it is time to wake again. Children, adults and elderly people show different patterns of sleep (see Figure 10.2). These have been recorded on EEG traces, as they are in sleep laboratories, which has given a great deal of information about what happens during sleep. In Figure 10.2 dreaming episodes are indicated by black bars. Note the deeper sleep of children and more frequent periods of waking in the elderly. Sleep stages are judged by EEG criteria. Long-term studies suggest that sleep experienced in a sleep laboratory (after the first night's 'settling-in') is typical of sleep outside the laboratory (Empson, 1989).

Stage 1

As the individual drifts into sleep, the EEG trace changes from recognizable alpha rhythm, which characterizes the relaxed waking state (see Figure 10.3), to the irregular trace of Stage 1 sleep. The EEG demonstrates low-voltage, slow waves (2–7 Hz, low amplitude). The individual is easily woken during this stage. Other physiological changes begin: the heart rate and breathing rate begin to slow down.

Stage 2

The EEG trace is of higher amplitude and shows characteristic 'spindle' patterns, of 13–15 Hz, which last for about 20 seconds. The reason for these is not known; they do not appear to correspond with any overt behavioural changes (such as turning over, for

---

GLOSSARY

REM (rapid eye movement) sleep Periods of sleep during which the eyes move rapidly and dreaming usually occurs. During REM sleep, motor neurons are inhibited and the limbs are effectively paralysed.

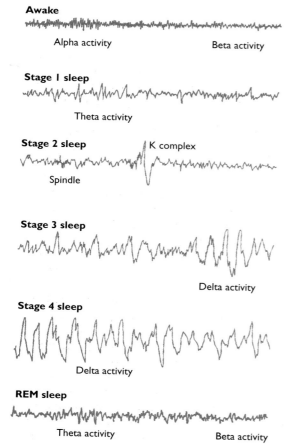

Figure 10.3 Typical EEG traces for (NREM) stages of sleep and REM sleep. Source: Horne (1988)

example). The individual is still quite easily awoken at this stage.

Stage 3

The individual is difficult to rouse during this stage, a behavioural indication of deeper sleep. A stimulus important to the individual will break the barrier; for example, a mother will hear her baby cry and wake up, whereas other stimuli of the same noise level may have no effect. The sleeper's heart rate and breathing rate are slow, and blood pressure drops. The EEG trace shows long, slow waves.

Stage 4

As for Stage 3, the sleeper can only be roused with difficulty, except for relevant stimuli. Heart rate and breathing rate are slow, and blood pressure is lowered. The EEG trace shows long, slow, rhythmical waves.

Within the first three and a half hours of a night's sleep, an individual has probably completed all the 'deep' sleep (Stages 3 and 4) that is likely to occur. Subsequent sleep cycles are likely to fluctuate between Stages 1 and 2. In most normal people, all sleep cycles include a period of REM sleep.

REM sleep and dreaming

Rapid eye movement (REM) sleep was first identified by Dement and Kleitman (1957). They observed subjects in a sleep laboratory who showed periods of sleep when their eyes could be observed rapidly moving under their lids. Eye movements can be monitored and recorded by an **electro-oculogram** (EOG), a process similar to an EEG but recording from near the eye socket.

If the volunteers were woken when their eyes showed rapid movements, they reported that they were dreaming. This happened 80 per cent of the time, whereas if subjects were woken during **NREM sleep**, they reported dreams only 15 per cent of the time. However, Beaumont (1988) suggests that subjects take longer to rouse from NREM sleep and may therefore have forgotten their dreams by the time they are fully awake and coherent.

Bursts of dreaming during REM may last for only a few seconds, with quiescent periods in between. In recall, however, we may link these bursts together, to form one dream, which may account for some of the inconsistencies and irrelevances we recall in our dreams.

Newborn babies spend much of their sleep time in REM sleep. Unfortunately, it is impossible to establish whether they experience dreams at this time and, if so, of what they are dreaming.

Faraday (1973) found that the rapidity of the eye movements correlated with the intensity of the dream. In addition, movements of the inner ear occur, which may be related to the auditory content of the dreams.

GLOSSARY

Electro-oculogram A process similar to an EEG but which gives a visual record of eye movements.

NREM (nonrapid eye movement) sleep A deeper level of sleep in which the cortex of the brain is less active (slow wave sleep).

Box 10.5   Sleep deprivation studies

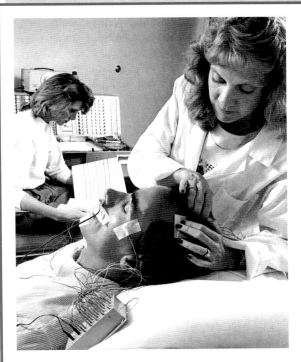

Hooking an EEG up to a sleep research patient

It has been found impossible to keep human participants awake continually. They take microsleeps, or even fall asleep standing up!

The longest recorded period of wakefulness was 264 hours. This was completed by a young disc jockey, who stayed on air for that period of time. He was carefully monitored for well-being during the experience. At no time did he lose touch with reality, although he experienced some minor illusions and psychological problems. After approximately 250 hours, his body temperature was 10 °C below normal and his skin temperature 10 °C below normal, indicating that the capillaries were constricting to conserve body heat.

Tests of mental functioning showed some decrement, especially speech and memory. Eye and motor control showed impairment at times. His circadian rhythm was still evident during deprivation.

His sleep was monitored for three nights following deprivation. Results showed that the first night's sleep showed a great increase in Stage 4 and REM sleep. This pattern was followed on the two subsequent nights, indicating that these are areas important in sleep.

This is, of course, a case study and may not generalize to the population at large. Other studies have tended selectively to deprive people of either REM or NREM sleep (Dement, 1960, 1972). Findings generally suggest that REM sleep is increased following a period of deprivation. Dement's earlier study suggested that REM sleep-deprived participants displayed a form of paranoia, but his later study did not find this.

Webb (1982) found that if volunteers were asked gradually to reduce their period of sleep from eight to four hours per night over a period of two months, they appeared to suffer no detrimental effect. In a previous experiment, Webb had asked participants to reduce their sleep abruptly to three hours per night for eight nights. Deterioration on cognitive and performance tasks was apparent by the seventh night.

It would appear from experimental studies that, while humans need sleep in order to function effectively, cognition and performance are unaffected by controlled sleep reduction. However, the volunteers are usually young, fit adults, and the experimental period is predetermined, which may enhance their motivation.

If people are deprived of REM sleep during one night, their following night's sleep will contain longer periods of REM, as though they have a need to 'catch up'. This phenomenon is known as REM rebound.

Participants woken during NREM reported shorter, less visual dreams. However, these were sometimes of the 'nightmare' type of dream, in which there was a strong emotional outburst. Sleepwalking (somnambulism) and sleeptalking occur during NREM sleep. Where dreams are sometimes 'acted out', these may be of the NREM variety, as they are usually linked to some highly emotional experience, and of course the motor neurons are not inhibited at these stages.

This may be why we sometimes incorporate external noises into our dreams.

As stated earlier, neurons in the locus coerulus fire during REM sleep. These prompt another important physiological mechanism, the inhibition of motor-neurones in the brainstem, in order to cut off physical activity from mental activity, so that individuals do not act out their dreams.

SELF-ASSESSMENT QUESTIONS

1. Describe some important physiological processes involved in sleep.
2. What are the differences between REM and NREM sleep?
3. Describe an example of an ultradian rhythm.
4. (a) What do sleep deprivation studies show?
   (b) Why must this information be viewed with caution?

Why do we sleep?

In this section, we shall be trying to answer the question of why we need to sleep and also to dream. These questions have been addressed by a number of researchers, who have formulated theories of sleep and dreaming. Given that we, as humans, need to rest in order not to exhaust ourselves, why do we need to sleep instead of just sitting or lying quietly?

All animals sleep, even though the process may leave them open to attack by predators. For example, the Indus dolphin, which is blind, sleeps for approximately seven hours a day – in 'naps' of 4–60 seconds (Pilleri, 1979). Other marine mammals exhibit similar patterns, suggesting that sleep is a physiological necessity.

Theories of sleep

Restoration theory

Oswald (1980) proposed that sleep is the period of quiescence necessary for the body and brain to replenish themselves, to repair any deterioration and damage sustained during the day. Body replenishment, he suggested, occurs during NREM sleep, and brain replenishment during REM sleep.

Physiological evidence is offered in support of this theory. In normal adults, growth hormone is only secreted during slow wave (NREM) sleep. In children, there is also some secretion occurring during the day. While growth hormone is obviously important in children (especially young babies), it also has a function in adults. Growth hormone increases the ability of amino acids (the constituents of proteins) to enter body cells. Assisting the process of restoration of body tissue is important, because cells need to be renewed regularly and frequently.

However, critics have pointed out that amino acids are only readily available for four hours after a meal, so not a great deal of protein synthesis will take place at night, during fasting. Studies have demonstrated that the rate of protein synthesis is higher during the day than at night (Clugston and Garlick, 1982). A human's metabolic rate is only 9 per cent lower during sleep than during quiet wakefulness; therefore a great deal of our potential for cell replenishment occurs by day.

The restoration of brain tissue during REM sleep would seem to imply the necessity for a period of quiescence in order for repair to be carried out, but, as we have seen earlier, the brain is extremely active during REM sleep.

Evolutionary theory

Meddis (1983) proposed that the need for sleep is rooted in our evolutionary past. Sleep is an advantage because it keeps the animal immobilized and inconspicuous for long periods of time. Because it is inconspicuous, it is therefore out of danger from predators.

Animals who are unlikely to be in danger from predators, such as lions, can sleep quite openly during the day. Other species, such as the Indus dolphin mentioned at the start of this section, have to adapt their sleep patterns. Humans, although predatory rather than hunted, sleep at night because human sight, unlike that of members of the cat family for example, is not specialized for seeing in the dark. Herd animals, such as zebra, usually sleep standing up (they do not fall over, as humans would, because they have a suspensory ligament in their legs that keeps them rigid during sleep). Many herd animals take microsleeps or short naps. Additionally, in a herd, there are usually some individuals awake while others sleep.

Because of this evolutionary predispositon to sleep, Meddis argues, people have maintained this behaviour, even though it may seem largely unnecessary in an urbanized society to be immobilized against danger. There are functional benefits, in that the long sleeps that babies have prevent their mothers from becoming exhausted.

This theory would seem to suggest that sleep is not necessary in a safe environment. Animal studies (for example Kleitman, 1927) showed that death eventually results from lack of sleep. Human sleep deprivation studies show that people deprived of sleep will sleep marginally more after deprivation, with a marked increase in the percentage of REM sleep, as though they need to 'catch up'.

Hibernation theory

Seemingly a variation on evolutionary theory, hibernation theory suggests that sleep evolved as a lesser form of hibernation, with the purpose of keeping humans and animals quiet and immobilized in the dark. Hibernating animals are also conserving energy and not using up food stores, or pointlessly looking for food in a season when none is available. If humans did not sleep at night, they would probably need to consume more food, which would deplete available resources.

There is not a great deal of support for hibernation theory. Other evolutionary behaviours that are not necessary for survival or lifestyle have been minimized or discarded by humans. It is unlikely that the species as a whole would seek to maintain a behaviour that occupies one-third of human life but has no real purpose.

Core sleep and optional sleep

Horne (1988) suggested that, while we need sleep, we mostly have more sleep than is necessary. He discounted Oswald's restoration theory on the basis that cell restoration takes place by day rather than at night. He also suggested that the increase in growth hormone at night might be related to the breakdown of fat rather than to protein synthesis.

Horne suggests that the first four hours of sleep are core sleep, which are necessary for rest, relaxation and restitution of the brain. The remaining hours of sleep he terms optional sleep, as these can be dispensed with, to no ill-effect.

Horne cites a study by Wilkinson, who allowed three groups of participants 4, 6 and 7.5 hours of sleep per night respectively, for six weeks. The cognitive functioning of participants was tested before and after this period of time. The 6- and 7.5-hour groups showed no decrement in cognitive functions, whereas the 4-hour group showed some decrement in memory. Horne concluded that no more than five hours of sleep was physiologically necessary. Any additional hours spent asleep were just an acquired habit.

If you refer back to Figure 10.2, you will see that, by the end of four hours' sleep, an adult has completed all

of the slow wave sleep for the night, plus less than half of the REM sleep. Horne would therefore seem to be suggesting that not all of the REM sleep is necessary. Most studies have shown that the long-term deprivation of REM sleep, when people are on sleeping tablets for example, is extremely detrimental and may result in hallucinations and other mental health problems.

Theories of dreaming

If one of the reasons why we sleep is to allow us to dream, we should examine the reasons why we dream. If a sleeper is woken during REM sleep, he or she can recall the ongoing dream, so the dream state cannot be far from conscious awareness; it is another level of consciousness. Researchers have not yet clarified whether REM sleep is solely for the purpose of dreaming, and also why we need to dream. We will look at a few theories.

Psychoanalytic theories

Freud's theory of dreams In perhaps the best known, yet least scientifically based theory, Freud suggested that dreams are wish fulfilment (see Chapter 30). Those things which we would like but cannot have in real life are the things we dream about. Some which we cannot admit, even to ourselves, are disguised and need interpretation by a therapist.

Jung's theory of dreams Jung suggested that dreams should be analysed in series rather than as individual dreams; a single dream would give little information on the dreamer's problems.

The lack of empirical data, or methods of finding empirical data, to substantiate psychoanalytic dream theories makes them difficult to accept. The interpretation of dreams by a therapist may be construed as being not entirely objective.

> **GLOSSARY**
>
> **Core sleep** Horne's (1988) term for the first four hours of sleep which he believes are necessary for rest, relaxation and restitution of the brain. The remaining hours (optional sleep) are not essential.

In addition, dreams can only be recorded by self-report, which is not an objective method. People may inadvertently add to their recalled dream, to include their current problem. Perhaps examining the content of dreams is not the most useful route to determining why we dream.

Neurological theories

Rose's neural theory Rose (1976) explained dreams as the output from the brain's random firings. These random firings may trigger memory sequences, which are then strung together as dreams. It is not really determined why some memory sequences and not others are triggered, or why dreams may contain hitherto unknown places or people.

Activation–synthesis model This model was proposed by Hobson and McCarley (1977). The high level of cortical activity during REM is not input from the senses but is internally generated, a form of 'neural noise'. This is the activation part of the model. Synthesis is the interpretation of this neural activity into dream sequences. Each individual synthesizes his or her dreams according to their unique experiences.

Genuine physiological input is incorporated into the dream. For example, the brainstem blocking of motor activity is recognized in the dream as trying to run away but being unable to do so. The authors propose that this process occurs during REM sleep. There seems to be no reason why the process is postponed during NREM. Random firings are probably still generated and passed to the cortex during NREM sleep, and may also be synthesized into dreams.

Forgetting theory Crick and Mitchison (1983) suggested that, during sleep, the cortex receives input from the brainstem during which synapses are modified so that unwanted connections are 'unlearned'. The function of REM, they suggest, is to sort and discard, or forget, unwanted learning. The

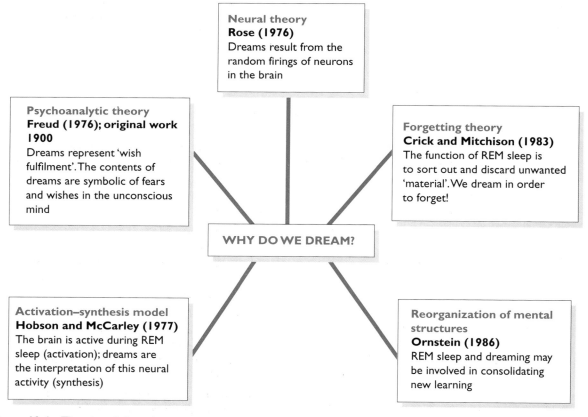

Figure 10.4 Theories of dreaming

exact mechanism for this selection and disconnection is as yet unidentified.

The perceptual content of our dreams corresponds with the activity generated in the perceptual cortex. The frontal lobes of the brain are probably involved in weaving this perceptual input into a story. This may account for why some people's dreams are more creative than others.

Hopfield (1984) carried out some computer-simulation experiments, with 'learning computers'. These simulate human learning processes, using connectionist models. Hopfield found that if a learning computer had been given superfluous information, it consolidated its necessary information more efficiently if given a period of unlearning of unnecessary information. This would seem to be similar to the process that Crick and Mitchison thought to occur in humans.

Reorganization of mental structures Ornstein (1986) suggests that REM sleep and dreaming may be involved in consolidating learning. This time is used by the brain to reorganize its mental structures into a memorable form. Support for this comes from experimental evidence that shows that REM sleep increases after people have been asked to learn complex tasks.

This process has been suggested, by some writers, as the reason why newborns spend so much time in REM sleep (50 per cent, as opposed to an adult's 25 per cent, of sleep time). This seems behaviourally unlikely, as a newborn may be awake for only half an hour, feeding, then asleep for a further three hours. That would give one and a half hours processing time for half an hour's information input. It seems unlikely that the function of a newborn's REM sleep is the same as that of an adult, unless the actual functions of REM are very different from those already proposed.

? SELF-ASSESSMENT QUESTIONS

1. (a) Describe the restoration theory of sleep.
   (b) What are the criticisms of this theory?
2. What other suggestions have been made for the reason why humans sleep?
3. What are the problems associated with the psychoanalytic theories of dreaming?
4. Briefly compare and contrast two neurological theories of REM sleep.

Chapter summary

■ When we speak of consciousness, we are describing a state of cortical awareness. This may be divided into focal attention, where the concentration lies, and peripheral attention, other things that can be brought into focal attention at will.

■ Altered states of consciousness are any that are different from those normally experienced. They include highly focused attention, dreaming, and awareness artificially altered by, for example, drugs or hypnosis.

■ Subconscious (or preconscious) processes may include not only an awareness of what is within our peripheral attention, but also habituated responses that we make, without reference to our conscious mind. These may be brought into consciousness at will.

■ Other processes, which we can only call subconscious for want of a better term, are those which cannot always be accessed by the conscious mind: for example, the problem-solving abilities described by Hilgard.

■ The unconscious state implies lack of consciousness. Unfortunately, this term is used to describe other states, so terminology needs to be standardized.

■ Unconscious states range from temporary loss of consciousness, to coma and vegetative states. PVS patients may show some brainstem activity, but little or no cortical functioning.

■ The human body exhibits innate biorhythms. Some are circadian rhythms, centred around the light/dark cycle; others are greater than a day, such as the menstrual cycle in women, or less than a day, such as stages within a night's sleep.

■ Disruption of body rhythms causes stress to the body, which has to readjust to new patterns.

■ Specific structures in the brain have been found to be involved with aspects of sleep. Activity in the cortex during sleep can be monitored noninvasively by EEG recordings. Differences in these traces indicate when sleep is changing from one stage to another.

■ Cycles of sleep (ultradian rhythms) last about 90 minutes and normally include several stages of sleep in each cycle. REM sleep usually indicates dreaming.

■ There seems to be evidence that sleep, rather than quiet rest, is necessary for human well-being. When volunteers are allowed less than four hours' sleep per night, their cognitive functions show decrement within a week. If this were to be prolonged beyond the usual experimental period, other problems might become evident.

■ REM sleep seems to be of particular importance: people deprived of REM sleep increase the proportion of time spent in REM on subsequent nights.

■ Some theories of sleep suggest that humans need sleep time for body and brain restitution. Others suggest that it is a behavioural carry-over from our evolutionary past.

■ As adults, humans spend approximately 25 per cent of their sleep time in REM sleep, which researchers have found to be associated with dreaming.

■ Reasons given for dreaming range from the emotional expression of wishes to the random firings of brain cells. Functions suggested for these random firings may be associated with learning: either the consolidation of learning or the sorting and forgetting of unwanted information.

■ Although a great deal of information has been uncovered on the physiological processes of sleep, answers to questions such as why we sleep and why we dream are as yet still open to discussion.

Futher reading

Farthing, G.W. (1992). *The Psychology of Consciousness*. Englewood Cliffs, NJ: Prentice-Hall. An interesting and readable overview of the problems of consciousness and its altered states.

Hilgard, E. (1979). *Personality and Hypnosis: A Study of Imaginative Involvement*, 2nd edn, Chicago: University of Chicago Press. A 'classic' text on hypnosis which offers accounts of methods, theories and experimental results.

CHAPTER 11

Stress and anxiety

Anxiety   219

Stress and stressors   220
- What is stress?   220
- What causes stress?   221

Models of stress   225
- Physiological model   225
- Arousal model   227
- Psychosocial stimuli model   227
- Transactional model   227

- Interactional model   227
- General facet model   228

Individual differences involved in stress   228
- Personality   228
- Racial/cultural factors   230
- Gender   231

Coping with stress   231
- Emotion-focused coping   231
- Problem-focused coping   232

Objectives

By the end of this chapter you should be able to:

- Discuss some factors which may cause stress;

- Describe physiological responses to stress;

- Outline a number of models of stress;

- Identify variables involved with individual experiences of stress;

- Discuss ways of coping with stress and managing stress.

Anxiety

Anxiety is an emotion that is distressing. Sometimes, it may have no specific cause, unlike fear, the cause of which can be seen and dealt with by fighting or running away. Anxiety produces the same physiological response as fear – an increase in sympathetic activity in the ANS – but this level may be maintained for some time if the individual cannot find a way of removing the source of anxiety.

This feeling of anxiety is frequently generalized from one situation or stimulus to another; Freud referred to this as 'free-floating anxiety'. If the individual does not relate the feeling of anxiety to one specific cause, it becomes extremely difficult to resolve satisfactorily.

Russell Davies (1987) suggests that anxiety states are often learned by classical conditioning (see Chapter 32). An anxiety-producing situation occurs at the same time as another stimulus (for example, a child may learn that pain is associated with a doctor), so that whenever the stimulus-object appears, anxiety is aroused. In the case of our example, the doctor is not the cause of the pain but the association has been made; each time the doctor appears, anxiety is renewed, even though the pain may be absent.

Avoidance of the stimulus is a method that individuals often use to reduce anxiety. However, this means that the real source of anxiety is never explored and conquered. Sufferers of social phobia (fear of social situations) or agoraphobia (fear of open spaces) avoid the anxiety-producing situations and convince themselves that life is normal, that they have no problems. When there is no escape from an anxiety-provoking situation, learned helplessness may be the response. This was identified by Seligman (1975): when a noxious stimulus or event is repeatedly presented, and there is no escape route available, the individual simply accepts all that is coming and goes on with his or her life after it has passed – until the

Stressors are not the same for everyone. What is stressful for one person might be quite manageable and even enjoyable for another

next time. This learned helplessness can be generalized from one situation to another, until the individual feels that he or she has little, if any, control over life events. This usually results in a state of depression.

Prolonged anxiety or depression can lead to a state of stress, which is a recognizable physiological condition, with psychological causes and outcomes of impaired physical and psychological abilities.

Stress and stressors

What is stress?

If you asked a number of people this question, you would be given a variety of responses. Some would interpret the word **stress** as relating to stressful situations, others would describe how they feel when stressed, and still others would describe how they dealt with stress. Psychologists, too, have defined stress in

different ways and some of the models put forward are discussed below.

The **stressor** is the situation, individual or object that causes a state of stress in the individual or an internal state of conflict that will cause stress (Figure 11.1). Stressors are not necessarily the same for all people; what appears stressful to one is merely a challenge, or all-in-a-day's-work, for someone else.

Stress responses or stress results are:

- ■ **physiological**, in that the body makes changes in order to respond to the stress state;
- ■ **behavioural** – the individual may change behaviour in order to deal with the stress;
- ■ **coping strategies**, which may or may not involve a change of overt behaviour (described later in the chapter).

Anxiety and stress may produce anger and aggression in some people, apathy and depression in others. So far, research has not positively identified why

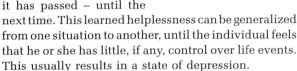

Stressor	Stress responses
Either external or internal	Physiological Coping strategies Behavioural

Figure 11.1   Stressors lead to stress responses

individuals of the same species may produce opposite responses to the same stimulus; differences may be due partly to personality, and partly to environmental variables.

What causes stress?

What causes you stress? The following may be factors:

■ **People**. Stress may be the result of conflict with parents, children, lovers or others with whom we come into conflict.

■ **Situations**. For instance jobs, driving or internal conflicts resulting from situations in which we find ourselves.

■ **Environmental events**. Noise or high temperatures, for example.

We would all undoubtedly produce a different list. Some stressors can be removed at source, others, for a variety of reasons, cannot and therefore have to be tolerated.

Other people

Frequently, the people who cause us stress are those we care about the most, and we would not want them 'removed'. We have to find methods of coping with the stress and anxiety caused, in order to continue living in close proximity with those whom we do not wish to leave.

Is this guy real? Fancy asking students if they know what stress is!

Box 11.1 Bullying

Bullying, whether at home, at school or in the workplace, is a source of severe stress from other people. Because it takes place in a 'closed' situation, usually without any moral or physical support for the victims, the 'flight' route is not open to them. Through physical or psychological weaknesses, the victim is precluded from the 'fight' response as well, and tends to try to avoid the bullies, by staying away from work or school, with long-term detrimental effects for the victim. Victims feel that they cannot tell others of their problem, for a variety of reasons. For example, they may believe they will be subjected to even greater abuse, or others will simply laugh and tell them to 'stand up for yourself'. (If they could do so, they would not be bullied in the first place.) Or they may be denying, even to themselves, that the problem exists, trying to pretend that the abuse is intended as fun. Various coping strategies are employed, most of which are ineffective. Usually, the victim needs outside help in order to resolve the problem permanently (Adams, 1992).

Bullying at home, whether it is abuse of a spouse or children, is an even more serious problem, because the victim can see no retreat from the situation. Women's refuges and children's helplines have been set up as initial responses. A full discussion of this problem is beyond the scope of this book.

Internal conflicts

Internal conflicts arise when an individual has to decide between two incompatible or mutually exclusive choices. These may be alternatives that are equally attractive, called **approach–approach conflicts** (Shall I join the soccer team or the basketball team? I don't have time to do both), or equally unattractive, called

---

> **GLOSSARY**
>
> **Stress** An unpleasant psychological or physiological state produced in response to a stressor.
>
> **Stressor** The situation, individual or object which can cause a state of stress in a person.
>
> **Approach–approach conflict** The conflict which arises when an individual has to decide between two alternatives that are equally attractive.

avoidance–avoidance conflicts (you don't want to take this dead-end job, but you don't want to starve).

Sometimes, the action you might wish to take has penalties attached (approach–avoidance conflicts), and you have to decide whether these are worth suffering (I would like to apply for a psychology degree, but I don't want to do the statistics necessary). Resolving inner conflicts can be very stressful; usually, the problems and alternatives are more serious than those suggested above.

Erikson (1980), in his theory of development, suggested some conflicts that arise when our inner motives are in opposition:

■ **Autonomy versus dependence**. We experience a desire to be independent, but it also feels safer to be dependent on someone we view as stronger than ourselves.

■ **Intimacy versus isolation**. We wish to be close to another, to share innermost thoughts and feelings, but fear we may be betrayed.

■ **Cooperation versus competition**. From childhood onwards, competition is encouraged in individuals, but they are also urged to cooperate and help others. Both at school and at work, this presents problems of deciding which course of action to take in which set of circumstances, and there are social penalties for making the wrong choice.

There are also cultural norms of behaviour and morality, which we are expected to observe. These often run contrary to our basic instincts: to fight or run away. A soldier may experience such fear that he would prefer to run, but society expects him to fight. A woman may want to thrash her husband's lover, but this would be condemned by many societies. Inner conflicts produced by blocking these actions lead to stress.

Life changes and daily hassles

Events that happen in our lives can also produce stress. Holmes and Rahe (1967) investigated the relative strengths of a number of these life events and produced a rating scale (the **Social Readjustment Rating Scale** (SRSS), see Figure 11.2), equating numerical values with a range of life events, from the most severe (death of a spouse) to lesser events, such as a change in eating habits. You may not rank these in the same order, but, on the whole, consensus is high (Holmes and Masuda, 1974).

Figure 11.2 Social Readjustment Rating Scale. Source: adapted from Holmes and Rahe (1967)

Rank	Life event	Mean value
1	Death of spouse	100
2	Divorce	73
3	Marital separation	65
4	Jail term	63
5	Death of close family member	63
6	Personal injury or illness	53
7	Marriage	50
8	Being fired at work	47
9	Marital reconciliation	45
10	Retirement	45
11	Change in health of family member	44
12	Pregnancy	40
13	Sex difficulties	39
14	Gain of new family member	39
15	Business readjustment	39
16	Change in financial state	38
17	Death of close friend	37
18	Change to different line of work	36
19	Change in number of arguments with spouse	35
20	Mortgage over £60 000	31
21	Foreclosure of mortgage or loan	30
22	Change in responsibilities at work	29
23	Son or daughter leaving home	29
24	Trouble with in-laws	29
25	Outstanding personal achievement	28
26	Wife begins or stops work	26
27	Begin or end school	26
28	Change in living conditions	25
29	Revision of personal habits	24
30	Trouble with boss	23
31	Change in work hours or conditions	20
32	Change in residence	20
33	Change in schools	20
34	Change in recreation	19
35	Change in church activities	19
36	Change in social activities	18
37	Mortgage or loan less than £10 000	17
38	Change in sleeping habits	16
39	Change in number of family get-togethers	15
40	Change in eating habits	15
41	Vacation	13
42	Christmas	12
43	Minor violation of the law	11

GLOSSARY

Avoidance–avoidance conflict The conflict which arises when an individual is forced to make a decision by weighing up the advantages and disadvantages of an undesirable situation.

Social Readjustment Rating Scale (SRRS) A scale developed by Holmes and Rahe (1967) to measure the levels of stress associated with particular life events.

To calculate the amount of stress experienced by an individual, over a given period of time (usually between six months and two years), the rank value of all that person's reported life events is totalled. This gives a life change score, which can be examined in conjunction with the individual's physical and mental well-being. Investigators have found that a high life change score is often followed by physical illness or psychological problems a year or two later (Rahe and Arthur, 1977). Presumably, the stress induced by life changes lowers the functioning of the immune system, causing illnesses to be contracted more easily.

Criticisms of the SRRS   Critics of the life events scale point out that it is difficult to separate other variables, which may be causes of the ill-health, from the apparent effects of life changes. For example, death of a wife may cause a man to change his lifestyle, to adopt an unhealthy diet, to drink and smoke more; it may be these variables that actually produce the breakdown in health.

Other critics suggest that the gradual breakdown in health may be the cause rather than the effect of the life events. Poor health may induce absenteeism or inefficiency at work, which may result in the loss of a job.

There is also a 'correlational effect' attached to mental ill-health: depressed people tend to report more negative events. It is difficult to say whether the depression or the reporting of the events is the cause or the effect. In addition, the scale does not allow for the fact that people's circumstances vary widely. What may be a traumatic event for one person may be a release for another; for example, individuals' responses to divorce vary widely.

Hassles and uplifts   Lazarus (1966) suggested that daily hassles cause more stress problems than do life events. Small daily problems can summate until we feel we cannot cope. DeLongis et al. (1982) found that daily hassles were a better predictor of ill-health than were life events. Lazarus also suggested that the effects of **hassles** were offset by '**uplifts**' – good events that happened in our day. These were balanced by the individual, providing an overall 'feel' to the day,

---

GLOSSARY

Hassles Daily problems which may cause stress, for example, arguments with partner, waiting in traffic jams, worrying about weight problems.

Uplifts The more positive things which may give us a good 'feel' to the day, for example getting on well with one's children, receiving an unexpected gift, completing a task.

Box 11.2   Occupational stress

It is increasingly recognized by employers that occupational stress is a worrying and expensive phenomenon. Some occupations, by definition, are more stressful than others: doctors, social workers and other caring professionals frequently suffer from high stress levels, with nurses top of the list (Wolfgang, 1988). Other professions, such as the police force, which may appear to be open to dangerous situations, have been demonstrated to suffer much lower levels of stress than expected. Jermier et al. (1989) reported stress emanating from overload of paperwork rather than fear of danger on the streets.

Stress at work may be due to a number of causes, some due to unpleasant physical environments (noisy or polluted) or incompatibility with other workers. Also, job strain is often produced by having too much – or too little – to do, or by having too difficult or too easy a job. French et al. (1982) suggested it is often attributable to a poor person–environment fit. This implies more than just the physical workspace, and involves a problem with the job itself, feeling like a square peg in a round hole. This produces stress in the person, who feels that he or she should change in order to do the job better but is unable to see how this can be accomplished. Inflexible work practices mean that the job task itself cannot be changed, so the result is impasse and greater stress.

Frustration at work, by not being able to achieve what the individual would like to achieve, through lack of facilities or other circumstances, produces stress and may lead to 'burnout'. This is a feeling of mental and physical exhaustion, a sense of futility and ultimately a lack of care for others (Maslach and Jackson, 1981). This syndrome has been reported among nurses and other care workers, who sometimes feel demoralized by their workload, compared with the resources they have available (see, for example, Jackson, et al., 1986).

Box 11.3 What influences the degree of stress felt?

Noise, pollution and extremes of heat or cold may account for feelings of stress. These are all subject to a wide variety of mitigating circumstances, and there is a great deal of difference between individual responses to these stressors. By and large, the factors that best predict how stressful these are seen to be are predictability and controllability.

Predictability

If we can predict when an event is likely to occur, it is perceived as being less stressful (Katz and Wykes, 1985). We find it very difficult to cope with uncertainty. Hunter (1979) found that women whose husbands were reported missing in action in the Vietnam war reported poorer health than those who knew they had been widowed; the uncertainty was more stressful than widowhood.

Controllability

Similarly, feeling that one has control over the events in one's life makes those events seem less stressful. Over the past ten years, surveys have been carried out with more than 20 000 civil servants. Questions were asked

concerning health-related behaviours, such as smoking and drinking, and work-related questions, such as perceived sources of pressure at work. Physiological measures were also taken, for example ECGs (to detect heart problems) and blood samples, to measure levels of, among other things, cholesterol. High levels of cholesterol have long been associated with coronary heart disease (CHD), so this was to serve as an indicator of those at risk.

It was found that there was a strong relationship between high cholesterol levels and grades of employment, but not in the direction that might be expected. The highest cholesterol levels were found among the lowest grades of civil servants, and a gradation continued until the lowest cholesterol levels were shown among the highest grades of civil servants. The lower the grade, the less control the individual has over work conditions and decision-making processes. It could be concluded that lack of control may have been causing stress, which related to increased cholesterol levels and the risk of heart disease (Brunner et al., 1993).

and changing the individual's perception of feeling stressed.

A man slogs through waist-deep mud after a mud slide swamped his home in Malibu, California, USA. Being involved in a serious accident or disaster such as this can cause post-traumatic stress disorder

Traumatic events

Situations outside the normal range of human experience are recognized as being highly stressful. These include earthquakes and floods; serious car, train or plane accidents; wars; or witnessing or being a victim of violent crimes, such as rape, assault or murder. Many survivors experience **post-traumatic stress disorder**, which may develop immediately after the disaster or some time later. Initially, sufferers may feel numb to the world, then may repeatedly relive the experience in 'flashbacks' or dreams. They may exhibit anxiety, depression or overalertness, and sometimes feelings of guilt that they have survived while others perished.

GLOSSARY

Post-traumatic stress disorder A pattern of symptoms which often occur after a traumatic event such as witnessing or being involved in a serious accident or being the victim of a violent crime.

SELF-ASSESSMENT QUESTIONS

1. Explain with some examples what is meant by the term 'stressors'.
2. For what purpose is the Social Readjustment Rating Scale (SRRS) used? How has this scale been criticized?
3. What are 'hassles' and 'uplifts' and how might these affect an individual's levels of stress?
4. Briefly outline some research findings which suggest that predictability and controllability may influence people's responses to stressful events.

Models of stress

A number of models of stress have been produced to explain and describe what happens to an individual in a stress state. We will examine some of these, commencing with a physiological model, which explains the body's responses to stress, but does not differentiate responses to specific stressors. We will then examine some interactional models, which look at the processes involved between stressor and stressed.

Physiological model

Physiological changes in response to stress are similar, although not identical, in all individuals. These changes were identified by Selye (1956), who called them the **general adaptation syndrome (GAS)**. He identified three stages of response (see Figure 11.3). When a stressor occurs, the body's resistance initially drops, then rises sharply. It stays high throughout the second stage of the response, but ultimately can be sustained no longer and falls in exhaustion. If a second stressor is added to the first (see lower dotted curve), resistance is lower throughout and exhaustion reached sooner.

Stage 1: Alarm

The body's 'fight or flight' responses are activated against the perceived threat. The hypothalamus sends impulses to the sympathetic division of the ANS, which increases heart rate, respiration rate and blood pressure, dilates pupils, releases glycogen, and brings about GSR (galvanic skin response: the electrical conductivity of the skin) changes through sweating.

The hypothalamus also prompts the endocrine system, via the pituitary, which releases ACTH (adrenocorticotrophic hormone). This travels to the adrenal glands, which release adrenaline and noradrenaline, thus perpetuating the responses implemented by the sympathetic division of the ANS. The corticosteroids (cortisone and hydrocortisol) are also released from the adrenals. These are also involved in the stress response, maintaining the body's responses.

Stage 2: Resistance

If the stressor is not removed, some of the immediate responses decrease in intensity. Sympathetic activity declines but maintains a level of constant readiness. Adrenaline levels remain high, however; the physical activity of fighting or running away has not been consummated, although the individual may perform other actions that are ineffective. High adrenaline levels are instrumental in depressing the body's immune responses. The immune system is responsible for warding off attack from external sources.

Chronic (long-term) stress leads to a depletion of the body's resources and a reduction in the effectiveness of the immune system. The number of white blood cells

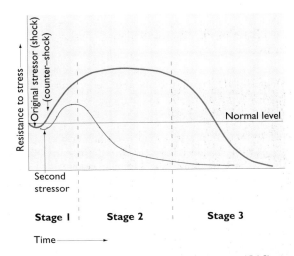

Figure 11.3 The general adaptation syndrome (GAS)

GLOSSARY

General adaptation syndrome (GAS) Selye's (1956) three-stage model which describes the body's physiological responses to stress.

(lymphocytes), which are essential to the immune system, is reduced under stress. Schleifer et al. (1979) reported that men whose wives had died from breast cancer showed depleted counts of lymphocytes within a month of the spouse's death, these remaining low for the following year.

Health problems that have been indicated as resulting from or being linked with stress include cancer, heart attacks, ulcers, colitis, asthma, hypertension (high blood pressure) and rheumatoid arthritis. In addition, depletion of the immune system leaves the body susceptible to attack by bacteria and viruses, which may cause a variety of illnesses (see Box 11.4).

Stage 3: Exhaustion

The body's resources are depleted; blood glucose levels drop because the stores of glycogen have been used, and the individual is probably eating inadequately to replenish them. The depletion of the immune system results in disease, which may lead to the psychosomatic illnesses outlined above (psychosomatic ill-

---

Box 11.4   Stress and the immune system

A relatively new area of research centres on psychoimmunology – the study of the effects of psychological factors such as stress on the body's immune system (see Chapter 1).

The immune system produces specialized cells known as lymphocytes which move through the bloodstream protecting the body from 'foreign bodies' such as bacteria, viruses and cancer cells. It affects the extent to which we are prone to infectious diseases, allergies, cancers and many other illnesses. It is not at present possible accurately to assess the overall efficiency of an individual's immune system, or immunocompetence. It is a very complex system with many interconnecting components. However, research has been carried out which suggests that stress can affect the ability of the immune system to protect the body against illness. Below is a selection of the findings from some of this research:

- In a study of men whose wives had died of breast cancer, Schleifer et al. (1979) reported that the functioning of the men's immune systems was significantly reduced during the month after their wives' deaths.
- Jemmott et al. (1985) showed that levels of antibodies in dental students fell in high stress situations such as taking exams.
- Cohen et al. (1991) injected a large number of healthy volunteers with either a common cold virus or an innocuous salt solution. All participants were also given a stress index based on their reports of the number of stressful events experienced in the previous year, the degree to which they felt able to cope and the incidence of negative feelings such as anger and depression.

Almost all the virus-injected participants showed signs of infection, but only about one-third actually developed colds. Moreover, the researchers found that even after controlling for factors such as age, cigarette and alcohol use, exercise and diet, the higher the stress index, the more likely were the participants to exhibit infection and cold symptoms (see diagram).

It was not clear how stress affected the body's resistance to the cold virus, since the two indicators of immunocompetence did not show any changes in response to stress.

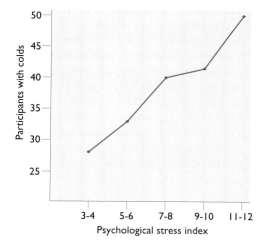

The percentage of virus-injected participants who developed colds in relation to the amount of stress reported (adapted from Cohen et al., 1991).

nesses are physical illnesses that are rooted in psychological problems). Death of the individual from one of these causes may be the result.

This depressing picture of stress responses is not an inevitable and unchangeable sequence. In the majority of people, the stressor is dealt with during Stage 1 or early Stage 2, and bodily responses return to normal. Frankenhauser (1983) suggests that there are gender differences in stress responses, in that women's responses show a higher increase than males', but return to baseline more quickly. This could be one of the factors underpinning the differences in resultant illnesses; men show a higher incidence of cardiovascular disease than women, which has been linked to long-term stress.

Arousal model

The concept of arousal, as described in conjunction with emotion in Chapter 9 and discussed in Chapter 12, was also applied as a nonspecific model of stress. Arousal was viewed as being beneficial to the individual's performance, up to an optimum level, but extremes of arousal produced stress and a corresponding decrement in performance (Yerkes–Dodson Law, see Figure 11.4). Performance increases up to an optimum level of arousal; if arousal continues to increase, performance declines. Stress may occur. A higher level of arousal is necessary for a simple, boring task, while a slightly lower level of arousal is better for a more complex task. Arousal levels vary between individuals. You may have noticed this phenomenon yourself: if you become too highly stressed before an exam, perhaps because you are desperate to do well, your performance is likely to be lower than you would expect of yourself.

The nonspecific idea of arousal would suggest that all stimuli would produce the same pattern of arousal; in real life, researchers have not found this to be so. As a model of stress, the concept of arousal has limited use.

Psychosocial stimuli model

Kagan and Levi (1975) suggested that psychosocial stimuli, such as life changes, prepare an individual for coping with stress. The extent to which they do so is influenced by genetic differences and learning experiences, which are subsequently reflected in the physiological stress response identified by Selye. However, even the authors admitted that this is a simple model; many facets began to be recognized as being implicated in stress.

Transactional model

Cox and Mackay (1976) suggested that stress is due to a dynamic transaction between the individual and the environment (see Figure 11.5). Important to this model is the individual's cognitive assessment of the perceived demands made on him or her, and that individual's perceived capability to deal with those demands. Stress is the result of the perceived demand outweighing the perceived capability. For example, an individual may perceive that the demand of taking four A levels in two years outweighs his or her capability. If the individual is pressured to do so, stress may result. This perception is influenced by a number of factors, such as personality, situational demands, previous experiences and any current stress state already existing.

Interactional model

The view of stress proposed by Lazarus (1976) included the suggestion that the individual's perception of capability interacted with cognitive appraisal of the threat. Again, a mismatch of the two resulted in

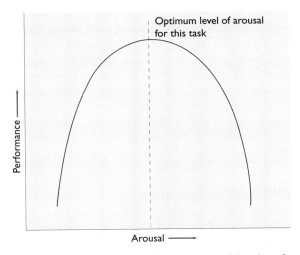

Figure 11.4 The relationship between arousal and performance

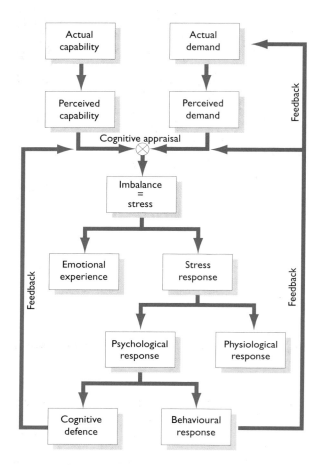

Figure 11.5 Transactional model of stress. Source: Cox (1978)

stress. Lazarus also looked at the role of frustration and conflict within the individual, in exacerbating stress.

General facet model

Beehr and Newman (1978) identified more than 150 variables involved in stress, giving recognition to the complexity of the problem. Their model is largely based on occupational stress. The organization referred to in the model is the workplace. This model gives recognition to changes occurring over time and feedback to the individual, which then results in personality and other changes. This is important in that subsequent reactions to stress may be influenced by these changes.

Individual differences involved in stress

There are a number of factors that cause people to experience and react to stress differently. Personality, race and gender may influence the way in which a person reacts to stress and which stressors are especially relevant to them. Some occupations are also recognized as being more stressful than others, although not to all individuals equally.

Personality

Once personality was recognized as having some bearing on individual experiences of stress, a number of different studies attempted to identify which particular characteristics were important. Some are described below.

Self-esteem

Self-esteem is the level of regard an individual has for him or herself (see Chapters 22 and 24). Extremely high levels of self-esteem may mean that the individual is overconfident and possibly unrealistic in expectations of self-efficacy. Self-efficacy is an individual's belief that he or she can perform required tasks and behaviours effectively. Low levels of self-esteem may indicate feelings of worthlessness, possibly resulting in depression and anxiety. A moderately high level of self-esteem has been shown to be associated with good mental health (Coopersmith, 1968).

Locus of control

The concept of locus of control was suggested by Rotter (1966) to identify how people saw the relationship between events and themselves. Each person has a locus of control that is either primarily external or primarily internal. We see our lives as being controlled by events outside the self if we have an external locus of control, or as being under the control of the self if we have an internal locus of control.

People with either an internal or an external locus of control can be subject to stress. Those who see themselves as recipients of all that life throws at them can come to view life as malevolent or depressing (this can be a precursor to Seligman's concept of 'learned helplessness'). Those who have an internal locus of control not only see themselves as being in control of their lives, but are also prone to blame themselves for things that go wrong. During a 'bad spell' (which we all have sometimes!) this self-blame can prove stressful. However, Johnson and Sarason (1978) found a higher incidence of depression and anxiety among those rated as high on external locus of control.

Type A/Type B

Type A personality was the phrase coined by Friedman and Rosenman (1974) to describe certain behaviour patterns displayed by patients in the USA who had developed coronary heart disease. Studies indicated that men who exhibited these patterns were two and a half times more likely to develop heart disease than were men who did not show these behaviours (Type B).

The type A personality may be at greater risk of heart disease than other people

Type A behaviours include being ambitious, competitive, alert, impatient and aggressive. Their speech is hurried, they gesture frequently and they have difficulty letting others finish what they want to say before interrupting. They are always in a hurry, to the point of appearing 'driven', showing chronically high levels of arousal. They exhibit 'deadline urgency' (having to get things done by a certain time) and extreme competitiveness, even in leisure pursuits. (See Exercise 11.1.)

Type B personalities may be equally ambitious, but do not appear 'driven'. Their job ambitions do not dominate their entire lives. They find time for family and friends, and tend to choose leisure pursuits that are less competitive than Type A's choice.

Type A people are often highly successful in their jobs, so their activities are not discouraged at work.

Exercise 11.1 Are you a Type A?

1. If you find you have 10 minutes to spare, do you:
   (a) squeeze in another job, or
   (b) have a cup of tea?
2. If you see someone struggling with a new task, do you:
   (a) take the job and do it yourself, or
   (b) just watch and encourage them?
3. If you are playing a game with a friend and you lose, do you:
   (a) feel angry with yourself,
   (b) shrug and go for a Coke?
4. When you finish a meal, do you:
   (a) get up and get going on the next job, or
   (b) sit at the table and chat?

Score

Three or four (a)s – take the heat off yourself, or life may be too short to worry!

Two (a)s – take life as it comes.

No (a)s – life could just pass you by!

GLOSSARY

Type A personality A pattern of personality characteristics, for example competitiveness, impatience, time-urgency, aggressiveness, which have been linked in the USA with the incidence of heart disease.

Ganster (1986) suggested that Type A behaviour may promote the risk of cardiac disease because it involves the system in the stress response. Organizations should weigh this risk against the desire for high performance from its Type A employees.

Other studies have found that the Type A personality appears to be involved in cardiovascular disease but is not a reliable predictor for this (Matthews, 1988).

These studies have all looked at men's responses, partly because at the time they were conducted, there were fewer women in executive and managerial positions and fewer women exhibiting cardiovascular disease. Currently, the incidence of both of these has risen, although women still lag behind on the managerial and heart disease fronts. The rises may not be directly correlated because there are other confounding variables. For example, more women have taken up smoking, which is a known causal factor in cardiovascular problems. Women may be resistant to 'executive stress', but if they smoke, it could be this which is causing the rise in heart disease, which may be wrongly correlated with stress.

'Hardy' personality

Some individuals seem to cope well with one stressful event after another, while others break down under very little pressure. Researchers have attempted to verify why this should be so; personality characteristics is one area of study.

Kobasa (1979) gave questionnaires to 600 executives or managers, asking them to itemize illnesses and stressful events they had experienced in the previous three years. Personality questionnaires were also completed. From the responses, Kobasa analysed two groups of responses. Both groups had scored above average on stressful events, but one group scored below average on illnesses, while the other group scored above average.

From the analysis it was found that the group of high stress/low illness group:

- felt more in control of their lives;
- were more actively involved in their work and social lives; and
- were more oriented towards challenges and change.

Critics of this study suggested that these characteristics could be the result, rather than the cause, of illnesses; for example, it is hard to become totally absorbed in your work or social life if you are ill. Subsequently, a longitudinal study (Kobasa et al., 1982) monitored executives for two years and identified that those who set out with positive attitudes were the ones who suffered fewest illnesses.

The personality characteristics of these hardy individuals include control, commitment and challenge. Control, as we have discussed earlier, has been demonstrated as a buffer to stress. Commitment may typify those with firm social support systems around them, while challenge involves cognitive appraisal of situations in order to reassess them benignly.

However, is this type of **hardy personality** available to everyone? If you have a low-interest job, you probably feel little commitment to it; it provides you with little challenge, and you almost certainly have no control over your area of work. You may argue that the essential characteristics could be assembled into interests outside work, but a 40-hour week at a boring job leaves people feeling stressed and therefore too tired to undertake challenging outside interests. It must be remembered that Kobasa's work was undertaken with executives and managers, who do not have exclusive rights to feeling stressed.

Racial/cultural factors

Constructs such as the Type A personality and rating scales such as SRRS have been criticized because there is no consideration of possible cultural differences in the kinds of stressors people are exposed to. Factors which cause stress in one culture may be nonexistent in another. Also, the additional stressors that people face in African, Asian or other ethnic minority communities within European and North American countries may not exist in the wider population.

Anderson (1991) identified three levels of stressors which are faced by African-Americans:

1. Chronic stressors such as racism, overcrowding and poor living conditions;
2. Major life events such as those listed in the SRRS;
3. Daily events or hassles.

GLOSSARY

Hardy personality A term used to describe individuals who appear to cope well with stress and to resist illness.

Anderson believes that while stress can exist at all three levels, it is likely to be most acute at level 3. This is largely because of the daily conflict and frustration experienced by African-Americans who are put under pressure to become assimilated into the mainstream white community but at the same time face barriers to their doing so.

Gender

Many facets of stress and stress responses show male/female differences. For example, while Type A behaviour may not be exclusive to males, the associated correlation with cardiovascular disease is much stronger in males than females.

There are also still differences in the ratio of males to females in a number of occupations; the resultant differences in stress levels may reflect these job differences.

Surveys have shown that, where both partners in a marriage or a household have full-time jobs, the female still takes more responsibility for home making and child rearing. This would appear to suggest greater stress on the female partner, trying to do 'two jobs'. Studies have demonstrated that women with children and full-time jobs show more instances of ill-health than do those without children.

Women often have stronger social support systems in place in their lives, which may mitigate the levels of stress experienced; this is discussed further in the next section.

? SELF-ASSESSMENT QUESTIONS

1. Describe a personality trait and say why it may produce stress in an individual.
2. Describe (a) a personality type likely to experience stress, and (b) a personality type resistant to stress.
3. How does either culture or gender influence the experience of stress?
4. Discuss whether occupation has any bearing on stress in the individual.

Coping with stress

Anxiety and stress are disturbing experiences, producing high levels of physiological arousal, which motivates the individual to try to reduce the stress level; this process is called 'coping'. Some coping processes will be briefly described here; they are relevant to physiological psychology in that they are instrumental in reducing autonomic arousal and thereby returning physiological processes to the baseline, but a full discussion of their application is outside the scope of this volume.

Lazarus and Folkman (1984) suggest there are two main forms of coping: **emotion-focused coping** and **problem-focused coping**

Emotion-focused coping

Emotion-focused coping involves an attempt to reduce the disturbing emotions which invariably accompany the experience of stress. Some examples are discussed below.

Social support

At home Social support processes are the network of friends and relatives willing to provide psychological assistance, even if only a willing ear, in times of stress. A number of studies have shown that where social support networks are strong, even extreme stress can be mitigated. Women often seem to maintain stronger social support networks than men, probably because of their primary involvement in childcare, a task that is made easier if shared among family or friends.

In the workplace Social support is also utilized in the workplace, frequently being stronger among shop-floor employees than at management level. While social support at home is seen as having a useful function, this does not always generalize to the work situation; in the same way, social support at work does not often carry over to the home (van de Pompe and de Heus, 1993).

GLOSSARY
Emotion-focused coping A form of coping with stress which involves attempts to reduce the negative emotions which often accompany stress (Lazarus and Folkman, 1984).
Problem-focused coping An attempt to reduce a stressful situation by trying to understand better its causes and to find possible courses of action.

Traumatic events Traumatic events, such as wars or earthquakes, produce strong feelings of camaraderie among those trying to help the survivors, thereby helping to reduce the stressful experience to a bearable level. This is another form of social support.

Defence mechanisms

Defence mechanisms were suggested by Freud as methods we employ to cope with anxiety and problems we do not wish to face directly. Inevitably they involve some distortion of reality. As such, these mechanisms prevent an individual from getting to grips with a problem and solving it, though they may give some temporary relief. Box 11.5 gives a brief description of some defence mechanisms.

Maladaptive coping methods

Taking drugs and heavy drinking are regarded as maladaptive, in that they mask the problem for only a limited time. When the effect wears off, the stressor is still there. This is not the same as taking one drink to relax. A small amount of alcohol will depress activity in the CNS, as discussed in Chapter 8. This will reduce temporary arousal effectively but does not deal with ongoing stress.

Problem-focused coping

Problem-focused coping involves trying to understand the problem situation better and taking action to deal with it. This kind of coping includes various forms of **stress management**.

Cognitive appraisal

This involves thinking about the stressful situation and trying to find ways of solving the problem. For example, driving to work down the motorway was proving very stressful; by leaving home five minutes earlier, I was able to drive to work along the B-roads, a much more pleasant way to start the day.

Time management

Not only trying to cram too much into a day, but also managing one's time ineffectively, can often be a source of stress. Individuals can be taught to look at what has to be accomplished in a day, or a week, and find

---

Box 11.5 Some defence mechanisms

Avoidance. The individual avoid the anxiety-provoking situation, in order not to experience stress. Social phobics avoids social situations, thereby fooling themselves that they have no problems.

Denial. When a situation is too painful to face, an individual may deny that it simply exists. The partner of a terminally ill patient may refuse to accept that there is anything wrong, despite having been given all the facts.

Repression. The problem is pushed into the unconscious so that it does not have to be dealt with.

Projection. The problem is projected to another person rather than being seen as one's own problem.

Rationalization. The individual looks for logical reasons for the stressful situation. In fact, these may not appear logical to anyone else.

Reaction formation. Other thoughts or feelings are substituted, which are diametrically opposed to the truth. For example, a man may be experiencing stress because he is strongly attracted to his best friend's wife. In order to deal with this, he develops a hatred for her; this feeling causes less stress than does the strong attraction.

---

efficient ways of working so that they are not constantly backtracking and thereby wasting time. Establishing priorities and working to these is an efficient method of time management.

Assertiveness

Assertiveness training helps people to learn to say 'no' when imposed upon. They learn to ask for what they want without being aggressive or self-effacing. It is often a highly effective technique to counteract low self-esteem. This counteracts stress in several ways: by learning to say no, people are not overworked or

---

GLOSSARY

Stress management A term used to describe a number of psychological techniques which are used to help people to reduce stress: for example, time-management, relaxation, biofeedback, cognitive restructuring (changing the way one thinks about the situation).

imposed upon; by asking for what they want, they are more likely to be happy with their situation; by seeing themselves as effective, they become more comfortable with themselves.

Relaxation and meditation

There is nothing really 'transcendental' about this. It is a specific technique that enables people to focus attention on specific thoughts. If attention is focused, it cannot wander and continually mentally 'rehearse' worries and anxieties, which would raise autonomic arousal levels. During relaxation, breathing is controlled, and heart rate and blood pressure are lowered.

Exercise

Exercise has been shown to be a highly effective form of stress management; even the physically unfit can reap the benefits by taking walks. It is thought that exercise shows two kinds of benefit in terms of relieving stress:

■ At the physiological level, it provides an outlet for the fight or flight responses, by providing physical activity.
■ At the situational level, it has the advantage of removing the individual from the stress-provoking situation.

Biofeedback

It has been suggested that by teaching people how to lower their blood pressure and reduce other bodily symptoms of stress, the harmful effects of stress may be counteracted (see Chapter 33 for a discussion of the techniques of biofeedback). To date, few studies have shown conclusively that the beneficial effects are maintained outside the laboratory situation. In addition, it has been argued that **biofeedback** is simply masking the experience of stress, not actually providing a respite.

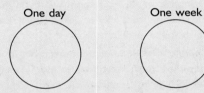

Exercise 11.2

Managing time effectively is one way of reducing stress. Try the following:

Draw two circles as below and complete these 'pies' with time you spend in one day and one week on work (college or other), hobbies, partner, housework, family, friends, self, etc.:

One day   One week

Show how you would like these 'pies' to be:

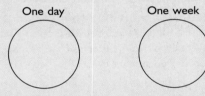

One day   One week

List the steps you will take in order to achieve these changes.

❓ SELF-ASSESSMENT QUESTIONS

1. Briefly explain what Lazarus and Folkman meant by emotion-focused coping and problem-focused coping. Give some examples of each.
2. Why are defence mechanisms unlikely to reduce stress in the long term?
3. In what ways may relaxation and exercise help to relieve stress?

Taking exercise can be an effective way of reducing stress

> **GLOSSARY**
>
> **Biofeedback** A psychological method where people are trained to lower their own blood pressure and reduce other bodily symptoms of stress.

Chapter summary

- Anxiety may lead to a state of stress, which is a physiological condition with both psychological and physiological consequences.

- A stressor is the situation, individual or object that causes a state of stress. Internal conflicts may arise when an individual has to decide between two incompatible choices. These may be approach–approach conflicts (alternatives that are equally attractive) or avoidance–avoidance conflicts (alternatives that are equally unattractive).

- Holmes and Rahe investigate life events that may evoke stress and produced a rating scale, the Social Readjustment Rating Scale (SRRS) which yields a Life Change Score. Investigators have found that a high Life Change Score is often linked to physical illness or psychological problems.

- Critics of the SRRS point out that other factors arising from the stressful situation, for example an unhealthy diet following a bereavement, may be the cause of ill health. Also, a breakdown in health could be the cause rather than the effect of particular life events.

- Lazarus suggested that daily hassles, small daily problems, cause more stress problems than do life events, and that the effects of hassles may be offset by 'uplifts', or pleasant events.

- Occupational stress is becoming a more common phenomenon, particularly among doctors, social workers, nurses and other caring professionals. Such people who experience a heavy workload may suffer 'burnout', a feeling of total mental and physical exhaustion.

- Research has shown that if an individual can predict when an event is likely to occur, it is perceived as being less stressful. Similarly, feeling that one has control over events makes those events seem less stressful.

- Models of stress include physiological models, which describe the changes taking place within the individual under stress. Selye's general adaptation syndrome describes three stages in the body's responses to stress.

- Psychoimmunology refers to the study of the effects of psychological factors such as stress on the body's immune system. Research findings suggest that stress can affect the ability of the immune system to protect the body against illness.

- The arousal model suggests that arousal is beneficial to an individual's performance up to an optimum level, but extremes of arousal produce stress and a deficit in performance. This model is useful only for identifying broad patterns of response rather than specific reactions.

- The transactional model suggests that the individual's perception of capability interacts with cognitive appraisal of the threat. A mismatch between the two results in stress.

- Early models fail to explain why some individuals experience stress in specific situations, while others do not. Later models take into account other factors, such as individual differences and localized environmental factors.

- Individual differences between people may explain why we do not all recognize the same experiences as being stressful.

- Many factors influence the things we find stressful as individuals and the way in which we respond. Personality variables, such as the 'type A' or 'hardy' personality, traits, such as self-esteem, and factors such as gender, race and occupation all have a bearing on the way we encounter stressors and the way in which we deal with them.

- Anxiety and stress are distressing experiences for the individual; coping processes are usually invoked to reduce stress levels.

- Levels of social support available and positive coping methods, such as problem-focused coping, assertiveness training, exercise and time management, may help to reduce the experience of stress.

Further reading

Cox, T. (1978). *Stress*. Basingstoke: Macmillan. A review of theories, causes and effects of stress in the light of empirical research.

Atkinson, R.L., Atkinson, R.C., Smith, E.E. and Bem, D.J. (1993). *Introduction to Psychology*, 11th edn. Orlando, FL: Harcourt Brace Jovanovich. Chapter 15 gives a very good introduction to all aspects of research into stress and looks at coping skills and stress management.

Epilogue

In this chapter, as throughout our discussion of the biological bases of behaviour, we have tried to give the reader some insight into the mind/body relationship, based on our current understanding of how the body 'works', together with how mental processes appear to relate to these physical processes. Through constraints of book size, it has been possible to look at only a few specific areas of knowledge. There are more, and it is hoped the reader's appetite will have been whetted to search these out.

- In some areas, the knowledge base is being extended almost day by day. There are exciting new developments occurring in physiological psychology and its associated fields of cognitive science and neuropsychology.
- The field of computer modelling of cognitive processes has been mentioned in this book. This area is giving useful insights to psychologists from many disciplines into the ways in which human learning may occur. Its premise has also been utilized to rehabilitate patients after brain injury. As human beings, we never stop learning; if the brain can be reeducated to process information in new ways, forming new neural networks to replace those which are damaged or useless, skills may be relearned which were previously thought impossible. This has tremendous implications for people injured in accidents – and their relatives.
- Increased knowledge of the biochemical functioning of the brain has led to advances in neuropharmacology. New drugs and new treatments are being used to treat people with mental problems that have demonstrable physiological causes. The quality of life is improved tremendously for a number of these people, which is what treatment is all about – not just sustaining life, but improving it.
- Increased knowledge of brain physiology and functioning has led to pioneering work in the field of neural transplants. Early work carried out in Sweden showed that Parkinson's disease (due to deterioration of the dopamine-producing neurons) could be alleviated by transplanting

such cells from a foetus into an adult brain. Foetal cells were used in order to overcome the problems of tissue rejection. However, if a healthy neuron could be removed from an individual, and perhaps grown in culture, and then retransplanted into that same person, both ethical questions and the practical problems of rejection would be resolved at the same time.

- These new fields, at the cutting edge of science, raise new practical, ethical and philosophical questions, which must be addressed. If it can be demonstrated that rehabilitation can be brought about even after severe brain injury, to provide an acceptable quality of life, what are the new criteria for keeping people alive on life-support machines? The practical implications of provision of treatment, and costs, will have to be considered, as must support systems to alleviate the psychological stress imposed on that individual's family.
- The same sorts of problem arise in individuals on drug therapies. Their treatments may be expensive; their families will now, of necessity, be involved in their care, as there are currently few long-stay psychiatric hospital places. Is there a more than an even chance that their quality of life will be improved by their treatment? With the advances made in science in recent years, the answer is 'yes', provided the practicalities of care can keep up with science.
- The ethical question of using aborted foetuses for neural transplants is one that raises many arguments. Emotively it is argued that these are living humans who should not be used for 'spare parts'. On the other hand, if they are to die anyway, should they not help to improve the quality of life for someone else? However, recent progress made in tissue cultures may remove the need to use foetal cells.
- New horizons in science – especially the human sciences – are bound to raise new ethical, practical and philosophical questions, which will need to be met as they arise. Meanwhile, the frontiers of knowledge are still being pushed back. We live in an exciting age.

PART 3

Cognition

Cognition refers to those aspects of behaviour (especially human behaviour) which are controlled by the higher centres of the brain, the cerebral cortex. It tends to be concerned with conscious rather than unconscious processes though there are exceptions to this, and voluntary rather than involuntary responses. In this part we are dealing especially with selective attention, perception, memory, thinking and language.

Contents

INTRODUCTION
Cognition 239
- What are cognitive processes? 239
- Historical background 239
- Some methods used by cognitive psychologists 240
- Cognitive science 241
- Some concepts in cognitive psychology 241

CHAPTER 12
Attention 244
- Selective attention 244
- Is attention conscious or unconscious? 251
- Vigilance or sustained attention 253
- Psychophysics 257

CHAPTER 13
Perception 261
- Sensation and perception 261

- Theories, models and principles 269
- Visual illusions 274
- Do we have to learn to perceive? 278

CHAPTER 14
Memory 288
- Early research 289
- Models of memory 290
- Real-life memory 303
- You too can have a better memory 307

CHAPTER 15
Thinking and language 316
- The nature of thinking 316
- Concept formation 319
- Problem solving 323
- Language and thinking 331

Cognition

What are cognitive processes?

Human beings (in common with other animals) function at various levels. At the most basic level, systems exist within the brain to control physiological functioning. The monitoring of bodily needs, such as the need for food and drink, for fresh air and sleep is part of the function of the lower brain. Cognitive processes, on the other hand, relate to those functions which have their control within the higher brain centres of the cortex. To an extent it is the development of a more complex cortical function to override and complement the lower brain which distinguishes human beings from animals. Cognition tends to be concerned with conscious rather than unconscious processes, though there is some overlap, and with voluntary rather than involuntary responses. The particular areas of cognition dealt with in this part include selective attention, perception, memory, language and thought.

Historical background

It is important to understand the historical background to the present study of cognition. Hearnshaw (1987) claims that cognitive psychology is both one of the oldest and also one of the newest areas of psychology. There is a full account in the Introduction to Part 1 of this book of some of the beginnings of psychology, and it might be useful at this point to read this chapter again.

Emergence of cognitive psychology

The factors that contributed to the emergence of cognitive psychology in the late 1950s and the early 1960s have included the following:

- The behaviourist approach, especially in the USA, seemed to be inadequate to explain complex human behaviour. Behaviourist learning theory, an approach based upon stimulus-response and reinforcement, was increasingly falling short of providing satisfactory explanations.
- Chomsky, researching language acquisition, rejected behaviourist explanations of it. The structure of language was too complex to be explained in behaviourist terms. His contention that humans have an inborn capacity to master language conflicted with behaviourists' belief in a *tabula rasa* (the notion put forward originally by John Locke in the 18th century that the human mind was a blank sheet at birth and that all human behaviour was learned).
- Piaget's constructivist approach to child development, which concentrated on the establishment of concepts, was causing something of a revolution in primary education in the 1950s and 1960s. It suggested that what he termed schemata were established, as children developed, as a result of what they experienced. These schemata represented the basic building blocks of intelligence. A fuller account of Piaget's research can be found in Birch (1997) and in Chapter 20 of this book.
- The advent of computers encouraged an information-processing approach in the communication and computer sciences which appealed to some psychologists.
- The needs of military technology were also providing a spur for development in this area. Much of the work done on attention and vigilance, described in Chapter 12, was the result of operational needs arising during the Second World War. For instance, Mackworth's researches into sustained attention (1950, p. 254) resulted from the need for radar operators and others to maintain their vigilance over long periods.

Some methods used by cognitive psychologists

Modelling

It is common for cognitive psychologists to attempt to build up a model of how the brain might be operating in a particular set of circumstances. The **modelling** hypothesis is an elaborate one, which is open to testing by means of experiment. An example of this is the template-matching model to explain pattern recognition. This model hypothesizes that when we see a face, in order to be able to recognize it we must mentally match it against the 'templates' of all the faces stored in our memory until we come upon one which fits perfectly. The model describes a theoretical process which might be going on in the brain and which can be tested experimentally. In this case the model turned out not to be a very satisfactory one, as will be explained in Chapter 13.

Advantages and limitations of modelling

Advantages On the positive side, modelling allowed researchers to come to grips in a meaningful way with the processes within the brain. Instead of saying, as behaviourists had done, that these were inaccessible to research, they could make an informed guess about what was happening in the brain which could be verified (or discounted) by empirical research.

Limitations On the minus side, it made great demands upon the creativity of researchers. The hypotheses to be tested resulted from speculation about what might be happening. If they were wildly adrift, much time and resources could be lost. However, if the informed guesswork was accurate, important insights might be gained.

Information processing

Information processing is an approach to the study of cognitive processes which has become increasingly popular among psychologists. It has two important components:

■ Mental processes are seen as a flow of information through various stages, which can be represented on a flow chart. This includes both the flow of information within a person's mind, and also the flow of information between the individual and the environment.
■ Mental processes may be better understood by comparing them with the operation of a computer with its three components: data, memory and program.

The information processing approach 'can be seen as an attempt to understand the software of a very complex computer' (Evans, 1983, p. 3). An example might make this clearer (see Exercise 31.1).

Exercise 31.1

Suppose you want to post a letter.

What are the stages you need to go through in this operation? As an exercise write down all the stages you need to go through in the process from the point when you have finished writing it. A suggested series of operational stages is at the end of this introduction. Check whether you identified the same number of stages.

At each stage there there will be collection of data from the environment, more data recovered from memory and a program (a set of instructions). The advantages and disadvantages of an information processing approach include the following:

■ **An advantage** is that each stage can be manipulated experimentally and observations made, especially of times taken for the stage.
■ **A disadvantage** is that you are looking at each little bit of the process on its own without much reference either to the rest of the process or to the individual participant. There are also severe limitations to the computer analogy which will be discussed further in Chapter 15 of this book.

GLOSSARY

Modelling The construction of a hypothetical model of what might be happening in the brain which can then be tested experimentally.

Information processing An attempt to understand cognition as the operation of the software of a very complex computer.

Ecologically valid methods

The results obtained in research need to hold good also 'in the real world'. Much research into memory, for instance, has been laboratory based and involved participants in memorizing unrelated words or nonsense syllables. This is not the kind of task we engage in in everyday life! By contrast, Bartlett in his research described in Chapter 14 (pp. 289–90) focused upon meaningful material and natural situations. Ecologically valid research attempts to mirror more accurately what happens outside the laboratory. This includes material used (Bartlett's story to be recalled is closer to reality than Ebbinghaus's nonsense syllables), the participants employed and the context. Research into eye-witness testimony, absent-mindedness or the ability of teachers to remember the names and faces of the members of their classes is likely to be more ecologically valid than laboratory research into recall of isolated words. However, it is not so easy to obtain good control of variables in this kind of research. Perhaps the way forward is a combination of ecologically valid and laboratory-based research. We have attempted to examine both.

Cognitive science

It is worthwhile to make a very brief mention of cognitive science, a developing discipline which relates to cognitive processing. Brown (1990) has suggested that this seems to take one of three forms:

- As a completely new discipline with its own subject matter (intelligent systems, both natural and artificial), its own methods and its own vocabulary. It suggests that mental states can be replicated and studied by using computers.
- As an umbrella discipline, providing a whole range of new tools for studying cognitive processes. These include: (a) The study of **artificial intelligence**, a branch of computer science that attempts to program computers to perform the kind of functions traditionally only associated with humans (language, for instance, or problem solving); and (b) **neuroscience**, which relates to attempts to find neurological explanations for mental processes. Examples might be the experiments of Hubel and Wiesel (1962) who used microelectrodes to pick up impulses from the visual cortex of a cat and found

that particular cells in the visual cortex responded to lines of specific orientations (see Chapter 7 for further details), or the study of evoked cortical potentials, electrical signals generated by neurons just below an electrode placed on the scalp. This is mentioned further in Chapter 12.

- As **ecocognitivism**, a view that rejects the notion that it is possible to study mental states independently of the ecology in which they occur: that is to say, their causes and effects in the real world.

Some concepts in cognitive psychology

It is worthwhile mentioning in this introduction some concepts which will crop up later in the book. These include distinctions made between top-down and bottom-up approaches and between serial and parallel processing.

You see, he's already into bottom-up processing

GLOSSARY

Artificial intelligence Involves attempts to program computers to mimic the operation of the human brain.

Neuroscience Attempts to find neurological explanations for mental processes.

Ecocognitivism The study of mental operations taking into account the 'real life' context in which they occur.

Top-down or bottom-up processing

Top-down processing starts with the broad context within which processing occurs – that is, the needs of the individual and the setting – and only after that considers the detailed characteristics of the stimulus being processed. For instance, a top-down approach to how children learn to read suggests that they first make predictions about what the text is most likely to mean from contextual and other clues. The hypotheses formed are then tested against the available evidence, which includes context as well as the words and finally letters making up the words on the page. **Bottom-up processing** starts with the stimuli and only after they have been processed do other factors come into play. To take the same reading example, in a bottom-up model of reading a child starts with letters and the sounds they represent, then words, their sound and their meaning and only after this the context and the sense of the whole.

Figure 3I.1 shows a distinction between top-down and bottom-up processing as it might be applied to the analysis of a musical symphony.

Note that top-down analysis begins with the entire work, while bottom-up processing begins with the notes.

Serial or parallel processing

In **serial processing** the assumption is made that each stage of the processing sequence must be completed

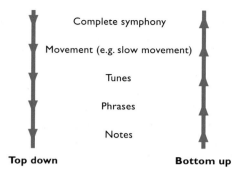

Figure 3I.1 An example of top-down and bottom-up processing as they might be applied to a musical symphony

before the next is begun. **Parallel processing**, on the other hand, implies that more than one stage of

---

GLOSSARY

Top-down processing Cognitive processing which takes account, first, of the holistic context of an operation, then deals with the detail of it.

Bottom-up processing Cognitive processing which deals first with details of an operation and then takes account of context.

Serial processing Completing one processing operation before commencing another.

Parallel processing Attempting to attend to more than one processing operation at the same time.

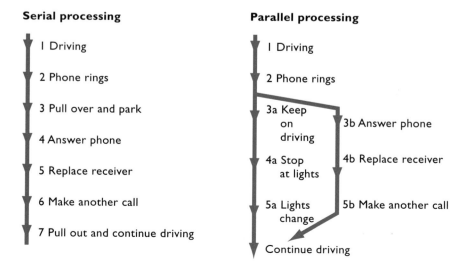

Figure 3I.2 An example of serial or parallel processing. A driver is going down a busy road and the car phone rings

processing may occur at any one time. For example, Allport and his colleagues suggested that it might be possible to pay attention to more than one thing at a time, provided that different senses were involved (Allport et al., 1972). This would involve parallel processing. Broadbent, however, suggested that there was a single channel-processing mechanism in which one item is attended to at a time. This is serial processing. Both Allport's and Broadbent's models are discussed in Chapter 14. Figure 31.2 attempts to illustrate this distinction. The flow chart shows what might happen in serial or parallel processing when you are driving down a busy road and the car phone rings.

 SELF-ASSESSMENT QUESTIONS

Self-assessment questions relating to this introduction are included on p. 257.

A solution to Exercise 31.1

1. Find an envelope.
2. Fold the paper on which the letter is written in such a way that it will go into the envelope.
3. Put the letter into the envelope.
4. Seal it.
5. Verify the address from your address book (or from your memory, if you are confident enough).
6. Find an appropriate stamp.
7. Stick it on.
8. Verify that the letter is ready to go (the address and the stamp are correct).
9. Find your way to the post box.
10. Ascertain that the post box is ready to receive the letter (i.e. that there will shortly be a collection).
11. Post the letter.

CHAPTER 12

Attention

Selective attention   244
▓ Advertising and attention   244
▓ Experimental studies of attention   245
▓ Models of attention   245

Is attention conscious or unconscious?   251
▓ Schneider and Shiffrin's experiments   251
▓ Feature integration theory   251
▓ Kahneman's capacity theory of
   attention   252

Vigilance or sustained attention   253
▓ Early research   253
▓ Theories of vigilance decrement   254

Psychophysics   257
▓ Thresholds of sensation   257
▓ Signal detection theory   259

Objectives

By the end of this chapter you should be able to:

▓ Describe what is meant by 'selective attention';

▓ Identify the problem of the 'cocktail party' phenomenon which Cherry investigated, and outline his conclusions;

▓ Show an understanding of the theories and models of selective attention formulated by Broadbent, Treisman, Deutsch and Deutsch, and Kahneman;

▓ Distinguish between unconscious and conscious attentional processes;

▓ Describe some of the factors which influence divided attention;

▓ Describe some of the research into sustained attention (or vigilance) and account for some of the findings.

Selective attention

Human beings are constantly bombarded by stimuli from the world in which they live, but can take in and use only a very small portion of this material. There exist, therefore, mechanisms which enable them to select and process stimuli which are valuable, or of interest, and to allow the rest to pass them by. This section will examine this process of selective attention.

Advertising and attention

To illustrate the way in which our attention is arrested and held, let us look at how advertisers attempt to attract our attention. Some of the characteristics of a stimulus which determine whether or not we will pay attention to it are the following:

▓ Its intensity: a bright colour will attract us more than a dull one.

■ Its size: a large thing is more likely to seize our attention than something small.

■ Its duration or repetition: a fleeting stimulus will not catch our attention as easily as one which persists or is repeated.

■ Its emotional content: a stimulus which carries emotional overtones for us will attract us more than a neutral one.

■ Its suddenness or novelty: a sudden or unexpected stimulus is likely to catch our attention more easily than one we have been expecting or that we have encountered before.

■ Contrasting stimuli will attract attention more readily than those which are similar to each other.

■ Something which moves is more likely to attract attention than something stationary. When a rabbit is in danger from a predator it freezes, thus avoiding attracting the predator's attention.

Focusing on one conversation amid a babble of noise at a party

of them. They were then questioned to find out how much of each message they had retained. Of the unshadowed message physical characteristics only were extracted, for instance:

■ whether the voice was male or female;
■ how loud or soft it was; and
■ if a tone replaced speech.

Regarding content, very little was picked up. Participants did not even notice if the speaker was using a foreign language, or if the speech was reversed. Processing of the unshadowed message seemed to be minimal.

Exercise 12.1

Take time to observe ten advertisements (on television or elsewhere). List the occasions when each of the above characteristics are evident. Assess which seem to be most used and most effective.

Experimental studies of attention

Cherry's cocktail party experiments

Cherry (1953) was particularly interested in what he called the **cocktail party phenomenon**. It applies to any kind of party situation. You have almost certainly experienced it. You are talking to someone in one part of the room and someone in another part of the room mentions your name or says something about you. You prick up your ears right away.

Cherry's aims were:

■ to examine how individuals can focus on one conversation amid a babble of noise (as in a party);

■ to ascertain how much of the unattended material is retained.

In his experiments, participants had two messages presented to them, one to each ear. They were asked to shadow (listen particularly to and repeat out loud) one

Models of attention

Broadbent's model of selective attention

Broadbent (1958) developed a model of selective attention as a result of his split-span experiments (Figure 12.1). These were experiments with **dichotic listening** (that is, listening to messages presented separately to each ear). An example of these is described in Box 12.1.

GLOSSARY

Cocktail party phenomenon A phenomenon described by Cherry where an individual may still attend to a message relevant to him or her while focused on another message in a crowded room.

Dichotic listening Listening to messages presented separately to each ear.

Box 12.1   An example of Broadbent's experiments on selective attention

Three pairs of digits were presented to each participant dichotically – three to one ear, three to the other – like this:

left	right
7	6
4	8
8	9

Participants found it much easier to recall all the digits from one ear then all from the other, rather than in pairs, as they had been presented: 748 then 689 rather than 76, 48, 89. When they were asked specifically to recall them in pairs they managed only 20 per cent correct recall.

Broadbent's explanation for this was that there is what he called a sensory buffer or filter. When two messages reach this filter together, one only can be processed; the other is reserved in the filter for future processing. The brain's limited processing capacity is thus not overloaded. Processing preference is determined by some physical attribute of the messages, in this case which ear received them first. Thus, the message to the right ear is reserved until all the left ear's message has been processed.

Other factors such as pitch or tone also seem to determine priority. Broadbent envisages information from the senses being held briefly in a short-term memory store before passing to a selective filter. This filter selects information on a physical basis, a high voice as opposed to a low voice or input from one ear as opposed to another. The selected information passes to a single-channel processor and from there to the output stage, whatever response is required. Unselected information is retained for future processing.

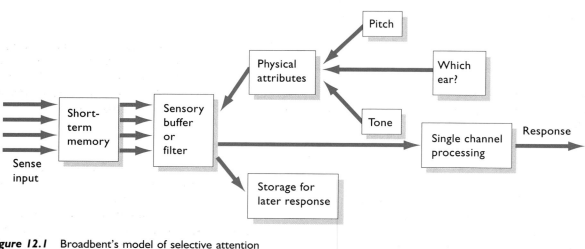

Figure 12.1   Broadbent's model of selective attention

Cocktail party phenomenon   While Broadbent's model dealt well with the phemonena which Cherry found in his shadowing trials, it had the limitation that it did not explain what he termed the 'cocktail party phenomenon'. An individual who has focused attention upon one conversation can nevertheless pick up relevant information from somewhere else in the room (a name for instance). This would indicate more than one level of selection. Moray (1959) tested this phenomenon by presenting a participant's name to the unattended ear while the participant was shadowing another message with the other ear. In nearly every case the name was picked up.

Other factors influencing processing include the following.

Experience of the participants   Underwood (1974) conducted similar experiments with participants who had had no experience of such tasks before, and compared their recall of pairs of digits with that of Moray, a researcher of great experience. While the naive participants could manage only 8 per cent recall, Moray managed 67 per cent.

The nature of the material   Allport et al. (1972) presented participants with different shadowing tasks. Passages from George Orwell's *Selected Essays* were presented to one ear to be shadowed, random words to be learned to the other. As might have been expected from Broadbent's model, very few words were recalled. However, when Allport replaced the words with a pictorial learning task, recall of the pictorial material was much better, suggesting that the dissimilarity of the two inputs was an important factor.

In an extension to this study, Allport et al. (1972) turned their attention to another kind of medium, music. Participants were all skilled piano players. They had again to shadow continuous speech, but in this case they had at the same time to sight-read piano music from a score. As with the first experiment, the second task did not interfere. They were equally good at sight-reading with or without the shadowing task. The sight-reading task also seemed to have no effect on the accuracy with which they performed the shadowing task.

Shaffer (1975), in two experiments, extended Allport's findings. In the first, a copy typist was made to shadow a piece of prose, heard over headphones while copy-typing a piece in German (a language she did not understand) from a visual presentation. In the second, the typist performed an audio-typing task, listening over headphones to material to be typed. She had at the same time one of two other tasks to perform: she had (a) to shadow a prose passage presented to the other ear; and (b) to read aloud a passage presented to her visually.

While the results in the first of these experiments showed little deterioration on the shadowing task, in the second there seemed to be considerable interference. These studies seem to lend some support to the view that separate channels are used to process different kinds of information.

Conscious or unconscious processing   Von Wright et al. (1975) suggested that failure to recall material presented to the unshadowed ear did not mean that it remained unprocessed. It may have been processed without conscious awareness. Their experiment was in two stages: first, a long list of words was presented to Finnish participants. When the Finnish word for 'suitable' was presented they sometimes received an electric shock. In the second stage of the experiment, participants shadowed one list of words while a second list presented to the other ear went unshadowed. In the unshadowed list was the previously shocked word, its synonym or its homonym (a word which either meant or sounded the same). When it was presented there was a noticeable change in galvanic skin response (GSR) (a measure of emotion). There had apparently been an emotional response to a word which had not been processed.

Meaning as a factor in selective attention   Gray and Wedderburn (1960) attempted to show that the meaning of messages to each ear had a bearing on which was selected. In a dichotic listening experiment participants were presented with digits interspersed with a coherent message. For example:

left ear	right ear
who	6
8	goes
there	7

Unlike participants in Broadbent's study, those in Gray and Wedderburn's experiment found little difficulty in recalling a coherent message 'Who goes there!' and then 687, even though the message had been presented partly to one ear, partly to the other.

Treisman's attenuation model

Treisman (1960, 1964a and b) used the shadowing technique originally developed by Cherry. An account of her experiments is in Box 12.2.

These experiments provide evidence that there is at least some processing of the unselected messages. The result of them was a revision of Broadbent's model of selective attention to what became known as the **attenuation** model. While one channel is still selected on the basis of its physical properties, the filter does not completely block the unselected messages but weakens them, so that a stimulus of higher intensity is needed for them to be processed. Instead of the all-or-nothing processing which Broadbent's model implies,

---

GLOSSARY

Attenuation A mechanism proposed by Treisman, whereby an unattended message is reduced, but may still be attended to if it reaches a threshold of intensity.

Box 12.2 Treisman's experiments on selective attention

Participants had to repeat the message coming into one ear, the 'shadowed message', while ignoring the other, the 'unattended message'. In one experiment, the shadowed message was in English, the unattended message was a French translation of it. The majority of participants recognized the meaning of the two messages as being the same, which supports Gray and Wedderburn's finding that meaning is important in the selection process. There must have been some processing of the unattended message for its meaning to be appreciated. In a second experiment, both the shadowed and the unattended messages were slightly jumbled English sentences like 'I saw the girl song was wishing' and 'me that bird jumping in the street'.

When the first of the sentences was presented to the shadowed ear and the second to the unshadowed ear, participants tended to produce a verbal response something like: 'I saw the girl jumping, wishing ...'. The word 'jumping' had intruded into the shadowed message in order to make more coherent sense of it. Where the shadowed sentence was already coherent sense, the intrusion did not occur.

In a further experiment, participants had to shadow a piece of normal prose, while the unattended ear received a string of words which only roughly resembled the structure of an English sentence. When the coherent message was switched without warning from the shadowed to the unattended ear, the response from the participants was to switch to shadowing the other ear. They were sometimes unaware that they had done this.

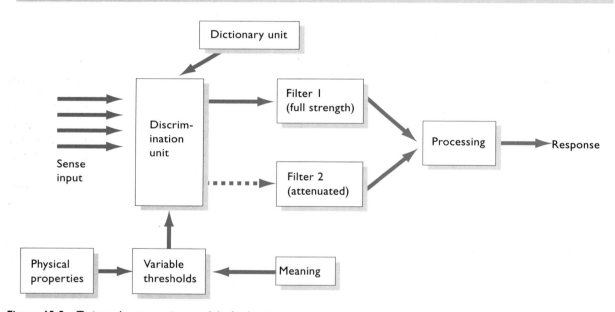

Figure 12.2 Treisman's attenuation model of selective attention

there is a focus on one input, while the others are weakened or attenuated. This attenuation model is illustrated in Figure 12.2.

You will see that besides the selected message there is also semantic processing of unselected material on the basis of what Treisman describes as a dictionary unit. This lists words and meanings each of which has a threshold (a minimum intensity at which that word will be recognized and used). The threshold will vary both in accordance with the importance an individual attaches to that word and also with expectations. The intruded word 'jumping' in her experiment could be processed because the listener expected it to be used rather than the words received in the shadowed ear. It thus had a lower threshold than other words received by the unattended ear.

Treisman's model clearly resolves some of the difficulties with Broadbent's model, for example:

- It demonstrates the processing according to meaning found by Gray and Wedderburn.
- It also provides an explanation for the 'cocktail party phenomenon', investigated by Cherry.

But there remain two difficulties:

- It is not clear what attenuation means. It is not that the stimulus becomes quieter, but that the information provided by the attenuated message is somehow reduced. It is hard to see how this works.
- Recognizing the meaning of a word or a passage requires extensive processing. The semantic analysis of the unattended messages would need to be nearly as complete a process as the full processing of the attended message.

Pertinence or late filter model of selective attention

Deutsch and Deutsch (1963) proposed a **pertinence** model of selective attention, which placed the filter much closer to the output end of the processing system. This was subsequently revised by Norman (1968, 1969, 1976) and essentially proposes that all information is initially analysed for its pertinence, or relevance, and is then passed on to a filter if found to be pertinent (see Figure 12.3).

Evaluation of the pertinence model   There appear to be various problems with this model.

Eysenck (1984) maintains this is a very uneconomical use of resources. It involves processing a large amount of material which is not going to be used.

Treisman and Geffen (1967) tested the model empirically. Participants in their study engaged in a shadowing task. They had to repeat the shadowed message aloud and also to indicate by tapping when they heard a certain target word (which might come into either ear). Deutsch and Deutsch's model would predict that the target word would be detected and would produce a response whichever ear it was presented to. The 'target' was, after all, pertinent. Treisman's (or Broadbent's) early filter model would predict that it would not be detected when it was presented to the unshadowed ear. Results supported Treisman – 87 per cent of the target words were detected in the shadowed, only 8 per cent in the unshadowed ear.

Deutsch and Norman (1967) rejected this as invalid. When the target was in the shadowed ear, participants had to shadow as well as tap; when it was in the other, they only had to tap. Treisman and Riley (1969) corrected this bias by telling participants to stop shadowing and tap as soon as they heard the target in either ear. There was still greater detection of shadowed than nonshadowed target words.

Limits to processing capacity

Broadbent, Treisman and Deutsch and Deutsch were all working on the basis that there was a limit to the processing capacity of the brain. Neisser (1976) disputed that such a limit existed. He said: 'There is no physiologically or mathematically established limit on how much information we can pick up at once' (Neisser, 1976, p. 96).

This limited capacity is not appropriate for an active developing structure such as the human brain. The

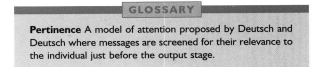

GLOSSARY

Pertinence A model of attention proposed by Deutsch and Deutsch where messages are screened for their relevance to the individual just before the output stage.

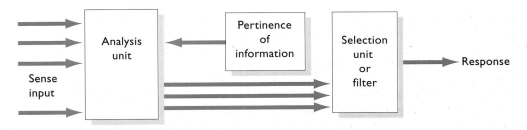

Figure 12.3   Late filter or pertinence model of selective attention

Box 12.3 An experiment to test Johnston and Heinz's resourced-based model of selective attention

Target and nontarget words were presented simultaneously to both ears of participants. Target words were 'shadowed'. There were two conditions:

(a) a low sensory-discrimination condition, where all the words were spoken by the same male voice;
(b) a high sensory-discrimination condition in which target words were spoken by a male voice, nontargets by a female voice.

The question at issue was this. In condition (b) it was possible to use sensory information based upon the voices used. In condition (a) only semantic information was available. There would be more complete processing of the nontarget words, but more resources would be used. If Deutsch and Deutsch were right, there would be complete analysis under both conditions. Participants were found to be more able to recall nontarget words in the low discrimination condition (a). This suggests that an early filter model such as Treisman's was more likely to be correct than Deutsch and Deutsch's late filter model.

Johnston and Wilson (1980) provided further backing for this. Participants had pairs of words which had at least two distinct meanings presented to them, one to each

ear. For example, 'bears' might be a target word under the category 'wild animals'. Each target was accompanied by a word which qualified it appropriately (say, 'brown') or inappropriately (say, 'suffers') or else by a neutral control word such as 'vehicle'. There were two conditions:

(a) a divided attention condition, in which the participant did not know to which ear the target word was to be presented; and
(b) a focused attention condition in which participants were told to which ear the target word was to be presented.

In the 'divided attention' condition (a) it was found that detection of targets was easier with an appropriate accompanying word – 'brown' with 'bears' – than with a neutral word, and even more difficult with an inappropriate word. In the 'focused condition' (b), the type of nontarget word made no difference to the rate of detection. Processing seemed in this case to be carried out according to the physical factor, the ear to which the target was presented. In the 'divided condition' (a) semantic processing had to occur.

brain contains millions of neurons (or nerve cells) which actively form interconnections with each other as stimuli from the environment reach it. While we may become inefficient when we try to do two things at once this becomes less so with practice.

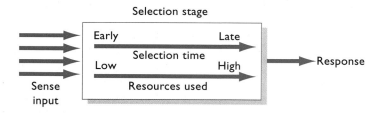

Figure 12.4 Johnston and Heinz's (1978) resource-based model of attention

A resource-based model of selective attention

Johnston and Heinz (1978) proposed a more flexible, resource-based model of selective attention. Selection might take place at different stages of processing, but more resources were used up when the selection occurred closer to the response. Figure 12.4 illustrates Johnston and Heinz's model.

There was thus a tendency for selection to occur as early as possible in the prevailing circumstances. Their experiment and that of Johnston and Wilson (1980) to test this, is described in Box 12.3.

SELF-ASSESSMENT QUESTIONS

1. What were Cherry's findings in relation to the 'cocktail party phenomenon'?
2. What did Treisman's model of selective attention succeed in explaining, which Broadbent's had not?
3. Describe the features of Deutsch and Deutsch's 'pertinence' model of selective attention.
4. In what way were Johnston and Heinz's conclusions a compromise between Treisman and Deutsch and Deutsch?

Is attention conscious or unconscious?

Schneider and Shiffrin's experiments

Schneider and Shiffrin (1977) distinguished between **controlled** and **automatic processing** in the following ways:

- Controlled processing is serial (one thing is processed after another).
- Automatic processing is parallel (more than one processing operation can occur at any one time).
- Difficult and unfamiliar tasks require controlled processing, simple and familiar tasks can be processed automatically.

Box 12.4 describes Schneider and Shiffrin's experiments.

A great deal of further research was inspired by Schneider and Shiffrin. Fisher (1984), for instance, suggested that there were clear limits to the number of items which could be processed simultaneously. This might not be much greater than the four items which Schneider and Shiffrin showed in each frame.

Feature integration theory

Treisman has taken this distinction between automatic and controlled attention further in what she calls feature integration theory. She distinguishes **preattentive processing** and **focused attention**.

Preattentive processing

With preattentive processing the individual scans and registers features right across the visual field, using parallel processing. This is, therefore, not unlike what Schneider and Shiffrin called automatic processing.

> **GLOSSARY**
>
> **Controlled processing** Serial processing of difficult or unfamiliar tasks.
>
> **Automatic processing** Parallel processing of easy or familar tasks.
>
> **Preattentive processing** Where a whole array is scanned and processed at once.
>
> **Focused attention** Where each item in an array is focused upon one at a time and processed.

Box 12.4   Experiments in controlled or automatic processing by Schneider and Shiffrin (1977)

Participants in Schneider and Shiffrin's experiments saw a rapid sequence of 20 pictures in each trial. In each picture (or frame) were four locations (see diagram), which could be occupied by a letter or by some dots. Participants had to look for and remember target letters in these frames.

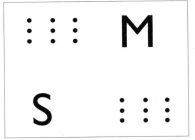

Example of a frame similar to those in Schneider and Shiffrin's experiments

Schneider and Shiffrin aimed to vary the difficulty of the task in various ways, through the number of the targets, the exposure time the participants received and through what they called 'consistent' and 'varied' mapping conditions. In the former, target and irrelevant items were from different categories, in the latter they could be from the same categories.

Results showed that in the consistent mapping condition it made little difference how many targets there were and how they were located. Only exposure time seemed to make a difference. Under the varied mapping condition the number of the targets and their locations made a difference as well. Schneider and Shiffrin's explanation was that in the consistent mapping condition the task was easy enough for automatic processing to be employed. In the varied condition participants had to use controlled processing, conducting a serial search through all the items in a frame.

Focused attention

In focused attention, by contrast, the individual identifies objects one at a time, by serial processing. Treisman and Gelade (1980) examined preattentive processing as compared to focused attention. Where there were isolated features to be looked for, where the target differed from surrounding irrelevant items in colour, size or orientation, it would seem to pop out of the display automatically. How many items there were altogether was immaterial. Try Exercise 12.2.

Exercise 12.2

Task A: Use marking pens with clear bright colours, say, red and green. On a plain piece of white paper make 30 red X's and one green X in a random array.

Task B: On a second sheet make 12 red X's and one green X.

Ask a friend to scan both sheets to locate the green X. Did it take longer to locate the target among 30 or among 12 irrelevant items?

Task C: Now make an array consisting of 15 red X's, 15 green O's and one green X.

Again ask your friend to locate the green X. Did it take longer to locate the target in this array?

In task A and task B in Exercise 12.2 the target would seem to pop out at you. It will not make much difference whether there are 12 or 30 items. You are looking for an isolated feature and can therefore use preattentive processing. However, in task C you are looking for a combination of two features, X and green. You cannot search at feature level but must search for a particular object, a more complex task. The more features there are, the longer it takes.

Kahneman's capacity theory of attention

It is clear from the above research that some tasks require more attention than others. In some cases there is automatic processing, in others attention has to be focused. Allport et al. (1972) and Shaffer (1975) in research described earlier suggested that attention might be divided. Shiffrin and Schneider (1977, 1984) suggested that the distinction might be between automatic and controlled (or focused) attention. Underwood's (1974) experiment, mentioned earlier,

had hinted that there was a distinction between practised and unpractised performance. In real life, we can see this distinction. Driving a car on an uncluttered road, we are often able to listen to the radio or hold a conversation at the same time as driving competently. However, when the road conditions become difficult we need to turn off the radio and stop talking to focus all our attention on the task of driving. There seems to be an overall limitation on our capacity for attention. Kahneman (1973) suggested that there exists a central processor to coordinate and allocate our attentional resources (see Figure 12.5).

Broadbent (1977) had suggested something similar in response to Allport's work, that there was what he termed a general executive controller. Kahneman's idea was that this central processor dealt with resource allocation. Instead of a single channel, processing one thing at a time, there was an array of processing resources to be deployed flexibly. The factors determining the allocation of resources include (a) the mental effort required; and (b) a person's level of **arousal**. More capacity was seen to be available when arousal levels were high. Arousal refers to a person's physiological state of alertness. This will be determined by the following factors:

- The overall level of stimulation in the environment at the time.
- A person's natural disposition (a neurotic person will be more easily aroused than a stable one).
- **Circadian rhythms**, or daily cycles of activity, within the physiological system. There are times in the day when physiological functions such as heart rate, metabolic rate, breathing rate and body temperature are at a maximum (often in the late afternoon and early evening) and times when they are at their lowest (usually in the early hours of the morning).
- Momentary intentions and enduring dispositions. The central processor is more likely to allocate resources to activities related to a person's immediate goals. Individuals will naturally turn their attention towards some external stimuli rather than others.

This seems to be a far more flexible system than that envisaged by Broadbent. In everyday life, there are both external and internal factors which determine whether we pay attention to something. An external stimulus, such as a cry for help, might grab our attention. But

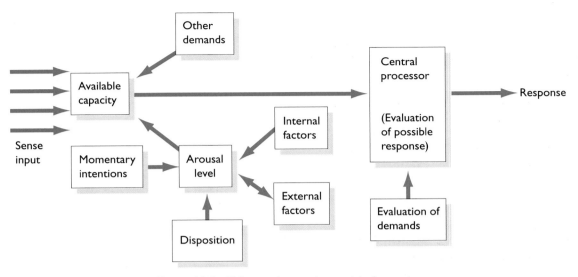

Figure 12.5 Kahneman's capacity model of attention

external demands will need to override the internal factors such as the immediate goals we have set ourselves to achieve and our enduring dispositions (the kind of people we are).

? SELF-ASSESSMENT QUESTIONS

1. What conclusions did Schneider and Shiffrin come to as a result of their experiments?
2. Describe Treisman's 'feature integration' theory. How did it extend Schneider and Shiffrin's work?
3. Kahneman introduced the idea of resource allocation into selective attention. What factors did he see as influencing this allocation of resources, and what factors influenced the amount of resources available at any one time?

Vigilance or sustained attention

The problem of maintaining attention on something we find boring is familiar to most people. Early research into vigilance performance originated in the 1940s. With the introduction of radar, performance decrement, as it became known, was obviously serious because it could endanger life. It is still the case that participation in a monotonous task is accompanied by lowered performance, which gets worse the longer one is engaged on it. Motorway driving, for instance, when it is uneventful can result in poorer driving skills.

Early research

Mackworth, in the 1940s, used three types of experimental technique to examine **performance decrement**:

■ **The radar test**. Participants were made to sit and watch a radar screen for occasional signals, visual blips, presented against a background of visual 'noise', that is, random, nonsignal visual events.
■ **An auditory listening task**. Participants were made to listen for sound tones, presented every 18 seconds for a duration of 2.5 seconds.
■ **The clock test**. This 'clock' had one pointer which moved in jumps at regular intervals, but every so often made a double jump. It could also be set to move continuously but occasionally speed up or slow down.

GLOSSARY

Arousal The state of alertness of an individual.

Circadian rhythms Daily cyclical changes in physiological state which effect arousal level.

Performance decrement The amount of worsening of performance on a vigilance task relative to the duration of a task.

Participants had to respond by pressing a button or reporting signals verbally when each of these 'events' occurred. Experimenters recorded the latency of responses (the delay between the signal and the operator responding to it), error rates, and finally evoked cortical responses (measurements of the brain's activity taken by means of an **electroencephalogram** (EEG)).

The factors which seemed to affect performance included the following:

- **Aspects of the signal itself**. This includes its intensity, rate of presentation, regularity, duration and spatial arrangement. Better vigilance performance resulted from increases in the intensity, frequency and duration of the signal. Presenting the signals regularly or near the centre of the display also improved performance.
- **Knowledge of results**. Where participants were given information on how well they had performed, even if this information was false, performance decrement was reduced.
- **Stimulation**. Having a telephone in the room ringing at intervals, or having other people in the room, especially if they were of high status, reduced performance decrement (for example, in a military context, having officers in the room, when the participants were 'other ranks').
- **Stimulant drugs**. These include amphetamines, and caffeine. Administered in moderate doses, they were found to reduce performance decrement.

- **Personality.** Highly introverted participants (as measured by Eysenck's Personality Inventory) showed almost no performance decrement.

Figure 12.6 illustrates some of the factors found by Mackworth to effect vigilance performance.

Theories of vigilance decrement

Pavlovian inhibition theory (Mackworth, 1950)

Pavlov had researched what became known as classical conditioning in the 1920s. Dogs were presented with meat powder which caused them to salivate. This was the unconditioned stimulus (UCS). The salivation was termed the unconditioned response (UCR). This UCS was then paired with (presented at the same time as) a second stimulus, a bell or a buzzer, perhaps, which was known as the conditioned stimulus (CS). After a number of such pairings, salivation was produced by presenting the CS alone. This was the conditioned response (CR), produced by the reinforcement of the CS by UCS. After a number of such single (unreinforced) presentations the CR tended to die away. Extinction had occurred. This conditioning process is fully described in Chapter 6.

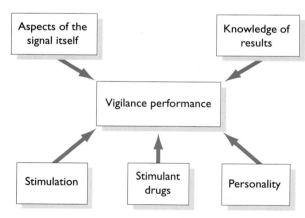

Figure 12.6 Some factors influencing vigilance performance (after Mackworth)

> **GLOSSARY**
>
> **Electroencephalogram (EEG)** A means of measuring electrical activity in the brain by means of electrodes attached to the scalp.
>
> **Pavlovian inhibition theory** Theory, based upon classical conditioning, developed by Mackworth and used to explain performance decrement.

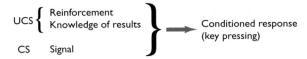

Figure 12.7 Mackworth's Pavlovian inhabition theory

Mackworth's **Pavlovian inhibition theory** attempted to place the phenomenon of vigilance decrement within this framework. The conditioned stimulus was the signal, the conditioned response was a key pressing response. Knowledge of results (KR) provided reinforcement. It was suggested that extinction occurred as a result of a prolonged period without KR. There is a full discussion of Pavlov and of classical conditioning in Chapter 6. Figure 12.7 illustrates Mackworth's theory.

Criticisms of Pavlovian inhibition theory Classical conditioning does not fit well with Mackworth's theory for several reasons:

▨ It is not easy to believe that KR would act as a stimulus to produce key pressing.

▨ Extinction in classical conditioning is the result of the inhibition of responses because UCS has not been paired with CS for a number of trials. In a vigilance task, vigilance decrement never reaches the point where there is no response to the signal at all.

▨ In Pavlovian conditioning a large number of unpaired (CS without UCS) trials produces extinction, whatever the timescale. In vigilance tasks, when the signal is presented more often the decrement declines.

Arousal level theory

It seems more plausible to link the performance decrement observed by Mackworth to participants' **arousal** level. In crude terms this is the degree of individuals' alertness. In physiological terms, though, it amounts to the level of activity in the brain (in the cortex, in subcortical structures such as the hypothalamus and in the autonomic nervous system).

Measurement of arousal level The degree of activity in the cortex may be measured by means of an electroencephalogram (EEG). Electrodes are attached to a person's scalp and the potential difference measured between two electrodes, amplified and recorded on a continuous roll. When a person is relaxing with the eyes closed, it is possible to detect what are known as **alpha rhythms** (regular waves at about 8–12 cycles per second). When the person is attending to the world with eyes open, beta rhythms can be detected (less regular waves of lower amplitude and a frequency of 12–30 cycles per second).

Stroh (1971) recorded the alpha rhythms of participants during a one-hour visual vigilance task. He wanted to find out the relationship between the level of alpha activity before a stimulus was presented and the likelihood of detecting it. If alpha activity is an indication of arousal level he could see whether arousal was a factor in vigilance decrement. Box 12.5 shows details of Stroh's experiment.

Factors influencing arousal level The factors which influence arousal level may be either endo-

---

Box 12.5 Stroh (1971) arousal level and vigilance decrement

Stroh had 24 participants in his study in three groups:

▨ Group A: those whose alpha activity before a missed signal was lower than before a detected signal;

▨ Group B: those whose alpha activity was lower before a detected signal; and

▨ Group C: those for whom there was no difference.

Looking for other ways in which the groups differed he discovered that Group A were younger and more neurotic (as measured on personality inventories). Group B were older and less neurotic. Alpha rhythms are replaced by more complex beta rhythms as attention is engaged. A decrease in alpha rhythms goes with an increase in cortical arousal. While a spontaneous increase in arousal seems to improve the performance of older and less neurotic people, the reverse is true in younger and more neurotic individuals.

GLOSSARY

Arousal The level of activity in the cerebral cortex.

Alpha rhythms Fairly regular brain waves recorded by EEG, characteristic of a relaxed state of wakefulness.

genous (coming from within the individual), or exogenous (those from outside the individual).

Endogenous factors include an individual's personality (particularly neuroticism and circadian rhythms (the natural daily variation in physiological and psychological performance).

Exogenous factors include:

- **Drives and incentives**. Hunger, thirst and pain are examples, as well as the anticipation of pleasure or pain.
- **Environmental circumstances**. Noise and bright lights may increase arousal (remember that Mackworth found that a telephone ringing occasionally lowered vigilance decrement). The higher the intensity, the greater the arousal. Colour may influence arousal also: blue is less stimulating than red.
- **Surprising or novel events**.
- **Drugs**. Amphetamines or caffeine may raise arousal; alcohol or barbiturates may lower it.
- **The difficulty of the task**. The harder a task, the greater the arousal.

Figure 12.8 illustrates the factors that may affect arousal.

Arousal and performance It has been suggested that there is an optimum level of arousal for effective performance. A variety of factors may influence arousal levels. A neurotic individual looking forward with anxiety to an examination misses the bus and arrives late. The supervisor appears annoyed and the paper is difficult. Such a level of arousal is piled up from various sources so that performance is drastically impaired.

The relationship between arousal and performance has become known as the Yerkes–Dodson Law (Yerkes and Dodson, 1908) and is discussed in Chapter 11. As arousal increases, so does performance up to an optimum level. If arousal continues to increase beyond this level performance deteriorates.

Individual differences and vigilance Other indices of arousal (besides EEG) include galvanic skin response (GSR), pulse rate and pupil diameter. As with EEG studies in relation to vigilance there is contradictory evidence. Sometimes there are higher, sometimes lower, GSR changes or pulse rates before a missed signal on a vigilance task. This can be explained in terms of individual differences. Kahneman (1973) has argued that pupil diameter is a good indicator of cortical arousal, but this has not been tested in relation to vigilance.

It has been suggested that extroverts are chronically underaroused and this is the reason why they perform less well on vigilance tasks. Their extroversion manifests itself in stimulus-seeking to spur on their reluctant arousal systems. When a vigilance task becomes monotonous and the novelty wears off, then their sustained attention is less.

Evoked cortical responses Evoked cortical responses (ECR) are tiny electrical changes which occur in the cortex when stimuli are presented to a person. They occur equally with all the senses. Haider et al. (1964) carried out an interesting study of ECR in relation to a vigilance task. Light flashes

> ### GLOSSARY
>
> **Endogenous factors** Factors internal to the individual which may determine arousal level.
>
> **Exogenous factors** Factors external to the individual which may effect arousal level.
>
> **Yerkes–Dodson Law** A law which relates performance on any of a variety of tasks to arousal level. This is a curvilinear relationship with optimum performance occurring at intermediate arousal levels.

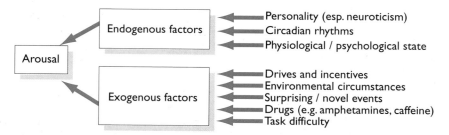

Figure 12.8 Factors influencing arousal level

were presented to participants at three-second intervals. Some of these flashes were dimmer than others and constituted the signals in the experiment. Participants responded by key pressing. As the experiment progressed, the latency (the time-gap between the signal and the ECR) of the evoked responses increased. Where signals were missed ECRs were smaller and their latency was greater.

Wilkinson et al. (1966) took this further. There seemed to be four components of ECR, two positive and two negative microvolt deflections. Before missed signals there seemed to be a larger second negative deflection and the first negative deflection had greater latency than in the case of detected signals.

? SELF-ASSESSMENT QUESTIONS

1. What is meant by an 'information processing' approach to cognitive processes? What are some of the advantages and disadvantages of this approach?
2. Distinguish between:
   (a) serial and parallel processing;
   (b) top-down and bottom-up processing.
3. List three views of the emerging discipline of cognitive science. Which seems to you to be the most useful?
4. What were the three types of vigilance test which Mackworth examined?
5. What factors seemed to reduce the vigilance decrement on a long and monotonous task?
6. Define what is meant by 'arousal'. What appears to be the relationship between arousal and performance on a vigilance task?
7. Describe two ways of measuring arousal.

Psychophysics

Thresholds of sensation

When you go into a dark cinema out of bright sunlight, you find yourself quite unable to see for a minute or two and then you accustom yourself to the low light levels and all is well. When you leave the cinema and return to the sunlight the same thing occurs. Your senses adapt and the threshold of your sensation alters to take account of external circumstances. The following exercise will demonstrate this.

Exercise 12.3

Close your eyes and ask a friend to present you with a piece of coarse sandpaper and a smooth piece of hardboard. Let the fingers of one hand run over the smooth hardboard and the fingers of the other over the coarse sandpaper for 30 seconds. Then replace both the hardboard and the coarse sandpaper with the reverse side of the hardboard, which will be intermediate in texture between the sandpaper and the smooth hardboard. What does it feel like? Is the sensation on the fingers of each hand the same?

Absolute threshold

When the intensity of a stimulus is small enough, you cannot detect it at all. There is a point where the intensity of a stimulus is just sufficient for you to be able to detect it. This is referred to as the **absolute threshold** of sensation. This will apply to all our senses, but it is not constant, however. As you can see from the cinema example above, your absolute threshold will be different when you have just come into the cinema from when you have been there a minute or two and your eyes have had time to adapt to the darkness. Because the nerve cells in your senses are never entirely without activity, there is not a single level of intensity below which you never detect a stimulus and above which you always do in any particular set of circumstances. There is always a certain amount of neural noise. This is the background activity against which you sense something. The brain has some difficulty in deciding when there is an external stimulus present or when the nerve impulses just represent neural noise.

Accordingly, there needs to be some convention concerning the measurement of the absolute threshold. In a darkened room, an individual is presented with a series of flashes of light of varying intensities and asked to report whether or not he or she sees a signal. The absolute threshold is the lowest intensity which is sensed 50 per cent of the time. Figure 12.9 represents this. The horizontal axis of the graph represents the

---

GLOSSARY

Absolute threshold That intensity of a stimulus which is the minimum that can be perceived 50 per cent of the time.

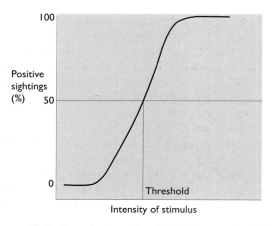

Figure 12.9 The absolute threshold of perception is the lowest intensity that can be seen 50 per cent of the time

intensity of the stimulus, the vertical the percentage of positive sightings. This will vary from zero (the signal is never seen) to 100 per cent (the signal is always seen). The absolute threshold is the 50 per cent point. A similar procedure may be adopted with the other senses.

Difference thresholds

A second threshold in which psychologists are interested is that which is termed **just noticeable difference (jnd)**. This is the minimum *difference* in intensity of a pair of stimuli for them to be perceived as dissimilar. This term was invented first by Gustav Fechner (1801–87). As with the absolute threshold, this is the minimum difference in intensity which can be perceived 50 per cent of the time. Both these thresholds will vary, not only for different people, but also for the same person under different circumstances. These circumstance may include differences in environmental conditions and also internal conditions such as motivation.

Weber's law

Weber (1795–1878) discovered a relationship between the absolute stimulus intensity and the jnd (**Weber's law**) The smallest difference in intensity which can be detected is proportional to the original stimulus intensity. Let us see how this might work. You are sitting at a table with just one candle. Someone comes in with a second candle and you will probably notice the difference immediately. But if you were in a room

Figure 12.10 Some of Weber's constants

Sense modality	Weber's constant
Vision (brightness of white light)	1/60
Kinaesthesis (lifted weights)	1/50
Pain (something hot on the skin)	1/30
Hearing (loudness of tone)	1/10
Pressure on skin	1/7
Taste (for salt)	1/3

lighted by three 100-watt electric light bulbs and someone brought in a candle you would not notice the difference. The ratio of the just noticeable difference to the background intensity will be constant. The formula Weber arrived at is as follows:

$$\frac{\Delta I}{I} = K$$

where ΔI is the increase in stimulus intensity needed to make a just noticeable difference, I is the background intensity and K is a constant, known as Weber's constant, which will vary widely with different sense modalities. Figure 12.10 shows some of the values of K.

Let us take another example. Suppose you are holding a 100-gram weight. You would need to add an additional 2-g weight before you would notice the difference. Weber's constant for lifted weights is 1/50, your background weight is 100 grams: 2/100 = 1/50.

Exercise 12.4

Take a glass of water and add three level teaspoonfuls of salt. According to Weber's Law the constant for saltiness in taste is 1/3. How much more salt would you need to add before you can taste the difference?

GLOSSARY

Just noticeable difference (jnd) That change in intensity of a stimulus which can be detected by an individual 50 per cent of the time.

Weber's law A law which governs the relationship between jnd and the background intensity of a stimulus against which a change occurs. The difference in intensity divided by the background intensity is equal to a constant (*K*) which is different for each sense modality.

Signal detection theory

There are two problems with the notion of thresholds as described above:

■ We are not always sure whether we can perceive a very weak stimulus.
■ Researchers cannot know for certain whether participants have actually perceived the stimulus which they say they have perceived.

To get over this difficulty researchers have introduced 'catch' trials when no stimulus was in fact presented. When a participant on one of these trials says he or she has seen a stimulus, researchers know that the participant is just guessing. How likely is it that participants are biased towards saying 'Yes, I have seen it' when in fact they are just guessing? In practical terms there are four alternatives:

■ To report correctly that the stimulus is there and they have seen it.
■ To report seeing a stimulus when there was none (a false alarm).
■ To report that there was no stimulus when in fact there was one (a miss).
■ To report correctly that there was no stimulus.

In **signal detection theory** (Green and Swets, 1966) it is possible to arrive at two measures of the participants' behaviour:

■ Their ability to perceive the stimulus correctly. This is referred to as d'.
■ Their willingness to commit themselves, to make a positive decision that they have seen a stimulus. This has been referred to as β.

This second measure, β, represents the participant's criterion of caution; in other words how likely they are to commit themselves. Either they operate with a lax criterion (β), in which case there are more false alarms or they operate with a strict criterion, in which case there are more correct detections and fewer false alarms. All kinds of factors may affect β; general motivation and guessing habits; specific motivations or incentives – there may even be 'pay-offs' – expectations and an appraisal of the kind of accuracy which is expected. Researchers are interested in two things; the proportion of correct detections as compared with the total number of times the signal has been presented and the proportion of false alarms. From this what has become known as the **receiver operating characteristic** (ROC) may be derived: that is to say, researchers may be able to measure the response bias and sensitivity of individual participants. This ROC may be important in real life too. Supposing a pathologist is concerned with assessing cervical cancer smears. It helps to be aware of how likely an individual might be to spot a problem correctly or to send out false alarms. This is what an ROC curve (a graph plotting proportions of correct detection against false alarms) may achieve.

SELF-ASSESSMENT QUESTIONS

1. What is meant by the absolute threshold of sensation? How has it been possible to mitigate the problem of neural noise in the measurement of absolute thresholds?
2. What are just noticeable differences (jnds)? What is the relationship between a jnd and the background intensity of a stimulus?
3. Define Weber's Law. State in your own words what it means in practical terms.

GLOSSARY

Signal detection theory A theory which aims to assess the degree to which an individual participant will report what he or she sees accurately and truthfully.

Receiver operating characteristic Characteristic of individual participants related to their truthfulness and accuracy in reporting what they see.

Chapter summary

- The issue of selective attention was first given prominence by Colin Cherry who described the phenomenon found in party situations where individuals could focus attention on a particular conversation and yet still pay attention to something which was said elsewhere in the room if it concerned them or mentioned their name. He used shadowing techniques where two messages were presented to participants, one to each ear. One message was to be shadowed (focused upon) and questions were asked about how much of each message had been retained. Only physical characteristics of the unshadowed message were retained.

- Broadbent used split-span experiments, using dichotic listening to build up his model of selective attention. He envisaged a sensory buffer through which only one message could pass at a time. Other messages were reserved for later processing. It did not address the cocktail party phenomenon.

- Various factors were found by Moray and others to influence selective attention. These included the experience of participants, the nature of the material used, whether the processing was conscious or unconscious and meaning.

- Other models which were developed included Treisman's attenuation model, Deutsch and Deutsch's pertinence model and resource-based models from Johnston and Heinz. Schneider and Shiffrin focused upon whether processing was controlled or automatic; Treisman developed feature integration theory and Kahneman a capacity theory in which attention was dependent upon external capacities, for instance what else was happening, and internal factors such as arousal.

- Mackworth was one of the earliest researchers to study sustained attention. He developed radar tests, auditory listening tasks and clock tests. He developed a Pavlovian inhibition theory which was not very convincing. Other theories developed have included ones based upon arousal levels (for example, Stroh, 1971), individual differences (Kahneman, 1973) and evoked cortical responses (Wilkinson et al. 1966).

- Discussions of thresholds of sensation have included study of absolute thresholds of perception. Because thresholds are not constant even for one individual under one set of circumstances, absolute thresholds have come to be based upon levels of intensity perceived 50 per cent of the time. Difference thresholds are based upon the minimum difference in intensity of a stimulus which can just be perceived, again 50 per cent of the time.

- The relationship between the background intensity of a stimulus and the difference threshold is the subject of Weber's Law which introduces a constant factor for each sense modality. Because both absolute and difference thresholds depend upon the truthfulness and accuracy of participants in reporting what they perceive, Green and Swets (1966) developed signal detection theory, the main feature of which has been the introduction of 'catch' trials where no stimulus was presented. Receiver operating characteristics (ROCs) were derived which estimated the response bias of individual participants.

Further reading

Matlin, M.W. (1989). *Cognition*. Fort Worth: Holt, Rinehart & Winston. There is a good comprehensive account of attention in Chapter 2 of this book. It includes accounts of research into the performance of two tasks at the same time, and the influence of practice upon such performance.

Eysenck, M.W. (1984). *A Handbook of Cognitive Psychology*. Brighton: Psychology Press. A very complete account of attention and performance including practical applications of theory.

Radford, J. and Govier, E. (eds) (1991). *A Textbook of Psychology*, 2nd edn. London: Routledge. Contains a good account of vigilance and sustained attention.

Eysenck, M.W. (1982). *Attention and Arousal: Cognition and Performance*. Berlin: Springer Verlag. Contains an account of research into vigilance.

CHAPTER 13

Perception

Sensation and perception   261
- Depth perception   262
- Perceptual constancies   264
- Pattern recognition   266

Theories, models and principles   269
- Gestalt theories of perception   269
- Gregory's theory of perception   270
- Gibson's theory of direct perception   270
- Neisser's cyclical theory of perception   271
- Brunswik's model   271
- Set as an explanatory concept   272

Visual illusions   274
- Illusions which distort reality   274
- Illusions resulting from ambiguous figures   276
- Processing strategies   277
- An overview of visual illusions and explanations for them   278

Do we have to learn to perceive?   278
- Neonate studies   278
- Deprivation and readjustment studies   281
- Cross-cultural studies   284
- Conclusion   286

Objectives

By the end of this chapter you should be able to:

- Distinguish between sensation and perception;

- Outline some of the factors (such as emotion and motivation) which may determine how the world around us is perceived;

- Describe how information about a three-dimensional world is processed and how we perceive depth;

- Describe how objects are perceived and recognized. In particular, indicate what is meant by 'perceptual constancy';

- Evaluate some of the evidence which indicates whether perception is innate or learned.

This chapter describes how information from the three-dimensional, 'real' world, received through our senses, is processed to provide a basis for our interaction with the environment. The focus will be upon visual perception, though much of what is discussed applies equally to the other senses. Perception can be said to be the process by which data from the environment is interpreted to allow us to make sense of it.

Sensation and perception

Sensation relates to the collection of data from the environment by means of the senses. Perception relates to our interpretation of this data. It takes into account experiences stored in our memory, the context in which the sensation occurs and our internal state (our emotions and motivations).

Gregory (1966) has described this process as one of forming hypotheses about what the senses tell us. This section will deal with some of the ways in which this interpretation of data results in perception of the world. It will include **depth perception, recognition of objects** and **perceptual constancy**. We will be concerned in this section only with visual perception, though similar mechanisms exist in relation to the other senses.

Richard Gregory described perception as a process of hypothesis forming

Depth perception

The world around us is three-dimensional, but the data collected about the world through our senses is in two dimensions (a flat image on the retinas of our eyes). The interpretation of this data within the brain results in three-dimensional perception. This perception of depth depends on the brain's use of a number of clues. Some of these cues, as they are termed, use data from both eyes (**binocular cues**). Others use data from one eye only (**monocular cues**). There is further discussion of some of these issues in Chapter 7.

Binocular cues to depth perception

Retinal disparity **Retinal disparity** refers to the slightly different view of the world registered by each eye. You can test this for yourself with Exercise 13.1.

The view of the object you get with your right eye is slightly different from that which you get with the left. Retinal disparity, therefore, provides two sets of data which, interpreted together in the brain, provide stereoscopic vision, an apparent 3D image.

Exercise 13.1

Hold a pencil (or any other small object) in front of your eyes about 15 cms away from them. First, close your left eye and look at the object with your right. Then change eyes and look at the object with your left eye. Compare the images you receive from each eye.

Convergence: **Convergence** is the movement of the eyes together so that each may focus upon an object. Try Exercise 13.2.

Exercise 13.2

Hold a pencil in front of your eyes and gradually move it in towards them, fixing your vision on it. Then move it away again.

You will feel your eyeballs turning inwards to follow its movement and the muscles of your eyes contracting. This sensation of muscle movement (**kinaesthetic sense**) provides data about how far the object is from your eyes, in other words about depth.

Monocular cues to depth perception

These monocular cues depend on data received from one eye only. Even with the loss of the sight of one eye, a person can still perceive the world in three dimensions. It is more difficult, though. You can appreciate this if you close one eye, go into another room and try to pick something up from a table. It will be more difficult to locate it.

Painters throughout history have used monocular cues to provide an impression of depth in a flat two-dimensional painting. These cues include:

Linear perspective Parallel lines appear to come together as they recede into the distance. Figure 13.1 shows a building. You know that the part of the building on the right is further away than that on the left, because the lines of the roof, doors, windows and base of the building converge towards the right.

Height in a horizontal plane Distant objects seem to be higher and nearer objects lower in the horizontal plane.

Relative size The more distant they are, the smaller objects will appear to be. A painter who wants to create the impression of depth may include figures of different sizes. The observer will assume that a human figure or some other well-known object is consistent in size and will see the smaller objects as more distant.

Superimposition of objects Where an object is superimposed upon another (partly hiding it) the superimposed object will appear to be nearer.

Clarity Objects which are nearer appear to be clearer and more well-defined than those in the distance.

Light and shade Shadow has the effect of pushing darker parts of an image back. Highlights bring other parts forward, thus increasing the three-dimensional effect.

Texture The coarser the texture of an image the closer it seems to be. If a pavement of bricks is to be depicted, the impression of depth is created by the texture of the bricks becoming finer as the pavement goes into the distance.

Motion parallax As you move, the apparent movement of objects past you will be slower, the more distant they are. On a wide open road, with few objects close at hand, a car will appear to those inside it to be going more slowly than on a narrow road with hedges or fences close at hand.

In the illustration (Figure 13.2) you can see several monocular cues. The texture of the wavelets on the sea appears finer as you go into the distance. Sailing boats appear smaller and higher in the horizontal plane the more distant they are, and where one partially obscures another it appears to be closer.

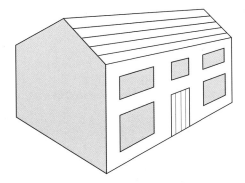

Figure 13.1 An illustration of linear perspective

Figure 13.2 Some monocular cues to depth perception

Primary and secondary cues

Primary cues relate to features of the physiology of the visual system. These include the binocular cues mentioned above (retinal disparity and convergence) together with **accommodation**. These are further discussed in Chapter 7.

Accommodation involves the lens of the eye altering its shape in order to focus the image more accurately on the retina. **Ciliary muscles** contract to elongate the lens and focus upon more distant objects, relax to allow it to become more rounded and focus upon nearer objects. Data are fed to the brain from kinaesthetic senses in these ciliary muscles, providing information about the nearness or distance of the object focused upon.

Together with the binocular cues (retinal disparity and convergence) accommodation relates to the physiology of our visual processes and so can be described as a primary cue. None of these cues operates in isolation and it is their combination which provides the information enabling us to form a hypothesis about the view in front of us.

Secondary cues relate to features in the visual field itself and include monocular cues described above.

Perceptual constancies

The world around us has the potential to provide total chaos and confusion as we perceive it. Images projected upon the retinas of our eyes from a single object vary so much that, if we depended only on data from this source, objects would have no constancy, but would appear to be different each time they were presented to us. That this does not occur is the result of perceptual constancy. Shape, size, brightness, colour and location are all areas of perception in which this concept of constancy applies. We shall take each in turn.

Shape constancy

Objects project different shapes on our retinas according to the angle from which they are viewed. Try Exercise 13.3.

The appearance of the cup in Figure 13.3 is totally different in each case. How do we recognize the images we receive? In the first view of the cup, there may be some difficulty in recognizing it as a cup, but less difficulty in the case of the side view. In each case, a hypothesis is made from the data received about what it is we are seeing. This hypothesis is tested and in most cases an appropriate response is made. Shape

Figure 13.3   An illustration of shape constancy

constancy enables us to recognize objects for what they are, even when the retinal image we receive varies.

In some cases, though, there may be ambiguity and an inappropriate response may be made. The basis for these hypotheses is our experience of perceiving similar things before. In ambiguous cases, two alternative hypotheses may be made and it may be difficult to decide between them. This results in a visual illusion. Illusions are discussed in a later section of this chapter.

Size constancy

Size constancy relates to the fact that although the image of an object projected on the retinas of our eyes becomes smaller the more distant the object is, yet we know the real size of the object from experience and scale-up the perceived size of the object to take this into account. Try Exercise 13.4.

Exercise 13.4

Hold a coin 30 cm away from your eyes and then move it away to arm's length. Does it appear to get smaller?

It is not noticeably smaller and yet the image it projects on the retinas of your eyes is smaller. We reach a compromise between the size we know the coin to be and the retinal size of it. How this compromise is arrived at depends on factors like our familiarity with the object and other cues, comparing it with another object the size of which we know, for instance.

The way we perceive size is determined jointly by the retinal size of an object, and what can be called the egocentric distance between the observer's eyes and the object, that is to say the distance as it appears to the individual observer (Wade and Swanston, 1991). The relationship between the egocentric distance and the retinal size is the subject of Emmert's Law, which is detailed in Box 13.1. You can test for yourself how this works in the following exercise.

The size of the after-image will vary proportionately with the distance from the eye. That is, if the distance

Exercise 13.5

Take a square of green coloured paper with a black dot in the centre. Stare fixedly at the dot for 30 seconds and then turn your gaze to a blank sheet of white paper. You will see a red after-image. After a few seconds, transfer your gaze to a white wall at a greater distance from you.

Box 13.1 Emmert's Law

The relationship between perceived size and retinal image may be summarized in the equation

$$S = s.D$$

where S is the perceived size of the object, s is the retinal size and D is the egocentric distance. This is called Emmert's Law.

between the eye and the first after-image was 20 cm, and the distance between the eye and the wall was 100 cm, the second after-image will be five times the size of the first. This is a demonstration of Emmert's Law. The perceived size of an object is related to the retinal size and the egocentric distance.

Brightness and colour constancies

The brightness of an object remains constant regardless of how it is illuminated. Experience tells us how light or dark an object is. Once we recognize it, experience will influence our perception of it. We know a piece of black velvet is dark and it will remain so, however it is illuminated. But if light is projected onto a piece of black velvet in such a way that there is no edge illuminated and we have no other cue to show that it is black velvet, it will appear light. Try Exercise 13.6.

Exercise 13.6

Take a grey piece of paper about 10 cm square and place it in the centre of a sheet of white paper. Take another sheet of the same grey paper and place it on a sheet of black paper. Put a sheet of tracing paper over each sheet. Which sheet of grey paper appears lighter?

The square on the black background will appear to be lighter than it really is, the other darker.

Similarly, whatever the illumination, the colour of an object will appear to be what you know it to be.

You know your beach ball is red. It will still appear red, even under coloured illumination, provided that you recognize it as your beach ball.

Location constancy

Location constancy is a similar phenomenon to brightness and colour constancies. We have become accustomed to the locations of things around us in relation to ourselves. When our heads move, objects around us do not move although the image projected on our retinas changes. Experiments with distorting goggles go some way to explaining this. The best known is that of Stratton (1897), who fitted himself with glasses which inverted his visual field. At first, he experienced confusion, but after a few days he seemed to adapt and his location constancy seemed to be restored. When he finally took the glasses off he again needed some time to readjust.

Pattern recognition

This is at the heart of the relationship between perception and sensation. It relates closely to depth perception and perceptual constancy. Recognition of a word written on a page, or perhaps even more basically than this, of Granny when we see her, depends on pattern recognition. There are four theories or models of pattern recognition. These are template matching theory, prototype models, distinctive features models and the scene analysis approach. This section will examine each in turn.

Template matching theory

In **template matching** theory, the stimulus is compared to a set of patterns stored in memory. It is then 'recognized' as the pattern it resembles most closely. For instance, it is suggested that we have a number of faces stored in memory of people we have met. When we meet someone, we mentally scan through these stored faces until we find one that closely resembles the face before us. Recognition then takes place. However, there are several problems with this theory.

Exact match The template has to fit exactly or the system will not work. Computer sorting operates in this way, but for it to work there have to be certain conditions:

- ■ The patterns have to be standardized. There are different ways of writing a letter A, as shown in Figure 13.4. For a computer to recognize it the letter must be written in exactly the form in which it has been stored in the computer.
- ■ The patterns also have to be very well differentiated. A number 1 that looks rather like a 7 will not do.

It is evident that the patterns which humans need to recognize are much more flexible. We need to be able to recognize Granny whatever she is wearing, whatever kind of hair-do she has. Pattern recognition theory needs to accommodate the fact that we are able consistently to recognize Granny, however she looks, and the letter A, no matter how it is written.

Figure 13.4 A number of ways of writing the letter A

The vast number of templates needed There would need to be an infinite number of templates stored for us to recognize all possible variations in letters, let alone faces and other shapes. There are clearly storage problems.

The time factor The procedure envisaged by the theory would be very time-consuming. In order to recognize a letter we should need to scan mentally through all the stored templates, and yet it is possible to read 200 words a minute. Supposing an average of five letters in a word, and, say, a dozen templates for each letter, there would be 12,000 templates to scan each minute, a formidable task.

Problems when images are rotated There are likely to be difficulties, also, when images are rotated. Pinker (1984) notes that when shapes are rotated the image on the retina changes drastically. Every time the shape was rotated, there would need to be another template. Yet Jolicoeur and Landau (1984) estimate that when an image is rotated 180 degrees it requires only 15 milliseconds of processing time to recognize it.

Recognition of part shapes There is also the problem of recognition of parts of shapes. It is possible to recognize a shape, even when only a fragment is registered on the retina. For this theory to work, there would need to be templates of a whole series of parts of objects.

Given all these problems, template matching theory does not seem capable of explaining the phenomenon of pattern recognition.

Prototype models

This seems to relate to Plato's theory of ideas (*Republic*, Book X). This suggests that objects in the world around are in a sense reflections of idealized prototypes and it

---

GLOSSARY

Template matching Theory of pattern recognition which hypothesizes templates stored in memory against which images may be matched.

is these prototypes which are stored in memory. When a shape is encountered it is compared with a prototype. If the match is close enough (it does not need to be exact), recognition takes place.

Research has shown this approach to be a more useful one than template matching. Franks and Bransford (1971) asked participants in their study to draw transformations of prototype designs which differed in varying degrees from the original. Shown the original prototype design, they were confident that they had seen it before, even though it had not been presented to them. This confidence varied with the closeness of the resemblance between the transformation and the prototype.

Prototype models do seem to get over some of the difficulties in the template theory. They explain how shapes may be recognized even with different orientations and representations, but it seems to be a philosophical approach rather than one based upon reality. Spoehr and Lehmkuhler (1982) suggested that there might be a need for templates of prototypes!

Feature-analysing models

In **feature-analysing** models, features of objects or patterns which have been encountered before are stored in memory rather than templates or prototypes. They have their origin in Selfridge's (1959) pandemonium model. This was a computer program originally designed to recognize the patterns of dots and dashes in the Morse code, and extended by Lindsay and Norman (1972) to form a model of how the brain might recognize letters. Selfridge hypothesized demons which 'shriek in the presence of the feature they represent'. Figure 13.5 illustrates Selfridge's pandemonium model. The first level of 'demons' represents line features, a vertical line for instance; the second level represents angles or the points where two lines meet; the third level of demons represent possible patterns; and finally there is a decision demon. The loudness of the demons' shrieks indicates the degree of certainty that the feature is present.

Gibson's (1969) research showed that people take longer to differentiate between similar letters such as B and R than dissimilar letters such as X and O. The former have many similar features, the latter relatively few. Garner's (1979) research into this phenomenon is described in Box 13.2.

Garner's research seems to tie up with the neurological research by Hubel and Wiesel described

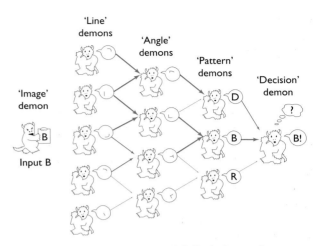

Figure 13.5 An illustration of Selfridge's pandemonium model

in Chapter 7 (Hubel, 1982; Hubel and Wiesel, 1965, 1979). They showed that individual neurons in the visual cortex responded to different line orientations. There are also some relationships with Treisman and Gelade's feature integration theory outlined in Chapter 12.

Box 13.2 Garner's (1979) research into feature analysing

Garner (1979) presented participants with one-letter targets followed by a series of letters one at a time. They had to press one key if the letter was the same as the target, another key if it was different. All 26 letters were used as targets with 50–75 trials for each target. Where letters had many different features, participants required a shorter time to make their decisions than where there were many similar features.

GLOSSARY

Prototype models Theory of pattern recognition which hypothesizes 'prototypes' of objects stored in the memory which are compared with objects encountered.

Feature analysing Theory of pattern recognition which hypothesizes features of objects stored in memory and scanned for recognition. An object is recognized when sufficient features are matched.

Scene analysis approach

There are characteristics both of feature analysis and prototypes in the **scene analysis** approach. As so often in cognitive psychology there has been an attempt to develop computer-based theories to accomplish the perceptual tasks that human observers perform. This use of computers to simulate human perception is known as machine vision. Computer scientists, interested in artificial intelligence (AI), have studied not only how perception occurs in humans but also how any organism or any machine perceives. At the present time, however, AI falls far short of full understanding of human perception. As Ullman says: 'The proficiencies of the human system in analysing spatial information far surpass the capacities of current artificial systems' (Ullman, 1984, p. 97).

Segmentation   Human perceivers are able to recognize incomplete objects in a way which is not possible for computers. An example of the scene analysis approach is Biederman's recognition by components theory (Biederman, 1987). Presented with an unfamiliar object or pattern people will segment it to see if any part is familiar. Biederman suggests that this process of segmentation occurs with any object we see, familiar or unfamiliar. There are three stages in the recognition of objects:

- Surface characteristics are registered, such as patterns of light and dark. A line drawing of the object can result.
- Segmentatation then occurs, particularly in the concave regions of the object.
- The component parts are then matched with representations in memory. Numerous possible representations may be scanned simultaneously by parallel processing. Matching may be either partial or complete.

This approach is a very complex one, too new as yet for much critical analysis to have been made, but clearly it initiates a change in the way in which pattern recognition is studied.

The importance of context in pattern recognition

In reality, shapes, objects and letters do not occur in isolation but in context and this context has an important bearing on their recognition.

Top-down or bottom-up approaches

In the introduction to this part we described differences between top-down and bottom-up processing. Most of the theories and approaches to pattern recognition have concentrated upon bottom-up processing. Emphasis has been on the stimulus, whether it is a template that needs to be matched or a set of features to be analysed. A top-down approach starts with people's concepts and expectations. Patterns can be recognized easily and rapidly, because we expect certain shapes to be found in certain locations. The process of reading illustrates this. If one or more letters are obscured or omitted altogether from a word in the text there is usually not much dif-icu-ty in re-di-g it. If an additional word is inserted we may not notice that it is there:

> DOGS ARE NOT
> ALLOWED IN THE
> THE PARK

The redundant THE is often not noticed at all. Some of the newer computer models of pattern detection (McClelland and Rumelhart, 1981, for example) allow the computer to change its mind in the light of the context. Where an obviously impossible word results from the system's analysis, it can backtrack to test whether the features might equally represent a less impossible word. But while it is possible for a computer to allow for context in a word, to do the same for a word in the context of a sentence is too difficult so far.

SELF-ASSESSMENT QUESTIONS

1. Briefly describe the distinction between 'sensation' and 'perception'.
2. List two binocular and three monocular cues to depth perception and describe each briefly.
3. What is meant by perceptual constancy? Describe the way in which size constancy scaling operates.
4. List four theories which have attempted to explain pattern recognition. Say which seems to you to be the most satisfactory. Give some reasons for your choice.

GLOSSARY

Scene analysis A computer simulation model of pattern recognition. An example is Biederman's recognition by the components model.

Theories, models and principles

This section discusses a number of theories which have been advanced about the relationship between sensation and perception. These theories will include Gestalt theories of perceptual organization, Gibson's direct theory of perception and Neisser's cyclical theory.

Gestalt theories of perception

The Gestalt psychologists, principally Köhler, Koffka and Wertheimer, working in the 1920s and 1930s, suggested that there existed within the brain an innate capacity for organizing perceptions, which followed certain rules. The 'whole' of perception was more than the sum of the parts, that is to say, the sum of all the individual sensations an individual receives. To begin with they were interested in exploring what makes figures stand out against a background (the **figure–ground** distinction). They maintained that there were laws of organization which determined the way in which individuals perceived things. Electrical fields within the brain were responsible for this organization, so that there was automatic perception of 'good' figures. Where the figure–ground distinction was ambiguous, the electrical fields switched from one interpretation to another. The basic principle on which Gestalt organization depended was the **Law of Prägnanz**. This may be defined as **good form**. Koffka (1935) expressed it as follows: 'Psychological organization will always be as "good" as the prevailing conditions allow.' There is further discussion of Gestalt approaches to psychology in the introduction to Part I.

Principles of Gestalt

Good form Perhaps this rather abstract notion of 'good form' may be interpreted as that which is intuitively satisfying.

The other principles (or laws) amount to explanation of the principle of Prägnanz. These laws rarely operate in isolation, frequently complementing or even opposing each other. They include the following:

Proximity Elements in an array which are close together are taken as belonging together. In Figure 13.6 you can see three groups of two vertical lines. They would not naturally be seen as six individual independent lines.

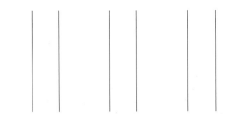

Figure 13.6 An illustration of proximity

Similarity Elements which are similar tend to be grouped together. In Figure 13.7 is a row of six circles. They will naturally be seen as pairs, two pairs of black circles and two pairs of white ones.

Figure 13.7 An illustration of similarity

Closure An incomplete figure will tend to be seen as a complete one. In Figure 13.8a is a square. At least, that is how it appears. It is still seen as a square in spite of breaks in each side. A word with one or more letters obscured can still be read as in Figure 13.8b, because the principle of closure will tend to complete it.

PERCEPTION

b

a

Figure 13.8 An illustration of closure

Continuity Where figures are defined by a single unbroken line they tend to be seen as an entity. In Figure 13.9 you will tend to see two continuous curved lines rather than two pointed figures meeting at A.

GLOSSARY

Figure–ground An organizing principle of perception suggested by Gestalt psychologists involving the distinction between figures and the background in which they are set.

Law of Prägnanz (good form) A Gestalt principle of perceptual organization that psychological organization will always be as 'good' as the prevailing conditions allow.

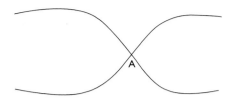

Figure 13.9 An illustration of continuity

Attempts to test Gestalt principles empirically

Attempts have been made to test these Gestalt laws empirically. In one experiment Pomerantz (1981) showed participants dots which they could join up as they liked. The prediction was that when the participants were shown patterns of dots suggesting simple figures of 'good form', all the participants would join them up in a similar way and the resultant figures would be 'good' ones which observed Gestalt laws of organization. Where the dot patterns did not suggest 'good' figures there would be much more variation in the ways in which they were joined up. This turned out to be the case.

Criticism of Gestalt

Eysenck (1984) criticizes Gestalt principles as being merely descriptive and having no explanatory power. They are also limited in that they are only directly applicable to two-dimensional representation.

Gregory's theory of perception

Gregory (1972a) took the view that the process of perception was an active one. Data received from the senses resulted in a **perceptual hypothesis** being set up. An individual's experience of the world and expectations resulting from that experience provided the means to test the hypothesis. The perceptual hypothesis was a 'first guess' at what the sensory data meant, based upon experience. For instance, experience suggests that more distant objects appear smaller. If there are cues in the sensory data to suggest something is distant (perspective cues, for instance, as in the Ponzo illusion, illustrated later in this chapter), and if the senses show it to be the same size as something apparently closer, then the perceptual hypothesis will be that it is larger, hence the illusion. Experience, context, motivation, emotional content all provide the means for us to test the provisional hypothesis which has been set up. This is a top-down process.

Gibson's theory of direct perception

Gibson (1986) has argued that there need not be processing stages interposed between the light falling on the retina and the responses made by the organism as a result. This is **direct perception**. The theory stressed the function of the senses as a means of providing for individuals all the information needed to enable them to interact with the environment. Individuals have what Gibson terms an **ambient optical array**, which consists of all the light rays which converge on the retina. For instance, as a person moves from a sitting to a standing position this ambient optical array will change, providing new information about the environment as a basis for action. Objects in the environment will appear larger or smaller and will have different textual gradients depending on distance. It is this ambient optical array which provides direct sensory information rather than there being a need for the brain to interpret incoming data in the light of experience. Processing of the information is not done cognitively but at a neural level. It is the whole array in front of you which provides the information necessary for you to act. When there is an illusion, it is just that the information in the array is insufficient for an appropriate response.

An evaluation of Gibson's approach

There are disadvantages with this ecological approach, as it has been called:

- Gibson concentrated on the activation of the visual system as a whole, but he did not make clear how the inputs were transformed into visual perceptions.
- It seems more suitable as an explanation of innately programmed reactions to environmental

---

GLOSSARY

Perceptual hypothesis Gregory's suggestion that data from the senses results in a hypothesis being set up which is then tested through experience.

Direct perception Gibson's theory of perception which suggests that the senses provide all the information needed for individuals to interact with the environment.

Ambient optical array A component of Gibson's perceptual theory consisting of all the light rays which converge on an individual's retina in a particular position. When this position changes the array will change.

circumstances. The visual array triggers stereotyped activity directly. A wasp buzzes against a closed window pane in reaction to a total visual environment.

■ Eysenck (1984) has suggested that the theory is in a sense too good. Visual stimulation provides so much information that perception should normally be perfect. But this is clearly not always the case. The tendency of large objects at great distances to look much smaller than they actually are is a case in point.

Neisser's cyclical theory of perception

Neisser's (1976) **cyclical theory of perception** could be described as a combination of top-down and bottom-up processing theory. He saw perceivers as starting with a perceptual model. On the basis of sensory cues, a person's expectations were used to build a model of probable objects. This perceptual model consisted of likely objects or events represented mentally. This model was then tested against sensory cues in the environment; the individual instituted an active search for cues which would either confirm or confound the model. This active search consisted of a bottom-up analysis of sensory information, as a result of which the model might need to be revised. There was thus an interaction between top-down or concept-driven processing, where the individual's concepts and expectations led, and bottom-up or data-driven processing.

Analysis by synthesis

The term which Neisser used for this approach is **analysis by synthesis**. The cycle consists of the generation of a perceptual model (synthesis), extracting information about the environment in order to correct and update the model (analysis) and repeating the process continuously to monitor the environment using expectations derived from previous experiences. Figure 13.10 shows this process.

Neisser combined the construction of hypotheses based upon experience and expectations of what the environment might be like, with the extraction from the environment of cues to enable the observer to correct the hypothesis in the light of data extracted.

Expectations are constantly changing. Neisser's models provide for a continuous exploration of the environment in order to confirm, modify or confound

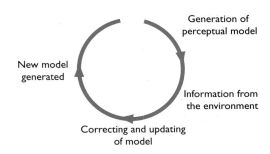

Figure 13.10 An illustration of Neisser's cyclical theory of perception

expectations. Gombrich (1960) spoke of the **beholder's share** in relation to the appreciation of works of art. Neisser's view has something in common with this. The sense that each person makes of the world is different from that of every other person.

Brunswik's model

Brunswik's (1956) model seems to have something in common with Gibson's theory in that it links perception very closely with action. Its central point, illustrated in Figure 13.11, is the organism (O). To one side are the inputs into the perceptual process, first distal inputs (c) which will include such things as a person's experiences, motivations, emotional states and personality disposition. Closer to the event,

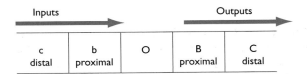

Figure 13.11 An illustration of Brunswik's model of perception

---

GLOSSARY

Cyclical theory of perception Neisser's perceptual theory which suggests a continuous process of analysis and synthesis.

Analysis by synthesis Neisser's perceptual model where information is extracted from the environment through the senses to correct and update impressions of what the environment might be like.

Beholder's share The contribution which an individual's personal value system and so on makes to his or her perceptions. The sense that each person makes of the world is different.

proximal inputs (b) include its context in terms of the physical objects surrounding it and the immediate sensory stimulation which constitutes the basis for perception (the interpretation of what has gone before). Beyond this perception, on the response side, is the establishment of a response set: for instance, the physiological changes which accompany any emotion generated by the event (increases in heart rate, muscular tension etc.). This is called a molecular response, and is followed by action (molar response) (B) and finally the future consequences of the event (C). These might include the emotional consequences, practical precautions taken, increased awareness, and so on.

Set as an explanatory concept

Set is a very general term for a whole range of emotional, motivational, social and cultural factors which can have an influence upon cognition. As such it helps to explain why we perceive the world around us in the way we do.

Set predisposes an individual towards particular perceptions. It may be induced by emotional, motivational, social or cultural factors. Its effects include:

- **Readiness**. Set involves an enhanced readiness to respond to a signal.
- **Attention**. Set involves a priority processing channel. The expected stimulus will be processed ahead of everything else.
- **Selection**. Set involves the selection of one stimulus in preference to others.
- **Interpretation**. The expected signal is already interpreted before it occurs. The individual knows beforehand what to do when the stimulus is picked up.

An athlete waiting for the starting gun hears 'get set' and each of the above effects come into play. There is enhanced readiness to move, enhanced attention and priority selection of the expected stimulus. The athlete has already interpreted the meaning of the starting gun and knows what action must be taken before it goes off.

Factors which influence set come under two headings:

- **Aspects of the stimulus**. These include the context within which it occurs and any instructions which may have been given.

- **Aspects which relate to the individual**. These include individual differences in personality or intelligence, past experience, motivation, emotional states and cultural factors.

Context and expectation

An example of the influence of context in inducing set is the experiment of Bruner and Minturn (1955). Participants were shown sequences either of letters or of numbers, for example:

C D E F G H or
8 9 10 11 12

When presented with an ambiguous figure/number ß which could be either B or 13, those who had seen the sequence of letters tended to perceive it as B, while those who had seen the numbers perceived it as 13. The context in which it was seen produced expectation and induced a particular set.

Another instance where past experience seems to have induced a particular set is in the experiment by Bruner and Postman (1949). Participants were presented tachistoscopically (over very short, measured durations of time) with playing cards with suit colours reversed, that is black hearts and diamonds, red clubs and spades. At very short exposures the cards were reported as being normal. However, as the exposures became longer, it became not uncommon for them to report purple or brown hearts. The stored experience of seeing playing cards had somehow begun to blend with the immediate stimulus information before them.

Motivation and set

There have been many studies of the effect of food deprivation upon perception. An example is that of Gilchrist and Nesberg (1952). Participants were deprived of food or water for varying periods. When they were shown pictures of objects relating to food or drink they perceived them as having enhanced brightness, and this brightness increased up to the point where they had been deprived for eight hours. After they were allowed to eat or drink as much as they wanted, brightness returned to base levels.

GLOSSARY
Set The predisposition of an individual towards certain cognitions. It manifests itself in perception and also in thinking.

Box 13.3　Perceptual defence

Perceptual defence could be regarded as an 'antiset': that is, a predisposition not to perceive something which may have unpleasant emotional overtones. The term was originally that of McGinnies (1949). In a classic study, participants were presented with either neutral words (such as 'table' 'apple' 'chair') or taboo words (like 'whore' 'penis' 'bitch'). Each of these words were presented very briefly to begin with, then for increasing lengths of time by means of a tachistoscope (a device which presents a very brief measured stimulus) until subjects were able to name them. This point was the recognition threshold. At the same time a measure of emotional response (galvanic skin response or GSR) was taken. It was found that the taboo words had a higher recognition threshold and were also accompanied by greater GSR.

There were problems, though, with this. It was pointed out by Howes and Solomon (1951) that the taboo words were likely to be less familiar, and also that difference might reflect, not difference in perception, but differences in response. Bitterman and Kniffin (1953) and Aronfreed et al. (1953) provided evidence that participants might feel embarrassed to utter the taboo words and might delay until they were completely sure.

Worthington (1969) attempted to resolve the matter by presenting 160 participants with two spots of light and asking them to say which was brighter. In fact there was no difference in brightness, but embedded in each spot was a word too dim to be consciously perceived (i.e. subliminal). The words had previously been rated for emotional content. Those words with high emotional rating were consistently perceived as dimmer. This does seem to back up McGinnies' idea of perceptual defence. Hardy and Legge (1967) also found evidence to support the idea.

A number of studies have shown the effect of other kinds of motivation upon the way in which things are perceived. Solley and Haigh (1958), for instance, asked children aged four to eight to draw pictures of Santa Claus during the month running up to Christmas. As Christmas approached, Santa became larger, nearer and more elaborate (a more decorated costume and a bigger bag of presents). After Christmas, Santa shrank and his present bag all but disappeared.

Emotion and perception

Emotional factors too may influence what is perceived as illustrated by experiments on **perceptual defence** described in Box 13.3.

Values, culture and personality

There is some evidence that an individual's value system may induce a set. Postman et al. (1948) rated participants on the Allport-Vernon scale of values. This divides values into six categories:

- theoretical,
- social,
- economic, and
- aesthetic,
- political,
- religious.

These categories represent the kind of things which individuals think are important. Words which related to highly rated value categories were found to be more easily perceived than lower-rated values.

Cognitive styles

Witkin (1949) identified two different cognitive styles, which were labelled **field-dependence** and **field-independence**. These relate to different ways of perceiving which are linked to personality characteristics. They represent differences in the abilities of individuals to separate background (or field) from figure. This was measured by means of a rod and frame test (RFT) or an embedded figures test (EFT). In the RFT, a rod was shown inside a square frame, tilted away from the vertical. The participant's task was to adjust

---

GLOSSARY

Perceptual defence A predisposition not to perceive something because of unpleasant emotional overtones.

Field dependence/independence A concept introduced by Witkin relating to different ways of perceiving the relationship between a figure and its background. It suggests that individuals have different abilities in this respect.

the rod so that it was vertical. Those who were field independent found this easier than field-dependent people who were more likely to line the rod up with the frame. You could argue that the latter had a perceptual set induced more easily by the context in which they saw things. Field dependence and field independence are discussed more fully in Chapter 29.

Cultural set

In Pettigrew et al.'s (1958) study, different racial groups of South Africans were assembled (English- and Afrikaans-speaking white people, Indians, Africans and people of mixed race). They were shown photographs by means of a binocular tachistoscope. Different pictures were presented to each of their two eyes. Pictures of a member of one race were shown to one eye, of another to the other simultaneously. Afrikaaners tended to exhibit a cultural set in that they saw all the pictures as either European or African without differentiating Indians and those of mixed race from the Africans. This seems to show evidence that their prejudices had had an effect upon their perception of the photographs. Their classification of everyone they encountered as either white or nonwhite was carried over into their perceptions.

From the above it can be seen that perceptions are influenced by a whole range of factors relating to the individual. These include cultural background and experience, personality, values, motivations (both extrinsic and intrinsic), the context in which something is perceived and the individual's expectations.

SELF-ASSESSMENT QUESTIONS

1. Make some comparison between:
   (a) Neisser's cyclic and Gregory's perceptual hypothesis theory of perception;
   (b) Brunswik's model and Gibson's theory of direct perception.
   In each case identify and comment on the differences and similarities.
2. Discuss factors that contribute to the establishment of set. Which of them are external, which internal to the individual?
3. List the Gestalt principles of perceptual organization.

Visual illusions

As has been seen, perception is a dynamic process of searching for the best available interpretation of the data received through the senses. It is not a passive reflection of sensations received, but an active process of testing hypotheses. Sometimes the data received is ambiguous, or at least the brain conceives it to be so, so that the interpretation is erroneous (an illusion), or vacillating (at one moment there is one perception, at the next another). The field of illusion is a wide one and this section will confine itself to a discussion of those visual illusions which contribute to an understanding of some of the issues already discussed in this chapter.

Illusions which distort reality

Perhaps the most famous (and most studied) illusion is the arrowhead illusion, first described by Franz Müller-Lyer in 1889 (see Figure 13.12).

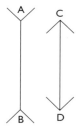

Figure 13.12   The Müller-Lyer illusion

An explanation of the Müller-Lyer illusion

The explanation given by Gregory (1968b) for the fact that the line between the outward pointing arrowheads (A–B) appears to be longer than that between the inward pointing ones (C–D) (though they are, in fact, the same length) relates to depth perception and size constancy scaling. If you see A–B as the furthest corner of the inside of a room, then the arrowheads might represent the floor and the ceiling. These are nearer than the corner (A–B). You might see C–D on the other

---

GLOSSARY

Size constancy scaling A perceptual process in which knowledge of the size of objects may modify the apparent retinal size of them at different distances. An object at a distance may thus appear larger than its retinal size.

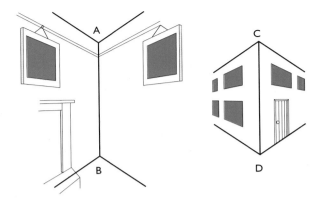

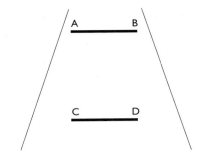

Figure 13.14 The Ponzo illusion

Figure 13.13 Gregory's explanation of the Müller-Lyer illustration. Line A–B appears longer than line C–D

A commentary on Gregory's explanation

What Gregory is claiming is that the internal processes of interpreting what we see use the apparent distance as a gauge of size. In the cases of figures such as the Müller-Lyer arrowheads or Ponzo's converging tracks, size constancy is applied wrongly. But then the question might be asked: Why do these figures appear flat, if the effect they have is as though they were 3D? Gregory (1970) suggested this was because they were lying on a flat surface. When they were presented in the dark as luminous two-dimensional outlines, Gregory claimed that they were in fact seen in 3D. But this 3D image does not seem to be seen by everyone. Stacey and Pike (1970) argued that instead of apparent distance determining the size, the size we see things determines the distance we think they are away from us.

Eysenck (1984) has noted that the Müller-Lyer illusion is still seen when circles or squares replace the fins (see Figure 13.15). This does not really fit with Gregory's explanation either. There is no size constancy scaling involved in this case. The difference in

hand as the nearest corner of the outside of a building. The arrowheads then represent walls receding into the distance (see Figure 13.13).

Experience of the relationship between size and distance encourages the observer to perceive A–B as more distant (and so smaller) than C–D. Sensory data, on the other hand, presents them as the same length. The brain, therefore, uses size constancy and scales up A–B to be longer than C–D.

A very similar effect is that of the Ponzo illusion, first described by Mario Ponzo in 1913 (see Figure 13.14).

The line A–B in this illusion appears to be longer than C–D. If we imagine the outer lines as a railway track receding into the distance, then linear perspective dictates that A–B must be further away than C–D and so should be shorter. But sensory data received shows the lines to be the same length. A–B is thus perceived as longer as a result of size constancy scaling.

Measurement of Müller-Lyer and Ponzo illusions

Gregory (1968) measured the extent of the illusion in each of these two cases by asking participants in his experiment to select a line which seemed to match lines at various positions between the converging outer lines (in the case of the Ponzo illusion). In the case of the Müller-Lyer illusion, the arrow angles were varied from 40° through to 170°. The amount of the illusion varied from the line being perceived as nearly 1 cm shorter than reality at 40°, to 1.5 cm longer at 150°.

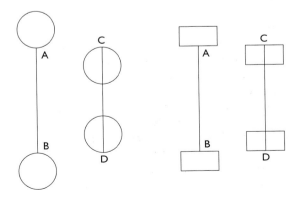

Figure 13.15 The Müller-Lyer illusion is still seen when circles or squares replace arrowheads

the apparent length may be related to whether it is seen as part of a large or a small object.

Day (1980) has suggested that more than one factor contributes to the Müller-Lyer illusion. The issue relates to whether what we perceive depends upon a detailed analysis of the information received through our senses (bottom-up processing) or whether it is primarily a matter of context and expectation (top-down processing).

Perhaps the factors which determine what we see include the conditions under which we view the figures. Gregory has tended to present the figures using a tachistoscope, which gives a brief exposure under controlled and perhaps not optimal conditions. In these circumstances it is not perhaps surprising that context and expectations become important. Gibson (1972), on the other hand, as the main proponent of bottom-up processing, has tended to use optimal viewing conditions.

Context and illusion

The circles illusion (Figure 13.16) illustrates well the effect of context upon perception.

The context of the outer circles, larger in one case, smaller in the other, leads us to exaggerate the size of the centre circle in A and reduce the size of the centre circle in B, although in fact they are the same size.

In all these cases we have misinterpreted the data available to our brains, which comes either from the senses directly, or from experiences of similar sensory experiences in the past stored in memory.

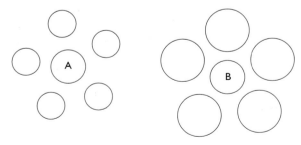

Figure 13.16   The circles illusion: circle A is the same size as circle B, but it appears larger

Illusions resulting from ambiguous figures

The Necker cube (see Figure 13.17) is a good illustration of an ambiguous figure. The data are

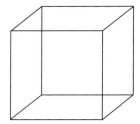

Figure 13.17   The Necker cube: at one moment we are looking down into the cube, at another we are looking up into it

insufficient to enable us to make an unambiguous interpretation of what our senses tell us, so that what is perceived seems to vacillate. At one moment we are looking down on a cube, at another up into it (Necker, 1832).

Paradoxical figures

Sometimes interpretation of the sensory data results in perceptions of impossible figures. The cues to depth perception (pp. 262–3) have been deliberately used by artists to provide false and impossible perceptions. Figure 13.18 shows Hogarth's use of false perspective in 1754 to provide an impossible scene. There is no way in which the man on the distant hill could light his pipe from the candle held by the woman leaning out of her upstairs window.

Exercise 13.7

Examine Hogarth's picture carefully. Count the number of false and impossible perceptions in the picture. In how many of these instances have false depth cues played a part? Make a list of them.

Figure–ground illusions

One of the most commonly found sets of illusions which either provide ambiguity or error in perception relate to figure and background. One of the organizing processes which has been discussed earlier under the heading of 'Gestalt theories of perception' is the distinction between figure and ground. Whenever a set of images is presented, it is necessary to distinguish what parts form the main focus of the images and what constitutes the background or context. Look at a picture

Figure 13.18 Hogarth's 'False perspective' provides an impossible scene

of cows grazing in a field and immediately the image will be organized in your mind as figure (the cows) and ground (the field and surrounding landscape). Well-known illusions occur when this organization becomes difficult. Examples include the woodcut by Mauritz Escher, 'Heaven and Hell' (Figure 13.19). The observer sees alternately either angels or devils.

Processing strategies

Much of what has been discussed in this section has related to what Coren and Girgus (1978) refer to as **processing strategies**, that is to say decisions taken by the brain about the data presented to it, in the light of such things as learning, past experience, motivations and expectations. A further explanation for some illusory effects are referred to by Coren and Girgus as **structural effects**. These are the result of the biological and optical construction of the eye. For example, the retina is not flat but concave, so that there is some distortion. Try Exercise 13.8.

Figure 13.19 Mauritz Escher's woodcut 'Heaven and Hell'; angels alternate in your perception with devils

Exercise 13.8

Cut a strip of paper 2.5 cm wide and 50 cm long. Make a mark in the centre of it and focus on it. What do you notice about the edges of the paper at the extreme ends? You should become aware of the barrel illusion. The paper will no longer appear parallel at the ends, but will bend inwards.

GLOSSARY

Processing strategies Explanations for perceived illusions which lay emphasis on the way in which information is processed in the brain.

Structural effects Explanations for illusions which emphasize optical features in the eye and neural effects in eye and brain.

With some illusions (for example, the Poggendorf illusion, Figure 13.20) the visual effects are due partly to processing strategies, partly to structural effects. Coren and Girgus (1978) showed that after five minutes of looking at the illusion the visual effects had decreased by 39 per cent. Processing strategies adapt after a period so that it is evident that 39 per cent represents the proportion of the illusion due to these strategies, while the remainder might be attributed to structural effects (optical features and neural effects in the retina and in the brain). This again relates to the debate concerning bottom-up or top-down processing in perception.

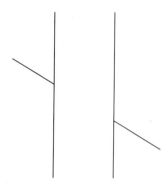

Figure 13.20 The Poggendorf illusion: the diagonal line intersects two verticals

The diagonal lines do in fact intersect the two vertical lines, though the left line appears higher than the right. Test this by putting a straight edge along the lines.

An overview of visual illusions and explanations for them

Visual illusions represent cases where the information presented to the brain through the senses is either incorrectly or ambiguously interpreted. There seem to be two explanations which can be offered for this.

■ A top-down processing explanation which emphasizes the ambiguity of the cues which help with interpretation. Factors involved here include: (a) the context in which the illusion is seen (the circles illusion illustrates this); (b) expectations resulting from past experience (Gregory's explanation for Müller-Lyer and Ponzo depend upon this as well as on size constancy and depth cues).

■ Structural explanations, which include optical features of what is seen and neural effects on the retina and in the brain. These can be said to be bottom-up processing explanations. The work of Coren and Girgus mentioned above illustrates this.

? SELF-ASSESSMENT QUESTIONS

1. Describe some explanations of visual illusions relating to processing strategies and show how illusions such as Müller-Lyer and Ponzo can be explained.
2. What is the role of experience in the perception of illusions?
3. Describe the ways in which top-down and bottom-up processing strategies have been brought in to explain illusions.
4. How do figure–ground illusions such as the Escher woodcut relate to Gestalt theories of perception?

Do we have to learn to perceive?

This section sets out the evidence for the origins of perceptual ability. It will be seen that the evidence does not point clearly either towards the overwhelming influence of innate ability or of learning, but rather that there is an interaction between innate endowment and environmental experience. The evidence comes from the following sources:

■ **Neonate studies**. These are studies using either newborn humans or animals. They show some perceptual ability even in newly born creatures.
■ **Deprivation studies**. Deprivation studies are those which examine, either with humans or with animals, the effects upon perception of deprivation of sensation, particularly sight and distortion of vision.
■ **Distortion studies**. Studies involving distortion of normal vision.
■ **Cross-cultural studies**. Studies which focus on differences in perception in different cultures which might indicate that perception has to be learned.

Neonate studies

Evidence from human neonates is often hard to interpret, as it has to be inferred from their reactions to stimuli placed before them. This inference is sometimes subjective.

Origins of figure–ground and shape perception

Fantz (1961) showed that babies were able to distinguish patterns, suggesting the possibility that figure–ground discrimination as well as some kind of form perception might be innate or at the least learned very early in life. Box 13.4 gives detail of Fantz's experiments with babies.

Maurer and Barrera (1981) used both Fantz's preference technique and also a habituation technique. Instead of measuring preferences as between pairs of stimuli (as Fantz had done), they presented one stimulus at a time and measured the time the babies fixated on it before looking away. They did this repeatedly until the child was bored with it and looked away after a very short time. Then an unhabituated image was presented. If the fixation time returned to what it had been initially, the babies clearly were able to discriminate between the two images. Stimuli included 'natural' faces, scrambled but symmetrical faces, and asymmetrical ones (see Figure 13.21). At one month old there was no significant difference in fixation times between any of the stimuli. At two months, however, there was a significant preference for a natural face.

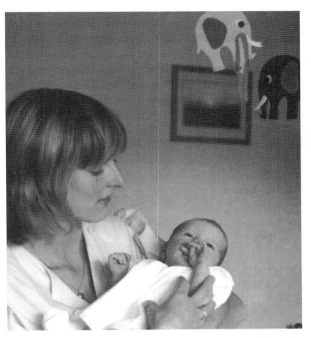

Is it an elephant? This six-week-old baby is attracted by the bright colours and movement of a mobile

Figure 13.21 Images used by Maurer and Barrera (1981). Babies showed a preference for natural faces by 2 months old

Maurer and Barrera's research seems to show that figure–ground discrimination is either learned within the first month of a baby's life or else that it is a matter of maturation: that is to say, it is a matter of normal development, independent of external stimulation. Some doubt is thrown on Fantz's conclusions.

The researchers also showed a development within infant perception. By two months old, babies were taking an interest in facial features (Maurer, 1983). By three to six months, they were discriminating between different facial patterns, between a smiling and a frowning face, for instance (Barrera and Maurer, 1981). Samuels and Ewy (1985) found that by the same age they could discriminate between attractive and unattractive faces.

Depth perception and size constancy

Bower et al. (1970) investigated responses of very young babies (6 to 20 days old) to a cube which loomed towards their faces. As it came close, they made defensive movements, such as throwing up their arms, moving their heads back or opening their eyes very wide. However, later studies such as that of Yonas (1981) only succeeded in establishing an eye-blink

---

GLOSSARY

Preference technique Technique used by Fantz to assess neonate perception based upon the preference an infant has for one stimulus over another.

Habituation technique A technique developed by Maurer and Barrera to assess neonate perception based upon the length of time the infants fixated on an object before becoming bored with it and looking away.

Maturation Development in infants and young animals which is dependent on age alone and not on learning.

Box 13.4 Fantz's studies with babies

The babies were placed in a specially designed looking chamber, illustrated in the photograph, which enabled observers to measure the time the babies spent looking at cards with various patterns. Figure A shows some of the images presented to babies in Fantz's experiments. Results included the following:

■ Babies as young as two days old spent longer looking at patterned cards than at plain grey ones.
■ Striped bullseye or checkerboard patterns were preferred to plain squares or discs.
■ Infants from four days to six months old preferred face-like patterns, even scrambled faces, to unpatterned stimuli containing the same amount of light and dark. In Figure B, babies showed a preference for (a) over (b) and (c).

Figure A

Fantz came to the conclusion that babies' preference for face-like patterns was innate. Moreover, the preference for face-like images was linked with their social needs. They clearly had a need to identify their caregivers. Some limitations of the study include:

■ The possibility that preference for the scrambled against the unscrambled face was because the former was asymmetrical. Studies with nonface patterns had shown babies to have a preference for symmetrical over asymmetrical patterns.

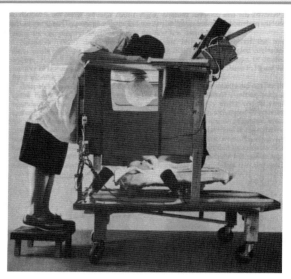

Apparatus used by Fantz

■ The preference technique adopted has limitations. It is better at showing what the babies like to look at than what they are able to discriminate.

(a)   (b)   (c)

Figure B

response to looming stimuli in infants of one month old. Accurate depth perception is indicated by the ability of babies to reach out and grasp objects which they can see and this ability is not achieved until about six months. However, Harris (1983) showed that there was some evidence of adjustment to distance by about three-and-a-half to four-and-a-half months.

In their classic experiment, Gibson and Walk (1960) used a visual cliff, illustrated in Figure 13.22. At one side of the central path the checkerboard pattern is covered by glass immediately above it; on the other there is an apparent drop with the checkerboard pattern several feet below the glass.

The researchers showed that six-month-old babies were reluctant to crawl over the 'cliff', even when their

mothers encouraged them to do so. Of course, babies old enough to crawl have already had time to learn to perceive depth, but the researchers also used newly born (or hatched) animals. Some, such as newly hatched chicks, are fully mobile almost as soon as they are hatched. Even as young as 24 hours old, chicks invariably hopped off on the 'shallow' side of the central runway and refused to move on to the 'deep' side. Similarly, kids and lambs (which can walk almost

GLOSSARY

Visual cliff Apparatus devised by Gibson and Walk to test the extent to which babies and small animals are able to perceive depth.

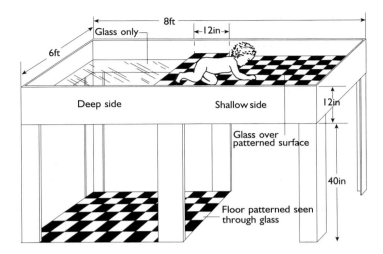

Figure 13.22 Gibson and Walk's (1960) 'visual cliff' (1 in = 25 mm approx; 1 ft = 300 mm approx)

as soon as they are born), always stepped on to the shallow, never on to the deep side, indicating that they can perceive depth.

Bower's (1965) experiments with size constancy are also interesting in this context and are described in Box 13.5.

Deprivation and readjustment studies

These studies include:

- Those which set out to deprive animals of early perceptual learning;
- Studies of humans, deprived of sight from birth, who have had their sight restored later in life;
- Studies with humans using distorting glasses.

Animal studies

In Riesen's (1950) experiments chimpanzees were deprived of light for the first 16 months of their lives (except for several 45-second intervals of light each day for feeding). When they were tested at 16 months old, they showed normal pupil constriction to light, but did not blink when threatening movements were made to their faces and showed no interest in their toys except through touch. However, Weiskrantz (1986) found that these visual problems were the result of poor development of the retina because of light deprivation. Another chimpanzee reared by Riesen in a translucent mask to mitigate this problem also showed poor visual

ability. The suggestion was that not only light but also patterned visual images are necessary for the proper development of sight.

Similar research by Hubel and Wiesel (1962) found incomplete development of receptive fields after kittens had been reared with full or partial blindfolds. Blakemore and Cooper (1970) reared kittens in a large drum which allowed them to see vertical stripes. When they were tested it was found that they responded to vertical, but not to horizontal lines. These experiments show only that proper development of physiological vision is dependent upon experience, not that perception (in the sense of the interpretation of what is presented to the senses) is innate. It has to be remembered that there are ethical issues in these studies. It is doubtful whether such experiments with animals are ethically acceptable, given the damage and distress which must inevitably have been caused.

Studies using human participants

Gregory and Wallace (1963) describe in some detail the case of a man (S.B.) who received a corneal graft at the age of 52 after having been blind from birth. While he made very good progress after the bandages were removed from his eyes and he was able to see, he had problems with things which he had not previously been able to touch. Where he was familiar with objects from touch, his judgments of size and distance were good. However, he became depressed with the drabness of the world around him, gradually gave

Box 13.5 Bower's experiments with size constancy

Bower reinforced a head-turning response in babies from 40 to 60 days old by a peek-a-boo response from an adult (Figure A). When this response was established, Bower only reinforced the babies when head-turning occurred in the presence of a 30 cm cube one metre away. Bower then presented four stimuli in counter-balanced order (Figure B):

1. The original 30 cm cube at one metre distant;
2. The 30 cm cube at three metres distant;
3. A 90 cm cube one metre away; and
4. A 90 cm cube three metres away.

The prediction was that if the babies did not have size constancy they would respond equally to (1) and to (4) (the retinal size was the same in both cases). If the babies had size constancy, they should respond to (2) (the same object) or to (3) (the same distance away). In the event there were 98 responses to (1), only 22 to (4) while (2) and (3) elicited 58 and 54 responses respectively. This indicated that at that age babies have some appreciation of size constancy. While this does not conclusively show perception to be innate, it shows that certain facets of it are at the least learned very early.

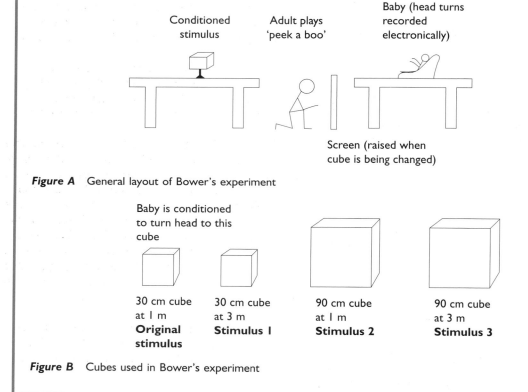

Conditioned stimulus   Adult plays 'peek a boo'   Baby (head turns recorded electronically)

Screen (raised when cube is being changed)

Figure A   General layout of Bower's experiment

Baby is conditioned to turn head to this cube

| 30 cm cube at 1 m **Original stimulus** | 30 cm cube at 3 m **Stimulus 1** | 90 cm cube at 1 m **Stimulus 2** | 90 cm cube at 3 m **Stimulus 3** |

Figure B   Cubes used in Bower's experiment

up active living and died three years later. There was clearly deep emotional disturbance.

This study does seem to show that S.B. depended upon the learning of touch perception which he had had to employ while he was blind and found it hard to learn to perceive visually, separately from this. It provides some evidence for the necessity of learning in perception, but again by no means conclusive

evidence. Other evidence regarding blind people who have regained their sight in adulthood comes from the archival studies of Von Senden, whose account of 65 such cases was analysed by Hebb (1949). His analysis included an assessment of:

■ Their ability to detect a figure or an object (Hebb terms this **figural unity**);

■ Their ability to name or identify the object (Hebb refers to this as *figural identity*).

He came to the conclusion that figural unity was innate, while figural identity had to be learned. These people seemed to be able to discriminate figure from background right away. Objects which were familiar to them from touch, however, and this includes faces, could not be identified by sight alone. They also showed little evidence of perceptual constancy (see the first section of this chapter). There are some problems related to these studies, however, which include the following:

■ Adults will have learned about the world through their senses. Loss of a sense modality is compensated for to some extent by the other senses. There is, therefore, a certain amount of unlearning needed of existing ways of experiencing the world. There will be a tendency for them to stick with what they know.
■ A radical alteration in someone's life (by having a new world of vision opened up, for instance) has emotional consequences for which there may have been little preparation. The depression Gregory's patient, S.B., exhibited seems to have been common in Von Senden's cases.
■ The years of blindness may have resulted in a deterioration of the visual system. It may be this, rather than the need for learning, which accounted for the problems encountered.
■ Von Senden's cases date from 1700 to 1928. The reliability of some of them, at least, may be suspect.

Studies involving distorted vision

Stratton's experiments on himself There are a number of studies involving the distortion of normal vision which provide some evidence for perceptual learning. Stratton (1897) wore an inverting lens on one eye (with the other one covered) for a period of eight days. He reported that he noticed the inversion less and less as the days went by. He could get around the house without bumping into things by the fifth day and his surroundings looked normal enough while he was moving about, but when he stopped and concentrated on what was about him things still seemed upside-down. When the inverting lens was removed he found the environment bewildering to some extent, but not upside-down. It is open to question whether it was his perception or his body movements which had adjusted to the glasses.

Ewart's experiments There have been many attempts to repeat Stratton's experiment. Ewart (1930) made participants in his experiment wear binocular inverting lenses for between 175 and 195 hours. He aimed to see whether perceptual adaptation did occur or whether the participants simply learnt to cope better. Two tests were administered on each day of the experiment:

■ Coloured blocks were presented to each participant in a line from an observation point. Participants had to name the colours of the nearest and the farthest blocks. Up and down and left and right judgments remained inverted throughout the experiment. There was no sign of adaptation.
■ He tested for motor adaptation and found progressive improvement in ability to locate things by touch. This seems to be improved coping ability rather than perceptual adaptation.

Köhler's studies Köhler (1964) used an optical device with a mirror which inverted the image vertically but not left to right. In his experiment, which lasted ten days, he found that the participants were able to see things the right way up provided that they moved about and touched objects in the environment. The more familiar objects became, the greater the likelihood that they would be seen upright. Moreover, when the inverting apparatus was finally removed, objects were sometimes seen to be upside-down, though only briefly.

Some conclusions from these studies If there seems to be a contradiction between the findings of Köhler and those of Ewart, several factors should be remembered:

■ The apparatus was different. Köhler's apparatus inverted vertically only, not left and right.

GLOSSARY

Figural unity Ability to detect a figure or an object, which Hebb claimed was innate.

Figural identity Ability to name or identify an object, which Hebb claimed had to be learned.

- Participants in Ewart's experiments were just given particular tests to carry out, whereas Köhler's had to practise a wide variety of perceptual-motor tasks, moving around the laboratory and picking things up.
- The number of participants was not very great (nine in all). There were likely to be considerable differences between the individuals in their reactions to what they were being asked to do. It is therefore very difficult to make any generalization.

The evidence provided by these studies seems to support the view that there is a strong element of learning in perception. If, for instance, participants in Stratton's, Köhler's or Ewart's studies found that when their vision was distorted in some way they were able gradually to adapt to the distortion, this adaptation seems to be a process of learning to come to terms with the new visual circumstance. Similarly, where individuals have regained their sight (as in the case of Gregory's S.B.) and found that they could not immediately see perfectly, there was a necessity for some unlearning of established patterns of perception (using other sense modalities than sight). This suggests that both the original mode of perception as well as the new one have had to be learned.

Cross-cultural studies

Cross-cultural studies also provide some evidence for the effects of different perceptual environments on the way in which individuals perceive the world. Several of these studies involve the presentation of illusions (such as those discussed in the previous section) to people with a different cultural background. Illusions such as the Müller-Lyer or Ponzo illusions seem to depend upon the 'carpentered' nature of the environment in which most Western people live. There is a preponderance of straight lines which may be viewed from different angles. The explanation given by Gregory (1968b) depends upon linear perspective as it is seen in a world of predominantly straight lines.

Studies involving visual illusions

Segall et al. (1966) reexamined a finding by Rivers at the beginning of the twentieth century that while non-Westernized people in Papua New Guinea were less susceptible to the Müller-Lyer (M-L) illusion, they were

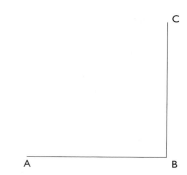

Figure 13.23 The horizontal–vertical illusion (distance from A to B is the same as from B to C)

more susceptible to the horizontal-vertical (H–V) illusion (see Figure 13.23) than English people. They suggested that while the M-L illusion depends upon the prevalence of right angles in the environment (a carpentered environment) the foreshortening of lines which fall on the retina vertically (the horizontal–vertical illusion) depends in part upon where people live. People living mostly outdoors in open, spacious environments would be more susceptible to it. Rain-forest dwellers on the other hand would be less susceptible. Segall et al. had M-L and H–V illusions presented to people in 13 different African countries and the findings largely supported their hypotheses. There have been criticisms of this study, though, which include the following.

First, Segall et al. did not consider the effects of Western education and other cultural variables. Jahoda (1966) has suggested that these might be very important.

Second, susceptibility to M-L decreases with age. If there is an impact by the environment on perceptual development it must occur at an early age. It is quite possible that the individuals tested spent their early years in quite a different environment (Weaver, 1974).

Third, size constancy also seems to be dependent on experience. Cole and Scribner (1974) report anecdotal evidence derived from Turnbull's (1961) study of pygmies in the Iturbi forest in West Africa. These were forest dwellers whose experience of perception at a distance was limited. A pygmy accompanied Turnbull out of the forest and saw cows grazing at a distance. Though the pygmy knew what cows were, he nevertheless thought he was looking at ants! Turnbull also reports that a Kpelle child raised in the jungle but taken to the capital city of Monrovia saw large tanker ships far out at sea from a high window of a hotel on a hill top.

Box 13.6 Research into pictorial perception by Hudson (1960) and Deregowski (1968, 1972a)

Hudson devised a pictorial perception test. He used three cues for depth perception, relative size, super-imposition of objects and and linear perspective. Other cues such as texture and clarity were not taken into account. Hudson's test was applied to people of a wide variety of tribal and linguistic groups in various parts of Africa. The people tested were then classified as having either two dimensional or three-dimensional vision. One of Hudson's test drawings is shown as Figure A. Participants were first asked to identify the objects in the drawing: the hunter, the antelope, the hill, the tree and the elephant. The man was clearly identified as a hunter about to throw a spear. Then they were asked questions such as 'What is the man doing?' Those who answered that the man was spearing the elephant (the nearest animal on a two-dimensional plane) were classified as two-dimensional viewers.

construct a model of this drawing using sticks and clay. Figure C shows some of these stick and clay models. The participants were found more often to construct two-dimensional models than were participants from Western cultures. The children were then asked to copy a two-pronged trident from a drawing (Figure D). Those classified as three-dimensional found more difficulty in doing this than did two-dimensional viewers.

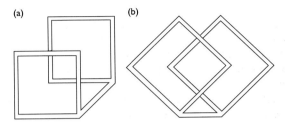

(a)   (b)

Figure B   Construction task figures used by Deregowski

Figure A   One of Hudson's test drawings

Support for Hudson's conclusions comes from a construction task designed by Deregowski. Zambian children were asked to look at a picture of two squares, one behind the other and joined by a single line (as in Figure B). The picture labelled (a) is usually seen by Western observers as three-dimenisional. When rotated 45°, as in (b), most Western observers see it as two-dimensional. The task the children were given was to

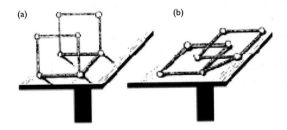

(a)   (b)

Figure C   Stick and clay models made (a) by 3D observers and (b) 2D observers

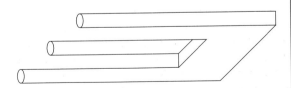

Figure D   The trident the children were asked to draw

The child commented on the bravery of people who would go out to sea in such small boats. There are problems with this kind of evidence, though:

■ Anecdotal evidence of this kind cannot be as valid as evidence that comes from a properly controlled study.

■ Vernon (1970) has pointed out that at great distances, especially with an intervening space, constancy is greatly reduced.

■ Especially in the second instance (the child and the tankers) there are insufficient cues to distance for the observer to be able to have a perceptual experience of size constancy. Instead, experienced observers would make an intellectual judgment on the basis of knowledge. The child, on the other hand, having no experience of tankers and few cues to distance, would have little to go on to make a correct judgment of size.

Pictorial perception and culture

The way in which pictures are interpreted within different cultures also contributes evidence as to the extent to which perception is learned. Hudson (1960) had discovered that some remote and illiterate groups in Southern Africa were unable to interpret monocular cues to perspective, such as superimposition of objects or height in plane (see pp. 262–3) in the same way that European observers conventionally do. All drawings are essentially meaningless abstract patterns unless the observers have learnt the conventions which allow them to intepret lines and shaded areas on a flat paper surface as recognizable objects. Descriptions of Hudson's studies and later research by Deregowski appear in Box 13.6.

Another cue to depth is retinal disparity (one eye does not see exactly what the other sees). This too was omitted in his tests by Hudson and contradicts the pictorial depth cues in Hudson's drawing. When you move your eyes superimposition of objects can sometimes disappear, for example.

Deregowski (1972a) succeeded in replacing this cue by the technique of asking observers to wear lenses of different colours over their two eyes and superimposing two images, appropriately displaced in the same two colours (each lens then filters out one image and only the other one reaches the eye). Most of the Kenyan schoolboys who had been tested using Hudson's picture and had interpreted it as two-dimensional, when tested again using this device saw the pictures as three-dimensional. Some, however, still saw the drawing as two-dimensional. Texture cues known as gradients of density were added to Hudson's drawings in a study by Kingsley et al. (unpublished) and a class of urban Zambian schoolchildren gave significantly more 3D responses than a similar class shown just the original drawing.

Conclusion

It is not possible to arrive at a definitive conclusion about the origins of perception. Some aspects, such as size constancy and figure–ground discrimination seem

(from the neonate studies of Bower and Fantz, for instance) to be present in very young children. Children and young animals also seem to be able to perceive depth very young, as has been shown in Gibson and Walk's experiments. What perceptual abilities are innate is much harder to prove. Maturation (the natural development of a baby independently of its environment) might go some way towards providing an explanation, but perhaps a more likely conclusion is that there are innate perceptual schemata that provide a basis for interaction with the environment and the development of other perceptual skills.

Distortion and deprivation studies also seem to be inconclusive. It is hard to compare human perception with that of chimpanzees or kittens, and in any case deficiencies in perceptual abilities in studies of young animals seem to be due more to deficient physiological development than to deficient psychological learning. The number of participants in studies such as those of Stratton, Ewart and Köhler does not allow generalization. There might well be individual differences among them sufficient to confound any overall effect. Gregory's and Von Senden's studies are also inconclusive, though there are indications that the sense-modality which has dominated an individual's life has a permanent and profound bearing on how he or she perceives the world when circumstances have altered. It does, therefore, provide some evidence for the influence of learning. Cross-cultural studies perhaps also provide evidence for learning. Where environmental conditions have been different, what is perceived is different (susceptibility to visual illusions, for instance).

❓ SELF-ASSESSMENT QUESTIONS

1. What evidence does the work of Fantz provide that perception is innate? Do you find it convincing?
2. Deprivation studies with animals provide some evidence for perception being learned. Does it seem satisfactory to you?
3. What evidence can be gained from cross-cultural studies that perception is learned?

GLOSSARY

Maturation The natural development of an infant independently of its environment.

Chapter summary

- To enable people to perceive the world in 3D, cues for depth perception are present in the system, binocular cues which depend upon both eyes, monocular cues which depend on only one. Primary cues for depth are those which are within the physiology of the eye and visual system with the brain; secondary cues are external, present within the visual field. Binocular cues include retinal disparity and convergence; monocular cues include linear perspective, height in a horizontal plane, relative size, superimposition of objects, clarity, light and shade, texture, motion parallax and accommodation. Of these accommodation is a primary cue, the rest are secondary.

- Perceptual constancies provide an element of stability in what we see. Retinal images vary according to the viewpoint from which we see objects, constancies allow us to recognize images regardless of their changing retinal appearance. Constancies include shape, size, location, brightness and colour.

- Recognition of patterns relates sensation to perception and is closely allied to depth perception and perceptual constancy. Theories of pattern recognition include template-matching theories, prototype models, feature analysis and scene analysis approaches. The context in which we see things is also very important.

- Theories of perception include Gestalt theories, which emphasize wholeness in perception; Gregory's theory, which lays emphasis upon formation of hypotheses; Gibson's theory of direct perception, which is an ecological approach dependent on what

he calls the ambient optical array; Neisser's cyclical theory, which involves analysis by synthesis; and Brunswik's model which relates proximal and distal inputs to the organism, which is central to the theory.

- Set is used as a useful term to explain the influence on perception of a whole range of emotional, motivational, social and cultural factors. Included in these are context and expectation, motivation, emotion, values culture and personality.

- Visual illusions are explained in terms of the relationship between size and distance, context, ambiguous figure and ground relationships and processing strategies adopted by individuals as they attempt to make sense of the world around them.

- The question of whether perception is innate or has to be learned is addressed by means of neonate studies, studies of very young children and animals who have not time to learn to perceive. The degree to which depth perception and size constancies are evident in very young creatures is the issue.

- Studies of animals deprived of early perceptual learning and humans who have regained sight after being born blind, and experiments using glasses that distort vision also contribute evidence as to whether perception is learnt.

- Cross-cultural studies provide evidence as to the extent to which culture and experience has influenced perceptual ability. In particular, studies of the extent of the perception of visual illusions such as Müller-Lyer and horizontal–vertical illusions illustrate the extent to which perceptual size scaling is dependent on particular visual environments.

Further reading

Wade, N.J. and Swanston, M. (1991). *Visual Perception.* London: Routledge. The core of this book is the function which visual perception serves for an active observer in a three-dimensional environment.

Gregory, R.L. (1996). *Eye and Brain,* 5th edn. Oxford: Oxford University Press. This has become a classic reference for the relationship between sensation and perception.

Serpell, R. (1970). *Culture's Influence on Behaviour.* London: Methuen. An excellent reference for cross-cultural studies into the nature or nurture of perception.

Smith, P.K. and Cowie, H. (1988). *Understanding Children's Development.* Oxford: Blackwell. Chapter 9 contains a very useful account of research into the development of perception.

CHAPTER 14

Memory

Early research   289
- Ebbinghaus's associationist approach   289
- Bartlett's constructivist approach   289

Models of memory   290
- More recent approaches to memory   291
- Information-processing models of memory   291
- The two/three-stage model of memory   291
- Immediate or sensory memory   292
- Short-term memory   294
- Long-term memory   295
- A commentary on the two/three-stage model of memory   299

- Some alternatives to the two/three-stage model   299

Real-life memory   303
- Autobiographical memory   303
- Remembering to do things   305
- Eyewitness testimony   305

You too can have a better memory   307
- Use of imagery   308
- Context and memory   310
- Recognition of people's faces   311
- Strategies that involve organization   311
- Revising for examinations   313

Objectives

By the end of this chapter you should be able to:

- Describe some of the early attempts to examine human memory, including research by Ebbinghaus and Bartlett;

- Make an evaluation of the merits of the two/three-stage model of memory;

- Identify what are meant by iconic and echoic memory and their relationship with short-term and long-term memory;

- Describe and evaluate alternatives to the modal model of memory including 'levels of processing' and 'working memory' models;

- Distinguish between episodic and semantic memory;

- Describe some of the research into ways in which long-term memory is organized;

- Identify ways in which memory research has been made more relevant to 'real life', including research into autobiographical memory, prospective memory and eyewitness testimony;

- Apply techniques practically which are aimed at improving your own memory, with an understanding of their basis in research.

This chapter examines the processes involved in the storage and retrieval of information. These include:

- The processes which enable human beings to store information just long enough to be able to use it (this might be termed either short-term or working memory).

- The storage of information for use in the longer term (long-term memory).

- The ways in which material is organized for storage and processes of retrieval from the long-term store.

- Some of the ways in which memory research has been conducted outside laboratories (ecologically valid, or 'real life' memory research).

■ Techniques and strategies for making the best use of memory.

Early research

Ebbinghaus's associationist approach

Ebbinghaus (1885) approached the subject of memory from an **associationist** standpoint. This was in the tradition of the empiricists of the seventeenth and eighteenth centuries, particularly Locke, Berkeley and Hume. This approach is discussed more fully in Chapter 1. When experiences occur together they will tend to be associated and so remembered together. Ebbinghaus used rigorously controlled experiments to explore the ways in which associations were formed and stored. Because of the importance of association, familiar and meaningful words could not be used as stimulus material. It was impossible to know how such words would fit into the existing web of a person's ideas.

The use of nonsense syllables

Ebbinghaus, therefore, created and used nonsense syllables, consisting of a consonant followed by a vowel followed by another consonant: **consonant–vowel–consonant trigrams** (or CVCs), such as BAZ, which he generated in hundreds and used as the material to be remembered. The associations formed between these CVCs were (theoretically, at any rate) entirely new ones unaffected by the individual's previous experience. His experiments were as carefully controlled as possible. He researched memory using himself as his own subject, varying systematically the number of times he read a list of CVCs over to himself, and the delay between reading the lists and recalling them.

Some results of Ebbinghaus's experiments

In one series of experiments he varied (between 20 minutes and a month) the delay between an initial learning of a list of CVCs and relearning them to the same standard of retention. Then he measured the number of relearning trials which were needed at each delay interval. As might be expected, the greater the delay, the more relearning trials were required. Forgetting was found to be very rapid at first, slowing down as the delay increased.

An evaluation of Ebbinghaus's contribution

Positive consequences of his approach The contribution which Ebbinghaus made to memory research lay in the development of a methodology of laboratory research; the use of nonsense syllables to control the effects of meaning; the use of free recall (recall in any order) or serial recall (recall of learned material in the order in which it was presented); and systematic manipulation of variables. Many of the methods he employed have been used in later research.

More negative consequences On the other hand, it could be said that he encouraged researchers to concentrate upon recall of meaningless nonsense syllables rather than upon more ecologically valid research.

Bartlett's constructivist approach

The **constructivist** approach focuses on meaningful material and more natural situations rather than lists of CVCs. Bartlett (1932) provided participants in his studies with stories to remember. Box 14.1 details an example of this approach.

An evaluation of Bartlett's contribution

Bartlett did not just use stories to illustrate how memory tended towards an active reconstruction of recalled events rather than a passive, almost photographic, reproduction of them. Participants in his experiments studied memory for faces, line drawings and ink blots. The most important determinants of human memory (in Bartlett's view) were the individuals' effort to find meaning in the context of their

---

GLOSSARY

Associationist An approach to explanations of psychological phenomena which emphasize links in the brain between stimuli. Ebbinghaus's memory research is an example.

Consonant–vowel–consonant trigrams (CVCs) Nonsense syllables, consisting of a consonant followed by a vowel followed by a consonant, used by Ebbinghaus in his research into memory.

Constructivist An approach to the explanation of psychological phenomena which emphasizes the construction of meaning from stimuli. Bartlett's approach to the study of memory is an example.

Box 14.1   An example of Bartlett's constructivist approach

Participants were presented with a story such as the one below, entitled 'The War of the Ghosts', invited to study it for 15 minutes and then recall as much of it as they could.

The War of the Ghosts
One night two young men from Egulac went down to the river to hunt seals, and while they were there it became foggy and calm. Then they heard war-cries, and they thought, 'Maybe this is a war-party'. They escaped to the shore, and hid behind a log. Now canoes came up, and they heard the noise of paddles, and saw one canoe coming up to them. There were five men in the canoe, and they said, 'What do you think? We will take you along. We are going up the river to make war on the people.' One of the young men said, 'I have no arrows.' 'Arrows are in the canoe', they said. 'I will not go along. I might be killed. My relatives do not know where I have gone. But you,' he said, turning to the other, 'may go with them.' So one of the young men went, the other returned home. And the warriors went on up the river to a town on the other side of Kalama. The people came down to the water, and they began to fight, and many were killed. But presently the young man heard one of the warriors say, 'Quick, let us go home; that Indian has been hit.' Now he thought, 'Oh, they are ghosts.' He did not feel sick, but they said he had been shot. So the canoes went back to Egulac, and the young man went ashore to his house and made a fire. And he told everybody and said, 'Behold, I accompanied the ghosts, and we went to fight. Many of our fellows were killed and many of those who attacked us were killed. They said I was hit but I did not feel sick.' He told it all and then became quiet. When the sun rose he fell down. Something black came out of his mouth. His face became contorted. The people jumped up and cried. He was dead.

(Bartlett, 1932, p. 65)

Comparisons were then made between the participants' versions and the original. Recalled versions tended to be shorter and contained distortions. Memory for the story was tested several times with different intervals of time between the study of the story and the recall. The longest interval was ten years. Changes in the recalled version embraced the following categories:

- **Omission**: detail tended to be omitted which did not fit in with the way in which the individual had conceived the story.
- **Rationalization**: new material was sometimes brought in to make the story more logical.
- **Emphasis**: the importance given in the story to particular aspects was sometimes altered. A theme (the ghost idea, for instance) might be made more central than it had been in the original.
- **Order**: the order of events was sometimes transformed.
- **Distortions**: individuals constructed their recall from their own attitudes, cultural background and their own emotional reaction to the story, which in turn reflected their individual experiences in life.

experience. This has proved to be very important when it came to the study of eyewitness testimony, which is more fully discussed in a later section. Where the meaning in something which a person is asked to recall is obscure, then meaning may be recreated. Perhaps this constructivist view of memory might be compared with Gregory's view of perception as an active effort on the part of perceivers to interpret the data coming to their senses in a way which has meaning.

Models of memory

This section will discuss some of the later approaches which have been adopted for the study of memory. These range from two- or three-process memory models which envisaged separate stores, a sensory buffer or visual information store (VIS), a short-term store (STS) and a long-term store, to the depth of processing approach of Craik and Lockhart (1972) and the working memory approach adopted by Baddeley and his colleagues (Baddeley and Hitch, 1974).

? SELF-ASSESSMENT QUESTIONS

1. What were the differences between the associationist and constructivist approaches to the study of memory?
2. List some of the changes that Bartlett found when his stories were recalled.

More recent approaches to memory

There have been three strands of development in later studies of memory, which are outlined below.

The information-processing approach

In much the same way that research into selective attention has concentrated upon models, memory researchers have produced flow-charts to illustrate the stages in which bits of information are processed. This might be described as an information-processing approach. It is essentially bottom-up. That is to say it concentrates upon the capacity of memory at each stage and on the length of time material might remain in a particular stage. It does not take much account of the individual or of the context within which the memory occurs. The distinction between bottom-up and top-down processing was discussed in the introduction to this part of the book (pp. 242–3).

The cognitive approach

A second approach makes a more top-down interpretation of memory. Individuals come into a memory situation with their own intentions, mental abilities and experience. The cognitive approach, as it can be termed, takes this context into account.

The ecological approach

What might be called an ecological approach to the study of memory has begun to be developed since the 1970s. As a result of Neisser's (1976) criticisms of much of the traditional laboratory-based research into memory (see pp. 306–7), more emphasis has been placed on how memory functions in everyday life. This tends to be a more functional approach concentrating upon memory for faces, names, birthdays and appointments rather than for nonsense syllables or line drawings.

Information-processing models of memory

The model of memory that underpins much of modern research concentrates upon three memory stages:

■ A **learning or input stage**. This deals with the way in which information enters the memory system and, of course, the factors which are likely to make this process easier or more difficult.
■ A **storage stage**. This is concerned with how information is organized within the memory system in order to be retained.
■ A **retrieval stage**. This is concerned with the processes involved in retrieving information from the memory for use.

The two/three-stage model of memory

This model contains features of a number of similar models, including that of Atkinson and Shiffrin (1968). It envisages separate immediate, short-term and long-term memory storage stages. Information flows through the system with recoding operating at each stage. This is designed to show how information is acquired, stored and retrieved.

A distinction is made between three kinds of memory:

Immediate memory This amounts to little more than a prolongation of the sensory stimulus, as it is received. Sperling (1960) called this the visual information store (VIS). Alternatively it has been called iconic memory (Neisser, 1967). A parallel process for the auditory modality has been called by Neisser an echoic store.

Short-term store (STS) This relates to the ability to retain information just long enough to use it. Typically it is the memory involved in retaining a telephone number just long enough to dial it after looking it up in a directory.

GLOSSARY

Ecological approach An approach which deals with 'real life' rather than laboratory settings.

Iconic memory (visual information store (VIS)) An immediate memory store which has the effect of prolonging the stimulus so that it can be processed for the short-term memory.

Short-term memory (STM) The ability to retain information just long enough to use it.

Long-term memory (LTM) The ability to retain information over indefinite periods.

Long-term store (LTS) This relates to the ability to retain information over almost indefinite periods of time. Figure 14.1 shows a flow diagram of this two/three-stage model of memory, whose elements are discussed in more detail below.

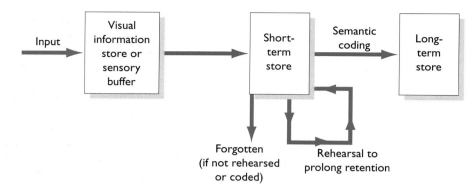

Figure 14.1 The two/three-stage model of memory

Immediate or sensory memory

Sperling (1960) developed what was termed the **partial report technique**, to establish the existence of the visual information store. Participants were presented with an array of three lines of four letters such as:

N	R	T	V
W	Y	D	A
P	L	H	U

This array was presented to them for 50 milliseconds.

At first (in the whole report method), participants had to report all they had seen. Participants were typically unable to report more than four out of twelve letters. Because Sperling did not believe that this represented a true picture of immediate recall, the partial report method was devised.

Immediately after the array had been presented, participants heard a tone: high, middle or low, indicating that they were to report top, middle or lowest lines respectively. Clearly they had no chance, before the array was presented, to concentrate on any one line. The assumption was that they would have been able to report an equal proportion of whichever line they had been asked to report. Thus, if a participant was asked (by means of the tone) to report, say, the top line and reported N T V it was assumed that three letters could have been reported in each of the three lines, nine in all as opposed to the four letters achieved in the whole report method.

By varying the delay between the presentation of the array and the tone to indicate which line was to be reported, Sperling was able to make an estimate of the duration of the iconic memory. If the tone was delayed by 500 milliseconds the response reverted to the four or five letters, which participants were able to report under the whole report method. This suggests that the duration of iconic memory is not more than 500 milliseconds (half a second).

Later research into immediate memory

After Sperling's research there was a spate of activity in this field, which generally supported the view that the icon lasted between 200 and 400 milliseconds after the stimulus disappeared: for example, van der Heijden (1981). Other research concentrated upon the characteristics of this iconic memory. Loftus et al. (1985), for instance, attempted to estimate what the iconic memory was worth in terms of memorization of a stimulus. Box 14.2 gives some details of this research.

However, Haber (1983a, 1983b, 1985) questioned the usefulness of iconic memory. His contention was that laboratory studies do not reflect what people do most of the time in real life. Most perception is of three-dimensional scenes and most involve movement. We are not often involved in trying to see things in brief flashes of light. However, it was pointed out that phenomena such as cinema films involve the integration into a moving whole of a series of brief light flashes. Ecological validity, while it is an important factor, needs to be balanced against scientific control of variables.

Echoic memory

Echoic memory is a term coined by Neisser to be the auditory equivalent of iconic memory. It amounts to a brief continuation of auditory stimulation after the actual sound has stopped. This was tested by Darwin et al. (1972). Detail of their research is in Box 14.3.

The duration of echoic memory (Crowder's research) The duration of echoic memory was measured in an experiment by Crowder (1982). Participants heard two artificially produced vowel sounds one after the other. Sometimes the vowel sounds were identical, sometimes merely similar. There were gaps between the presentations which ranged from 0.5 to 5 seconds. Participants had to report whether the vowel sounds were the same or not. An index of discrimination ability was produced which showed how accurately people were able to report whether the two sounds were different. Performance was most accurate at intervals of less

---

Box 14.2 Research into iconic memory by Loftus et al. (1985)

Participants were presented with colour slides of landscapes for durations varying from 62 to 1300 milliseconds under three conditions:

- A 'mask' condition where the presentation of the stimulus was immediately followed by a second slide showing a jumble of black and grey lines on a white background to prevent the formation of an icon.
- A 'delayed mask' condition where there was an interval between the landscape slide and the mask.
- A 'no mask' condition.

To test recall, the 72 landscape pictures together with 72 other slides, not previously seen, were shown and participants asked to indicate whether each slide was old or new. Participants' accuracy rates were interesting. For instance, where there was immediate masking it took 370 milliseconds exposure of the original slide to achieve the same accuracy (69 per cent) which had been achieved without masking with a 270 millisecond exposure. It might be said that iconic memory was worth 100 milliseconds exposure time.

Box 14.3 Research into echoic memory by Darwin et al. (1972)

The researchers presented participants with an auditory display and indicated to them which part of it was to be reported by means of a visual signal. This was the reverse, in fact, of Sperling's procedure. Special headphones presented three groups of items – digits and letters – one to the right ear; one to the left ear; the third recorded on both right and left channels so that it seemed to come from in between the other two. Then participants were given a visual cue as to which of the three sequences of letters and numbers they should report.

Results
Results were similar to those of Sperling except that the capacity of echoic memory seemed to be about five items, as against nine for iconic memory. There might have been some difficulty for the participants in separating the three input channels. The duration, too, was different, two seconds approximately, as opposed to half a second for the iconic memory.

---

than a second and accuracy deteriorated as the interval increased up to about 3 seconds, after which there was no change. Crowder surmised from this that the limit of duration of echoic memory seemed to be about 3 seconds. This was not very different from Darwin et al.'s estimate of 2 seconds.

Neuroscientific evidence for echoic memory Naatanen (1986) has summarized several pieces of research using **evoked cortical response (ECR)**. There was mention of this technique in Chapter 12. Participants were told to concentrate on reading a book. While they were doing this, a tone of a specified frequency was repeatedly presented to them. On some trials this frequency was slightly different. Researchers found that there was a change

---

GLOSSARY

Echoic memory An immediate memory store for the auditory sense modality. It prolongs auditory stimuli so that they can be processed for the short-term store.

Evoked cortical response (ECR) The brains response to a stimulus measured by means of electroencephalogram recordings.

in wave pattern about 200 milliseconds after the different tone was presented. This possibly indicates a duration of echoic memory of this length.

Cowan (1984) has suggested that there might be two kinds of echoic storage: (a) a short auditory storage of less than a second, and (b) a long auditory storage of several seconds' duration. During the latter there might be some partial analysis and transformation of material. This might particularly apply to the spoken word, which needed to remain longer in storage to pick up additional cues coming later in a sentence.

Short-term memory

The original proposal in the model, described above, was that short-term memory (STM) contained material which needed to be kept in store for not longer than 30 seconds as opposed to long-term memory (LTM), which was a more durable permanent store.

Memory span

Once material has been selected by means of the immediate memory processes (the iconic or echoic memories) the model proposes that it passes into STM. Miller (1956) has suggested that the capacity of this store is limited to seven, plus or minus two items. In order to identify what this means in practice, conduct a brief test to identify your own memory span (Exercise 14.1).

Exercise 14.1

Get a friend to present to you a series of digits at about the rate of one a second. Start with three digits. When they have been presented, immediately repeat them in the correct order. Then go on to four, then five, then six digits and so on in the same way. Your memory will be that number of digits which you can correctly repeat on 50 per cent of attempts.

Most people find that their memory span for digits is somewhere between five and nine (that is, seven plus or minus two). This holds good for groups or 'chunks' of numbers, letters or even larger units of information like words or phrases. Thus, while it is possible to recall only about eight or nine unrelated digits, it is not too hard to recall a London telephone number: for example, 0171 234 5498. These 11 digits would normally be beyond most people's span but because

they are grouped, the number is little more difficult to recall than three items would be.

Duration of STM

Unless it is possible to rehearse material to be recalled (that is, to keep repeating it silently or out loud) it will very quickly be forgotten. Peterson and Peterson (1959) did some experiments to test the duration of STM, using a technique which has become known as the Brown–Peterson Technique.

Participants were given groups of three consonants to recall. This should be well within their memory span. They were asked to repeat the consonants after intervals of 0, 3, 6, 9, 12, 15, or 18 seconds. In order to prevent participants from rehearsing the consonants during the interval (which would have extended the duration of the STM) they were asked to count backwards aloud in threes from a three-digit number they were given. It is worthwhile trying this. The sequence is shown in Exercise 14.2.

Exercise 14.2

First get a friend to present a trigram to you (three unrelated letters: for instance, N H W) immediately followed by a three-digit number such as 456. Count backwards from that number in threes aloud (456, 453, 450, 447 etc.) until your friend gives you a signal (a tap on the table will do) for you to recall the trigram. Then repeat the three letters. Repeat this with various time lapses such as those above. It will be hard to recall the letters after more than a 6 second interval.

The trace decay theory of forgetting   The Petersons found that correct recall was high after short intervals such as 3 or 6 seconds, but by 18 seconds' interval participants were recalling only about 10 per cent correctly. They suggested that the duration of STM was only about 6 to 12 seconds if unrehearsed. There was a memory trace within the brain which decayed gradually. This was the trace decay theory of forgetting.

GLOSSARY

Memory span The amount of material that can be stored in the short-term memory at any one time.

Box 14.4 Conrad's (1964) experiments to test acoustic coding in STM

387 participants were shown sequences of six letters on a screen and were told to write them down as they appeared. However, they were presented too fast for the participants to keep up, so that they had partly to be held in memory. In some cases, participants substituted wrong letters. Conrad did an analysis of these errors and concluded that in most cases participants substituted letters which sounded similar (B for V or X for S, for example). These acoustic confusion errors suggested that STM was coded acoustically, even when the original material had been presented visually. There must be a means of recoding material, presented visually, for it to be registered in the sound-based STM.

Interference theory of forgetting An alternative explanation for this phenomenon was that forgetting occurred when other material interfered with memorization. The Petersons found that while the first set of consonants in a series of trials was not often forgotten, in later trials participants began to mix up the trigrams they were asked to recall. This was an interference theory of forgetting.

Coding in STM

It is clear that immediate memory is either iconic or echoic, depending on whether the information was received visually or aurally. Evidence has been produced by Conrad (1964) that STM is coded acoustically: that is to say, what matters is what the material to be recalled sounds like. Box 14.4 gives some details of his experiments.

Visual coding in STM Den Heyer and Barrett (1971) have, however, produced evidence for visual or visuospatial coding in STM. Participants in their experiment were presented with a grid pattern with letters on it at random. Figure 14.2 gives an example of the kind of grid they used.

Participants had to recall two things: (a) the letters on the grid, and (b) the position in the grid where letters occurred. As with the Petersons' experiments, there were tasks interposed between the presentation of the array and the recall (either a 'counting backwards' task or else a visual 'matching patterns' task). While the 'counting backwards' task disrupted recall of the letters

B		D		E	
	Y		Z		
	A			M	
		B			

Figure 14.2 An example of the kind of grid used in Den Heyer and Barrett's experiments

on the grid, recall of the positions of letters on the grid was interfered with most by the 'visual matching' task. The conclusion they reached was that the letters were coded verbally, whereas the positions were coded visually.

Long-term memory

This is the final stage in the modal model. While it is possible to characterize short-term memory in terms of its duration, its capacity and its coding it is much more difficult to do this for long-term memory. There seem to be no known limits to the duration or to the capacity of long-term memory storage. It is important that semantic connections (that is to say, understanding of meaning) are involved in the process of coding for long-term memory, but that is not the only way in which it is organized. There is great diversity, not only in what is stored – all kinds of knowledge and beliefs, objects and events, people and places, plans and skills – but also how it is stored.

The following will examine some of the factors involved in organization and retrieval in long-term memory, including distinctions between episodic and semantic memory, interference effects and the ways in which it seems that material is organized within our memory systems. It is worthwhile to remind readers of the stages involved in memory, because recall or forgetting may be influenced at each or any stage. These are the input or encoding stage, the storage stage and the retrieval stage.

Episodic and semantic memory

The model of memory proposed by Tulving (1972) suggests a distinction between **episodic memory** and **semantic memory**. The distinction seems to be as follows.

Episodic memory The storage of information about events and the relationships between them has been described as episodic memory. Here are some examples:

■ There was a gale last winter and tiles crashed down from the roof on to the patio.
■ At Easter, we visited our friends, who were staying in Yorkshire.
■ Unfortunately, I had left the lights of the car on, and when I returned the battery was flat.

Each of these examples are episodes which describe personal experiences. Memory for them is related to other experiences. Leaving the car lights on is related, for instance, to coming back to find the battery flat and the car refusing to start.

Exercise 14.3

Think of two different examples of episodic memory. Remember that they must concern events and relationships, related to personal experience.

Semantic memory While episodic memory is memory for fairly transitory events in your experience, semantic memory can be described as memory for more permanent items of knowledge, usually involving language, such as: (a) it is usually warmer in the summer than in the winter; (b) a starling and a robin are birds, but a bat is a mammal which flies; or (c) 2+2=4.

Tulving has defined semantic memory as:

A mental thesaurus, organised knowledge a person possesses about words and other verbal symbols, their meanings and referents, about relations among them, and about rules, formulas and algorithms for the manipulation of these symbols, concepts and relations. Semantic memory does not register perceptible properties of inputs, but rather cognitive referents of input signals. (Tulving, 1972, p. 386)

The distinctions that Tulving made between these forms of memory involve a wide range of characteristics. Tulving (1983) lists 28 different distinctions. Episodic memory, for example, is based upon sensations, semantic memory upon understanding; episodic memory is time-related, semantic memory is related to concepts; episodic memory is very subject to forgetting,

semantic memory is less so; semantic memory tends to be more useful to an individual than episodic memory.

Some criticisms of Tulving's distinction Johnson and Hasher (1987) contend that episodic and semantic memory have not been shown empirically to be separate systems which can be isolated from one another. Wood et al. (1980), in support of Tulving, have shown that there were different bloodflow patterns in the left cerebral hemisphere for participants in their experiment who were engaged on an episodic memory task from that for other participants who were engaged on a semantic memory task. However, it was pointed out by critics (Baddeley, 1984; McKoon et al., 1986) that any two different tasks, even two semantic tasks, might be accompanied by different bloodflow patterns. It did not imply that there was a distinction between semantic and episodic memory.

Some of Tulving's distinctive characteristics were also called into question by McKoon and her colleagues. Tulving had claimed, for instance, that semantic memory was conceptual; episodic memory was time-related. Ratcliff and McKoon (1978) showed that even in episodic memory conceptual relationships may be as important as time relationships.

Interference effects

One of the factors that seem to influence whether something is forgotten or not is interference. Where there is some similarity between one lot of material remembered and another, recall can be affected. Interference effects can be of one of two kinds.

■ Retroactive interference. Retroactive interference occurs when what you learn later interferes with previously stored material. You have perhaps learned the times of the trains to London and then you look up in a train timetable when trains leave for Birmingham. This new learning may interfere with the old and cause you to forget it.

GLOSSARY

Episodic memory The storage of information about events and the relationships between them.

Semantic memory The storage of information about permanent items of knowledge, usually involving language.

Retroactive interference Interference with earlier memory caused by subsequent learning.

■ **Proactive interference**. Proactive interference works the other way around. The stored memory you have for the times of trains to London may interfere with, and cause you to forget, train times to Birmingham.

McGeoch and Macdonald (1931) demonstrated retroactive interference effects in an early experiment, described in Box 14.5.

Box 14.5 Retroactive interference: an experiment by McGeoch and Macdonald (1931)

Participants were divided into five experimental and one control group. All groups were given a list of words to learn. The five experimental groups were then given another learning task. They had to learn either: (a) numbers, (b) nonsense syllables, (c) words unrelated to the original list, (d) synonyms of the words in the original list, (e) antonyms of the words in the original list.

The control group had no intervening task. When recall of the original list was tested, success varied from 4.5 for the control group to 1.25 for those who had to learn synonyms. There seemed to have been more interference where the material was similar. More words were remembered by the group which had to learn numbers (3.68) than nonsense syllables (2.58), unrelated words (2.17) or antonyms (1.83).

Organization in long-term memory

There will inevitably be a very complex mass of information stored in LTM. Without some organization, much of this material will become inaccessible to recall. It seems likely that items in the long-term memory are grouped together according to their meanings. Free-recall studies allow participants to recall material in any order they wish. It is then possible for experimenters to see how material is grouped in the memory.

Grouping of material Bousfield (1953) gave participants 60 items to learn in a random order. The list included 15 names of animals, 15 names of people, 15 professions and 15 vegetables. They were asked to recall the list in any order they liked.

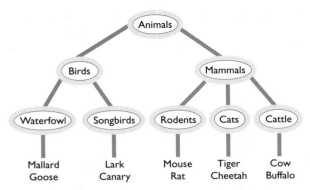

Figure 14.3 Organization of words into hierarchies increases learning efficiency (Bower et al., 1969)

Participants tended to remember them in clusters, belonging to the same category. Once they had remembered one animal, for instance, several others tended to follow. Bousfield suggested that there must be some kind of semantic organization in long-term memory.

As well as semantic categorization there seems also to be some organization into hierarchies. Bower et al. (1969) divided participants into two groups and asked them to learn a list of 112 words. Under one condition, the words were already organized into different conceptual hierarchies as illustrated in Figure 14.3.

In the other condition participants received the same words, arranged in a similar pattern, but the words were not organized into hierarchies. In the first learning trial the first group remembered 65 per cent of the words as opposed to 18 per cent for the other group. After three trials recall was 100 per cent for the first group as compared with 47 per cent for the other group. Organization into a hierarchical form seems to have a dramatic effect upon recall.

Hierarchical network model of semantic organization

An extension of this has been Collins and Quillian's (1969) network model of semantic memory. A network consists of a series of nodes with links between them. A name is linked to some characteristic. For instance, 'bird' is linked to 'has wings' or 'can fly'. The network is hierarchical in the same way that Bower et al.'s conceptual hierarchies are. An example of Collins and Quillian's hierarchical organization model is illustrated in Figure 14.4.

Collins and Quillian were able to make predictions about the time needed to retrieve information from the long-term store. A technique employed consisted of presenting participants with a number of statements to be judged as true or false. These included true statements like the ones above and also some false ones like 'canaries have gills'. Response times were measured. It was found that the time taken to verify whether the statement was true varied with the number of levels of the hierarchy the search has to pass through. You could predict, for instance, that 'a canary can sing' would take less time to verify than 'a salmon has gills'. In the first case, there is just one level involved, in the second case two. A statement such as 'a shark has skin' would take longer still to verify as there are three levels involved. It seems that in the last case the memory search has to pass through three stages 'a shark is a fish', 'a fish is an animal', and 'an animal has skin'.

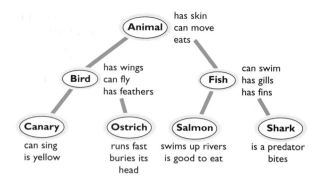

Figure 14.4 An example of Collins and Quillian's hierarchical model of memory organization

share many links and lie close together so that the paths between them are short. 'Bird' and 'wings' and 'sparrow' would probably lie close together in memory storage and would have many interconnecting links. 'Shark' and 'yellow' and 'feathers' would not lie so closely together and would not have so many links. The important points about this model seem to be the following:

- Speed of access depends on the length and strength of the links.
- Strength of linkage depends on frequency of use.
- Activation of memory about concepts spreads outwards to adjacent concepts (from 'birds to 'wings' to 'feathers', for instance).
- As the distance increases so the strength of the activation decreases. There is no indefinite spread of activation. No matter how long you took over it, it is unlikely that thinking about roses would lead you to think about lions! The paths between are too long and too indirect.

Exercise 14.4

Using Collins and Quillian's network model, which of the following statements would take longest to verify:

An ostrich eats
Salmon spawn in rivers
Birds breathe?

Typicality effect   There is a problem with Collins and Quillian's model in that it seems to work very well with a typical member of a category (a cod is a fish, for example) but less well for untypical members of a category (a penguin is a bird, for example). It has been found that a statement about a typical member of a group may be verified faster than one about an untypical member.

Spreading activation model

Problems such as the above have led Collins and Loftus (1975) to suggest a different kind of network model. They termed this a spreading activation model. In this model concepts are grouped in interconnected clusters rather than hierarchically. Closely related concepts

Advantages of the spreading activation model
This model has distinct advantages over the earlier network models. Typicality is not a problem. It also links in very well with what is already known about how information is represented in the brain. Activation of a concept can be thought of as activating a

neuron (or nerve cell). The activation then spreads to other neurons producing a pattern of excitation. While such patterns do not last long, there is also evidence for longer-term changes in the ways in which nerve cells are linked to each other, their synaptic connections. These may make particular links easier or harder to excite.

A commentary on the two/three-stage model of memory

There are several points that need to be made about this model of memory.

One-way flow of information

The model implies that there is a one-way flow of information, from immediate memory to short-term and finally to long-term stores. But this is not necessarily the case. Suppose that you were registering the letter V in the short-term memory (from a spelling of a name in a phone conversation perhaps). You would need to equate the letter V with the sound 'vee'. That relationship you would have stored in your long-term memory. There must therefore be a link back from LTM to STM.

Nature of information stored

The model emphasizes the amount of information which is stored. Common sense would suggest that it is at least as important to consider what kind of material has to be remembered. Some things are easier to remember than others. Information which is funny, familiar, distinctive or which has some particular association for us (a self-reference perhaps) is more easily recalled. Meaningful material is remembered much more readily than that which has no meaning for us.

Individual differences

The model ignores the fairly crucial point that there are enormous individual differences in the way we operate our memories.

Functions of memory

Another vital point is that the model pays no attention to the function of memory. While emphasizing what memory does and how it works it ignores what it is for. A later section in this chapter will look at the operation of memory in everyday life, the ecology of memory.

Short-term/long-term memory distinction

There is not universal acceptance of a distinction between short-term and long-term memory storage. Depth of processing theories, for example, which will be discussed later, blur this distinction. However, clinical evidence from patients suffering from Korsakov's syndrome (where chronic alcoholism produces a combination of dementia and amnesia) or from those who have sustained a severe head injury, shows that STM can sometimes be severely impaired while LTM remains intact.

Complexity problem

The model understates the complexity of LTM.

Some alternatives to the two/three-stage model

Working memory model (Baddeley and Hitch, 1974)

The model of memory which we have been considering up to now envisages passive storage of information. Immediate, short-term and long-term stores have storage durations which vary, as well as having varying capacities. The working memory model takes a more active view of memory. It is concerned with the storage of information which is being used actively and about which we are currently thinking. This may come from two sources: (a) new sensory information; and (b) old information stored in the long-term memory.

For instance, if you were replacing the sparking plugs in your car you would use new sensory information to locate the spanner over the plug and old stored information as to which way to turn the spanner to unscrew it.

Baddeley (1981) has suggested that working memory consists of several parts as illustrated in Figure 14.5.

■ **An articulatory loop.** An articulatory loop stores material in verbal form and allows for verbal rehearsal (the inner voice).

GLOSSARY

Working memory model Baddeley's memory model which included a primary acoustic store, an articulatory loop and a visuospatial scratchpad.

Articulatory loop An element in Baddelely's working memory model that allows for rehearsal of material heard.

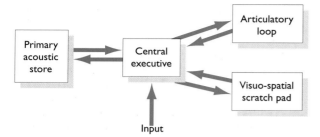

Figure 14.5 An illustration of Baddeley's working memory model

■ **A primary acoustic store**. This is of limited capacity and accepts material either directly as it is heard or via the articulatory loop (the inner ear).
■ **A visuospatial scratchpad**. This allows for intake of visual information and for visual and spatial rehearsal.
■ **A central executive**. This is free of sense modality.

To relate the working memory model to what has been discussed under the heading of short-term memory, consider the articulatory loop as explaining how seven (plus or minus two) items of information can be stored for a brief period (6–12 seconds), unless rehearsal takes place. The loop allows for this rehearsal. Baddeley experimented with articulatory suppression. Participants were made to mutter some words or phrases to occupy and suppress the articulatory loop, while at the same time performing another task such as learning a list of words. Where it was found that this procedure of concurrent verbalization impaired performance of the task, it was assumed that the articulatory loop was employed in the task. This is not unlike the Petersons' technique for preventing rehearsal. The visuo–spatial scratch pad is the visual equivalent of the articulatory loop and explains Den Heyer and Barrett's findings, mentioned above (p. 295).

An evaluation of the working memory model
There are positive and negative points to be made. On the positive side, it can be said to come much closer to explaining how memory actually works than the Atkinson/Shiffrin model does: for instance, by the suggestion that there are different ways of dealing with different kinds of information (sound-based, verbal, visual or spatial). It is also useful to see a common source of resources in the central executive

used in widely different cognitive tasks. It begins to be possible to see how memory systems may operate in such diverse tasks as reading and doing mental arithmetic. In reading, the articulatory loop has been seen to be involved alongside the central executive which oversees semantic analysis and the comprehension of the material (Baddeley and Lewis, 1981). It is an active rather than a passive system and has more ecological validity as it can be seen to involve real-life tasks.

There are, however, two unresolved problems. First, it is not very clear exactly what role the central executive plays. It is claimed to have a limited capacity yet there has been no measurement of that capacity. It is said to be modality-free, but how it operates has not been defined.

Second, the clear distinctions which have been made between the various components seem rather unrealistic. Baddeley and Lewis (1981) in their investigation of the operation of working memory in reading found that the speed and accuracy of judgments about the sounds of words and nonwords was unaffected by articulatory suppression. This kind of processing of sounds was taking place somewhere other than in the articulatory loop.

Levels of processing

A second alternative is the levels of processing model proposed by Craik and Lockhart (1972). Their thesis is that information memorized is processed at different levels which relate to what is done with the material. Processing is either shallow or deep and this processing level determines how well the material is retained

Shallow processing Shallow processing consists simply of coding the material (structurally) in terms of its physical characteristics; such things, for example, as whether a word is written in upper- or lower-case type or acoustically (according to its sound). This could be, for instance, whether the voice is that of a man or a woman.

Deep processing Where the processing involves some semantic manipulation (that is, manipulation which relates to its meaning) then there is a deeper level of processing. For instance, answering the question of whether 'bear' means the same as 'carry' would involve some semantic processing. It focuses on the meaning of the words.

It is assumed that the retention of material is dependent directly upon the depth at which it has been processed. It is not realistic to make a sharp distinction between short-term and long-term memory. Stimuli undergo successive processing operations, at first in terms of physical characteristics (the letters and the typeface of a printed word or the sound of a spoken word), then at a deeper level in terms of meaning. It is perhaps interesting to compare this with some of the ideas developed about attention, discussed in Chapter 12, which separate processing of physical characteristics from deeper semantic processing. Rehearsal of material to be remembered can also be at different depths:

- Simple repetition is shallow and is termed **maintenance rehearsal**.
- When rehearsal explores meaning, it is termed **elaborative rehearsal** and involves deep processing.

While shallow processing leads to short-term retention, **deep processing** leads to longer-term retention. Box 14.6 describes some experiments on depth of processing.

It's all right, Mum, they say you remember things much better when there's been deep processing

Box 14.6 Some experiments on depth of processing

Elias and Perfetti (1973) gave participants in an experiment a list of words. For some of the words they were asked to find rhymes, for others they had to produce synonyms. While they were not specifically asked to memorize the words, they were subsequently tested on how many they could recall. It was found that they could recall significantly more of those words for which they had had to produce synonyms. This, of course, involved semantic processing, while finding rhymes involved just the sound of the words and so was shallow processing.

Craik and Tulving (1975) found that people who had answered questions about a word's meaning were about three times as likely to recall it later as they would be if they had simply answered questions about the word's physical characteristics.

Other forms of memory, too, seem to be affected by this deep/shallow processing distinction. Groups of participants in an experiment conducted by Fiske and Schneider (1984) were each given different instructions for dealing with stimuli with which they were presented:

- Some had to press a button whenever they detected a word which represented the name of a vehicle (semantic processing).
- Others had to press the button whenever the word contained the letter G (graphic processing).
- Others again were told to ignore the words altogether (control).

After participants had seen all the stimuli, Fiske and Schneider asked them to estimate how many times they had seen each of the words. There was a clear relationship between estimates and processing instructions. A word actually presented 20 times was reported in the vehicle-naming condition to have been presented 18 times, in the graphic processing condition only 5 times, and in the 'ignore' condition 0 times.

GLOSSARY

Maintenance rehearsal Shallow rehearsal involving no more than simple repetition.

Elaborative rehearsal Deeper rehearsal involving meaning.

Deep processing Processing of material to be memorized which involves a semantic or meaning element and is therefore more durable.

Originally Craik and Lockhart had concerned themselves only with the encoding end of memory and not with retrieval. A later piece of research, however, suggested that the same distinction should also apply to retrieval (Moscovitch and Craik, 1976). The reasons why deep processing seems to influence recall relate, in the view of Craik and Lockhart (1986), to two factors:

■ **Distinctiveness,** which describes the extent to which a stimulus is different from other memory traces in the system.
■ **Elaboration,** that is, how rich the processing is in terms of meaning.

Let us take some examples: Suppose you want to remember the word 'chicken'. If processing involved the notion of a chicken strolling down the motorway dodging the cars as they raced by, that would provide a more distinctive memory trace than, say, a chicken sitting on a nest and laying an egg. If this image was elaborated upon by suggesting that the chicken on the motorway had a bare behind because it had lost all its tail feathers and was being chased by an irate farmer brandishing a pitchfork it would be very memorable!

Research by Craik and Tulving (1975) emphasizes the importance of elaboration. Participants were asked to read sentences and decide which words were appropriate in the sentences. Some were simple, such as:

She cooked the - - - -

Others were more elaborate like:

The great bird swooped down and carried off the struggling - - - -

The accompanying words were either appropriate (rabbit) or inappropriate (book). Recall was much better where the sentence frame was more elaborate.

All this research seems very much divorced from the reality of anything you might ever have to remember. Palmere et al. (1983) have shown that it need not be so. Participants were asked to read a 32-paragraph essay on a fictitious African nation. Each paragraph contained just one major idea and consisted of four sentences, one 'main idea' sentence and three others which provided examples of the main idea. As they were presented to participants, eight of the paragraphs were intact, eight had one example sentence removed, eight had two example sentences removed, eight had all three example sentences removed. Participants read the essay and were tested on their recall of the main ideas. The greater the elaboration, the more examples, the greater was the recall of the main ideas.

Self-referencing effect   Recall of material seems to be better when there is self-reference, that is to say when individuals can relate it to themselves. This has been regarded as an extension of the levels of processing approach to the study of memory.

Rogers et al. (1977) asked participants in their study to process lists of words with much the same kinds of instructions as in other research into levels of processing. There were instructions which related to the physical characteristics of the words (capital or small letters, for instance), instructions which related to acoustic properties of the words (rhyming perhaps), instructions which demanded that participants consider the meanings of the words, and also self-referencing instructions. These required participants to decide whether a particular word could be applied to themselves.

It was found that the greatest number of words recalled were those which had self-referencing instructions. For the rest, the results were predictable, the next best recall being for words with semantic instructions, then acoustic and finally physical instructions.

There are clearly possible practical applications for this. Apart from the obvious one that a good way of remembering material presented to you is to relate it to yourself, there is a suggestion in a study by D'Ydewalle et al. (1985) which suggests that products might be better remembered by inviting consumers to consider how they might use the product themselves.

An evaluation of the depth of processing approach   Several points have been made in evaluating this approach. It has been suggested that the approach represents an oversimplification of what is in fact a very complex reality. We have seen that there are several different ways in which 'depth' can be interpreted, the amount of effort which is put into it, for instance. Tyler et al. (1979) had participants in their experiment solving two sets of anagrams, easy ones or more difficult ones. While the level of processing in each case seemed to be the same, they remembered more of the difficult anagrams than of the easy ones. We have already seen that others have highlighted factors such as elaboration or distinctiveness.

Eysenck suggests that the arguments might be circular ones.

> In view of the vagueness with which depth is defined, there is danger of using retention-test performance to provide information about depth of processing, and then using the putative 'depth of processing' to explain retention test performance. (Eysenck, 1978, p. 159)

Craik and Lockhart have tended to use only free recall as a retention test. Morris et al. (1977) have used either a standard recognition test or else a rhyming recognition test, where participants had to select words which rhymed with the words in the list. While the standard test produced results which were in line with what the depth of processing hypothesis would predict, the rhyming recognition test showed that more words were recognized where the instructions involved processing the words acoustically. This could be, for instance, asking 'does the word rhyme with - - - -?' rather than when the instructions involved semantic processing (for example, asking 'does the word mean the same as - - - -?'). Shallow processing seemed to be producing better memory for the words than deep processing.

Morris et al. (1977) suggested that different kinds of processing led learners to acquire different kinds of information. Retention depends on whether the information acquired is relevant to the kind of test used.

It has been assumed that deeper levels of processing are associated with more durable memory for information. It is not possible to test whether this is true without ensuring that the amount of learning at different depths of processing is the same. This has not usually been done. However, when Nelson and Vining (1978) manipulated the number of learning trials so that there was equal learning at deep and shallow levels of processing there was the same rate of forgetting with deep as with shallow processing.

Real-life memory

In this section we shall examine memory for events in one's own past (autobiographical memory), remembering to do things and eye-witness testimony. All these things are more closely related to reality than the laboratory studies discussed up to now.

Autobiographical memory

We have considered the way in which semantic memory seems to be organized. Autobiographical memory is concerned with episodic memory. It is the memory for events in a person's life. Research into autobiographical memory tends not to deal with lists of words or nonsense syllables. It also tends to be conducted not in laboratories but 'in the field'. There is emphasis on ecological validity.

Parallel to Ebbinghaus's studies of his own memory in the last century (see beginning of this chapter) Linton (1982, 1986) tested her own memory for events that had occurred in her own life. Each day she recorded two events that had occurred during the day and each month tested her memory for those events. She looked at each brief description of events and attempted to recognize exactly the event described, together with its date. In six years she accumulated

Autobiographical memory Memory for details of a person's own life events.

Ecological validity Relevance to what happens in the 'real world'.

![?] **SELF-ASSESSMENT QUESTIONS**

1. What are the three stages in Atkinson and Shiffrin's model of memory? How do they differ:
   (a) in terms of coding?
   (b) in terms of duration?
2. Does Craik and Lockhart's 'depth of processing' theory seem to you to replace the need to assume separate short-term and long-term memory stores?
3. Describe Baddeley's 'working memory model'. Do you feel it gets over the problems thrown up by the two/three-stage model?
4. How did Tulving distinguish between semantic and episodic memory. List two distinctions.
5. Distinguish between retroactive and proactive interference.
6. Compare the models of memory organization of Bower et al., Collins and Quillian and Collins and Loftus. How do the main features of each differ?

5500 events. She found that her memory for real-life events faded only about 5 per cent a year. Pleasant memories were easiest to recall with about 50 per cent correctly recalled; about 30 per cent of unpleasant events and 20 per cent of neutral ones were correctly remembered.

Accuracy of recall

The accuracy with which we recall events in our lives depends on several things:

- The time that has elapsed since the event;
- The type of event, whether pleasant, unpleasant or neutral; and
- Whether the event occurred to oneself or to another person.

Other factors that have been researched include search strategy, the position of an event in a longer sequence and the cues used to trigger recall (Loftus and Fathi, 1985). Seaching one's memory, starting with most recent events and working backwards, seems to be more accurate than the other way around. Pillemer et al. (1986) found that students recalled events which occurred early in the college year more accurately than those later in the year. Rubin et al. (1984) found that odours evoked unique memories more than other cues.

Lapse of time

Thompson (1982) found that accuracy in dating events decreased by more than a day for each week that passed. For instance, after two weeks had passed people were inaccurate by about two days, but after 10 weeks this inaccuracy had increased to 12 days.

Pleasant or unpleasant events

Thompson (1985) also noted that pleasant events were recalled more accurately than unpleasant ones (but then, they were also rated as being more memorable).

Self-reference effect

There seems to be a self-reference effect in memory for life events as well as for words. Thompson et al. (1987) found that where events actually happened to them, individuals remembered dates more accurately than if they occurred to someone else.

Flashbulb memory

The term 'flashbulb memory' has been used to refer to our memory for the situation in which we first learned of an outstanding event. For instance, people are said to have very accurate memories of what they were doing when they heard that President Kennedy had been shot.

Brown and Kulik (1977) attempted to investigate this by questioning people to see whether certain national events triggered this kind of memory. They listed six kinds of information which were likely to be listed in flashbulb memories for national events:

- the place;
- the event that was interrupted by the news;
- the person who gave them the news;
- their feelings;
- the feelings of others;
- the aftermath.

Think about the flashbulb memories that are triggered in your own mind when reference is made to the Dunblane massacre, the death of Diana, Princess of Wales, or some other major event. Do the kinds of information you recall tally with those listed above?

Exercise 14.5

Consider an event, either a national occurrence or else one that was much more personal to you and list the 'flashbulb' information in your own memory.

Brown and Kulik found that what determined the triggering of flashbulb memories included first and foremost a high level of surprise, a perception of the importance of the event and the high level of emotional arousal which accompanied it.

More recently Pillemer (1984) asked people to recall the attempted assassination of President Reagan on 30 March 1981. First, a month after the event, and then again six months later, participants were asked where they were at the time of the assassination attempt and who told them about it. There was quite vivid recall of individuals' personal situation at the time of the attempt. There were strong visual images. The amount of the emotion which the event aroused in individuals seemed to be positively related to the vividness, elaboration and consistency with which the detail was recalled.

Rubin and Kozin (1984) also studied vivid memories for events in people's lives. Participants were asked to describe the three clearest memories from their past. The categories of memories they reported were interesting: 18 per cent concerned accidents or injuries to themselves or their friends. Other frequently reported memories included sports, love affairs, animals and things which happened to them in their first weeks at college. National events figured in only 3 per cent of memories. The most vivid memories were the most surprising and the ones which were most rehearsed.

Exercise 14.6

What are the three clearest memories you have of things which have happened to you? Do they match at all the categories which Rubin and Kozin found? You might go round all your friends and ask them the same question. Put the results of your survey in an order of frequency.

Schematization of autobiographical memory

Schemata represent generalizations abstracted from a large number of specific events in our lives and serve to summarize important attributes in the events. Suppose you developed a schema for lunchtimes. Attributes might include where you consistently tend to sit to eat lunch, who you tend to eat with and the topics of conversation which arise. This schematization provides organization so that we can summarize events in our lives. Single events are not readily distinguishable. If you are asked to recall details they are likely to be reconstructions of the generic or schematic memory.

Repisodic memory You may recall events which never happened, but which are similar to the schemata you have developed. Neisser (1981) has termed this inaccurate memorization of events **repisodic memory**. This is an example of cognitive processes actively reshaping our memories. Barclay (1986) has provided some empirical evidence for this. Three graduate students were asked to keep records of three memorable events a day. At a later date they were presented with accounts of events which were either exactly what they had written or a 'foil', a similar but unfamiliar event. Approximately half of these foils were recognized as having occurred.

Remembering to do things

While there has been much research into **retrospective memory**, that is, memory for things previously learned, **prospective memory** or memory for future actions already planned (remembering to do things) has been much less well-researched. One area which has received some attention is **absent-mindedness**. Reason (1984) notes that these kinds of slips of memory are more likely to occur:

- In familiar surroundings;
- If you are preoccupied;
- If there are other distractions;
- If there is pressure of time; and
- If a well-established routine is changed. For instance, if you have decided to have croissants for breakfast instead of toast and they are all ready for you, you may still automatically make your customary pieces of toast!

Box 14.7 gives some detail of a study carried out by Meacham and Singer (1977) on prospective memory.

Eyewitness testimony

The unreliability of testimony in court from those who have been eyewitnesses to an event is well-attested. However, juries still seem willing to trust the testimony of eyewitnesses. Perhaps they should be more careful. There are two problems:

- Being able to recognize faces accurately.
- Associated with this, the difficulty of recall of other information relating to an event.

The first section of this chapter included discussion of Bartlett's study of reconstructive memory. Some of the issues involved are similar to those relating to eyewitness testimony. Detail tends to be rationalized to fit the way in which the individual has conceived the event.

GLOSSARY

Repisodic memory Term used by Neisser for inaccurate memorization of events, either events which never happened or events similar to schemata already developed.

Retrospective memory Memory for events in the past.

Prospective memory Memory for events scheduled to occur in the future.

Absent-mindedness Slips of memory relating to things that need to be done.

Box 14.7 Prospective memory: some research

Meacham and Singer (1977) gave students eight postcards to send back to the experimenter one a week for eight weeks. There were two conditions:

■ Some participants had instructions that they should send them back every Wednesday.
■ Others had to send them back on a specified different day each week.

In each of these two groups some were told they would receive payment ($5) for remembering to send back the cards, while others received no payment. While the 'every Wednesday' group were no better at remembering to return them than the 'random day' group, a promised payment did make a difference. In each group those who were paid remembered more often than those who were not. A further study (Harris, 1984) indicated that the interval between being given instructions and carrying them out made little difference. People instructed to return cards two days later were no more reliable than those who had a 36-day delay.

Recognition of faces

In Chapter 13 there was a discussion of pattern recognition and, in particular, feature-analysing models of pattern recognition (pp. 266–8). This is relevant here. There have also been studies which have dealt particularly with the problems of recognizing faces. Shapiro and Penrod (1986) collated the results of 128 studies of facial recognition in order to see whether any particular variable seems to have an effect on accuracy of recognition. The following factors seem to have a bearing on this:

■ **Race**. People seem to recognize members of their own race significantly better than members of another race.
■ **Time and attention paid to the face**. The more time and attention which is spent upon looking at a face, the greater the accuracy of recognition.
■ **Distractions**. Accuracy of recognition is likely to be reduced where something distracts attention from the face.
■ **Importance of the upper part of the face**. The upper part of a person's face determines

recognition of it to a markedly greater extent than the lower half of the face.

■ **Depth of processing**. Some of the factors discussed in the section on depth of processing also seem to apply here. Where it has been necessary to make some judgment about a face, recognition is likely to be more accurate than when a person simply looks at a face.
■ **Irrelevancy of training**. Training does not seem to influence accuracy of recognition.
■ **Time intervals**. The length of time which has elapsed does not seem to influence accuracy of recognition automatically. Depth of processing and the distinctiveness of the face seem more important in increasing accuracy. What has happened in the interval also matters. Presenting other pictures of faces, or photo-fits, substantially reduces accuracy.

Recall of circumstances

Witnesses to motor accidents are frequently asked to recall the details of what happened. Loftus and Palmer (1974) showed that the wording of a question relating to what a witness had seen could make a substantial difference to the accuracy of testimony. Box 14.8 shows detail of two of Loftus and Palmer's experiments.

How can distortions of eyewitness testimony be avoided?

Attempts have been made, in the two studies below, to find out how people can be made to resist information which may distort their memory:

Prior warning Greene et al. (1982) showed that warnings about the possibility of misinformation, when responding to a questionnaire, may increase accuracy. The time taken to read the questionnaire also seems to have a bearing on this.

Taking time Tousignant et al. (1986) found that those who took their time to read the questionnaire were more likely to be accurate than those who did it hastily.

This section has contained some of the more ecologically valid pieces of research which have emerged as a result of Neisser's strictures about memory research (Neisser, 1982) in a speech in which he refers to the 'thundering silence' for the previous hundred years on real memory.

Box 14.8 Eyewitness testimony: experiments by Loftus and Palmer

Participants in their study were shown a film of a multiple car accident. After being asked to describe what happened in their own words they were asked specific questions. There were three groups:

- Some were asked, 'About how fast were the cars going when they smashed into each other?'
- Others were asked, 'About how fast were the cars going when they hit each other?'
- A control group were not asked any question about the speed of the cars.

The first group's mean estimate of the cars' speed was 10.5 mph, the second group's estimate was 8.0 mph. The wording of the question had affected the recall of the motor accident. A week later all the participants were asked the question: 'Did you see any broken glass?' Even though there was no broken glass shown in the film of the accident, 32 per cent of the first group said that there was broken glass, compared to 14 per cent of the second group and 12 per cent of the control group. Eyewitness evidence is easily distorted by information presented subsequently. The explanation that participants may simply have been responding to the experimental situation, arguing that cars that smash into each other would inevitably produce broken glass, has been refuted by a later experiment.

Several groups of participants in an experiment by Loftus et al. (1978) saw slides of a sports car which stopped at an intersection and then turned and hit a pedestrian. Of these groups:

Group A saw a 'stop' sign at the intersection.
Group B saw a 'yield' sign.

Twenty minutes to one week later participants were asked questions about the accident. A critical question contained information which was either (a) consistent, or (b) inconsistent with the detail of what they had seen on the slides. Alternatively, the detail was not mentioned in the question. For instance, members of the group which had seen the 'stop' sign were asked, 'Did another car pass the red Datsun while it was stopped at the yield sign?' (inconsistent). Other members of the group were asked, 'Did another car pass the red Datsun while it was stopped at the "stop" sign?' (consistent). Still other members of the group had a question which did not include the sign at all. Then they were shown slides, one with a 'stop' sign and one with a 'yield' sign and asked which they had seen. Those who had had an inconsistent question tended to choose the information contained in the questionnaire rather than that on the original slides. Those who had had a consistent or a neutral question produced more correct responses. Later information does influence the responses of eyewitnesses.

You need only tell a friend, not himself a psychologist, that you study memory. Given a little encouragement, your friend will describe all sorts of interesting phenomena: the limitations of his memory for early childhood, his inability to remember appointments, his aunt who could recite poems from memory by the hour, the regrettable decline in his ability to remember names, how well he could find his way around his home town after a thirty years' absence, the differences between his memory and someone else's. Our research has, of course, virtually nothing to say about any of these topics.

(Neisser, 1982)

The concluding section of this chapter will contain some practical ideas for the improvement of memory skills.

? SELF-ASSESSMENT QUESTIONS

1. List some of the factors found by Linton to influence the accuracy of memory for events in our lives.
2. What are some of the factors which seem to have a bearing on ability to recognize faces accurately?
3. In what ways can later information distort memory for events of which a person has been an eyewitness?

You too can have a better memory

This section is devoted to techniques that may improve recall of information. For the most part it is firmly based upon research and what is known about the way in which memory works. There are two broad categories in which these techniques lie, first the use of **imagery** and second the employment of organizational strategies.

Use of imagery

Imagery involves creating in the mind mental pictures of things which are not physically present. Clearly, it is much easier to represent some things with mental pictures than others. Concrete objects, such as a 'house', a 'chair' or an 'envelope' (high imagery material) are much easier to picture than abstracts such as 'justice' or 'inflation' (low imagery material). Paivio (1968) showed that people will ordinarily recall high imagery material twice as well as low imagery material. Bower (1972) also conducted experiments into the use of imagery. Details of one of these are in Box 14.9.

How can you use imagery?

One way, therefore, to improve memorization, is to create mental images of things which have to be remembered and then associate these with other mental images. These can either be things which you wish to remember as associated ('liberty' perhaps, represented by the torch on the Statue of Liberty), or, alternatively, it is possible to create a list of items which are memorable to you in some way and then pair each item in that list with something that you want to remember, making a careful mental picture in your mind of each pair together. The more bizarre and

---

Box 14.9 Using imagery to assist memorization. An experiment by Bower (1972)

Bower asked participants in his experiment to memorize pairs of unrelated words. One group (the experimental group) was asked to make mental images of the pairs of words (for instance, if the two words were 'shoe' and 'orange' the mental image created might show a shoe with an orange prominently attached to the toe). The control group was merely asked to memorize the words. The experimental group showed significantly better recall of the pairs of words. Bower also noted that the more unusual the images were, the better was the recall.

---

elaborate the images you create the more memorable they are likely to be. Try to make sure, as well, that there is reference back to yourself.

A list of ten items that has been much used and is well known to most people rhymes the numbers 1–10:

one	bun	
two	shoe	
three	tree	
four	door	
five	hive	
six	sticks	
seven	heaven	
eight	gate	
nine	line	
ten	hen	

It is easy enough to remember the rhyming words and then to create images which associate each with an item you wish to remember. This can be extended almost indefinitely, by, for instance, creating an alphabetical list of, say, animals:

A is for antelope
B is for bear
C is for cat
D is for dog

and so on. The alphabetical list will be comparatively easy to learn and then images of each animal can be placed in your mind alongside images of the things you have to remember. There can, of course, be many alphabetical lists. It has been suggested that this kind of imagery will be assisted if the images created are as bizarre as possible. The research evidence on this is not clear-cut.

GLOSSARY

Imagery The process of forming mental images of things or events you need to remember. Material to be remembered may have high or low imagery value.

Bizarreness of images

Wollen et al. (1972) found that it mattered more for recall that the images created interacted with each other than that they were bizarre. Other studies such as that of Webber and Marshall (1978) found that bizarreness did make a difference, especially when there was some delay in recall.

The applications of this kind of imagery are wide-ranging. It has been used by Patten (1972) with patients with memory disorders. It has been used extensively in the teaching of foreign languages. Atkinson and Raugh (1975) asked students to think of English words which resembled each of the Russian words they were trying to teach and then create images of the English word interacting with the meaning of the Russian word. Bull and Wittrock (1973) found that imagery helped children extend their vocabulary. Children had to draw pictures of the new words and then write definitions of them.

Exercise 14.7

List ten items which you need to memorize. Go through each in turn and create an image in your mind, associated in some way with the rhyming list above. At the end of the day try to recall what 'one' is, what 'two' is and so on.

Method of loci

Cicero, a Roman orator of the first century BC, was known to have used the **method of loci** to remember names and other facts he needed to remember in his speeches. He visualized the people and facts which he needed to remember; in particular, locations around the room in which he was speaking. More recently, Bower (1970) has outlined how this technique might be used. The first stage is to identify and commit to memory a number of specific locations. You might use the route followed as you go from home to college. Along this route will be landmarks that can be used for locations (the point where you have to turn off the main road onto a footpath, for instance). At each of these locations, mentally recreated in imagery in your mind, place an image of something which you need to remember. Then all that is needed is to traverse the route in your mind and the objects which you have placed along it will come to mind. Groninger (1971) tested this technique experimentally. Details are in Box 14.10.

Box 14.10 Method of loci. Groninger's experiment to test its effectiveness

Participants in this study operated under two conditions. In the experimental condition, they had to think of 25 locations in order. Then items on a 25-word list were mentally pictured at each of these locations. Participants in the control condition were free to use any method they wished to memorize the 25-word list in order. There was to be no further rehearsal of the word list. Then, after intervals of one week and five weeks, both groups were tested. Recall of the word lists was significantly better for those who used the method of loci than for the control group, particularly after five weeks.

Exercise 14.8

Visualize a route which you frequently take, preferably walking. Identify salient points along this route; places where you have to turn, perhaps, or landmarks, like a prominent building of some kind. At each of these points make a mental image of something you want to remember and place the image you have created at the location along the route. Later, retrace your route in your mind and see if you can recall the items you wanted to remember.

Extensions of this method have been tried by Bellezza (1983). Words on a page, set out, each with a distinctive arrangement on the page, were learned more easily than if they did not have this distinctive arrangement or pattern on the page. In a later study, Bellezza (1986) found participants learnt abstract psychology terms more easily if they were superimposed on a picture. For example a cue word, 'depth' for instance, in 'depth perception', could be illustrated by a drawing of a steep cliff with someone at the top and the bottom of it. Associated words like relative size, light and shade and texture could be arranged around it.

GLOSSARY

Method of loci A mnemonic technique or memory aid that involves visualizing material to be remembered in particular locations.

Arrangement of material on a page

Lovelace and Southall (1983) found that students remembered material better when it was presented to them typed on pages with numbers and space at the top and bottom of the page. Knowledge of where the material was and on what page helped provide cues for its recall. By contrast, when the material was typed on a continuous scroll with no pages or page numbers, recall was reduced by 25 per cent. All this relates to the context in which something is learned. Recall is easier if the context can be reconstructed as well as the actual material.

Exercise 14.9

As you make your notes from lectures and class activities, be very careful about the look of each page. Put page numbers at the top left-hand corner, highlight and underline headings and key words. Then, when you come to revise your work recreate the patterns and layout on your original notes. The content should become easier to memorize.

Context and memory

Not unrelated to the above is what is known as the encoding specificity principle. Tulving (1983) suggests that recollection of an event occurs if and only if the properties of the trace of the event found in memory are sufficiently similar to the properties of the cue information presented at the time of retrieval. In practice this means that recall is likely to be best when the context in which learning takes place is the same as that in which testing is done. Box 14.11 details an experiment by Smith et al. (1978) concerned with this.

It is hard to see how this encoding specificity principle can be made to operate in practice. Clearly, it is likely that formal examinations, taken in a large impersonal hall with unfamiliar invigilators, by students who have done their learning in small informal groups with teachers they know well, are likely to put students at a disadvantage. Administrators should take note.

Students should perhaps be encouraged not to do their final revision at home, in a bedroom, perhaps with music playing, but in a classroom which comes as near as possible to the conditions they will encounter in the exam room.

Box 14.11 Encoding specificity. An experiment by Smith et al. (1978)

Participants were asked to learn material in two very different settings. On one day they had to learn words in a windowless room with a large blackboard and no cabinets, where the experimenter was formally dressed in a jacket and tie. On another day they learned a different set of words in a tiny room with two windows with the experimenter dressed in open-necked shirt and jeans. Then on the next day they were tested on both sets of words, half of them in the windowless room with the formally dressed experimenter, the other half in the tiny but well-lit room with the casually dressed experimenter. Recall was best of material learned in the same setting as the original learning, with those tested in the same context recalling an average of 13.6 words, while those tested in a different context recalled an average of only 9.1 words.

Mood congruence and state-dependent memory

Context refers not only to the physical context in which something is committed to memory but also to an individual's physiological context when something is learned. This can include affective states (emotional and motivational states, for instance) and also factors such as states induced by drugs or alcohol. Memory appears to be better if there is a congruence between the material to be learned and the individual's mood. This is mood congruence. When pleasant material has to be learned, it is best learned in a pleasant frame of mind, while someone in an unpleasant mood will be better able to learn unpleasant material. Blaney (1986) reviewed 29 cases where mood had been experimentally induced and showed that, in 25 of these, mood congruence had a bearing on memory. However, it is not easy to see how this can be made to operate in a study situation.

GLOSSARY

Encoding specificity principle Recollection of material is easier if the context in which attempts to recall are similar to the context in which memorization took place.

Mood congruence Involves the matching of the affective content of what has to be memorized to the mood you are in when you memorize it.

State-dependent memory may be more relevant, though, to your situation. It is suggested that what people remember is at least partly determined by the physiological state they are in. The state during encoding needs to match that during recall. However, Blaney's review of the literature, mentioned above, casts some doubt on this. A significant number of studies have failed to show evidence of state-dependent memory.

Recognition of people's faces

Putting names to faces and recognizing people when you see them can be important. People are often pleased and flattered when you meet them and greet them by name. How can we make sure that we recognize people we meet?

The section in Chapter 13 on pattern recognition concerned ways in which we are able to recognize what we have seen before, whether this is a printed letter or word or the features of a face. This has also been discussed in connection with eyewitness testimony. A teacher in front of a classroom full of children has this problem, as has a doctor faced with a succession of patients, each of whom only visits the doctor very infrequently. Imagery can help here too. This is what you can do:

- On introduction, make careful note of the person's name, repeat it out loud and create a mental image for it if at all possible.
- Suppose, for example, the name is Sean Miller, a mental image might be created of a windmill and the miller going about his business of grinding corn. This particular miller has a closely cropped haircut (is shorn).
- Then look at the features of the individual in front of you, superimposing them on your 'shorn miller' (nose, eyes, ears and any other distinctive feature). Remember that the top of the face – eyes particularly – are the most distinctive part.
- If any of these features remind you of some well-known person he or she too can be incorporated into your image, probably in caricature. Similarly, if the features remind you of a friend or a relative he or she can go into the image. When you meet the individual again, the image will recur and with it the name.

Strategies that involve organization

As has been seen in the sections on short-term and long-term memory, disconnected or random material is much harder to commit to memory than material which has a pattern to it. First, the process of breaking material into chunks is important. Remember that the capacity of short-term memory is around seven, plus or minus two, items (Miller, 1956). But each item can be a single letter or a digit, a group of letters or digits or a word.

Elaboration and self-referencing

We noted in the section concerned with levels of processing that deeper processing with more elaboration and with self-referencing is likely to result in more accurate recall. The more active the manipulation of representations of what you are trying to remember, the more effective the recall. It is also important to note that long-term memory is very dependent upon organization. Things are better remembered linked together than unrelated. It might be well to refer back to the section on long-term memory organization on p. 297.

Chunks and meaning

As an example, let us take UK postal codes. These are normally two letters followed by two figures, then as a second group a figure followed by two letters. BS232XG is a collection of seven letters and digits with no meaning to it. It is hard to memorize. Break it up into BS23 2XG and it immediately becomes easier, a chunk of four and a chunk of three. It becomes easier still when the pattern for postal codes is known. You understand that BS refers to Bristol. A random collection of letters and numbers has been organized into fewer and more meaningful chunks.

There is evidence that the time spent in organizing material so that it connects together and is meaningful is time well spent. To some extent this organization is spontaneous. Tulving (1962) found evidence for such spontaneous organization and this is described in Box 14.12.

GLOSSARY

State-dependent memory What individuals remember is at least partly determined by their present physiological state.

Box 14.12 Spontaneous organization. Studies by Tulving (1962) and Rubin and Olson (1980)

Tulving asked participants in his study to recall the same list of words in each of 16 trials. As trials progressed, there was increasing spontaneous organization. This was rather a sterile process. Not many people are asked to memorize the same list of words 16 times.

A more ecologically valid study was conducted by Rubin and Olson (1980). Undergraduates were asked to list members of the staff in their faculty. There was spontaneous organization in the way they had remembered and listed the names. Those who taught the same subjects tended to be grouped together.

Hierarchical organization

Hierarchical organization has also been shown to be effective. This is a system where items are arranged in classes. It has already been seen that there is hierarchical organization in long-term memory. It might be useful to look back to p. 297.

Hierarchical organization can be visualized as a kind of family tree. At the summit of a family tree are the two individuals from whom all those below are descended. Each generation becomes more numerous. In the same way, hierarchical organization of information starts with a few broad classifications and subdivides into more specific and still more specific classes. When writing notes for this section, there are broad categories of techniques for memory improvement, imagery and organization, for instance. Within each are more specific techniques. Under the classification of imagery there is the method of loci and under this again a specific technique for memorizing items along a path you regularly travel.

How to use hierarchical organization   Linking this discussion of organization with the previous section on imagery, there are ways in which you might reorder your notes so as to be able to remember them more accurately.

Lovelace and Southall (1983) showed that patterns on a page can be important for memorization. Start with the key idea in a box in the centre of the page. Highlight it by drawing and perhaps by colour. Round it, like the legs

of a spider, let lines radiate on which subordinate ideas are written. Outwards from these are attached the lower and more specific items in the hierarchy. Figure 14.6 illustrates the kind of pattern which might result. Then, when you come to revise for an examination, take a blank sheet of paper and attempt to recreate the pattern.

Exercise 14.10

You might like to try Lovelace and Southall's technique for yourself. The trick is to establish key words as memory joggers and to work out from the centre. Try to create a pattern like this for a section from elsewhere in the book and see if it helps your recall of the material.

Meaningfulness and memorization

The section on levels of processing (p. 300) clearly contains practical ways of improving memorization. It is evident that where material has been processed so as to focus upon its meaning, recall becomes better. After all, focusing on the meaning amounts to semantic processing and this is deep and therefore effective processing in terms of memory. Learning facts by rote is a less helpful way of preparing for an examination than working to tease out the meaning behind the words. Part of your revision programme needs to be devoted to making sure you understand everything. Understanding involves putting things in your own words. If you put into your own words what you are hoping to be able to recall, you force yourself to come to terms with its meaning and so process it more deeply. Elaborating on it and trying to make it more distinctive, by, for instance, creating unusual and elaborate examples will help still further. The key processes are:

understanding → recasting material in your own words → elaborating on it → finding unusual and distinctive examples.

Mnemonic techniques involving mediation

Mediation techniques involve finding a simple mediator which will help you remember something

---

GLOSSARY

Mediation The use of a link between what you need to remember and something already established in memory.

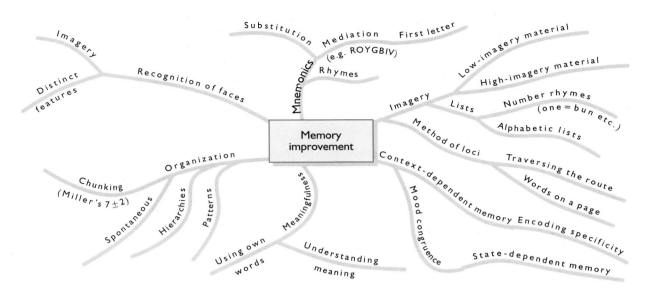

Figure 14.6 Example of the use of patterns to help memorization

long and complex. Extra words or images are used to make material more memorable. The sentence 'Richard Of York Gained Battles In Vain' has been used by generations of schoolchildren to help them to remember the colours of the spectrum in order: Red, Orange, Yellow, Green, Blue, Indigo, Violet. The first letter of each word that you want to remember is used to make up a more meaningful sentence, preferably one that has possibilities for imagery. Alternatively, first letters can be used to form a nonsense word which is memorable through its very bizarreness. Such a word is SOHCAHTOA, which still remains in my memory from schooldays. In full, it relates to trigonometrical rules for computing the angles of triangles: 'Sine is the Opposite over the Hypotenuse, Cosine is the Adjacent over the Hypotenuse, Tangent is the Opposite over the Adjacent'.

Morris (1978) showed that this technique was useful where the order of items to be remembered was important, less so when this was not the case. However, it remains one of the most popularly used techniques.

Some other mnemonic techniques

Substitution The techniques described above are useful for verbal material, but where numbers are involved it is difficult, if not impossible, to use them. In these circumstances a letter can be substituted for

a digit. Then mediation techniques such as the creation of words or sentences can be used. Alternatively, words may be substituted for digits, each having the same number of letters as the digit it represents. For example, if you had to remember a particular security number such as 4294 then a sentence such as 'Jane is available soon' could be substituted: 'Jane' 4 letters, 'is' 2 letters, 'available' 9 letters, 'soon' 4 letters, hence 4294. Clearly there are problems in creating and decoding such mnemonics but they are effective.

Rhymes Rhymes are much used to help us remember. Most of us remember the number of days in each month of the year by the rhyme 'Thirty days hath September, April, June and November' and so on.

These are just some of the mnemonic techniques which have been employed to enable us to use memory more effectively. The most useful way forward for you as individuals who want to improve their memory is to try some of them, and if they seem to work for you then use them.

Revising for examinations

Examinations are a fact of life for most students and it is worthwhile at this point to say a little bit about them. In a sense, revision for examinations should go on right

In complete silence, nearly 3000 students concentrate on their examination in Nice, France

throughout the period of study, but there will almost inevitably be a period leading up to the examination which is a revision period. The question will always arise, 'Will I remember it all in the examination room?' Perhaps some pointers for success are appropriate.

- **Understanding**. You will not easily remember what you do not understand. As you go through whatever course you are engaged upon make sure you understand everything as you go along. Your learning must not be a passive process of absorbing the notes you are given, but of creating your own in terms that *you* can understand.
- **Images**. Remember that pictures speak louder than words. As you go through the course, sit down after each class and devise your own diagrams, figures and pictures.
- **Linkages**. Think of your memory system as a gigantic set of hooks, where everything is linked to everything else. If you have not been given the linkages between things, seek them out for yourself. In many cases these linkages will be hierarchical, rather like a family tree. As you study your notes do it actively, creating these hierarchies, starting with a central theme and branching out and branching out again.

- **Active learning**. Remember Craik and Lockhart's levels of processing theory (p. 300). Process everything you have to learn deeply, delve into meanings and write down your notes again in a new form.
- **Rehearsal**. The more often you rehearse what you have to learn the better it will stick. That is why revision really should begin from the beginning of your course, building each bit on what went before.
- **Panic**. How do you cope with the panic of approaching examinations? The answer is that there is no substitute for preparation. Last-minute swotting is not really the answer.

? SELF-ASSESSMENT QUESTIONS

1. Describe two mnemonic techniques which involve imagery.
2. How can you make sure that you remember people's names?
3. In what ways does it help memorization to organize the material you want to learn more carefully?
4. What is meant by mediation in memorization?

Chapter summary

- The earliest studies of memory were those of Ebbinghaus in the 1880s and Bartlett in the 1930s. Ebbinghaus concentrated upon association and used nonsense syllables to study how short-term memory worked. Bartlett discovered that we construct our own memories, fitting new material into what is already in our minds.

- Atkinson and Shiffrin produced a two-stage model of memory (short-term storage and long-term storage). To this was added immediate memory, in effect an extension of the stimulus so that it lasted longer. This was termed iconic or echoic memory. So there is a two/three-stage model.

- Other models included the levels of processing theory. This suggested that long- and short-term memory were not separate but that the length of retention depended on what was done to the material, how it was processed. Deeply processed material was retained longer than shallowly processed material.

- Baddeley and Hitch developed a 'working memory model' which consisted of a primary acoustic store together with an articulatory loop for rehearsal and what they termed a visuospatial scratchpad for nonverbal memory. There was a central executive to control the input of material.

- Organization in long-term memory is envisaged by Collins and Quillian as being a hierarchical network.

- Collins and Loftus modified this model into a spreading activation model. Concepts are grouped in interconnected clusters. Access to memory depends upon strength and length of links which in turn is dependent on frequency of use.

- Ecologically valid studies of memory include auto-biographical memory. The accuracy with which people remember what happens to them depends upon the length of time which has elapsed, whether the event was pleasant or unpleasant and the degree of self-reference.

- Prospective memory includes the study of absent-mindedness. Slips of mind are more likely to occur if surroundings are familiar and if there are distractions and pressure of time.

- The study of eyewitness testimony includes the ease or difficulty of remembering faces and the rationalizing of events to fit preconceived views of events. Recall of the circumstances of events can be influenced by the wording of questions put to witnesses.

- There are two broad categories of ways in which memory may be improved, the use of imagery and the employment of organizational strategies. Meaning has a strong influence upon recall. The use of mnemonic techniques is useful, but not a substitute for meaningful learning.

Further reading

Baddeley, A.D. (1990). *Human Memory: Theory and Practice.* Laurence Erlbaum Associates. A valuable work for all aspects of memory.

Buzan, T. (1974). *Use Your Head.* London: BBC Publications. Contains the substance of a series of TV programmes on memory improvement and study skills.

Eysenck, M.W. (1984). *A Handbook of Cognitive Psychology.* Brighton: Psychology Press. Covers all aspects of memory research to considerable depth.

Matlin, M. (1989). *Cognition.* Fort Worth,: Holt, Rinehart & Winston. Particularly useful for aspects of real-life memory.

CHAPTER 15

Thinking and language

The nature of thinking   316
- Autistic and rational thinking   317
- A Freudian view of thinking   317
- Piaget's view of thought   317
- A Gestalt model of thinking   318
- A behaviourist model of thinking   318
- Cognitive approaches to thinking   318

Concept formation   319
- Concept formation studies   320
- Later studies of concept formation   321

Problem solving   323
- Understanding problems   323

- Representing the problem   324
- Strategies to solve problems   326
- Factors that may influence problem solving   328

Language and thinking   331
- Linguistic relativity   331
- Restricted and elaborated codes of language   332
- Thought as subvocal speech   332
- The influence of thought upon language   333
- Thought and language as independent   333

Objectives

By the end of this chapter you should be able to:

- Identify various interpretations of what is meant by thinking, including Freudian, Piagetian, Gestalt and behaviourist views;

- Describe what are meant by 'concepts', together with some of the research into their formation;

- Demonstrate an understanding of some of the cognitive processes involved in solving problems

and factors which may facilitate or inhibit problem solving;

- Identify various theories about the relationship between language and thought including linguistic relativity theory, Vygotsky's and Piaget's views;

In this chapter we are concerned with thinking. Problem solving and concept formation are two of the particular topics dealt with, as are various models of thinking. Additionally, the chapter is concerned with language and its relationship with thinking. The acquisition of language and theories related to this are discussed fully in Chapter 20. Attempts which have been made to teach human language to animals are discussed in Chapter 17.

The nature of thinking

Thinking has been defined as the process involved in manipulating information, either collected through the senses or stored in memory from previous experience, so as to be able to respond to the immediate situation. In this section, we shall examine various models of thinking. These include Freudian approaches, distinctions between autistic and rational thinking,

Piaget's view of thinking and that of the behaviourists and the Gestalt psychologists.

Autistic and rational thinking

McKellar (1972) draws a distinction between **autistic thinking** and **rational thinking**. Autistic thinking has no rational purpose. It is the brain's manipulation of the information available to it, from the senses or from stored material, without any particular purpose. Daydreaming is an example of autistic thinking. Rational thinking, on the other hand, is logical and rational and directed towards a purpose. When you are solving the clues in a crossword puzzle you are engaging in rational thinking.

A Freudian view of thinking

For Freud and the psychoanalysts, thinking is closely related to their view of basic human motives. For them, the basic human motive is the satisfaction of bodily needs. Where these needs are not fully satisfied, memory of them is brought into play. This memory is associated with the kind of excitation that actual food, warmth and contact evoke. For example, a hungry infant hallucinates about food, but this hallucination is not in itself satisfying. Some of the energy released is devoted to solving the problem, to changing the environment so that the food, the warmth or the contact is obtained. This is essentially autistic thinking, driven by emotional rather than by rational processes. Freud makes a distinction between primary and secondary thought processes. While secondary thought embraces rational conscious thought of which we are normally aware, primary thought processes are normally unconscious. There seem to be three separate levels of thinking:

- **Preconscious thought**, which comprises those thoughts and ideas which are not engaging our consciousness at the moment, to which we are currently not paying attention but which nevertheless exist for us.
- **Conscious thought**, to which we are currently paying attention and on which we are engaging our minds.
- **Unconscious thought**, which remains inaccessible to our consciousness but which nevertheless plays a part in determining our behaviour.

A more complete discussion of Freud's theory can be found in Chapter 30.

Piaget's view of thought

The building blocks of an individual's intelligence Piaget termed **schemata**. They are continually being modified or added to by contact with the environment so that the individual's adaptation to that environment becomes more complete. The process involved is one of **equilibration**. When something new manifests itself in an individual's environment his or her mind is thrown into a state of imbalance or disequilibrium. This is uncomfortable, so there is motivation to find a new balance. This new balance occurs through adaptation, which takes the form either of **assimilation** or else of **accommodation**. With assimilation, an object or an

Varying degrees of attention in a maths exam. Daydreaming is an example of autistic thinking

idea is understood in terms of the concepts or actions (schemata) which the child already possesses. With accommodation, concepts and actions are modified to fit the new situation. A fuller discussion of Piaget's theories is found in Chapter 20 or in Birch (1997).

A Gestalt model of thinking

There is a classic account of a German psychologist Wolfgang Köhler, interned on the island of Tenerife during the First World War, who set problems for a chimpanzee named Sultan. This has been fully described in Chapter 6. Köhler saw the principle concerned here as one of **isomorphism** the notion that the mind always attempts to restructure the elements of a problem so that the brain fields adopt **good form**, or Prägnanz, as the Gestalt psychologists described it. There is an inborn tendency within the brain to seek order out of chaos. This is in accordance with the Gestalt 'laws of organization', which have already been mentioned in Chapter 6.

A behaviourist model of thinking

Behaviourists found some difficulty in explaining thinking. It did not seem to accord well with their principle that all mental processes were essentially the forming of associations between stimuli. There is full discussion of behaviourist approaches to psychology in Chapter 1. Watson (1913) viewed thinking as subvocal speech. The process of thinking inevitably (as Watson saw it) involved inner language. This was a motor theory of thought. Some work was done with deaf mutes. It might be expected under Watson's theory that they would move their fingers more than a normal group of adults when they were thinking: they used their fingers for sign language, after all. There did seem to be a higher correlation between motor activity in the fingers and thinking than in a hearing group of adults. Skinner later viewed thinking as private behaviour as opposed to overt behaviour, and believed that it was similarly subject to stimulus control and reinforcement. In his book *Verbal Behavior* (1957) he attempted to show that both overt behaviour and thinking were controlled by operant conditioning. In overt behaviour, there was an interaction with someone else, while, with thinking, individuals are their own listeners. There is in effect an interaction with themselves.

Cognitive approaches to thinking

Cognitive approaches to thinking have attempted to examine the mental processes which occur during thinking. Miller et al. (1960) identified what they referred to as **heuristic strategies**. These were models which enabled them to simulate the way in which the mind solved problems. The complexities of a problem might be simplified by working out a series of rules of thumb. These could then be applied one at a time. Though this did not guarantee that a solution to the problem could be found, it reduced the problem to manageable proportions. A computer could then be programmed to deal with it. For example, in programming a computer to play chess, a set of instructions had to be devised such as 'check that the king is safe' or 'make sure that the queen cannot be taken'.

Newell and Simon (1972) attempted to mirror human problem solving and behaviour in a heuristic way. To validate the models set up, they relied on individuals' verbal reports of what was going on in their heads while they attempted to solve problems. In this way, computer models were constructed of how problems were solved. Within these models the program was analogous to the set of rules or instructions within which a person operated; the computer memory was analogous to the memory of the individual, and the input and output from the computer represented the problem posed and the solution found.

However, because human brains are not computers and cannot be so rigidly controlled there were difficulties, including the following:

■ It is not very useful to think of human beings as machines. Any analogy is bound to be partial only, as we do not fully understand the principles on which the human brain operates.

■ Computers, while they are very accurate and efficient calculators and solvers of logical

---

GLOSSARY

Isomorphism A term used by Gestalt psychologists for the tendency of brain fields to adopt good form. They have envisaged electrical fields within the brain which determine patterns of perception and thought.

Good form (Prägnanz) Relates to a tendency (described by Gestalt psychologists) for the brain to seek order out of chaos through isomorphism.

Heuristic strategies 'Rule of thumb' strategies employed to solve problems based upon what amounts to a 'hunch'.

problems, are not capable of original and creative thinking.

■ Computers are not susceptible to human emotions. They do not get tired, anxious, angry or afraid.

We shall return to a discussion of heuristic strategies at a later point.

The structure of knowledge

There is also quite extensive work by cognitive psychologists into the structure of knowledge. Generalized knowledge can be encoded in what have been called schemata. Unlike Piaget's use of the term, schemata here rejects the clusters of similar items of knowledge. This is related to the use of the term in the context of social cognition (see Part 6 Introduction). They provide expectations about what should occur in relation to procedures, sequences of events and social situations and allow us to make predictions about new situations. These are also extensively referred to in Part 6 of this book. To take an example used by Eysenck (1984), suppose you were in an unfamiliar house and needed to use the toilet. The schemata you possess about houses would lead you to rule out the living room as a place to look. However, it is just possible you might be in error and the toilet might be next to the living room.

Scripts are a particular kind of schema. They are standard sequences of events which by repetition have become predictable. Someone might develop a script related to going to work in the morning. You kiss your family goodbye, pick up your briefcase and a neatly furled umbrella, go out of the door and make for the station. On the way you stop at the newsagent and buy a

copy of the *Guardian* before arriving at the station two minutes before the train is due to leave. This is a relatively strong script in that the order of events is rigidly programmed. Weak scripts do not necessarily prescribe a rigid order of events, yet the events are sufficiently stereotyped to provide expectation that they will occur.

The work on concept formation described in the next section of this chapter also comes within this category of cognitive approaches to thinking.

Concept formation

When individuals form concepts, they are abstracting the essential characteristics from something they perceive. They can then place it in a category alongside other items with similar characteristics, label it and respond appropriately.

Walking alongside a river, I saw in the water an animal moving about and occasionally a black head appeared. The appearance and characteristics of what I saw enabled me to place it in a category. It was clearly a mammal, not a fish, and furthermore its behaviour, size and appearance made me suppose it must have been an otter. Accordingly, my appropriate response was to tell my companions that there was an otter in the river. From descriptions, definitions and previous encounters I had formed the concept of an otter and this conceptualization had enabled me to respond in an appropriate way. Without concepts every encounter with everything in our environment would have to be on a trial and error basis.

Concept formation can be seen as rational thinking. An assortment of information, either perceived by the senses or stored in memory from previous experience, is directed towards a clear goal (the attainment of the concept) according to preordained rules.

The information involved consists of **attributes** of the stimuli before us. A London bus, for instance, has various attributes: it is red, it has two decks, it is large, on wheels and carries a great many passengers. All these

? SELF-ASSESSMENT QUESTIONS

1. What is the distinction between autistic and rational thinking?
2. The Gestalt psychologists used the term 'isomorphism' to describe the way in which the brain operates. Explain briefly what the term implies.
3. In what way did behaviourists get over the difficulty they had in explaining thinking?
4. List some of the difficulties involved in computer simulation of thinking.

GLOSSARY

Scripts Standard sequences of events which have become predictable because of frequent repetition. These are stored in memory for use when there is an appropriate trigger.

Attributes Elements of stimuli before us which are abstracted to enable us to form concepts.

attributes are relevant to its conceptualization as a London bus. It may also have attributes which are not relevant to the concept of 'London bus', which do not mark it out as a London bus particularly. It may be driven by a red-haired woman, it may have graffiti scrawled on it, but this does not make it any more or any less a London bus. Attributes will also vary in their **salience**: that is, the ease with they are noticed. The colour of the bus may be a very obvious (i.e. salient) attribute, the name painted on the side is much less salient.

Concept formation studies

Most of the studies done by psychologists into concept formation are concerned to measure how efficiently participants learn concepts and/or what strategies they adopt to do so. Efficiency may be measured by the number of trials required to guess a concept correctly, or perhaps the number of wrong guesses before the correct one.

Bruner's studies

A classic study was that of Bruner et al. (1956). This is described in Box 15.1.

Bruner and his colleagues found that participants made use of four main strategies to identify concepts: **conservative focusing**, **focus gambling**, **successive scanning** and **simultaneous scanning**.

Conservative focusing This involves focusing on the first positive instance, and then selecting a card which differs in one attribute only. With a negative response you know that that attribute is relevant. Suppose the concept was all the cards with green crosses (whatever number) and the first positive instance had two borders and one green cross, you might select a card with two borders and a single black cross. The negative response would confirm that colour was a relevant attribute. But suppose you selected a card with two borders and two green crosses (varying just the number of crosses), the positive response would indicate that the number of objects was not relevant. In this way you could test all the attributes and eventually arrive at the answer.

Focus gambling Focus gamblers fix on the first positive example and then, when asked to select a card, choose one where two or more of the attributes are different. Suppose the concept was all cards with

green crosses, and the first positive example is a card with two borders and one green cross you might select a card with two borders and two black crosses, thus varying two attributes at once. You would have lost your gamble, because the negative response would not tell you whether it was borders or colours that were relevant. On the other hand, if you selected a card with three green crosses and three borders you would get a positive response, would have won your gamble and know that both numbers and borders are irrelevant.

Successive scanning This strategy starts with a hypothesis and selects cards that are relevant to that hypothesis. Take the concept of all cards with green crosses and the initial positive example of two borders and one green cross; a successive scanner would start with a hypothesis relevant to that, say, all cards with two borders, and pick a card with two black crosses and two borders. Getting a negative response, the successive scanner rejects this hypothesis and tries another, changing one attribute at a time. If, on the other hand, a card with two borders and two green crosses was selected and a positive response obtained, the hypothesis could be maintained and a guess made at the answer.

Simultaneous scanning This is the least effective and most difficult strategy. It is similar to successive scanning except that instead of scanning for one attribute at a time the simultaneous scanner attempts to remember all the attributes at once, a difficult feat of memory.

Try Exercise 15.1 to see how Bruner's procedure works.

Exercise 15.1

Link up with a friend and simulate Bruner's procedure in the following way: Take a pack of playing cards which has attributes of suits (hearts, diamonds, spades and clubs), colours (black and red) and numbers (ace to ten, Jack, Queen and King). Ask your friend to select a concept and

⟶

GLOSSARY

Salience Feature of particular attributes which makes them prominent so as to attract immediate attention.

Box 15.1   Bruner et al. (1956). A concept formation study

The researchers devised a set of 81 cards, which varied in four ways:

■ *In their borders*: the cards had one, two or three borders.

■ *In the numbers of objects*: the cards had one, two or three objects on them.

■ *In the kinds of objects*: the cards had one of three objects depicted on them – a square, a circle or a cross.

■ *In the colour of the objects*: the objects could be green, red or black.

Examples are shown below.

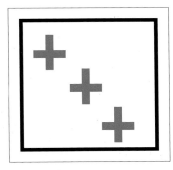

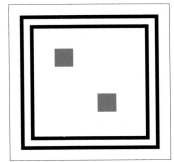

Examples of cards used by Bruner et al. (1956)

The procedure for the participants was as follows. Participants worked in pairs. One of the pair (A) was invited to think of a set of attributes: for instance, all those cards with red objects on them and three borders. This constituted a concept. Then, with all the cards displayed, A pointed to a positive instance of the concept. The other participant (B) was then invited to select another card and ask, 'Is this one of them?' When the answer was 'No', they merely proceeded to another card, but if the answer was 'Yes', they were entitled to guess what the set of attributes (the concept) was. A measure of the ease or difficulty of attainment of a concept was the number of guesses required to reach the correct answer. The researchers also identified the strategies employed by participants.

Bruner and his colleagues identified several types of concept:

■ **Conjunctive concepts**, where a card had to possess all of a set of attributes (for example, all those cards with two borders, and green crosses).

■ **Disjunctive concepts**, where the card had only to have one or more of a number of attributes (for example, all those cards with either crosses on them, or with two borders).

■ **Relational concepts**, where the concept relates one attribute to another (for example, all those cards with more borders than objects).

In real life you could identify a conjunctive concept as, say, a cricket ball. To be a cricket ball it needs to be round, hard, red, made of leather and to possess a seam. If it lacks any of these attributes it is not a cricket ball. A disjunctive concept might be the idea of 'out' in cricket, where one of a number of things has to occur: for instance, the ball is bowled and hits the stumps; the ball hits the batsman's pads when they are in front of the wicket; the batsman hits the ball and a fielder catches it; and so on. A relational concept might be that of a quorum for a meeting: that is, where the number of people present at the meeting is smaller than a number previously fixed.

go through Bruner's procedure. First get your friend to point out a positive example of the concept selected, then select further cards and for each ask, 'Is that one?'. Take each of the strategies described in turn and decide for yourself which is the most effective.

Later studies of concept formation

A more recent study of concept formation was that of Levine (1975) which resulted in his theory of hypothesis testing. The technique which he employed, the blank trials procedure, is as follows:

1. The participants are presented with a card on which there are two figures, differing in respect of four attributes, colour (black or white), size (large or small), shape (X or T) and position (left or right) and guess which figure is correct. This will, of course, be a wild guess, as there is very little to go on. The experimenter answers 'right' or 'wrong'.

2. The experimenter presents the participant with four new cards. Participants choose again, but this time the experimenter gives them no feedback. These are the 'blank trials'. While the participants learn nothing from these 'blank trials' the experimenter can analyse the responses and determine which attribute the participants believe to be correct.

3. There is a further 'feedback' trial, followed by a further four 'blank trials' and so on.

Figure 15.1 shows a flow chart for Levine's experiment.

The experimenter can tell from the participants' choices on the blank trials which hypotheses they are forming. If, for example, a participant has consistently chosen the right-hand position, the experimenter can infer from this that the hypothesis has been formed that the 'right' position is correct. This, then, is a way in which private thoughts can be made more public. It is, however, very slow and time-consuming.

Working hypothesis Levine suggested that at the outset participants started with a pool of hypotheses (in the case of the example above, a possible eight hypotheses: X, T, black, white, large, small, left and right). From this pool participants would choose a smaller number of hypotheses (any number from one to eight) which seemed to them to be likely. From this smaller number of hypotheses, a **working hypothesis** would be selected. It is on this working hypothesis that the immediate response would be based. If feedback supported the chosen hypothesis, there would be no reason to change it. If, on the other hand, feedback did not support the hypothesis formed, the participant tried to remember as much as possible of previous trials before forming another working hypothesis.

Global focusing strategy Levine suggested that people keep track of a number of other possible hypotheses, while using a current working hypothesis. If a participant had perfect memory, he or she would be able to keep track of all the hypotheses which were consistent with the feedback and would not adopt any hypothesis which had already been rejected. Given eight possible hypotheses, this marvellous person should be able to work out the answer after only three trials. Levine termed a strategy where participants keep track of as many hypotheses as possible at the same time a **global focusing strategy**. Intelligent adults seem to adopt a global focusing strategy where the task is a comparatively simple one. Where the task is more difficult or where memory skills are more limited other strategies may be adopted.

The use of introspection

An alternative way of finding out what people are thinking when they are forming concepts involves **introspection**. The think aloud method involves

---

GLOSSARY
Working hypothesis A hypothesis relating to a concept in Levine's studies. Responses would be based upon this. Feedback might either support it or not. While there remained support for it the hypothesis need not be altered.
Global focusing strategy A strategy adopted in Levine's concept formation trials by many intelligent adults which involves keeping track of as many hypotheses as possible at the same time.
Introspection A technique which involves a person saying out loud what he or she is thinking in response to a stimulus. It has been used in the study of concept formation by Dominowski.

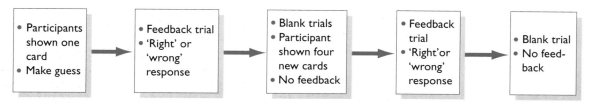

Figure 15.1 Flow chart illustrating Levine's (1975) experiment

getting participants to say out loud what they are thinking, usually in response to a stimulus. Dominowski (1974) used this method in studying concept formation, but there are problems.

First, introspection changes thinking. It seems inevitable that saying out loud what you are thinking will result in your performing the task differently. It may encourage people to use particular strategies or methods, or it may result in simply working more carefully.

It is uncertain to what extent we have complete access to what we are thinking. Nisbett and Wilson (1977) suggested that much of our thinking is unconscious. Participants in several studies (for example, Storms and Nisbett, 1970) seemed to be entirely oblivious to the processes which determined their behaviour:

> When people are asked to report how a particular stimulus influenced a particular response, they do so not by consulting a memory of the mediating process, but by applying general causal theories about the effects of that type of stimulus on that type of response.
>
> (Nisbett and Wilson, 1977, p. 248)

However, cognitive psychology has depended upon introspection. Experiments on visual illusions or on memory would be difficult without it. Ericsson and Simon (1980) have suggested some criteria to help us distinguish between valid and invalid use of introspection:

■ Reports should be obtained during, and not after, the performance of a task as retrospective reports are likely to be faulty.

■ Introspections about what participants are attending to or thinking are likely to be more accurate than those which involve interpretation or speculation.

■ The involvement of attention is a prerequisite of introspection. Only information in focal attention can be verbalized.

? SELF-ASSESSMENT QUESTIONS

1. What is meant by a concept? How does the formation of concepts assist people to react appropriately to the world around them?
2. What were the three types of concept which Bruner identified?

3. Outline in your own words the 'hypothesis testing theory' of Levine.
4. What are some of the problems inherent in using introspection to find out what people are thinking? Do Ericsson and Simon's criteria for valid use of introspection seem to you to be useful?

Problem solving

Almost every day-to-day activity involves solving problems. They may be as simple and routine as making a cake using a recipe in a book, or as complex as finding the reason for the car not starting in the morning. It is useful to think of three elements of a problem:

■ **The original situation**: for example, that of having invited people for coffee and having nothing to offer them to eat.
■ **The goal situation**: for example, to have a tasty cake to offer when the visitors come.
■ **The rules**: for example, nothing is to be used except what is in the cupboards.

This section aims to examine problem solving and to describe some of the research into it. This will include ways of understanding problems, methods of representing the elements of problems and strategies for solving them.

Understanding problems

Before a problem can be solved there must be understanding of it. Understanding involves creating internally (in your head) a representation of the elements of the problem. Greeno (1977) suggests that this involves three requirements: coherence, correspondence and relationship to background knowledge.

Coherence

For instance, in the cake-making example, quoted above, there needs to be **coherence**. The list of ingredients and the method described in the recipe need to fit together. If there is some element which does not fit, then the problem becomes difficult to solve. For instance, if the list of ingredients includes items not mentioned in the description of the method, then there is no coherence. The whole thing does not fit properly together.

Correspondence

There also needs to be a close **correspondence** between the internal representation and the material involved in the problem. The internal representation (the way in which we perceive the elements involved) may be inaccurate or incomplete. Instructions to beat eggs into the cake mixture will assume an internal representation of what this involves. Lack of correspondence between an individual's internal representation of this process and the assumption made in the instructions might result – to take a rather far-fetched example – in attempts to beat the eggs in, shells and all!

Relationship to background knowledge

This is fairly closely related to the third criterion for understanding, the **relationship to background knowledge**. Instructions for baking a cake need to be in different terms for someone who is a complete novice at cooking and for someone who is already an accomplished cook. Vocabulary and concepts need to be familiar and at the right level.

Representing the problem

Once the elements of the problem are established, it becomes necessary to find a way of representing them, a kind of shorthand which makes manipulation of the elements more manageable than it would be in the original form. There are several alternative ways of doing this:

■ Symbols,
■ Lists,
■ Matrices,
■ Hierarchical trees,
■ Graphs, and
■ Visual representations.

Symbols

When we learnt to solve problems in algebra, they were represented in symbols. To take a typical example:

Mary and Jane are friends. Mary is five years older than Jane. Five years ago Mary was twice Jane's age. How old are they now?

A common way to solve problems like this is to represent what is not known by symbols. In the above example:

Let Mary's present age be m and Jane's be j, then

$$m = j + 5$$

represents the first sentence of the problem.

The second sentence is represented by

$$2(j - 5) = m - 5$$

So we can substitute $(j + 5)$ for m in the second equation and get $2(j - 5) = (j + 5) - 5$

$$\therefore j = 2j - 10,$$

$$\therefore j = 10, m = 15.$$

You can then check that you are right by translating back into the terms of the original problem. Mary is 15 and Jane is 10 (five years younger). Five years ago Mary was 10 and Jane was five, half her age.

The difficulty often encountered with symbols is that of oversimplification. A problem solver may misrepresent the problem when it is transformed into symbols.

Lists

This translation into symbols cannot always be done, though, and sometimes a list is an easier way to represent the problem. Here is the well-known 'orcs and hobbits' problem:

Orcs and hobbits problem   There are three orcs and three hobbits who want to cross a river. There is a boat which will carry only two creatures. If ever there are more orcs than hobbits on either bank of the river, the orcs will immediately kill and eat the hobbits.

GLOSSARY

Coherence In relation to problem solving, when the elements of the problem and the method of its solution do not fit it will prove hard to solve the problem.

Correspondence In relation to problem solving, when there is a problem to be solved there needs to be a close match between our internal representation of the problem and the elements involved.

Relationship to background knowledge When a problem has to be solved, vocabulary and concepts employed need to be at the right level for solvers and familiar to them.

How can both hobbits and orcs get across the river without this happening?

A list could be made as follows:

Right bank	Left bank
3 hobbits + 3 orcs	none
3 hobbits + 1 orc	0 hobbit + 2 orcs
3 hobbits + 2 orcs	0 hobbit + 1 orc
3 hobbits + 0 orc	0 hobbit + 3 orcs
3 hobbits + 1 orc	0 hobbit + 2 orcs
1 hobbit + 1 orc	2 hobbits + 2 orcs
2 hobbits + 2 orcs	1 hobbit + 1 orc
0 hobbit + 2 orcs	3 hobbits + 1 orc
0 hobbit + 3 orcs	3 hobbits + 0 orcs
0 hobbit + 1 orc	3 hobbits + 2 orcs
0 hobbit + 2 orcs	3 hobbits + 1 orc
0 hobbit + 0 orc	3 hobbits + 3 orcs FINISH

This can be cumbersome and not very helpful. In this case, it does not show clearly who crosses and returns on each trip.

Matrices

One way of representing all the possible combinations is a matrix. This makes it easier to keep a track of the alternatives at each point. The hobbit and orc problem could be represented in this way:

	Boat	Right bank	Left bank
1st crossing	2 orcs	3H + 1O	0H + 2O
1st return	1 orc	3H + 2O	0H + 1O
2nd crossing	2 orcs	3H + 0O	0H + 3O
2nd return	1 orc	3H + 1O	0H + 2O
3rd crossing	2 hobbits	1H + 1O	2H + 2O
3rd return	1 hobbit	2H + 1O	2H + 2O
4th crossing	2 hobbits	0H + 1O	3H + 2O
4th return	1 orc	0H + 2O	3H + 1O
5th crossing	1 orc	0H + 0O	3H + 3O
			FINISH

This matrix makes it possible to see the results of each move as well as the move itself. Simon and Hayes (1976) found that at least 50 per cent of participants in their study used a matrix of some kind.

Hierarchical trees

Where a problem is concerned with probabilities, then a hierachical tree may be the best representation of it. Take this as an example:

There is a bag full of marbles, half of which are plain glass, half are silver. The bag is shaken and a marble is drawn out. If three marbles are drawn what is the chance of getting three silver ones?

Figure 15.2 shows a hierarchical tree diagram which might make the problem easier to solve. From the diagram it is comparatively easy to see what the possible outcomes are:

silver silver silver	silver 3 glass 0
silver silver glass	silver 2 glass 1
silver glass silver	silver 2 glass 1
silver glass glass	silver 1 glass 2
glass silver silver	silver 2 glass 1
glass silver glass	silver 1 glass 2
glass glass silver	silver 1 glass 2
glass glass glass	silver 0 glass 3

So you can see that there is one chance in eight of obtaining three silver marbles (12.5 per cent).

Graphs

Sometimes it makes it easier if the problem is represented visually by a graph. The problem described below is perhaps best represented by a graph:

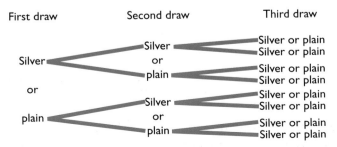

Figure 15.2 A hierarchical tree may make a problem easier to solve, especially where probabilities are involved

A walker set out to climb a mountain up a steep and winding path towards the top. He climbed slowly at times, at times more quickly and sometimes he rested. At the top there was a mountain hut where he spent the night, before starting down again along the same path. Though he walked faster coming down, his speed was variable and again he rested occasionally. Prove that there must be a spot on the path which the walker will pass at the same time of day, climbing up or going down.

By plotting the time on the base axis of a graph and the height of the path on the vertical axis you can plot his progress going both ways. The lines are bound to intersect at some point as is shown in Figure 15.3.

Visual representation

It may sometimes help to use some other kind of visual representation, as may be shown in the following problem which you have probably come across before:

There are two stations 100 km apart. At precisely the same time two trains leave, one from each station. Train A is a goods train travelling at 40 km/h; train B is a passenger train which goes a little faster, at 60 km/h. Overhead there is a bird flying along the track, starting from train A and not stopping until it reaches train B where it wheels around, flies back along the track to train A, where again it wheels around and returns. What distance will it need to fly at a steady 80 km/h before the trains meet?

A visual illustration such as that in Figure 15.4 might help solve the problem. The answer is at the end of this section (p. 329).

It is clear that there is no one best way to represent a problem. Symbols, lists, matrices, hierarchical trees, graphs and visual representations can all be used. Schwartz (1971) has shown that there is a relationship between the representation of the problem and its solution. Those who did not use any particular mode of representation were found to be successful only 25 per cent of the time.

Strategies to solve problems

Once the problem has been understood and represented in one of the ways described above, strategies must be devised to arrive at a solution. These may include: (a) random search strategies, or (b) heuristic search strategies.

Random search

A problem solver may occasionally use trial and error to solve a problem. That is to say, all kinds of possible solutions are tried but no attempt is made to be systematic or to keep records of the attempts which have been made. This is a very inefficient way to go about finding a solution to the problem which could be described as unsystematic random search.

Alternatively it is possible to engage in a systematic random search. Supposing you knew that a friend of yours lived in a particular street, an unsystematic random search might involve knocking on doors at random and asking whether he or she lived there. A systematic search would involve adopting some system to make sure no possibilities were overlooked. In the case above, this might be to knock first at number 1, then 2, then 3 and so on till the end of the street. If your friend did live in the street, you would be bound to find him or her but it might take a long time.

Heuristic strategies

Newell and Simon (1972) claim that to employ more sophisticated heuristic

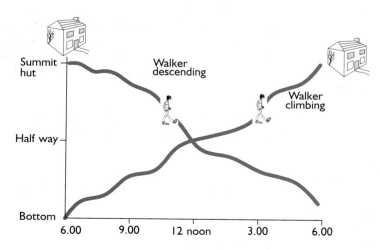

Figure 15.3 A graphical representation of the problem of the walker

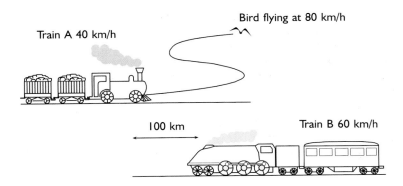

Figure 15.4 A visual representation of the train problem

strategies, is likely to result in a saving of what they term **problem space**: that is, all the possible solutions of which the problem solver is aware. Heuristic strategies involve looking at a large portion of the problem space at first, and then by applying relevant information gained about the problem, narrowing down the search area until it becomes more manageable. Thus, with the problem of finding your friend's address, mentioned above, you may have been told that there is a wonderful view across the town from the back windows of the house. So, you could eliminate all the houses on one side of the street, because none of them have that kind of a view. Your friend might also have told you that he or she lives in a bungalow, so that a further group of possible solutions to the problem can be eliminated. To take another example, suppose you have an anagram to solve while doing the crossword in the newspaper: certain combinations of letters do not occur, or occur only very rarely in English, so it is not necessary to plod through all the possible combinations of letters.

Kinds of heuristic strategies include: (a) means–end analysis, (b) planning strategies, and (c) backwards searching.

Means–ends analysis Another way of approaching the solution of problems is known as **means–ends analysis**. The problem is broken down into smaller elements. Each of these subproblems can then be dealt with in the following way. First, identify the ends or goals which you want to achieve and then work on ways in which these ends can be reached. Sweller and Levine (1982) have drawn attention to the fact that means–ends analysis concentrates the

solver's mind upon the essentials, the difference between the present state and the goal state.

In the hobbits and orcs problem, described above, there could be said to be an overall problem (to get three hobbits and three orcs from one side of the river to the other) and subproblems such as the viciousness of the orcs (they will kill hobbits whenever they outnumber them) and the size of the boat (it will take only two at a time). Each of these subproblems can be thought of in terms of means and ends and solutions found. The orcs' viciousness can be neutralized by ensuring that at no time are there more orcs than hobbits on either side of the river. The size of the boat can be got over by making several trips and returning the boat between trips. These two subproblems will sometimes mean that backwards moves have to be made, ferrying orcs or hobbits back from the left to the right side of the river.

Newell and Simon (1972) developed a computer program called General Problem Solver (GPS) based upon means–ends analysis. It attempted to ape the ways in which humans tackle problems. The advantage was that it forced researchers to be clear and unambiguous about the processes used to solve problems. Computers have no tolerance of ambiguity. The program was then tested against the steps taken by humans when solving problems, to develop a theory to predict how humans solve problems.

GPS has been important in that it was the first program to simulate human behaviour. It was used to solve problems such as the hobbits and orcs problem, letter/number substitution problems, grammatical analysis of sentences, proofs in logic and trigonometry problems.

Planning strategy Other heuristic strategies include planning strategy which involves disregarding

> ### GLOSSARY
>
> **Problem space** Consists of all the possible solutions of which a problem solver is aware.
>
> **Means–ends analysis** A problem is broken down into small elements. In each a goal is identified and problems in reaching that goal systematically worked out.

some aspects of a problem to make it simpler. Once the simpler problem has been solved, the complications can be reintroduced. For instance, when dealing with the hobbits and orcs problem, a solver might disregard the viciousness of the orcs in the first instance, and concentrate upon getting all the creatures across on a boat which would take only two at a time. Only after a solution to this simpler problem had been found would the more complicated one be tackled. Planning strategies include **analogies** (where an earlier problem is used to compare with that currently being solved) and **problem isomorphs**, sets of problems with the same structures and solutions, but with different details and contexts.

Backwards search   A further heuristic strategy is that of backwards searching. This involves starting at the goal and working backwards from there. Consider the game of Solitaire. This is composed of a circular board on which there are holes for 33 marbles or pegs as laid out in Figure 15.5. The player removes the centre marble and play proceeds as follows. A marble next to the vacant centre space may be 'jumped' and removed by one behind (or next to) it. The jumping and removal continues with the object of one marble finally being left in the centre space. A backwards search, starting with one marble in the centre, may be one way towards solving what can be a very difficult problem.

Try this problem. A backwards search strategy may prove useful here:

Exercise 15.2

A lily doubles its size every day. If in 30 days it covers half the pond how long will it take to cover the whole pond. (The answer is at the end of the section on p. 330.)

Factors that may influence problem solving

Factors that may adversely affect a person's ability to solve a problem can be termed mental set. This amounts to a disinclination of the problem solver's mind to move away from certain preconceived assumptions about the elements of the problem. This 'set' may take several forms:

◼ **Operational set**. A preconceived assumption that the problem will be solved by means of a particular operation or set of operations.
◼ **Functional set**. An assumption that the elements of a problem have a fixed function.
◼ **Rule set**. The preconceived notion that there are certain rules, within the constraints of which the problem will have to be solved.

Operational set

When a person's mind assumes a fixed pattern of operation and will not shift to an alternative pattern this can be termed operational set. Luchins (1942) illustrated this with his water jar problem. This is detailed below.

> There are three jars A, B and C, and an unlimited supply of water to fill them. In a series of problems,

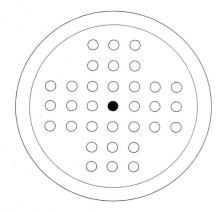

Figure 15.5   A solitaire board

Luchins listed the capacities of each of the jars, as well as the amount of water which has to be drawn in each case (the goal).

	A	B	C	Goal
1.	21	127	3	100
2.	14	46	5	22
3.	18	43	10	5
4.	7	42	6	23
5.	20	57	4	29
6.	23	49	3	20
7.	15	39	3	18

Try the problems yourself. By the time they come to problem 6 most people have worked out a way of solving the problems, by filling jar B, then filling A from it and finally filling C twice. What is left in B is the goal amount. When they come to problem 7, they do the same thing, even though there is a much easier way of arriving at the required amount. See the end of the section (p. 330).

Functional set

A similar phenomenon is functional set, sometimes termed functional fixedness. This amounts to having in your mind a fixed notion of what each element in a problem is for. The ring and peg problem described by Scheerer (1963) illustrates this well. Box 15.2 sets this problem out.

Set of rule

Below are two problems.

1. Take 6 matches and assemble them to form four equilateral congruent triangles each side of which is equal to the length of the matches.
2.

```
    •   •   •

    •   •   •

    •   •   •
```

Nine dots are arranged in the form of a square (as illustrated). Draw four continuous straight lines to connect them all without lifting your pencil from the paper.

Answers are at the end of this section (p. 330).

When assumptions are made that a problem has to be solved within the constraints of certain rules, though no such rules have been imposed, it can be termed a set of rule. This is what may happen here. With the match problem there is no imposed constraint that the triangles must be in two dimensions. In the nine dots problem there may be an implicit constraint that you need to keep within the square.

A question of insight

Insight refers to a sudden flash of inspiration in relation to the solution of a problem. Gestalt psychologists suggested that the elements of a problem, which initially had seemed unrelated, suddenly come together to form coherence, a sudden cognitive reorganization. Weisberg and Alba (1981) examined the nine dots problem described above. Participants in their experiment were each given 20 blank sheets of paper on which to attempt solutions of the problem. If they had not solved it after ten attempts they were divided into four groups:

1. A control group who were given no further help with the problem.
2. A group who were told that once they had exhausted all the possibilities within the square, they would have to go outside it.
3. A group who were also told to look outside the square but in addition were shown where to put the first line.
4. A group who were shown where to put the first two lines.

While none of the control group was successful in solving the problem, in group 2, 20 per cent were, in group 3, 60 per cent were and in group 4, 100 per cent were successful. This seems to indicate that it is not really enough simply to remove the unwarranted assumption that they had to stay within the square. Group 2 did not do spectacularly well.

Answers to problems

The train problem
The goods train is travelling at 40 km/h, the passenger train at 60 km/h. They are therefore closing the gap at 100 km/h, and will meet in one hour. During this time the bird will have flown 80 km.

Box 15.2 Ring and peg problem (Scheerer, 1963)

Participants were required to put two rings on a peg from a position two metres from the rings and the peg. They could not do this without a tool to extend their reach. When they were not actually engaged in picking up the rings and placing them on the peg they were allowed to move freely around the room and use anything they saw there. There were two sticks but neither was long enough to bridge the gap alone without joining them together. The only piece of string in the room was that by which an object was hanging from a nail on the wall. It was in clear view.

The first 16 participants (the control group) had the string hanging alone on the nail and they had no difficulty in taking it down, tying the sticks together and solving the problem. Experimental groups of participants found the string performing various functions. Group A found the string hanging up things which had no function (an out-of-date calendar, a blank piece of cardboard or a cloudy mirror). Group B found the string was hanging up objects such as a 'No Smoking' sign, a current calendar and a clear mirror. In all cases the string was tied with a square knot in plain sight above the nail.

All the group A participants succeeded in using the string to solve the problem. Of group B 56 per cent failed with the current calendar, 69 per cent with the clear mirror and 53 per cent with the 'No Smoking' sign. In interviews afterwards, none thought they were forbidden to take down the string, but they did not think of doing so.

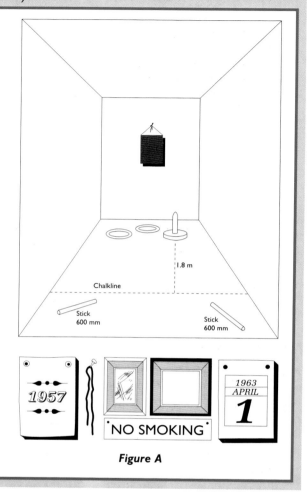

Figure A

Lily pond problem

Thirty-one days. It covered half the pond in 30 days and then during the next day doubled in size to cover the whole pond.

Jar problem

Fill A and C and pour into the empty B.

Match problem

The three equilateral triangles form a pyramid. There is nothing in the problem which suggests that the answer has to be in two dimensions.

The nine dots problem

There is nothing in the question which suggests that the solver has to remain within the square.

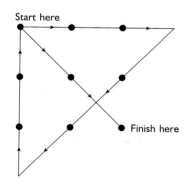

1. List three ways of representing a problem. What are the limitations of each?
2. Means–ends analysis is an important heuristic strategy. What is meant by a heuristic strategy?
3. What is meant by 'set' in relation to problem solving? How does it relate to perceptual set, described in Chapter 13?

Language and thinking

This section is concerned with the relationship between thought and language. There are essentially four views taken on this relationship:

▪ That language determines thought;
▪ The behaviourist view that thought is internal speech;
▪ That thinking determines linguistic development;
▪ That the two are independent of one another, but each has an influence upon intellectual development.

The first of these viewpoints is represented by the Whorf–Sapir linguistic relativity hypothesis, the behaviourist view is represented by Watson, the third is Piaget's viewpoint and the fourth represents Vygotsky's view.

Additionally, this section will examine the theses of Bernstein and Labov which relate to language and social class in the first case and language and race in the second.

Linguistic relativity

The linguist Benjamin Lee Whorf (in Carroll, 1956) and the anthropologist Edward Sapir suggested that the language people used determined their perception of the world and consequently their thought. As evidence, they cited the language of the Hopi Indians in North America. Unlike most European languages the Hopi language has no grammatical forms, constructions or words for time. This suggests that the Hopi do not think about time in the way we do. They also have no separate words for insect, aeroplane or pilot. Is it feasible to suggest that they do not differentiate between them? Eskimos have a great many different words for snow, differentiating snow suitable for making igloos from snow suitable for sledging, for instance. Whorf suggests that this is evidence that their thinking about snow is more complex than ours is.

Evidence for linguistic relativity

Some support for **linguistic relativity** comes from a study of the Navajo Indians by Carroll and Casagrande (1958). They studied three groups of participants:

▪ Those who spoke only Navajo;
▪ Those who spoke Navajo and English;
▪ American children of European descent who spoke nothing but English.

The form of things is very important to the Navajos and this is reflected in their language. Different verbs are used for handling long, flexible objects from those used for handling long rigid objects, for instance. American children develop object recognition in this order; *size*, then *colour* and finally *form or shape*. If Whorf and Sapir (1947) are right, you would predict that Navajo-speaking children would develop recognition of objects by their form at an earlier stage than American children. This is what Carroll and Casagrande found.

The difficulty with linguistic relativity is a chicken and egg problem. There is no way of being sure which comes first, the environment or the language. Whorf and Sapir assumed that in the beginning there was language and it was language which determined the way in which people perceived and thought about things. But it could equally well have been the other way around. The hundreds of camel-related words in Arabic or the 92 words for rice used by the Hanuxoo people of the Philippines simply reflect the nature of the worlds they live in and the things that are important to them. It is likely that language simply highlights differences in the environments of different people and provides labels to store these differences in memory.

There is also a problem which relates to the flexibility of language. It is not static, but new terms, relating perhaps to new technology or perhaps to the use of jargon, are continually being introduced. This seems to indicate that thought is the parent of language rather than the other way around. If it were not so, but if thought always needed to reflect language there would be no means to introduce fresh thinking. Changes in language use would not by themselves suffice to bring about change. The spur, as in new technology, must be original thinking.

Restricted and elaborated codes of language

Hess and Shipman (1965) have proposed that there are differences in the ways in which language is used in low status and high status families. They suggested that in high status (middle class) families language conveys meaning. It describes, explains and expresses feelings. In low status (working class) families language tends to be used more to give orders to the child, who is thus deprived of the same access to meaning as higher status children.

Bernstein (1961) claimed that working-class and middle-class children use different language codes:

■ **Restricted code of language**, used by working-class children, is syntactically crude, has short, grammatically simple sentences, a restricted vocabulary and is context-bound (that is to say, meaning depends to a high degree upon the context in which it is used).

■ **Elaborated code of language**, used by middle-class children, employs a larger vocabulary, more complex and flexible grammar and syntax and allows abstract thought to be expressed more easily.

A parent of children on a bus, who insist upon getting up and walking around, might simply say 'Sit down and keep quiet!' or, if they persisted, 'Sit down and keep quiet or I'll hit you!' but if using an elaborated code of language might say 'You had better sit down in your own seats or the bus might suddenly stop and you would be thrown violently on the floor and hurt yourselves'.

This seems to point to there being a link between the kind of language used by individuals and the thought processes and intellectual development of these individuals. Bernstein claimed that the lack of an elaborated code of language is a barrier to working-class children developing their full intellectual

potential. Additionally, the pattern of learning in schools is based upon the use of an elaborated code. Teachers are, after all, generally middle-class and certainly equipped with elaborated codes of language. They may not communicate adequately with some of the working-class children in their charge.

It has been suggested that the terms 'restricted' and 'elaborated' are value-laden and that middle-class language is in some way regarded as superior. This is perhaps misleading. It is likely that most people employ what Bernstein would regard as a restricted code for some of the time. There is certainly some upper-class language usage which is just as restricted. Educated people have access to an elaborated code which they can use when they need to. Some less well-educated people do not. This places them at a disadvantage intellectually.

In a similar way, researchers such as Labov (1970), Houston (1970) and Williams (1972) have studied the dialects used by black Americans. They have found them to be profoundly different from 'standard' English. Children often employ two distinct modes of speech, one for home, one for school. The school mode is not well developed and thoughts are not so easily expressed. Consequently, it has been frequently asserted that the children are intellectually inferior. However, Williams (1972) developed a Black Intelligence Test, written in a dialect in which black children were more skilled. They performed much better on this test, while Genshaft and Hirt (1974) found that white children performed poorly on it.

Thought as subvocal speech

A more extreme view has been taken by behaviourists and in particular by Watson (1913). His suggestion was that thinking was **subvocal speech**. The assumption was made that when someone attempted to solve a

---

GLOSSARY

Restricted code of language Code of language used, according to Bernstein, by working-class children. It is syntactically crude, grammatically simple, restricted in vocabulary and context bound.

Elaborated code of language Code of language used, according to Bernstein, by middle-class children. It employs a large vocabulary, has complex and flexible grammar and syntax and is suited for the expression of abstract ideas.

problem it necessarily involved some kind of inner language. When individuals struggle with a problem, especially in stressful conditions, they frequently talk to themselves. If you enter an infant classroom, there will often be a buzz evident, of children vocalizing their thoughts. But this is not the same as saying that it is necessary for them to vocalize in order to think. A study carried out by Smith et al. (1947) would seem to indicate that it is not. Smith was given a curare derivative which paralysed him totally. He was kept alive on an artificial respirator. Subvocal speech was impossible. Thought should also (according to Watson's hypothesis) have been impossible. Nevertheless, he later reported that he was able to understand and think about what people were saying while he was paralysed.

The influence of thought upon language

Language as one of a number of functions

Piaget claimed that language was just one among a number of symbolic functions. Others included symbolic play and imagery. He maintained that: 'Language and thought are linked in a genetic circle . . . in the last analysis, both depend upon intelligence itself, which antedates language and is independent of it' (Piaget, 1968).

Piaget has taken an opposite view of the relationship between thought and language to Whorf and Sapir. For him, intellectual development comes first, and without it language is little more than meaningless babble. As an illustration of this, Sinclair-de-Zwart (1969) studied children who had acquired the concept of **conservation of volume** (a level of intellectual development where children can appreciate that the volume of a liquid remains constant even when it is poured from a tall slender container to a short squat one). He found that they understood the meaning of words such as 'more', 'bigger', 'as much as'. Those children who had not reached the stage of conservation of volume found it hard to use such words correctly even when given specific linguistic training.

Language and thought as separate

For Bruner, language and thought are separate. He postulated three ways in which a child can retain and use information from the environment:

- Through **enactive representation**: that is to say, by means of physical manipulation of the environment.
- Through **iconic representation**: that is, picturing the environment mentally.
- Through **symbolic representation**, particularly through language.

Nonlinguistic thought comes first (what he terms enactive or iconic representation of the world). After language has developed, thought is amplified and accelerated in symbolic representation. These ideas of Bruner's are more fully explored in Chapter 20 (p. 000).

Thought and language as independent

Vygotsky (1962) held that language had two distinct aspects:

- As a monitor and controller of a person's private thoughts (**inner speech**).
- As a means of communicating those thoughts to others (**external speech**).

He believed that in infancy, thinking and language are independent. To begin with, a child's attempts to use language represent purely social speech, with no inner thought. Simultaneously, the child is developing primitive forms of thinking and reasoning, which do not involve language. Then, at about the age of two the

---

GLOSSARY

Subvocal speech The view of thinking taken by Watson and other behaviourists that thought was speech which was not vocalized.

Conservation of volume An ability to understand that the volume of material remains constant even when its appearance changes.

Enactive representation According to Bruner, the simplest way in which a child gains information about the world, by physical manipulation of the environment.

Iconic representation According to Bruner, a nonverbal means of obtaining information by picturing the environment mentally.

Symbolic representation According to Bruner, a means of obtaining and manipulating information about the environment through symbols, particularly language.

Inner speech An aspect of language, described by Vygotsky, as a monitor and controller of thinking.

External speech An aspect of language, described by Vygotsky, as a means of communicating thoughts to others.

social speech and the primitive thinking begin to come together. Words begin to act as symbols for thoughts. Vygotsky would agree with Piaget that the earliest thought is independent of language but where they part company is that Vygotsky believed that language plays an essential part in a child's intellectual development after about the age of two. Later, after about the age of seven, language and thought again separate, with language having two distinct functions:

- Internal language for the child itself as an aid to thought (**egocentric speech**). But children under about four or five frequently express this egocentric speech aloud, as do older people in situations of stress.
- External language as a means of communicating thought to others.

Luria and Yudovich (1956) studied a pair of twins. Up to five years old they had played almost exclusively together and had developed only the most rudimentary form of language. Then they were placed in separate nursery schools and the researchers reported as follows:

The whole structure of the mental life of both the twins was simultaneously and sharply changed.

Once they acquired an objective language system, the children were able to formulate the aims of their activity verbally and after only three months we observed the beginnings of meaningful play.
(Luria and Yudovich, 1956)

? SELF-ASSESSMENT QUESTIONS

1. Describe the theory of linguistic relativity. What were its weaknesses?
2. What are the essentials of Vygotsky's view of the relationship between thought and language? How convincing do you find them?
3. Does the work of Bernstein and Labov seem to you to support the notion that language determines thought?

GLOSSARY

Egocentric speech Internal language used as an aid to thinking. Vygotsky's notion of inner speech. However, in young children and in adults under stress this egocentric language is often expressed.

Chapter summary

- McKellar drew a distinction between autistic and rational thinking. Autistic thinking was purposeless, simply the brain's manipulation of information stored, while rational thinking has a purpose and is logically directed to that purpose.

- Freud divided thought into three levels, preconscious, conscious and unconscious thought. Primary thought was roughly equivalent to autistic thought and secondary thought was rational. Both primary and secondary thought might be at any of the three levels. Piaget, on the other hand, saw thought as part of the development of schemata, the building blocks of intelligence.

- Gestalt psychologists took the view that thinking was a restructuring process in the mind, an attempt to create isomorphism. Behaviourists had some problem

explaining thought and envisaged it as inner behaviour, subvocal speech. Cognitive psychologists have tried to simulate the workings of the mind with computer analogies. Human beings are not computers, however, and these simulations have not been entirely satisfactory.

- Concepts are collections of attributes of stimuli before us which we take together and label. Bruner and his colleagues identified three kinds: conjunctive, disjunctive and relational. They also explored strategies adopted in forming concepts. Levine used working hypotheses to explore concept formation and Dominowski and others employed introspection.

- Problem solving will involve understanding and representing the problem before a solution can be found. Representation of the problem can be materially helpful in solving it. Strategies used to solve problems include random search and heuristic strategies, which include means–ends analysis and backwards searching. Set, in various forms, may also have an effect upon ease of solution of problems.

■ The views taken of the relationship between language and thought include linguistic relativity, the view that language influences thought; the behaviourist view of thought as subvocal speech; Piaget's and Bruner's view of language as a symbolic function dependent on the development of intelligence; Vygotsky's view that language has two separate functions, as an aid to thinking and as a means of communication.

Further reading

Birch, A. (1997). *Developmental Psychology: from Infancy to Adulthood*, 2nd edn. Basingstoke: Macmillan. For further discussion of language acquisition and children's development of language skills.

Bruner, J.S. (1983). *Child's Talk: Learning to Use Language.* Oxford: Oxford University Press. This is particularly concerned with the social functions of language.

Matlin, M. (1989). *Cognition.* Fort Worth, TX: Holt, Rinehart & Winston. Takes the discussion of thinking and problem solving further. Chapter 8 is particularly concerned with problem solving and creativity.

Newell, A. and Simon, H.A. (1972). *Human Problem Solving.* Englewood Cliffs, NJ: Prentice-Hall. Provides a computer simulation approach to thinking and problem solving.

PART 4

Animal behaviour

This part of the book is concerned with the study of animal behaviour. Psychologists have from a very early time been interested in studying the behaviour of animals in the hope that insights might be afforded into the behaviour of humans. This study has been called 'comparative psychology' and it is under this title that it appears on some examination syllabuses.

The emphasis in this book is on a sociobiological approach to the study of animals. Sociobiology is the term given by Wilson (1975) to the study of the ways in which the behaviour of animals is determined by that which promotes fitness. Fitness is seen as adaptation to the environment so that the genes which an animal carries may be passed on to succeeding generations. Natural selection determines that behaviour which is well adapted will allow the animal to grow to maturity and reproduce, while genes that detemine less well adapted behaviour will not be passed on. There is discussion of the relationship between instinct and learning and of gene-culture coevolution which has allowed the development of the human species to far outstrip that of any animal species.

Contents

INTRODUCTION
Comparative psychology   339
  Rationale for comparative psychology   339
  Continuity or discontinuity   340
  Fields of study   345
  Methods of study of animal behaviour   348

CHAPTER 16
Instinct and learning   350
  Adaptation to the environment   350
  Development of behaviour within the individual   355
  A comparative study of learning and memory   363

CHAPTER 17
Animal communication   372
  The bases of communication   372
  Social communication   377
  Teaching human language to animals   382

CHAPTER 18
Social behaviour of animals   395
  Social organization   395
  Territory and social organization   400
  Social dominance   407
  Parents and offspring   409

Epilogue to Part 4   418

Comparative psychology

The term 'comparative psychology' does not reflect well present thought on animal behaviour, but yet it remains a frequently used title of this area of work. Accordingly, it is perhaps as well to set out the rationale and perspective from which we have approached the area in this text. All behaviour, certainly among animal species, and probably among human animals as well, is driven by an overarching need, that of the individual animal to pass its genes on to succeeding generations. Behaviour which does not contribute to this end will tend to die out, to be replaced by behaviour which does more to ensure that the genes an individual carries are transmitted to offspring.

It is important to stress that this does not imply any *motivation* on the part of individual animals to maintain their species; indeed, there are instances where the need of individuals to perpetuate their genes has led to species diversification.

At a later point we shall discuss the origins of the sociobiological approach to the study of animal behaviour and its implications for human animals. We have refrained from extrapolating to too great an extent from animal to human behaviour, but the reader is invited to draw conclusions, bearing always in mind that there are vast differences between animals and humans – as well as some surprising similarities. Comparative psychology does, after all, imply comparison!

Rationale for comparative psychology

Why study animals?

It is possible to suggest several cogent reasons.

Pure interest   Animal behaviour is interesting for its own sake. This is particularly true for psychologists, as their interests lie in studying behaviour.

Insights into human behaviour   Knowledge gained from the study of animal behaviour can often provide fresh insights into human behaviour.

Contexts of interaction between humans and animals   There are many contexts where the lives of humans and of animals interact – in farms, for instance, or in zoos. For example, some zoos no longer keep polar bears in captivity as studies of their behaviour have shown that they sometimes become mentally disturbed.

Convenience and practicality   There is also the practical point that studying animals' behaviour is sometimes more convenient than studying humans. There are two main reasons:

- They reproduce more rapidly so that their behaviour can be easily studied across more than one generation.
- They are more controllable. Experimentation is about the control of variables and where animals are subjects this control is more easily achieved. It needs to be borne in mind that control has an ethical side to it and this will be discussed later in this chapter.

339

Practical spin-offs of the study of animal behaviour

It is often expected that scientific study will have practical applied spin-offs. Here are some of them which relate to comparative psychology.

Interaction with animals

On farms, animals are managed to serve our own purposes, to produce wool, dairy products and meat, for instance.

At home, many of us have pets, and again it is not hard to see that an understanding of animal behaviour may contribute not only to our own but to the animals' comfort, health and well-being.

In zoos and wildlife parks as well as in the wild, humans have an interest in conserving the habitats of animals and making sure they are successful, particularly that they breed and reproduce. If we understand their normal mating behaviour in the wild, it will be easier to provide the right conditions for them to reproduce in the somewhat artificial conditions of the zoo or the wildlife park. In the case of some endangered species this may be the only way in which the species can survive.

Development of new methods of study

By the study of animals, experimental and observational methods may be developed which may then be used in the study of humans. To take a specific example, Kaye and Brazelton (1971) did a detailed study of what went on in feeding sessions between a human mother and her baby. In particular, they studied the relationship between the jiggling a mother does with her baby and the baby's sucking. It appears that jiggling actually lengthens the pauses between bursts of sucking which occurred when the jiggling stopped. The method adopted was not unlike the close, detailed study of animal behaviour which has been termed ethology. Kaye and Brazelton's study could be said to fall into the category of human ethology, the close observation and study of human behaviour in the natural environment.

Transfer of concepts from animals to humans

Besides the *methods* of animal ethology it has been possible sometimes to translate some of the *concepts*

also from animal to human study. For instance, the concept of imprinting was studied by Lorenz (1958) among others (it is described in greater detail in Chapter 16 in relation to young birds). This might be related to the concept of attachment explored by Bowlby (1969) with human children in Chapter 19.

Extrapolation from animals to humans

Books such as *Manwatching* by Desmond Morris (1977) have attempted to extrapolate from animal to human study. In this case the nonverbal behaviour of humans is related to animal behaviour. However, it is open to question whether this extrapolation is legitimate. At all events it must be done with caution.

Continuity or discontinuity

A crucial point concerns the concept of continuity between humans and animals. This is a philosophical and religious issue. The question is whether humans and animals are one creation with continuity of development between them or whether humans and animals are separate and unrelated creations. The Book of Genesis puts it like this:

> And God made the beast of the earth after his kind, and cattle after their kind and every living thing that creepeth upon the earth after his kind: and God saw that it was good. And God said 'Let us make Man in our own image, after our likeness.'
>
> (Genesis 1: 25–6)

This has been interpreted to mean that there were separate creations for each species of animal and for human beings. That is to say there was discontinuity between animals and humans. If discontinuity were accepted, there would be little point in studying animals to find out more about humans.

In 1859 Charles Darwin published *The Origin of Species*, which suggested there was an evolutionary

---

GLOSSARY

Continuity The proposition that humans and animals are one creation differing only in the stage of evolution each has reached.

Discontinuity The belief that humans and animals are separate creations. This has been based upon a literal interpretation of the Bible.

link between humans and animals, that they were in fact one creation with different species occupying different places on the evolutionary tree. Not unnaturally, this caused a furore among those who regarded the Bible as the literal and inspired word of God but at the same time it opened the way for scientific research to compare the behaviour of animals with that of humans.

Charles Darwin suggested that there was an evolutionary link between humans and animals

The mechanisms of genetics and evolution

Genetics

The mechanism of genetics refers to the way in which characteristics are passed on from parents to offspring within a species. Any organism which reproduces sexually possesses a biological inheritance determined by its genes. Many vital characteristics are determined in this way and the totality of these characteristics is known as its genotype. An individual's environment (the food it eats, its habitat and the social context in which it lives) interacts with its genes to determine its phenotype, the characteristics and behaviour which are evident for all to see. What happens in the case of a simple organism such as a plant may make this clearer. The kind of leaves it has, its flowers and its fruit, are

determined by its genotype. Its potential maximum and minimum height are also determined genetically, but within these limits the actual height it attains, the amount of fruit or flowers it bears and whether it grows perfectly and without defect may be determined by the environment. This is perhaps an oversimplification because even susceptibility to attack by pests and diseases may be the result of genetic inheritance. A plant may even have a genetic defect which prevents it using the available soil fertility for growth so that it does not thrive even in the very best of environments.

An example of interaction between genes and environment In human terms, the phenomenon of phenylketonuria (PKU) illustrates this interaction. PKU is a genetic defect that prevents certain individuals from producing an enzyme whose function is to metabolize phenylalinine, which is a common constituent of certain foods, especially dairy products. The build-up of phenylalinine in the bloodstream is toxic, causing mental retardation and eventually death. The toxic effects can be prevented, however, by careful observation of a low protein diet. By itself there are no harmful effects from this genetic defect but sufferers are going to need to observe a very particular diet to avoid problems.

The way in which these genetic principles operate is like this. Every cell in the body contains the same genetic material, produced by the union of two germ cells, one from each parent. This genetic material is carried on chromosomes, which come in pairs. In human beings there are 23 pairs of chromosomes. Each chromosome carries two tightly linked strings of DNA molecules, segments of which have been identified as the genes which determine biological features. It functions like this:

GLOSSARY

Genes Determinants of physical and behavioural characteristics inherited by individuals from parents.

Genotype The totality of the genes inherited by an individual, including both dominant and recessive genes.

Phenotype Characteristics, behavioural and physical, inherited by an individual which are openly displayed by that individual.

Chromosomes Tightly linked strings of DNA molecules, carried in every cell in the body and inherited in pairs from each parent. Genes are carried on chromosomes.

When cells divide, a process called mitosis occurs, which duplicates the genetic material in the cell and sends a copy into each new cell. The genes which each of a pair of chromosomes carry are not always identical.

Each member of a pair of genes is called an allele. These alleles provide alternative blueprints for characteristics. For instance, an individual may possess one allele for blue eyes and one for brown eyes, inherited, one from each parent.

Genes may be dominant or recessive. Characteristics determined by dominant genes will be displayed in the phenotype even if only one parent has passed it on; those determined by recessive genes will not occur unless there is inheritance from both parents. It is important to note that characteristics in an individual are frequently the result of an interaction between several genes. Each gene will determine certain characteristics of form or behaviour. These characteristics do not exist in isolation but in conjunction with each other. For instance, dyslexia is thought to be a genetically based abnormality which adversely affects an individual's ability to read and to write. This abnormality interacts with other genetically determined characteristics which relate to intelligence. A dyslexic person is not lacking in intelligence because of being dyslexic, but the impairment of the ability to read and write may impede the development of intellectual capacities if steps are not taken to mitigate the problem. Dyslexic individuals frequently find themselves placed in classes for 'slow learners'.

When conception occurs, a single germ cell from the father (a sperm cell) merges with a single germ cell from the mother (an ovum) to form a zygote. This is the single cell from which the whole organism will develop.

The sperm cell and the ovum are exceptional in that they do not have 23 pairs of chromosomes as does every other cell, but 23 single unpaired chromosomes which are called gametes and are formed by a process called meiosis. The pairs of chromosomes first duplicate as in mitosis, then the cells divide twice and produce four cells each with 23 chromosomes. On fertilization both mother and father contribute one gamete so that there are again 23 pairs of chromosomes in the zygote. Then the zygote divides by mitosis to form all the specialized cells of the body.

Other important factors in genetic inheritance are crossover and mutation. Crossover occurs when sections of chromosomes split off and exchange places before meiosis so that the combination of alleles on the chromosomes is shuffled. This increases the number of possible gametes. Mutation occurs when the copying process is imperfect and new characteristics or behaviours appear.

Figure 4I.1 is an illustration of this mechanism.

Evolution

The mechanism of evolution works like this:

Most species produce far more offspring than are needed to maintain numbers. It is inevitable, if the balance of numbers is to be maintained, that a high proportion of their young will fail to reach maturity.

Adaptation means that those which do succeed in reaching maturity are those best adapted to

---

GLOSSARY

Mitosis The process of copying genetic material in each cell and transferring a copy into each new cell.

Allele Term used for each member of a pair of genes.

Dominant gene A gene which displays the characteristics it determines when either allele possesses it.

Recessive gene A gene which displays the characteristics it determines only when both of a pair of alleles possess it.

Zygote The union of a single germ cell from the mother (ovum) with a single germ cell from the father (sperm).

Gamete Single unpaired chromosomes formed by meiosis.

Meiosis Process whereby single unpaired cells divide twice to provide four cells each with a full complement of chromosomes.

Crossover The splitting off and shuffling of portions of chromosomes before meiosis, thus increasing the possible number of gametes.

Mutation Imperfect copying of genetic material at mitosis, resulting in variations in characteristics.

Adaptation Fitness of genes to survive in the environment in which they find themselves, thus ensuring individuals reach maturity and reproduce.

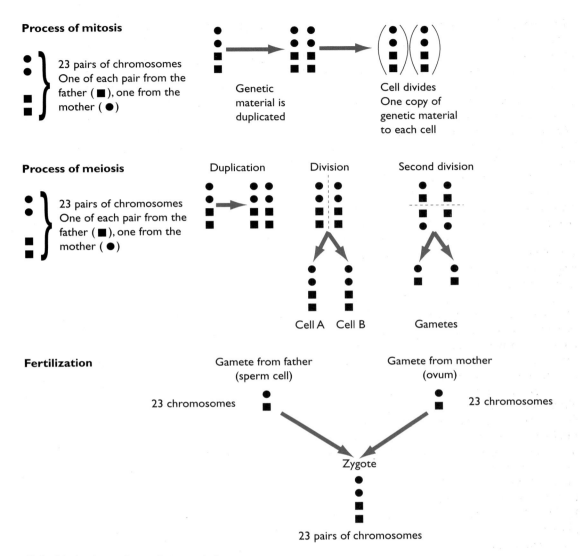

Figure 41.1 Mechanisms of genetic transmission

survive in the environment in which they find themselves. Their genes (the innate blueprint which determines their characteristics) are those which ensure survival. Individuals in a species that carry genes which are less well adapted to survival are less likely to be able to pass on their genes to succeeding generations.

■ When there are changes in the environment individual organisms may need to change too, if they are to survive. The important point is not so much the survival of the individual but the survival of the genes.

■ Where mutation occurs one individual may be better adapted to the environment than another, so that particular characteristics or behaviour are passed on into succeeding generations.

■ So, the population of a species as a whole changes over generations to become better adapted to survive. If it is unable to do this it will eventually face extinction. Any given species, then, is continuously undergoing modifications in its characteristics and its behaviour. An example might make this clearer and this is included in Box 41.1.

Box 4I.1   The example of the peppered moth

The peppered moth has wing colourings which vary from very light to very dark. Whether individuals in that species have light or dark colouring is determined by their genetic make-up (the individual's gene blueprint). This blueprint is passed on into the next generation through the individual reaching maturity, mating and producing offspring. The environmental conditions in which some of these moths live have changed. Industrial development has resulted in heavy smoke deposits on trees and buildings. In these conditions, light-coloured moths stand a much greater chance of being spotted by predators than darker ones. Dark-coloured moths have better camouflage, are less easily spotted and so stand a better chance of passing on their genes (including that for dark colouring) to their offspring. The predominant colouring of the moths changed in this way from light to dark.

So much then for the mechanism of evolution. What are the implications of Darwin's theory for the study of behaviour? Given discontinuity, there was no point in studying any organism other than human beings in order to find out more about human behaviour. They represented, after all, a unique creation. Once Darwin's thesis was accepted the situation changed. It became possible to look not only at the ontogeny of a species, that is to say the changes that occur in that species with development and maturation, but also at the phylogeny, the point it has reached in evolutionary terms.

Social Darwinism

The introduction of Darwin's ideas on natural selection (Darwin, 1859) provided for some people at the time a seeming justification for a 'laissez-faire' or 'market forces' approach to politics.. If the development of animal species better adapted to survive is the result of evolution through natural selection, then the same set of forces could be seen to be at work within human behaviour. Those individuals within the human species who succeeded best could be seen to have done so in accordance with the natural order of things. Their genes had been responsible for behaviour which was better adapted to their environment and so it was right that they should prosper and pass on this genetic

advantage to their heirs. It was not right to try to 'buck the market' by introducing artificial ideas of social justice or reform. Herbert Spencer, in his treatise entitled *Social Statics* (1851), put it like this: 'Inconvenience, suffering and death are the penalties attached by nature to ignorance, as well as to incompetence … If to be ignorant were as safe as to be wise, no one would become wise' (Spencer, 1851).

Similarly, in 1884 Spencer used Darwinism to defend competitive individualism. So far as Spencer was concerned there were close parallels between economic competition and natural selection. Social evolution could take place most easily in a condition of laissez-faire. Social reform should be limited to charitable benevolence. There was no room for state intervention. Spencer replied to criticisms of him made by T.H. Huxley in these terms:

Because I hold that the struggle for existence and the survival of the fittest should be allowed to go on in society, subject to those restraints which are involved by preventing each man from interfering with the sphere of action of another, and should not be mitigated by governmental agency, he, along with many others, ran away with the notion that they should not be mitigated at all. I regard proper benevolence as adequate to achieve all those mitigations that are proper and needful.

(Spencer, 1884)

Fields of study

Ethology

Ethology is essentially the study of behaviour in the natural environment. Within the field of ethology there has been development not only in the ways in which behaviour is studied but also in what behaviour is studied. There are broadly three areas within ethology:

Crook (1970) applied the label comparative ethologists to those who studied behaviour in the same way as they studied any other animal characteristics. Differences not only in physical characteristics but also in behaviour may be related to differences in their ecology; that is to say, the environments in which they live, the sources of their food and the predators which they have to avoid.

Crook also described the study of animal society as social ethology. Social ethologists attempt to understand individual animal behaviour in relation to the social environment in which they live. This new approach by social ethologists, particularly Wilson (1975) and Dawkins (1976), has became known as sociobiology and has been seen as the kind of scientific revolution described by Kuhn (1962). Kuhn explains that when a previously held set of assumptions about a subject, its paradigm, is challenged so strongly by new evidence that it has to be abandoned, a new paradigm takes its place. This kind of revolution occurred in physics, for instance, with Einstein's theory of relativity. In sociobiology animal societies could be treated as biological entities and understood in terms of evolution and natural selection. In terms of method, the question to ask of any behaviour studied is this: 'Will the gene survive which produces that behaviour in an organism living in a particular environment, more especially, a particular social environment?'

In addition there are behavioural ecologists, interested in the way in which the behaviour of an animal interacts with the environment in which it exists. For instance, the establishment of territories by animals is one way in which they can give themselves exclusive access to resources. Territoriality is discussed more fully later in this book (Chapter 18).

Sociobiology

The introduction of sociobiology, providing as it did a basis for the study of the genetic and evolutionary origins of behaviour, not only of animals but also of the human species, was seen by some academics as reactionary. A group calling themselves 'Science for the People' campaigned vigorously against the new study of sociobiology on the grounds that any attempt to provide a biological basis for social behaviour would lead to social Darwinism. Human applications of sociobiology were to be condemned because of the political dangers posed by such thinking:

> These theories provided an important basis for the enactment of sterilization laws and restrictive immigration laws in the United States between 1910 and 1930 and also for the eugenics policies which led to the establishment of gas chambers in Nazi Germany.
>
> (Jonathan Beckwith and 14 cosigners of a letter in *New York Review of Books*, 13 November 1975)

This was clearly an extreme reaction but the reasoning behind these condemnations of sociobiology is flawed. Scientific discovery should not be judged for its possible political consequences, it was suggested. What matters was truth. Knowledge provided a better basis than ignorance for combating reactionary attitudes. The more that became known about the relationship between biological mechanisms and behaviour the more possible it was to deal with abnormal human behaviour.

A further group of individuals maintained that there was an incoherence in the idea of sociobiology. The natural sciences had a fundamentally different subject matter and intention from that of the social sciences or humanities. What is unique, most richly structured

---

GLOSSARY

Ethology The study of behaviour in the natural environment.

Comparative ethologists Those who study behaviour in animals in the same way as other characteristics.

Ecology The context in which animals or people live.

Social ethology Attempts made to understand animal behaviour in the context of their social environment.

Paradigm An essential uniting characteristic of a study or a science.

Behavioural ecology Attempts made to understand how animals' ecology (the context in which they live) interacts with their behaviour.

Sociobiology The treatment of animal societies as social entities to be understood in terms of natural selection and evolution.

and most interesting about human existence was permanently beyond biological investigation. Because human beings had free will they were able to reflect upon the consequences of their actions and they were able to create cultures which diverged. There was enormous variation in culture from one society to another which put it beyond the scope of the traditional reductionist biological analysis. These were much more valid criticisms. Free will, cultural diversity and consciousness were the stuff of what being human was about. The challenge faced was to incorporate mind and culture into evolutionary theory.

Culture

At this point, it might be useful to identify clearly what is meant here by culture. It can be said to be an amalgam of all those behaviours which result not from genetic programming but from interaction with the environment. In human terms, the way in which we live, the kind of houses we build, the sort of work we do and the way in which we treat each other are a part of our culture. That we use knives, forks and spoons to eat our food, while Indians use a hand, is a cultural difference between us. That we walk upright on two legs, while animals mostly go on four, represents a genetic difference between humans and most species of animal.

Gene–culture coevolution

The result of this challenge has been a continuing pursuit of the ways in which genetic evolution has come together with culture to create the people we are. In their book *Promethean Fire*, Lumsden and Wilson (1983) have outlined some of the ways in which this **gene–culture coevolution** works. The human species (*Homo sapiens*) has its behaviour determined neither entirely by its genetic make-up, nor entirely as a result of the culture in which individuals live. There is a discussion of their arguments in Box 4I.2.

Evidence from less developed societies than our own suggests that the assumption that children do in general enjoy a well-ordered social world is false. Their behaviour is not governed wholly, or even for the most part, by instructions from adults, and they are left to fend for themselves even more than in advanced societies. But in spite of this, they become socialized into their own group. Their speech, the skills they need in daily life, their facial expressions, their under-

standing of the lore and ritual of the tribe and other patterns of behaviour become well-developed. It seems evident that this could not occur from free will alone but that there must in addition be a set of genetically determined rules and principles which enable them to learn their world speedily. The suggestion is that those who possess a set of innate clues to help them to master the world into which they are born are likely to adapt to it more quickly and more successfully than they would if they were just endowed with problem-solving mechanisms of a very general kind. Those who are most successful in their adaptation leave more of their genes to succeeding generations.

The conclusions reached in *Promethean Fire* have been summarized by Lumsden and Wilson as follows:

All domains of human life, including ethics, have a physical basis in the brain and part of biology; none is exempt from analysis in the mode of the natural sciences.

Mental development is more finely structured than has been generally appreciated in the past; most or all forms of perception and thinking are biased by processes in the brain that are genetically programmed.

The structure in mental development appears to have originated over many generations through a specialized form of evolution (gene–culture co-evolution) in which genes and culture change together.

The biases in mental development are only biases; the influence of the genes, even when very strong does not destroy free will. In fact the opposite is the case; by acting on culture through the epigenetic rules, the genes create and sustain the capacity for conscious choice and decision.

The predispositions originate from an interaction of particular sets of genes and the environment; they can be altered in a precise manner if the appropriate information about them is available.

Ethical precepts are based on the predispositions, and they too can be altered in a precise manner.

One result of a strong human science might be the creation of a sophisticated form of social en-

---

GLOSSARY

Gene–culture coevolution The coming together of genetic evolution culture to allow the human species to develop more rapidly than other species.

Box 41.2 Gene–culture coevolution

Lumsden and Wilson have illustrated their arguments by imagining species of intelligent creatures which they have christened *eidylons* and *xenidrins*. The former, while brilliant and formidable, have their entire thought and behaviour pre-programmed into their genetic makeup. The latter, equally brilliant and formidable, have no constraints at all on their thought and behaviour placed upon them by their genes.

Among *eidylons*, while their behaviour reflects the circumstances in which they find themselves and they react to what goes on around them, the way in which they react has been genetically predetermined. A festival inspires the singing of a ritual hymn but every last note and inflection has been fixed. An accident occurs and those who witness respond with appropriate expressions of shock and grief. But these are entirely invariant. One appropriate response has been preprogrammed into them to every stimulus they might encounter. There are no alternative or optional ways of responding. Even the ways in which they pass their culture on to succeeding generations has been preordained. The young are genetically programmed to hear and receive just one appropriate response.

Xenidrins, on the other hand, have entirely free will. In any set of circumstances any response is possible so that their minds and their behaviour are entirely the products of the accidents of their history, where they live, what they have to eat and what other species of flora and fauna they encounter. This *xenidrin* world is that which has frequently been postulated by philosophers such as John Locke in the eighteenth century who believed the human mind to be a *tabula rasa*, a blank slate upon which each person's experience writes to determine how he or she will behave and respond.

The way in which humans have developed and evolved is different from either of these hypothetical species. If humans had been *eidylons* there would have been no development except as a result of genetic evolution. Differences among individuals in behaviour arising from gene structure or mutations result in differential adaptation to the environment and differential survival and reproductive rates. Where the genetic structure was better adapted, individuals would be more successful in passing on their genes. Humans are faced with continual choices to make as the environment in which they exist changes and, unlike the *eidylons*, they have a degree of free will in making these choices. If this were not the case, if their behaviour were entirely predetermined genetically, responses to the changing environment would have been too slow to account for the massive advances which have taken the species *Homo sapiens* rapidly so far ahead of other primates.

If, on the other hand, humans had been *xenidrins*, whose behaviour was entirely governed by free will, it is hard to see how their genetic make-up would have remained unaffected by the choices made. It is inevitable that some choices made will result in greater success in adapting to the environment and consequently greater reproductive ability. The genes which encouraged those choices become more widely spread in the population. New genetic mutations and recombinations will arise to predispose individuals to make these better-adapted choices. The *tabula rasa*, then, is not such a blank sheet as it was.

gineering, one that touches the deepest levels of human motivation and moral reasoning.

(Lumsden and Wilson, 1983, pp. 181–2)

Methods of study of animal behaviour

Ethological methods

Ethology refers to the study of animals in their environment. This may be pure observation free from any manipulation of the environment or it may be experimental, that is to say it may involve some deliberate manipulation of variables in order to be able to observe the results of this manipulation. In Chapter 16, for instance, the observations made by von Frisch (1967) of honeybees are described. He suggested that the elaborate 'dances' they perform indicate to other members of the hive where the food is to be found. This was the result of close and careful observation without manipulation of the environment. Later, Michelsen (1989) constructed a brass model which could be inserted into the hive and made to perform the dance. This amounted to an experimental manipulation of the bees' environment so that the results of this manipulation could be observed.

The studies described were laboratory experiments where variables were deliberately manipulated to examine the results of this manipulation. The advantage of experimentation of this kind over observation is that besides the closer control of variables it was possible to identify cause. Konishi was able to identify feedback (or the lack of it) as determining whether or not the characteristic birdsong of the white-crowned sparrow developed. Contrast this with some of the accounts in Lorenz's (1952) *King Solomon's Ring* which are of observations of natural behaviour.

Laboratory study of animals

The behaviour of animals can be studied either in their natural environments or in laboratories. Laboratories enable scientists to exercise greater control. Experimentation is easier with this kind of control. An experimenter can manipulate one or more of the variables in the study in order to observe and to measure the effect of this manipulation on other variables. Perhaps an illustration will make the distinction clearer. Experiments performed by Marler

and Tamura (1964) and Konishi (1965) are detailed in Box 41.3.

Laboratory studies of conditioning

The above studies, whether in the laboratory or in the natural environment, and whether observational or experimental, are primarily concerned with learning more about animals. Work done by Pavlov, at first on classical conditioning, and later by Thorndike and Skinner on instrumental and operant conditioning is less concerned with animal behaviour, and more with the notion of learning and conditioning as a psychological phenomenon. The use of animals was convenient to this end. In the studies of both classical conditioning and operant conditioning the laboratory environment of the animals was totally controlled. Conclusions drawn are about the nature of learning and conditioning and were intended to be applicable to any species, though more recent studies quoted have highlighted the importance of species-specific characteristics (that is, those characteristics which are peculiar to a particular species). Differences in such characteristics are reflected in different conditioned behaviour. A full account of these and other studies of learning is in Chapter 6.

Conclusion

To sum up, then, methods used in the investigation of animal behaviour have included the following:

■ The study of animals in their natural environment in order to find out more about animals. This may be observational or else may include some experimentation.
■ Laboratory study in carefully controlled environments with the same object.
■ Laboratory study using animals with the purpose of investigating psychological phenomena which are as much applicable to humans as to animals. This may be because animals are more convenient to study than are human participants for some of the reasons outlined earlier in this chapter.
■ Physiological study of animals. This might include study of the hormonal changes which occur in relation to motivation or perhaps the role which the hypothalamus (a structure in the lower brain) plays in the control of feeding.

Box 41.3   Experiments by Marler and Tamura (1964) and Konishi (1965)

Marler and Tamura (1964) investigated the way in which the song of the white-crowned sparrow, a native of the Pacific coast of America, was affected by early experiences. Different groups of birds were subjected to different early experiences with the object of exploring the contributions made by instinct, on the one hand, and environmental circumstances, on the other, to the way in which their characteristic song developed.

■ Group A were isolated from other members of their species and never allowed to hear the mature adult song.
■ Group B were similarly isolated but exposed to the song of other species when juvenile.
■ Group C were exposed to the song of adults of their species as juveniles.

Group A and Group B ended up singing a song that was recognizably that of their species but simpler and without the regional 'dialects', while Group C when they began to sing did so with a recognizable local dialect. It was noticed that this happened where they were exposed to tape recordings of adult song before they were three months old but not when the exposure was later (say, beyond four months).

In later experiments (somewhat dubious ethically), Konishi (1965) deafened groups of birds by removing the cochlea from the inner ear at various stages in their development. Those who were deafened as juveniles produced only disconnected notes with no phrasing, which was not recognizable as the song of the white-crowned sparrow. This was true even when the birds who were deafened had been exposed to adult song but had not themselves begun to sing. However, once they had begun to sing, deafening left their song unchanged.

The flow chart below illustrates what was done in these experiments.

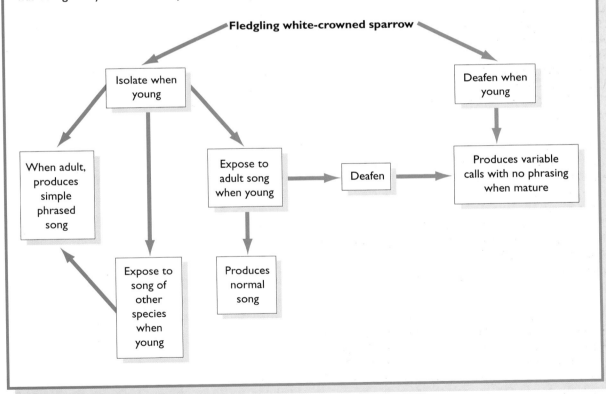

CHAPTER 16

Instinct and learning

Adaptation to the environment 350
- Phylogeny 350
- Ontogeny 352
- The interplay of phylogenetic and ontogenetic adaptation 354
- Optional foraging theory 354

Development of behaviour within the individual 355
- Imprinting 355
- Maturation 358

- Behavioural patterns and external stimuli 358
- Complex situations 362

A comparative study of learning and memory 363
- Problems in comparative research 363
- Evidence from comparative studies 363
- Can animals think? 365
- The study of memory 368

Objectives

At the end of this chapter you should be able to:

- Understand and evaluate key terms such as ritualization, parallel evolution and instinct;

- Be familiar with the interaction of factors in the decisions made by animals when foraging;

- Understand and evaluate the importance of early experience in learning situations, such as imprinting, and the interaction of sign stimuli with fixed action patterns;

- Assess evidence for the phenomena of thinking and memory in animals.

Adaptation to the environment

As suggested by Darwin's theory, discussed in the introduction to this part, adaptation will occur over time, with the result that new species will evolve and existing species will adapt and change, in order to obtain optimum advantage from changing environments; that is to say, to have the greatest chance for genes to survive into succeeding generations. This adaptation of a species over time, by natural selection, is called **phylogenetic adaptation**.

In addition, changes also occur within the lifetime of an individual member of a species. These changes reflect what members of the local population find advantageous and possible. This is known as **ontogenetic adaptation**.

Phylogeny

Evolutionary theory allows for some members of a species not only to evolve into a species distinct from those existing, or those yet to come, but also to continue evolving, as they constantly adapt to the ever-changing pressures of their environment. This differentiation may have benefits, in evolutionary terms, by fitting the new species to a changed environment; for example, lower or higher environmental temperatures, the disappearance of a source of food, could mean extinction for that species unless it adapts to these changes. If environmental temperatures decrease, genes which permit tolerance to lower temperatures will survive as opposed to those which do not.

Differentiation within species

By studying the behaviour patterns of closely related species, it is possible to identify how certain patterns have evolved and where differentiation has occurred. For example, Morris (1959) described evolutionary changes in courtship patterns of tropical grassfinches. Male zebra finches (*Taeniopygia guttata*), when courting a female, 'bow' forward on their perch and wipe the bill across the perch as though cleaning it. In two related species, the spice finch (*Lonchura punctulata*) and the striated finch (*Lonchura striata*), the males of both perform the 'bow' and hold the head low over the perch for some seconds, but do not wipe the beak. Morris suggests that the courtship bow of these two species has evolved from an ancestor who did perform beak-wiping during courtship, much as the present-day zebra finch still does. We do not know what change in evolutionary circumstances promoted this differentiation. Perhaps their diet changed from sticky to a nonsticky food, but the innate residual pattern of behaviour still remained and was incorporated into courtship activity.

Ritualization

Huxley (1914) identified a particular example of evolutionary behaviour which he termed **ritualization**. Ritualization consists of responses which have no specific function, except to serve as a signal. For instance, Huxley described a component of the courtship display of the great-crested grebe (*Podiceps cristatus*). At one point both partners rise out of the water, presenting nest-building material to each other (see Figure 16.1). While this behaviour derives from elements of the nest-building behaviour of the species, it does not in this context seem to have much to do with nest-building.

Ritualization as a form of communication One of the uses of ritualization is for members of a species to

Figure 16.1 The courtship display of the great-crested grebe: an example of ritualization

recognize and respond to signals from other members of the same species; in this way it can be regarded as a form of communication. (For further discussion of communication, see Chapter 17.) If the initial signal is understood and a 'correct' response is given, the interaction proceeds. If an 'incorrect' response is given, aggression may result (chasing away the intruder, as the individual is now regarded). Even more seriously, in the case of some species of spider, the smaller male spider may be eaten, instead of mated! This illustrates the reason why ritualized responses are timed to a fraction of a second, in order that no mistake is made as to their meaning.

> **GLOSSARY**
>
> **Phylogenetic adaptation** The adaptation of a species over a period of time by a process of natural selection.
>
> **Ontogenetic adaptation** Changes in behaviour occurring within the lifetime of an individual of a species which are advantageous to its survival.
>
> **Ritualization** Behavioural responses which have no specific function except to serve as a signal.

Parallel evolution

Lorenz (1950) suggested that it would be difficult to identify the origins of many display postures, if these were not identifiable in less ritualized forms in related species. However, we must be careful not to assume that all close similarities in behaviour between species are due to the same causes; they may in fact be due to parallel evolution. For example, the development of the forelimbs in bats, birds and pterodactyls evolved independently, though each resulted in flight.

Ontogeny

As an animal develops, its behaviour changes. This section examines how this behaviour changes and the extent to which the changes depend on environmental influences. Ontogenic adaptation is closely linked to the causes of these changes. For example, a nestling bird, which as far as maturation and motivation is concerned is not ready to mate, may still behave in a way which indicates that it is about to mate. This behaviour may be regarded in the same light as 'play' behaviour exhibited by mammals: that is, as training for what it must do later in life. For example, kittens chase and pounce on a toy or a small moving object; later in the cat's life those same movements may be used to stalk and capture prey. In the same way, at a later stage in its development, the bird may produce elements of copulatory behaviour. The full-blown process of copulation, however, requires the coming together of internal and external stimuli.

Internal stimuli for the mating process may include:

- Maturation,
- Internal hormonal states.

These may need to be prompted by external stimuli such as:

- Extended day-length, as in spring for birds;
- Triggers such as warming water, in the case of sticklebacks;
- The presence of a sexually available partner.

Successful mating may contribute to the organism's chances of reproduction which, of course, are crucial to the animal's chances of passing on its genes.

Interaction of genetic and hormonal factors

The interaction of genetic and environmental factors can be extremely complex, as shown by Dagan and Volman (1982). A newly hatched cockroach (*Periplaneta americana*) turns away from a puff of air as accurately as an adult cockroach, in spite of having only four sensory hairs on its cerci instead of 440, as an adult has (a cercus is an antenna-like structure on the cockroach's rear; there are two cerci, one either side: see Figure 16.2). This shows that the fully fledged response is available from hatching. Yet if an adult loses one of its pair of cerci, its escape behaviour is initially impaired, and it will even turn into the wind instead of

> **GLOSSARY**
>
> **Parallel evolution** Similar behavioural or physical evolutionary changes in different species resulting from dissimilar causes.

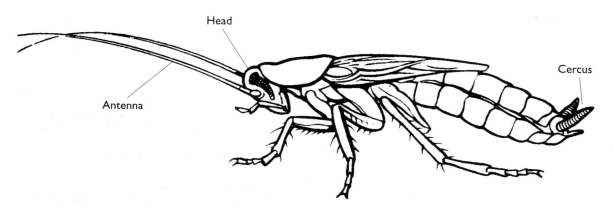

Figure 16.2 The cerci of a cockroach, used in detecting air movements

Head

Cercus

Antenna

away from it. After 30 days, with or without practice, the accurate escape behaviour returns. Somehow its nervous system has altered in order to respond to the remaining intact cercus, demonstrating that adaptation is possible, even after maturation and even when the fully functional behaviour was available from the time of hatching.

Instinctive behaviour

There was a move in the 1970s to discontinue use of the word 'instinct' in comparative psychology, as it had become debased by common usage. Numerous types of behaviour had been loosely or inaccurately described as 'instinctive'. However, tacit agreement seems to have prevailed. The term **instinctive behaviour** is used in its strictly ethological sense as referring to **species-specific behaviour** which is not controlled by conscious decision-making processes, and has a genetic basis.

An example of such species-specific behaviour would be the egg-rolling behaviour of the greylag goose (*Anser anser*) (Lorenz and Tinbergen, 1970). If an egg rolls out of the nest of a greylag goose, she stands up and stretches her neck, hooks her beak over it and attempts to roll it back into the nest; even if attempts are unsuccessful she never tries using her feet or wings. Both Lorenz and Tinbergen labelled this behaviour as 'instinctive' but realized that while this was descriptive, it was not sufficiently explanatory. This led to the suggestion that various species evolved fixed action patterns (described in the next section), stereotyped behaviour patterns, species-specific and genetically driven.

Cultural evolution

In most species higher than invertebrates on the **phylogenetic scale** (the scale which identifies how far one species has evolved relative to other species), behaviour is learned from parents, peers or other adults of the same species; not all behaviour is genetically preprogrammed. Learned behaviour may complement instinctive behaviour. For example, in birds the *instinct* to migrate is present, but the young birds learn the *route* to a suitable winter habitat by following the older birds initially. Once learned, this information is then passed on by them to the next generation and the next. Inevitably, minor adaptations to this knowledge have to be made by individuals or generations, as rain forests are cut down or floods wash away deltas. New learning occurs by experience.

Cultural transmission of behaviour This cultural transmission of behaviour occurs among species who have the ability to modify their behaviour. Japanese macaques (*Macaca fuscaca*) of Koshuma island were observed picking up sweet potatoes which were caked with earth. One day a female monkey washed her potato in the stream, before eating it. This behaviour was copied by other members of the troop, and the washing of muddy fruit before eating became an established behaviour pattern. This individual monkey had changed the behaviour pattern of her troop. This change may spread to other troops of the same species, or even to related species. In all probability chimpanzees may have learnt to use tools in the same way. Chimps will use a stick to poke into narrow termite holes too small for their hands. When the stick is covered with termites, the chimp will withdraw it from the hole and eat the termites (McGrew et al., 1979). Chimps of other bands may use grass stems of leaves instead of twigs. Such behaviour has been observed in a wide range of habitats and the learned behaviour has presumably been available for some time (Schiller, 1957).

The importance of parental care and lifespan development

From the above examples it can be seen that species more likely to enlarge their repertoire of behaviour by passing on learned skills are those which

- Form groups,
- Have protracted parental care,
- Have contact with others of the same species.

These learned skills are built on to the genetic components of behaviour. The longer the expected

---

GLOSSARY

Instinctive behaviour Species-specific behaviour which is not controlled by conscious decision-making processes and which has a genetic basis.

Species-specific behaviour Instinctive behaviour which is found only in a particular species.

Phylogenetic scale The point to which a particular species has evolved is represented by its position on the phylogenetic scale.

lifespan of an individual, the more they may be expected to learn, and in the higher primates, including humans, learning may appear to overshadow the genetic components of their behaviour. However, there are other constraints. Elephants live longer than chimpanzees, but do not have the same manual dexterity. Their size, strength and bulk also make it less necessary for them to employ stratagems in order to obtain food. Their learning skills, therefore, may only progress as far as is necessary.

The interplay of phylogenetic and ontogenetic adaptation

As you will have realized by now, there is no fixed and immovable division between behaviour which is genetically driven and that which is learned. What is termed 'instinctive' behaviour is constantly being refined by learning, and much learned behaviour is underpinned by evolutionary factors. An attempt to divide behaviour between nature and nurture is altogether too simplistic, and not really very useful. What is useful, however, is to have an understanding of the evolutionary basis of behaviour (where it is coming from) and how learning has changed that behaviour. The circumstances in which animals find themselves may alter behaviour in either of two ways.

■ There may be environmental constraints upon them.
■ New opportunities may present themselves.

Not only vertebrates are capable of learning, of course. What members of a particular species learn is dependent upon what they need and the characteristics of learned behaviour in any one species are associated with their needs and what instinctive behaviour they have inherited. The advantage of acquiring a new behaviour through learning is that it assists the individual to survive and reproduce successfully. Its genes survive to be passed on. The ecological niche which it occupies has become more favourable. It has adapted.

Optimal foraging theory (OFT)

All animals feed. Birds peck, cats pounce and bite; each species feeds in its own specific way. Learned components of behaviour are added to genetic components. For example, an animal may have to

learn *where* is the safest or most fruitful place to feed. These two instances may not be one and the same. Where food is most plentiful may not be the safest place. The animal must then make decisions as to what course of action to take. It must obtain as much as it can with least risk. It is no use to an individual to go to rich pastures to feed, if the end result is being eaten by a larger predator!

A bird foraging in a depleted area may in fact do more for its energy reserves by staying in that area, if the next area for feeding is some distance away. Energy will be expended getting to the new feeding grounds. However, before the current patch drops below a viable level (where the energy expended on finding food is not balanced by the poor amount of food found) the bird will make the decision to expend energy and fly to a new site (Krebs and Davies, 1987). It is unlikely that it is *consciously* weighing up the pros and cons, but optimal foraging theory (OFT) provides a useful working description of behaviour. Possibly the animal has had previous experience of moving to a new patch if it has failed to find food after a certain length of time. It does not work out travel time and energy losses and balance these against the benefits to be found in the new area.

In a similar way, humans sometimes behave without conscious thought. For example, if someone throws you a ball, you probably catch it, even if you have no understanding of the laws of physics for flight and aerodynamics. If you stopped to calculate these, you would probably miss the ball!

Various factors influence animals' foraging behaviour, including:

■ Economic decisions,
■ Risk taking,
■ Food availability.

Economic decisions

Individuals of a species have to make economic decisions when foraging. Bees, for example, have been observed returning to the hive with less than a full load of nectar, even when more was available. Schmid-Hempel et al. (1985) found that the further bees had to fly back to the hive, the smaller the load they collected. Full loads were only collected when reasonably close to the hive. In other words, bees were maximizing their efficiency by collecting a full load when they could easily manage to transport it to the hive, and a smaller load when they had further to fly, to ensure they had enough strength and stamina for the journey.

For starlings (*Sturnus vulgaris*), collecting leather-jackets to feed their young, there may be a time constraint. Their young need visiting and feeding frequently. Kacelnik (1984) carried out a series of studies which showed that starlings in fact increased their load size, the further they had to fly to their nest. Of course the 'load-weight' which can be carried by bees is a constraining factor. A starling is obviously not so constrained by its carrying capacity.

Risk-taking behaviour

The more hungry an animal is, the more risks it will take when foraging. This is why hitherto shy birds are seen on the bird table in winter. Milinski and Heller (1978) found that hungry sticklebacks (*Gasterosteus aculeatus*) will accept the danger of lurking predators in order to obtain high intake rates of food. Werner et al. (1983) added bass to a pond of bluegill sunfish. The small sunfish were in danger of being eaten by the bass. Subsequent observation showed that the small sunfish fed only in sheltered, low-risk areas, until they grew large enough not to be someone else's dinner. There is clearly a balance to be struck between hunger and the risk of predation.

Food availability

For many species the food available varies seasonally. Territories may be extended in periods of shortage, or even totally changed, as in the case of nomadic habits of herds of antelope or other herbivores. Individuals or groups have to make decisions as to whether it is best to drive away intruders, in order to keep all the available food for themselves, or whether the costs of sharing provide useful benefits, such as providing early warning of, or a distraction to, predators.

Elgar (1986) studied house sparrows. The first sparrow from a flock to find a food source gives a 'chirrup' call to the remainder of the flock, before flying down to feed. Sparrows in flocks spend less time scanning for predators and consequently more time feeding, therefore the costs of sharing are outweighed by the benefits. But if the food source is indivisible, the individual sparrow does not call the flock, but flies down and feeds alone.

? SELF-ASSESSMENT QUESTIONS

1. Identify and describe an example of evolutionary change in a species.
2. Describe an example of the cultural transmission of behaviour.
3. Discuss how animals make decisions when foraging.

Development of behaviour within the individual

Imprinting

The importance of early experience in the young organism, including parental care in species where this occurs, makes it essential that the young recognize the parent who will be responsible for them. (We shall be returning to this in Chapter 18.) While there may be genetic elements in this recognition, Lorenz (1952) showed that, in birds and poultry at least, this recognition occurs through an **imprinting** process which takes place early in the new organism's life. Imprinting provides for the

- feeding,
- protection,
- warmth,
- comfort and
- early learning

of the young of a species. It ensures a bond between parent and young, usually for a comparatively brief period of time, while parental care is necessary.

Lorenz demonstrated in a series of experiments that young birds will follow something which is presented to them immediately after hatching. This, in the normal run of events, would be the parent bird, but these experiments included a range of unlikely articles such as an orange balloon, as well as Lorenz himself. The

---

GLOSSARY

Imprinting A mechanism of attachment of the young of a species, especially praecocial birds, to their parents. They will follow the first moving thing they see shortly after hatching.

essential elements to imprinting were, Lorenz suggested:

■ that the objects moved (inanimate objects were on a turntable);
■ that they should be presented within a **critical period**, usually within 24 hours of hatching.
■ that imprinting was irreversible once it had taken place.

Lorenz also suggested that imprinting would later influence the choice of sexual partners for mating, but this secondary purpose of imprinting has been called into question by other researchers, for a number of reasons. For example, in a species which exhibits **sexual dimorphism** (where males and females are different in size or coloration), females would expect to mate with other females on maturity, if imprinting had influenced the choice of partners.

Critical/sensitive period

Other researchers, such as Guiton (1959), found that this critical period could be extended if the newly hatched birds were kept in the dark until their exposure to the item on which they were to be imprinted. This called into question the concept of a critical period for learning to occur, and the term was modified to **sensitive period**.

This implies that learning will occur more easily at a specific time, but does not rule out the possibility of it ever occurring outside a time as specific as the critical period. The concept of critical period was applied to human bonding by researchers such as Bowlby (see Chapter 19), but needed to be modified in the light of subsequent research such as Guiton's. In addition, humans have greater powers of rationalization and cognition than other animals, and are therefore more likely to be able to overcome deficits in early experience. The idea of a critical or sensitive period was thought to have implications for human learning. Children who were not given the opportunity to learn to speak, read or socialize at times when children normally do these things, would remain disadvantaged. However, care must be exercised in extrapolating into such a complex area as human learning from such basic beginnings. Many studies have shown that skills can be acquired at later periods in life, probably because humans are very adaptable, and also because motivation plays such a large part in human learning.

Components of imprinting

Hess (1972) carried out a series of experiments, to try to clarify the essential components of imprinting. These are described in Box 16.1.

Hess therefore proposed that imprinting was most likely to occur when the bird was strong enough to move around and follow the parent, but before the fear of large moving objects developed. Both auditory and visual components are important; auditory stimulation may occur before hatching. Laboratory imprinting may be reversed; imprinting in the natural environment is likely to be irreversible.

Functions of imprinting

Obvious functions of imprinting:

■ It ensures that the young of a species knows whom to follow for food.
■ It ensures that the young of a species knows where to retreat for warmth or protection.
■ There may be some truth in Lorenz's suggestion that for some species the imprinted model may serve as a model for mating, on achieving maturity.

In addition, imprinting may prepare the young for recognizing kin or siblings. These individuals would then not be subject to aggression as might others of the same, or a similar, species. Holmes and Sherman (1982) showed that ground squirrels (*Spermophilus beldingi*) recognized as 'siblings' those who were reared with them in the nest. This discrimination continued into adulthood. This illustrates the importance of learning in early experience, but imprinting is not the only mechanism in use. There also seems to be some kind of phenotype matching available, as litter mates who were full sisters (same mother, same father) were more cooperative and less aggressive to each other than half-

---

GLOSSARY

Critical period Period after hatching when Lorenz claimed imprinting had to occur, about 24 hours.

Sexual dimorphism Differences in size and/or coloration between males and females of a species.

Sensitive period Period after hatching (birth) during which imprinting or other forms of attachment are most likely to occur. A modification of Lorenz's critical period.

Box 16.1 Hess's experiments on imprinting

Hess's first experiment identified that a moving object was necessary (as Lorenz had already suggested); ducklings would follow a model of a female mallard (*Anas platyrhynchus*) on a turntable when it was set in motion.

He found that as well as the visual stimulus of a moving object, there were also auditory components to imprinting; ducklings would follow a quacking model of a male mallard, on a turntable, in preference to a silent model of a female. (Male and female mallards can be differentiated by plumage; the female is cryptic brown, while the male is more colourful, with blue, green and white flashes.)

Hess used field studies (1972), as well as laboratory experiments, and found that sound responses in mallards begin before hatching, between mother and incubating ducklings. Pre-hatching sounds may facilitate the recognition of maternal calls which are given after hatching. Early imprinting experiments did not include this auditory experience. Imprinting on humans may have occurred more easily, as the visual stimulus took on an enhanced importance, in the absence of appropriate auditory stimuli.

In addition the only sounds available were human ones. The need to control the variables (hatching birds in incubators, for example, in order to control conditions) may actually have constituted deprivation and thereby confounded the results. In this instance, preliminary field studies could have pointed the way for increased accuracy in laboratory experiments.

Hess also found that although imprinting could occur within one hour of hatching, it was strongest between 12 and 17 hours after hatching. If no dark-rearing was involved, imprinting was unlikely to occur if no stimulus was presented within 32 hours.

The phenomenon of laboratory imprinting was found to be reversible. Ducklings who had imprinted on a human were subsequently allowed to follow a female mallard. After an hour and a half they showed no signs of following a human being again. When the experiment was tried the other way around there was no transfer; the ducklings did not follow a human, once imprinting had occurred on the female mallard.

The diagram shows the layout of some of the apparatus used by Hess.

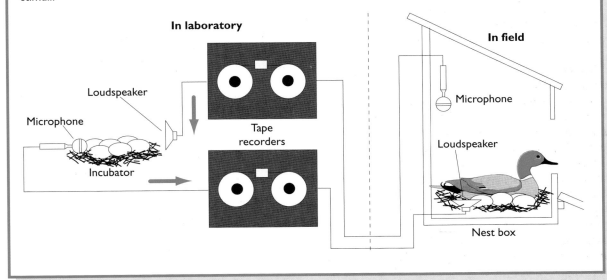

sisters (same mother, but different fathers, due to multiple mating).

These complex recognition patterns indicate that it is unlikely that imprinting is the whole story of how one individual recognizes another. Imprinting is not a full learning process, but is more accurately viewed as a preparedness for learning. Even then, as Guiton's and others' experiments have shown, it is an adaptable preparedness, which enables the individual to adapt to changed environments.

Maturation

Maturation is the biological process through which any organism progresses to become an adult of its species. Biological maturation is an inevitable process, though it is sometimes hindered by insufficient nutrition or forestalled by premature death. The organism does not have to work towards maturity. Maturity is genetically preprogrammed to occur, although individual rates of achieving maturity may vary between individuals of a particular species, owing to intervening variables such as food availability.

As the young of any species matures, behaviour which was present from birth mature into their adult pattern. For example, the type of 'play' aggression directed previously at litter mates becomes the full-blown response, now directed at a potential intruder.

External environmental opportunities may interact with the internal changes brought about by maturation. For example, as the young animal matures, hormonal and other biological changes occur within the body, promoting growth and, later, reproduction. External stimuli such as warmer weather and longer day-length may interact with the ability to produce hormones necessary for the reproductive process to take place, but until maturation, day-length and warmer weather will not have this effect.

Behavioural patterns and external stimuli

Early ethologists such as Tinbergen and Lorenz identified species-specific behaviour patterns in which there were few if any variations between individuals of a species. This lack of variation showed them to be genetically programmed and so they were termed **fixed action patterns (FAPs)**.

Lorenz (in Lorenz and Tinbergen, 1970) suggested that FAPs possessed specific characteristics. These were defined by Lea (1984) and are detailed in Box 16.2.

Some FAPs do have the rigid quality which Lorenz describes. For example, the 'head-throw' of the goldeneye drake (*Bucephala clangula*), used in court-ship rituals, has an average time of 1.29 seconds and variations of only hundredths of a second occur between individuals of the species (Dane *et al.*, 1959). However, while not all behaviour patterns are so rigid in their display and timing, they are still easily recognizable by others of the species. For this reason the more neutral term 'behaviour patterns' is used in descriptions nowadays.

Box 16.2   Characteristics of fixed action patterns (FAPs)

Universality
FAPs occur in all members of a defined group within a species. For example, nesting geese display the egg-rolling behaviour mentioned in the previous section, but goslings, ganders and nonnesting geese do not. Egg-rolling is therefore an FAP of nesting geese.

Stereotyping
The behaviour always occurs in the same form, with a small allowance for variation.

Independence of individual experience
If a member of a species is reared in isolation its fixed action patterns will not be significantly different from any other members of the same species.

Ballistic nature of response
Even if circumstances change once the response is initiated, the response itself will not change.

Single-purpose response
Each FAP has only one function and is not adapted or used for any other similar or different purpose. For example, the actions involved in egg-rolling are not used by the greylag goose for any other purpose.

Identifiable trigger stimuli
There is a specific stimulus or set of stimuli which reliably trigger a specific FAP.

Marler demonstrated by his experiments with white-crowned sparrows (see Box 4I.3 on p. 349) that a subspecies might modify or add to a basic FAP. Learned regional variations were added to the basic song pattern (FAPs) of sparrows in various areas along the Pacific coast of the United States.

Maturation The biological process of development through which any organism passes to become adult. It does not imply learning.

Fixed action patterns (FAPs) Species-specific behaviour patterns, genetically programmed and triggered by a stimulus or set of stimuli.

Sign stimuli

Many behaviour patterns need a specific external stimulus as a trigger; for example, the 'gape' of a nestling bird is the stimulus for the parent bird to regurgitate or feed the young. Triggers such as this have been termed **sign stimuli**. They can be of two kinds: (a) excitatory, promoting behaviour, as in the case of the nestlings, whose gaping beaks prompt the parent to feed them; and (b) inhibitory, as in the case of young turkey chicks (*Meleagris gallopavo*), who constantly emit a high-pitched sound which prevents the mother from killing them. This is an aural sign stimulus. Deaf turkeys may kill their young (Schleidt et al., 1960), because the mother does not hear the appropriate signal (cheeping), and responds with aggression. The excitatory and positive visual stimulus of young turkeys (actually being able to see her young) is ignored in the absence of the inhibitory auditory stimulus, and the young are killed as though they do not belong to her.

Attributes of sign stimuli Tinbergen (1951) studied sticklebacks (*Gasterosteus aculeatus*) to find out what stimuli encouraged the male to mate with a female, and to drive other males away from his territory. Using a series of experimental stimuli he showed that the red underbelly of the male was the stimulus to attack, whilst the swollen (grey-brown) underbelly of a female was the stimulus for mating.

Supranormal stimuli Even when they were **supranormal stimuli** (that is to say, exaggerated stimuli which are more effective than normal stimuli in eliciting a response), the same behaviour occurred. A red underbelly (however large) still provoked attack, while an abnormally large 'female' underbelly promoted repeated enthusiastic attempts at mating. Rowland (1989) demonstrated that a male stickleback directed courtship to a 'dummy' female with an abnormally large abdomen in preference to a 'dummy' female of normal proportions. In the real-life situation, courting the fattest female would result in more eggs laid in the male's nest, thereby optimizing his chances of passing on his genes. In the same way, if a greylag goose (*Anser anser*) is presented with a much larger (but correctly coloured) egg outside her nest, the goose will attempt to retrieve it by egg-rolling.
  This may cast some light on the question of why host birds will accept cuckoo eggs, which are often larger than their own, and the cuckoo nestling, which is often larger than the 'adoptive parents' themselves.

Displacement activities

As Tinbergen (1951) has described, recognizable behaviour was sometimes seen to occur in totally irrelevant contexts or situations. For example, an animal might break off from a threat display and begin to preen, or a male stickleback who has been attempting unsuccessfully to court a female, might break off his activities and swim to his nest-site, performing the 'fanning' movements with which he would ventilate eggs in the nest except that the eggs have not been laid! This type of 'irrelevant' behaviour Tinbergen called a **displacement activity**. What function does displacement behaviour perform?

Protracted conflict It has been suggested that stress or conflict causes displacement activities. Rowell (1961) suggested they occur when the animal is in a protracted conflict situation and inappropriate responses may be made.

Stress It has also been suggested that extremes of displacement activities can be produced in animals suffering severe stress or conflict, such as the bar-biting exhibited by sows in farrowing crates and the head-swinging movements of polar bears and elephants in captivity. In the natural situation there is usually an escape route from severe conflict; appeasement gestures can be offered, or flight, to terminate fights, or a new mate can be found if courtship does not proceed.

Time and space Displacement activities may simply fulfil the function of breaking off an unsuccessful pattern of behaviour and giving the animal time and space to find an appropriate response.

GLOSSARY

Sign stimuli Behaviour patterns providing a specific trigger for FAPs. The 'gape' of a nestling bird, for instance, is a trigger for parent birds to regurgitate food to feed it.

Supranormal stimuli Exaggerated stimuli which are more effective than normal stimuli in eliciting a response.

Displacement activity Apparently irrelevant behaviour, interposed into normal behaviour (courtship, for instance, or threat displays) resulting from conflict or stress.

Approach–avoidance conflict When a conflict of motives occurs, between, say, the need to gain access to food or water and something which gets in the way of satisfying that need (another animal, perhaps), then an animal will be in a state of stress. Time is needed for the animal to gather information so as to come to a decision. When there is an encounter between one animal and another, internal conflict may arise as to whether flight or attack is the best course. There may not be sufficient information immediately available about the other animal's fighting capacity or willingness to fight. In these circumstances displacement activity may occur. Masserman (1950) attempted to produce stress experimentally. Cats, trained to open a box for food, sometimes received a strong blast of air. Their behaviour became quite disturbed. Some became hysterical, others became depressed. Physiologically they showed all the signs of acute stress, raised blood pressure, gastric problems and hair erection.

Vacuum activities When the normal activities towards which animals are motivated are frustrated by the absence of suitable stimuli, animals may engage in **vacuum activity**. That is to say, they may still engage in what amounts to FAPs, even though the appropriate trigger for these patterns is missing. A hen would normally engage in dustbathing (scratching out and then wallowing in a patch of bare earth or dust). Even when confined to a cage with a wire floor the hen may go through the motions of scratching and wallowing. Vestergaard (1980) called this vacuum dustbathing. This animal is displaying very high motivation to perform a frustrated activity.

Displacement activities among human beings In his book *Manwatching: A Field Guide to Human Behaviour*, Morris (1977) describes how humans engage in displacement activities under stress:

> social occasions are, not surprisingly, riddled with displacement interjections. The host, as he crosses the room, is rubbing his hands together (displacement handwashing); one of his guests is carefully smoothing her dress (displacement grooming); the hostess is shifting some magazines (displacement tidying); another guest is stroking his beard (displacement grooming again); the host is preparing drinks and the guests are sipping them (displacement drinking); the hostess is offering round small tidbits and the guests are nibbling them (displacement eating).
>
> (Morris, 1977, p. 180)

Have you ever combed your hair, tied a shoelace, lit a cigarette, not because you needed to do these things but simply because you felt embarrassed or did not know how to respond to someone, and needed time to gather your thoughts?

Physiological concomitants of stress and frustration

Stress in animals may result from a variety of causes including frustration, overcrowding, extremes of temperature or the inability to escape from a position of apparent danger. Fraser and Broom (1990), in describing the physiological changes which accompany stress, point out that most are attempts to restore the delicate balance of the animal's metabolism.

Moderate stress In cases of moderate stress the activity of the autonomic nervous system is heightened. Adrenalin is released and other physiological changes take place:

- Sweat glands of the skin begin to secrete.
- Hair becomes erected.
- There is an increase in heart rate.
- Breathing becomes more rapid.
- Blood is redistributed towards the muscles.

These physiological changes apply not just to conflict situations but also where there is strong arousal, attack, escape or sex.

More severe or persistent stress Where the stressful situation persists, adrenocorticotrophic hormone (ACTH) is released by the pituitary gland, which prompts the adrenal cortex to release steroids. Under chronic stress animals may suffer from gastric ulcers, loss of hair or tumours of the pituitary gland; they may become ill enough to die.

In the natural environment there is nearly always the option of escape from a conflict situation as a last resort. The physiological results of prolonged stress do

---

GLOSSARY

Vacuum activity FAPs which occur even when there is no trigger stimulus.

not seem to be adaptive and no mechanism exists to deal with chronic conflict. Animals in captivity or human beings, however, may find themselves the victims of chronic stress or conflict.

Conflict and display

In some cases the conflicts which occur are connected to display. Red deer (*Cervus elephas*) may remain in a state of conflict: for example, while an assessment is made of an opponent's ability to fight. Roaring and walking up and down are part of the assessment process for stags. When a stag hears his opponent producing a high number of roars per minute he will assume his adversary is fit and strong and may retreat. The conflict situation will not persist.

(a)

(b)

Figure 16.3 Threat (left) and appeasement (right) in the lesser black-backed gull

Threat and appeasement Darwin (1872) described what he called the **principle of antithesis**. A species may exhibit two completely opposed postures to members of the same species. The first is the **threat posture** and the second the **appeasement posture** (Figure 16.3). Tinbergen (1959) has illustrated these postures in relation to the lesser black-backed gull (*Larus fuscus*). In the threat posture the bird moves towards its rival with its neck stretched upwards and forwards, its bill and head pointing down and its wings lifted clear of the body; its plumage is slightly raised. The appeasement posture is almost the complete antithesis. The head is held low and the bill points upwards. The wings are pressed close to the body. There is no way in which the bird is going to engage in attacking its opponent, which would involve beating with its wings and attempting to peck down on him.

Evolutionarily stable strategies (ESS)

Maynard-Smith (1982) developed a 'game theory' approach to these problems. This implies that an animal will develop strategies which have the best chance of enhancing life expectancy and reproductive capacity. Maynard-Smith called these **evolutionarily stable strategies (ESS)**. Once an aggressor has received an appeasement signal from his opponent his best strategy is to call off the fight. After all, if the fight continues there is the risk (albeit a small one) that he will lose, or else the greater risk that he may receive injury such as to impair his life expectancy or reproductive chances.

Furthermore, while he is engaged in the fight, time and energy are being lost which could more profitably be spent gathering food or protecting mates. Appeasement in the face of a stronger rival or the acceptance of appeasement from a weaker one is likely to confer an advantage in terms of passing on one's genes to the next generation. The genes which determine this behaviour

---

GLOSSARY

Principle of antithesis Darwin's description of the opposed postures adopted by members of the same species signifying threat or appeasement. A threat posture by one individual may trigger an appeasement posture from another.

Threat/appeasement postures Postures adopted by animals to indicate either a threat to another animal or an appeasement response to that threat.

Evolutionarily stable strategies (ESS) Strategies, described by Maynard-Smith, adopted by aggressors and opponents which have the best chance of enhancing life expectancy and reproductive capacity in each.

rather than fighting on in the face of damage and injury are more likely to be successful. Only if aggression can be carried through without serious risk would it be to the advantage of the individual not to accept appeasement if offered, or not to offer it in the face of greater strength. Evolutionary stability is unlikely to result either from consistently aggressive or from consistently subservient behaviour.

Complex situations

Sign stimuli and resultant behaviour patterns may be adequate in simple situations, but where decisions have to be made the direct responses may have to be adapted or modified. For example, Seeley (1985) describes the complex assessments of honeybee (*Apis mellifera*) scouts looking for new quarters. Premises are considered suitable only if they conform to a number of prerequisites. For instance, the volume of the cavity has to be between 15 and 80 litres, it has to have a south-facing entrance, smaller than 75 square centimetres, the nest site needs to be several metres above ground and between 100 and 400 metres from the parent nest. Seeley showed that the scout walked round and round the interior to assess its cavity. All other factors must also be weighed up and coordinated.

Davies and Brooke (1989) found that species which are currently host to cuckoo eggs (reed warblers, meadow pipits and pied wagtails) showed some degree of discrimination between their own eggs and model eggs. If the model eggs were similar to their own they would be accepted. Consequently, different cuckoos specialized in different hosts and laid eggs similar to their chosen hosts. In Figure 16.4 the top row shows cuckoo eggs from a reed warbler nest, meadow pipit nest and pied wagtail nest. The bottom row shows eggs from species often parasitized by cuckoos. From left to right: reed warbler, meadow pipit, pied wagtail, sedge warbler, robin. (Note the size difference, showing lack of discrimination in host birds.) Some species, such as flycatchers and reed buntings, would also make suitable hosts, as they have similar diets and nesting sites, but are not parasitized by cuckoos. These species, when tested, rejected all model eggs. Davies and Brooke suggest that they were once parasitized by cuckoos but their egg-discrimination skills became so good, they were no longer used as hosts. On the other hand, species which are no use to cuckoos, by virtue of unsuitable diet or location, appear not to have sophisticated egg-discrimination skills.

It would seem that while the basic genetic sign-stimuli prompts remain fairly consistent, when circumstances demand there can be many kinds of

| Reed warbler | Meadow pipit | Pied wagtail | Sedge warbler | Robin |

Figure 16.4 Examples of bird's eggs mimicked by cuckoos. Top row: cuckoo eggs found in reed warbler, meadow pipit and pied wagtail nests. Bottom row: eggs from species often parasitized by cuckoos

modification. Learning plays a part, not just in the individual's behaviour, but in that of the entire species.

❓ SELF-ASSESSMENT QUESTIONS

1. What are the processes and functions of imprinting? Support your answer with appropriate evidence from studies.
2. Define and give examples of (a) sign stimuli, (b) fixed action patterns, (c) displacement activities.
3. Describe an example of a genetically programmed component of behaviour which has been modified to accommodate a complex situation.
4. What are meant by evolutionary stable strategies? Describe an example of ESS.

A comparative study of learning and memory

As we noted at the beginning of this chapter, comparative psychology has a long history. Initially, a wide range of animals was investigated, even though studies of the rat and pigeon became by far the most common. Psychologists have always been interested in the study of learning and recently those with an ethological interest have started to investigate differences in learning ability between species. Thus, there is a reasonable amount of data that may provide evidence of evolutionary changes.

This section will examine some of the evidence from comparative studies of learning along with some of the problems encountered, will explore the question of whether animals can think and will consider some research which has investigated memory mechanisms in animals.

Problems in comparative research

Manning and Dawkins (1992) draw attention to the following pitfalls in comparative research:

■ **Human vanity**. Our essential vanity about human intellectual ability invariably leads us to search for an upward progression among animals, with human beings placed firmly at the top of the hierarchy. This has sometimes led to a failure to consider that there may be a number of possible hierarchies, each of which uses a different set of criteria. The question arises: should honeybees be judged by the same criteria as monkeys?

■ **Overemphasis on laboratory studies**. In the past, there has been an overemphasis on laboratory studies of learning, with less effort being made to investigate the role that various kinds of learning play in the natural life of different animals.

■ **Diversity among animals**. Different animal groups vary widely in their sensory capacities and manipulative ability. It is therefore not easy to devise truly comparable situations for testing different animals. For example, the procedures necessary to measure discriminative conditioning in an octopus, a honeybee and a rat need to be very different and it is not always possible to be sure that problems set are of equal difficulty or that the animals perceive them in the same way.

Motivation and reinforcement also represent problems. These are discussed fully in Chapter 9.

Because of the difficulties outlined above, some researchers have questioned the validity of any comparisons at all of intellectual ability between different animals (Macphail, 1987). However, others have attempted to devise valid comparative tests and some of the evidence collected is noted in the following subsection.

Evidence from comparative studies

Comparisons of brain development

Many studies have sought to examine the correlation between brain development and learning in animals. The main question considered is whether there is a link between the structure of the brain and the degree of complexity in the animals' behaviour. The factors which have been considered include brain size and the growth of the cerebral cortex.

Brain size   The prevalence of learning, the capacity to process information and the general complexity of behaviour are greater in mammals and birds than in fish and reptiles. These differences are thought to be linked to the evolution of a large brain – or encephalization (Jerison, 1985). However, brain size

---

GLOSSARY

Encephalization The extent to which a species has evolved a brain of large size.

is not the only important factor: whales and elephants have larger brains than humans but less learning capacity.

Growth of the cerebral cortex In vertebrates, the upper part of the brain, the cerebrum, is divided into two symmetrical cerebral hemispheres, linked together with a series of fibres at the corpus callosum. The outer covering of the hemispheres, known as the cortex, is a sheet of nerve cells arranged in layers. It is in the cortex that 'higher mental functions' such as thinking, reasoning and problem solving are thought to occur. The amount of cerebral cortex relative to the rest of the brain varies in different animal groups, with humans possessing the greatest amount. However, there is no simple link between the cerebral cortex and learning ability. For instance, birds have been underestimated in the past because the cortex is small relative to the size of their brains. In fact their learning ability has been found to be second only to that of the primates (see the account in Chapter 17 of the capacities of a grey parrot by Pepperberg, 1990a, 1990b). Birds have evolved along a separate line to that of mammals for over 200 million years and they have developed a different type of brain structure.

It is clear that brain structure alone is not a sufficient guide to learning abilities. Comparative studies of the behaviour of animals have added more to our understanding.

Behavioural tests

Simple learning capacity There is no reliable evidence that speed of learning in simple behavioural tests varies between vertebrates or between them and invertebrates. However, there is evidence that *what* is learned does systematically vary. Gellerman (1933) described a series of experiments in which two chimpanzees and two two-year-old children were learning that a food reward was associated with a white triangle on a black square and not with a plain black square. One child learned in a single trial but the other took 200 trials and both chimpanzees took over 800. Most rats took 20–60 trials. However, though the chimpanzee might take longer than the rat to learn this simple discrimination task, it learnt *more* about 'triangularity'.

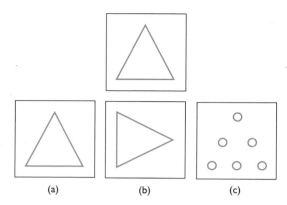

Figure 16.5 The concept of triangularity (Hebb, 1958). Trained to respond to the top shape, a rat makes random responses to any of the lower figures. A chimpanzee responds to (a) and (b) but makes random responses only to (c). A two-year-old child recognizes a 'triangle' in all three lower figures.

Learning sets It was once assumed that only more advanced mammals were capable of forming learning sets (see Chapter 6, p. 134). However, in a review of comparative studies, Warren (1965) suggested that all vertebrates with the exception of fish could do so. In more recent research, Mackintosh et al. (1985) showed that goldfish can form repeated reversal sets such as those described on p. 134, as can the octopus.

The speed with which learning sets are acquired differs dramatically between different animal groups. For example, Mackintosh (1983) compared rats and goldfish in a simple reversal experiment. Both learned the original reversal with roughly the same number of errors, suggesting that both animals found the problem of equal difficulty. However, afterwards, rats improved much more quickly than goldfish. In more difficult discrimination tasks, rats performed more slowly than dogs, cats or primates. No study has demonstrated that fish can ever improve their speed of learning in this situation.

Conclusions on comparative studies of learning

Manning and Dawkins (1992) suggest that we can cautiously conclude that cats and dogs show more signs of 'intelligence' than rodents and that primates do show greater superiority. However, they point out that many learning experiments do not do justice to the enormous flexibility and ingenuity of animals such as chimpanzees. Also, we may be influenced by their similarity to ourselves, especially as they can manipulate objects in the same way as we do.

It is possible that we underestimate the intelligence of other animals because they do not have good hands and good eyesight. Because their structure and environment is so different from our own, it is only recently that we have become aware of the exceptional intelligence of dolphins. Chapter 17 includes detail of research into the abilities of dolphins to comprehend language.

Can animals think?

No-one who has kept a pet or who has observed animals closely in the wild can have failed to wonder whether they 'think', 'reflect' on their actions or have a 'mind' and 'consciousness'. These words are in inverted commas because though we are all aware that these phenomena exist in ourselves, it is quite difficult to define them precisely; it is even more difficult to find evidence that they exist in animals. The information about these issues tends to be unsystematic and often anecdotal. Nonetheless, it is of considerable interest to many psychologists who study animal behaviour.

Some errors which may bias these arguments

Before discussing the question of whether animals have higher mental processes, it is important to be aware of some of the errors which can occur when interpreting animal behaviour.

Lloyd Morgan's canon and anthropomorphism A principle which has generally guided comparative psychologists in their work with animals is known as Lloyd Morgan's Canon. In the early twentieth century, Lloyd Morgan, one of the pioneers of comparative psychology, proposed that animal behaviour should not be interpreted as arising from higher mental processes if it could be interpreted in terms of simpler mechanisms. Morgan's guiding principle has enabled comparative psychologists to avoid some of the more absurd explanations of animal behaviour proposed in the past. Two examples of such explanations are relevant. These are included as Box 16.3.

These two, clearly absurd, claims about the thought processes of animals are classic examples of anthropomorphism – the tendency to attribute to animals

---

Box 16.3   Examples of absurd explanations of animal behaviour

Around the beginning of the twentieth century in Germany, Baron von Osten claimed that his horse (nicknamed 'Clever Hans') could actually count and calculate sums. On being presented with a sum, for example 5 + 6, the horse would give an answer by beating the ground with its hoof the correct number of times. It transpired that the horse was simply responding to unconscious changes in its owner's facial expression when it arrived at the correct answer.

Around the same time, Lewis Morgan (not to be confused with Lloyd Morgan) claimed that beavers possessed a complex understanding of hydraulics which enabled them to construct dams and channels.

---

human characteristics for which there is no real evidence.

Psychologists who study animal behaviour generally work hard to develop objective techniques and to avoid anthropomorphism. However, in doing so, researchers may fail to recognize that some animals might well be capable of thinking, reflecting and planning.

Animal thinking or anthropomorphism?

Manning and Dawkins (1992) describe three examples of animal behaviour which may indicate true 'thinking', and these are described in Box 16.4.

Manning and Dawkins (1992) have made a number of interesting observations about the examples in Box 16.4, whilst bearing in mind that they are 'one-off' situations, which makes generalization difficult.

The descriptions of the orang-utan and the sheepdog are isolated cases; the behaviour observed may not be seen again. However, this does not make them any less

---

GLOSSARY

Lloyd Morgan's Canon A principle proposed by Lloyd Morgan that animal behaviour should not be interpreted as arising from higher mental processes if it can be interpreted in terms of simpler mechanisms.

Anthropomorphism The attributing to animals of human characteristics for which there is no real evidence.

Box 16.4 True thinking in studies of animal behaviour

'Insight' in an orang-utan

Alfred Russell Wallace, the famous biologist who collaborated with Charles Darwin in his original theory of evolution, made some observations at the end of the last century. Whilst visiting the island of Borneo, Wallace studied a captive orang-utan. Close to the cage, a number of domestic chickens foraged for food. The orang repeatedly attempted to catch one, but they always managed to escape. On one occasion, Wallace saw the orang scatter grain from its food dish outside the cage, scattering some seed very close to the bars. It then sat quietly as the chickens discovered the grain and pecked their way right up to the cage. In a flash, the orang shot out its arm, caught one of the birds and killed it. (Compare this to Köhler's example of the ape, Sultan, on p. 132.)

'Problem-solving' in a sheepdog

Vines (1981) describes how a sheepdog dealt with the problem of a stubborn ewe, which refused to join the main flock. After a number of unsuccessful encounters with the ewe, the dog returned to the main flock, cut off several sheep and shepherded them over to the stubborn ewe. The ewe immediately joined this group, whereupon the dog shepherded them all back to the main flock.

'Anticipation' in honeybees

A number of people have recorded, rather than studied, some interesting behaviour in honeybees. Honeybees are known to communicate with each other about the nature and location of food by performing an intricate 'dance' system. (See Chapter 17 for a detailed account of this form of communication.) When studying communication in honeybees, it is often necessary to train them to forage at a dish several metres from the hive. For example, in one study described in Chapter 17, Esch et al. (1965) found variations in the speed of the dance depending upon how far from the hive the food was placed. Typically, in such studies, a dish of sugar solution is colour-marked and placed on the board of the hive. Once the bees start to feed, the dish is moved further out and then further. Initially, moves of more than a metre or two cause some difficulty, but as the day passes it is possible to move the dish 20 metres or more. At this point, researchers have reported an extraordinary occurrence. Often, as they move the dish to a new position, they find bees already there flying around looking for the food. Colour markings show that these are not newcomers attracted by the 'dance' and searching haphazardly in the same general direction; they are the original bees 'anticipating' the next position of the food source.

interesting or important. Some animal observers will argue that to have observed such behaviour at all significantly enlightens our view of animals. Others are more cautious: perhaps the orang spilt its food accidentally; Wallace's belief that he had witnessed true insight could be misguided. A question mark is thus raised both over the accuracy of the observations and over their interpretations.

Similar comments could be applied to the behaviour of the sheepdog. Dogs often have trouble with individual sheep. Nothing was known about the past experiences of this dog and it might simply have imitated the behaviour of older dogs during its training.

The example of the honeybees is extraordinary because the behaviour came from an insect. We are usually reluctant to consider the possibility that insects might think about the future or work out that a food dish may next appear in a particular location. However, this may well be the correct explanation. It is

as well to note, though, that in the paragraphs which follow, an alternative explanation is proposed.

Griffin's study of animal thinking

Griffin (1984) in an important book entitled *Animal Thinking* argued that although animal behaviour is not easy to interpret, it must now be accepted that true thought processes and some kind of consciousness must exist in some mammals and birds. From an evolutionary perspective, it is hard to accept that mind and consciousness in human beings have not arisen from similar processes in those animals from whom we have descended. However, even if this argument is accepted, we should not accept that honeybees have such capabilities without attempting first to eliminate other possible explanations.

In attempting to interpret the behaviour of the honeybees cited above, Griffin suggests that there might be a simple explanation. In their normal lives, honeybees sometimes follow a food supply which extends out in one direction. This occurs when the sun rises and the shadow of a hill or trees moves gradually off a flower crop; the flowers begin to open and emit nectar as they are warmed by the sun. This allows the bees to extend their feeding range as the shadow moves. It might follow from this, that the ability to move out along a line of food dishes may be a function of some inborn ability. Some kind of automatic and unconscious 'rule' might be operating as it appears to in the bees' amazing dance communication referred to earlier. We shall be returning to this, as has been mentioned, in Chapter 17.

A theory of mind

As was noted in the previous subsection, it is possible that an unconscious and automatic 'rule' might operate to affect behaviour in some animals. However, such a proposition is not sufficient to explain the behaviour of others. For example, Premack and Woodruff (1978) carried out a series of experiments which were designed to investigate thought processes in chimpanzees. A major aim was to try to discover whether the animals were capable of recognizing that individuals other than themselves had thought processes which are similar to their own. Such an understanding has become known as a **theory of mind**. If it were shown that animals do possess a theory of mind, it could be assumed that they should be capable of inferring wants, beliefs and intentions in others. Box 16.5 describes one such study.

The research provoked a lively debate about the existence of a theory of mind in animals. Astington et al. (1988) drew attention to the views of one participant in the debate, Dennett (1978). Dennett was not convinced that Premack and Woodruff's research methods had succeeded in demonstrating that chimpanzees possess a theory of mind and made the following observations (as quoted in Astington et al., 1988):

The spirit of Dennett's list of minimal requirements is simply that

- one should refrain from attributing a theory of mind to any organism whose own way of going about things can be just as easily understood without such mentalistic assumptions; and

Box 16.5 Studies involving theory of mind (Premack and Woodruff, 1978)

In one study, the researchers set up a situation where a chimpanzee was shown video pictures of a human being who clearly had a need for something. For example, one picture portrayed the person as huddled and shivering with cold in a room which had an unlit heater; another revealed the person vainly trying to open a locked door. The chimpanzee was then shown pictures of a series of objects (familiar to the animal), each of which could provide a remedy for the situation shown in the video, for example a burning wick for the heater; a key for the door. The researchers reasoned that to select the right picture, the animal would need to (a) anticipate the need of the person as distinct from itself, and (b) choose a solution as it might do so for itself.

In fact, the chimpanzee appeared to be capable of performing these mental operations. One chimpanzee chose the 'correct' picture seven times out of eight. Premack and Woodruff claimed that their experiments demonstrated that chimpanzees do possess a theory of mind.

- any candidate who is suspected of having such a theory of mind but cannot openly persuade us of this fact in his or her own words, must be set some behavioral task that makes the having or not having of such a theory explicit.

(Astington et al., 1988, pp. 393–4)

Clearly, Dennett did not believe that Premack and Woodruff's research had fulfilled these requirements.

It is important to note that Premack and Woodruff's original research report and the debate which followed stimulated a flurry of research into children's understanding of the minds of others. Such research has gathered momentum and theory of mind is currently a major focus in developmental psychology. There is a

GLOSSARY

Theory of mind The ability to understand the mental states of others; an appreciation that other individuals have wants, beliefs and intentions.

full discussion of theory of mind as it relates to the development of children in Chapter 20.

The study of memory

Learning could not occur without memory. To learn, it must be possible to store the results of experience and recall them to advantage later. As with learning itself, comparative research has been carried out into memory mechanisms. Important evidence has been collected from certain molluscs, the honeybee and some mammals. The study of human memory has provided many rich insights. Unlike animals, humans can report what they can and cannot remember, though their recollections are not always dependable. (See Chapter 14 for further discussion of memory.)

The nervous system and memory

Manning and Dawkins (1992) have argued that the study of memory clearly must include an investigation of the neurophysiological and biochemical aspects of how the nervous system can store some kind of representation of past experiences, in some cases for a lifetime. Despite much research, how memories of events are stored in the nervous system is still a matter of some speculation.

Two possible explanations of how the nervous system records memories of events are:

- The nervous system works by the transmission of electrical activity in neurons (nerve cells) along defined pathways. It is likely that the process of learning causes increased activity in those pathways which record stimulation of the sense organs. However, it does not seem likely that increased activity *per se* could constitute memory and that a memory could be recorded in the form of continuous flows of neural impulses moving around the same pathways for long periods of time.
- A more likely explanation is that when a memory is formed, some kind of structural change occurs in the nervous system so that some channels are made more accessible. It is now generally thought that this is the case. This explanation suggests that memory storage must be represented in a physical form.

Whilst accepting that one should investigate the biological basis of memory, Manning and Dawkins (1992) argue that the most important evidence for memory must be found by observing behaviour. What an animal does shows what it has learnt, stored and then recalled; from these observations it is then possible to infer memory mechanisms and then check them physiologically and biochemically.

Different kinds of memory

It is well established that not all our experiences are stored in the same way in memory. We can look up a page number in the index of a book and then find it impossible to remember it five minutes later; on the other hand, we can recall the addresses of friends even after many years. It has been suggested that the former is an example of short-term memory and the latter of long-term memory.

Evidence for two different memory stores Evidence for the existence of these two different memory stores comes from many sources. One source which is relevant to the study of memory in animals takes account of clinical studies of amnesia. People who have sustained a head injury or a severe shock are often unable to recall events that preceded the injury, though their short-term memory may be intact. This phenomenon is known as retrograde amnesia. Interestingly, where recovery occurs, the most distant memories tend to return before the recent ones. The condition of retrograde amnesia can also be created in animals. This is demonstrated in studies carried out by Andrew (1985) which are described below.

Manning and Dawkins have suggested that the process by which events are transferred to long-term

---

GLOSSARY

Short-term memory Memory for material required only on a short-term basis (for instance, memory of a telephone number retained long enough to dial it).

Long-term memory Memory for events and experiences stored on a long-term basis (for instance, recognition of someone you have not met for a long time).

Retrograde amnesia Inability to recall events before a head injury or other trauma while short-term memory remains intact.

memory is more labile and sensitive to disturbance than the store itself. Support for this conclusion comes also from studies with rats and chicks using drugs which affect the functioning of the nervous system. For example, low doses of strychnine or pecrotoxin which are powerful stimulants can actually enhance the early stages of memory if they are administered just before or just after a new task is learned. However, if a drug which blocks protein synthesis – for example, puromycin – is given at the same stage, memory of the new task does not consolidate and fades rapidly, though long-term memories are not affected (Andrew, 1991; McGaugh, 1989).

In studies using these techniques, the animal is presented with a task which can be recalled accurately after a single trial. For example, a chick learns not to peck at a coloured bead after finding on just one occasion that the bead is coated with a very bitter substance. In a study using the kind of task described, Andrew (1985) showed that there are drugs, for instance onabain and sotalol, which affect memory specifically at each of three time phases: short-term, intermediate-term and long-term. They are ineffective if used earlier or later (see Figure 16.6). Andrew suggested that this indicated three types of memory.

Corresponding to these periods of drug sensitivity, the ability to recall fluctuates precisely. Figure 16.6 shows these fluctuations. First, chickens pecked at a coloured bead coated with a bitter substance. Then, different batches of chickens were tested for their reaction to the beads. Initially recall was good; they avoided beads similar to the bitter one. After 14–15

minutes, however, memory faded. This was not normal 'forgetting' because recall returned a minute or so later. Fifty-five minutes after the initial event, a second dip in recall occurred. Finally, memory recovered more permanently.

Similar studies with rats also showed two dips in recall before long-term memory was established, although the timing was slightly different. There were parallel findings too with honeybees; their recall fell sharply after a learning experience and then recovered to a sustained level by ten minutes (Erber, 1981).

Manning and Dawkins believe that the studies described show the following:

- The precise timing of their ability to recall events suggests that animals retrieve their memories from different stores in turn. A dip in recall seems to result from the process of moving from a store that is fading to the next one which is forming.
- The nature of these processes remains to be investigated as does an explanation of how the different phases of memory interact with each other. Does each phase play a part in the formation of the next phase or does each form and fade concurrently, possibly interacting and conveying information as it fades and the next phase develops?
- However they interact, each phase must contain a representation of what has been learned. Long-term memory is shown to be formed in around an hour. As mentioned earlier, the formation of long-term memory probably results in changes in the structure of the brain which create neural impulses along new pathways. The processes involved in establishing short-term and intermediate memory probably involve nervous activity alone. This could explain why they eventually fade and why they are susceptible to physical shock and to drugs.

The study of memory is an exciting and relatively new area of research in comparative psychology. Studies by Mishkin and Appenzeller (1987) have further investigated the three phases of memory referred to above. Other research has considered the nature of long-term memory. Horn (1985, 1990) has reviewed the work of Bateson, Horn, Rose and colleagues, who studied imprinting by newly hatched chicks as a learning and memory system.

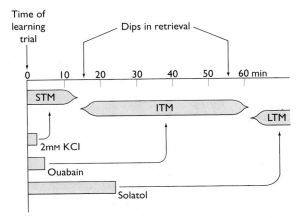

Figure 16.6 A scheme for the three stages of memory storage proposed by Andrew (1995)

SELF-ASSESSMENT QUESTIONS

1. Discuss some of the problems encountered when comparative research is carried out.
2. Evaluate some of the evidence drawn from attempts to compare intellectual ability between different animal species.
3. How would you respond to the question 'Can animals think'?
4. Briefly outline two likely explanations of how the nervous system may record memories.
5. Discuss some research which has provided evidence of three stages of memory storage in animals.

Chapter summary

- Adaptation to the environment enables animals to survive and to pass their genes on to succeeding generations. This adaptation occurs in two ways: by means of natural selection (phylogenetic adaptation), and also by changes brought about by learning during the lifetime of individuals (onogenetic adaptation).

- Within a species, differentiation of behaviour occurs as individuals adapt their behaviour to meet the environmental circumstances they find themselves in: for instance, changes in diet or location. This too can change through natural selection or through learning. Some behaviour becomes ritualized, particularly behaviour serving as a signal to communicate important information: for instance, concerning courtship and mating.

- Ontogenetic adaptation may be prompted by internal stimuli: maturation and changes in hormonal states and external stimuli such as the lengthening of days as spring comes. Genetic and hormonal factors interact to provide the ideal circumstances for reproduction and so the survivial of the genes.

- Optimal foraging theory describes how animals may balance the safest and most fruitful places to feed against the energy expended in getting to a better (safe from predators or more abundant in food resources) areas some distance away. Economic decisions have to be taken, relating to such factors as load-carrying capacity, the frequency with which young need to be fed, risk taking, and food availability.

- Early experience in young organisms to recognize and form attachments to parents is essential for their survival. Imprinting is one way in which the young may form attachments. Researchers such as Guiton and Hess have made discoveries about critical and/or sensitive periods during which this attachment may occur.

- Fixed action patterns and sign stimuli represent stereotyped behaviour patterns, which have particular characteristics described by Lea. They serve to excite or to inhibit behaviour so that individuals become better adapted. Displacement activities may occur when fixed action patterns may occur in irrelevant contexts or when there are no triggers available for this behaviour (vacuum activity). This is particularly evident in cases of stress or conflict.

- Evolutionarily stable strategies are described by Maynard-Smith: in these, aggressors and opponents behave in ways that have the best chance of enhancing life expectancy and reproductive success.

- Problems inherent in comparing learning and memory capacities between species relate to diversity of species, human vanity and an overreliance on the use of laboratory study. Brain size and encephalization as well as particular tests of learning capacity (studies of learning sets, for instance) do provide evidence that primates have more 'intelligence' than cats or dogs and that they in turn are more 'intelligent' than rodents.

- There is some evidence of thinking in animals, though there is danger of anthropomorphizing. There is also some evidence of a theory of mind among chimpanzees.

- Evidence from studies of memory in animals indicate that there are separate short, intermediate and long-term stores on which animals draw in turn. The nature of these stores and the ways in which they are used is as yet not fully explored.

Further reading

Hinde, R.A. (1966). *Animal Behaviour*. London: McGraw-Hill. A detailed account of animal behaviour from a biological standpoint.

Krebs, J.R. and Davies, N.B. (1993). *An Introduction to Behavioural Ecology*. Oxford: Blackwell. An up-to-date text on behavioural ecology.

Lea, S.E.G. (1984). *Instinct, Environment and Behaviour*. London: Methuen. This is a very readable introduction to the study of animal behaviour, which takes a broadly sociobiological approach.

Manning, A. and Dawkins, M.S. (1992). *Animal Behaviour*, 4th edn. Cambridge: Cambridge University Press. This book takes a broadly biological approach and links ethology with comparative psychology and physiology. An updated version of a key text in this area.

CHAPTER 17

Animal communication

The bases of communication   372
- The sensory world of animals   373
- Sign stimuli   374
- Social signals   374

Social communication   377
- Modes of communication   377
- Message or meaning   378

- Effectiveness of social communication in animals   379

Teaching human language to animals   382
- What is language?   382
- Teaching human language to other primates   384
- Experiments with other species   387

Objectives

By the end of this chapter you should be able to:

- Identify several ways in which animals respond to stimuli;

- Appreciate the importance for animals' adaptation of innate releasing mechanisms;

- Make an assessment of the effectiveness of intentional social communication;

- Evaluate the significance of von Frisch's description of the honeybee dance;

- Identify some of the criteria for language described by Hockett and others;

- Evaluate attempts to teach language to apes and other animals, including dolphins and a parrot.

The bases of communication

Animals respond in a wide variety of ways to their environment. Features within this environment may have one or more of several effects, including:

- Orientation,
- Eliciting a response from other animals,
- Arousal.

  Orientation refers to the means whereby an animal responds to the basic physical characteristics of its environment. It perceives light, gravity, air, water currents and similar things and responds so as to be in the right relationship to them. A fish rests with its head into the current. Even in total darkness, rats have a righting reflex which keeps them upright in respect to gravity. Honeybees guide themselves using the sun as a compass.

> **GLOSSARY**
>
> **Orientation** In relation to animal behaviour, orientation may represent the responses of an animal to the basic environmental situation. For instance, a fish rests with its head upstream.

Eliciting of responses refers to the way in which responsive behaviour occurs in relation to what an animal perceives. Specific behaviour by another animal or a specific feature in the environment is related to particular behaviour on the part of an animal.

Less specific responses relate to changes in level of **arousal**. Each incoming sensory pathway has collaterals which connect to the **reticular formation**. This is a collection of nerve fibres at the base of the brain which connect via nonspecific pathways to all the higher centres of the brain with the purpose of arousing them to action. An example is the 'priming' of responses found in the courting of doves. When a female dove sees a male courting, she undergoes hormonal changes which make her more ready to engage in nest building. However, this effect is not immediate. Her perceptions need to be repeated and to build up over several days before she comes to reproductive condition. Responses, first hormonal and then behavioural, are being made, not only specifically, in that the courtship results in nest building eventually, but also in terms of her arousal in a much more general sense. She becomes more receptive to what she perceives. Adler (1974) has provided examples of this phenomenon. He refers to '**pumps**', which act over a long period to increase receptivity, and '**triggers**', which produce an immediate and specific response. Suckling provides the 'trigger' to make the female rat produce milk for her offspring while the pregnant female's activity in licking and grooming her nipples has encouraged mammary gland growth. This is a 'pump' effect.

The sensory world of animals

Insect senses

It would be wrong to think of the world of animals as being the same as ours from the point of view of the sensory information they receive. In some instances the sensory world of animals extends beyond ours; in others not so far. Insects, for instance, have compound eyes which provide them with very different sensa-

Sensitivity of bee's visual system (left picture) as compared with human's (right picture).

tions from our own. Image formation is very rudimentary, but at the same time they have a very wide field of view and highly developed ability to detect movement. They can see colour but they have greater sensitivity into the ultra-violet end of the spectrum, with less sensitivity at the red end. Red is confused with black or dark grey. Bees are sensitive also to the plane of polarization of light and can use this sensitivity to locate the sun's position even when it is obscured by cloud. Our own flicker fusion frequency is about 50 cycles per second. This means that any light which flickers faster than this is seen as a steady light. Insect eyes may have a flicker fusion frequency of up to 250 cycles per second. This means that a fluorescent tube, working on alternating current (AC) mains supply at 50 cycles per second, is seen by us as a steady light while insects will be able to perceive the flickering of the tube.

The sensory systems of mammals

So much for the sensory world of insects, but mammals also have a different sensory world. A cat or a dog gains more of its information through smell. Griffin (1958) has shown that bats use an extraordinarily sensitive system of echo-location to locate objects and to hunt insects while they are flying.

Sign stimuli

The use of sign stimuli enables animals to pick out of the available array of sensory information available to them at any one time those features to which they must respond. This is discussed fully in Chapter 16. Examples include:

■ A male stickleback's responses to red colouring and to the swollen underbelly of the female.
■ Hen turkeys' responses to the cheeping sound of their chicks. When they hear it they accept the chicks; deafened birds kill the chicks.
■ Minnows' panic reaction when any fish is scratched or wounded and there is blood in the water.

There are several things to be borne in mind about sign stimuli:

■ The fact that something has been called a sign stimulus does not mean that the normal response to it occurs *only* in response to that sign stimulus.
■ There may be more than one sign stimulus which will elicit a particular response. For instance, as well as red colouring, a head-down threat posture by a male stickleback in another's territory will evoke an aggressive response. This provocative position is added to the colouring to provoke an even stronger response than either of them separately. This additive effect is termed heterogeneous summation.
■ Where animals rely upon inherited behaviour, it is more important for the survival of the animal that it never misses making a response to the stimulus than that there should occasionally be false responses. Driving away rival males from its territory was found by Tinbergen (1951) to be so important to a male stickleback that it showed extreme responsiveness to red colouring, even to the extent of showing aggression towards red flowers falling on to the surface of the water, or towards a passing red bus.

■ Similarly animals must never fail to respond to sign stimuli provided by a predator or to the alarm calls of other individuals. The alarm calls of other species too may provide early warning of impending danger. The ideal alarm call needs to carry as far as possible as well as giving the predator the least chance of locating the author of the alarm call. This will mean a constant pitch and a graduated beginning and ending.

Social signals

Releasers

Animals are frequently responsive to sounds, scents and colours in other animals. Lorenz has suggested that these sounds, scents and colours have specially evolved in order to evoke these responses (Lorenz, 1958). The term he used for them was releasers. The point he made was that the releasers and the animals' responses to them have become mutually adapted to each other in the course of evolution, so much so that these social signals have almost become a form of language.

Experiments with social signals

Baerends (1957, 1959) conducted a series of experiments which demonstrated the way in which herring gulls determine which eggs are there to be incubated and which might provide food to eat. So far as incubation is concerned, there is a strong preference for green colouring, but even more important than the colour of the egg is its speckling. The more speckled an egg is and the greater the contrast between the speckling and the background, the more the gull is impelled to roll the egg into the nest and incubate it. Other characteristics such as shape are unimportant. Square or cone-shaped 'eggs' are rolled into the nest,

---

> **GLOSSARY**
>
> **Sign stimuli** Signals to which an animal must respond. For instance, a male stickleback is programmed genetically to respond to the swollen underbelly of a female.
>
> **Heterogeneous summation** The additive effect of more than one sign stimulus which provokes a much stronger response than one sign stimulus only.
>
> **Releasers** Term used by Lorenz for those stimuli in the environment (sounds, scents and colours) which have evolved to elicit responses in animals.

just so long as they are speckled. Green colouring and speckling are the releasers for incubating behaviour. In contrast to this, where gulls are engaged in robbing nests to eat the eggs a red or a blue background colour becomes the releaser. Eggs with a green background colouring are the least likely to be eaten, even though they may be just as conspicuous. In the same way, speckling is not nearly as attractive to feeding gulls as it is to incubating ones.

Exaggerated characteristics

Ethologists have adopted the technique of creating mock-ups of stimuli and then systematically changing characteristics of these stimuli to see which ones seem to be the most important in evoking responses. Frequently it has been discovered that where some characteristic has been exaggerated, the response to it also becomes stronger. Tinbergen (1951) found, for instance, that an oyster catcher will attempt to brood a giant egg in preference to its own. The larger an egg is (within limits) the more it seems to stimulate incubation.

Another example is that of the silver-washed fritillary butterfly (*Dryas paphia*), studied by Magnus (1958). As they fly by, females of this species display a flashing orange wing pattern which attracts the males. Magnus devised a revolving drum which flashed the requisite orange wing pattern and thereby attracted the male fritillaries. The normal wing-beat speed of the butterfly is about eight beats per second. Magnus found that the faster the wing beat simulated on the drum the more attractive it was to the males, up to as high as 75 beats per second.

But, of course, the characteristics which provide releasers are not just for this purpose and the evolution of supranormal stimuli might militate against these other purposes so as to provide for stronger responses. Increasing the wing-beat speed of fritillaries might make the females of this species more attractive to the males but at the expense of less efficient flight. Perhaps the increased response to exaggerated stimuli simply reflects an increase in general arousal evoked by the larger stimulus rather than a specifically stronger releaser.

Selectivity in responses

An animal must inevitably have evolved a system to enable it to respond to certain stimuli within its environment and to ignore the rest. The discussion of sign stimuli above implies a filtering system which operates to separate those stimuli to which it will be genetically programmed to respond from those which will be passed over. Besides, it is quite beyond the capability of any animal's brain to process all the information presented through its senses. Barlow (1961) has calculated that there are roughly three million sensory nerve fibres entering the brain.

Filtering of information to the senses Assuming that each of these nerve fibres represents a switch which can either be 'off' or 'on', the number of possible combinations of sensory input is astronomical. The brain has to economize in handling sensory information and this implies that there must be a filter system. This filtering can occur at one of two points.

There may be **peripheral filtering** at the point where the information impinges upon the organism, through its senses. In humans this filtering in part takes the form of limitations in the sensitivity of the senses. We cannot hear sounds, for instance, above a frequency of about 20 kilohertz. It has already been noted that the sensitivity of human eyes falls short of being sensitive to ultra-violet light while honeybees have greater sensitivity. That is to say, the peripheral filtering system of the honeybee is different from ours.

There may also be **central filtering**. Selection of what stimuli are to be responded to, may be in the central rather than the peripheral nervous system, the brain rather than the senses. Lorenz (1937) has suggested that there might be a specific mechanism responsible for filtering out those stimuli to which the animal is genetically programmed to respond. He termed this the innate releasing mechanism (IRM).

Innate releasing mechanisms How an IRM operates can be illustrated by an example. Tinbergen and Perdeck (1950) studied the pecking responses of gull chicks. An adult gull's bill is yellow with a red patch on the lower mandible. The aim of Tinbergen and his colleague was to establish what characteristic of this

---

GLOSSARY

Peripheral filtering Limitations in the sensitivity of the senses so that an animal may select those stimuli to which it must respond and pass over other stimuli.

Central filtering Selection of which stimuli to respond to which takes place in the brain rather than in the senses.

bill provided the stimulus for the chicks to peck at it and for the adult to regurgitate the food brought back to the nest. Box 17.1 gives details of their experiment.

Results showed the patch on the mandible to be the crucial attribute. Contrast was important. Grey bills with black or white patches were responded to more than plain bills. Red colouring was important. A plain red bill attracted more responses than any other colour, and a red patch was responded to more than a black one even where there was less contrast. Head colour and head shape made no difference to the response. The central filter system seems to filter out redness and contrast and ignores bill colour, head shape and head colour. It is, however, still possible that filtering is peripheral. There is some evidence that blue light appears darker to birds' eyes than an equivalent quantity of red light and so might be more likely to seize the chick's attention.

Alarm responses

A factor which may contribute to the survival of a species is its ability to recognize and respond to the presence of possible predators. Certain species of birds – ducks, geese, pheasants and turkeys, for instance – raise alarm calls when a bird of prey passes overhead. Individuals with young can then respond by providing shelter. Turkey hens spread their tails as they give the alarm signal and the young chicks come and find shelter beneath them.

Box 17.1 Tinbergen and Perdeck's experiment to show the nature of an IRM

A number of cardboard models were made which varied the following attributes:

- head colour
- head shape
- bill colour
- the colour of the patch on the lower mandible
- the degree of contrast of the patch on a medium grey bill

Care was taken to present these models to the chicks in a standardized manner. First, each type of model was presented to an equal number of chicks which had not seen a model or a real adult gull before. Then the order of presentation was randomized.

Insect alarm signals In other species alarm signals may take different forms. Among insects, alarm systems are often chemical. Maschwitz (1964, 1966) surveyed 23 species of *Hymenoptera* and found evidence of alarm pheromones in all of them.

Chemical signals among mammals Carl (1971) in his study of arctic ground squirrels (*Spermophilus undulatus*) found that it was impossible to come close to groups of animals who set up waves of alarm calls which increased in intensity and duration as an intruder approached. On the other hand, he was able to approach to within three metres of an individual squirrel. They clearly found safety in numbers. There is some evidence that an alarm pheromone exists among rodents. Carr et al. (1970), among others, found that house mice produce an odour when they are under stress which causes avoidance by some other animals.

Responses to alarm signals Responses to alarm signals differ markedly between species, some displaying aggression and some panic flight. Wilson and Regnier (1971) found both of these reactions among formicine ants. Some species orient themselves aggressively towards the source of the problem while others scatter in all directions in panic.

Relationship between senders and receivers of alarm signals The chances are that the recipients of these alarm calls will be related to the caller. The apparent altruism of an animal drawing attention to itself to give warning of an intruder serves to enhance the chances of some of the animal's genes surviving. If the warning enables more than two of its brothers or sisters to survive, or more than eight of its cousins (a brother carries 50 per cent of its genes, a cousin 12.5 per cent), then the sacrifice of the calling animal's life will have been worthwhile in evolutionary terms. This is fully discussed in Chapter 18.

? SELF-ASSESSMENT QUESTIONS

1. Describe three ways in which an animal may respond to the physical nature of its environment. Discuss some of the functions of these responses.
2. In what ways is the sensory world of animals different from our own?
3. Describe some of the main functions of sign stimuli.

4. In what ways have animals become mutually adapted to one another? How do the social signals they employ contribute to this adaptation?

5. What seem to be the main functions of innate releasing mechanisms?

Social communication

So far in this chapter we have been concerned with the way in which animals respond to what they perceive in the environment in which they live. To say that an animal is communicating requires also that there is an element of purposiveness. An animal must *intend* to pass information to another, rather than simply receiving and responding to a signal within its environment. This does not necessarily mean that the intention needs to be conscious; it involves a mutual adaptation between the communicating animals to the benefit of both.

Communication will often be between members of the same species, but it does not need to be confined to this. When a skunk raises its tail and presents its hindquarters to a potential predator it passes information to it; as the saying goes – *'Nemo me impune lacessit'*, which roughly translated means 'No one gets away scot-free with harassing me'!

Even within this overall definition of what is meant by social communication there can be variants. Altmann (1962) has a broad definition: 'a process by which the behaviour of an individual affects the behaviour of others'.

This clearly applies to the skunk. Hinde and Rowell (1962) limit their definition somewhat to those visual signals which clearly had evolved for the purpose of affecting the behaviour of others.

Modes of communication

Different groups of animals seem to have specialized modes of communication which relate to the evolution of their sense modalities. These can include tactile communication, sound, chemical and visual signals.

Tactile communication

Tactile communication is important among many invertebrates, for instance among earthworms emerging from their burrows at night to mate, or among social insects. Among higher species, when one monkey spends time grooming another it is conveying general information about the social relationship which exists between the animals. There are clearly limitations on tactile communication. It can, by its nature, be used only at close range. Feeler range is about as far as it can go. It is not uncommon among humans as Figure 17.1 shows. The touch on the back is gently guiding the man's companion in the direction desired.

Sound signals

Where it is advantageous to communicate over longer distances and perhaps through obstacles, such as dense vegetation, sound is a more appropriate mode. Hooker and Hooker (1969) have described the way in which the African bou-bou shrike use low flute-like calls. While remaining concealed in dense vegetation the male and the female of this species conduct a kind of duet of alternating calls to one another. Low notes seem to have the characteristic of carrying through the

Figure 17.1 An example of tactile communication between men. A man gently guides his companion in the direction desired

undergrowth over great distances. The study by Payne and McVay (1971) into the 'song' of humpback whales has suggested that their communication can be received hundreds of miles away. Water is a better medium for sound communication than is air.

Chemical signals

Both insects and mammals use chemical communication, though there are limitations. Patterning is not possible, as it is with sound or visual signalling, and it is not easy to turn the signal off and on quickly. The information conveyed in this way needs to be relatively stable as well as relatively simple. 'This is my territory' is the message conveyed by mammals marking the limits of their territory; or 'I am ready to mate' when female animals secrete special chemicals to indicate their receptivity to the male.

These chemical signals referred to as **pheromones** are supposed to stimulate reproductive urges. It is believed that they are important in human communication also. Indeed, one kind have recently been incorporated into scent marketed by a cosmetics firm. Wilson (1965) has described the way in which chemical signals are adapted to their purpose. Pheromone and territorial signals need to persist well, so they consist of chemicals which are not too volatile. Where some insects use chemicals to signal alarm, persistence needs to be less. Consequently they can be more volatile.

Visual signals

The range of visual signals must inevitably be fairly short. Alarm signals often involve flashes of white which can be seen over quite long distances. The white underside of the tails of rabbits are an instance. Colour is quite important among fish, reptiles and birds, though less important among mammals, with the exception of primates, including humans.

Message or meaning

There are a number of separate issues related to message and meaning, including:

■ **Purpose and intention**. A male bird singing in its own territory may be conveying information about his present condition.
■ **Interpretation**. How the receiver interprets the message may be more than this. It may include

information not only about the sender's state but where he is, whether he has a mate and even who he is.
■ **Consciousness**. Some of this information may be consciously conveyed, other information unconsciously conveyed. In a similar fashion, humans convey certain information by what they say, and more information by nonverbal signals (what they are wearing, what postures they adopt, what gestures and what tone of voice they use).

Information conveyed includes:

■ **Sexual information**. Pheromones, for example, convey information about the transmitter's state.
■ **Information between parents and offspring**. Food calls or alarm signals are examples.
■ **Contact signals**. These are important for animals who live in groups: such calls are made by geese in flight. Lorenz (1952) describes the way in which a flock of geese on the ground take the decision to fly. One bird (or a few) begins to call. If this call to flight is taken up generally, then the flock will take to the wing. If too few respond the flock remains on the ground.

Metacommunication

Where the intention of a message is to qualify other signals which follow it, this has been termed meta-communication. Some carnivores (lions or dogs, for instance) invite their young to play with them. Forequarters are lowered as an indication that all apparently aggressive movements which follow are in fact only in play. Dogs sometimes also wag their tails during play fights. This kind of playful rehearsal of aggression is evolutionarily necessary. Young animals can be trained to stalk and attack without the risk of engaging in real fighting. Figure 17.2 shows a lion's lowered forequarters in play.

GLOSSARY
Pheromones Chemical signals which are said to stimulate reproductive urges.
Metacommunication So far as animals are concerned, communication which is designed to qualify or modify other signals. Forequarters are sometimes lowered by carnivores in apparently aggressive play to show that it is not 'for real'.

Figure 17.2 An example of metacommunication. The lion lowers its forequarters as a preliminary to play with its cubs

Pumps or triggers

Some signals are 'all or nothing', while others allow for a graded response. Brown (1964) found that Steller's jays (*Cyanocitta stelleri*) provide information regarding the amount of resistance which may be expected in case of an invasion of territory by the way in which their crests are held. If the bird intends to flee or if the approach is part of courtship then the crest is held flat. Otherwise the higher the angle at which the crest is held, the greater the resistance which is to be expected. Leyhausen (1956) attempted to grade the facial expressions of cats according to their aggressiveness and to their fear (see Figure 17.3).

The problem with this kind of signal is that it can be ambiguous to the receiver. In many cases it makes better sense to have a stereotyped signal. Alarm calls need to be of a fixed kind, as do sexual signals in many cases. Many signals have a pump effect in that they may be repeated on many occasions and over successive days, so that their effects gradually increase and make the receiver more likely to respond. Animals lacking as they do the resources of a symbolic language system have to rely upon context and upon the way in which signals are combined to convey their meaning. Attempts have been made, which will be described in detail later, to teach symbolic language to primates. However, in the wild, in spite of the fact that their social interactions may be quite complex, they exhibit very few gestures. While human beings frequently attempt

Figure 17.3 Expression of fear and aggressiveness in cats (after Leyhausen, 1956)

to deceive those with whom they are communicating, this seems nearly impossible for animals. Where there seems to be deceit, as in the case of the moth with eye spots, these spots are simply visual releasers, evolved to deceive predators.

Effectiveness of social communication in animals

The only way to be certain that animal communication works is to be able to measure responses to it. We have already seen some examples of the measurement of communication in animals. Tinbergen's experiments with the red spot on a herring gull's bill, mentioned above, are illustrative of attempts to measure visual communication. Clearly, the response of the chicks to various stimuli presented to them shows whether or not the communication has been received.

Noble (1936), studying yellow-shafted flickers (*Colaptes auratus*), a type of American woodpecker in which the only obvious difference between males and females is a small black mark or moustache beside the bill, captured the female of a pair of flickers and stuck a moustache of black feathers on to her. When she was returned to her mate she had a very rude reception. She was promptly attacked and driven from the male's territory, not to be accepted again until the moustache had been removed. The moustache was clearly a communication to the male of this species of woodpecker that here was a rival who had to be driven from the territory.

It is difficult to measure how effective a signal has been. For instance, if there is no response it may not simply mean that that signal is ineffective. There may be one of several reasons; for instance:

■ The receiver may have received the message but failed to respond for some reason.
■ The signal was not perceived.
■ The signal may act not so much as a trigger to set off a preconditioned response (as with the herring gull chicks), but as a 'pump' which has the effect of altering the perceiver's receptivity to subsequent signals.

Honeybee dance

Research by von Frisch (1967) on the **honeybee dance** has stimulated a great deal of discussion on the subject of animal communication, particularly relating to problems of measurement. It was known for a long time that bees must have some form of communication relating to flower crops, but it was von Frisch's careful observations which elaborated upon the dance system which bees seem to use to convey information about the nature and whereabouts of food sources. Box 17.3 provides details of von Frisch's study.

Some qualifications of von Frisch's findings - While von Frisch and his coworkers were convinced that the bee dance represented a form of communication between foraging bees and those which

Box 17.2 Experiments by Wells and Wenner designed to modify von Frisch's conclusions

Their hypothesis was that the dance merely stimulated bees to go out and forage. The food source was then located by smell. While they did not disagree with von Frisch's observations with regard to the form of the dance and the apparent relationship to the distance and direction of the food source, they asserted that this information is not communicated to the other bees in the hive. They paid more attention to the scents which adhered to the bodies of foragers from the food source and to the wind direction. Bees in the hive were given a choice of food source.

■ Some dishes were scented and placed at sites some distance from the hive. These had previously been visited and indicated by dances even though the scent had now been lost.
■ Other dishes, placed also at some distance away from the hive, were scented, but had not previously been visited or indicated by the dance ritual.

remained in the hive, Wells and Wenner (1973) have disagreed with this interpretation. Their experiment is described in Box 17.2 above.

It was predicted that if a large number of bees made the second of these choices, Wells and Wenner's olfactory theory was a more likely explanation than von Frisch's dance-language theory. This turned out to be the case. Additionally, it turned out that the direction of the wind was significant and this was not noted in von Frisch's experiments.

The important point about this in relation to animal communication is that it is very hard to show that communication has occurred unless the recipients of the message respond. Wenner's research seemed to show that the bees were not responding to the dances but to other cues. If Wenner's explanation is accepted then the relationship between the food source and the

GLOSSARY

Honeybee dance Dance described by von Frisch by means of which a foraging bee indicates to others in the hive the direction and distance of a food source.

Box 17.3   The honeybee dance

Von Frisch marked foraging bees as they drank from prepared dishes of sugar syrup and then observed their behaviour as they returned to the hive. For the purposes of this experiment, glass-sided observation hives were used. On its return to a hive, a forager contacted other bees on the surface of the comb and gave up its cropful of sugar syrup to them. Then the dance began. If the food source was within 50 metres of the hive, the bee performed what has become known as the round dance. Staying in approximately the same place on the comb, the bee moves alternately to the right and to the left over a circular path. Other bees face the dancer, sometimes in contact with her through their antennae. This round dance seems to be the signal which conveys the information: 'Leave the hive and search within 50 metres'.

When the food source (in von Frisch's experiments, his dishes of sugar syrup) was moved beyond 50 metres, the forager's dance changed its form. Between the turns to left and to right a series of short runs was incorporated with the bee waggling its abdomen rapidly from side to side. It is from this waggle dance – von Frisch claims – that much more information is transmitted and read back by other bees who follow every move the dancer makes, Work by Esch et al. (1965) suggests that bees also produce bursts of high-pitched sound during the waggling dance. The waggling dance remains essentially the same whether the food source is 100 metres distant or 5 kilometres. Distance is indicated by the tempo of the dance. There are nine to ten complete cycles of dance per 15 seconds when the food is 100 metres away, and this speed of dance falls off steeply at first and then more gradually until at 6 kilometres there are only two cycles of dance per 15 seconds. In addition to this there are correlations between the distance the food source is away, the number of waggles and the duration of each waggle. As the distance increases, both the number of waggles and the duration of each waggle increase.

However, it is perhaps the way in which the *direction* of the food source is indicated which is the most remarkable. Von Frisch discovered by means of repeated observations at different times of the day that bees, as they forage, record the direction of the food source relative to the sun. As they perform their dances on a vertical comb when the sun is not visible, this angle to the sun is transposed to the same angle relative to gravity. The waggle run is, for instance, 10 degrees to the left of the vertical where the angle of the food source relative to the sun is 10 degrees to the left of it. It follows that as the sun apparently moves across the sky, so the angle of the bees' dance, relative to gravity, will change.

The illustrations show the honeybee dance. Picture (a) shows the waggle dance. Picture (b) shows the sun's bearing on a vertical comb surface.

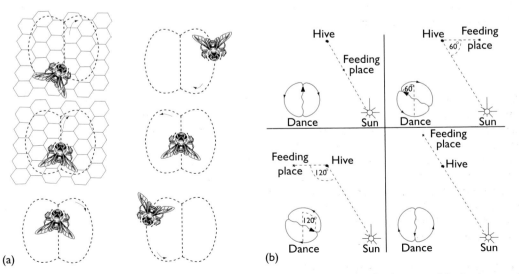

(a)

(b)

The honeybee dance. (a) The waggle dance. The straight-line part of the dance indicates the direction of the food source. The duration indicates the distance from the hive. (b) The relationship between the sun's angle and the direction of the dance

nature and form of the dance (which seems to be proven) does not have any obvious function.

Gould et al. (1985) have produced a very elegant solution to the problem. It was discovered some years ago that if there was a small point of light to the side of a vertical comb, the bees took this to be the sun. When dancing, a bee will treat this point of light in exactly the same way as it would treat the sun. A food source at, say, 10 degrees to the left of the sun is indicated by a waggle-run at a similar angle in relation to the point of light. If this light is not available then the bees orient their dances in relation to gravity. Gould blacked out the ocelli (simple eyes) on the dorsal surface of the bees' heads, so they then required a much stronger light source before they could respond. Gould made ocelli-blackened bees perform their dances on a comb with a very dim light source, so that they behaved as though there were no light and related their waggle-run to gravity. Watching bees with undamaged sight could therefore be misled (they took the light source, invisible to the dancers, as the sun) and would appear at dishes set out in a fan array according to the apparent angle indicated. The light on the comb was moved every 30 minutes. The angle apparently indicated therefore moved also. Gould also had all the ocelli-blackened dancers anaesthetized as they arrived at the dishes.

The results of this experiment showed clearly that Wells and Wenner's olfaction theory was mistaken and that von Frisch's dance-language hypothesis was correct. As the light source was moved so the new recruits among the bees shifted their attention to dishes displaced by an equivalent angle. It appears fairly certain that communication does occur by means of the dance. The important point is that measurement of whether communication occurs must depend upon the observed behaviour of those receiving the communication.

More recently still, Michelsen and his colleagues have gone further towards demonstrating that von Frisch was right (Michelsen, 1989; Michelsen et al., 1989). They constructed a brass model which they placed in the hive and allowed to become covered with beeswax. In this way it acquired the odour of the colony. The model could be moved through the waggle dance in simulation of the bee dance and even had an artificial 'wing' which simulated the acoustic field around the real bee dancer when it was vibrated. It was successful in that foragers were induced to visit dishes of food not previously visited and the directions they move in and the distances they travel correspond to the

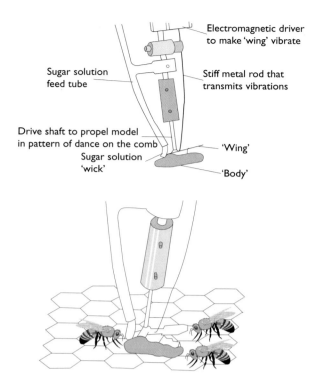

Figure 17.4 The dancing bee model of Michelsen et al. The upper diagram shows detail of its construction, and the lower diagram its position in the hive

'dance' pattern of the model. The model is illustrated in Figure 17.4.

❓ SELF-ASSESSMENT QUESTIONS

1. In what ways may animals purposively convey information as a form of social communication?
2. What sorts of information are conveyed in this way?
3. What evidence have we for the effectiveness of this kind of social communication?
4. Make some assessment of the significance of von Frisch's investigation of the honeybee dance.

Teaching human language to animals

What is language?

Before discussing attempts which have been made to teach human language to animals, it is as well to be clear about what constitutes language. Is it just communication, as described in the earlier parts of this chapter? Or is it a wholly different order of things? Brown (1973) has claimed that language has been a critical attribute of human beings for between one and three million years. This is quite impossible to establish beyond doubt. There are no fossil remains (or indeed other remains) which provide evidence of *spoken* language going back to an early date. Writing systems (which can of course leave remains) go back some six thousand years.

Clark and Malt (1984) have suggested that a fully fledged language has to have the following attributes:

- It has to be reasonably regular in form so that it can readily be learned by children.
- Because spoken words disappear so quickly from our echoic memory (the most immediate and most basic form of retention) it must be possible to interpret what is spoken very rapidly.
- It must be capable of capturing those ideas which people want to convey. It follows that there is a very close relationship between the context in which people live and the language which they speak. To take an example of this, human beings are sensitive (because of the nature of their visual system) to four primary colours – red, green, blue and yellow. Where language has a limited number of terms to depict colours, these four colours are always included.
- Language must be able to function in a social setting. It must be an aid to the social relationships between people.

Hockett (1959, 1960) proposed a number of criteria for defining human language. First there were several 'design features', as he termed them, which seem appropriate enough for human spoken language, but are less applicable to written language or to other nonspoken forms of human language (for example, sign language as used by the deaf, semaphore or morse signalling systems or perhaps even the 'ticktack' code used by bookies on race courses). These are detailed in Box 17.4.

Brown (1973) has selected three of these features as essential for language: semanticity, productivity and displacement. We shall discuss further the extent to which those who have attempted to teach human language to apes and other species have been successful in meeting these criteria.

How far do these criteria go towards suggesting that animal communication is in fact the use of language?

Box 17.4   Hockett's 'design characteristics' of language

- **Vocal/auditory character**: Language is seen as carried by sound, made vocally and received auditorily.
- **Broadcast transmission and directional reception**: Language is broadcast and the receiver must be able to tell where it comes from.
- **Rapid fading**: Vocal language fades rapidly.
- **Feedback**: It must be possible for someone using language to hear what he or she is saying.

Hockett also included a number of design features which have become accepted as criteria by which language production by animals may be judged. These include the following:

- **Interchangeability:** Language is a two-way process of communication with speakers able both to send and receive information.
- **Specialization:** The speech function is for communication only and is not a by-product of any other form of behaviour.

- **Semanticity:** Language conveys meaning.
- **Traditional transmission:** This refers to the possibility of transferring language skills from one generation to the next.
- **Learnability:** Language can be learned.
- **Discreteness:** Information is coded not by the length of the utterance but by the position of the phonemes (the units of utterance).
- **Displacement:** This involves the ability to convey information about things which are not present in time or place.
- **Duality of patterning:** There is a double pattern to language. Words are made up of phonemes, sentences of words.
- **Productivity:** A user of language is capable of generating an infinite number of novel utterances.
- **Prevarication:** Language can be used to talk about impossible things or things that are not true.
- **Reflexiveness:** Language can be used to talk about language.

Much of what has been discussed so far in this chapter is not so much language as signalling. It falls down especially on the criterion of displacement. Von Frisch's account of the honeybee dance, however, does seem to be an exception. Information is passed to other worker bees about the location of nectar which may be at some distance from the hive. But even if it passes the criterion of displacement, other of Hockett's criteria do not seem to apply. For example, there is no evidence for prevarication. Bees convey information about where the sources of food are, not where there are no sources of food. Productivity also is lacking. The dances are set patterns and there is no way in which an infinite number of novel utterances may be generated.

Teaching human language to other primates

The Kelloggs and the chimpanzee 'Gua'

Attempts have been made over many years to show that the use of language was not a species-specific attribute of humans but was a result of human intelligence. It was argued that if this was the case it ought to be possible to teach animals who were close to humans on the phylogenetic scale (chimpanzees and gorillas particularly) to use language. An early attempt by the Kelloggs (Kellogg and Kellogg, 1933) was a complete failure. The chimpanzee 'Gua' was not able to utter a single word despite being brought up with the Kelloggs' own child and treated exactly alike. She was, however, capable of understanding about 70 words or commands.

The Hayes and 'Vicki'

Keith and Cathy Hayes (Hayes, 1951; Hayes and Hayes, 1952) used operant conditioning to teach their chimpanzee, Vicki, to talk. This too seems to have been a failure. The problem was that chimpanzees lack the vocal apparatus to make the sounds of human speech. Taking account of this, a number of researchers began a different approach.

The Gardners and 'Washoe': attempts to use sign language

Gardner and Gardner (1969) used American Sign Language (ASL) as a medium. They appear to have had much greater success with 'Washoe', a female chimpanzee, than the previous researcher. ASL uses gestures to represent words and there are also devices to indicate verb tense and other grammatical structures. The Gardners created an environment for Washoe that was as close as possible to that which might obtain in a household where the parents were deaf. They signed to Washoe and to each other in her presence and rewarded correct gestures by the chimp. By the time Washoe was four she had mastered 160 signs. The following positive results were obtained:

■ She was able to generalize. A sign representing a particular object or activity might be used for a similar one. She even overgeneralized as young children often do.

■ She also began at a fairly early stage to string signs together; at first, just two signs together. Braine (1963) has described the way in which young children string words together in terms of pivot and open words. For example, in utterances like 'milk allgone' and 'Sarah sleep', 'allgone' and 'sleep' are pivot words which can be combined with a number of different open words. Washoe combined signs in a similar fashion.

■ There was even some evidence of displacement in Washoe's signing. There were times when she seemed to be referring to objects which were not physically present.

■ She was even able to recombine signs to express new meanings. She was shown a swan and was asked 'What's that?' She replied 'Water bird'.

An evaluation of the Gardners' attempts At first sight it seems that Washoe developed a 'language' which met at least some of Hockett's criteria, but there does need to be some caution:

■ There is a danger of anthropomorphizing (treating Washoe's behaviour as though it was that of a human). While she used some of the signs used by a deaf person there is no way of knowing whether they had the same meaning to her as they would have had to a human. Semanticity is difficult to prove.

■ Many of the gestures which she learnt were those which were natural to apes in any case. There is a great deal of overlap in the gestural repertoire of Washoe and of untrained apes.

Two of Washoe's signs: left, signing 'sweet' for lollipop; right, signing 'hat' for woollen cap

- Washoe mastered only the hand configurations of American Sign Language. Signs used in ASL are defined in terms of four parameters – hand configuration, movement, orientation and location. The Gardners seem to have focused only on the first of these.
- In relation to syntax, Washoe seems to have developed a consistency in the way in which she combined signs which might indicate an understanding of syntax. However, Terrace et al. (1979) carried out a detailed analysis of the 35 multisign sequences which Washoe used in the film *Teaching Sign Language to the Chimpanzee, Washoe*. All of them were preceded by a prompt from the teacher, so the ordering of signs might have been purely imitative and not due to a mastery of syntax.

The success of the Gardners with Washoe prompted others to make similar efforts to train primates to use forms of language. Patterson (1978) trained Koko, a gorilla, and made the claim that 'language is no longer the exclusive domain of man'.

The Premacks and 'Sarah': attempts to use symbols

An alternative approach was adopted by Premack and Premack (1972) who developed an artificial language of symbols (plastic shapes which could be attached to a magnetic board) and taught it to an ape, Sarah. She made significant progress. She certainly seemed to have some understanding of the relationship between the symbols and the meanings they represented. She also seemed to understand the significance of word order in expressions like 'red on green' or 'green on red'. She could arrange coloured cards to correspond with a sentence or construct a sentence to describe the way the cards were arranged. She could construct sentences containing the verb '*be*', and use the conjunction '*and*' as well as terms for colour, shape and size. She was able to follow commands from a sentence of symbols that represented such things as 'Sarah, put the banana in the pail and the apple in the dish'. When she was shown two objects, a key and a pencil for instance, and the symbols for them, she could pick the correct symbol for 'same' or 'not same' 80 per cent of the time.

Savage-Rumbaugh, 'Lana' and 'Kanzi': attempts to transfer training from one chimp to another

A chimp, Lana, was taught to communicate on a computer keyboard by punching symbolic keys. More recently, Savage-Rumbaugh et al. (1983) studied a pygmy chimp called Kanzi who learned symbols by watching other chimps being trained. Kanzi learned to combine symbols, make statements and ask for things. When another chimp, Austin, was removed from Kanzi's compound he typed the symbols for Austin and TV and was then quite happy to watch a videotape of Austin (*New York Times*, 1985). There is some evidence that all these animals have acquired complex skills. It is much more difficult to assess whether this amounts to language acquisition.

Terrace and Nim Chimpsky

Terrace (1979) attempted to teach language to a chimpanzee called Nim Chimpsky (a pun upon the name of Noam Chomsky, the linguist who has been foremost among those who claim language to be a species-specific capacity in humans). Between the ages of 18 months and three years Nim was observed to have used more than 19,000 'utterances' consisting of two or more signs. Analysing these two sign combinations, Terrace and his colleagues found that of combinations consisting of a verb and either 'me' or 'Nim' the chimpanzee chose in 83 per cent of cases to put the verb first – 'hug Nim' rather than 'Nim hug'.

Comparisons with human children's speech In Chapter 20 there is an account of children's acquisition of language. An analysis of children's speech when they start to produce two-word combinations has shown that in about 80 per cent of cases their utterances are in one of eight semantic categories: action + object, for instance 'drink milk', or object + beneficiary, 'food Sarah'. Terrace found that 84 per cent of Nim's 'utterances' fell into one of these semantic categories.

So far it looks as though Nim's utterances show a striking similarity to those of young children. However, while children rapidly develop throughout the period between two and four years old from producing two-word utterances to stringing sentences together of four words or more, Nim remained stuck with two-word utterances. While children's three- or four-word utterances extend the meaning of what they are trying to say beyond what they could say in two words, Nim's three-word combinations often did little more than repeat or emphasize. So you find not 'Give Nim banana' but something more like 'banana Nim banana Nim'. Videotaped interactions of Nim's utterances revealed further differences between the chimp and the average child at a similar stage of language development.

Far more frequently than with human children, Nim's utterances interrupted signs which his handlers had been making. Instead of the turn taking which Trevarthen, among others, had noted in small children from babyhood (Trevarthen, 1974a, 1974b), Nim did not appear interested in making conversation.

When small children start to talk, about 20 per cent of their utterances are imitative of their parents' expressions, and about 30 per cent are spontaneous and not in response to something an adult has said. With Nim the proportions were 40 per cent imitative and only about 10 per cent could have been regarded as spontaneous. Nim used language in a markedly less creative and more imitative way than human children do.

Evaluation of attempts to teach human language to apes

The question at issue is this. Can it be said with any degree of assurance that language is not a species-specific capacity in humans? Or is it a function of intelligence which is related in turn to the position animals occupy on the phylogenetic scale? The answer rests in part upon the extent to which workers have been able to impart language (as defined by Hockett's criteria) to animals close to us on the phylogenetic scale. Of these criteria some are clearly not relevant to the use of ASL as a 'language' and can be discounted. The main design features with which we are concerned are therefore the following:

- Interchangeability,
- Displacement,
- Productivity,
- Traditional transmission,
- Prevarication, and
- Reflexiveness.

Interchangeability There is some evidence that chimps in a colony set up by Roger Fouts in Oklahoma (Fouts, 1972) showed **interchangeability**. Washoe went there after she left the Gardners. The animals freely gave and received signs among themselves even when there were no humans present.

Displacement Washoe would sign 'time eat', which suggested she had a concept of time, and Fouts designed an experiment to demonstrate **displacement**. One chimp is taken out of the sight of the others and shown two hidden 'presents', one pleasant

---

GLOSSARY

Interchangeability The two-way nature of language where each party to a communication may send and receive information.

Displacement The ability of language to convey information about things which are not present in time or place.

and one unpleasant (food, perhaps, and something chimps dislike (a stuffed snake, for instance). Then the chimp is taken back to the other chimps and left for a while. Evidence of displacement was found in that the chimps managed to convey where the 'presents' were.

Productivity   Evidence from Terrace (1979) does not seem to back claims for apes' **productivity**, but Koko, Patterson's gorilla (Patterson, 1979), seems to have devised her own form of swearing, 'You big dirty toilet!'

Traditional transmission   There does seem to be evidence that Washoe succeeded in passing her signing skills on to her children (**traditional transmission**). Certainly, chimps seem to be able to learn signs from each other when they are living together.

Prevarication   Patterson described what she claimed was evidence for prevarication. When she puts a stethoscope to her ears Koko smirked and put her hands over her eyes.

Reflexiveness   Patterson described how Michael, a gorilla who lived with Koko, correctly copied signs made by Koko and was rewarded by Koko signing 'Good sign, Michael'.

All this seems rather inconclusive. The conclusion which Terrace has drawn is 'I can find no evidence confirming an ape's grammatical competence, either in my own data or those of others that could not be explained by other processes' (Terrace, 1979, p. 67).

The researchers themselves seem to be convinced that there is evidence for interchangeability, productivity, reflexiveness and prevarication. In an attempt to avoid bias in their results the Gardners used double blind techniques. Washoe had to make an appropriate sign for a series of photographic slides shown to her in random order. Another researcher who could see the slides was asked to record the signs which Washoe made. It is clear that if the signs made were clear enough for the observer to understand and this seemed to be the case, then Washoe must have understood the meaning of the signs and could name objects correctly. There is evidence of displacement in the account given by Patterson of a conversation with her gorilla, Koko, which took place three days after Koko had bitten Patterson:

Me: What did you do to Penny?
Koko: Bite.
Me: You admit it.
Koko: Sorry, bite, scratch. Wrong bite.
Me: Why bite?
Koko: Because mad.
Me: Why mad?
Koko: Don't know.

(Patterson, 1979, p. 459)

There remains the problem that apes do not seem to sign without prompting. Many apparently original signs made are in fact responses to questions or they are straightforward imitations of signs made to them. Their signs could be chains of operant responses which the apes use to get what they want from their trainers.

Experiments with other species

These include marine mammals such as dolphins and an African grey parrot. Batteau and Markey (1968) attempted to introduce an artificial language to dolphins and succeeded in testing the ability of dolphins to respond to simple commands given by artificially generated whistle words. However, owing to the death of Batteau, this project was not completed and such detail as exists appears only in an unpublished government report.

Comprehension or production of language

Researchers in this area appear to have had a comprehension approach in mind, as opposed to the production approach adopted by the experimenters with apes, mentioned above. Herman and his colleagues (Herman et al., 1984) have claimed that there is merit in concentrating upon comprehension rather than production as a critical measure of sentence processing. It is hard to assess the production of language by apes quantitatively or to be objective in the interpretation of what is produced. This is true even of the production of language by human children. The assumption that production implies comprehension is not necessarily valid.

GLOSSARY

Productivity The ability of a language user to generate an infinite number of novel utterances.

Traditional transmission A characteristic of language that it is possible to transfer the skills involved from one generation to the next.

Echolalia   The production of speech without meaning is a feature of some psychotic behaviour and has been termed echolalia. It involves the meaningless repetition of the last word that was heard. Production may easily be prompted by nonlinguistic cues, as Terrace (1979) noted in his criticisms of the Gardners' work. He regarded grammatical structure as part of the essential definition of language and suggested that the Gardners had not conclusively shown Washoe's understanding of this. Much of what he observed in his detailed analysis of the Gardners' film of their work with Washoe could be explained by operant conditioning. A key human linguistic skill is the tacit use of grammatical features of a language to produce and comprehend sentences, including ones that are novel to the user. Chomsky describes this 'mysterious ability' in the following terms: 'Having mastered a language, one is able to understand an indefinite number of expressions which are new to one's experience and one is able with greater or less facility to produce such expressions on an appropriate occasion' (Chomsky, 1972, p. 100).

Teaching dolphins to comprehend language

Experiments with Kea   In parallel with research where attempts were made to teach sign language to primates (Gardner and Gardner, 1969; Patterson, 1979; Terrace, 1979 etc.), Herman et al. (1984) taught dolphins to respond by using a 'language' which did not necessitate them having to produce the sounds of human speech. There were two versions of this 'language'. Their original experiments began in January 1977 with a dolphin (*Tursiops truncatus*) Keakiko ('Kea'). Sounds were generated by computer to represent each of three objects (a ball, a life ring and a styrofoam cylinder) and each of three actions (to fetch, to touch and to mouth). Kea was able to learn these. She was also able to respond immediately to new objects which were instances of the class of old objects (new balls of different colours and textures, for example). She was also able immediately to generalize her action responses to new (and unnamed) objects introduced into the tank.

The way it worked was something like this. Two-word sentences were produced consisting of object + action (e.g. 'ball fetch'). The naming of the object first provided a bridge on which the action signal that followed was contingent. Kea was quite quickly able to respond flawlessly to each of the nine possible two-word

sentences. Unfortunately, the project came to an abrupt end with the abduction of Kea. She and Puka, another dolphin in the same tank, were abducted and taken in a small van to a remote location where they were abandoned in the open sea. It is doubtful whether long-domesticated dolphins would be able to survive the stress of removal from familiar surroundings to the wild.

Akeakamai and Phoenix   A new project was begun in 1979 with two new female dolphins, Akeakamai and Phoenix. Akeakamai was taught to comprehend an acoustic language, while Phoenix was taught a gestural language. The 'languages' had a lexical component (words) together with a set of syntactical rules. 'Sentences' were composed of a sequence of words which expressed a unique semantic proposition and ranged in length from two to five words.

In English, word order may drastically alter meaning and this was the case also in the artificial dolphin languages. The language which Akeakamai was taught was produced by computer-controlled wave-form generators and consisted of short whistle-like sounds. Phoenix was trained to use a gestural 'language' composed of unique movements of her trainer's arms and hands. The vocabulary of these languages consisted of words which could easily be combined with other words to form meaningful sentences. With a comparatively small vocabulary hundreds of sentences could be produced. While some of the words were used for training purposes, others were set aside for the testing of the comprehension of novel sentences and syntactical forms. A sentence might be novel lexically in that while the syntactical pattern is familiar, there are new lexical items (words). Alternatively, a syntactically novel sentence is one where the words are familiar but a new sentence form is introduced for the first time. A sentence might be reversible syntactically: 'Take the frisbee to the surf board' or 'Take the surf board to the frisbee'. To find out whether the dolphins had constraints on their ability to use word-order information, the researchers trained Phoenix to use an inverse grammar rule ('to surf board, frisbee take'), while Akeakamai was trained to use a more straightforward left-to-right grammar ('frisbee take to surf board').

Cognitive capabilities of dolphins

Quite apart from examining the sentence-processing abilities of dolphins, Herman and his colleagues were aiming at studying the cognitive capabilities of the dolphins. Complex information processing was, they claimed, in part a skill which could be improved by education. In a similar way, the full realization of human potential is largely dependent upon long-term special education. Knowledge structures are greatly enriched through education, which serves to expand the ability to recognize and solve problems.

Box 17.5, on the following page, shows the vocabulary which Phoenix (P) and Akeakamai (A) were able to comprehend.

An evaluation of Herman et al.'s attempts to teach language to dolphins

Herman and his colleagues claim that their study has demonstrated that dolphins can understand imperative sentences and that this understanding involves the use both of the semantic and the syntactic elements of language. Phoenix and Akeakamai used two different modes, acoustic and visual, and two different sets of rules, in relation to word order. Regarding semantics, both dolphins found it easy to generalize from one example of a class to others which they had not previously met. Not only were they able to understand lexically novel sentences (ones that contained words

which they had not previously met) but structurally novel ones as well. This understanding of structural innovation included the integration of linked action words (that is, turning more than one command into an integrated response). What these dolphins were able to demonstrate was far more than a set of stimulus–response chains as occurs with operant conditioning. There was more reliance upon the understanding of sets of recombinable lexical elements held together by syntactical rules than upon contingencies between stimulus, response and reward.

It was claimed that the dolphins' ability to understand that arbitrary symbols could be made to stand for real-world objects encouraged researchers to look more creatively at natural communication among animals.

Special, intensive and protracted education was seen as having dramatically enhancing effects upon the dolphins' cognitive and knowledge structures. They became more capable, in a general sense, as a result of the training they received. This has profound implications for human formal education.

Herman's work with dolphins represents a radical departure from the language work with apes carried out by researchers such as the Gardners, Patterson and Savage-Rumbaugh in that it concentrates upon comprehension rather than production of language. McNeill (1970) outlined reasons for studying comprehension rather than production in humans in the following terms: 'In comprehension the investigator knows what the input to the process is – it is the sentence comprehended. Thus when comprehension fails, the source of the trouble can be located. The same cannot be said of production' (McNeill, 1970, p. 11).

As regards Hockett's criteria for language, much of it seems to be geared to the production of language rather than its comprehension, but there was evidence for displacement and semanticity in some of these studies with dolphins. The dolphins certainly understood meaning, and they both searched for missing objects which had been referred to and 'reported' their absence using the NO symbol.

Parrot talk

It has long been assumed that the ability of parrots and similar birds to mimic human speech is simply that, mimicry, and does not imply that they are capable of using language with any degree of understanding. But Irene Pepperberg (1983, 1987, 1990a, 1990b) has been conducting studies with an African grey parrot

Box 17.5 Comprehension vocabulary of dolphins (Herman et al., 1984)

Comprehension vocabulary of Phoenix (P) and Akeakamai (A); if only one dolphin understands a listed word it is followed by the initial of that dolphin

Objects

Tank fixtures

GATE (divides portion of tank; can be opened or shut) (P)
WINDOW (any of four underwater windows) c
PANEL (metal panel attached underwater to side of tank) (P)

Relocatable objects a

SPEAKER (underwater)
WATER (jetted from hose)
PHOENIX (dolphin as object) (A)
AKEAKAMAI (dolphin as object) (P)
NET c, d

Transferable objects b

BALL
HOOP
PIPE (length of rigid plastic pipe)
FISH (used as object or reward)
PERSON (any body part or whole person in or out of water)
FRISBEE
SURFBOARD
BASKET

Actions

Take direct object only
TAIL-TOUCH (touch with flukes)
PECTORAL-TOUCH (touch with pectoral fin)
MOUTH (grasp with mouth)
(GO) OVER
(GO) UNDER
(GO) THROUGH
TOSS (throw object using rostrum movement)
SPIT (squirt water from mouth at object)

Take direct and indirect object
FETCH (take one named object to another named object)

IN c, d (place one named object in or on another named object)

Agents

PHOENIX or AKEAKAMAI (prefix for each sentence; calls dolphin named to her station; indicates to dolphins which is to receive fish reward)

Modifiers

RIGHT or LEFT (used before object name to refer to object at that position) (A)
SURFACE or BOTTOM (used before object name to refer to object at that location) (P)

Other

ERASE (used in place of action word to cancel the preceding words – requires the dolphin to remain at station or to return immediately)
YES (used after correctly executed instruction)
NO (sometimes used after incorrectly executed instruction – can cause emotional behaviour)

Key

a Objects whose locations may be changed by trainers.
b Objects that may be moved by dolphins – all names represent classes of objects with multiple exemplars.
c Added to Akeakamai's vocabulary after completion of the majority of testing reported in data tables.
d Added to Phoenix's vocabulary after completion of the majority of testing reported in data tables.

(*Psittacus erithracus*) for about ten years and the studies seem to indicate that there is a degree of understanding behind the mimicry. She taught the parrot to make same/different judgments about the shape, colour and material of objects. She also provided some evidence that the parrot was capable of object classification according to concepts, that is to say he was able to make classifications of objects according to relatively abstract criteria which were not based upon any single perceptual feature. This process of conceptualization lies at the back of much language as opposed to the mere imitation of sounds.

Conditions for vocal learning There has been a considerable amount of research into the vocal abilities of mimetic birds going back to the 1940s, but though the birds were trained to reproduce language sounds they could not attach meaning to the sounds they produced. Pepperberg and her students were able to devise a vocal code for her parrot Alex which enabled her to examine his cognitive capabilities. She has outlined three conditions which facilitate exceptional vocal learning:

■ The subject must have the capacity to produce the sounds of human language. It is on this that the Kelloggs and the Hayes found difficulty with apes and it is this which led the Gardners to use ASL.
■ The subject must have the cognitive capacity to recognize that human sounds have a functional significance at least equivalent to their own sounds.
■ The subject must be given contextual support to learn the human sounds.

The first two of these conditions Pepperberg found relatively easy to meet using the parrot Alex. He was a good mimic and found no difficulty in reproducing the sounds of English. He had natural cognitive abilities which suggested that he would be able to recognize parallels between the language system he was being taught and his own natural communication system. Piaget (1952), Vygotsky (1962), Bandura (1971) and Todt (1975) have described the kinds of contextual support which facilitate the transfer of knowledge acquired in one domain to another.

A concept or behaviour may be more readily learned if it is functional. Piaget has suggested that functionality may play a part in assimilation. He has used this term to describe the way in which children take in

information and fit it into their existing knowledge. The function that information serves for the individual affects the case with which it is assimilated. Todt demonstrated that African grey parrots learned their vocalization most easily in a context of social interaction. A technique was developed by which humans play the roles of a young parrot's peers. In the wild, parrots engage in complex vocal duets and juvenile parrots observe these. Todt was able to set up a laboratory situation in which the young parrots observed humans engaged in the types of vocal exchanges which were to be learned. This greatly facilitated and speeded up the learning of parts of these exchanges.

Model/rival training Based upon this, Pepperberg and her students developed what she termed model/rival training (M/R). For instance, the parrot observed two human trainers handling objects in which the parrot has shown interest. One human (the trainer) shows the object to another human who acts as model for the bird's responses and rival for the trainer's attention. The trainer asks the model/rival questions about the object(s) and rewards correct responses with praise and the object itself. Box 17.6 shows an excerpt from a model/rival training session.

These techniques have had significantly greater success in developing communication skills than have programmes of operant conditioning such as have been used in some of the ape studies (for example, the Gardners and Washoe). On some occasions, when Alex had earned his reward he was able to reject the object about which the questions had been asked and correctly answered and to specify something else. However, his trainers would not respond to any such request as 'I want key' until a reward had been earned by successfully completing a task.

Avoidance of unconscious trainer cueing Terrace had criticized the Gardners' procedures (Terrace et al., 1979) on the grounds that there was evidence of 'trainer cueing', albeit unconscious cueing, and Pepperberg has taken precautions against this possibility. For instance, neither the trainer nor Alex was able to predict the questions which would be asked on a particular day. The principal trainer would list all the possible questions about the objects to be presented. The student trainer who was administering the test then formed the questions and deter-

Box 17.6 M/R training used with parrot, Alex (Pepperberg, 1983)

Excerpt from M/R training session, 30 April 1979

I: Kim, what colour? (Holds up a green triangular piece of wood.)

K: Green three-corner wood.

I: (Briefly removes object from sight, turns body slightly away.) No! Listen! I just want to know colour! (Faces back toward K; presents object again.) What *colour*?

K: Green wood.

I: (Hands over exemplar.) That's right, the colour is *green*; *green* wood.

K: OK, Alex, now you tell me, what shape?

A: No.

K: OK, Irene, *you* tell me what shape.

I: Three-corner wood.

K: That's right, you listened! The shape is three-corner; it's *three-corner* wood. (Hands over exemplar.)

I: Alex, here's your chance. What colour?

A: Wood.

I: That's right, wood; what *colour* wood?

A: Green wood.

I: Good parrot! Here you go. (Hands over exemplar.) The colour is green.

Note: I refers to the principal trainer, Irene Pepperberg; K to Kimberley Goodrich, one of the secondary trainers; and A to the parrot, Alex. This segment of the session lasted about 5 minutes.

mined test order randomly. Test questions were then interspersed into training sessions on unrelated topics. The chance for any particular object to show up in a test might only occur once a week and so could not be predicted. No student who had trained Alex on a topic tested him on it as well.

Avoidance of expectation cueing The intermingling of different types of question during tests or training on some other topic obviated expectation cueing. Alex was never tested successively in one session on similar questions. Only if the response was incorrect was the question repeated.

Scoring procedures To evaluate Alex's cognitive capacities on various tasks, test scores were arrived at. There were two ways of scoring:

■ The total of correct responses was divided by the number of presentations required to arrive at an overall score.

■ Percentages of first correct trials (that is, where only one presentation was required) were arrived at for comparison.

Some comparisons with nonhuman primates The tasks on which Alex succeeded demanded a similar level of abstract information processing to those given to nonhuman primates such as Premack's Sarah. On a same/different task, for instance, he had to:

■ Pay attention to multiple aspects of two different objects.
■ Determine from a question posed vocally whether the response demanded an assessment of similarity or one of difference.
■ Determine which attribute was 'same' or 'different'.
■ Produce vocally a label for the category which represented this attribute.

Language behaviour of an African grey parrot

Pepperberg has claimed her prime purpose to be the examination of Alex's cognitive capabilities rather than his language competence. She did not, unlike Herman's study described earlier, focus upon syntax (for example, word order). Alex was not trained to use his communication code for self-reference, to express emotions or to attribute intentions to others. While Herman and his colleagues tested their dolphins using commands to which the correct response was compliance, Pepperberg used questions to elicit the production of vocal responses. Some of these vocalizations, acquired during training, were later heard used in *private* monologue speech. This is similar to behaviour observed in young children in the early stages of language acquisition. Pepperberg justifies this limitation of the scope of her investigation by the assertion that to examine linguistic competence *per se* would perhaps muddy the waters when the prime object is to examine the parrot's cognitive abilities.

As it relates to Hockett's criteria for language the above limitation makes assessment difficult. Like Herman, Pepperberg has claimed that the language training Alex received has enhanced his cognitive abilities. Concepts can be learned which Alex would otherwise have been unable to learn. She suggests, however, that training affects the ease with which learning can occur more than whether it can occur at all.

 SELF-ASSESSMENT QUESTIONS

1. What are the defining features of language, described by Hockett, which are relevant to whether apes can be said to be capable of learning language?

2. Describe two unsuccessful attempts made to teach apes to talk.

3. Discuss some of the attempts to teach apes nonvocal forms of language.

4. How does the work of Herman and his colleagues with dolphins and Pepperberg with an African grey parrot enhance our understanding of the nature of language?

5. Make some assessment of how far you think it right to say that language is no longer to be regarded as a species-specific capacity of humans alone.

Chapter summary

- A basic element of communication is response to the environment. This could involve orienting responses, the eliciting of responses from another animal or arousal. These responses may be all at once, or trigger responses slowly increasing receptivity: a trigger or a pump effect.

- The sensory systems of animals are different from our own, so that the information they receive is in some ways more extensive than ours. Insects have a different sensitivity to light, more sensitive at the ultra-violet end of the spectrum less sensitive at the infra-red end. Some mammals, such as dogs or cats, have greater olfactory sensitivity and sight that is less sensitive to colour.

- Some animals exhibit sign stimuli which enable them speedily to pick out from the array of stimuli before them signals to which they must respond. Some of these are releasers, social signals and responses to them which have developed in the course of evolution. The colour of a gull's egg is important so that it knows what response to make to it, to eat it or to incubate it. Where these signals are exaggerated the response to them may also be intensified.

- There exist filtering mechanisms, both peripherally through the sensitivity of the sensory system, and centrally within the central nervous system. Alarm signals and responses to them are essential for the survival of individuals threatened by predators. They may be audible, visual or chemical in nature.

- Social signals among animals may be tactile, audible, chemical or visual, each of which media have their own characteristics. Sound signals travel long distances, visual signals are of short duration and do not carry so far. Messages contained in these signals include those which convey information about the intentions and condition of the sender, and may be conscious or unconscious. Most frequently they concern sexual information or information of concern to parents and offspring. Metacommunication may qualify other communications which acompany them.

■ Von Frisch's descriptions and interpretations of the honeybee dance have been well researched by Wells and Wenner, by Gould and by Michelsen. The type of 'dance' and the relationship of the dance to light sources and to gravity accurately show where sources of food may be found. Wells and Wenner were sceptical of von Frisch's claims, saying that the source of food was discovered by smell, but research by Gould et al. and by Michelsen tended to confirm von Frisch's findings.

■ The value of attempts to teach human language to animals depends to an extent upon definition of what language is. Hockett's criteria for language are a useful yardstick in evaluating such attempts. Early attempts to teach language to chimpanzees failed because of chimps' vocal deficiencies. Later attempts used sign language or symbols and were more successful. Terrace concluded, however, that chimps use language in a less creative way than small children.

■ Attempts to teach human language to dolphins concentrated upon comprehension rather than production of language. Herman et al. had considerable success with Akeakamai and Phoenix. The training they were given greatly enhanced the dolphins' cognitive skills.

■ Pepperberg's attempts to teach human language to an African grey parrot were based upon model/rival training. These had greater success than operant conditioning programmes with chimpanzees. Pepperberg's prime aim was the assessment of the parrot's cognitive skills and again it was claimed that training enhanced these skills.

Further reading

Herman, L.M. (ed.) (1980). *Cetacean Behavior: Mechanisms and Functions*. New York: Wiley InterScience. A fascinating account of attempts to establish skills of comprehension of human language in dolphins.

Lea, S.E.G. (1984). *Instinct, Environment and Behaviour*. London: Methuen. A clearly written account of communication among animals, ranging from insects to mammals and birds. There is particular attention paid in Chapter 6 to comparative intelligence in animals and language skills especially.

Manning, A. and Dawkins, M.S. (1992). *An Introduction to Animal Behaviour*. Cambridge: Cambridge University Press. Chapter 3 concentrates upon communication and in particular has an excellent discussion of von Frisch's research with honeybees.

Pepperberg, I.M. (1990a). 'Conceptual abilities of some non-primate species with an emphasis on an African grey parrot', in S.T. Parker and K. Gibson (eds) *Language and Intelligence in Monkeys and Apes: Comparative Development Perspectives*. Cambridge: Cambridge University Press. A good first-hand account of work done to establish the cognitive skills of an African Grey parrot, with particular reference to its language skills.

Wilson, E.O. (1975). *Sociobiology: The New Synthesis*. Cambridge, MA: Harvard University Press. An account of animal behaviour from a sociobiological standpoint.

CHAPTER 18

Social behaviour of animals

Social organization   395
- Forms of social organization   396
- Advantages of grouping   396
- Costs of group living   398
- Caste systems among social insects   398
- Social organization among primates   399

Territory and social organization   400
- Forms of territorial organization   400
- Territory, organization and mating behaviour   401

- Aggression   402

Social dominance   407
- Dominance and subordination among primates   407

Parents and offspring   409
- Sexual selection   409
- Instinctive mechanisms of care   412
- Kin selection   413
- Evolutionary interests of parents and offspring   415

Objectives

By the end of this chapter you should be able to:

- Demonstrate ways in which animals' social grouping has advantages in relation to their survival;

- Show what evolutionary functions follow from social behaviour of animals;

- Describe the social organization among insects such as honeybees and termites;

- Describe and comment upon the forms of social organization among primates;

- Show some understanding of conflict behaviour, its origins and manifestations (for example, territorial conflict, threat displays, appeasement and displacement behaviour);

- Demonstrate an understanding of courtship, mating and parenting behaviours.

Social organization

One of the most striking features of all animals – and this includes humans – is their tendency to be social. This social behaviour can take various forms. Sometimes animals exist in pairs, sometimes in larger groupings, flocks, herds or schools. This chapter sets out to show how these forms of social organization can be the result of natural selection and the genes that individual animals carry. It can be an advantage to a species to group together with others. Animals that carry genes which tend to make them interact with others in particular ways will, in the right circumstances, have an advantage and the genes they carry will be passed on.

Forms of social organization

By social organization we are referring to the ways in which individual members of a species interact with each other. Some forms of social organization will be rigid and species-specific – among social insects, for instance – while others will be much more fluid, dynamic and dependent upon prevailing conditions. The diversity of forms of social organization will include its permanence as well as the purposes for which it exists. These social groupings include:

- **Societies.** These can be described as extremely stable relationships where individuals live in the same group for prolonged periods. Female elephants may live in the same family for 40 or 50 years.
- **Flocks of birds or schools of fish.** These are less complex and less durable forms of organization. Individual birds, however, or fish may stay together for some months.
- **Aggregations.** These are the least permanent and durable forms of social organization. Most commonly, aggregations occur when large numbers of members of a species gather at a common food source. Fruit flies, for instance, aggregate on a piece of rotten fruit. They are attracted to a common food source. Even here, though, there is some social organization in that they react to each other, spacing themselves out so that they do not touch one another.

Among humans you can see the way in which certain rules of aggregation are adhered to when large numbers of people come together. Even in a crowded street they will go to some lengths to prevent contact, stepping off the pavement into the road, for instance. Morris (1977) describes this maintenance of personal space:

> If a man enters a waiting room and sits at one end of a long row of chairs it is possible to predict where the next man to enter will seat himself. He will not sit next to the first man, nor will he sit at the far end, right away from him. He will choose a position about halfway between these points. The next man to enter will take the largest gap left and sit roughly in the middle of that and so on . . .'.
>
> (Morris, 1977, p. 130)

A waiting room. It is possible to predict where any newcomer will take his or her seat

Advantages of grouping

Individuals who group themselves together do so because they are likely to be better off than they would be on their own. Better off implies being better adapted, more able to survive and pass on their genes: that is to say, fitter.

There are three ways in which we can discover what the advantages amount to:

- **Experimental methods.** We can use experimental methods. Some members of a species may be separated so that they are on their own, while others remain together. We can then observe how well the separate individuals and the groups succeed.
- **Observation.** We can observe naturally occurring variations within a given species, those that group or those that do not.
- **Comparisons.** Comparisons can also be made between species that are naturally solitary and those which are social.

It is also possible to argue from a purely theoretical standpoint, as Hamilton (1971b) does, that grouping

---

GLOSSARY

Societies Stable relationships where animals live together in the same group for prolonged periods.

Flocks (of birds)/schools (of fish) More temporary and less stable relationships between animals than societies, but which may last for several months.

Aggregations Impermanent relationships between animals which do not last longer than the immediate cause of their coming together: for instance, for a common food source.

together is inevitable. He has shown that if each individual animal tries to place at least one other animal between itself and a potential predator, the result will be tight groupings.

At a very basic level, Allee (1938) set out to discover the benefits gained by individuals even in loose aggregations. Water-fleas cannot survive in alkaline water. The respiration of a large number of them together was sufficient to make the water acid enough for them to survive. While individuals alone perished, groups survived.

Advantages of grouping for birds and fish

Flocks of birds or schools of fish provide the following advantages for their members:

Physical advantage Emperor penguins huddle close together against the cold as they incubate their eggs in the Antarctic winter. Thus the available heat is conserved and the outside penguins move more than those in the centre so that heat is generated in that way.

Protection against predation Lazarus (1979) compared the responses of red-billed weaver birds to a predatory goshawk alone and in flocks with other birds. While the solitary birds failed to make any response at all, those in groups were much more likely to spot the predator. Using a hawk model, starlings were found by Powell (1974) to spend much more of their time in surveillance and a much smaller amount of their time feeding when they were on their own than when they were in groups of ten or more. This finding is echoed by Elgar's (1989) review of more than 50 studies of both birds and mammals. The bigger the groups they are in, the greater proportion of their time they are able to spend feeding. Macdonald (1986) studied the habits of meerkats (*Suricatta suricatta* which post lookouts while the rest of the group feeds.

Defence against attack Predators have been found to be very reluctant to attack a group but instead to adopt the stratagem of attempting to make them scatter so that they can then single out isolated individuals (Hamilton, 1971b). Göttmark and Andersson (1984) showed that gulls have much greater success in warding off predators in large groups than singly or in small groups. They band together to mob the predator.

Better utilization of food resources Sources of food found by one member of the group may be exploited by the group as a whole. C.R. Brown (1986) found that when individual cliff swallows had located a rich source of insect food they were followed on their next foray by less successful members of the group. The original finders were not put at a disadvantage by this because the cache of food was so plentiful. Gannets are frequently found fishing in groups. Nelson (1980) suggested that the reason for this was that the fish become disorientated by the birds diving at them together and so are more easily caught.

Facilitation of sexual activity The presence of other birds of the same species has the effect of stimulating sexual activity. This has been termed the **Fraser Darling effect** after the researcher who described it:

> Though the immediate mate of the opposite sex may be the most potent excitatory individual to reproductive condition, other birds of the same species, or even similar species, may play a decisive part if they are gregarious at the breeding season. Without the presence of others the individual pairs of birds may not complete the reproductive cycle to the limit of rearing young to the fledgling stage.
>
> (Darling, 1938)

Smaller colonies of herring gulls start laying eggs at a later date and have a longer breeding season than large colonies. Consequently they are more exposed to predation by enemies. Darling claimed that in larger colonies the breeding season was shorter owing to social facilitation. The fact of social living makes breeding easier. Breeding is compressed into a shorter period of time when most other birds are also producing chicks. Predators are likely to be well fed at this time (with plenty of prey about) and they will be more likely to ignore individual chicks than they would

---

GLOSSARY

Fraser Darling effect Phenomenon noted by Darling where the grouping of indidviduals of a species together stimulates sexual activity and therefore reproduction.

be if they confronted a breeding pair on its own. Any particular chick therefore has a greater chance of survival.

Group hunting among predatory species

Among mammals a number of predatory species (for example, lions, hyenas and hunting dogs) hunt in groups. They may drive their prey towards others hidden under cover or take turns to run their quarry to the point of exhaustion. Kruuk (1972) has described how the size of a pack of hyenas hunting their prey will vary with the size of their quarry. Hunting zebra, the mean number of hyenas in a group is 10.8, hunting adult wildebeest it is 2.5 and young gazelle fawns 1.2. When they are in an inappropriately sized group they ignore prey which in other circumstances they would attack.

Packer has suggested that the motives in this kind of group hunting are not entirely cooperative (Packer, 1986). The advantage lions gain in hunting together lies in being better able to protect the kill from scavengers and thieves rather than in making the kill in the first place.

A review of the literature by Martinez and Klinghammer (1970) has indicated that among marine mammals, killer whales (*Orcinus orca*) hunt in packs for sea-lions, whales and other dolphins.

Costs of group living

But group living has costs as well. These include:

■ **Competition for food**. Living in a group will inevitably mean that individuals will have to compete for food.
■ **Disease**. The risk of transmission is likely to be greater.
■ **Cannibalism**. Where the young are crowded together, there is some risk to the young from their own species.

As in many situations, a balance needs to be struck in terms of survival. If the benefits of group living, which have been mentioned, outweigh the costs in terms of the individual animals surviving to pass on their genes, then social living traits will prevail at the expense of the genes which determine that animals live alone.

Hoogland and Sherman (1976) have listed a number of disadvantages which face bank swallows as a result of their communal nesting. There is greater risk, for instance, of their picking up fleas. There is also a greater likelihood of the burrow's collapsing because of large numbers of other birds nesting in it. However, it does appear that the advantages of communal living outweigh the potential risk.

Caste systems among social insects

While some insects lead what are perhaps the most solitary lives of all (the mason wasp, for instance, has contact with members of its species only for the briefest of periods during mating), some ants, bees and wasps have evolved complex social relationships which can be termed caste systems. Individuals are divided into workers, soldiers and reproductives. The members of each caste not only have quite discrete functions or roles within their group but have evolved anatomical differences as well. Wilson (1971) has described in some detail the social divisions within these colonies of social insects. He has defined the traits such insects exhibit as eusocial.

Eusociality is defined by the common possession of three characteristics:

■ Cooperation among individuals of the same species in caring for the young.
■ Division of labour in reproduction. Sterile workers support fecund nestmates.
■ An overlap of at least two generations of life stages. Offspring will contribute to the support of their parents during some period of their life.

Determinants of caste

Nutrition It is interesting that the caste of an individual insect is determined as much by what it is fed on, as by any genetic determinant. Potentially, larval bees are all equal. Most get a restricted diet and develop into workers. Reproductive classes have an enriched diet.

GLOSSARY

Caste Among animals castes represent complex social relationships which are characterized by discrete functions or roles and sometimes by anatomical differences as well. They tend to be permanent and unchangeable.

Eusociality Beneficial characteristics among social insects, involving cooperation, division of labour in reproduction and an overlap between generations for life support.

Pheromones **Pheromones** (chemical signals released into the air) are secreted by the insects themselves and coordinate development and social behaviour. A queen bee produces pheromones which suppress the reproductive capabilities of the workers. The supply of pheromones has to be maintained. Where a honeybee colony loses its queen the behaviour of some of the workers in the brood area begins to change. Emergency queen cells begin to be constructed, and some of the youngest workers begin to be fed royal jelly and are destined to become queens. Where queen substance falls below a critical level (through dilution as the size of the colony grows) there is a greater likelihood of swarming, which is the main means whereby new colonies are formed. Among honeybees a single queen founds a colony, constructing the nest and rearing the first batch of workers. Then the workers take over foraging and extending the colony while the queen remains in the nest laying eggs.

Tasks within caste systems

These are rigidly differentiated. Among honeybees, workers have the following duties:

- Foraging;
- Rearing the young;
- Nest construction;
- Attending the queen; and
- Guarding the colony.

Among termite or ant colonies there are similar duties for the workers except there is sometimes an additional caste of 'soldier'. Soldiers have the sole function of guarding the colony and develop enlarged jaws and other weapons. Function is very closely linked to nutrition. The functions of queens and other castes within the colony are also carefully defined. A relatively simple set of responses to particular stimuli enable the insects to have control over their environments and successfully adapt to them. There is a carefully evolved system of responses with limited flexibility. This is adaptiveness rather than intelligence.

Social organization among primates

Because humans are themselves primates there has been great interest in the way in which primates organize themselves socially. The majority of primates are social animals with relatively stable and cohesive social groups. Jolly (1966) in her study of ring-tailed lemurs (*Lemur catta*) showed them to move around in troops of around 12–20 animals which included both adult males and breeding females. They are also territorial. Troops occupy territories marked by scent. Mothers and infants have close contact with each other, and as the infants grow older other adults approach and play with them as well. This seems to characterize a typical primate organization. In human families the closest contact in the initial period after birth is between mother and child. Other adults play an increasing role as the child grows older. Between species, the size of troops varies widely, from baboons whose troops are sometimes very large to almost solitary orang-utans.

Intercommunication among primates

A feature of primate social organization is the way in which individuals within a group are constantly attentive to other members of the group. Posture, gestures, movements and calls all provide means of communication and responses to each other. Primate groups are highly complex for a number of reasons.

Long infant dependency There is a long period in their life cycle during which the young are dependent.

Longevity Larger species of primates can live for 20-30 years and humans much longer than that. Within a group, therefore, every individual is likely to know every other individual from long experience.

Intelligence Primates are intelligent animals with high levels of learning ability. As the social situation within a group changes, the responses each individual makes to that situation are highly flexible. Humphrey (1976) has suggested that it is the complex demands of the primates' social life which has led through evolutionary selection to growth in the size of primate brains, and in turn the growth in brain size

---

GLOSSARY

Pheromones Chemical signals released into the air to coordinate development and social behaviour.

offered greater flexibility and complexity in their relations with each other. The apotheosis of this development is, of course, the human brain. Gene–culture coevolution, described in some detail in the introduction to this part, is a major contributor to the phenomenal development of the human species.

? SELF-ASSESSMENT QUESTIONS

1. What are some of the forms of social grouping among animals? List the characteristics of each.
2. Explain some of the advantages and disadvantages of social grouping.
3. Describe the caste system of social organization among insects. In what way does this system seem to you to have evolutionary advantages for the species concerned?
4. Can you account for the complexity of social relationships among primates?

Territory and social organization

Defence of territory is important in the social organization of many vertebrates. Territoriality represents a way in which animals can minimize competition for food, mates and nesting sites. Some animals are territorial during some parts of the year and gregarious at others. Great tits vigorously defend territory during the nesting season, which means that at this important season they have an assured food supply, while in the winter they join together in large flocks, the better to locate scarcer food resources and protect them against predators. Defending a territory is not without its costs.

Brown (1969) has introduced the notion of **economic defendability**. Whether an animal will defend its territory will be determined by the value of the resources within it and whether it can be defended without the expense of too much energy. This idea of economic defendability has been examined by Gill and Wolf (1975). Nectar-feeding sunbirds in East Africa defend their territory vigorously against intruders. Gill and Wolf calculated the energy they expended defending this territory and matched it against the increased levels of nectar available to them in their 'private' flowers. They found territorial defence to be a very worthwhile use of energy.

Forms of territorial organization

The lek

This is found in some species of grouse and other birds and in a few mammals. Males gather in a tight group or **lek**. Within this lek each male defends a small territory of his own. The sight of so many males displaying together lures females from far and wide who come and choose their mates on the basis of this fashion parade. Henley or Ascot might be seen also as a similar 'marriage market' for the human species. Gibson and Bradbury (1985) have shown that among grouse the males who display for the longest time and the most vigorously are most likely to be chosen by females. The sole purpose of this lek area seems to be that of a marriage market, because the females once mated go off on their own to raise their young. The males offer them no assistance at all but continue to attract other females.

Nest sites

Pied fly-catchers have a different use of territory involving **nest sites**. Males arrive about a week ahead of females at breeding grounds in Northern Europe, beginning with the oldest males with the blackest plumage. These birds have the pick of the best territories. The success they have in attracting a mate could be due to either of the following factors:

■ That they have the best sites.
■ That they are individually the most attractive. Black is clearly beautiful.

An ingenious experiment by Alatalo et al. (1986) aimed to separate the above two factors and is described in Box 18.1.

GLOSSARY

Economic defendability In relation to territory occupied by an animal, the balance between the value of the resources within a territory against the energy necessary to defend it.

Lek A form of territorial organization found in some species of birds and also in a few mammal species. Males form a tight group and display together. This conglomeration of males acts as a lure for females, who come to choose a mate.

Nest sites A form of territorial organization used particularly by pied fly-catchers, based upon the establishment of the best sites in which to set up nests. Males establish sites ahead of the arrival of the females who are attracted by their success in doing this.

Box 18.1   An experiment by Alatalo et al. (1986) into the nest site behaviour of pied fly-catchers

Pied fly-catchers (*Ficedula hypoleuca*) will regularly nest in artificial nest boxes. The researchers restricted the number of nest boxes available at any one time, only putting up more when the first were occupied. When the females arrived, the researchers carefully noted the order in which the males found a mate. They discovered that it was the quality of the territory which was most attractive to the females rather than individual characteristics such as age or blackness of plumage. In terms of fitness this makes excellent sense. The survival of the brood is more dependent on cover and food supply than upon handsomeness of plumage or age. It seems more important for the bride that the bridegroom should be well endowed with this world's goods than that he should be handsome!

The 'sexy son' hypothesis

The 'sexy son' hypothesis has also received some attention. This involves females choosing handsome young males because their sons will also be handsome and so will find it easier to find mates.

Territory, organization and mating behaviour

There is an established relationship between the type of social or territorial organization of members of a species and the mating system adopted (that is, the relationships and roles of the two sexes in reproduction). Factors include the following.

Mating systems and territory

Where there are 'lek'-type territories, animals tend to be polygamous, while animals which have to defend large territories are either monogamous or have just two or three females to each male. Jarman (1974) found interrelationship between diet, territory, body size and mating system in different species of antelope. With smaller antelope, duikers or dik-dik for instance, the male lives with a single mate in a territory which he defends to provide food for her and their offspring throughout the year. Larger antelopes, gazelles, water-buck and impala have a social organization involving large groups, ranging from six to more than a hundred animals. They do not stay in the same area all year but males defend territories vigorously against other males and attempt to mate with any females entering it. Males are promiscuous, mating with as many females as possible as they enter their territory, while females wander from territory to territory in search of food, mating as they go.

Access to potential mates

A factor which determines the kind of social organization of a given species may be the control of access by others to potential mates. Emlen and Oring (1977) have shown that polygamy may evolve where males defend a group of females to provide them with the food they need.

Scarcity of food resources

Crook (1965) has suggested that there is a relationship between the scarcity or otherwise of food resources and the mating system adopted. Among weaver birds, forest species are solitary nesters, monogamous and insectivorous; savannah species, on the other hand, nest in colonies, eat seeds and are polygynous (that is, one male to several females). Monogamy seems to be favoured when there is scarcity of food, polygyny when it is plentiful. In the latter case it does not seem to be so essential that there should be a male at hand for each female to help with the rearing of the brood. However, Crook's conclusions have not been universally accepted. Haartman (1969) has suggested other factors which could have an effect upon mating systems – the kind of nest sites available, for instance. In any case, Crook's findings with weaver birds do not seem to hold with other species.

Survival chances of the young

The mating system adopted will be that which provides the greatest chance for the young of the species to survive. The need for both parents to be at hand to feed and care for the young indicates that monogamy is desirable, while in cases where one parent is quite capable of rearing the young on her own, polygyny offers the chance for the male to pass on his genes to a larger number of offspring. Polygyny or promiscuity are the most common mating systems among mammals except where the male makes a substantial contribution to the upbringing of the young. With birds, things are different. Incubation demands the attention of both parents, as does the collection of food for the young, so that a high proportion of bird species are monogamous.

The polygyny threshold model

A model has been developed by Verner and Wilson (1966) and Orians (1969) which has become known as the **polygyny threshold model**, which relates the need for the male to care for the brood to the desirability (from the male's point of view) of having several families and so passing on his genes to more offspring. It may pay a female, too, to settle for a lower level of care for the brood by the male in return for a higher quality of territory, rather than mate monogamously with a male who has only a poor territory. On good territory a female may have better success in raising her brood, in spite of the competition of other females, provided there are not too many of them. Beyond a certain threshold of numbers, she might do better in a monogamous mating on poorer territory.

However, Davies (1989) has pointed out that the model does not always fit the data. What is best for males may not always be what is best for females. The mating system which evolves may be a compromise. Catchpole et al. (1985) showed that among great reed warblers where migrating females arrive later than the males, the fine characteristics of a particular male's territory may occasionally attract several females to settle there. The polygyny threshold model would suggest that their breeding success ought to be at least as good as that of monogamous birds on poorer territory. But it does not happen like that. The later arrivals do significantly less well. The males benefit, but the females are worse off than if they had a single unmated male on a poorer territory.

Contributions made by males

The contribution made by males of a given species to the upbringing of the brood is correlated with differences between the sexes in their appearance and displays. In species in which the male mates many times but contributes nothing to the brood except his sperm there are the greatest differences in size and appearance between the sexes. A peahen is a very dowdy creature in comparison with the magnificent plumage of the peacock. His courtship ritual is spectacular but he does not care for his young at

A peacock displays his tail feathers as part of his courtship display

all. Male elephant seals are some three or four times the size of the female, but the responsibility for raising the pups rests entirely with the female. Intense competition between the males of such species as elephant seals and red deer allows the female to choose that male which is likely to contribute the best (that is, the most well-adapted) genes (his sole contribution), and the successful competitor can then assemble a large entourage of females. Among elephant seals, in some seasons as few as 4 per cent of the males are responsible for 85 per cent of the matings (Le Boeuf, 1974). Such males are very successful in passing on their genes and here again the 'sexy son' phenomenon operates. Females choose the 'likeliest lads' to father their offspring in the expectation of handsome offspring who will find no difficulty in attracting females.

Aggression

In animals other than humans, some main functions of aggression have been identified. These include:

■ Defence of territory,
■ Competition for mates,

■ Defence of offspring,
■ Status in the social order of the species.

While these may well be applicable to humans, human motivational processes are more complex and difficult to analyse.

Aggressive behaviour can take different forms, for different reasons, but can roughly be divided into three main areas: offensive, defensive and predatory. These are controlled by different brain mechanisms, which would seem to confirm them as separate mechanisms which are related behaviourally although they do not follow identical patterns.

Environmental influences on aggression

Environmental influences shown to increase aggression include:

■ Overcrowding,
■ Isolation, and
■ Territory changes.

Overcrowding In both laboratory and field studies, overcrowding has been shown to be linked with aggression. Calhoun (1962) found that laboratory rats who were living in overcrowded conditions were more aggressive than rats of the same strain who had ample space. Pulliam (1976) and Caraco et al. (1980) observed that as the size of flocks of yellow-eyed junco increased, so did the proportion of time spent in aggression.

Isolation Where animals have been kept in total isolation they have been found to be very aggressive. Kruijt (1964) found this to be the case with jungle fowl, where after months of isolation birds would even resort to long battles with their tails.

Territory A frequent cause of aggression between animals is the defence of territory. This is often carried out as a precursor to mating behaviour; in the case of the stickleback as a means to ensure a place for the courted female to lay her eggs. Hawks and many other birds defend their territories in order to safeguard their supply of food. Other species defend their territories for food, courtship areas or places to rear their young. Baboons are nomadic, but defend their temporary territories against intruders until food stocks are depleted, before moving on to a new area.

While one's own territory will always be defended, from time to time an animal needs to expand its territory; for instance, in winter, food may not be so readily available, so the animal needs to range wider, causing conflicts with neighbours, who may also be seeking to expand their territories.

Definitions of aggression in human terms tend to look only at offensive aggression, as though defensive and predatory behaviours do not exist. Yet current thinking on the increasing problem of aggression among car drivers suggests that it is a defensive reaction, defending one's personal (road) space. In speaking of wars, defence of territory is viewed as permissible, even laudable, but not road space. By looking at examples of animal aggression we can remove the moral and cultural complications, which render some of the definitions of aggression inadequate when applied to humans.

Physiological factors

Whether an animal wins or loses an altercation, the body's responses are the same. In aggression the same mechanisms are involved as during stress (described in Chapter 11); when aggression or stress subsides the body's responses return to baseline again (homeostasis). Balance is restored in the autonomic nervous system and the hormonal system.

High adrenalin levels and high testosterone levels are hormones implicated in aggressiveness. Many studies have shown that a high level of testosterone, the male hormone, is implicated in aggression. Albert et al. (1989) demonstrated that castrated male rats treated with testosterone fought and dominated other male castrates who were untreated.

It has been suggested that specific brain areas are involved in aggressive behaviour, as with other forms of motivation. Again, these may not only be different from one species to the next, but between male and female of the same species.

Is aggression innate?

Lorenz, in his book *On Aggression* (1966), defined aggression as 'the fighting instinct in beast and man which is directed against members of the same species'. It is useful for our purposes that we confine aggression to attacks on members of the *same* species. The problem many ethologists and others have with Lorenz's definition is that the word 'instinct' implies that it is innate and genetically preprogrammed into us – man and beast. While many people will accept it is in the 'beast', they prefer to think of 'man' as having free will.

Lorenz suggested that an individual of a species avoids a fight to the death with another of the same species through the recognition of appeasement gestures which inhibit the final death blow, as the death of an individual would be detrimental to the species by diminishing the gene pool. For example, dogs will roll on to their backs, exposing their soft underbelly and the vulnerable part of the throat; this action says 'I give in.' In humans, cringing, pleading, smiling or crying act as appeasement gestures. Although humans do not have large canine teeth or other equipment for killing others of the same size of the same species, their cognitive abilities are advanced enough to devise weapons for that purpose. Lorenz's claim that an animal's aggression stops short of killing its own species has been undermined by numerous studies. Lea (1984) points out that infanticide is one of the more common forms of aggression among animals; instances among lions are well documented. Goodall (1968) reported warfare among two bands of chimpanzees which resulted in the death of all adult males from one band. It would appear therefore that irrespective of appeasement gestures, provision or lack of physical weapons to kill, the killing of animals of the same species does occur. Whether this is innately preprogrammed, or culturally devised and learned, has not been clearly demonstrated.

Postaggression recess?

Lorenz's psychohydraulic model of motivation (Figure 18.1) would suggest that after a fight or aggressive behaviour, there would be less motivation on the part of the animal to exhibit aggressive behaviour again for some time. Conversely, in the absence of opportunities for aggressive behaviour, aggression would build up within the individual, to be released at the first opportunity. In fact the reverse of both these extremes has been found by a

number of researchers. Heiligenberg and Kramer (1972) tested an aggressive species of cichlid fish (*Tilapia pelmatochromis*). Males were kept on their own with no opportunity to meet other males, and components of aggressive behaviour diminished over a number of days, rather than building up.

Wilz (1970) found that male sticklebacks would deliver more 'bites' (the measure of aggression used) towards a test tube containing another male at the end of a ten-minute period than at the beginning. Even when the test-tubed intruder was removed from the territory, the stickleback still showed aggressive behaviour. It even attacked a female (which would not be expected), and seemed unable to respond sexually for some time. However, one could possibly argue that the level of aggression was falsely maintained as the consummatory behaviour of fighting was never achieved, although the intruder was removed eventually, or 'driven away'. The cause of aggression could have shifted from 'territory defence' to 'frustration'.

Irritable aggression

Irritable aggression caused by pain, anxiety, negative stimuli and frustration, whilst potentially equally as damaging as any other form of aggression, does not

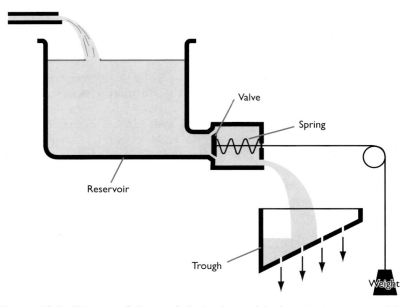

Figure 18.1 Diagram of the psychohydraulic model of motivation proposed by Lorentz (1950). The analogy is with water filling a tank: when it reaches a high level it makes the water flow

serve a function, such as the defence of territory, nor a proximal cause, such as the presence of an intruder.

Frustration is often considered to be a cause of aggression in humans as well as other species, and this may be due to any number of causes. In species which have hierarchical social organizations (see p. 408), aggression may be due to attempts to rise in the dominance order of the social hierarchy. Patterns of aggression shown to potential predators or intruders of other species may contain similar elements to aggressive behaviours within a species, but are not always identical.

Learning and aggression

A number of studies have shown that early learning affects the level of aggression shown by an individual. Male and female rats reared in isolation are more aggressive than rats of the same strain which have been gently handled by humans when young. Namikas and Wehmer (1978) found that male mice reared in litters with male siblings were less aggressive to other males in adulthood than males who had been reared solely with female siblings.

While it would be most unwise to generalize these findings to humans, there may be implications worthy of attention. The human species has much greater potential for learning than rats – or indeed than any other animal. It also lives longer than most. If there is such a thing as a basic instinct for aggression, perhaps it might be controlled or enhanced by learning. If high levels of testosterone are implicated in human aggression, these are at their highest during adolescence. It could be argued that humans are, by then, socialized enough (through learning) to be able to control or redirect their aggression to some extent. Perhaps those who do not have missed out on a degree of socialization? Or perhaps their learning suggested to them that aggression was permissible, even laudable (Bandura, 1971)?

Individual influences in aggression

Specific factors have been shown to influence the level of aggressive behaviour demonstrated by an individual in a species. These include:

- The size of the individual relative to others;
- The size of the individual's natural 'weapons';
- Past experiences;
- 'Badges' of seniority;
- Displays of dominance.

Individual size The size of an animal relative to others of its species will often determine whether an animal will initiate an attack. Smaller animals are more likely to offer appeasement gestures or run away.

Natural weapons Likewise the size of an animal's natural 'weapons' (horns, antlers or canine teeth, for example) also have bearing on aggressive behaviours.

Past experiences Past experiences, especially if one individual has previously lost an encounter with the one now offering aggression, is going to affect decisions whether to fight or run away.

Badges of seniority 'Badges' of seniority are recognized by individuals who live in social groups. However, Rohwer and Rohwer (1978) showed that it takes more than just the badge to determine dominance. Dominant birds in flocks of Harris sparrows have dark head and breast feathers. When subordinate birds were painted with black paint, they did not rise in status, because their behaviour did not match their plumage. However, when they were also injected with testosterone a change in behaviour was observed along with a rise in status.

Dominance displays Displays of dominance discourage aggression from others: for example, the roar of a stag, or the chest beating of a male gorilla, actively discourage aggression from others of the species, thereby avoiding the necessity for actual fighting. This is as well, since the assertion that death will be avoided in intraspecies encounters does not always hold true. Wilkinson and Shank (1977) suggested that 5 to 10 per cent of adult musk ox bulls may die each year in fights over females. Stags fight for females during the rutting season; their antlers may inflict wounds which could be fatal. Clutton-Brock et al. (1982) observed that two animals of equal size will tend to prolong their fight, neither being willing to give in or offer the appeasement gesture of leaving the arena.

Natural populations of some species differ in their levels of aggression. Maynard-Smith and Riechart (1984) demonstrated that desert spiders (*Aegelopsis*) are very aggressive. They fight over access to web sites.

Fear and aggression alternate during encounters between two spiders. Factors involved include ownership of the disputed site, relative bodyweight of the two contestants, quality of the territory involved and genetic factors. Some populations of spiders are more aggressive than others. Even where the external situation is the same, some will withdraw more readily than others.

Evolution of fighting

The reason that individuals in a species do not fight to the death was suggested by Lorenz to be a mechanism designed to avoid the reduction of the gene pool available to the species. If this were so, one might argue, where was the usefulness in evolving fighting behaviour at all, if it promoted the inevitable risk that some individuals might accidentally be killed, as in the case of the musk ox bulls. The costs and benefits model developed by Maynard-Smith (1976) suggests that aggression may be used by an individual if the resultant benefits appear to outweigh the costs. Evolutionary stable strategies (ESS), discussed in Chapter 16, emerge from the interaction of genetically programmed behaviour plus the animal's experiences in previous similar situations, possibly with the same adversary. The decision to attack or retreat is made. Ecological circumstances such as the availability of food, mates, status or territory and the number of competitors, will determine the pay-offs.

Is aggression a male prerogative?

Research would seem to suggest that the answer to this is yes – or is it that there has been little research into female aggression? Certainly higher levels of androgens (male hormones) seem related to aggressive behaviours; these hormones are present in smaller, but varying amounts in females. Vom Saal and Bronson (1980) found that female rats who had been situated between two male siblings in the uterus, had significantly higher levels of testosterone than other females who were next to only one male or all female siblings. When tested as adults, these females showed higher levels of interfemale aggression than other rats, although there was no difference in their fertility or maternal behaviour.

Female hamsters are always more aggressive than males. Their aggressiveness does not seem to be hormone-dependent, but is inhibited during oestrus, when both progesterone and estradiol are present. Injections of either hormone alone does not inhibit aggression.

Some primates, such as rhesus monkeys and baboons, become more aggressive around the time of ovulation (Saayman, 1971). In humans, researchers have found that aggressive behaviour decreases around the time of ovulation, but increases prior to menstruation; increased irritability has been noted as a symptom of pre-menstrual tension, which in less controlled individuals could spill over into acts of aggression. This may be related to hormonal changes prior to menstruation or retention of fluid which causes pressure within the brain.

It is usually the males of the species which have evolved the 'weaponry'. The antlers of the stags, or the large claw of the fiddler crabs, for instance, have evolved by a process of natural selection; the victor of a battle for a female will have passed on his genes, which included those for the growth of large antlers or claws. Females, as the 'resource' in this scenario, had no necessity to evolve these – although they could be useful in defending young. Many cows, female wildebeest and goats have horns, and will use them for this purpose. On the other hand, females of many species cooperate with other females, especially in areas such as rearing young; probably antlers or horns would inhibit this cooperation.

In most species, females with young are aggressive if threatened. Maternal aggressiveness in mice may become apparent during pregnancy, where it appears to relate to a rise in progesterone levels (Mann et al., 1982). However, these levels drop at parturition. The stimuli for maternal aggression after birth seems to be the sight and the smell of the pups (Svare and Gandelman, 1976). Calhoun (1962), in his study of overcrowding in rats, identified instances of infanticide by females. Other females known to kill their young include sows, and sometimes cats and dogs. Infanticide is more likely to be carried out by males, as a precursor to impregnating the mother, in order to propagate their own genes. Two reasons have been suggested for female infanticide: to decrease crowding and to attain an optimal litter size.

Female spiders will kill a male who makes a mistake in the courtship pattern, or sometimes after mating, simply as a source of food. However, the female spider of many species is often larger than the male. The female praying mantis does not wait for the male to finish the act of copulation, but bites off his head before the act is finished; reflexes ensure that fertilization ensues.

In Greek mythology the Amazons, a tribe of women, were reputed to be fierce and warlike; as there were no men in the tribe, women took on the role of warriors, and cut off their right breast in order to draw a bow. Whether there was any historical evidence for a tribe of aggressive women, or whether it was mere fantasy, we shall probably never know, but the legend serves to suggest that the concept of 'aggressive women' was not viewed as implausible in classical times.

Current female aggression is complex and probably culturally and socially influenced; for example, female circumcision is carried out by other females, although probably originally instigated by males. Whether female circumcision is an act of aggression can be debated. Certainly there is no hygienic reason, as there is with male circumcision; reasons given seem wholly punitive rather than practical.

We have instanced some examples of female aggression; undoubtedly there are others, although it is the more flamboyant displays of male aggression which are researched more often.

There is further discussion of aggression in Chapter 25, in a social psychological context.

? SELF-ASSESSMENT QUESTIONS

1. What are some of the advantages of territoriality in terms of evolutionary success?
2. What is meant by a lek? What are the characteristics of lek-type organization?
3. What relationship seems to exist between scarcity or otherwise of resources and mating systems among animals?
4. Among species where polygyny is the norm there is often great disparity between the sexes. Can you identify an evolutionary reason for this?
5. Discuss some of the reasons put forward for aggressive behaviour among animals.

Social dominance

As long ago as 1935, Schelderup-Ebbe developed notions of **social dominance hierarchies**. He observed 'pecking orders' among flocks of hens. In any flock there emerged one who was dominant and could

displace all others. Below her was a second bird who was able to displace all but the first, and so on until at the bottom of the hierarchy was a bird displaced by all. This is an alternative form of social organization to territoriality but not clearly distinguished from it. Animals cannot be categorized as either territorial or hierarchical. For some the social system is seasonal. Fraser Darling's account of the social organization of red deer (1935), and Clutton-Brock and Albon's (1989) more recent study of this species on Rhum in the Hebrides, showed that outside the breeding season males and females live apart. Among males there is a clear linear social dominance hierarchy. The larger stags become dominant and are able to displace the smaller ones, lower placed in the hierarchy, from the best feeding spots. Hierarchy does not have the same importance among hinds. The pattern changes in the rutting season, though. Males go off singly to display areas and roar to attract hinds. The stags then defend the group of females they have collected during the few weeks of the rutting season. Thereafter they return to their former separate herds.

Dominance and subordination among primates

Dominance and subordination are important features of the social relationships among primates. As with other species, dominance involves the threat of displacement or even attack, though as rank becomes established it becomes increasingly less necessary to carry through threats or attacks. Grooming is an important manifestation of dominance. Dominant individuals allow themselves to be groomed by a subordinate as a placatory gesture. Sexual presentation is also used as an appeasement gesture. Among baboons and chimpanzees it is a frequent response to a threatening and dominant animal. Having a high rank within a group implies that a dominant individual's behaviour is not limited by other individuals. In all species, including humans, high-ranking, dominant individuals have greater freedom to act than low-

| GLOSSARY |

Social dominance hierarchy Pecking orders which are found among some animals (flocks of hens, for instance, or among red deer herds). There is a dominant animal, to whom the others defer, a second who is able to displace all but the first and then a third and so on.

ranking, subordinate ones. Choice is not for all equally, but is greater for dominant individuals. In almost all primate groups there seems to be a hierarchy of rank which determines the behaviour of individuals.

Rowell (1974), however, has disputed this analysis. She has suggested that dominance hierarchies are largely the result of the crowding and unnatural stress which exists among *captive* groups. Dominance hierarchies, she found, are not common among wild groups of primates, and where they do exist are more a matter of deference by subordinates than aggression by the dominant. Displays of threat are less common than displays of deference. When obvious evidence of dominance hierarchies existing in the wild has been shown, it could be the result in part of human interference. Goodall (1968) found that when she placed caches of food for her chimpanzees, the dominant males sat in the best places and the rest of the group spaced out according to rank. Where the food had to be searched for individually, the influence of rank was less obtrusive. Others, however, have found clear evidence of hierarchies in wild and undisturbed primate colonies. Deag (1977), for instance, found a linear hierarchy among a troop of Barbary macaques.

Survival functions of hierarchies

Hierarchies of this kind have an important survival function. There are clear advantages, not only for high-ranking but also for low-ranking individuals. They include the following:

- **Cohesion**. It is vital for the survival of all the members of a troop that it should stay together.
- **Predictability of social interactions**. It is to the benefit of all members of the troop, not only of the high but of the low rankers as well, that they should be able to predict how other members of the troop will react to them.
- **Avoidance of stress**. There is likely to be less fighting and stress when the outcome of conflicts can be predicted in advance. Less favoured animals will be likely to keep clear of those to whom they will inevitably lose in any competition.
- **Fluidity of hierarchies**. Rankings are not fixed for all time. As circumstances change and dominant animals become older, subordinate animals will take over.

Primate social structures are complex, however, and hierarchies may not always be linear. Studies by van der Waal (1989) in Arnhem Zoo, of free-ranging rhesus monkeys on Cayo Santiago Island (Colvin, 1983) and of African vervet monkeys (Cheney, 1983) show dynamic structures, with alliances formed, broken up and re-formed among individual animals.

Dominance and sex

Males frequently breed outside the group in which they were born but females tend to remain in the group along with mothers and sisters. For males, their rank in a group is largely determined by size. As they become sexually mature they frequently leave the group into which they were born, and this results from disputes over dominance. With females the hierarchy is different. The rank the mother holds determines the position of her daughters, the youngest mature daughter ranking immediately behind the matriarch with her sisters in reverse order of age. Gouzoules and Gouzoules (1987) have demonstrated that this is evolutionarily sensible. The youngest daughter gets most support from her mother because she has the longest reproductive span ahead of her and so has the greatest chance of passing on her genes – that is, once she has surmounted the perils of infancy and come to maturity.

Permanence of relationships between the sexes varies between species. In those just discussed, several adult males and adult females live together with no permanent male–female bonds. In other species, the family group tends to consist of just one adult male, a harem of females and their offspring. The surplus males form all-male troops, whose members occasionally challenge a male in a family group. Kummer's studies with hamadryas baboons give insight into these relationships (Kummer, 1968; Bachmann and Mummer, 1980). Baboons were caught from the wild and set up in cages. Where two unattached males were caged together and a female introduced, threats and sometimes fighting ensued until the female became attached to one of the males (usually the dominant one). Sometimes, the subordinate male was first caged singly with the female who was allowed to interact and pair with him. Then when they were put all together, the dominant male made no overtures at all to the female, if she were strongly paired already to the other male. There seemed to be the same social inhibition against poaching someone else's girl as is evident in human society.

SELF-ASSESSMENT QUESTIONS

1. Describe what is meant by a 'social dominance hierarchy'.
2. What evidence is there of social dominance hierarchies among primate species?
3. Describe the evidence for there being a relationship between the sex of primates and dominance.
4. Can it really be said that one sex is dominant over the other?

Parents and offspring

The previous sections of this chapter have alluded to the relationships between the upbringing of offspring and patterns of social and sexual relationships. This section aims to tie up some loose ends. There are various questions to be considered:

▨ What means are employed to ensure that members of a species find the most evolutionarily advantageous mating system? In other words, how does sexual selection operate?
▨ To what extent are interactions between parents and offspring governed by natural selection?
▨ What evolutionary role is played by imprinting and other forms of bonding between adults and young?
▨ How does this tie in with what is known about mother–infant interactions in the human species?
▨ How do issues such as altruistic behaviour relate to relationships between parents and offspring?

Sexual selection

There needs to be a means whereby males and females of a species find each other and remain together long enough to copulate. This can pose quite a problem for species which are solitary or widely dispersed. What is more, the chances need to be high that the offspring from copulation will be successfully reared. Females, which contribute not only genes but also some store of food in the ovum, need to be relatively sure that it is a male of the right species which copulates with her, so that her investment will not be wasted. Hybrids are infertile. As we have seen, visual displays such as that of the peacock, and audible displays as with the red deer, contribute to this insurance.

Promiscuity may be associated with female care for the young. Chimpanzee females come into oestrus only infrequently (maybe once in two years). Then all the males in the group will copulate with her. Care of the young is almost entirely in the hands of the females.

Anisogamy

Because of **anisogamy** (the fact that males and females do not have equal contributions to make, but female gametes accommodate the store of food mentioned above), females are virtually assured of finding a mate. Males, on the other hand, contribute relatively little. Consequently, it is in their interest to make their contribution in as many places as they can, to invest in as many females as they can. The exceptions are those species where the male makes a large contribution to the rearing of offspring. In these cases, the females have to compete for a mate. In a classic experiment Bateman (1948) documented the effects of anisogamy among fruit flies (*Drosophila melanogaster*). The flies had chromosomal markings which enabled Bateman to identify individuals. Groups of five males were introduced to five virgin females. Each female thus had five males to choose from and each female had to compete with four other rivals. Only 4 per cent of the females, but 21 per cent of males failed to find a mate. Even the unlucky 4 per cent of females were vigorously courted and most of the males repeatedly attempted to mate. In terms of success the most successful males produced almost three times as many offspring as the most successful females.

Parental investment

Trivers (1972) developed a **theory of parental investment**. According to this theory there is a relationship between parental investment (defined

---

GLOSSARY

Promiscuity Polygamous relationships where there is no pair bond.

Anisogamy The fact that males and females do not make an equal contribution to parenthood; the male contributing only sperm, the female contributing also some store of food in the ovum.

Theory of parental investment Trivers' account of the relationship between the investment a parent makes towards the upbringing of offspring and reproductive success.

as any behaviour toward the offspring which increases the offspring's chances of survival) and reproductive success (the number of offspring surviving). The sex with the smaller per-offspring investment will have a greater variance in reproductive success and so there will be more competition among members of that sex. Consequently, greater intrasexual display and more techniques of sexual selection will evolve. In most cases the sex with the greatest contribution to make towards raising offspring will be the female. But in some species the females are the more competitive sex. In those cases the females indulge in the most conspicuous display.

Exclusivity in sexual behaviour

The male of a species which fertilizes by insemination (and this includes all mammals, birds and reptiles) cannot be certain that the offspring which his mate is bringing up are in fact his own. It is to his advantage, from the point of view of passing on his genes, to have exclusive access to the unfertilized eggs of the female. There are various ways in which this exclusivity can be brought about:

■ Dominance systems are one way of avoiding sperm competition. The dominant male will have first access to the available females.

■ In monogamous birds (that is, birds who have just one partner) exclusivity is ensured by a time lag between bonding and copulation. This acts as a quarantine period to allow alien sperm to be detected. It is interesting to speculate whether betrothal serves the same purpose in human societies. Couples may become engaged as a preliminary bonding to ensure that there has been no infidelity prior to marriage.

Adulterers have had harsh treatment in many human societies. Among Eskimos, Australian Aborigines and Bushmen murder or fighting resulting in death often seems to be the result of retaliation for actual or suspected adultery. In more sophisticated human societies there have been very harsh penalties meted out to females found to be adulterous – stoning, for example, among the Jews of Biblical times.

DNA and exclusivity   Another dimension has been added to the issue of sexual exclusivity (among humans, at least) by the introduction and use of DNA 'fingerprinting'. This is described in Box 18.2.

Box 18.2   The use of DNA fingerprinting

Short sequences of the DNA message are repeated within the double helix which forms the genetic blueprint in every organism. The number of times a sequence is repeated and the position in which these repeats occur are peculiar to a particular individual. DNA fingerprints are part of the genetic inheritance of each of us, and have been used by the agency that has been set up to track down fathers reluctant to pay proper maintenance for their children, the Child Support Agency (CSA), to prove paternity in cases where an errant father has disputed his responsibility. It is also used extensively in criminal cases as an alternative to fingerprints, because any single trace of DNA will suffice to provide the evidence, particularly in cases of rape where a trace of sperm will be sufficient to provide a DNA fingerprint.

There is a full discussion of the issue of DNA fingerprinting in Jones (1993), *The Language of the Genes*. While it was at first supposed that this method of identification was as near to being infallible as it could be (in one American court the chance of being wrong on a DNA identification was described as one in 738 million million) it is not now considered to be quite so foolproof. Human beings are not infallible and there have been mistakes in labelling and also in the comparison by eye of the stained bands of each sample.

Courtship, then, has a betrothal role to play among animals, apart from its more obvious functions of ensuring choice of the right sex and species before copulation, overcoming aggression and arousing responsiveness in the partner.

Some definitions of mating behaviour

Wilson (1975) claims polygamy to be natural for all animals. Monogamy, where it occurs, is the result of evolutionary pressure to equalize the parental investment in the rearing of offspring. This forces the establishment of sexual bonds. The evidence for his claim depends to an extent on definition of terms. **Monogamy** implies that one male and one female join to rear at least one brood. Sometimes it extends for a lifetime. **Polygamy** covers any form of multiple mating. A form of polygamy where one male mates with several females is termed **polygyny**. The converse (where one female mates with several males) is **polyandry**. There is both simultaneous and **serial polygayny**: matings may take place in succession or more or less at the same time. Where simultaneous polygyny occurs it can be referred to as **harem polygyny**. In most cases there is at least a temporary **pair bond**, even in polygamous species. Where there is not this bond polygamy can be said to be promiscuous. Even in promiscuous relationships, according to Selander (1972), matings are not random but highly selective.

Conditions promoting polygamy

Wilson (1975) lists five general conditions which promote polygamy:

- Local or seasonal superabundance of food.
- Risk of heavy predation.
- Precocial young.
- Sexual bimaturism (males and females of some species come to maturity at different ages) and extended longevity.
- Nested territories due to niche division between the sexes.

Many of the details of the above conditions have been mentioned earlier in this chapter, but it is appropriate to summarize here.

Superabundance of food The condition of superabundance of food relates to the polygyny threshold model of Orians (1969) and Verner (1965) (sometimes termed the Orians–Verner model). This links polygyny to the availability of easy food resources, or conversely, monogamy to comparative scarcity.

Predation Where there is heavy predation on a species there will be a greater chance of offspring being raised if both parents are there to provide protection. This favours monogamy. Von Haartman (1969) relates polygyny to the nest sites preferred by particular species. Where these are well protected, males may spend more time courting additional females.

Precocial young In species which have **precocial young**, which can move around and fend for themselves very early, there is less need for male participation in the upbringing of offspring and they

can devote more of their energies to display and to fighting for additional mates. Polygynous species with precocial young include pheasants, partridges and the like, but the relationship between precocity in the young and polygyny is certainly not invariable. Exceptions include swans, geese and ducks.

Sexual bimaturism and extended longevity

Sexual bimaturism refers to the fact that in some species males and females mature at different ages. Among these and among long-lived species there is a tendency to defer reproduction until they are large and mature enough to gain dominance. During their first year adult males do not mate, though females breed freely. The dominance gained by this forbearance leads to the insemination of more than sufficient females to make up for the loss during the first year. Bimaturism is widespread among polygynous species of birds and mammals. Examples include elephant seals (*Mirounga leonina*) (Carrick et al., 1962), mountain sheep (Geist, 1971) and red-winged blackbirds (Peek, 1971).

Nested territories Where species breed within the confines of a feeding territory and the female is smaller than the male (or for some other reason requires less space) and if she cares for her offspring on her own, a given feeding territory will be able to support more than one female. Thus lizards (*Anolis*) and geckos (*Gehyra variegate*) have evolved poly-

---

GLOSSARY

Monogamy The union of one male and one female of a species to rear at least one brood. exclusively.

Polygamy Any form of multiple mating, which includes both polyandry and polygyny.

Polyandry The mating of one female with several males.

Polygyny The mating of one male with several females.

Serial polygayny A mating system where a male mates with several females, one at a time.

Harem polygyny A mating system where a male has several females to mate with at the same time.

Pair bond An attachment between a male and a female of a species which may be either permanent or temporary.

Precocial young Offspring of a species which are able to move around and fend for themselves very early in life. These include pheasants, swans and ducks.

Sexual bimaturism The maturation of males and females of a particular species at different ages.

gamous mating behaviour (Schoener and Schoener, 1971; Bustard, 1970).

Instinctive mechanisms of care

The important thing is that the offspring should survive to reach adulthood. In many instances this means that some parental care is necessary. The very young have not had the time to learn from experience what they have to do to be cared for, so that much of their behaviour must be instinctive. There is instinctive behaviour on both sides of the interaction between adult and young as the following examples show.

Parent herring gulls are instinctively ready to open their beaks to regurgitate food when chicks peck at them (Tinbergen and Perdeck, 1950).

A comparison has been made between the feeding rituals of razor bills and guillemots. While the guillemot parent presents the chicks with a single fish tail first, sheltering the fish at the same time with its wings and feet, the razor bill presents the fish in its bill openly for the young to peck at. Each species evolved ritual instinctive behaviour with which to ensure the survival of their own chicks. When eggs were transferred from the nest of one species to that of the other, many of the chicks died before they could adapt to the foreign feeding rituals of the other species. Parents and offspring in either case had mutually adapted to the responses of their own young.

Trevarthen (1975) has investigated the interactions of human babies with adults. He coined the term 'prespeech' to describe the mouth movements he observed during these interactions. He suggested that babies were endowed at birth with quite complex abilities. Similarly, Condon and Sander (1974) analysing video recordings of babies' interactions with their caregivers reported that they appeared to synchronize their movements to the rhythms of the speech of adults. This synchrony they saw as the prototype of the turn-taking which is part of adult conversation.

Imprinting

The phenomenon of **imprinting**, described in Chapter 16, represents yet another set of interactions between offspring and adults. Environmental circumstances are clearly involved as well. Species which are able to move around as soon as they are born or hatched, such as ducklings or goslings, face the problem of the mutual recognition of parents and offspring. This can particularly prove a problem where animals live in groups. They need to make sure they are caring only for their own offspring. Imprinting is a rapid form of learning. The young animal is predisposed by instinct to respond to any object it sees or hears during a fairly short 'sensitive' period after hatching. Lorenz (1952) had greylag goslings follow him wherever he went, even into the lake to teach them to swim. Many imprinting experiments have been done which have shown young birds 'imprint' on many different bright, noisy moving objects.

Mechanisms of attachment in mammals

This kind of mechanism for mutual attachment of adults to offspring does not seem to be restricted to birds. Goats and sheep need to see and smell kids or lambs shortly after birth or they will reject them. Farmers attempting to make a sheep accept a lamb which does not belong to it sometimes impregnate the lamb with its foster-mother's smell by rubbing it with its bedding straw. The mechanism seems to be a matter of instinct, but it depends upon triggers in the environment to become operative.

Even in the case of humans, though we are not a species which is mobile at birth as birds and sheep or goats are, there still seem to be mechanisms which attach the baby to its mother at a very early stage. MacFarlane (1975) has shown that babies will respond selectively to their own mother's bra-pads as young as three days old and there is selective response to her voice by 30 days old (Mehler et al., 1978).

Bereavement

Goodall (1974), in her observations of chimpanzees in Tanzania, records the death of Flo, one of the chimpanzee mothers she was observing. Flo had a son, already eight years old and independent, but such was his depression following his mother's death that he stopped eating and died shortly afterwards. Among humans, too, bereavement is an important cause of illness and even death. Parkes (1972) has identified three stages of reaction to bereavement:

GLOSSARY
Imprinting Mechanism whereby offspring of precocial species form attachments to their parents.

1. **Denial**, during which stage the bereaved person refuses to see the death as 'real'.
2. **Pining**, which involves intense longing for the dead person, restlessness or even hallucinatory sightings of the deceased in a crowd or at a distance.
3. **Depression**, which includes feelings of apathy, self-blame and anguish.

Care from fathers and others

Among animals, as well as among humans, the care of the young does not come exclusively from the mother. Fathers also provide care, exclusively in the case of sticklebacks, partially in the cases of several kinds of monkey. Among titi and some marmosets, males carry the infants most of the time when they are not actually feeding (Mitchell, 1964). In other species the mother provides most of the care for the first year but when there is a new infant born the father takes over, at least to some extent. Rowell et al. (1964) describe what they call 'aunting' among some troop-living primates. Juvenile females who have not yet given birth themselves find any new-born animal of intense interest. They will pick the infant up, pass it round and even run off with it. The chances are that they will be related to the mother. If by taking over in this way they relieve the mother then they are increasing the chances of successful rearing of offspring to carry on the line. They are also giving themselves experience which will stand them in good stead when they come to raise their own infants.

Kin selection

Kin selection is also a factor where birds such as moorhens lay more than one clutch of eggs in a season. In such cases the young of the first brood stay with their mother throughout the season and help feed the second brood which are, of course, their siblings.

Altruism and selfishness

The issue of **altruism** or selfish behaviour provides a good illustration. Wilson (1975) provides the following definition of altruistic behaviour:

> Blood relatives bestow altruistic favors upon one another in a way that increases the average genetic fitness of the members of the network as a whole, even when this behavior reduces the individual fitnesses of certain members of the group. The members may live together or be scattered throughout the population. The essential condition is that they jointly behave in a way that benefits the group as a whole, while remaining in relatively close contact with the remainder of the population. This enhancement of kin-network welfare in the midst of a population is called kin selection . . . When a person (or animal) increases the fitness of another at the expense of his own fitness, he can be said to have performed an act of altruism.
>
> (Wilson, 1975, p. 117)

What appears on the surface to be social behaviour aimed at promoting the good of the species, sometimes at the expense of individual members of it, is in fact behaviour which promotes the '**fitness**' of the genes which members of the group share. For instance, within a hive of honeybees a large part of the population is related to the queen's daughters, who share 50 per cent of her genes. It makes evolutionary sense, therefore, for workers to be prepared to sacrifice themselves for the queen. They are sterile and so will leave no offspring to inherit their genes. The queen will pass on the workers' as well as her own genes. The explanation of such altruistic behaviour rests on the concept of kin selection.

Wilson identifies three levels of behaviour in this context: altruism, selfishness and spite.

Altruism Altruism (self-sacrifice for the fitness of another) cannot really be said to be altruistic *genetically*, though in the conventional sense it is. If individuals sacrifice themselves for their offspring, the offspring may have their reproductive life ahead of them, while that of the parent may well be over (or, at the least, shorter than theirs). Ensuring the survival of 50 per cent of one's genes is preferable to none of them being passed on.

GLOSSARY

Kin selection Support and help offered by kin to kin within a species in order to increase the chances of the survival of the kin and so of the genes which they share.

Altruism Helping behaviour or self-sacrifice without any apparent benefit to the individual behaving altruistically.

Fitness Successful adaptation to the environment so that an individual reaches maturity and reproduces, thus passing on its genes.

Selfishness Selfishness involves individuals in seeing to their own 'fitness' at the expense of that of others. While this is not laudable, it is at least understandable. However, if the others happen to be two brothers it may, in evolutionary terms, prove to be profitable. A brother will have 50 per cent of the same genes. Two brothers may be capable of passing on as many of an individual's genes as that individual is.

Spite Spite is demonstrated when individuals lower the 'fitness' of unrelated competitors with no compensating benefit to their own 'fitness'. This too may evolve if the benefits (in terms of 'fitness') for close relatives (brothers or sisters, perhaps) compensate.

Inclusive fitness

In these discussions the term 'fitness' has been used in the way in which Wilson uses it: that is, in terms of genes which are better adapted to survive. Hamilton (1964, 1970, 1971a, 1971b, 1972) has developed the concept of **inclusive fitness**. This amounts to the sum of an individual's own fitness plus the effects of his or her behaviour on the fitness of all his or her relatives.

In Hamilton's model, a coefficient of relationship r represents the fraction of an individual's genes held through common descent by two individuals. Accordingly, an individual and his or her brother have $r = 1/2$ in common, an uncle $r = 1/4$, first cousins $r = 1/8$, and so on. For altruistic, selfish or spiteful behaviour to evolve, the loss of an individual's fitness must be more than compensated for by gains in fitness made by relatives. So, if first cousins benefited only by apparently altruistic behaviour, k (Hamilton's symbol for the ratio of gain in fitness by the relatives to loss of fitness by the individual) would need to be greater than 8. That is to say, there would need to be eight times the benefit to the relatives (or benefit to eight relatives). Where the altruistic behaviour has an effect upon combinations of relatives the number of relatives of each kind are taken into account, together with their coefficients of relationship.

Hamilton deals with selfish behaviour and spiteful behaviour in a similar way. Where an animal acts selfishly this usually results in a gain by that animal in fitness. But this may not be the case if the selfish animal shares too many genes with those animals which lose by the selfish behaviour. Spiteful behaviour, too, needs to result in an *overall* gain for the genes of the spiteful individual.

Reciprocal altruism

Trivers (1971) extends these ideas further with what he terms **reciprocal altruism**. The example he uses is that of 'Good Samaritan' behaviour in humans. A man dives in to save another from drowning. The drowning man has a 50:50 chance of dying. The chances of the rescuer dying in the attempt are perhaps one in 20. If at some future date the roles are reversed and the rescuer becomes the rescued, both will have benefited. Each will have traded a 1:2 chance of dying with a 1:10 chance. Where a population at large engages upon such reciprocally altruistic behaviour, the individuals in that population will have enhanced their personal genetic fitness.

There are problems with this argument, though. What if the rescued man does not bother to reciprocate? But if cheating tarnishes a person's good name, the momentary advantage gained by cheating on a moral obligation will be outweighed by the later adverse effects on life and reproduction chances.

But while human behaviour is full of examples of altruistic behaviour, reciprocal altruism is rare in the behaviour of animals. However, Wilkinson (1984) describes a remarkable example of reciprocal altruism among vampire bats (*Desmodus rotundus*). A bat needs to find food regularly, making an incision in the victim's skin with its sharp teeth and sucking its blood; if it fails on three successive nights to find food it may die from starvation. But a bat that has not found food will often be fed by another bat regurgitating its blood meal to it. Bats feed their kin in this way but they also feed unrelated animals, especially those which are starving. The criteria for affording such help include the following:

■ They are sensitive to whether a bat is starving or well fed and can assist a starving animal at a cost to itself which is not too high. A starving bat loses weight at a greater rate than a well-fed one. Consequently, the transfer of sustenance from a

---

GLOSSARY

Inclusive fitness The sum of an individual's fitness (adaptation to the environment) together with the effect of his/her behaviour on relatives carrying some of his/her genes.

Reciprocal altruism Altruistic behaviour without any immediate benefit to relatives in the expectation that benefits will be reciprocated at a future time.

well-fed donor to a starving recipient gives the recipient more time than the donor loses.

■ Bats associate with particular other individuals over a long period of time and so remember benefits given them.

■ Bats may find themselves short of food at any time so that altruism acts as a kind of insurance policy.

■ Those who donate food will be more favourably placed than others to receive when times are hard. Altruism has a background of selfishness to it.

Some other examples of altruistic behaviour

In troops of baboons (*Papio ursinus*) dominant males position themselves in exposed locations to watch while others forage. When predators approach, the watchers bark to warn the foraging troop and even threateningly approach the intruders (Hall, 1960).

Meerkats take turns to go up to a high look-out point to keep watch for predators (exposing themselves to danger) while other members of the group feed (Macdonald, 1986).

A meerkat keeps watch for predators

Birds engage in distraction displays to attract the attention of an enemy away from eggs or young. The female nighthawk (*Chordeiles minor*) will fly conspicuously at low level away from it when an intruder approaches her nest, finally settling on the ground in front of the intruder, wings drooping and outstretched (Gramza, 1967) as though she were injured. Alarm calls (described in Chapter 17) attract the attention of an enemy away from other members of the species and towards the caller.

Recognizing kin from nonkin

Clearly if kin selection is to operate, then there has to be some means whereby the animals can distinguish kin from nonkin. Holmes and Sherman (1982) studied Belding's ground squirrels (*Spermophilus beldingi*). In some cases there were females which had been fertilized by more than one male, so that in one litter of young there may well be siblings and half-siblings. In spite of having been born from the same mother and having grown up in the same burrow, the young were more aggressive towards half-siblings than to full siblings. The researchers transferred baby squirrels to new litters when they were very young and found that they were less aggressive towards their foster siblings than to strangers but also less aggressive towards their full genetic siblings from their original litters. Not only does familiarity play a part, but there seems also to be a way in which they can recognize their full siblings even when they have not been brought up with them.

Inclusive fitness is about success in leaving offspring, and this may include individuals aiding the offspring of relatives who may be more rewarding reproductively than they can be themselves. This relates to the discussion of altruism and kinship selection.

Evolutionary interests of parents and offspring

If we have taken as the theme the ways in which the genes may best be passed on, there is clearly a balance to be struck between the numbers of young produced and the care which is afforded to each one. A human being may produce two or perhaps three children and devote a great deal of care and attention to them, sometimes for the best part of 20 years. In the past, families produced more children, perhaps as many as 15 or 20, fully expecting that not all of them would survive, and this is still the case in less-developed societies. Similarly, among animal species it is not unknown for parents to stop feeding the weakest of a litter when times get hard, and even feed it to its siblings (Polis, 1981).

Trivers (1974) has suggested there is an apparent conflict of interest between parents and offspring. While the adults have an interest in dividing the available food resources fairly, so that all the offspring may have a good chance of surviving (notwithstanding the special case mentioned above), each individual offspring has an interest in getting as much as possible. While its siblings do share some of its genes, they do not share all of them.

Again there can be a conflict when the time comes for the offspring to become independent. In human terms, it is not infrequent to find adolescents lingering on in the protected environment of home, perhaps pursuing yet another course of study, just so long as the parents will fund it. So far as passing on the genes is concerned, he or she would be better off finding a mate and rearing a new family. But of course there is always the problem of finding the resources to be able to bring them up. Where animals produce young serially, one at a time, as

is the case with cattle, for instance, there is a stage of conflict when the parent abandons the young animal which has now reached maturity, in favour of producing and caring for the next.

Much of the contents of the preceding paragraphs has juxtaposed human and animal behaviour to emphasize that to an extent we are all animals and much of animal behaviour has resonances for us too.

? SELF-ASSESSMENT QUESTIONS

1. What is the 'theory of parental investment'? How does it link parental investment in offspring with competition for sexual selection?
2. What are some of the ways in which interactions between adult and offspring are instinctive?
3. Attachment of young to adults is clearly important in a wide range of species. To what extent does it appear to be due to learning?
4. What sources of conflict of interest exist between parents and offspring?

Chapter summary

■ Animals, including humans, interact with each other in diverse ways, combining themselves together to form tight or less tight groupings. There are evolutionary advantages to this grouping which include physical protection from cold or from predation, defence, better utilization of available food resources, facilitation of sexual activity (Fraser Darling found that sexual activity was enhanced by the presence of other individuals of the same species) and cooperation in hunting for prey. Disadvantages (for nothing is free of cost) include competition for food, spread of disease and cannibalism.

■ Some insects are organized according to a caste system. There is cooperation in rearing the young as well as division of labour, with sterile workers helping to rear the next generation of individuals who share at least some of their genes. Generations overlap so that while parents support offspring, they will in turn

be supported at a later stage of life. There is rigid demarcation into castes, determined by such things as nutrition and pheromones. Each caste has specific functions within the group such as foraging, rearing young, guarding the colony and attending the queen. Members of castes are anatomically differentiated also.

■ Forms of territorial organization are closely linked to mating behaviour. The lek might be compared to a fashion parade. Nest sites form another territorial division which influences success in breeding and rearing young. There is a close relationship between the scarcity or plentifulness of food and the mating system adopted. The polygyny threshold model developed by Verner and Wilson links polygyny with availability of food resources.

■ There is a link between territorial behaviour and aggression in animals. Physiological and other factors combine to suggest that aggression has an innate component. While it is more common among males, it is not exclusively a male trait.

■ Among some species (red deer and hens are examples) there exists a social dominance hierarchy, with the strongest individuals becoming dominant and having best choice of mate. This seems to have evolutionary advantages. The strongest individuals are likely to produce the strongest offspring, most likely to be successful.

■ Mating systems and the rearing of young also have a bearing on evolutionary success. Trivers' theory of parental investment has suggested a relationship between parental investment (any behaviour by parents which enhances the offspring's chances of success) and variance in reproductive success.

Polygamy is likely to be associated with five general conditions, according to Wilson: seasonal super-abundance of food, risk of predation, precocial young, sexual bimaturism and nested territories.

■ Some mechanisms for the care of offspring are instinctive. Examples include gull chicks pecking at their parents' bills so that they regurgitate food, as well as the behaviour of human babies as they interact with their mothers. Imprinting seems to be a special case of a mechanism for attachment to the species.

■ The evolutionary interests of parents and offspring are not identical. Altruism and kin selection relate to the sharing of genes between close relatives. An individual child has an interest in survival while its parent may have an interest in its siblings too surviving.

Further reading

Lea, S.E.G. (1984). *Instinct, Environment and Behaviour.* London: Methuen. Makes some very useful comparisons between human and animal behaviour, particularly in the area of parenting and the upbringing of offspring.

Manning, A. and Dawkins, M. (1992). *Animal Behaviour*, 4th edn. Cambridge: Cambridge University Press. Contains a good account of mating systems and social organization within a number of species, and provides an excellent account of animal behaviour from a biological standpoint.

Epilogue to Part 4

This chapter, and the whole of our discussion of animal behaviour, takes a sociobiological approach. Natural selection is the guiding principle. This involves the way in which one allele (one of a pair of genes, each of which determines a particular sort of behaviour or characteristic) survives into the next generation because it is 'fitter' or better adapted than the alternative allele. But this is by no means the whole story. Culture and learning are important also. The culture and the environment in which a creature lives and its capacity for learning have a crucial impact upon its behaviour and its behaviour in turn will influence its chances of survival. Gene–culture coevolution, which has been referred to in the introduction to this part, goes some way towards accounting for why humans have developed at a much faster rate than animal species.

The sociobiological approach has not been without its critics and some of the initial hostility towards the ideas it espouses have also been outlined in the introduction to this part. Some of these criticisms are listed here:

▨ Rose et al. (1990) castigate it as just another example of genetic determinism, ignoring other levels of explanation (for example, social, cultural or cognitive explanations). However, Lumsden and Wilson (1983) have gone some way towards meeting this criticism.

▨ Sociobiologists, additionally, are using the term 'gene' rather differently from the way in which it is used by geneticists. Dawkins (1976) refers to it as a 'unit of natural selection' without fully explaining the biological processes which go on in the cell. Hayes (1986) has criticized this as being circular and misleading.

▨ Gould (1981) has also criticized the methodology employed by sociobiologists in trying to explain particular instances of animal behaviour in terms of their evolutionary significance, rather than endeavouring to discover the principles and mechanisms which underlie behaviour.

▨ Hinde (1987) has argued that while the biological perspective taken by the sociobiologists is important it is only one of several ways of explaining human behaviour. Extrapolating from animal to human behaviour is dangerous. Humans have different levels of cognitive ability from animals and have capacity for language. Animal species are also enormously diverse, as Wilson (1992) has demonstrated in his book *The Diversity of Life*. However, if this account provides insights into the behaviour of humans and animals then it will have served its purpose.

PART 5

Human development

Developmental psychology involves the study of the psychological changes that take place in people between birth and old age. The most dramatic changes occur in childhood. Therefore, most research has focused upon childhood and adolescence. This is also, in part, because the two most significant theorists to influence our thinking about development, Freud and Piaget, concentrated on the period up to adolescence.

The study of adults did not emerge to any great extent until after World War II. Even today there are relatively few psychologists who study adulthood per se, and only the study of the aged has received substantial attention from researchers. Nonetheless, research interest in adult development is growing and that interest will be reflected in this part of the book.

Contents

INTRODUCTION
The study of development 421
- Influences on development 421
- The ecology of development 422
- Cultural influences on development 424
- Research designs and methods 425
- Ethical considerations 426
- Theoretical approaches in the study of development 426

CHAPTER 19
Early socialization and attachment 428
- Developing social relationships 429
- The development of attachment 436
- Attachment, separation and deprivation 445
- Children's play 451

CHAPTER 20
Cognitive development 459
- Piaget's theory of cognitive development 460
- Cognitive development in a social context 468

- Information-processing approaches to cognitive development 474
- Language acquisition 478

CHAPTER 21
Intelligence – its origins and measurement 487
- The measurement of intelligence 487
- Alternative views of intelligence 492
- Origins of differences in IQ 496

CHAPTER 22
Social behaviour 502
- Cognitive-developmental theory and social cognition 502
- Moral development 504
- Development of gender 513
- Understanding self and others 524

CHAPTER 23
Adolescence and adulthood 535
- Adolescence 535
- Lifespan development: the study of adulthood 543
- Young adulthood 547
- Middle adulthood 552
- Late adulthood 557

The study of development

Influences on development

Traditionally, psychologists have related developmental processes to age. For example, the reasoning ability of a typical five year old is very different to that of a nine year old. A developmental psychologist may wish to investigate the processes involved in this progression. What experiences and interactions have influenced the child's development? However, in 1980, Baltes, a German psychologist, wrote an influential paper emphasizing the lifespan nature of development and pointing out that factors other than age influence the developmental process (Baltes et al., 1980).

Baltes proposed that there are three important influences on development (see Figure 5I.1). He called these influences normative age-graded, normative history-graded and nonnormative life events.

- **Normative age-graded influences** are those which are strongly related to chronological age.

For example, the way in which children develop language ability is very closely linked to their age, a two year old having far less mastery of language than a five year old.

- **Normative history-graded influences** are those related to events happening at a particular time and affecting most members of a given generation (or 'cohort'). Examples might be the civil war in the former Yugoslavia or the famine in Rwanda.

- **Nonnormative life events** are those which may influence the development of individuals at particular times and at different ages. Examples might be the effects of divorce in a family or a severe accident resulting in physical disability.

Baltes pointed out that each influence is determined by an interaction of biological and environmental factors (see Box 5I.1), though one or the other may be the more dominant in particular circumstances.

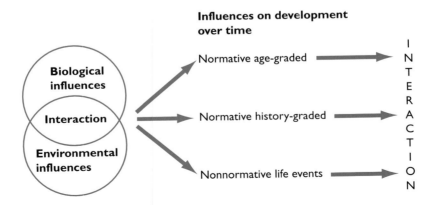

Figure 5I.1 Influences on development (Adapted from Baltes, 1980)

Box 5I.1   The interaction of biological and social factors

It has been said that development is about how the 'biological' infant turns into the 'social' adult. Throughout the history of psychology, there has been a tradition of separating out 'heredity' and 'environment', 'nature' and 'nurture', 'biology' and 'society' in attempts to explain how a child develops particular qualities and capacities. (See Chapter 2 for a detailed discussion of the heredity–environment issue.) It is now generally accepted that development occurs through an interaction of biological factors (genetic programming) and social factors (the quality of the environment). This is by no means a simple proposition. There are two ways in which this interaction could be considered.

On the one hand, we could look at the skills a child is born with and watch how these skills develop and are influenced by particular experiences as the child matures. This is the general approach taken by those who have studied perceptual development and language development.

Alternatively, we could look for ways in which the same environment might have different effects on children who are born with different characteristics. One important approach of this kind has involved the study of vulnerable and resilient children.

Horowitz (1987, 1990) sees the 'vulnerable' child as starting life with a particular handicap such as premature birth or 'difficult' temperament. The 'resilient' child will start life with a particular advantage, such as a sunny disposition. Horowitz proposes that a child's inborn vulnerability or resilience interacts with the 'facilitative-ness' of the environment. A highly facilitative environment is one where the child has loving and sensitive parents and is provided with rich and stimulating experiences.

It might be supposed that the most favourable consequences would occur for resilient infants brought up in highly facilitative environments, the least favourable for vulnerable infants in unsatisfactory environments, with other combinations falling somewhere in between. However, Horowitz suggests that a resilient child may do quite well in a poor environment. Similarly, a vulnerable child might do quite well in a highly facilitative environment. According to Horowitz's model, it is only the vulnerable child in a poor environment who experiences extreme disadvantage.

Horowitz' model of development is receiving support from a growing body of research. For example, low-birthweight children brought up in middle-class homes tend to have normal IQs, as do normal-weight children reared in poverty-level homes. However, children who are low-birthweight *and* reared in poverty-level homes are most likely to have very low IQs (Werner, 1986). Psychologists are beginning to realize that the same environment can have very different effects on development, depending upon the inborn characteristics of the child.

The ecology of development

Recent researchers into human development have emphasized the importance of studying the **ecology of development** – or development in context. By 'ecology' is meant the environmental conditions which a person experiences or is affected by, directly or indirectly. This is an approach based on the work of the American psychologist, Urie Bronfenbrenner (1979).

Bronfenbrenner believed that the environment within which an individual develops is much more complex than was originally thought. It is much more than just 'the immediate, concrete setting containing the living creature' though this may be an appropriate way to think of it in relation to animal behaviour. Bronfenbrenner proposes that the ecological environment consists of a set of four nested systems: the microsystem, the mesosystem, the exosystem and the macrosystem (see Figure 5I.2).

■ At the heart is the **microsystem**, stemming from an individual's experiences in a particular setting. For example, one system a young child experiences is the pattern of activities and interactions in the home environment with parents and siblings. As the child grows older, he

> ### GLOSSARY
>
> **Development** All the physical and psychological changes that take place between birth and old age.
>
> **Ecology of development** The study of development in the context of the environmental conditions a person experiences or is affected by, directly or indirectly.

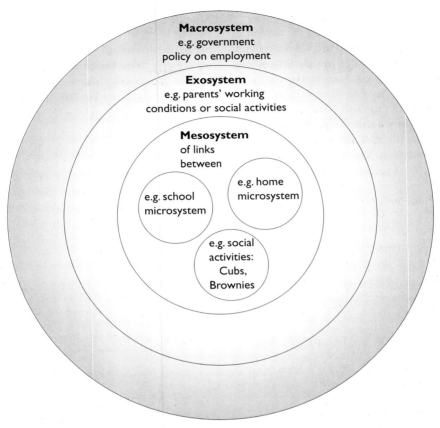

Figure 51.2 The ecology of development: development in context (Bronfenbrenner, 1979)

or she is influenced by other microsystems, in settings such as playgroup, school, church and so on. Most psychological research has been carried out from the perspective of the microsystem: for example, patterns of play in the nursery school or interactions between mother and child in the home.

- At the next level is the **mesosystem**. This involves the relationships between the various settings the developing individual participates in. For example, for a child, this might be the links between the home and school environments; for an adult those between family and work settings.
- The third level, the **exosystem**, refers to settings in which children do not actively participate, but which do affect them. For example, the parents' work or their social activities may influence the kind of care given to children.

- The final level, the **macrosystem**, consists of the organization of the social institutions and the ideologies that exist in the society of which the individual is a part. Factors such as generally accepted working hours, rates of unemployment, social mores about working mothers or the availability of child care may affect parents' well-being in the work situation which in turn will affect a child's microsystems and mesosystems.

An evaluation of Bronfenbrenner's model

The value of Bronfenbrenner's model lies in showing us the importance of recognizing all these systems as well as the links between them, when we conceptualize and design psychological investigations – not just the microsystems which have most commonly been studied.

Bronfenbrenner suggests that developmental psychologists should strive to understand the ecological environment as it influences the child's development. For example, events such as starting nursery school, having a new sibling, going to university and, more indirectly, factors such as parental unemployment or divorce, present individuals with challenges to which they must adapt. In this way, development takes place. Bronfenbrenner believes that the best way to understand people is to look at how they cope with and adapt to change.

Criticisms of ecological theory

Thomas (1992) has argued that Bronfenbrenner's theory does not lead to very precise and testable hypotheses. This may in part reflect the fact that existing developmental research had tended to neglect the role played by ecological factors as represented by Bronfenbrenner. However, Thomas holds that, notwithstanding this point, the theory is imprecise about important factors such as the relationships between microsystems. (For example, how does involvement in the family relate to involvement at school?) Thomas concludes that though there has been insufficient research carried out to test and develop the theory, it remains a very important framework for developmental psychology since, unlike some theories, it attempts to address the real world directly.

Cultural influences on development

In studying the ecology of development, Bronfenbrenner does not examine the concept of **culture**. However, if we are to understand development we must examine cultural influences as part of the environment in which the child is growing up (see Box 51.2).

GLOSSARY

Culture A system of meanings and customs, relating to such things as values, attitudes, laws, protocols, kinds of dwellings, and so on, shared by some identifiable group.

Box 51.2 Cultural influences on development

While there is no generally agreed definition of the term, culture basically refers to a system of meanings and customs, including values, attitudes, goals, laws, beliefs, morals, physical artefacts such as tools, kinds of dwellings and so on (Bee, 1995). In order to be called a culture, this system of meanings and customs must be shared by some identifiable group and transmitted from one generation of that group to the next (Betancourt and Lopez, 1993).

Culture clearly has an impact upon the way families socialize their offspring. It is important to realize that actions or events that appear to be the same on the surface may have totally different meanings in different cultural contexts. (See Chapter 19, where cross-cultural differences in attachment behaviour in young children is considered.) For example, smacking a child might be acceptable in one culture but be considered a brutal form of abuse in another.

Bee (1995) argues that there are two main reasons why studying culture is important to the understanding of development:

- If we are to discover those aspects of development which are truly universal, it is not sufficient to study white, middle-class children from Western cultures and assume that what is observed applies to all children.
- If we are to understand fully how the environment influences a child's development, it is important to understand culture as part of that environment. We need to consider how different cultural beliefs influence the way people experience their lives. For example, it has been argued that the heavy emphasis in Western cultures on independence, achievement and freedom of the individual leads to a higher level of tolerance of aggression and violence than is evident in other cultures (Lore and Schultz, 1993). This could be one explanation for the growing violence in Western cultures.

So far in developmental psychology, there has been insufficient truly cross-cultural research to draw on, with most studies restricted to just a few cultures which have much in common, such as European and North American. However, the database is expanding and this book will refer to the findings from cross-cultural research wherever possible.

Research designs and methods

In order to study human behaviour scientifically, developmental psychologists use a number of different research designs and methods. Those most commonly used are summarized below.

Where the aim is to observe age-related changes in some area of psychological functioning, two principal designs have been used to gather information about individuals at different points in their development: **cross-sectional** and **longitudinal design**.

Cross-sectional design

In a cross-sectional design, groups of individuals of different ages are compared at the same point of time. For example, researchers who wish to compare moral values held during early adulthood with those held during middle age will make observations or carry out tests on groups of both young and middle-aged adults at one time. Conclusions will then be drawn about moral values at these two age levels. The strengths of cross-sectional design include:

- It is quick and relatively inexpensive;
- It can be easily replicated;
- It can identify differences between age groups and general trends in development which may then be studied more intensively.

The limitations of cross-sectional design include:

- Because behaviour is observed at only one time, it tells us nothing about development within individuals;
- People of widely differing age groups will have received different social and cultural experiences, and observations might reflect these differences rather than differences due to age.

Longitudinal design

In a longitudinal study, a single group of individuals will be studied over a period of time, usually a number of years. Observations and tests will be carried out at various time intervals. Thus, a study of moral values during adulthood might involve testing one group of adults every ten years between the ages of 20 and 60. The strengths of this design include:

- It provides a view of the development of individuals over time;

- Questions can be answered about the stability of behaviour;
- It may be possible to determine some of the effects of earlier experience and conditions on later development.

Its limitations include:

- It requires a very large investment of time and money;
- Participants may be lost or drop out, and those who remain may form a biased group;
- Changes in societal influences at different points in time may result in some rather dated conclusions being drawn. When the study was originally designed, it may have asked research questions that are no longer relevant or interesting. For example, the effects of divorce on a child's psychological adjustment might be very different now that divorce is more socially acceptable than it was, say, 30 years ago.

Cohort design

Baltes's model of three major kinds of influence on development, referred to earlier, led to other kinds of research design for studying development, in addition to the cross-sectional and longitudinal ones already considered. One of these is cohort design, in which different samples of children born in different years are compared at the same ages. This, of course, involves studying the samples at different points in time. It therefore combines some of the features of cross-sectional design with some of longitudinal design and capitalizes on the strengths of both.

An extension of this is **cohort-sequential design**. Here, it would be possible to study, say, the effects of particular educational policies on children born in 1985, 1990 and 1995. Each cohort would be followed

---

GLOSSARY

Cross-sectional design A research design which involves groups of individuals who vary on a particular dimension, often age, being compared at the same point in time.

Longitudinal design A research design which involves a single group of individuals being studied over a period of time.

Cohort-sequential design A research design which combines features of cross-sectional design with those of longitudinal design by studying samples of different ages and then comparing them over a period of time.

through longitudinally from, say, age 3 to age 16. This would provide both cross-sectional and longitudinal data and would allow researchers also to assess the impact of historical changes over a period of time.

Because of their complexity and the time involved, cohort-sequential designs have not yet become widely used except as small-scale studies. One example is a study by Olweus (1989) into the problems of school bullying in Norway.

Figure 5I.3 summarizes the characteristics of cross-sectional, longitudinal and cohort designs.

Methods of study

Within the overall research designs discussed above, a wide range of different methods can be used to make observations and collect data. These include experimentation, observation, clinical interview, survey, correlational techniques and case study. All of these methods are described and evaluated in Chapter 34 and it can be seen that each has particular strengths and weaknesses. The method chosen by an investigator will depend largely upon what aspect of development is being studied. Ideally, a number of different methods should be used within one study. If these different methods produce similar findings, confidence can be placed in the conclusions drawn.

Ethical considerations

Any research into human behaviour raises some ethical questions. If we go into someone's home to observe parent–child interaction, we are invading the family's privacy. Parents may even feel that there is an implication that something is wrong with the way they

are bringing up their children. If we test adults or children in a laboratory situation, some will perform worse than others; there is a risk that some participants may react badly to what they perceive as a poor performance. Some ethical issues are considered in Box 5I.3.

Theoretical approaches in the study of development

Three major theoretical approaches have been used in the study of development:

■ The **psychodynamic approach**, which arises from Freud's theory of personality development and has been upheld by neo-Freudians such as Erikson;

■ The **learning theory approach**, which is based on the work of the early behaviourists such as Watson, Pavlov and Thorndike and more recently the work of Skinner and that of the social learning theorist, Bandura, and others.

GLOSSARY

Psychodynamic approach An approach to the study of development which is based upon Freud's theory of personality development.

Learning theory approach An approach to the study of development based upon behaviourist learning theory and social learning theory.

Cognitive-developmental approach An approach to the study of development derived initially from Piaget's theory of cognitive development.

Figure 5I.3 Characteristics of research designs

Cross-sectional Different samples	Studied at different ages	At the same point in time
Longitudinal One sample	Studied at different ages	At various points in time
Cohort Different samples born at different times	Studied at the same ages	At various points in time

Box 51.3 Ethical issues in developmental research

In the UK the British Psychological Society has issued guidelines on ethical questions in research (BPS, 1990) (see Chapter 5 for a detailed discussion of ethical issues). In the USA, similar guidance is offered by the US Department of Health and Human Services, which all recipients of grants must adhere to.

The most fundamental guideline is that participants in research must be protected from possible mental or physical harm. More specific guidelines include the following:

Informed consent

Participants must agree in writing to take part in the investigation. In the case of research involving children, informed consent must be obtained from the parent or guardian. The procedures to be used and their possible consequences should be described. For example, if you intended to study relationships between adolescents and their parents, you might wish to observe individual families as they discussed some area of conflict between them. Before starting the study, it would be essential to explain to each family exactly what would be involved and to point out that the scenarios to be observed might sometimes promote tension. After the procedure, you would need to debrief the families and offer support to any who found it particularly stressful.

Research with children

Ethical guidelines are particularly important in research involving children. Any child who is reluctant to take part must not be tested or observed; any child who becomes distressed must be comforted; potential risks to a child's psychological well-being must be avoided.

The informed consent of children presents some problems. Even if they can reasonably be expected to understand fully what it is they are agreeing to, it is important to make sure that the consent of a parent or guardian is obtained.

■ The **cognitive-developmental approach**, which was initially derived from Piaget's theory of cognitive development, but recently has encompassed work by other theorists such as Kohlberg, Bruner and Vygotsky. The study of social cognition, ways in which children perceive, understand and conceptualize about other human beings and about social relationships, can also be included within this approach.

Each of these approaches has been considered in detail in Chapter 1. Social learning theory is addressed in detail in Chapter 6 and social cognition is discussed in Chapter 22.

? SELF-ASSESSMENT QUESTIONS

1. Describe the three main influences on development proposed by Baltes (1980).
2. Discuss Bronfenbrenner's (1979) theory relating to the ecology of development.
3. Why is it important to study cultural influences on development?
4. Which research design, cross-sectional, longitudinal or cohort sequential, do you consider would be the most appropriate for the study of children's patterns of play behaviour at different ages? Give reasons for your answer.
5. Discuss some ethical considerations that might arise in developmental research.
6. What are the main theoretical approaches used in the study of development?

CHAPTER 19

Early socialization and attachment

Developing social relationships   429
- Early social interactions   429
- Parenting   431
- Siblings   434
- Grandparents   435

The development of attachment   436
- Early attachment and later development   436
- Bowlby's theory   436
- Security of attachment   439
- Criticisms of the attachment construct   442
- Attachments after infancy   443
- Early attachment and later relationships   445

Attachment, separation and deprivation   445
- Bowlby's 'maternal deprivation' hypothesis   446
- A reassessment of maternal deprivation   447
- Care outside the home: childminding and day care   448

Children's play   451
- What is play?   451
- Some theories of play   452
- Studies of play   453
- What is the value of play?   455

Objectives

By the end of this chapter, you should be able to:

- Understand the concept of socialization;

- Describe some of the major milestones in the social and emotional development of infants and consider early social interactions both with parents and other family members;

- Describe the views of Bowlby and other researchers concerning the nature and significance of attachment;

- Describe and assess the importance of the Strange Situation procedure for measuring attachment in infancy and consider some measures of attachment in older children and adults;

- Critically evaluate Bowlby's views on maternal deprivation in the light of subsequent re-assessments of his work;

- Assess the importance of early experience for later social and emotional development in the light of the available evidence;

- Discuss the nature and functions of play in early childhood.

Socialization is a concept which is used to describe and explain how children acquire the behaviour necessary to enable them to fit in with their culture or society. It is the process by which people acquire the rules of behaviour, the systems of beliefs and attitudes

---

GLOSSARY

Socialization The process by which people learn the ways of a given society or social group, so that they can function within it.

of a given society or social group, so that they can function within it.

In infancy, the socialization process is influenced most by the parents, who act as models for acceptable behaviour, provide loving support and decide on which behaviours to restrict and which to allow. However, increasingly, research findings indicate the importance also of a young child's relationships with people other than the parents: for example, siblings and grandparents.

It is important not to think of socialization as unidirectional (moving in one direction) – something which is imposed on children by other people. Babies are not passive beings waiting to be moulded into a particular kind of personality. They are active individuals, each with its own genetic potential, who are capable of influencing the way other people react to them. Most parents of more than one child will be able to testify to the differences between their infants – what was effective with one child did not necessarily work with another. Therefore, we should take a bidirectional (two-way) view of the socialization process.

While the term socialization used to be applied exclusively to the developing behaviour of the child, it has over the past few years widened to consider the adjustments and changes which take place through life. This chapter will be concerned mainly with some of the processes which influence social and emotional development in infants and young children, and will consider in particular the development and significance of the intimate attachments which are formed between children and the adults who care for them. However, it will also briefly consider the attachment process in older children and adults.

Developing social relationships

Before considering children's social development in detail, it is important to note a number of events – or milestones: – which occur during the first year of life (Bornstein and Lamb, 1988). Box 19.1 outlines four of these milestones: **social smiling, stranger anxiety, separation anxiety** and **social attachment**.

Early social interactions

There have been a few rare instances where a child has been found in a state of extreme deprivation and has had little or no interaction with other human beings. For example, Davis (1947) described the case of a little girl, Anna, who was found at the age of six in an attic where she had been kept with no social contact since she was a baby. When she was discovered, Anna could not speak or feed herself and was totally apathetic. What she had in common with other children found in similar circumstances was that she was completely lacking in the normal skills of social interaction, in fact was considered to be 'barely human'.

What cases such as Anna's show is that children's development takes place to a large degree through social relationships. Other people's behaviour towards the child and the child's behaviour towards them influence the development of personality, cognition (perception, memory, thinking) language, emotion and, of course, social behaviour.

Mutual reciprocity

Schaffer (1977) drew attention to what was termed the **mutual reciprocity** (giving and receiving) of the infant–mother relationship. He described the sensitive and finely balanced patterns of interaction which occur as each responds to the activities of the other and each influences the behaviour of the other. So how do these crucial early social interactions take place and what are the factors which help the development of social interactions between an infant and other people?

Smith and Cowie (1991) describe a number of characteristics which can be observed in the young baby's repertoire of behaviour. These include:

GLOSSARY

Social smiling The voluntary smiles that an infant starts to produce around four to six weeks old, usually prompted by an overture from an adult.

Stranger anxiety (wariness) The wariness or distress which a child displays from about eight months of age when faced with a strange adult.

Separation anxiety The protest or distress exhibited by a child from about the age of eight months when separated from an attachment figure.

Social attachment A bond of affection directed by a child towards a specific individual.

Mutual reciprocity Schaffer's (1977) term for the reciprocal patterns of interaction which occur between an infant and caregiver.

Box 19.1 Milestones in social and emotional development

Social smiling

A necessary precursor to the socialization process is the existence of communication, or 'social signals', between child and adults. One such signal which has been investigated is social smiling. Although newborn infants often produce facial expressions which look like smiling, these expressions seem to represent involuntary reactions to the child's physical state, for example tiredness or discomfort. Voluntary smiling, often smiling which occurs in response to overtures from an adult, usually starts when the infant is around four to six weeks old. Smiles are initially prompted by a variety of things, including faces, bells and bullseyes (Emde and Harmon, 1972). Gradually, however, they are reserved for social contexts, with the human face being the most likely stimulus to encourage smiles. From the second and third months, the child seems capable of recognizing particular faces and thereafter is most likely to smile in response to familiar people, such as members of the family or regular visitors. Less familiar individuals will bring forth only weak smiles. Infant smiles appear to serve as a powerful mechanism which are designed to attract the attention of adults and encourage them to come closer.

Stranger anxiety or wariness

At about the age of eight to nine months, a child will often exhibit what Spitz (1965) has described as 'eight months anxiety'. This refers to the wariness or open distress which the young child displays when faced with a strange adult. The phenomenon of 'stranger anxiety' has been extensively studied by Ainsworth (1969; Ainsworth et al., 1974). It will be considered in greater detail later in this chapter.

Separation anxiety

In the early weeks of life, a baby will not discriminate between different people. If you pick it up it will respond no differently to you than it would to anyone else. At around six to eight months, babies begin to protest if they are separated from specific people, usually the parent. If the separation continues, the reaction changes from distress and anger (Bowlby, 1973, 1980, called this the 'protest' stage) to apparent depression and dejection (the stage of 'despair'). Finally, the child apparently recovers, adjusts to the situation and becomes responsive again to social overtures (the stage of detachment). A child under the age of six months who experiences a long-term separation from the parent may appear to be unsettled by new routines and approaches. However, this cannot be compared to the extreme distress and misery that has been observed in older infants who have experienced similar separations (Yarrow, 1964).

Social attachment

Attachment may be defined as a bond of affection directed towards a specific individual. In a young child, the first strong attachments appear to form around eight months and tend to coincide with the emergence of separation anxiety as described above. Once a baby becomes mobile, it is possible to observe the kinds of behaviour which signal that an attachment has been formed. These include:

- moving towards and staying close to the parent (or main care giver), particularly when distressed or afraid;
- protest when separated from the adult;
- clinging and using the adult as a 'secure base' from which to explore.

John Bowlby (1969), a key theorist in attachment research, believed that these behaviours have survival value and are designed to encourage physical (and later psychological) closeness to the mother. Bowlby's theories and research will be considered in more detail later in this chapter.

The ability to learn From a very early age, babies pay attention to human faces and voices in preference to other stimuli. To the delight of parents, they learn to distinguish between the familiar voice of the mother or father and other less familiar voices (Mehler et al., 1978). Behaviour such as this is likely to make parents feel 'special' and become even more responsive.

Behaviours which invite social responses For a very young baby, smiling or crying does not have any social meaning. A baby cries if hungry or uncomfortable and often seems to smile quite randomly. However, parents tend to respond to these signals as if the child were trying to initiate social interaction. If babies cry, they are likely to pick them up and talk to them; if they smile, they tend to smile back and talk to them. Gradually the baby learns the social consequences of crying and smiling because of the social importance parents attach to them. As Newson (1979) observed: 'Human babies become human beings because they are treated as if they already were human beings.' Lock (1980) suggests that a whole range of behaviours that initially do not have any social significance for the infant take on an intended social meaning through the child noting their effects on the mother and then deliberately using them to produce this effect.

Enjoyment of 'contingent responding' in others
Contingent responding refers to the response made by a parent following quickly upon an action instigated by the baby – a sort of 'answer' to the baby's action. For example, with a very young baby, contingent responding is given when the parent reacts quickly and appropriately to the child's smiles or coos. Later, this enjoyment of contingent responding develops into games such as 'peek-a-boo' which are at first initiated by the adult and then later develop into genuine interactions which involve anticipation and turn-taking.

Social referencing

Studies have shown that babies of around one year old are actually quite good at gauging a parent's emotional response in a particular situation before deciding how to react themselves. This is known as **social referencing**. It seems to occur in situations which are ambiguous in some way and where the infant is not sure how to respond. The baby scrutinizes the mother's face for emotional cues and, if she is not there, will do the same with other adults. For example, Klinnert (1984) observed how infants reacted to some unfamiliar toys. They often turned to their mothers as if to gauge her reaction. Where the mother responded positively, so did the baby. If the mother's response was negative, so was the baby's. This early social referencing is thought to be the beginning of a baby's ability to empathize with others.

Parenting

What all this tells us, is that these aspects of infant and parent behaviour help the child to develop appropriate skills of social interaction. Babies seem to be programmed to behave in certain ways and parents, by their responses, provide frameworks for them to learn and

develop. Kaye (1984) calls these frameworks '**scaffolding**' or 'framing' and suggests that the infant is like an apprentice who is learning the skills of social interaction from an expert. (See also Chapter 20 for a discussion of scaffolding.) Kaye explains that good parents provide these frameworks in a number of different ways:

- **Nurturing for physical and emotional needs**. They nurture children by providing for their physical and emotional needs. This paves the way for communication and a mutual understanding to develop.
- **Protection**. They protect children from danger, though allow them to try out things which they are not yet quite capable of.
- **Helping**. They act as helpers either by doing things for children that they cannot yet manage for themselves or adapting the particular activity or object so the child can cope with it.
- **Feedback on behaviour**. They give children feedback on their actions to help them to improve their performance or to avoid danger.
- **Modelling**. They act as models by demonstrating skills and attitudes.
- **Encouraging discourse**. They encourage discourse (talk or conversation) and this promotes understanding and sharing.
- **Acting as memory**. They act as a memory for the child, which helps the child to organize information and accomplish plans.

Figure 19.1 summarizes some of the mechanisms which influence the development of social behaviour in infancy.

Fathers

Until relatively recently, most of the research into early relationships focused on the mother–infant relationship and parenting was assumed to be carried out by a

---

GLOSSARY

Contingent responding The response made by a caregiver following an action instigated by the baby – an 'answer' to, for example, the baby's smile.

Social referencing The process of gauging another person's emotional response to an ambiguous or uncomfortable situation before responding oneself.

Scaffolding The supportive framework provided by caregivers and within which a child can learn and develop.

Box 19.2   Infant imitation

A very important way in which infants learn is through imitation. Many studies have shown that even newborn babies will imitate certain mouth movements like mouth opening or sticking out the tongue (Meltzoff, 1985). This is quite an amazing feat for a newborn, since not only must the baby pay attention to the other person's mouth movement, but must then match its own mouth movements to fit. This occurs simply through feedback from the baby's own muscle movements, since it cannot see its own face.

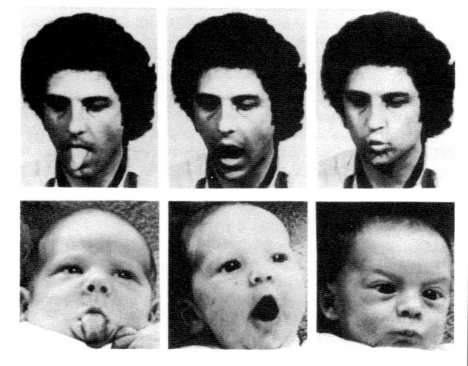

Modelled expressions and infant's imitation (from Meltzoff and Moore, 1977)

Research by Kaye and Marcus (1978, 1981) showed that babies imitate social stimuli from around the age of six months. The researchers performed various actions such as clapping their hands in front of the child or adopting exaggerated facial expressions. The infants invariably tried to imitate the actions themselves, with their efforts improving as they got older.

Meltzoff (1985) (cf. Meltzoff and Gopnik, 1993) believes that infants are socially attuned from birth and have an innate ability to relate their actions to those of other people. He argues that infants' ability to imitate indicates a much more complex process at work than has generally been acknowledged. Imitation, he believes, is a 'double edged' activity which has both social and cognitive implications. In order to imitate, the child must:

▉ perceive the action to be copied;
▉ represent the action mentally;
▉ translate the action into similar actions of his or her own (this involves a realization that in some ways the other person is 'like me');
▉ organize his or her motor behaviour so that it fits with the content and sequence of the other person's action.

Bremner (1988) argues that not only is imitation in infants an index of social awareness, it is an important source of information about the infant's understanding of the world. In particular, it demonstrates their understanding of the relationship between self and other people.

A large amount of research has been carried out into infant imitation. There have been some disagreements and discrepancies in the findings of different workers, some of which probably arise from methodological differences. Nonetheless, we can conclude that the existence of the ability to imitate has important implications for the infant's social development, since it provides a mechanism for learning human behaviour.

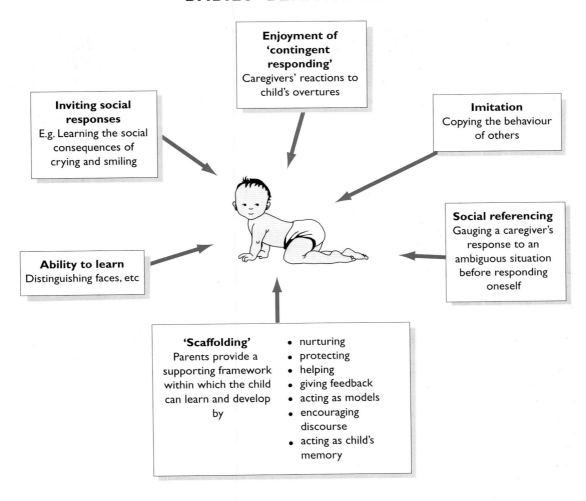

Figure 19.1   Some mechanisms that influence the development of social behaviour in infancy

female. But what of fathers? Over the last two decades or so, research has been carried out into infant–father interactions and relationships.

In an early study carried out in a maternity ward, Parke and O'Leary (1976) showed that there was little difference between the reactions of mothers and fathers towards their babies. Kotelchuk (1976) demonstrated that infants were equally upset in the presence of a stranger whether mother or father left the room. Lamb (1977) detected few differences in signs of attachment when children played alone, first with one parent and then the other. However, when both parents were present, most children were likely to display stronger attachment to the mother.

As research interest in the role of the father grew, attention was given to the different ways in which mothers and fathers interact with children. Lamb (1977) found that, typically, fathers played more vigorously with their children than mothers did; they did not sit as close and they talked to them in more adult language. Mothers tended to interact with their infants in a gentler, more low-key fashion.

It is often suggested that the role of fathers has changed in recent years, with males becoming more involved in caring for their infants. Research carried out in a number of different societies has shown that fathers are as capable of performing the parenting role as are mothers. Typically, however, mothers tend to play a larger part in childrearing and domestic tasks than do fathers (Lamb, 1987). Studies by Lewis and Cooper (1988) and Frankenhauser et al. (1991) show that where both parents go out to work, fathers generally take a greater responsibility for child care. However, the mother usually takes the main responsibility. So perhaps the idea of the new, nurturant father is a little premature.

Sibling relationships may influence the developmental process

Exercise 19.1

Visit some homes where there is a young child (from about four months to about two years). Get permission to observe or play with him or her for a short time. Behave in a relaxed, friendly way.

As soon as possible afterwards, record the visit:

■ What was the child's initial response to you? Was he or she wary or friendly?

■ With babies, did you observe any tendencies such as imitation or social referencing or did you try out 'contingent responding'?

■ How were the responses of babies under 12 months different from those of older children?

Siblings

The majority of children grow up in a family where there are other brothers and sisters. Usually the age difference between siblings is quite small, so they are usually similar enough in age and developmental stages to become important social companions for each other within the home environment. Unfortunately, there is only a limited amount of information available on sibling relationships or what effects interaction between siblings might have on the developmental process.

The most extensive research into sibling relationships within the home was carried out by Dunn and her colleagues (Dunn and Kendrick, 1982; Dunn, 1984). Initially, 40 firstborn children were observed in the home. In each family, a new baby was expected in about a month and in the majority of cases the first child was around two years old. After the birth of the new baby, visits were made to the home when the child was one month old and then eight months and 14 months. The natural behaviour between the siblings and with their parents was observed and parents were interviewed. Some of the findings are as follows:

■ Inevitably, interaction between firstborns and their parents decreased when the new baby arrived. As might be expected, many older children showed signs of jealousy because the new arrival received more attention. Parents did usually try to include the firstborn in activities such as feeding sessions and sometimes fathers were able to pay more attention to the older child while the mother was involved in activities with the new baby.

■ Few firstborns were overtly hostile towards the infant, though some were hostile, often through language. For example, 'Baby, baby. Monster, monster'. The large majority of the firstborns were affectionate towards, and interested in, the new sibling.

■ There was a wide variety of responses from firstborns when the baby cried. Fourteen of them were usually concerned and anxious to help, ten were ambivalent, five were sometimes gleeful and ten actually tried to increase the baby's distress.

Dunn and Kendrick concluded that:

■ Sibling relationships involve deep emotions, both of love and envy.

These deep and powerful relationships may be the means through which individuals learn to understand and influence others. Even children under two years old seem to be learning how to frustrate, tease, placate, comfort and influence the behaviour of their brother or sister. The same is true also of the younger ones as they grow up.

Family dynamics

The behaviour geneticist Sandra Scarr points out that although siblings share around 50 per cent of their genetic inheritance and many similar experiences within the family, they differ in intelligence, personality and most kinds of mental disorder almost as much as unrelated people do (Scarr and McCartney, 1983). This suggests that it is important to investigate how a 'family environment' may affect different family members in different ways and how siblings may influence each others' development. It is possible that siblings may often try to be as different as possible from each other (Lamb and Sutton-Smith, 1982). Schachter (1982) calls this 'sibling de-identification'. It may also be that siblings seek out different 'roles' for themselves within the family situation. What is needed is more data on family dynamics and on what actually happens in the home.

Studies of only children show that they generally do well in achievement and intelligence tests and do not appear to have any deficiencies in adjustment or sociability (Falbo and Polit, 1986). This and other studies into the effects of family size seem to suggest that relationships between children and adults are still the most important to many aspects of development.

Grandparents

Relatively few grandparents share the same home as their grandchildren, though many live fairly close and those who live further away tend to keep in touch through letters, phone calls and visits. In the 1930s and 1940s, there were many negative stereotypes of grandparents. In particular, some psychiatrists and social workers regarded grandmothers as too strict and punitive and likely to have a harmful effect on their grandchildren. At other times, grandparents were thought of as too lenient with their grandchildren (Townsend, 1957). More recently, the more positive aspects of child–grandparent relationships have been recognized. For example, a grandparent may act as a

A grandparent can be an important part of a child's social world

companion and become an important part of a child's social world. Many grandparents provide emotional support, particularly where a child is in conflict with the parents.

As with sibling relationships, there has not been a large amount of research into child–grandparent interactions and relationships. However, studies that have been carried out indicate that grandparents can considerably influence the behaviour of their grandchildren.

Tinsley and Parke (1984) examined both direct and indirect influences. Indirect influences are those which occur without there necessarily being any direct interaction. For example, the way parents interact with their children will be influenced by the way they themselves have been brought up by their parents: that is, the children's grandparents. Grandparents may also provide financial and emotional assistance to the parents which will be of great value at times of family stress.

Direct influences can vary in intensity. The strongest influences will occur in situations where a grandparent acts as a surrogate parent, perhaps looking after children while the parents work. Usually, it is the maternal grandmother who performs this role. However, Radin et al. (1991) suggest that grandfathers can also be influential. They found that grandfathers had a beneficial effect on young grandchildren of teenage mothers. This was particularly the case for grandsons.

Do early attachment relationships influence a child's later development?

SELF-ASSESSMENT QUESTIONS

1. Outline some of the milestones in social and emotional development that occur during the first year of life.
2. Describe some of the mechanisms that contribute to the development of a young child's social relationships.
3. Discuss some research which has examined a child's relationships with parents, siblings and grandparents.

The development of attachment

As we saw in the previous section, **attachment** can be defined as an enduring bond of affection directed towards a specific individual. Traditionally, research into attachment has been heavily influenced by Freud's psychoanalytic theory (see Chapter 30) and has stressed the importance of the infant–mother relationship. Bowlby (1969) and other researchers influenced by the psychoanalytic tradition believed that the attachment bond which develops between an infant and its mother forms the basis of all interpersonal relationships in later years. More recent research, however, has also stressed the importance of attachments which form with other adults, particularly the father.

Some questions that have been tackled by researchers include:

■ How is the relationship between a child and parent formed and maintained?
■ Is continuity of care necessary for the formation of attachments or is the quality of the relationship the crucial feature?
■ How do we distinguish between 'good' and 'bad' relationships. What features of the parent–child interaction are important?

Early attachment and later development

Running throughout most research is the question: What is the relationship between early attachment and later development? For example, what are the consequences for later social and emotional development if a bond does not form?

Interest in the last question was prompted in the 1940s and 1950s by evidence concerning the effects of institutionalization on social and emotional development. Children who had grown up in institutions frequently seemed to display listlessness and troubled behaviour and showed no interest in social interaction (Bowlby, 1951).

Bowlby's theory

Many early theories explained attachment as operating to satisfy some kind of innate need or drive. Environmental-learning theorists favoured the explanation of secondary drive theory: the mother, as a source of food, satisfied the child's basic physiological

---

GLOSSARY

Attachment The bond of affection which forms between a child and specific caregivers. The strongest attachments occur from the age of about eight months onwards.

Box 19.3 Harlow's studies of deprivation in monkeys

Harlow (1958, 1969), a prominent investigator of animal behaviour in the USA, carried out a series of controlled experiments with rhesus monkeys over a period of some 20 years. Harlow's experiments took several forms.

Infant monkeys were removed from their mothers shortly after birth and were placed alone in a cage with a surrogate (substitute) mother. The surrogate mothers were of two kinds: either a 'cloth mother' which consisted of a cylinder of wood covered with soft, terry towelling material, or a 'wire mother', which was simply a wire cylinder. Both were of the same size and general shape as an adult monkey. Each 'mother' was equipped with a feeding bottle so that the infant could nurse from it. Each monkey had the opportunity to gain access to the other surrogate mother.

The finding was that, irrespective of which 'mother' provided the nourishment, each infant spent most of its time clinging to the cloth mother. Harlow concluded that baby primates need a source of warmth or 'contact comfort', in addition to the source of food.

Observation of the monkeys' behaviour when they were later introduced to the company of other, normally reared monkeys revealed a bleak picture. Most could not interact adequately with other monkeys; many were either aggressive or indifferent; males were unable to mate successfully; those females who did mate and produce offspring were cruel and inadequate mothers. Harlow concluded that infant mothers cannot develop normal behaviour without the presence of a live mother. However, later experiments showed that brief exposure to other juvenile monkeys each day greatly reduced the abnormal behaviour of deprived monkeys. Could inter-action with age-mates compensate for the lack of a mother?

In an attempt to assess the total importance of a mother, whether real or surrogate, Harlow and Harlow raised infant monkeys in complete isolation from both humans or other monkeys. The later behaviour of these monkeys was even more bizarre than that of the surrogate-raised monkeys. They clutched their own bodies and rocked compulsively. When later they were exposed to other, normally reared monkeys, they were usually apathetic and often became aggressive towards both others and themselves, biting their own arms and legs. The extent of the abnormal behaviour reflected the length of the isolation.

As a result of these experiments, Harlow claimed in 1971 that mothering is crucial for normal development in all primates.

Later research questioned Harlow's earlier claims. Novak and Harlow (1975) raised infant monkeys in total isolation for a year. When the monkeys were later introduced to younger, 'therapist' monkeys, who played and interacted with them, the behaviour of the deprived monkeys became much more normal and they were able to participate effectively in all social situations. It was concluded that the effects of deprivation are not irreversible.

Ethical issues

When these studies were conducted, it was felt that the distress and damage caused to the monkeys could be justified because of the important insights which were gained into human behaviour. However, critics questioned both the cruelty of the procedures and the relevance of the findings in relation to humans. Given the much stricter guidelines and regulations which now exist in relation to research with animals (see Chapter 5), it is doubtful that the experiments would be carried out today.

---

needs. The primary drive was towards satisfaction of basic needs, the secondary drive was attachment to the mother in order to satisfy these needs. However, this theory was largely overturned by the work of Harry Harlow who investigated the effects of maternal deprivation on infant monkeys in the late 1950s and 1960s (see Box 19.3). Harlow showed that given the choice between an artificial wire 'mother' which offered milk and one covered with soft terry towelling cloth which did not offer food, the young monkeys chose the cloth 'mother', and became attached to it rather than to the one that offered nourishment.

Though Bowlby was influenced initially by psychoanalytic theory, he also become heavily influenced by concepts from **ethology** (see Box 19.4) and particularly

> **GLOSSARY**
>
> **Ethology** The study of natural behaviour, often in the natural environment.

the work done by Tinbergen (1907–88) and Lorenz (1903–89) into **imprinting** in animals (see Chapter 16). Through imprinting, the young of many species form early attachments to parents. A manifestation of this attachment is the young animal's tendency to stay close to the parent whenever the parent moves. Remember that Bowlby believed that the various kinds of attachment behaviour shown by human babies (see p. 430) are designed to maintain proximity between mother and baby.

Box 19.4 Insights from studies of imprinting

Ethologists study the behaviour of animals, often in their natural habitat, from the standpoint of biology. Such naturalistic observations are considered crucial to the understanding of important behaviours such as aggression and sexual relations. Ethologists are guided by specific hypotheses in their work, and once their hypotheses have been tentatively supported from a study of the animals' natural behaviour, a specific experiment may be devised.

Konrad Lorenz (1935), an important figure in ethology, showed that young animals such as geese and ducks follow their mothers from an early age and become permanently bonded or imprinted on her. This 'attachment', he contended, is of crucial importance to the animals' later social and mating behaviour. Lorenz showed, during the course of his experiments, that if animals become imprinted upon a human or on some inanimate object instead of the parent, their later mating behaviour becomes seriously disrupted. He also suggested that such abnormal behaviour was irreversible.

In addition to studying the process and effects of imprinting, Lorenz also investigated the time during which imprinting behaviour emerged. He proposed that there was a critical period or fixed time, during the first three days of life, when imprinting must occur if a lasting attachment is to result.

Later researchers such as Sluckin (1965) and Bateson (1964) were less convinced of the existence of such a rigid critical period in the development of imprinting. They preferred to speak instead of a sensitive period, a more flexible time during which imprinting is most likely to occur.

Bowlby's theory contains a number of concepts drawn from biology. Attachment behaviour was seen as a system which evolves in order to provide the infant with protection as occurs in other mammals – in other words it is adaptive (has survival value). The tendency to remain close to adults offers protection against predators and reduces the likelihood that the child will become separated from the adult on whom he or she depends for survival. Bowlby suggests that this mechanism can only be understood in terms of the primeval human environment (the very early stages of human development). This is because changes in the fairly recent history of human development have been too rapid for evolutionary mechanisms to keep up.

Bowlby stressed that attachment behaviours are not designed to maintain proximity with any adult. As the child develops, its attention becomes increasingly directed to one person in particular, the primary caregiver (usually the mother). Though the child may form other attachments, Bowlby believed that there is always one which is qualitatively different from the others. This aspect of Bowlby's theory is usually referred to as **monotropy**.

Bowlby's three publications (1969, 1973, 1980) on 'attachment and loss' revolutionized concepts on what is involved in the development of social relations, and his ethological-based theory dominates this field of research (Rutter and Rutter, 1993).

Is monotropy correct?

Bowlby's views, particularly on monotropy – the idea of attachment to just one caregiver, usually female – have attracted controversy and criticism. A naturalistic study which provided contradictory evidence was carried out by Schaffer and Emerson in 1964.

Schaffer and Emerson observed the attachment behaviour of 60 babies in the home situation. They observed that:

■ The first strong attachment to a particular person occurred around the age of seven to eight months.

GLOSSARY

Imprinting A form of learning observed in some animals soon after birth, which results in attachment to a parent.

Monotropy A theory proposed by Bowlby that an infant forms a strong attachment to just one caregiver, usually the mother.

■ Most children formed attachments with many people in addition to the mother. Attachment figures included fathers, siblings, grandparents and family friends. The researchers described a small group of infants whose strongest attachments were with their fathers.

■ By the age of 18 months, only 13 per cent of the babies had just one attachment figure. The remainder had formed multiple attachments.

Schaffer and Emerson concluded that 'mother' can be male or female and 'mothering' can be shared by several people. Any person who provides a great deal of stimulation and interaction can become an attachment figure, even if they are not providing food. These findings were supported in research carried out in the USA by Cohen and Campos (1974) and by **cross-cultural studies** of attachment.

Cross-cultural studies of attachment Ainsworth (1967) spent several months observing patterns of attachment in infants of the Ganda tribe in Uganda. Her study provided striking support for Bowlby's description of the course of attachment behaviour. Most of the babies were clearly attached to their mothers by around six months; most began to fear strangers during the last three months of their first year. However, the babies were cared for by several adults in addition to their mothers and most formed attachments simultaneously with several people.

In Israeli kibbutzim, from early infancy children spend most of their waking time being cared for in a children's house by a *metapalet*, or children's nurse. Research suggests that the infants appear to form strong attachments both to their mothers and to the *metapalets* (Fox, 1977). The babies also develop strong bonds with their own infant peers, which leads to much greater social involvement than is usually observed in such young children.

Security of attachment

Much research into attachment behaviour in babies has been carried out by Mary Ainsworth (1967, 1973). She has described behaviours such as smiling and vocalizing preferentially to the mother, crying when the mother leaves the room, following the mother and lifting arms to her, using the mother as a secure base from which to explore in a strange situation and as a refuge to retreat to when frightened.

Ainsworth developed a method for observing and assessing the attachment behaviour babies display towards their mothers. This method is known as the **Strange Situation** and it has been widely used with 12–24-month-old babies in Britain, in the USA, Germany, Holland, Israel and Japan. It is essentially a method for assessing how far a baby would use the mother as a secure base from which to explore and how the child would react to the mother's absence and return when placed in a slightly stressful situation (see Box 19.5).

Research into attachment types

Some interesting findings have emerged from studies where babies were first assessed using the Strange Situation procedure:

Attachment type related to other aspects of development Lewis et al. (1984) found that 'secure attachment' at 12 months correlated with:

■ The quality and sensitivity of mother–child interaction at 6–15 weeks;
■ Curiosity and problem solving at age two;
■ Social confidence at nursery school at age three;
■ Lack of behaviour problems (boys) at age six.

Browne (1989) found that 'insecure/avoidant' attachment appeared to be linked to the likelihood of infant maltreatment or abuse. In one study, 70 per cent of maltreated babies were found to be insecurely attached to the parents.

Advantages of Type B Many studies have found that infants categorized as Type B appear to have many advantages over their peers categorized as Type A or Type C. These advantages have revealed themselves in terms of more positive play (Wartner et al., 1994), greater autonomy, interpersonal competence, eagerness to learn during the preschool and early school years (Youngblade and Belsky, 1992) and greater responsiveness to unfamiliar adults at school

---

GLOSSARY

Cross-cultural studies Studies in which similarities and differences between different cultures are examined.

The Strange Situation A procedure developed and used by Ainsworth for observing and assessing the attachment behaviour babies display towards their mothers.

Box 19.5   The Strange Situation (Ainsworth et al., 1978)

The procedure is a kind of controlled observation (see Chapter 34) and is carried out in a comfortably equipped laboratory situation. It involves eight short episodes, during which the child successively experiences playing in a strange room in the mother's presence, being left alone there, the mother's return and then departure, the entry of a stranger, and so on. The procedure is designed to provoke a response in the baby which will indicate the baby's attachment to the mother and the sense of security and comfort felt in her presence. Particular attention is paid to the baby's behaviour in the reunion episodes to see if it is adequately comforted by the mother.

It was hypothesized that in an effective attachment relationship, the child would use the mother as a base to explore, but would be distressed by her absence and would seek closeness on her return. The 'mother absent' episodes are curtailed if the baby is excessively distressed or if the mother wishes to return more quickly.

On the basis of the findings from studies using the Strange Situation procedure, Ainsworth has identified three main attachment types: **Type A** insecure (anxious/avoidant); **Type B** secure; **Type C** insecure (ambivalent).

Type A babies' behaviour

During the mother's absence, their babies do not appear distressed. In the reunion episodes, they avoid closeness or interaction with the mother; they ignore mother on her return or greet her casually, switching between this and avoidance responses such as turning away.

Type B babies' behaviour

These babies explore actively in mother's presence and show distress in her absence. They seek closeness, interaction or bodily contact in the reunion episodes.

Type C babies' behaviour

These babies are anxious before separation from the mother and distressed during separation. They are ambivalent during the reunion, when they both seek and avoid contact with the mother.

Most research on attachment types has been based on the above three categories. However, subsequent research by Main and colleagues suggested that a fourth category might exist: **Type D** disorganized/disorientated.

Type D babies' behaviour

Main and Solomon (1986) found in their research that a small proportion of babies did not appear to have a coherent strategy for coping with the stresses of the Strange Situation. Their behaviour seemed to be totally disorganized and disoriented; this was characterized by incomplete movements and reactions, sometimes wariness of stranger, sometimes of mother.

(Turner, 1993). Though there have been some disparities in the literature, it is generally agreed that the quality of attachment is an important aspect of parent–child relationships, one which can predict other social and cognitive aspects of development over the next few years.

Stability of security of attachment over time   The significance of research findings depends very much on whether security of attachment is stable over time. There would be little point in drawing conclusions from a measure which might simply reflect the child's emotional state at the time of testing. Therefore, studies have been carried to examine test–retest reliability. (The same group of infants are assessed twice with a suitable time lag between the tests.)

Waters (1978) found an almost exact agreement between babies Strange Situation classification at 12 and 28 months, and Antonucci and Levitt (1984) found good reliability between seven months and 13 months. Main et al. (1985) found a strong relationship between security of attachment at 18 months and at six years. However, it has been shown that when a child's home circumstances changed – for example, parental divorce, moving house, starting nursery school – security of attachment often changed also either from secure to insecure or the other way round (Thompson and Harris, 1983).

In sum, most research found stability over time in security of attachment except in some cases where there was a marked change in the child's home circumstances.

Parental responsiveness   In a follow-up study Ainsworth et al. (1974) found that when observed in the home, babies' behaviour was very similar to that observed in the laboratory situation. Further-more, there appeared to be a link between the attachment types assigned to the babies and the behaviour of their mothers as follows:

- Babies classified as 'securely attached' cried the least and had mothers who were sensitive and responsive to their needs.
- Mothers of babies classified as 'anxious/avoidant' tended to be unresponsive to the babies' social signals and were often relatively cold and rejecting.
- Mothers of 'ambivalent' babies were inconsistent in their responses to the babies' needs, sometimes responding warmly, at other times ignoring the child's social signals.

Ainsworth's early research has been supported by a great deal of more recent research set up to test the hypothesis that sensitive caregiving produces securely attached children. Sroufe and Fleeson (1986) argue that the common factor in the lives of securely attached babies seems to be contingent responsiveness from the parents to the child (see previous section of this chapter). That is, parents are sensitive and match their responses to the babies' needs.

When very unfavourable family situations have been studied – for instance, homes where there are highly stressed, neglectful or abusive parents – serious problems have often been found. For example, parental stress and depression have been found to be linked to the development of insecure attachment in the child (Jarvis and Creasey, 1991). Carlson et al. (1989), studying a sample of neglected and badly treated infants found that about 80 per cent of them fell into the Type D (disorganized and disoriented) category. It seems likely that the highly stressful and inconsistent regime in an abusive home may interfere with the organization of an effective attachment system. The child's instincts are to seek proximity to the parent; however, because of ill-treatment and rejection, he or she ends up feeling confused about, and distrustful of, attachment figures.

Despite the above findings, the research carried out has not succeeded in producing a consistent or conclusive pattern which enables us to be sure what features of parental behaviour are most important to the development of secure attachment (Lamb et al., 1984). There are many other factors that may be important, for example the quality of the relationship between parents, the degree of stress in the home and other possible factors.

Characteristics of the infant Research findings seem to indicate a strong link between the quality of caregiving and attachment. However, many studies which have claimed such a link have been correlational and one must not overlook the problem of causation which exists in correlational studies (see Chapter 34). Campos et al. (1983) point out that differences in maternal behaviour may be due at least in part to the characteristics of the child. A mother may appear to be insensitive because her child is unresponsive, so significant correlations found between maternal responsiveness and security of attachment may not necessarily indicate that causality is from mother to child.

Some researchers have argued that it is differences in temperament, widely thought to be inherited, that determine how attachment develops. Belsky and Rovine (1987) found that newborns who showed more temperamental instability (frequent tremors, startle more easily) tended to fall into certain subtypes associated with distress in the Strange Situation. However, Belsky and Rovine propose that both parental responsiveness and infant temperament are important. Children of different temperamental characteristics present different challenges to their caregivers, but also the caregiver's style of responding to the child may determine the kind of attachment relationship which develops between them. In other words, it is a two-way process.

Cross-cultural variations In studies carried out in the USA, around 65–70 per cent of babies tend to be classified as Type B (securely attached to their mothers), some 20 per cent as Type A (insecure/avoidant) and around 10 per cent as Type C (insecure/ambivalent). However, some German researchers have found around 40–50 per cent to be Type A (Grossman et al., 1981). In Japan, Miyake et al. (1985) classified 35 per cent of babies as Type C. A very substantial contribution to the debate about cross-

GLOSSARY

Temperament Basic behavioural characteristics: for example, sociability, responsiveness, distractibility, which are widely believed to be innate: that is, inborn and not resulting from environmental influences.

cultural differences was made by two Dutch researchers, van Ijzendoorn and Kroonenberg (1988). They carried out a **meta-analysis** of 32 studies which had used the Strange Situation methodology in eight different countries. There were three main findings:

- There were some noticeable **intracultural differences** in the way the types were distributed. For example, one of two Japanese studies showed a high proportion of Type Cs but no Type As at all while the other yielded a distribution very similar to that found in Ainsworth's original studies. Overall, van Ijzendorn and Kroonenberg found intracultural differences to be 1.5 times as large as cross-cultural differences.
- When the distributions from different cultures were aggregated, the pattern which emerged was very close to Ainsworth's 'standard'.
- While Type Bs were the most common in all cultures, Type As were relatively more frequently found in West European countries, while Type Cs were more common in Israel and Japan.

These findings raise the question of whether 'insecure attachment' is a less satisfactory style of development, as Ainsworth and others believe. Or does it simply reflect different styles of interacting? (See Box 19.6.)

Criticisms of the attachment construct

Meadows (1986) argues that definitions of terms such as 'attachment behaviour' and 'adequate mothering' need further consideration. Different researchers have sometimes included different criteria in their definitions. For example, Main and Weston (1982) include angry behaviour such as tantrums; other researchers have included 'minutes of crying' or 'number of frowns or smiles'. However, a number of studies indicate that the different behaviours may not be related and may vary from time to time and in different situations (Rutter, 1981).

A number of criticisms of the construct of attachment have centred on the way attachment has been measured and, in particular, the use of the Strange Situation procedure to determine attachment types.

- The laboratory procedure of introducing a 'stranger' who would approach and make overtures to the baby at set time intervals and without considering the baby's behaviour has been described as unnatural. Bronfenbrenner

Parent–child relationships may vary according to styles of child rearing in different cultural groups

(1979) argues that the Strange Situation provides an ecological setting which might influence the very behaviour being investigated. Rheingold and Eckerman (1973) found that in more natural settings, where a child could approach a stranger in his or her own time, the child often smiled at and sometimes moved towards the stranger. Nonetheless, despite these findings, it is generally recognized that infants do react differently to people they do not know and are wary of strangers even in familiar surroundings. Also, as we have seen, whether or not it is ecologically valid, the Strange Situation does provide a reliable basis for predictions about other aspects of a child's development.

GLOSSARY

Meta-analysis A statistical technique which is used to aggregate and analyse the results of a number of independent studies in relation to a particular hypothesis.

Intracultural differences Differences which exist *within* a culture.

Lamb et al. (1984) have criticized the fact that the attachment typing arrived at from the Strange Situation procedure was initially based on only 26 American babies. They argue that the classification system was arrived at too quickly using an inadequate sample.

Box 19.6 Cross-cultural differences in attachment types

Takahashi (1990) argues that interpretations of the Strange Situation types should be very carefully thought through, particularly when they are applied to different cultures. He pointed out that Japanese babies were particularly upset by the 'infant alone' episode because usually, in Japan, babies are never left alone at one year old. Therefore, fewer babies were classified as 'securely attached'. Also, it would be difficult for Japanese babies to be assessed as 'insecure/avoidant' since Japanese mothers typically moved immediately towards and picked up their baby.

Sagi and Lewkowicz (1987) suggest that the *meaning* of the Strange Situation may be different for different cultures. The nature of the parent–child relationship varies according to the backgrounds, assumptions and expectations of different cultural groups. For example, German parents perceived some of the behaviour of securely attached babies as hallmarks of a 'spoiled' child. Harwood and Miller (1991) compared Anglo-American and Puerto Rican mothers' reactions to observations of infants who exhibited types A, B or C behaviour. The former perceived independence in babies more favourably while the latter favoured characteristics of obedience and relatedness.

Bretherton (1992) argues that attachment theorists will have to rethink the scope of their work to take account of ecological differences. However, despite misgivings about the usefulness of the Strange Situation in measuring attachment cross-culturally, it could be argued that the differences between cultures add further support to the idea that there is a relationship between caregiving style and the formation of attachments. As different cultures have different styles, it might follow that there would be variations in attachment types.

The assertion that the 'secure attachment' classification is 'normal' must be viewed with caution in the light of studies which have showed variations between cultures (see p. 441).

Smith and Cowie (1991) point out that the Strange Situation procedure measures the relationship between the child and the mother. It cannot be assumed to measure some characteristic of the child. In studies which have used the procedure to assess father–child attachment, it has been found that the attachment type arrived at is often different from that which exists with the mother.

Despite the above concerns and criticisms, the Strange Situation is commonly used internationally and it does seem to allow predictions to be made between the quality of attachment and a whole range of later social and cognitive functions. Lamb et al. (1984) argued that the Strange Situation procedure has become the most powerful and useful procedure ever available for the study of socio-emotional development in infancy.

Attachments after infancy

Until the last few years, almost all research into attachment was concerned with very young children. However, it is clear that selective attachment is not something that applies only to infants. If attachment is thought of in terms of the kinds of relationships that reduce anxiety and provide emotional support when we are stressed, it is clear that attachment is in evidence right through all stages of life, including old age (Rutter and Rutter, 1993).

There has been considerable research interest in the factors that may influence stability or change in attachments and also the extent to which early infant–parent attachment may influence a child's later relationships, not just with parents but also with siblings, friends, marriage partners or their own children.

The measurement of attachment after infancy

A major problem to face researchers has been how to measure attachment in the years following infancy. As we have seen, it is fairly straightforward in infancy because separation followed by reunion tends to produce very distinctive reactions in the child and because the seeking of closeness is such a widespread indicator of attachment.

Several studies have attempted to measure attachment in older children. For example, Main and Cassidy (1988) successfully used a variation on the Strange Situation with children from three to six years. For older children and adolescents, a procedure known as the Separation Anxiety Test has been used. In this procedure, the youngsters are asked to respond to photographs showing separation experiences. A procedure known as the Adult Attachment Interview can be used to measure attachment in adults (Main et al., 1985; Pratt and Norris, 1994). The individual is interviewed about his or her early relationships with parents. A technique which has been used to demonstrate the importance of attachment in adulthood is known as the Social Convoy Diagram (Levitt, 1991). This is illustrated in Box 19.7.

Internal working models

The concept of **internal working models** was originally proposed by Bowlby (1969). It refers to representations in children's minds of relationships they have with parents and other key individuals or attachment figures. These are thought to exist in the form of cognitive structures which are said to contain memories of interactions the child has had with the attachment figure (Bowlby, 1988). These cognitive structures are often referred to as 'schemas' or 'event scripts' which influence the child's interactions with the attachment figure in the light of previous interactions.

Bowlby (1980) argues that though the working model of attachment can change, it is not in a constant state of flux. Once it is developed, it will influence a child's behaviour, affecting memory and attention. Thus the models children build of the relationships they have with parents will regulate how they feel about each parent and how they behave towards them.

Box 19.7   Social convoy diagram (adapted from Levitt, 1991)

This is a technique which demonstrates the importance of attachment in adulthood.

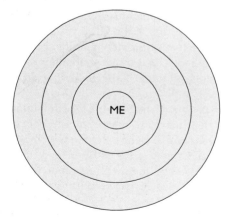

Draw some circles and consider this for yourself.

In the inner circle, nearest to yourself, place the names of those people to whom you feel 'so close that it's hard to imagine life without them.'

In the middle circle, place those people who are 'not quite as close but still very important'.

In the outer circle, place those who don't quite belong in the inner circles but nonetheless are 'close enough and important enough' to have a place in your social network.

Now consider who are the people in your life who provide you with the most support and reassurance – those you would be most likely to confide in, who would look after you if you were ill, who would offer you advice or financial help. It would be very surprising if these were not the people you have placed in the inner circle.

Levitt (1991) carried out a series of studies with people at different stages of the lifespan from young adulthood to old age and from different cultural groups. He found a marked consistency among responses. Most people enter a small number of individuals in the inner circle, usually family – spouse or life partner, parents, children. In-laws are rarely found there, though they often appear in middle or outer circles along with other family and friends.

Levitt (1991) claims that the existence of at least one close relationship seems to be associated fundamentally with personal well-being.

Bowlby sees attachment in the school-aged child as being characterized not by the seeking of proximity (closeness) but by more abstract characteristics such as approval and affection. These features, he suggests, become internalized in the child as part of that child's internal working model.

Parent–child pairs of differing attachment types would be expected to have different working models of the relationship. For example, a boy classified as having an insecure/ambivalent relationship with his mother may have an internal working model of her which leads him not to rely on consistent support and comfort when he is upset.

Early attachment and later relationships

Rutter and Rutter (1993) propose that although there is not a lot of solid evidence that early attachment experiences are directly linked to particular attachment relationships in later life, there are some indications that this is so.

> . . . it seems that the experience of selective attachments may in some fashion underlie the development of a range of close relationships in adult life (friendships, sexual love relationships and parent–child relationships) even though the security-providing qualities that characterize attachment in infancy are lacking.
>
> (Rutter and Rutter, 1993, p. 125)

They go on to suggest that individuals' experience of selective attachments seems to improve their capacity to be effective parents. In support, they cite research including a 36-year longitudinal study carried out by Franz et al. (1991). This study showed that the experience of warm and affectionate parenting in early childhood was associated with having a long, happy marriage and close relationships at 41 years of age. However, though these findings suggest continuity in relationships over time, they do not show without doubt that the determining factor was the quality of early attachment.

Other studies also indicate continuities in relationships. They showed that adults who experienced poor parenting themselves when young tended themselves to have children who were insecurely attached (Parkes et al., 1991). However, there are exceptions. There are many examples of people who are excellent parents and have children who are securely attached, despite their own insecure upbringing. Main et al. (1985) found

that such mothers, in contrast to those with insecure infants, were able to describe and analyse their own unhappy earlier experiences in a rational way and were able to draw out positive aspects of their own childhood experiences. Mothers who had experienced an unsatisfactory childhood and who themselves had insecure children were unable to discuss their own experiences so rationally. Main suggests that it may be important for people who have experienced an unsatisfactory childhood to develop a balanced perspective and to try to adopt a positive view of themselves which will pay off in later relationships.

❓ SELF-ASSESSMENT QUESTIONS

1. Outline Bowlby's theory of the nature and functions of attachment. What does Bowlby mean by monotropy?
2. Outline Ainsworth's Strange Situation procedure for measuring the quality of attachment in infancy. Briefly describe the resulting attachment 'types'.
3. In what ways have our understanding of social and emotional development been enhanced by research into 'secure' and 'insecure' attachment? Are these terms culturally valid?
4. Consider some ways of measuring attachment in older children and adults.
5. What is known about the links between the quality of early attachment and later relationships?

Attachment, separation and deprivation

An ongoing concern which began in the late 1940s and early 1950s and still stimulates controversial debate is whether very young preschool children suffer emotional deprivation if they spend time in day care or childminding situations rather than being brought up in conventional family settings. The debate centres largely on whether mothers of young children should work or should stay at home to look after their children until they are of school age. It has been suggested that very young children should not be deprived of contact with a mother during a particularly sensitive period when the primary attachment relationship is forming. The idea became known as the 'maternal deprivation' hypothesis and it was first proposed by John Bowlby in a paper to the World Health Organization in 1951.

Bowlby's 'maternal deprivation' hypothesis

Bowlby was concerned about the symptoms observed in institutionalized or hospitalized children. Many exhibited disturbed behaviour, were intellectually retarded and seemed unable to form close relationships with other people. Bowlby believed that a child deprived of the opportunity to form an attachment with a mother or permanent mother figure during the early years of life would develop social, emotional and/or intellectual problems in later life.

Influences on Bowlby

Research findings Among many studies which influenced Bowlby's views were his own account of 44 juvenile thieves in a child guidance unit compared to 44 juveniles who were emotionally disturbed, but who had not been accused of a crime. Bowlby observed that the former group contained many individuals who suffered from so-called 'affectionless psychopathy' (an inability to feel affection for or care about the well-being of others). Moreover, over half of the first group compared with only two of the second had been separated from their mothers for a period of at least a week during the first five years of life. Bowlby concluded that maternal deprivation was the cause of their delinquency and severe emotional disability (Bowlby, 1944).

He was also influenced by Goldfarb's (1943) comparison of two groups of children aged between 10 and 14, 15 of whom had spent the first three years of life in an institution and 15 of whom had spent the same period in foster homes. Compared to the 'fostered' group, the 'institutionalized' group scored lower on tests of intelligence, language and sociability. Goldfarb concluded that the lack of opportunity for the institutionalized children to form an attachment with one person during the first three years of life led to their intellectual and social retardation.

Subsequent researchers drew attention to the methodological flaws in these two studies, largely arising from problems of sampling and the lack of appropriate control groups.

According to Bowlby, maternal deprivation could also lead to such conditions as depression, enuresis (bed wetting) and dwarfism (stunted physical growth).

Ethological theory As we saw in the last section, Bowlby later interpreted many of his earlier observations in the light of ethological theory. He emphasized the survival function of the human infant's need to stay close to and form an attachment with its mother. He likened this attachment process to imprinting in birds (see Box 19.4).

A major aspect of Bowlby's maternal deprivation theory was his proposal that there was a **critical period**, or optimal time, during the first three years of life when this primary attachment should occur (see Chapter 16 for a discussion of critical and sensitive periods in imprinting).

Harlow's work with monkeys Bowlby's 'maternal deprivation' theory was also influenced by the work of Harlow and his associates (1958, 1969) into the effects of deprivation in infant monkeys (see Box 19.3). In early studies, Harlow's research showed that infant rhesus monkeys who were separated from their mothers and raised in isolation suffered abnormal social and mating behaviour when they were later placed in the company of other monkeys. As a result of these experiments, Harlow claimed that mothering is crucial for normal development in all primates.

Despite many criticisms of his theory, Bowlby's work has had some very worthwhile effects. His work and that of other researchers has led to a much greater awareness of the emotional needs of young children. Also, in a practical sense, it led to many improvements in the care of children in institutions and a move towards fostering and adoption rather than institutional care. It also led to more enlightened care of young children who need to be hospitalized and a recognition of the need for parents to have better access to their children.

> **GLOSSARY**
>
> **Maternal deprivation hypothesis** Bowlby's theory that very young children should not be deprived of contact with a mother during a particularly sensitive period when the primary attachment relationship is forming.
>
> **Affectionless psychopathy** A syndrome proposed by Bowlby to describe an inability to feel affection for others or to form social relationships.
>
> **Critical period** A genetically determined time when a particular kind of development must occur; otherwise it will not occur at all.

A reassessment of maternal deprivation

Rutter's findings

Bowlby's theory stimulated a large amount of research into the infant–mother relationship and much of it criticized and challenged his more extreme views. In a major review and reassessment of Bowlby's work, Michael Rutter (1972, 1981) supported the view that distortion of early child care could have adverse effects on psychological development. However, he strongly criticized Bowlby's use of the concept of 'maternal deprivation' to cover what is probably a wide range of different problems. Rutter urged researchers to seek more precise descriptions of 'bad' care and 'bad' effects and to examine more closely the probable links between them.

Rutter distinguished between the short-term and long-term effects of a child being separated from the parent.

Short-term effects By short-term effects, Rutter meant the child's immediate response to a depriving experience and to the behaviour shown over the following few months. In relation to the short-term effects of separation, he made the following points:

- Rutter agreed with Bowlby's description of the three stages of distress usually exhibited by a baby who is separated from the parent: protest, despair and detachment (look back at p. 430). These three phases are often referred to as the 'syndrome of distress'.
- The other syndrome likely to result from maternal deprivation, according to Bowlby, is that of developmental retardation, or slowing down of developmental growth, particularly in language and social responsiveness.
- After considering the evidence on many factors which are likely to influence a child's response to deprivation (such things as age, sex, temperament, previous mother–child relationship, other separation experiences), Rutter concluded that the syndrome of distress is likely to be due to the disruption of the attachment process, but not necessarily with the mother. Retardation, he believed, can best be explained by the absence of appropriate stimulating experiences.

Long-term effects Long-term was used to refer to effects seen some years later, either following a brief period of separation or after prolonged separation.

After reviewing a wide range of studies (some of them described in Box 19.8), Rutter concluded that:

- Most of the long-term effects of so-called 'maternal deprivation' are likely to be due to the lack of something (**privation**), rather than to any kind of loss (**deprivation**).
- Failure to develop bonds with anyone, not just the mother, in early childhood is the main factor in the development of 'affectionless psychopathy'.
- Family discord and the lack of a stable relationship with a parent are associated with later anti-social behaviour and delinquency.
- A lack of stimulation and necessary life experiences are likely to be responsible for intellectual retardation.
- The evidence does not support Bowlby's views concerning the special importance of the bond formed with the mother. The chief bond need not be with a biological parent and it need not be with a female. Rutter stressed the importance of a child's relationships with people other than the mother, in particular the father.

Rutter's conclusions In his review described previously, Rutter concluded that the evidence overwhelmingly supported the importance of deprivation and disadvantage as adverse influences on children's psychological development. The worst effects are experienced by children who have experienced multiple caretaking in early life and have been unable to form strong attachments. However, it appears that humans are far more flexible than Bowlby suggested. While the first few years of life do appear to be important for bond formation and social development, a single, female mothering figure is not essential to healthy development.

Rutter argued that the concept of 'maternal deprivation' should be abandoned. Researchers should try to investigate the different kinds of inadequate childcare and look carefully at their separate effects. It

---

GLOSSARY

Privation The lack of something which had never been experienced; in attachment theory, the lack of opportunity to form an attachment bond.

Deprivation The loss of something; in attachment theory, it relates to the loss of an attachment figure.

Box 19.8 Research findings which challenged Bowlby's views

Below is a brief outline of some of the research findings which have contradicted or challenged some of Bowlby's views.

Rutter (1972) carried out a study in which he compared a large number of boys aged 9–12 on the Isle of Wight with a similar group in London. All the children in both groups had been separated from their parents for a variety of different reasons at some point in early childhood. Some of the boys went on to become disturbed and delinquent; others did not. Rutter believed that the crucial factor which made the difference was what happened to the boys after the separation. Where separation was caused through the illness or death of a parent, the children tended to recover and lead normal lives after the traumatic incident. Where parental separation came about through family discord or divorce, the child often became maladjusted and delinquent. Rutter argued that it is the discord often present in separating or divorcing families and the subsequent difficulties in the family which lead to later behaviour problems, rather than the actual separation from a parent.

Freud and Dann (1951) studied six three-year-old orphans who had spent most of their lives together in a German concentration camp. In the absence of either a mother- or father-figure, the children appeared to have formed very close and warm attachments with each other. Moreover, although their behaviour was disturbed in some respects, there was no sign of the 'affectionless psychopathy' that had been predicted by Bowlby to occur where children are deprived of mother-love.

Unfortunately, there was no follow-up study of the children's adult lives. Also, it should be borne in mind that this is a case study and therefore lacks the objectivity and precision of stricter methods of study (see Chapter 34).

Clark and Clark (1976) documented much evidence which runs counter to Bowlby's claims that infancy and early childhood years have a special overriding importance in social and emotional development. They proposed instead that the whole of development is

important, with the infancy period no more so than middle or later childhood.

Tizard and her colleagues (1978; Hodges and Tizard, 1989), in a longitudinal study, followed the progress of a group of institutionalized children who were later adopted after the age of four. The group was compared to a similar sample of children who were reared at home. The researchers' aim was to try to discover whether early institutional experience would affect the children's later social and emotional behaviour even if they were adopted.

At the age of eight, it was reported by most of the adoptive parents that the children had formed strong attachments to them. However, many parents reported that the children had some emotional problems. They were often difficult to manage and at school were quarrelsome and unpopular with their peers. These findings were reflected also in the follow-up study when the children were 16.

Tizard concluded:

- Most children had formed attachments with adoptive parents and there was little to support Bowlby's claims of an early critical period for the formation of attachments.
- The first two years of life did appear to be critical in shaping some aspects of later development; the early institutional experiences of the children seemed to have caused some problems of social and emotional adjustment.
- Harlow's later research with infant monkeys (see Box 19.3) showed that his early studies may have confused the effects of maternal deprivation with the effects of total isolation. Novak and Harlow (1975) showed that the disturbed behaviour of deprived monkeys was much reduced when they were allowed to interact with other 'therapist' monkeys. This seemed to show that the effects of early deprivation were not irreversible and interactions with peers could be as effective as those with parents in easing the effects of social isolation.

is important, also, to look at individual differences in children's responses to stress and deprivation and discover why it is that some children develop normally despite adverse experiences, while others do suffer psychological damage.

Care outside the home: childminding and day care

This section started by raising the ongoing (often heated) debate about whether preschool children will

Box 19.9 Early experience and its later effects

This seems to be a good point at which to summarize some of the insights which have been drawn from research into the effects of early experience on later development.

There is a long history of research which proposes that children's early experiences with their parents determines what they are like in later life. Many of the earlier accounts of child development, particularly those arising from a psychoanalytic tradition, implied also that once the roots of development were established in early infancy, change was difficult or impossible later on. We now know that this is not correct, or at least that the link between early experience and later effects is far more complex than was originally thought. The work of Rutter discussed above and that of other researchers have highlighted a number of methodological and conceptual problems.

Perhaps the most important point is that the long-term outcome attributed to a particular early experience may not be directly due to the experience itself. It may be the outcome of the continuing effects of its short-term consequences. Or it may be the result of a severe and pervasive problem which caused both the disturbing early event and the longer-term effects. An example may make this clearer.

It has long been accepted that children from broken homes are more likely to have later problems such as unsatisfactory social relationships and delinquency and to underachieve at school. Many explanations stressed the painful effect on the child of being separated from one parent. It now seems to be a more plausible explanation to attribute children's behaviour problems to family discord both before and after the divorce, loneliness and changes in discipline. Also, the changed circumstances of the single parent left responsible for the child, for example lowered income or having to go out to work, are likely to have an impact on the child's behaviour (Rutter, 1981).

Distinguishing between different causes of childhood problems is very important, since different preventative measures and different treatments may be important.

suffer psychological harm if they are cared for in a day centre or by a childminder whilst their parents are at work. It is clear from the research findings considered above that children do not need to be cared for 24 hours a day by a 'single, female mothering figure' as Bowlby suggested. However, related research has considered the quality of alternative care such as childminding and nursery-based day care and the probable effects on young children. Some of this research evidence is outlined below.

Care in a day centre

Most studies of day care have been carried out in the USA. Generally, research suggests that there will be no adverse intellectual or emotional effects on the child, provided the quality of the care is high. Factors such as a stimulating, well-organized environment, committed and caring staff, a high ratio of staff to children are all important (Belsky and Steinberg, 1978).

However, in the late 1980s, a further controversial debate began. After reviewing a number of recent studies, Belsky and Rovine (1988) showed that infants placed in full-time day care during the first year of life had higher levels of insecure attachment, as measured by the Strange Situation, than those brought up at home or where the mother worked part-time. They concluded that placing infants under one year old in

Preschool children in a nursery school setting

day care for more than 20 hours a week could adversely affect the child's emotional well-being.

These findings do raise concerns. However, there are a number of ways they could be interpreted:

■ It is possible that babies placed in day care during the first year of life are at real risk.

■ Alternatively, it is possible that the higher rate of insecure attachment shown in the infants arises because they have not been in day care for very long. Blanchard and Main (1979) found that the longer babies had been in day care, the less likely were they to show symptoms of insecure attachment. The highest levels were shown by those babies who had been in day care only a short time. Therefore, it is possible that the effect may 'wear off'.

■ Clarke-Stewart (1989) has suggested that the Strange Situation procedure may not be appropriate for babies of working mothers, since these babies experience more systematic separations than babies looked after at home. Therefore Belsky and Rovines' conclusions may, at least in part, be inaccurate.

It is clear that much more research must be carried out in order that these issues may be resolved. Incidentally, researchers are generally agreed that Belsky and Rovine's findings do not apply to infants who are placed in day care after the age of one year.

Childminding

There is a mandatory requirement in Britain for those who look after other people's children in their own homes (childminders) to be registered with the local authority, who will monitor the conditions in which children are cared for. However, it is generally accepted that there are many unregistered childminders. Studies of childminding include the following.

Mayall and Petrie (1977, 1983) carried out a naturalistic observation study of 39 childminders in the London area. The researchers were highly critical of the bad housing, cramped conditions and unstimulating care that children were exposed to. Many of the children appeared insecure and showed deficits in cognitive and language skills. However, since there was no control group for comparison, it was not clear whether the children's problems arose from the childminding or from other factors arising from the home environment.

Bryant et al. (1980) combined methods of survey, interview and naturalistic observation to study childminding in Oxfordshire. Though there were no examples of inadequate conditions, and in general carers were conscientious and affectionate, few carers considered that their job was to provide stimulation for the children. About 25 per cent of the children appeared to be thriving. However, many of the remaining children were unnaturally quiet, passive and detached and about 25 per cent of the total were either disturbed or in distress or had inadequate cognitive and language skills. However, once again, it is not clear the extent to which these problems arose from the childminding situation or from problems in the home situation.

Jackson and Jackson (1979) found that many unregistered childminders provided poor conditions and little affection or stimulation. Moss (1987) argues that there is a need to provide childminders with training courses and improved facilities and resources.

A study which compared the behaviour of children who were cared for either by relatives or by childminders or in private day care was carried out by Melhuish (1990). It was found that at the age of 18 months, language ability was highest for children cared for by relatives and lowest for those in nursery care. However, there were no noticeable differences between the three groups in attachment behaviour towards the mother or in cognitive development. Interestingly, the nursery care group showed more prosocial behaviour, such as cooperation and sharing. So while care by relatives would seem to be the preferred situation, care in a nursery setting may have some advantages.

SELF-ASSESSMENT QUESTIONS

1. What did Bowlby mean by 'maternal deprivation'?
2. Discuss some research which has challenged Bowlby's concept of 'maternal deprivation'. How useful, or otherwise, has this concept been in helping us to understand the effects of early deprivation?
3. Outline some of the conceptual and methodological problems inherent in trying to link early experience to later development.
4. Outline the findings from research which has examined the care of children outside the home.

Children's play

As with many other young mammals, play is a characteristic part of the behaviour of all normal, healthy children. A dominant view in psychology has been that play has important implications for a child's psychological development. This section aims to consider the nature and functions of play and its role in development.

" PERSONALLY, I THINK THAT NURSERY SCHOOL PUTS **TOO** MUCH EMPHASIS ON CREATIVE PLAY WITH TOY MONEY ! "

What is play?

A number of problems arise when psychologists attempt to define what they mean by play. One of the main problems is in deciding what to include under the umbrella term of 'play'. Do we confine ourselves to what children do or should we include the activities of adults who enjoy a game of bingo or go down to the pub to play darts. And if we do confine ourselves to the behaviour of children, what range of activities should be included: painting, playing with bricks, experimenting with sand and water, kicking a football, exploring a new object? Should all these be subsumed under the heading of 'play'?

The range and diversity of all the above activities have presented psychologists with a dilemma in seeking to describe and explain behaviour associated with play, particularly during early childhood. There is much disagreement about the activities that should be categorized as play. There seems to be no simple definition.

Defining features of play

Some theorists have looked at the general characteristics and functions of play. For example, Garvey (1977) provided one list of characteristics:

- Play is essentially enjoyable and associated with positive affect (feeling good).
- It is an activity done for its own sake, is rewarding in itself and does not depend on the attainment of goals outside the play situation.
- It is spontaneous and voluntary and is not instigated or controlled by someone else.
- The player needs to be actively involved.
- It is not the same as 'real life' and should not be taken literally.

While intuitively this list of characteristics has appeal, looking at play in terms of an idealized list of features is not as simple as it might appear. There are some features which all play seems to share; we can probably all agree that people play for the sake of enjoyment rather than for externally imposed reasons. However, there are other features which are not necessarily shared by all kinds of play. For example, Sluckin (1981) has suggested that much of what goes on in school playgrounds is anything but free/voluntary/spontaneous since it is strongly influenced by other children (and sometimes adults). Also, there is often evidence of play that does not have 'positive affect' and is characterized by aggression and tears rather than pleasure.

Purposes of play

Gardner believed the purposes of play in the development of the child to be:

greater mastery of the world, more adequate coping with problems and fears, superior understanding of oneself and one's relationship to the world, an initial exploration of the relations between reality and fantasy, an arena in which intuitive, semi-logical forms of thought can be freely tested.

(Gardner, 1982, p. 255)

You will recognize many of these functions of play in the theories and studies which follow.

Some theories of play

Numerous theories of the nature and purposes of play have been developed, some dating back to the end of the last century. This section will briefly consider a selection of the more recent theories.

Piaget's theory of play

Piaget firmly linked the development of play with the development of thought (see Chapter 20) and contended that children's developmental level may be inferred in part from their play. He proposed three broad stages of play activity:

Box 19.10 Social aspects of play

Parten (1932) proposed that socially there is a clear developmental sequence in a child's style of play, particularly in the early years.

- Until the age of 18 months, there is much **solitary play** with objects such as toys.
- The three year old is more likely to engage in **parallel play**, playing alongside other children, sometimes watching and imitating the other child but not truly interacting.
- Around the age of four, children increasingly engage in **social play** and simple interactions take place. Initially these interactions are quite rigid, but they soon involve 'give and take' in the form of turn-taking and cooperation.

Many subsequent researchers have confirmed and used Parten's categories. However, Cohen (1987) argues that social categorizations of play such as this have limited usefulness since most children mix many different kinds of play. She points out that typically these categories have been derived from observing children in playgroups or nursery schools, whereas much of the play children engage in actually occurs within the family. Therefore, it is likely that such play will involve children of different ages playing together, and also children playing with adults, and the patterns of interaction will vary.

- **Mastery play** corresponds to the sensorimotor stage of development (birth to two years, approximately). The emphasis is on practice and control of movements, and on exploration of objects through sight and touch. Children's play activity contains many repetitive movements which are indulged in for the simple pleasure of demonstrating their developing mastery of the skills involved.
- **Symbolic play** coincides with the preoperational stage (approximately two to seven). The child employs fantasy and make-believe in play and delights in using one object to symbolize another – so a chair may become a motor car, a sheet a fashionable dress.
- **Play with rules** characterizes the operational stages (from about seven onwards). The child's developing thought processes become more logical and play involves the use of rules and procedures.

Piaget proposed that play is an expression of the process of **assimilation**, where children are attempting to take in knowledge of the world around and change it to fit in with their own understanding and experience.

Psychodynamic views of play

Freud's psychodynamic theory of development (see Chapters 1 and 30) viewed play as a means of relieving pent-up emotions. Children may use play to explore and cope with their feelings about life and work out their fears and anxieties (**catharsis**) in a safe situation.

GLOSSARY

Mastery play The first of Piaget's stages of play activity (sensorimotor), where a child of up to about two years spends time exploring and manipulating objects through sight and touch.

Symbolic play The second of Piaget's stages of play activity (preoperational) where a child begins to use fantasy in play and uses objects to stand for something different.

Play with rules The third of Piaget's stages of play activity (concrete and formal operations) where the child begins to play increasingly complex games with rules.

Assimilation The process described by Piaget, where children attempt to fit knowledge of the world around into their existing understanding and experience.

Catharsis Freud's notion of a 'cleansing' of emotional fears and anxieties, in order to overcome problems associated with them.

Play can thus be seen both as a defence against problems and as a coping behaviour. Erikson (1963), a neo-Freudian, contended that: 'The child's play is the infantile form of the human ability to deal with experience by creating model situations and to master reality by experiment and planning.'

The psychodynamic approach to play is characterized in the use of **play therapy** to treat disturbed children. The basic assumption is that the child's play is a reflection of his or her unconscious mind. During therapy, the child is encouraged to play in a safe, undemanding situation with objects such as dolls, buildings and so on. Through play sessions, the child can act out and come to terms with anxieties.

A pioneering figure in the development of play therapy was Melanie Klein, a leading figure in European psychoanalysis. An account of her approach is contained in Chapter 1.

Vygotsky and play

Vygotsky (1967) saw play as a leading contributor to overall development. He emphasized particularly the rules of play. Confronted with a problem, the child unconsciously devises a make-believe situation which is easier to cope with. Such a 'game' involves the use of a set of rules and procedures which enable the child to take an object from its familiar context and believe that it is something else – so a broom handle can become a horse and the 'rules' of the game allow the child to behave in a manner which is removed from everyday reality.

Vygotsky believed that play creates a 'zone of potential development' (see Chapter 20) where children can operate at a level which is above that for their normal age: for instance, performing some of the movements of writing for the first time. One way of assessing a child's potential development at a particular time, Vygotsky believed, is to note the distance between the levels of activity reached during play and those of his or her customary behaviour.

Bruner's views on play

Bruner et al. (1976) stressed the learning potential of play. They viewed play as a means of attaining physical and cognitive skills in young children. Play involves experimentation with smaller actions which may later be combined into a more complex, higher order skill. Thus, a two year old given a set of construction toys,

Playing with construction toys is likely to help young children to develop important spatial skills

will initially explore and handle the individual pieces. Over a period of time, the child will experiment with possible uses and combinations until eventually he or she will be able to assemble complete constructions with confidence. This kind of play allows a child to understand such things as spatial relations and mechanics in a relaxed, nonthreatening setting. Thus, play contributes to problem solving and an understanding of the use of tools.

Studies of play

Much of the theorizing about the importance of play has been done without any real evidence to support claims about its value in development. Nonetheless, over the last 20 years or so, a range of empirical studies

---

GLOSSARY

Play therapy A therapeutic technique based on psychoanalytic principles, often used by therapists to treat children who are emotionally disturbed.

have been carried out. It is intended to look at two 'classic' studies in some depth and to look more briefly at a range of others.

Play and cognitive development

Sylva et al. (1980) carried out a naturalistic observational study of the play of preschool children in Oxfordshire playgroups and nursery schools. This was part of a large project under the directorship of Jerome Bruner. The researchers were particularly concerned to investigate how play may contribute to cognitive development.

The researchers identified what they called **elaborated play** – rich play which challenges the child and stimulates more complex activity involving the child's fullest capacities. Elaborated play has two important characteristics:

■ It has a clear goal and some means for its achievement;
■ It has 'real world' feedback, that is, the child is able to assess his or her own progress without referring to anyone else.

The main findings of the study were as follows:

■ It was proposed that the richest, most elaborated and extended play occurs in building and construction activities, drawing and art and doing 'school readiness' puzzles. These activities also encourage the child to concentrate for longer periods of time.
■ Somewhat behind these activities in importance is play involving pretending, small-scale toys, sand and dough.
■ Less elaborated play such as informal, impromptu games and 'horsing around' appear to serve the functions of social contact and release of tension.
■ Young children play longer and better when they operate in pairs rather than alone or in larger groups. The presence of an adult nearby for assurance or brief comment, but not managing the situation, improves the quality of play.

Sylva et al.'s study has important implications for the organization and staffing of nursery schools and playgroups. It emphasizes play which offers cognitive challenge. However, by implication, perhaps it underplays the importance of the social challenge found in, for instance, pretend play.

In considering a range of studies that have examined the contribution of play to cognitive development, including the Sylva et al. one discussed above, Meadows (1986) concluded that there are problems in comparing studies. One such problem arises from differences in how the 'quality' of play was assessed. However, she found that, on the whole, the researchers agreed in two important ways:

■ The general level of cognitive complexity of children's play was disappointing. Much of what they did was simple, undemanding and uninventive.
■ Where teachers were more than casually involved and the children used a range of materials which made it easy to define a goal and move towards it (for example, in art activities) children did show higher levels of play.

Exploration

Hutt (1966) carried out a study in which she investigated exploratory behaviour. **Exploration** has often been confused with play. However, Hutt's experiment made the distinction clear. Exploration is explained as an activity during which children may investigate objects and events in the environment and/ or features of their own physical ability.

Children aged from three to five were presented with a novel and complex object in the form of a red, metal box with four brass legs and topped with a lever which, when moved, activated various novel auditory or visual stimuli. Typically, at first, the children concentrated on trying to find out what the novel object could do. This was followed by an attempt to use the object as part of a game. Once the children had become familiar with the object, they would investigate it further only if a new feature, for example a new sight or sound, was discovered.

Hutt distinguished between the earlier exploratory behaviour and the later play behaviour. Exploration was characterized as fairly serious and focused,

---

GLOSSARY

Elaborated play A term used by Sylva to describe the kind of play which challenges and stimulates and is most likely to enhance a child's cognitive development.

Exploration Activities where children investigate objects and events or aspects of their own physical ability.

essentially asking 'What does this object do?' Play was characterized as being more relaxed and involving a range of activities, essentially asking 'What can I do with this object?'

Though the study was strictly an experiment, it involved some degree of natural observation.

What is related to playfulness?

In a follow-up to Hutt's study above, Hutt and Bhavnani (1972) revisited 48 of the children whose exploratory behaviour had been studied. They found that nonexploring in early childhood related to lack of curiosity and adventure in boys, and to problems of personality and social adjustment for girls. Those children who had been earlier categorized as more imaginative explorers were more likely to be judged as independent and curious by their teachers and more likely to score highly on tests of creativity. Hutt proposed a relationship between one form of exploratory play (as investigated in her study) and subsequent personality, creativity and cognitive style. However, this was a correlational study, so we cannot assume that there is a causal link (see Chapter 34) – we must not assume that imaginative play causes a child to develop creativity. The imaginative play of some of the children in Hutt's original study might be a by-product of their essential creativity rather than a cause of it.

Connolly and Doyle (1984) found that the amount and complexity of fantasy play in preschool children was significantly and positively correlated with measures of social competence. Johnson et al. (1982) found a positive correlation between the level of constructive play in four year olds and their intelligence scores. This is in accord with the findings of Sylva et al.'s study of the value of elaborated play. Again, however, we must be aware of the problem of causality in these correlational studies.

What is the value of play?

So what can be concluded about the value of play and its significance in childhood development? The truth is that there is little conclusive evidence that play is essential to healthy development. In some cultures, children seem to play very little, yet they develop normally. The pervading feeling among researchers seems to be that while play may have benefits, they are unlikely to be of crucial importance. Other activities may fulfil the same functions. However, Meadows

Box 19.11   Play tutoring

As in other areas of developmental psychology, there has been a trend towards studying children's play in more ecologically valid ways. This means paying more focused attention to the social context in which play happens over a sustained period of time.

A group of studies in the USA have highlighted the benefits of play tutoring with deprived preschool children. Play tutoring is a technique pioneered by Smilansky (1968) and summarized by Christie (1986). It involves adults engaging children in play, usually with verbal guidance and suggestions and sometimes acting as role models in fantasy play. Several studies found that play tutoring encouraged cognitive, language and social development in children. However, a study by Smith et al. (1981) compared play tutoring to skills tutoring, where adults interacted with children in structured activities such as jigsaws and sorting shapes. Groups of four-year-old children in a nursery school experienced equal amounts of either play tutoring or skills tutoring. Both groups showed improvements on measures of social, cognitive and language skills and neither group was superior to the other. The researchers concluded that the crucial factor that caused the improvements was adult involvement, particularly verbal stimulation, and this may have accounted for the findings of earlier studies of play tutoring.

(1986) argued that play cannot be written off as useless. It is a source of enjoyment and pleasure which probably contributes to a child's emotional well-being. 'It is a potential source of feelings of competence and achievement, and so a contributor to the child's self-esteem and feelings of self-efficacy. It is part of the child's social worlds of peers and of adults' (Meadows, 1986, p. 30).

Exercise 19.2

Visit a preschool playgroup. Identify different kinds of play as in Sylva's study. Observe the role of the adults in children's play and in encouraging language development.

? SELF-ASSESSMENT QUESTIONS

1. What do you understand by 'play'? Outline some difficulties experienced by psychologists in their efforts to define 'play'?

2. List some differences you might observe between the play of three-year-old children and that of eight-year-old children.

3. Discuss theory and evidence which suggest that play contributes to cognitive development.

4. What is 'exploratory play'. Briefly outline the findings of a relevant study.

5. What do you conclude about the value of play and its significance in childhood development?

Chapter summary

■ Four important milestones in the social and emotional development of children are social smiling, stranger anxiety or awareness, separation anxiety and social attachment. Interactions with other human beings are hugely important for development and constitute what Schaffer calls mutual repricocity.

■ Characteristics which can be observed in a young baby's repertoire of behaviour include the ability to learn, behaviour which invites social response and enjoyment of contingent responding by others. At about one year old babies are quite good at social referencing (gauging a parent's emotion response in a particular situation).

■ Parents provide frameworks (scaffolding) for infants to learn the skills of social interaction by providing for their physical and emotional needs, protecting them from danger, helping where infants are not yet able to manage for themselves, adapting activities to bring them within the capacity of the infant, giving them feedback on their actions, acting as models, encouraging conversation and acting as the child's memory.

■ Imitation is a very important means of development from the earliest stages and is an index of the infant's social awareness and an important source of information about the child's understanding of the world.

■ While mothers have been the focus of investigation into the development of infants, there is evidence that fathers also play a part in the development of attachment. They have been found to be as capable as mothers of performing the parenting role.

■ Social development is also influenced by interactions with siblings and deep emotions are involved both of love and of envy. Siblings may try to be as different as possible from each other and seek out different roles for themselves within the family.

■ While in the 1930s and 1940s there was a negative stereotype of the role of grandparents, more positive aspects have recently been recognized. Their influences on children may be both direct and indirect, acting sometimes as surrogate parents when parents work and providing a model (from the way in which parents themselves were brought up) for parenting skills.

■ Attachment may be defined as an enduring bond of affection towards an individual. Theories of attachment have been heavily influenced by psychoanalytic theory. Harlow, in his research with rhesus monkeys, showed that the need was not primarily the satisfaction of basic physiological needs, for instance for food, but the satisfaction of emotional bonding needs.

■ Ethological studies of imprinting, such as those of Lorenz, have been influential to the understanding of the role of attachment in animals and particularly of the importance of critical periods during which attachments are most easily formed.

■ Bowlby's theory contains concepts drawn from biology, especially the concept that attachment has adaptive value. His theory stresses the attention given to the primary caregiver, usually the mother, and that attachment is qualitatively different with her than other attachments. This 'monotropy' has been disputed by other researchers, who have claimed that attachment may be with a male or a female and that there may be a sharing of attachment.

■ The method of assessing attachment in babies developed by Ainsworth, known as the Strange Situation, has been widely used in the USA, Germany, Holland, Israel and Japan as well as in the UK. Using this method Ainsworth has identified three attachment types, A insecure (anxious, avoidant), B secure and C insecure (ambivalent). A fourth category, Type D disorganized and disoriented, has been added as a result of research by Main and Solomon. Infants in category B were found to have advantages, including greater positive play, greater autonomy, interpersonal competence and eagerness to learn during preschool and early school years.

■ There is also a link found between attachment types and the behaviour of mothers. Type B infants cried least and had mothers who were sensitive and responsive to their needs. Parental stress and depression have been found to be linked to insecure attachment; 80 per cent of neglected and badly treated infants fell into type D.

■ There is evidence that temperamental differences determine how attachment develops. Different temperaments present different challenges to parents, but the way in which the caregiver responds to the child may determine the type of attachment. There is some cross-cultural variation on the distribution of attachment types as well as intracultural differences.

■ Criticisms of the construct of attachment have centred on measurement using the Strange Situation. The introduction of a stranger technique has been criticized as unnatural and likely to alter the natural behaviour of the infants. Furthermore, the initial study was carried out on a very small sample of American children (i.e. small and atypical).

■ While most research has concentrated upon very early attachment, it is clear that attachment does not only apply to infants. Attachment is in evidence at all stages of life and tests have been devised to measure attachments in older children and adolescents, including the Separation Anxiety Test. The Social Convoy Diagram has been used to assess attachment in adulthood.

■ There is evidence that early attachments are linked to later attachment relationships. The development of friendships, sexual and loving relationships and parent–child relationships in adult life may be affected by early attachments.

■ Bowlby was concerned with disturbed behaviour exhibited in institutionalized or hospitalized children and suggested that children deprived of the chance to form an early attachment with a mother or permanent mother-figure suffer later social, emotional and intellectual problems. He used the evidence from his own study of 44 juvenile thieves and Goldfarb's study of institutionalized children, though later researchers have noted methodological flaws in these studies.

■ Rutter carried out a major reassessment of Bowlby's work and distinguished between short-term and long-term effects of deprivation of attachment. Privation (lack of attachment) was more likely than deprivation to be responsible for the condition described as affectionless psychopathy. Family discord and lack of a stable relationship with a parent was likely to be associated with antisocial behaviour and delinquency, while lack of stimulation and necessary life experiences were responsible for intellectual retardation.

■ Other researchers who challenged Bowlby's views included Freud and Dann, Clark and Clark and Tizard and her colleagues. Rutter argued that the concept of 'maternal deprivation' should be abandoned and researchers should look at differences in children's responses to stress.

■ The quality of care afforded to children when they are not in the care of their parents is seen as important and the relative merits of childminding and nursery day care have been studied. It has been found that children placed in full-time day care during the first year of life had higher levels of insecure attachment than those whose mothers do not work or who work part-time. A comparison of children in the care of childminders, cared for by relatives and in nurseries, found that language ability was highest in the group cared for by relatives and lowest in the group which had nursery care. While childminders were generally conscientious and affectionate there was often insufficient stimulation. In these circumstances some children were found to be passive or detached and others distressed or disturbed.

■ Gardner has claimed that play has for its function greater mastery of the world, coping with problems and fears, understanding of oneself and one's relationship to the world, exploration of reality and fantasy, and the testing of intuitive and semilogical thought. There is a developmental sequence in the kinds of play in which children indulge, first solitary play, then parallel play and then social play.

■ Piaget saw mastery play as coinciding with the sensorimotor stage of development, symbolic play with the preoperational stage and play with rules with the operational stages of development. Play was seen as an expression of assimilation.

■ Freud and his followers saw play as a means of catharsis. Vygotsky saw play as contributing in a major way to overall development, creating a 'zone of potential development'. Bruner, too, saw the learning potential of play, a means of attaining cognitive and

physical skills through experimentation with smaller actions.

■ Sylva's naturalistic observational study of play found that the richest forms of play were building, construction, drawing and art. Pretend play and small-scale toys, sand and dough was less rich while informal play served the purpose of social contact and tension release. Young children play best in pairs. The presence of an adult can improve the quality of play.

■ Hutt investigated exploratory behaviour and distinguished exploratory from later play behaviour. Play was more relaxed and involved a range of activities. Connolly and Doyle found a relationship between the complexity of fantasy play and social competence.

Further reading

Bowlby, J. (1988). *A Secure Base: Clinical Applications of Attachment Theory*. London: Tavistock/Routledge. A collection of lectures given by Bowlby since 1979. Though it focuses mainly on attachment from a clinical perspective, it gives an outline of the main features of attachment theory and describes relevant research.

Durkin, K. (1995). *Developmental Social Psychology: From Infancy to Old Age*. Oxford: Blackwell. Chapter 2 looks at social life in infancy and Chapter 3 gives an excellent overview of attachment theory, including up-to-date research findings from North America, Europe and Australia

on the emergence of attachment in older children and measuring and categorizing attachment.

Rutter, M. (1981). *Maternal Deprivation Reassessed*, 2nd edn. Harmondsworth: Penguin. A classic text which presented a challenge to Bowlby's 'maternal deprivation' hypothesis; it raises many relevant conceptual issues in relation to the problems of attempting to link early experience to later development.

Smith, P. K. (ed.) (1986). *Children's Play: Research, Developments and Practical Applications*. London: Gordon and Breach. An interesting and accessible series of articles on children's play.

CHAPTER 20

Cognitive development

Piaget's theory of cognitive development 460
- Schemas and operations (variant cognitive structures) 461
- Adaptation to the environment (invariant functions) 461
- Piaget's developmental stages 462
- Evaluation of Piaget's theory 465
- Cross-cultural studies of Piagetian ideas 467

Cognitive development in a social context 468
- The influence of Vygotsky 469
- Bruner's theory 470

- Educational implications of Vygotsky's and Bruner's theories 470
- Conclusions 473

Information-processing approaches to cognitive development 474
- Developmental aspects of information processing 474
- Study of individual differences in information processing 476
- Evaluation of the information-processing approach 476

Language acquisition 478
- Sequence of language acquisition 478
- Some studies of language acquisition 480
- Theories of language acquisition 481

Objectives

By the end of this chapter you should be able to:

- Describe and evaluate Piaget's theory of cognitive development;
- Discuss the psychometric approach to cognitive functioning;
- Have an appreciation of other approaches to cognitive development, including those of

- Vygotsky, Bruner and information-processing theorists within cognitive science;
- Consider the educational implications of theories of cognitive development;
- Critically evaluate research and theories of language acquisition.

The term 'cognitive', which is derived from the Latin *cognosco* (to know), refers to all those psychological activities involved in the acquisition, processing, organization and use of knowledge – in other words, all those abilities associated with thinking and knowing. The cognitive processes of perception and memory have been the most widely studied. See Part 3 of this book for a detailed consideration of cognitive processes.

Cognitive abilities also include a child's measured intelligence, levels of thinking and even, to some extent, creativity and the way interpersonal relationships are conducted. Since language is the medium through which thinking usually takes place, and since much intelligent and creative activity is expressed through language, this, too, is usually regarded as a cognitive activity.

Two key questions dominate the study of cognitive development:

- What changes in cognitive functioning occur as the child grows older?
- What factors may be responsible for these changes?

The best known and most influential approach to these questions is that of the Swiss biologist turned psychologist, Jean Piaget (1896–1980). Piaget's theory focuses mainly on logical thinking, reasoning and problem solving, and is less directly concerned with processes such as perception and memory. Piaget's theory will be considered in some detail and the chapter will also include a brief review of three other theoretical approaches drawn from the work of Vygotsky (1978), Bruner (1966b, 1986) and theorists within the information-processing approach of cognitive science (see the Introduction to Part 3). Chapter 21 will examine factors associated with the development of intelligence test performance – the psychometric approach to cognitive functioning.

Piaget's theory of cognitive development

Most psychologists would agree that Jean Piaget was the most influential developmental psychologist of the twentieth century. Largely as a result of his work, cognition has been a major focus in child development research since the late 1950s when his work was translated from French into English.

For over half a century Piaget made detailed observations of children's activities, talked to children, listened to them talking to each other, and devised and presented many 'tests' of children's thinking. His methods of study, which included the **clinical interview** and naturalistic observation (see Chapter 31), were in sharp contrast to the rigorous and strictly controlled methods used by the behaviourists. In his studies, Piaget did not manipulate variables in the manner of formal experiments. His early research programme attempted instead to describe the kinds of thinking characteristic of children up to adolescence. Further, Piaget's interest was not in the uniqueness of

---

Box 20.1   Children's concepts

A concept is the idea an individual has about a particular class of objects (including animate objects) or events, grouped together on the basis of the things they have in common. It is through concepts that we are able to think about and make sense of the world. Thus a small child will have a concept of 'daddy', 'dog' or 'table', of 'softness' and 'hardness', of 'small things' and 'large things', of 'more than' and 'less than'. When children encounter new objects and experiences, they try to make sense of them by fitting them into their existing concepts. Consider the two-year-old girl who has formed the concept of 'bird' as an object that flies in the sky. One day she sees her first aeroplane and tries to link it to her concept of 'bird'. But the noise, the size and the shape do not fit her existing concept. If she questions her parents, they will provide a new word and explain the differences between birds and aeroplanes, therefore allowing the child to create a new concept.

---

individual children, but rather in the similarities between children of roughly equivalent ages.

Piaget's findings led him to propose a theory of how children form the concepts involved in thinking – that is, a theory which suggests that children develop more sophisticated ways of thinking mainly as a consequence of maturation. Box 20.1 gives some examples of concept formation in childhood. Chapter 15 contains additional discussion of concept formation.

Piaget believed that the way in which we are able to form and deal with concepts changes as we move through childhood into adolescence. A child's thinking is not simply a less well informed version of an adult's, but differs from it in a number of important ways which are discussed below.

GLOSSARY

Cognitive processes All the processes involved in thinking and knowing, including perceiving, interpreting, reasoning, remembering, using language.

Clinical interview A method used by Piaget to study children in an informal setting, by asking them questions and setting them tasks.

Schemas and operations (variant cognitive structures)

Piaget saw the structure of the intellect in terms of schemas and operations.

A **schema** (plural schemas or schemata) is the internal representation of some specific physical or mental action. The newborn child, Piaget believed, is endowed with a number of innate schemas which correspond to reflex responses: for example, the looking schema, the grasping schema, the sucking schema and so on. As the child develops, these innate schemas integrate with each other and become more elaborate, and entirely new schemas are formed as the child responds to the environment.

Fundamental to intelligence are schemas consisting of knowledge about objects/events and knowledge of how to do things. In any intellectual or physical act, there is always a schema of some kind of present, a kind of cognitive plan which the individual uses to deal with a particular problem.

An **operation** is a higher order mental structure which is not present at birth, and is usually not acquired until middle childhood. An operation involves the child in knowing more complex rules about how the environment works. It has the characteristic of **reversibility**. This means that an operation can be regarded as a mental activity which can be reversed – done backwards, so to speak. The rules of arithmetic involve operations which are reversible. For example, a child of five will readily understand the process of addition ($2+3=5$) but will not appreciate that this process is reversible by subtraction ($5-3=2$). The older child who is capable of operational thinking will recognize that addition is reversible by subtraction and division is reversible by multiplication.

Look at Figure 20.2 on page 463 and read the account of Task 1 set for children by Piaget. When asked the final question, 'Does the "sausage" have the same amount of Plasticine as the "cake"?', the answer given by a child of four or five is usually very different from the answer given by a child of seven or eight. The older child will usually reply without hesitation 'of course they are the same'. The younger child typically says that the 'sausage' now contains more Plasticine than the 'cake'. Younger children's thinking seems to be dominated by the appearance of objects. Moreover, they are not capable of performing the mental operation of reversibility, or mentally reversing the moulding of the 'sausage'.

Children's cognitive structures change as they grow older. Hence, Piaget terms 'schemas' and 'operations' **variant cognitive structures**.

Adapatation to the environment (invariant functions)

Piaget based his theory firmly within a biological framework, and **adaptation** is a key concept. In order to survive, every individual must adapt to the demands of the environment.

Intellectual development is seen as the adaptation of cognitive structures (schemas and operations) to meet the demands of the environment. Such adaptation takes place through the processes of **assimilation** and **accommodation**. Assimilation refers to the process whereby a new object or idea is understood in terms of concepts or actions (schemas) that the child already possesses. Accommodation is a complementary process which enables all individuals to modify concepts and actions to fit new situations, objects or information.

Consider again the example described in Box 20.1 of the child who first encounters an aeroplane. Her initial interpretation of it as a bird is an example of assimilation – she assimilates the aeroplane into her schema of 'bird'. On acquiring new information about

---

GLOSSARY

Schema Piaget's term for an individual's internal representation, a kind of cognitive plan, of some specific physical or mental ability: for example, grasping an object or understanding how to do multiplication.

Operation Piaget's term for a more advanced mental structure that allows an individual to perform a mental action in reverse.

Reversibility The ability to mentally reverse thought processes and arrive back at the original starting point.

Variant cognitive structures Piaget's term for cognitive structures such as schemas and operations which change as a child grows older.

Adaptation Piaget's key concept relating to the way in which individuals adjust their behaviour to cope with the environment.

Assimilation The process of taking new information or experiences into existing schemas in order to cope with the environment.

Accommodation A process, complementary to assimilation, which enables an individual to deal with totally new concepts or experiences by modifying existing schemas or developing new schemas.

the characteristics of an aeroplane, she accommodates to the new situation and consequently develops a new schema.

The twin processes of assimilation and accommodation continue throughout life as we adapt our behaviour and ideas to changing circumstances. Assimilation is the process that enables an individual to deal with new situations and new problems by using existing schemas. Accommodation, on the other hand, is the process which involves the changing of existing schemas or the development of new schemas. It is because of the unchanging nature of these processes that Piaget referred to assimilation and accommodation as **invariant functions**.

Before a child has acquired new knowledge, she or he is in a state of what Piaget called equilibrium (or cognitive harmony). When this state of equilibrium is disturbed – that is, when something new or demanding is encountered – the processes of assimilation and accommodation function to restore it. Piaget proposes a process of **equilibration** which acts to ensure that accommodation is consolidated via assimilation, and that a balance is maintained between the two. In this way, mental structures change and cognitive ability gradually progresses.

Piaget's developmental stages

Piaget has identified a number of distinct stages of intellectual development. He proposed that children move through each of these stages in turn, in the sequence and at approximately the ages shown below. The speed at which children move through each stage, although influenced by each child's particular experiences, is essentially controlled by biologically determined maturational processes. The process cannot be hastened – a child must be maturationally ready before progressing to the next stage. At each stage, new, more sophisticated, levels of thinking are added to the child's cognitive repertoire.

Stage 1: Sensorimotor (approximately birth to two years)

In this stage the child experiences the world mainly through immediate perceptions and through physical activity, without thought as adults know it. For example, not until about eight months does a child have any concept of **object permanence**. Until then, out of sight is out of mind, and children will not attempt to look for a previously visible object which is placed out of sight as they watch. Their thinking is dominated by the 'here and now'. With the acquisition of the object concept and when other means of knowing, such as memory and language, are available to them, the sensorimotor stage is at an end. The child can now anticipate the future and think about the past.

Stage 2: Preoperational (approximately two to seven)

This is the stage that has been most extensively studied by Piaget. It marks a long period of transition which culminates in the emergence of operational thinking. With the development of language the child is now capable of symbolic thought, but Piaget argues that the child's intellectual capabilities are still largely dominated by his or her perceptions, rather than by a conceptual grasp of situations and events.

Piaget described a number of limitations to a child's thinking which exist at this stage of development. These limitations – **egocentrism**, **centration** and irreversibility – are discussed below.

Egocentrism This refers to children's inability to see the world from anything but their own point of view. They are not capable of understanding that there can be viewpoints other than their own. Thus, if a small boy is asked to say what someone sitting on the other side of a room is able to see, he will describe things from his own perspective only; a little girl may tell you that she has a sister, but will strenuously deny that her sister has a sister.

GLOSSARY

Invariant functions Piaget's term for the cognitive processes which do not change with maturity: for example, assimilation and accommodation.

Equilibration A process which acts to ensure that accommodation is consolidated via assimilation and that a balance is maintained between the two.

Object permanence The belief that objects continue to exist even when they are not visible.

Egocentrism The inability to see an object or situation from anything but one's own point of view.

Centration A characteristic of the thinking of young children, where the child may focus upon one feature of the environment, while ignoring others, however relevant.

Figure 20.1 illustrates Piaget's famous 'three mountains task' which was designed to illustrate the egocentrism of young children. Children are asked to select from a series of photographs of the model landscape one that corresponds to a view different from their own. Children under eight do not seem to be able to imagine what other views would be like.

Centration   This involves attending to (centring on) only one feature of a situation and ignoring others, no matter how relevant. The child's inability to decentre is apparent in Piaget's famous **conservation** tasks, some of which are described in Figure 20.2.

In Task 1 the younger preoperational child will exhibit an inability to conserve – that is, will be unable to grasp the fact that the amount of Plasticine remains the same even though the appearance of one may change. Similarly, in Task 2, even though the child has agreed that the two 'fat' beakers contain the same amount of liquid, when the contents of one are poured

Task I   **Conservation of substance**

The child is shown two identical balls of Plasticine and is asked 'Are these two "cakes" the same?'

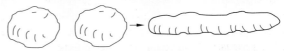

The experimenter rolls out one ball of Plasticine into a 'sausage' shape. The child is asked 'Does the "sausage" have the same amount of Plasticine as the "cake"?'

Task 2   **Conservation of volume**

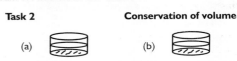

The child is shown is shown a short, 'fat' beaker (a) containing milk, and is asked to pour milk from a jug into a second identical beaker (b) until it has the same amount of milk as the first beaker. The child agrees that the amount of milk in each beaker is identical.

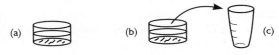

The child is then shown a tall 'thin' beaker and is asked to pour the contents of one of the original beakers into it. The child is then asked 'Is there the same in (c) as there is in (a)?'

Task 3   **Conservation of number**

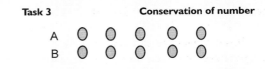

The child is shown counters placed in two identical rows (A and B). The child agrees that the two rows have the same number of counters.

The experimenter 'bunches up' the counters in row B. The child is asked 'Do the two rows still contain the same number of counters?'

Figure 20.2   Typical Piagetian conservation tasks

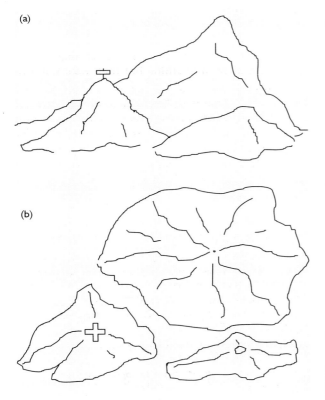

(a)

(b)

Figure 20.1   Piaget's 'mountain task' (Piaget and Inhelder, 1956) showing three mountains viewed (a) from the front and (b) from the top

into a tall, thin beaker, the child will now usually contend that we have more liquid than before, simply because the level has risen higher. This illustrates an inability to conserve volume.

In Task 3, the preoperational child will claim that the two rows in part 2 of the experiment do not now contain the same number of counters.

All these conservation tasks are the same in that they first involve a phase in which the child is presented with two entities and is asked to agree that they are 'the same'. Then the appearance of one entity is transformed while the child watches. The child is then asked to judge whether the two things are still the same. Piaget carried out similar tasks with area, length, weight and so on.

Irreversibility The conservation experiments also show the inability of preoperational children to work backwards mentally to a starting point. Look back to page 461 and reread the discussion of the importance of reversibility to the development of operational thinking.

Stage 3: Concrete operations (approximately 7–11 years)

The main features of this stage are:

■ the acquisition of reversible thinking, and
■ the ability to decentre.

Hence, children confronted with conservation tasks are capable of understanding the concept of invariance, partly because they realize that the transformation of shape, volume, spatial distributions, and so on are capable of being reversed, and partly because their thinking is no longer dominated by only one feature of a situation.

Piaget maintains that conservation takes place in a definite order, with the conservation of number coming first at approximately six or seven years and conservation of volume being achieved last at about 11 or 12 years of age. The child also becomes less egocentric, and is now capable of seeing objects and events from the viewpoint of another.

Another important feature of this stage is the child's increasing ability to handle such concepts as **classification** – the ability to group objects together logically in terms of their common characteristics – and **seriation** – the ability to arrange items in rank order in terms, for example, of their colour or size.

The stage of concrete operations is so called because the child needs to manipulate and experiment with real objects, in order to solve problems in a logical way. For example, children at this stage will have difficulty dealing with the verbal problem 'Joan is taller than Susan; Joan is smaller than Mary; who is the smallest?' in their heads, but would have no difficulty if given three dolls to represent Joan, Susan and Mary.

Stage 4: Formal operations (approximately 11 years onwards)

This stage marks the emergence of the ability to reason in the abstract without having to rely on concrete objects or events. Children's thinking increasingly resembles that of adults: they are able to solve a problem in their head by systematically testing out several propositions, by isolating such propositions and at the same time considering their interrelatedness.

Figure 20.3 illustrates Piaget's 'pendulum task', which was used to investigate formal operational thinking.

Children are given several weights and a length of string suspended from a hook. They are told they can vary the length of the string, change the weight and vary the strength of 'push'. Their task is to find out which of these different factors affects the time taken to complete one swing of the pendulum.

The preoperational child typically thinks the strength of 'push' is the only important factor.

The concrete operational child will attempt to investigate the different factors – different weights, shorter or longer string etc. – but does so randomly rather than systematically.

The formal operational child systematically tests each factor and sets up a hypothesis that one or the other factor is important, testing it out until all possibilities have been investigated.

Figure 20.3 Piaget's 'pendulum task' designed to investigate formal operational thinking

GLOSSARY

Classification The ability to group objects together in terms of common attributes.

Seriation The ability to arrange things in order.

Figure 20.4 contains a summary of Piaget's stages of development. Piaget proposed that all children move through the stages in the sequence shown. The ages given are approximate and may vary depending upon intelligence, cultural background and socioeconomic factors.

Evaluation of Piaget's theory

Methodological considerations

Piaget's reliance on the clinical interview method has been criticized. It has been suggested that because there were no set questions and no standard method of presentation, there may have been a tendency to 'lead' children into views that were not strictly their own. Piaget himself was aware of these problems and much of his later work employed more strictly controlled methods.

Bryant (1974) argued that the design of many Piagetian tasks made it very difficult for children to give correct answers. Piaget, he felt, may have underestimated the language and memory skills of young children. By a slight rewording of a Piagetian question or the use of a more realistic example, Bryant showed that children under five were capable of more sophisticated thought than Piaget claimed.

Cognitive abilities in infancy

A great deal of modern research into infant cognition shows that Piaget underestimated some of the cognitive abilities of babies. The following studies are among those which have challenged some of his assumptions.

Piaget's belief that a child has no concept of the permanence of objects until the age of eight or nine months was challenged by Bower (1981). In a series of experiments with babies, Bower showed that infants as young as four to six weeks have some ability to appreciate the existence of objects that disappear from view. When the babies were presented with a moving object which disappeared behind a screen and then re-appeared at the other side, many of them moved their eyes to follow the anticipated movement of the object. However, later experiments appeared to suggest that the same object moved to a number of different positions, is perceived by babies under five months as a series of different objects. Bower concluded that up to about five months of age, a child does not understand that place and movement are linked.

Piaget proposed that during the sensorimotor period, a baby's thinking is dominated by the 'here and now' and shows no evidence of the internal representation of objects and events. However, studies of memory in very

Figure 20.4 Piaget's stages of cognitive development

Stage	Characteristics
1. Sensorimotor (Birth to 2 years)	Experiences the world through motor activities and sensory impressions
	Differentiates self from the external world
	Acquires object permanence (the understanding that objects exist even if not visible)
2. Preoperational (2–7 years)	Becomes able to represent something through images and language
	Thinking is egocentric; has difficulty taking another's viewpoint
	Inability to decentre; cannot attend to more than one feature of a situation
	Irreversibility; cannot work backwards mentally to a starting point
3. Concrete operational (7–11 years)	Able to think logically and reverse thought processes, but needs to manipulate real objects to solve a problem
	No longer egocentric
	Can conserve number (age 6), mass (age 7), weight (age 9), volume (age 11)
4. Formal operation (11 years onwards)	Can reason in an abstract sense
	Can systematically test out several propositions
	Becomes concerned with ideas and beliefs

young babies by Rovee-Collier (1993) show that they may be capable of some kinds of internal representation long before Piaget suggested. Rovee-Collier demonstrated that babies as young as three months could remember for as long as a week kicking actions they made to move a mobile placed over their cots.

Egocentrism

Piaget's 'mountains task' was designed to assess whether a child can take the point of view of another person. Using this model, Piaget claimed that children under about eight years do not perform the task successfully. Margaret Donaldson (1978) described a series of experiments, carried out by her colleagues, which shows that young children between three and a half and five years old are quite capable of appreciating the viewpoint of another person. Figure 20.5 contains a description of the 'boy and policeman task' carried out by Hughes (1975).

Why should the experiment described by Donaldson produce findings which were so different from those of Piaget when he used the 'mountains task'? First, in Donaldson's experiment, a great deal of care was taken to ensure that the children fully understood the task, and, in particular, the meaning of 'to hide'. Secondly, Donaldson claimed that the 'policeman' task 'made sense' to the child and that its realism and interest value captured the child's imagination.

> the task requires the child to act in ways which are in line with certain very basic human purposes (escape and pursuit). It makes human sense . . . in this context, he shows none of the difficulty in 'decentring' which Piaget ascribes to him . . . the 'mountains task' is abstract in a psychologically very important sense, in the sense that it is abstracted from all basic human purposes and feelings and endeavours.
>
> (Donaldson, 1978, p. 24)

Conservation

Many psychologists have contested Piaget's claim that children in the preoperational stage are unable to conserve. It has been pointed out that it is by no means certain that young children use and interpret words in the same way as adults do and failure in conservation tasks may, in some cases, be accounted for in terms of the difficulties children experience with word meanings: for example, 'less than' and 'more than' and so on.

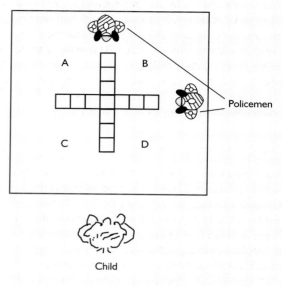

1. Two 'walls' are set up to form a cross.

2. A 'policeman' doll is placed on the model so that he can see the areas marked A and C, but cannot see B and D because they are obstructed by the wall.

3. The child is given a 'boy' doll and asked to place it on the model where the policeman cannot see it.

4. The task is repeated several times using two policeman dolls which are placed in varying positions on the model. On each occasion the child is asked to place the boy where the policeman cannot see him.

5. Ninety per cent of the children tested placed the 'boy' doll correctly so that neither 'policeman' could see it.

Figure 20.5 The 'boy and policeman' task (Donaldson, 1978)

As in the 'policeman' task, context too may be an important factor in conservation experiments. In a replication of one of Piaget's number tasks, McGarrigle (reported in Donaldson, 1978) found, as did Piaget, that few children under six appeared to understand conservation of number (refer back to Task 3 in Figure 20.2). However, the task was repeated, but this time a 'naughty' teddy bear was introduced, who proceeded to rearrange one row of counters while 'messing about'. When asked on this occasion if both rows contained the same number, a large proportion (63 per cent) of the children gave the correct answer, indicating their ability to conserve number.

Why should 'naughty teddy' have made such a difference? Donaldson argued that in the earlier experiment, the child may have thought that because the experimenter (an important adult) had rearranged the counters, it seemed reasonable to assume that something must have changed. However, a study by Eames et al. (1990) failed to replicate the 'naughty teddy' findings. The researchers suggested that experimenter effects in the McGarrigle study might have been responsible for the discrepancy.

Formal operational thinking

Some research has shown that the kind of abstract thinking described by Piaget as occurring at the formal operational stage is not attained by all teenagers or adults. A study by Lewis (1981) showed that only 50–60 per cent of 17 year olds used formal operational logic in problem-solving tasks. Keating (1980) suggests that only about 50–60 per cent of 17–20 year olds in Western countries ever use formal operational thinking and, if they do so, it is not consistently employed.

The concept of stages

Piaget proposed that the development of the intellect occurs in 'clear cut', qualitatively different stages, each of which builds upon and replaces the level of adaptation reached in the previous stage. Some later investigators claimed that their findings supported this view of stage-like changes in cognitive behaviour (Neimark, 1975). Other investigators have been more critical and argued that discontinuous, step-like changes in cognitive development are unlikely and that development proceeds in a continuous manner (Keating, 1980).

Bee (1995) argues that the evidence does not support Piaget's notion of development occurring through a number of coherent, general stages. She feels that development is a much more gradual process where skills which existed at an earlier age in a more rudimentary form are gradually improved.

Despite the criticisms of Piaget's theory, it is worth noting that the vast majority of critical studies contain a tribute to the man whose great intellectual scope provided such a monumental contribution to our understanding of child development.

Cross-cultural studies of Piagetian ideas

Several cross-cultural studies have supported Piaget's view that the stages of cognitive development are the same for children in many different countries and cultures. For example, conservation tasks were set for groups of 7–11-year-old children from the Meru of Tanzania (Nyiti, 1976), from the Themne of Sierra Leone, and from the Kamba of Kenya (Kiminyo, 1977). In all these cultures, the average age at which the children were able to solve the conservation tasks was very similar to that for children from Europe and North America. As Piaget's theory would predict, some 11 to 12 year olds who had not attended school, had more difficulty solving conservation of volume tasks than children of the same age who had attended school.

Findings from a study by Jahoda (1983) were consistent with the idea proposed by Donaldson that the context and relevance of the tasks set have an important bearing on a child's cognitive ability. Jahoda found that nine-year-old children in Harare, Zimbabwe, showed evidence of abstract thinking when playing a shopping game with a mock shop. In particular, they demonstrated a greater understanding of concepts such as profit and loss than did British children of the same age. The Harare children were highly involved in their parents' small businesses and Jahoda argued that because of this, they had grasped principles of trading at an early age. The shopping game was therefore more relevant and interesting to them.

Exercise 20.1

Explore the ability to conserve in young children between the ages of three and seven.

Take some counters or sweets and lay them out in front of the child in two identical rows with about six in each. Ask the child, 'Do these two rows each have the same number of sweets?' Wait until the child agrees that they are the same before going further.

Take one row and bunch the sweets together while the child watches. Ask, 'Now does each one have the same number of sweets?' Record the child's answer and ask her or him to explain it.

Repeat the activity with several children of different ages.

Compare your findings with those of Piaget.

Box 20.2   Implications of Piaget's theory for education

Although Piaget's theory was not directly concerned with what goes on in the classroom, his work has had a major impact on the way children are taught, particularly at the primary school level. Some of the educational implications of his theory are outlined below.

The concept of 'readiness'
Because of Piaget, parents and teachers are aware that a child's intellect is *qualitatively* different from that of an adult. Therefore, it is important that teachers should be sensitive to children's level of development and their ability to understand and deal with concepts of varying kinds. For example, it would not make sense to expect a child of six to be able to grasp a problem which involved conservation of volume. Asking children to cope with tasks or solve problems before they are ready to deal with the concepts involved will result in confusion and distress and may prevent them from ever fully appreciating some concepts.

Active involvement in a stimulating environment
Piaget emphasized the importance of *active* participation and interaction with the environment. It is now generally recognized that active involvement in learning leads to greater understanding and retention. Therefore, teachers should provide an appropriate environment in the form of rich and varied materials and activities which will

stimulate children's natural curiosity and help them to make the transition to a new stage of development. Opportunities to learn by discovery will encourage children to explore the environment and to learn through their own activities.

Questioning children
Questioning children also encourages them to be active in their own learning. Where an incorrect answer is given, the teacher should look for clues which may provide insight into the child's thought processes.

Use of concrete materials
Children below the formal operational level should be introduced to new concepts through concrete objects, building up gradually, where appropriate, to more abstract reasoning.

Assimilation and accommodation
In order for children to accommodate new ideas and experiences, the teacher should allow them first to assimilate them. New concepts should therefore be linked to what children know and have experienced already. (See also Donaldson's work – page 466 – and Jahoda's study – page 467 – on the importance of context and relevance to a child's thought processes.)

 SELF-ASSESSMENT QUESTIONS

1. Briefly describe Piaget's methods of investigating children's thought processes.
2. Define the terms 'schema' and 'operation' as used by Piaget. Why are these known as 'variant cognitive structures'?
3. Briefly explain the processes of assimilation, accommodation and equilibration.
4. List the key features of children's thought processes at each of Piaget's developmental stages. What factor did Piaget believe principally governs the speed at which children progress through these stages.
5. Evaluate Piaget's theory in the light of more recent research.
6. Discuss some of the educational implications of Piaget's theory.

Cognitive development in a social context

As we have seen, Piaget's view of cognitive development assumed that there are psychological structures in people's minds which affect their thought processes and which become increasingly more sophisticated with age. Cognitive development is thought of as individuals constructing their own internal mental model of external reality, relatively independently of other people. However, many developmental psychologists have also investigated *social* influences on a child's developing thought processes. This approach takes the view that children develop more sophisticated ways of thinking because adults are available as teachers and models to guide them through increasingly more demanding situations. The work of Vygotsky (1896–1934) and Bruner (1915–) is highly influential in the study of cognitive development in a social context. Both will be discussed below.

The influence of Vygotsky

The work of Vygotsky, a Russian psychologist, was unknown in the West until it began to be translated in the 1960s. Even in Russia, much of his work was denigrated or censored by the oppressive Stalinist regime following the Russian revolution.

Lev Vygotsky (1896–1934)

Like Piaget, Vygotsky (1978) saw children as curious, problem-solving beings who play an active part in their own development. Where he differed from Piaget was in his view of the importance of the role of other, more knowledgeable people in children's development. Vygotsky argued that children acquire the mechanisms of thinking and learning as a result of the social interactions between themselves and the adults around them. The child's knowledge and skills develop because of this cooperative process involving 'experts' and a 'novice'. The more expert person is seen as providing a framework or scaffolding within which a child works towards greater understanding. In the early stages of learning something new, the adult provides plenty of props and verbal prompts. An example might be a situation where a very young child is learning to handle a construction toy for the first time. Initially, the parent gives the child much help and models what is required. As the task becomes more familiar and easier to handle, the parent leaves more and more for the child to do until eventually he or she can cope with the whole task alone. Butterworth's (1987) studies into infant–parent interaction see scaffolding processes at work as the mother engages the child in ritual language games and rhymes and encourages turn-taking. The concept of scaffolding will be considered again later in this section.

The importance of language and culture

As so much of social interaction, both in the home and in school, involves language, Vygotsky saw language development and cognitive development as closely interrelated. It is through language, he believed, that an individual organizes his or her perceptions and thought processes. Thus he placed more emphasis

than did Piaget on the importance of language development, though he stressed that this should be seen in the context of the individual's culture and the help and support available in that culture.

Vygotsky stresses the importance of three major elements in the process towards fully developed cognitive ability:

- First, children respond to the world through **action**. This often does not require the use of language.
- Secondly, children are able to reflect upon their own thought processes through **language** and may use strategies such as talking themselves through a problem.
- Thirdly, understanding is reached through cooperation with others in a wide variety of **social settings**. These will involve interactions with parents, peers, teachers and other people significant in children's lives. They will also involve children in learning through elements of their own culture – through art and language, explanations and comparisons, songs and play.

Vygotsky stresses the importance of cultural experiences and the social interactions that occur within the child's culture. It is within this cultural framework that children construct their understanding of the world.

The zone of proximal development (ZPD)

An idea central to Vygotsky's theory is the zone of proximal development (ZPD). This is the area between the child's actual developmental level and the potential developmental level which could be

> **GLOSSARY**
>
> **Scaffolding** A framework provided by adults or more knowledgeable peers within which a child may develop a greater understanding of a mental or physical activity.
>
> **Zone of proximal development (ZPD)** Vygotsky's term to describe the area between a child's actual developmental level and the potential level which could be achieved with the help of adults or more experienced peers.

achieved with the help of adults or more experienced peers. For example, a child may attempt to emulate and master activities such as writing performed by older siblings, and this may act as a stimulus to the child's own development.

Unlike Piaget, Vygotsky did not believe that it was necessary for children to be 'ready' before they were able to learn something new. He argued that adults could and should provide children with activities above their developmental level, far enough above to provide challenge, but not so far that it would demoralize or confuse'. In other words, in helping children to learn, adults should provide experiences that fall within the ZPD, so that children might achieve something they would not do alone.

Box 20.3   Bruner's three modes of representation

Bruner described three ways in which children represent the world to themselves. The earliest to emerge is the **enactive mode**, where thinking is based entirely on physical actions and uses neither imagery nor words. For a baby playing with a toy, the movement involved becomes its internal representation of the toy. Enactive representation operates throughout life and is apparent in many physical activities – for example, throwing a ball, swimming, cycling – which we learn by doing and which we do not represent internally through language or images.

Between the ages of two and six, when a child becomes capable of representing the environment through mental images, **iconic representation** is possible. These mental images may be visual, auditory, olfactory or tactile. They provide a means whereby children may experience and build up a picture of the environment, even though they may be unable to describe it in words.

Finally, the transition from the iconic to the symbolic mode occurs at around the age of seven and the child is able to represent the environment through language and later through other symbolic systems such as number and music. **Symbolic representation** leads to thought of a much more flexible and abstract kind, allowing the individual not only to represent reality but to manipulate and transform it.

Bruner's theory

The American psychologist, Jerome Bruner (1966b, 1986) has been heavily influenced by the work of Vygotsky and has extended and applied his ideas in education.

Bruner suggested that children develop three main ways of internally representing the environment to themselves on their way to acquiring the mature thought processes of the adult. These three modes of representation are the enactive, the iconic and the symbolic (see Box 20.3).

A classic experiment by Bruner and Kenney (1966) exemplified the limitations of iconic thinking. Children from five to seven were shown an arrangement of glass tumblers which were placed on a board in order according to height and diameter (see Figure 20.6). When the glasses were removed, all the children were capable of replacing them in the correct positions. Then the glasses were removed and one glass was replaced on the board, but in a different position. The children were asked to replace the rest of the glasses so as to retain the original pattern. The older children, who were capable of symbolic thought, were able to complete the task satisfactorily, whereas the younger, iconic representers, were not. Bruner and Kenney suggested that the younger children were unable to restructure and transform their original image of the array to enable them to cope with the new situation.

Educational implications of Vygotsky's and Bruner's theories

There are a number of practical implications of Vygotsky's theory which have been taken up by modern researchers and applied to educational settings. These are discussed below.

GLOSSARY

Modes of representation In Bruner's theory, the different ways in which children internally represent the environment to themselves as their thought processes develop.

Enactive representation According to Bruner, the simplest way that a child thinks by physically manipulating the environment.

Iconic representation According to Bruner, a kind of thinking which is based on the use of mental images.

Symbolic representation According to Bruner, thinking which involves the representation of the world through symbols such as language or number.

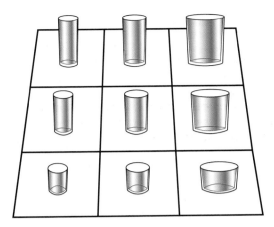

Figure 20.6 Bruner and Kenney's experiment

Interactions with others

Vygotsky's view suggests that meaning is socially constructed and arises from the interactions between a child and more experienced peers and adults. This departs quite strongly from the child-centred model of education which arose from Piaget's theory and from traditional, more didactic methods of teaching. Teachers influenced by Vygotskian theory would not view children solely as individuals who develop mental competence through their own actions, even though this may be an important experience. Rather they would offer abundant opportunities for children to develop concepts and skills through interaction with others, particularly more expert others.

Scaffolding

The notion of scaffolding is particularly important in educational settings. Failure by teachers to provide appropriate supporting frameworks for children's learning or to build upon the knowledge and experience that children bring to the classroom may well result in a failure to achieve their full potential. Box 20.5 illustrates how scaffolding may enhance learning.

Using language

The importance of language is central to both Vygotsky's and Bruner's theories. In the school setting, children should be provided with opportunities not just to listen, watch and do, but to engage in discussion and conversation both with teachers and with peers. By

Box 20.4 Comparisons between Piaget and Bruner

Bruner's modes of representation have obvious similarities with Piaget's stages of development. However, a major difference arises from Bruner's insistence that, although we acquire these modes sequentially during childhood, the adult retains and uses all three throughout life. We do not 'pass through' the earlier modes, and although adult thinking employs mainly the symbolic mode, we also employ enactive and iconic thinking when the need arises.

Like Vygotsky, Bruner places greater emphasis than did Piaget on the part played by experience. He stresses that cognitive growth is significantly influenced by such variables as culture, family and education. In particular he stressed the value to the developing thought processes of a child of instruction by expert adults.

In contrast with Piaget, Bruner stresses the importance of language to the child's developing thought processes. Children who still depend upon iconic thought are dominated by the images they perceive; their ability to restructure and reflect upon these images is limited. Parents and teachers should encourage children to describe problems and events by talking and writing about their experiences in order to encourage symbolic rather than iconic representation.

encouraging children to use language to express their thoughts, teachers can help them to move beyond their immediate perceptions towards greater understanding.

Parent–teacher links

Close links between parents and teachers can enhance a child's opportunity to learn and make it more relevant and interesting. Wells (1985) suggests that some of a child's most important learning experiences occur at home where parent and child interact and have shared goals.

Teacher intervention

Piaget emphasizes the teacher as a facilitator who provides the right environment and materials for children to 'discover' their own learning. Both Vygotsky

Box 20.5 Scaffolding in educational contexts

Bruner and his colleagues carried out a number of research studies to examine the role of scaffolding in learning. In one, carried out by Wood et al. (1976), the researchers suggested that there are a number of factors which characterize effective scaffolding when a tutor attempts to develop a child's learning:

■ **Recruitment**. The tutor's initial goal is to capture children's interest and motivate them to attempt the task.
■ **Reduction of degrees of freedom**. The tutor must simplify the task and break it down into manageable steps in order for the children to achieve success.
■ **Direction maintenance**. In the early stages of the task, the tutor should encourage the children and motivate them to succeed. Later on, the children should find the task motivating in its own right.
■ **Marking critical features**. The tutor should emphasize relevant aspects of the task, in order that the children may judge how far their end-product differs from a correct solution.
■ **Demonstration**. The tutor should demonstrate a correct solution, or where the child has already produced a part solution, should offer explanations of any discrepancy. This should lead to children imitating and then improving their effort.

The above is based on data from an observational study carried out by the researchers with three-, four- and five-year-old children. A tutor taught each individual child to build a three-dimensional structure, a task the children would have been unable to do on their own. It was agreed in advance that the tutor would allow the children to complete as much as possible by themselves and would offer verbal help before demonstrating the task. The tutor's behaviour at each stage of the task was dependent upon the child's success or failure. This study illustrates well the process of scaffolding. The tutor guided the children through a task, at each stage allowing the child's level of achievement to determine the next level of tutoring. She worked within the ZPD (zone of proximal development), the area between what the children could do on their own and what they could achieve with help.

and Bruner believe that the intervention of the teacher is crucial to a child's learning. However, this intervention should be tailored to the child's level of development and ZPD. Help and encouragement should be freely available. However, where children are succeeding in a task, relatively little help need be given and they should be allowed to learn how to work independently. And even where children are not succeeding, they may have sufficient knowledge for the teacher to direct them to another activity which is within the ZPD. In this way, the demands placed upon children will not be so simple as to become boring, nor so complex that they become demoralized and give up (Wood, 1988).

Vygotsky's theory emphasizes the importance of adults being aware of a child's ZPD and moulding their scaffolding behaviour to suit the child's existing knowledge and developmental level. However, this could be difficult in a school situation, where teachers are frequently responsible for the learning of 30-plus pupils. So how might it be possible for teachers to handle this situation?

Peer tutoring

There is a growing body of research which suggests that **peer tutoring** may be one answer. Foot et al. (1990) have used Vygotsky's model in explaining how peer tutoring operates. One child (the tutor) is more expert than the other (the tutee) on the task in hand. Each child is aware that the aim is for the 'expert' to improve the knowledge or skills of the 'novice'. However, the expert is only slightly ahead of the novice and is therefore better able to understand the difficulties involved and to scaffold the novice effectively within the latter's ZPD. Thus the tutoring is effective when it is only slightly beyond the tutee's capabilities and falls within the ZPD.

Cooperative group work

A body of research findings is growing on ways in which children in a classroom situation can examine and negotiate meanings through processes such as conversation, active participation and carrying out tasks of particular relevance to themselves (for example, Cowie and Rudduck, 1988, 1991; Salmon and Claire, 1984). Bennett and Dunne (1989) found that cooperative group work was effective in encouraging children to anticipate and respond appropriately to the behaviour of other children. The researchers found that those children who had engaged in cooperative group work – activities within small groups where children were required to cooperate with each other and to discuss the activity – were less competitive, less concerned with status and more likely to display logical thinking than were children who had worked alone. However, the value of cooperative group work depends very much on the way the learning is structured. Some researchers have argued that not all cooperative group situations enhance a child's cognitive development. Slavin

(1987) has stressed the value of motivation and intergroup competitiveness. Brown and Palincsar (1989) have emphasized that much depends on the child's initial ability and social status. They argue that the benefits of cooperative learning will be felt most by children who have only an incomplete understanding of the situation and who are faced with a situation which they can take seriously, but which conflicts with their own views.

Conclusions

Meadows (1995) concludes that:

> The best candidate for social experience affecting cognitive development that a theory offers is Vygotsky's idea of 'scaffolding' . . . There is some evidence that parenting that is notably lacking in scaffolding and child-contingent discussion is associated with later difficulties in concentration and the development and elaboration of activities.
> (Meadows, 1995, p. 30)

However, she points out that, as yet, we know very little about how common scaffolding is in adults' dealings with children, whether there is an optimum amount of scaffolding that is effective, whether cultural differences that influence language development apply also to cognitive development, whether there are alternative ways of achieving the same result (some cultures do not appear to engage in scaffolding, as it is recognized in Anglo-American settings). Also, it is not known how scaffolding affects children: among other things, it may provide models of cognitive skills or of self-scaffolding (the process through which more mature learners may guide themselves through difficult tasks). She argues that further research is necessary in order to clarify these and other issues.

❓ SELF-ASSESSMENT QUESTIONS

1. What are the most important differences between Vygotsky's theory of cognitive development and that of Piaget?

Does working cooperatively in groups enhance a child's cognitive development?

GLOSSARY

Peer tutoring A learning situation where a child (the tutee) is tutored through the learning of a task by another child (the tutor) who is slightly more proficient at the task than the first child.

2. What does Vygotsky mean by the 'zone of proximal development'?
3. Outline some of the main features of the concept of 'scaffolding' in relation to Vygotsky's theory.
4. Briefly discuss the three major ways in which, according to Bruner, individuals represent the environment to themselves.
5. Discuss some of the educational implications of Vygotsky's and Bruner's theories.

Information-processing approaches to cognitive development

The information-processing approach to the study of cognitive development has gathered momentum over the last two decades, particularly in the United States. Information-processing theorists, while in some cases influenced by Piaget, do not subscribe to a single, unifying theory in their work. Their aim is to understand how an individual interprets, stores, retrieves and evaluates information. Typically, this approach has included the following:

■ A detailed study of processes such as perception, memory, the use of strategies, reaction times, the efficiency with which attention can be allocated and so on.
■ An attempt to understand what aspects of information-processing change with age and which are relatively stable. For example, it is known that children's ability to handle several items of information at one time increases with age and that their performance will suffer if this capacity is overloaded.

Information-processing theorists tend to view the human mind as being similar to a computer. The physiology of the brain, with the nerves and connective tissues, are seen as the 'hardware' of cognition, with the processes occurring during cognition being viewed as the 'software' or 'programs'. Typically, information-processing theorists present people with problem-solving tasks and then investigate the strategies used to solve them. Often, computer simulation techniques are used (computer simulation refers to attempts to replicate human thinking by using computers).

Within the information-processing approach to children's thinking, there currently exist two main strands:

■ **Study of developmental structures and processes**. This approach, without necessarily implying that distinct stages of development exist, assumes that children's thought processes develop in a clearly sequential way.
■ **Study of individual differences**. Researchers in this field are interested in identifying the kinds of basic information-processing capacities or strategies that might underlie differences between people in relation to their cognitive functioning.

Aspects of these two approaches are discussed below. There is further discussion of information processing in Part 3.

Developmental aspects of information processing

The work of Case (1978, 1985) exemplifies this approach. Some of his propositions can be summarized as follows:

■ **Sequential development**. Cognitive development occurs in an orderly sequence, during which the child's information-processing capacities become increasingly more proficient.
■ **Working memory**. The crucial concept in explaining development was thought to be the amount of 'working memory' or 'M-space' (roughly equivalent to short-term memory) the child possesses at a particular time. Case argued that tasks that the child encounters can be described in terms of the amount of M-space they require. As children develop, the amount of working memory increases and this is responsible for their increasing ability to handle cognitive tasks, such as problem solving and remembering things.

GLOSSARY

Information-processing approach An approach which considers the human brain to be analogous to a computer and aims to understand how people interpret, store, retrieve and evaluate information.

Computer simulation The use of computers to replicate and understand human thought processes.

'M-space' A term used by information-processing theorists to describe working memory (roughly equivalent to short-term memory).

Meadows (1995) argues that although it is feasible that the size of the memory stores increases as children grow older it does not follow that this is responsible for the increasing proficiency that occurs in memory and information-processing skills as the child develops. More important, she suggests, are the changes that occur as a result of the child's increasing experience of handling cognitive tasks. Dealing with knowledge, studying and exploring in school lead to the child becoming more 'expert' at remembering things and solving problems.

Other research has examined a wide range of information-processing phenomena. Some of this research is outlined below.

Efficiency in information processing

Clearly information processing becomes more efficient as children grow older. The best evidence for this is that they become *faster* at solving problems and performing other cognitive tasks. Kail and Park (1992) found increases with age in children's performance in a wide range of activities such as simple perceptual motor tasks (for example, tapping), reaction times to a stimulus (for example, pressing a button when a light is flashed) and simple addition. Results with children in Korea were very similar to those for children in the United States, which adds some cross-cultural validity to this proposition. Hale et al. (1993) argue that efficiency in information processing is brought about by physical changes in the brain which allows increasing speed of both responses and mental activity.

Use of rules

Some researchers have found that in addition to an increase in speed of information processing, children increasingly acquire a basic set of rules when solving problems. As the child grows older and gains more experience, these rules are applied to a wider and wider range of problems. Siegler (1981) studied children solving a range of different problems. Figure 20.7 shows a balance scale similar to that used by Siegler in his experiments. The scale has a series of pegs on either side of the centre piece, and weights can be placed on the pegs. Children are asked to predict which way the balance will fall depending on the number and location of the weights. Siegler concluded that almost all but the very youngest children behaved as if they were following one of four rules:

- **Rule 1**, where children paid attention to only one aspect of the problem set (usually the number of weights) and seemed incapable of handling other dimensions.
- **Rule 2**. Here children still paid attention only to the number of weights unless there was an equal number on each side. In this case they also took account of the distance of the weights from the central point.
- **Rule 3**, where children attempted to take account of more than one aspect of the problem but did not do so systematically and often ended up making a guess at the solution.
- **Rule 4**. Here, the child was able systematically to test out different possibilities and arrived at the correct solution (comparing distance times weight for each side).

Siegler proposed that children developed the rules in an orderly sequence, starting with Rule 1. It is clear that the sequence has many similarities with Piaget's description of children's development of problem-solving abilities. However, Siegler proposed that whether a child uses a particular rule depends not so much on age, but on the child's experience of solving particular kinds of problems and the extent to which the child has been able to practise aspects of the task concerned. This is in keeping with the findings from the cross-cultural study by Jahoda (1983) discussed previously, which highlighted the importance of experience to cognitive development.

Metacognition

Metacognition refers to children's knowledge and understanding of cognitive processes, particularly

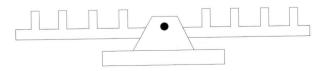

Figure 20.7 Siegler's balance scale

> **GLOSSARY**
>
> **Metacognition** An individual's awareness of his or her own thought processes: for example, remembering or understanding something.

their own cognitive skills – knowing about knowing, if you like. Here are some examples:

- A girl who says, 'I won't be able to solve this problem because I don't remember how to convert from fractions to decimals' is demonstrating her awareness of the limits of her own cognition in relation to a particular task.
- When children can describe the best ways of studying or explain why they find one particular kind of mental arithmetic task more difficult to do than another they are showing awareness of their own cognitive processes. Such awareness of one's own cognitive processes, or metacognition, is part of a larger category of cognitive skills that information-processing theorists call **executive processes**. These include contemplating different strategies and planning how to solve a problem.

Metacognition and the idea of a central executive system have played a dominant part in the information-processing approaches already described (for example, those of Siegler, 1981, and Case, 1985) and theorists see cognition as becoming increasingly proficient and controlled as a child develops and receives more and more education.

Study of individual differences in information processing

Whilst some researchers have been studying developmental changes or sequences, others have concerned themselves with individual differences. In general, their strategy has been to compare performance on standard IQ tests with some measure of information-processing skill. Some of these measures and tentative findings are as follows.

Speed of information processing

A number of researchers have found that individuals with faster reaction times or speed of performance on an assortment of tasks also have higher IQ scores on standard tests (Vernon, 1987). Further, some studies have linked speed of processing both to IQ and to the functioning of the central nervous system. For example, it is now possible to measure speed of conduction of neural (nerve cell) impulses such as those in the nerves of the arm. Vernon and Mori (1992) found that there was a relationship between this measure and measures of IQ.

Comparisons of normal-IQ and retarded children

DeLoache and Brown (1987) compared searching strategies used by two-year-old children who were developing normally with those of children of the same age who appeared to show delayed development. In a task where the children were set to search for a toy hidden in the room, the search strategies and skill of the two groups did not differ. However, when the experimenter discreetly removed the toy from its location before the children started to search there was a difference. The normally developing children searched in various other locations, whereas the delayed-development children continued to search in the place where they had first seen the toy hidden. It appeared that they were not able to change their strategies. This and other studies suggest that flexibility in the use of information-processing strategies may be another key factor underlying individual differences in cognitive ability.

Evaluation of the information-processing approach

As we have seen earlier in this chapter, before the information-processing approach was developed, there were two main approaches to studying cognitive development. The first – the psychometric or IQ approach (discussed in Chapter 21) – was concerned solely with measuring cognitive ability. The other approach, exemplified by the theories of Piaget and his followers, focused on the development of cognitive structures and processes.

The information-processing approach has complemented and provided some important links between the other two approaches. It now seems likely that while there are some basic inborn strategies which develop with age (such as noting differences and similarities) some of the changes in cognitive ability that Piaget attributed to changes in structure are heavily influenced by experience. For example, the more often children play with coloured shapes, the more proficient they will become at classifying objects. Therefore, individual differences in cognitive ability

---

GLOSSARY

Executive processes A category of cognitive skills, which includes metacognition, and involves organizing and planning strategies.

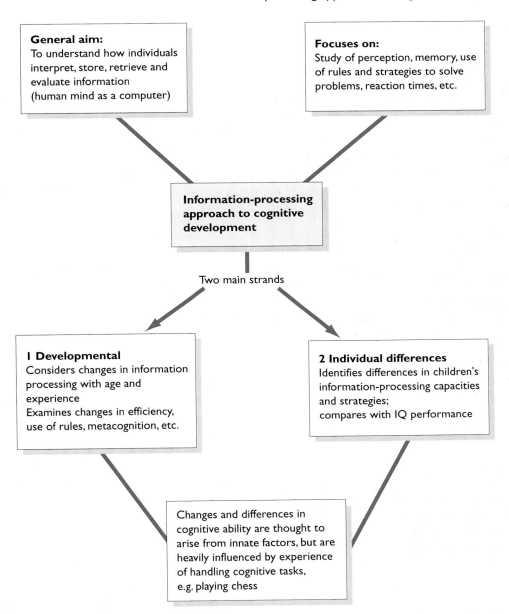

General aim:
To understand how individuals interpret, store, retrieve and evaluate information
(human mind as a computer)

Focuses on:
Study of perception, memory, use of rules and strategies to solve problems, reaction times, etc.

Information-processing approach to cognitive development

Two main strands

1 Developmental
Considers changes in information processing with age and experience
Examines changes in efficiency, use of rules, metacognition, etc.

2 Individual differences
Identifies differences in children's information-processing capacities and strategies;
compares with IQ performance

Changes and differences in cognitive ability are thought to arise from innate factors, but are heavily influenced by experience of handling cognitive tasks, e.g. playing chess

Figure 20.8 Flow chart illustrating the scope and aims of the information-processing approach to cognitive development

can be thought of as arising from inborn differences in the efficiency of basic cognitive processes coupled with differences in experience.

There are some practical applications of the information-processing approach. For example, studies of recognition memory in infancy provide a means for the early identification of retarded children or those that may be at risk of later problems. This could lead to

the identification of particular kinds of training that would be helpful to children with learning difficulties.

The information-processing approach, then, shows much promise and is an important addition to other approaches to the understanding of cognitive development. However, this approach is not yet sufficiently well developed to explain all the differences that are observed among children on Piagetian tasks. Additionally, there are not yet any tests of information-processing ability that could justifiably replace the use of IQ tests in educational and clinical settings.

1. How does the information-processing approach to cognitive development differ from that of Piaget?
2. Outline some of the research which has examined developmental aspects of information processing.
3. Briefly indicate some findings from research which has been concerned with individual differences in information processing.
4. Outline the main strengths and weaknesses of the information-processing approach to cognitive development.

Language acquisition

The basic units of a language are words and each word is made up of sounds, known as **phonemes**, which correspond roughly to the letters of the alphabet. Phonemes combine together to form **morphemes** which are the smallest units of language to have a grammatical purpose. For example, the word 'pins' is made of four phonemes p-i-n-s, and two morphemes, 'pin', which is a word, and 's', which serves the purpose of converting the word to the plural.

" I WAS LIKE YOU — THOUGHT I KNEW IT ALL — THEN THEY STARTED ON THINGS CALLED **WORDS** ! "

In the remarkably short time span of about three years, young children progress from speaking their first word at approximately 12 months, to producing fluent, grammatically correct speech. Without any deliberate training, children are able to acquire a working knowledge of grammar, particularly **syntax** (the grammatical rules that determine how words are combined in sentences) by the time that they are about four and a half. At the same time, their understanding of the meaning of words and sentences (**semantics**) and their appreciation of how language is used in different social contexts (**pragmatics**) develops rapidly.

Psychologists are interested in a number of questions about language acquisition. These include the following:

▪ What accounts for the rapid progress in mastering such a complex and intricate system as language? To what extent does language acquisition depend upon biological factors and to what extent upon learning?
▪ How far is it important to examine the child's developing competence in various social contexts?
▪ What role is played by adults in providing the kind of environment within which the child's language development will flourish?

These and other questions will be explored below.

Sequence of language acquisition

There are three main phases of early language acquisition: **babbling**, one-word utterances and early sentences.

GLOSSARY

Phonemes The basic sounds that are combined to form words.

Morphemes The smallest unit of language to have a grammatical purpose.

Syntax The grammatical rules that determine how words are combined in sentences.

Semantics The meaning of words.

Pragmatics In relation to language, how it is used in different social contexts.

Babbling The syllable-like sounds produced by a baby from about six months on.

Babbling

The first sounds made are cries, which reflect the child's physical state of well-being, followed soon by gurgles, coos and chuckles, which are not strictly speaking language, but are thought to represent what Vygotsky called the 'pre-intellectual' stage. At about six or seven months, the child begins to babble, producing syllable-like sounds, for example, 'gaga', 'dada'. All babies, including those who are deaf, in all cultures, produce these same speechlike sounds. This suggests that maturation, rather than learning, is responsible. A major, longitudinal study of children's language by Wells (1985) confirmed that there appears to be 'a universal sequence of development, at least in general outline' (p. 224). Towards the end of the first year, the sounds made begin to resemble the particular language that is spoken around the child. Parents seem to spend a lot of time interpreting the meaning intended in a baby's actions and vocalizations (Snow, 1977). Indeed, they often go beyond the actual meaning, for example:

Baby: dadadada
Mother: Yes, that's Daddy. He has gone to work.

This is another example of 'scaffolding'.

One-word utterances

At about 12 months, a child produces the first understandable words: for example, 'mama', 'dog', 'no'. Children's active vocabulary by the age of 18 months is, on average, about 30 words, though they will understand and react correctly to many more that they cannot yet utter.

Early sentences

At about the age of 18 months to two years, children begin to put two words together to form simple sentences: for example, 'Mummy go', 'Teddy fall'. These words are not randomly linked, but appear to be 'telegraphic' versions of adult sentences, in which essential nouns, verbs and occasional adjectives are uttered (see Brown's work discussed in Box 20.6). From the start, it seems, the child is capable of following simple rules of grammar. At this stage, children seem to be adept at interpreting other people's responses. For example, if the word 'milk' is not understood, they may change it to 'give' or 'want it' (Wilcox and Webster, 1980).

Shortly after the age of two years, a child can consistently produce three- and four-word utterances. This is followed by a rapid increase in the use of grammatical rules and a child is able to alter the word arrangement in a sentence to change the meaning: for example, 'Lucy is singing' becomes 'Is Lucy singing?' By the age of three, children begin to use more complex sentences and their language is generally understood by adults, even outside the family. By about the age of four and a half, the child's language is very similar to that of an adult.

Figure 20.9 An overview of the sequence of language development

Age	Characteristics	Example
4–9 months	Babbling	Gagaga Dadada
Around 12 months	One-word utterances	Mummy Dog No
18 months to 2 years	Two-word sentences	Daddy go Teddy fall
Between 2 and 2½ years	Three- or four-word sentences	What are you doing? Put my teddy down
	Rapid increase in use of grammatical rules. Word order can be changed to change meaning	'Jamie is playing' becomes 'Is Jamie playing?'
Around 3 years	Longer, more complex sentences	
Around 4½	Adult-style language	

Some studies of language acquisition

Trevarthen (1974a) studied babies from birth to six months with the aid of recording devices. He noted a particular kind of behaviour in babies as young as six weeks which he termed 'pre-speech'. He suggested that this was a primitive attempt at speech by moving the lips and tongue, sometimes vocally, at other times soundlessly. He noted also that as early as two months, babies make soft, low vowel sounds in response to others. This responsive vocalization may be the beginning of 'taking turns' as children and adults do in conversation later on.

Gelman and Shatz (1977) found that adults usually speak differently to children than they do to adults. Typically, they use shorter sentences, speak in a high-pitched voice and emphasize key words and phrases. The length and complexity of the sentences used are also adjusted to suit the child's level of comprehension. This simplified form of speech used by adults when talking to children is known as the **Baby Talk Register (BTR)**. (It used to be known as 'motherese' but this term is now considered to be sexist.) It is thought that the way parents adjust their language to suit a child's level plays an important part in the acquisition of language. Gelman and Shatz also tape-recorded four year olds presenting a new toy to adults and to younger children. The four year olds used shorter, less complex sentences when they were speaking to the two year olds, showing that even at this early age, they had acquired the skill of adjusting their use of language to suit their listener's linguistic level.

Cazden (1965) found that a group of children whose utterances were *commented* upon on a regular basis over a period of three months showed more progress in language development than a similar group whose utterances were *expanded upon* and imitation of correct language encouraged. The following is an example:

Child's utterance	Expansion by adult	Comment by adult
Me play	You are playing	What are you playing with?

These findings were confirmed by Nelson et al. (1973) who compared children whose utterances were *recast* (commented upon in the same context) with those whose utterances were *expanded upon*. Children whose utterances were recast used more complex

Box 20.6 An early naturalisic study of language development

In a pioneering, longitudinal study lasting ten years, Brown and Bellugi (1964) used naturalistic observation techniques to study the development of language in three children under two and a half, Adam, Eve and Sarah. The children were visited in their homes and tape-recordings made of conversations between child and mother. The tape-recordings were later transcribed and analysed by Brown and his colleagues. The following are among the insights obtained from Brown's work:

■ Early sentences produced by young children up to about two and a half are short and incomplete grammatically. However, the words retained are 'telegraphic' in that they preserve the meaning of the message, while the smaller 'functor' words, which are not essential to the meaning, are left out, for example, 'baby highchair', meaning 'Baby is in the highchair'. Correct word order is invariably retained.

■ Children up to the age of four or five have difficulty in correctly expressing a negative (I will not walk), past tenses (I shouted), irregular plurals (mice).

■ Early sentences are much the same whatever language children speak. Whether they are English, Russian or Chinese, the same variety of meanings are expressed: for example, statements about location ('spoon table'), possession ('my doll'), actions ('Mummy dance').

Brown's then innovatory approach to the study of language acquisition produced a vast amount of data which has provided material for many further studies. However, the study had some limitations. Because of the nature and size of the sample, it was difficult to generalize findings to all children. Also, child speech was analysed from a typed transcript of the recordings. It was noted by Robinson (1981) that features of the language used, such as intonation, pitch and stress, were not included and the caretaker's utterances and the context in which the utterances were made were often left out.

Baby Talk Register (BTR) The simplified form of speech used by adults when talking to children (formerly known as motherese).

grammatical forms of language than did children whose language was just expanded.

Exercise 20.2

Get permission to visit some homes where there is a young child between 18 months and three years. Ask if you can play with and talk to the child for a short time alongside the parent or other adult. If possible, tape-record the sessions.

Note down any instances of the characteristics of language described in studies of language acquisition; for example:

■ The use of 'telegraphic' sentences by the child;
■ Errors by the child when using negatives;
■ 'Virtuous errors' such as 'I seed' or 'mouses', where the child is applying 'correct' rules;
■ Corrections of grammar, expansions or recastings by the adult;
■ The use of BTR by the adult.

Theories of language acquisition

Traditionally, two broad theoretical approaches have been taken in an attempt to explain language development. These are learning theory and nativist theory. Each of these will be considered in turn. In addition, approaches will be discussed which have emphasized the importance of social interaction on the development of language.

Learning theory

Learning theorists view reinforcement and imitation as the principal mechanisms governing a child's acquisition of language. Skinner (1957) distinguishes three ways in which speech may be encouraged.

■ The child uses **echoic** responses: that is, imitates sounds made by others, who immediately show approval. In line with the principles of operant conditioning (see Chapter 6), this reinforcement increases the likelihood of the word being repeated on future occasions in the presence of the object.
■ The child produces a **mand**: that is, a random sound, which then has a meaning attached by others; for example, on hearing 'dada' the parent uses it to form a word and encourages the child to repeat it.
■ A **tact** response is made, where the child utters a word, usually imitated, in the presence of the object, and is rewarded by approval.

Gradually, through the processes of imitation, trial and error and reinforcement, children develop and refine their language until it matches that of the parents.

Limitations of the learning theory approach

Learning theory cannot explain:

■ The remarkable rate of language acquisition. An impossible number of utterances would need to be imitated/reinforced if these were the only mechanisms responsible.
■ The many different responses that may be made to the same verbal stimuli;
■ The creative and novel utterances made by children. 'Mouses', 'I seed', 'He goed' – all common childhood utterances – are unlikely to have been acquired though imitation and reinforcement. Herriot (1970) argued that these 'virtuous errors' arise because the child is actively trying to apply 'correct' grammatical rules, and has not had sufficient experience to remember the irregular morphemes.

The learning theory explanation relies heavily on the role of the caretaker in acting as a model for the child's speech and providing reinforcement. However, Brown and others observed that parents rarely correct a child's grammar or reinforce grammatically correct statements. Rather, they tend to be interested in the truth or accuracy of the utterances. McNeill (1966a) showed that when parents do attempt to correct a child's speech the results are often disappointing, as the following dialogue demonstrates:

Child: Nobody don't like me.
Mother: No, say 'nobody likes me'.
Child: Nobody don't like me.
After eight repetitions:
Child: Oh, nobody don't likes me.

Dodd (1972) studied babies' utterances during the babbling stage and found there was no imitation of sounds made by an attentive adult, though the amount of babbling increased.

Imitation and reinforcement clearly play a part in language acquisition since children end up speaking the language they hear around them, but learning theory does not appear to provide the whole explanation as the studies by Gelman and Shatz (1977) and those by Cazden (1965) and Nelson et al. (1973) suggest. These studies appear to show that the involvement of adults and older children who use an appropriate form of BTR and who recast a child's utterances in an accessible form provide an environment in which language will develop effectively.

Nativist theory

Chomsky (1968a) strongly opposed Skinner's learning theory explanation of language acquisition and stressed the likelihood of some biologically based predisposition to acquire language. He maintained that humans possess an inborn brain mechanism which he terms a **'language acquisition device' (LAD)**. The language acquisition device contains certain information about the structure of language which is progressively used as the child matures.

At some level, all languages share common elements. Chomsky calls these common features 'linguistic universals'. One sort of 'universal' relates to the existence of nouns, adjectives and verbs, which are common to all languages. These 'universals' exist at the '**deep**' structural level in languages. Through the language acquisition device the child has an innate awareness of these universals. The differences that exist between the various languages, Chomsky suggests, exist at the '**surface**' structure. Put at its simplest level, the surface structure represents the actual words and phrases which make up a sentence, while the deep structure corresponds more or less to the meaning of the sentence. The understanding of how to transform this deep structure into the surface structure is what Chomsky terms **transformational grammar**. When children are exposed to language, they are able to 'scan' what is heard, extract the underlying grammatical rules and apply them in new situations and in varying forms (transformations).

Here are two examples which make this clearer.

1. Take these two sentences:
   John was chased by a bull.
   A bull chased John.
   The surface structure of these two sentences is very different. Every word has a different position, the form of the verb has changed and the subject is different in each case. Yet the deep meaning of the two sentences is the same.

2. Now look at these sentences.
   Some children are easy to please.
   Some children are anxious to please.
   One word only has changed, but the deep meaning is quite different. In the first sentence, the children are the object who are easily pleased; in the second, they are the active subject, wanting to please.

Arguments in support of Chomsky's theory include:

■ The existence of 'linguistic universals' must point to an innate capacity of language in humans. Chomsky argues that this predisposition is not shared by other species. However, studies aimed

Noam Chomsky maintained that language is the result of innate cognitive structures in the mind

---

GLOSSARY

Language acquisition device (LAD) Chomsky's term for an inborn brain mechanism which 'programmes' a child to be able to learn language.

Linguistic universals Features which are common to all languages: for example, the use of nouns and verbs.

at investigating whether nonhuman primates can acquire language have cast some doubt on this assertion since they suggest that chimpanzees appear to be able to use human language, albeit in a limited form (see Chapter 17).

- The fact that children acquire language so competently in such a short time span is quite remarkable, particularly in view of the fragmented and often distorted samples of speech they are exposed to in the home. Such a feat could not be accomplished without the existence of an inborn capacity for language. However, it should be remembered that a child does not acquire language in isolation from the social context in which it occurs. It is likely that speech heard by the child is interpreted in conjunction with its social context (see Box 20.7).

- All human beings possess common physiological features related to language, such as finely tuned vocal chords, and language areas in the cortex of the brain. Furthermore, virtually all children, regardless of their intellectual ability, acquire language at approximately the same age and in the same sequence (Lenneberg, 1967).

- The findings of studies by Brown and Bellugi (1964), Herriot (1970) and McNeill (1966a) previously referred to, suggest that children appear to have an inborn capacity to use 'rules' of language. This is illustrated in their language through their production of 'errors' (for example, 'I wented'). This would be consistent with the existence of a LAD. However, some psychologists have suggested that the use of rules by children in their early speech is the result not so much of an inborn LAD, but of the child's **prelinguistic knowledge**. By this is meant that, before children are capable of using language, they are able to communicate and understand the communications of others through gestures, facial expressions and actions.

Criticisms of Chomsky's theory include the following:

- It has been suggested that Chomsky's theory overemphasizes the structure of sentences, while neglecting their meaning. For example, the theory cannot explain single- or two-word utterances since they contain no (or very little) grammatical structure. Bloom (1970), researching childhood

utterances, maintained that the meaning of the utterance must be taken into account. One of the children she studied produced the utterance 'Mummy sock' in two different contexts, one where her mother was putting a sock on the child's foot, the other while picking up her mother's sock. The intended meanings are very different.

- Language acquisition is not just about knowing the structures or the rules, but also about learning the social functions of language (see Box 20.7). You cannot divorce language from the context in which it is used. Bruner (1983) saw language as 'a by-product (and a vehicle) of culture transmission'.

- The theory tends to ignore the fact that parents modify and simplify their language to help their child's understanding. (Look back at the references to the BTR on page 480.) Chomsky is suggesting that the environment is inadequate for language learning.

- The theory appears to suggest that children's linguistic achievements proceed quite separately from their intellectual development, that learning to talk about something is separate from forming a concept of it.

A child's early interactions with others are an important forerunner to the development of language and the skills of communication

---

Box 20.7 Language and social interaction

The learning theory approach to language acquisition suggests that language is acquired through the influence of the environment. This is thought to occur in the form of parents' modelling and reinforcing appropriate language. Nativist theory implies that the environment is of less importance. What is crucial is the child's innate tendency to acquire language. A third approach highlights the importance of the social interaction which occurs between children and the people around them. Essentially, this view suggests that children begin to master the social context and then later add language to their repertoire.

Some of the research already discussed supports this social interaction hypothesis: for example, studies by Gelman and Shatz (1977) into the influence of the BTR and by Nelson et al. (1973) into the effectiveness of adults recasting a child's sentences.

Another line of research has focused on the development of **joint attention** and mutual understanding of gestures. Joint attention relates to the communication that occurs through the shared understanding of gestures between a child and adult when they are focusing together on an object. Butterworth (1987) has described how, as early as six months, babies will follow the mother's gaze to look at something and by about nine months will start pointing to direct the mother's attention to an object. Often the mother names the object or comments on it. This form of nonverbal communication between a child and adult together with the experiences of 'turn taking' and the mother's verbal comments seem to be an important forerunner to the development of language and the skills of communication. Bruner (1983) has called these early interactive processes and later 'scaffolding' the **Language Acquisition Support System (LASS)**.

? SELF-ASSESSMENT QUESTIONS

1. Outline the main phases of language acquisition in children.
2. What insights did the studies of Brown and his colleagues provide about language acquisition? What were the shortcomings of this research?
3. Explain what is meant by the Baby Talk Register.
4. Briefly outline both the learning theory and the nativist approach to language acquisition. Comment on the strengths and weaknesses of each.
5. Outline the findings of research which shows that early social interaction plays an important part in the acquisition of language.

GLOSSARY

Joint attention The term used to describe the communication that occurs through the understanding of gestures between a child and adult when they are focusing on something together.

Language Acquisition Support System (LASS) Bruner's term to describe the process of nonverbal communication which occurs between an infant and adult and which encourages the development of the child's language.

Chapter summary

Piaget's influence on the understanding of children's cognitive development has been profound. He used clinical interview and naturalistic observation. Children's thinking is not simply a less well-informed version of an adult's but differs in a number of important ways. The intellect is structured in terms of schemas (schemata), internal representations of physical or mental actions and operations, higher order mental structures.

■ Development occurs in the context of adaptation to the environment. This takes place through assimilation and accommodation, which are the invariant functions of development. The process of equilibration acts to ensure that accommodation is consolidated via assimilation and that there is a balance between the two.

■ Stages of development were proposed: the sensorimotor stage, the preoperational stage, the concrete operational stage and the formal operational stage. Within the sensorimotor stage immediate perceptions and physical activity allow infants to develop object permanence. In the preoperational stage the child's thinking is limited by egocentrism and by centration. The younger preoperational child is characterized by inability to conserve. Piaget developed conservation tasks to test this ability. Within the concrete operational stage a child learns to decentre and acquires reversible thinking. Classification is also an ability acquired at this stage.

■ The formal operations stage is characterized by an ability to reason in an abstract way without manipulating and experimenting with real objects as was necessary in the concrete operational stage. Propositions can be formulated and tested in the child's head in the same way as with an adult.

■ Later researchers have modified Piaget's conclusions and have been critical of his methods. The lack of object permanence in the sensorimotor stage has been contested in experiments carried out by Bower. Donaldson and her colleagues carried out a number of experiments which showed that egocentrism is acquired much earlier than Piaget had suggested. The suggestion that preoperational children are unable to conserve has also been contested by researchers including McGarrigle.

■ The abstract thinking Piaget describes in the formal operations stage has been shown not to be attained by all teenagers and adults. Keating suggested that only 50–60 per cent of 17–20 year olds use formal operations. Other researchers have been critical of Piaget's notion of discrete stage-like changes as development occurs and have suggested that development is more continuous than the above implies.

■ Cross-cultural studies have in general supported Piaget's view that the stages of development are the same for all cultures.

■ Piaget's research has had profound implications for education, particularly the notion that children's thinking is qualitatively different from adults'. The concept of readiness has arisen from this. Piaget emphasized the importance of active involvement in learning. Discovery learning has encouraged children to explore the environment and engage their natural curiosity. Questioning children is used to a greater extent so that children can be active in their learning. The use of concrete materials before the formal operational stage (about 11 years old) has come before more abstract reasoning. The linkage between what is already known has been stressed. Assimilation precedes accommodation.

■ Vygotsky stressed the importance of other more knowledgeable people in the development of children, who provided a scaffolding within which the child can gain greater understanding. He stressed also the importance of language. Three elements contributed to the process of development: action, language and the social setting. He developed the idea of a zone of proximal development (ZPD), an area between a child's actual and potential development level. Adults should provide children with experiences which fall within the ZPD.

■ Bruner suggested that children develop three main ways of representing the environment to themselves: enactive, iconic and symbolic. Enactive representation is based on physical actions, iconic representation is based upon the creation of mental images and symbolic representation is based upon the use of language. Children develop from enactive to iconic to symbolic modes of representation. Vygotsky and Bruner lay greater emphasis than Piaget on the role of experience in development. Culture, family and education are of paramount importance.

■ Vygotsky's emphasis on scaffolding has highlighted the role teachers must play in schools, and the need for close links between parents and teachers who together provide scaffolding. Adults need to be aware of the child's ZPD. Peer tutoring and cooperative group work have been found to be appropriate means of providing scaffolding behaviour within a classroom.

■ Information-processing approaches to development see the human brain as analogous to a computer. It is suggested that cognitive development occurs in an orderly sequential way. Capacity for processing information increases as children develop, especially the amount of working memory (M-space). Children become faster at solving problems as they grow older because information processing becomes more efficient. Children increasingly acquire a set of rules to apply when solving problems as well as greater knowledge of their own cognitive processes (metacognition).

■ There has been research into individual differences in the speed with which children process information. Links have been made between speed of processing and IQ. Comparisons have also been made between normally developing and retarded children in the use of searching strategies. The information-processing approach has complemented and provided links between other approaches to development.

■ The acquisition of language is central to the development of children's abilities. Children acquire in a relatively short time a working knowledge of syntax, semantics and pragmatics. There are three main phases in language acquisition: babbling, one-word utterances and early sentences. Trevarthen investigated prespeech and Gelman and Shatz studied the simplified form of speech used by mothers with their infants (the Baby Talk Register).

■ Children whose use of language was commented upon by an adult in a systematic way made more progress in language development than others whose language was expanded upon.

■ Theories of language acquisition include learning theory, nativist theory and a social interaction approach. Learning theory approaches stress reinforcement and imitation. Skinner outlined three ways in which language is encouraged, through echoic responses, through mands and through tacts. Learning theory does not explain the rapidity with which language is acquired, the many different responses to the same stimulus and the use by children of creative and novel utterances.

■ Nativist theory centres around Chomsky's notion of a language acquisition device (LAD), an inborn brain mechanism, which contains information about the structure of language. He stresses linguistic universals at the deep structural level and differences between languages at the surface level. His view is supported by the existence of linguistic universals, the rapidity with which all human children acquire language and the fact that all human beings possess physiological features related to language. Children also appear to have an inborn capacity to use the 'rules' of language.

■ A third approach emphasizes the importance of social interaction to the development of languages.

Further reading

Bee, H. (1995). *The Developing Child*, 7th edn. New York: HarperCollins. Part 4 of this introductory, American text gives a good, up-to-date overview of a range of different approaches to the study of cognitive and language development and includes an examination of cross-cultural perspectives. It covers Piaget's theory, the measurement of intelligence and the information-processing approach to the understanding of cognitive development.

Donaldson, M. (1978). *Children's Minds*. London: Fontana. In its time, a revolutionary text, which is very readable and provides a challenge to Piaget's views on the power of logical thinking in the child.

Meadows, S. (1995). Cognitive development. In P.E. Bryant and A.M. Colman (eds), *Developmental Psychology*. Harlow: Longman. This provides a brief overview of the 'state of the art' in the study of cognitive development.

Smith, P.K. and Cowie, H. (1991). *Understanding Children's Development*, 2nd edn. Oxford: Blackwell. An excellent British text which considers many different aspects of development. It includes a very good description and critique of Piaget's theory, an overview of theory and research in language development and very good coverage of the theories of Vygotsky and Bruner on social aspects of cognitive development.

CHAPTER 21

Intelligence – its origins and measurement

The measurement of intelligence   487
- What is intelligence?   487
- Intelligence tests – a historical sketch   488
- The relationship between intelligence and IQ   489
- Problems with the use of IQ tests   490

Alternative views of intelligence   492
- Gardner's theory of multiple intelligences   492

- Sternberg's triarchic theory of intelligence   492

Origins of differences in IQ   496
- The heredity–environment issue   496
- Nature–nurture: an interactionist approach   500

Objectives

By the end of this chapter, you should be able to:

- Appreciate the complexity of attempting to define intelligence;

- Understand the nature and functions of intelligence tests and be aware of the controversies surrounding their use;

- Have a knowledge of a range of theories of intelligence and their implications for intelligence testing;

- Appreciate the issues surrounding the heredity–environment controversy in intelligence and evaluate different kinds of evidence used by psychologists to reach a conclusion;

- Discuss the interactionist approach used by psychologists in assessing the relative influence of heredity and environment on intelligence test performance.

The measurement of intelligence

Before considering the measurement of intelligence, it is important to look at the concept and examine some different definitions.

Traditionally this approach to studying cognitive functioning, or intelligence, has focused on individual differences in performance on specially devised tests. Often referred to as the psychometric approach (discussed in Chapter 4), it has a major weakness in that it focuses on the measurement of intelligence but does not examine its development.

What is intelligence?

The idea of 'intelligence' or 'ability' is a far-reaching and powerful concept in everyday life. It is used freely to describe differences between people and to explain why individuals behave as they do. Terms such as 'bright', 'quick-thinking', 'dull' and 'slow' are frequently used to label people as being of a certain type. Despite the confidence with which these terms are used, finding a precise definition of intelligence that all psychologists can agree upon is very difficult (see Box 21.1). Some early definitions implied that intelligence is an entity – something one has a lot or a little of. More recent definitions have stressed the idea of intelligent behaviour which is aimed at successful adaptation to the environment. But what is intelligent behaviour? One child may have an exceptional talent for music while another is particularly good at solving mathematical problems; yet another child may excel at creative writing. Which child is the more intelligent? In the next section, we shall examine a range of different theories about the nature of intelligence.

Sternberg (1984) argues that any definition of intelligence must recognize the cultural context in which the definition is being applied. What is classed as intelligent behaviour in one culture may not be so highly regarded in another. This idea will be considered later.

In Western societies, the definition of intelligence is often closely linked to the notion of **intelligence quotient (IQ)**. This is the score derived from an intelligence test and it will be discussed later. IQ tests have traditionally emphasized powers of reasoning and verbal and mathematical abilities. Since intelligence is often equated with the ability to do intelligence tests, some psychologists have suggested that intelligence is 'what the tests measure', a rather circular definition.

Box 21.1   Some definitions of intelligence

'The ability to carry on abstract thinking' (Terman, 1921)

'Innate, general cognitive ability' (Burt, 1955)

'To judge well, to comprehend well, to reason well . . .' (Binet and Simon, 1905)

'Intelligent activity consists in grasping the essentials in a situation and responding appropriately to them.' (Heim, 1970)

Intelligence tests – a historical sketch

The earliest examples of intelligence tests were provided at the end of the nineteenth century by Sir Francis Galton in England and J. McK. Cattell in America. These early tests, which were based on the measurement of simple sensory processes such as the speed of reaction times and judging the difference between two weights, did not prove useful as measures of intelligence.

Simon–Binet test

The first tests to resemble modern intelligence tests were devised by the French psychologist Alfred Binet and his co-researcher, Theodore Simon. In 1905, Binet was requested by the French government to devise tests which would identify children who needed special educational help. Using the judgments of school teachers on what constituted 'average' performance on a range of tasks involving reasoning and judgment, Binet first undertook to identify the 'mental level' of the 'normal' child in various different age groups. From this work, a number of age-related scales were devised based on the concept of **mental age**. Thus, a seven-year-old child who satisfactorily completed all those items normally completed by the average eight-year-old was said to have a mental age of eight; the ten-year-old who was able to complete only those tasks expected of eight-year-olds would also be assigned a mental age of eight.

The result of this work was the Simon–Binet (1905) test, which is generally regarded as the first intelligence test.

Intelligence quotient

Later researchers contended that in order for a more complete assessment to be made of the ability levels of children of different age groups who exhibit the same

---

mental age, some account should be taken of the child's chronological, or actual, age. In 1912, Stern introduced the idea of an intelligence quotient (IQ) which could be calculated as follows:

$$IQ = \frac{\text{Mental age (MA)}}{\text{Chronological age (CA)}} \times 100$$

It can be seen that when MA and CA are the same, using this calculation, IQ is 100, that is, average. This way of calculating IQ is not used any longer. Today, a child's test performance is compared directly to norms (average scores) drawn from a large group of children of the same age during a standardization process (standardization is discussed in Chapter 34). However, an IQ of 100 is still used as the average score.

Stanford–Binet

In 1916, the Simon–Binet test was revised by Lewis Terman of Stanford University. The Stanford–Binet test, as it became known, was originally designed for children but was later extended to measure IQ in adults. The Stanford–Binet Intelligence Scale was revised many times, the most recent revision being in 1986. Before the 1986 revision, the IQ score was derived from an amalgam of all the items and would not reflect differences between a child's performance in, for example, numerical ability compared to verbal ability. (See Box 4.5 in Chapter 4 for an example of items similar to those used in the Stanford–Binet Intelligence Scale for six to eight year olds.)

Wechsler

The most widely used test of adult intelligence, the Wechsler Adult Intelligence Scale was devised in 1939 and this was followed later by the Wechsler Intelligence Scale, for Children (WISC). Both these tests have subsequently been revised. Because it was felt that the Stanford–Binet scales relied too heavily on language ability, the Wechsler scales provide measures not just on a verbal scale but also a nonverbal performance scale, which requires the manipulation or arrangement of blocks, pictures and other displays.

British Ability Scales

The Stanford–Binet and Wechsler tests were designed mainly for use with American populations. An

---

Box 21.2   Infant tests

In 1969 the Bayley Scales of Infant Development (revised in 1993) were constructed. Since a child under two years old has limited or nonexistent spoken language, these were designed primarily to measure sensory and motor skills such as reaching for a dangling ring (designed for a typical three month old), putting cubes in a cup on request (nine months) or building a tower from three cubes (17 months). Tests of this kind have been useful for identifying infants and toddlers who may not be developing normally. However, in general, the scores derived from these tests do not correlate highly with later scores drawn from tests such as the Stanford–Binet or WISC. It seems, therefore, that these tests are not tapping the same kinds of abilities as those measured by the common childhood or adult intelligence tests (Colombo, 1993).

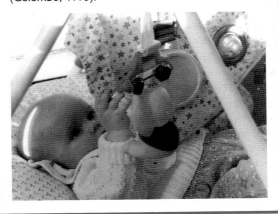

important milestone so far as Britain is concerned is the British Ability Scales designed for 2 to 17 year olds (Elliott et al., 1983). This test, in addition to using traditional items concerned with reasoning, short-term memory and so on, measures aspects of development and moral reasoning.

The relationship between intelligence and IQ

Though IQ scores purport to be a measure of intelligence, the relationship between 'intelligence' and 'IQ' cannot be considered in the same way as, for example, that between 'weight' and 'pounds and

Box 21.3   Predictive ability of IQ scores

Crucial questions about IQ tests are whether they are stable and whether they predict anything helpful in relation to a child's later development. Before dealing with these questions directly, it is necessary to reexamine the concepts of reliability and validity (see also Chapter 4 and Chapter 34).

Reliability

In order for it to be considered reliable, a test given to the same individual on two or more occasions should yield the same or nearly the same score; in other words, it should be consistent. This can be assessed using the test–retest method. The test is given to the same group of individuals on two different occasions, with a suitable time-lag to prevent them from remembering the test items (or two different versions of the same test may be used). The technique of correlation (see Chapter 34) is applied to the two sets of scores to examine the degree of similarity between them. The resulting correlation coefficient, known as a reliability coefficient, should be in the region of 0.90 (that for the Wechsler Intelligence Scale is 0.91). A perfect match between two sets of scores would yield a correlation coefficient of 1.00.

Validity

It is necessary also to demonstrate that the test is measuring what it claims to measure: that is, intelligent behaviour. This is its validity. One way of doing this is to examine the test's predictive validity. For example, children's scores on an IQ test can be correlated with some future measure of intelligence, such as school achievement or a different IQ test. The stronger the correlation, the more likely it is that the two measures are tapping the same abilities.

There are other kinds of reliability and validity which are established when a psychometric test is being developed. For an account of these, please see Chapter 34.

Stability of test scores

As has already been pointed out, scores on infant IQ tests such as the Bayley do not correlate highly with later IQs. A typical correlation coefficient between scores on the Bayley at one year old and scores on the Binet at four years old is only about 0.2 to 0.3. From the age of about three onwards, reliability in IQ test performance increases. Typically, the correlations between IQ scores in middle childhood are in the region of 0.80 (Honzik, 1986). The older the child the more stable the IQ score becomes.

What do IQ scores predict?

When psychologists have compared children's IQ scores with tests of their school performance, the correlation consistently found is around 0.60 (Carver, 1990). This is a strong but by no means perfect correlation (remember that a perfect correlation would be 1.00). It tells us that for the majority of children, the higher their IQ score, the more likely they are to achieve well in school. However, there will be some children with high IQ scores who do not excel at school while some with lower IQ scores do. This is an important point to remember.

---

ounces'. Whilst we accept a numerical value expressed in pounds and ounces as an objective and exact indication of the weight of something, because of the complexity and uncertainty surrounding definitions of intelligence, the same cannot be said for an IQ score in relation to intelligence. Continuing the analogy between weight and intelligence, claiming that some-one who weighs 60 lbs is half as heavy as someone who weighs 120 lbs is legitimate; arguing that someone with an IQ of 70 is only half as intelligent as someone with an IQ of 140 would be nonsensical.

Problems with the use of IQ tests

Advocates of psychometric tests have drawn attention to the great value of IQ testing as a reliable and standard means of comparing individuals to others (see Box 21.3). The results of tests, it is claimed, can be a valuable source of information in a wide range of situations from diagnosing children's learning diffi-culties to helping individuals to make educational and career choices. However, there have been a number of criticisms associated with their use and these are fully discussed in the last section of Chapter 4. You should reread this section now.

Box 21.4 Culture and IQ tests

One of the most controversial issues in IQ testing is the question of whether tests are biased in favour of white, middle-class people. If so, their use with groups whose social or cultural experience is very different would seem to be unfair. This is a particularly important issue with verbal tests that require competence in a particular language. A child whose first language was not English could not be expected to score as highly on verbal items as a child from a solely English-speaking home. And even where English is the first language, the vocabulary used may differ significantly between middle-class and working-class homes. One of the most widely used tests thought to be relatively culture-free is Raven's Progressive Matrices which uses nonverbal items in the form of shapes and symbols. However, cultural factors, it has been claimed, can also influence performance on nonverbal items depending upon the particular experi-

ences of test-takers and how familiar they are with the materials and content of the tests (Irvine, 1966; Simon, 1971). Vernon (1969) reflects the view of many psychologists when he argues that there can be no such thing was a truly culture-fair test.

The importance of social and cultural influences on IQ testing was illustrated by Warburton (1951) who described some of the difficulties encountered in devising ability tests for Gurkha recruits. Brought up in a less competitive society than our own, they were not motivated to succeed in what appeared to be irrelevant, abstract tasks and they were unaccustomed to working within a set time limit. Consequently, their achievement, even on 'performance' tests was thought not to be a reflection of true ability. The messages from this study are still relevant today.

Boys hunting from an outrigger canoe in Irian Jaya, Indonesia. In their culture, these skills are highly valued as a sign of intelligence

SELF-ASSESSMENT QUESTIONS

1. How would you define intelligence'?
2. Briefly describe some widely used IQ tests.
3. How is an IQ score currently arrived at?
4. What are thought to be the main benefits of IQ testing? Discuss some of the controversies arising from the use of IQ tests.

Alternative views of intelligence

Early attempts to clarify the nature of intelligence tended to rely on the statistical analysis of people's scores on intelligence tests (see Box 21.5). Over the past decade or so, a number of psychologists have attempted to go beyond the traditional psychometric approach to intelligence with its heavy emphasis on verbal and reasoning skills. Gardner (1983) and Sternberg (1985, 1988) have attempted to understand intelligence in terms of a complex interaction of various cognitive and other systems. Each theory will be briefly discussed below.

Gardner's theory of multiple intelligences

Gardner's theory of multiple intelligences (1983) is based partly upon the results of tests and partly on research from neuropsychology. The theory has three fundamental principles. The first is that there exists seven distinct intelligences, as follows:

■ **linguistic** (language skills such as reading, writing, speaking and listening);
■ **logical-mathematical** (numerical skills);
■ **spatial** (understanding relationships in space as in driving or playing chess);
■ **musical** (skills such as singing or playing an instrument);
■ **bodily kinaesthetic** (using the body as in dance or athletics);
■ **interpersonal** (understanding and relating to others);
■ **intrapersonal** (understanding oneself).

The second principle is that the intelligences are independent of each other. They operate as modular systems without a 'central control' to coordinate them. In other words, a person's abilities as assessed under one intelligence should in theory be uncorrelated with the person's abilities as assessed under another intelligence.

Finally, Gardner believes that though they are separate and independent of each other, the intelligences interact and work together whenever the need arises; for example, solving a mathematical word problem would require linguistic and logical-mathematical intelligence to work together.

Gardner believes that each intelligence resides in a separate portion of the brain and that a particular intelligence could be isolated by studying brain-damaged patients. Damage in one area of the brain could impair one intelligence leaving the others intact. The phenomenon of severely retarded individuals who have one exceptional skill, such as playing a musical instrument or manipulating numbers, provides evidence for the independent existence of one particular intelligence (see Box 21.6).

The first three intelligences proposed by Gardner are very much in line with those measured in conventional IQ tests. However, Gardner's inclusion of the other abilities as part of intelligence represents a new and interesting approach, as does his attempt to explore the roles of physiological and cognitive processes in intelligence.

Among criticisms made of Gardner's theory is that the kinds of intelligences he proposes are not easily measurable. However, Gardner replies that while the intelligences he proposes may not be measurable by conventional IQ tests, they can be assessed through the activities engaged in by children at school, such as composition or athletic activities (Gardner and Feldman, 1985).

Sternberg (1990) suggests that whilst Gardner's theory is at present too vague to be substantiated in detail, it represents an important contribution to understanding the human mind and intelligence.

Sternberg's triarchic theory of intelligence

Sternberg's **triarchic** (governed by three systems) **theory of intelligence** (Sternberg, 1985, 1988) seeks to explain the relationship between:

| GLOSSARY |

Gardner's theory of multiple intelligences Gardner's theory that there exist seven distinct intelligences, which are independent of each other, but which interact and work together whenever the need arises.

Box 21.5 Early theories of intelligence: general intelligence or specific abilities

The debate about whether we possess one intelligence or a number of separate abilities is centuries old. This debate can be seen in some of the early theories about the nature of intelligence, two of which are outlined below.

Spearman's two-factor theory

Charles Spearman (1863–1945) was one of the pioneers of mental testing. He proposed that an individual's performance on tests of intelligence was determined by a common factor which he called g (general intelligence) and factors which were specific to different kinds of test, which he labelled s (specific factor). Thus a person's measured intelligence would be made up mainly of g, which he saw as roughly equivalent to the ability to see relationships between things. Yet they would vary also according to their specific abilities (s) in that one person might perform better on tests which measured mathematical reasoning, where another would excel at verbal reasoning. During the 1940s and 1950s, Spearman's ideas were extended further by Cyril Burt and Philip Vernon. Burt and Spearman were agreed that g was inherited and unchangeable, whereas s could result from training.

Since this model of intelligence proposes that there is a g factor which dominates performance on all tests, an individual's IQ would be arrived at by amalgamating scores from a range of tests, for example verbal ability and numerical ability, and calculating a single, overall IQ score.

Thurstone's multifactor theory

Spearman, Burt and Vernon (sometimes known as the 'London line') put forward a model of intelligence based on the existence of a general factor which affected all aspects of human functioning. However, in the United States, other researchers were developing models which proposed that intelligence consisted of a number of different and basically unrelated skills. The most notable of these models was that of Thurstone (1938) who proposed seven primary mental abilities (PMAs). All were equally important, he believed, and none correlated highly with any other. The PMAs were as follows:

- Verbal ability,
- Perceptual speed,
- Numerical reasoning,
- Rote memory,
- Word fluency,
- Spatial ability,
- Inductive reasoning.

Since this model denied the existence of a g factor which affects all areas of functioning, each PMA is assessed by a different test. Performance yields a profile of seven scores, rather than a single g score.

Gould (1981) drew attention to the political and educational implications of the debate. He strongly criticized Burt's model with its assumption of a dominating 'innate' g factor. The influence of this model in the 1940s on the development of the 11-plus examination to select children for grammar school education was not supportable. Thurstone's PMAs, he believed, whilst still open to criticism, represented a less entrenched and rigid view of a child's abilities.

- Intelligence and the internal world of the individual: that is, the mental mechanisms that underlie intelligent behaviour (the **componential subtheory**);
- Intelligence and the external world of the individual: that is, the use of these mental mechanisms in everyday life in order to adapt to the environment in an intelligent way (the **contextual subtheory**); and
- Intelligence and experience or the role played by life experience in linking the individual's internal and external worlds (the **experiential subtheory**).

The componential subtheory

Sternberg proposes that intelligent functioning, for instance trying to solve a mathematical problem, involves three basic information-processing mechanisms or components. These are:

GLOSSARY

Triarchic theory of intelligence Sternberg's theory which sees intelligence as governed by three systems: componential, contextual, experiential.

Box 21.6   Exceptional talents in individuals who have learning difficulties

There are a growing number of instances in the literature of individuals who have learning difficulties in some way but who possess remarkable intellectual talents. Many published instances are of individuals who have exceptional numerical ability, such as being able to do mental arithmetic very quickly or identify the day of the week of a specific date over the past or future few hundred years.

Other cases involve exceptional artistic or musical talent. For example, Stephen Wiltshire, a young boy who is autistic, is capable of producing complex and detailed drawings of buildings after seeing the buildings only once or twice. Harriet, who had little general knowledge and had an IQ of 73, was an outstanding pianist who was

capable of reproducing complex classical pieces from memory. She also had a detailed knowledge of classical music and could talk about it with confidence, using words that she otherwise would not use.

Self described 11 case studies of individuals who had learning difficulties in some way but who had an exceptional talent.

The view that intelligence is one entity which is controlled by a general factor is seriously challenged by these cases, since they show that it is possible for exceptional intellectual abilities to be present in individuals who have been categorized as 'of low intelligence'. They offer support for Gardner's model of intelligence which proposes that individuals possess a number of intelligences that are distinct and separate from each other.

This skilful drawing of a cockerel is one of a series produced by an autistic girl called Nadia when she was only six years old

---

- **Metacomponents**, which include higher order processes involved in identifying the nature of the problem, developing a strategy for its solution and evaluating the success of the solution;
- **Performance components**, which include lower order processes involved in actually solving the problem according to the plans laid down by the metacomponents;
- **Knowledge-acquisition components**, which include processes involved in learning new material, such as sifting out relevant from irrelevant information.

Other components have been considered by Sternberg. These include **retention components** – processes involved in retrieval of information from memory – and **transfer components** – processes involved in generalizing (transferring information from one situation to another).

The components function together in a highly interactive way and are not easy to study in isolation from each other. Metacomponents activate perfor-

mance and knowledge components, which in turn provide feedback to the metacomponents.

Understanding the nature of the components, Sternberg argues, is not sufficient to allow an understanding of the nature of intelligence, as there is more to intelligence than a number of information-processing components. Nor is it sufficient to assess an individual's intelligence solely through IQ tests. The other two aspects of the triarchic theory go some way to explaining the other elements of intelligence which contribute to individual differences in intelligent behaviour – outside of testing situations as well as within them.

The experiential subtheory

The information-processing components discussed above are always applied to tasks and situations where the person has some level of previous experience. The essence of the experiential aspect of the triarchic theory is that an individual's intelligence can only be understood if account is taken not just of the components but of his or her level of experience.

Intelligence is measured most effectively where the tasks being undertaken are either relatively novel (not totally outside the individual's understanding, but close to the limits) or in the process of becoming automized (performed automatically).

Novelty Different sources of evidence suggest that assessing the ability to deal with relative novelty is a good way of measuring intelligence. In studies with children, Davidson and Sternberg (1984) found that those who were intellectually gifted had the ability to deal with novelty in a problem-solving situation without being given helpful cues, whereas less gifted children benefited from help. Sternberg contends that the various components of intelligence that are involved in dealing with novelty in particular situations provide apt measures of intellectual ability.

Automization Equally, Sternberg believes that the ability to automize information, as in skilled reading, is a key aspect of intelligence. Poor comprehenders are often those who have not automized the elementary processes of reading and therefore have not the resources to allocate to more complex comprehension processes. Thus, the ability to automize allows more resources to be devoted to novelty. Similarly, if one is able to deal effectively with novelty, more resources are available for automization.

The contextual subtheory

According to this aspect of the theory, intelligence is not a random mental activity that happens to involve certain information-processing components. Rather, it is purposely directed towards one or more of three behavioural goals – adaptation to an environment, shaping of an environment and selection of an environment.

Adaptation The components of information processing and the importance of dealing with novelty and automization of information processing are seen by Sternberg as universal in that they operate in the same way for individuals in one culture as they do for those in all other cultures. However, the way these components show themselves in the experience and behaviour of individuals will vary from culture to culture. What is intelligent in one culture may be seen as unintelligent in another.

Shaping This involves adapting the environment to one's own preferred style of operating rather than the other way round. Sternberg sees this as a key feature of intelligent thought and behaviour: 'In science, the greatest scientists are those who set the paradigms (shaping) rather than those who merely follow them (adaptation)' (Sternberg, 1990, p. 281).

Selection This involves renouncing one environment in favour of another. It sometimes occurs when both adaptation and shaping fail. For example, if one has failed to adapt to the demands of a particular job or to shape the nature of those demands to make them fit in with one's needs, the intelligent thing to do may be to select a new environment by changing one's job.

Assessment of Sternberg's theory

It can be seen that a major feature of Sternberg's theory is his emphasis upon the need to go further than studying intelligent behaviour as represented by typical problems in IQ tests. Bee (1989) argues that standard IQ tests have failed to assess many of the kinds of abilities featured in Sternberg's contextual and experiential subtheories and which are so relevant to intelligent functioning in the 'real world'. However, Sternberg himself is developing a test based on his triarchic theory of intelligence. In addition to providing scores for componential skills, it will also assess coping with novelty skills, automization skills and practical intellectual skills.

❓ SELF-ASSESSMENT QUESTIONS

1. Contrast the views of intelligence proposed by Spearman, Burt and Vernon with that of Thurstone. What are the implications of these two approaches for IQ testing?
2. Outline Gardner's theory of multiple intelligences. How are Gardner's views supported by the study of retarded individuals who possess an exceptional intellectual skill?
3. Outline Sternberg's triarchic theory of intelligence. What are the implications of this approach for intelligence testing?

Origins of differences in IQ

The heredity–environment issue

The question of the origins of differences in IQ has inevitably centred around disputes about nature versus nurture. During the nineteenth century, Francis Galton (1869) studied the relative effects of heredity (nature) and environment (nurture) on the development of intelligence. Subsequently, this issue developed into probably the most controversial and divisive debate to be encountered in psychology. General issues in relation to the heredity–environment debate are fully discussed in Chapter 2. You should reread that section now.

The question that concerned psychologists was 'Which is the more important influence on the development of differences in intelligence: heredity (that is, genetic inheritance) or environment (usually defined as all the experiences an individual is exposed to from the time of conception)? Psychologists now know that this is far too simplistic a question. Differences in intelligence are the result of an interaction between heredity and environment. No psychological characteristic can be entirely one or the other. Some aspects of development, for example temperament, may initially be inherited, but they can be influenced by such things as the parents' style of childrearing. Nonetheless, there is still a good deal of disagreement about the relative importance of each. Let us examine some of the available evidence.

Family and twin studies

An important source of evidence relating to the inheritance of intelligence came from studies which correlated IQ scores between people of varying degrees of genetic relationship: for example, parents paired with children, siblings (including twins) paired with each other, cousins paired with each other. Figure 21.1 shows the **correlation coefficients** arrived at from three individual studies (Newman et al., 1937; Shields, 1962; Burt, 1966) and from a survey which examined 111 studies on familial resemblances in measured intelligence (Bouchard and McGue, 1981).

Of particular interest is the data relating to twin studies. But first some facts about twins. Twins are of two different kinds; **monozygotic** (MZ) or 'identical' twins and **dizygotic** (DZ) or 'fraternal' twins. DZ twins have developed from two separately fertilized ova and

Figure 21.1 Family studies of intelligence showing IQ correlation coefficients

| Relationship | Name of study | | | |
	Newman et al. (1937)	Shields (1962)	Burt (1966)	Bouchard and McGue (1981)*
Monozygotic twins				
Reared together	0.91	0.76	0.94	0.86
Reared apart	0.67	0.77	0.77	0.72
Dizygotic twins				
Reared together	0.64	0.51	0.55	0.60
Siblings				
Reared together				0.47
Reared apart				0.24
Single-parent offspring				
Reared together				0.42
Reared apart				0.22
Cousins				0.15

*Median correlation.

are no more alike genetically than any two children of the same parents. MZ twins have developed from a single fertilized ovum and are thought to start life genetically identical. Differences in behaviour between identical twins must, it is thought, be attributed almost entirely to the effects of the environment.

Examining the data in Figure 21.1, a number of points can be made:

■ Overall, the data clearly show that the closer the family relationship, the higher is the average correlation coefficient between IQ scores and

---

GLOSSARY

Correlation coefficient A statistic which describes the degree of relationship between two variables: for example, the IQs of children compared with the IQs of their mothers.

Monozygotic (MZ) twins 'Identical' twins who have developed from a single fertilized ovum and are thought to be genetically identical.

Dizygotic (DZ) twins 'Fraternal' twins, who have developed from two separately fertilized ova and are no more alike genetically than any two children of the same parents.

therefore the more similar are the IQ scores. It also shows, of course, that correlation coefficients rise as the *environments* become more similar.

- The highest correlation coefficients relate to MZ twins reared together, indicating that they have more similar IQs than any other pairs. Hereditarians would attribute this to the greater degree of genetic similarity between MZ twins. However, it is probable that they were also *treated* more similarly than DZ twins.
- Even MZ twins reared apart have more similar IQs than DZ twins reared together. Hereditarians claimed this as powerful support for genetic influences on intelligence.

Evaluation of twin studies   As noted above, hereditarians claimed that the evidence from twin studies overwhelmingly supported the role of genetic inheritance in intelligence. However, environmentalists have made a number of criticisms of twin studies:

- Different studies used different intelligence tests; it is therefore difficult to make a valid comparison between them.
- Many of the MZ twins reared apart were in fact brought up in very similar homes. This suggests that their environments may have been quite similar (Kamin, 1977). An example in one study (Newman et al., 1937) where an MZ pair were brought up in very different environments revealed an IQ difference between the twins of 24 points.
- Some of the earlier studies are likely to have suffered from sampling inaccuracies because, at that time, there was no reliable method of identifying true MZ twins.
- Herman (1984) pointed out that families who produce twins may not be typical of the general population. Therefore, generalizations from twin studies should not be made.
- The data produced by Burt is open to doubt since the results of at least some of his twin studies are thought to have been faked. (Burt's data are not included in the Bouchard and McGue review.)

Adoption studies

A large number of studies have compared the IQs of adopted children with those of both their adoptive parents and their natural parents. The assumption is that if heredity is the more important influence the correlation between children's IQ scores and those of their natural parents will be higher than the correlation with their adoptive parents.

Two early adoption studies (Burks, 1928; Leahy, 1935) found very low correlations of 0.13 and 0.18, respectively, between the IQs of children and their adoptive parents. The correlation for children and natural parents living together is about 0.50. It seems from these figures that environment is important, though less so than heredity.

Hereditarians claimed that foster/adoption studies offer powerful support for a high heritability component to IQ. However, environmentalists argued that there are major flaws in the early studies cited by hereditarians. For example, Kamin (1977) drew attention to the process of selective placement practised by adoption agencies. He made two main points.

First, selective placement involves placing children in homes which resemble as closely as possible the home environment of their natural parents. Thus the children of 'bright' mothers may be placed in homes with high-IQ adoptive parents, whereas the children of less 'bright' mothers may be placed in homes where the adoptive parents' IQs resemble those of the natural parents. Therefore, selective placement could account for the similarity between the IQ of adopted children and their natural parents even if they have not lived together.

Kamin's second point was that the correlation between the IQ of children and adoptive parents is likely to be artificially lowered because of the nature of adoptive parents as a group relative to parents in general. Because of the conditions laid down by adoption agencies, adoptive parents are likely to be emotionally stable, financially secure, not alcoholic, and so on. Also, there is likely to be less variance in their IQs than that of the children they adopt. This could artificially reduce the correlations between the IQs of the two groups.

Later studies attempted to avoid some of the problems in the early adoption studies and concentrated on parents who had brought up both adopted and natural children (Scarr and Weinberg, 1977; Horn et al., 1979). In both studies, the correlation of mother–natural child IQs was very similar to the correlation of mother–adoptive child IQs (0.22 and 0.20, respectively, in the Scarr study). This provides no support for the high heritability of intelligence since the second relationship did not involve similar genes.

A study which supported the environmentalist case in highlighting the effects of a 'good' environment on IQ was carried out by Schiff et al. (1978) in France. They studied 32 children born to parents of low socio-economic status who were adopted before they were six months old by parents of high socioeconomic status. A comparison was made between the children's IQs and those of their biological siblings who had been reared by their natural mothers. The average IQ of the adopted group was 111 while that of the 'naturally reared' group was 95.

Environmental influences

After much research, there appears to be a general consensus on the environmental conditions that enhance the development of an individual's intellectual potential: these conditions include good prenatal and postnatal nutrition and health care; intellectual stimulation; a stable emotional climate in the home; parental encouragement and support. Box 21.7 outlines some of the research findings which have contributed to this view.

Environmental enrichment

Because children from underprivileged homes tend to be at a disadvantage intellectually, a number of programmes have been mounted which aimed to provide greater intellectual stimulation for these children. The first and best known of these programmes is **Project Headstart**.

In 1965, funds were allocated in the USA to provide enriched learning experiences for preschool children from deprived homes. A variety of approaches was used. In some, teachers visited children and their parents at home to provide intellectually stimulating activities of the kind that children from 'better-off' homes tend to receive from their parents. In other programmes, the children attended classes where they took part in special learning activities.

Early follow-up studies showed that the project had not been as successful as had been hoped in that no lasting IQ gains were found in children who had participated compared to those who had not. However, later follow-up studies highlighted some lasting benefits. Compared to a control group of children who had not received pre-school enrichment, participants in Headstart at age 15 were a full grade ahead, scored higher on tests of reading, arithmetic and

---

Box 21.7 Studies of environmental influences on intelligence

A classic longitudinal study carried out by Skeels (1966) studied a group of children brought up in an unstimulating orphanage environment. At 19 months, their mean IQ score was 64. Some of the children were removed from the orphanage and given individual attention. At age six, the latter group showed a mean IQ of 96, compared to 60–70 in the institutionalized group.

Studying 12-year-old children, Fraser (1959) found a strong, positive correlation between high IQ and factors such as the level of parental encouragement, general family atmosphere and the amount of bookreading in the home.

Wiseman (1964) found a strong correlation between the standard of child care and IQ.

Bayley (1970) contended that IQ differences between children of low and high socioeconomic status become progressively greater between birth and entrance to school, suggesting that the quality of the environment amplifies any genetic differences present at birth.

---

language use and exhibited less antisocial behaviour (Zigler and Berman, 1983; Lee et al., 1988). Significantly, programmes that actively involved parents in stimulating their child's intellectual development have tended to produce the greatest benefits (Darlington, 1986).

Even larger and more lasting benefits are found when an enrichment programme is started in infancy. Ramey (1992, 1993) reported a study which followed the progress of a large sample of infants (6–12 weeks) who had been randomly allocated to one of two groups. One group received specially enriched day care up to their entrance to kindergarten and the other (a control group) received medical care and nutritional supplements but no enriched day care. At all ages, the average IQ scores of the children in the 'enriched' group were higher than those of the control group; 44 per cent of the

---

GLOSSARY

Project Headstart A programme in the USA which aims to provide enriched learning experiences for preschool children from deprived backgrounds.

Box 21.8 Race and IQ

A lively and often bitter debate has developed over the years. The question arose as to whether or not genetically determined differences in intelligence existed between different racial groups. It is an undisputed fact that using standard IQ tests, black Americans score on average approximately 15 points below the average of the white population (Shuey, 1966); the controversy arose from how this information was interpreted.

The debate began in 1969 with the publication of an article by Arthur Jensen in the USA in which he claimed that genetic factors were strongly implicated in the average Negro–white intelligence differences found. He based this view on an 80 per cent heritability estimate, which was calculated from studies of the white population. (Heritability refers to the proportion of a trait's variance *within a particular population* that can be attributed to genetic differences.) He added that the evidence did not support the possibility of strong environmental influences. In view of the implications of this view for social policy and in particular the allocation of resources for such enrichment projects as Headstart, a heated exchange began between hereditarians and environmentalists. There follows a summary of some of the more important points made:

■ Jensen's use of an 80 per cent heritability estimate is based on *within-group* differences, that is, differences within the white population. It does not follow that conclusions can be drawn about *between-group* differences, or differences between black and white populations (Mackenzie, 1984).

■ Tobias (1974) pointed out Jensen's failure to take account of the possible cumulative effects of generations of environmental deprivation suffered by American blacks in the form of poverty, malnutrition,

prejudice and lack of educational opportunity. It is well known that the effects of poverty and malnutrition can persist for at least two generations after improvements in conditions have taken place.

■ Kamin (1977) argued that the complex interaction between genetic factors and environmental influences is not well understood. No study has yet been able to estimate the extent to which different environments can affect intellectual development.

■ Fontana (1988) argues that a starting point for the debate must be the difficulties in defining and measuring intelligence. Concepts of intelligence and the methods for measuring it in Western white societies are culture-bound: that is, they may not be valid for other cultures.

■ Race, like intelligence, has no agreed definition though most commonly it refers to a group sharing a common gene pool. However, known differences in gene structure are greater *within* a racial population than *between* such populations (Bodmer, 1972).

■ Where black or mixed-race children are adopted before they are a year old and reared by well-educated, high-income white families, they score an average of 15 IQ points higher than underprivileged black children reared in their biological families (Scarr and Weinberg, 1977).

■ Fontana (1988) suggests that '. . . there are no conclusive grounds for supposing genetic differences in intelligence exist between races. Such measurable differences as do exist would seem to be far too strongly contaminated by environmental variables to allow us to explain their origins with any confidence' (p. 102).

control group children had IQ scores classified as borderline or retarded (scores below 85) compared to only 12.8 per cent of the 'enriched' group. Additionally, the 'enriched' group achieved significantly higher scores on reading and mathematics tests at age 12. These findings show that the intellectual power of disadvantaged children can be significantly increased if such children are given stimulating experiences early in life.

An additional and very contentious issue has been that of the relationship between IQ and race. Box 21.8 summarizes some of the evidence relating to this debate.

Exercise 21.1

Talk to as many people as possible of a variety of ages and backgrounds about what they understand by 'intelligence'. Ask them what characteristics a highly intelligent person would have.

Record the replies and try to organize them into different categories.

Compare the categories with Gardner's multiple intelligences on page 492. Were all seven of Gardner's 'intelligences' referred to in the responses? If not, why do you think this is? Do you think people's replies were influenced by factors such as age, level of education, cultural or socioeconomic background?

Nature–nurture: an interactionist approach

As we have seen, the nature–nurture debate in intelligence was concerned with the role of genes and environment in determining measured intelligence. Much of the research discussed has served to highlight the complexity and, some would argue, the futility, of trying to unravel the relative contributions of each. Consequently, psychologists are now much more likely to be concerned with addressing the question 'How do heredity and environment interact?' If you look back at the discussion in Chapter 2, you will see that Anastasi and others have used the concept of **norm of reaction** in relation to the question of how heredity and environment may interact. This explanation sees genetic structure as imposing a top and bottom limit on an individual's potential behaviour. Where within this range the individual behaviour (in this case, IQ) will fall is determined by the kind of environment experienced.

Because of the difficulty of assessing genetic potential and the interaction with various environments, the usefulness of 'norm of reaction' is at present limited. Moreover, recent developments in genetics suggest that genetic structure is more flexible than had been thought. Rigid upper and lower limits may not exist. Nonetheless, until more conclusive evidence is available, it serves to remind educationists and social policy makers of the complex interaction between heredity and environment and the need to ensure that all individuals receive the best possible environmental conditions. It may also encourage researchers to develop more searching studies of the social and educational practices which might reduce IQ differences between groups.

? SELF-ASSESSMENT QUESTIONS

1. Critically evaluate some evidence which offers support for the role of 'nature' in the heredity–environment debate.
2. Referring to evidence, discuss some environmental factors which are likely to enhance the development of the intellect.
3. Briefly discuss the main issues arising from the controversy surrounding race and IQ.
4. Discuss the interactionist approach to the heredity–environment debate in relation to intelligence.

GLOSSARY

Norm of reaction The upper and lower limits of genetic potential within which an individual will develop.

Chapter summary

- Definitions of intelligence have included 'The ability to carry on abstract thinking' (Terman) and 'Intelligent activity consists in grasping the essentials in a situation and responding to them' (Heim). Intelligence has been associated with IQ and with intelligence tests.

- Early tests centred upon the notion of mental age (MA) and the ratio between mental and chronological age (CA). IQ (intelligence quotient) was calculated as mental age divided by chronological age multiplied by 100. Earliest tests were those of Simon and Binet later revised by Terman of Stanford University and known as Stanford–Binet tests. Because Stanford–Binet relied heavily on verbal ability, Wechsler tests were devised. In the UK, British Ability Scales have been devised for 2 to 17 year olds.

- The measurement of intelligence is complex and uncertain and cannot be considered as analogous to other physical measurements such as weight in kilograms and grams. IQ has value as a means of comparing individuals but criticisms have been made, discussed in Chapter 4.

- Questions are raised about reliability, validity, especially predictive validity, and stability. IQ scores correlate reasonably highly with school performance but by no means perfectly. A particular problem with

IQ tests has always been that they are not culture-fair, favouring white middle-class people.

■ Theories of intelligence include Spearman's two-factor theory which proposed two factors *g* (general intelligence) and *s* (specific intelligence) and Thurstone's multifactor theory which proposed seven primary abilities. The assumption of a dominating *g* factor in Spearman's model has had profound educational and political implications.

■ Gardner's theory posited seven distinct intelligences, linguistic, logical mathematical, spatial, musical, bodily kinaesthetic, interpersonal and intrapersonal. These are independent and separate, though they interact. Sternberg introduced a triarchic theory of intelligence, componential subtheory, contextual subtheory and experiential subtheory.

■ The origins of differences in IQ centre round the nature–nurture debate discussed in Chapter 2. Evidence comes from family and twin studies where IQ scores of individuals with various genetic relationships have been correlated. Twin studies have been of particular interest and controversy. MZ twins reared together have been found consistently to have more similar IQs than DZ twins or siblings, but there have been problems with the data.

■ Adoption studies have compared IQs of adopted children with both that of their adoptive and their natural parents. These studies also lend some support

to the notion that heredity is an important factor, though attention has been drawn to the fact that placements for adoption tend to be selective. Environment, therefore, is also important.

■ There is cogent evidence of the effect of a good environment in raising IQ levels, both from adoption studies by Schiff et al. and a longitudinal study by Skeels. The Headstart programme in the USA provided enriched learning environments for de-prived preschool children, especially when the enrichment programme started in infancy. Average IQ scores were higher than a control group and reading and mathematics scores significantly higher at age 12.

■ A more important question is how heredity and environment interact. Anastasi has used the concept of 'norm of reaction'. The genetic structure imposes a top and bottom limit on potential behaviour; environment determines where, within these limits, behaviour including IQ will fall.

■ A further issue which has been raised, and which has aroused bitter controversy, is that of race and IQ. The fact that black Americans score on average 15 IQ points lower than whites has been used to indicate a genetic inferiority, but Jensen in particular has ignored factors such as cumulative deprivation, the culture-bound nature of IQ and tests for it, complex interactional factors between heredity and environment, and the lack of an agreed definition of intelligence.

Further reading

Sternberg, R.J. (1990). *Metaphors of Mind: Conceptions of the Nature of Intelligence*. Cambridge: Cambridge University Press. This gives a first-hand account of Sternberg's triarchic theory of intelligence. It is fairly difficult, but rewarding, reading.

Kail, R. and Pellegrino, J.W. (1985). *Human Intelligence: Perspectives and Prospects*. New York: Freeman. This provides a very readable account of different approaches to the study of intelligence, including Piagetian theories, information-processing approaches and the measurement of intelligence.

CHAPTER 22

Social behaviour

Cognitive-developmental theory and social cognition   502
- Social cognition   503
- Evaluation of the cognitive-developmental approach   504

Moral development   504
- Psychodynamic approach   505
- Social learning approach   506
- Cognitive-developmental approach   506

Development of gender   513
- Masculinity and femininity   513
- Sex differences in behaviour   514
- Factors that influence gender role development   516
- What can we conclude?   523

Understanding self and others   524
- The nature of self   524
- The influence of social factors   524
- Developmental trends   524
- Self-esteem   526
- Theory of mind   528

Objectives

By the end of this chapter you should be able to:

- Appreciate the scope of cognitive-developmental theory and the study of social cognition;

- Discuss psychodynamic, learning theory and cognitive-developmental approaches to moral development;

- Evaluate these approaches to moral development in the light of empirical evidence;

- Discuss research into (a) the effects of parental style (b) peer group influences and (c) wider social influences on moral development;

- Describe and assess the findings from research into gender role development;

- Evaluate alternative explanations of the origins of gender role behaviour;

- Discuss findings from studies of the development of self-concept and factors affecting self-esteem;

- Consider findings from research into the development of a child's theory of mind.

Cognitive-developmental theory and social cognition

Psychoanalytic theories centre almost exclusively on children's emotional development and the impact on development of their relationships with a few key people. The learning theory approach emphasizes the central role that reinforcement plays in children's development and also the importance of imitating appropriate models. Cognitive-developmental theory emphasizes the importance to social and emotional behaviour of the child's developing thought processes and the exploration of objects. Traditionally, this approach centred upon Piaget's theory (see Chapter

20). However, other theories of cognitive development have also been considered in Chapter 20 and all may be said to have contributed to the cognitive-developmental approach.

Over the past 25 years or so, it has been recognized that children's personal and social development is strongly influenced by the way in which they think and reason about themselves and other people. A relatively new term has entered the psychological literature, that of social cognition (see also the Introduction to Part 6).

Social cognition

The first thing to note is that the term **social cognition** means different things to different researchers. Durkin (1995) distinguishes between individual social cognition, the most widely used approach to social cognition, and cognition as a product of social interaction. These two approaches will be briefly considered below:

Individual social cognition

This approach focuses on people's perceptions, thinking and reasoning about other human beings and about social relationships. Developmental psychologists have addressed a number of questions in this area of social cognition. These include the following:

- How do children understand and conceptualize the social world – the people around them, relationships between themselves and others?
- What changes take place in such reasoning and concepts as children develop?
- What is the relationship between cognition and social behaviour?

The following areas are among those that have been studied:

- Children's perceptions of themselves and the development of the self-concept;
- Conceptions of relationships between themselves and other people: for example, authority relations and friendships;
- Development of moral reasoning;
- Gender role development;
- Many areas drawn from social psychology: for example, person perception and attribution theory (see Chapter 24).

Initially, a good deal of research on individual social cognition was strongly influenced by Piaget's work. Therefore, many of the underlying principles were based upon his theory. For example:

Stages of development Children's social thinking and reasoning develop through a sequence of stages. All children pass through these stages in the same order and at approximately the same age. Each new stage incorporates and builds upon the characteristics of preceding stages.

Developing thought processes Various features of children's thought processes at different stages of development have an effect on how they perceive and understand social situations. As a child develops, thought processes change:

- From simple to complex: that is, from their tendency to focus on only one feature of a situation or problem to their ability to take account of many considerations at one time;
- From concrete thinking (where reasoning must be linked to something concrete) to abstract thinking (the ability to think and reason in one's head);
- From rigid to more flexible thinking.

These ways of thinking affect a child's understanding of social situations and relationships.

Taking someone else's perspective Piaget considered that children below the age of about six or seven are egocentric. He believed, therefore, that they are incapable of **perspective taking**: that is, seeing a problem or a situation from the point of view of another person. As noted in Chapter 20, more recent studies indicate that very young children may not be as egocentric as Piaget believed. Nonetheless, it is clear that the ability to take someone else's perspective (sometimes called role-taking ability) becomes more skilful and sophisticated as a child develops.

> ### GLOSSARY
>
> **Social cognition** Cognitive processes and structures that influence and are influenced by social behaviour.
>
> **Perspective taking** The ability to understand a problem or situation from someone else's point of view.

This ability influences the way the child perceives and reacts to social situations.

While experimental methods have been used to study individual social cognition, these have often appeared unduly constraining and unrealistic in the context of children's social understanding and behaviour. More often, variations on Piaget's clinical interview method have been used. Typically, a child is told a story about an imaginary social or moral situation. The interviewer then attempts to elicit the child's understanding of the motives and behaviour of characters in the story. Examples of this approach can be seen in Kohlberg's (1969) work on moral reasoning and Selman's (1976) work on perspective taking and friendships in children.

Cognition as a product of social interaction

This has been a less widely used approach to the study of social cognition. It is concerned with the ways in which interactions with other people – adults or children – influence, enhance and guide the development of cognitive abilities. It takes the view that social cognition is a social process; that is, something which occurs as people interact with each other. This is in contrast to the individual approach to social cognition, which tends to emphasize that development occurs as a result of activities within the individual.

Paradoxically, this second approach to social cognition has also been influenced by Piaget. Piaget's belief in the relevance of social interaction to cognitive development has tended to be overlooked. In the 1970s, neo-Piagetian researchers working in Geneva reestablished this aspect of his theory and drew on concepts from social psychology to reinterpret it. However, a discussion of this research is beyond the scope of this chapter.

Another important influence on the 'social' approach to social cognition comes from Vygotskyan theory and this was considered in some detail in Chapter 20. As we saw in that account, Vygotsky argued that the child acquires the mechanisms of thinking and learning as a result of social interactions with adults and peers. To explain how these interactions may guide and enhance a child's cognitive development, he proposed the concepts of the zone of proximal development – the area between a child's actual developmental level and the potential level achievable – and of scaffolding – a supporting framework provided by adults and sometimes peers (see Chapter 20).

Many of the early parent–child social interactions, such as contingent responding and social referencing, discussed in Chapter 19, might also be considered under the heading of social cognition.

Evaluation of the cognitive-developmental approach

The cognitive-developmental perspective is fast becoming the most important influence on the study of development. It links behaviour to the kind of cognition or thinking ability expected at the age or level of development a child is at. As we have seen, Piaget's theory of cognitive development was the starting point, though the approach is not necessarily tied directly to Piaget's ideas. For example, the work of Kohlberg has been influential in the field of moral development and gender role development. A general criticism has been that most research carried out from a cognitive-developmental perspective has viewed development from the standpoint of individual social cognition, emphasizing the individual's perceptions and reasoning about other people and the environment, while neglecting the influence of the surrounding culture. The environment is taken as fixed and the child is thought to develop an understanding of the world because of emerging cognitive processes, which are the same for everyone. However, more and more cognitive-developmental research is starting to be carried out into how aspects of development are influenced by the social interactions and relationships a child experiences. Some of this research will be referred to in the remaining sections of this chapter.

? SELF-ASSESSMENT QUESTIONS

1. Briefly explain your understanding of the cognitive-developmental approach to social behaviour.
2. What do you understand by 'social cognition'?
3. Briefly distinguish between two different developmental approaches to social cognition.

Moral development

The study of moral development has been a topic of research in psychology for over 60 years. An investigation of how children develop moral values involves looking at the processes through which children adopt and internalize the rules and standards of behaviour that are expected in the society that they grow up in. Internalization may be defined as the process through which standards and values become a part of one's own motive system and guide behaviour, even in the absence of pressure from others.

The major theories that have arisen from the study of moral development fall into three main categories:

- the psychodynamic approach arising from Freud's theory;
- the social learning view which draws on the work of Skinner and Bandura; and
- the cognitive-developmental approach characterized by the theories of Piaget, Kohlberg and Eisenberg.

Each of these approaches focuses on a particular aspect of the child's experiences and largely ignores other important considerations. For example, psychodynamic theory emphasizes the emotional aspects of moral development, whereas cognitive-developmental theories stress the links between children's levels of moral reasoning and their stage of cognitive development. Learning theorists emphasize the role of reinforcement, punishment and observational learning.

Each of these three theories will be discussed, together with a brief account of Gilligan's theory of moral orientations and research into child-rearing styles and peer-group influence.

Psychodynamic approach

The first complete theory of moral internalization was Freud's (see the account of Freud's theory in Chapter 30). The central thrust of the theory, which is concerned with the development of the superego or moral arm of the personality, is as follows.

During the phallic stage of psychosexual development, the boy encounters the Oedipus complex. Overwhelmed by feelings of love for his mother and fear of retaliation from his father, the boy identifies with his father. This involves the child taking over all his father's beliefs, values and attitudes, and through his father, the moral standards and values of the culture in which he is growing up. Thus the superego is born.

A similar process exists for a girl as she encounters the Electra complex. Freud, however, though aware that the theory was less well-defined for girls than for boys, believed that females develop a weaker superego and consequently are less moral than men. This has, not unexpectedly, angered modern-day feminists.

The superego

The superego, which is unconscious, consists of two distinct parts: the ego ideal and the conscience.

- The ego ideal is concerned with what is right and proper. It represents the child's image of the sort of virtuous behaviour the parents would approve of.
- The conscience, on the other hand, watches over what is bad. It intercepts and censors immoral impulses from the id and prevents them from entering the consciousness of the ego.

The superego, then, represents the child's internalization of rules and prohibitions, initially imposed by the parents, but later adopted by the child in the form of self-discipline independent of parental approval or displeasure. Thus children become capable of controlling their own behaviour and preventing themselves from indulging in the sorts of behaviour forbidden by their parents. Transgression of moral rules is likely to be followed by feelings of guilt and anxiety.

Psychodynamic theory predicts that the individual with a strong superego is likely to experience greater feelings of guilt in a situation involving a moral dilemma than does the individual with a weaker superego, and is therefore less likely to transgress the

---

> **GLOSSARY**
>
> **Moral development** The process through which children adopt and internalize the rules and standards of behaviour that are expected in the society they are growing up in.
>
> **Internalization** The process through which standards, beliefs and values become part of one's own motive system.
>
> **Superego** Freud's term for that part of the personality which is concerned with morality.
>
> **Ego ideal** That part of the superego which is concerned with the sort of 'good' behaviour that parents would approve of.
>
> **Conscience** That part of the superego which is concerned with preventing immoral impulses from entering the conscious mind.

rules. This theory is widely accepted by psycho-analytic theorists, with minor variations, although its main support comes from scattered observations of adult patients (Hoffman, 1984). However, Hoffman questions whether a largely unconscious, internalized control system can account for all the complexities of moral behaviour. Other researchers have suggested that, although the superego persists during childhood, it is disrupted in adolescence by hormonal changes, social demands and new information about the world that may contradict it (Erikson, 1970).

Social learning approach

Social learning theorists typically avoid terms such as 'moral internalization' and concern themselves solely with observable behaviour. However, in attempting to explain moral behaviour, they do describe a similar phenomenon: the individual's ability to behave in a moral way, or refrain from violating moral rules in conditions of temptation, even when no other person is present.

Social learning theory states that initially a child's behaviour is controlled by rewards and punishments from the parents. Because of a history of experiences where a child is punished for transgressing the rules, painful anxiety will subsequently be experienced whenever the rules are broken, or in situations involving temptation to behave amorally, even if no other person is present. This explanation has much in common with the concept of the superego.

Bandura's work on observational learning also contributes to the social learning view of moral development. It is assumed that one way children learn moral behaviour is by observing and emulating models who behave in a moral way. Observation of models who are punished for amoral behaviour is said to cause the child to experience vicarious punishment, resulting in the child avoiding that behaviour.

A great deal of research has been inspired by social learning theory, but much of it has serious drawbacks. Perhaps the biggest shortcoming arises from the frequent use of controlled experiments in which a single adult–child interaction is used to indicate the presence or absence of moral behaviour in the child. Such a situation cannot adequately reflect the complexities of the 'real life' socialization process.

A study by Bandura and MacDonald (1963) which claims support for the social learning view will be discussed later in this chapter (see Box 22.1).

Cognitive-developmental approach

Piaget emphasized the cognitive aspect of moral development, believing that children's moral thinking is linked to their stage of cognitive development. Using his own type of clinical methodology, Piaget investigated children's attitudes to rules in the game of marbles and their responses to right and wrong and judgment, as depicted in a series of short stories. A well-known example of the latter is the story where children are asked to judge who is naughtier, a boy who accidentally breaks several cups or a boy who breaks one cup while trying to steal jam from the cupboard.

After analysing the responses of numerous children of varying stages of cognitive levels, Piaget concluded that there are two broad stages of moral thinking.

■ The stage of **heteronomous morality** or moral realism: in this stage, the child complies strictly with rules, which are viewed as sacred and unalterable. Right and wrong are seen in 'black and white' terms and a particular act is judged on the size of its consequences, rather than the intentions of the actor. Thus, the child who broke several cups is 'naughtier' than the child who broke only one cup, irrespective of the intentions involved.

■ The shift to the second stage, referred to as **autonomous morality**, or moral relativism, occurs around the age of seven or eight. Rules are viewed as established and maintained through negotiation and agreement within the social group. Judgments of right and wrong are based on intentions as well as consequences. Hence the child who broke a cup in the course of stealing is seen as committing the more serious offence.

Piaget believed that both cognitive development (and therefore maturation) and social experience, particularly interactions with the peer group, play a

GLOSSARY
Heteronomous morality (moral realism) Piaget's first stage of moral realism, where children comply strictly with rules and base judgments about moral issues on consequences rather than intent.
Autonomous reality (moral relativism) Piaget's second stage of moral reasoning which begins to develop around seven. Judgments of moral issues are based on intentions as well as consequences.

Box 22.1 Cognitive versus social learning theory

A basic objection was raised to Piaget's cognitive theory of moral development by Bandura and MacDonald (1963) who doubted the relevance of concepts such as 'stages of development'. In an attempt to explain children's moral judgment through social learning theory they carried out the following experiment.

Groups of children, all of whom had previously taken Piagetian-style tests of moral reasoning, were exposed to a number of conditions in which adult models responded in various ways to similar dilemmas. Results showed that, in general, children imitated their model's responses, even where these responses conflicted with their own usual style of reasoning, as revealed by the earlier Piagetian test. These findings presented a strong challenge to the cognitive approach, which predicts that:

■ children at a particular stage of development would be unlikely to imitate responses which conflicted with their level of moral reasoning;

■ children in a higher stage of development would be unlikely to revert to a lower level of moral reasoning.

Critics of the study have commented on the deficiencies of the experimental design and report, and on Bandura and MacDonald's failure to pay attention to children's reasons for their judgments.

Langer (1975), in a replication of the experiment, found that:

■ the moral judgments of half the children remained the same even after viewing the model;

■ where children's choices did change, the explanations they gave did not.

Langer concluded that the techniques used in Bandura and MacDonald's experiment confused the children, resulting in imitation of the model without true understanding of the reason for the judgment. Hoffman (1979) suggests that children did not merely imitate the model. They were aware that moral acts may not be intentional, but placed less emphasis on intentions because the stories used, like Piaget's, portrayed more serious consequences for accidental rather than intended acts. Perhaps if consequences for accidental and intended acts had been equal the children's responses would have been different.

---

role in the transformation from one stage to the next. In the earlier, heteronomous stage, the child's moral reasoning is influenced by (a) egocentricity (inability to view events from the point of view of others), and (b) dependence on the authority of adults.

Kohlberg's universal stage model

Building upon Piaget's work, Kohlberg (1969, 1976) attempted to produce a more detailed and comprehensive account of moral development. Like Piaget, Kohlberg focused on an individual's reasoning when presented with a series of moral dilemmas in the form of short stories (see an example in Box 22.2). Kohlberg's 'moral stories' have been presented to thousands of people of all ages, intelligence levels and socio-economic backgrounds.

Kohlberg sees moral development as occurring at three levels: preconventional morality, conventional morality and postconventional (or principled) morality; each level contains two distinct stages. Figure 22.1 gives a brief description of the six stages. He stated that these stages are fixed and that everyone passes through them in the same order, starting at the lowest level. The end product of progression through these stages is a mature and reasoned sense of justice.

Many studies have provided supporting evidence of the links between children's moral reasoning and their stage of cognitive development. However, Kohlberg's theory has also generated much controversy. Debate centres on the main tenets of Kohlberg's theory, that is, that moral reasoning is linked to cognitive development and the stage sequence is the same for everyone,

GLOSSARY

Preconventional morality The first level of moral reasoning proposed by Kohlberg. Rules are kept so that punishment is avoided and judgments are dominated by what is favourable to oneself.

Conventional morality Kohlberg's second level of moral reasoning, where children's values are influenced by society's rules and norms.

Postconventional morality (principled) Kohlberg's final level of moral reasoning, where values are dominated by principles of equality, justice and individual rights.

Figure 22.1 Kohlberg's six stages of moral development

Level 1: Preconventional (Middle childhood)

Stage 1: Punishment and obedience orientation

Rules are kept in order that punishment may be avoided. The consequences of an action determine the extent to which that action is good or bad.

The interests and points of view of others are not considered, i.e. the child is egocentric

Stage 2: Instrumental relativist orientation

A 'right' action is one that is favourable to oneself rather than to others. Some consideration is given to the needs of others, but only where the result is favourable to oneself.

Level 2: Conventional (Approximate age 13–16 years)

Stage 3: 'Good boy/girl' orientation

An action is judged as right or wrong according to the intentions of the actor. Socially acceptable standards of behaviour are valued, and 'being good' is important.

Stage 4: 'Law and order' orientation

There emerges a profound respect for authority, and a belief that society's rules must be kept.

Consideration is given to the point of view of the system that makes the rules, in addition to the motives of the individual.

Level 3: Postconventional or Principled (Approximate age 16–20)

Stage 5: Social-contract legalistic orientation

What is right is judged in relation to the majority opinion within a particular society. 'The greatest good for the greatest number' is the general rule. It is recognized that moral and legal points of view sometimes conflict with each other.

Stage 6: Universal principles of conscience

Self-chosen ethical principles now dictate one's actions: the equality of human rights and respect for the dignity of human beings as individuals are of paramount importance. When laws conflict with these principles, one acts in accordance with the principle.

It is likely that these young people, taking part in an anti-racism march, have reached the principled level of moral reasoning

Box 22.2 The story of Heinz

One of the most famous of Kohlberg's stories relating to a moral issue involves the dilemma of Heinz:

> In Europe, a woman was near death from a special kind of cancer. There was one drug that the doctors thought might save her. It was a form of radium that a druggist in the same town had recently discovered. The drug was expensive to make, but the druggist was charging ten times what the drug cost him to make. He paid $200 for the radium and charged $2000 for a small dose of the drug. The sick woman's husband, Heinz, went to everyone he knew to borrow the money, but he could only get together about $1000 which is half of what it cost. He told the druggist that his wife was dying, and asked him to sell it cheaper or let him pay later. But the druggist said, 'No, I discovered the drug and I'm going to make money from it.' So Heinz got desperate and broke into the man's store to steal the drug for his wife.
>
> (Kohlberg and Elfenbein, 1975, p. 621)

After listening to the story, the person is asked some questions. For example: 'Should Heinz have stolen the drug?'; 'Would anything be different if Heinz didn't love his wife?'; 'What if the person dying was a stranger to Heinz? Should he still steal the drug?'

On the basis of people's answers to dilemmas such as this one, Kohlberg concluded that there are three main stages of moral reasoning, each having two stages within it (see Figure 22.1).

While the ages at which people attain different levels varies, participants' responses to Kohlberg's moral dilemmas indicate that, in general, children in middle childhood are preconventional (level 1), younger adolescents (13–16 years) are at the conventional level (level 2), and about half of older adolescents (16–20 years) attain the principled level (level 3). Cross-cultural studies have revealed that the same sequence of stages exists in certain other cultures (Kohlberg, 1969).

Critique of Kohlberg's theory

Research evidence Rest (1983) reviewed a dozen cross-sectional and longitudinal studies and reported that participants did generally develop moral reasoning in the direction proposed by Kohlberg's theory. However, some participants showed no improvement in moral reasoning over time and one in 14 participants who were in school actually moved back to an earlier stage. In a strict interpretation of stage theory, participants should continue to move to higher stages and regression to an earlier stage should not occur.

Principled reasoning (level 3) has not been found at all in some groups. Moran and Joniak (1979) showed that scores on moral judgment tests were closely linked to the sophistication of language used. Therefore, those people whose command of language, particularly the use of abstract terms, is poor may be wrongly judged to be operating at a lower level of moral reasoning than they are actually capable of.

Cross-cultural evidence Kohlberg claimed that the six stages of moral reasoning exist in all cultures. His own study (1969) found that children in Britain, Mexico, Taiwan, Turkey and the USA showed similar sequences of development. Gardner (1982) questioned whether it is appropriate to apply Kohlberg's approach to other cultures, since moral judgments in other cultures may be based on very different values and priorities from those in Western cultures.

In a review of 44 studies completed in 26 different cultures around the world, Snarey (1985) concluded that there is much support for the cross-cultural universality of Kohlberg's theory. Edwards (1986), in a review of a large number of cross-cultural studies, drew similar conclusions.

Moral reasoning and moral behaviour A major criticism of Kohlberg's work concerns the extent to which there is a positive relationship between moral reasoning and moral behaviour. In general, there is evidence of a link between the two. The following studies are relevant.

In one study (Milgram, 1974) participants were led to believe that they were administering severe shocks to another person. It was later found that those participants who refused to administer shocks when instructed to do so by an authority figure were more likely to be at the principled level of moral reasoning

and on the relationship between Kohlberg's stages and moral *behaviour*. A brief discussion of some relevant research follows.

than were those who did administer shocks. However, these findings might have been the result of other factors not examined in the study, such as intelligence level or naivety about psychological experiments.

Many more recent studies have found a positive relationship between moral reasoning as tested by Kohlberg's model, and moral behaviour. However, rarely has a strong link been established (Kutnik, 1986).

Richards et al. (1992) found that children classified as either Stage 1 or Stage 3 were less likely to be rated by their teachers as exhibiting conduct disorders than those classified as Stage 2. Kohlberg's theory would predict a consistent trend towards better behaviour with increasing moral maturity.

The relationship between moral reasoning and moral behaviour is clearly a complex one which further research findings may clarify.

Exercise 22.1

Try out one of Kohlberg's 'moral stories' (e.g., the Heinz dilemma in Box 22.2) on children and adults of a range of different ages. Record their answers and see how well they fit in with Kohlberg's stages of moral reasoning (Figure 22.1).

Box 22.3   Social contexts of moral development

The family context

Since children's first and most pervasive exposure to moral regulations takes place within the family context, it is to be expected that the beginnings of morality are to be found here. Many researchers have argued that the attachment process in infancy (see Chapter 19) is of crucial importance and have noted that securely attached infants have been found to comply favourably to parents' rules (Speicher, 1994). Observational studies by Kagan (1989) and Dunn and Brown (1994) found that rudimentary moral awareness was apparent in children as young as 21 months and was very closely tied to social interactions within the family. Durkin (1995) argues:

> A serious limitation of both Piaget's and Kohlberg's theories of moral development is that they under-estimate the knowledge and abilities of the preschooler, and fail to incorporate the early social developmental contexts of morality into their models.
>
> (Durkin, 1995, p. 489)

There is a large body of research which suggests that the type of parental discipline administered in childhood affects moral development. In a review of the research, Hoffman (1978) draws attention to two contrasting styles of discipline used by parents:

■ the use of 'inductions', that is discipline techniques which encourage children to reflect on their behaviour and consider the effects of wrongdoing on other people;
■ 'power assertive' discipline, which involves the use of force, threats and withdrawal of privileges.

The central finding is that the frequent use of inductions fosters a personality who behaves morally even when there is no pressure from others to do so, and who is likely to experience strong guilt feelings when she or he does transgress. In contrast, the use of power assertive techniques by parents is associated with individuals who behave morally solely to avoid punishment.

It has been pointed out that most of the studies were correlational, and therefore prevented inferences about a causal link (see Chapter 31) between type of discipline and moral internalization. However, Hoffman argued that the weight of evidence is such that it must be assumed that style of parental discipline does strongly influence moral development.

Peer influences

Despite its undoubted importance, there has been little research on how interaction with peers affects a child's moral development. Correlational studies have shown a negative relationship between early comfortable and frequent interactions with peers and rates of delinquency during adolescence (Conger and Miller, 1966).

Experimental research reviewed by Hoffman indicates that if a child observes a peer who behaves aggressively and is not punished, there is an increased likelihood of that child also behaving aggressively.

The role of peers in moral socialization, and the influence of school experiences (an area which has been neglected), await further research.

If this child is encouraged to think about the feelings of others when he has transgressed, he is more likely to behave better in the future

Eisenberg's model of prosocial reasoning

Kohlberg's moral dilemmas tended to be concerned with misdeeds such as stealing or disobeying laws. They do not investigate children's reasoning in relation to **prosocial behaviour** (actions that are intended to help or benefit another person). Eisenberg and her colleagues (Eisenberg, 1986; Eisenberg et al., 1987) have examined this issue by asking children to respond to stories in which a choice has to be made between self-interest and helping another person. In a typical story, a child is on his way to a birthday party when he comes upon another child who has fallen and hurt himself. If he stops to help he might miss the party food. What should he do?

Eisenberg found a clear developmental sequence in children's responses to stories like this. Typically, preschool children were concerned with the implications for themselves rather than with moral considerations. They say things such as 'I wouldn't stop because I might miss the party' or 'I'd stop and help because he might help me sometime'. Eisenberg calls this **hedonistic reasoning**. Gradually, children begin to display what Eisenberg calls **needs-oriented reasoning**. Here the child expresses concern for the well-being of the other person even if the need is in conflict with the child's own wishes. A typical statement might be 'I'd help because he'd feel better'. There is no attempt to express generalized principles or values; the reaction is one of responding to need. Figure 22.2 contains a brief overview of Eisenberg's stages of prosocial reasoning.

Figure 22.2 Eisenberg's stages of prosocial reasoning

Stage 1 Hedonistic, pragmatic orientation
Children are concerned with their own selfish goals rather than moral issues. 'Good behaviour' is whatever helps them to meet their own needs.

Stage 2 Needs of others orientation
There is concern with the needs of others, even though these may be in conflict with one's own needs.

Stage 3 Approval and interpersonal orientation and/or stereotyped orientation
Thinking is dominated by stereotyped ideas of how 'good people' and 'bad people' behave.

Stage 4a Empathetic orientation
At this stage, there emerge some signs of sympathetic responding, concern for others and/or feelings of guilt or positive feelings in relation to one's own behaviour.

Stage 4b Transitional
There is some evidence of the internalization of values, norms, duties or responsibilities in relation to helping others.

Stage 5 Strongly internalized
This is similar to Stage 4b, but the existence of internalized values etc. is much more obvious. The individual is concerned with a desire to meet obligations in relation to other individuals and society, and with a conviction about the rights and equality of all other people.

Later, in adolescence, children typically say they will do helpful things because it is expected of them. For example, a typical response might be 'Society would be a better place if we all helped each other'. In general, young people at this stage show that they have developed and internalized clear guiding principles in relation to prosocial behaviour. The pattern here is very similar to that shown at Kohlberg's level 3 (principled reasoning). Eisenberg has reported that similar sequences have been found among children in West Germany, Poland and Italy.

Though there are obvious similarities between the pattern of prosocial reasoning found by Eisenberg and Kohlberg's levels of moral reasoning, researchers have not found a strong correlation between the two. Though the stages are similar, children seem to move through them at different rates.

Though it has not changed the fundamental principles of Kohlberg's theory, Eisenberg's research has provided for a broader and more complete view of the nature of children's moral and prosocial reasoning.

(Note that altruism and prosocial behaviour are discussed also in Chapters 18 and 26.)

Gender and morality

An area of controversy currently surrounding Kohlberg's theory concerns the possibility of gender differences in moral reasoning. Archer (1989) argues that to some extent boys and girls develop in different social worlds. They experience different opportunities and different constraints and social expectations. Durkin (1995) asks whether these differences lead to different kinds of morality.

Much research evidence suggests that there are differences between males and females when Kohlbergian measures of moral reasoning are used (Holstein, 1976). For example, findings from a longitudinal study of adolescents by Holstein revealed that the most frequent score for boys was around Stage 4, while girls' scores tended to be around Stage 3. One possible interpretation of these findings is that moral reasoning in females is inferior to that of boys. Unsurprisingly, this argument has provoked a heated and emotive debate.

Gilligan's 'moral orientations'

Gilligan (1977, 1982) has challenged the very basis of Kohlberg's theory. She has argued that his focus on the development of concepts of justice is based on male ways of viewing life and therefore his measures of moral reasoning are biased against females.

Gilligan's arguments include the following:

■ There are two distinct **moral orientations**: justice and care. Each has its own inbuilt assumption –

not to behave unfairly towards others (justice) and not to ignore someone in need (caring). Males and females learn both of these principles, Gilligan hypothesizes, but boys are more likely to operate from an orientation of justice, while girls are more likely to operate from an orientation of caring.

■ Boys are brought up to be independent and achievement-oriented and are therefore concerned with issues such as equality of treatment and applying abstract principles to resolve conflicts of interest. In contrast, girls are encouraged to be caring and concerned for the well-being of others.

■ The gender differences described, Gilligan argues, may result in boys and girls using different criteria when judging moral dilemmas.

Gilligan's model generated a lot of debate and stimulated a number of research studies designed to examine possible gender differences in reasoning about moral dilemmas. Some studies of adults have found that there is a tendency for males to use 'justice' reasoning and females 'care' reasoning (Lyons, 1983). However, this pattern has not been replicated in studies of children. For example, Walker et al. (1987) applied Kohlberg's justice scheme and Gilligan's criteria for a care orientation to participants' responses to moral dilemmas. He found no gender differences among children and only adults produced the pattern that would be expected by Gilligan.

Gilligan's proposals are by no means proved. However, the value of her work lies in the fact that a new debate has been opened up about possible gender differences. There is no conclusive evidence that males take a justice orientation in moral reasoning and females a caring orientation. However, this does not mean that there are no differences in the assumptions that males and females bring to moral judgments. Further research might be enlightening.

> **GLOSSARY**
>
> **Moral orientations** Gilligan's term for two distinct styles of responding to moral issues: justice and care. Boys are more likely to operate from an orientation of justice, while girls are more likely to operate from an orientation of caring.

? SELF-ASSESSMENT QUESTIONS

1. Outline both the psychodynamic and the social learning theory approaches to moral development.
2. According to Piaget, what would be the main differences in moral reasoning between a five-year-old child and a nine-year-old child?
3. Discuss two similarities between the work of Piaget and that of Kohlberg in the area of moral development.
4. Briefly evaluate Kohlberg's theory, referring to relevant research evidence.
5. What are the central findings from research into parental discipline and moral development?
6. In what ways has Gilligan's theory of 'moral orientations' challenged the findings from Kohlberg's work?

Development of gender

The study of how individuals develop a gender role (or sex role) has been a central concern of developmental psychologists for many years. Gender role development has been an important focus of debate within the major theories of psychology, and is a frequent target of the nature–nurture controversy.

The study of gender role development is beset by a proliferation of similar, often confusing terms. 'Sex' and 'gender' are defined in many dictionaries as synonymous and are often used as such. Thus, different researchers may refer to 'sex-role' or 'gender role' and mean essentially the same thing – behaviour considered by society to be appropriate for males and females. Because the term 'sex' has a number of meanings and is usually associated with biological/genital differences, there has been a trend towards using 'gender' to refer to the psychological/cultural aspects of maleness and femaleness. (Huston, 1983, has produced a detailed account of sex role taxonomies and definitions.)

Masculinity and femininity

Throughout history, men and women have been perceived as psychologically different in many important ways. These differences have usually been accepted as 'natural' and closely linked to the roles played by the sexes in society. Over the last two decades, however, following the emergence of the women's liberation movement, a great deal of research has raised doubts about the 'natural' nature of these differences and has questioned why it is that women's roles are typically of lower status than those of men.

Research into differences between the sexes has generally posed one of two types of question: first, what characteristics do typical males and females possess and how do they differ? Secondly, to what extent do individuals perceive themselves to be masculine or feminine? The first question deals with gender stereotypes. The second deals with gender identity.

Gender stereotypes

This refers to rigid beliefs about what males and females are like. Numerous studies have identified characteristics which can be said to form stereotypes of males and females and there appears to be strong agreement between them. One example is a study carried out by Spence et al. (1975) in which the researchers used an instrument known as the Personal Attributes Questionnaire with large samples of college men and women. Some of the characteristics attributed to males and females were as follows:

Males	Females
Independent	Emotional
Assertive	Warm to others
Aggressive	Creative
Dominant	Excitable
Like maths and science	Feelings easily hurt
Mechanical aptitude	Need approval

GLOSSARY

Gender role (sex role) Behaviour, attitudes and activities that are considered by a particular society to be appropriate for males and females.

Sex The term used to denote biological/genital aspects of being male or female.

Gender Usually used to refer to psychological/cultural aspects of males and females.

Gender stereotype (sex stereotype) Excessively rigid beliefs about what males and females are like and how they should behave.

Gender identity Perception of oneself as masculine or feminine.

Ruble (1988) suggested that stereotypes of males and females had changed little in the last 20 years, at least among college students, despite the feminist movement and growing concern with equality between the sexes. In the USA, Bergen and Williams (1991) found a very high correlation (0.9) between stereotyped perceptions of the sexes in 1972 and those in 1988. Other research, for example Williams and Best (1990), has found that the overall gender stereotypes revealed in American research tend to exist also in countries in Asia, Africa and Europe.

Gender identity

This refers to people's perceptions of themselves as either masculine or feminine. Early research into gender identity tended to place a high value on sex-typing. An important aim of the research was to look for ways of helping males and females to acquire appropriate sex-typed attitudes and behaviour in order to promote their psychological well-being. Masculinity and femininity were seen as representing opposite ends of a continuum, and it was assumed that an individual would exhibit either masculine characteristics or feminine characteristics, but not both.

More recently, Bem (1974) and others have criticized this bipolar approach, claiming that both so-called masculine and feminine characteristics may develop in the same individual. For example, a person may be both assertive (a characteristic generally associated with masculinity) and sensitive to the needs of others (thought of as a feminine characteristic) and still function effectively. Bem has used the term **androgynous** to describe people who possess both masculine and feminine characteristics.

Bem's research stimulated a large number of studies which attempted to determine whether androgynous individuals are more psychologically healthy and well-adjusted than are individuals who are rigidly typed as either masculine or feminine. Though there have been a few inconsistencies, most research has confirmed that this is in fact the case. For example, several studies have reported that androgynous individuals score higher on measures of self-esteem than do individuals who are rigidly sex-typed (S.L. Bem, 1983). However, several researchers have found weak or no differences between androgynous and masculine-typed individuals on measures such as self-esteem. Also, it has been suggested that masculine characteristics tend to be more highly valued in Western societies than are

feminine characteristics and it may be mainly the masculine aspects of an androgynous personality that are positively related to psychological flexibility and adjustment.

Sex differences in behaviour

Many studies have attempted to discover whether commonly held beliefs about the characteristics of men and women are borne out by the way in which people actually behave. A comprehensive review of the literature was published by Maccoby and Jacklin in 1974 (see Box 22.4).

Reviews using meta-analysis

Later reviews of sex differences attempted to avoid some of the methodological problems found in Maccoby and Jacklin's review (see Box 22.4) by using a technique called **meta-analysis**. Meta-analysis is a way of aggregating and statistically analysing the results of a number of independent studies in relation to a particular hypothesis.

Studies using the technique of meta-analysis, for example Eaton and Enns (1986), have found reliable sex differences in activity level, aggression, influencability, empathy, mathematical reasoning and spatial ability. Brownmiller (1984) found differences in language ability in favour of females. Generally, however, the sex differences found in research have been very small – accounting for less than 5 per cent of the variance – or they have been confined to studies which used particular methods. It is worth noting also that the more recent meta-analyses of cognitive sex differences have shown females to be performing better relative to males than in earlier studies.

The influence of situational factors

Before we leave the question of whether in reality there are genuine psychological differences between males

---

GLOSSARY

Androgynous Used to describe individuals who possess both masculine and feminine characteristics and whose behaviour does not conform rigidly to that for either males or females.

Meta-analysis A statistical technique which is used to aggregate and analyse the results of a number of independent studies in relation to a particular hypothesis.

Box 22.4   Maccoby and Jacklin's review

Maccoby and Jacklin (1974) investigated over 2000 studies of sex differences in personality or intellectual abilities, comparing studies which reported statistically significant sex differences with studies which did not find statistically significant differences. Maccoby and Jacklin reported the existence of sex differences in only four areas: aggressive behaviour and mathematical, spatial and verbal abilities. Specifically, they observed:

■ From the age of around eight or nine, girls score higher than boys on tests of verbal ability, whereas boys perform better on mathematical and spatial tasks from puberty onwards;
■ Boys are more physically aggressive than girls. This difference is evident at all ages from about two years on, and across many different cultures.

In other areas where sex differences have been claimed, Maccoby and Jacklin could find no reliable supporting evidence.

Maccoby and Jacklin's findings provoked a great deal of controversy, largely centring on the methodology used in their review. A number of points have been made.

■ Some of the studies reviewed were methodologically weaker than others, employing smaller sample sizes and less powerful statistical analyses. Such studies are less likely to find true sex differences. Maccoby and Jacklin's approach in giving each study equal weight could lead to an underrepresentation of true sex differences.
■ Studies which do detect sex differences are more likely to be published than those which show no significant difference. Therefore an overrepresentation of sex differences could be present in Maccoby and Jacklin's review.
■ The way studies were categorized may have obscured sex differences. For example, broad categories such as 'social sensitivity' may include characteristics such as role taking, nurturance and empathy. So: for example, a large number of studies with a 'no differences' finding in role taking might obscure a true difference in, say, nurturance or empathy.

and females, we should note the possible effect of situational factors in the studies carried out. Particular features of a study may differentially influence the way males and females respond, which could lead to contamination of the results. For example, subtle influences such as the sex of the researcher, the relative number of males and females in the room and the topic under investigation may encourage participants to behave in line with current stereotypes of males and females. And researchers themselves may subconsciously be influenced by their own stereotypic beliefs. For example, it is interesting to note that studies of conformity carried out by women are less likely to find sex differences than those conducted by men (Eagly and Carli, 1981). However, Eagly (1987) discusses this 'sex of researchers' effect and concludes that it is not a robust one.

What can we conclude about sex differences in behaviour?

On the basis of current evidence, little justification can be found for existing gender stereotypes and it seems that males and females are much more similar than has generally been thought. So why has there been so much empirical and theoretical attention given to the development of gender roles and gender identity? One reason is that whether or not basic characteristics of males and females are similar, their roles in society are very different. In general, adult men and women have very different roles and responsibilities in the home, and in the workplace they operate in very different fields of activity: women represent the majority of secretaries, nurses and teachers, while men account for almost all engineers, carpenters and mechanics. In the so-called higher professions of medicine and law, whilst women are gaining ground in terms of their overall representation, they are grossly underrepresented in the more prestigious, senior posts.

Gender differentiation   Gender differentiation begins very early on. As young as two or three, boys can be seen playing in different ways from girls: boys are more likely to be found playing with construction toys and to engage in considerable 'rough and tumble' play; girls are more likely to be found playing with dolls or household toys. By adolescence, distinctive roles are established both in behaviour and in

From an early age, there are gender differences in the choice of toys

interests and occupational choices. So, differentiation between the sexes is pervasive and the study of developmental processes can help us to understand why. And not just to satisfy our scientific curiosity: a knowledge of the processes involved can help our understanding of those factors which may lead to atypical development such as transsexualism. It also informs our ability to make decisions about whether to recommend clinical intervention for an individual who is mentally disturbed. On the other hand we may wish to use our understanding to promote gender equality. Gender differentiation may be seen as wholly unacceptable because it limits the scope of opportunities available to males and females. For example, social sanctions are often imposed on men who want to stay at home to look after their children and on women who do not.

Given that gender differentiation exists from a very early age, what are the factors which cause boys and girls to behave differently and to have particular beliefs about sex-appropriate behaviour? This question has been approached from a number of different theoretical perspectives.

Factors that influence gender role development

Biological factors

There are two main types of physical characteristics which may play a part in gender role differences and which have been considered by researchers.

- **Chromosomal sex**. Males and females differ in one pair of chromosomes. Prenatally, the presence of a Y chromosome in males leads the embryo to develop testes; the absence of the Y chromosome in females results in the development of ovaries.
- **Hormonal differences**. Hormones affect prenatal sex differences in anatomy and brain differentiation. Though males and females can produce the same range of hormones, males produce far more androgens than females, the most important androgen being testosterone. Females produce mainly oestrogen and progesterone.

It is thought that these two physical characteristics, chromosomal and hormonal differences, affect the genetic blueprint which determines masculinity and

---

Exercise 22.2 Investigating stereotypes

Make a list of about 15 adult occupations or activities. Give a copy of the list to a number of adults, asking them to indicate for each item whether it is suitable for males, females or equally appropriate for both sexes.

Record the responses and decide whether they indicate the existence of any definite masculine and/or feminine stereotypes.

Repeat the investigation with children of different ages. Are there any obvious similarities or differences between these responses and those from the adult group?

You could carry out a similar investigation using a list of children's toys and activities.

femininity. (There may also be differences between the two sexes in the way the brain is organized, though as yet there is no firm evidence.)

The question arises as to what extent these obvious biological differences also extend to psychological development. What clues can be found about the extent to which biological factors may influence gender role behaviour? One line of enquiry has been to make cross-cultural comparisons.

Cross-cultural studies   The underlying rationale of this approach is that the sex differences which exist in many different cultures ought to imply that there is a biological basis. In nearly all cultures women are the main caretakers, while men are the warriors and protectors. There is evidence, too, of consistent sex differences across cultures in characteristics such as dominance, aggression and interest in infants. Though these findings suggest biological influences, caution must be exercised in drawing firm conclusions. Cross-cultural similarities in sex roles might be explained by similarities in socialization practices across different cultures. Also, there are some notable examples of differences between cultures (see Box 22.5).

Despite the lack of firm evidence from cross-cultural studies, a suggestion does exist of consistent sex differences in aggression and parenting which may result from biological influences, possibly combined with socialization.

Hormonal influences   Numerous animal studies have provided evidence of the effects of hormones on behaviour. Typically, male and female rats are injected with hormones appropriate to the opposite sex during a sensitive period early in development. Such animals later exhibit behaviour characteristics of the opposite sex. Behaviour studied includes aggression, parenting, rough and tumble play and mating behaviour. These findings suggest that hormonal influences in nonhuman mammals are responsible for the animals behaving in a masculine or feminine manner. However, the effects of hormone manipulations may vary from species to species, and how relevant such findings are to the understanding of sex differences in humans remains a matter for debate.

For obvious ethical reasons, it is not possible experimentally to manipulate the hormonal state of humans. Nevertheless, some studies have been carried out on humans who, for various reasons, develop

---

Box 22.5   Gender roles in New Guinea (Mead, 1935)

Probably the best known example of differences in gender role development between cultures can be found in Margaret Mead's classic study of three primitive tribes in New Guinea (1935).

- In the Arapesh tribe, both males and females exhibited gentle nonaggressive, affectionate characteristics, behaving in ways traditionally associated with femininity in Western cultures.
- Among the Mundugumor tribe, both males and females behaved in what we would call a 'masculine' way – aggressive and assertive.
- The Tchambuli tribe completely reversed sex roles as we know them. Women were assertive, made decisions about the economic organization of the tribe and looked after the collection of food; men, on the other hand, took few decisions and spent a lot of time following artistic pursuits.

Mead concluded that sex roles are culturally, rather than biologically, determined. However, Mead has been accused of exaggerating the differences between the Arapesh and Mundugumor tribes. Also, in a later book, she adopted the view that there were 'natural' differences between males and females, females being more nurturing and intuitive than males.

---

abnormal hormonal conditions. For example, a foetus can be exposed to unusual hormone levels if a mother receives hormone injections for medical reasons during pregnancy.

Several studies have indicated that females exposed to male hormones before birth often later exhibit more masculine gender-role behaviour than matched control groups of girls who were not exposed to the hormone (Money and Erhardt, 1972; Hines, 1982). This suggests that hormones may control sex-related behaviour in humans as it does in animals. However, the interpretation of these findings is not so straightforward as might appear. Children exposed to abnormal hormones before birth are often born with some abnormality of the genitals. It is possible, therefore, that a girl's more masculine behaviour reflects her own, her parents' and possibly the investigator's reactions to her more masculine appearance. This research highlights the difficulty of separating out the effects of biological factors from socialization processes.

In general, research into the effects of prenatal hormones in humans suggests that sex hormones may have some effect on behaviour. For example, it is possible that during normal foetal development, sex hormones predispose boys to become more physically active and interested in rough and tumble play. However, while it is impossible to conclude that biological factors do *not* play an important part in any thorough explanation of sex differences, they cannot by themselves explain the process of gender role development.

Biosocial theory

Money and Erhardt argue that in most cases social learning can override biological processes; gender identity is usually consistent with the sex of rearing rather than genetic sex. Money and Erhardt's argument is often referred to as the biosocial approach.

The biosocial approach is based on extensive study of individuals whose genetic endowment is at odds with the way they have been reared. One very striking example of such a case is that of a monozygotic (produced from a single egg) twin boy who was reared as a girl because of an accident to his penis during a circumcision operation (Money and Erhardt, 1972). At 17 months, the child was given surgery to create a vagina and then was given steroids. According to the parents, this reassignment of sex was very successful. Studies like this and the many studies where an individual has been born with a genetic abnormality, such as **hermaphroditism**, suggest that the effects of the socialization process are very powerful indeed. (Hermaphroditism refers to a condition in which a person has functioning sexual organs of both sexes.) Money and Erhardt suggested that provided a clear and consistent gender assignment is made by around the age of three, there will be no problems of adjustment to gender reassignment.

Socialization influences

Biological factors may predispose males and females to adopt particular gender behaviour. However, most investigators agree that cultural influences and socialization processes are the main determinants of an individual's gender role identity and roles. Debate continues, however, about how the child learns gender identity and when during development this learning occurs. Two theories will be briefly considered.

Freud's psychoanalytic theory (see Chapter 30) suggests that during the phallic stage of development, the child encounters the Oedipus/Electra complex. Satisfactory resolution of the conflict results in the child identifying with the same-sex parent. Thus the sex-appropriate attitudes and behaviour of the parent become internalized during the child's socialization.

As has already been noted, psychoanalytic theory is open to much criticism and controversy, and verification of the existence of the Oedipus/Electra complex has not been empirically established.

Social learning theorists (see Chapter 6) maintain that gender role identity and behaviour are, like all behaviour, learned through the processes of reinforcement and modelling. Children are said to be shaped towards male or female roles. Children learn by being rewarded for sex-appropriate behaviour and punished for inappropriate behaviour, and by imitating the behaviour of male and female models such as their parents (initially).

Thus, if we look at reinforcement, boys may receive approval for aggressive behaviour, whereas girls would be penalized for the same behaviour; dependency may be encouraged in girls but frowned upon in boys. One problem with this explanation is that although we know that reinforcement does affect behaviour, it is not always easy to know what is reinforcing. Take the example of the toddler who throws a tantrum in the supermarket and is reprimanded by her father. If the child's behaviour is aimed at attention seeking, then her father's anger will be reinforcing and the behaviour will be repeated.

Huston (1983) claims that there is little firm evidence that children are more likely to imitate a model of the same sex rather than of the other sex. He suggests that the role of observational learning in the development of gender roles may be oversimplified. The modelling process is likely to be affected by such things as the characteristics of the model and the extent to which the model reflects the young person's own characteristics (Duck, 1990) The child's perception of the situation and of the importance of gender are also

---

GLOSSARY

Hermaphroditism A condition where a child is born with functioning sexual organs of both sexes.

important factors. (See also Box 22.5, Gender roles in New Guinea.)

There is a wealth of research which indicates that boys and girls receive different socialization experiences. Below is a selection of that research.

Studies of socialization influences

Maccoby and Jacklin (1974) found little evidence that boys were reinforced for aggression and girls for dependency. They concluded that infant and toddler girls and boys were treated very similarly. However, Maccoby and Jacklin may have failed to detect subtle differences in treatment.

Smith and Lloyd (1978) have shown that boys are encouraged in more physical activities than are girls. Several other studies have shown that adults are more likely to offer a doll to a child they think is a girl and toys such as trucks or blocks to a child they think is a boy.

Parke and Suomi (1980) showed that fathers are more likely to engage in physical rough and tumble play with their sons than with their daughters.

Fagot (1978) found that parents consistently show more approval when children behave appropriately to their sex and react negatively when girls or boys behave in an inappropriate way.

Langlois and Downs (1980) found that both boys and girls are put under pressure by parents to behave in gender-appropriate ways, but this is particularly true of fathers. It seems, also, that boys are put under more pressure than girls.

Eccles-Parsons (1983) argued that many studies show that parents' expectations of achievement, particularly mathematical accomplishment, are lower for girls than for boys.

There is considerable evidence that people do respond differently to boys and girls on the basis of the expectations of what girls and boys are like. In one study by Rubin et al. (1974) parents were asked to describe their newborn babies as they would to a close friend. Even though boys and girls were very similar in health and in size and weight, they were described very differently. Boys were generally depicted as more alert, stronger and better coordinated than girls. Girls were described as smaller, softer and less attentive than boys.

Cognitive-developmental theory

Social learning theory stresses the influence of external pressures on children's developing gender identity and behaviour and these influences clearly play a major part. However, the effect of these influences cannot be fully understood without a consideration of internal factors within the child. In applying cognitive-developmental theory to the development of gender roles and identity, Kohlberg (1966) believed that the most important factor is the child's level of cognitive development.

Development of gender constancy Kohlberg argued that early in life the child is labelled as 'boy' or 'girl' and this categorization leads to the child's perception of him or herself as masculine or feminine. This gender self-concept coupled with the child's growing knowledge and understanding of gender, directs and organizes his or her activities and ways of thinking. Thus, a girl may in effect say to herself, 'I am a girl and I must behave like a girl'. A key stage in the process involves the child's acquisition of gender constancy. This refers to the child's knowledge and understanding that gender is a consistent and stable characteristic and that gender is constant even if a person wears opposite-sex clothes or takes part in opposite-sex activities. Though children appear to be able to apply gender labels to themselves and other people from around two years old, it is thought that gender constancy is not fully acquired until around five or six years old. (It is thought to coincide with the child's understanding of the constancy of objects as illustrated in Piaget's conservation tasks.)

The link with levels of cognitive ability A central feature of cognitive-developmental theory is that the child's growing cognitive abilities lie at the heart of gender role development. The theory suggests that as children's conceptual awareness increases, so they are motivated to search for more information about gender role. One way of doing this is to look for models of gender-appropriate behaviour. This aspect of cognitive-developmental theory has something in common with social learning theory in that it

---

GLOSSARY

Gender constancy A child's understanding that gender is a consistent and stable characteristic despite changes in appearance, dress or activity.

Box 22.6   Gender and the media

Development of gender roles, like the acquisition of other complex behaviour, is unlikely to be the result solely of differential treatment and reinforcement. Therefore, many researchers have concerned themselves with how children may learn masculine or feminine behaviour by imitating same-sex models in the media. There is a growing body of research into this issue.

Male and female stereotypes abound in the literature and television as well as in the 'real' world. In most areas of television, whether light entertainment programmes or documentaries, males outnumber females 7:3 (Durkin, 1985). Males are usually represented in more dominant roles with higher occupational status, while females are often shown in subordinate roles and in traditional feminine occupations, such as housewife, nurse or secretary. In TV commercials, women are more likely to be shown using products, particularly domestic products, while men are generally seen as receiving their services or commenting on the quality of the products. These sorts of findings have been found repeatedly in research in North America, Britain, Australia, Italy and other countries (Davis, 1990; Furnham and Bitar, 1993). And sex stereotypes exist also in other media to which children are exposed, including radio advertisements, the lyrics and style of pop music videos, and the content of teen magazines.

The above findings are remarkable, but how influential are these models during gender role development? Is there a relationship between viewing such material and the acquisition of particular behaviour and attitudes? Research findings are not always clear.

Some studies have reported a positive correlation between the amount of television children watch and the likelihood of their subscribing to stereotyped beliefs (Levy, 1989). However, these findings do not present such a clear picture as they appear to. First, in the majority of studies the correlations found were rather small. Also, it should be remembered that the technique of correlation does not imply causation (see Chapter 34). It might be that children who are already strongly sex-typed prefer to watch a lot of television because it supports their own stereotyped beliefs. In Levy's (1989) study, it was found that girls who preferred educational TV programmes showed much more gender role flexibility than other girls.

Interestingly, one investigation, a large-scale field experiment, found that children sometimes change their stereotyped attitudes when they are presented with counter-stereotyped television programmes (Johnson and Ettema, 1982).

It seems that media content might be implicated in gender role development, but the findings of research are by no means conclusive.

---

suggests that modelling plays an important part. However, unlike social learning theory, the suggestion here is that modelling the behaviour, attitudes and values related to a particular gender role takes place as a result of the child's developing cognitive processes. Information about gender-appropriate attributes is *actively* sought out rather than *passively* acquired (Martin, 1991).

Self-socialization   A wealth of research supports the claim that children's gender role awareness becomes more accurate and complete with age and that as development proceeds they search for more information and structure their own gender role behaviour accordingly. This process has been referred to as self-socialization (Ruble, 1987). This

aspect of cognitive-developmental theory offers a more complete account than has been available previously of the possible role of media in gender role development (see Box 22.6). It may be important to consider what children themselves bring with them to reading books or TV viewing (including their own stereotypes) rather than simply considering the stereotypes that are to be found there (Calvert and Huston, 1987).

Self-socialization In relation to gender role, the process whereby as children develop they become increasingly aware of behaviour associated with both sexes and structure their own behaviour appropriately.

Box 22.7 Gender schematic processing theory

Another cognitive developmental theory – gender schematic processing theory – also emphasizes the child's active processing of gender-related information (Martin, 1991). However, this theory differs from Kohlberg's in an important respect. It is proposed that children do engage in an active process of finding out about their own gender, but this process starts when they discover their own sex rather than when they attain gender constancy as suggested by Kohlberg (Martin and Halverson, 1987).

This theory suggests that once children have a gender identity, they increasingly search the environment for information with which to extend and enhance the relevant gender schema – an internal body of knowledge about the characteristics and behaviours associated with a particular gender. The schema enables the child to interpret what is happening in the environment and to select and attend to appropriate kinds of behaviour. In this way, children's perceptions of themselves become sex-typed.

Martin and Halverson explain how gender schematic processing may occur:

- Initially, children learn which objects and activities are appropriate for each sex.
- Subsequently, they concentrate on learning more about the activities that are appropriate to their own sex and pay less attention to activities associated with the opposite sex. For example, boys become aware that playing with dolls is 'for girls' so they avoid dolls and learn little more about them. Thus appropriate gender-related behaviour becomes a part of a child's gender schema.
- Information that is consistent with the child's schema is taken on board and information that is inconsistent is disregarded or rejected. For example, if children encounter an adult who is taking part in an activity that is associated with the opposite sex, they may fail to take in the information. In support of this idea, a number of experiments have shown that when young children are shown pictures or films of adults engaged in stereotypical opposite-sex activities (such as a female as a doctor and a male as a nurse) they tend to either disregard the information, miss the point or forget it completely, insisting that the woman was the nurse and the man the doctor (Liben and Signorella, 1993).

Exercise 22.3 Gender and the media

Watch a number of TV advertisements over a couple of hours at the same time of the evening for about a week. List the main participants and note their sex.
Make notes on the following questions:

What occupation or status does each participant in the advertisement have? Is there a tendency for one sex to play more dominant roles while the other sex is depicted mainly in subordinate roles?

Who is most likely to be seen

- serving food
- using a domestic product carrying out repairs
- commenting on the benefits of insurance or banking services (or similar)
- demonstrating the attributes of a particular make of car?

Do you feel that TV advertisements do or do not promote masculine and feminine stereotypes?

You could design a similar investigation using the advertisements that appear during children's programmes or observing the content of drama or situational comedy programmes.

How important is gender constancy to gender role development?

As we have seen, Kohlberg (1966) argued that the acquisition of gender constancy (at around five or six) is a central influence in the development of gender role. This view has been supported by many experimental studies: for example, those by Ruble et al. (1981) and Frey and Ruble (1992). In Ruble et al.'s (1981) study, the researchers administered a measure of gender constancy to preschool children and then divided them into 'low' or 'high' levels of gender constancy. The children were subsequently shown a series of TV

Social learning theory

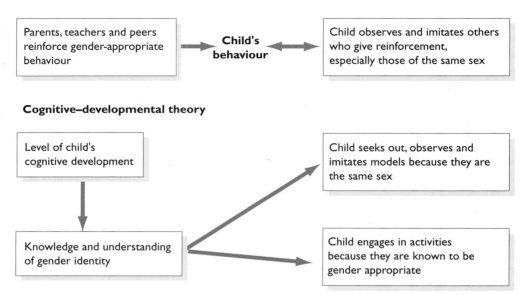

Cognitive–developmental theory

Figure 22.3 A summary of the social learning and cognitive developmental approaches to gender role development (after Smith and Cowie, 1991)

commercials which presented some attractive toys as either for girls or for boys. It was found that the 'high gender-constancy' children were more likely to respond to the underlying message of the advertisements. This affected their judgment of which sex the toys were appropriate for and whether they were inclined to play with the toys or not.

Self-evaluation Other studies have not found a clear relationship between gender constancy and sex-typing or preferences (Bussey and Bandura, 1984). Bussey and Bandura (1992) argue that gender development starts as a result mainly of external sanctions from parents. Gradually a shift then occurs towards a process of self-regulation which is organized by the child's perceptions of the likely consequences of particular attitudes and behaviour. According to this proposal, the main mechanism to influence this process is **self-evaluation** – judging one's own attitudes and behaviour (see Box 22.8).

Some problems with cognitive-developmental theories

Cognitive-developmental approaches are currently the most influential in the study of gender role development. However, they have a number of limitations:

- Like social learning theory approaches, cognitive-developmental theory does not explain *why* the sexes are valued differently (Bem, 1993).
- In contrast to social learning theory, cognitive-developmental theory has little to say about the precise links between the child's development and the surrounding culture (Bem, 1993). The environment is taken as fixed and the child is thought to acquire information because of developing cognitive processes which are the same for all.

GLOSSARY

Self-evaluation The process through which an individual makes a judgment about his or her own attitudes and behaviour.

Box 22.8 Gender constancy and self-evaluation

To investigate the relative importance of gender constancy and self-evaluation, Bussey and Bandura (1992) asked preschool children whether they would feel 'happy' or 'unhappy' if they played with a number of same-sex or opposite-sex toys. The findings were as follows:

- Both boys and girls between the ages of three and four showed approval for same-sex behaviour and disapproval for opposite-sex behaviour.
- By the age of four, boys were very happy to play with dump trucks and robots, but not comfortable with dolls and kitchen sets. Girls' preferences were the opposite of this.

- Across a number of tasks, children's judgments of their own preferences and likely behaviour (self-evaluation) served to predict gender-linked behaviour, whereas gender constancy and gender knowledge scores did not.

Bussey and Bandura concluded that, early in life, children learn the sanctions against opposite-sex behaviour and start to organize their own behaviour accordingly. (It is interesting to note that Bussey and Bandura were coming from a social learning theory perspective.)

- Lloyd and Duveen (1993) argue that most cognitive-developmental models argue from the basis of individual social cognition emphasizing the individual's perceptions of what is happening in society. Since we now know that cognitive development itself is influenced by social interactions (see Chapter 20), there is a need to study gender role knowledge as being acquired in a social context.
- There appears to be a problem with the relationship between cognition and behaviour (Huston, 1985). Huston argues that if cognitions are major determinants of gender role development, then after the early years we would expect to find a positive relationship between gender concepts and sex-typed preferences in behaviour. These relationships do not appear to be strong and there is a marked difference between males and females. For example, both boys and girls appear to develop their gender role cognitions in the same order and at around the same pace. However, boys tend to have stronger gender stereotypes than girls and are less likely to engage in opposite-sex activities. Further, boys increasingly tend to display preferences for masculine activities and masculine self-images throughout childhood, while girls actually move away from feminine preferences and identity during middle childhood (Archer, 1989). Huston argues that there is a need for research to concentrate less on concepts and cognitions and more on behaviour, activities and interests.

What can we conclude?

It seems clear that no single process is responsible for the development of gender roles and all the major theoretical approaches have something to offer to our understanding. The process probably works something like the following:

- It seems likely that sex hormones and other biological factors predispose young children towards masculine or feminine characteristics.
- It is probable that, at the same time, these naturally occurring differences are heightened by factors such as reinforcement from adults and other children for gender-appropriate behaviour and the imitation of gender-stereotyped models in the family, school and media. And right from birth, other people's gender-stereotyped expectations are likely to exert their influences.
- These biological and social factors probably interact at various points in development and are organized by the child's own perceptions and growing understanding of gender and their selective attention to behaviour and attitudes which are relevant to their own gender.

These are very general conclusions and it is clear that the acquisition of gender role is a complex process which cannot yet be fully explained. There is a great deal more to be discovered, particularly about the importance of the social context in which children develop a gender role.

SELF-ASSESSMENT QUESTIONS

1. Explain, giving examples, the terms 'gender stereotypes', 'gender identity' and 'androgyny'.
2. Are there psychological differences between males and females? Refer to research evidence.
3. Outline the biological explanation of gender role development. Evaluate a study that has been used to support the biological approach.
4. Briefly describe some research which suggests that the development of gender roles is influenced by (a) parental treatment and (b) the media.
5. Outline two cognitive-developmental approaches to the study of gender role. What problems are associated with these approaches?
6. Given the available evidence, what conclusions would you draw about the development of gender roles?

Understanding self and others

One of the most important areas of research in social cognition is that concerned with the child's developing understanding of the self. In the first part of this section, we shall explore the main findings of research into development of the self and factors affecting self-esteem. (Perception of the self is also discussed in Chapter 24.) The second part of the section will be concerned with the development of the child's understanding of others and in particular the emergence of a 'theory of mind'. Theory of mind refers to the child's understanding of the thoughts, feelings and beliefs of other people.

The nature of self

One of the most crucial processes of the child's early years is the development of a sense of self. What do we mean by a sense of self? What characteristics exist in the child who has a well-developed sense of self? Gardner (1982) suggests that there a number of factors. Children should:

■ be aware of their own body, its appearance, state and size (body image);
■ be able to refer to themselves appropriately through language and be able to distinguish

descriptions which apply to self and those which do not;
■ be aware of their own personal history, experiences they have had, skills and abilities acquired, their own needs and wishes.

Such a knowledge of self involves the ability to see oneself as others do and to develop a sense of self-awareness by taking account of the attitudes and perspectives of others. In addition to these ingredients, a mature sense of self includes a feeling of self-worth or self-esteem – an acceptance of and contentment with what one is like. Self-esteem is that part of the self-concept in which we judge our own competence in comparison to some internalized standard or expectation.

The influence of social factors

Early writers such as Cooley (1902) and Mead (1934) have highlighted the influence on the development of self of interactions with other people. This proposal has been confirmed in more recent research (Fogel, 1993; Youniss, 1994). Through these interactions the child becomes aware of the judgments parents make: for example, 'naughty', 'good', 'bright', 'a bit slow', 'very feminine', 'a real boy'. It is from these labels that children develop a sense of who and what they are – the **self-concept**. Cooley called this the 'looking glass self', since it reflects what other people think of us.

Kuhn (1960) showed that as a child develops, the sense of self becomes less physically oriented and increasingly influenced by social factors. Groups of children and young adults were asked to respond to the questions 'Who am I?' Only 25 per cent of statements made by seven year olds related to social roles such as 'I am a son', compared to 50 per cent of statements made by 24 year olds.

Developmental trends

In the early months of life, children do not distinguish themselves from the things around them. Gradually, however, they develop an awareness of their own body as an entity separate from the environment. This

---

GLOSSARY
Self-concept A general sense of who and what one is, including feelings of self-worth.

distinction between 'self' and 'not self' seems to develop gradually from about the third month of life and is well-established between 12 and 15 months. Lewis and Brooks-Gunn (1979) described this distinction of oneself from others as the '**existential self**'. This sense of 'separateness' is established through the pattern of interactions babies have with those around them. Interestingly, Lewis and Brooks-Gunn link this awareness of 'separate self' to the understanding of object permanence as described by Piaget (see Chapter 20).

During the second year of life, a second aspect of 'self' develops – what Lewis (1990) refers to as the more objective '**categorical self**'. This refers to the characterization of oneself in terms of categories such as age, gender, attractiveness, ability and so on. The categories used may vary between cultures or historical period or they may be universal. Also, they may remain constant over a lifetime or they may change, depending upon an individual's experiences. Meadows (1986) explains these features by describing her own 'categorical self':

This girl, at three years old, is not remotely concerned about her body image. However, during adolescence, her body image will become very important

including the ability to use language appropriately to refer to themselves. By the time they are three, children are able to refer to a wide range of self-characteristics, including feelings and perceptions, appearance and opinions (Schatz, 1994).

Some of the basic landmarks in this early, very rapid development of the self can be seen in the findings from research studies carried out (see Box 22.9).

Adolescence has been recognized by many researchers as a time of particular importance in the development of self. Erikson (1968) described the 'identity crisis' which occurs during the teenage years. Faced with dramatic body changes and pressures arising from the need to make career and other important choices, adolescents try out different roles in order to 'find themselves'. All the young person's cognitive and emotional capacities are brought to bear on the task of forming a coherent sense of who and what one is. At adolescence, too, many studies have highlighted the special importance of the body image as an aspect of the sense of self. (Development during adolescence will be considered in greater detail in the next chapter.)

> . . . my own categorical self would include the following categories, all relative and not in any order of importance: 'tall', which appeared early, will remain constant and could be universal; 'female', also early, universal and constant, although the defining attributes and connotations of 'female' have undergone historical and cultural changes . . .
>
> (Meadows, 1986, p. 146)

By the age of two, children appear to have acquired many of the basic components of a sense of self,

Box 22.9 Development of the self – some studies

Some of the basic elements in the development of the self can be seen in the findings of research:

Lewis and Brooks-Gunn (1975) carried out a series of studies of the emergence of a sense of the self in infants. Confronted with pictures of themselves, one-year-old babies generally call themselves 'baby'. Shortly before they reach two, most children start to use their own name and can verbally express their own mental state; by two and a half they can use personal pronouns such as 'I'; by the age of three, almost all children can refer to themselves in pictures using both their names and the correct personal pronouns.

In addition to using language correctly to refer to oneself as subject (the sense of 'I'), a sense of self involves the ability to recognize oneself as object (the sense of 'me' that is perceived by others) One aspect of the 'me' that has attracted much research attention in relation to infancy is the physical self. Lewis and Brooks-Gunn (1979) investigated infants' reactions to their own reflections in a mirror. A child's nose was secretly coloured with rouge and she or he was placed in front of the mirror. It was assumed that children who recognized the reflection as themselves might well touch their own nose. The findings were that few 9–12-month-old children touched their own noses, while about two-thirds of 21-month to two-year-old children did so. The older children also acted coy or touched the mirror image. The researchers concluded that an awareness of one's own person emerges around the age of about 18 months.

Bannister and Agnew (1977) also illustrated children's increasing self-awareness with age. Groups of children of school age were asked a variety of questions about themselves and their home and school lives. The answers were tape-recorded and then rerecorded in different voices to disguise the identity of the original speakers. Four months later, the same children were asked to listen to the recordings and identify which statements were their own and which were not, and to give reasons for their choices.

Findings indicated that the children's ability to recognize their own statements increased with age. It was notable, also, that the children's explanations for their decisions reflected a growing knowledge of and confidence in their own feelings and beliefs. Thus, five-year-old children tended to rely on memory and simple clues contained in the statements: for example, 'That girl likes swimming and I swim, so I must have said that'. Nine year olds tended to use more complex methods for determining which statements were theirs and which were not. One child insisted that the statement 'I want to be a soldier when I grow up' was not his, because 'I don't think I could kill a human being so I wouldn't say I wanted to be a soldier'.

Self-esteem

As we saw earlier, **self-esteem** is that aspect of the self which is concerned with how we evaluate ourselves as people. It has been claimed that a major factor in the development of psychological disorder is some individuals' feelings of inadequacy and unworthiness. The classic work of Coopersmith (1968) has shown marked variations in the behaviour of children who differ in self-esteem (see Box 22.10).

Self-esteem and different domains

A more recent measure of self-esteem contains four subscales designed to measure three different aspects of a child's feelings of self-worth – cognitive, social and physical skills together with general feelings of self-esteem (Harter, 1982). Studies which have used this scale reveal that children often rate themselves very differently in these domains. Thus, their evaluation of their physical skills may differ from an evaluation of their cognitive skills. Marsh et al. (1991) found that, from about the age of eight, children have the cognitive and emotional maturity to be able to integrate information from several different domains of their lives into a general assessment of their self-worth.

Harter (1987) asked children to rate themselves in five areas (scholastic competence, athletic competence, social acceptance, physical appearance and behavioural conduct) as well as completing a more

---

GLOSSARY

Self-esteem That part of the self which is concerned with how we evaluate ourselves as people.

Box 22.10 Coopersmith's studies of self-esteem

Coopersmith (1968) studied a group of children from the age of ten until early adult life. Using the results of a battery of tests and self-ratings, the sample was divided into three groups which were labelled 'high', 'medium' and 'low' self-esteem. The findings were as follows:

- **High self-esteem** boys showed themselves to have a positive and realistic view of themselves and their own abilities. They were confident, not unduly worried by criticism and enjoyed participating in things. They were active and expressive in all they did and were generally successful academically and socially.
- **Medium self-esteem** boys had some of these qualities but were more conformist, less confident of their own worth and more in need of social acceptance.
- **Low self-esteem** boys were described by Coopersmith as a sad little group who were self-conscious, isolated, reluctant to participate in activities; they constantly underrated themselves and were oversensitive to criticism.

All the boys came from the same socioeconomic background (middle class) and there were no significant differences between the groups in such characteristics as intelligence and physical attractiveness.

A major difference between the three groups arose when the researchers investigated the characteristics and behaviour of the boys' parents. In general high self-esteem boys tended to have parents who were also high in self-esteem. These parents, in contrast with the parents of low self-esteem boys, were more affectionate and showed greater interest in and respect for their children as individuals. Parents had higher and more consistent standards than did those in the other groups. Methods of discipline were consistent and relied upon rewards for good behaviour and withdrawal of approval rather than physical punishment for bad behaviour.

Discipline in the homes of low self-esteem boys was inconsistent. It varied between highly punitive and overpermissive styles and less clear guidance was given to the boys, who were rarely sure where they stood. Low self-esteem boys often regarded their parents' behaviour as unfair.

A follow-up of the sample into adult life showed that the high self-esteem boys were more successful than low self-esteem boys, both educationally and in their careers.

Limitations of Coopersmith's study

One must be cautious when drawing conclusions from Coopersmith's study. Self-esteem is notoriously difficult to measure accurately. Asking children questions about how they evaluate themselves is a procedure which is open to biased responses; children may not want to admit they have undesirable characteristics. Also, Coopersmith did not investigate the influence of socioeconomic background or sex upon self-esteem; all the participants were boys and from middle-class backgrounds.

However, more recent research – notably Rosenberg (1985) – has tended to support Coopersmith's findings that the key factors which appear to be related to high self-esteem appear to be firm, consistent but reasoned control, positive encouragement of independence and a warm, loving atmosphere.

There is evidence to suggest that children from lower socioeconomic backgrounds typically exhibit lower self-esteem than do those from homes higher up the socioeconomic scale. In general, too, girls tend to have lower self-esteem than boys. Even in primary schools where they often outshine boys, girls are inclined to underrate their own abilities. Girls tend, also, to set themselves lower goals in life and to rate themselves lower on written measures of self-esteem than do boys. This is probably the result of cultural factors and the general lower status of women in society (Fontana, 1988).

---

general assessment of their self-worth. The main findings were as follows:

- Where children made a low assessment of themselves in an area which was important to them, the more likely it was that their general self-esteem would be low; however, where children perceived themselves as not very competent in an

area which was relatively unimportant to them, their high self-esteem tended to be maintained. For example, if children who consider athletic competence to be relatively unimportant perceive themselves as incompetent in this domain, they are unlikely to suffer a serious threat to their general self-esteem. However, in a domain which they consider to be important: for example, mathematical competence, perceived incompetence may adversely affect general feelings of self-worth.

■ One domain which appears to be especially important to children is that of physical appearance. Both boys and girls who were unhappy with the way they looked tended to have low self-esteem.

Why should such a relatively superficial aspect of the self, such as external appearance, affect a child's general feeling of self-esteem when aspects such as conduct or competencies may not? To answer this, psychologists point to the importance of the real world social context (Jackson, 1992; Erwin, 1993). For example, good looks are highly valued in most cultures and it seems that conceptions of what constitutes attractive physical appearance are established early in life.

The research findings in relation to domain specificity of self-esteem are important and should be understood by teachers and other people who work with children. Improving children's feelings of self-worth about their athletic competence will not necessarily make them feel good about their academic performance or improve general feelings of self-worth.

Whether self-esteem is affected by performance depends more on whether individuals value the sport than on their actual success

Theory of mind

As we saw in Chapter 20, Piaget focused on cognitive development in children. He believed that a special quality of human beings is their scientific and technological potential. Given the enormous scientific and technological advances that have taken place over the past centuries, his assumption would seem to be correct. However, the question has been asked as to whether that potential is the only highly developed human quality, or whether there is some other important quality which is closely linked to our social development.

As human beings we live and interact in groups. A feature of human social behaviour that distinguishes us from many nonhuman animals and insects such as ants, who also operate in groups, is our capacity to interact together in work and play in a reciprocal way. This seems to require a capacity to appreciate what other people are thinking and feeling. Such a capacity has become known as a **theory of mind**. Mitchell (1992) asks: 'What do we have instead of the ants' instincts that enables us to be such proficient creatures? We have

a "theory of mind" and this could be the most important feature of human cognition' (p. 36).

The idea behind possession of a theory of mind is that human beings are natural psychologists who collect evidence about other people's emotions, beliefs and wishes. On the basis of this evidence, they construct a theory which enables them to predict and explain the behaviour of others.

The ability to understand that other people have minds which are similar to our own, but which see the world from their own unique perspective, is something we take for granted. In many of our interactions, we are very preoccupied with what is going on in the other person's mind. In a game like chess, a large part of the skill of playing is to try to assess how your opponent is thinking of moving or what he or she is thinking about your play.

So far as young children are concerned, we must not take the possession of a 'theory of mind' for granted. It appears that a theory of mind is not present in the child's repertoire of cognitive abilities until the age of about four. (Theory of mind in relation to animals is discussed in Chapter 16.)

Consider the following scenario which has been enacted in many experimental situations:

■ Suppose we show a young child, Jennie, aged three, a Smarties tube that in fact, unbeknown to the child, actually contains pencils. If we ask Jennie what is in the tube, it would not be unreasonable to say that she would be sure to answer 'Smarties', since she cannot see inside the tube.

■ We then open the tube and show Jenny that it contains pencils.

■ Next, we tell Jennie that we are going to call her friend Lucy into the room and ask her what is in the Smarties tube. If we ask Jenny to tell us what she thinks her friend Lucy will say when we ask her what is in the Smarties tube, Jenny, at three years old, is almost certain to say 'pencils'. She has not yet developed a theory of mind – the ability to appreciate the perspectives, beliefs and feelings of other people – which would enable her to realize that Lucy will be misled in the way she was herself.

The 'Smarties' procedure and other similar procedures have been used in many studies into theory of mind (Perner et al., 1987; Gopnik and Astington, 1988). Studies found that the great majority of children under four, when asked the question 'What do you think Lucy will say when we ask her what is in the tube?', answered 'Lucy will say "Pencils"'. Children of four and above were quick to appreciate that Lucy would be misled because of the nature of the tube and the fact that she had not seen it before. They were aware that Lucy would have a false belief and would give the answer 'Smarties'.

False beliefs

A central feature of a theory of mind is being able to understand that people sometimes entertain false beliefs. If children can appreciate that people can have false beliefs, then they are able to understand that the way someone's mind represents the world may be different from the way the world really is (Mitchell,

What is in the Smarties tube?

1992). In such circumstances, we would conclude that the child had acquired a theory of mind. If, on the other hand, a child was unable to grasp that people can have false beliefs, then it would be assumed that he or she had not yet acquired a theory of mind and thinking was restricted to the way the world really is.

'False belief tasks', as they have come to be called, have been of particular interest to developmental psychologists because they have provided a format for discovering whether or not a child possesses a theory of mind. Box 22.11 outlines the rationale which underlies the tasks set for children in many theory of mind experiments. What these studies show is that while a four year old understands that people have beliefs and that these beliefs can be different from the way the world really is, the three year old does not.

Debate in the study of theory of mind

How does theory of mind develop? There is currently much research interest into how theory of mind develops in children and the age at which a child possesses a theory of mind. This has generated a great deal of debate and sometimes disagreement. Some of the ideas arising from research are outlined below:

GLOSSARY

False belief task A task set up to discover whether a child possesses a theory of mind. The task requires the child to understand that another person may entertain a belief that is not actually true.

Many researchers have proposed that the three year old has a conceptual deficit that is overcome at around four. This is known as the **'magic age' view**. The 'magic age' view generally reflects a tendency to see the development of a theory of mind as dependent upon cognitive development. It tends to ignore social and environmental influences in the developmental process.

Hobson (1990) has suggested that perhaps the development of a theory of mind is dependent not on innate mechanisms, as might be suggested by linking it to cognitive development, but occurs when a certain level of understanding has been gained through relevant experiences.

Harris et al. (1989) argued that it is children's awareness of their own mental state which enable them to appreciate the mental states of other people. This occurs through the child using an 'as if' or pretence mechanism: being able to understand someone else arises from imagining yourself in their situation.

Leslie (1987) agreed with Harris that pretence is important, but she believes that it is only one example of the child using what she calls second-order representations or metarepresentations, which emerge at around 18 months.

Box 22.11 Theory of mind experiments

Experiments into theory of mind:

- Test children's understanding of belief and particularly false belief;
- Require that a child attributes a false belief to another person;
- In order to demonstrate that children attribute beliefs to another, they must show that they can ascribe to the other beliefs different from their own.

The procedure is as follows:

- A situation is arranged so that the child's beliefs are true and another's beliefs are false;
- The child is asked what the other person will think or do.

If children can recognize that the other person will act on the basis of his or her own false beliefs, we conclude that they can attribute beliefs to the other.

Box 22.12 Theory of mind and egocentrism

You may be thinking that a young child's problems understanding what is going on in someone else's mind is similar to Piaget's idea that young children are egocentric. Piaget's view of egocentrism was that young children understand their own mental perspective on a situation, but cannot understand that another person's mental perspective of the same situation might be different (see the description of Piaget's 'three mountains task' in Chapter 20). This is similar to the idea that young children cannot appreciate other people's false beliefs and therefore have no theory of mind. However, there is an important difference between the two concepts. Egocentrism refers to ignorance about other people, whereas the idea that young children lack a theory of mind implies that they know nothing about minds at all, including their own.

In support of the idea that young children have no notion about their own minds, Gopnik and Astington (1988) carried out a variant of the Smarties experiment. As before, the child was shown a Smarties tube and when asked what was inside it replied 'Smarties'. Then it was revealed that the tube really contained pencils. After closing the lid of the tube, the child was then asked: 'When you first saw the tube before we opened it, what did you think was inside?'

As before, the large majority of children of about four and above correctly replied 'Smarties', whereas the great majority of children under that age answered 'pencils'. Moreover, the children who gave this wrong answer were generally the same ones who had given an incorrect answer when they were asked to judge another person's false belief. Astington (1994) argues that three year olds simply do not understand that their own beliefs may change: when they find out they are wrong, they are unable to remember their own earlier false beliefs.

GLOSSARY

The 'magic age' view The view that possession of a theory of mind is linked to a child's cognitive development and does not occur in a child under four years of age.

■ A first-order representation involves symbolizing something in your own mind, for example a book or a toy or a state such as thirst.

■ A second-order representation, or **metarepresentation** includes children's ability to understand their own thoughts by adding pretence or imagination. For example, a child playing with a doll will be able to think about the actual doll (a primary representation). In the context of play, the child may pretend that the doll is a real baby and imagine scenarios that are relevant to looking after a baby (metarepresentations). Leslie considers that the cognitive ability of metarepresenting is the most important factor underlying the theory of mind. The ability to metarepresent is observable in a child's pretend play, talking about mental states and understanding false beliefs.

■ Perner (1991) disagrees with Harris's view on the importance of pretence and uses the term 'metarepresentation' rather differently. Perner argues that the ability to metarepresent involves modelling mental states and this does not occur until the child is four. It is then that they possess a theory of mind and can succeed in false belief tasks.

■ Lewis and Osborne (1990) argued that it was possible that some of the standard false belief tasks used in earlier experiments demanded too much of a younger child's language skills. For example when, in the 'Smarties' procedure described on page 529, the child is asked 'What will Lucy say when we ask her what is in the tube?', does the child really understand that this question refers to a time before Lucy finds out what is really in the tube? The researchers set up an experiment using the 'Smarties' procedure. However, they changed the question 'What did you think was in the tube?' to 'What did you think was in the tube *before I took the top off?*' and the question 'What will (friend's name) think is in the tube?' to 'What will (friend's name) think is in the tube *before I take the top off?*' This amended procedure resulted in a clear improvement in the performance of three year olds. A clear majority of three year olds now gave the correct answer.

Theory of mind and autism

Autism is quite a rare developmental disorder. It affects

Box 22.13   False belief and reality

Mitchell and Lacohee (1991) proposed that young children do know about false beliefs, but are loath to acknowledge anything which is not based in reality. By definition, understanding another person's false belief does not have a basis in reality.

The researchers endeavoured to set up an experiment that would provide a false belief with a basis in reality, yet would preserve its 'false' status. A sample of three year olds were shown a Smarties tube and asked to mail a picture of what they thought was in the tube in a special post box. All the children posted a picture of Smarties and the pictures were kept in the post box out of sight until after the next stage of the experiment. Next, the children were shown that the tube really contained pencils. The pencils were returned to the tube, the lid was closed and the children were asked the modified question, 'When you posted your picture, what did you think was in the tube?'

Tested in this situation, a majority of the three year olds correctly answered 'Smarties'. The researchers argued that their study showed that young children can understand false belief when it is based in something real (the picture in the post box).

---

about two in every 10,000 people. It is usually diagnosed from about three years onwards and is very disabling. It sometimes, but not always, involves mental retardation. Behaviour in children suffering from autism is usually characterized by poor communication skills and a complete unresponsiveness to other people.

A large body of research findings is accumulating which suggest that a central feature of autism is the inability to appreciate the minds of other people: that is, a deficit in theory of mind. A leading scientist in this field is Simon Baron-Cohen from Cambridge University. Some of this research is discussed in Chapter

---

GLOSSARY

Metarepresentation The ability to think about and understand one's own thoughts.

Autism A rare developmental disorder which is usually detected in early childhood. The sufferer exhibits severe limitations in language and an inability to relate to other people.

32, where the phenomenon of autism is more fully discussed. You may wish to look at this now.

SELF-ASSESSMENT QUESTIONS

1. What characteristics exist in a child who has a well-developed sense of self?
2. Outline some studies which demonstrate children's increasing self-awareness with age.
3. What factors may influence the level of a child's self-esteem?
4. Outline the findings from Harter's research into self-esteem and domain specificity.
5. Explain what is meant by a 'theory of mind'. Outline the findings of some studies into a theory of mind in young children.
6. What is meant by the 'magic age' view in relation to the development of a theory of mind? Does research support this view?

Chapter summary

■ Research into individual social cognition, which has been influenced by the work of Piaget, focuses on people's perceptions, thinking and reasoning about others and about social relationships. An alternative approach to social cognition, which also encompasses the work of Vygotsky, centres on ways in which interactions with other people may influence the development of a child's cognitive ability.

■ Study of moral development centres upon the way in which children adopt and internalize rules and standards of behaviour demanded by society. Approaches to moral development include psycho-dynamic, social learning and cognitive developmental approaches. While psychodynamic theories empha-size emotional aspects, social learning emphasizes reinforcement, punishment and observational learn-ing, and cognitive development approaches empha-size levels of cognitive development in relation to moral reasoning.

■ In Piaget's theory of moral development children progress from heteronomous morality to autono-mous morality where judgments of right and wrong are based on intentions as well as consequences. Kohlberg produced a more detailed and compre-hensive account building on Piaget's work focusing on an individual's reasoning. He sees moral development in three levels, each having two stages. Level 1 is preconventional, level 2 conventional and level 3 postconventional or principled.

■ There has been some criticism of Kohlberg's work. The idea of progression and of absence of regression

to previous stages was contested by Rest. Gardner has questioned whether Kohlberg's stages applied cross-culturally. The extent of a relationship between moral reasoning and moral behaviour has also been contested.

■ The type of parental discipline has been found to have a bearing on moral development. Power-assertive discipline tends to produce personalities who behave morally merely to avoid punishment, while the use of inductions produces a personality who behaves morally even without pressure to do so.

■ Eisenberg has produced a model of prosocial reasoning and distinguishes hedonistic reasoning from needs-oriented reasoning. In the latter children express concern for the needs of others, in the former the implications for themselves are the most important thing.

■ It is possible that there are differences between genders in moral reasoning. Gilligan suggested there were two distinct moral orientations, justice and caring. Boys are more likely to operate from the justice orientation, girls from the caring orientation. Gilligan's suggestions are by no means proved, but a new debate has been opened up.

■ Masculinity and femininity relate to gender stereo-types, characteristics attributed to males and females. These have changed little in the last 20 years. Gender identity refers to individuals' perception of them-selves as masculine or feminine. Masculine and feminine characteristics may develop in the same individual. The term androgynous has been applied to those with both masculine and feminine character-istics. Bem confirmed that androgynous individuals were more psychologically healthy and well adjusted than those more rigidly masculine or feminine.

■ Boys from the age of about eight or nine score higher in tests of mathematical and spatial ability, while girls perform better at verbal tests. Boys are physically more aggressive than girls. The review of the literature by Maccoby and Jacklin, however, gave equal weight to all the studies reviewed, though some were methodologically weaker. This may have caused underrepresentation of gender differences. Meta-analytical studies have found reliable sex differences in activity level, aggression, influenceability, empathy, mathematical reasoning, and spatial ability. However, in general, sex differences are small.

■ Gender differentiation begins as young as two or three. By adolescence there are distinctive beha-vioural, interest and occupational choice differences. Sex differences in behaviour may arise from biological factors including chromosomal sex differences and hormonal differences. Cross-cultural studies have in large part found consistent gender differences across cultures. There is evidence that hormonal differences have an effect upon behaviour. Females exposed to male hormones before birth exhibit more masculine gender role behaviour later. However, gender role tends to be consistent with sex of rearing rather than genetic sex. Money and Erhardt have found that the effects of socialization are very powerful.

■ Freud's psychoanalytic theory suggests that the phallic stage of development results in satisfactory gender role identification. Social learning theorists claim that gender role, like all behaviour, is learnt through social reinforcement and modelling. There is much research which suggests that boys and girls are socialized differently. The ways in which males and females are represented on the media clearly play a part in this. There has been found to be a correlation between the amount of TV watched and the strength of stereotyped gender role beliefs.

■ Kohlberg's cognitive-developmental theory suggests that gender-role development is heavily influenced by a child's level of cognitive development. Labelling as 'boy' or 'girl' early in life leads to children's perception of themselves as male or female. Gender self-concept directs and organizes activities and ways of thinking. The development of gender constancy at or around five to six years old has been found to be a key stage.

Self-socialization develops with age and allows children to structure their own gender role behaviour.

■ Once children have a gender identity, gender schemas begin to develop as children search the environment for objects and activities appropriate for their sex. Children may fail to take in information which shows adults engaging in activities which are thought appropriate for the opposite sex.

■ The development of gender constancy at age five or six is seen as central to the development of gender role. Bussey and Bandura found that self-evaluation served to preserve gender-linked behaviour as early as four years old.

■ Self-awareness involves seeing oneself as others do. Self also includes a sense of self-worth or self-esteem. Cooley and Mead have highlighted the importance of interactions with others in the development of self-concept. As children develop, their self-concept becomes less physically oriented and increasingly influenced by social factors. During the early years of life children develop an awareness of themselves as an entity separate from the environment. This has been termed existential self and has been linked to Piaget's concept of object permanence. During the second year of life a categorical sense of self develops. By three years old a child is able to refer to a wide variety of characteristics of self. Experiments by Lewis and Brooks-Gunn have explored the emergence of a sense of self.

■ Adolescence has been recognized as a particularly important time in respect of the development of self-concept. Erikson has described the identitiy crisis of teenage years. Coopersmith studied the self-esteem of a group of children between 10 and adulthood. While those with high self-esteem had a positive and realistic view of themselves, those with medium self-esteem were more conformist and less confident of their worth. Those with low self-esteem were self-conscious, isolated and reluctant to participate in activities. Differences also reflected differences in parents' self-esteem and the ways in which discipline was imposed.

■ Children frequently rate themselves differently in different domains of self-esteem: cognitive, social and physical. Where they had low self-esteem in an area which was important to them it was more likely their general self-esteem would be low. Physical appearance is especially important. Where boys and girls were unhappy with the way they looked they tended to have low self-esteem.

■ Possession of a theory of mind implies a capacity to appreciate what other people are thinking and feeling. Theory of mind may not be present in children until the age of about four.

■ A central feature of theory of mind involves an ability to realize that other people may have false beliefs.

Studies of theory of mind have used 'false belief tasks' to discover whether or not children possess a theory of mind.

■ Debate centres around the age at which children develop a theory of mind and the mechanisms involved in its emergence. Research findings indicate that many sufferers from autism fail to develop a theory of mind.

Further reading

Archer, J. and Lloyd, B. (1985). *Sex and Gender*. Cambridge: Cambridge University Press. This gives a useful review of gender differences in both children and adults.

Astington, J.W. (1994). *The Child's Discovery of the Mind*. London: Fontana. This gives a good introduction to the study of 'theory of mind'. There is an interesting chapter on whether a child with autism possesses a theory of mind.

Durkin, K. (1995). *Developmental Social Psychology: From Infancy to Old Age*. Oxford: Blackwell. This book considers a range of different areas of social development, presenting theories and up-to-date research findings from North America, Europe and Australia. There are excellent chapters on social cognition, self-concept, moral and prosocial development and the development of gender.

CHAPTER 23

Adolescence and adulthood

Adolescence   535
- Late and early maturation   536
- Adolescent identity   537
- Two views of adolescence   539
- Studies of adolescent turmoil   540
- Aspects of adolescent experience   541

Lifespan development: the study of adulthood   543
- Erikson's theory of psychosocial development   544
- Levinson's seasons of a man's life   546

Young adulthood   547
- Growth trends   547
- Life events   548

Middle adulthood   552
- Personality and social development   552
- Developmental theories of middle adulthood   554
- Unemployment   555

Late adulthood   557
- Senescence   557
- Cognitive functioning in late adulthood   557
- Theories of personality development and adjustment   559
- Successful adjustment to ageing   559
- Retirement   560
- Death and bereavement   562

Objectives

By the end of this chapter you should be able to:

- Identify and discuss physical and psychological changes that take place during adolescence;

- Assess alternative views of the factors which influence personality and social development during adolescence;

- Discuss the findings from a range of empirical studies into aspects of adolescence;

- Assess theories and studies of development and change during early, middle and later adulthood;

- Discuss the impact of particular life events during adulthood: for example, marriage, parenting, divorce, unemployment, retirement, bereavement and death.

Adolescence

Sometime after the age of 10, humans mature sexually and become capable of reproducing. The period of time during which the reproductive processes mature is known as puberty. Although the most obvious signs of development during puberty are physical, changes also

> **GLOSSARY**
>
> **Puberty** The period of time during which the reproductive processes mature and secondary sex characteristics develop.

occur in cognitive functioning, social interactions, emotions and the sense of self. **Adolescence** is a longer period of time, and is generally defined as the period from the onset of puberty up to adulthood.

Adolescence has traditionally been considered a time of conflict and turmoil. G. Stanley Hall, the first person to study adolescence scientifically, described it as a period of 'storm and stress' as well as of great physical, mental and emotional change. Currently, many clinical psychologists and psychoanalytic theorists still describe adolescence as a time of psychological disturbance, though some recent studies of typical adolescents suggest that the extent of adolescent disturbance has been exaggerated (Coleman, 1995).

Late and early maturation

As noted above, the age at which young people reach puberty varies. Late or early maturation appears to

have few lasting psychological effects in girls. However, in males the picture is different. Boys who mature early are likely, because of their greater strength and size, to have an advantage in sports. They are also likely to develop earlier self-confidence in relationships with girls. The reverse is likely to be true for late-maturing boys. As a result, there are likely to be some personality differences between late and early maturing males. A large number of studies have indicated that late-maturing males are likely to be more tense and self-conscious, less socially adept and to have greater feelings of inadequacy and rejection. In contrast, early maturers appear to be more self-assured and at ease with themselves. Follow-up studies indicate that these differences can persist into adult life. At age 33, most late maturers appeared to be less self-confident and controlled and more in need of support and help from others (Clausen, 1975).

As we have seen, early maturation seems to be advantageous for boys. However, the impact on girls is less extensive and more variable (Crockett and Petersen, 1987). Initially, early-maturing girls tend to be more dissatisfied with their body image, more moody, listless and discontented and more disorganized when under stress. They are often less popular with their same-sex peers than are late-maturing girls and are more likely to perform poorly in school (Simmons et al., 1983). However, they also appear more independent and are more popular with opposite-sex peers. By late adolescence and adulthood, however, the picture is very different. The formerly discontented early-maturing girl tends to become more popular with her peers of both sexes, is more self-possessed and better at coping.

How can this transformation be explained and why is early maturation clearly more favourable for boys than for girls? Simmons et al. (1983) suggest a number of factors that may be important, including the following:

■ Early-maturing adolescents are in the minority among their peers.
■ While society tends to view early maturation in boys favourably, the messages are more ambiguous for females. For boys, greater strength

---

Box 23.1 Physical changes during adolescence

During puberty, hormonal secretions from the pituitary gland, which lies at the base of the brain, begin to stimulate the ovaries in females and testes in males, and the adrenal glands in both sexes. In males, reproduction depends upon the production of sperm cells, an event which usually occurs between 12 and 15 years. In females, the onset of the first menstrual flow, usually between the ages of 11 and 14, signals the production of ova. Certain changes which occur during puberty are known as **primary sexual changes**: ovulation in females is accompanied by an increase in the size of the vagina, clitoris and uterus, while in males enlargement of the penis and testes coincides with the production of sperm. In addition to these primary changes, a number of **secondary sexual changes** occur. These include, for both sexes, the development of pubic hair and changes in the shape and proportions of the body. In females, the breasts develop and in males the voice deepens and facial hair begins to appear. Both sexes experience the '**growth spurt**', a substantial and rapid increase in height. The growth spurt in boys generally begins about two years later than it does in girls, and lasts for a longer period of time.

GLOSSARY

Adolescence Generally defined as the period of development from the onset of puberty up to adulthood.

and physical prowess is more socially desirable. Among girls, early maturation may mean being temporarily taller and heavier than their female peers and taller than boys of their own age. In our society, early maturing girls may also be the target of more conflicting sexual messages than is so for males.

Adolescent identity

Erikson (1968, 1980)

According to Erikson, adolescence is the stage of development during which the individual is searching for an identity. (See the next section for an outline of Erikson's theory of lifespan development.) The crisis he called 'identity versus role confusion', encountered during adolescence, is seen by many psychologists as the central crisis of all development. The major goal of the adolescent at this time is the formation of a secure and enduring **ego identity**, or sense of self. Erikson sees ego identity as having three important components:

- a sense of unity, or agreement among one's perceptions of self;
- a sense of continuity of self-perceptions over time; and
- a sense of mutuality between one's perceptions of self and how one is perceived by others.

In order to arrive at a coherent sense of identity, adolescents typically 'try out' different roles without initially committing themselves to any one. Thus, stable attitudes and values, choices of occupation, partner and lifestyle gradually come together and make sense to oneself and others around.

Failure to achieve a firm, comfortable and enduring identity results in **role diffusion**, or a sense of confusion over what and who one is. Overstrong pressure from parents and others may cause the young person to become bewildered and despairing, resulting in withdrawal, either physically or mentally, from normal surroundings. In the most extreme cases of role diffusion, adolescents may adopt a negative identity. Convinced that they cannot live up to the demands made by parents, the young people may rebel and behave in ways which are the most unacceptable to the people who care for them. So the son of a local Tory dignitary may join a left-wing group, or the daughter of an atheist may become a devout member of a religious group.

Erikson's views arise mainly from clinical observations of both normal and troubled adolescents.

Marcia (1966)

Marcia extended and elaborated on Erikson's account of adolescent identity and identified four different kinds of identity status in adolescents (Figure 23.1):

- **Identity diffusion**. An identity status which is characterized by a lack of commitment and indecision about important life issues such as vocational choices, ideology and religion.
- **Identity foreclosure**. A status of initial commitment and development of values, but overshadowed by a hesitant acceptance of the values of others (for example, parents or teachers) rather than by self-determined goals (for example, choosing 'A'-level subjects or job options because an adult advises that they are desirable).
- **Moratorium**. A status of extreme identity crisis when an individual rethinks his or her values and goals but has difficulty making firm commitments.
- **Identity achievement**. A status where individuals have resolved their crises and have made firm commitments to particular values or choices in life, for example religious commitment or vocational choice.

Marcia believed that in order to reach a fully achieved personality, the young person must both have assessed his or her values and have made a firm commitment.

Study of Marcia's statuses Meilman (1979) studied a group of American males aged between 12 and 22 years. He found that there seemed to be a broad age-related trend in relation to the statuses identified by Marcia. For example, younger participants tended to be categorized as experiencing identity diffusion or foreclosure, while from the age of 18 on, increasing numbers of young men were categorized as identity achievers. However, the status of moratorium – the

---

GLOSSARY

Ego identity Erikson's term to describe the sense of self, a secure feeling of who and what one is.

Role diffusion Erikson's term to describe the sense of confusion about the self that is often experienced by adolescents who have failed to achieve a secure ego identity.

Degree of crisis

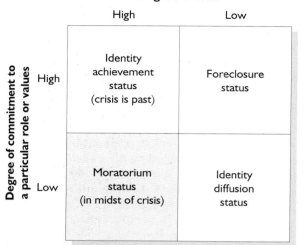

Figure 23.1 Marcia's four identity statuses (after Marcia, 1980)

most extreme crisis – was found in only a very small number of participants, whatever their age.

Female identity An important question arises from Meilman's research and the work of Erikson and Marcia. Are researchers making the assumption, as has so often been done in the past, that male development is the standard against which females are to be judged? The picture of identity development so far as females are concerned is not clear. Though some research has included female participants,

The development of an identity in females may take a different course from that in males

there does seem to have been some bias towards issues of male identity. Erikson argued that females develop differently because they postpone their identity development until they have found a male partner, whose name they will accept and whose occupation determines their social status. Marcia (1980, p. 178) concedes that Erikson's model and the identity status approach can be applied to females 'only more or less'.

Parental styles and identity

Parents play a significant part in determining how successful adolescents are in achieving an untroubled and enduring sense of identity. It has been shown that adolescents who are poorly adjusted and suffer a wide range of psychological problems are more likely to have experienced parental rejection or hostility than acceptance and love (Rutter, 1980). In particular, the style of parental control is an important factor in the parent–child relationship. A number of studies have shown the following:

- Democratic, but authoritative, parents are most likely to have children who, as adolescents, have high self-esteem and are independent and self-confident. Democratic/authoritative parents, while respecting the young person's right to make decisions, expect disciplined behaviour and give reasons for doing so (Elder, 1980). Such rational explanations are important to adolescents who are approaching cognitive and social maturity and preparing to take responsibility for their own behaviour.
- In contrast, more authoritarian parents expect unquestioning obedience from their children and feel no need to explain reasons for their demands. Adolescents with authoritarian parents are likely to be less self-confident and independent, and more likely to regard their parents as unaffectionate and unreasonable in their expectations (Elder, 1980; Conger and Petersen, 1984).

What can we conclude about adolescent identity?

In general, research evidence provides little support for the idea that the majority of adolescents experience a serious identity crisis, though this may be the case for a small minority (Feldman and Elliott, 1990). Hill (1993) suggests that the question of whether everyone experiences a total moratorium remains unanswered.

Adams et al. (1994) reviewed research findings which point to the influence of family styles on development of a sense of identity. He concluded that youths suffering role diffusion tend to come from rejecting and detached families, while those who achieve a secure sense of identity appear to come from warm, supportive families that encourage independence and initiative.

Durkin (1995) argues that what emerges from research in this area is that identity development is not a short-term process but one which extends beyond adolescence and at least into young adulthood and depends heavily on interactions between young people and their social contexts.

Two views of adolescence

The 'traditional' view

The 'traditional' view of adolescence is that of a period of development beset by turmoil and personal upheaval. Adolescence is characterized by extreme physical, emotional and cognitive changes, developing sexual urges, the need to make vocational and other choices, coping with pressure to conform to peer group expectations. All these factors exert pressure and contribute to the turmoil experienced by many young people.

The notion of adolescence as a time of storm and stress is taken for granted in many developmental theories, especially psychoanalytic theories. Anna Freud (1958), for example, described the adolescent as experiencing renewed sexual feelings and strivings. The intensity of inner drives, she believed, leads to excessive emotional upset as the adolescent tries to cope with these impulses and desires. However, this view has been challenged by many researchers into adolescent experience, starting with the classic study of adolescence in Samoa by Mead (1939) (see Box 23.2).

The sociological view

Mead's views on the problems experienced by adolescents in Western societies have been reflected more recently in sociological theory. The **sociological view of adolescence**, like the psychoanalytic approach, involves a belief in the concept of 'storm and stress'. Where these two theoretical approaches differ is in their explanations of the causes of the trauma.

" I BLAME MY PARENTS — THEY NEVER SET ME ANY STANDARDS WORTH REBELLING AGAINST. "

Sociological theory suggests:

- Both socialization and role changes are more significant during adolescence than at any other time during development. Aspects of adolescence such as the increasing independence from parents and other authority figures, greater involvement with peers coupled with a heightened sensitivity to evaluations by other people all serve to hinder the process of role change from childhood to adulthood.
- Major environmental changes such as changing schools, going to university or college, leaving

---

GLOSSARY

'Traditional' view of adolescence Adolescence is seen as a time when stress and turmoil are inevitable. This view is prevalent among psychoanalytic theorists, who see internal factors such as the intensity of inner drives and sexual feelings as a causal factor.

Sociological view of adolescence This approach takes the view that 'storm and stress' during adolescence is caused mainly by external factors such as socialization and role changes, peer pressure, environmental and social changes, the mass media.

Box 23.2   Adolescence in Samoa

The anthropologist, Margaret Mead (1939), challenged the traditional view of adolescence, questioning whether the Western portrayal of adolescence as a troubled and tumultuous time was applicable in other cultures. Mead's study of life among preliterate peoples in the island of Samoa in the South Seas suggests that adolescent turmoil may result from cultural pressures that exist in industrialized, Western societies.

In Samoan life, boys and girls become familiar at an early age with the facts of life, death and sex. Sexuality is treated in an open, casual manner, and, by adolescence, young people freely engage in sexual and love relations. Samoan adolescents therefore experience less guilt and shame than their Western counterparts, and are spared the anxiety and confusion often faced by Western adolescents.

Focusing on the course of adolescence in Samoan girls, Mead describes the process as smooth and natural – in sharp contrast with the adolescent years experienced in our society. Growing up in Samoa is easier because life in general is less complicated. Emotional relationships are treated casually, child rearing is treated lightly, competitiveness and ambition are almost nonexistent. Consequently, adolescence is uneventful. In contrast, Western adolescents experience lives filled with opportunities,

ambitions, pressures to achieve, and thus the stresses which accompany such lifestyles. Mead saw the wide range of opportunities and the pressure to make choices as fostering conflict and stress in adolescents of more 'civilized' societies.'

Mead did not conclude that we should try to remove the stresses that beset adolescents in our society. Rather, we should find ways of more adequately preparing young people for the range of personal and societal choices that they must face.

Mead's study has been criticized by some contemporary anthropologists. Freeman (1983): for example, claimed that her account of life in Samoa was inaccurate and misleading. He attributed her 'errors' to a lack of understanding of the Samoan language and to her decision to live with American ex-patriates on the island rather than with the people she was studying.

Freeman's other argument was that both earlier and later studies provided views of Samoa which conflicted with those of Mead. However, he based his arguments mainly on his own work in Samoa in the 1940s and 1960s. It may be that Samoan society has changed greatly since the 1920s because of the influence of Christian missionaries and American military bases.

---

home, starting a job, all demand the formation of a new set of relationships and this in turn leads to different and often greater expectations and major reassessment of the self.

■ The effects of competing socialization agencies, including the family, the school, the peer group, the mass media and so on, present the adolescent with a wide range of values and ideals from which to choose. This may result in uncertainty and conflict (Brake, 1985; Marsland, 1987).

■ Many of those writing from a sociological perspective believe also that social changes that have occurred since the early 1970s have presented young people with increasingly stressful situations.

Studies of adolescent turmoil

Masterson (1967) found evidence of anxiety in 65 per cent of a sample of normal adolescents aged between 12

and 18 years. Similar findings were reported by Rutter et al. (1970). Almost half of their sample of 14–15 year olds showed symptoms of emotional upset, such as depression or extreme misery.

In contrast, some studies failed to find evidence of stress or turmoil in adolescents. For example, Offer (1969) reported that for the majority of adolescents, changes in identity and in relations with parents and peers occurred gradually and without trauma. Dusek and Flaherty (1981) investigated the stability of self-concept in adolescents during a three-year longitudinal study. Responses to self-report questionnaires indicated that adolescent self-concept does not appear to undergo excessive change. The changes that were noted in subjects appeared to occur gradually and uneventfully.

Coleman and Hendry (1990) found that in most situations, peer-group values appeared to be similar to those of important adults rather than in conflict with them.

Overwhelmingly, research into adolescence indicates that though a small minority may show some disturbance, the large majority of teenagers seem to cope well and show no undue signs of stress or turmoil. Coleman (1995) contends that support for this belief can be found in every major study that has appeared in recent years.

Conflict between theory and research

As we have seen, research provides little support for the 'storm and stress' view of adolescence proposed both in psychoanalytic theory and in sociological theory. Coleman (1995) suggests the following reasons for this mismatch.

- It has been pointed out by many writers that psychoanalysts and psychiatrists see a very select sample of the population. Their views on adolescence may well be unduly influenced by the experiences of the individuals they meet in clinics or hospitals.
- Sociological theorists may, it has been argued, fail to disentangle the concepts of 'youth' or 'the youth movement' from assumptions about the young people themselves. Youth is frequently seen by sociologists as in the forefront of social changes in the established values of society. This may lead to a view which confuses radical forces in society with the beliefs of ordinary people (Brake, 1985).
- Some adolescent behaviours such as hooliganism, drug-taking or vandalism are extremely threatening to adults. It may be that the few who are engaged in these anti-social activities therefore attract greater public attention than the majority who do not. Sensational accounts in the mass media may result in adolescent misdeeds being seen as more common than they actually are. The behaviour of the minority comes to be seen as the norm for all young people.

Coleman argues that all three of these factors may contribute to an exaggerated view of the stress and turmoil that may be expected during adolescence, thus leading to the gap between theory and research widening. This does not mean that the two traditional theories have no value. Perhaps the most important contribution made by the theories is that they have provided a framework for an understanding of those young people who do experience problems and a wider knowledge of those who belong to minority groups.

Coleman says of the theories:

> . . . it must be recognised that they are now inadequate as the basis for an understanding of the development of the great majority of young people. The fact is that adolescence needs a theory, not of abnormality, but of normality.
> (Coleman, 1995, p. 61)

He believes that a viable contemporary theory must incorporate the findings of empirical studies.

Aspects of adolescent experience

Cognitive growth

In his theory of cognitive development, Piaget (see Chapter 20) defined a new level of thinking which emerges around puberty – formal operational thought. Formal operational thought, you will remember, requires the ability to reason and systematically to test out propositions in the abstract without reference to concrete objects. It is considered by Piaget to be the high point of human development.

According to Piaget, the adolescent, faced with a scientific problem to solve, is capable of reasoning hypothetically and taking account of a wide range of differing alternatives, as well as understanding the underlying scientific law. This change in adolescent thought has been described as a shift of emphasis from the 'real' to the 'possible'. However, many studies have shown that true operational thought is found in our culture in only a minority of adolescents. For example, Shayer and Wylam (1978), testing a very large sample of British schoolchildren, found that only about 30 per cent of young people aged 15 or 16 had achieved 'early formal operations'. Therefore, Piaget's claims do not seem strictly to apply to the majority of adolescents. It is nonetheless clear that significant cognitive changes do occur during the adolescent years. Adolescent thought processes become more analytical and reflective than in younger people. Adolescents are more likely to use complex techniques as aids to memory, and are more likely to be capable of anticipating and developing strategies to deal with problems, both academically and in relation to social situations.

Kohlberg's work on moral development (see Chapter 22) has drawn attention to the way in which cognitive changes influence moral reasoning during adolescence. Moral values in the young child at the preconventional level, are typically linked to external sources such as punishments and rewards. At the conventional level, in early adolescence, moral thinking is dominated by concern for the family, society or national standards. Older and more experienced adolescents and adults, during the postconventional or principled level, characteristically base moral judgments on the dictates of their own conscience.

In general, studies have broadly supported Kohlberg's proposal that, with increasing age, young people tend to reach higher levels of moral reasoning (Rest, 1983).

Peer relationships

Peers play an important role in socialization during adolescence. As young people become less influenced by family ties, they develop a greater affinity with others of the same age group. This trend was clearly illustrated in a study by Sorensen (1973). Sixty-eight per cent of his sample believed that their personal values were in accord with those of most other adolescents. Also, 58 per cent of the sample were more likely to identify themselves with others of the same age rather than with others of the same gender, community, race or religion.

A classic study by James Coleman (Coleman et al., 1961) drew attention to the so-called **adolescent subculture** which existed in Western societies. Such a subculture, Coleman believed, was substantially different from the adult culture and was responsible for orientating adolescents towards their peers and

alienating them from their parents or the academic goals of their school.

More recent observers have been critical of the stereotyped view of adolescent society portrayed by Coleman. McClelland (1982) suggested that, while many adolescent groups may distinguish themselves from adults through common tastes in clothing, hairstyles, music and so on, not all these groups are necessarily in revolt against adult norms. According to Hartup (1983), adolescents are more likely to be influenced by parents than peers in such areas as moral and social values. Berndt (1992) concludes that most experts agree that for the majority of teenagers today, peers have far less influence than had previously been believed.

Exercise 23.1

Talk to a number of 15–17 year olds of both sexes about adolescent experience (or develop a simple questionnaire that they can complete anonymously – be sure to note their gender).

Questions you might put are:

■ Do you consider adolescence to be a period of stress and turmoil relative to childhood? If so, what kinds of problems arise and what do you think are the reasons for them?

■ Do you think that most people experience feelings of uncertainty about who they are and what they stand for (identity crisis) during adolescence?

■ If you have a personal problem, are you more likely to discuss this with your parents or with a friend of your own age? Why?

Record the answers and consider whether there is support for any of the theories and research findings discussed in this chapter.

Look to see if there are any clear differences between male and female respondents.

Peer relationships become very important during adolescence

GLOSSARY

Adolescent subculture A term used by Coleman (Coleman et al., 1961) to describe the existence among adolescents of a culture that was separate to the adult culture and which tended to orient young people towards their peers and alienate them from adults.

Box 23.3   The functions of peer relationships

Dunphy (1963) believed that peer relationships during adolescence tend to fall into three main categories: cliques, the crowd and individual friendships.

- ■ **'Cliques'**, or small, intimate same-sex, and later both-sex, groups tend to be made up of young people of similar age, interests and social backgrounds. The clique is thought to provide the framework for the sorts of intimate personal relationships that formerly existed in the family setting.
- ■ Around the clique exists the **crowd**, the larger, more impersonal and loosely defined group. The crowd comes together mainly on the basis of similar social interests or future life-expectancies or career orientations. For instance, university-bound or career-minded 'A'-level students might loosely constitute one crowd, while students who are training for skilled, manual jobs might constitute another.
- ■ As well as belonging to cliques and crowds, adolescents usually have one or two close friends. **Friendships** involve more intense and intimate relationships than do cliques, and provide a setting

for young people to 'be themselves' and to express their innermost feelings, hopes and fears. Adolescents put a high premium on loyalty and trustworthiness in friends. Of almost equal value, especially for girls, is that a friend will listen and respond sympathetically to confidences. Berndt (1982) believes that adolescent friendships can enhance self-esteem by allowing individuals to feel that others respect and are interested in their ideas and feelings. Also, intimate friendships are likely to enhance young people's periods of development by contributing to their social skills and sense of security.

There is agreement between theorists that the peer group offers the young person a 'safe' environment in which to make the shift from unisexual to heterosexual relationships. First, 13 or 14 year olds can practise their new relationship skills within the protected context of the crowd or the clique. When greater confidence is acquired, they can then move towards dating and later the formation of more committed heterosexual pair relationships.

? SELF-ASSESSMENT QUESTIONS

1. Briefly describe the physical changes which take place at puberty. Explain some of the psychological effects of late and early maturation.
2. Outline the views of Erikson and Marcia on the adolescent's search for an identity. Does research evidence support their views?
3. Discuss some different theoretical views on the nature of adolescence.
4. Why do you think there is a conflict between theory and research in relation to the existence of 'storm and stress' during adolescence?
5. What cognitive changes occur during adolescence?
6. In what ways are peer relationships of importance during adolescence?

Lifespan development: the study of adulthood

Until relatively recently, few developmental psychologists paid attention to the course of development during adulthood. This has been partly because two of the most important thinkers in the field, Piaget and Freud, did not consider the adult years; adolescence was treated as the last major period of development. More recently, however, research has been carried out into the nature and quality of adulthood, particularly old age. Investigations have viewed the adult years as a series of 'phases' linked both to age and to various milestones in life, or **critical life events** such as marriage, parenting, divorce, unemployment, retirement, bereavement and death.

GLOSSARY

Critical life events Events or phases in life – for example, marriage, parenting, unemployment – which induce stress and cause some psychological adjustment to take place.

Few theories of adulthood have been proposed. However, a major theory which has embraced **lifespan development** from birth to old age is that of Erik Erikson (1963). Erikson has written extensively not only on childhood and adolescence, but on the developmental changes that take place during adulthood.

Erikson's theory of psychosocial development

Erikson's (1963) theory attempts to provide a framework within which development throughout the whole lifespan may be viewed. A practising psychoanalyst, Erikson was strongly influenced by the ideas of Sigmund Freud (see Chapter 30). However, whereas Freud described psycho*sexual* stages of development, Erikson emphasized the *social* forces which influence development. He described a sequence of **psychosocial stages** which he claimed are applicable to individuals in different cultures and societies. A brief account of Erikson's stages is set out in Figure 23.2. It includes an indication of the approximate ages covered by each stage of the lifespan.

Erikson sees each stage of life as marked by a crisis, or struggle, which the individual must confront and attempt to resolve. (Note that the stages are named in relation to the opposite extremes of the crisis; for example, during the first stage the crisis is 'trust versus mistrust' indicating the individual's need to develop a sense of trust in the environment.)

The level of success with which the crisis is managed will determine that individual's psychological well-being at a particular time. The person who is unable to deal satisfactorily with a crisis will continue to experience problems in later stages and thus progress will be impaired. However, Erikson believed that it is possible to compensate later for unsatisfactory experiences at a particular stage. Similarly, satisfactory negotiation of a crisis at an early stage could be diminished if the individual suffers deficiencies later in development.

Erikson's claim that the eight psychosocial stages of development are applicable universally to individuals in different societies is open to some doubt. The validity of the crises described at each stage, and agreement about what constitutes a desirable outcome, may depend heavily upon the norms and values of a particular culture (Booth, 1975). For example, stage 4, industry versus inferiority, may apply only in cultures

such as ours, which place heavy emphasis on competitiveness and which frown upon children who do not succeed in particular skills at a given time.

A further examination of Erikson's views on adulthood will appear in the following sections on young, middle and late adulthood.

Box 23.4 Some studies of Erikson's theory

Central to Erikson's theory is the notion that personality change arises in relation to the different crises that characterize each developmental stage. A study by Ryff and Heinke (1983) asked the question 'Do people perceive their own personality changes in this way?' Perceptions of personality change were studied in three adult groups: young, middle-aged and old-aged. Participants completed a number of personality scales including two which related to the Eriksonian concepts of integrity (related to old age) and generativity (related to middle age). Concurrent, retrospective and prospective self-reports were obtained. Support for Erikson's theory was found in that all age groups perceived themselves as being most generativity-oriented at middle age and having higher integrity at old age.

A series of studies by Block (1971, 1981) have offered support for Erikson's belief that personality changes occur during the adult years and that adolescence is a critically important time in personality development.

A longitudinal study by Kahn et al. (1985) found support for Erikson's proposition that establishing an identity in adolescence is crucial for later successful intimate relationships. Students' identity scores taken in 1963 were related with their marital status some 20 years later. Interesting sex differences emerged: women with low identity scores were more likely to be divorced or separated; men with low identity scores were found more often to remain single.

GLOSSARY

Lifespan development Development which occurs throughout life, from birth to old age.

Psychosocial stages Erikson's term for the stages of personality development through which an individual passes during life.

Figure 23.2 Erikson's stages of psychosocial development

Life crisis	Favourable outcome	Unfavourable outcome
First year: Trust v mistrust Children need consistent and stable care in order to develop feelings of security	Trust in the environment and hope for the future	Suspicion, insecurity, fear of the future
Second and third years: Autonomy v shame and doubt Children seek a sense of independence from parents. Parental treatment should not be too rigid or harsh	A sense of autonomy and self-esteem	Feelings of shame and doubt about one's own capacity for self-control
Fourth and fifth years: Initiative v guilt Children explore their environment and plan new activities. Sexual curiosity should be sympathetically handled by parents	The ability to initiate activities and enjoy following them through	Fear of punishment and guilt about one's own feelings
Six to 11 years: Industry v inferiority Children acquire important knowledge and skills relating to their culture	A sense of competence and achievement. Confidence in one's own ability to make and do things	Unfavourable reactions from others may cause feelings of inadequacy and inferiority
Adolescence (12–18 years): Identity v confusion The young person searches for a coherent personal and vocational identity	Ability to see oneself as a consistent and integrated person with a strong personal identity	Confusion over who and what one is
Young adulthood (20s and 30s): Intimacy v isolation The adult seeks deep and lasting personal relationships, particularly with a partner of the opposite sex	The ability to experience love and commitment to others	Isolation; superficial relationships with others
Middle adulthood (40–64): Generativity v stagnation The individual seeks to be productive and creative and to make a contribution to society as a whole	The ability to be concerned and caring about others in the wider sense	Lack of growth; boredom and overconcern with oneself
Late adulthood (65+): Integrity v despair The individual reviews and evaluates what has been accomplished in life	A sense of satisfaction with one's life and its accomplishments; acceptance of death	Regret over omissions and missed opportunities; fear of death

Levinson's seasons of a man's life

Levinson (1978, 1986) formulated an influential account of adult development based upon the notion of a series of phases said to occur in each person's life cycle. The account was initially based upon detailed interviews with 40 American men between the ages of 35 and 45. Each participant was asked to review his life so far and to comment on critical choices and their consequences.

From his participants' responses, Levinson proposed four life periods or 'seasons':

- childhood and adolescence;
- early adulthood (from approximately 17–45 years);
- middle adulthood (approximately 40–65 years); and
- older adulthood (from 60 onwards).

Early and middle adulthood

Levinson claimed that though each individual person is unique, everyone goes through the same basic sequence. Each season has its own character and a person's life experiences will be influenced by the biological and social changes associated with that phase of life.

Levinson's account of early and middle adulthood described the self-perceptions and social orientations of a group of men. However, he claims that a broadly similar pattern exists for women.

Early adulthood is seen as the stage where the individual seeks independence from parents and becomes the basis for what Levinson calls **the Dream** – a vision of his goals in life which provide motivation and enthusiasm for the future. For example, a man at this stage of his life might anticipate achievement in his career, sporting achievement or the accumulation of personal wealth, and so on. How the individual relates to his Dream is seen by Levinson as crucial, in that if the Dream does not become a part of his life, it may die and he loses his sense of purpose and responsiveness to life.

Around the age of 28–33, the individual faces the **age 30 transition** when he goes through a period of self-questioning before he finds his niche in life and makes a commitment to a particular career. A key feature of the early adulthood season is the existence of a mentor, an older and more experienced colleague or boss who provides help and advice on career advancement.

Middle adulthood is viewed as a time for the consolidation of interests, goals and commitments. Somewhere between the early 30s and about 40, people begin to 'settle down'. Stable commitments are made to family, career, friends or some special interest. The transition to middle life occurs around 40 and lasts for about five years. This transition period forms a link between early and middle adulthood and according to Levinson is a period of crisis when people evaluate themselves. This reevaluation involves measuring their achievements in the light of earlier goals – the Dream – and, where necessary, readjusting these goals. Levinson believed that the individual must come to terms with discrepancies between what was aimed for earlier in life and what the reality is now. If this acceptance is achieved the individual will experience stability during middle adulthood. Levinson notes that qualities such as wisdom and compassion often emerge during middle adulthood.

Levinson's model is useful in that it illustrates the scale and complexity of adult development. However, it was initially based upon the collection of data from a small group of males in a particular country, who were experiencing development within a particular social, economic and political climate. Critics have stressed the need for cross-cultural research and studies into female development. In relation to the latter, subsequent researchers have studied women's lives in order to discover the extent to which Levinson's framework fits (see Box 23.5).

? SELF-ASSESSMENT QUESTIONS

1. Briefly outline Erikson's theory of lifespan development. How far do you think his model can be applied to all human beings?
2. Outline and evaluate Levinson's model in relation to the study of early and middle adulthood.
3. How far do Levinson's 'seasons' of adulthood apply to the development of females?

GLOSSARY

The Dream Levinson's term for the significant vision an individual develops early in life in relation to, for example, career or sporting goals for the future.

Box 23.5   Seasons of women's lives

Roberts and Newton (1987) have reviewed four studies (unpublished doctoral dissertations) carried out by female investigators with a total sample of 39 females. Their aim was to discover whether Levinson's model of adult development was also applicable to women. A danger, of course, with this kind of research is that attempting to view women's lives through a structure which emerged from a study of men might overlook some important dimension of women's lives or view the developmental progress of women as inferior against a male criterion. However, if anything, the results appear to point to greater complexity in female development.

Roberts and Newton (1987) concluded that, in general terms, the age-related developmental progress of women's lives was very similar to that which Levinson found in men. For example, the early adulthood phase involved the same preoccupation with the 'Dream' and almost all the women experienced an age 30 transition.

However, there were some subtle but important differences:

- For women, the Dream involved different priorities. Very few placed occupational goals as high on the list. Even a group of lawyers, who did place importance on their careers, considered them secondary to marriage. Women's Dreams were generally more complex and diffuse than men's and reflected a conflict between their personal goals and their obligations to others. For many participants, part of their Dream was their husbands' success.
- Levinson stressed the crucial role played by a mentor in men's lives. Roberts and Newton suggested that, for women, such a person was difficult to find. Even women who had professional careers, and who did identify role models, tended not to find a mentor from whom they could receive advice and support in relation to career development.
- The age 30 transition was found to be as important in women's lives as it was for the men in Levinson's study. However, the nature of this transition tended to be influenced by what had gone before. For example, women who had in their 20s placed more emphasis on marriage and motherhood, tended now to develop more individualistic goals. Those who had been career oriented during their 20s, now focused on marriage and starting a family.
- The 30s seemed to be less clearly defined for women and few saw this as a time for 'settling down'. Durkin (1995) suggests that for women the establishment of seniority in a career may be more uncertain, thus providing a less objective basis for 'settling down'.

As with Levinson's research, the studies described by Roberts and Newton are based upon a small sample drawn from an American population. However, in general, women do seem to experience the 'seasons' of adult life described by Levinson. However, the priorities of women's lives are often different from those of men's. Greater emphasis is placed on relationships than on careers, and there seems to be a greater willingness to orient their goals and dreams around other people.

Young adulthood

Growth trends

Following the sometimes turbulent and uncertain period of adolescence, the young adult is usually preoccupied with self-growth in the context of society and relationships with others. According to Sheehy (1976) the central concern of 'Who am I?' during adolescence shifts to questions such as 'How do I put my aspirations into effect?' or 'Where do I go from here?' during adulthood.

White (1975) identified five **growth trends** observed during young adulthood.

- **Stabilization of ego identity**. Ego identity – one's feelings about oneself – is more firmly embedded than at any previous time during development. The ego cannot be seriously damaged, as it might have been during childhood or adolescence, by being called a failure, for example. Greater commitment to social roles, such as occupational

---

GLOSSARY

Growth trends White's term for the general developmental characteristics which have been observed during young adulthood.

role, and to other people, helps the individual to define and maintain a stable and consistent sense of self.

■ **Freeing of personal relationships**. Development of a stable view of themselves results in young adults becoming less concerned about themselves and able to develop strong personal relationships with others. This freedom allows them to be more responsive to another person's needs.

■ **Deepening of interests**. Young adults develop more commitment, and consequently achieve greater satisfaction, from interests such as hobbies, study, occupation, or personal relationships than do younger people.

■ **Humanizing of values**. During this period young adults increasingly view moral and ethical problems in the light of life experiences. They are therefore more likely to be aware of the human aspects of values and the way these values apply in society.

■ **Expansion of caring**. A much more general concern for the well-being of others develops during early adulthood. This concern extends not only to particular individuals known personally to them, but in the wider sense to the deprived and suffering in society at large.

White emphasizes that these growth trends represent the ideal goals of development during youth and young adulthood. Most people make some progress through the dimensions, though it is doubtful whether everyone fulfils all these goals.

Life events

Another way of considering adult development is to look at the way in which people adjust to important life events. A life event can be any 'happening' or phase in the life of an individual which requires that individual to change the pattern of life. Some life events, such as marriage or starting a job, are experienced by most adults. Others, such as imprisonment or suffering a disabling accident, are experienced by relatively few people. Life-event theory suggests that all life events, whether good or bad, can induce stress and therefore require some psychological adjustment.

Lowenthal et al. (1975) found that, as might be expected, young adults are in general exposed to more life events than are middle-aged and older adults. The latter two groups report more negative stresses, while young adults report more positive stresses. Lowenthal et al. point out that the impact of a life event on an individual is not determined simply by the actual occurrence of the event. The critical factor in assessing the level of stress appears to be the individual's perception of the event. Two people might experience a similar life event (divorce, for example) but perceive it in very different ways. One person might feel bereft, while another might feel liberated.

Marriage

In modern Western societies, over 90 per cent of adults marry at least once. Although there is an increasing tendency for younger people not to enter into formal marriage, the majority of people who do not legally marry still enter into long-term pair-bonding relationships which resemble those of a husband and wife (Reibstein and Richards, 1992).

Marital adjustment Many studies have examined the changes and adjustments that people undergo when they marry:

■ Vincent (1964) found that in a group of married people significant changes occurred in such traits as dominance and self-acceptance. Traditionally, greater adjustments to marriage have been made by women. Women often relinquish a career to become housewives and mothers and this may result in less contentment in marriage for women than for men.

■ Unger and Crawford (1992) found that more women report dissatisfaction with their marriages than do men. Marriage appears, however, to have a beneficial effect on men.

■ Veroff and Feld (1970) found that married men reported that they were happier than single men. They were also healthier and lived longer.

■ Teachman et al. (1994) found that in the USA married men spent less time unemployed than single men and were more likely to take a job than single men.

■ As with all relationships, marriage is not static (Reibstein and Richards, 1992). Both partners develop and change and the nature of the relationship changes as a result. For some couples this change is for the worse, though for others marital satisfaction is maintained or increased throughout life.

Box 23.6   Marital roles

There are many different kinds of marriage, each of which may sustain different roles for the husband and wife. Duberman (1973) identified three main types of marriage.

- The traditional marriage operates on the assumption that the husband is the main force and decision maker. While the wife may have authority over such matters as childcare and domestic matters, all other areas are controlled by the husband.
- The companionship marriage places the emphasis on equality and companionship. Male and female roles are not differentiated and either partner may make decisions and assume responsibilities in any area.
- The colleague marriage is similar to the companionship marriage in that heavy emphasis is placed upon sharing and personal satisfaction. However, role differences are accepted, and each partner becomes responsible for different areas of married life, according to their interests and abilities.

Companionship and colleague-type marriages are becoming increasingly common among middle-class couples. Many marriages, of course, do not fit neatly into any of these categories, and many features overlap.

Current social pressures regarding roles in marriage are less rigid than they were. Far more young people subscribe to the idea of shared roles in marriage, as compared to their parents' generation. As more women work outside the home, their husbands make greater contributions to household chores and childcare. Below is a selection of research findings:

- Bahr (1973) reported that husbands of working wives perform significantly more household chores than husbands of nonworking wives. However, Walker (1970) compared the work activity of husbands and wives in the home and showed that women spent far more time on household tasks than men (five hours a day compared to one and a half hours a day).
- Presland and Antill (1987) found that where both partners were working, there is a slight increase in the amount of time men spend on housework and a more substantial decrease in the amount of time women devote to it. However, women tend generally to retain the overall responsibility for household chores.
- Matlin (1993) argues that traditionally in marriages, women and men generally divide up the household tasks according to how much physical strength may be required and whether the tasks are performed inside or outside the home. For example, women have tended to do the cooking, cleaning and baby tending, while men have washed the car, done the gardening and taken out rubbish.
- A study by Booth (1977) showed that husbands of working women tended to be happier and under less stress than husbands whose wives were full-time homemakers.
- It is interesting that Wright et al. (1992) found that Swedish men were considerably more involved in housework than American men. This suggests that deliberate social policy changes have influenced domestic gender behaviour. Since the 1970s, the Swedish Government has pursued a policy of commitment to gender equality in areas such as tax systems, childcare provision and family support which has not been paralleled in America or in other European countries.

- Bengston et al. (1990) found that in general patterns of marital satisfaction tended to follow a U-shaped curve, high in the early and later stages but dropping in the middle.

(See also the discussion of love and marriage in Chapter 25, and in Malim (1997))

Divorce

Recent statistics indicate that more than one in three marriages will end in divorce. Most of these divorces will occur during the first seven years of marriage (Reiss, 1980). Teenage marriages are almost twice as likely to end in divorce as marriages that take place when couples are in their 20s.

The fact that marriages that break down tend to do so in the early years, and that teenage marriages are more likely to end in divorce, suggests that there may be some underlying developmental cause. One or the other of the marriage partners may not have firmly established a coherent identity independent of parents, or have succeeded in making a commitment to an occupation.

Adjustment to divorce   Studies suggest that divorce is highly stressful and ranks second only to the death

As more women work outside the home, their partners make greater contributions to household chores

of a spouse in terms of the readjustments which the individual must make in his or her life (Holmes and Rahe, 1967). Emotional reactions to divorce will vary according to the events that preceded the break (Kelly, 1982). For the unsuspecting, previously contented person, the reaction may be shock; the person who has suffered years of conflict and misery may well experience relief. However, evidence suggests that both will suffer distress and will experience a period of 'mourning' for the relationship.

Wiseman (1975) reports that many divorced people experience an identity crisis as they reorganize their lives. This is particularly true for a woman who married young and whose identity was dominated by that of her husband.

Bohannon (1985a, 1985b) proposes that there are six components involved in the process of divorce. These components are not sequential and may overlap. Bohannon suggests that it is important to understand these components in order to cope with the emotional chaos which divorce may bring:

■ **Emotional divorce**. This component typically begins before the decision is made to divorce. It is characterized by a failing marriage and involves a wide range of negative feelings and behaviours, including betrayals, accusations and lack of affection and support.

■ **Legal divorce**. This relates to the legal process of severing the civil ties of marriage. Many couples are unprepared for the complexities of divorce and the amount of psychological energy needed to cope.

■ **Economic divorce**. Decisions must be made about how couples will divide up their money and possessions. Almost invariably, this process involves resentment, anger and hostility.

■ **Coparental divorce**. Where there are children, the courts will decide which parent will receive custody. This is done on the basis of what is best for the children. Access rights for the parent not given custody must also be determined. During this stage, worry and distress is often expressed about the effects of the divorce on the children.

■ **Community divorce**. This relates to the changes which occur in a divorced person's status in the surrounding neighbourhood. Many divorced people feel isolated and lonely and may experience some social disapproval. Sometimes, relationships with friends are changed and some divorced people regret that divorcing a spouse involves also a 'divorce' from their in-laws.

■ **Divorce from dependency**. The shift from being part of a couple to becoming single requires considerable psychological adjustment. As might be expected, those individuals who maintained a high degree of independence in their marriages are likely to become autonomous more quickly than those marriage partners who were dependent upon one another.

Bohannon's components should not be seen as a precise and rigid framework that is the same for everyone who is going through divorce. As noted previously, reactions to divorce may vary from person to person, depending upon the events that went before. However, the main value of Bohannon's work is that it highlights the complexity of divorce and provides a framework which helps us to understand the changes that people face when going through this painful process. There is also discussion of the breakup of relationships in Chapter 25.

Parenting

In Erikson's model of psychosocial development, the young adult experiences the crisis of **intimacy** versus isolation. The need to feel love for and make a commitment to another person is the main goal of this stage. Following the resolution of this crisis, the first stirrings of the crisis of generativity occurs as couples confront feelings and make decisions about parenthood. Generativity – the desire to care for others and contribute to the growth and well-being of future generations – may be achieved through having children (see also the section on 'Parents and offspring' in Chapter 18).

Fertility motivation Many factors influence a couple's decision to have children. Researchers on fertility motivation – people's motives for having or not having children – have cited a number of factors which may contribute to the decision: social pressure, particularly from their own parents; a need for the emotional security that offspring may give in later life; a desire to pass down one's own characteristics and values; a love of children for their own sake.

Parenthood as a developmental process Many researchers believe that, for both parents, having a child contributes to the developmental process in that it allows them to relive the earlier developmental crises through which they themselves have passed. Erikson (1968) believes that pregnancy allows a woman to use the 'productive inner space' which lies at the centre of female fulfilment. Benedek (1959), a psychoanalyst, suggested that a woman's maternal instinct arises from her early identification with her own mother. Memory traces retained from her own childhood allow her to reexperience the pleasures and problems of infancy as she looks after her own child. Dinnerstein (1976), however, believed that a woman's feelings about mothering would be different if childcare were shared more evenly with the father.

Adjusting to parenthood A major task of parenthood is to socialize the infant. The parents, in turn, are socialized by the child. As the parents help the child to acquire good eating, toilet and social habits, they learn how to respond to the child and make it comfortable and secure.

Parenthood has been described as a crisis point in the life of a couple. In a study of over 2,500 adults, Dohrenwend et al. (1978) found that the birth of the first child was rated the sixth most stressful life event in a list of 102 possible events. This may be at least in part because people receive little preparation for parenthood from society.

Many studies have indicated that marital satisfaction tends to decrease with the arrival of the first child (Reibstein and Richards, 1992). Schulz (1972) found that young parents talk to each other only about half as much as couples without children, and then the conversation is often about the child. In some marriages, however, particularly if children are planned, they can strengthen the marital relationship.

Parenthood invariably leads to the couple relating to society in a new way. New mothers enjoy the company of other new mothers; young parents seek out the company of their own parents for advice and emotional support, and for babysitting. Social institutions which previously have had little significance in the lives of the couple will be reevaluated. Parks, libraries and schools will be assessed, and active involvement may occur in causes such as the promotion of road safety or opposition to TV violence (Brodzinsky et al., 1986).

There is strong evidence that the quality of the relationship which existed between the parents before the child was born is important. Their relationship has implications first for how the parents will meet the challenge of parenthood and secondly for the quality of their interactions with the child (Cox et al., 1989; Heinicke and Guthrie, 1992). Heinicke and Guthrie found that parents who showed the most positive prebirth interactions and who were able to deal with any conflicts in a mutually respectful way were more likely to adjust well to the birth of a child. Cox et al. (1989), reviewing the literature, concluded that the extent to which couples establish a confiding relationship was related to maternal warmth and the husband's feelings about his role as a father.

GLOSSARY

Intimacy According to Erikson, a critical psychosocial achievement, characterized by the feeling of love and commitment to another person.

Isolation According to Erikson, a feeling that one is disconnected from others in the absence of a true intimate relationship.

Fertility motivation People's motives for having or not having children.

Box 23.7 Attachment behaviour in parents

We saw in Chapter 19 that typical behaviour indicating attachment in infants included wanting to stay close to the attachment figure, distress at absence, feelings of security in the presence of the attachment figure. These characteristics are also to be found in the new parent who experiences a close attachment to the child (Newman and Newman, 1988). However, the parents' experience of attachment has some additional features: for example, a strong sense of responsibility for the child's well-being, satisfaction on meeting the child's needs, and anxiety and stress when those needs do not appear to be met. Also, the parent experiences a new social capacity: the opportunity and obligation to exert authority. How this is incorporated into family life has important implications for the child's development and the parent–child relationship.

There appears, also, to be a sense of continuity in attachment relationships. Feeney et al. (1994) and Main (in press) found that new parents' reports of their own personal attachment histories were closely related to the attachment types found in their own infants. These findings offer some support for Benedeck's (1959) views referred to earlier on the implications of a woman's identification with her own mother. (See also Chapter 19.)

Exercise 23.2 Marital roles

Interview several young couples who have been married for a year or two about the 'style' of their marriages and the roles and responsibilities that each partner assumes. Questions you might ask are:

■ To what extent do you have your own specific roles and responsibilities?
■ What factors determine the responsibilities each partner will have – issues of equality? interests and abilities? traditional gender-role expectations?
■ To what extent are household chores and/or childcare shared? Who has the most overall responsibility for these aspects of marriage?

Record the answers and consider the evidence in the light of Duberman's three main types of marriage and the research findings on marital roles in Box 23.6.

Middle adulthood

There are two conflicting interpretations of the nature of middle age. One view is that it is a time of conflict and crisis. Researchers have used the term **midlife crisis** to describe the time when middle-aged people become conscious of, and often depressed about, the changes which are taking place in their lives, such as the physical and psychological effects of ageing, occupational adjustments and the departure of children from the home (see Box 23.8). A more optimistic view emphasizes that middle age is a time when people are more accepting of themselves and are ready to approach life with renewed vigour.

Which of these two interpretations is adopted by middle-aged people depends upon how they perceive themselves and their lives. So, too, does the timing of the advent of middle age. Some people perceive themselves to be young or middle-aged well into their sixties, whereas others consider themselves middle-aged at 35.

Personality and social development

An important question that has been addressed by researchers is 'Do aspects of personality, such as values and beliefs, change systematically as people move from young adulthood to middle and old age, or is personality stable throughout?' Unfortunately, the

? SELF-ASSESSMENT QUESTIONS

1. Describe White's account of development during young adulthood.
2. What do you understand by the term 'life events' as used in psychological literature?
3. Discuss some of the research carried out into the impact of either marriage or divorce.
4. What psychological adjustments must be made during parenthood? To what extent are parents socialized by the child?

Box 23.8   Does the midlife crisis exist?

As was noted earlier, Levinson reported that men of between 40 and 45 experienced a crisis as they moved through the transition period from young to middle adulthood. He believed that these feelings of turbulence and self-evaluation are a normal part of development and allow the individual to reach a new stability in life.

As a result of Levinson's work, the notion of a 'midlife crisis' was widely taken up by newspapers both in the USA and in Britain. It was not always remembered that Levinson's sample was small and restricted to particular kinds of men in just one society. Subsequent research has raised doubts about how far Levinson's findings can be generalized to everyone:

■ Vaillant (1977) argued that most periods of life are experienced as difficult by some people.
■ Baruch et al. (1983) found that doubt about the direction of one's life and the value of achievements is often experienced in early career, rather than during middle age.
■ Several studies found that large numbers of middle-aged people actually feel more positive about this stage of their life than earlier ones (Long and Porter, 1984).
■ Farrell and Rosenberg (1981), using larger samples than Levinson, found that while many people report that they experienced some reevaluation during middle age, only about 12 per cent felt that they had experienced a crisis.

To summarize, the midlife crisis does not seem to be as widespread as Levinson indicated. Durkin (1995) suggests that the time and degree to which people experience uncomfortable self-evaluations are likely to vary depending upon personality and social context.

Overall, midlife is a period of change and readjustment but . . . the nature and consequence of the changes are integrally interwoven with the individual's social relationships and roles.

(Durkin, 1995, p. 638)

in general, empirical evidence supports the notion of stability of personality in adulthood.

Longitudinal studies, in particular, note that some of the most stable characteristics include values (social, political, economic, religious and aesthetic) and vocational interests. Neugarten (1977) reported that in cross-sectional studies the findings are less clear-cut, with some studies, though not others, finding differences between age groups in personality characteristics such as rigidity, cautiousness, conservatism and self-concept. (See the Introduction to Part 5 for an indication of the strengths and limitations of long-itudinal and cross-sectional studies.)

Stability of personality

Studies of personality over time have distinguished between relative stability and absolute stability.

■ **Relative stability** refers to the rank order of personality scores of a sample of participants over a period of time. A personality dimension would be relatively stable if the rank order among participants remained similar from one period to another, irrespective of whether there was an overall increase or decrease in the scores.
■ **Absolute stability** refers to whether participants maintain the same score on a personality dimension from one occasion to another. For example, it is known that people increase their level of self-awareness between childhood and middle age. The absolute stability of this personality dimension is therefore low.

Box 23.9 contains an account of some of the findings from Haan et al.'s (1986) longitudinal study of personality and physical and mental health from adolescence to middle age.

GLOSSARY

Midlife crisis The term used to describe the time during middle age when people become conscious of, and often depressed about, their life situation.

Relative stability Whether the rank order of participants' scores on a characteristic such as personality remain the same relative to each other over a period of time.

Absolute stability Whether participants in a study maintain the same score on a test of a characteristic such as personality from one occasion to another.

answer to this question is not easy to obtain. Personality is a very complex aspect of human beings, and not easy to measure accurately over time. However,

Box 23.9   Stability of personality over time

Haan and colleagues (1986) carried out a major longitudinal study of personality and physical and mental health in several cohort groups from adolescence to middle age. Participants' personality ratings were correlated across the adolescent, young adult and middle adult years. Results showed the following.

- Generally, personality dimensions were relatively stable: that is, participants rated high on particular dimensions on one occasion tended to be rated high on a later occasion.
- Greater stability existed between adolescence and young adulthood, and between young adulthood and middle adulthood, than between adolescence and middle adulthood.
- Those personality dimensions most concerned with the self (for example, self-confidence) tended to be the most stable.
- Women's personalities tended to be more stable than men's.
- Men's personalities changed most during the period from adolescence to young adulthood, as they developed careers and financial independence.
- People increased in cognitive investment, openness to self, nurturance towards others and self-confidence from adolescence to old age; that is, there is a low degree of absolute stability in these dimensions.

It seems that while some developmental change does occur, adult personality is not subject to large and pervasive changes in relation to beliefs, attitudes and values. Haan et al. (1986) suggest that transformations in personality that do occur probably arise from circumstances that force a person to change. This supports the idea suggested in the last section that people adjust their personalities in response to life events such as marriage or parenting.

Developmental theories of middle adulthood

Erikson

Erikson (1963) considered the central conflict of the middle years to be that of generativity versus stagnation. The individual becomes concerned with contributing to and guiding the next generation. Erikson explains that this drive does not always necessarily relate to one's own children, but may take the form of creative contributions or guidance and counselling with young people. The person who does not achieve generativity will experience a sense of personal impoverishment and an excessive concern with self.

Peck

Peck (1968) described four major psychological adjustments which face middle-aged people.

- They must learn to value wisdom more than physical power and attractiveness. This involves accepting as inevitable the decline in physical powers and gaining satisfaction from the wisdom that comes from experience, knowledge and mental ability.
- Men and women must value each other as individual personalities rather than as primarily sex objects.
- They must develop the capacity to shift their emotional investment from one person or activity to another. Emotional flexibility is particularly important in middle age. As children leave home, relatives or friends die, and certain activities such as strenuous sport are no longer possible, it is important to be able to focus on and gain satisfaction from different people or activities.
- It is important at middle age to remain mentally flexible and receptive to new ideas and ways of doing things.

Levinson

As we saw earlier, Levinson (1978, 1986) suggested that from the age of approximately 40–45, an individual moves through a midlife transition which forms a bridge between early and middle adulthood. A major task of middle adulthood is to evaluate success or

---

GLOSSARY

Generativity versus stagnation According to Erikson, the most significant psychosocial crisis of middle age. An individual becomes concerned with contributing to and guiding the next generation (generativity). If this does not occur, the individual experiences a sense of impoverishment or stagnation.

Midlife: a time for change, or perhaps even a new life?

failure in meeting the goals established during young adulthood. This self-appraisal arises from a heightened awareness of one's own mortality and a desire to use the remaining time wisely. A second task of middle adulthood is to take steps to adjust the more negative elements of one's life and establish the basis of a new life structure. The amount of change made at this time will vary greatly from person to person. For some, a drastic change may occur, such as divorce or a major change in occupation. Some individuals may experience change in their social outlook, personal values or inner convictions.

Erikson, Peck and Levinson each describe a different facet of middle age. A common theme exists in that each agrees that middle adulthood is a period of significant challenge, during which individuals must adjust to changes both within and outside of themselves.

Unemployment

Unemployment is an extremely stressful occurrence for adolescents and adults of all ages. However, the unemployment rates caused by recession are likely to have more serious outcomes for older adults. Middle-aged and older adults, once unemployed, are likely to remain so for up to 70 per cent longer than younger workers (Entine, 1976). The psychological consequences for middle-aged adults are also likely to be serious. Family responsibilities will probably be very demanding and the need to save and build up financial security for old age is likely to be at its most pressing.

Unemployed adults appear to progress through four psychological stages during a prolonged period of unemployment:

■ **Relaxation and relief** occurs after the initial shock. Individuals experience a feeling of contentment with their new, more relaxed status. Feelings of hope and confidence in their ability to find new employment lead to phase 2.

■ **A concerted effort** is made to secure a new job. At this stage, most are becoming bored with their increased leisure time, but are still optimistic about job prospects. As efforts to find work are continually frustrated, the jobless person enters a third phase.

■ **Vacillation and doubt**. The individual begins to experience self-doubt and efforts to find work are irregular. Relations with family and friends become strained.

■ **Malaise and cynicism**. The last phase is characterized by feelings of apathy and listlessness. Many of the people studied claimed that they felt helpless and inadequate and had difficulty in imagining themselves ever working again.

Jahoda's thesis

While there appears to be agreement about the damaging psychological effects of unemployment, there is less of a consensus on the mechanisms that may bring this about. Probably the most influential account of the processes which underlie the link between unemployment and psychological well-being has been proposed by Jahoda (1982). Jahoda suggested that employment, however difficult, fulfils a number of important functions:

■ It gives people a clear time structure to the day and provides a compulsory pattern of activity.
■ It provides a source of social contacts outside the home.
■ It allows people to experience a feeling of participation in a wider collective purpose.
■ It is a source of identity and social status.

Jahoda's account focuses on the importance of a life structure and of ties with the community. She argued that in an advanced capitalist society, it is only through employment that such experiences can be provided.

Jahoda's explanation stimulated a sustained debate in the literature and a number of possible inadequacies were pointed out. For example, Fraser (1981) argued that Jahoda greatly underestimated the significance of sheer financial hardship. Gallie et al. (1994) argued that

Box 23.10 Studies of the psychological impact of unemployment

An in-depth study of the lives of unemployed men was carried out by Marsden in 1975. Marsden found that the men were beset by difficulties in sleeping, by loss of appetite and by tiredness during the day. As the length of unemployment grew, they tended to lose a sense of meaning in their lives and often their sense of identity.

It was difficult to be sure from Marsden's study how typical these experiences were of unemployed people in general. However, in the 1980s a major programme of research into the psychological consequences of unemployment was set up by Peter Warr of the Social and Applied Psychology Unit at Sheffield. The studies showed that unemployment led to increasing levels of psychological distress among men. It could be argued that it was not possible to disentangle cause and effect in the studies. However, a longitudinal study by Warr and Jackson (1985) indicated that once people were reemployed, there was a noticeable improvement in their psychological well-being, suggesting that unemployment was the causal factor.

Research by Gallie and Vogler (1994) showed that the currently unemployed had a lower level of psychological well-being than any labour market group, other than currently nonactive people who had been unemployed previously or who had an unemployed partner.

There has been markedly less research interest in the psychological consequences of unemployment for women. However, Kelvin and Jarrett (1985) have suggested that women's experiences of unemployment may differ from those of men in the following ways:

- In general, women are typically to be found in less-skilled and less well-paid work, with fewer opportunities for career enhancement. Thus, many women may perceive their work as less enriching and therefore the loss of a job is not so traumatic.
- Many women often bear the double burden of a job and domestic work. The loss of paid employment doubtless eases this demanding workload.
- The domestic role many women play may offer an alternative set of activities and source of identity, which shield them from some of the worst effects of unemployment.

Jahoda's proposals do not adequately address the possible differences between men's and women's experiences or whether other roles outside employment can provide compensatory benefits for the loss of employment-based experiences.

A small-scale study by Miles (1983) has provided some support for Jahoda's thesis. However, it focused only on men in one particular region (Brighton), the sample was not randomly selected and there was only a very small control group of employed people.

Following Jahoda's thesis, Gershuny (1994) examined two aspects of unemployment: first, whether unemployment does cause psychological distress through changes in the individual's environment other than those brought about by financial loss; secondly, the extent to which different patterns of sociability and domestic situation may alleviate the effects of unemployment. His provisional conclusions are as follows:

- The categories of experience described by Jahoda do seem to be strongly associated with paid employment.
- There is a significant, though small, relationship between opportunities to experience these categories and levels of psychological adjustment. This applies both to men and women, though the relationship is rather smaller for women.
- Activities outside of employment can to some extent provide experiences of the kind that Jahoda saw as vital for psychological health. However, in general, they do not appear to be an adequate substitute for employment itself.

? SELF-ASSESSMENT QUESTIONS

1. What do you understand by the term 'midlife crisis'? Does it exist?
2. What conclusions would you draw from research carried out to investigate the stability of personality over time? Distinguish between absolute and relative stability.
3. Outline one developmental theory of middle adulthood.
4. Briefly discuss Jahoda's (1982) thesis in relation to the psychological impact of unemployment. How far is the thesis supported by research evidence?

Late adulthood

Old age is the last phase of the lifespan. Researchers in the field of **gerontology** have attempted to define when exactly the period of old age begins. Some distinguish between 'elderly' and 'advanced' old age. Early old age is said to occur between the ages of 65 and 74, and late old age from 75 on. However, a chronological definition of ageing can be misleading. The adage 'You are as old as you feel' is subscribed to by many older adults. This implies that subjective or psychological factors are more important in defining whether or not a person is old, than is noting the number of years lived.

The study of older adults has gathered momentum over the last 20 years or so. As life expectancy increases, older people have become the focus of attention by psychologists, medical practitioners, urban planners and politicians. Among gerontologists, many disagreements arise about late adulthood. Some find that intellectual ability declines with age; others refuse to accept that this is so. Some believe that successful adjustment to old age is brought about by the individual's disengagement from society; others believe that continued activity actually enhances adjustment in later years.

Senescence

Senescence, or primary ageing, refers to the period of life when the degenerative processes of ageing set in. It is a normal part of growing older and usually occurs gradually. The timing and effects of senescence vary from person to person.

Researchers have identified many different aspects of senescence. These include physiological, biochemical and behavioural changes. As people age there is a loss of neural tissue; the heart, lungs and nervous system become less efficient; and the body's resistance to disease breaks down. Older people are thus more likely to become ill and have greater difficulty in recovering. Many of the external signs of senescence begin to appear during middle age: grey hairs, skin wrinkles, weight gain, diminishing muscle strength and agility, sight and hearing difficulties are all outward manifestations of the changes which occur with increasing age.

Cognitive functioning in late adulthood

Certain aspects of intelligence appear to decline with age.

Exercise 23.3 Stereotypes of the elderly

The evidence outlined in Box 23.11 suggests that some negative stereotypes about elderly people exist in our society. How far does the media promote the continuation of these stereotypes?

Watch a random selection of TV shows at peak viewing time over a two-week period.

Note in particular the roles and behaviours of older adults in the programmes, as well as other people's attitudes and behaviour towards them.

From your observations, draw some conclusions about the role of TV in perpetuating negative stereotypes about older people.

Are there any subgroups of older adults who are more likely to be stereotyped than others?

Longitudinal studies indicate that performance on IQ tests is relatively stable up to the age of around 60. After this, a steady decline is often noticeable in areas which measure psychomotor skills, attention, memory, inductive reasoning and quickness of response. However, social knowledge, verbal-conceptual ability and mathematical reasoning do not appear to be affected by the ageing process (Horn and Donaldson, 1980).

Decreases in intellectual functioning do not seem to be experienced equally by all people. A study by Schulz et al. (1980) found that those who had kept themselves mentally active throughout their lives, experienced little, if any, decline. Schaie (1983, 1990) found that older people who continue actively to use a skill or ability often perform better than younger people who have had less practice.

Studies of memory processes during old age indicate that short-term memory – that is, the recall of immediate information that is still being attended to – suffers some decline. There appears to be little difference between older and younger adults in the number of items that can be held in short-term memory.

GLOSSARY

Gerontology The scientific study of the elderly and the ageing process.

Senescence The period of life when the degenerative processes of ageing set in.

Box 23.11   Attitudes towards the elderly

Cultural variations

Attitudes to increasing age vary considerably across cultures. In many traditional societies, chronological age is not an important factor, partly because the years are not counted. However, Keith (1990) found that in advanced industrial nations, chronological age promotes social differentiation. Historical and anthropological evidence reviewed by Fry (1985) and Tout (1989) shows that, in many societies, elderly people retain their status, authority and social involvement.

Even within Western societies whose economic status is similar, policies and attitudes towards the elderly vary. For example, in Greece there is a general view that people retain their vigour well into their late 70s and should be cared for and involved in the family (Amira, 1990). In Denmark, there is a policy of state-funded, institutional support which ensures the care of the elderly, but which also results in their separation from relatives and greater problems of loneliness (Jamieson, 1990).

These old men in Greece are still active leaders in their society, gathering together daily to discuss important issues in village life

Stereotypes of the elderly

In British and American societies, attitudes towards the elderly are somewhat paradoxical. On the one hand, we respect the wisdom and experience of many professional people, such as judges and politicians, who are past the normal age of retirement. On the other hand, there are many negative attitudes associated with ageing and stereotypes abound in many areas of life. Schmidt and Boland (1986) found a range of different stereotypes, from 'perfect grandparent' at the positive end to 'bag lady' and 'vagrant' at the negative.

Stereotypes of the elderly tend to contain some negative components, whatever the age group of the perceivers (even older people themselves). However, the most negative stereotypes appear to be held by children and adolescents (Goldman and Goldman, 1981). Over 800 children aged 5–15 from Australia, England, Sweden and the USA were interviewed about their perceptions of old age. Though there were some variations among interviewees, there were two general patterns of response:

- Children of all ages were more likely to say negative things about the elderly than positive; this kind of response was more likely as the age of the respondents increased. Over 90 per cent of 15 year olds described elderly people in negative terms.
- The researchers commented on the revulsion and often disgust expressed about old age. Remarks about physical attributes (wrinkled skin, feebleness, sickness, etc.) and psychological characteristics (bad-tempered, slow to react or understand, etc.) were common.

There may be many reasons why old age is perceived in such a negative way. Jackson (1992) suggests that diminishing physical attractiveness may be one reason. Attractiveness is highly prized in many societies. Durkin (1995) proposes that another reason may be the older person's changing status both within the family and in the world of work. When people retire, they no longer have a clear economic role, their income is reduced and their authority diminished.

As we have seen, there is compelling evidence that stereotypes exist in relation to the elderly. However, on a positive note, it seems that few people extend the stereotypes to all the people that they actually *know*. For example, most studies find that grandparents are generally valued and described in positive terms by children and adolescents (Werner, 1991).

The older adult, however, is likely to be more susceptible to distraction and less able to recall memorized information in a different form.

So far as long-term memory is concerned, research indicates that older people have more problems remembering material that they have ceased actively to focus upon, though they will have little difficulty remembering knowledge and experiences that they recall frequently. As with general intellectual functioning, well-educated and mentally active individuals do not experience the same memory decline as those people who do not exercise their minds.

Many researchers stress that although some aspects of cognitive functioning do show decline, this should not lead to an overly pessimistic view of old age. As people age, deficits in physical and mental functioning are often compensated for by greater wisdom arising from experience and breadth of knowledge.

The cognitive quality of wisdom incorporates such characteristics as intuitiveness, experience, introspection, empathy, understanding, patience and gentleness. Clayton and Birren (1980) note that most adults associate these characteristics with old age.

Pratt et al. (1987) compared young, middle-aged and older adults' responses to moral dilemmas and found no decline with age but noted evidence of increasingly complex reasoning among 60–75 year olds.

Theories of personality development and adjustment

Late adulthood is seen by many theorists as a time of continuing psychological growth. The developmental tasks of the older adult include adjusting to declining physical powers and health, coping with retirement and limited income, and adjusting to the death of a marriage partner.

Erikson's theory

During old age, according to Erikson (1968), the individual must resolve the crisis he describes as ego integrity versus despair. As people approach the end of their lives they tend to look back and evaluate the decisions they have made and the actions which have influenced their lives. This review should ideally lead to feelings of satisfaction and acceptance that the life one has lived is meaningful and important. Such feelings lead to high ego integrity. The person whose life review reveals feelings of regret and disappointment that life has been unsatisfactory and unfulfilling will experience despair.

While most people will experience both these psychological states at various times, the person who achieves a greater degree of integrity over despair will experience a feeling of well-being and a sense of purpose even in the face of death.

Peck's theory

Peck (1968) believes that continued psychological growth during late adulthood depends upon how well individuals cope with three major developmental tasks.

- They must come to terms with **vocational retirement**. This involves developing feelings of self-worth and satisfaction in areas other than the job of work which has been a central influence in earlier stages of life. People able to express their personalities in ways not connected with their work role are more likely to lead happy, interesting and well adjusted lives in later years.
- **Physical decline** is inevitable in old age. People who have relied upon physical well-being for satisfaction and pleasure may become very preoccupied with the state of their bodies and depressed about their declining physical powers. Peck believes that it is important that older people should shift their attention away from bodily concerns and learn to value satisfying relationships with others and creative mental activities.
- The final adjustment that older adults must make is related to **human mortality**. Each individual must recognize and accept that death is inevitable. Such acceptance should include the knowledge that their lives can be significant after death through children, through friendships and through contributions they have made to society.

Successful adjustment to ageing

What constitutes successful adjustment to old age has been the subject of some debate. There are two prevalent, largely conflicting, theories: disengagement theory and activity theory.

Disengagement theory proposes that as individuals approach their last years of life, they gradually

GLOSSARY

Integrity versus despair According to Erikson, the most significant crisis to be overcome in late adulthood. If people feel content and accepting of their lives, integrity is achieved; despair results if it is felt that life has been without real meaning.

Disengagement theory A theory which suggests that during late adulthood the gradual detachment of an individual from work and social activities will lead to psychological well-being.

withdraw from social contacts and activities. They also become less concerned with the problems of the outside world and detach themselves from complicated emotional interactions with other people.

Studies (Neugarten, 1973, 1977) suggest that older people increasingly take less part in family and community activities. This does not mean that friends and social relationships are not important to them. In fact, friendships can often provide valuable support and compensate for losses experienced in old age. Therefore, friendship and social interaction can help the adjustment process during ageing (Tesch, 1983).

Disengagement theory was first proposed by Cumming and Henry (1961) who maintained that the gradual disengagement of the individual from society will lead to psychological well-being and contentment. However, premature disengagement caused by ill health or early retirement is likely to lead to problems in adjustment.

Activity theory, developed by Maddox (1964), suggests that successful adjustment during old age is brought about by the individual remaining productive and active. Psychological well-being is maintained where an individual can find substitute activities for those that are ending. For example, retirement from work will require the individual to find new interests and activities to fill the gap.

Activity theory has received little empirical support and has been criticized as an over-simplification of the issues involved. Some individuals clearly prefer to maintain a high level of involvement in social activities and relationships, while others are more contented with disengagement.

The activity theory of ageing suggests that it is important for elderly people to find new interests and activities – here, helping to run a charity shop, for example

Studies by Reichard et al. (1962) indicate that personality factors are important determinants of whether a person will adjust successfully to old age. Therefore, they argue that neither disengagement nor activity theories alone can adequately explain successful ageing. Also, factors other than personality or the ageing process may partially determine whether an individual disengages from society or continues to lead an active life. Lack of money, reduced mobility, societal attitudes towards old people may all militate against an individual leading an active, independent life in old age.

Durkin (1995) argues that two factors stand out as being critical to well-being and satisfaction in later years: personal control and social involvement. These are the same factors which are important throughout the lifespan from infancy onwards. Pratt and Norris (1994) found that higher self-efficacy (seeing oneself as having control over one's life) is associated with well-being among the elderly. When asked to identify the most important factors to affect the quality of life, older people consistently tend to place relationships, social networks and health at the top of the list (Ferris and Branston, 1994).

Retirement

Most people retire from full-time work during their 60s. The exact age at which people retire is usually determined by our social security system which decrees that 60 for a woman and 65 for a man are the appropriate ages. However, there is an increasing tendency for people to retire earlier. This, coupled with the fact that life expectancy is increasing, means that the proportion of retired people in the general population will steadily increase. By the beginning of the twenty-first century, it is expected that a person will generally live another 25 years after retirement. (National Center for Health Statistics, 1992). While some people approach retirement with pleasurable anticipation and relief, others consider themselves not yet ready to relinquish what is often a meaningful and important part of their lives.

> **GLOSSARY**
>
> **Activity theory** A theory that suggests that successful ageing during late adulthood is brought about by the individual's continuing to be active and productive; the opposite of disengagement theory.

Psychological impact of retirement

Because of the emphasis placed on the importance of work in our culture, retirement presents most people with a substantial sense of loss. It involves moving from a role which is clearly defined and economically productive to one which is more ambiguous and economically-unproductive (Ransom, et al., 1991). Loss of identity, social role, financial security and prestige require that significant psychological adjustments are made. However, research has indicated that, contrary to popular belief, retirement is not generally associated with decline in health and psychological well-being. For example, Streib and Schneider (1971)

Box 23.12   The retirement process

Retirement is often thought of as a life event which happens suddenly, usually in late adulthood. However, some researchers view retirement as a developmental process which takes place gradually over a period of time.

Atchley (1977, 1991) suggests that the process of retirement involves seven phases (see diagram) though not all people necessarily pass through every stage.

- **Phase 1** – The **remote phase** usually occurs during middle adulthood. At this time most working adults are fully immersed in their jobs and may have only vague thoughts about retirement. Little or no preparation for retirement is made at this time.
- **Phase 2** – As the time for retirement approaches, people enter the **near preretirement phase**. At this time much active thought and planning for retirement occur. The individual gradually disengages from some of the duties and responsibilities of the job.
- **Phase 3** – The actual retirement is often accompanied by feelings of pleasure and anticipation – **the honeymoon phase**. Many of the activities previously planned can now be engaged in.
- **Phase 4** – Retirement activities often prove to be less satisfying than expected. When this happens the individual enters the **disenchantment phase** and feels depressed and 'let down'.

- **Phase 5** – Disenchantment is usually followed by a **reorientation phase** during which people face up to the reality of retirement. The individual contemplates the future and attempts to develop a realistic view of its alternatives.
- **Phase 6** – There next follows what Atchley terms the **stability phase** when people settle to the routines of retirement with realistic awareness of their own capabilities and limitations. In the stability phase, people can be said to have fully adjusted to the role of the retired person.
- **Phase 7** – The **terminal phase** occurs when for one reason or another the retirement role ends. This may happen because individuals become ill or disabled and can no longer care for themselves. For some people the role of retiree is terminated when they seek out employment once again.

Atchley's phases of retirement may not apply in the same form and sequence to everyone. Individual differences in personality, variations in the age at which people retire and the reasons why they retire will all influence the process of retirement. However, his model aids our understanding of the developmental tasks which are faced by most older people who are making the transition from the role of worker to that of nonworker.

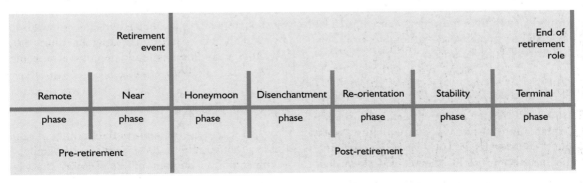

Atchley's phases of retirement

Box 23.13   Kübler-Ross's stages in the dying process

Kübler-Ross (1969) studied over 200 terminally ill people. On the basis of her observations and interviews with the patients, she proposed that the dying process consists of five stages through which the dying person passes as death approaches.

1. **Denial**. Most people, on learning that they are terminally ill, react with shock followed by a sense of disbelief. They may assert that there has been an error in diagnosis and that the doctors are incompetent. Denial can be observed in almost all patients and is considered to be a fairly healthy way of coping with the initial shock.

2. **Anger**. As denial becomes difficult to sustain, the dying person typically experiences anger at his or her condition and resentment of the healthy. 'Why me?' is a common cry. Kübler-Ross believes that it is important for the person's caretaker to understand why and how the anger originates, and to empathize with the patient.

3. **Bargaining**. At this stage the person adopts a different approach and attempts to bargain with God for an extension of life or a period of time without pain and discomfort. A patient may promise: for example, a life dedicated to the Church, or donation of organs to medical research in return for a postponement of death.

4. **Depression**. When terminally ill patients can no

longer deny their illness and when more severe physical symptoms occur or hospitalization is necessary, a sense of deep loss is experienced. Kübler-Ross distinguishes between two kinds of depression which occur at this time. Reactive depression results from the loss already suffered (for example, loss of physical strength or job) while preparatory depression relates to the loss that is to come (for example, loss of loved ones and treasured possessions). Kübler-Ross believed that encouragement and reassurance are helpful to people suffering reactive depression. However, patients suffering preparatory depression must be allowed to express emotions and prepare for impending loss.

5. **Acceptance**. In this final stage, the dying person accepts death. If they have been allowed time to work through the earlier stages and have been given some assistance to do so, they will feel no anger or depression. Quietness and gentle companionship are appreciated and they appear emotionless and detached.

Not all terminally ill people move through the stages described by Kübler-Ross. For example, a person may die in the anger stage because he or she is psychologically incapable of moving beyond it, or because the rapid progression of the illness does not allow the time to do so.

---

observed that, except for people who are compulsorily retired, it does not appear to lead to low morale. Troll (1982) notes that for many people, health improves in the early post-retirement years. Bosse (1991) found that for those men and women who were forced to retire for reasons of poor health or redundancy or whose health or financial circumstances deteriorated, retirement became a stressful experience.

Death and bereavement

In Western cultures the subject of death is a sensitive issue which, in the past, has been frequently avoided. Metaphors such as 'passed away' or 'no longer with us' have been used to describe the occurrence of death. Over the past two decades there has been a considerable shift in attitudes towards dying. Doctors and psychologists have attempted to view death, not as a

distinct event which terminates life, but as an important process in the life cycle.

Previously, doctors and family members have tended to withhold the truth from a dying person, on the basis that it was kinder to do so. Today, however, most doctors recognize that a dying person needs to be aware of his or her condition in order that the necessary psychological adjustments and practical arrangements may be made (Schulz, 1978).

Care of the dying

Box 23.13 summarizes some of the findings of Kübler-Ross's (1969) study of 200 terminally ill people.

One important outcome of Kübler-Ross's study is the realization by doctors and other medical workers that people who are dying need sensitive care as they prepare for death. Many terminally ill patients face death alone in a sterile and impersonal hospital ward without the support and companionship of family and friends.

A more humane approach towards the care of the dying is slowly gaining ground with the emergence of the **hospice** movement. A hospice is an establishment which provides a homelike and emotionally supportive setting for terminally ill people. The emphasis is on keeping the patient comfortable and free from pain and providing companionship as the patient prepares for death. Family and friends are encouraged to help with the care of the patient. The hospice movement arose from the work of the British doctor, Dame Cicely Saunders, in the 1960s.

Bereavement

Bereavement is the condition or state of loss and is most often experienced when someone close to us dies. However, bereavement may result from other losses such as loss of a close relationship through divorce or the loss of a job because of redundancy.

Grief is a person's emotional response to bereavement. The grieving process involves psychological suffering. However, it has been suggested that it is a necessary process and people who do not grieve are unlikely to recover from their loss.

Clayton et al. (1971) identified the 'symptoms' most commonly associated with the grieving process. In a study of 109 recently bereaved widows, the most common symptoms reported by more than 80 per cent of the respondents included crying, depression and insomnia. Over half suffered from loss of appetite and had difficulty concentrating. It is generally recognized among researchers that loss of a spouse during later adulthood provides one of the most serious threats to the health and well-being of the surviving partner (Wortman and Silver, 1990). Box 23.4 outlines some of Crosby and Jose's views on dysfunctional methods of coping with grief.

The loss of a child is also traumatic and parental bereavement is just as powerful for young parents as it is for those in their 60s. Their dreams and plans may be as strong for a young baby as they are for an adult or teenage offspring. Loss during pregnancy, too, promotes intense grief among parents (Smart, 1992).

Research indicates that bereavement can produce changes in nervous, hormonal and respiratory systems and can weaken the immune system (National Academy of Sciences, 1984). Bereaved persons are therefore at greater risk of suffering physical or mental illness.

Stages of bereavement Bowlby (1980) identified five stages in the grieving process:

- concentration on the deceased person;
- anger towards the deceased or other people;
- appeals to others for help;
- despair, withdrawal, disorganization;
- reorganization and focus on a new object of interest.

Cavanagh (1974) suggested seven stages of bereavement:

- shock,
- disorganization,
- violent emotions,
- guilt,
- loneliness and loss,
- relief,
- reestablishment.

GLOSSARY

Hospice An establishment which provides a homelike and emotionally supportive setting for terminally ill people.

Bereavement The condition or state of loss, usually brought about by the death of someone close.

Grief A person's response to bereavement, which involves psychological suffering

Box 23.14   Coping with grief

Coming to terms with complex feelings and the many demands and pressures of bereavement results in a wide range of behaviours. Some of these will be helpful and constructive; others will not and will only increase the psychological distress of the bereaved person. Crosby and Jose (1983) discuss functional (helpful) and dysfunctional (unhelpful) ways of coping.

Dysfunctional methods of coping

Three different kinds of behaviour have been observed:

- **Avoidance**. This is often known as the 'keep busy' strategy. Though many people believe that avoidance is therapeutic and helpful, if it is adopted over a prolonged period, it often becomes dysfunctional in that it encourages the denial of a loved one's death and prevents the bereaved person from coping. Similarly, getting away from home on a trip too soon after the death may result in the bereaved person failing to come to terms with the first stages of grief. Returning home is then more difficult to cope with and the grief process has been disrupted.
- **Obliteration**. This is a process which goes beyond avoidance and denial. It involves an attempt totally to erase all memories of the deceased person. This may involve disposing of all clothing, pictures, hobbies and other possessions.
- **Idolization**. This is the opposite of obliteration. Here, the survivor glorifies the memory of the deceased person, who is perceived to be impossibly perfect. This appears to be an attempt to hold on to the belief that the deceased is still present.

Functional methods of coping

Crosby and Jose see the key process here as good communication within an accepting and positive network of support. The bereaved person's energies need to be directed at the actual loss, as experienced collectively and individually. There should be no scapegoating, blaming and feelings of guilt about the deceased. Within this network, survivors should feel free to express their feelings but should recognize that feelings are often the result of irrational or illogical internalized beliefs. Thus, they should also be prepared to challenge their own beliefs and the beliefs of others.

Open communication allows unlimited opportunities for grief reduction. Where feelings are shared, survivors can often be helped to see the sometimes irrational assumptions they make about their own role in events that were actually far beyond their control. Often, survivors reason that if they had done something differently, the death would never have happened. This then leads to prolonged grieving, where grief becomes mixed up with guilt.

? SELF-ASSESSMENT QUESTIONS

1. What has research told us about attitudes towards the elderly in different cultures?
2. To what extent does cognitive functioning decline with age?
3. Outline two theories of personality development during late adulthood.
4. Contrast two theories concerned with successful adjustment to late adulthood.
5. Discuss research which has investigated the psychological impact of retirement.
6. In what ways can the findings of psychological research be of help to those who care for the dying?
7. Discuss some of the physical and psychological effects of bereavement.

Chapter summary

- Adolescence is normally reckoned to be the period from the onset of puberty until adulthood. It has been considered to be a period of turmoil and conflict. It is a time of physical change when primary and secondary sexual changes occur in both males and females as well as growth spurts in boys and girls.

- Maturation may occur either earlier or later than the norm in both sexes. In boys early maturation can be advantageous, while late-maturing males are often tense and self-conscious, with feelings of inadequacy and rejection which may persist into adulthood. Early maturation in girls is less advantageous. They can be dissatisfied with their body image, moody and listless. They appear more independent and popular with their peers of the opposite sex. By late adolescence they are more popular, more self-possessed and contented.

■ Erikson has identified adolescence as a crisis point of identity versus confusion. The main goal is the establishment of a clear ego identity. Failure can result in role diffusion. Marcia identified four different kinds of adolescent identity status: identity diffusion, identity foreclosure, moratorium and identity achievement.

■ The picture of female identity achievement is not so clear as that of males. Erikson argued that women postponed identity development until they had found a male partner. Marcia conceded that Erikson's model is only partially applicable to females.

■ Parents play a significant part in determining how successful adolescents are in achieving trouble-free and enduring identity sense. Democratic but author-itative parents foster high self-esteem in their children who become independent and self-confident, while authoritarian parents foster less self-confident and independent adolescents.

■ The traditional view of adolescence is that of a time of turmoil and stress. Psychoanalytic theorists particu-larly believe that the renewal of sexual urges and their intensity leads to emotional upset in coping with them. The sociological view of adolescence reflects Margaret Mead's belief in storm and stress. Socio-logical theory suggests that socialization and role changes are at their most significant during adoles-cence.

■ Studies by Rutter et al. and by Masterson have found anxiety in 65 per cent of normal adolescents while almost half their samples showed emotional upset, depression and misery. The latest research by Cole-man, however, has found that the large majority of teenagers cope well. There is a mismatch between theory and research which provides little support for the storm and stress view of adolescence put forward by psychoanalytic and sociological theory.

■ Piaget has described formal operational thought as emerging at about the onset of puberty. Many later studies have revealed that it is found only in a minority of teenagers, Shayer finding that only about 30 per cent achieve it by age 15 or 16.

■ Kohlberg's work suggests that adolescents base their moral judgments, in the early stage of adolescence, on the conventional level but during later adolescence on the postconventional or principled level of moral reasoning.

■ Peer groups play a role in socialization during adolescence with an adolescent subculture emerging in Western societies, which is different from adult culture and orients adolescents towards their peers. This subculture may have the effect of alienating adolescents from their parents and from the academic goals of school. More recent research suggests that for the majority of teenagers adolescent subculture is not as important as had been thought when Coleman did his research in 1961. Peer relationships fall into three categories: cliques, the crowd and friendships.

■ Erikson provided a framework of psychosocial development throughout life which sees each stage in life marked out by a crisis. Successful management of the crisis will determine psychological well-being at the time. There is some empirical support for Erikson's framework, but there is doubt whether it is equally applicable to all societies and cultures.

■ Levinson proposed four life seasons in a person's life cycle: childhood and adolescence, early adulthood, middle adulthood and older adulthood. It was, however, based on a small sample of males from a particular culture. Subsequent researchers have studied women's lives. In general, women experience Levinson's seasons, though priorities are different, with greater emphasis on relationships than on careers and greater willingness to orient their goals and dreams around other people.

■ White identified five growth trends for young adulthood: stabilization of the ego identity, freeing of personal relationships, deepening of interests, humanizing of values and expansion of caring. Adjustment to life events is a further way of considering adult development, and young adults are exposed to more life events than middle-aged or older adults.

■ Over 90 per cent of adults marry at least once. Duberman has identified three kinds of marriage: traditional marriage, companionship marriage and colleague marriage, the last two becoming increas-ingly common among middle-class couples. Adjust-ments are made by each partner in a marriage, traditionally greater by women than by men, and women report greater dissatisfaction with marriage

■ than men. In general, married men are happier than single ones, are healthier and live longer. Roles in marriage are less rigid than they were, with men taking a greater part in household chores than hitherto, but still significantly less than women. Swedish men have been found to be significantly more involved in household work than American men.

■ Divorce is extremely stressful and there is evidence that both partners will suffer 'mourning' for the relationship which has gone. Bohannon lists six components in divorce: emotional divorce, legal divorce, economic divorce, co-parental divorce, community divorce and divorce from dependency.

■ Becoming parents is a typical young adult experience. Motivation for becoming parents includes Erikson's concept of generativity and findings from studies into fertility motivation. Parenthood can be seen as a developmental process. Children can cause a decrease in marital satisfaction, but can strengthen the relationship where the quality of the relationship was good before the birth of the child. Parents' experience of attachment is extended to include responsibility for the child's well-being and there is an enhanced sense of continuity in attachment.

■ Middle age has been characterized by the existence of a midlife crisis, but this does not seem to be as widespread as Levinson indicated.

■ Personality remains in general stable during adulthood, though distinctions have been made between absolute and relative stability.

■ Erikson's crisis for middle age is between generativity and stagnation. Four psychological adjustments have been identified for middle age: valuing of wisdom above physical strength or attractiveness, valuing by men and women of each other as personalities, emotional flexibility, and mental flexibility and receptivity. A major task of this period of life is self-appraisal and adjustment to the more negative elements of life.

■ Unemployment represents a stressful event for middle-aged people particularly. Unemployed adults pass through four stages: relaxation and relief, a concerted effort to find another job, vacillation and doubt, and malaise and cynicism. Those currently unemployed have been found to exhibit a lower level of psychological well-being than any labour market

group. For women, the loss of a job is often not seen as so traumatic as it is for men.

■ Jahoda has outlined four important functions of employment: to give a structure for the day, to provide social contacts outside the home, to give a feeling of participation and to provide a source of identity. It has been suggested that Jahoda has underestimated the impact of financial hardship and she does not adequately deal with differences between men's and women's experiences.

■ Researchers have identified different aspects of senescence: physiological, biochemical and behavioural. There is loss of neural tissue; heart, lungs and nervous system become less efficient. Illness becomes more likely and recovery slower. External signs of ageing appear in middle age and progressively become more severe.

■ There is considerable cultural variation in attitudes to old age. While there is social differentiation in industrial societies, in many societies old people retain their status, authority and social involvement. Attitudes to the elderly contain negative stereotypes, especially held by children and young people. Reasons for this include loss of physical attractiveness and changing status.

■ Performance on IQ tests is relatively stable until age 60 and thereafter there is a gradual decline though this is not experienced by all people equally. Those who have kept mentally active do not experience deterioration. Short-term memory suffers some decline. There is sometimes difficulty in recalling material in long-term memory which is not regularly focused upon. Such deficits are compensated for by wisdom.

■ Erikson's crisis for old age is between ego integrity and despair. Older people look back and evaluate their decisions and can have satisfaction in a meaningful and important life. Likewise there will be times of despair. The balance between these feelings will determine the feeling of well-being and purpose, even in the face of death.

■ Peck outlines three major developmental tasks for older people: coming to terms with vocational retirement, physical decline and human mortality.

■ Disengagement theory suggests that older people gradually withdraw from social contacts and activities, though friends and social relationships remain important. Activity theory suggests that remaining productive and active brings about successful adjustment. However, there is not much empirical evidence for this view. Personality factors are important in determining successful adjustment. Two factors stand out as being critical: personal control and social involvement.

■ Retirement from work presents people with a sense of loss. There may be loss of identity, of social role and financial security which require psychological adjustments. For many people health improves in early retirement except where retirement is forced upon them, when that can be stressful. Atchley has identified seven stages of the retirement process: the remote phase, near preretirement, the honeymoon phase, the disenchantment phase, the reorientation phase, the stability phase and the terminal phase.

■ Kübler-Ross has identified five stages in the dying process after study of 200 terminally ill people: denial, anger, bargaining, depression and acceptance. A result of her work has been the realization of the need for sensitive treatment of the dying, and hospice care is gaining ground.

■ Bereavement occurs when someone close to us dies and grief is the emotional response to it. Symptoms of grieving include crying, depression and insomnia. It may produce changes in the nervous, hormonal and respiratory systems and can weaken the immune system. Bowlby identified five stages in bereavement: concentration on the deceased, anger, appeals for help, despair withdrawal and disorganization and finally reorganization and refocusing. Kavanagh suggests seven stages: shock, disorganization, violent emotion, guilt, loneliness, relief and reestablishment.

■ Crosby and Jose have outlined functional and dysfunctional ways of coping with grief. Dysfunctional ways include avoidance, obliteration and idolization. Functional ways include good communication, acceptance of support, freedom to express feelings, and absence of guilt, blame and scapegoating.

Further reading

Bryant, P.E. and Colman, A.M. (eds) (1995). *Developmental Psychology*. Harlow: Longman. J.C. Coleman in Chapter 4 gives a very good overview of psychoanalytic and sociological theories in relation to adolescence, as well as presenting up-to-date research evidence. The chapter also considers cognition in adolescence and relationships with adults. Chapter 5, written by J.C. Cavanaugh, considers a range of cognitive, social and personality issues in relation to ageing.

Durkin, K. (1995). *Developmental Social Psychology: From Infancy to Old Age*. Oxford: Blackwell. Chapters 18 and 19 consider theories and research into young, middle and late adulthood.

Turner, J.S. and Helms, D.R. (1995). *Lifespan Development*, 5th edn. Orlando, FL: Harcourt Brace. An interesting and comprehensive account of theory and research into development through the lifespan. The chapters on adulthood are particularly useful and consider a number of critical life events such as marriage, parenting and divorce.

PART 6

Social psychology

Social psychology relates to the behaviour of humans in relation to their social interactions with each other. No human can be entirely isolated from contact with other people and all such contact may have an effect upon behaviour. In particular, this affects social cognition, the perceptions of people and events stored in memory and drawn upon when similar people or events are encountered again. The contents of this part are as follows:

Contents

INTRODUCTION
Some perspectives on social psychology   571
- Social role perspective   521
- Learning perspective   571
- Social cognition perspective   573

CHAPTER 24
Self and others   575
- Social schemata   575
- Attribution   581
- The perception of self   587

CHAPTER 25
Relationships with others   594
- Affiliation   594
- Friendship, love and marriage   602

CHAPTER 26
Conflict and cooperation   614
- Intergroup relations   614
- Aggression   623
- Prosocial behaviour   636

CHAPTER 27
Attitudes   648
- The nature and function of attitudes   648
- Measurement of attitudes   659
- Prejudice and discrimination   662

CHAPTER 28
Social influence   677
- Conformity and compliance   677
- Leadership and followership   687
- Group decision making   690
- The influence of the crowd   696

Some perspectives on social psychology

Social psychologists attempt to provide a framework within which to understand the interactions between people. Perspectives which have been taken correspond quite closely to those adopted in other branches of psychology. They include social role perspective, learning perspective and social cognition perspective.

Social role perspective

The idea of **role** is probably the oldest perspective on the ways in which people interact. It envisages a world in which everyone plays a part, or, more likely, several parts. In every part or role a person plays, expectations are aroused in terms of behaviour. Let us take an example.

Jane is a mature student who has come back into college, now that her children are at school. She plays a whole series of interrelated roles. Figure 6I.1 shows a few of them, together with some of the expectations which are aroused as she plays out these roles. In each case there will also be a role partner or role partners who observe her from the outside and interact with her.

Learning perspective

A second perspective is that of learning, which concentrates upon stimulus and response. This goes back to behaviourist theory and in particular to the work of Watson (1913) and later to Skinner (1953) and others. A stimulus can be defined as an event which results in a change in someone's behaviour. This may be either internal or external. As far as a social stimulus is concerned it is most likely to be something which someone else does or says. **Reinforcement** is a further important element, a favourable outcome related to the stimulus which makes a particular response more

---

GLOSSARY

Role A part or parts played by an individual which involve obligations towards and expectations from another individual (the role partner).

Reinforcement A term used in learning theory for that stimulus which strengthens a particular response and so causes it to recur.

Figure 6I.1 Roles and expectations

Role	Role partner(s)	Expectations
Wife	Husband	Loving, caring, nurturing
Mother	Children	Loving, providing
Student	Tutor	Paying attention, doing assignments etc
Student	Other students	Joining in, supplying mutual help
Badminton club member	Other members, the team	Good play, cooperation, training, enthusiastic playing

likely to recur. This seems highly technical but in practice it is simple enough. Suppose your boss comes to you and remarks how well you dealt with that difficult customer. Your behaviour has been reinforced and you will be more likely to treat a future customer in a similar way. Learning has occurred. If, however, your behaviour goes unrewarded there will be no such impulse to behave in the way you did.

Generalization

If the same positive outcome results from more than one social stimulus you will be likely to group these social stimuli together as having some common feature. Being polite to a difficult customer, trying to see his or her point of view and not responding in kind to abuse come to be generalized. Stimulus generalization is very useful in allowing learning theorists to explain behaviour which otherwise might be difficult to explain if each behaviour had to be reinforced separately.

Discrimination

Discrimination occurs when you learn to respond differently to different stimuli. Perhaps a different tone might be adopted towards a customer with a legitimate grievance from that shown towards someone who is just 'trying it on'. Different reinforcement in each set of circumstances results in learning to discriminate between one stimulus and another.

Learning theorists tend not to be much concerned with what is going on in the mind of the learner, but just with relationships between stimuli and responses, the argument being that they can see different stimuli and can observe and measure different responses but there is no way to account for what thoughts are going through the mind. It is all the language of cause and effect.

Examples of the use of a learning perspective

These include the following:

- ■ The work of Miller and Dollard (1941) who explained the socialization process in young children in terms of stimulus-reward and reinforcement.
- ■ From this basis Bandura (1973) developed social learning theory, claiming that learning can occur

Box 6I.1 Learning theory and social learning theory

As a reaction to introspective and psychoanalytic methods which were employed in the early years of this century, Watson attempted to apply scientific method to the study of psychology. Publicly observable behaviour became the proper subject matter for psychology. Watson and the other 'behaviourists', as they became known, rejected consideration of the internal mechanisms of the mind, concentrating instead upon observable behaviour.

Skinner (1974) was a leading exponent of this approach who developed operant conditioning. A key principle of operant conditioning was that where behaviour is reinforced (that is, where people are rewarded when they behave in a particular way) it will tend to be repeated under similar circumstances.

Bandura (1969) extended this by proposing that imitation plays a significant part in human learning. People learn by observing what others are doing. Thus a social learning approach to human behaviour proposes that the main determinants of an individual's behaviour are not any internal characteristics or traits that individuals may possess but what happens to that individual in the environment, both observing the behaviour of others and finding that particular kinds of behaviour are reinforced. Observed behaviours may be stored and only introduced when individuals feel that they will be reinforced. Thus Bandura reintroduced some element of cognition: that is, the build-up of patterns in the mind though stored experience.

by observing the behaviour of a model: that is, by imitation as well as by reinforcement.

- ■ Homans's (1958, 1974) social exchange theory and Thibaut and Kelley's (1978) development of it are manifestations of learning theory as applied in social psychology. According to this theory, social behaviour can be explained in terms of costs and rewards. Any interaction with another person (a dyad) depends on the rewards it offers and the costs it incurs. Box 6I.1 distinguishes the approaches which have been employed.

Social cognition perspective

The social cognition perspective has tended to be the dominant one in recent years as it seems to have greater applicability to a wider range of topics within social psychology than do the others. It is this perspective which we have used to provide a unifying framework for this Part. It is analogous to ideas put forward by Tolman and others (Tolman, 1948) relating to cognitive maps.

The suggestion is that an internal representation is built up, through learning and memory, which provides a framework for our understanding of external events. Altman and Chemers (1980) investigated cognitive mapping in the physical sense. The places in which we spend the most time are 'mapped' in the greatest detail and are used as a kind of shorthand for orientation. Cognitive maps are, in essence, personal, reflecting our own experiences as individuals. Milgram (1977) took a structured approach to cognitive mapping. New Yorkers were shown colour slides of their city and asked to identify locations. This revealed that people had a very uneven picture of their city – just enough of a map for them to get by – and reflecting their individual needs and experience. For British people cognitive maps of the world tend to show Britain and Europe dominant against a background of the rest of the world and looking larger than, say, Africa or South America, in spite of the fact that Africa is five times the size of Western Europe, and South America is three times the size. This illustrates the point that the pictures built up in cognition represent what is important to us as individuals from the point of view of our experience.

Schemata (schemas)

Similar processes are at work when people interact with others. Patterns are developed which provide some consistency in the way in which they behave. It is almost as though they were actors playing their parts on a stage. In the same way that you would not expect a performance in the theatre to be impromptu and unscripted, so one way in which social psychologists attempt to impose order upon the apparent chaos which is people's interactions with each other is to visualize them as performing a role and following a script. In very much the same way as an actor learns his or her 'lines' and then rehearses them, an individual acquires a cognitive framework of social interaction with others over the course of a lifetime.

Crocker et al. (1984) have described the structure of knowledge which results as networks of schemata. They may be representations, stored in memory, of types of people, of social roles to be played out or of events to be reenacted.

Functions of schemata

Interpretation

When we meet someone else and he or she either says something or behaves in a particular way, how do we know how to react? We will draw upon our stored schemata to make sense of it. At a very simple level, suppose we meet someone and in response to the usual, 'Hello, how are you?' he or she says, 'Much better now, thank you', we draw upon our knowledge, gained from previous encounters, that the individual concerned has been in hospital and is now recovering. If, however, the response is, 'I'm OK now, no thanks to you', different schemata are drawn upon, involving memory of some less than totally pleasant incident. They help us to interpret more effectively and with greater speed the social events which we encounter.

Inference

The schemata are also gap-fillers. They not only provide us with a means to interpret stimuli, but also the context within which that stimulus occurs; a set of inferences which allow us to arrive at judgments about people and about social events. Schemata allow us to fill in the gaps in information which we acquire in social encounters. We are thus able to build up much more rapidly a more complete picture of the context in which an encounter occurs than would be possible if we were to rely just on the stimuli in front of us.

Scripts

Schemata do not arrive singly, but in battalions. Scripts could be described as sequences of schemata. How do children in school know how to behave? They develop a 'classroom script', a set of rules governing what you

---

GLOSSARY

Schemata (schemas) Social cognition cognitive processes and structures that influence and are influenced by social behaviour.

do when you are in a classroom. If the script developed is a good one, this might involve sitting quietly in one's place, putting a hand up and waiting to be asked before volunteering an answer and so on. On the other hand a script might develop that was unhelpful to the progress of learning, a 'shouting out' script or even a 'baiting the teacher' script. The idea of cognitive **scripts** developed by Schank and Abelson (1977) and Abelson (1981) takes the social cognition perspective further. A 'script' relates to a set of rules for behaving in a particular context or class of context.

Langer (1978) draws a distinction between mindful and mindless behaviour. Behaviour which conforms to an established script is mindless, carried out and responded to without conscious thought. The pattern has been set according to a cognitive map and becomes automatic. Unscripted behaviour, on the other hand, requires more thought.

Prototypes

In the same way that a script is a sequence of schemata, a prototype is a cluster of schemata relating to an individual person or a group of individuals. For instance, you might have developed the prototype of a 'yuppie'. The prototypical yuppie might display a number of characteristics: trendiness in dress, perhaps, an ostentatious display of prosperity and a particular style of life. An observer who establishes a prototype of a yuppie – that is, a particular pattern in his or her mind that represents in shorthand form all the characteristics experience has shown represent 'yuppie' – would classify him/her as a yuppie after identifying at least some of the characteristics. Once the yuppie is identified, the observer might ascribe to him or her other 'yuppie' characteristics: pushiness, perhaps or self-advertisement. In much the same way as schemata and scripts speed up and facilitate the responses made to situations we may find ourselves in, prototypes enable us to make judgements and responses easily and quickly about individuals or groups of people on the basis of experience.

The idea behind prototypes, as behind scripts and schemata, is that by establishing a pattern or framework in knowledge and memory, individual social interactions become easier to manage.

We shall continue to compare different explanations of social phenomena and relate them back to these three perspectives, though increasingly the social cognitive perspective is tending to predominate.

GLOSSARY

Script A framework or structure in the mind formed through experience, relating to behaviour in a particular set of circumstances and brought into play when those circumstances recur.

CHAPTER 24

Self and others

Social schemata   575
- Impression formation   576
- Social stereotypes   577
- Implicit personality theories   579
- Implicit social theories   579
- Personal construct theory   580

Attribution   581
- Correspondent inference theory   581
- Kelley's covariation model   582
- Bias in attribution   584

- Some applications and extensions of attribution theory   586

The perception of self   587
- Schemata and self   587
- A humanistic view of self   588
- Self and attribution   588
- Self-esteem   590
- Culture and self   590
- Social identity theory   590

Objectives

By the end of this chapter you should be able to:

- Describe how people store information about themselves and others as schemata;

- Outline the self-perception theories put forward by Bem, Weiner and others;

- Identify what is meant by the attribution process in the judgment of a person's character;

- Describe models of the attribution process as they apply to a person's perception, both of self and others;

- Describe some of the influences of social cognition in how we perceive ourselves and others.

In this chapter we shall review the social cognitive approach to the way in which we perceive other people, including the use of schemata, scripts, prototypes and exemplars. There is a full account in the introduction to this part of the book of social cognition. It may be useful to refer back to it. There is also reference to social cognition in Chapter 22.

Social schemata

It is necessary for us to be able quickly to make sense of persons, events, situations or places which we meet in our lives. The building up of schemata fulfils this need. Effectively, we are making a cognitive plan of whatever or whoever it is we meet to represent our knowledge of it. This plan will include the characteristics we are aware of and the interrelationships between these characteristics. This forms a schema, stored in memory and activated by a particular cue.

Let us put flesh on some of these rather nebulous ideas. You meet and get to know someone. Characteristics of that individual register in your memory; for instance, that he or she is very intelligent, fond of reading serious books, but at the same time is something of an adventurer who likes to go to wild and sometimes dangerous places to walk and to climb. At the same time, he or she is politically quite aware and has a very active social conscience. All these traits and pieces of information are stored away and form a schema. Every time you meet this person the schema of old information is activated by some cue (perhaps the recognition of his or her face) and new information is added. Then gaps are filled in by means of prior knowledge or preconceptions, both about this particular individual or those you have met with similar characteristics. This pattern fits all the different kinds of schemata, the most common of which include:

■ **Person schemata**. This is what has been mentioned above. These amount to impressions formed of either a particular person of whom we have personal knowledge, a friend, a neighbour or a workmate, or someone well known to us of whom we may not have personal acquaintance, a politician, perhaps, or a television personality.

■ **Role schemata**. Schemata structure the knowledge we have about the occupants of particular roles. Teachers, for example, may have been categorized in your mind as having certain defined characteristics. This pattern of characteristics is formed from experiences you may have had of teachers, either first-hand or via information from someone else. Some cue will trigger this teacher schema (perhaps meeting someone carrying a pile of books) and inferences are made about the way in which this particular teacher will behave. Gaps in this pattern of knowledge are continually being filled through direct experience. The schema of 'teacher' is thus modified in the light of what you know.

■ **Scripts**. Scripts are schemata about events. You will perhaps have developed a schema relating to going to a restaurant for dinner which might involve waiting for a waiter to seat you at a table, being presented with a menu and so on. This schema has developed as a result of your stored experience of restaurants and what happens in them. The fact that you know what is going to happen when you go to a restaurant makes it much easier for you to cope. In situations where these established scripts do not exist there can easily be disorientation or frustration. You might, for instance, have been invited to a royal garden party at Buckingham Palace. You have no script for such an event, so it is difficult for you to cope. If, however, you were the Queen, a royal garden party script would be well developed through long experience.

Impression formation

Social psychologists have a long history of attempts to make sense of the impressions we form of those we meet. When we meet someone for the first time, physical appearance is probably the first source of information we have about that person. Gender and race are usually evident immediately. It may not even be necessary to get a good look at someone to determine gender. Berry (1990) has suggested that the way in which people walk or the way in which they move their faces and heads while talking enables us to decide whether they are male or female. Then we notice other physical features, such as height, weight or facial expression. These initial pieces of information about race or gender or about outward physical appearance enable us to categorize a person as belonging to a particular kind of schema. For any category of people, from very broad categories like male or female, young or old, black or white, or narrower categories such as teacher or doctor perhaps, a set of characteristics come to mind.

Exercise 24.1

As you walk down the street, take a good look at five individuals you pass. Analyse your impressions of them. Consider such categories as gender, race, social class and status. What made you come to your conclusions about these five people?

Prototypes

These characteristics represent a prototype, a fairly fuzzy and ill-defined set of images we have of people belonging to a particular category. Though usually the prototype represents the average member of a category

---

GLOSSARY

Prototype A fairly fuzzy image we make of people whom we identify as belonging to a particular category.

of people, Chaplin et al. (1988) have said that there are occasions where the prototype is the ideal or perhaps an extreme member of a category. An individual who is concerned deeply about animals might form a prototype of a vivisectionist as a person who derives satisfaction or even pleasure from inflicting pain on animals. The prototype is what immediately comes into your mind when you think of a category of people. Particular instances you meet will not fit your prototype exactly, because your prototype of some category of people or other is something you have constructed in your mind, but all instances are more or less prototypical.

Finally, there will be considerable similarity between the prototypes formed about a particular category of people by members of a particular social group. For instance, the prototypes formed of 'teacher' by a group of schoolchildren are likely to be very similar.

Exemplars

There is a suggestion that as people become more familiar with a particular category of people they tend to alter their mental representation of the category from the fairly fuzzy prototypical representation towards a more clear-cut representation of the group in terms of exemplars (specific instances of the category which they have met). Brewer (1988) takes this view, while Judd and Park (1988) suggest that as far as in-groups are concerned, that is to say, members of a group of which the observer is a member, mental representation is in terms both of prototypes and exemplars fairly indiscriminately, while out-groups (groups of which the observer is not a member) use only exemplars.

There is a great deal in common between schemata, prototypes and exemplars. They are all part of the network of mental representations of the world based upon memory and experience which enables us to respond quickly and easily to people and events which we meet.

Social stereotypes

Prototypes and exemplars are essentially personal. Each individual's network of social cognition is different from that of each other individual and is firmly based in the experience of that individual. There are cases, however, where the prototypes established by individuals are widely shared. In these cases it can be said that there is a social stereotype. The term originates from Lippman (1922), who described stereotypes as 'pictures in our heads'. This seems not unlike the schemata which we have been discussing, with this distinction: whereas schemata tend to be neutral, stereotypes often have a pejorative connotation. Lippman saw stereotypes as a means whereby people protect their relative standing in society. In a white-dominated society, for instance, white people may use negative stereotypes of black people to justify their dominance. However, it would not be correct to say that all stereotypes are negative.

A stereotype will reflect the whole range of our information about a particular group of people. This information is likely to be positive and neutral as well as negative. Deaux and Lewis (1983) studied stereotypes of men and women. Commonly men were stereotyped as being independent and competitive; women warm and emotional. Whether these characteristics are regarded as positive, negative or neutral reflects the attitudes of the individuals who are making the judgment.

Formation of stereotypes

Stereotypes are easily developed and can be pervasive in their effects. Hill et al. (1989) found that they were able to create stereotypes in a very short time. A description of their study is in Box 24.1.

Quite often stereotyping embraces national characteristics. Linssen and Hagendoorn (1994) studied European students' stereotypes of Northern and Southern European nations. Participants in this study were 277 16–18-year-old students in Denmark, England, the Netherlands, Germany, France and Italy. A questionnaire was administered to participants by means of which 22 characteristics were identified which clustered into four general dimensions:

GLOSSARY

Exemplar A representation of a category of people personified in an image of a particular person in that category.

In-groups/out-groups The group to which the individual belongs is an in-group. Out-groups are all the rest.

Social stereotype theory Reflection of the whole range of information we possess about a group of people, encapsulating our impression of their characteristics.

Box 24.1 Formation of stereotypes. A study by Hill et al. (1989)

Participants in the study were shown six videotaped episodes, each less than two minutes long. A voice-over indicated that the person speaking had a personal problem related to the episode, but none of the participants knew the nature of the problem. Half the participants were shown episodes where it was always a man who had the problem; the other half were shown episodes where the person with the problem was a woman. Two weeks before they saw the episodes, and again two weeks after the viewing, participants were asked to rate on various traits including 'sadness' such people as their boy- or girl-friends or other men and women they knew well. Results, illustrated in the diagram, showed that before the viewing participants did not feel that the men and women they rated differed in 'sadness'. After they had seen the videotaped episodes, however, there was an apparent difference. Those who had seen episodes where there was a male voice-over which seemed to be sad, rated males they knew as sadder; those who had seen episodes where there was a female voice-over which seemed to indicate sadness rated the females they knew as sadder. Participants were interviewed afterwards and indicated that they had not even realized that it was men or women who had more problems in the episodes they watched. In spite of this, the viewing of manipulated gender differences between people who were quite unknown to them, had altered their judgments about people they knew well.

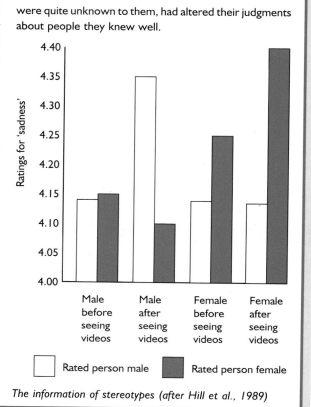

The information of stereotypes (after Hill et al., 1989)

■ **Dominant** – proud, assertive, aggressive.
■ **Empathic** – helpful, friendly.
■ **Efficient** – industrious, scientific, rich.
■ **Emotional** – enjoying life, religious.

Participants were asked to indicate the proportions of each national group who possessed each of these characteristics.

Results showed a polarization between Northern and Southern nations. The Northern nations were characterized as being more efficient; the Southern ones as being more emotional.

Exercise 24.2

As you talk to your friends, get them to indicate their stereotypical characteristics of a German, a Russian and an American. How closely do they match?

Hogg and Vaughan (1995) have identified a number of clear findings which result from research into stereotyping going back several decades. These are as follows:

■ People show an easy readiness to characterize vast human groups in terms of a few crude common attributes.
■ Stereotypes are very slow to change.
■ Stereotype change is generally in response to wider social, political or economic changes.
■ Stereotypes are acquired at a very young age, often before the child has any knowledge about the groups which are being stereotyped.
■ Stereotypes become more pronounced and hostile when social tensions and conflict arise between groups, and then they are extremely difficult to modify.

"THEY'RE PERFECTLY HARMLESS — I'VE LOCKED THE HOUSE AND THE GARAGE, AND NOTIFIED THE LOCAL POLICE."

■ Stereotypes are not necessarily inaccurate or wrong; rather, they serve to make sense of particular intergroup relations.

Implicit personality theories

As a result of socialization during childhood, as well as through experiences later, each of us arrives at his or her own **implicit personality theory**. This comprises a set of unstated assumptions about which personality traits will tend to go together. Frequently these implicit personality theories are extended to include beliefs about what sort of behaviour goes with particular personality traits. It is important to note that these theories are rarely made explicit, or stated in formal terms; quite frequently we are not consciously aware of them at all. In spite of this they dominate the way in which we make judgments about other people. Rosenberg and Sedlak (1972) found that college students, when they described people they knew, used only a limited number of terms: intelligent, lazy, self-centred, ambitious and friendly. However, they were unlikely to use all these terms to describe the same

person. 'Intelligent' frequently went with 'friendly', rarely with 'self-centred'. So that individuals have an implicit personality theory where intelligence goes with friendliness, but not with self-centredness.

Rosenberg and Jones (1972) used archival methods (that is to say, analysis of archival material – see Chapter 34) in an analysis of *A Gallery of Women* by Theodore Dreiser (1929), a collection of sketches of 15 women. In their analysis, the investigators tabulated all the trait descriptions which Dreiser used in his sketches. By means of statistical analysis they arrived at three basic dimensions of personality used by Dreiser – hard/soft, male/female and conforms/does not conform. Hardness was found to go together with maleness (though they were not identical traits), but maleness/femaleness were not closely associated to conformity/nonconformity (see Figure 24.1).

Implicit social theories

In much the same way as we have developed implicit personality theories or constructs about the people we meet, so we develop implicit social theories which inform our behaviour. Typically, implicit social theories embrace cause-and-effect relationships, ex-

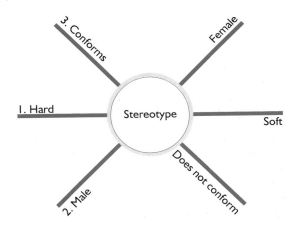

Figure 24.1 Rosenberg and Jones' (1972) three basic dimensions of stereotype

GLOSSARY
Implicit personality theory Unstated beliefs or assumptions about what characteristics (of people) tend to go together.

planations as to why events happen. For instance, a social theory might embrace the relationship between lack of discipline in schools and the rise in crime; or alternatively, unemployment and the rise in delinquency. This has been investigated by Anderson and Sechler (1986). These implicit theories are different in at least two ways from more formal social theories developed by social psychologists:

◼ They are unstated and so are not subjected to public scrutiny in the way in which formal theories are.
◼ While formal theories are based firmly in logic and tested in research, implicit social theories are based upon casual observation. They are essentially personal and idiosyncratic.

When we have only a limited amount of information to go on we tend to fill in the gaps to make people and events more comprehensible. Anderson and Sechler found that when presented with two random events and asked to imagine a link between them, people more often than not found a relationship. Both implicit personality and implicit social theory help individuals to make sense of what is otherwise a chaotic world.

Personal construct theory

Kelly (1955) devised yet another approach, which has some similarities to implicit personality theory. He suggested that individuals construct a cognitive theory which mediates the way in which they see the world (and this, of course, includes other people). **Personal constructs**, as he termed them, represent each individual's guide to interpreting the world. Kelly's view was that we are all scientists, struggling to understand and predict events. To this end we build up constructs (sets of assumptions which form the basis for our view of the world). What motivates us primarily is validation of our construct systems. We need proof that the way in which we view the world is the right one. Kelly rejected the possibility that there might be some absolute or objective truth, in favour of a phenomenological approach. This suggests that the world does not have any meaning outside our own perception of it. He thought of constructs as having bipolar dimensions. For instance, an individual might have developed a construct of *disciplined* as an expression of personality; the opposite pole to this

might be *scatterbrained*. Impressions formed of other people would use this dimension (amongst others). When we meet people they are categorized according to where they seem to be on this dimension. The effect is to impose some kind of framework on what otherwise might be chaotic impressions formed of other people. But it is an idiosyncratic order; no one person's constructs are likely in total to be the same as any other person's. Moreover, it is not just impressions of other people, but every facet of life which is affected by our construct system. Let us take one example. You are in the market to buy a car. Within your construct system you have established certain constructs about cars: for instance, you might have the following bipolar dimensions:

> fast – slow
> cheap to run – costing a lot to run
> keeping its resale value – depreciating quickly

These are the terms in which you see the cars you are in the market to buy, ignoring, perhaps, someone else's constructs which might include:

> providing a smooth ride – giving a harsher ride
> having soft seating – having firm seating
> resistant to corrosion – prone to rust.

Kelly developed a way in which personal constructs might be uncovered, and this has been extensively used in a wide variety of fields. It is known as the Repertory Grid Technique. A fairly large number of the people, events or objects under investigation are assembled and arranged in threes. Participants are asked in what way two of the three are the same and the third one different. From the responses, constructs (the ways in which two are the same) and opposites emerge. Taken together they provide a picture of the participant's personal construct system as it relates to what is under investigation. There is a full discussion of Kelly's theory in Chapter 30, with particular reference to personality.

> GLOSSARY
>
> **Personal construct** The notion proposed by Kelly that every individual constructs his or her own way of seeing the world and, in particular, other people.

Exercise 24.3

Imagine that you are about to look for a car to buy. Make a list of 12 makes and models of car. Taking three of them at a time, list ways in which two of them are the same and the third one is different. Now make some analysis of the constructs you have come up with and describe what seems to you to be important in a car. Now show your list of cars to a friend and get him or her to do the same, taking three at a time and saying how two are the same and the third different. How closely do your constructs match those of your friends?

❓ SELF-ASSESSMENT QUESTIONS

1. What are meant by social schemata? In what way do the social schemata we have developed affect the impressions we form of people?
2. What is a script? Describe some of the ways in which scripts serve to facilitate our interactions with other people.
3. How are social stereotypes formed? How does stereotyping influence the perception we have of others?
4. Describe the basis for personal construct theory. What practical means have been developed to uncover an individual's personal constructs?

Attribution

This section deals with the ways in which we draw inferences about people we meet from the behaviour we observe. Human beings operate as scientists, trying continually to find explanations for observed phenomena. This enables us to attempt to predict the behaviour of people and maybe exert some influence over it. In this way we are more in control of our lives and less prone to be blown randomly this way and that. To find causes for things is quite a powerful tool in our attempts to control events. If a tower block collapses it is immensely valuable to find out the cause of the collapse if we are to stop it happening again. Much the same applies to human behaviour. If we understand why people behave in the way they do it might be possible to predict and control behaviour. This is what lies at the root of attribution processes.

Heider (1958) believed that, left to themselves, most people attempt to construct their own theories about the causes of human behaviour. The following principles lie behind Heider's ideas:

■ **Motivation**. Human behaviour is motivated. If we can discover their motives we can predict how people are likely to behave.
■ **Causation**. The search for causes for things pervades most human thought. In an experiment Heider and Simmel (1944) asked participants to describe the movements of abstract geometric figures. The researchers found that participants did this as though the figures were humans with intentions to act in particular ways.
■ **Prediction**. We are trying all the time to predict and control elements in the environment which may impinge on us. Because of this we look for causes which are stable and enduring, personality characteristics in people which are consistent in many situations, and stable environmental circumstances.
■ **Internal and external bases of behaviour**. When we attempt to explain why people behave as they do, we distinguish between internal and external causes. Internal causes include such things as individuals' personality characteristics or abilities; external causes include social pressures or environmental circumstances. An individual is caught shoplifting. Internal causes might include the suggestion that he or she is dishonest or not very bright. External causes might be that he or she is out of work or has lost his or her home through repossession.

Correspondent inference theory

Jones and Davis (1965) and Jones and McGillis (1976) claimed that individuals make correspondent inferences. That is to say, the assumption is made that the behaviour we are witnessing is the result of a corresponding dispositional trait. The brusque behaviour of someone we meet is explained by inferring that the individual concerned is naturally grumpy or irritable. Irritability is a stable trait which enables us to explain his or her behaviour and allows us to predict how that individual will behave next time we meet him or her. In this way we are able to control our world better.

For people to make a correspondent inference about someone's behaviour, Jones and Davis suggest that they need to take account of the following:

■ **Free choice**. How freely chosen is the behaviour? Clearly, if there are external constraints upon behaviour (threats or inducements, for instance) it is less easy to infer that the behaviour is due to some dispositional cause.

■ **Commonness**. Does the behaviour observed have noncommon effects? These effects have been defined as those which could only be achieved by behaving in this particular way. In other words, does the observed behaviour have effects in common with other behaviour? If that is the case, then it is going to tell us less about the disposition of the individual than would be the case if there were few behaviours which might produce the same effect.

Take an example. It is your girlfriend's birthday. There is a variety of things you could do: send her a bunch of flowers, take her out to dinner, arrange a surprise party and so on. But you met at a performance of *Carmen* and you know that is special to her. So you take her to the opera to see *Carmen*. It is this behaviour on your part which demonstrates your love for her in a way in which none of the other possibilities could. It has the fewest noncommon effects.

■ **Social desirability**. How socially desirable is the behaviour? If it is socially desirable it may be social roles (that is, what society demands of you in the particular role you are playing) which produce it rather than your disposition. Correspondent inference is more easily made if the behaviour observed is 'out of role'. Edward comes to a funeral dressed in a flowery shirt, shorts and sandals. He is behaving out of role and that fact will tell observers more about his disposition than if he arrives in a dark suit. Edward's role as 'mourner' carries certain social expectations and obligations (see Introduction). This includes dressing soberly. Jones et al. (1961) found that where people behaved 'out of role' (in a way which did not fit with what was expected) more inferences were made about their disposition than when they conformed.

■ **Hedonic relevance**. Correspondent inferences are more likely to be made about behaviour which has hedonic relevance. How does the behaviour which we are observing affect us? It has hedonic relevance if it involves rewards or costs for the observer. An extension of this may be referred to as personalism: that is, where the intention of the person performing the action we observe is to help or to harm us.

One difficulty with this correspondent inference theory is that a great deal hinges upon intention. Yet an equally strong source of correspondent inference is unintentional behaviour. A person could easily be characterized as slapdash as a result of acting in a careless manner. It is unlikely that he or she would intentionally behave in a careless or slapdash manner. Nisbett and Ross (1980) and Ross (1977) have highlighted a problem with the issue of noncommon effects. People do not pay regard to behaviour which is not observed: that is, all those other ways in which an individual might have behaved. The issue of whether there might be other behaviours which would produce the same effect simply does not arise.

Kelley's covariation model

This is probably the best known model of attribution. Kelley (1967, 1973) maintained that people use the principle of covariance to decide whether to attribute behaviour they observe to internal (dispositional) causes or external (environmental) causes. Kelley refers to the **actor** as the individual who is behaving in a particular way and the **observer** as the individual who is affected by this behaviour, who observes it happening. When a particular action and a cause are seen to covary (or occur together) repeatedly in the case of a specific person, conclusions tend to be drawn about that person. For instance, whenever there is a party Charlie is found sitting in a corner drinking by himself. There is co-occurrence of action (sitting alone, drinking in a corner), a specific person (Charlie) and a possible cause (extreme shyness). Attributions which are made by an observer depend upon three factors:

■ **Consistency**. Does Charlie always go off into a corner at parties or only at this particular one? If

---

GLOSSARY

Actor The individual who initiates a piece of behaviour.

Observer The individual who observes someone doing something and draws inferences from that action.

there is high consistency (it happens every time or at least most times), the observer will tend to attribute this behaviour to Charlie's disposition (shyness). If there is low consistency (it is only at this party that Charlie behaved like this) the potential cause (shyness) will tend to be discounted and the observer will look for some other cause.

■ **Distinctiveness**. Is it just at parties that Charlie behaves in a shy manner (high distinctiveness) or does he display the same kind of behaviour in all kinds of environments (low distinctiveness). In the former case the observer will tend to discount shyness and look for another cause.

■ **Consensus**. Does everyone behave like this or is it just Charlie? A strange party perhaps, where everyone goes off by themselves, but if that did occur there would be high consensus. If it were just Charlie it would be low consensus.

Figure 24.2 shows Kelley's covariation model.

Discounting or augmentation of cause

In general terms behaviour is likely (in Kelley's model) to be attributed to Charlie's disposition where the following apply:

■ Consistency is high,
■ Consensus is low,
■ Distinctiveness is low.

Augmentation Kelley's model also allows for what he terms the **augmentation principle**. The way he expresses this is as follows: 'When there are known to be constraints, costs, sacrifices or risks involved in taking an action, the action is attributed more to the actor than it would be otherwise' (Kelley, 1973, p. 114).

What this means is that where the action that is observed has costs involved for the actor, an observer would be more likely to attribute it to the disposition of the actor than to some environmental circumstance. Let us consider an example of how this might work. There is a strict embargo in the office against any one of the secretarial staff releasing details in advance of proposed redundancies, on pain of dismissal. Mary knows that James's wife is expecting her first baby and they have just bought a new house. The list for redundancies is going before the board the next day and James's name is on it. In spite of the extreme risk involved, Mary leaves James's name off the list the Chief Executive Officer (CEO) has drawn up in the hope that it will not be noticed, and James will get a reprieve. Because of the risk involved to herself, an observer would be much more likely to attribute this to Mary's sympathy for James than to any other cause.

Discounting The opposite effect is termed discounting, which results in one possible cause being reduced in importance by other plausible causes. Suppose there are several possible causes for an action which is observed. Mary might have been very tired at the end of a long day and have left James's name off the list inadvertently. Two of the names the CEO gave Mary might have been very similar and

> **GLOSSARY**
>
> **Augmentation principle** Where costs are involved for the actor, the action is attributed more to the actor's disposition than it would otherwise be.

Figure 24.2 Kelley's covariation model of attribution

Consistency	Distinctiveness	Consensus	Attribution
Low		⟶	Discounting Look for another cause
High	High	High ⟶	Attribution to an environmental cause
High	Low	Low ⟶	Attribution to a person's disposition

James's name might have been left off because Mary could not read the CEO's writing. The CEO might have confused the issue. He might have listed James Sturt rather than James Stewart when there was a John Sturt working for the firm. This situation represents what Kelley terms a multiple sufficient cause schema. A number of factors are there in the observer's mind, any of which might be sufficient to be the cause of James's name being left off the list. Which cause we select depends upon the information we have available. Mary might have expressed concern at James's possible inclusion. The CEO might have made a habit of getting names wrong and getting very cross when mistakes are pointed out to him. Mary's expression of concern might cause the observer to discount the CEO's mistake or Mary's tiredness.

Causal schemata

In common with other schemata, mentioned earlier, causal schemata are mental representations built up as a result of experience and stored memories. In this case, to use Kelley's words, 'a causal schema is a conception of the manner in which two or more causal factors interact in relation to a particular kind of effect' (Kelley, 1973, p. 125). In the course of our observations of people we have developed certain beliefs about causes and effects. These beliefs then form the basis for our explanation of a particular person's behaviour.

As well as the multiple sufficient cause schema, mentioned above, we might have a multiple necessary causal schema which could be applied. More than one cause might be necessary to explain the event. A combination of the CEO's confusion of names and Mary's tiredness at the end of the day, perhaps.

Bias in attribution

There is evidence that attribution is biased towards dispositional explanations of behaviour. Unless there is some situational cause staring us in the face we tend to attribute observed behaviour to some internal characteristic of the individual observed. Jones and Harris (1967) showed that even where students had been clearly told that the author of a particular essay had been assigned to take a particular political viewpoint, they made inferences about the author's political attitudes from the content of the essay.

Fundamental attribution bias

Fiske and Taylor (1984) have called this pervasive tendency to explain behaviour in terms of disposition fundamental attribution bias. Gilbert (1989) has claimed that it is automatic for us to attribute behaviour to disposition and we cannot avoid doing it. All we are able to do is to amend it once we have made the attribution. Miller and Lawson (1989) go so far as to maintain that fundamental attribution bias can only be overcome when additional, objective information convinces us that the disposition of the actor could not possibly be the cause of the action. People in Western society have a very strong sense of personal responsibilty, according to Jellison and Green (1981). People have to be held accountable for their actions so that internal attributions of cause are much more highly valued than external ones.

Cross-cultural evidence for attributional bias

While American children were found by Miller (1984), as they grew older, to place increasing reliance upon disposition as an explanation of events they observed, the Hindu children of India by contrast based their attributions more on situations. This suggests that the fundamental attribution bias may not be universal.

Actor–observer effect

Another explanation of the fundamental attribution bias is that it depends upon whose perspective it is taken from. While Jones and Nisbett (1972) confirmed that as far as the observer was concerned dispositions play a much more central role in explanations of behaviour than situational factors, actors place more emphasis upon the situation. This has become known as the actor–observer effect. This is illustrated by an experiment by Storms described in Box 24.2.

GLOSSARY
Causal schemata Mental representations, based upon experience, of the way in which two or more causes interact to explain an individual's action.
Fundamental attribution bias A pervasive tendency to explain behaviour in terms of disposition.
Actor–observer effect An explanation of 'fundamental attribution bias' which claims that observers place more emphasis on disposition, actors upon the situation.

Box 24.2　The actor–observer effect

Storms (1973) conducted an experiment which provided strong confirmation of the actor–observer effects. Pairs of participants (the actors) were asked to converse while another pair of participants (the observers) watched on closed-circuit television. The actors were found to place greater emphasis upon the situation when the conversations were rated, while the observers placed more emphasis upon disposition. There was an apparent actor–observer effect. When Storms showed the actors a videotape of their conversation (in other words turning them into observers of their own conversation), greater emphasis was placed upon disposition. Subsequent investigations as to why this should happen have concentrated upon self-focus. Gibbons (1990) reviewed this research. What seemed to happen was this: in normal circumstances we tend to pay more attention to the situation than to ourselves. However, when we are watching ourselves on videotape we tend to focus more on ourselves. The interpretations of behaviour we then make are those which best confirm our self-concept. So long as the behaviour observed is consistent with the way in which we see ourselves we are likely to attribute it to dispositional rather than situational causes. But if we observe ourselves acting in a way which is inconsistent with our concept of ourselves then the situation becomes more important when we come to attribute cause.

False consensus

As we have seen, alongside information about consistency and distinctiveness 'consensus' information helps us to attribute cause to the behaviour we observe in people. Ross et al. (1977) have demonstrated that we do sometimes create our own consensus effect. We regard our own behaviour as typical. Given the same set of circumstances, we assume, anyone else would behave in the same way. Ross demonstrated this false consensus effect experimentally. Students were asked to walk around their campus for 30 minutes wearing a sandwich board proclaiming 'Eat at Joe's'. Those who agreed to do so estimated that 62 per cent of their peers would also have agreed. Those who refused estimated that 67 per cent of their peers would also

have refused. Why does this happen? Marks and Miller (1988) have suggested several possibilities:

- Consensus is artificially inflated by the habit people have of associating with other people who have similar views. In one group of people, the consensus might be that it is lax discipline in schools which is the root cause of the upsurge in crime. Because they tend to meet only people with similar views they assume that everyone thinks the same. There is consensus. Among a different group, the rise in crime is thought to be due to unemployment. Again there is consensus because they tend not to associate with people who think differently.
- Another possible explanation is that our own views are so salient as to displace any consideration of alternatives.
- Yet a third possibility is that exaggerating the consensus behind our own views justifies us in maintaining they are correct.

In this way we manage to maintain a stable perception of reality – at least of reality as we see it. Factors that research has thrown up which appear to influence false consensus include:

- How important beliefs are to us and how certain we are about them (Granberg, 1987);
- External threat;
- Status as a member of a minority group.

Cause and effect – we get what we deserve

Another source of bias lies in the rooted belief that the world is essentially a just place. This is the **just world hypothesis**. Lerner (1966) put it like this: 'There is an appropriate fit between what people do and what happens to them' (p. 3).

When we see apparent injustice happening – that is, something which threatens our belief in a just world – we make attempts to put the situation right. This may involve one or more of several expedients:

GLOSSARY

Just world hypothesis The hypothesis that whatever happens to an individual is related to what that individual deserves.

- We may compensate the victims, raising money to alleviate suffering – Band Aid for instance.
- We may attempt to mete out justice to those who are to blame, trying to ensure that someone is convicted of a bombing outrage, for instance.
- We may try to convince ourselves that no injustice has in fact occurred. A girl is attacked and raped late at night in a sleazy part of town. 'Why was she out at night in that neighbourhood alone? It was just asking for trouble. There was no injustice; she had only herself to blame!'

We make attributions of cause to support our belief that we live in a fundamentally just world. There must be a logical explanation for injustice occurring. Symonds (1975) interviewed hundreds of rape, assault and kidnapping victims. Many received no help and sympathy, but censure from friends, family and the police.

Some applications and extensions of attribution theory

Cognition and emotion

In an experiment which has now become very well known, Schachter and Singer (1962) demonstrated that there were two separate components in emotion:

- The arousal which produces such effects as an increased heart rate, changes in breathing patterns and in the distribution of the blood and similar physiological effects. These have been well described in Chapter 9.
- The cognitive component which allows us to interpret the physiological changes we are experiencing as feelings of fear, of anger or of other emotions.

Box 24.3 shows the detail of Schachter and Singer's experiment.

Misattribution paradigm Schachter and Singer's work led Valins (1966) to test what was termed the misattribution paradigm. Where we experience physiological arousal which does not particularly indicate a cause, we will search for a cause to attribute to it. Valins saw therapeutic implications in this. For instance, if someone feels depressed for no apparent reason then by supplying a plausible cause for the

---

Box 24.3 Attribution of emotion. An experiment by Schachter and Singer (1962)

Schachter and Singer injected some student participants with epinephrine (adrenalin) which had the effect of inducing physiological arousal. Others were injected with a placebo (a saline solution which had no physiological effect and so acted as a control). Four groups of participants were given different information about what they would experience as a result of the injections they had been given as described below:

- For one group, the effects of an adrenalin injection were accurately described (though they were not told it was adrenalin, but a drug called suproxin which was supposed to improve their visual acuity).
- For a second group the information given was that they would experience numbness and itchiness.
- A third group were given no information as to what they would feel.
- The fourth group (which had the placebo injection) were also given no information.

A confederate then attempted to produce feelings of euphoria in some of the participants and anger in others as they waited in an anteroom.

Results

The misinformed group experienced the strongest emotional feelings. The informed group searching for an explanation for their physiological state attributed it to the injection they had had. The misinformed group and the uninformed group had no such explanation and so attributed their bodily changes to strong emotion (anger or euphoria). In the absence of a situational cause, a dispositional cause came to the fore.

---

feelings experienced we can alleviate them by a process of reattribution. However, Valins's initial hopes have not been fully realized. There are two reasons for this:

- Maslach (1979) has shown that it is not as easy as was first thought to manipulate emotional feelings. Unexplained arousal is not easily explained by superimposing environmental cues. Because it is not pleasant to feel emotionally aroused, there is a stong tendency to attribute negative causes for it.

- The misattribution effect which Schachter and Singer and Valins noted seems to be confined to the laboratory and it was in any case short-lived.

? SELF-ASSESSMENT QUESTIONS

1. Outline two models of the attribution process.
2. List some of the sources of error in causal attribution.
3. What is meant by 'fundamental attribution error'?

The perception of self

The way an individual perceives himself or herself is immensely important. The information we store about self represents our self-concept. We have already come across self-schemata in the introduction to this part, where they were used to illustrate the social cognitive approach to social psychology. They have been applied to the way in which self-concepts are built up.

Schemata and self

In much the same way that schemata influence the way in which we perceive and react to social events, established schemata relate also to our perceptions of ourselves. Markus (1977) has referred to **self-schemata**. Networks of knowledge about ourselves are built up and come together to form the self-concept. Markus distinguishes between people who are **schematic** in relation to certain attributes of themselves and those who are **aschematic**. Schematic individuals are intensely concerned with a particular aspect of themselves and have therefore built up very well-formed schemata in relation to these aspects. Markus et al. (1982) have applied this to masculinity and femininity. They classified individuals as:

- **Schematic**. Those whose self-concept was stereotypically masculine (masculine schematics) or stereotypically feminine (feminine schematics). These were people for whom being

masculine or feminine assumed an overwhelming importance in the way which they perceived themselves.

- **Androgynous**. Those with a strong set of schemata relating to masculinity or femininity, but whose self-schemata included a combination of masculine and feminine attributes.
- **Aschematic**. Those without a strong set of schemata relating to masculinity or femininity; those who were effectively neutral.

Self-schemata as a context-specific network

Breckler et al. (1991) have portrayed these self-schemata as a net composed of nodes which are context-specific. In some contexts of their lives people have developed very clear concepts of themselves; in other contexts their self-concepts are nothing like as clear. To put this in terms of schemata, they are aschematic in some contexts of their lives, schematic in others. It all depends upon what is important to an individual: that is, his or her own value system. Some people, for instance, set great store on sporting prowess and on sporting interest. Sport occupies a prominent place in their value system. It is likely that they would be schematic in that area of their lives; they would have developed a very clear concept of themselves within the context of sport as a result of their life experiences. These same individuals might very well find that the appreciation of fine art was much less important to them. They would be likely to be self-aschematic within this context; no very clear view of themselves would have developed.

Complexity in self-schemata

Most individuals' self-concept is complex. There are a relatively large number of self-schemata. Linville (1987) has suggested that this fact is beneficial in that it provides a buffer to limit damage to a person's

---

GLOSSARY

Self-schemata Schemata which relate to an individual's concept of self.

Schematic (aschematic) Relates to the extent to which self-schemata concerning certain characteristics (e.g. masculinity/femininity) have been developed. A schematic person has well-developed self-schemata; an aschematic person does not.

self-concept resulting from negative life events. If your self-esteem takes a knock in one area of your life (maybe you are thrown out of the football team in which you were playing), this is much less damaging if there are a large number of areas in your life which are important to you. An individual whose whole life seemed to revolve around playing football (a person with a very limited number of self-schemata) would find it much more damaging.

Self-schemata and aspiration

It is just as important that self-schemata indicate what we aspire to as what we are at the present time. Higgins (1987) has suggested that we have three types of self-schemata:

- **Actual self** – that is, how we currently see ourselves to be;
- **Ideal self** – how we would like to be;
- **Ought self** – how we think we should be.

Where there are discrepancies between these sets of self-schemata, motivation to change may come to reduce the discrepancy. If efforts are made to reduce the gap which are not successful, then emotional difficulties may arise. Failure to resolve the gap between actual and ideal could result in disappointment, dissatisfaction or sadness. Failure to close the actual/ought gap results in emotions such as fear, anxiety or anger.

A humanistic view of self

This is not dissimilar to the view of self-concept taken by Rogers (1951, 1961). In his view, a person's self-concept arose from his or her interactions with other people which resulted in internalized conditions of worth. It was necessary for psychological health for people to receive **unconditional positive regard** from others. Where this unconditional positive regard was there, the ideal self and the actual self were not too far apart. On the other hand, where this unconditional positive regard was not forthcoming, the fear was always present that their behaviour might not receive approbation from others and their self-development was impaired. The conditions of worth which they internalized were reflections resulting from other people's reactions to them. To put this into simpler terms, they were always 'looking over their shoulders'

at what others were thinking of them rather than being secure in their knowledge of their own self-worth. They had very low self-esteem.

Rogers's solution was **client-centred therapy**. This nondirective therapy allowed clients to explore themselves without any sense that the therapist was directing them to think or behave in a particular way. This is described in Chapters 30 and 33.

Self and attribution

Locus of cause

Attribution theory, which has been more fully described in the previous section, refers to the way in which we observe the behaviour of those with whom we come into contact and from our observations make inferences about what they are like. For instance, we might characterize an individual as 'mean' on the basis of his or her reluctance to contribute a full share of the cost of an outing. The behaviour we have observed is said to have an internal locus of cause. It results (we surmise) from a character trait. Bem (1967, 1972) has suggested that this attribution process might equally be applied to the judgments we make about ourselves.

Bem's self-perception theory

This self-perception theory proposes that there is no essential difference between judgments arising from self-attribution and the attributions of character we make of others. We are aware of what we do and as a result of that awareness we make judgments about the kind of people we are. For instance, you go jogging every morning and quite frequently find yourself in the gym having a 'workout'. It is quite possible that someone whose opinion you care about has remarked that you are getting fat. In that case, the self-perception theory does not apply. But in the absence of any such external locus of cause you would infer that it is a facet of your character to like to keep yourself in trim.

GLOSSARY

Unconditional positive regard Relates to Rogers's contention that individuals need the esteem of others without conditions.

Client-centred therapy A form of therapy developed by Rogers where the client (patient) is central and the therapist acts as a facilitator rather than an initiator.

Self-attribution and motivation

Bem's theory has quite strong implications for motivation. You can either do something because there is an external pressure exerted on you to do it or because you enjoy it and are committed to it. There is evidence (Deci and Ryan, 1985) that in the latter case motivation increases, while in the former, motivation to perform is reduced. Your employer offering you a large bonus as an inducement to finish a job on time or, alternatively, threatening to sack you if you do not, does not result in your being as strongly motivated as you would be if you were doing it simply because you liked doing it. There is even evidence (Condry, 1977) that being given an external reward for doing something which had previously been done because enjoyment was obtained from it actually worsens performance. This has been termed the overjustification effect.

Weiner's extension to self-attribution

Weiner (1979, 1985, 1986) was interested in success or failure on a task and the causes and consequences of attributions which are made relating to this success or failure. There are three factors which may have a bearing on future performance on the same task:

- **The locus of cause**. Did you fail your driving test because you were not yet ready for it (in your estimation)? This would be an internal locus of cause. Or because you had a poor instructor? Or again because the traffic on the day of the test was horrendous? These would be external causes.
- **The stability of the cause**. You could hire another instructor next time; you could make sure that the test was not held in the rush hour; you could prepare yourself extra well by masses of practice. Each of which indicate a cause which is not stable. It can change. If, on the other hand, you feel you failed because you were so nervous you could not control what you were doing, that would be a much more stable cause.
- **Controllability**. If the traffic on the test route was always horrendous, that might be beyond your control. If you were subject to panic attacks that too might be beyond your control.

It could be argued that controllability and stability are really two facets of the same thing. But Weiner claims that these three dimensions are independent of one another and can help individuals understand their successes and failures. However, it is at least doubtful whether we actually undertake an analysis like this of the cause of our success or our failure outside the confines of a social psychology laboratory.

Locus of control

Rotter (1966) did some work in this area on what was termed attributional style. The suggestion was that individuals differ in the amount of control they feel they have over the outcomes of their actions. A distinction is made between those with external locus of control and those with internal locus of control. Internals have a tendency to attribute the outcomes of actions (in particular, rewards or punishments) to some facet of their own character; externals, on the other hand, impute causes of these outcomes to external factors.

Internal or external locus of control Let us consider how this might work. Two individuals, Jeremy and John, take their psychology examination and fail. Jeremy, having an external locus of control, claims that he had a very poor teacher, the paper was exceptionally difficult, and not only that but all through the examination there was a pneumatic drill digging up the road outside the hall where the examination was taking place. John, with an internal locus of control, blamed failure on the fact that he had always had difficulty understanding the subject – after all he had always been regarded as a borderline candidate.

Two other candidates, Janet and Jane, passed with flying colours. Jane, whose locus of control was external, said it was a very easy paper and, besides, all those questions which she had just revised came up. Janet realized that it was all down to the hard work she had put in during the previous months, and in any case she always did well in examinations. She had an internal locus of control. Just consider the differences in their self-concepts. The externalizers, Jeremy and

---

GLOSSARY

Locus of control (internal or external) Rotter's differentiation between those who see their behaviour dictated by forces outside themselves (external locus of control) or whose behaviour is the result of internal factors, such as disposition or ability (internal locus of control).

Jane, saw themselves as so much flotsam, tossed hither and thither by the storms of life. There was little that they could do to influence events. John and Janet were able to take much more active control of the outcomes.

Self-esteem

Yet another facet of self-concept is self-esteem, the value which we place on ourselves. There are two sides to this. Self-image is factual. You may see yourself as fat or thin, clever or not so clever, athletic or not athletic. There is a basis in fact for this. You came last in the race. You can no longer get into the clothes you bought for yourself last year.

But this is only half the story. If you see being fat as something disgusting, and you dislike yourself for it, your self-esteem is low. But if you see being fat as something comfortable or cuddly you have a positive view of yourself.

Coopersmith conducted experiments into self-esteem with a group of ordinary American 10- to 11-year-old boys (Coopersmith, 1968). This experiment is described in Chapter 22 where there is a full discussion of the development of self-esteem.

Culture and self

It is difficult to divorce what an individual conceives himself or herself to be from that individual's cultural context. Culture is quite a complex thing. It might be related to something as local and individual as membership of a family group which defines an individual's aspirations and values. On a broader level, it could embrace religious affiliation or social class. From a different perspective, gender or ethnicity are important elements in culture. There is little doubt that African culture, Japanese, Chinese or Hindu cultures are distinct and different from one another and in their turn distinct and different from that of Western Europe or America.

Hsu's multilayered model of culture

Hsu (1985) has described self as embedded in a multilayered model, a series of concentric rings, depicted in Figure 24.3. The outermost ring represents the influence upon self of the 'outer world' in a very general sense and the innermost level represents the influence of the unconscious mind in a Freudian sense: that is, that part of an individual's mind which

determines his or her behaviour without conscious awareness of it (this is itself set in place through the experiences of very early childhood). At intermediate levels within this model, society and culture exert strong influence upon self-concept. Hsu claims that the third level of intimate society and culture is particularly resistant to change.

Divergent concepts of self in different cultures

Hayes (1993) has described some of the divergent concepts of self in particular cultural contexts. In Africa, self is intricately linked to the tribe. The context within which an individual's self exists is that of the tribe. Mbiti (1970) points out that in many African tribes it was traditionally forbidden to count people. They could not be separated from the society (the tribe) to which they belonged. Individuals effectively did not exist except as corporate members of the tribe. In African thought, the guiding principles are 'to be at one with nature' and to ensure 'the survival of the tribe'. This contrasts, strongly in the view of Nobles (1976), with the European view which is 'to control nature' and 'the survival of the fittest'.

Bharati (1986) has described how Hindus equate a person's innermost self not with community or social contexts but with the oneness of God. Access to this innermost 'self' can only be through meditation and self-discipline.

Devos (1985) describes how the self in Japanese culture is intimately linked with social interaction and social relationships. Perhaps this is the influence of Buddhism which sees each and every one of our actions and experiences as linked in a chain of cause and effect. If we commit some injury to another, a bad karma will be the result and we shall reap the reward for it, if not in this life, then in a future incarnation (Gruber and Kersten, 1995). Japanese children learn from a very early age to be aware of the effect that their actions will have on others. In this way the Japanese have their ultimate satisfaction in belonging to a group. Their sense of self is intimately associated with an awareness of the way in which what they do impinges on others.

Social identity theory

Tajfel (1978, 1982) (also Tajfel and Turner, 1986) has developed what he calls social identity theory.

The outer world
Wider society and culture
Operative society and culture
Intimate society and culture
Expressible conscious
Inexpressible conscious
Preconscious (Freudian)
Unconscious (Freudian)

Figure 24.3   Hsu's model of the impact of culture on self (after Hsu, 1985)

According to this theory the social groups we belong to are an integral part of our self-concept.

Abrams and Hogg (1990a) have maintained that social categories (a nation, perhaps, or a religion in terms of large entities or smaller groupings such as clubs) are instrumental in providing their members with a social identity. This social identity does two things:

■ It defines and evaluates them. It is fairly commonplace to find an individual defined as a Scot or as Welsh, as a Catholic or a Protestant (particularly in places such as Northern Ireland) or perhaps as a member of the local amateur operatic society or a walking group.

■ It prescribes appropriate behaviour. Characterizing someone as a Protestant in Northern Ireland conjures up a picture of marching with orange sashes, but it also acts as an evaluating tool. The individual is evaluated by others as a Northern Ireland Protestant who thinks and behaves as Northern Irish Protestants characteristically behave – perhaps as fanatically loyal to the Union and as somewhat inflexible in thinking. But it is not only others who define a person in this way, but individuals define and evaluate themselves in similar terms. They think and behave in charactistically Northern Irish Protestant ways. It is a part of their self-concept.

❓ SELF-ASSESSMENT QUESTIONS

1. Distinguish between schematic and aschematic individuals. How do the contexts in which we perceive ourselves acting have an effect upon self-concept?

2. Bem has developed an attributional theory of self. Describe in simple terms how this attributional process works.

3. What did Carl Rogers conceive of as being the source of mental well-being? What did he mean by unconditional positive regard?

4. What is meant by self-esteem? How do you think that Rotter's locus of control theory relates to self-esteem?

5. Outline ways in which self-concept may be different in the context of different cultures. How do you see gender or ethnicity affecting the way in which we see ourselves?

6. What is social identity? What does it add to the concept of self?

Chapter summary

■ Social schemata are means by which we rapidly make sense of persons, events, situations or places we meet. We may develop person schemata, role schemata or scripts which might be described as event schemata.

■ Impressions we make of other people depend in the first instance on physical appearance. These first impressions enable us to categorize people and relate them to prototypes we have formed of such categories and perhaps to a particular exemplar of them (specific instances we have met of a particular category).

■ While prototypes and exemplars are personal, stereotypes are shared perceptions of an out-group among members of an in-group. They often have a pejorative overtone. Vast human groups may be characterized in terms of a few common attributes. Stereotypes serve to make sense of intergroup relations.

■ Implicit personality theories are sets of unstated assumptions about what traits of character tend to go together. Similarly, implicit social theories imply unstated assumptions about cause-and-effect relationships which will inform behaviour.

■ Personal constructs, described by Kelly, represent each individual's guide to interpreting the world. The world does not have any meaning for Kelly outside an individual's own perception of it. Constructs will have a bipolar dimension (a construct and a contrast)

which determine the terms in which we see things. For instance, a teacher may be categorized as a good disciplinarian (construct) or unable to keep order (contrast).

■ Attribution processes are those which relate behaviour to personality characteristics or disposition. Correspondent inference theory makes the assumption that individuals infer that behaviour witnessed is the result of some dispositional trait. There are limitations on this direct relationship centring on how freely chosen the behaviour is, how socially desirable, what hedonic relevance it has and whether such behaviour is noncommon.

■ Kelley's covariation model links causes of behaviour to its consistency, distinctiveness and consensus. It also allows for augmentation and discounting of cause when there are constraints, costs and sacrifices involved. Bias in attribution of cause is towards attribution of cause to disposition rather than situation (fundamental attribution bias). Moreover, the observer is more likely than the actor to emphasize disposition rather than situation as the cause of behaviour. Other sources of bias include consensus (people tend to associate predominantly with those who hold similar views) and the just world hypothesis. Schachter and Singer applied attribution theory to attributions of the causes of emotional feelings.

■ Self-schemata taken together form the self-concept (the perception a person has of himself or herself).

Schematic individuals are intensely concerned with a particular aspect of themselves, for instance masculinity or femininity. Being male (or female) has assumed paramount importance in relation to their self-concept. Other individuals may be aschematic in this regard: masculinity/femininity plays no great part in the valuation they make of themselves.

■ Rogers has placed emphasis in relation to self-concept on unconditional positive regard as being necessary for psychological health. The actual and the ideal self should not be too far apart. Where these conditions of worth are not met Rogers believed self-esteem would be low and the solution might be client-centred therapy.

■ Bem applied attribution theory to people's self-concept. Individuals might have an internal or an external locus of cause. We either attribute our behaviour to dispositional factors (internal locus of cause) or to situational factors (external locus of cause). This has implications for motivation. Weiner related success or failure to self-attribution and Rotter extended this idea to include locus of control (the degree to which we have control over outcomes in our lives). Self-esteem links perception of ourselves in a factual way (self-image) to evaluation of those attributes which we see ourselves possessing.

■ An individual's cultural context is difficult to divorce from self-concept. Our social identity prescribes behaviour we consider appropriate. African, Hindu or Japanese cultures link self-concept closely with particular behaviour.

Further reading

Deaux, K., Dane, F.C. and Wrightsman, L.S. (1993). *Social Psychology in the 90's*, 6th edn. Pacific Grove, CA: Brookes-Cole. Chapter 3 of this book describes some of the research on self-concepts, including gender identity, self-perception theory and social comparison. Chapter 4 contains a good account of person perception including an excellent outline of social cognition.

Hogg, M.A. and Vaughan, G.M. (1995). *Social Psychology: An Introduction*. Hemel Hempstead: Prentice-Hall/Harvester Wheatsheaf. Chapter 3 of this book contains a good basic account of attribution theory, including biases in attribution, together with some extensions and applications.

CHAPTER 25

Relationships with others

Affiliation   594
- Patterns of affiliation   595
- The propinquity factor   595
- Similarity   596
- Complementarity of needs   596
- Pleasantness   597
- Physical attractiveness   597

- Repricocity   597
- Theories of attraction   598

Friendship, love and marriage   602
- Friendship   602
- Love   603
- Mate selection   606
- Break-up of relationships   607

Objectives

By the end of this chapter you should be able to:

- Describe why it is that humans have a need to affiliate;

- Identify some of the factors which influence our choice of people with whom to affiliate;

- Show an understanding of balance theory and social exchange theory in relation to affiliation;

- Distinguish between friendship and love and between different kinds of love;

- Understand how relationships develop;

- Appreciate some of the factors which may lead to the break-up of a relationship and the consequences of such a break-up.

Affiliation

No man is an island entire of itself.
                    (Donne 1571–1631: *Devotions*)

Human beings have a need to affiliate. There is some evidence that we cannot easily cope with being out of contact with other human beings for prolonged periods. Schachter (1959) conducted a study in which participants (five male students) volunteered to put themselves into a situation where they had no contact at all with other people. One of these students lasted in his isolation cell a mere 20 minutes before he had an uncontrollable desire to leave. Isolation did not affect them all equally but even one who remained isolated for eight days admitted feeling nervous and uneasy.

Schachter put forward four possible reasons why we should have such a strong urge to affiliate with others:

- **Lessening of anxiety**. Anxiety is less when we are together with other people; we feel more secure in a group. Cutrona (1986) found that there was a significant relationship between social interaction and stress.

- **Lessening the importance of our own concerns**. Our own immediate concerns assume less importance to us, which again reduces the anxiety we feel.

- **Cognitive clarity**. We have need of the information which association with others can provide; it provides us with cognitive clarity. Our minds become clearer. Kirkpatrick and Shaver (1988) have noted that when people are in a stressful situation they look for someone to help them cope with stress: either a competent intelligent person who will help them assess the situation clearly, or somebody warm and supportive.

■ **Self-evaluation**. Being with others provides us with a yardstick against which we can evaluate ourselves. Self-evaluation is a mechanism for anxiety reduction.

These students are part of the same social network

Patterns of affiliation

Social networks

We develop systematic links with other people so that a social network is formed. Berscheid (1985) has used this term to refer to those people with whom an individual is in actual contact. Social networks are not static, particularly when people move. New people join and some of the old associates drop out of the picture. Much of the research which has been done in this area has been done on college campuses. It is necessary to bear in mind that samples of college students are not typical of people as a whole. Nevertheless these kinds of studies do provide insights. Hays and Oxley (1986) studied differences in affiliation patterns between first-year students who remained at home and commuted to college and those who lived in. In American universities this generally means dormitories. Commuting students generally retained connections with friends and relatives more easily and their relationships tended to be more intimate. The social networks established by the resident students included many more new acquaintances and centred more upon what was going on in the university. You could say that resident students integrated more deeply into the life of the university than those who retained links with home by living there.

Gender differences in social networks Hays and Oxley found some gender differences too. Men included more friends of the opposite sex. Women provided more social support for their friends, both informational and emotional. These gender differences did not obtain in the nonresident students in their contacts with friends and relatives outside college. The origins of these gender differences have been studied by Wheeler et al. (1983) who suggested that women have been socialized to express their emotional feelings more than men. They found that interactions between women were more 'meaningful' measured by such things as self-disclosure, intimacy and pleasantness than those between men.

Choice of relationship

The question which needs to be answered is this: on what basis do we choose those with whom we affiliate? What makes someone attractive to us? Deaux et al. (1993) have listed six factors which may influence choice:

■ Proximity, the propinquity factor;
■ Similarity in beliefs, values and personality characteristics;
■ Need complementarity;
■ Pleasantness or agreeableness;
■ Physical attractiveness;
■ Reciprocation of attraction.

The propinquity factor

It is suggested that when everything else is considered we like people better with whom we are frequently at close quarters than those at a distance. Festinger et al. (1950) showed that people who lived on the same floor of an apartment block liked each other better than people who lived on other floors or in another building. Even architectural features such as the location of a staircase can have an influence upon the way we choose our friends. Hogg and Vaughan (1995) have highlighted several reasons why this should be the case:

Familiarity. If we are physically close to someone, we are likely to see him or her often. This leads to feeling comfortable with him or her and then to familiarity. This has even been extended to strangers. Jorgensen and Cervone (1978) found that the more we see people, the more we like them.

Availability. When it requires little effort on our part to interact with someone the social cost to us is low. It requires much more effort to keep in touch with someone who has moved away.

Expectation of continued interaction. If we expect that we are going to have to interact with someone over an extended period we make an effort to like him or her. For instance, if people move in next door we try to get on with them. We can predict that it will be uncomfortable not to.

Similarity

Newcombe (1961) offered free board and lodging to students who were prepared to participate in his study, giving details of their attitudes and values and filling in numerous questionnaires over the course of the first semester at university. Attraction between students was measured as well as changes in attitudes. During the first few weeks the propinquity factor was important. As time went on, though, similarities in attitudes before the term began became more closely related to degree of attraction.

Byrne's law of attraction

Byrne (1971) went as far as to formulate a 'law of attraction'. This stated that there was a linear relationship between the degree of attraction and the proportion of attitudes in common (Clore and Byrne, 1974). In other words, the more attitudes individuals share, the more likely they are to be attracted to one another.

However, Byrne's studies were conducted in a laboratory setting and based upon hypothetical descriptions of people. This gives them less ecological validity (they were less closely related to reality) than Newcombe's study or that of Kandel (1978).

Attitudes, values and attraction

Kandel (1978) conducted an extensive study with over 1800 male and female adolescents aged 13 to 18. Each

student's attitudes and values were measured by means of questionnaires and compared with the attitudes and values of his or her best friend. She obtained strong confirmation that similarity was an important factor. The process seems to work both ways. Not only are we attracted to those who share our attitudes and values, but we are repelled by those with opposing attitudes and values. Those with different attitudes and values challenge beliefs and threaten our self-concepts. However, the evidence shows that the similarity-attraction process is more likely to occur than dissimilarity-repulsion (Byrne et al., 1986; Dane and Harshaw, 1991).

Sometimes, though, we do not dislike those with dissimilar attitudes and values. We may even prefer them to have such values and attitudes, especially when a person has been stigmatized (Novak and Lerner, 1968) or is perceived to be of a lower status (Karuza and Brickman, 1978). This happens because too much similarity to an otherwise undesirable person threatens our own self-image.

Complementarity of needs

Winch et al. (1954) have claimed that people choose relationships so that their basic needs may be mutually gratified. This is the theory of **need complementarity**. The evidence for this is ambiguous. Kerckhoff and Davis (1962) have suggested that it only operates in the long term. Similarity of values is more important in the initial stages of a relationship. Need complementarity comes later. Brehm (1992) has suggested that it only relates to certain dimensions of behaviour such as dominance and submissiveness. For instance, a dominant person will tend to be attracted to a submissive one and vice versa. Lipetz et al. (1970) did find, however, that complementarity was related to marital satisfaction. This seems to support the notion that it is a long-term thing, rather than relating to initial attractiveness.

> **GLOSSARY**
>
> **Ecological validity** An assessment of the extent to which a test or experiment is relevant to what happens in the 'real world'.
>
> **Need complementarity** A relationship between two partners is more likely to be sustained if the needs of each are complementary to those of the other.

Pleasantness

It seems to be self-evident that we like people who are pleasant. We find positive traits more attractive than negative ones. However, in evaluating the traits we observe in other people as positive or negative, we are concerned to consider what these traits mean for us (Clore and Kerber, 1978). When we say that someone is 'kind', we are implying that we are likely to be on the receiving end of that 'kindness'. The yardstick of that evaluation is the way it affects us. On the negative side, 'dishonesty' in another person is likely to be assessed according to how likely it is that that person will cheat us.

Physical attractiveness

Cultural/sociobiological differences

Beauty is clearly in the eye of the beholder or perhaps is dictated by the demands of fashion. Cunningham (1986) has put an interesting sociobiological slant on this personal or ephemeral view of physical attractiveness (sociobiology relates to the biological basis for behaviour, particularly the need to pass our genes on to succeeding generations). American men found 'cute' faces attractive. 'Cute' equates to 'childlike' (eyes large and set well apart, small nose and chin). 'Childlike' implies youthfulness which, in turn, has implications for the individual's potential to produce offspring.

First impressions and evaluations

Physical attractiveness is closely related to the first impressions we have of someone we meet. We will make an immediate evaluation of that person on the basis of their physical attractiveness. Attractive individuals are less likely to be adjudged maladjusted or disturbed, more likely to be offered a job at interview and likely to have their written applications more positively evaluated than those who are seen as less physically attractive (Cash et al., 1977; Dion, 1972; Dipboye et al., 1977). Landy and Sigall (1974) conducted an experiment to test this last point. Male students were asked to grade two essays of different quality written by female students. An independent assessment had previously been given of the essays by someone who had no knowledge of the authors. A good essay was presented to the students together with a photograph of an attractive woman, with a control photograph or with a photograph of a relatively unattractive woman. In a similar procedure the poor essay was paired with photographs of attractive and less attractive women as well as with control photographs. The more attractive woman had her essay more highly assessed, both in the case of the good and the poor essay.

Physical attractiveness and success

This preference given to physically attractive people carries over into many spheres. Dion et al. (1972) demonstrated that physically attractive people are seen as happier, more successful and more likely to get married than less attractive people. It even extends into the courts. Sigall and Ostrove (1975) found that jurors take an easier view of attactive women defendants. In a study of criminal trials in Pennsylvania attractive male defendants received lighter sentences and were twice as likely to avoid imprisonment as less attractive people (Stewart, 1980).

Reciprocity

What has been termed the **reciprocity** principle applies in attraction. We like those who like us, and dislike those who dislike us. Dittes and Kelley (1956) showed, as a result of an experiment conducted with students, that members of a discussion group were more attracted to the group if the group apparently liked them.

Reciprocity and self-esteem

Self-esteem seems to be a crucial factor in this reciprocation of attraction. Where someone has a high self-esteem he or she is less influenced by others' liking or disliking them. Where people have low self-esteem, whether someone else likes them or not assumes much greater importance. Dittes (1959) found that where the group appeared to like an individual who had low self-esteem, that individual liked the group a lot. Similarly where the group apparently showed dislike, a low self-esteem individual would take a strong dislike to the group.

GLOSSARY
Reciprocity Relates to the idea that feelings we have for others depend to an extent on the feelings which they express for us.

Theories of attraction

Balance theory

Agreement between people strengthens bonds between them and also involves positive feelings (that is, liking). Disagreement between people who like each other produces tension. This is a state of imbalance. This is not a comfortable state and there will be attempts made to restore balance. Either one or both the parties concerned will alter their attitudes or their beliefs (their cognitions about whatever or whoever is causing the disagreement) to restore the agreement and so the balance.

If, on the other hand, two people dislike each other when they first meet because there is dissimilarity in their cognitions there will be imbalance which neither will have incentive to change. No balance exists to be restored, so that there is no feeling of discomfort. Heider (1958), who formulated balance theory, proposed that there were two possible relationships between people, a unit relationship (belonging together, being members of a group or having something in common) and a liking relationship. Both come into play in relations between people. Members of a group, say members of a Conservative Club, will assume that other members share many of their beliefs, attitudes and opinions. A liking relationship will be likely to exist between members so long as nothing changes this assumption (Spears and Manstead, 1990). Balance will exist. Discovery of a major source of

difference in beliefs produces imbalance. If X believes that taxes should be raised to pay for school improvements, while Y believes in reducing public spending to pay for tax cuts, this will produce a negative affect in X and Y which may be restored to balance by either of them, or both altering their view. Liking will be difficult while there is imbalance. Figure 25.1 illustrates Heider's balance theory. In A, P represents one individual, O represents another. X is a third person or an activity, perhaps. A is a balanced state: + represents positive affect (liking), – represents negative affect (disliking). B shows an unbalanced state.

This is in essence a cognitive theory, based on the notion that there is pressure to achieve and to maintain cognitive consistency.

Reinforcement/affect theory

Put very simply, we like people who reward us; dislike those who punish us. Byrne and Clore (1970) use a learning theory model to explain interpersonal attrac-

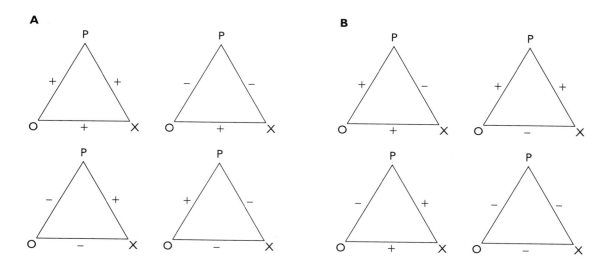

Figure 25.1 Heider's balance theory (Heider, 1958). P represents one individual, O another, and X is a third entity (a person, perhaps, or an activity). + and – signs represent positive or negative feelings (affect)

tion: **reinforcement/affect theory**. Assuming that most stimuli are either rewarding or punishing, we like those we associate with rewarding stimuli and dislike those associated with punishment. The more positive or negative affect we experience, the greater the feelings of liking or disliking. If neutral stimuli are associated with positive or negative affect, similar feelings result.

How does this work in practice? Someone is kind to us. This is a positive, rewarding experience (positive affect) and so we evaluate that person positively (that is, we like him or her). We also tend to like people and objects which we associate with the rewarding situation. Not only are we well disposed to the person who has been kind to us, but we like the place where the kindness happened and those other people who happened to be there at the time. There is a contagion in liking or disliking.

Figure 25.2 illustrates Byrne and Clore's reinforcement/affect theory.

Social exchange theory

The **social exchange** theory of Clark and Mills (Clark and Mills, 1979; Mills and Clark, 1982) and the interdependence theory of Thibaut and Kelley (Kelley and Thibaut, 1978; Thibaut and Kelley, 1959) take reinforcement theory further. Each person in a relationship associates certain costs and certain benefits with that relationship. Attraction is a two-way process and the behaviour and the perceptions of both individuals must be taken together. In different kinds of relationships, costs and benefits are defined differently. We treat relationships with strangers or business associates differently. A strict minimax strategy may be adopted. We aim to minimize costs and maximize benefits. Reciprocity is important. There needs to be a balance between what a person gives to a relationship and what he or she gets from it.

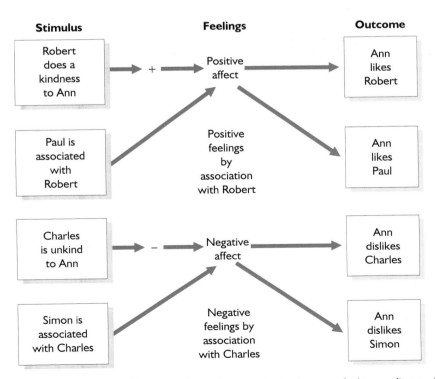

Figure 25.2 Reinforcement/affect model (Byrne and Clore, 1970). We like those we find rewarding, and dislike those who are associated with punishment. These feelings are contagious

This is an exchange relationship. In communal relationships, on the other hand, it is a bit more flexible. With family members and close friends we do not concern ourselves quite as much with balancing every input and outcome. Costs and benefits still come into the equation, though. You help a friend in trouble without expecting anything in return. However, if in the longer term your friend only contacts you when he or she needs help and ignores you the rest of the time, the quality of the relationship will deteriorate and eventually your appraisal of it will alter. Figure 25.3 illustrates social exchange theory. In a relationship such as those of Jane and Bill and Sarah and Tom, every activity they engage in is assigned a value: positive for benefits, negative for costs.

Clark (1984) illustrated the distinction between exchange and communal relationships with an ingenious experiment. This is described in Box 25.1.

This experiment recognized the fact that costs and benefits may be defined differently in different relationships. The distinction made was between *exchange* and *communal* relationships as described above.

Thibaut and Kelley's interdependence theory

The interdependence theory of Thibaut and Kelley (1959, 1978) is similar to social exchange but includes

Box 25.1 Clark's experiment with record keeping in relationships

Participants were pairs of students, either two friends or two strangers. The task they were set was as follows:

In a 15 × 26 matrix of numbers the two participants had to search for specified sequences of numbers. They had to take turns looking for a sequence, then circling it in ink when they found it. There was a choice of pens, one with red ink, one with black. They were promised a joint reward for the task, which they could divide as they wished. The dependent variable was the choice of pen. The independent variable was the kind of pair of participants, friends or strangers.

In an exchange relationship, it was argued, the two participants would need to keep a tally of each one's contribution so as to be able to divide the reward according to the relative contribution of each. So different coloured pens would be chosen. In a communal relationship the friends would be more likely to use the same pen. That was how it turned out. The pairs of strangers chose different pens in significantly more cases; the pairs of friends chose the same pen significantly more often.

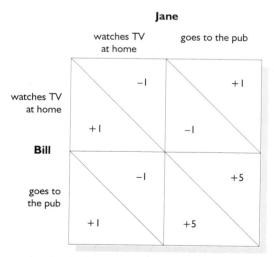

Jane's relationship with Bill is likely to be compatible. The positive values outweigh the negatives

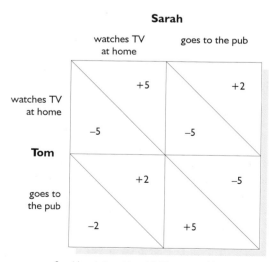

Sarah's relationship with Tom is not likely to be compatible. Negative values outweigh the positives

Figure 25.3 Social exchange theory. Every activity of Jane and Bill, or of Sarah and Tom, has a value assigned to it: positive for benefit, negative for cost

more detail. Indeed, it also has sometimes been referred to as social exchange. An important further concept is comparison level. This is the common standard against which all relationships may be judged. Rewards are compared with what the individuals concerned have come to expect. This is where social cognition comes in. Everyone has stored schemata relating to what is to be expected from a relationship. This is based upon past experience and represents the measure of comparison for any present relationship. Only if the gains to be had exceed the comparison level will the relationship be judged to be satisfactory. As with all schemata, this comparison level is not static but can change with experience and age; as we get older we tend to demand more from a relationship. Comparison level is also situation-specific. Expectations, based upon experience, will vary according to the circumstances. A similar evaluation is made of the costs involved in the relationship, again against a comparison level of costs. Only if the rewards outweigh the costs is the relationship likely to continue.

Evaluation of alternatives A further element which enters into the calculations in interdependence theory is that there is also evaluation (conducted in the same way) of the alternatives. Jogging along nicely in a relationship with a friend, the costs and rewards are pretty well in balance. Then you meet an exciting new stranger. The potential rewards of this new relationship are greater; the costs are less. In all probability you will abandon your present relationship for the new one. However, if your present relationship is an excellent one, with rewards that greatly exceed the costs, then you would be likely to be in much more of a quandary.

An evaluation of social exchange How useful is social exchange? Clearly, it is a very subjective process involving much speculation. It is also hard to maintain the notion that social relationships are based solely upon cost/benefit analysis on a personal level. The influence of the broader community in which we live also counts for something, though it might be argued that this is part of the costs and the benefits. For example, suppose you want to develop a relationship with someone of a different ethnic background in a racially intolerant community. The intolerance of the community might be said to impose additional costs, which might sway the balance.

Reinforcement theory bases itself solely upon learning theory, while social exchange or interdependence theory brings in an element of social cognition.

Equity theory

Equity theory modifies social exchange, stressing the importance of perceived fairness in what is going on between people. It is summarized by Walster et al. (1978) in terms of the following:

- **Minimax principle**. Maximization of reward and minimization of cost.
- **Consensus**. There is more than one way in which rewards can be shared out, but there must be agreement on a fair system.
- **Avoidance of distress**. An inequitable relationship produces distress; the more inequitable the more distress it causes.
- **Need to restore equity**. Someone who is in an inequitable relationship will try to restore it to equity. The losing partner will put in as much effort as seems necessary to restore equity for as long as there is a chance to do so.

Adams (1965) dealt with two main situations in relation to equity:

- A mutual exchange of resources;
- The distribution of limited resources.

According to Adams, equity exists between two individuals A and B when A's outcomes plus A's inputs equal B's outcomes plus B's inputs. The ratio of inputs to outcomes is first estimated. Then a comparison is made of the ratio between inputs and outcomes for the other person. If these ratios are equal people feel they are being treated fairly (equitably). This rule of distributive justice was originally propounded by Homans (1961). If there appears to be inequity we are

---

GLOSSARY

Equity theory Stresses the importance of *perceived fairness* in a relationship regarding the benefits which each partner receives and the costs each incurs.

Minimax principle The notion that an individual will strive to minimize costs and maximize benefits in a relationship.

motivated to do something about it. There are two possible ways of going about this. We can:

■ alter the inputs and/or the outcomes;
■ alter our *perceptions* of the inputs and outcomes, so that it no longer *appears* that the relationship is inequitable.

Norms of distributive justice Adams claimed that when neither of the above methods works, the relationship is likely to end. In practice, society operates on the basis of norms. These include:

■ **An equity norm:** the rule of distributive justice, for instance (see above);
■ **A social welfare norm:** a rule which maintains that resources should be distributed according to people's need;
■ **An equalitarian norm:** a rule that everyone gets an equal share.

Adams claimed that people will always prefer the equity norm when allocating resources, but more recent research by Deutsch (1975) and Mikula (1980) has modified this. It seems that the circumstances and the situation have a bearing on the norm chosen. Various points have been made:

■ **Differences in evaluation.** Lamm and Kayser (1978) suggest that a *friend's* inputs into a relationship are differently evaluated from those of a stranger. Where a friend is concerned you will tend to take into account not only the resources which you perceive that friend as able to contribute, but also the effort which goes into that contribution. With a stranger, on the other hand, it is just ability that matters.
■ **Gender differences.** Gender makes a difference too; women are likely to allocate resources on an equalitarian norm, men tend to use an equity norm (Kahn et al., 1980; Major and Adams, 1983; Major and Deaux, 1982).
■ **Women's role.** Kahn makes the point that the traditional role of women is that of maintaining group harmony. This may best be achieved by adopting equalitarian norms in allocating resources.

? SELF-ASSESSMENT QUESTIONS

1. Why do people need to affiliate with others? List three advantages which may stem from affiliation.
2. Make a list of factors which affect our choice of those with whom we form relationships. Which seems to you to be the most important and why?
3. Social exchange and interdependence theories go some way towards explaining why we choose to form a relationship with one person rather than another. Do these theories seem to you to be convincing? Explain your answer.
4. Equity is claimed to be an important basis for forming and maintaining a relationship. How do you see Adams's equity theory operating in practice? Illustrate with an example.

Friendship, love and marriage

Friendship

What do you expect from a friend? Can you say that there is some behaviour which is incompatible with friendship? Argyle and Henderson (1985) have attempted to answer these questions by setting out four criteria for a friendship rule:

■ **Agreement.** People should generally agree the behaviour specified in the rule is important for friendship.
■ **Difference in rule application.** The rule should be applied differently to former friends as compared to current friends.
■ **Failure to adhere to the rule.** Nonadherence is often cited as a reason for the break-up of a friendship.
■ **Close friends and acquaintances.** The rule should differentiate behaviour between close friends and not-so-close friends.

They then proceeded to question students in England, Italy, Japan and Hong Kong about friendship and attempted to apply the above criteria to the responses they gave. They were able to identify six rules which met the above criteria completely, together with three more which did not meet the last criterion though they met the others. These are listed below:

1. Share news of success with a friend,
2. Show emotional support,
3. Volunteer help in time of need,
4. Strive to make a friend happy when in each other's company,
5. Trust and confide in one another,
6. Stand up for a friend in his or her absence,
7. Repay debts and favours,
8. Be tolerant of other friends,
9. Do not nag a friend.

Development of friendships

Interaction between friends Hays (1985) has shown that when acquaintances begin to develop into friends, there is a great deal of interaction to begin with. Then this tends to ease off as the two individuals concerned begin to concentrate more on other things. But the amount of interaction is balanced by the increase in its quality. It becomes more intimate.

Gender differences There is a difference in emphasis between male-male friendships and female-female friendships. Because females tend to be more verbally oriented, communication plays a considerable part, as well as self-disclosure. Confidences are more often exchanged. Males, on the other hand, are more activity-oriented so that friendships develop out of shared activities and interests. An interesting study by Derlega et al. (1989) is described in Box 25.2. This highlighted gender differences in the ways in which friendship was expressed.

Girls expressing friendship on meeting. Females exhibit higher levels of intimacy and touching than males

Box 25.2   Gender differences in the expression of friendship (Derlega et al., 1989)

Participants (dating partners, mixed-sex pairs of friends, male friends and female friends) were asked to role-play meeting and greeting their friendship partners at an airport where one of them was coming back from a trip. Greetings were photographed and scored for levels of intimacy and touching. Results showed male–male pairs using minimal touching, while mixed pairs of friends and female friends reached a higher level of intimacy and touching. Seven mixed pairs and eight female pairs reached the most intimate levels of touching. But of the dating couples, all reached the most intimate level, engaging in some combination of hugging and kissing.

Love

Loving and liking

There seems to be general agreement that love is different from liking. Intuitively, we feel that there is a qualitative difference between liking someone and loving him or her. It is more than simply a matter of degree. Rubin (1973) distinguished 'liking' and 'loving' and developed scales to measure each separately. Hatfield and Walster (1981) went further and separated passionate love from companionate love. Their definitions are as follows:

> Passionate love is an intensely emotional state and a confusion of feelings: tenderness, sexuality, elation and pain, anxiety and relief, altruism and jealousy. Companionate love, on the other hand, is a less intense emotion, combining feelings of friendly affection and deep attachment. It is characterized by friendship, understanding and concern for the welfare of the other.
>
> (Hatfield, 1987, p. 676)

Most people would accept that there are other people with whom we certainly cannot say we are 'in love', but with whom we enjoy sharing time and whom we find it pleasant and comforting to be with. Argyle and Henderson (1985) have claimed that passionate love is a first stage. Couples who have been together a long time have said that the first passionate love evolves over time into something at once deeper and less violently emotional: a relationship characterized more by attachment and affection than by sexual excitement. This is illustrated in a longitudinal study by Simpson et al. (1986), described in Box 25.3.

Falling in love

Can you say that there is a state of 'being in love'? Milardo et al. (1983) suggest that you can fall in love. It

---

Box 25.3   Simpson et al.'s study of love

Participants in this study were asked: 'If a man (woman) had all the qualities you desired, would you marry this person, even if you were not in love with him (her)?' There were three samples taken at intervals between the 1960s and the 1980s. There were more people in the earlier samples who said they would be willing to marry without falling in love, with just under 80 per cent of women willing to marry without love in 1967 as compared to less than 20 per cent in 1984. For men, the proportions were much lower in 1967 (less than 40 per cent), and much more nearly similar to the women's sample in 1976 and 1984. Perhaps the security offered to women by marriage was a more important factor in 1967. By 1984, they felt themselves to be more independent economically, so that the romantic side of marriage assumed greater importance.

---

really is comparable to some kind of accident over which we have little or no control. The lover becomes the total focus of a person's life. Other friends are excluded. It is very intensely emotional. There is a very strong desire on the part of both individuals to spend as much time as possible in each other's company.

Culture and falling in love   However, there is some evidence that we need to have been brought up in a culture which believes in this kind of romantic love; where young people are taught that it exists both in fiction and in real life. Perhaps Romeo and Juliet have something to answer for! If we did not see people 'in love' in films, TV and plays or read about it in fiction, we should not expect it to happen to us. Furthermore, the more you think about love the more likely you are to 'fall in love' and if you really do believe in 'love at first sight' there is a much greater chance that it will happen to you (Tesser and Paulhus, 1976; Averill and Boothroyd, 1977).

Three-factor theory of love

Hatfield and Walster (1981) proposed that there were three factors responsible for the experience of 'love':

- **Cultural exposure**. An individual needs to have been exposed from an early age to the idea of love and being in love.
- **Physiological arousal**. Being sexually aroused in a physiological sense at a particular time.
- **Appropriate love object**. There needs to be an appropriate love object present: an attractive (to

you, at least) person (usually) of the opposite sex and of similar age.

Again we return to the cognitive explanation of emotion put forward by Schachter and Singer (1962) described earlier in Chapter 9 (p. 199). Cognitively we need to find an explanation for the physiological changes we experience. The label we attach to the feelings experienced when the three factors above are there is 'love'. Figure 25.4 illustrates this three-factor theory of love.

This is an interesting theory, but the evidence for an external labelling of internal feelings of this kind is not conclusive. While the evidence of Schachter and Singer's study clearly support the idea, Marshall and Zimbardo (1979) are not so sure. External labelling seems to be just one factor in what is quite a complex process.

You might equally well explain it using the reinforcement/affect theory mentioned earlier. The arousal which is experienced in the 'love object's' presence is associated with that person. This positive emotional feeling is reinforcing. In effect you learn to be in love.

Attachment theory of love

Hazan and Shaver (1987, 1990) and Shaver and Hazan (1987, 1988) used the **attachment theory** first propounded by Bowlby (1969, 1973, 1980) to explain the various types of love. This has its roots in the evolutionary need to develop an attachment mechanism to keep infants secure in the face of danger. This goes back to studies of imprinting in precocial birds by Lorenz (1937) and others. Box 25.4 shows Hazan and Shaver's attachment theory of love.

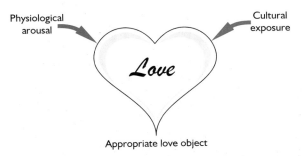

Figure 25.4 Three-factor theory of love (Hatfield and Walster, 1981)

Cognition and love

In common with most other social experience, cognition plays a considerable part in love. In the first place, experience sets the culture within which we relate to other people. Our childhood experiences of attachment of other people establish patterns of cognition, which, while they may be modified by experience at any time in life, nevertheless colour our perceptions of what love is.

Sexual orientations

We have tended to ignore the gender of lovers in this discussion. While heterosexual love has been the major focus (the research is very much greater here), love experiences do not appear to be very different for people with different sexual orientations. Hazan and Shaver did not find any differences between heterosexual and homosexual individuals.

Sternberg's triangular theory of love

Sternberg (1986) saw love as a triangle with three components: intimacy, passion and commitment. Intimacy relates to the feelings of bonding and attachment just mentioned – the desire to be close to someone else; passion relates to the sexual and romantic aspects of a relationship, and commitment has two aspects – decision to unite with someone else and commitment to remain with that person. In different individuals these three components are present in different strengths and this results in different kinds of love. Liking involves a strong dose of intimacy but little passion or commitment; infatuation involves high levels of passion but not so much commitment or intimacy; empty love is mostly commitment with little passion or intimacy; romantic love is strong on passion and intimacy but there is little commitment. In the centre of the triangle, Sternberg puts consummate love. Figure 25.5 illustrates this theory.

> **GLOSSARY**
>
> **Attachment theory of love** Relates to the suggestion that links between two individuals in a relationship have similar functions to the supportive functions of attachment in young children or animals.

Box 25.4 Hazan and Shaver's attachment theory of love

The researchers used with adults the three main styles of attachment identified by Ainsworth et al. (1978) in respect of infants: secure, avoidant and ambivalent (this is discussed in the context of children's development in Chapter 19). They argued that love was a form of attachment. A person's adult romantic attachments should therefore have some relationship to other attachment experiences. They characterized them as follows:

■ **Secure attachment:** I find it relatively easy to get close to others and am comfortable depending on them and having them depend on me. I don't often worry about being abandoned or someone getting too close to me.

■ **Avoidant:** I am somewhat uncomfortable being close to others; I find it difficult to trust them completely, difficult to allow myself to depend on them. I am nervous when anyone gets too close, and often love partners want me to be more intimate than I feel comfortable being.

■ **Anxious/ambivalent:** I find that others are reluctant to get as close as I would like. I often worry that my partner doesn't really love me or want to stay with me. I want to merge completely with another person, and this desire sometimes scares people away.

(Hazan and Shaver, 1987)

Hazan and Shaver obtained extensive information from more than 1200 people's romantic experiences and reactions. The reported histories of their relationships with their parents were related to their different adult attachment styles.

More particularly in the context of love, 'secure' lovers believed that their relationships were going to have their ups and downs; the extremely intense feelings which accompanied the beginning of the relationship (the falling in love part) can reappear. Second honeymoons are quite on the cards. Indeed, in some relationships romantic love does not fade at all. Their romantic relationships were happy, with great friendship and trust. There was no fear of becoming close to someone else.

'Avoidant' lovers tended to believe that the fictional kind of romantic love was only fictional and did not exist in real life. People rarely found real love. The relationships of avoidant lovers tended to include high levels of jealousy and low levels of acceptance.

The 'anxious/ambivalent' lovers agreed that real love was rare. However, they did believe that to 'fall in love' was possible – indeed easy – and they had started to fall in love quite often. Their relationships tended to go to extremes: excessive preoccupation with sexual attraction, desire for union and love at first sight.

Mate selection

Economic advantage has been considered to be of overwhelming importance in choosing a mate. It used to be said, 'You do not marry for money, but you marry where money is.' In Jane Austen's *Pride and Prejudice*, Mrs Bennett's preoccupation was that her daughters should marry 'well'. Considerations were entirely those of wealth and expectations. However, the novel makes plain that this preoccupation did not coincide well with that of the daughters themselves. Personal characteristics were seen as more important. A series of studies going back to the 1940s have consistently highlighted such traits as dependability, emotional stability, pleasing disposition and mutual attraction (Hill, 1945; McGinnis, 1959; Hudson and Henze, 1969; Silva, 1990). Buss and Barnes (1986) conducted a study in which the participants were married people aged between 18 and 40. The following ten characteristics were listed as being most important:

■ good companionship,
■ considerateness,
■ honesty,

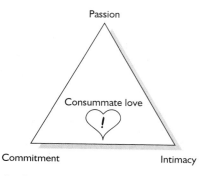

Figure 25.5 Sternberg's triangular theory of love

- affection,
- dependability,
- intelligence,
- kindness,
- being understanding,
- loyalty,
- being interesting to talk to.

On the other hand the respondents valued least highly the following characteristics:

- dominance,
- agnosticism,
- being a night owl or being an early riser.

Assortative mating

Buss (1984) has stressed the importance of similarity in mate selection. The ethological concept of **assortative mating** seems to apply as much to the choosing of a mate by humans as to animals. We tend to choose a mate who has similar characteristics or who engages in similar forms of behaviour. Lesnik-Oberstein and Cohen (1984) found that married couples tended to share similar characteristics: susceptibility to boredom, for instance, a desire to seek out new experiences or impulsivity. Buss found similarities in choice of activities, willingness to display intimacy and tolerance of quarrelsomeness. It has to be borne in mind, of course, that psychologists tend to question couples about these things after they have been together for some time so that the ones who do not share these characteristics may no longer be together to be questioned.

Development of love

A close and intimate relationship does not just happen overnight, but develops fairly slowly and through a number of stages. Kelley et al. (1983) have identified some of them. These are detailed in Box 25.5.

Rempel et al. (1985) identified increasing trust as one of the crucial ways in which behaviour and feelings change as a relationship develops. Trust involves three separate ways in which one partner in a relationship views his or her partner:

- **Predictability**. Each partner can predict more easily what the other will do.
- **Dependability**. Past evidence and experience leads each partner to develop assumptions about the disposition and characteristics of the other, which leads him or her to be able to depend upon the partner.
- **Faith**. This involves each partner in looking ahead to outcomes which are becoming more certain.

Break-up of relationships

The fairy story version of relationships involves the couple 'living happily ever after'. However it frequently does not work out like this. Hill et al.'s (1976) longitudinal study followed 231 couples in Boston over two years. By this time, 103 had broken up, 43 were married, 9 were engaged, 65 others were still courting and the remaining 11 could not be contacted. Going back to an initial questionnaire given to the couples at the beginning of the study, it emerged that those who felt closer in 1972 were more likely to be together in 1974. Also, as has been mentioned earlier, women appeared to be more influential than men in maintaining the relationship and their feelings were a more sensitive index than men's of the health of the relationship. Similarities were an important factor in determining whether a couple stayed together. Figure 25.6 shows correlation coefficients on age, education, verbal test score, numerical test score, attractiveness and views on sex roles between partners. Those who stayed together were clearly more highly correlated on these measures than those who did not.

Another factor is the man's need for power. Men who showed a high need for power in the first questionnaire were much less likely still to be in the relationship after two years: 50 per cent of these relationships had broken up by 1974 compared to 15 per cent of the relationships in which the man had a low need for power. As far as women's need for power was concerned there was no relationship between this measure and the success or failure of the relationship.

Timing of relationship break-ups As is so often the case in social psychological studies, a high proportion of the couples studied were college students. Intensive interviews conducted as part of

---

GLOSSARY

Assortative mating Suggests that a successful union between two individuals is most likely when the two partners have similarities in characteristics or in behaviour. This is a concept borrowed from ethology.

Box 25.5   Kelley et al.'s stages of love

Stage 1 Acquaintanceship

Two people get to know each other and begin to interact. In the case of many contacts we make it never gets any further than this. We meet someone casually at a party, get on all right but there it ends.

Stage 2 Discovery

Increasing degrees of interdependence emerge at this stage and both partners become more willing to disclose information about themselves. A fair amount of energy is expended on the relationship at this stage. The activities of each of them as individuals are brought together and coordinated and they each look forward to future rewarding interactions. The attractiveness of each partner is accentuated in the eyes of the other and other people are correspondingly downgraded in attractiveness. This is cognitive dissonance in action (see Chapter 27). When you have made your choice in anything, that choice assumes greater attractiveness; all other alternatives become less attractive.

Stage 3 Build-up

The course of true love does not always run smoothly. Circumstances and problems unfold at this stage, which may increase tension. The idealization which has occurred in Stage 2 comes up against the reality of your partner's less than ideal characteristics. Sacrifices may also be needed in order to respond to the needs of your partner and this produces further strains (Brehm, 1988; Holmes, 1989).

Metts (1989) has noted that patterns of deception change too at about this time. In the early stages of a relationship we tend to tell little white lies (or sometimes even bigger ones) to protect our self-concept. At the build-up stage deception may be used to protect the relationship rather than ourselves. You have a Valentine card from someone other than your partner and say nothing about it because it might cause problems for the relationship.

Jealousy also grows as commitment grows. Research has suggested that jealousy arises out of two factors: a desire for exclusivity in the relationship and feelings of inadequacy.

However, causes of jealousy are different in men and women; in men it is related to self-esteem. A man's partner is a source of self-esteem. His manhood depends to some degree upon maintaining a relationship with her and also, if he holds fairly traditional views about gender roles, she is part of his territory on to which someone else may be encroaching. Women, on the other hand, believing that the relationship holds more rewards for them than any available alternative, are jealous in protecting it. For men it is a matter of status; for women it is the nature of the relationship itself which is at stake. This determines the ways in which jealousy shows itself according to a study by Shettel-Neuber et al. (1978): men become angry and are likely to engage in activities which could endanger the relationship; women, on the other hand, are likely to become depressed and also to try to improve the relationship.

Stage 4 Commitment develops

Even in the case of arranged marriages which have started with a formal agreement, emotional involvement and love can follow. The important thing, according to research by Blais et al. (1990) is the motivation behind the commitment at this stage. Where motivations to remain committed are intrinsic and self-determined, people take a positive view of behaviour related to maintaining the relationship and, because their view of the relationship and behaviour related to it is positive, they remain happy with it. Each partner's perceptions of the relationship are likely to affect the other's. Blais and his colleagues found, however, that this was more true of women than of men, so that it seems that women have a greater role to play in the development of a relationship than men.

the second stage in the study (after two years) provided insights into when break-ups were likely to occur. Relationships were most likely to break up at the beginning of the autumn term and at the ends of the autumn and spring terms. It seemed that the partner who was less committed to the relationship tended to take advantage of natural break points in

the year to end it. By contrast when the more committed partner chose to end the relationship the break up usually came in the middle of the year.

Who decides to end it? Most break-ups seem to come from a decision by one partner or the other to end it. This was the case in 85 per cent of both the

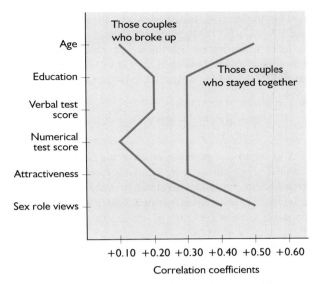

Age

Education

Verbal test
score

Numerical
test score

Attractiveness

Sex role views

Those couples
who broke up

Those couples
who stayed together

+0.10 +0.20 +0.30 +0.40 +0.50 +0.60

Correlation coefficients

Figure 25.6 Similarity and relationship break-up (Hill et al.,
1976)

women and the men. Both men and women were
more likely to say that it was they who wanted to end
it rather than their partner. Thus self-esteem is
protected. Hill et al.'s data also support the view that
it was more likely to be the woman who decides to
break it up. What is more, when it was the man who
decided to end it, the couple often remained 'good
friends'. When it was the woman who broke it off,
this was much less likely to happen.

Role complementarity and break-up

It is very important for the maintenance of a relationship, either inside or outside marriage that there should
be **complementarity of roles**. Whenever there is a
change in the roles within a relationship there needs to
be renegotiation. Suppose a man is made redundant
and begins to work from home, the wife who has had
control within the home, perhaps for a long time now,
has to share this control. Unless there is careful renegotiation tensions will build up until a break-up
becomes possible. Even without such dramatic
changes as redundancy or retirement, role changes
may gradually occur. Children growing up and leaving
home, for instance, will alter the wife's role of mother
and care-giver to them, perhaps. In any case a
redefinition of the role of women has taken place in
the second half of the twentieth century. The role strain

which has developed because of this is not unrelated to
the increase in marriage break-ups.

Equity and break-up

Equity theory has been discussed earlier (p. 601). It
suggests that people have a notion of what they deserve
from a relationship. This will be based at least in part on
comparisons with what they see their partners getting
from the relationship. When one partner feels that the
relationship is out of balance, he or she will try to
restore the balance, either actually or psychologically,
changing inputs or outcomes or else perceptions of
input and outcomes. Dissatisfaction will arise whenever the relationship appears to be out of balance; this
will apply not only to the individual who appears to be
underbenefiting, but also to the partner who sees
himself or herself as gaining too much. Sprecher (1986)
has reported feelings which include hurt and resentment on the part of men, sadness and frustration on the
part of women. When men feel they have under-
benefited they feel anger; when they overbenefit, guilt.
Women become depressed when they see themselves
as underbenefiting; angry when they are overbenefit-
ting. When the imbalance becomes too great, equity
theory would predict break-up. Berscheid and Walster
(1978) tested this prediction; the details of their
research are in Box 25.6.

Duck's model of relationship break-up

Duck (1988, 1992) has produced a detailed relationship dissolution model. There are four phases, each of
which incorporates a threshold. When this threshold is
reached certain behaviours are predicted to follow.
Figure 25.7 illustrates this model.

Psychological consequences of relationship break-
up

With divorce becoming so common that it is no longer
considered to be deviant, the consequences of
separation and divorce in psychological terms have

GLOSSARY

Complementarity of roles Relates to the idea that two
individuals are most likely to form a satisfactory relationship if
the role one partner adopts within the relationship complements that of the other partner.

Box 25.6 Equity and relationship break-up (Berscheid and Walster, 1978)

A total of 511 men and women at the University of Wisconsin were interviewed about their relationships. Initially they were asked to evaluate their relationships by assessing the contributions and benefits of each partner. Four estimates were made:

■ All the contributions each partner considered he or she made to the relationship were rated on a scale +4 to −4. These included personality, emotional support, help in decision making and so on.
■ Then each partner was asked to rate his or her partner's contributions in the same way.
■ Similarly, benefits received from the relationship were rated, such as love, excitement, security or having a good time.
■ The partner's benefits were finally rated in the same way.

The investigators were thus able to determine how equitable the relationship was perceived to be. Then three months later couples were interviewed again and asked whether they were still going out with the same partner and how long they expected the relationship to last. Those whose relationships were equitable at the first session were both more likely to be going out with the same individual but also more likely to predict that the relationship would last.

The important things seem to be whether they *perceive* themselves to be close to someone else, so as to be on intimate terms with them and whether their total network of contacts with others is satisfactory in two ways:

■ In terms of regularity;
■ In terms of control; were their contacts regulated by themselves or by others?

You could instance someone living in a residential home for the elderly being intensely lonely. There may be plenty of contacts with others on a regular basis, but no intimacy at all and a total lack of control over contacts with others.

Transactive memory disruption

Transactive memory, described by Wegner et al. (1991), refers to the way in which couples or groups have a common memory which is greater than their individual memories. Memory load is shared, with each individual being responsible for remembering only a part of what the couple or the group needs to

---

GLOSSARY

Transactive memory Relates to the situation in a close relationship where two partners in a relationship may jointly have greater memory than either has individually.

---

to be considered. Loneliness is one of these consequences, not only after the separation and divorce but during the break-up. Williams and Solano (1983) have suggested that it is the *quality* of relationships which is a factor in feelings of loneliness, not just the presence or absence of them. There was no difference in their study between the number of friends which lonely and nonlonely people had, but there was a difference in the intimacy of their relationships. Maxwell and Coeburgh (1986) have identified four predictors of feelings of loneliness:

■ How close individuals were to the closest person in their lives;
■ How many close friends they had;
■ Degree of satisfaction with their relationships;
■ Whether they had daily contacts with others.

Depression can follow the break-up of a relationship

Figure 25.7 Duck's (1988) relationship dissolution model

Phase	Threshold	Behaviour
Intrapsychic phase Brooding with little outward show Needing partner Seeking third party to voice concern	Partner's behaviour unbearable	Assessment of partner's behaviour Assess negative features Assess positive features Assess withdrawal costs
Dyadic phase Justify withdrawing What can be done? Attributing responsibility	Shall I withdraw?	Confrontation or avoidance dilemma Negotiate Repair and reconciliation Assess withdrawal costs
Social phase Negotiate with friends for social support and reassurance of rightness	Decision to withdraw	Negotiate postwithdrawal state with partner Discussion among friends Create face-saving/blame-placing stories
Grave-dressing phase Division of property Access to children Protection of reputation for reliability Socially acceptable version of the life and death of the relationship	Withdrawal inevitable	Activity to do with getting over it Retrospection: post mortems Publish own version of break-up

know. It is a shared system of memory encoding, storing and retrieval. When couples break up, either through separation or divorce or through death, transactive memory is disrupted. The consequent loss of memory for each partner is debilitating.

Social support

Depression can be the consequence of the disruption of the social support system which has been established. Brown and Harris (1978) did an extensive study of mental health and close relationships among 458 women in south London. Of those who reported having a stressful experience in the last year only 10 per cent of those who had a supportive husband suffered depression as compared to 41 per cent of those who did not have this support. The evidence of Stroebe and Stroebe (1983) is that men suffer even more than women because they find it more difficult to establish a new support network quickly.

Physical/health consequences of relationship break-up

Furthermore, there are actual health risks accompanying loneliness. There is quite a lot of anecdotal evidence for dying of a broken heart. It frequently occurs that couples die within a short period of one another. Obviously, some of these deaths are chance but research by Raphael (1985) has indicated that disruption of the support network could at least be partially responsible. Where this was replaced by regular counselling sessions the surviving widows coped much better with the loss of their husbands. Those who did not receive counselling showed a substantial impairment in health. There is some evidence that there may be immune system damage following an extended period of grieving (Jemmott and Locke, 1984).

? SELF-ASSESSMENT QUESTIONS

1. What discrete categories of love have been identified?

2. Identify and describe three theories of love. Which of them seems to you to provide the best explanation of it? Why?

3. List some of the factors which might lead to the break-up of a relationship.

4. Describe Duck's model of relationship break-up. Do you think it portrays accurately the stages a couple might go through?

Chapter summary

- Human beings have a need to affiliate to one another. This is dictated by anxieties, by the need for cognitive clarity and by the need for self-evaluation. Factors which influence the selection of someone else to affiliate with include propinquity, similarity, need complementarity, agreeableness, physical attraction and reciprocation.

- Among theories of attraction are balance theories, which involve agreement among individuals who are attracted to each other. Byrne and Clore's reinforcement/affect theory emphasizes what each party gets out of the relationship. This has similarities with social exchange theory and interdependence theories which depend upon fairly mechanistic assessments of the costs and benefits relating to a relationship. Equity theory modifies these theories and emphasizes the norms on which a broader society depends, including equity, social welfare and equalitarian norms.

- Friendships depend on the maintenance of certain rules which govern the interactions between people. These rules include agreement on behaviour, differentiation between current and former friends on the basis of how rules are applied, differentiation between rules of behaviour which apply to close friends and to acquaintances. When rules are not adhered to, this may be cited as a cause of break-up of a friendship. Friendships develop out of acquaintanceships through continued interaction.

- There clearly exist different types or levels of love. These include passionate love and companionate love. Passionate love will over time tend to moderate to become companionate love. Falling in love is certainly possible. This involves another person becoming the entire focus of someone's life. It is an intensely emotional state over which the individuals concerned have no control. There is, however, a cultural side to this. Romantic love of this kind has to be a part of the culture of individuals who fall in love.

- Three factors seem to be responsible for love: physiological arousal, cultural exposure and the presence of an appropriate love object. Hazan and Shaver link the need for attachment found in children to adult romantic attachments. The three styles of attachment in children – secure, avoidant and ambivalent attachment – apply equally to romantic love in adults.

- Love has three components according to Sternberg: passion, intimacy and commitment. Different types of love depend upon the relative strengths of each of these components. Economic advantage as well as similarities in behaviour, characteristics and choice of activity are likely to lead to successful mating.

- Kelley outlines the stages in the development of love from acquaintance and discovery to build-up and eventually commitment between the partners. As relationships develop so behaviour changes. Increasing trust manifests itself in three ways: in predicability, in dependability and in faith in a person's partner.

- Relationships may break up as a result of decisions by either partner. Commonly break-up occurs where need complementarity is not maintained or it is perceived that there is no longer equity between the partners. The psychological consequences of the break-up of a relationship include loneliness, disruption of transactive memory, depression and health consequences. A broken heart is not impossible.

Further reading

Deaux, K., Dane, F.C. and Wrightsman, L.S. (1993). *Social Psychology in the 90's*, 6th edn, Pacific Grove, CA.: Brookes-Cole. Chapter 9 contains a full account of research into affiliation, social networks, attraction, love and the development and ending of relationships.

Duck, S. (1995). Repelling the study of attraction. *The Psychologist*, 8, 60–3. This article in a special edition of *The Psychologist* devoted to relationships suggests that the study of personal relationships has advanced well beyond merely looking at what makes one person attractive to another.

Hogg, M.A. and Vaughan, G.M. (1995). *Social Psychology: An Introduction*. Hemel Hempstead: Prentice-Hall/Harvester Wheatsheaf. Provides an excellent account of affiliation, attraction and love in Chapter 12 of this book.

Kitzinger, C. and Coyle, A. (1995). Lesbian and gay couples: speaking of difference. *The Psychologist*, 8, pp. 64–9. This article in the same edition of *The Psychologist* discusses the differences and similarities between lesbian and gay relationships and those of heterosexual couples.

CHAPTER 26

Conflict and cooperation

Intergroup relations 614
- Social identity 615
- Ethnocentrism 616
- Ultimate attribution bias 618
- Social representations 618
- Relative deprivation 619
- Realistic conflict theory 620

Aggression 623
- Explanations of aggressive behaviour 623
- Factors influencing aggression 626
- Violence on TV 631

- Pornography and aggression 634
- Control of aggression 634

Prosocial behaviour 636
- Helping others and altruism 636
- Theories relating to helping behaviour 637
- Culture and altruism 638
- Empathy 639
- Deciding whether to help 640
- Influences on prosocial behaviour 642
- Towards a more prosocial society 645

Objectives

By the end of this chapter you should be able to:

- Identify what is meant by group identity and highlight the distinction between out-groups and in-groups;

- Describe what is meant by social identity and appreciate the effect social identity has on the way in which we interact with other people;

- Describe and evaluate some of the theories relating to aggressive behaviour, including psychoanalytic theories and learning theories;

- Identify factors which may cause people to be aggressive, including environmental and situational factors;

- Evaluate the evidence linking violence on television and aggressive behaviour;

- Describe and evaluate some theories and models which account for altruism and prosocial behaviour, including empathy–altruism models and arousal–cost reward models;

- Describe Latané and Darley's research into bystander behaviour and identify some of the factors which may inhibit people from helping.

Intergroup relations

Margaret Thatcher had a habit of enquiring, concerning any individual whose name cropped up, 'Is he/she one of us?' Any group to which an individual belongs can be referred to as an **in-group**; a group to which an individual does not belong is an **out-group**. In-groups and out-groups are defined entirely in terms of the individual's membership. Margaret Thatcher's 'one of us' referred to the in-group to which she belonged, a group of people who shared her political analysis and attitudes. All the rest constituted an out-group. This again can be explained by social cognition. Experiences have been transformed into mental representations which in turn play a part in determining behaviour. Margaret Thatcher's experience of the miners' union coming close to unseating a Conservative government in 1984/5 were transformed into representations of the miners as subversive and hostile which in turn coloured her behaviour in relation to them.

Social identity

Categorization leads to assumptions of similarity among those who are categorized together. The differences which exist between members of a group are minimized; the differences between groups are accentuated (Brewer and Kramer, 1985; Wilder, 1986). Members of a group, viewed from outside, are relatively homogeneous. But, from within the group, the same homogeneity does not exist. It depends also upon how well acquainted we are with group members. Those we know very well we will tend to discriminate between and categorize on finer criteria than when we are considering members of a group we know less well. When all are members of the same group, some additional criteria, other than group membership, are needed to discriminate between people. This does not apply when we are judging members of another group. Group membership itself is an important discriminator. The out-group will be stereotyped and this stereotypical information extends our relatively meagre knowledge of the members of the group. We have assumed a **social identity** and this is the standpoint from which we view other people.

Activation of group identity

The presence of members of an out-group serves to trigger in-group social identity. Perdue et al. (1990) demonstrated that activation of group social identity is a spontaneous cognitive process. Their study is detailed in Box 26.1.

This is another manifestation of social identity theory, outlined by Tajfel (1978, 1982) and Tajfel and Turner (1986). The groups to which we belong are a part of our self-concept. You, as an individual, are motivated to maintain or enhance self-esteem and

Box 26.1 Activation of group identity. An experiment by Perdue et al. (1990)

The experimenters flashed adjectives onto a computer screen and asked participants to say whether they could be used to describe a person (any person). There were three categories of adjectives:

- positive adjectives which could be applied to people (e.g. good, kind, trustworthy);
- negative adjectives which could be applied to people (e.g. bad, cruel, untrustworthy);
- control adjectives such as draughty or brick, which were not usually applied to people.

Before each adjective was presented, a 'prime' appeared on the screen. This is something presented so rapidly that the participant does not have time to process its meaning consciously. Even though no conscious cognitive processing occurs, the prime has the effect of spontaneously increasing the cognitive accessibility of related concepts for a brief period. This effect has been verified by Fowler et al. (1981). Three such 'primes' were used in this case: we, they and XXX. Perdue and his colleagues found that participants took significantly less time to decide that positive traits were applicable, and more time to decide that negative traits applied when primed with 'we' than when primed with 'they' or 'XXX'. Even such very general references to social identity as 'we' were enough to trigger positive associations in memory so that it was easier to decide that positive adjectives applied. To be reminded of your group, social identity gives you a positivity bias which enables you to discriminate in favour of your own group.

the discrimination mentioned above in favour of your own group helps this maintenance or enhancement. As van Knippenberg and Ellemers (1990) have put it, if the

GLOSSARY

In-groups/out-groups The group to which an individual belongs is an in-group: out-groups are all the rest.

Social identity The groups to which we belong represent part of our self-concept. This is social identity and it contributes to self-esteem.

status of group X is higher than that of group Y, then as a member of X an individual will share in that status.

Ethnocentrism

Sumner (1906) described how out-groups are evaluated from the standpoint of an in-group. Your own group is the centre of everything and all others are rated by reference to it:

> Each group nourishes its own pride and vanity, boasts itself superior, exalts its own divinities and looks with contempt upon outsiders. Each group thinks its own folkways are the only right ones, and if it observes that other groups have their own folkways these excite its scorn.
>
> (Sumner, 1906, p.13)

This was termed **ethnocentrism**. Sherif (1962, 1966) believed that the origins of ethnocentrism lie in the nature of intergroup relations. Where groups compete for scarce resources there is conflict and ethnocentrism arises. Three field experiments were conducted using as participants young boys in summer camps.

Summer camps are a very usual phenomenon in the USA and Sherif and his colleagues used this institution to conduct experiments. There were three separate experiments in group conflict, each lasting about three weeks. The third, in 1954, became known as the Robbers' Cave after the location in Oklahoma where it took place. This is detailed in Box 26.2.

Ethical issues raised by Sherif's experiments

Sherif's experiments raise a number of ethical issues. In particular:

■ There are ethical issues which arise from the very fact that questionable attitudes were deliberately induced in the children.

GLOSSARY

Ethnocentrism The process by which our own group is placed at the centre of our consciousness and other groups are sidelined. Defined by Sumner as the 'view of things in which one's own group is the centre of everything, and all others are scaled and rated with reference to it'

A huge crowd assembles in the Lustgarten, Berlin in 1939 to hear Hitler's May Day speech: a graphic demonstration of the power of ethnocentricism

Box 26.2 Sherif et al.'s Robbers' Cave experiment (1962, 1966)

Twenty-two boys took part, carefully selected so that no initial prejudices were likely. Three bases were chosen for selection:

- They had no prior acquaintance with one another. They came from different schools and neighbourhoods.
- The boys were healthy and well-adjusted with no neurotic tendencies, members of stable families with both parents living at home. They had no record of past disturbances in behaviour. Minority group members were not included.
- They came from stable white Protestant families of the middle socioeconomic level. They showed the normal range of individual differences but were matched as far as possible for size and skills when the groups were formed.

Stage one – spontaneous personal choices

All the boys were housed at first in one large bunk house. Activities were camp wide and full opportunities were given for friendships to be formed. They were asked who their best friends were. Then they were divided into two cabins; about two-thirds of best friends were separated and allocated places in different cabins. This stage was omitted in the 1954 Robbers' Cave experiment on the grounds that the previous two experiments had provided sufficient information about friendships formed on the basis of pure personal preference.

Stage two – group formation

At this stage activities were on a cabin basis. Within each cabin they were independent, camping out, cooking, improving swimming places, transporting canoes over rough terrain to water and playing various games. Different individuals assumed different responsibilities and displayed different skills. In the 1954 experiment the groups were named Rattlers and Eagles. They became cohesive groups with low ranking and high ranking members. Each group developed its own jargon, special jokes and special ways of performing tasks. This stage lasted one week.

Stage three – intergroup conflict

In the 1954 study the groups were not even aware of each other's existence until just before this stage began. A tournament of games was arranged apparently at the boys' own request, soon after they became aware of each other's existence. There was friendly rivalry to begin with, then animosity. Members of each group began to call members of the other 'sneaks', 'cheats' and 'stinkers'. The Eagles burnt a banner left behind by the Rattlers. Next morning the Rattlers seized the Eagles' flag and there were scuffles. Each group had negative feelings towards all members of the other group. Within each group solidarity, cooperativeness and morale increased, but this did not extend to members of the other group.

Stage four – intergroup cooperation

In an earlier experiment (Sherif, 1951), the introduction of a common enemy was found to be means of reducing conflict. Common goals seemed to afford a means to promote cooperation. The first opportunity for this arose when there was an (arranged) breakdown in the water supply. First, each group explored the pipeline separately to find the cause of the problem and then they came together and jointly located the source of the difficulty. Second, an opportunity came to see a film which both groups had high on their list of preferences. They were told that the camp could not afford it, but the groups got together, worked out how they could jointly get the money together and finally enjoyed the film together. The third opportunity arose when the groups were due to go on an outing to a lake some distance away. The lorry which was to have transported the food refused to start (this too was arranged). The boys got a rope and all pulled together to get it to start.

Finally, when the time came to go home, the boys were given the choice of travelling on separate buses or on the same bus and they opted for the latter. A stop was made for refreshments on the way home and one group had five dollars it had won as a prize. They chose to spend it on the whole group, inviting their former rivals to be their guests for a malted milk.

- There was certainly a problem of informed consent. Where children are concerned, parents should have been fully informed of the true purposes of the study before the experiment took place. It seems unlikely that a cross-section of middle-class parents would have given their consent to prejudice deliberately being induced in their children.

- The children had no inkling as to what the whole thing was about. They were manipulated.
- There is no evidence that any of these children could have withdrawn from the experiment at any time during it.
- There is no doubt at all that pain and stress were caused at various stages in the experiment.

The experiment was justified by the experimenters in that a great deal of insight was gained into the way in which intergroup tensions arise and that it all ended happily. There did not appear to have been any permanent damage done. However, there clearly were risks which it is hard to justify.

Ultimate attribution bias

Pettigrew (1979) refers to **ultimate attribution bias**. In-group members attribute their own desirable behaviour to internal stable factors, while the out-group's desirable behaviour is attributed to factors within the immediate situation. Where undesirable behaviour is at issue, the opposite occurs; a group's own undesirable behaviour is attributed to the situation while the other group's undesirable behaviour is the result of disposition.

Social representations

A group will also construct and transmit to its members explanations of what are complex and unfamiliar ideas in much more familiar and straightforward terms. What starts out as being a specialist and technical explanation of some phenomenon is given public attention and by a process of simplification, distortion and ritualization becomes a 'common sense explanation' which is then accepted as orthodoxy. The process is illustrated in Figure 26.1.

The original theory of **social representations** was formulated by Moscovici (Farr and Moscovici, 1984; Moscovici, 1988). Let us take an example of the way in which social representations operate. Moscovici has explored the way in which the technical and scientific ideas about psychoanalysis have become simplified and familiar from being complex and unfamiliar. People are commonly referred to as having a 'complex', suffering from 'repression' or being 'neurotic', in very much the same way as you might describe someone's medical condition, 'He's got flu' or 'She's broken her leg'. The original set of ideas put forward as theory by

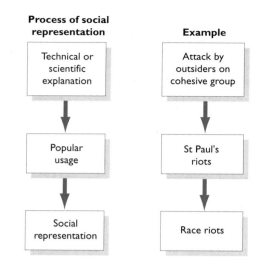

Figure 26.1 Moscovici's theory of social representations

Freud and others have become simplified, distorted and familiar. Similarly social representations may distort and simplify perceived events or phenomena. There arises a kind of 'group think' about something which happens. This is discussed in Chapter 28. For instance, Reicher (1984) conducted an analysis of the causes of the riots which took place in the St Paul's district of Bristol in the spring of 1980. St Paul's is the main residential area of the black community in Bristol, a relatively deprived inner city area, but one with a certain cohesion as a community. The conclusion that Reicher came to relating to the rioting which took place was that the community saw themselves as a cohesive in-group, threatened by outside forces (the police raid on a social centre for the community, the Black and White Café). The police and their cars were the only real target. The common view taken of the riots was that they were 'race riots' or else that they were the response of a deprived group to 'government cuts'. Litton and Potter (1985) have contrasted the popular conception of the cause of the rioting – the social representation of it – with Reicher's analysis.

In a similar way you could contrast the 'social representation' of electricity as a source of heat or light emanating from a socket with the technical/scientific description of electricity in terms of electrons moving within conductive material.

Relative deprivation

Berkowitz (1962, 1972) argued that subjective rather than objective frustration was the source of hostility and aggression. Deprivation is never absolute, but relative. Deprivation and frustration only become apparent when there is some standard against which to measure it. Primitive peoples living in what would be to us extreme deprivation do not feel deprived until they have an external standard to measure their situation against. **Relative deprivation** occurs when a person's own experiences are compared with his or her expectations. Davies (1969) produced a J-curve hypothesis of relative deprivation. People's past and current attainments determine their future expectations. Where attainments suddenly fall short of expectations there is acute relative deprivation. Figure 26.2 illustrates this J curve.

What seems to happen is that when there is a long period of rising prosperity expectations rise. Then, when there is a sharp drop in fortunes, people's expectations continue to rise while their fortunes do not. This leads to circumstances where collective violence is more likely to occur. Davies cites various examples:

- The French revolution,
- The Russian revolution,
- The American Civil War,
- The rise of Nazism in Germany,
- The growth of black power in the USA in the 1960s.

However, the theory does not seem entirely to fit the facts. It is hard to claim that French or Russian peasants had rising expectations. They were simply downtrodden to the point where they had little more to lose. It is perhaps more appropriate in the case of the American Civil War, where cotton plantation owners in the South felt their way of life threatened by an antislavery movement based mainly in the North, and saw secession from the Union as a way of maintaining their prosperity. The rise of Nazism in Germany followed a period of extreme unemployment and hyperinflation resulting from reparations exacted by the Allies after World War I. It is hard to say that there were rising expectations unless you go back to the prewar period. Finally the Black Power movement was the *result* of discrimination and prejudice. There was hardly much sign of rising expectations among the blacks who were discriminated against. Moreover, systematic tests of Davies's predictions such as that of Taylor (1982) did not show that expectations were constructed from immediate past experience or that dissatisfaction was based upon a mismatch between people's actual situation and what they had confidently anticipated.

Berkowitz's (1972) view is that aggressive behaviour results from an array of aversive events of which frustration is one and which might include such things as a long, hot summer. There might be perceived relative deprivation, poor housing and overcrowding, hot weather with little relief from air conditioning or green vegetation in the hot city streets, aggressive stimuli such as violence from armed police which leads to individual acts of violence and thence to collective rioting. Runciman (1966) distinguished two forms of relative deprivation:

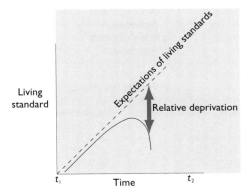

Figure 26.2 Davies's J curve of relative deprivation

■ **Egoistic relative deprivation**. This occurs where an individual feels deprived relative to other similar individuals.

■ **Fraternalistic relative deprivation**. This occurs where individuals make comparisons with members of other groups or individuals dissimilar to themselves.

Figure 26.3 illustrates the idea of relative deprivation put forward by Runciman (1966).

Walker and Mann (1987) made a study of unemployed workers. Where there was fraternalistic relative deprivation there was likely to be militant protest, demonstrations and damage to property. You could cite the poll tax riots in Britain in the late 1980s, where individuals collectively felt that they were carrying an unfair share of the burden of the cost of local government in comparison with people who were clearly much better off than they were. Where individuals felt themselves to be egoistically relatively deprived, symptoms of stress were reported, such as headaches and sleeplessness rather than militancy. In French Canada, for instance, there was extreme dissatisfaction on an individual level about discrepancies between salaries of French-speaking as compared to English-speaking Canadians. There was fraternalistic deprivation which resulted in militancy (Guimond and Dubé-Sinard, 1983). Inter-

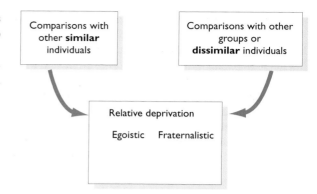

Figure 26.3 Runciman's analysis of fraternal or egoistic relative deprivation

group comparisons which lead to conflict and militancy seem to be most common between dissimilar groups.

Realistic conflict theory

Out of these experiments arose realistic conflict theory (Sherif, 1966) (see Figure 26.4). Sherif argued like this:

■ Where individuals share goals which require them to be interdependent in order to achieve

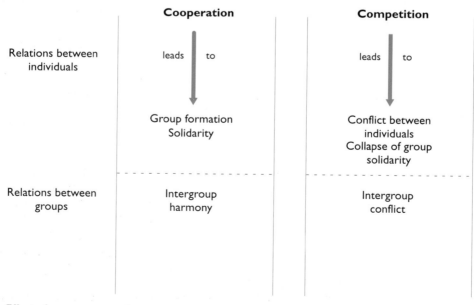

Figure 26.4 Effect of group cooperation or competition on group behaviour (after Sherif, 1966)

them, then they will tend to cooperate and form a group.

- Where individuals' goals are mutually exclusive (as, for instance, in a competitive game) the inter-individual competition prevents a group from forming and may result in an existing group collapsing.
- Where groups have mutually exclusive goals (where, for instance, one football team competes with another) realistic intergroup conflict is likely to be the result with ethnocentrism, prejudice and discrimination the likely outcome.
- Where the achievement of shared goals demands intergroup interdependence, conflict will be reduced and there will be increased harmony.

Naturalistic experiments reported by Fisher (1990) have supported realistic conflict theory as have experiments conducted earlier by Blake and Mouton (1961). A series of 30 studies were conducted across the USA involving more than 1000 business people on management training programmes. There is also support cross-culturally for Sherif's conclusions from Diab (1970) in the Lebanon and from Andreeva (1984) in the former Soviet Union. However, Tyerman and Spencer (1983) in Britain attempted a replication in Britain involving Boy Scout patrols as participants. Competition between patrols did not produce as much hostility as Sherif's model would have predicted and it proved easy to foster intergroup cooperation, even where there was no superordinate goal. Tyerman and Spencer's explanation for this lies in the ethos of the Scout movement which provides its own super-ordinate goals.

The focus in realistic conflict theory lies in the relationship between the cooperative or competitive nature of human behaviour and people's goals. This has been explored in a very abstract way using games devised for two or more people to play. The problem, with this, though, has been with its ecological validity – that is to say, the extent to which it reflects what happens in 'real life': we shall describe the most frequently used of these games, the Prisoner's Dilemma (PD).

The Prisoner's Dilemma (PD)

This is based upon an anecdotal 'real life' situation where two prisoners found themselves being questioned by detectives. They are clearly guilty, but the detectives only have enough evidence to convict them

on a lesser offence. The confession of one of them would tip the balance. So they are questioned separately and persuaded to confess by offers of more lenient sentences. If one confesses, then he or she will get immunity; the other will be convicted of a more serious offence. If neither confesses they will both get light sentences. The dilemma facing them can be illustrated in terms of a matrix (Figure 26.5).

When the game is played out in a laboratory situation, participants have two choices:

- To confess (C),
- To inform on the other (i.e. to defect) (D).

Experimenters in the hundreds of experiments which have been carried out using PD have focused on:

- Strategies employed,
- The rewards on offer,
- Opportunities to communicate,
- Encouragement of cooperation.

Experimenters have tried to identify those factors which might make players more cooperative and less competitive.

Strategies employed It frequently happens in the laboratory that one of the players is a stooge, a confederate of the experimenters, who plays a predetermined game. This might be:

- 100 per cent competition (D). This has the effect of forcing the participant to compete in self-defence.
- 100 per cent cooperation (C). This produces more cooperation from the participant.
- Tit for tat (i.e. whatever the participant does, the stooge does the same). This rewards the participant for cooperation and punishes defection. Cooperation rates consequently rise.

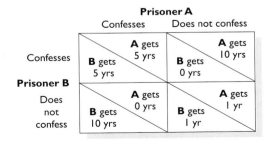

Figure 26.5 A typical matrix for the Prisoner's Dilemma game

Rewards on offer Where the game is played in a laboratory the actual pay-offs are often merely in the form of points. These sometimes have no significance other than in the game, or else the points represent minimal amounts of money (e.g. 1 point = 1 penny). With only these negligible rewards you may be effectively taking away any incentive to cooperate. McClintock and McNeel (1966) found that there was more cooperation where there were greater real rewards (i.e. actual money).

Opportunities to communicate The lack of opportunity to communicate may reduce cooperation between players. This may be for no other reason than to maintain the simulation of prisoners being separately interrogated. It is reasonable to assume that greater opportunity to communicate will lead to greater cooperation. Scodel et al. (1959) gave participants a discussion period midway through the game and found greater cooperation. Voissem and Sistrunk (1971) allowed some participants to pass notes in a standard form, expressing their intentions and/or expectations before each trial of a 100-trial PD game and found that cooperation progressively increased as compared to other participants who were not allowed to communicate at all. Where partial communication was allowed there were intermediate levels of communication.

Encouragement of cooperation Deutsch (1958) established cooperative, individualistic and competitive conditions for participants.

- **Cooperative condition**. Participants were encouraged to feel concerned about how well the other player was doing.
- **Individualistic condition**. Participants were told that they should be concerned only about their own outcomes.
- **Competitive condition**. Participants were told to make as much money for themselves as they could and do better than any other player.

Under each condition participants were made to feel that the other player had the same goals.

In each condition participants were sometimes allowed to exchange notes beforehand and sometimes not. There was an increase in cooperation in each condition when communication was allowed.

- The individualistic condition showed the greatest increase, from 35.9 per cent to 70.6 per cent.
- The cooperative condition showed an increase from 89.1 to 96.9 per cent.
- When participants were allowed to exchange notes beforehand, the percentage of cooperative responses increased from 35.9 per cent with no communication to 70.6 per cent in the individualistic condition.
- In the cooperative condition the increase was from 89.1 per cent with no communication to 96.9 per cent when communication was allowed.

In the competitive condition the increase was from 12.5 per cent to 29.2 per cent.

Exercise 26.1

Play the Prisoner's Dilemma game with a friend. Use the matrix illustrated and conduct 100 trials. Each person independently and without any collusion chooses either C or D on each trial. First use 'points' as a reward, then try 1p a point. Then test to see the effect of various strategies (e.g. tit for tat, 100 per cent cooperation or 100 per cent competition). You do not, of course, tell your friend what strategies you are adopting.

The commons dilemma

Hardin (1968) has described the 'tragedy of the commons'. The **commons dilemma** is that when villagers used the common pasture of the village to graze their animals, provided that there was moderation the common supported the animals grazed on it and replenished itself. But supposing an individual villager decided to double the number of the animals grazed to increase profits, this might not *by itself* affect the outcome. But when others, lured by the first villager's rewards, decided to do the same, the common can no longer replenish itself and is destroyed.

This represents a paradigm for many of the problems of environmental conservation. Canadians, worried

---

> **GLOSSARY**
>
> **Commons dilemma** The appropriation of resources by an individual or a group, which might be to the detriment of others if other individuals or groups did likewise.

about the depletion of fish stocks, implement a voluntary restriction on catches, and even lay up some of their vessels. But when Spanish trawlers invade their waters, catching even immature fish, there is conflict and the stocks are depleted. However, there do seem to be circumstances where the common good is supported through voluntary cooperation. Brewer suggests that this is likely to happen when individuals identify closely with the common good: that is, where they derive their social identity from it. For instance, where villagers identify closely with the village, self-interest becomes subordinate to the common good (Brewer and Kramer, 1986; Brewer and Schneider, 1990; Kramer and Brewer, 1984, 1986).

? SELF-ASSESSMENT QUESTIONS

1. What are meant by the concepts of in-group and out-group? Illustrate these concepts by using examples.
2. What is meant by social identity? What effect can this have upon the cognitions of individuals?
3. Moscovici has developed a theory of social representation. Describe how this may result in a sort of 'group think' which may colour the perception which individual members of a group may have of events.
4. Explain how games such as Prisoner's Dilemma may assist explanation of competitive or cooperative behaviour. What is the limitation of such games?

Aggression

It is as well at the outset to make clear what is meant by aggressive behaviour. For the purposes of this book it is defined as behaviour which is intended to cause harm to another living organism. Intention is important. Where a person is knocked down by a car because he or she steps off the pavement, there is no aggression; but if the car mounts the pavement in order to knock the person down then that *is* aggressive. The idea of a living organism is also crucial. If you fly into a temper and kick the cat, that is aggression; but if in your temper you slam the door so hard that the glass in it shatters that is not aggressive behaviour. You have not intended to harm another living organism.

Explanations of aggressive behaviour

Explanations of aggression fall roughly into three:

▓ Biological explanations,
▓ Biosocial explanations,
▓ Social learning explanations.

Biological explanations

Again there are three categories of explanation:

▓ Those which are based upon the psychoanalytic theory of Freud and his successors.
▓ Those which are based upon ethology (the study of animals in their natural environment).
▓ Those which have their basis in sociobiology (the study of the biological basis for social behaviour).

Psychoanalytic theories of aggression Freud (1930) proposed that there were two opposed instinctive forces at work in humans, eros and thanatos, the former a life instinct, the latter a death instinct, self-preservation as opposed to self-destruction. In humans aggression was related to the second of these forces, self-destruction, and this instinct is directed outwards towards others, to cause harm to them. The important point is that aggression is for humans a natural and instinctive urge which has to find expression, either prosocially through activity, or antisocially through causing harm to others. A young man may give vent to his aggression by a hard game of rugby football. A vigorous debate may allow aggression to be expressed verbally, but within what is socially accepted. Alternatively, there may be verbal insults or fighting aimed at harming someone else. This urge is considered to be innate, inevitable and needing to be tamed.

Ethologically based theories of aggression Ethologists study the normal behaviour of animals. It is suggested that there is a build up of energy which finds expression in **fixed action patterns** (Crook, 1973). The release of this energy is dependent on the

---

GLOSSARY

Fixed action patterns Patterns of behaviour in animals which are triggered by a releaser (e.g. aggression triggered by invasion of territory).

presence of a trigger, which Hess (1962) has called a releaser. The threatening behaviour of another animal (bared teeth, for instance) may act as the trigger, or the invasion of territory. The protection and preservation of territory allows each animal to have the resources it needs to survive. There is also a purpose served in sexual selection. Within a species, aggression allows the stronger members of a species to mate and so to produce stronger offspring. The losers in such contests signal appeasement so that injury or death rarely occurs in these conflicts. The problem with humans is that such appeasement gestures have not been developed (there was no need in a harmless omnivorous creature) so that they deploy the killing power of weapons to cause death and destruction.

Sociobiology   Wilson (1975) defined sociobiology as the study of the biological base of social behaviour. He has extended the Darwinian theories of evolution. Aggression (or indeed any behaviour which survives) must be **adaptive**. This means it must make it more likely that an individual member of a species exhibiting that behaviour will reproduce and so pass on its genes. Neo-Darwinists, as they have been called, are not so much concerned with the species as with the genes which determine an individual's

A cat will defend its territory against invasion

patterns of behaviour. Such genetically based behaviour will continue if it serves to 'increase the genetic fitness (i.e. reproductive success) of the individual or of close relatives who carry the genes for that behaviour' (Cunningham, 1981, p. 71). Aggression may enable an individual to acquire or to preserve more resources or to defend and protect relatives, all of which make it more likely that the individual (or its close relatives) will be able to pass on its genes and so perpetuate the behaviour they determine. We are not talking about the preservation of the species but the success of individuals or groups within that species. It has to be remembered that aggression also carries a potential cost, severe injury or death, which may prevent its aims being realized so that gains have to be balanced against costs. The development of aggression is bound to be selective (Krebs and Miller, 1985).

The assumptions of all the biologically based explanations of aggression centre upon it being instinctive and innate. It is a basic part of the condition of all animals, including humans.

Biosocial explanations

These explanations include the **frustration/aggression hypothesis** and also Zillman's **excitation/transfer theory**.

Frustration/aggression hypothesis   Dollard et al. (1939) proposed that aggression was always caused by some frustrating event or situation. On the other hand frustration does not inevitably lead to aggression. This theory was welcomed as not involving the kind of psychoanalytic 'mumbo-jumbo' prevalent at the time. Frustration was defined as anything which interfered with the realization of a goal. When someone expects to be able to buy an electric light bulb from a shop, but finds it closed, that is frustrating even when there is a supermarket half a mile away. Frustration may come from the difficulty of the task itself or from interference from someone else.

While there is evidence that aggressive behaviour may sometimes have its roots in frustration (Azrin et al., 1966; Rule and Percival, 1971) the link is by no means as strong as Dollard had suggested. Buss (1961, 1967) suggested that the link only existed when the aggression had instrumental value (that is, when aggression might help to get over the frustration). The amount of the frustration is important too. Mild frustration does not seem to result in aggressive behaviour. Harris (1974) carried out some field studies, cutting in on people who were queuing for the theatre or in a store. When she cut in on someone who was second in line, she was often met with verbal abuse, while someone who was 12th in line responded much less aggressively. Interference when you are close to your goal is more frustrating than when you are further away.

Berkowitz (1965) has suggested that frustration creates a readiness for aggressive action. Frustration creates anger which may or may not be translated into aggression. There is an interaction between the cognitive and emotional states engendered and the environmental cues. In the example above, you feel cross that someone has cut in on you and you react to the whole situation.

Excitation/transfer theory Zillman has developed an excitation/transfer model of aggression (Zillman, 1979, 1988). This attempts to link the affective and the environmental elements. Zillman's model suggests that there are three factors which determine whether aggression is expressed in action:

- Learned aggressive behaviour;
- Arousal or excitation from another source;
- The individual's interpretation of the aroused state.

Excitation might occur from a wide variety of sources. You might just have played a stimulating game of squash where you won in a close fought contest. You might just have had a row with someone at work and there is residual excitation or arousal. Someone cuts in on you at a traffic intersection. You are much more likely to react with 'road rage' than you would be if you were not aroused. Figure 26.6 illustrates the excitation/transfer theory.

Social learning explanations

Learning to be aggressive Bandura (1973, 1977) has suggested that aggressive behaviour is largely learned. Both prosocial and antisocial behaviour may be learned, though there is certainly some biological component. The experiences through which it is learned can be either first-hand or vicarious. Socialization into aggressive behaviour may be through a straightforward conditioning process or else through observational learning. These ideas are also discussed in the introduction to this part of the book.

Direct experience Behaviour is established and maintained through rewards and punishments. Suppose a child wants a toy which his sister is playing with. He attacks her and seizes the toy. When no one intervenes to stop him he has been rewarded for his aggression. He has the toy. Conversely, when an adult intervenes with harsh words every time he tries to gain his way through aggressive behaviour, socialization will reduce natural aggressive tendencies (Figure 26.7).

The range of possible reinforcements for aggressive behaviour is very large. It might be social status or social approval (Geen and Stonner, 1971; Gentry, 1970). Money is a reinforcer for adults; sweets for children (Buss, 1971; Gaebelein, 1973; Walters and Brown, 1963). In cases of extreme provocation it may be reinforcing to watch a victim suffer (Baron, 1974; Feshbach et al., 1967). It has been suggested as a reason why serial killers commit their crimes.

Aggressive behaviour may have its roots in frustration

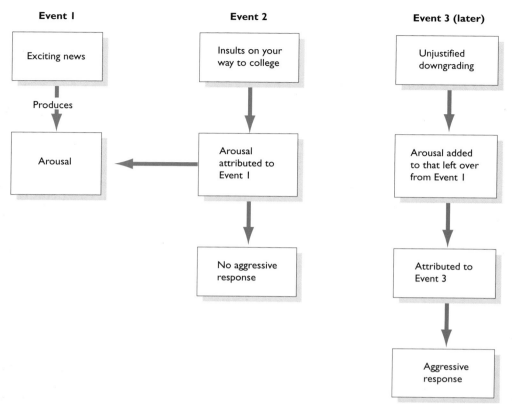

Figure 26.6   An illustration of Zillman's (1979) excitation/transfer model of aggression

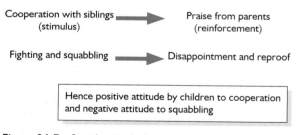

Figure 26.7   Socialization helps reduce aggressive tendencies

Observational learning and modelling   Bandura and his colleagues conducted a series of experiments into the ways in which aggressive behaviour is learned through observation and modelling. These are described in Box 26.3. Observational learning is discussed more fully in Chapter 6.

Factors influencing aggression

Among those factors which have been found to influence aggressive behaviour are:

■ Personal factors including individual differences;
■ Environmental factors such as hot weather or poor air quality;
■ Situational variables such as the presence of weapons or of provocation of some kind.

It is not easy to separate such factors and there is bound to be interaction between them. However, it is worthwhile to discuss each factor on its own so long as it is borne in mind they are never going to be discrete.

Individual differences

The idea of an 'aggressive personality' is quite an attractive one. If it were possible to measure the aggressiveness of people's personalities you might be able to determine how likely it was that a violent offender might reoffend. Age, gender, culture and personal experiences combine to make some people more likely to behave violently than others.

Box 26.3 Experiments on observational learning (Bandura, 1973, 1977)

A child of nursery school age was brought into a room by an adult and introduced to making pictures using potato prints and colourful stickers. After a short time another adult came into the room and was shown a corner where there was a mallet, a large inflatable 'Bobo' doll, as well as some other toys. The experimenter set up two conditions:

■ A nonaggressive condition where the second adult plays quietly for ten minutes.
■ An aggressive condition where the second adult attacks the Bobo doll, hitting it, kicking it, pounding its nose and yelling aggressive comments.

Then the child was taken into another room where there was the child's favourite toy as well as a Bobo doll and some other toys, aggressive and nonaggressive. The child was forbidden to play with the favourite toy, but could play with anything else in the room.

Bandura and his colleagues were interested to see how the adult's behaviour in the first stage of the experiment affected the child's choice of playthings. Children who had watched the aggressive model were found to choose more aggressive playthings and to play with them more aggressively than those who had watched the adult playing nonaggressively or indeed than a control group who had had no initial session. It has to be remembered that the Bobo doll is inanimate, so that strictly it falls outside our definition of aggression, but there does seem to be a link between aggressive behaviour in a play situation and in other contexts. Among adults most people know how to be aggressive but there is evidence that the presence of an aggressive model serves to remove some of the inhibitions which prevent people from behaving aggressively.

Type A personality There is evidence that there exists a pattern of behaviour which has been described as a **Type A personality** (Matthews, 1982). Those who exhibit this pattern of behaviour have been found amongst other things to be more prone to coronary heart disease. They are hyperactive and very competitive in their interactions with other people. They are also more aggressive towards those who are perceived as competing with them on an important task (Carver and Glass, 1978). Dembroski and MacDougall (1978) found that such individuals were happier to work alone than with others so that they could be in control of the situation and not have to endure the incompetence of others. Within an organization Baron (1989) found that Type A personalities were more frequently in conflict with their subordinates and with their peers, though not with their superiors. In this they appear to have something in common with the authoritarian personality described by Adorno et al., 1950 (see p. 670). Strube et al. (1984) found that Type A personalities were more likely to engage in child abuse than other personality types. There are suggestions that the aggressive tendencies of Type A personalities are inherited (Rushton et al., 1986). Twin studies have been used to support these conclusions. Identical (monozygotic) twins have the same genetic make-up, while fraternal (dizygotic) twins are no more alike genetically than other brothers or sisters. If pairs of identical twins are more alike in their tendencies towards aggression than pairs of fraternal twins, you might suppose that there was an inherited factor. This has been found to be the case.

Gender and socialization Maccoby and Jacklin (1974), in their extensive review of the literature on gender differences, suggested that females are less aggressive than males. Later research by Eagly and Steffen (1986) casts some doubt on this. While men do seem to be more aggressive, the differences are small and not always consistent. While the issue is solely physical aggression it is undoubtedly true that men are more aggressive, but when psychological or verbal aggression are added into the equation, gender differences are not clear-cut at all. However, there are substantial differences in the way in which men and women view aggressive behaviour. Women are much more guilty and anxious about behaving aggressively,

GLOSSARY

Type A personality A pattern of behaviour which includes a high degree of competitiveness which, it is suggested, might lead to aggression.

more concerned about the harm they may be causing to their victims and worried about possible danger to themselves.

Dodge and Crick (1990) reviewed the literature on aggression in children and came to the conclusion that individual differences in aggression may reflect differences in the ability to process information about social situations. There were three specific areas of difference:

■ Differences in ability to interpret social cues and the meaning of other people's behaviour;

■ Difference in ability to generate alternative possible responses in social situations;

■ Differences in ability to decide which response to adopt.

Aggressive children and adolescents appear to Dodge and Crick to have what they refer to as a hostile attributional bias. That is to say, they are more likely than nonaggressive children to attribute hostile intent to others' actions.

Environmental factors

Environmental factors in aggression include noise, air quality and heat.

Noise Donnerstein and Wilson (1976) found that there was evidence of a greater tendency towards aggression in conditions of high noise levels. It has to be borne in mind that their experiment was laboratory-based and involved participants being prepared to deliver higher levels of shock to a partner in high noise conditions than in low noise or no noise at all. Noise itself did not provoke violence, but lowered the threshold when an instigation to violence was present. However, this kind of study may not be very valid ecologically. How often in 'real life' do you deliver shocks to other people?

Air quality In an archival study Rotton and Frey (1985) matched reports of family disturbances with levels of ozone in the atmosphere and revealed a correlation between weather conditions and violent crime. Days when the temperature was high and the winds were low (when air quality was at its worst) tended to precede violent episodes.

Heat When there have been civil disturbances media reports have emphasized the 'long, hot

summer' effect. In fact the US Riot Commission (1968) cited hot weather as a cause of riots, although the relationship between high temperatures and aggressive behaviour is not quite as simple as that. Research has found that while it is true that heat increases the tendency towards aggression it is not a linear relationship (Baron, 1977). It appears that aggressive tendencies are mediated by the amount of discomfort people feel and that the relationship between discomfort and aggression is curvilinear. The highest levels of aggression are found when discomfort is at an intermediate level, with lower tendencies towards aggression both when there is little discomfort and when it is very high. Figure 26.8 illustrates Baron's conclusions.

Other research has corroborated these findings. Palmarek and Rule (1979) in a laboratory study used two conditions of ambient temperature, one of high temperature (96° Fahrenheit) and one of comfortable temperature (73° Fahrenheit). In the course of the tasks participants were asked to perform, various levels of insult were used against them. Greater aggression occurred when there was moderate arousal, caused either by the excessive heat or by the insults. But when there was no such arousal or when there was extreme arousal as a result of both insults and heat there was less aggression. However, Anderson and Anderson (1984) have suggested that these findings were the

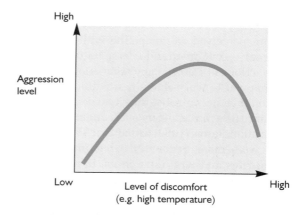

Figure 26.8 Baron's conclusions on relationships between physical discomfort and aggression

GLOSSARY

Hostile attributional bias The tendency for an individual to attribute hostile intent to other people's actions.

result of the experimental procedures. Participants may have guessed what the experiment was about and consciously tried to resist being aggressive. Laboratory studies such as those of Baron and of Palmarek and Rule are bound to be artificial and therefore less ecologically valid than field studies might be. However, Baron and Ransberger (1978) found support for the curvilinear relationship in an archival study. Instances were collated of communal violence in the United States and matched with records of temperatures on the days when the violence occurred. As it got hotter, riots became more likely, but only up to a point. It seems it sometimes gets too hot even for causing trouble.

However, Anderson has more recently (1989) reviewed a wide range both of field and laboratory studies in this area and drew the following conclusions: 'Temperature effects are direct: they operate at the individual level. Temperature effects are important; they influence the most antisocial behaviours imaginable' (Anderson, 1989, p. 94).

Influence of the situation

Arousal Zillman's excitation/transfer model, which has been discussed earlier, illustrates the importance of an aroused state in relation to aggression. This may come from a direct verbal or physical attack, from an emotional state from some other source or from expenditure of energy and stimulation (anything from watching an exciting sporting contest to a couple of hours spent Scottish dancing).

Provocation and aggression Much more obviously than in Zillman's model, aggression is likely to result from provocation of some kind. Someone makes a direct verbal or physical attack and you retaliate. There is a much stronger link between aggression and provocation than between frustration and aggression. Geen (1968) demonstrated that this was the case in an experiment. Participants were either frustrated in attempts to complete a jigsaw puzzle or were allowed to complete the task unhindered. In this second condition, after the task was completed, a confederate of the experimenter's insulted both the participant's intelligence and motivation. The aggressive behaviour which ensued was far stronger than in the frustration condition.

The perception a person has of another's intention in attacking has an effect on retaliatory action. If we believe that someone has *intentionally* tried to harm us then we are much more likely to retaliate. In addition, Lysak et al. (1989) showed that the avoidability of harm which is caused is also important. Where we perceive that another person could have foreseen the consequences of his or her actions then we place blame upon that person and may retaliate even though there was no intent to cause harm. In fact the actual harm caused does not appear to be as important as intent or foreseeability. Where there is advance knowledge of some mitigating circumstance this can reduce the likelihood of retaliation.

Instigation from third parties It happens not infrequently that witnesses or bystanders become involved in confrontations between people. Borden (1975) suggested that even inactive bystanders may influence events. The presence of a male observer may be the cause of a higher level of aggressive behaviour than if the observer were female. Society norms implicitly suggest that women are less likely to approve of violence than men are. Milgram's experiments, which will be fully discussed in Chapter 28, showed that external pressure was influential in persuading individuals to administer apparently massive shocks to others (Milgram, 1963, 1965, 1974). If the bystanders perceive that their urgings are having an effect they will urge even more aggression; while if the individual being attacked refuses to retaliate they will give up their instigation (White and Gruber, 1982).

Disinhibition, deindividuation or dehumanization Disinhibition refers to any reduction in the social forces which restrain us from acting in an aggressive manner. Inhibitions against aggression are part of the socialization process. In most societies people are brought up to regard aggression and violence as undesirable and to be avoided. Shame and guilt are attached to behaving in an aggressive way. However, several factors may reduce or even eliminate these inhibitions. These include deindividuation and dehumanization.

Deindividuation involves the individual who is

GLOSSARY

Disinhibition A reduction in those forces which restrain people from behaving in an aggressive manner.

Deindividuation A feeling of anonymity which results in individuals not taking responsibility for their behaviour.

perpetrating violence or aggression, feeling that he or she is somehow anonymous; that as individuals no shame or blame can be attached to them. Examples of this kind of disinhibition include the effects of military service. In the My Lai incident during the Vietnam war a platoon of soldiers entered a Vietnamese village and slaughtered men, women and children indiscriminately. Hersh (1970), commenting on this incident, has suggested that a climate in which it was legitimate to shoot anything which moved had grown up. Soldiers no longer thought of themselves as individuals who were individually responsible for their actions and who might be punished for them, but as anonymous soldiers. The wearing of uniforms serves to promote this feeling of anonymity. In war crimes trials at the end of World War II it was a frequent defence that those on trial were only obeying orders. Middlebrook (1980) has suggested that the hoods worn by Ku Klux Klan members or the stocking masks which armed robbers wear serve this same purpose.

Dehumanization works in a similar way, with the same effect of anonymity in relation to the victims of violence. Reports of military encounters refer to units of the enemy being 'taken out'. Individual human beings were not perceived as being killed, but units of the enemy fighting force were being eliminated. Cohen (1987) demonstrated the way in which the use of nuclear weapons in war might be made acceptable. Victims were referred to as 'targets' and the wholesale death and destruction which accompanies the use of nuclear weapons is referred to as 'collateral damage', even though this might refer to thousands of human casualties. The references made by Bosnian Serbs in the war in the former Yugoslavia to 'ethnic cleansing' disguise genocidal acts by sanitizing them.

Alcohol and drugs The use of drugs and alcohol may have the same disinhibiting effect. It is common to see images of drunks engaged in violence. At the same time it has been suggested that the use of cannabis has the opposite effect of minimizing tendencies towards aggression. Taylor and his colleagues conducted a series of laboratory studies to verify this (Myerscough and Taylor, 1985; Shuntich and Taylor, 1972; Taylor, 1986; Taylor and Gammon, 1975; Taylor et al., 1976). These were laboratory experiments where participants had to compete with a partner in a reaction time trial. Each trial winner had the chance to administer a shock to the loser at a level of his or her choosing. Different amounts of either

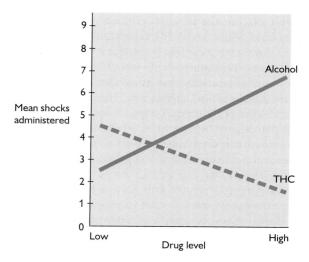

Figure 26.9 Aggression and drugs: a comparison of the effects of alcohol and THC (cannabis) (Taylor et al., 1976)

alcohol or THC (tetrahydrocannabinol), the major active ingredient of cannabis, were administered to participants. Levels of aggression were measured by the mean shock settings used by winners against losers. Small amounts of alcohol reduced aggression levels, but those who had had larger amounts were found to be progressively more aggressive. THC, on the other hand, had no effect in small doses, but decreased aggressive behaviour when larger doses were administered. Figure 26.9 shows the findings of Taylor et al. (1976).

Anger and aggression Berkowitz (1983a, 1983b) developed a model of the relationship between anger and aggression which he termed the cognitive/ neoassociationistic model. In this model aversive stimuli of a wide variety of kinds, ranging from the discomfort of excessive heat or noise to frustration of one's achievement of a goal or to the insults or attacks of another individual, produce negative emotional feelings (dislike). These are not specific but are

> **GLOSSARY**
>
> **Dehumanization** The effect of anonymity in relation to the victims of violence so that they are no longer regarded as humans.
>
> **Cognitive/neoassociationistic model of behaviour** A model of behaviour which links stimuli of various kinds to emotional feelings and thence to action.

interpreted in the light of other cues which may be available. What we *do* about these negative feelings may be either avoidance or attack. Which way it turns out depends among other things upon the network of associations which exist in memory between anger and aggression. If, in similar circumstances before, feelings of anger have been associated with aggressive behaviour, this may have the effect of **priming** (or making more accessible) thoughts about aggression. These images of violence or aggression may be real or they may be fictitious. This is interesting as a cognitive explanation of the linkage between media violence and aggressive behaviour. In a similar way experiences of prosocial behaviour (discussed in the following section) may 'prime' helping. You watch a film of someone coming to the assistance of someone in distress; that event is stored in memory and makes more accessible to you (that is, primes) prosocial behaviour at a later date. It is as well to note that this operates in two directions. Thinking about anger/sympathy may prime aggressive/prosocial behaviour; equally, thinking about aggression/helping may prime anger/sympathy. Figure 26.10 illustrates the neoassociationistic model.

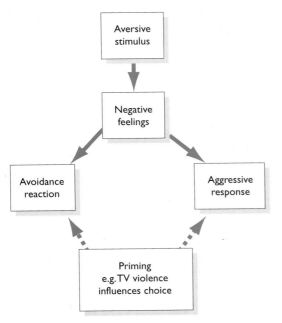

Figure 26.10 Berkowitz's neoassociationistic model of the relationship between feelings and actions

Violence on TV

While the influence of violence and aggressive behaviour on the media and in particular on TV has received attention, it has proved more difficult to establish causal links in a formal laboratory situation, while there have been many reports of individuals copying violent attacks seen on TV or video. The two children involved in the murder of the toddler James Bulger in northern England recently are a particular case. Geen and Donnerstein (1983) have conducted a review of such studies. The following points are made:

- The TV violence to which participants in laboratory experiment were exposed was often of a fairly mild kind and of short duration.
- The violence to which actual viewers are exposed is much more extended in time and much less mild.
- Violence to which people are exposed has the effect of disinhibiting and sanitizing violence.
- Violence and aggression is often portrayed as not being harmful to the victims. Injuries received are underplayed.
- In many instances the aggressor is seen as the 'good guy' and is only rarely portrayed as being punished for his or her violence.

Research in the USA has shown that on children's Saturday morning television there is a violent act every two minutes. By the time a child is 16 it will have witnessed more than 13,000 killings on television. (Liebert and Schwartzberg, 1977). While there are more constraints in the UK over children's exposure to TV violence (the 9 o'clock watershed, for instance) children are exposed to violence consistently and over a prolonged period. The availability of videocassette recording and of satellite and cable TV has increased this. In addition, news programmes often report violence. During the Gulf War, for instance, there were regular reports of bombs and missiles destroying Iraqi installations. The war in Bosnia and reports of violence and massacres in Rwanda are other instances.

> **GLOSSARY**
>
> **Priming** The process by which emotional feelings (e.g. anger or sympathy) make thoughts about aggressive (or prosocial) behaviour more accessible.

The attempts which have been made to study links between TV violence and aggression have taken several forms:

- There have been artificial experiments using material specially produced for the purpose, as in the case of Bandura's Bobo doll experiments (reported earlier). Then there were experiments using actual TV or film material.
- There were also field studies using quasi-experimental designs (naturalistic studies) and actual TV viewing patterns, as well as correlational studies, such as those of Eron and Huesman.

Laboratory studies

Studies (Berkowitz and Alioto, 1973; Geen and Stonner, 1971; Josephson, 1987; Liebert and Schwartzberg, 1977; Turner and Berkowitz, 1972) have identified various factors which modify the link between TV violence and aggressive behaviour including:

- **Justification**. Only where the film justifies the violence it shows is aggressive behaviour likely to follow.
- **The initial aggressiveness of the viewer**. Only where there was a high initial level of aggression was exposure to violence likely to lead to it.
- **Identification**. The link between TV violence and aggression is valid only to the extent to which the viewer identifies with the aggressor in the film.
- **Redeeming features of the aggressor**. Where the aggressor is portrayed as having redeeming features, aggression is more likely to follow.
- **Cues to violent episodes**. Aggression is more likely to occur where there are cues which remind viewers of violent episodes.

Field or naturalistic studies

An example of a study conducted in a more natural setting is that of Leyens et al. (1975). This is described in Box 26.4.

Conclusions from a number of such studies suggest that there is a relationship between violence on TV and aggressive behaviour, but this is by no means proved. It remains a contentious issue. Sheehan (1983) correlated children's TV viewing habits and the levels of

> **Box 26.4** A naturalistic (quasi-experimental) study of the link between watching films and aggression (Leyens et al., 1975)
>
> The participants were boys who lived in four small dormitories in a boarding school in Belgium. In two of the dormitories aggressive behaviour tended to be high and in the other two low. A particular week was designated as 'Movie Week', during which the investigators were able to manipulate the amount of violence shown in television films. The television sets the boys ordinarily watched were disconnected and special films shown. In two of the dormitories (one high aggression, one low aggression) films were shown that were saturated with violence. In the other two dormitories (again, one high aggression, one low aggression) only nonviolent films were shown. During the week and in the week that followed, each boy's aggressive behaviour was monitored and rated. Physical aggression increased in both the dormitories which had been shown the violent films, but verbal aggression only increased in the high-aggression dormitory. In the other there was actually a decrease in verbal aggression.

their aggressive behaviour. Participants in his study were middle-class boys and girls in Australian primary schools aged between five and ten years old. Some were age cohorts tested more than once during the years 1979–81. Aggression was measured by peer ratings of incidents of behaviour by each child which caused physical injury or irritation to another child. Correlations between the viewing of violent TV programmes and aggression measured in this way were significant among eight to ten year olds but not among the younger children. It has to be remembered that correlational data of this kind does not imply cause. It has also to be said that there has been considerable criticism of the methodology of many of these studies. Durkin (1995) makes the following points:

- **Demand characteristics.** Many of the studies suffer from 'demand characteristics' (see Chapter 34).
- **Unbelievable analogies.** Some of the analogies made with real life violence are less than totally believable.

"IT'S REALLY HOMEWORK — I NEED TO PREPARE MYSELF FOR THE PUNCH-UP IN THE PLAYGROUND TOMORROW."

- **Confounding variables.** There are frequently confounding variables which may have been overlooked.
- **Alternative explanations**. There are sometimes alternative explanations for the findings of these studies which have not been fully examined.

He says 'The topic is contentious and the widely cited proof of the effects of media violence is at least open to criticism – a point which is overlooked in many orthodox treatments of the topic' (Durkin, 1995).

Perhaps we should be cautious in the way in which we interpret these studies, particularly in view of the fact that there may be a political motive behind some of the conclusions which are drawn. It may be easier for government to blame the media than to tackle the root causes of violence, the social problems of our time: poverty, for instance, deprivation and the growth of inequality between rich and poor.

However, there have been other longitudinal studies done by Eron (1982) and by Huesmann et al. (1984) which have shown not only that there is a causal link but that it is bidirectional. Children as young as eight

were observed, their aggressiveness assessed as well as the amount of time they spent watching TV. Then some years later aggressiveness was again assessed, together with TV viewing time. Eron came to the conclusion that the amount of time the eight year olds spent watching TV is linked to how aggressive these will be by the time they reach the age of 18 (Eron, 1980).

Reasons for the link between TV violence and aggression

Two sets of explanations for the link have been advanced:

Observational learning or modelling   As we watch television we are assimilating models of behaviour which can be imitated at a later time. How effective this learning is depends upon such things as:

- The degree to which children watching violent TV shows really believe that this is what 'real' life is like.
- The degree to which the child identifies with the aggressive characters in the film (Huesmann et al., 1984).

Cognitive explanations   These are dependent upon thinking and memory processes rather than associative learning. Where children have frequently watched violence on film, aggressive scenarios become more accessible in memory. TV may become a priming device in Berkowitz's neoassociationistic model (described earlier). Bushman and Geen (1990) extended this to include adults and Berkowitz demonstrated that desensitization occurred. People who see a great deal of violence become less concerned about the possible harmful consequence of their actions. However, Josephson (1987) has shown that the priming effect may work in the opposite direction also. Violence may prime social norms to *reduce* the extent to which naturally non-aggressive children act out the aggressive themes they see on TV. Bushman and Geen (1990) found similar effects with adults. Where there was high hostility, viewing even moderate levels of violence increased violent cognitions, but among those whose personality showed low levels of hostility the effect was the opposite. Violent cognitions decreased.

Pornography and aggression

Pornography has been defined as a particular type of erotic material in which sexual and aggressive elements combine to portray force and coercion being used to accomplish the sexual act. Freud (1938) suggested that there was a close link between aggression and sexuality. Later psychoanalysts have maintained the existence of this link. Stoller (1976) has stated: 'Hostility, overt or hidden, is what generates and enhances sexual excitement and its absence leads to sexual indifference and boredom' (Stoller, 1976, p. 903).

Kutchinski (1973), in a study carried out in Denmark, measured the frequency of sex offences before and after restrictions were lifted on the sale of pornographic material. Sex crimes were found to have declined markedly after the lifting of restrictions. This gave rise to a theory which suggested that pornography acted as a safety valve. Now that it had become easier to obtain sexual materials, Kronhausen and Kronhausen (1964) argued, potential sex offenders get their 'kicks' from such materials and do not have to resort so much to sex crimes. However, this was an initial reaction. Bachy (1976) found that once pornographic materials were readily available the incidence of rape increased rather than decreased. These were correlational studies, though, and great caution is necessary before cause is inferred.

A more extensive programme of research, which included experimental work, was carried out by Donnerstein (Donnerstein, 1982; Malamuth and Donnerstein, 1982, 1984). They concluded that men who are exposed to pornography will become more aggressive towards women. The important point seems to be that the material to which they are exposed should be pornographic rather than simply erotic (see definition above). Unless anger is involved erotic material has little effect on aggression, while intense provocation or more arousing erotic material *will* result in increased aggression (Donnerstein et al., 1975; Ramirez et al., 1982). Zillman and Bryant (1982) found that men became more callous in their dealings with women when they were exposed over a long period to such materials.

Control of aggression

For theorists who believe that aggression is an innate urge (for instance, psychoanalysts who see aggression

as the expression of *thanatos* or death instinct), it is not possible to eliminate aggression. The aim must be to channel it into acceptable ways. Sporting events or other competitive activities provide an outlet.

Similarly, ethologists such as Lorenz (1966) do not believe that it could be possible to eliminate aggressive behaviour entirely. If we can identify the cues which trigger aggressive behaviour then it might be possible to control it.

Instrumental learning depends upon the reinforcement of behaviour. If aggressive behaviour is not reinforced, theory suggests it should die away. Brown and Elliot (1965) found that a person who is not rewarded for displays of aggression is less likely to acquire or maintain aggressive behaviours. Punishment of aggression is more problematical. Baron (1977) has suggested that punishment is effective in reducing aggression only in certain conditions:

- It must be predictable. Where a parent or a teacher is attempting to control aggressive behaviour, he or she above all needs to be consistent.
- It must follow the aggression closely. It is not effective for there to be delay as it depends upon the association of the punishment with the behaviour.
- It must be legitimized by the existing social norms.
- Those who administer punishment must be seen as nonaggressive models.

The threat of punishment is even less certain in reducing aggression. Baron suggests that it is effective only when:

- The person threatening is not especially angry.
- The punishment which is threatened is quite severe.
- The aggressor sees it to be very likely that the threat will be carried out.
- The aggressor has not much to gain by his or her aggression.

These very considerable limitations on punishment and the threat of it as a means to reduce aggressive behaviour must mean that it is not a very effective means. Davies (1980) used archival information to highlight some relevant points. He used records of murders and executions in London between 1658 and

1921. During the weeks immediately following the well-publicized execution of a murderer, the incidence of homicide decreased by about 35 per cent, but about six weeks later returned to what it had been before. While capital punishment may be a deterrent in the short term, in the longer run there is little evidence of deterrence.

Social learning theorists are more optimistic. They believe the answer lies in replacing violent and aggressive models with nonaggressive ones. Baron (1971) has found that the influence of a nonaggressive model can neutralize the effect of aggressive models. This suggests that even if it is not possible to remove all potentially aggressive models, providing nonaggressive models will be some help.

Incompatible responses

It has been suggested that as it is difficult to do two things at once, a means of controlling violent responses might be to provide conditions which induce responses that are not compatible with aggressive ones. Baron and Ball (1974) used humorous cartoons, while Rule and Leger (1976) attempted to foster empathy. In both cases participants in their studies were found to be less aggressive when there was an alternative non-aggressive response available.

Discouragement of aggression

It is sometimes possible to defuse retaliation and reduce the chance of aggression in response to attack by explaining why the attack was beyond the aggressor's control: that is, providing mitigating circumstances. This was most effective if the information was available before the act of aggression and if it is accepted as reasonable (Zillman et al., 1975: Zillman and Cantor, 1976).

Reducing frustration

If frustration is a major factor in aggression (see above), it ought to be possible to look to ways of controlling frustration in order to reduce aggression. Ransford (1968) found that those blacks in Los Angeles with the most profound feelings of frustration were those who were most liable to resort to violence. If some of the social and economic frustrations can be removed, then there is a chance that there will be less violence. It is possible to see the growth in unemployment and in the numbers of disadvantaged people in the UK as linked to the growth of violent crime since the early 1980s.

Catharsis

Catharsis refers to the release of pent-up aggressive energy through other forms of behaviour. It has been suggested that fantasy might provide a means whereby catharsis might occur and aggression might be reduced. However, while it has been found that aggression works to reduce aggressive fantasies, there does not seem to be much evidence that it works the other way round. There is more support for efficacy of behavioural catharsis in reducing subsequent aggression. This refers to the opprtunity to express aggression at the time the frustration occurs (Konečni, 1975).

Cognitive means of aggression control

It was noted earlier that Berkowitz's neoassociationistic model points to a link between the priming effect of experiences, whether direct or by means of film or television, to make the memory of earlier experiences more accessible. When a link is built up between aggression and feelings of anger, aggression becomes more likely. Alternatively, if a cognitive link can be established between nonviolent responses and emotional arousal this may make an aggressive response less likely. Accordingly, the presentation of non-aggressive responses on film or on television may serve to 'prime' nonviolent behaviour. Berkowitz (1989) has pointed to measures which:

- Reduce aversive stimuli (by, for instance, ensuring adequate food and shelter).
- Strengthen social norms against aggression (by rewarding nonaggressive responses and not rewarding aggressive ones, for instance).
- Reduce the accessibility of aggressive actions in memory by reducing overall exposure to aggressive models. In this way feelings of anger will not be so likely to 'prime' aggressive action.

GLOSSARY

Catharsis Refers to the release of pent-up emotional energy.

? **SELF-ASSESSMENT QUESTIONS**

1. Describe some of the different explanations of aggression, including biological, biosocial and social learning explanations. Is it possible to say that any one approach provides a complete explanation?
2. Is it plausible to say that some individuals are *naturally* more aggressive than others?
3. List some factors which seem to contribute to aggressive behaviour. Is there good evidence for the 'long, hot summer' factor?
4. Is there convincing evidence that watching violence on TV may make children more aggressive?
5. Identify some ways in which aggressive behaviour may be reduced. Do you think that Berkowitz's neoassociationistic model might contribute to this?

Prosocial behaviour

Wispé (1972) defined prosocial behaviour as behaviour which has social consequences which contribute positively to the psychological or physical well-being of another person. This encompasses a very wide spectrum of behaviour. At this time consideration will be limited to the following:

■ Helping behaviour,
■ Altruism – giving or sharing with no obvious self-gain,
■ Bystander intervention – that is, the likelihood that bystanders will intervene to help others in trouble.

Helping others and altruism

There are three approaches which have been taken to explain human helping behaviour:

■ Biological approaches,
■ What might be termed biosocial approaches,
■ Social learning approaches.

Biological and biosocial explanations

Biologists take the view that just as there is an innate need in humans to eat or to drink, there is also a need to help others and that this has been taken as one explanation for the comparative success of the human species. In particular, sociobiologists have drawn attention to the evolutionary benefits of altruistic behaviour (Krebs and Miller, 1985; Wilson, 1978). As we have seen in Part 4 of this book, sociobiologists approach human (as well as animal) behaviour from the point of view of genetic and evolutionary survival. The basic proposition is that humans, in common with all animals, have one preeminent goal, the survival of the genes. Human beings will be predisposed to help relatives because in so doing they are furthering the survival of the genes which they share with those relatives. Your son, because of his parentage, shares genes with you. If your paramount interest lies in ensuring that your genes are passed on to succeeding generations, you have vested interest in your son's survival. Not quite as much as in your own, perhaps, but more than an unrelated stranger's. Then again, if you yourself have passed the time of life when you can yourself reproduce, gene survival may be ensured to an even greater extent if you can ensure your son's survival. Hence there may be circumstances when you will sacrifice yourself for your children.

Reciprocal altruism Reciprocal altruism takes this one stage further. Trivers (1971) has used reciprocal altruism as an explanation for 'Good Samaritan' behaviour. A man dives into a river to save another from drowning. The man has a 50:50 chance of drowning. The chances of the rescuer dying in the attempt are perhaps one in twenty. If at some future date the roles are reversed, both will have benefited. Each will have traded a 1:2 chance of dying for a 1:10 chance. Within the population as a whole such reciprocally altruistic behaviour will have enhanced each individual's personal genetic 'fitness'. There is a fuller discussion of altruism, including reciprocal altruism, in Chapter 18.

The main problems with this sociobiological approach to helping behaviour are:

■ That there have been no good studies done with human participants which have supported the biological explanation of helping,

---

GLOSSARY

Altruism Helping others without any expectation of personal gain.

Reciprocal altruism An apparently altruistic act performed in the expectation that at some time in the future someone else will do the same for oneself.

■ That the extensive research done by social learning theorists into helping behaviour has been ignored.

Learning theory approaches to helping behaviour

These can be divided into two, those based upon basic learning theory and those which depend upon social learning and modelling. Both of these approaches contend that there is no innate tendency to help others but that this behaviour needs to be learned. Classical conditioning and instrumental learning represent the basic learning theory approach; observational learning and modelling the social learning approach. These processes of learning are part of the socialization process during childhood. Straightforward telling, reinforcement and modelling each have a part to play. Grusec et al. (1978) have found that it increases a child's helpfulness just to tell him or her what the right behaviour is. Children learn to expect people to be helpful. But to instruct children to help others is less helpful unless there is evidence that the instructor is practising what he or she preaches.

Reinforcements such as praise also work as Fischer (1963) found. Where children were praised or reinforced with bubblegum for sharing what they had, they learnt to share with other children. Vicarious reinforcement also plays a part. Where children saw another person behaving generously to a third person they tended to imitate.

Modelling behaviour There is evidence that people learn to be helpful by observing others helping. Grusec and Skubisky (1970) found that where children won tokens in games and then saw an adult giving away tokens to a needy child they were more likely to behave generously. Children's attitudes to prosocial behaviour also improved where they watched prosocial behaviour on television (Coates et al., 1976). An experiment described in Box 26.5 illustrates this modelling effect.

Vicarious experience The outcomes, so far as the model is concerned, have been found by Bandura (1973) to make a crucial difference. Where the model is seen to have been reinforced for helping, the model is much more likely to have been effective in influencing behaviour; where the outcomes are negative, models will be much less effective. This

---

Box 26.5 Modelling prosocial behaviour (Bryan and Test, 1967)

Bryan and Test (1967) demonstrated that adult behaviour as well could be influenced by modelling. They set out to test whether the presence of a model would influence the number of motorists who stopped to help a woman who had had a puncture. This was an experiment where there were two conditions:

■ In the experimental condition motorists first passed a car by the side of the road whose driver (a woman) was being assisted to change a wheel by a male motorist who had stopped to help her. A short way along the road there was another car with a puncture, again with a woman driver. In this case she was alone and clearly needed help.

■ In the second condition (control) there were only the second car and its woman driver. There was no model.

Results showed that more than 50 per cent more motorists were prepared to stop and help in the experimental condition (i.e., where there was a model).

---

was borne out in an experiment conducted by Hornstein (1970). Participants who observed an individual returning a lost wallet and having a good reception were found to be more likely to help on another occasion than those who witnessed someone returning the wallet and having either an indifferent or a hostile reception.

Theories relating to helping behaviour

Attribution processes

In the section on 'self' in Chapter 24 we discussed Bem's theory of self-attribution (p. 588). In the present context it is suggested that individuals may develop self-attributions of helpfulness. A person may see himself or herself as helpful and this self-attribution will serve to focus behaviour on the helping option where there is a choice of possible behaviours. An old man slips on a loose paving stone and falls. The choices available to you, as a passer-by, are either to assist or to leave it to someone else. If your self-attribution leads you to see yourself as a helpful person you will be more likely to take the choice of helping rather than leaving it to someone else. Grusec and Redler (1980) found that such self-attributions of helpfulness provided a stronger reinforcement for helpful behaviour than external reinforcements such as verbal praise. Perry et al. (1980) found that children experience bad feelings when they fail to live up to their self-imposed standards of helpfulness.

'Just world' hypothesis

According to the 'just world' hypothesis developed by Lerner (Lerner, 1977; Lerner and Miller, 1978) there is a strong link between cause and effect (see Chapter 24). People have the feeling that you get what you deserve. This is allied to the Buddhist teaching of karma. Whether it happens now or later your sins (and your good deeds) will find you out. In these circumstances people will be less likely to come to someone else's assistance. After all 'they must have done something to deserve it!' And, of course, this is convenient as well. In rape cases it has sometimes been said of the victim, 'she had it coming to her'. Either she was out too late at night, or she was dressed provocatively. This just world hypothesis is a learned attribution and is acquired in childhood. However, this is very much the view of a small minority of people. Evidence of undeserved suffering gives the lie to it. A class of infant school-children were attacked by a psychopath in the gymnasium of their school in the Scottish town of Dunblane. He opened fire with an arsenal of guns and killed a large number of the children together with one of their teachers. Is this really evidence of a 'just world'?

Social norms of behaviour

In childhood social norms of behaviour are acquired through learning. These norms specify what behaviour is expected as normal and what is abnormal. They are the product of the culture in which we have grown up and they lay down what behaviour is expected within that culture. In almost every culture there is a norm which specifies that to be selfish is wrong; to be helpful is right. In most cultures it is prescribed that we do what we can to help other people.

Two social norms in particular have been cited as responsible for altruism:

The principle of reciprocity   This is the 'do as you would be done by' norm. Individuals have an obligation to reciprocate help which has been given them; the more so, if the help given is freely given and involves some sacrifice. The greater the sacrifice the greater the obligation it lays on us to reciprocate (Tesser et al., 1968; Wilke and Lanzetta, 1970).

The social responsibility norm   People have a social obligation to give help to those who need it. Membership of a community imposes an obligation upon individuals to help, without any expectation that this help will be reciprocated or rewarded. Such help is frequently given anonymously. Charity collectors call at your front door and if you do not give to them there are feelings of guilt. Of course, the just world hypothesis lays down that you give the most help to those whom you perceive as being in greatest need of help. You are more likely to contribute generously for poor children than to support a local football team. You are less obligated to help in the rehabilitation of drug addicts, perhaps, than in the support of disabled people. The former might be seen as having brought their misfortunes on themselves and so are less deserving. The concept of the deserving poor, prevalent in Victorian times and reemerging more recently, reflects this.

Culture and altruism

It is evident that some cultures are far more prosocial than others. Child-rearing practices, religious training and education (in the broadest sense) may determine the extent to which people are motivated to help others. If people are led to believe that there is 'no such thing as society', but just individuals looking after their own interests, prosocial behaviour will not readily be fostered. Eisenberg and Mussen (1989) summarized cross-cultural research on children's prosocial tendencies and concluded that American children typically were less kind, considerate and cooperative than those reared in Mexican villages, Hopi Indian children reared on reservations or Israeli children reared in kibbutzim. There seem to be two separate kinds of cultures in this respect:

■ **Individualist cultures**, such as the USA, Canada, Australia and some European countries, where less emphasis is placed upon the responsibility each individual has for the welfare of others; more on the freedom individuals have to pursue their own goals.

■ **Collectivist cultures**, which include Japan and some other Asian countries, those from the former Communist bloc, many Latin American and native American cultures where the good of the group is held to be more important than individual wishes.

Empathy

Empathy, the vicarious experiencing of another's emotions, and its relationship with altruism has been the basis for the empathy/altruism hypothesis developed by Batson and his colleagues (Batson, 1987, 1990; Batson and Oleson, 1991; Coke et al., 1978). Batson has suggested that empathy can produce genuinely altruistic motivation to help, as distinct from egoistically motivated helping. You may be 'personally distressed' at seeing the suffering that someone else is experiencing and your motivation for helping may be an egoistic one, to relieve your own distress. Alternatively, there may be genuine empathy, a sympathetic focus on the other person's suffering and a motivation to reduce it. Batson and his colleagues have demonstrated several times in experiments that participants who are genuinely aroused empathetically continued to help, when they could quite easily have relieved their own distress by escaping from the situation. The difficulty is to rule out other egoistically based motives for helping (how you appear to other people, for example, or the good feelings which assisting someone in trouble may give you). Batson's later studies cast some doubt on whether apparently genuinely empathetic people might have such ulterior motives as these.

Cialdini's negative-state relief model

An alternative to the empathy/altruism hypothesis is Cialdini's negative-state relief model (Cialdini et al., 1973, 1987). This model (Figure 26.11) has suggested that people learn in childhood that it is gratifying to help and this gratification can help them to overcome sadness and guilt (that is, personal distress at the suffering of others and guilt that they are all right while someone else is suffering). These feelings of sadness are experienced also by those who empathize with the victim, but they help in order to reduce their own sadness rather than through an altruistic desire to relieve the victim's suffering. Cialdini's experiments, described in Box 26.6, were designed to test whether other means of lifting the negative feelings (sadness) – aroused by watching someone else suffer – might break the altruism/empathy link.

> **GLOSSARY**
>
> **Empathy/altruism hypothesis** The hypothesis put forward by Batson that empathy with someone who is in trouble may provide a genuine motivation for helping.
>
> **Negative-state relief model** The model which suggests that people learn in childhood that it is gratifying to help.

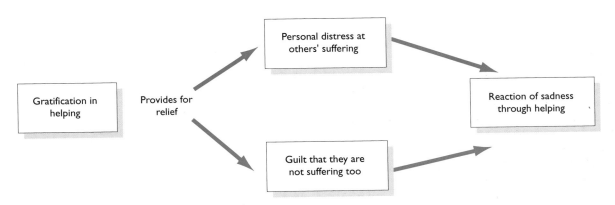

Figure 26.11 An illustration of Cialdini's negative-state relief model

Box 26.6   Experiments to test Cialdini's negative-state relief model

Cialdini arranged for participants to receive – in one condition – an unexpected gift of money or, in another, lavish praise. In yet another study participants were led to believe that their mood of sadness had been 'fixed' by a drug, so that even helping the victims would not relieve it. Schaller and Cialdini (1988) tried to relieve the 'sadness' using a comedy tape. The results of these studies challenged the empathy/altruism hypothesis. While the surprise gift of money did not make any difference, the other attempts to relieve negative arousal states (lavish praise, belief that the feelings had been fixed or a comedy tape) did lessen the motivation to help. Schroeder et al. (1988), however, found with highly empathetic individuals none of such mood-relieving strategies altered their motivation to help.

It has to be said that some of these studies are of somewhat doubtful ecological validity. Not only Cialdini's, but also Batson's studies involved laboratory tests, where students (not, perhaps, a typical sample of the population at large) watched other students being given electric shocks (not something you see often everyday in real life). However, his research has led Batson to say that if research continues to suggest that empathetically aroused people often help for altruistic rather than egoistic reasons, present views about human nature and human capacity for caring need to be revised radically. That said, genuine concern for others is a 'fragile flower, easily crushed by egoistic concerns' (Batson et al., 1983, p. 718). When highly empathetic people were asked to take a victim's place to receive painful shocks, but were perfectly free to leave if they wished to, 86 per cent opted to leave (Batson et al., 1983).

Deciding whether to help

Two processes operate side by side to determine whether or not we give help when it appears to be needed:

- **Cognitive processes**. These include an evaluation and interpretation of the situation, weighing up the consequences of alternative courses of action.
- **Emotional processes**. These act as motivators to spur people on to action.

Piliavin's bystander calculus model

Piliavin et al. (1981) have developed an arousal/cost–reward model (also termed a bystander calculus model) to explain what happens when decisions are taken whether to give assistance in emergencies (Figure 26.12). This consists of five distinct stages:

Awareness   Becoming aware that someone needs help. This may be something quite clear-cut such as screams, cries for help or smoke billowing out of an upstairs window in a house. But often the cues are ambiguous. It may be quite difficult to decide whether the noise you hear from within a house represents an emergency situation.

Emotional arousal   Having become cognitively aware that there is an emergency and someone may need help, there will be a degree of emotional arousal. Physiologically, this will represent itself by a quickened pulse, butterflies in the stomach and the other manifestations of strong emotion. (There is a full discussion of emotion in Chapter 9 of this book.)

Interpretation   You will need to interpret the physiological changes which you experience, using cues from within the total environment. Piliavin stresses that arousal is a distressing thing which you are motivated to reduce. This is egoistic motivation rather than altruism. However, arousal might be due to empathy with the distress of the victim, which accords with Batson's empathy/altruism hypothesis. Arousal and your interpretation of it are important in determining whether or not you go and help. The more highly aroused you are the quicker you are to help, as evidenced by a staged emergency by Gaertner and Dovidio (1977). Chairs appeared to have crashed down on a woman in the next room. Those bystanders who were most highly aroused (those

---

GLOSSARY

Bystander calculus model Embodies Piliavin's suggestion that it is distressing to see someone suffer, which causes arousal. The decision as to whether or not to help amounts to a cost–benefit analysis as to whether the relief of distress is worth the costs involved..

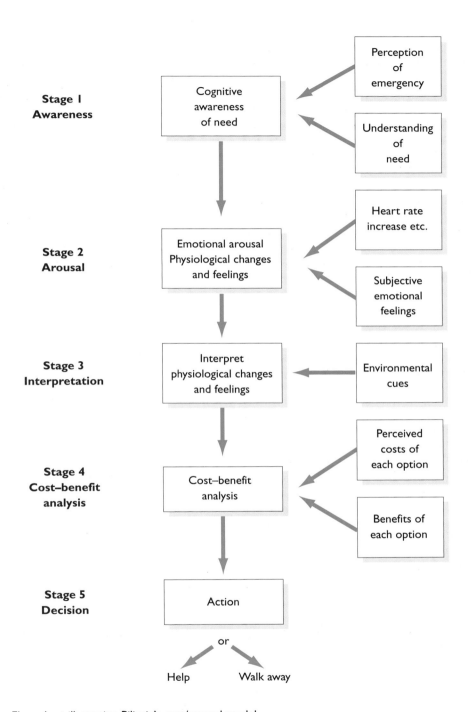

Figure 26.12 Flow chart illustrating Piliavin's cost/arousal model

who had the fastest heart rate and said that they felt most upset) were the quickest on the scene to help. But the arousal had to be labelled as a response to the 'emergency'. Gaertner and Dovidio tested this by giving one group of the bystanders a 'drug' (in fact a placebo) and telling them it would cause them to be aroused; while another group were told that the 'drug' they were given would not cause them to be aroused but might give them a dull headache. The former group attributed their arousal to the drug and were slower to help.

Cost–benefit analysis What are the likely consequences of either helping or not helping? Costs might include some of the following:

■ Effort and time expended;
■ Loss of resources, including any benefits or rewards you might have to forego (you might, for instance, have a train to catch).
■ Risks involved – of actual harm, of embarrassment, of social disapproval or emotional reaction to interacting with the victim.

On the other side of the balance sheet you weigh up the rewards:

■ Monetary rewards for heroism;
■ Increased self-esteem which comes from living up to the moral standards you have set yourself;
■ Social approval.

And what about helping indirectly rather than directly (phoning the police or the fire service rather than going in yourself) or escaping from the scene? You weigh up the potential costs and benefits of these options as well, as you perceive them.

The perceptions people make of the costs and benefits are individual ones, influenced perhaps, by knowledge of their own abilities. There may also be some distortion, exaggerating the costs of helping or of not helping.

The decision stage You decide whether or not to help.

A commentary on Piliavin's model There is doubt whether people really do calculate in this detached way when there is an emergency. Latané and Darley (1970) have said that the very nature of most

emergencies is that they are dangerous and unforeseen and consequently produce very high levels of arousal. Bystanders are less likely to take account of all the cues in the situation and then calmly weigh up costs and benefits than to act in an impulsive fashion, doing what to someone not directly involved might be seen as irrational. There is a distinction to be drawn between routine help and what happens in cases of emergency. There is not a great deal in common between, for instance, a routine commitment you may have taken on to get your elderly relative out of bed every morning and reacting to smoke billowing from the windows of a house you happen to be passing.

Influences on prosocial behaviour

These include:

■ Situational influences; what kind of a need is it?
■ What is the relationship between the helper and the helped?
■ What other people do.
■ Personal influences. (For instance, are men or women more helpful? Do people receive more help in towns or in the country?)

Influences of the situation

The Kitty Genovese episode Latané and Darley conducted a series of experiments to determine what the situational factors might be which determine bystander intervention in emergencies. The stimulus to this research was the shocking affair of Kitty Genovese. In a respectable neighbourhood of New York city, Kitty Genovese was on her way home from work late at night. She was suddenly attacked by a man with a knife. At first her screams alarmed the man and he ran off. But when no one came to her aid, he returned, sexually assaulted her and stabbed her eight times. In the half hour that the attack lasted no one came to help her. After about half an hour an anonymous resident called the police but would not give his name because 'he did not want to get involved'. The next day police interviewed neighbouring residents. No fewer than 38 people admitted hearing the screaming. The affair became a cause célèbre, exciting the attention, not only of the media, but of social psychological researchers. Apathy, callousness, indifference and a loss of concern for others were cited (Latané and Darley, 1976).

Cognitive model of Latané and Darley

Latané and Darley (1970) developed a cognitive model to determine whether or not bystanders decide to help in emergency. This too had five stages:

1. **Noticing the event** and realizing that help may be needed.
2. **Interpretation.** Is the event a serious emergency? Are there cues which indicate distress: screaming, for example?
3. **Responsibility.** Is it anything to do with me? Does the bystander accept responsibility? This may include factors such as other witnesses to the event and also perception by the bystander of his or her competence to deal with the situation.
4. **Decision.** This may include direct intervention, indirect intervention (calling the police, perhaps), escape or doing nothing.
5. **Action.** This will depend on the nature of the situation (emergency or not), knowledge of what to do and the behaviour of other people.

Figure 26.13 is a flow chart illustrating Latané and Darley's model. Latané and Darley's development of this model led to a series of experiments which are described in Box 26.7.

Latané and Darley (1976) set out in their most elaborate experiment to test each of these three issues. This became known as the 'three-in-one experiment' and is detailed in Box 26.8.

Individual differences in helping behaviour

Latané and Darley (1970) did not find any personality measure which accurately predicted whether someone would help. Attempts by other researchers (Bar-Tal, 1976; Schwartz, 1977) to single out Good Samaritans from the rest of the population have not been successful. There is some evidence though that there is a relationship between possession of specific skills and willingness to use them to help others (Midlarsky and Midlarsky, 1976; Schwartz and David, 1976). In a more general sense the possession of emergency skills (first aid training, for instance) makes it more likely that someone will intervene in an emergency.

Leadership There is some evidence that some people are more likely to take the initiative in all kinds of action than others. There is clearly a skills component in this but, apart from this, Baumeister et al. (1988) have identified a more specific quality of leaders: that they do not suffer to the same degree as do followers from diffusion of responsibility (see p. 644). But leadership and followership is the subject of a section in Chapter 28.

Gender and helping Males are more likely to help females than vice versa. Cars are more likely to stop for a female than a male hitchhiker, or for a male and

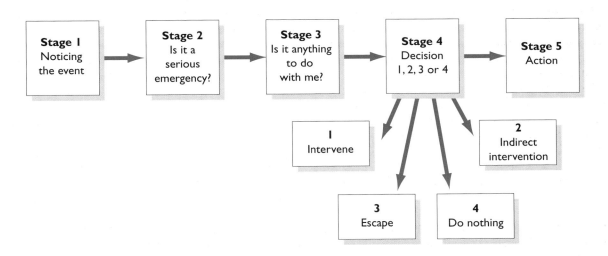

Figure 26.13 Latané and Daley's cognitive model of bystander intervention

Box 26.7 Latané and Darley's experiments on bystander intervention

In the first of these, participants (male students) were interviewed ostensibly about problems which they faced as students in a large university. They were given, to begin with, a questionnaire to complete and while they were doing this smoke began to pour from a vent in the wall. This continued for six minutes by which time the room was full of smoke. In relation to the question of what influence other people have on decisions taken in such situations there were three conditions:

- Participants were alone;
- They were with two other participants whom they did not know;
- They were with two confederates of the experimenter who ignored the smoke.

The hypothesis was that in such situations other people present exercise a crucial influence on decisions which are taken. Results suported this hypothesis. Of those who were alone, 75 per cent took positive action, reporting the matter. Of those in the company of two other strangers only 38 per cent took action. In the third condition, where there were two other people present who had had instructions to ignore the smoke, only 10 per cent took action.

Latané and Darley suggested that the presence of other people inhibits action; the more people, the more inhibition. Where those who were present obviously ignored what was happening the inhibition was greatest of all. There appear to be three issues which affect the decisions taken:

- **Diffusion of responsibility**. In a group people will offload their responsibility on to others (social loafing). In an emergency the fact that there are others watching provides an ideal opportunity for social loafing. In fact they do not even have to be there watching or visible. The knowledge that others are around somewhere is enough.
- **Audience inhibition**. The presence of other people has another effect as well: to make people afraid of appearing foolish. They become self-conscious and frightened that they are going to make a mistake.
- **Social influence**. People will look to others as models for what they should do. Chapter 28 will deal in greater detail with issues of social influence.

female pair (Pomazal and Clore, 1973). Those who are more physically attractive are more likely to get help. Przybyla (1985) manipulated the sexual arousal of participants by showing them sexually explicit videos. Seeing an erotic video made a male participant more likely to help a female in trouble, while when it was a male who was in trouble participants were less likely to help and spent less time on it. Females, on the other hand, when aroused by an erotic video spent less time helping anyone, male or female.

The type of situation which presents itself makes a crucial difference. In dangerous emergencies men are more likely to intervene. It is conceived as part of the male role to act heroically in dangerous situations (Eagly and Crowley, 1986). Moreover, because men are in general stronger and more likely to have relevant skills, they perceive the costs of intervening as being lower than women do. However, women are more likely to provide help where emotional support is needed (Brody, 1990; Eagly and Crowley, 1986).

Town and country   There seems to be something in the crowded noisy hectic environment of the big city which inhibits helping. Milgram (1970) proposed what he termed the urban overload hypothesis to explain why people in rural areas and in small towns are more helpful than those in big cities. In large cities people had to be selective in the help they gave. The general levels of stimulation were so high that they had sometimes to ignore people in need and to be choosy about those they helped. Amato (1983) studied helping behaviour in different sizes of communities and found that as the population of a community increased so helping decreased.

Mood and helping   All kinds of things may put you into a 'good mood', being successful in something, having some good fortune, being happy or even good weather. Isen (1987) manipulated the success factor and showed that it did indeed make participants more likely to help. George (1991) found that happy

Box 26.8 Latané and Darley's (1976) three-in-one experiment

Four conditions varied the communications between the participants and other bystanders

- Where they could see and be seen,
- Where they could see but not be seen,
- Where they could not see but be seen,
- Where they could neither see nor be seen.

These conditions were achieved by means of television monitors and cameras. Participants were recruited to take part in a study of repression. The props used were a supposedly antique and unreliable shock generator. An emergency situation was created when the experimenter apparently received a violent shock from this generator, screamed, jumped into the air, threw himself against the wall and then fell to the floor out of camera range with his feet sticking up. Then he began to moan softly until help arrived or for about six minutes. The conditions used were as follows:

- **Control or baseline condition**. No one is present with the participant. The video camera in the participant's room is pointed at the ceiling (the participant cannot be seen) and the monitor shows the ceiling of the second room (the participant cannot see).
- **Diffusion of responsibility**. The participant knows

there is another person there but otherwise the same conditions apply (the camera points to the ceiling, the monitor shows only a ceiling).

- **Diffusion plus social influence**. The participant can see in the monitor another person working on a questionnaire. The camera still points to the ceiling (the participant can see but not be seen).
- **Diffusion plus audience inhibition**. The camera points to the participant (who knows he or she can be seen) but the monitor just shows the next room ceiling.
- **Diffusion plus social influence plus audience inhibition**. Each person is visible to the other via cameras and monitors.

Results

The results showed a cumulative effect. Where the participant was alone there was the greatest readiness to help. With just diffusion of responsibility there was slightly less readiness. With diffusion as well as inhibition (or influence) there was still less readiness. With diffusion as well as inhibition and influence there was least readiness of all.

The results supported Latané and Darley's suggestion that the factors of diffusion, influence and inhibition were additive.

---

salespeople were more likely to go beyond the call of duty to be helpful. There is no doubt that the present trend towards more aggressive management and consequent unhappiness and insecurity do not make for helpful people. If you focus on your own good fortune you are more likely to be helpful, but if the focus rests on someone else's fortune then that makes you less helpful. Rosenhan et al. (1981) found that happiness at a good posting (to Hawaii) increased helpfulness; but the thought of a friend getting the posting actually decreased it.

Bad mood or ill fortune do not seem to have the same effect. A feeling of guilt may stimulate helping behaviour (Carlson and Miller, 1987). As has been seen (p. 639), sadness can motivate people to help (Cialdini et al., 1973). But if you are preoccupied with your own woes you will not be likely to help anyone else (Aderman and Berkowitz, 1983). What seems to matter is where the focus of attention is. If you focus on the misfortunes of others you will be more likely to

help; but if you focus on your own unhappiness then you will not help others.

Towards a more prosocial society

How can we have a more prosocial society? Maybe we need to start with how children are brought up. Young children are naturally egoistic but may become more prosocial as they grow up. They discover that adults approve of children who help others. Also, as they grow up they become more able to empathize with others, as their cognitive abilities improve. Piaget saw children becoming less egocentric as they grew older (Birch, 1997). Children can be encouraged to act more prosocially if they are reinforced for prosocial behaviour. But they need to develop intrinsic motives, and rewarding all good behaviour may inhibit this intrinsic motivation. Parents are the ideal models. Where they practise what they preach and clearly set out the norms of behaviour which are expected they will encourage children to be prosocial (Eisenberg and Mussen, 1989). In the same way that violence on television may foster aggression so television portrayals of people behaving prosocially may increase prosocial behaviour (Liebert and Sprafkin, 1988; Roberts and Maccoby, 1985). Children should have real opportunities to help, looking after younger brothers or sisters, helping with the cleaning and the washing up and so on. We have already noted that individualist cultures foster less prosocial behaviour than do collectivist ones.

Adults too can be encouraged to be more prosocial. The ways in which charity fund-raisers increase the rewards of helping behaviour while minimizing the costs could be studied. They give us little prizes and opportunities to win things. They make it easy. Just phone up with a credit card number. They put us in a good mood by putting on a show (Bob Geldof's 'Band Aid' and the BBC's 'Children in Need' appeal are examples). Social approval can be mobilized. Jason et al. (1984) found that on a campus 31 per cent of students volunteered to give blood if they were directly approached by friends, while only 14 per cent volunteered when approached by people they did not know. When they do give blood, a good experience initially will encourage them to do it again until they become intrinsically and altruistically motivated.

SELF-ASSESSMENT QUESTIONS

1. Describe the sociobiological explanation of altruism. Do you find it convincing?
2. Outline and compare Batson's empathy/altruism hypothesis with Cialdini's negative-state relief model. Which of these seems to be the best explanation of why people help others?
3. List the factors which Latané and Darley found inhibit bystanders from helping in emergencies. Does their complex 'three-in-one' experiment support the view that these factors are additive?
4. Is it possible to identify ways in which prosocial behaviour may be encouraged?

Chapter summary

■ Most people tend to categorize others with whom they interact as 'one of us' – belonging to the 'in-group' – or not one of us – belonging to the out-group. These categorizations play a part in determining behaviour through the social cognitions which are involved. They also contribute to social identity. In-group differences are played down; differences between groups are accentuated. In-group membership in turn makes a contribution to self-concept.

■ Ethnocentrism is nourished by in-group identity and in-group feeling, so that members of our own group are favourably evaluated, out-group members unfavourably. This leads to ultimate attribution bias. Desirable behaviour from members of the in-group is attributed to their disposition. Undesirable behaviour is attributed to situational causes. The opposite is true of out-groups. Their undesirable behaviour is down to disposition, desirable behaviour to situation.

■ Moscovici formulated a theory of social representation. Perceived events may become simplified and distorted so that a kind of group think arises about what has actually happened. Technical terms also become simplified and distorted as they become familiar currency within a group.

■ Subjective rather than objective frustration and deprivation are sources of aggression and hostility. They are measured against what others are perceived to endure.

■ Realistic conflict theory has arisen from the need to examine whether a policy of cooperation between groups or competition between them was best in order to achieve the goals set by individuals and groups. It looks at the relationship between the competitive and cooperative sides of human nature. This has been explored in a very abstract way by researchers using games where the strategies individuals adopt can be seen to have a bearing on the outcome. Prominent among these games has been the 'Prisoner's Dilemma' which has been extensively used in this context.

■ Aggression is explained in a number of ways including biological, biosocial and social psychological explanations. Included in the biologically-based explanations are those of Freud and the psychoanalytic school as well as ethological and sociobiological theories. Biosocial explanations include the aggression/frustration hypothesis put forward by Dollard in the 1930s and more recently Zillman's excitation transfer model. Explanations based upon learning theory include those of Bandura.

■ Factors influencing aggression include dispositional ones such as the notion of an aggressive personality. Type A personalities have been identified in this context as well as the authoritarian personality described by Adorno. Gender is a factor in aggression with males more heavily involved in physical aggression than females, though when psychological and verbal aggression is included there does not appear to be much difference between genders. Environmental factors considered include noise, air quality and heat, while situational factors may include arousal and provocation. Disinhibition may play a part, as may alcohol and/or drugs. Anger may act as a primer to make overt aggression more likely to occur.

■ The issue of TV violence has been researched not only in the laboratory but in naturalistic settings. Some links have been found between TV violence and aggression. Explanations include learning and cognitive factors (e.g. Berkowitz's neoassociationistic model). However, the issue is contentious, and by no means proved.

■ Practical strategies to reduce aggression include punishment, though this is of limited efficacy.

■ Incompatible responses to a situation, such as humour or empathy, may be used to defuse potential aggression. Frustration may be reduced, which in turn will limit aggressive behaviour. Behavioural catharsis, and the presentation of nonaggressive responses to films or TV in place of the more usual violent ones may serve to 'prime' nonviolent rather than violent behaviour.

■ There may be biological or sociobiological explanations for prosocial behaviour including apparent altruism. Learning and modelling also have a part to play. Batson has developed an empathy/altruism hypothesis. Cialdini's model suggests a need to reduce the negative feelings produced by seeing others suffer, particularly where people have been brought up from childhood to think that it is gratifying to help. Piliavin's bystander calculus model is essentially based on a cost/benefit analysis of alternative responses to a given situation. As a result of the Kitty Genovese affair, Latané and Darley examined possible factors which might inhibit helping behaviour. These included diffusion of responsibility or social loafing, audience inhibition and social modelling.

■ Factors found to influence prosocial behaviour include leadership qualities, gender, mood and what Milgram has termed urban overload. Those who live in large cities had to be selective in the help they gave while those in the country need not be so choosy. This goes to expain why country people appear to be more helpful than urban dwellers.

Further reading

Deaux, K., Dane, F.C. and Wrightsman, L.S. (1993). *Social Psychology in the 90s*. 6th edn. Pacific Grove, CA: Brooks-Cole. Contains an excellent chapter on aggression and violence, including collective violence (warfare, for example) and societal violence.

Hayes, N. (1993). *Principles of Social Psychology*. Hove: Lawrence Erlbaum. Chapter 6 of this book provides an alternative view of aggression and altruism.

Hogg, M.A. and Vaughan, G.M. (1995). *Social Psychology: An Introduction*. Hemel Hempstead: PrenticeHall/Harvester Wheatsheaf. Chapter 13 of this book provides a very full account of research into prosocial behaviour, including some applied situations such as cheating in examinations, reporting shoplifters and the prevention of crime.

Malim, T., Birch, A. and Hayward, S. (1996). *Comparative Psychology*. Basingstoke: Macmillan. Chapter 1 of this book contains a discussion of altruism and selfishness from an ethological viewpoint. Chapter 2 discusses aggression from a similar standpoint.

CHAPTER 27

Attitudes

The nature and functions of attitudes   648
- Functions of attitudes   649
- Attitudes and behaviour   650
- Attitude formation   653
- Balance theory   654
- Cognitive dissonance theory   655

Measurement of attitudes   659
- Likert scales   659
- Thurstone's scale of attitude measurement   659
- Osgood's semantic differential   660
- Bogardus's social distance scale   660
- Unobtrusive measures of attitudes   660

- Bogus pipeline technique   661
- Expectancy-value technique   661

Prejudice and discrimination   662
- Definitions of prejudice and discrimination   662
- Sexism   663
- Racism   664
- Ageism   665
- Other forms of prejudice   665
- How do prejudice and discrimination manifest themselves?   666
- Causes of prejudice   666
- The reduction of prejudice and discrimination   671

Objectives

By the end of this chapter you should be able to:

- Define what is meant by attitudes and identify the three components of an attitude;

- Describe some theoretical models of attitudes including Pratkanis and Greenwald's socio-cognitive model and Ajzen's theory of planned behaviour;

- Identify some theories which relate to the formation of attitudes, including conditioning and cognitive theories;

- Describe some theories relating to changing attitudes, including balance and cognitive dissonance theories.

- Describe and evaluate attempts which have been made to measure attitudes;

- Identify some of the bases for prejudice and discrimination;

- List some of the emphases which have been adopted in the study of prejudice;

- List some of the ways in which prejudice and discrimination might be reduced.

The nature and function of attitudes

Since Allport (1935) referred to attitudes as the most indispensable concept in social psychology, the study of them has remained central. According to him an attitude is 'a mental and neural state of readiness, organized through experience, exerting a directive and dynamic influence upon the individual's response to all objects and situations with which it is related' (Allport, 1935, p. 810).

McGuire (1989) has linked attitudes to a tripartite view of human experience which has ancient roots in philosophy:

> The trichotomy of human experience into thought, feeling and action, although not logically compelling, is so compelling in Indo-European thought (being found in Hellenic, Zoroastrian and Hindu philosophy) as to suggest that it corresponds to something basic in our way of conceptualization, perhaps . . . reflecting three evolutionary layers of the brain, cerebral cortex, limbic sytem and old brain.
>
> (McGuire, 1989, p. 40)

Thus attitudes are widely held to have three components (Figure 27.1):

- **Cognitive**, which includes perceptions of objects and events or reports or beliefs about them: for example, the belief that to live by a main road is likely to be noisy and dangerous.
- **Affective**, which includes feelings about and emotional responses to objects and events. For example, I may be continually worried and fearful about the effect that living on a main road is going to have on my family.
- **Behavioural or conative** components. This concerns intentions and predicts the way in which an individual may behave in relation to an object or event. For example, 'I am going to sell my house because I do not want to go on living on a main road'.

This three-component model has had wide acceptance, but more recently doubt has been cast upon the behavioural component. It is hard to see how knowing someone's attitude towards something may realistically help us to predict his or her behaviour. Ajzen (1988) has suggested that people do not always behave in ways which are consistent with their attitudes. They may, for instance, be faced with conflicts between contradictory attitudes.

Functions of attitudes

Attitudes function in much the same way as schemata or scripts. They represent packaged and memorized responses to people, events and situations, short cuts to the necessity of working out each time how we should

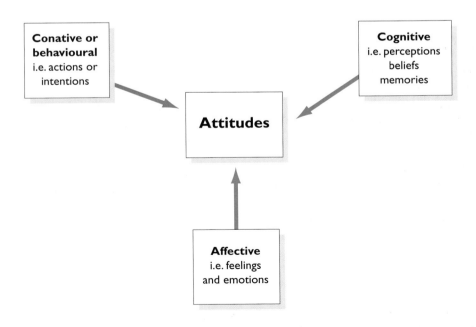

Figure 27.1 Three components of attitudes: cognitive, affective and conative

respond. We no longer have to figure out from scratch how we should relate to objects, events and situations each time we come across them.

Fazio (1989) has suggested that one of the main functions of attitudes is to facilitate evaluation of objects. If I have a hostile attitude towards abortion, for example, it enables me to come to an instant appraisal of someone who is intending to undergo an abortion, without the necessity for a full appraisal of all the facts of the case. This may or may not be a good thing.

A sociocognitive model of attitude function

Pratkanis and Greenwald (1989) have developed their sociocognitive model of attitude structure. This might be described as a definition of attitude structure which draws upon ideas from social cognition. You will remember that social cognition centres around the storing in memory of social experiences which may be drawn upon at a later time to facilitate responses to particular situations (see Chapter 22). In Pratkanis and Greenwald's model, the object, person or event towards which you have a particular attitude is represented in memory by three elements:

■ **A label** for that object, person or event together with rules for applying that label;
■ **An evaluation or appraisal** of the object, person or event;
■ **A knowledge structure** to support that appraisal: that is to say, a cognitive basis for it.

The most important element in this is appraisal. It has to be borne in mind that there are two elements in evaluation. Breckler and Wiggins (1989a, 1989b) have made some attempt to clarify the distinction between these two elements:

■ **The emotional reaction** to the object,
■ **Thoughts, beliefs and judgments** made about the object.

While the first of these two elements is clearly in the affective domain and relates to emotional responses (the second of the three components of attitudes mentioned above), the second is cognitive, relating to knowledge and thought. The behavioural component is not dealt with in their model. This omission is discussed below. Figure 27.2 represents Pratkanis and Greenwald's model.

An information-processing approach to attitudes

Anderson (1971, 1980) stresses that we receive information about objects, people and events and as a result of that information attitudes are formed. The nature of the attitudes we form depends upon the way in which this information is received and combined. Some items of information will be received before others; some items will receive more emphasis than others. The importance that is attached to different pieces of information, and the order in which they are received, will materially affect the formation of attitudes. We receive all the information as it comes in, make an evaluation of it and then combine it with what is already stored. Anderson complicates this somewhat by the suggestion that individuals assemble a number of items of information, attach values to them and take the average of these values in order to form attitudes.

Attitudes and behaviour

It is important to note that neither Pratkanis and Greenwald nor Anderson have dealt with the third component we mentioned, the behavioural element. The problem of trying to predict how people will behave by measuring attitudes in some way (measurement of attitudes will be dealt with in the next section) is full of pitfalls. La Pière (1934) conducted a classic study into the relationship between attitudes and behaviour. He was interested in attitudes towards the Chinese, and in particular towards two Chinese friends of his. Travelling right across America with his Chinese friends they visited 66 hotels, autocamps and tourist homes as well as 184 restaurants and were only refused service once. Six months later he sent a questionnaire to all the places they had visited, asking 'Will you accept members of the Chinese race as guests in your establishment?' The replies he received indicated that 92 per cent would not accept Chinese customers.

This study has stimulated a huge amount of research into the relationship between attitudes and behaviour. In particular, Ajzen and Fishbein (1980) have argued that what La Pière and others were doing was to attempt to predict *specific* behaviour from *general* attitudes: that is, general attitudes towards Chinese people and specific attitudes towards these two specific Chinese on these particular occasions. As a result they developed their theory of reasoned action (Fishbein and Ajzen, 1974; Ajzen and Fishbein, 1980).

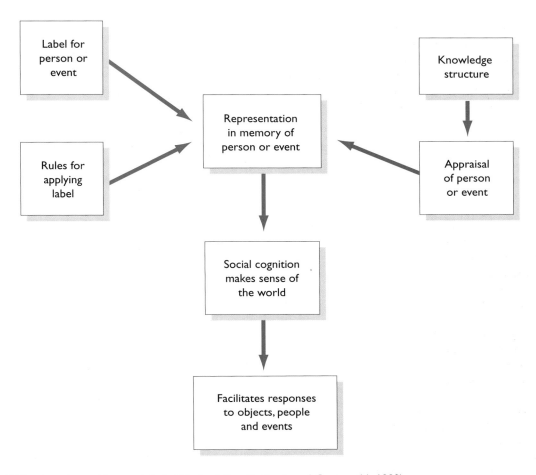

Figure 27.2 A sociocognitive model of attitudes (after Pratkanis and Greenwald, 1989)

Theory of reasoned action

Ajzen and Fishbein's model contains the following components:

- **Subjective norm**. This is a guide to what is considered to be the 'proper thing to do'. It is arrived at by means of a perception of what 'significant others' believe.
- **Attitude**. For example, 'I do not like to serve Chinese people'.
- **Behavioural intention**. This amounts to a decision taken internally not to serve Chinese people.
- **Behaviour (in a specific case)**. What actually happened.

A specific action will be performed if:

- The attitude is favourable:
- The social norm is favourable: people who are important to you approve your action.
- Perceived behavioural control is at a high level: that is, you perceive that there is a high degree of freedom to choose how to behave in a specific set of circumstances.

Theory of planned behaviour

The third element in this model, conscious behavioural control, has assumed paramount importance in Ajzen's (1989) extension of it. This involves the extent to which it is easy or difficult to perform the action. This extension Ajzen referred to as a theory of planned behaviour. An example might help to make this clearer.

Example to illustrate the theory of planned behaviour A student has a favourable attitude towards the examination; the attitudes which 'significant others' (parents, teachers and peers) take towards the examination are favourable; perceived behavioural control is determined by his or her ability in relation to the task, how good the teaching and preparation for the exam is and perhaps the content of the actual paper, things which he or she perceives as being only partially within his or her control. Behaviour (passing the exam) and attitude are therefore only conditionally related. If he or she gets in with a group of ne'er-do-wells (the social norm is not favourable), if it transpires that his or her ability does not match up to the task or if the teaching

is poor then behavioural intention will not be closely linked to outcome. Figure 27.3 illustrates how these factors are related in this model.

Exercise 27.1

Put yourself in this position. You are a young person thinking of buying your first car. Taking Ajzen's theory of planned behaviour into consideration, detail the factors you bear in mind before you come to a positive attitude towards buying the car. How are attitudes (to having a car) and behaviour (the decision to buy one) related?

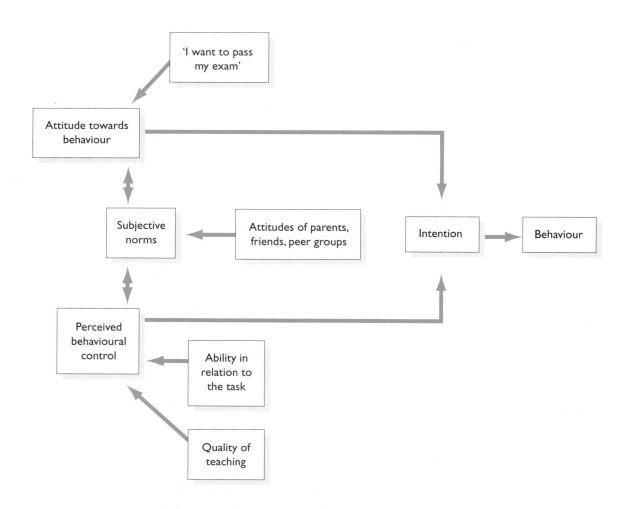

Figure 27.3 Theory of planned behaviour (Ajzen, 1989)

Other factors linking attitudes to behaviour

Other factors which may influence the relationship between an attitude and a person's behaviour include accessibility (how easily an attitude is called to mind (Fazio, 1986); strength of attitude (Fazio et al., 1986) (claims that only a strong attitude may be automatically translated into action), personality and situational variables.

Attitude formation

Means whereby individuals form attitudes include the following:

- Direct experience,
- Classical conditioning,
- Instrumental (operant) conditioning,
- Observational learning and modelling,
- Cognitive development.

Direct experience

In a great many instances the attitudes we hold are the result of direct experience of the object of the attitude. It might be the result of a traumatic event or of direct exposure. Stroebe et al. (1988) focused upon changes in attitudes which resulted from student exchanges with foreign countries. Fishbein and Ajzen (1975) have suggested that these kinds of changes result from the information gained about the attitude object which leads to beliefs and then influences the extent of our liking or disliking the object.

Mere exposure effect Zajonc (1968) has identified a mere exposure effect. The number of times you meet an attitude object will affect the evaluation you make of it. Repeated exposure strengthens the response you make to something or someone, whether that is a dish you have in a restaurant or a member of parliament (MP) standing for election. This gives a sitting MP, a familiar dish, or a place you know well from many visits to it, an advantage over the unfamiliar or the new. It may, of course, work in either direction. Familiarity or exposure may equally strengthen negative as well as positive attitudes. When Margaret Thatcher became Prime Minister the level of exposure to her on the media was such that attitudes to her became polarized. You either adored her or abhorred her.

Classical conditioning

Under classical conditioning a repeated association between one stimulus and another may cause a previously neutral stimulus to elicit a reaction which was previously confined to another, nonneutral stimulus (see Chapter 6). For instance, you may form a romantic attachment with someone who is passionately fond of curries, to which you had been indifferent. Every occasion on which you go out with this person you go to a curry house. An association is formed between this individual and curry. Your liking for the individual is transferred to a liking for curry so that even when you are with someone else you will tend to choose curry. This might be said to be an extension of Zajonc's mere exposure effect or perhaps an explanation of it. To take another example, you grow up with great respect and fondness for your father who happens to be an ardent socialist. Long association may cause you to have similar positive attitudes towards socialism as he has. Figure 27.4 illustrates how this process might work.

Instrumental/operant conditioning

This is a second form of associative learning of attitudes. To put it at its simplest, responses which are reinforced (that is, followed by favourable outcomes)

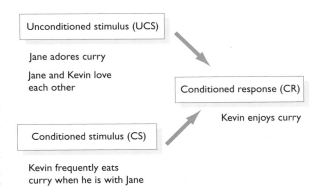

Figure 27.4 Classical conditioning of attitudes

GLOSSARY

Mere exposure effect Zajonc's contention that the amount of a person's exposure to an attitude object will have an effect upon his or her attitude to it.

are strengthened, those that are not reinforced tend to die away. Parents use this form of conditioning to form the attitudes of their children. They try to ensure that acceptable behaviour, children's cooperation with their siblings, for instance, wins praise; conflict and fighting with them does not. Hence a negative attitude is formed towards fighting and a positive one towards peaceful cooperation. Figure 27.5 illustrates this process. Operant conditioning is fully discussed in Chapter 6.

Observational learning or modelling

The work of Bandura (1973) has already been discussed in other contexts. Suppose that you had a very happy childhood with your mother staying at home full-time to devote her time to the family. You have modelled your positive attitude to mothers staying at home on the successful outcome you experienced. Observational learning and modelling is also discussed in Chapter 6. Figure 27.6 illustrates this.

Cognitive development of attitudes

Cognitive approaches to formation and changing of attitudes give weight less to the external outcomes or reinforcements associated with a particular attitude and more with what is going on internally, in the mind. Heider's **balance theory** or Festinger's concept of **cognitive dissonance** are instances.

Balance theory

Balance theory stems from Heider (1946). It is concerned with the balance between three elements which form a triad:

■ a person (P),
■ another person (X),
■ an attitude object (O).

Balanced and unbalanced states

These triads may be either 'balanced' or 'unbalanced'. The relationships between the elements may be positive (+) or negative (−). A 'balanced' state exists when there are either three positive relationships or when there are two negatives and a positive, as in Figure 27.7.

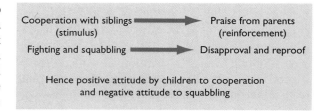

Figure 27.5 Operant conditioning of attitudes

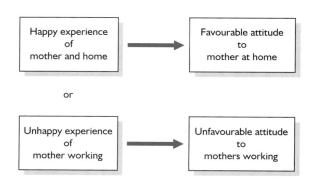

Figure 27.6 Observational learning/modelling of attitudes

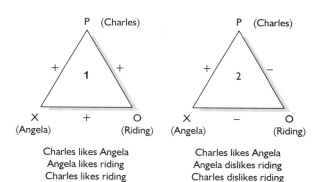

Figure 27.7 An illustration of Heider's balance theory (balanced states)

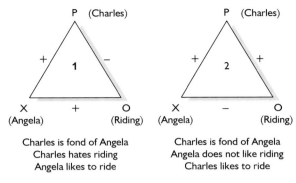

Charles is fond of Angela
Charles hates riding
Angela likes to ride

Charles is fond of Angela
Angela does not like riding
Charles likes to ride

Figure 27.8 An illustration of Heider's balance theory (unbalanced states)

Other combinations are unbalanced, as in Figure 27.8.

Heider suggested that where unbalanced states occur there is tension. Wherever there is an odd number of negative relationships there is an unbalanced relationship. Forces are likely to build up to restore balance. For instance, Charles may try to (or profess to) overcome his dislike of riding in 1, or may give up riding in 2. The tensions are thus resolved.

Balance theory in action: an example

Heider's balance theory has been used to explain the way in which people vote in elections. People try to achieve a balance between:

- their attitude towards an issue,
- their attitude towards a candidate,
- the candidate's attitude towards an issue.

If there was a balanced relationship they would be more likely to vote for the candidate. For instance, if an individual felt that a particular politician held a positive attitude towards European integration and he or she liked the politician, the voters would be likely to vote for that politician if he or she had a positive attitude towards European integration.

Cognitive dissonance theory

A second theory relating to consistency in attitudes is cognitive dissonance theory. This was proposed by Festinger in 1957. Cognitive dissonance exists when there is a conflict between two related cognitions (thoughts, beliefs or attitudes). This might also include

behaviour. For example, if an individual was a member of a church which was strongly committed to Sunday observance, that is to say, it was opposed to anyone working on Sundays and in particular to shops opening and was personally committed to these views, there might be dissonance if circumstances (the arrival of an unexpected guest, for example) made it necessary for him or her to purchase provisions at the supermarket on Sunday morning. Attitudes to Sunday observance are at odds with behaviour and this is uncomfortable. Festinger talks about cognitive elements which may be:

- consonant,
- dissonant,
- irrelevant.

Figure 27.9 illustrates the concept.

The size of the conflict (and therefore of the tension it produces) is related to:

- **The importance** to the person of the elements.
- **The ratio** of consonant to dissonant elements. The greater the number of dissonant elements the greater the dissonance.
- **The amount of cognitive overlap**. The less two events have in common the greater the potential dissonance. For example, a choice between going to the theatre and going fishing would create greater dissonance than one between the theatre and the cinema.

Motivation to change

The importance of this theory is that dissonance is uncomfortable, so that there is motivation to alter one or more of the elements in order to restore consonance between the elements. An extension of the basic idea is the notion of forced compliance. The suggestion is that pressure of some kind to adopt a public attitude which is at odds with another thought, belief or behaviour will reduce the amount of the dissonance and so of the discomfort that results.

Box 27.1 shows details of a classic experiment by Festinger and Carlsmith (1959) which aims to test this notion.

A debate about Festinger and Carlsmith's experiment

This evident exception to what has become a very basic rule of learning, that the stronger the reinforcement,

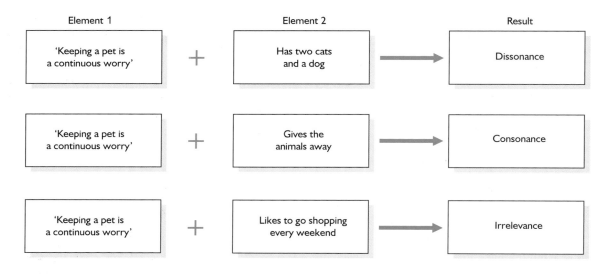

Figure 27.9 Examples of cognitive dissonance (Festinger, 1957)

Festinger and Carlsmith (1959) paid participants either a small amount of money ($1) or a larger amount ($20) to promote publicly a position which they did not hold privately. After being asked to spend a long period on a very boring and meaningless task they were paid to represent it to other potential participants as interesting and very worthwhile. Those who were paid the larger sum altered their *private* opinion of the task much less than did the group who had received only $1. Presumably, the larger sum of money was sufficient to justify their behaviour, lying to the other participants; those who were offered only a trifling sum had to find some other justification and this was that they really did find the boring task interesting and worthwhile. It was clear that there might be circumstances where a smaller reward produced a larger attitude change. This runs quite counter to the accepted laws of reinforcement that a greater reward will produce a greater change in behaviour.

attitudes are determined from behaviour. We are aware of what we are doing and so get to 'know our own attitudes, emotions and other internal states . . . partially by inferring them from observations . . . of overt behaviour' (Bem, 1972). Bem described Festinger and Carlsmith's study to participants in a study of his and asked them to predict the results. Their predictions were not unlike the results of the original experiment; $1 was not enough money to persuade someone to lie, so that participants had looked back at the experiment and decided that they had enjoyed it. After all they had *said* they had enjoyed it.

The controversy between Festinger on the one side and Bem on the other raged for some considerable time, with each side mustering empirical support. Finally, the debate ended with a review of the research by Fazio et al. (1977) which concluded that there was right on both sides. It all depended how great the discrepancy was between attitudes and behaviour. In most ordinary situations where the discrepancy was fairly small, Bem's self-perception theory was right, but where the discrepancy was very large Festinger's dissonance theory provided the better explanation.

A review of the evidence A further review of the research on dissonance by Cooper and Fazio (1984) led them to state that dissonance arousal depends upon two criteria: aversive consequences and personal responsibility.

the greater the change in behaviour will be, has been challenged by Bem (1967, 1972). Bem's self-perception theory, described in Chapter 24, proposed that

The consequences of the behaviour must be aversive. That is to say, it has to result in an event that runs counter to self-interest; as Cooper and Fazio say, 'an event that one would rather not have occur'. For example, in the instance mentioned above, you are on your way to the supermarket on Sunday morning, already uncomfortable because you are doing something which is contrary to your beliefs, and you meet the pastor of your church.

There has also to be an assumption of personal responsibility. A person has to attribute the event to some personal internal factor. You feel personally responsible for not having made adequate provision for the possibility of someone coming to lunch. This is most likely to occur when the individual has some choice in the matter and can foresee the consequences.

When these two criteria are met, dissonance may be aroused, provided that the behaviour involved is not inconsistent with an individual's self-concept (Scher and Cooper, 1989). In very nearly every case where attitude change has resulted from dissonance reduction, Steele (1988) argues that behaviour is involved which is inconsistent with a person's self-concept. When there is a threat to your self-concept from behaviour you perceive yourself to be engaged in, lying to someone else, for instance, acting in a foolish way or arguing against your own self-interest, there are really only two alternatives:

- to change your self-concept, which is not likely to happen, or
- to change your attitudes to make them more consistent with the behaviour you are engaged in.

Self-affirmation

Thus we have seen members of government who see themselves as honourable men and who certainly would not conceive themselves to be liars, justifying telling less than the truth (it has been termed 'being economical with the truth'). They have not altered their concept of themselves as honourable men who would not lie, but they have altered their attitude to truth. This attitude change occurs as a result of **self-affirmation**. They have responded to a threat to their self-esteem by enhancing some other aspect of the self-concept, perhaps a concern for security. It has to be borne in mind that the conclusions Steele has come to were arrived at in a laboratory setting. This might not be the

same as what would happen 'in real life'. He provided alternative means for self-affirmation where participants found themselves engaged in activities inconsistent with their attitudes by, for instance, completing questionnaires about values. Figure 27.10 provides as an algorithm, an updated version of cognitive dissonance theory, incorporating the modifications of Cooper and Fazio and of Steele.

"SPEED, A QUICK START, COMFORTABLE SUSPENSION — EVERYTHING PROVES IT'S MUCH BETTER THAN THE ONE I *NEARLY* BOUGHT!"

Postdecisional dissonance

When you make a decision – perhaps an agonizing one between alternatives of nearly equal attractiveness – dissonance is likely to arise beween your attitude to the nonchosen alternative and your behaviour in choosing the other one.

GLOSSARY

Self-affirmation The response to a threat to a person's self-concept as a result of cognitive dissonance, involving enhancing some aspect of the self-concept.

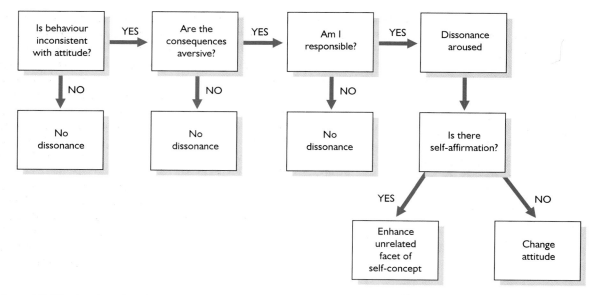

Figure 27.10 An algorithm that updates cognitive dissonance theory, incorporating the work of Cooper and Fazio (1984) and Steele (1988)

Box 27.2 shows details of an experiment by Knox and Inkster (1968) into **postdecisional dissonance**.

You go into a car showroom in a state of ambivalence about the merits of two models of car. Finally, you make up your mind to select one of them, which stirs up dissonance. This is uncomfortable so that attempts are made to reduce it. Emphasis is placed on the good points of the one chosen, while highlighting the disadvantages of the other. This process will even go so

---

Box 27.2 Postdecisional dissonance. An experiment by Knox and Inkster

Knox and Inkster (1968) went to a racecourse in Vancouver to interview those waiting to place their bets. Most admitted not being very confident that the horse they had chosen would win. However, interviewed again after they had placed their bets, they were much more certain that their choice was the right one. The suggestion was that the act of deciding upon one horse rather than another created dissonance which motivated people to alter their attitudes, not only to the chosen horse but also to the nonchosen one. By boosting the merits of the chosen option, dissonance is reduced and reduced still more by downgrading the other choice.

SELF-ASSESSMENT QUESTIONS

1. Identify the components of an attitude. Why is it true to say that the link between attitude and behaviour is a fragile one?

2. List some of the ways in which attitudes are formed. Which of these seems to you to be the most convincing?

3. Describe what is meant by balance in relationship to attitudes. How does imbalance generate attitude change?

4. Cognitive dissonance theory has been influential in explaining some of the ways in which attitudes may change. What are the important elements of dissonance theory? Identify some of the practical implications.

5. List some of the ways in which dissonance theory has been updated since Festinger's original formulation of it.

GLOSSARY

Postdecisional dissonance Dissonance which arises after a person has made a decision. It may be reduced by enhancing the positive aspects of the decision taken.

far as **selective exposure**. You seek out information which supports your choice and avoid information which does the opposite.

Measurement of attitudes

It is not an easy thing to measure attitudes. They are not directly observable. There is not even a very clear relationship, as we have seen, between attitudes and behaviour or between what is measured and what happens in real life. However, because they are so central to social psychology and have been central for so long, techniques have been developed to measure them. They are related to one or other of the components of attitudes which have been discussed earlier.

Likert scales

To measure the cognitive component of attitudes, rating scales have been developed. Perhaps the most well known and widely used of these are **Likert scales** (Likert, 1932). A number of statements are produced relating to the attitude in question and respondents are asked to indicate the extent of their agreement or disagreement with each statement. Supposing, for example, that you wanted to measure the attitudes of a sample of people to the use of nuclear power to generate electricity. You might produce statements such as:

1. *Nuclear power stations are potentially very dangerous both to those who work in them and also to the neighbourhood in which they are located.*
2. *Nuclear energy is a safe, cheap, inexhaustible and nonpolluting means of generating power.*
3. *The cost of decommissioning nuclear power stations represents a massive burden, not only on the present generation, but also on their children and grandchildren.*
4. *The damage to the environment through global warming and the destruction of the ozone layer is much less using nuclear energy than fossil fuels.*

and invite participants to say whether they:

strongly disagree	1
disagree	2
undecided	3
agree	4
strongly agree	5

The numbers alongside would not, of course, be included in what was presented to the respondents but would be used to attach a numerical value to responses; in this case the highest numerical value represents the strongest unfavourable attitude towards nuclear power.

As you can see, the statements are balanced, half in favour of nuclear energy, half against, and the scoring of responses is done accordingly, so that 'strongly disagree' would be scored 5 on statement 2 and so on. The maximum unfavourable attitude score would be arrived at by endorsing 'strongly agree' on statements 1 and 3 and 'strongly disagree' on statements 2 and 4. This balancing is done to avoid **acquiescence response set**, a tendency simply to agree with all the items. Responses to some statements correlate less well with the total for perhaps 20 items than others and these can be dropped and replaced by statements, where the responses correlate more highly (i.e. which are more effective measures of the attitude concerned).

Thurstone's scale of attitude measurement

This also attempts to measure the cognitive component. Thurstone assembled 130 statements representing favourable and unfavourable attitudes. These statements were then given to a large number of judges to arrange them in 11 categories labelled A to K. F represented a neutral position. The 20 statements which had the greatest agreement from the judges constituted the final scale. Each was given a value, arrived at by averaging all the judges' ratings. Participants were presented with the statements in a random order and asked to indicate those with which they agreed. The numerical values attached to these statements were then averaged and a measure of the participant's attitude was thus obtained.

An evaluation of Thurstone's scale

■ **Its cumbersome nature**. Large numbers of judges have to rate vast numbers of attitudinal statements.

GLOSSARY

Selective exposure In cases of postdecisional dissonance a person may reduce dissonance by seeking out evidence which supports the decision taken.

Likert scale A method of attitude measurement involving the construction of a number of attitude statements with which respondents had to agree or disagree.

Acquiescence response set A tendency in attitude measurement scales for respondents to agree with all items indiscriminately.

■ **Ambiguity.** It is quite possible for two participants to end up with identical attitude scores, even though they had each endorsed a completely different set of statements.

■ **Subjectivity.** There was much subjectivity. The values attached to the statements depended on the particular judges used. Thurstone himself contended that objectivity would come from the sorting process, but a study by Hovland and Sherif (1952) did not support this. They found a definite bias in the way in which black judges or those who were sympathetic to black people sorted statements as compared to those who were unsympathetic to black people.

■ **Level of measurement.** Finally, Thurstone assumed that the data obtained from this procedure were interval scale data (the assumption was made that a score of 6, for instance, was twice as favourable as a score of 3). In fact, because the judges are not totally objective we have only an ordinal scale of measurement, that is, putting participants into a rank order. Chapter 35 contains a full discussion of levels of measurement.

Osgood's semantic differential

The **semantic differential** (Osgood et al., 1957) focuses upon the affective component of attitudes, the emotion or feeling attached to a word or concept. The focus of the attitude is rated on a seven-point bipolar scale. Pairs of adjectives are produced, as shown in Figure 27.11.

The respondent places an X at a point on the seven-point scale. Three dimensions are represented by the pairs of adjectives chosen: evaluation (good, clean), potency (strong) and activity (active, fast). This approach does have the advantage that the researcher does not have to make up a series of statements, but can use a fairly standard set of adjectives. It yields a great deal of information and is generally reliable, but does demand careful analysis.

Bogardus's social distance scale

Bogardus's scale (1925) was an early attempt to measure attitudes from behaviour. It is based upon the degree of intimacy with which respondents feel comfortable in contacts with other racial or social groups. Statements such as:

Figure 27.11 Osgood's semantic differential: an example of pairs of adjectives that might be used

	1	2	3	4	5	6	7	
Fair	-	-	-	-	-	-	-	Unfair
Large	-	-	-	-	-	-	-	Small
Bad	-	-	-	-	-	-	-	Good
Clean	-	-	-	-	-	-	-	Dirty
Valuable	-	-	-	-	-	-	-	Worthless
Weak	-	-	-	-	-	-	-	Strong
Active	-	-	-	-	-	-	-	Passive
Cold	-	-	-	-	-	-	-	Hot
Fast	-	-	-	-	-	-	-	Slow

■ *I would accept these people to close kinship through marriage,*
■ *I would accept these people as visitors only to my country,*
■ *I would exclude these people from my country,*

are taken as indications of attitude to members of other races or social groups and are assigned numerical values to provide an attitude measure. This technique is obviously quite limited in application, though Triandis (1971) has used it to measure attitudes to religion and race.

Unobtrusive measures of attitudes

Webb et al. (1969) suggested that attitudes might be inferred from watching what people do, from archival records and from physical traces. For instance, it might be possible to count the number of noseprints on a museum display case to determine the attitude of the visitors to that particular display and measure the height of the noseprints to give some indication of the ages of the interested visitors. By examining the changes in roles played by male and female characters

---

GLOSSARY

Semantic differential A method of measuring the affective component of attitudes devised by Osgood.

in children's books, changes in sex role attitudes might be inferred. The kinds of books people borrow from libraries are another source of information about people's attitudes. After the introduction of TV more nonfiction books were borrowed but fewer fiction, indicating a change in people's attitudes to books. A successful television version of a book, *Middlemarch*, for instance, or *Pride and Prejudice*, might increase the popularity of the book from which the adaptation came as evidenced from demands to borrow from the library. The way in which people seat themselves in a room can also be an index of attitudes. When there is good feeling between people they will tend to sit closer together.

Bogus pipeline technique

There have been attempts to get over the reluctance of people to reveal their true feelings, which has made it hard to measure attitudes. Jones and Sigall (1971) introduced what has become known as a **bogus pipeline technique** to overcome this problem. Participants in their studies were connected to a machine resembling a lie detector and were told that the machine could measure the strength and direction of their true attitudes so that there was no point in lying. Cialdini et al. (1981) successfully used the technique in investigating cognitive dissonance. They were attempting to ascertain whether the attitudes they reported were genuine or whether they reflected impression management: that is to say, attempts to appear to others to be consistent.

Expectancy-value technique

It was noted earlier (p. 651) that Fishbein and Ajzen had debated the relationship between attitudes and behaviour and had arrived at what they termed a theory of planned behaviour. They suggested that attitudes and behaviour might be linked more closely if there was an evaluative as well as a belief component. Fishbein developed an **expectancy-value technique** for measuring attitudes which incorporated this. He combined a rating scale with a scale of evaluation. For instance, in investigating attitudes towards the use of nuclear energy for power generation he might instruct participants to rate nuclear power stations with the instruction: 'Rate the degree to which you believe the following statements to be true or untrue' (0 = not true at all, 10 = absolutely true):

Nuclear power stations are:

	0	1	2	3	4	5	6	7	8	9	10
safe	□	□	□	□	□	□	□	□	□	□	□
economical	□	□	□	□	□	□	□	□	□	□	□
sustainable	□	□	□	□	□	□	□	□	□	□	□
environmentally unfriendly	□	□	□	□	□	□	□	□	□	□	□

'Now rate the value you place upon each of the attributes' (−10 = extremely undesirable, 0 = neutral, +10 = extremely desirable):

safe	−10	0	+10
expensive	−10	0	+10
sustainable	−10	0	+10
environmentally unfriendly	−10	0	+10

The strength of the belief can then be combined with the value attached to provide a numerical value for the attitude strength.

Exercise 27.2

Canvass attitudes to a prominent issue of the day. First, use a Likert scale technique, devising six pro and six anti statements, and then approach ten people, to indicate their degree of agreement/disagreement. Then employ Fishbein and Ajzen's 'expectancy-value technique' to measure the same set of attitudes by the same people. Compare the results.

The measurement of attitudes is difficult. The approaches used have been linked to the components of attitudes and this is part of the problem. It is hard to separate cognitive from affective components or either of these from the behavioural aspect. There is little

GLOSSARY

Bogus pipeline technique The technique adopted by Cialdini and others of connecting respondents to attitude tests to what appeared to be a lie detector so that they would believe there was no point in answering other than truthfully.

Expectancy-value technique A method of attitude measurement devised by Fishbein and Ajzen, incorporating a value rating scale with more conventional Likert-type statements of attitude.

certainty that holding a particular attitude is inevitably linked to a particular sort of behaviour. In addition there is a problem of interpretation. The assumption is frequently made that everyone will interpret the question in the same way. This is not always the case. Nevertheless, it remains a worthwhile enterprise to make the attempt, because so many of the choices we make in everyday life are linked to the attitudes we adopt.

? SELF-ASSESSMENT QUESTIONS

1. Describe the measurement of attitudes by means of a Likert scale. Which component of attitudes does this measure?

2. What measures have been adopted to attempt to measure the behavioural component of attitudes? What do you think are the limitations of these attempts?

3. Do you feel that the Fishbein expectancy-value scale solves the problem of the fairly tenuous link between behaviour and attitude?

Prejudice and discrimination

Definitions of prejudice and discrimination

Prejudice refers to the making of assumptions about people's characteristics (usually to their detriment) on the basis of the identification of a salient characteristic and behaving in accordance with these assumptions. For instance, a Bosnian Serb might identify someone as being a Muslim and immediately characterize that individual as being asssociated with a supposed Islamic threat to take over their country. Discrimination follows from this and implies that simply on the basis of an identification made, an individual is treated differently from the way in which someone not so identified might be treated. Behaviour such as that known as ethnic cleansing might well follow. An employer might, for instance, have a prejudiced view of the abilities and commitment of members of ethnic minorities. In evaluating the abilities and experience of applicants for a job it may be assumed that members of an ethnic group would not be suitable so that once identified they are ruled out of contention.

While most people would consider prejudiced behaviour and discrimination unacceptable behaviour – indeed, it is used as a term of abuse to call someone bigoted – nevertheless prejudice is extremely pervasive. It is a part of the social cognitive structure of each individual that experience and learning has built up in us which allows us to take short cuts in our judgments about people and things.

It is usual to consider prejudice to be an attitude towards a particular set of people, objects or events. Allport (1958) has said that attitudes have three component parts:

■ **Cognitive**. This amounts to a set of beliefs about the object of prejudice;
■ **Affective**. Feelings or emotions related to the person or object in question;
■ **Conative**. Intentions to behave in a particular way towards the person or object.

In more general terms, prejudice refers to *negative* emotional responses to particular people and the consequent intolerant, unfair and unfavourable attitudes towards them. We have already considered stereotyping (Chapter 24) which consists of assigning a range of characteristics (usually negative) to a group as a whole. Once an individual has been identified as belonging to that group it is assumed that he or she possesses these characteristics.

Devine (1989) has shown that the primary difference between prejudiced and unprejudiced people may rest in the way in which unprejudiced people are able to inhibit or to disregard negative stereotypical beliefs. Where a stereotypical belief exists, it will be spontaneously triggered upon identification of a member of the group which is the subject of the stereotypical belief. Elimination of stereotypical beliefs is likely to be a difficult and protracted process, but conscious control may allow people to inhibit or disregard negative beliefs, so that prejudiced behaviour does not occur (see Figure 27.12).

Note that in this model there are two stages:

■ The unconscious stage, where identification triggers the existing stereotype.
■ The consciously controlled stage, where a nonprejudiced person may inhibit prejudiced beliefs to prevent a prejudiced response, while a prejudiced person will allow these beliefs to be transferred into responses.

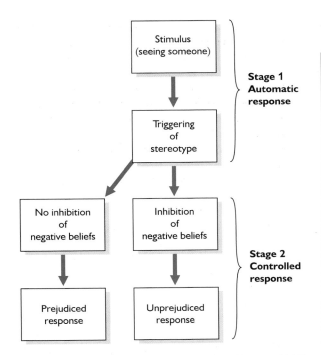

Figure 27.12 Devine's model of prejudice (Devine, 1989)

There are a number of specific manifestations of prejudiced behaviour, including sexism, racism and ageism, and we shall deal with each of these separately.

Sexism

Sexism refers to prejudiced behaviour towards one sex, most usually prejudiced behaviour by men towards women. There is a widespread belief that men are more competent and independent, while women are warmer and more expressive. These stereotyped beliefs are attested by Broverman et al. (1972) and Spence et al. (1974). Deaux (1985) has provided evidence that these social stereotypes of men and women are held across a wide cross-section of people in Europe, North and South America, parts of the Middle East and Australia. Box 27.3 shows detail of a study by Broverman et al. (1972).

Why should this be so? Maybe there is some truth in the stereotype, and males and females really do have different personalities. But this does not seem as likely as that males and females have adopted different sex-role behaviours and males who have more power have perpetuated and maintained this role assignment and the differences in characteristics which go with it.

Certain occupations – secretaries, nurses, babysitters and so on – have been designated 'women's work'. Consequently these occupations are less highly valued than occupations such as lawyers, doctors, engineers and accountants in which there have been until fairly recently more men than women. Now that there are an increasing number of women lawyers, doctors and dentists, perhaps this gender role stereotyping will diminish.

Social identity theory

Social identity theory (see Chapter 24) determines how individuals are perceived, not only by others but also by themselves, and what their roles and the appropriate behaviour which goes with those roles will be (Abrams and Hogg, 1990b). Some analysis of the ways in which these gender role categorizations arise in school has been made by Lloyd and Duveen (1992). What was implicit in the personal relationships in the home becomes explicit in school. Registers are divided by sex and boys' names are called first; groups of children tend to be all of one sex or the other, there are boys' toys and games and girls' toys and games as well as 'boyish behaviour' and 'girlish behaviour'. To refer to a girl as a tomboy or to a boy as a cissie is to indicate that they are not behaving according to their gender role stereotype. Forceful, assertive behaviour belongs to boys; submissive behaviour to girls.

Face-ism

Another facet of sexism relates to the different levels of attention paid, particularly by the media, to men and to women. It was noted by Archer et al. (1983) that when males are depicted, prominence is given to the face; on the other hand when females are depicted, the media focus upon the upper body. It is as though women are regarded primarily as decorative objects. This phenomenon was termed face-ism.

A further and rather subtle form of sexism has been described by Ng (1990). When people are being referred to generically, masculine pronouns tend to be used (he, him etc). Similarly sex-role stereotypes are reinforced by the use of words such as 'chairman'. Accordingly, in books such as this we have endeavoured to use nonsexist language. The fact that doing this sometimes makes the language appear clumsy serves to reinforce the fact that sexist language is very firmly entrenched, as though humanity was essentially male and to be female was somehow an aberration. The way in which language is used is important in that it is through language that the world is represented and prejudiced language reflects prejudiced thought. This again is social cognition. Life experience has established patterns of thinking about people which can be hard to change.

Differences regarding success or failure

The way in which success or failure is differentially attributed to men and to women is another manifestation of the way in which people have been programmed to think. Deaux and Emswiller (1974) found that on tasks which traditionally might be regarded as 'male' tasks, success was attributed overwhelmingly to ability or to effort in the case of a man, but to luck or to the fact that it was an easy task in the case of a woman. On traditionally female tasks this difference in attribution did not occur.

There is evidence, however, that efforts to reduce sex stereotyping and sex discrimination have had some effect. In the 1960s, for instance, Goldberg found that identical pieces of work were differently evaluated when attributed to a man as compared with a woman (Goldberg, 1968). A replication of this study done by Swim et al. (1989) found that this differential evaluation was no longer evident.

Racism

In Germany in Hitler's time, Jews were subjected to gross prejudice and discrimination culminating in the Holocaust. More recently in Rwanda, prejudice and discrimination by one tribal group towards another resulted in mass genocide. Similarly, in Bosnia there has been genocide by Serbs against Muslims and Croats and violence by all three groups. Whereas in places such as these, racism has resulted in many deaths and vast numbers of people being displaced from their homes, elsewhere in Western countries laws enacted against discrimination have done something to reduce the more blatant forms of racism. However, it is still widespread in a less blatant or more covert way. Pettigrew (1987) has examined the very pervasive way in which racism persists even among those who have made conscious efforts to resist it. The automatic stereotypical reactions which Devine (1989) reported are hard to eradicate:

> Many Southerners have confessed to me . . . that even though in their minds they no longer feel prejudice towards blacks, they still feel squeamish when they shake hands with a black. These feelings are left over from what they learned in their families as children.
>
> (Pettigrew, 1987, p. 20)

Symbolic racism

This has been termed symbolic racism (Kinder and Sears, 1981) or modern racism. Individuals who hold deep-seated attitudes based upon racial fears and upon stereotypes learned very early in life to express these attitudes in more socially acceptable ways. For instance, schemes established to give preference in awarding public contracts to firms run by and

---

GLOSSARY

Face-ism The emphasis placed in men upon depicting their faces while the emphasis in women is on the upper body. An aspect of sexism.

Symbolic racism A deep-seated form of racism, developed as a result of upbringing, expressed in socially acceptable ways.

employing black workers are opposed on the grounds that they interfere with the free operation of the marketplace. Symbolic racial attitudes have been harder to measure than blatant racism. One technique used involved some of the methods of cognitive psychology. Gaertner and McCloughlin (1983) paired positive and negative descriptive adjectives with racial labels (e.g. black or white) and asked participants to say whether they fitted together. They predicted that where the pairing represents an existing attitude participants would respond more quickly than where the trait is not associated with an existing racial group. There was a tendency for positive adjectives paired with 'white' to be responded to more rapidly than negative adjectives. Similarly when 'black' was paired with negative adjectives there was also a more speedy response.

Ageism

In countries such as the UK, Canada, the USA and in some European countries such as the Netherlands the extended family has to a large extent been replaced by nuclear families. Instead of there being uncles and aunts and grandparents living close at hand and supplementing the support given to children by their parents, in these countries families typically tend to be nuclear; that is, mother, father and children only. Youth tends in these societies to be very highly valued; old age

The system of apartheid, which separated the population of South Africa into blacks, whites and other races for more than 40 years, was a dramatic example of institutionalized racism

is much less highly valued. Increasingly unfavourable stereotypes are being attached to older people. Indeed ageism, as this prejudice against older people may be termed, starts earlier and earlier. In competition for some jobs to be over 40 is now considered to be too old. Brewer et al. (1981) have shown that older people are treated as relatively worthless and powerless members of the community.

Other forms of prejudice

Other focuses of prejudice include homosexuals and people with various kinds of disability. The prejudice which exists against homosexuals can be seen in the refusal by senior officers in the armed services to allow those who have been discovered to be homosexual to continue serving. In the USA, President Clinton faced great opposition to his proposal that there should be no bar to homosexuals serving in the US armed forces. The HIV epidemic and AIDS have focused attention upon homosexuals and there has been some increase in prejudice against them, though in most communities they are not considered deviant and immoral in the way they once were. Oscar Wilde would not have been thrown into Reading gaol had he lived a hundred years later. However, a survey done in the United States in 1974 by Levitt and Klassen did show that a majority of people thought that homosexuals were 'sick'.

Similarly there has been marked change in the level of prejudice against disabled people of all kinds. Once they were regarded as freaks and kept out of sight as a family secret. Hitler's 'Final Solution' embraced not only Jews but mentally ill people as well. There is an island in Greece where mentally handicapped people are incarcerated in appalling conditions. Mentally handicapped children in Romania were found after the fall of the Ceaucescu regime to be living like animals in a bleak castle. Szasz (1967), in his book *The Myth of Mental Illness*, argues that labels are important. If a person is labelled as 'mad', prejudice and discrimination follows. Not until mental illness is treated in exactly the same way as any other illness will this be diminished. Where there is a physical cause then it is just an illness. Where there is not it is just 'a problem of living'.

How do prejudice and discrimination manifest themselves?

Subtle discrimination

As we have seen, blatant prejudice and discrimination against individuals and groups is not common and is often illegal. What is much more common is subtle discrimination. For example, a landlord may turn away a potential tenant on discovering that he or she is black on the pretext that the flat has already been let. In effect discrimination is operating against either women or single parenthood where single mothers cannot find work because the flexible working hours are not available which would allow them to take a job.

Tokenism

Sometimes a trivial movement is made towards helping members of a group which is being discriminated against in order that more meaningful help can be written off as unnecessary. Rosenfield et al. (1982) had participants in their study do a small favour for a black stranger. Subsequently, when asked to participate in more demanding forms of helping they were more reluctant to do so than other people who had not already 'helped'. This is **tokenism**.

Reverse discrimination

Positive (or reverse) discrimination is where a positive step is taken to reverse what is seen to be the results of prejudice. The Labour Party in the UK has taken the step of insisting on all-women shortlists for some of its most winnable seats in Parliament. This step was taken because there was felt to be discrimination against women trying to enter Parliament. It may well have a positive effect in getting more women elected. But Fajardo (1985) has demonstrated that this kind of reverse discrimination can have negative effects as well, particularly on the self-esteem of the individuals on the receiving end. In this study, identical essays attributed to black students were marked more leniently than when they were attributed to white students. Self-esteem was damaged when reality impinged on them. In the same way women elected to Parliament from all-women shortlists might feel that they had somehow got elected too easily, with consequent loss of self-esteem.

Causes of prejudice

Allport (1958), in his book *The Nature of Prejudice*, identified six emphases or approaches to causal theories of prejudice (Chapter 13). These are displayed graphically in Figure 27.13.

- The historical or economic approach,
- The sociocultural approach,
- The situational approach,
- The approach via personality dynamics and structure,
- Phenomenological approach,
- Approach via stimulus object.

Historical/economic approach

Historians have suggested that we cannot properly understand the causes of prejudice without examining

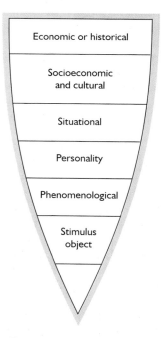

Figure 27.13 Emphases in causal theories of prejudice (after Allport, 1958)

GLOSSARY

Tokenism The token acknowledgment of sexism or racism by means of a trivial gesture so that more meaningful steps may be written off as unnecessary.

the history which surrounds any particular conflict. For example, prejudice against black people in the United States has its roots in slavery. Slave owners in the South of the USA treated their slaves like chattels. The prejudice of Protestants in Northern Ireland towards Catholics stems from what happened when William III of Orange overcame James II at the Battle of the Boyne in 1690. The Protestants then became 'top dogs' in Ireland and identified closely with the Protestant regime in England. These are just two examples but it might be argued that virtually all cases of prejudice have a historical root.

Exploitation theory In many instances the economic circumstances are determinants of the roots of prejudice. Cox (1948) has summarized the exploitation theory of prejudice in these terms:

> Race prejudice is a social attitude propagated among the public by an exploiting class for the purpose of stigmatizing some group as inferior, so that the exploitation of either the group itself or its resources may be justified.
> (Cox, 1948, p. 393)

Prejudice against native populations rose to a peak during the period of European colonial expansion in the nineteenth century, Cox has claimed, because there was need for justification of the way in which indigenous populations were treated. People in colonial territories were variously described as 'inferior', 'requiring protection', belonging to a 'lower form of evolution' or being 'a burden' which the colonialists had to bear altruistically. Sexual and social taboos (for example, 'clubs' for colonialists which native people were not allowed to enter except in the capacity of servants, or a complete ban on intimate relationships) reinforced the inequality. It allowed colonialists to rationalize exploitation – 'Orientals only need a handful of rice a day'; 'Some of these people are so primitive they would not know how to use money if they had it! They would only use it for drink'.

There are flaws in this argument, though. There are many examples of prejudice which do not fit this exploitation theory:

- Jews cannot really be said to be victims of economic exploitation. The cause in this case seems to be jealousy; they were altogether too successful in prospering when others had

economic difficulties (e.g. in Germany in the 1930s).
- Quakers and Mormons were at various times victims of prejudice without being exploited. It was their difference which made them victims.
- Immigrant groups such as the Irish in the USA suffered exploitation but did not suffer the same prejudice as did the Jews and the black population of America. White tenant farmers suffered exploitation as 'sharecroppers'.

Community pattern theory A network of historic hostilities exists in Europe where cities and lands have changed hands. You could cite the hostility of Lithuanians, Latvians and Estonians towards the Russians who came to live among them when the USSR included the Baltic States. The native Baltic people see them as intruders. There is hostility among Poles in Silesia towards the Germans, and among Germans in what was once East Prussia towards the Poles and the Russians. Closer to home, some of the animosity between the two communities in Northern Ireland stems from the fact of settlers from Scotland being brought in and given privileged status over the indigenous population.

Sociocultural emphasis

This is the causal explanation favoured by sociologists and anthropologists. Factors which are cited include:

Urbanization, mechanization and the increasing complexity of life Ill-educated people flocked to the cities, when times were hard on the land: for example, during the depression years in the United States or at the time of the potato famine in Ireland. There they were capable of doing only menial work. At the same time, advertising encouraged a desire for more goods and more luxury. The poor were not able to reach the standard of material possessions which was considered the norm. They were therefore treated with contempt.

Materialism in the city 'We hate the city and its materialist values'. These are personified in dislike of those who have done well; those who may be dishonest, sneaky, too clever by half, vulgar and noisy. Jews have received opprobrium as the symbol of all that is hated in the city; hence anti-semitism.

Upward mobility of certain groups There are feelings of condescension towards those who have not 'made the grade'.

Increases in population coupled with limitations on housing and available usable land It was the clamour for *Lebensraum* which led to Hitler's rise.

Inability among many people to develop their own standards internally They relied for leadership upon others and conformed to the behaviour of these others (for example, in Nazi Germany).

The role and function of the family changed and also the standard of morality altered There is prejudice in some British cities against immigrants from Asia or the Caribbean because their family values and patterns of living are not the same as those of the original population: for example, Asian girls coming to school wearing shalwars under their skirts or being sent back to India, Pakistan or Bangladesh for an arranged marriage; West Indian families holding noisy parties late at night; many individuals crowded into one dwelling.

Situational emphasis

This is the individual level of explanation which tends to be favoured by psychologists as opposed to sociological or historical explanations. It focuses upon conformity to others as being a strong influence on the growth of prejudice. Stereotypes of national or of racial groups tend to change according to situational changes. For instance, stereotypes of Russians during the period of the 'Cold War' tended to see them as hostile and prepared to go to almost any lengths to inflict damage on the Western powers. Since the overthrow of the communist regime in Russia they have been seen as muddled, confused and in need of help. The situational emphasis is what is left after we have removed the historical element from the sociocultural perspective. Allport (1954) highlighted the importance of *atmosphere*. He recounted an incident which illustrates the impact of atmosphere upon attitudes:

> An inspector of education in a British African colony wondered why so little progress was made in learning English in a certain native school. Visiting the classroom he asked the native teacher to put on a demonstration of his method of teachng English. The teacher complied, first making the following preface to the lesson in the vernacular which he did not know the inspector understood: 'Come now, children, put away your things, and let us wrestle for an hour with the enemy's language'.

> (Allport, 1954, p. 208)

Other situational theories may place emphasis upon such things as:

The employment situation It is necessary, it might be argued, to discriminate against those over 50 because they are no longer as quick on the uptake as they were and would not allow the firm to compete in the current economic situation. Ageism is therefore justified as situationally necessary.

Upward or downward social mobility Those on the way up separate themselves from those they have left, no longer frequenting the same venues and so becoming prejudiced against those who do. 'Spending an evening at Bingo is not something that people like us do!' Bingo is therefore characterized as mindblowingly dull and those who go to Bingo as stupid.

The types of contact between groups Those who like to spend their time going to concerts or to the theatre and who meet their friends there, often look down on those who frequent football matches or spend evenings in pubs. There is, they claim, a lack of intellectual stimulus from the people they meet there.

The density of groups You might hear it said, 'I cannot see how they stand the crush of shopping in the superstore on a Saturday'. Those who prefer to shop at more select high street shops show prejudice against the crowds shopping at a superstore.

Figure 27.14 illustrates this situational emphasis.

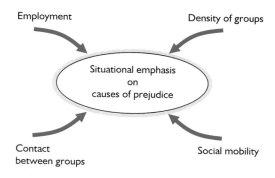

Figure 27.14 The situational emphasis in the causes of preduice

Psychodynamic emphasis

This is to do with conflict. Again, it is essentially a psychological emphasis and concentrates on such things as stress. Within this area is the frustration theory of prejudice. Allport quotes from Bettleheim and Janowitz (1950) to illustrate the violent prejudice of a World War II veteran:

> When asked about possible employment and a future depression he replied: 'We'd better not have it. Chicago'll blow wide open. On South Park the niggers are gettin' so smart. We'll have a race riot that'll make Detroit like a Sunday school picnic. So many are bitter about the part the Negro played in the war. They got all the soft jobs – the quartermasters, engineers. They're no good for anything else. The white got his ass shot off. They're pretty bitter. If both whites and niggers get laid off, that'll be bad. I'm gonna eat. I know how to use a gun'.
>
> (Bettleheim and Janowitz, 1950, p. 82)

Deprivation or the frustration of not being able to get work is causing or intensifying prejudice. Hostility boils up and if it is not controlled will burst out against ethnic minorities. These minorities become demons against whom feelings of anger are directed. The frustration of not being able to get a job has caused and intensified prejudice.

Scapegoat theory

This frustration theory has sometimes been termed a scapegoat theory. The anger which has been engendered as a result of the frustration or deprivation suffered is displaced upon a logically irrelevant victim. Two problems with this 'scapegoat' theory are:

- It does not explain why the pent-up hostility is vented upon a particular victim;
- It does not explain why it is that in many personalities no such displacement occurs, no matter what the frustration.

The authoritarian personality

A second explanation for prejudice within the psychodynamic emphasis centres upon the character structure of the prejudiced individual. It seems that only certain types of people develop prejudice as an important feature of their lives. At the end of World War

II the atrocities of the Nazis in the Holocaust were revealed and it was felt that no one could have perpetrated these atrocities unless they had dysfunctional personality structures. In particular, the authoritarian personality was put forward by Adorno et al. (1950) as an explanation of prejudice. There existed, in their view, a prejudiced personality, and only those who possessed this element in their personalities would be prejudiced. Some people are bigots, prejudiced against all minorities. The same individuals who were found to be anti-semitic would also be prejudiced against black people. This authoritarian personality was defined by a group of personality characteristics which included the following:

- Respect for and deference to authority and authority figures;
- An obsession with rank and status;
- A tendency to displace their anger and resentment on to weaker others;
- An intolerance of ambiguity and uncertainty;
- A need to maintain a rigidly defined world;
- Problems with achieving intimacy with other people.

Origins of the authoritarian personality Adorno et al. argue that the authoritarian personality has its origins in childhood. Where parents adopt an excessively harsh and disciplinarian regime in order to enforce on their children emotional dependence and obedience, children develop a love/hate relationship with their parents. This conflict between love and hate is stressful and there is a need to resolve it. The hatred is repressed through fear and guilt and finds its outlet through displacement on to those who are weaker; while the power and the authority of the parents is idealized and generalized to all authority figures. The basis on which this theory rested was the original research of Adorno et al. (1950), described in Box 27.4.

An evaluation of the 'authoritarian personality' theory There has been an enormous amount of interest and research into the authoritarian personality. There remains the difficulty that it lays too little emphasis upon sociocultural and situational factors. Pettigrew (1958) in a cross-cultural study found that although whites in the Southern United States and in South Africa were significantly more racist than those from the Northern United States there was no

Box 27.4 Research into the authoritarian personality (Adorno et al., 1950)

A questionnaire was distributed to 2000 members of organizations in California, which aimed at discovering:

- Anti-semitism;
- General ethnocentrism: that is to say, feelings about race in a more general way;
- Political and economic conservatism;
- Potential for fascism.

In addition, some of these 2000 were given projective tests and interviewed about their childhood. In spite of some encouraging results suggesting that the authoritarian personality originates in early childhood, the study has been severely criticized for its methodology by Brown (1965). In particular there were the following problems:

- An artificial correlation between the scales produced to measure the above four characteristics could have occurred because of an acquiescence response set. There was a tendency for respondents to agree with items because of their agreement with other items.
- The interviewers knew both what the hypothesis was and also the test scores of those they interviewed.
- Bias could have occurred because of experimenter expectancy. Rosenthal (1966) has claimed that belief about what results should be obtained from a study may well influence the results obtained.

difference in terms of how authoritarian their personalities were. While the personality of individuals might predispose them to be prejudiced in some contexts, there had to be a culture of prejudice and norms within a particular society legitimizing prejudiced behaviour for prejudiced behaviour to develop. Stephan and Rosenfeld (1978) found that racial attitudes among children were determined more by how much contact they had with members of other races than by the way in which they were brought up by their parents. You could reduce prejudiced behaviour in Northern Ireland more by ensuring that children were educated together in mixed Protestant/Catholic schools than by any

attempt to change children's upbringing in their home surroundings.

A further problem is the notion that, once engendered in childhood, authoritarianism remained a permanent personality style. All the evidence is that there can be sudden and dramatic changes in people's attitudes in the light of events. In Germany, extreme anti-semitism arose during about 12 years (the period of Nazi dominance from 1932 to 1945). This is far too short a period for parents to adopt new child-rearing styles which might form the basis for authoritarian personality.

Other examples include attitudes towards the Japanese after the bombing of Pearl Harbour in 1941; attitudes towards the Argentinians after the invasion of the Falkland Islands in 1982 and attitudes towards the French as a result of the resumption of nuclear testing on Muroroa atoll in 1995. As situations change, so prejudices alter.

Dogmatism

Within the same psychodynamic field and closely allied to the authoritarian personality is Rokeach's (1948, 1960) **theory of dogmatism**. Rokeach focused upon cognitive style. The characteristics of the dogmatic personality include:

- Isolation of contradictory belief systems from one another;
- Reluctance to change beliefs in the light of new information;
- Appeals to authority to justify the correctness of existing beliefs.

The scales which Rokeach used to measure dogmatism are reliable and correlate highly with measures of authoritarianism, but the same problems remain. It overlooks the sociocultural and situational influences. What is essentially a group phenomenon is reduced to individual personality predispositions.

Belief congruence theory

At the same time as his dogmatism theory Rokeach produced, separately, a **belief congruence** theory of prejudice. Individuals use their belief systems as anchoring points. When others agree with your beliefs it confirms and validates them. This congruence of beliefs is therefore reinforcing. You tend to be attracted to and to have positive empathy with people who share your beliefs. The converse also applies. You have negative feelings towards those whose beliefs are not congruent with yours. As far as Rokeach was concerned prejudiced behaviour and social discrimination are more likely to be caused by incongruity in beliefs than ethnic or racial differences.

However, there are problems with this. First, Rokeach excludes circumstances where prejudice is institutionalized or where the prejudice has received social sanction. In those cases, it is a matter of group membership. This excludes many of the most obvious manifestations of prejudice.

Second, the research on which Rokeach's theory has been based is quite seriously flawed. Participants in his study had to rate their attitude towards a number of individuals in a repeated measures design. Some of these individuals were of the same race, some of different race. All had different beliefs. There was therefore no homogeneity of belief within the racial groups and no separation of belief between groups. The focus was therefore on individual differences, with participants responding not as members of a racial group but as individuals. The research design has therefore written out in advance racial or ethnic group membership as an explanation, which leaves only the belief variable.

Phenomenological emphasis

This is the holistic emphasis. The overall impression created by the stimulus object or person is what matters. You may label a person or a group of persons as 'dirty' or 'stupid' and that is a defining label. Clearly the historical and cultural background from which perceptions originate contributes to the perception. A couple of examples might make this clearer.

- You come from a background where cleanliness is a paramount virtue. To use Kelly's (1955) term it is a 'personal construct' which helps you to make sense of the world. When you meet someone or a group of people, perhaps a group of 'travellers', they are identified as 'dirty' and that is the overriding and defining perception. Negative feelings towards that person or that group arise from that source. You feel hostility and are prejudiced against them.
- The context from which you perceive the world is that of passive and compliant women and more aggressive and assertive men. You meet a woman

whose behaviour is more assertive than most, even though it is less assertive than that of most men. You are more hostile to her than you would be towards a man behaving in exactly the same way. You are prejudiced and discriminate against her.

Emphasis on earned reputation

The focus here is on the minority groups who are the object of prejudice. It suggests that the characteristics of the groups which are the objects of prejudiced and discriminatory behaviour may have provoked that hostility. Both Triandis and Vassiliou (1967) and Brigham (1971) have come to the conclusion that there is a 'kernel of truth' in stereotypes. The traits which identify a particular group tend to be commonly agreed upon by different respondents. That is not to say that stereotypes are *justified* even though they may be relatively accurate. Let us take some examples. Asians tend to display emotions facially less than do Europeans; hence they tend to be stereotyped as impassive and unemotional (Ekman et al., 1987). La France and Mayo (1976) found that black people make less eye contact with others than white people; hence there exists a stereotype of shiftiness. This may help understanding of the origins of prejudice and discrimination.

The reduction of prejudice and discrimination

In the discussion of prejudice a wide variety of emphases have been brought in, and the strategies that may reduce prejudice relate to these. It is evident that prejudice is extremely complex so that attempts to combat it must be multifaceted. We shall not attempt to disentangle the facets. Education must inevitably play a great part. Formal education in schools can have only a marginal impact if the children are subjected to bigotry at home. It helps to reinforce prejudice if the historical victories of one group are celebrated and remembered. This is what happens with such events as the Apprentice Boys parades in Northern Ireland. Men

---

GLOSSARY

Theory of dogmatism Personality characteristics described by Rokeach involving rigidity of thinking.

Belief congruence The use of acceptance by others of a person's beliefs to strengthen and validate them.

adorned in orange sashes march through the city to commemorate events which took place in 1688 when apprentice boys closed the gates of the city against the Catholic King James.

Box 27.5 details experiments on prejudice.

Superordinate goals

Sherif's summer camp studies, which are fully discussed in Chapter 26, showed that by imposing superordinate goals on groups which had become hostile to one another intergroup tension might be

---

Box 27.5 Experiments on prejudice

Blue eyes and brown eyes experiment

One way in which children may be helped to feel what it is like to be a victim was demonstrated in an experiment conducted by Jane Elliot, a teacher with a third-grade class in Iowa, and reported by Zimbardo (1979). She announced to the class that it was a well-known fact that blue-eyed children were brighter and generally superior to those with brown eyes. The brown-eyed children were told that they were inferior and had to look up to and respect the blue-eyed ones. They were forced to sit at the back of the class, use paper cups instead of drinking from the drinking fountain, to stand at the end of the line and wear special collars to enable the blue-eyed ones to identify them immediately, even from behind. Blue-eyed children were accorded special privileges, such as second helpings at lunch and extra time at break. After the first hour the effects began to show up. The school work of the brown-eyed ones deteriorated; they became angry and depressed and began to describe themselves as stupid. To quote Zimbardo: 'What had been marvelously cooperative, thoughtful children became nasty, vicious discriminating third graders' (Zimbardo, 1979, p. 638).

The next day Elliot informed the children that she had made a mistake. It was really the brown-eyed children who were brighter and blue-eyed children were inferior. Almost at once there was a switch in attitude and behaviour. Brown-eyed children's work began to get better and the blue-eyed children began to lose their self-confidence.

Orange and green experiment

A second experiment was reported by Weiner and Wright (1973) which closely follows Elliot's experiment. White children in a third-grade class were assigned randomly to be either green or orange people. They wore orange or green armbands to distinguish them. To begin with the orange people were regarded as superior. They were told that they were brighter and cleaner than the greens. The greens were regarded as inferior and denied privileges. The second day the situation was reversed. The group which was discriminated against lost self-confidence, felt inferior and did poorly in their schoolwork. Then at a later date the children who had been through the experiment were asked if they would like to go on a picnic with black children from a nearby school; 96 per cent agreed, as compared with only 62 per cent of a control group who had not been through the orange/green experiment.

These experiments mirror the experiences of black people, especially in the Southern states of the USA who had historically first been slaves and then had been regarded as inferior.

Equal status contact can help. When people are made aware that members of minority groups share their goals, ambitions and feelings, prejudice may be reduced. There needs to be personal contact between groups on an equal footing (Cook and Pelfrey, 1985).

Summer camp experiment

Clore (1976) set up a unique summer camp for children. It was administered by one white and one black male and one white and one black female. Blacks were equally divided in power, privileges and duties. Instead of always seeing blacks in a servile, or subordinate, role (which of course harks back to the historical fact of slavery) there was contact between the races on an equal basis. Tests showed that children attending the camp had significantly more positive attitudes towards other race children after attending the camp than they did before.

Ethical implications

There are ethical implications in these experiments. The manipulation of children's feelings and attitudes is not really ethical. It is perhaps worthwhile to look back to the section on ethics (Chapter 5) and make your own assessment as to the extent to which these experiments breach ethical guidelines.

reduced. The problems with the water supply at the camp was not solvable by either of the groups on their own but by cooperating they were able to overcome the problem. Cooperation in turn reduced prejudiced and discriminatory behaviour. There are superordinate goals to be achieved. Worchel et al. (1977) artificially created cooperative, competitive relationships between two groups and then imposed superordinate goals which were either achieved or not. Relations between the group improved except where there had been competition and the superordinate goal was not achieved. In this case relations actually got worse. Where the failure to achieve the goals can be attributed to the other group, rightly or wrongly, then intergroup relations worsen. If there are external reasons for the failure then intergroup relations may improve. Hogg and Vaughan (1995) have suggested that this might have been the case in Argentina in 1982 at the time of the Falklands War. The junta controlling Argentina was suffering factional conflict and the invasion of the Falklands was introduced as a superordinate goal. Its failure could be blamed on the junta and so the factional conflict worsened and the junta fell.

Contact

Taking the situational emphasis, prejudiced or discriminatory behaviour which results from high unemployment (ageism, for instance, or discrimination against ethnic minorities) might be changed by altering the situation; by creating more jobs, for instance, where unemployment is high. Increased contact between groups is important in this context. Groups may be separated by a wide range of differences: educational, cultural, occupational and material. The suggestion is made that greater intergroup contact might reduce prejudice and conflict. Stephan and Stephan (1984) have claimed that ignorance is a factor. Allport (1954) proposed the contact hypothesis. However, he has stressed that the *nature* of the contact is important. He discussed six different kinds of contact.

Casual contact Where an individual lives in a place where members of a minority group also live, for example, in Bradford (a city in the north of England where there is a high concentration of people of Asian origin), people may say that they know Asian people because they meet so many of them. But it is a superficial contact. Alternatively,

where there is segregation it may be frozen into relationships between subordinates and those in positions of authority. The evidence is that such contacts do more to increase prejudice than dispel it. The reasoning behind this is as follows. Perceiving a member of an out-group casually triggers rumour, hearsay, tradition and stereotypes linked to that out-group. The greater the frequency of the casual contact, the more the adverse mental associations are strengthened and we are sensitized to perceive signs that confirm the stereotype. If a dozen Asians are behaving impeccably in a Bradford street and one is not, we will select the one who is misbehaving to confirm our preconceptions. Allport quotes an imaginary instance to illustrate this process:

> An Irishman and a Jew encounter each other in casual contact . . . Neither, in fact, has any initial animosity towards the other. But the Irishman thinks, 'Ah, a Jew; perhaps he'll skin me, I'll be careful'. The Jew thinks, 'Probably a Mick; they hate the Jews; he'd like to insult me.' With such an inauspicious start, both men are likely to be evasive, distrustful and cool. The casual contact has left things worse than before.
>
> (Allport, 1954, p. 252)

Acquaintance True acquaintance lessens prejudice. Gray and Thompson (1953) found that there was a uniform tendency to rate higher on an acceptability scale (the Bogardus social distance scale, mentioned earlier) those groups in which people had five or more acquaintances. A way, therefore, of reducing prejudice is to increase knowledge. There are various ways of doing this. One is through academic teaching in schools. Anthropological facts can be taught as well as reasons why different customs have developed in other ethnic groups.

Another way is through social travel. This is aimed at giving students direct experience with other groups. Smith (1943) has evaluated an experiment in social travel, where 46 graduate students travelled to Harlem for a weekend, were entertained in black people's homes there and met prominent black doctors, editors, writers, artists and social workers. Twenty-three students were unable to travel and so acted as a control. Attitudes towards blacks were measured both before and after the weekend. Even after a year had elapsed only 8 out of the 46 failed to show more favourable attitudes towards black people. This was not the case with the control group. It is worth noting that all the black people in this study were of high status (at least as high as the visitors' status).

A third method of increasing knowledge is through intercultural education, which may involve role play. A white adult with antiblack attitudes might be asked to play the role of a black musician trying to get a room in a hotel and being refused by the receptionist when it is known to both that rooms are free.

Residential contact   The question here is whether integrated housing serves to increase or to lessen prejudice as compared to segregated housing. As has been seen in Northern Ireland, segregation in housing means segregation in schooling, shopping, medical facilities and so on. Friendships across group residential boundaries become very hard to form.

A minority group becomes much more visible if it is segregated. Black people represent a mere 10 per cent of the metropolitan population of New York. If they were randomly distributed they would not seem significant, yet concentrated in Harlem they are seen as a dangerously expanding threat.

It is at the boundaries of segregated areas that tension is likely to occur, particularly if there is pressure from within the segregated area from an expanding population. Integrated housing removes barriers to effective communication. Once these barriers are removed fallacious stereotypes are reduced and realism replaces fear and autistic hostility.

Occupational contact   Black people tend to be near the bottom of the occupational ladder. This may have its roots in the historical fact of slavery. With menial jobs come poor pay and low status. Similarly, women have historically been seen to have their place at home rather than at work. When they enter the job market it is frequently in jobs with low pay and low status. Occupational contacts with members of outgroups who are of equal status are important for the reduction of prejudice. Equal opportunities legislation can help, but there is also a task of persuasion to be

done. Those who have authority should lead by example.

Members of minorities which have been victims of prejudice have contact on an equal basis once they have been appointed to posts in the higher echelons of employment and this will help to break down prejudice.

Pursuit of common objectives   Occupational contacts of the kind referred to above are fine, but suffer from an inherent limitation. Contact, even if it is on an equal status basis, may remain dissociated from prejudiced behaviour at a more generalized level unless it leads people to do things together. A multi-ethnic team have a common goal, and so its ethnic composition becomes irrelevant. Common participation and common interests are more important than mere equal-status contact.

Goodwill contacts   Goodwill contact with minority groups is likely to achieve very little unless there are concretely defined objectives. DuBois (1950) was establishing a neighbourhood festival and invited members of ethnic minorities (Armenians, Mexicans, Jews and so on) to recollect what each used to do in autumn festivals in their childhoods. Universal values common to all ethnic groups were in this way brought out and grounds for acquaintance established. An agenda for the improvement of community relationships was evolved which might be strengthened by cooperative endeavour.

Conclusion

So far as the psychodynamic emphasis is concerned, some of the frustrations which lie at the root of scapegoat theory can be alleviated. Poverty, poor housing and lack of employment opportunities are capable of remedy. The authoritarian personality seems to be the result of particularly harsh child-rearing practices and so may be reduced in time with patient education. Indeed there is evidence that child rearing has become more liberal, so that perhaps it is reasonable to expect authoritarian and dogmatic personality structures will become less common.

SELF-ASSESSMENT QUESTIONS

1. List the various emphases which have been employed in attempts to explain prejudice and discrimination. Can it realistically be said that the emphasis used depends upon the discipline of the observer: psychologists favouring psychodynamic explanations, historians and sociologists favouring historical/economic or sociocultural explanations and so on?

2. Describe the authoritarian personality. Is it realistic to explain prejudice in terms of a natural disposi-

tion to be prejudiced? Where do the flaws lie in this explanation?

3. Allport has put forward a contact theory for prejudice reduction. Specify which kinds of contact between groups are likely to be most helpful in reducing prejudice.

4. Superordinate goals have been suggested as a way of reducing prejudice and hostility. Explain how such goals may be used in a practical way to reduce conflict.

Chapter summary

■ Attitudes have three components: cognitive, affective and behavioural/conative. They function much in the same way as do schemata or scripts, allowing us to produced packaged and memorized responses to people, events and situations.

■ There has been some discussion as to the extent to which the behavioural element is useful as a means of predicting behaviour. Ajzen and Fishbein developed a theory of reasoned action which attempted to link attitudes with behaviour. This was later extended by Ajzen to form what was termed a theory of planned behaviour. This takes into account not only a person's own attitudes, but also those of significant others as well as the amount of control a person may have over his or her behaviour.

■ Attitudes may be formed in a variety of ways, by direct experience, through conditioning processes, through observation and modelling and through cognition. Attitude change may come as a result of the existence of cognitive imbalance. There is strong motivation to maintain balance between attitudes. Festinger developed the theory of cognitive dissonance to explain how conflict (and therefore tension) between attitudes and behaviour may induce attitude or behaviour change. Steele and Cooper and Fazio have updated this concept to include the effect on self-concept of dissonance – self-affirmation.

■ Cognitive dissonance also operates whenever we make a decision, to enhance the attractiveness of the

chosen option, and to detract from the attractiveness of the nonchosen option.

■ The ways in which attitudes have been measured are linked closely to the three components. Thurstone's and Likert's scales of measurement are aimed at measuring the cognitive component; Osgood's semantic differential aims to measure the affective component, and the behavioural component has been measured by Bogardus's social distance scale and by unobtrusive measures, such as the kinds of books borrowed from libraries. What has been termed a bogus pipeline technique has been introduced to overcome the reluctance of people to reveal their true feelings.

■ Fishbein developed what was termed an expectancy-value technique to link closely the evaluative and belief components in attitudes. This arose out of the theory of planned behaviour.

■ Prejudice represents a particular set of attitudes (usually hostile) towards people which has become pervasive. It manifests itself in sexism, in racism and in ageism, particularly, though other groups too may be objects of prejudice, such as homosexuals or disabled or mentally handicapped people.

■ Prejudice may manifest itself in overtly hostile behaviour, but more common are incidents of subtle discrimination or tokenism. The causes of prejudice are multifaceted ranging from historical and economic to sociocultural and situational explanations. More individual causes centre upon making scapegoats out of target groups or individuals to obviate frustration or upon the personality characteristics of individuals – the authoritarian personality.

■ Similarly Rokeach has produced a theory of dogmatism, represented by a particular cognitive style characterized by reluctance to alter belief in the face of new information, isolation of contradictory beliefs and appeals to authority to reinforce the correctness of existing beliefs. People will use their belief system as anchoring points and will tend to be attracted to those who hold similar views. This reinforces the existing view.

■ There is also a holistic phenomenological aspect. People tend to use 'personal constructs' to help them make sense of the world. Hostility and prejudice may arise from the use of these constructs as overriding and defining perceptions. Gypsies may be characterized as dirty or women as compliant. The defining labels attached to that group influence the way in which all members of that group are perceived. Stereotypes of groups may contain a kernel of truth. Black people, for instance, tend to make less eye contact than white people and so there tends to be a perceived stereotype of shiftiness.

■ The reduction of prejudice may be achieved by establishing superordinate goals which may be achieved by cooperation between groups or else by means of enhanced contact. These may include casual, social, academic and occupational contacts as well as integrated housing or the pursuit of common objectives.

Further reading

Allport, G.W. (1958). *The Nature of Prejudice*. Garden City, NY: Doubleday Anchor. This represents the seminal text on prejudice and discrimination.

Deaux, K., Dane, F.C. and Wrightsman, L.S. (1993). *Social Psychology in the 90's*. 6th edn. Pacific Grove, CA: Brookes/Cole. Chapter 7 deals well with attitudes and attitude change. It also covers the issues in persuasion very well.

Eiser, J.R. (1986). *Social Psychology: Attitudes, Cognition and Social Behaviour*. Cambridge: Cambridge University Press. Part II of this book goes into attitudes and social influence at considerable depth.

CHAPTER 28

Social influence

Conformity and compliance 677
- Conformity 678
- Why do people conform? 679
- Individual differences in conformity 680
- Compliance 681
- Obedience 683

Leadership and followership 687
- The personalities of leaders 688
- Situational factors 688
- Behavioural factors 688
- Fiedler's contingency model of leadership 690

Group decision making 690
- Characteristics of groups 691
- Communication networks 692
- Roles in groups 693
- Norm formation 693
- Decision making in groups 693

The influence of the crowd 696
- Freudian explanation of crowd behaviour 696
- Deindividuation 696
- Emergent norm theory 697
- Social identity theory and crowds 697

Objectives

By the end of this chapter you should be able to:

- Distinguish between conformity and compliance;

- Describe some of the research on conformity to social norms by Asch and others;

- Identify what is meant by foot-in-the-door, door-in-the-face, that's-not-all and low-ball techniques;

- Describe and comment upon Milgram's experiments on obedience, particularly in respect of the ethics involved;

- Indicate the relative importance of situation and personality in the emergence of leadership;

- Describe Fiedler's contingency model of leadership;

- Describe the effects on decision making of different communication structures within an organization;

- Identify what is meant by deindividuation in relation to crowds of people.

Conformity and compliance

The distinction made here between these two terms, which have frequently been used interchangeably is this. While **conformity** relates to responses to indirect pressure, **compliance** relates to how we respond to direct requests. Conformity would be involved in dressing appropriately for whatever situation we may

> **GLOSSARY**
>
> **Conformity** The tendency for members of a group, to behave in a similar way to other members of the group.
>
> **Compliance** Acceding to a request made by another person.

" HEY ! REMEMBER THE BAD OLD DAYS, WHEN THEY MADE US WEAR SCHOOL UNIFORM ? "

find ourselves in, because of the pressure exerted on us by others to do so. You appear at a wedding in your best clothes, because to appear in jeans and trainers would be frowned upon. However, if the invitation stipulated formal morning dress you would comply with that request.

Conformity

When an individual is part of a group, the individual is influenced by that group in relation to the way in which he or she responds to stimuli. The earliest studies of conformity include the work of Sherif (1936). He studied the responses of individuals, in groups of various sizes and also alone, to what is known as the autokinetic effect. You are in a darkened room and there is a stationary pinpoint of light at the far side of it. If you try it, you will see that the light will appear to move. Your eyes have no other reference point. Sherif believed that where there was ambiguity, social norms

tend to emerge to reduce the uncertainty. Participants in Sherif's study made a large number of judgments about how far the point of light had moved. Over a number of trials a frame of reference or a range of variation emerged within which the estimates were made, each individual working alone developing a different frame of reference so that they gradually, over the course of about 100 trials, narrowed the range of their estimates of how far the light had moved. However, when participants were together in a group calling out their estimates, other participants' estimates began to be used as a frame of reference so that eventually they were giving virtually identical estimates. Their individual estimates had converged on a group norm. This group influence was powerful enough to remain with the individuals when they later made estimates on their own. It had become internalized.

Uncertainty and ambiguity

Later, Asch (1951) argued that it was the uncertainty and ambiguity which made people conform to a norm. If the stimulus had been entirely unambiguous, judgments made would be entirely individual and not influenced at all by other people. To test this, he set up what has become a classic experiment. Male students were recruited for what they thought was a visual discrimination task. Seated round a table in groups of between seven and nine they were presented with a card on which were a test line and three comparison lines (as in Figure 28.1), A, B and C. A standard line was shown to them and they took it in turns to call out which of the comparison lines was the same length as the test line. In reality, all but one of the 'students' were confederates of Asch's, primed to give wrong answers on 12 of the trials, in six cases picking a line that was too short and in six one that was too long. In each of the 18 trials the real naïve student answered second to last. To control for ambiguity, there was also a condition where participants made their judgments privately with no group influence. There were less than 1 per cent errors in this condition.

The results were not as Asch had predicted. While there were 25 per cent of participants who relied on their own judgment throughout and were not influenced by others at all, 50 per cent conformed to the judgment of the erroneous majority on six or more trials out of the 12 where there had been manipulation by confederates, and 5 per cent

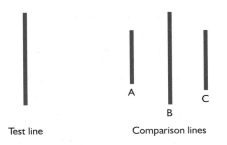

Test line   Comparison lines

Figure 28.1 Sample lines in Asch's study of conformity

conformed on all 12 trials. The average conformity rate was 33 per cent.

When they were debriefed, participants gave various reasons for conforming to the erroneous majority. Initially they experienced uncertainty and self-doubt. They had, after all, a disagreement on what was a straightforward perceptual judgment. Then there was fear of social disapproval, anxiety and loneliness. Some really thought that they had perceived the lines in a different way from the others, that the group was right and their eyesight must in some way be defective. Others simply went along with the majority so as not to 'rock the boat'. There were even some who maintained that they actually saw the lines as the majority.

Why do people conform?

Deutsch and Gerard (1955) suggested that there were two different kinds of influence which persuaded people to conform:

- **Informational influence.** The other people in the group provide a source of information in a case of ambiguity and uncertainty – such as in the Sherif studies.
- **Normative influence.** Where there was little ambiguity, as in Asch's experiments, group norms and a strong social pressure not to be deviant, not to be the odd one out, persuaded people to conform. Deutsch and Gerard replicated the Asch studies and found that when participants were explicitly identified as group members, normative influence ensured that 'conformity' was greater.

More recently Abrams and Hogg (1990a) have proposed another influence which may operate to underpin both the above influences, **self-categorization.** As soon as we know a little about someone we

meet we tend to place him or her in a category or categories. It may be 'male' or 'female', 'young' or 'old', 'well-educated 'or 'badly educated' or we may perhaps put a class label on them. Abrams and Hogg are suggesting that the same processes operate as far as we ourselves are concerned. Membership of a group is very important to us and what we do has to be consistent with membership of the group. Even something as transitory as being on a panel helping with an experiment confers membership of a group. We identify with the group in order to maintain our self-concept – and membership of the group is included as part of that. We need to conform.

This self-categorization theory provides us with an explanation of why some people remain independent and why some people are anticonformists, trying desperately hard not to be like everyone else. It may be part of someone's self-concept that he or she is not like everyone else, either fiercely independent, not taking any account of what others do, or fiercely different, taking account of others' behaviour but deliberately not conforming to it. Abrams and Hogg (1990b) used a situation similar to that used by Sherif. There were six participants in a darkened room, three of whom were confederates of the experimenters. Using Sherif's procedures, the confederates consistently estimated the movement of the point of light as 5 cm greater than the rest of the group, thus creating the impression that there were two subgroups. The researchers then set up a competitive task, pitting the three confederates against the other three participants, so that explicit groups were set up. In this situation the discrepancy between the estimates (of light movement) were significantly greater than in the nonexplicit group set up (the original situation).

Thus self-categorization operates to strengthen both informational and normative conformity as well as anticonformity and independence (as Deutsch and Gerard found).

GLOSSARY

Informational influence The influence that results from the provision of information that reduces ambiguity.

Normative influence Influence to change behaviour as a result of pressure to conform to the behaviour of other members of a group.

Self-categorization The process described by Abrams and Hogg by which people identify with a group in order to maintain and enhance their self-concept.

Factors which influence the degree of conformity include the following.

Group size

As the size of a group increases so does its influence. The larger the group the greater the number of reasons they are able to provide for conforming. Also, as Insko et al. (1985) found, the chances become greater that there will be someone in the group with sufficient power to exert pressure to comply. But group members must be seen to be acting as individuals.

Group cohesion

Wilder (1977) showed that the more closely (in an Asch-type situation) the 'confederates' are seen as cohering, the less the conformity is likely to be by a single individual who does not see himself or herself as belonging to that cohesive group. Conformity is greater when there are, for instance, four individuals making erroneous judgments, apparently independently of one another, than when they are seen as a single group. In that case the pressure to conform is little more than it would be with a single individual making erroneous judgments. But notwithstanding that, when the individual sees himself or herself as *belonging*, the pressure is greater.

Unanimity

Where there is not unanimity among those making erroneous judgments, but rather a clear majority and minority view, then conformity becomes much less. The minority itself becomes a source of influence. This happens in the case of jury deliberations when a unanimous verdict has to be arrived at. A single individual who cannot make up his or her mind has pressure exerted from either side, from those who would vote for conviction as well as from those who favour acquittal. But the pressure will be greater from those who are in the majority. As more of the jury decides to convict, the pressure on the one undecided juror to convict increases, as Campbell et al. (1986) showed.

Individual differences in conformity

Crutchfield (1954) replicated Asch's research but with significant modifications. Participants in his study were military men attending a three-day assessment programme. They did not confront one another, however, but were in individual cubicles in which were electrical panels. They responded to questions, projected on the wall using these panels and received feedback on other participants' responses via the panels, which were in fact connected not to the other participants' panels but to the experimenter's. The apparent order in which the responses appeared (from the display of lights) to be made could be varied by the experimenter, as well as the proportions of agreement or disagreement. The questions were wider, involving amongst other things, attitudinal statements such as 'I believe we are made better by the trials and hardships of life' or 'Free speech is a privilege rather than a right; it is permissible to suspend free speech when a society feels threatened' as well as perceptual questions like those of Asch. The results were similar to those in Asch's experiments.

Personality characteristics of conformers

Crutchfield found that conformers and nonconformers showed different personality characteristics. Nonconformers were higher than conformers in the following traits:

■ Intellectual effectiveness,
■ Ego strength,
■ Leadership ability,
■ Maturity in social relationships,
■ Efficiency,
■ Ability to express themselves,
■ Naturalness,
■ Lack of pretension,
■ Self-reliance.

Conformers were found to be:

■ Submissive,
■ Narrow,
■ Inhibited,
■ Lacking in insight.

Gender differences

It has also been suggested in early research that females are more conforming and also more conservative than men. However, later research, such as that of Zimbardo and Leippe (1991) and Cacioppo and Petty (1980) has found that much of this difference is due to the particular research setting, where men had an informational advantage. Where women know less about the subject they conform more, but men also conform more than women when they know less about the subject. Eagly and Carli (1981) found that in face-to-face interaction, women conform more than men. This, they suggested, is because women are socialized to a greater extent to regard harmony as important, so that they are likely to go along with the group and yield to pressure rather than risk disharmony.

In general, the consensus seems to be that situational, rather than individual, factors are of greatest importance.

Compliance

As has been mentioned, conformity refers to indirect pressure, compliance to responses to direct requests. Suppose you have been invited to a wedding. There is pressure to conform to particular standards of appearance. Men are likely to wear suits, probably with a carnation in their buttonholes; women will wear smart dresses or suits and probably a hat. However, the invitation might specify 'formal dress' which is a direct request for men to wear morning suits and a top hat. To go along with such a direct request is compliance. This happens all the time. You are buying a house. The solicitor calls and asks you come to his or her office to sign some papers. You do so. Your friend asks you to buy something for him or her while you are in town. You buy it.

Foot-in-the-door effect

Much of the research into compliance relates to sales techniques. The **foot-in-the-door** effect relates to the notion that once you have been induced to comply with a small request you will be more likely to comply later with a larger demand. Freedman and Fraser (1966) sent undergraduate experimenters to present women in their homes with a small request, to sign a petition about road safety or to place a small notice in their window. Then two weeks later different experimenters approached the same women with a more substantial request, to put a large billboard on their front lawn to promote road safety. Others approached a control group (who had not had the first request) with the same request. Those who had had the 'foot in the door' were much more likely to comply.

Self-perception De Jong (1979) suggested that the reasons behind the foot-in-the-door effect relate to self-perception. Complying with the first request leads people to see themselves as basically helpful people. Then at the second request they are reluctant to lose this image of helpfulness which is seen as a positive one, even if complying with the request is irksome. It is suggested that there are two necessary conditions to produce this effect:

- The first request has to be sufficiently large that the individual thinks about it before complying. What are the implications of complying?
- There has to be free choice. If there were any external pressure applied to comply there is no longer any reason why the individual should attribute compliance to being helpful (that is, the self-perception of a positive disposition). If women were offered money to grant the first request, Zuckerman et al. (1979) found that that was sufficient justification in itself and the effect was lost.

Door-in-the-face effect

The **door-in-the-face** effect is in effect the obverse of the foot-in-the-door effect. Cialdini et al. (1975) suggested that there were occasions when refusal of an initial request actually made it *more* likely that a second request would be acceded to. In their study college students were approached with a very demanding request – to serve as voluntary counsellors in a juvenile detention centre for two years. In nearly every case this initial request was refused. However, when the same people were approached a second time with a much less onerous request – to chaperon juveniles on a trip to the zoo – there was much greater compliance, 50 per cent complied compared to 17 per cent where there had been no larger first request. De Jong's self-perception explanation would suggest that there should be less compliance on the second request. They have already refused one request and so have

---

> **GLOSSARY**
>
> **Foot-in-the-door** The process whereby compliance with a small request makes compliance with a larger or less desirable one more likely.
>
> **Door-in-the face** The process where compliance with a request follows refusal to comply with a larger request.

begun to see themselves as unhelpful. This should, in theory, have coloured their response to the second request and they should have been less likely to accede to it. Again, it has been suggested that there are two conditions which have to be met for the door-in-the-face effect to operate:

■ The initial request has to be sufficiently onerous for them not to think badly of themselves if they refuse it.
■ The second request has to be made by the same person who made the first one. According to Cialdini and his colleagues, the second request is then seen as a concession and complying with it is seen as a reciprocal gesture.

When you put your hand into icy water and then into lukewarm water, the lukewarm water feels hot (you can try this for yourself). This contrast effect, it is suggested, lies behind the door-in-the-face phenomenon. You go into a car showroom to buy a used car. The salesperson asks you how much you want to spend. You say, perhaps, £2000. You are shown a few very well used and high mileage vehicles for around your price before the salesperson shows you a much better-looking car for £3000. It appears so much better a bargain that you cannot pass it by. That is the door-in-the-face technique in action.

That's-not-all technique

Allied to the door-in-the-face is the that's-not-all technique. In this technique you go into the showroom and are shown a car at around your price and before you have the chance to say 'yes' or 'no' the salesperson says you can have it for £500 less than the advertised price and you will get free insurance as well. According to Burger (1986), the difference between this and the door-in-the-face is that the consumer does not have the chance to refuse an offer before a more favourable one is made. Burger's comparison of the two techniques showed 'that's not all' to be the more effective. In both techniques there is a concession made.

Low ball technique

Cialdini et al. (1978) investigated a technique prevalent among dealers in new cars. This low ball technique consists of offering a much better deal than any of the competitors, a discount on the list price or a very high trade-in price for your old car. You agree to the deal and

'That's not all', 'low ball', 'lure' techniques – all these weapons may be found in the armoury of the successful car salesman

all the papers are prepared when the salesperson goes to check with the boss. Then he or she comes back and apologizes that the boss will not agree to the deal. You can have the car for the list price. In many cases the customer will still go ahead with the deal. You are committed and reluctant to back out.

Cialdini demonstrated the low ball technique by getting students to agree to take part in an experiment and only then telling them that they had to be there by 7 a.m. Others, told initially of the early start, were much less likely to agree to take part. Cialdini (1985) suggested reasons for the effectiveness of low ball techniques. When people receive the initial offer or request and make a commitment, they develop justifications for that commitment. When one of the justifications (the low price, for example) is removed the remaining justifications still remain.

The lure

A variation on the low ball technique is the **lure**. You go to buy a pair of shoes and you see just what you want on the shelf for a very attractive price. You tell the salesperson you would like this pair but in a different size and colour. The salesperson goes out to the back to look for a pair the right size and returns to apologize that the size (or colour) which you want is not available

---

GLOSSARY

Lure A technique where an enticing offer, found to be unavailable, is used to ensure acceptance of a less favourable offer.

but you can have another similar pair in the right size and colour but it is not 'in the sale'. Because you have made a commitment and justified that commitment to yourself you go ahead with the purchase. Joule et al. (1989) set out to test this. Students were asked to volunteer for a boring hour-long study which involved memorizing numbers. No payment was mentioned. Only 15 per cent agreed. A second group were asked to volunteer to take part in an interesting half-hour study which involved watching a film. They would be paid 30 francs (about £4); 47 per cent agreed. When they arrived to take part they were told that the study which they had agreed to take part in had been completed the day before. They could take part in the boring memory study, though, but unfortunately they could not be paid for it. They all accepted. They had made a commitment to take part in an experiment and stood by that commitment.

Theory of politeness

Brown and Levinson (1987) developed what they termed a theory of politeness to explain why people comply. It relates to impression management. What matters is to give the best impression to people you meet. Goffman (1967) referred to face saving in this context. When you ask someone to do something for you, you are asking to be allowed to impose your will on the other person. The person may lose 'face' if he or she complies. Similarly, when you ask someone to do something for you and the person refuses, that may involve loss of face on your part. Polite requests involve less face threatening than more peremptory demands and so are more likely to be complied with. Brown and Levinson developed a hierarchy of strategies to obtain compliance. Those which might involve loss of face (force, threats, bribery, deception) are likely to be less successful than those which do not (such as polite requests, invoking personal reasons or expertise or bargaining for a favour).

Power bases

Whether we are able to induce someone to comply with a request may depend upon the power which we can exercise. French and Raven (1959) identified five types of power:

■ **Coercive power**. This amounts to the ability to administer punishment of some kind. A teacher,

for example, or a parent has sanctions which can be applied to ensure compliance.

■ **Reward power**. The ability to reward someone for compliance. A parent may reward a child for doing what he or she is asked, for example.

■ **Expert power**. This stems from superior knowledge, ability or expertise.

■ **Referent power**. Power may be exercised because you look up to, identify with or wish to emulate someone.

■ **Legitimate power**. If you are elected or appointed to an official position you may exercise power by virtue of that. A headteacher exercises power over pupils and staff because of his or her appointment to that position.

Raven (1965) added an additional source of power, informational power. If you know that your boss has been claiming expenses to which he or she was not entitled, for example, and your boss knows that you know, this can be very influential in gaining compliance to requests. It is very hard sometimes to separate sources of power. In fact several sources may be exercised at the same time. A teacher may have legitimate power because of being a teacher; expert power because of possessing knowledge; referent power if a pupil identifies with him or her; reward or coercive power because of having the ability to administer rewards or punishment. The circumstances will often determine the likelihood of compliance. When a parent or a teacher is there, coercive power may be more effective than when they are not. Legitimate power is vested in the position an individual holds; referent power depends upon the dispositional characteristics of the individuals concerned. All these factors carry over into the discussion of obedience, which is a special case of compliance.

Obedience

Where there is legitimate power there is pressure to comply. Where requests are put in the form of an order, compliance becomes obedience. When a police officer tells you to do something, you do it because of his or her official position. If you are in one of the armed services you obey your superior officers. They have legitimate as well as coercive power over you. There may be a conflict between what you know to be right and the legitimate orders you are given. At the Nuremburg trials after World War II, Nazis justified genocide by claiming that they were only following orders. After the massacre of My Lai in Vietnam, where a whole village was exterminated by American forces, Lieutenant Calley was able to claim that he was only doing what he had been ordered to do. The question at issue is the extent to which ordinary individuals will do what they are told to do even when doing so puts the lives of other innocent people at risk.

Milgram (1963) set out to determine how far ordinary individuals would go in obedience to orders. An instruction from a legitimate authority would be obeyed, and this was the most important factor in relation to obedience. He conducted a series of experiments which are detailed in Box 28.1.

Replications of Milgram's work carried out elsewhere produced similar results. Mantell (1971) in Germany found an even higher rate of obedience. Shanab and Kahya (1977) in Jordan found 80 per cent

obedience in children. High levels of obedience were also found in Australia by Kilham and Mann (1974).

A question of ethics

Much of the debate which centred around Milgram's research into obedience has been concerned with the ethics of what he did. While participants in his studies did not *actually* inflict pain or suffering on the supposed 'victims', they thought they were doing so and this caused stress. On the other hand, there is no evidence that any of them suffered psychological harm and in fact, at a later date (Milgram, 1992) 83.7 per cent of them indicated that they were glad they had taken part. Only 1.3 per cent had any misgivings.

The ethical questions in this research centre upon three issues:

Box 28.1 Milgram's experiment on obedience

He advertised for and paid 40 men of various ages and occupations for participation in a series of 'trials'. What then ensued involved a series of deceptions.

First deception

Participants were introduced to an individual whom they were led to believe was another participant, but who was in fact an accomplice of the experimenter.

Second deception

Participants were informed that the purpose of the experiment was to assess the effects of punishment on learning. In fact the aim was to find out the extent to which participants would obey.

Third deception

Participants drew lots to determine who was to be the learner and who the teacher, but in fact the ballot was so rigged that the accomplice was always the 'learner'.

Fourth deception

The 'lesson' was a verbal learning task. The teacher was instructed to administer a shock to the 'learner' every time there was a wrong answer. He was instructed to increase the level of shock by one increment each time. The 'learner' was strapped to a chair in an adjoining room with electrodes attached to his wrist. There was an impressive-looking 'shock generator' with 30 switches. Participants were given to understand that

the switches controlled electric current which increased by increments of 15 volts from 15 to 450 volts. At the low end there was a label 'slight shock'; at the high end 'DANGER: SEVERE SHOCK' and finally 'XXX' at the end. In fact the equipment was a sham and the accomplice was a good actor who never received any shocks at all.

The experiment proceeded and for each wrong answer the experimenter instructed the 'teacher' to increase the shock by 15 volts. At 300 volts the 'learner' began to pound the wall and no longer answered any questions. The 'teacher' turned to the experimenter for guidance and was told that the experiment must continue. Failure to answer was to be taken as a wrong answer. Milgram was trying to find out how many participants would continue to administer all the shocks in the series. Of 40 participants, 26 (65 per cent) continued right to the end. None stopped before 300 volts, at which point five refused to continue. In all, a total of 14 defied the experimenter and backed out before the end. The conclusion which Milgram drew was that obedience to instructions was an extremely powerful force in society. The graph shows some detail.

In later research (Milgram, 1965, 1974) Milgram investigated the situations in which people would or would not obey. There were various factors studied, for example:

Box 28.1 continued

Proximity of the victim

The closer the 'victim' was to the person administering the shock, the more likely that person was to refuse to administer it. Where the 'victim' was in the same room and only 18 inches away only a third of participants would go the whole way.

Proximity of the authority figure

Where the experimenter (Milgram himself or an assistant) was not physically there but gave orders by telephone or tape recording the experimenter's authority was frequently defied. In these circumstances obedience was reduced to 20.5 per cent. Where the

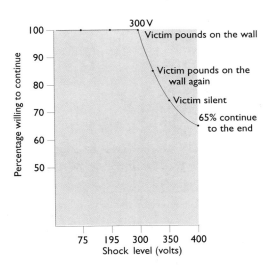

Milgram's studies on obedience. The graph illustrates the percentage of participants who were prepared to go on administering shocks as the intensity of the shocks increased

experimenter gave no orders at all and the participants were entirely free to choose, only 2.5 per cent persisted until the end.

Group pressure

Where there were two disobedient 'teachers' (in fact, confederates) who appeared to revolt and refused to administer shocks after the 150 volt to 210 volt range, obedience dropped to 10.5 per cent. On the other hand, where the two confederates continued to obey to the end obedience increased to 92.5 per cent. This finding relates to the issue of conformity discussed earlier in this section.

Legitimacy of the authority

The original experiments were conducted in the very prestigious Yale University and the scientists present wore white lab coats. Milgram ran one experiment in a run-down inner city office block. Obedience dropped in these surroundings to 48 per cent. Bushman (1984, 1988) tested the effect of the legitimacy of authority and so the possibility that participants might be able to abdicate responsibility for what they do. The scenario was someone fumbling for change by a parking meter. Bushman had confederates, variously dressed, in uniform, in a neat suit or in shabby clothes stop passers-by and order them to give the person change for the meter. Seventy per cent obeyed the uniformed confederate, compared with 50 per cent of those who were not in uniform and even fewer of those who were shabbily dressed. When questioned as to why they had obeyed, those who obeyed the uniformed confederate said they did so 'because they were told to', while the reason given for obeying the nonuniformed confederates was more frequently that they wanted to be helpful.

- **Stress**. Can the amount of stress to which the participants were subjected be justified in terms of the importance of the research itself and its outcomes?
- **Freedom to withdraw**. Were the participants free to withdraw at any time? While they were free in the sense that no one tied them down, it was never made explicit to them that they could withdraw, although withdrawal was a large part of what was being measured. The fact that they were paid also places a certain obligation upon them not to back out.

- **Informed consent**. The third issue is about whether they gave 'informed consent' to what they were about to be asked to do. As part of the design of the experiment the participants had to be naïve about its true purpose. They could not therefore give *informed* consent.

  Some further points have been made in Chapter 5 in the context of a discussion of ethics in a more general sense. Milgram's defence to charges of ethical misconduct centre around precautions taken beforehand to ensure that none of the participants was in any way

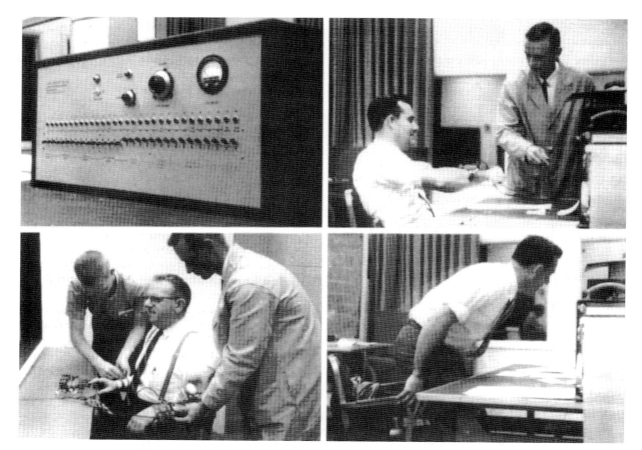

Milgram's experiment on obedience. Top left: the apparatus for delivering 'shocks'. Top right: the 'teacher' receiving a sample shock. Bottom left: the 'learner' is attached to the shock generator. Bottom right: the teacher breaks off the experiment (from Milgram, 1963)

unstable and around the care taken in debriefing them afterwards. Nevertheless, Bettelheim, quoted in Miller (1986) was moved to say, 'These experiments are so vile, the intention with which they were engaged is so vile, that nothing in these experiments has any value' (Miller, 1986, p. 124).

One of the results of this debate is a set of guidelines for psychological research which makes it unlikely that the exact procedures of Milgram's research could now be replicated. The code of practice includes three key points:

■ That there must be informed consent.
■ That participants must be explicitly told that they are free to withdraw at any time, without any repercussions.
■ There must be full and honest debriefing at the end.

Generalizability

It was also suggested by Baumrind (1964) among others that it was not possible to generalize these findings into 'real life'. There was the prestigious nature of the institution to be taken into account as well as the fact that the participants were paid volunteers. It is known that volunteers do not constitute a typical sample.

Other studies involving obedience

Other studies into obedience include the work of Hofling et al. (1966). The researchers looked at nurse–doctor relationships in a hospital setting. Nurses were instructed by telephone to give 20 mg of the drug 'Astrofen' to a patient, Mr Jones. The doctor would come to see the patient in ten minutes and would sign for the

Box 28.2 Zimbardo's prison experiment

Twenty-five volunteer participants were selected, after extensive psychological tests, to take part in an experiment for a generous fee. The context was a simulated prison and the participants were to role play being either prisoners or guards. The toss of a coin determined which role each person would play. To start with, the 'prisoners' were arrested, charged with a felony and underwent all the procedures associated with this. They were deloused, strip-searched, given a prison uniform, with a number front and back and a manacle on one ankle. The 'guards' on the other hand were given military-style uniforms, reflective sunglasses to prevent eye contact, clubs, whistles, handcuffs and keys. They were encouraged to shout orders and push the 'prisoners' around. Anything was allowed short of physical violence. While the 'prisoners' were locked up for 24 hours a day, the 'guards' worked eight-hour shifts. In quite a short time a perverted relationship began to develop between 'prisoners' and 'guards'. Aggression increased by 'guards'; 'prisoners' became more passive. Within 36 hours one 'prisoner' had developed symptoms of depression and had to be released. Soon others also showed symptoms of stress and the whole experiment had to be called off after six days, though it had been scheduled to last a fortnight.

Once again it might be useful to reread the section on ethics in Chapter 5 and make your own assessment of the degree to which any of these experiments breached ethical guidelines.

SELF-ASSESSMENT QUESTIONS

1. Describe Asch's experiments on conformity. Comment on their ecological validity (how far do they seem to you to mirror what happens in 'real life')?
2. List some of the techniques used to ensure compliance. Comment upon their effectiveness.
3. Were the samples in Milgram's experiments representative? If not, why not?
4. What were the factors which caused participants in Milgram's experiments to obey, even when they were apparently inflicting pain on others?
5. List some of the criticisms made of these experiments. Do you think they were justified?
6. Make some comparison of Milgram's work with either that of Hofling or of Zimbardo. Can you draw any conclusions about human nature from these experiments?

drug then. Twenty-one out of 22 nurses complied, in spite of the fact that three rules were broken:

■ The maximum dose for this drug was 10 mg;
■ Written authority was required for its administration;
■ Nurses were required to check the genuineness of a doctor.

Zimbardo et al. (1973) conducted an experiment into social power in a more general sense. Details of their experiment are in Box 28.2.

Zimbardo was subjected to similar criticisms as to the ethics of his experiment as Milgram had been. It remains unclear whether the dubious ethics of the programme was justified by the uncovering of normal human beings' propensities to behave in an evil manner.

Leadership and followership

We shall now be considering why it is that some individuals become leaders in whatever they become involved with, while others are content to follow the lead of others. This division between leaders and followers seems to subsist as much in teams, committees, gangs and so on, as in the larger context of countries, political parties and councils. It seems at least possible that there are factors which can be isolated which provide a clue as to why this should be the case. These factors include:

■ **Personality**. Can it be said that those who persistently emerge as leaders in whatever field possess certain personality traits which mark them out so that it can be predicted who will lead?
■ **Situation**. Is it the situations in which individuals find themselves and the requirements of those situations which allow certain individuals to emerge as leaders, while others are content to be led?

■ **Behaviour or style**. Do leaders behave consistently in ways which might be termed *leaderlike* while others adopt the behaviour of followers?

The personalities of leaders

The question here is whether there is such a thing as a 'great person' personality and, if so, is it a trait or traits which are inherited? Stogdill (1974) and others have reviewed attempts to link the personality traits of leaders to their effectiveness and identified a number of personality characteristics which correlated with leadership, albeit weakly. Leaders tend to be above average in size, health, physical attractiveness, intelligence, self-confidence, talkativeness and the need for dominance. Mann (1959) found intelligence to be a reliable factor, Mullen et al. (1989) isolated talkativeness. Intelligence would seem to be needed because leaders have to be able to think and respond quickly and develop the ability to gain access to information quickly and accurately. Being talkative makes you the centre of attention so that everyone looks to you for a response to the situation. However, the search for the personality of the great leader has not been successful. Correlations among traits and between traits and effective leadership have been low. Great events in history, however, have by popular consent been associated with 'great' individuals. People talk about the 'Thatcher years' when referring to the changes which took place in Britain in the 1980s. Churchill is identified with standing alone against the world in 1940; Hitler is identified with the phenomenon of Nazism in Germany in the 1930s. Similarly, great trends in thought and in science are associated with particular individuals. Plato, Socrates, Freud and Isaac Newton spring to mind. It makes easier sense for people to interpret complex events and ideas in a straightforward way, and what could be more straightforward than to lay them at the door of particular individuals?

Situational factors

If it is not easy to predict who will assume leadership from personality traits, then perhaps there are features in situations which will allow us to predict who will emerge as leader. Different situations call for different qualities of leadership.

Task-oriented or socioemotional leadership

Bales (1950) identified, as part of his analysis of interactions among people in groups, two distinct functions of leaders within groups, **task-oriented leadership** and **socioemotional leadership**. In the former the task of a leader is primarily to ensure that the job in hand gets done, that the objectives are reached; in the latter, that relations between the individuals in the group remain buoyant and happy. In some cases the leader will perform both of these functions, not only ensuring that the job gets done but also that the members of the group get on well with each other while doing it. In other cases there may be one person providing task leadership and another socioemotional leadership. Their functions may be complementary. In Sherif's studies of boys' summer camps, described in Chapter 26 (Sherif et al., 1961; Sherif, 1966), it was found that when the situation changed from one of establishing group cohesion (Stage 2) to one of intergroup conflict, leadership changed and a person more capable of leading the group in these circumstances emerged. On a national scale, when a war situation arose in 1939–40 the individual who had led failed attempts to maintain the peace, Neville Chamberlain, was replaced by Winston Churchill. During the previous decade Churchill had been relegated to a backwater of politics and then emerged as the right leader in the right place at the right time. After the war was over in 1945 the situation changed to one which demanded different qualities and Churchill was rejected in his turn.

Behavioural factors

If it is possible to separate one's personality from one's behaviour then perhaps leadership is related to the ways in which individual people behave towards one another. Lippitt and White (1943) studied leadership in the context of after-school activities in clubs for boys. The parameters of effectiveness studied were morale,

---

> **GLOSSARY**
>
> **Task-oriented leadership** A style of leadership, described by Bales, where the leader is more concerned with the attainment of group goals than with relationships between members of the group.
>
> **Socioemotional leadership** A style of leadership which places emphasis upon the relationships between the members of a group.

Box 28.3 An experiment in leadership style (Lippitt and White, 1943)

The leaders of the clubs were confederates of the experimenters who had been trained to exercise three distinct leadership styles:

- **Autocratic leadership**. The prime focus was on achievement. The leader issued orders, praised or censured boys without giving reasons, discouraged communication between the boys and behaved in an aloof and impersonal way towards them.
- **Democratic leadership**. The leader helped the boys plan their projects by means of discussion, allowed them to choose their own workmates and communicate freely with each other. When comments were made they were fully explained and the leader joined in group activities.
- **Laissez-faire leadership**. The boys were left very much to themselves. Advice and help were only given when the leader was directly asked for it and no praise, blame or other comment was offered at all.

Each group was assigned a particular leadership style. One confederate was the leader for seven weeks and then the confederates swapped round. It was important that each group was exposed to only one leadership style, though to three leaders. In this way Lippitt and White were able to separate leadership style from a specific leader who was behaving that way. They were thus able to rule out personality explanations of differences in leadership outcomes.

The democratic style of leadership led to the boys liking their leaders more than in either of the two other styles. The atmosphere engendered was friendly. Productivity was relatively high and the boys got on with their tasks whether the leader was there or not. In the case of the autocratic leadership style the atmosphere engendered was quite different. It was aggressive but dependent and self-oriented. Productivity was high but only while the leader was there. The laissez-faire style of leadership created a friendly but play-oriented atmosphere. Productivity was low and increased only when the leader was not there.

Initiating structure or consideration

While the Lippitt and White experiment was a valuable addition to what was known about leadership, it was limited in that it was concerned only with juveniles, and only boys at that. Studies done at Ohio State University focused upon the distinction between task-oriented and socioemotional aspects of leadership. Distinctions were found as a result of questionnaires completed by military and industrial participants between the initiating structure of leadership and consideration structure. This roughly corresponds to the distinction Bales (1950) drew in his Interaction Process Analysis (IPA) between task area interactions and socioemotional interactions. There seemed to be two distinct types of leader: a task-oriented and a socioemotional type. In the Ohio study the distinction was as follows:

- **Initiating structure**. This relates to the leader's behaviour in defining the relationship between himself or herself and the members of the group, establishing patterns of organization, channels of communication and methods of procedure (Halpin, 1966). The leader has the task of motivating the group towards its defined goal. This may also involve identifying and agreeing on the goal.
- **Consideration structure**. Halpin sees consideration as behaviour indicative of friendship, mutual trust, respect and warmth in relation to other group members.

The flaw in this approach is that it concentrates solely on the behaviour of the leader. Deaux et al. (1993) have suggested that these researchers had fallen prey to fundamental attribution bias (see Chapter 24), in they overemphasized the importance of the dispositional characteristics of leaders as opposed to situational factors.

Recognition of this failing and the need for an interactionist approach has led to the development of

task achievement and group atmosphere. Box 28.3 details the experiment carried out by Lippitt and White.

what have been called contingency models of leadership. These were developed by Fiedler (1964, 1967) and have received considerable empirical support from, for example, Chemers (1983, 1987).

Fiedler's contingency model of leadership

There are four components of the model, the first related to disposition, the other three to situation.

The personality of the leader Fiedler devised an instrument called the least preferred coworker (LPC) scale. Participants using the scale were asked to think of all the people with whom they had ever worked and identify the one person they found most difficult to work with. Eighteen bipolar scales were used for this (for example, pleasant/unpleasant, boring/interesting, friendly/unfriendly and so on). High LPC scores indicated that the leader had a favourable attitude towards the least preferred coworker; low LPC scores indicated an unfavourable attitude. In more explicit terms a low LPC score indicated a task-oriented leadership style; a high LPC score a relationship-oriented one.

Relations between the leader and the members of the working group These could range from very good to very poor. The leader might be liked and respected or disliked, distrusted and rejected.

Task structure There were three elements here:

■ **Task definition**. Some tasks were very clearly defined in terms of goals, while others were much less clearly structured. The tasks before workers on an assembly line in a factory were likely to be much more clearly delineated than, for example, those before members of a committee working out policy for the factory.
■ **Solution specificity**. This related to whether there was more than one solution to the problem or more than one way of completing the task.
■ **Verifiability**. How easy it was to determine whether the decisions taken were the right ones.

What power and authority were vested in the leader? Could he or she hire and fire? Had the leader the authority to raise the pay and status of an individual worker? What backing did the leader get for decisions made? To take examples: if you are

responsible for a group of canvassers in an election campaign, they are volunteers and the leader would ordinarily be able to exercise very little positional authority over them; whereas the commanding officer of a military unit would have extremely high positional authority.

There were thus eight situational variables, as illustrated in Figure 28.2. In Category I the situational control was at its highest; in Category VIII at its lowest. A low LPC resulted in the most effective leadership where situational control was either very high or very low: at intermediate levels of situational control a high LPC score produced maximum effectiveness.

This model goes some way towards explaining why it has proved difficult empirically to show that particular personality characteristics or particular behavioural patterns explain effective leadership. It seems clear that effective leadership is the result of fairly complex interactions between personality, behaviour and situational factors.

❓ SELF-ASSESSMENT QUESTIONS

1. What personality traits have been found to be associated with effective leadership?
2. What differences did Lippitt and White find in the effectiveness of different styles of leadership in the context of boys' clubs?
3. Do you feel that Fiedler's contingency model of leadership adequately solves the problem of whether effective leadership is associated with the personality, the behaviour of leaders or the situation in which leadership is needed? Explain your answer.

Group decision making

Following on from the previous section on leadership, this section aims to examine the influence of group membership on the behaviour of members of the group, with particular reference to the way in which decisions are taken.

GLOSSARY

Contingency model A model of leadership devised by Fiedler in which situation and leadership style interact.

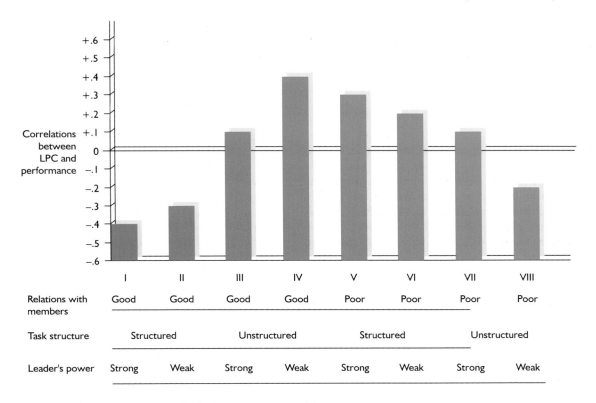

Figure 28.2 Situational variables in Fiedler's contingency model

Characteristics of groups

First, it is necessary to be clear what a group is. Perhaps Bales's (1950) proposal is relevant so far as size is concerned:

> Provided that each member receives some impression or perception of each other member, distinct enough . . . that he can give some reaction to each of the others as an individual person then a collection of people can be termed a small group.
>
> (Bales, 1950)

Johnson and Johnson (1987) have identified seven features of a group:

- **Interaction**. A group is a collection of individuals who are interacting with one another.
- **Perception of belonging**. A group consists of two or more persons who perceive themselves to belong to a group.
- **Interdependence**. Group members are interdependent.
- **Common goals**. A group is a collection of individuals who join together to achieve a goal.
- **Need satisfaction**. Individuals who belong to a group are trying to satisfy some need through membership of it.
- **Roles and norms**. Members of a group structure their interactions by means of roles and norms. Roles consist of sets of obligations and expectations. The role of 'student', for example, embodies obligations to attend class, listen to the teacher and attempt to do what is asked of you; it also embodies expectations that the teacher will provide the means to achieve the goals set. Norms imply established ways of behaving: that is, uniformities among people in the ways they behave.
- **Influence**. A group is a collection of individuals who influence each other.

Group size

For our purposes, a group, therefore, is not just a collection of people waiting for a bus; most of the features listed above would not apply. There is certainly a limitation in size. You cannot interact with each of the members of a group of 200 people. Most experimental research has concentrated on groups of between three and ten people.

Group cohesiveness

Group cohesiveness relates to the way in which members of a group hang together; how tightly or how loosely knit it is; what degree of mutual support or uniformity of behaviour there is. Where there is very low cohesiveness a collection of individuals almost ceases to be a group. Festinger et al. (1950) defines cohesiveness in terms of the attractiveness of the group to its members and the attractiveness of members of the group to each other and the degree to which the group satisfies the goals of individual members and acts on those members.

Communication networks

Most of the features of a group mentioned above presuppose communication between its members. The relationships between members of a group depend upon the channels of communication which exist between them. The pattern of these channels may in turn be determined by a number of factors, for example:

■ **Location**. The physical relationship of one group member to another (they may be in different buildings most of the time, for example) may have an effect on ease of communication.
■ **Formal rules or chains of command**. In military units, individuals may not communicate direct with, for example, the commanding officer but need to go through a chain of command – platoon commander, company commander and so on.
■ **Personal factors**. This may include personal liking or dislike. Two members of a group may not be on speaking terms and communication between them may be solely through intermediaries.

Leavitt (1951), Shaw (1964, 1978) and Steiner (1972, 1976) are among those who have studied communication networks. Leavitt used some of the networks shown in Figure 28.3 to investigate the relative efficiency of five-person groups with different structures in solving simple identification problems.

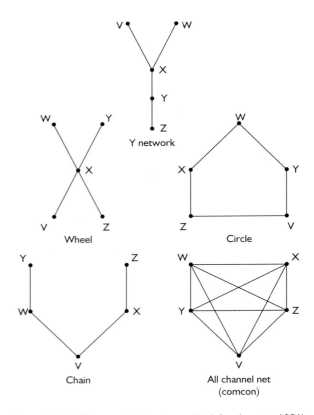

Figure 28.3 Communication networks (after Leavitt, 1951)

The form of communication links is important in that it determines the way in which the group functions. Wheel, Y and chain networks tend to lead to a centralized organization because the person at the centre of the wheel, the intersection of the Y or the middle of the chain is pivotal. The central person is likely to emerge as leader. By contrast, in less centralized communication patterns such as circle or all channel net (comcon), where everyone can communicate with everyone else, the structure of communication does not influence who emerges as leader. Individuals' personalities and skills become more important. It also makes full advantage of the contributions which each member of a team may make. Where a particular individual or individuals are absent, the negative impact of this is less, because channels of communication are less likely to be interrupted. Romzek and Dubnick (1987) have reported that a factor which led to the loss of the Challenger space shuttle was that concerns about the performance of a key component, the O-ring seals, were not channelled to the appropriate individuals because two key members of the communication network had left.

Roles in groups

Within a group the roles to be occupied by individuals emerge and develop. This includes the leadership role, which has been explored in the previous section. This process of role differentiation has been explored by Forsyth (1983). Where there is a new group, one individual may assume the task leadership role (keeping the group working towards a goal) and another may assume the morale leadership role, corresponding to the initiating structure and consideration elements mentioned earlier. Where the group has been in existence for some time and a member of the group leaves, a newcomer may be specifically assigned to take over the role – whatever it might have been – of the leaver. The new person will probably modify the role in the course of time. But to begin with, the role is associated with the position to be filled rather than with the individuals who fill them (Katz and Kahn, 1976: McGrath, 1984).

Norm formation

As the group develops so also do the expectations members have about what rules and procedures might be appropriate to develop. This is the process of the establishment of group norms. For example, during Sherif's studies of conformity in relation to the autokinetic effect (described earlier in this chapter), where judgments were made by members of a group they were much less variable than those made by individuals, and this 'group norm', once established, persisted even when those who had established the norm left the group to be replaced by others. Among the norms which develop in this way are status characteristics. These involve rules or expectations concerning the characteristics of individuals who will be accorded the highest status and authority within the group. For example, experience might be conceived of as the most important characteristic of group membership, so that individuals with the most experience are accorded the highest status within the group.

Status characteristics model

Berger et al. (1980) have developed a model called status characteristics theory to explain how these principles emerge. Within this model, status characteristics may be specific or they may be diffuse. In the former case, the characteristics of an individual which

cause him or her to be accorded status and authority within the group may be closely linked to the task in hand. Suppose a group has been convened to plan for the establishment of a new laboratory for a school. Within the group are individuals with specific knowledge and experience of laboratory work in a school context, perhaps the head of the science department, alongside members of the governing body and perhaps the head teacher. This individual is likely to have high status *within* the group, though maybe not outside it, in recognition of his or her expertise (his or her *specific* status characteristics).

Diffuse status characteristics

At another level there are individuals who have *diffuse* status characteristics. These are less closely linked to the task in hand, but nevertheless throw up expectations about performance. The head teacher, in the group mentioned above, might be a case in point. Within this category of status characteristics can be included considerations of gender, perhaps, or race. Suppose the group mentioned above is planning for an engineering laboratory, the female members of the group might be accorded lower status than the male ones because of the assumption that women have less skill in domains that include mechanical and mathematical abilities. On the other hand, were the group planning a nursery rather than an engineering laboratory, the female members of the group might have higher status on the unwritten assumption that small children are women's domain.

Decision making in groups

Social decisions schemes

Given that one of the most important functions which groups perform is that of decision making, it is worthwhile to spend a little time on the processes by which decisions are reached within groups. Davis (1973) in a model called **social decisions schemes** has related the strictness of the rules adopted in discussions leading to the forming of decisions, to the

---

GLOSSARY

Role differentiation The emergence in a group of particular roles assigned or adopted by individual members of the group.

concentration of power. Where there is maximum strictness (as, for example, in cases where a unanimous decision is to be reached; in a jury situation for example) there is least concentration of power. Egalitarian rules such as unanimity tend to spread power among all the members; authoritarian rules concentrate it on one or on a few members. Majority decision-making rules concentrate more power. Where the final decision is left to the chair there is maximum power concentration.

Generating ideas

The ability of a group to generate ideas is important to decision making. Osborn (1957) popularized the technique of brainstorming to achieve this end. Members of a group are encouraged to put forward as many ideas as they can irrespective of quality and to build upon others' ideas where they can. However, there is no evidence that brainstorming is effective in producing more novel ideas than the individual members of the group might produce on their own. Paulus et al. (1993) have suggested three reason for this:

■ **Evaluation apprehension.** Individuals tend to censor their ideas because they are concerned to make a good impression. Productivity is therefore reduced.
■ **Social loafing.** Individuals have a tendency to leave it to others. It has been suggested that the larger the group, the greater the amount of social loafing.
■ **Production blocking.** The difficulty of having to deal with the ideas produced by others at the same time as generating your own has been termed production blocking.

Group memory

As a result of experiments carried out, Clark and Stephenson (1989) have concluded that groups recall more material than individuals and more than the individual in the group with the best memory. There do seem to be qualifications about this, however. Where the material to be memorized is simple and artificial, group superiority in memory is greater than for complex and realistic tasks.

Transactive memory A quite different and separate aspect of the advantages of groups over individuals in terms of memory lies in Wegner's ideas about **transactive memory** (Wegner, 1986; Wegner et al., 1991). Individuals within a group can share a memory load so that each individual is responsible for memory of part of what is needed to be recalled. When a group is formed individual members are assigned, on the basis of stereotypes, domains of information related to their social categorization. One member, for example, categorized as a technical expert, might remember technical details; while another might recall organizational facts, the programme of events for instance. Areas of expertise may be assigned explicitly or implicitly.

Groupthink

In most cases groups come together in order to work out the best solution to the problems that confront them. It may be that they are ad hoc groups set up as 'working parties' to deal with specific problems or they are committees set up to run an organization: the academic board of a college, for example, or the board of directors of a firm. Groups may differ in the degree of their cohesiveness. Cartwright (1968) has described 'cohesiveness' as the total of all the forces attracting members to a group. When all or nearly all the members of the group are strongly attracted to it, the group is highly cohesive; less cohesive groups may be those with a number of members who are *ex officio* or who feel that their interests ought to be represented. Janis (1982) defined **groupthink** as 'a mode of thinking that people engage in when they are deeply involved in a cohesive in-group when members' striving for unanimity overrides their motivation to realistically appraise alternative courses of action'. Five antecedent conditions of groupthink have been described by Janis and

---

GLOSSARY

Evaluation apprehension A situation where productivity within a group is impaired because of individuals' apprehension of how their contributions will appear to others.

Social loafing The tendency within a group to leave it to others.

Transactive memory Relates to the situation in a closer relationship where two partners or members of a group may jointly have greater memory than as individuals.

Groupthink A term used for the situation where a group places unanimity of decision ahead of the search for a realistic solution to a problem.

Mann (1977) and more recently McCauley (1989) has added a sixth. These are:

- High cohesiveness;
- Uncertainty of approval;
- Insulation;
- Lack of methodical procedures for search and appraisal;
- Highly directive leadership;
- High levels of stress and low levels of hope of finding a better solution than the one advocated by the leader or by other influential persons.

Uncertainty of approval refers to the extent to which a group member feels able to count on the acceptance of his or her ideas by other members of the group.

Insulation relates to the extent to which the group is cut off from outside influence. A board of directors, for example, insulates itself from the judgment of qualified outsiders because they are not members of the board. McCauley relates this insulation to two events which happened during the time President Kennedy was in power: the abortive invasion of Cuba, which became known as the Bay of Pigs episode; and the Cuban Missile Crisis, when Soviet missiles were discovered to have been based in Cuba, targeted on American cities. In the former, decisions were taken by a cohesive group around the President himself, with disastrous consequences. American forces were forced into a humiliating retreat. In the latter, Kennedy encouraged debate, appointed a 'devil's advocate' and brought outsiders with differing opinions into his discussions on the crisis. The US was able to face down the threat and the crisis was averted.

The above antecedent conditions lead to symptoms of groupthink becoming apparent. These include:

- Mind guards. The conscious protecting of the group from information which might shatter its complacency and lay it open to doubt;
- The illusion of invulnerability;
- Collective rationalization;
- Belief in the inherent morality of the group;
- Unfavourable stereotyping of out-groups;
- Pressure applied directly on dissenters;
- Self-censorship;
- The illusion of unanimity.

Closed-mindedness of groupthink The closed-mindedness described above is destructive of efficient decision making. Alternative policies are not ade-

quately explored, objectives are not fully surveyed, the risks inherent in the chosen policy, not fully examined, information is only partial, the processing of it is biased, and contingency plans are not worked out. Most of us can identify cases where groupthink has resulted in poor decisions being taken, sometimes with disastrous consequences. However, Hogg (1992) and Turner et al. (1992) have suggested that groupthink has not been fully explained. For one thing, group cohesiveness has not been defined precisely enough. It could amount to a group consisting of close friends with strong emotional and friendship ties to each other. It could merely imply that members of the group get on reasonably well together. It has also been suggested that groupthink is not a discrete phenomenon at all but merely a specific case of 'risky shift'. This is explained below.

Risky shift phenomenon

Contrary to what appears to be common sense, the outcome of group discussions appears to be more extreme than the sum of the views of the members would lead you to suppose. There is a **group polarization** which takes place during discussion. Stoner (1961) found, in some very important research, that group decisions were riskier than ones taken by individuals on their own. For example, a committee looking into the spending of a large sum of money on a new laboratory is likely to be less cautious than a single executive might have been, making the same decision. This finding became known as the **risky shift phenomenon**. This term is, however, something of a misnomer. Research over the years between Stoner's original research and the present has suggested that the shift resulting from group discussion was not necessarily in the direction of greater risk, but in the direction of the initial opinions of the group. This might well be towards a more conservative line. Kaplan (1987) has explained this phenomenon in terms of two types of influence:

GLOSSARY

Group polarization A tendency for members of a group to take more extreme attitudes and/or decisions than individual members would.

Risky shift phenomenon A term used for group polarization coined before it was realized that polarization might result in more conservative decisions.

Normative influence Within a group individuals have a chance to assess the opinions of others. Pressures to conform encourage them to move towards a position of perceived agreement. This may be for one of two reasons:

- Desire for a favourable evaluation by group members;
- A concern for self-presentation.

A bandwagon effect may also be evident whose influence depends on the extent to which individual members see themselves as 'belonging' to the group.

Informational influence Learning results from exposure to the group discussion itself. Members are persuaded to change their opinions by the arguments advanced by other members of the group.

Both of these influences may operate on a group at any given time. Where the emphasis is upon getting the job done, and on right answers to problems, informational influences are stronger. Where the emphasis is upon the group rather than the task and where there is no one right answer but solutions depend upon judgment, then normative influences come to the fore. Unanimous decisions (such as jury decisions, for example) are the result of both normative and informational influences (Kaplan and Miller, 1987). Members need to convince others holding different opinions to change them and this involves informational influence. At the same time the unanimity rule means that there is emphasis on group harmony and this brings normative influence into play.

? SELF-ASSESSMENT QUESTIONS

1. Describe two types of communication network within groups. What effect is each of these likely to have on the influence exerted by particular members?
2. What is transactive memory? How may this operate to make groups more effective than individuals?
3. Describe the phenomenon of the risky shift. Is this really a proper description of it and why does it occur?

The influence of the crowd

LeBon (1908) observed events during a period of great social turmoil in France, read accounts of crowd behaviour in the French Revolution of 1789 and in the Paris Commune in 1871 and claimed that 'the crowd is always intellectually inferior to the isolated individual . . . mob man is fickle, credulous and intolerant, showing the violence and ferocity of primitive beings'.

This primitive behaviour was attributed to three things

- **Anonymity.** Individuals cannot be easily identified in a crowd;
- **Contagion.** Ideas and emotions spread rapidly and unpredictably;
- **Suggestibility.** The savagery which is just below the surface is released by suggestion.

Freudian explanation of crowd behaviour

Freud (1921) saw the crowd as unlocking the unconscious mind. The socialization process has submerged the id as the ego and the superego develop. The leader in a crowd acts as a hypnotist, replacing the superego. In Freud's terms the id represents a person's basic animal impulses, the ego the modification of these impulses as a result of the impact of those around us and the superego is the internalized sense we develop of right and wrong. The primitive impulses of the id come under the leader's control because each of us has the instinct to regress to the 'primal horde'. McDougall (1920) believed strongly in the instinctive motives within human beings. Fear and anger are the strongest and most widely shared of these instincts. Where these strong primitive instincts are brought to the surface there is wide consensus so that they spread and strengthen in the crowd as each individual provides stimulus to the others. The effect is, as LeBon has suggested, a lowered sense of responsibility and anonymity.

Deindividuation

Festinger et al. (1952) were the first to use the term **deindividuation** for the loss of personal responsibility and the anonymity which come upon people in a crowd situation. In a series of experiments by Festinger himself and by Zimbardo (1970), participants were deindividuated by being made to wear uniform laboratory coats or, in Zimbardo's case, cloaks and hoods reminiscent of the Ku Klux Klan or dressed as prison guards in a simulated prison (for a full account of this experiment see the first section of this chapter). In each study participants were found to be ready to behave in ways which were quite foreign to their normal behaviour, making negative comments about their parents in Festinger's study, or behaving quite brutally to 'prisoners' in Zimbardo's study.

Diener (1976) had children engage in 'trick or treat' activities wearing costumes which concealed their identities. Children were invited into homes in Seattle where they were asked to take just one piece of 'candy' from a plate. Some of them were asked their names and so were individuated to an extent; others were not. As many as 80 per cent of the deindividuated children took more than one piece of candy as opposed to 8 per cent of the individuated ones. It is questionable whether this was an ethical experiment in terms of what was discussed in Chapter 5.

Self-awareness

People are normally aware of themselves as individuals and, as a consequence, monitor their own behaviour. When a person is deindividuated, this self-awareness is reduced and the monitoring process no longer operates to ensure that restraints on behaviour are in place. He or she is no longer concerned about what others may think. In many instances this loss of restraint leads to aggression and antisocial behaviour, though this is not inevitable. It might equally manifest itself in the kind of euphoria that was evident in the rally held in Sheffield by the Labour Party in the UK before the 1992 general election. Those present, while not aggressive, behaved in an unrestrainedly euphoric manner.

Other researchers, including Carver and Scheier (1981), have distinguished public and private deindividuation. It is only when you become less attentive to how you want others to evaluate you and do not care any longer what others think, that behaviour begins to be released from the social norms which restrain it and may become antisocial.

Emergent norm theory

Turner's (1974) explanation takes a somewhat different approach. A crowd of people probably have no common prior association with each other and have come together just on this one occasion for a particular purpose. For example, the crowds that rioted in British cities in protest at the imposition of a flat rate of 'poll tax' in the late 1980s, which paid no regard to individuals' means or ability to pay, brought together very diverse people with little in common and so few preexistent common norms of behaviour. There was nothing to tell them how to behave, so that norms of behaviour begin to emerge which were peculiar to that particular crowd. Attention was drawn to individuals who stood out from the crowd and to their behaviour and they began to supply the norms of behaviour. There was pressure on the previously inactive majority in the crowd to conform to these emergent norms.

There are some difficulties with emergent norm theory, though. Diener (1980) claims that the emergence of norms implies self-awareness. People do not need to comply with norms unless they feel that they are identifiable. Mann et al. (1982) conducted an experiment which supported this view. Participants were found to be more aggressive when anonymous, irrespective of what norms had been established, but when the norm established was an aggressive one, this aggression increased.

Reicher (1982, 1987) rightly states that crowds do not usually come together except with a specific purpose (to demonstrate against the poll tax, for example), and this purpose implies shared norms. You do not usually find a crowd coming together for no purpose at all. Any purpose, whether it be supporting a football team or demonstrating against a perceived injustice, in itself establishes norms.

Social identity theory and crowds

As often as not crowd behaviour involves confrontation, one group against another: striking miners against the police, for example in the miners' strike in Britain in the early 1980s (miners went on strike against threats to their jobs and police were used to prevent pickets stopping strike-breakers getting into the mines, so that

---

GLOSSARY

Deindividuation A feeling of anonymity which results in individuals not taking responsibility for behaviour.

Emergent norm theory Emergence norms of behaviour in crowd situations where people involved have nothing obvious in common except the purposes for which the crowd has come together.

confrontation ensued); supporters of one football team confronting those of another. Reicher (1982, 1984) relates social identity theory to crowd behaviour. This has been discussed earlier (p. 615) in a different context. So far from losing their identity, members of the crowd replace their idiosyncratic personal identities with a social identity as a crowd member (or perhaps, more correctly, a faction member within the crowd). They categorize themselves as, for example, supporters of the England football team and identify others as 'the enemy', supporters of Italy, for example. Group membership produces group norms of conduct, very often mediated by leaders or prominent individuals. The police in a strike confrontation may behave in one way governed by their norms of conduct; strikers in another, governed by their norms. Reicher has used the theory to explain what happened in the riots in St Paul's in Bristol in the early 1980s (see Chapter 26). The following points emerged:

- ■ **Selective nature of attacks**. The rioters were selective in their attack, attacking police, the bank and entrepreneurial merchants, who were seen as representing the power of the state.
- ■ **Containment**. The crowd did not stray from the boundaries of St Paul's.
- ■ **Social identity**. A strong sense of social identity was engendered as members of the St Paul's community.

The riot was a protest against the government by a community which felt itself to be deprived. There was particularly high unemployment in St Paul's even in a time of national high unemployment.

Football crowds

Marsh et al. (1978) conducted an ethogenic (see p. 835) study of football crowds. They observed social behaviour and analysed the accounts which football fans gave of what was going on. The conclusions which they arrived at suggested that violence, when it occurs, does not come from a deindividuated mob. There is a great deal of ritualized aggression but little actual damage. While fans might talk about the opposition getting their 'heads bashed in', actual aggression was limited to chasing the opposing fans back to the railway station, being careful not to catch them up.

Ritualized aggression   It was the chase and the ritualized aggression which was important. This has

Football hooligans at a Euro 96 match. Violence among football fans is often ritualized aggression

its parallels in the animal world where defence of territory may result in **ritualized aggression** which stops short of actual injury, which would be counterproductive. Actual conflict involves the risk of injury or even death to either party. A severely injured animal is likely to be unable to pass on it genes. Marsh suggested in the context of football crowds that outbreaks of uncontrolled violence are more likely to occur when the ritual is upset by the interference of outside authority. Excessive control removes the known pattern of ritualized behaviour and replaces it with a much less well-controlled violence. The 'hooligans' of the football terraces are in fact part of a well-defined and structured social pattern.

Social disorder

Most political demonstrations are peaceful affairs which pass off without injury or violence. However, there are occasionally violent altercations. The St Paul's riot in Bristol has already been mentioned, as well as the poll tax riots. A specific event, such as the raid by the police on the Black and White Café in St Paul's, provided a flashpoint from which more generalized violence erupted. But to say that such flashpoints *caused* the violence is too simplistic.

> ### GLOSSARY
> **Ritualized aggression** A stereotypical display of aggression, serving to communicate a message, but stopping short of actual injury.

Waddington et al. (1987) have proposed a model which might be used to analyse different kinds of social disorder. In their model there are six levels of analysis.

Structural Wider issues of social structure need to be considered. For instance, in the St Paul's area there was very high unemployment among the black people, which led to frustration and alienation.

Political or ideological A particular sector of society might feel aggrieved about a piece of legislation which has imposed social controls on them to unacceptable levels. The recent Police and Criminal Justice Act in Britain has provided this focus of discontent for 'travelling' groups.

Cultural Social representations (see Chapter 26) are ways in which we see the world and include such things as beliefs about rights. A different cultural group within a society may have different social representations of the elements of a problem. The police, for example, in St Paul's, see the world quite differently from young unemployed black people. The problem will be defined quite differently. As far as the police were concerned it was about drugs. So far as the community of St Paul's were concerned it was an invasion of territory.

Contextual This includes the particular time when the incident occurs and the sequence of events which have led up to this particular one.

Spatial This includes the physical setting in which the confrontation has occurred, the layout of open spaces and buildings and the symbolic significance any of these may have for the participants. The Black and White Café, for example, represents a focus for the black community in the St Paul's area, and so has importance as a centre of the community's 'territory'. In the eyes of the police, on the other hand, the café was a centre for drug dealing.

Interactional This concerns the nature of the interactions which took place between the people involved. It might be argued that the police overstepped the established norms of behaviour in dealing with a particular community. Was a 'raid' on the Black and White Café an appropriate way of responding to a suggestion of drug dealing? The arrest or the rough treatment of a prominent member of the community, a local politician or a trades union official might be seen as 'out of order'. Waddington et al. stressed that interpersonal style could be as important as the political context.

Waddington et al. conducted an analysis of two public rallies which took place during the miners' strike in 1984, one of which was disorderly and involved violence between the police and demonstrators. The second, in a similar context, was peaceful. Researchers used participant observation (see p. 830), both while the events were taking place and in the run-up to them. They used the model above and concluded that at the structural, ideological and cultural levels there was no difference between the two events. The differences were at the situational, contextual and interactional levels. The second, peaceful, event was carefully planned with consultation with the local police. The setting was carefully organized so as to channel the crowd's responses into peaceful activity, with entertainments laid on. To control the movements of the crowd without recourse to police intervention, barriers were erected beforehand. The control of the crowd was undertaken by the organizers themselves, the police carefully avoiding any confrontation.

As a result of this work, Waddington's team concluded that crowd violence was not unpredictable. Action can be taken at any or all of the above levels to ensure that it does not occur. On a practical level Waddington outlined five steps which can be taken to ensure peaceful crowd control:

- **Self-policing**. Confrontation is more likely to be avoided if the control of the crowd is left in the hands of the organizers of the rally.
- **Liaison**. There should close cooperation and liaison between the organizers and the police both before and during the event.
- **Minimum force**. A policy should be adopted of the police using minimum force. For them to be deployed in riot gear presupposes they expect trouble.
- **Training in interpersonal skills**. Those involved in managing and controlling crowds should have had appropriate training.
- **Accountability**. Police and law enforcement agencies should be seen as wholly accountable for their actions. The use of overalls which deliberately conceal the numbers of individual officers to give them anonymity is not acceptable.

1. Describe what is meant by deindividuation. What are its causes and results?
2. What is meant by emergent norm theory? How far is it reasonable to say that a group of people is without common norms of behaviour at any time?
3. Can it reasonably be said that crowd violence is an unpredictable thing which cannot be prevented? What steps does the evidence suggest may be taken to avoid it occurring?

Chapter summary

■ The distinction between conformity and compliance lies in this: conformity is the response made to indirect social pressure, while compliance is concerned with acceding to direct requests. The earliest studies of conformity concerned the tendency to conform to the norms of those around where there was uncertainty or ambiguity. You do not know how to respond so you take your cue from others. Two separate influences cause people to conform: informational and normative influences. Self-categorization strengthens each of these influences.

■ Factors which influence the degree of conformity exhibited include the size of the group, the cohesion of the group and unanimity shown by group members. Crutchfield found specific differences in personality traits between conformers and nonconformers. Nonconformers showed greater intellectual effectiveness, ego strength, maturity and efficiency than conformers. They were also more self-reliant, natural, able to communicate effectively and lacking in pretension.

■ Compliance has been much researched in relation to selling. The foot-in-the-door technique shows that initial compliance with a small request may lead to compliance with a larger one. On the other hand, refusal of an initial request can make it more likely that a subsequent request will be acceded to (door-in-the-face technique). Techniques to ensure compliance known as 'that's not all', low ball and lure are also employed by salespeople.

■ The degree of compliance can depend upon the type and degree of power exercised by the parties. Types of power include coercive power, reward power, expert power, referent power, legitimate power and informational power.

■ Obedience relates to compliance with direct orders. Milgram's experiments suggested that individuals would obey orders even when to do so might cause actual harm to someone else. While his experiments have been criticized for their dubious ethics they throw considerable light on how people will behave. Other studies confirm some of the conclusions he reached.

■ Personality, situation and behaviour all contribute to leadership. There appear to be separate task and socioemotional leadership traits. Fiedler produced a contingency model of leadership which drew all these elements together. The most effective leadership is manifested where situational control is either very high or very low.

■ Groups have clearly defined characteristics. Members must interact with each other, have some perception of belonging, be interdependent, have common goals, satisfy some need by membership, adhere to certain roles and norms within the group and exert influence on other members. In practice this implies group size of between three and ten.

■ The communication links between members of a group will determine the way in which a group functions. Centralized structures place more emphasis upon the leader. Within a group individuals assume particular roles and this role differentiation will separate those who exert leadership by initiating new procedures while others are more concerned with the morale of the group as a whole.

■ Decision making within groups has its own characteristics. Brainstorming is a useful way of generating ideas, but is subject to individuals' feeling evaluation apprehension, which may inhibit them. There is also a danger of social loafing, where certain individuals remain passengers. Transactive memory relates to the sharing of memory load among members of a group so that total memory is more efficiently utilized.

■ Groupthink is a phenomenon where membership of a close-knit group may inhibit realistic appraisal of alternative choices, because of the apparent need to strive for unanimity. The risky shift phenomenon implies that a group might be less cautious in making decisions than individuals within the group. This polarization of ideas tends to be towards the initial opinions of the group, which may equally be less or more cautious.

■ Members of crowds tend to be fickle, credulous and intolerant. Individuals lose their identities and deindividuation occurs and there is reduced self-awareness.

Diverse people brought together at random in a crowd tend to develop their own norms of behaviour – emergent norms.

■ There seems to be a parallel between the actions of football crowds acting aggressively towards opposition fans and the behaviour of animals defending territory. Their aggression often stops short of actual injury as this is not in the interests of either group.

■ Demonstrations are generally peaceful. It is usually possible to channel feelings of protest into peaceful action unless other forces are introduced which adopt a hostile role towards the demonstrators. Control of the crowd is best left to the organizers of the demonstration themselves.

Further reading

Deaux, K., Dane, F.C. and Wrightsman, L.S. (1993). *Social Psychology in the 90's*, 6th edn. Pacific Grove, CA: Brookes-Cole. Chapters 12 and 13 of this book contain a good account of group processes, including polarization and 'group think'.

Hayes, N. (1994). *Foundations of Psychology*. London: Routledge. Chapter 15 contains an excellent account and discussion of crowds and of social disorder.

Waddington, D., Jones, K. and Critcher, C. (1987). Flashpoints of public disorder. In G. Gaskell and R. Benewick (eds), *The Crowd in Contemporary Britain*. London: Sage. An analysis of the miners' strike and other incidences of public disorder, suggesting reasons why some crowds may be disorderly while others are not.

Personality and abnormal behaviour

Part 7 looks at two dimensions on which people may differ from each other: personality and abnormal behaviour. It begins by examining what we mean by personality and exploring some of the issues and assumptions which exist in various theoretical approaches to the study of personality. We then look at the theories in greater depth and explore ways in which personality is assessed.

The rest of Part 7 focuses on atypical development and abnormal behaviour and includes a discussion of a number of forms of atypical development, critical evaluation of the problems which arise when attempts are made to distinguish 'abnormal' from 'normal' behaviour, some of the characteristics and possible causes of various mental disorders and a range of different therapies used to treat them.

Contents

INTRODUCTION

Definitions and issues in personality theory and abnormal behaviour   705

■ What do we mean by personality?   705

■ Assumptions made about personality   705

■ Atypical development and abnormal behaviour   707

CHAPTER 29

Type and trait approaches to personality   709

■ Multitrait approaches   710

■ Is personality consistent?   718

■ Single-trait theories   722

CHAPTER 30

Psychodynamic and person-centred theories of personality   727

■ Freud's psychoanalytic theory   727

■ Person-centred approaches to personality   734

CHAPTER 31

Atypical development   744

■ Learning difficulties   745

■ Physical and sensory impairment   748

■ Emotional disturbances and behavioural difficulties   751

CHAPTER 32

The classification, diagnosis and causes of mental disorder   762

■ Normality and abnormality   762

■ Diagnosis and classification of mental disorders   776

■ Classifications and descriptions of mental disorders   776

■ Possible causes of mental disorders   783

CHAPTER 33

Treatments and therapies   790

■ Somatic treatments   791

■ Behavioural therapies   795

■ Cognitive-behavioural therapies   800

■ Psychoanalytic therapies   801

■ Humanistic-existential therapies   803

■ Treatment effectiveness and patient care   804

Definitions and issues in personality theory and abnormal behaviour

What do we mean by personality?

Describing and making assumptions about the personalities of others is something we all do in everyday life. Phrases such as 'She has lots of personality' and 'He has no personality' are typically used. In a psychological sense, however, these phrases are meaningless. All people have a personality and they differ not in the amount, but in the kind of personality they have.

Separately studying psychological processes such as perception, thinking, motivation and emotions makes it very difficult to describe the person as a whole. The concept of personality attempts to encompass all the different psychological processes and present a coherent picture of the individual's characteristic ways of thinking, feeling and behaving. Like intelligence, personality is notoriously difficult to define and there is no one definition that all psychologists would subscribe to. For example, some psychologists use the term 'personality' to refer to all the various ways in which individuals differ from each other, including social behaviour, emotions, intellectual functioning, and so on, where others limit the term to account only for social and emotional aspects of behaviour. Hall and Lindzey (1978) carried out a review of personality theories and concluded that: 'no substantive definition can be applied with any generality... the way in which given individuals will define personality will depend completely upon their particular theoretical preference' (p. 9).

Hampson (1988) suggests that the following definition of personality by Child (1968) is one which is considered acceptable by many psychologists: 'more or less stable, internal factors that make one person's behaviour consistent from one time to another, and different from the behaviour other people would manifest in comparable situations' (p. 83).

Assumptions made about personality

Theories of personality vary in terms of the assumptions made about psychological functioning in humans and about appropriate methods used to study personality. Below is a brief indication of some of the issues and controversies which concern psychologists who study personality. From this the reader should begin to appreciate the complexity of this field where many theories exist relatively independently of each other and offer diverse and often contradictory viewpoints. Chapters 29 and 30 will attempt to explore some of these theories in greater depth, along with a number of different ways in which personality is assessed. It should be noted that the concepts of reliability and validity (discussed in Chapters 21 and 34) are as important a consideration in personality assessment as they are in intelligence and other psychometric testing.

Issues and controversies in personality research

Idiographic versus nomothetic approaches

A major difference between personality theories is the way in which they emphasize the uniqueness of the individual – idiographic theories – as compared to the similarities which exist between people – nomothetic theories.

GLOSSARY

Idiographic theories A belief that human beings are unique and can only be understood through the use of techniques, for example, case studies, which are designed to reflect that uniqueness.

Nomothetic theories These theories assume that the same traits or dimensions of personality apply to everyone in the same way, though people will differ in the extent to which they may possess a characteristic. Nomothetic approaches to the study of personality have been carried out by Cattell and Eysenck, already referred to, both of whom have attempted to discover the major dimensions of personality which are present to some extent in everyone but on which individuals will differ. The work of these two theorists will be examined in Chapter 29.

Idiographic theories These theories are person-centred. Idiographic theorists aim to build up a detailed picture of each individual's personality and generally believe that the study of similarities between people is of limited value. Gordon Allport is probably the main advocate of this approach, though paradoxically in addition to studying individual traits (unique personal characteristics) he also considered the existence of common traits (basic characteristics which apply to all members of a particular social or cultural group). The humanistic psychologist Carl Rogers also represents the idiographic approach as does George Kelly with his personal construct theory. The theories of Allport, Rogers and Kelly will be examined in Chapter 30.

Freud's psychoanalytic theory was developed from clinical case studies of his patients. To this extent, his theory is idiographic. For Freud, personality structure consisted of three interrelated systems – the id, ego and superego. A key element of his theory rests in his notion of an unconscious mind harbouring repressed ('forgotten') memories which influence conscious thoughts and behaviour. Freud's theory is considered in Chapter 30.

Type and trait approaches

Many theorists make use of the concept of traits, as referred to above, in describing personality. Traits are considered to be stable and enduring aspects of personality which are reflected in people's behaviour. Examples might be 'liveliness' or 'even-temperedness'. Cattell is considered to be a trait theorist.

Other theorists subscribe to the view that individuals may be categorized into distinct personality types. Probably the earliest type theory was the Greek physician Hippocrates' division of human beings into sanguine, phlegmatic, melancholic and choleric temperamental types. It was thought that the personality was dominated by a particular body fluid, namely blood, phlegm, black or yellow bile.

Types differ from traits in that a person cannot be said to possess a type to varying degrees; the person either is or is not categorized as a particular type. Traits, on the other hand, are factors that are thought to be normally distributed throughout the population and are therefore represented in everyone, but to varying degrees.

By far and away the most famous and prolific personality theorist was H. J. Eysenck, who died in 1997. Eysenck's theory proposes two major dimensions of personality as continuums along which each individual can be placed. These dimensions are introversion–extraversion and neuroticism–stability. Both Cattell and Eysenck arrived at their theories through analysing the scores from large numbers of personality questionnaires and other data such as direct observations of behaviour. Both Eysenck and Cattell are known as multitrait theorists. These two theories will be examined in greater depth in Chapter 29 along with more recent multitrait theories. Chapter 29 also considers some single-trait theories – approaches which have focused upon one particular aspect of personality.

Consistency versus situational specificity

Trait approaches view the individual's personality as being generally consistent. Thus, it is thought that people will usually react in similar ways in many different situations: the person who is honest at work will also be honest in dealing with friends; the aggressive person may be expected to behave aggressively in a number of different settings. The notion of personality traits as consistent has been challenged by Mischel who argued that behaviour is more likely to be

> **GLOSSARY**
>
> **Nomothetic theories** Based on the idea that there are laws of behaviour which are applied to everyone and can be used to compare people with each other.
>
> **Trait** A term used to describe stable and enduring personality characteristics such as 'liveliness' or 'aggressiveness'.
>
> **Type** In relation to personality, a term used to classify people into an 'all or none' category, for example 'extravert'.

influenced by the situation a person is in than by that person's temperament: a view termed situational specificity.

Mischel criticized traditional personality theories which use the concept of trait both on conceptual and statistical issues. His challenge led to the situationist approach which holds that behaviour is largely determined by the situation in which it occurs. More recent research, not surprisingly, has concentrated on the interaction between a person's temperament and characteristics of the situation in which he or she is operating. Thus, the interactionist approach provides a compromise between the trait and situationist stances. The issue of consistency of personality will be examined in Chapter 29 and will include a discussion of both situationist and interactionist positions.

What makes a good personality theory?

Bearing in mind the controversies and disagreements which exist between personality theorists, is it possible to say what should be expected of a good personality theory? Many theorists would agree that a good personality theory should:

- be consistent and logical and put forward assertions which are capable of being tested empirically;
- be supported by valid scientific evidence;
- be able to describe and explain human behaviour in terms which make 'real world' sense. For example, how far is the theory useful in terms of predicting suitable career choices or understanding possible causes of psychological disorder?

The reader may wish to keep these criteria in mind while considering the personality theories which follow and consider to what extent each one meets the criteria.

Atypical development and abnormal behaviour

Atypical development

With the exceptions of Chapters 31–33, most of this book has considered the normal processes of psychological development and functioning. Occasionally development does not follow the usual pattern. This

Do these two heads of state possess personality traits that are consistent across different situations, or are their personalities likely to be influenced by the situations they find themselves in?

results in what is termed atypical development or development which is not typical of the human species. Some childhood conditions which arise from atypical development are described and discussed in Chapter 31: for example, certain kinds of learning difficulties, physical and sensory handicaps and emotional/behavioural problems.

Normality and abnormality

A major issue to be faced by those who study and treat abnormal behaviour lies in the question 'When does behaviour become abnormal?' There is no dividing line separating 'normal' people from 'abnormal' people and the decision about whether an individual's behaviour departs sufficiently from the norm to require help in changing it is often a difficult one. Chapter 32 considers

GLOSSARY

Situational specificity In relation to personality, the view that people's characteristics are not necessarily fixed and may vary depending on the situation in which they find themselves.

Atypical development Development which does not follow the usual pattern of development for human beings.

different ways in which both normality and abnormality might be defined in general terms. More specifically, Chapter 32 also looks at models of abnormality that are espoused in the five major theoretical approaches in psychology: psychoanalytic, learning theory, cognitive, humanistic and physiological.

Mental disorder or mental illness

Psychopathology is the scientific study of mental disorders. The immediate problem this poses is what constitutes a mental disorder and should this be regarded as a 'mental illness'? This point is discussed more fully in Chapter 31 along with an evaluation of the 'medical model' – or 'mental illness' – approach to abnormal behaviour.

Chapter 32 examines the way mental disorders are classified and diagnosed using the International Classification of Diseases (ICD) and, in the USA, the Diagnostic and Statistical Manual of Mental Disorders (DSM). Some of the problems of diagnosing mental disorder are considered, along with some of the techniques used.

Categories and descriptions of mental disorder

Approximately one in ten men and one in seven women will be treated for mental disorder during their lifetime. For the majority, these are brief periods, possibly of depression or an obsessional state. For some, the problem may be more severe and long-lasting, for example schizophrenia or acute depression.

Some of the more common mental disorders, such as schizophrenia and anxiety disorders, are briefly described in Chapter 32, which also considers the major areas of research into their possible causes.

Treatments and therapies

Mental disorders are treated mainly by psychiatrists, doctors who specialize in the study and treatment of mental abnormality, and clinical psychologists, professionals with a first degree in psychology who have completed postgraduate training in the assessment and treatment of mental disorder. In a clinical setting a

psychiatrist and a clinical psychologist will often work together in helping an individual to overcome a mental disorder.

A range of different kinds of treatments are considered in Chapter 33. These are generally categorized in relation to the theories or assumptions of the five main approaches to psychology, as mentioned above.

Largely because of the practical and ethical problems involved in defining abnormality and diagnosing mental disorders, the treatments are not so clear-cut as treatments often are for physical complaints. And a major problem arises in deciding when the treatment has been effective. The idea of what constitutes a 'cure' for mental disorder is considered in Chapter 33, and some research into treatment effectiveness is also considered.

SELF-ASSESSMENT QUESTIONS

1. Briefly explain some ways in which psychologists have defined personality.
2. Distinguish between idiographic and nomothetic approaches to the study of personality, referring to the work of one theorist who exemplifies each approach.
3. What do you understand by type and trait approaches to the study of personality?
4. What issues arise in relation to the consistency of personality?
5. What do we mean by 'atypical development'?
6. What contentious issues arise when
   (a) distinguishing abnormal from normal behaviour;
   (b) finding suitable treatments for mental disorder?
7. What classification systems are used to diagnose mental disorders?

GLOSSARY

Psychopathology The scientific study of mental disorder.

Psychiatrist A medical doctor who is trained in the study and treatment of mental disorders.

Clinical psychologist Someone who has successfully completed a first degree in psychology followed by postgraduate training in the assessment and treatment of mental disorder.

CHAPTER 29

Type and trait approaches to personality

Personality types   709

Multitrait approaches   710
- Eysenck's theory   711
- Cattell's theory   715
- The 'Big Five'   717

Is personality consistent?   718
- Mischel's attack on traditional personality theories   719

- Situationism   719
- Interactionism   720
- What can we conclude about consistency of personality?   721

Single-trait theories   722
- Field dependence–field independence (FD-I)   722

Objectives

By the end of this chapter you should:

- Be able to evaluate the following approaches to personality: multitrait, situationist and interactionist, single-trait;

- Have examined and made an assessment of some of the ways in which personality has been assessed.

Personality types

As was noted in the Introduction, some personality theorists have categorized people into personality types on the basis of distinctive personality characteristics. Personality types are an all-or-none phenomenon – if a person is assigned to one category, he or she does not fall into any other category within that system.

Reference has already been made to the Greek physician Hippocrates who assigned individuals to one of four types of temperament on the basis of a predominance of particular body fluids. Other type theories have centred around proposed links between temperament and body physique, the most noteworthy by William Sheldon (1942). Sheldon assigned people to one of three categories dependent on their somatotypes (or body build), endomorphic, ectomorphic and mesomorphic:

Body type	Personality
Endomorphic (fat, soft, round)	Relaxed and sociable, fond of eating
Ectomorphic (long, thin, delicate)	Introverted, intellectual, uninterested in consuming food and drink
Mesomorphic (muscular, strong)	Energetic, hearty, assertive, insensitive

Sheldon's type theory is interesting but cannot be substantiated and has not been found to predict people's behaviour. People come in all shapes and sizes and cannot be categorized easily into one of Sheldon's somatotypes.

Type theories have intuitive appeal, as witness the popular tendency to describe fat people as 'jolly' and thin people as 'sensitive'. However, little empirical evidence can be found in support of the links between body type and temperament. Other type theories have categorized people into purely psychological categories. For example, Jung (1923) the psychoanalytic theorist (see the introduction to Part 1) proposed that people are predominantly either 'introverts' or 'extraverts', the introvert being shy and withdrawn and the extravert confident and outgoing.

The notion of types is tempting because of its simplicity. However, research evidence suggests that people differ in the degree to which they exhibit a particular characteristic or dimension of behaviour rather than slotting neatly into a distinct type. Hampson (1988) argues that individual differences cannot be adequately captured by placing people into a few all-or-none categories. Much recent research in personality has centred on the concept of traits.

Multitrait approaches

Though there are many definitions of traits which differ in detail, in general they are seen as 'broad, enduring, relatively stable characteristics used to assess and explain behaviour' (Hirshberg, 1978, p. 45). Thus, one person's personality may characteristically reveal dominant traits such as thoughtfulness and friendliness; another may typically display greater shyness and sensitivity.

Multitrait theories are designed to convey a picture of the whole personality. They aim to identify the range of traits that are central to the human personality and to produce tests of these traits which will indicate the extent to which people differ. They assume that individuals all share the same basic personality structure but will differ from each other in the extent to which they exhibit particular traits.

The two best known multitrait theorists are Eysenck (1947) and Cattell (1965) and their theories will be discussed in this section. The personality tests produced by Eysenck and Cattell are widely used today and it is useful to understand something of the theories which led to their development. Both theorists used the statistical technique of **factor analysis** to

---

> **GLOSSARY**
>
> **Multitrait theories** Theories which aim to identify the range of traits that are central to personality and which convey a picture of the whole personality.
>
> **Factor analysis** A complex statistical technique which is used to find the common factors underlying the scores from a number of different measures (for example, intelligence or personality tests).

Box 29.1   The use of factor analysis

Factor analysis is a statistical technique which is used to find the common factors underlying the scores from a number of different tests or measures (for example, intelligence or personality tests). It uses the statistical technique of correlation (see Chapter 34) and involves reducing a large amount of data to a much smaller amount made up of overlapping characteristics, or factors. (Eysenck and Cattell correlated people's scores on personality questionnaires or objective tests as well as assessments of their observed behaviour in order to arrive at the traits they believed were central to personality.)

The mathematical principles of factor analysis are beyond the scope of this book. However, it is important to note that the factors emerging statistically must be interpreted and named by the investigator and should be carefully justified. For example, Eysenck named the factors arising from his use of factor analysis 'extraversion' and 'neuroticism'. These will be discussed later.

Criticisms of factor analysis are:

- In some cases, the rather subjective nature of the labels attached to the various factors has been questioned.
- Gould (1981), writing about the use of factor analysis in intelligence testing, draws attention to the fallacy of reification (the tendency to see abstract concepts such as 'verbal ability' as concrete entities). A factor is just a statistic. The fact that it has been given a label does not 'prove' its objective existence.
- There is more than one method of factor analysis. The number of factors revealed in an investigation may depend upon which method is used, as well as the number and variety of tests analysed and the kind of sample (Eysenck and Cattell used two different methods of factor analysis).

arrive at the major dimensions which characterize the human personality (see Box 29.1).

The remainder of this section will explain the theories of Eysenck and Cattell and will conclude by referring to other more recent multitrait approaches.

Eysenck's theory

Eysenck (1947) used the technique of factor analysis to analyse personality data drawn from his study of 700 battle-fatigued soldiers diagnosed as neurotic. His analysis led him to propose that personality can be sufficiently described by two dimensions: **extraversion–introversion** and **neuroticism–stability**. The two dimensions are thought to be normally distributed in that the majority of people can be placed in the middle of the dimension and relatively few at either extreme. He does not use these dimensions to suggest that people may be categorized into distinct types, as in the classical type theories discussed earlier. Rather, he suggests that there are general differences between, for example, extreme introverts and extreme extraverts, but does not claim that the categories are totally distinct from each other.

Figure 29.1 illustrates Eysenck's dimensions of personality and the traits associated with each. Note the relationship to Hippocrates' typology: melancholic, choleric, phlegmatic, sanguine. Eysenck's work was influenced by these categories. Below are some of the characteristics Eysenck associated with the extreme positions on his two dimensions.

Extraversion–introversion (E)

Typical **extraverts** are sociable, thrive on human company, frequently seek exciting activities and are willing to take risks. They are impulsive, restless, optimistic and not always reliable.

Introverts are typically more serious and reserved individuals who prefer solitary activities to people. They are more cautious, pessimistic, orderly and restrained.

Neuroticism–stability (N)

Highly **neurotic** individuals tend to be more prone to worries and anxiety and are often touchy and irritable. They are more likely to complain of headaches and to suffer from eating and sleeping difficulties.

Highly stable individuals are less likely to make strong emotional responses and tend to be relatively calm, even-tempered and controlled.

Remember that these descriptions relate to the extreme ends of the dimensions and that very few people would fit them exactly. The majority of individuals would fall somewhere in the middle.

Eysenck's later factor analytical studies led him to identify a third personality dimension, psychoticism.

Psychoticism (P)

Psychoticism is unrelated to E and N. High scorers on the psychoticism scale tend to be solitary and lack feeling for others. They are also likely to be insensitive, aggressive and hostile.

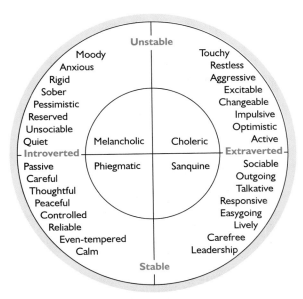

Figure 29.1 Eysenck's dimensions of personality

> **GLOSSARY**
>
> **Extraversion** One of the dimensions of personality identified by Eysenck; it is characterized by a number of traits, such as sociability and impulsiveness.
>
> **Introversion** One of the dimensions of personality identified by Eysenck; it is characterized by traits such as reserve, cautiousness and a reluctance to socialize.
>
> **Neuroticism** One of the dimensions of personality identified by Eysenck. Neurotic individuals tend to be more prone to worry and anxiety and are often touchy and irritable.

Box 29.2 Measurement of Eysenck's personality dimensions

Initially Eysenck's dimensions were assessed using rating scales based on observer data. Later, he and his colleagues devised a series of questionnaires designed to measure E and N. The present version is the **Eysenck Personality Inventory (EPI)** (Eysenck and Eysenck, 1964). This is a self-report questionnaire made up of a number of questions to which respondents are required to reply simply 'yes' or 'no'. The EPI contains a 'lie scale', which assesses an individual's tendency to give socially acceptable answers. More recently the Eysenck Personality **Questionnaire (EPQ)** has been produced and this contains a scale designed to measure P (Eysenck and Eysenck, 1975).

The EPI and EPQ are intended to be used primarily for research purposes rather than to make diagnoses in individual cases. On the whole, they have been found acceptable in terms of reliability and validity. Barrett and Kline (1982) found that the EPQ factors emerged with 'remarkable clarity' in three different samples of people. However, as in other studies, the P dimension was less clearly defined than E and N and this remains the most controversial of Eysenck's dimensions.

Eysenck's personality questionnaires (like those of Cattell referred to later) are further examples of psychometric tests (see Chapter 4). Like intelligence tests, they have been exposed to the processes of reliability and validity.

Unlike E and N, psychoticism is not normally distributed in the population. The distribution of P is highly skewed with the majority of people falling at the 'low' end of the scale (Eysenck and Eysenck, 1976). There is some evidence that criminals and schizophrenics have high psychoticism scores (Hampson, 1988).

The hierarchical structure of personality

As we have seen, Eysenck claims that the structure of personality comprises just three different dimensions. In support of this claim he offers a hierarchical model of personality (see Figure 29.2) which neatly illustrates the processes involved in factor analysis.

The lowest level relates to numerous specific pieces of behaviour, such as talking to someone in a supermarket or reading a book on a bus. At the next level, his analysis reveals habitual responses, which are typical ways of behaving made up of clusters of specific responses. Habitual responses can be explained by the traits contained at the third level. For example, in Figure 29.2, 'sociability' includes the habitual responses of 'going to parties' and 'taking part in team games'. At the top of the hierarchy is the type level; in Figure 29.2 this is extraversion. E contains several subcomponents, sociability and risk-taking being just two of them. (Though Eysenck refers to the top of the hierarchy as the 'type' level, remember that E, N and P are dimensions rather than types, since individuals possess all three to varying degrees and are not assigned into rigid categories.)

According to Eysenck, knowing a person's score on one of the dimensions at the type level makes it possible to predict that person's traits, habitual responses and specific responses in relation to that particular dimension. Eysenck claims support for this assertion from his use of criterion analysis. Criterion analysis involves the use of the **Eysenck Personality Inventory (EPI)** and **Eysenck Personality Questionnaire (EPQ)**

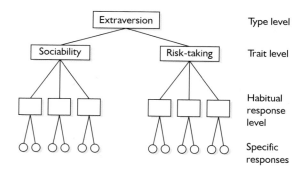

Figure 29.2 Eysenck's hierarchical model of personality in relation to extraversion (adapted from Eysenck, 1947)

The individual on the left might be described as a typical introvert, the individuals on the right as extraverted

with groups of people who are already known to differ on the dimensions of E, N and P. The logic is that people who, for example, have been identified clinically as highly neurotic would be expected to score highly on N compared with nonneurotics.

The physiological basis of personality

Eysenck's theory offers no firm support for the biological basis of P. However, he proposes that differences in E and N between people are related to the types of nervous system they possess. Below is a summary of some of the more important points made in this aspect of his theory.

Cortical arousal The concept of cortical arousal, or alertness, is related to E. Extraverts are considered to be less aroused than introverts and to seek stimulation constantly in order to increase their arousal level. Conversely, introverts are seen to be generally overaroused and are therefore likely to look for strategies to avoid excessive stimulation.

ARAS Cortical arousal is controlled by activity in a particular part of the brain known as the ascending reticular activating system (ARAS), which is easily activated in introverts, but responds more slowly in extraverts. Eysenck suggests that extraverts have 'strong' nervous systems – the ARAS is biased to inhibit neural impulses (chemical 'messages' within

the nervous system: see Figure 32.5 in Chapter 32 for a brief explanation of neural transmission) which 'dampens down' the effects of stimulation to the brain. Conversely, introverts have 'weak' nervous systems where the ARAS provides strong excitation, or boosting, of incoming stimulation, thereby increasing its effect. Put very simply, for introverts a little stimulation will have a relatively powerful effect, while extraverts may need a large amount of stimulation before any effect is felt (hence their tendency to seek extra stimulation).

Autonomic nervous system Eysenck proposes that the physiological basis of N is to be found in the autonomic nervous system (ANS) (discussed fully in Chapter 8). The sympathetic division of the ANS is active when emotion is felt and it controls bodily changes associated with strong emotional reactions: for example, increased pulse and heart rate, sweating and churning stomach. In neurotics, the ANS reacts more quickly and strongly to stimulation, causing them more readily to experience anxiety than their less neurotic counterparts.

Box 29.3 contains some of Eysenck's views on personality and conditioning.

Is there support for the biological theory?

In looking for support for Eysenck's biological theory, four kinds of evidence have been considered: genetic

Box 29.3   Personality and conditionability

As we have seen, Eysenck believes that biological factors can explain differences between introverts, extraverts, neurotics and stable individuals. One of the most significant psychological effects, he believes, relates to the relative ease or difficulty with which individuals become conditioned.

Introverts, because of their sensitivity to stimulation, will condition more quickly and strongly than will extraverts. This difference was demonstrated by Franks (1956, 1957) who found that introverts could be conditioned to produce eye-blinks in response to a buzzer more quickly than could extraverts. The biological explanation suggests that since introverts produce a higher level of arousal than extraverts, their nervous systems are more likely to form the necessary associations.

It has been suggested that this difference in conditionability also partly explains the characteristically different patterns of behaviour shown by introverts and extraverts. Shackleton and Fletcher (1984) suggest that the introvert, whose social conditioning has been more effective, is likely to be more conformist and cautious than the extravert.

evidence, laboratory studies, clinical data and 'real world' behaviour. A selection of the findings appears below.

Genetic evidence   Shields (1976) showed that identical twins (identical genetic structure) were significantly more similar in E and N than were nonidentical twins (different genetic structure).

Laboratory studies   Eysenck's biological theory predicts that introverts will differ from extraverts in their levels of cortical arousal. Traditionally, cortical arousal has been assessed using the electroencephalogram (EEG), a mechanism for measuring the electrical activity of the brain. Gale (1981) reviewed 30 studies which attempted to relate EEG activity to personality measures. Only half of them showed significant differences between introverts and extraverts with the better designed, more recent studies doing so more frequently. Gale, however, pointed out that the laboratory conditions themselves may influence cortical activity in that extraverts are less likely

to be influenced by the presence of others than are introverts. Clearly, effective control must be exercised in experiments if findings are to be meaningful.

Clinical data   Studies which have used psychiatric samples have shown that individuals scoring high in N exhibit a wide variety of physical responses such as increased sweating and heart rates. They often also fail to habituate (become accustomed to and stop responding) to external stimuli, which implies that they may have a poorly functioning ANS (Lader, 1975). Whilst these findings apply to patient groups, there is generally no evidence of links between N scores and these measures of autonomic functioning in nonpatient groups. Thus, no unequivocal support exists for Eysenck's suggested association between ANS functioning and N.

'Real world' data   The Eysenck Personality Questionnaire is quite a good predictor of behaviour outside the laboratory. In a study of participants' choices of leisure activities, Furnham (1981, 1982) found that extraverts tended to search for stimulating social situations involving competitiveness, intimacy and assertiveness. He regarded this as an indication that extraverts strive to raise their arousal level. Neurotics tended to avoid social interaction and competitiveness, while high psychoticism scorers chose situations where they were able to manipulate people.

Evaluation of Eysenck's work

■ As has already been noted, there is no firm support for many aspects of Eysenck's theory. Criterion studies do seem to give validity to his dimensions of E and N and to a more limited degree, P. However, a crucial element of the theory, his proposal that introverts condition more easily than extraverts, has received only limited support. Consequently, his application of this element to social conditioning and likely differences in social behaviour between extraverts and introverts seems precarious.

■ Kendrick (1981) suggests that clinical applications of Eysenck's theory have been limited and that few clinicians have made use of predictions arising from the theory when treating patients. Lanyon (1984) claims that the EPQ has not been sufficiently well validated on clinical

Box 29.4 Eysenck's theory of criminality

Eysenck (1964) proposed that because of the poorer conditionability and thus poorer socialization of extraverts, the incidence of crime would be higher in that group. Furthermore, a combination of high E with high N would produce a strong drive level resulting in a tendency towards antisocial behaviour. Eysenck's 'typical' criminal, therefore, would be a neurotic extravert. Later, criminality was linked also to high levels of P (Eysenck and Eysenck, 1970).

Research evidence has been equivocal. Two studies have found that delinquent boys had higher P scores than controls (Edmunds and Kendrick, 1980; Farrington et al., 1982). Rushton and Chrisjohn (1981) found that E and P, though not N, were related to self-reported delinquency. Many studies have produced findings which undermine Eysenck's claims. In a review of studies which compared prisoners' scores on the EPI to those of controls, Cochrane (1974) concluded that though prisoners were higher on N, they were no higher on E. In summary, there is no convincing evidence that offenders are more extraverted than nonoffenders, though there is some evidence that they are more psychotic and more neurotic.

samples to demonstrate firmly its practical usefulness.

- Critics have questioned whether such a simple instrument as the EPI with its inflexible 'Yes/No' questions is adequate to measure the complexities of human personality (Heim, 1970).

- Whilst acknowledging its shortcomings, Shackleton and Fletcher (1984) pay tribute to Eysenck's theory and point out that it has generated a vast amount of research and has provided an invaluable model for personality investigations. Of Eysenck himself they say that 'almost every problem to which he has addressed himself has benefited from the debate his attention invariably stimulates' (p. 53).

Cattell's theory

The work of Cattell (1965) resulted in a complex personality theory which postulates that the basic structure of human personality is made up of at least 20

traits. His research addressed aspects of human functioning often ignored by other personality theorists (for example, ability, emotion, motivation and learning). Like Eysenck, his work led to the development of a questionnaire designed to measure personality, the **16PF** (see Box 29.5). A brief account of the main elements of his approach and findings follows.

The structure of personality

Cattell started by devising a technique to ensure that every possible aspect of personality would be investigated. Using a standard English dictionary, he collected 18,000 words, or traits names, which could be used in everyday language to describe personality. His aim was to reduce this vast amount of data to more manageable proportions, using the technique of factor analysis as already described. The main stages in his analysis were:

1. Groups of individuals were observed and rated on the trait names. Factor analysis of this data revealed that 15 first-order factors (known by Cattell as primary traits) could encompass all the terms used to describe human personality. The 15 primary traits were referred to by Cattell as L Data (life data).

2. This stage involved the construction of questionnaires based on the 15 source traits. After administering them to groups of people, the resulting scores were analysed. Sixteen factors emerged and 12 of these closely resembled the source trait derived from the earlier analysis. Thus, three of the earlier factors did not reappear but four new ones emerged. The resulting factors (known as Q data) form the basis of the widely used 16PF (personality factors) questionnaire (see Figure 29.3), which will be discussed later. The first 12 factors lettered A to O are found in L data and Q data while the last four are identified from Q data only.

3. At the third stage of the project, a number of objective tests were administered to large groups of people. These tests involved observing indivi-

GLOSSARY

16PF A rating scale devised by Cattell to assess the structure of personality based on 16 factors.

Figure 29.3 Factors measured by Cattell's 16PF (after Cattell, 1965)

Low score description	Factor	High score description
Reserved, cool, detached	A	Outgoing, warmhearted
Less intelligent, concrete thinker	B	More intelligent, abstract thinker
Emotionally unstable, easily upset	C	Emotionally stable, calm, mature
Humble, mild, submissive	E	Assertive, aggressive, stubborn
Sober, cautious, serious	F	Happy-go-lucky, impulsive, enthusiastic
Expedient, disregards rules	G	Persevering, conscientious
Shy, restrained, timid	H	Adventurous, socially bold
Tough-minded, self-reliant	I	Tender-minded, clinging
Trusting, adaptable	L	Suspicious, self-opinionated
Practical, careful	M	Imaginative, unconventional
Simple, natural	N	Shrewd, calculating
Self-assured, confident	O	Insecure, self-reproaching
Traditional, conservative	Q^1	Experimenting, liberal
Group-dependent	Q^2	Self-sufficient
Undisciplined, self-conflict	Q^3	Controlled, socially precise
Relaxed, composed	Q^4	Tense, frustrated

duals in structured situations (a more unusual one was blowing up a balloon, which identifies timid people) in order to make predictions about their behaviour in different situations. Twenty-one factors emerged from this data (known as T data) and a number of them were found to coincide with the second-order data drawn from the questionnaire data.

Thus, Cattell used a comprehensive range of different measures of human behaviour in his search for the basic structure of human personality. Unfortunately, the three sources of data described above did not reveal exactly similar structures. Whilst there seems to be considerable agreement between the factor structure found in L and Q data, T data appears to expose a somewhat different aspect of personality. Twenty factors have emerged from T data, but Hampson (1988) points out that the relationship between these factors and those located in L and Q data is yet to be fully established.

Practical applications of Cattell's theory

Cattell has applied aspects of his theory to many different situations, some of which are outlined below:

■ **Abnormal psychology**. The 16PF questionnaire has been used in clinical situations, largely for

research purposes as its validity is insufficiently well-established for use in individual diagnoses (Williams et al., 1972). The Clinical Analysis Questionnaire has also been developed for psychiatric settings.

■ **Occupational selection and counselling**. Cattell has provided profiles derived from personality scores for different occupational groups such as accountants and lawyers. These have been used in vocational counselling.

■ **Education**. His tests for use with young children and adolescents, as described earlier, have been widely used in educational settings. His work on intelligence has led to the development of a 'culture-fair' test which attempts to measure intelligence uncontaminated by cultural factors (see Chapters 4 and 21).

Evaluation of Cattell's work

■ While a good level of support exists for Cattell's surface traits, particularly what he calls exvia (extraversion) and anxiety, a relatively large number of studies have failed to support the validity of his source traits (for example, Eysenck and Eysenck, 1969; Vagg and Hammond, 1976; Saville and Blinkhorn, 1976; Browne and Howarth, 1977). However, Kline (1981b) argues that this may be partly accounted for by the fact

Box 29.5 Cattell's measurements of personality

A number of questionnaires have been developed by Cattell and his colleagues; as already noted, the best known one is the 16PF (Cattell et al., 1970) which is intended for adults. The 16PF measures the factors shown in Figure 29.3. Versions of the 16PF are also available to assess the structure of children's personality.

All the above tests are appropriate for normal groups. Unlike Eysenck, Cattell believes that the abnormal personality is qualitatively different from the normal personality (Cattell, 1973). Therefore, although the 16PF can distinguish between neurotics and normals, additional factors are included to distinguish psychotics, who are considered to possess personality traits not found in normal groups.

Twelve abnormal factors were presented by Cattell and Kline (1977). Seven of these were associated with depression.

Though Cattell believed that general personality factors and abilities remain relatively constant over time, he recognized that a number of different situations and body states may temporarily influence the way people behave. For example, states such as tiredness, elation, fear or drunkenness may all cause a person to act 'out of character'. Therefore, trying to predict behaviour on the basis of trait factors without taking account of moods or states in particular situations could be deceptive.

Thus Cattell, to a greater extent than Eysenck, upheld the importance of temporary fluctuations in behaviour in the light of particular circumstances. This led him to develop the Eight State Questionnaire which measures mood and state factors such as depression, arousal, anxiety and fatigue. These are thought of as short-term phenomena as, for example, when a usually composed individual becomes agitated after a road accident.

---

that different researchers have used different, sometimes inadequate, techniques.

■ Peck and Whitlow (1975) argue that if Cattell's theory is to be widely accepted amongst psychologists, it must be demonstrated that the data used are appropriate and are capable of producing a stable number of primary factors. Also, these factors should be seen to have psychological, as well as mathematical, validity.

■ Though disagreements exist between Eysenck and Cattell about the best methods for arriving at a theory of personality structure, paradoxically, the agreements between them about some of the second-order factors lend some validity to the theories and personality questionnaires of both researchers.

The 'Big Five'

It has been seen from the work of Eysenck and Cattell that the former prefers to describe the structure of personality broadly in terms of his three personality dimensions (neuroticism, extraversion and psychoticism) where the latter favours a more detailed view (between 16 and 23 factors). It has been shown that, despite these differences, many aspects of their theories are essentially the same. What can be concluded? A consensus seems to be emerging among

trait researchers that five factors may provide a compromise between the conclusions of Eysenck and Cattell. An outline of relevant research findings and views in the **five-factor approach to personality** appears below:

■ The most influential findings arose from a series of studies carried out by Tupes and Christal (1961) and Norman (1963). The researchers factor-analysed data drawn from a range of different samples using Cattell's (1947) trait-rating scales. Despite differences in the samples, a common picture emerged of five factors which seemed to form the basis of personality structure. The factors were labelled extraversion, agreeableness, conscientiousness, emotional stability and culture. They have since become known as the Big Five. These are displayed in Figure 29.4, together with some of the trait scales which characterize each of the five factors.

GLOSSARY

Five-factor approach to personality An approach which presents a compromise between Eysenck and Cattell and proposes that five factors (the 'Big Five') form the basis of personality structure.

Figure 29.4 The five factors forming the basis of personality structure (after Norman, 1963)

Factor name	Representative trait scales
Extraversion	Talkative – silent Frank, open – secretive Sociable – reclusive
Agreeableness	Good-natured – irritable Not jealous – jealous Mild, gentle – headstrong
Conscientiousness	Fussy, tidy – careless Responsible – undependable Scrupulous – unscruplous
Emotional stability	Poised – nervous, tense Calm – anxious Composed – excitable
Culture	Artistically sensitive – artistically insensitive Intellectual – unreflective, narrow Polished, refined – crude, boorish

■ The five factors have now been identified in many different studies using samples of children (Digman and Inouye, 1986) and adults (McCrae and Costa, 1985, 1987). However, some disagreement exists regarding the exact nature of one of the five factors. McCrae and Costa (1985) have proposed a new, important personality factor called **openness to experience**, which distinguishes individuals who are open to experience as indicated by their artistic and intellectual pursuits, creativity, liberal views, untraditional values, independence and impracticalness. Eysenck and Eysenck (1985) disagree that openness is a new factor and argue that it is at the opposite end of the continuum to psychoticism. Hampson (1988) proposes that openness to experience could be a form of the Big Five factor called 'culture' rather than a new factor. Currently, researchers believe the five factors to be as follows (Costa and McCrea, 1993): **extraversion, agreeableness, conscientiousness, neuroticism** and **openness to experience**.

■ The five factors are not related to a particular theory. They are easy to understand because they are described using everyday language.

■ Hampson (1988) concluded: 'Although the debate over the definitive structure of personality ratings is far from over, the Big Five represents a reasonable compromise between the extreme positions offered by Eysenck and Cattell' (p. 71).

■ Costa and McCrae (1993) point out that the five factors have been replicated across many different cultures using many different kinds of data.

■ Goldberg (1993) proposes that the five factors can account for all the personality structures derived from trait ratings by the various multitrait theorists. This is disputed by Cattell (1995) who questions the validity of Goldberg's interpretation of the statistical techniques which led to the development of the five-factor theory.

? SELF-ASSESSMENT QUESTIONS

1. For what purpose did Eysenck and Cattell use the technique of factor analysis in their study of personality?
2. Briefly outline the major dimensions of personality identified by Eysenck. What techniques are used to assess them?
3. Summarize the main claims made by Eysenck about the physiological basis of personality. Is this aspect of his theory supportable?
4. Identify some of the ways in which Cattell's theory differs from that of Eysenck.
5. What are some of the practical applications of Cattell's theory?
6. Outline some relevant research findings and views suggesting that personality structure can be described by five factors (the Big Five).

Is personality consistent?

The concept of consistency is central to the view of personality put forward by trait theorists. Trait theorists propose that personality is made up of a number of stable, internal factors (e.g. extraversion, neuroticism and psychoticism in the case of Eysenck's theory) which are consistent and therefore cause individuals to behave in similar ways on different occasions and in a range of different situations. Thus, it is expected that a person who is generally aggressive or very shy will be so in a wide variety of different

SHE'S NOT REALLY AGGRESSIVE, YOU KNOW, IT'S JUST THE SITUATION SHE'S ALWAYS FINDING HERSELF IN.

situations. The most harmful criticism of trait theories, if it were upheld, would be to weaken their claims regarding the consistency of behaviour. Such a criticism was made by Mischel (1968), a social learning theorist. A social learning theory approach to human behaviour (see Chapter 6) proposes that the main determinants of an individual's behaviour are not any consistent, internal characteristics or traits the person may possess, but what happens to that individual in the environment, through observing the behaviour of others and receiving patterns of reinforcement. Observed behaviours may be 'stored' and only introduced when individuals feel they will be rewarded.

Mischel's attack on traditional personality theories

In a book called *Personality and Assessment*, Mischel (1968) strongly attacked the concept of personality and traits in particular. He argued that traditional personality theories, such as Freud's psychoanalytic theory (see Chapter 30) and trait theories had greatly overstated the case for behavioural consistency. He proposed instead that it is particular situations which may cause an individual to behave in certain ways: for example, calmly or aggressively. Consistencies in

behaviour must therefore arise from similarities between situations in which people find themselves.

In reviewing the evidence for behavioural consistency, Mischel was considerably influenced by a long-standing study by Hartshorne and May (1928) which used several thousand children as participants. The aim of their investigations was to examine the concept of a trait of honesty. It was thought that someone who is basically honest will consistently behave with honesty in many different situations, regardless of whether there is any pressure upon them to be honest or dishonest. Hartshorne and May found, however, that children who were honest at home were not necessarily so at school and vice versa. They concluded that honesty is not a consistent behaviour which is determined by a personality trait, but is mainly a function of situational factors.

Despite the evidence from the honesty studies and several other investigations, Mischel conceded that behaviour may be consistent over time in similar situations. However, he argued that if the situations vary, the behaviour may also change. He did not regard consistency of behaviour in similar situations as sufficient evidence for the existence of stable personality traits.

Situationism

Following Mischel's criticisms of traditional personality theory, interest was renewed in psychology over the long-standing issue of which has the more important effect on people's behaviour: characteristics within themselves or the situation they find themselves in. Mischel, as has been noted, subscribed to the latter view, which became known as situationism.

Research is available which has vividly portrayed the compelling effect of the situation on behaviour (see Box 29.6). However, despite evidence in support of it, intuitively people feel uncomfortable with the extreme version of situationism. Logic tells us that, in general, people are recognizably the same in different situations.

GLOSSARY

Situationism In relation to personality theory, the view of Mischel and others that characteristics within people (traits) are less important than the situations in which they find themselves.

Box 29.6   Does the situation influence behaviour?

Zimbardo et al. (1973) carried out the classic 'prison' experiment (fully discussed in Chapter 28) in which student volunteers with no known antisocial tendencies were kept in a prison setting. Some were randomly allocated to be 'prisoners' while others became 'guards'. After only a few days, the 'guards' displayed extremely aggressive and brutal behaviour, whilst the prisoners became passive and dependent, several of them showing symptoms of severe emotional disturbance. It is important to note that all the participants had originally been judged as emotionally stable, physically healthy and 'normal to average' in relation to personality tests.

This experiment offers powerful support for the effect of situation on behaviour.

Criticisms of situationism

Bowers (1973) pointed out the weaknesses of pure situationism by drawing attention to its failure to acknowledge the ability of individuals to determine their own course of action. He argued that it is misguided to attribute the causes of behaviour either solely to situations or solely to internal traits. The foolishness of such approaches is illustrated by the ease with which it is possible to find supporting evidence for either. For example, driving in city traffic can provide support for situationism in that the majority of people comply with traffic lights. Alternatively, when driving on the motorway, individual preferences (and perhaps personality traits) may determine driving speed more so than does the situation. Bower concludes that the dispute about traits versus situations should be discontinued in favour of an interactionist approach which takes both into consideration.

Mischel himself moved towards an interactionist position by proposing that situations alone cannot account for people's behaviour. The same situations may have different 'meanings' for different people, depending on what he referred to as 'person variables' arising from their previous learning experiences. Person variables were seen as an alternative to traits and included such things as competence, expectancy

and values. Thus, different people may respond quite differently in the same situation.

Interactionism

Interactionism provides a compromise between the trait and situationist approaches to personality. Pervin and Lewis (1978) argue that not only should an interactionist approach address internal characteristics of people and features of the situations in which individuals operate, but it should also pay attention to the process through which one influences the other. A large amount of research has been carried out from an interactionist perspective. Some examples appear in Boxes 29.7 and 29.8.

Criticisms of interactionism

- Olweus (1977) suggested that a significant interaction does not reveal anything about the process underlying that interaction. Nor does it tell us much about why people behave as they do. He adds that a study of the way personality interacts with situations can only be meaningful in the context of a sound theory of personality dispositions.
- Mischel (1981) stresses that the concept of 'interaction' must be clearly defined and analysed. Otherwise, interactionist research may result only in statements of the obvious.
- Cronbach and Snow (1977) draw attention to the difficulties arising from the virtually unlimited number of possible interactions that could be studied and the number of other variables which may intervene to modify the particular interaction studied.
- A major problem in interactionism has been in defining precisely what is meant by 'situation'. Though psychologists have tried to develop taxonomies (classifications) for different kinds of situations, they have encountered many difficulties. For example, disagreements exist on

---

GLOSSARY

Interactionism In relation to personality theory, the view that an individual's personality is influenced by an interaction between internal characteristics (traits) and features of situations in which they operate.

whether situations can be defined objectively without allowing for people's perception of the situation. Thus, the word 'situation' is often used in a vague, poorly defined way.

Hampson (1988) argues that interactionism was a paradoxical solution to the consistency problem since it emphasized the importance of both personality traits and situational variables. Whilst it has succeeded in restoring confidence in the concept of personality, it has not resolved the fundamental problem of whether people's behaviour is consistent.

Box 29.7   The interaction of person and situation

McCord and Wakefield (1981) tested the hypothesis that introverts would perform better in arithmetical tasks than extraverts in classes where punishment prevailed, whereas extraverts would achieve more in situations where rewards predominated. Findings indicated that this was the case, indicating that personality (introversion–extraversion) interacts with the kind of situation (punishment-oriented or reward-oriented). It should be noted that this kind of interaction is 'one-way', the situation affecting the individual rather than the other way round.

A study by Moos (1969) is an example of an investigation which attempted to estimate the extent of the influence of characteristics of the person, situation factors and their interaction on behaviour. Psychiatric patients were observed in a number of different situations (for example on the ward, in the chapel, having occupational therapy) and their behaviour (such as smoking, talking, listening) was noted. Moos found that situation factors accounted for 10 per cent of the observed differences in behaviour, characteristics of the person accounted for 12 per cent and their interaction for 21 per cent. Thus, the interaction was seen to influence behaviour to a greater extent than either person or situation factors studied alone.

Many other studies have demonstrated the effects on behaviour of the interaction of person factors and situation factors. Much of it has been criticized for failing to demonstrate fully the highly complex nature of this interaction.

Box 29.8   Person-centred approaches to consistency

Over the last decade or so, a number of new approaches have attempted to resolve some of the issues in the consistency debate. One such approach is known as the person-centred approach, which centres on people's own perceptions of the consistency of some of their own personality traits. It suggests that consistency does exist but only for some kinds of people and certain kinds of behaviour in certain situations (Bem, 1983).

A study which greatly influenced the person-centred approach was carried out by Bem and Allen (1974). They investigated friendliness and conscientiousness in a group of college students. Bem and Allen found that when participants were asked to rate themselves on consistency of these two traits, those who saw themselves as consistently friendly did in fact behave in a friendly way in a large number of situations (supported by direct observations and by ratings from peers and parents). Students who rated themselves as inconsistently friendly were indeed found to be friendly in some situations and not others. Similar findings emerged for the trait of conscientiousness. Thus it seems that the traits of friendliness and conscientiousness may not be characteristic of all individuals. However, those for whom it is characteristic can be expected to act in a consistent way in a wide range of situations.

As a result of Bem and Allen's research, the importance of self-assessed consistency as a predictor of consistency in behaviour has been widely acknowledged.

Bem and Allen's findings have been supported by Kenrick and Stringfield (1980), though not by Chaplin and Goldberg (1984).

What can we conclude about consistency of personality?

Evidence suggests that a pure trait approach to personality does not provide sufficient support for the idea that people's behaviour is invariably consistent. However, the opposite view, situationism, has also proved inadequate. Intuition, supported by research evidence, tells us that the way we behave is influenced both by who and what we are and the situations in which we find or place ourselves. Research goes on into the issue of the consistency of personality and new solutions continue to be sought.

 SELF-ASSESSMENT QUESTIONS

1. Explain Mischel's situationist view of the nature of personality. In what way does this view challenge the beliefs of trait theorists?
2. What does Bowers (1973) suggest are some of the weaknesses of a pure situationist view of personality?
3. What are the main tenets of an interactionist approach to personality? Refer to some relevant studies.
4. What insights does the study by Bem and Allen (1974) provide into the issue of consistency of personality?
5. What conclusions can you draw about the consistency of behaviour?

Single-trait theories

The major personality theories considered so far have attempted to describe the whole of personality and to predict behaviour in a wide range of situations. **Single-trait theories** emphasize the role played by one particular aspect of the personality in influencing behaviour. One example that has already been discussed is the theory of **internal–external Locus of Control** (Rotter, 1954). Research has focused on the extent to which people perceive themselves as being able to influence and control their own lives (internality) or, in contrast, to attribute what happens to them with regard to such factors as luck, fate, other people, etc. (externality) (see Chapter 24).

Need for achievement (n Ach) (McClelland et al., 1953) is an area of research that has examined influences on people's need to attain success or some standard of excellence. It was developed further by Atkinson and Feather (1966), who added the related motive fear of failure.

Another single-trait theory that has already been discussed is **Type A Personality** (Friedman and Rosenman, 1974). This deals with a particular pattern of behaviour and the likely consequences. Type A behaviour is characterized by impatience, aggression,

competitiveness and a sense of 'deadline urgency'. A large amount of research evidence has revealed a link between Type A behaviour and coronary heart disease (see Chapter 11).

Though single-trait theories are generally less comprehensive than their multitrait counterparts in that they address more limited aspects of human personality, increasingly they are becoming an important focus for research into personality.

The single-trait theory to be discussed here focuses on the trait of field dependence–field independence. This has been chosen because of the vast amount of research it has generated over the past 40 years or so. Reviews of this and other single-trait theories can be found in London and Exner (1978).

Field dependence–field independence (FD-I)

Cognitive styles

FD-I is an example of a **cognitive style**. Cognitive styles relate to the manner in which people think, remember, perceive and generally process information. It relates not only to the sorts of tasks generally thought of as 'cognitive' such as solving problems or remembering factual information, but also to how people deal with their social worlds. Thus the study of cognitive styles has its roots in both cognitive psychology and personality theory. Messick et al. (1976) described 19 separate cognitive styles that have been the focus of research, of which field dependence–field independence has been the most widely studied.

Origins of FD-I

FD-I has the distinction of being discovered accidentally by Herman Witkin in 1949. Witkin and his colleagues were investigating perceptual processes in human beings and in particular the use of internal (within the body) and external (in the outside world) cues when perceiving and judging whether a straight

---

GLOSSARY

Single-trait theories of personality Theories which focus on one aspect of the personality, rather than attempting to convey a picture of the whole personality.

Cognitive style This relates to the manner in which people think, remember, perceive and generally process information.

rod was vertical when set in different positions. Two imaginative tests were devised to separate out these external and internal cues: the Rod and Frame Test and the Body Adjustment Test.

In the **Rod and Frame Test (RFT)** participants were seated in a completely darkened room facing a tilting luminous frame within which was a luminous rod. They were required to adjust the rod to a vertical position when the rod and frame were tilted, sometimes in the same, sometimes in the opposite directions. The degree of difference of the rod setting from the true upright constituted the participants' score. Those who relied heavily on external cues tended to set the rod in line with the frame; those who relied on internal cues set the rod more closely to the true vertical. The former were described as field-dependent and the latter as field-independent.

The **Body Adjustment Test (BAT)** took place in a small tilted room. Participants, who were seated, were required to adjust their body to the upright position while the room remained tilted. Field-dependent people, relying on external cues, tended to misjudge the situation and adjust their bodies to the angle of the room, whilst field-independent people, relying on internal cues, were able to make a more accurate judgment and adjust their bodies to the true vertical.

Witkin's hope of separating out the relative importance of internal and external cues in perceiving the vertical was never achieved, since he found wide individual differences between people. Some consistently depended upon internal cues while others relied on external cues. Consequently he abandoned his research into perception of the vertical and concentrated instead on investigating individual differences in a range of tasks and exploring the possible psychological basis for them. The most extensively studied of these tasks was the **Embedded Figures Test (EFT)**. In this, participants are required to pick out simple figures which are embedded within more complex designs. Figure 29.5 contains a likely example. Those described as field-independent were found to locate the figures quickly and easily while field-dependent people were distracted by the complexity of the surrounding 'field'. A group version of the EFT, the **Concealed Shapes Test**, devised by Gardner et al. (1960), has also been widely used to assess FD-I.

Witkin found that there was a high correlation between participants' scores on the RFT, BAT and EFT. What all three measures of FD-I have in common, it seems, is that they each require the participant to

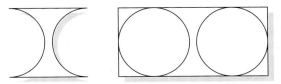

Figure 29.5 An item similar to those in the Embedded Figures Test (Witkin, 1950)

disembed an item from its context, or 'field'. For some people the field exerts a strong influence, making it difficult for them to extract and interpret the constituent parts (**field dependence**). Others can more easily analyse and interpret the constituent parts of the whole field (**field independence**). It is important to note that many people are neither extremely field-dependent nor highly field-independent, but fall somewhere on the continuum between these two extremes.

Individual differences in FD-I

Witkin maintained that there is a close relationship between FD-I and personality:

> Field dependence–independence is a manifestation in the perceptual sphere of a broad dimension of personal functioning which extends into the sphere of social behaviour and into the sphere of personality as well.
>
> (Witkin, 1976, p. 44)

A large amount of research has been carried out into differences between field-dependent and field-independent people. This has explored links between FD-I and such diverse areas as problem-solving skills, career choices and social sensitivity among others. A sample of some of this research is described below.

GLOSSARY

Field dependence A cognitive style. A field-dependent individual finds it difficult to concentrate on an object, problem or situation while ignoring distracting features of the surrounding context.

Field independence A cognitive style. A field-independent individual views the world analytically and is able to concentrate on an object, problem or situation without being distracted by its context.

Cognitive skills Studies of cognitive skills have tended to investigate people's performance in problem-solving tasks. The field-independent person is usually found to be more successful in such tasks than the field-dependent person. For example, Frank and Noble (1984) found that field-independents solved both easy and difficult anagrams more quickly than did field-dependents. This could not be explained by differences in verbal intelligence since the groups did not differ significantly on this factor.

Career choices Witkin (1977) proposed that, because they rely on their own internal cues, field-independent people are logical and analytical. They tend to be found in occupations such as engineering, science and experimental psychology. They are often regarded by others as ambitious, distant and inconsiderate. Field-dependent people, however, are more attentive to the environment and tend to be very good with people. They are usually thought of as friendly, warm and sensitive. They tend to gravitate towards occupations which involve dealing with people, such as social work, primary school teaching and clinical psychology. A study by Quinlan and Blatt (1973) showed that a group of very successful surgical nursing students were significantly more field-independent than equally successful psychiatric nursing students, who tended to be field-dependent.

Social differences Research in the social domain has tested the hypothesis that the extremely field-dependent person would tend to be more responsive to social cues and would rely more heavily on the attitudes and judgments of others than the field-independent person. Linton (1955) tested this hypothesis by investigating the relationship between field dependence and conformity. She found a significant (+0.6) correlation between these two factors.

A study by Ruble and Nakamura (1972) examined the relationship between FD-I and attention given to social stimuli, which in this case was represented by the amount of time spent looking at others. In a problem-solving task, field-dependent children were found to look at the experimenter's face more than did field-independent children. However, this did not improve their performance in a follow-up trial. It could be assumed that it would have been more helpful to watch how the experimenter solved the problem rather than looking at her face. In a second task, where

children were asked to choose from three possible correct solutions, looking at the experimenter's face was more useful. In this case, the experimenter provided social cues by looking at and leaning towards the correct example. This resulted in field-dependent children performing better than field-independent children.

Evaluation of FD-I

Witkin's theory received a great deal of supporting evidence from a wide range of sources, For example, Wapner (1976) believed that the study of FD-I provides a creative and novel approach to some central problems of education. Chickering (1976) suggested that Witkin's studies of FD-I are important to higher education in particular, in that they offer valuable insights on how institutions may adapt educational environments and practices to suit students with varying cognitive styles. However, a number of criticisms of Witkin's theory have been made:

FD-I and intelligence Witkin has argued that FD-I cannot be equated with intelligence. Unlike the scores on IQ tests, he argued, measures of FD-I provide a value-free picture of an individual's functioning in that it is neither better nor worse to be either field-dependent or field-independent, since each has both strengths and weaknesses. Some investigators, for example Vernon (1972), have argued that tests of FD-I do not measure anything which is not revealed by IQ tests, and, therefore, FD-I is not distinguishable from intelligence. It is known that between the ages of 8 and 17 years, people become more field-independent. Since IQ also increases with age, the view that FD-I is merely an aspect of intelligence is supported.

However, research into sex differences in FD-I reveal that, from the age of 12 up, males tend to be more field-independent than females (Maccoby and Jacklin, 1974). Since there are no known sex differences in general intelligence it does not seem likely that FD-I and intelligence are equivalent.

Links with personality As already noted, Witkin (1976) argued that FD-I is a perceptual manifestation of personality and social behaviour. Gruen (1957) challenged Witkin's claims of a direct link between perception and personality. He claimed that Witkin's procedures focus too much on people's perceptions of a task without taking account of processes within the person which may be involved in their perceptions: for example, their attitudes towards or feelings about particular testing situations. Gruen suggested that the same score in an FD-I task might reflect quite different processes in different individuals.

SELF-ASSESSMENT QUESTIONS

1. What do you understand by single-trait theories? Give some examples.

2. What is the relationship between perception and the cognitive style field dependence–independence?

3. How might an extremely field-dependent person be identified through the use of the Embedded Figures Test?

4. Give some examples of likely personality differences between field-dependent and field-independent people.

5. Critically evaluate the usefulness of the concept of field dependence–independence.

Chapter summary

Typologies include those of Hippocrates. He assigned temperaments to individuals based upon the predominance of one of four humours: blood (a sanguine temperament), phlegm (a phlegmatic type), black bile (a melancholic type) and yellow bile (a choleric type). Sheldon used somatotypes to divide individuals into endomorphic, ectomorphic and mesomorphic types. Jung divided people into introverts and extraverts.

Multitrait theories aim to convey a picture of the whole personality in terms of a range of traits. The best known multitrait theorists, Eysenck and Cattell, used factor analysis to arrive at traits or dimensions along which individuals may vary.

Eysenck proposed two basic dimensions, neuroticism–stability and introversion–extraversion. At a later stage he added a third, psychoticism. These dimensions were measured by means of questionnaire-type personality inventories. Individuals show a hierarchical structure of personality in their behaviour from specific pieces of behaviour to habitual ways of behaving and finally to types of personality, which were linked to Hippocrates' temperaments.

Eysenck saw these dimensions as having a physiological basis. The basis of extraversion–introversion was seen to be in cortical arousal, while the basis for neuroticism rests in the sympathetic division of the autonomic nervous system. He claimed that introversion–extraversion had a bearing on the ease with which individuals could be conditioned. Introverts were more easily conditioned than extraverts.

Eysenck has presented evidence of several kinds to support his theory, including genetic evidence from studies of twins, laboratory studies of cortical arousal, clinical studies of habituation as well as 'real world data'.

Cattell's factor analysis resulted in at least 20 traits or dimensions of personality. These included 15 primary traits (L data) and four factors known as Q data. These formed the basis for the 16PF questionnaire, which has received wide use. Additionally, objective tests identified what were known as T data. Twenty factors emerged from T data. The relationship between these and the L and Q data has not been finally established. Cattell's tests have been widely used in abnormal psychology, in occupational selection and counselling and in education.

A consensus view is emerging as a result of both Eysenck's and Cattell's work that there are five personality factors: extraversion, agreeableness, conscientiousness, emotional stability and culture. To these factors McCrae and Costa have added 'openness to experience'.

The concept of consistency has become central to views of personality. Mischel subscribes to the view that the most important factor influencing people's behaviour is situation. Disposition is seen as less influential. This is in opposition to the views of Eysenck and Cattell.

■ A compromise position between these views is that of Pervin and Lewis. This is the interactionist position which stresses the interaction between disposition and situation. The evidence is that a pure trait approach is insufficient to explain behaviour. Equally, situation by itself is inadequate to provide explanations for behaviour. Research continues into consistency of behaviour.

■ Single-trait theories concentrate upon one aspect of personality. These include internal–external locus of control, need for achievement, Type A personality and field dependence–independence. Internal–external locus of control emphasizes the extent to which individuals feel they are in control of their own life; need for achievement emphasizes the extent to which individuals have an overriding need to achieve success or to avoid failure, and Type A personality identifies a particular pattern of behaviour and its likely consequences.

■ Field dependence–independence focuses upon cognitive style. Witkin devised tests of field dependence including the Rod and Frame Test, the Body Adjustment Test and the Embedded Figures Test. Individual differences in field dependence have been found to have a bearing on problem solving and upon career choices. There is also a relationship between field dependence and responses to social cues. According to Witkin, field dependence is a perceptual manifestation of personality and social behaviour, unlinked to intelligence.

Further reading

Fonagy, P. and Higgitt, A. (1984). *Personality Theory and Clinical Practice*. London: Methuen. This book discusses five of the major theoretical approaches to personality and examines their clinical applications. It also considers the debate about the consistency of personality.

Hampson, S. (1988). *The Construction of Personality: An Introduction*, 2nd edn. London: Routledge. A widely-acknowledged and authoritative text which looks at a range of different approaches to the study of personality, including multitrait and single-trait approaches, self-theories and implicit personality theories. It also considers issues relating to situationism and interactionism.

CHAPTER 30

Psychodynamic and person-centred theories of personality

Freud's psychoanalytic theory 727
▧ The structure of the personality 728
▧ Defence mechanisms 730
▧ Three levels of the mind 730
▧ Development of the personality 731
▧ Evaluation of Freudian theory 732

Person-centred approaches to personality 734
▧ Allport's trait approach 736
▧ Carl Rogers: 'self' theory 737
▧ Kelly's personal construct theory (PCT) 738
▧ Idiographic approaches: some conclusions 741

Objectives

By the end of this chapter you should:

▧ Be able to describe and evaluate Freud's psychoanalytic theory of personality;

▧ Have considered the nature of projective tests and the case for and against their use in assessing personality;

▧ Be able to describe and evaluate some person-centred (idiographic) approaches to personality;

▧ Be aware of a number of assessment techniques used in person-centred approaches to personality;

▧ Have completed an activity based on Kelly's Repertory Grid technique.

Psychodynamic theories of personality propose an account of human behaviour which relies heavily on the notion that personality is motivated by dynamic inner forces which regulate and control behaviour and arise from past experiences (see also Chapter 1). All psychodynamic theories are based to varying degrees on the psychoanalytic theory of Sigmund Freud (1856–1939). Other psychodynamic theorists, such as Jung, Adler (briefly discussed in the introduction to Part 1), Erikson (discussed in Chapter 23), Anna Freud and Melanie Klein (considered in Chapter 1) adapted and modified Freud's original ideas. Freud's psychoanaly-

tic theory has been outlined in the Introduction to Part 1. His theory is now described and evaluated in greater depth.

Freud's psychoanalytic theory

Freud trained as a doctor in Vienna, where his interest in neurology led him to specialize in the treatment of nervous disorders. He noted that many neurotic symptoms exhibited by his patients appeared to stem from earlier traumatic experiences rather than from

Sigmund Freud (1856–1939)

negative, in that he believed the contents were repressed because they were painful or threatening; burying unacceptable memories in the unconscious, therefore, is likely to make our conscious existence less painful. For most people this is a healthy defensive process but for some it may lead to psychological disorder (see the later discussion of defence mechanisms).

■ The existence of instincts which motivate and regulate human behaviour even in childhood: for example, **Eros** (a general life instinct made up of life-preserving and sexual drives) and **Thanatos** (a death instinct which involves aggressive and destructive drives). The source of these instincts is psychic energy and the most dominant, the libido, is sexual in nature. Freud regarded the libido as a force which compels humans to behave in ways which are likely to reproduce the species. He proposed that the amount of psychic energy for a particular individual is fixed and that energy could be linked to objects, people, thoughts and actions. He called this process cathexis.

The structure of the personality

Freud held that the personality encompassed three major parts, the id, the ego and the superego. Each part

physical complaints. Freud gradually developed his now famous psychoanalytic treatment of emotional and personality disorders. A major technique used was that of free association, where patients were encouraged to relax and express the free flow of thoughts entering their minds. (See Chapter 33 for an examination of psychoanalysis as a therapeutic treatment.) The aim of free association was to penetrate the unconscious mind of the patient and reveal thoughts, feelings and motivations of which the patient had not hitherto been aware. It was from this early work in a clinical setting that Freud developed his theory of the human mind and personality, a theory which continued to grow and develop throughout his life.

Central to Freud's theory was his belief in:

■ The existence of an unconscious mind harbouring repressed memories which motivate and influence conscious thoughts and behaviour. Freud's view of the unconscious mind was largely

---

NOW'S OUR CHANCE TO GET A GLIMPSE OF HIS UNCONSCIOUS MIND.

has its own function, and in the healthy, mature personality the three parts produce well-balanced, integrated behaviour. Note that these parts of the personality should in no way be thought of as tangible biological entities.

The id

The id is biologically determined and is the most primitive part of the personality. It represents all the instinctual drives: sexual, aggressive and those concerned with the satisfaction of bodily needs. It operates on the **pleasure principle**: that is to say, it seeks to obtain pleasure and avoid pain. Unsatisfied desires create tension, so release must be sought either through real solutions or through fantasy. The id is irrational and impulsive and is unaffected by social restrictions. In the newborn baby, all mental processes are id processes.

The ego

As the infant develops and attempts to adapt to the demands of the outside world, the ego emerges. It operates on the **reality principle**: that is to say,

gratification of needs are postponed until the appropriate time and place. For example, the young child learns that hunger will only be satisfied when someone is available to prepare food. This does not imply that the ego is concerned with what is 'right' or 'good', only that it takes account of the constraints and restrictions of the outside world. The ego is often said to be the 'executive' or 'manager' of the personality, in that it attempts to strike a balance between the realities of the outside world and the irrational, self-seeking drives of the id.

The superego

Around the age of four to six the third part of the personality, the superego, emerges. The superego represents the individual's own internal framework of what is 'right' and 'wrong' as represented by the moral sanctions and inhibitions which exist in the surrounding culture. Largely unconscious, it has two components: the **ego ideal** and the **conscience**. The ego ideal is concerned with what is right and proper. It represents the individual's view of the sort of virtuous behaviour that would be rewarded by others, initially the parents. The conscience, on the other hand, watches over what is bad. It intercepts and censors immoral impulses from the id and prevents them from entering the consciousness of the ego. Psychoanalytic theory predicts that the individual with a strong superego is likely to experience greater feelings of guilt in a situation involving a moral dilemma than is a person with a weaker superego and is therefore less likely to transgress the rules (see Chapter 22 for a discussion of the psychoanalytic approach to moral development).

Freud believed that the three parts of the personality are in continual conflict, with the id trying to attain gratification of impulses and the superego setting often unreasonably high moral standards. The ego is obliged to maintain an appropriate balance between these two opposing forces and the external demands of social reality.

Unresolved conflict results in anxiety which may show itself in:

■ **Dreams**, which Freud believed are the disguised fulfilment of suppressed wishes. Dream interpretation became a major strategy used by Freud when treating his patients.

■ **Neurotic symptoms**, such as extreme anxiety attacks, irrational fears or in some cases physical symptoms, such as paralysis or blindness.

Defence mechanisms

During the development of his theory, Freud identified a number of **defence mechanisms** and these were later refined and elaborated by his daughter Anna Freud (1936).

Defences are unconscious strategies used by individuals to protect themselves from painful anxiety or guilt. Such feelings may occur in one of three ways:

■ through moral conflict (ego versus superego, e.g. temptation to commit a crime);
■ through conflict over impulses (ego versus id, e.g. a desire to inflict harm on an opponent);
■ through external threat (ego versus reality, e.g. severe family conflict).

The short-term use of defence mechanisms is thought to be a 'normal' and healthy device for coping with life's pressures; where they are excessively used on a long-term basis they are considered to be dangerous and unhealthy.

Defence mechanisms are probably the most widely accepted aspects of Freud's theory, partly because they are described in relatively precise terms and partly because they receive intuitive credibility from the personal experiences of many people. Numerous defence mechanisms have been proposed by psychoanalysts; a number of them are briefly explained in Box 30.1.

Three levels of the mind

Freud distinguished three modes of thinking, each of which operates at one of three levels. These he termed **conscious**, **preconscious** and **unconscious**. The term 'levels' is meant to convey how far particular thoughts are available to us, rather than the existence of different regions of the mind.

■ **Conscious**. The conscious part of the mind represents all the thoughts and feelings we are aware of at a given time. It manifests itself in the ego and is organized in terms of logic and reason. Its main function is responding to external reality, avoiding danger and maintaining socially

---

Box 30.1 Freudian defence mechanisms

Repression. Forcing painful or frightening memories, feelings, wishes, and so on, out of conscious awareness and into the unconscious ('motivated forgetting'): for example, repressing the memory of a harmful experience or an unacceptable truth or feeling. According to Freud this is the most basic and important defence mechanism which is often supported by other defences.

Denial. Refusing to accept reality, for example that you are seriously ill or that a partner is unfaithful. This is considered to be the most primitive defence.

Regression. Reverting to behaviour characteristic of an earlier stage of life when no conflict or threat was present: for example, a two-year-old child faced with a newborn brother or sister may wish to be a baby again and insist on wearing nappies or being bottle fed once more.

Displacement. Redirecting feelings or behaviour onto a substitute object or person because you cannot express them towards their real target: for example, shouting at your partner after a disagreement with the boss.

Sublimation. A variant of displacement where unacceptable impulses are channelled into a substitute activity: for example, rechannelling the desire to handle faeces into artistic activities or redirecting aggressive impulses into sporting activities. Psychoanalysts believe this to be a positive and beneficial defence mechanism.

Projection. Assigning your own unacceptable feelings or characteristics to someone else: for example, saying 'She hates me' when your true feeling is 'I hate her'. (See also the discussion of the paranoid personality in Chapter 32.)

GLOSSARY

Defence mechanisms Unconscious strategies, often involving the distortion of reality, used by people to protect themselves from painful anxiety or guilt. Defence mechanisms include repression, denial, projection, displacement and regression.

Preconscious Part of the mind which contains thoughts and memories which may not be conscious at a given time but which are accessible to us.

acceptable behaviour. Anxiety is thought to occur if the conscious part of the mind is dominated by impulses which seek to satisfy unconscious desires.

- ■ **Preconscious**. The preconscious contains thoughts which may not be conscious at a given time but which are accessible to us. It acts as a kind of filter, censoring unacceptable wishes and only allowing them through to consciousness if they are sufficiently disguised to avoid recognition of their unconscious roots.

- ■ **Unconscious**. The unconscious operates at the deepest level and is largely inaccessible except through psychoanalytic techniques such as free association or dream analysis. It is thought to be made up of repressed material, including desires and impulses which are largely sexual and sometimes aggressive.

Figure 30.1 illustrates the relationship between the three levels of consciousness and the id, ego and superego.

Development of the personality

Freud proposed that in the course of development children pass through a series of stages. During each stage satisfaction is gained as the libido (or sexual energy) is directed towards a different part of the body. He referred to 'sexual instincts', though in attributing this term to children, he used the term 'sexual' in a rather special way to mean something like 'physically

During the oral stage, a child gains satisfaction from sucking and biting objects

pleasurable'. Each stage entails a set of problems to be overcome in relation to later development. Failure to negotiate satisfactorily a particular stage results in **fixation**, or halting of development at that stage. Fixation causes the individual to retain some of the characteristics of that stage in later life and in severe cases results in neuroses in adult life.

Below is a brief description of Freud's **psychosexual stages**.

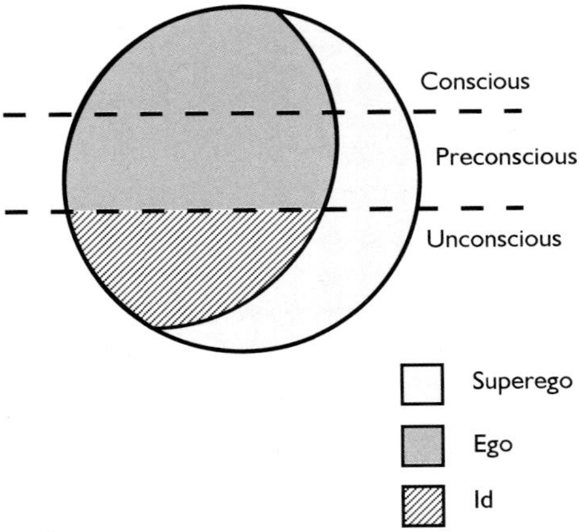

Oral stage (birth to 1 year)

The id is dominant. Libidinal energy is centred on the mouth and the child gains satisfaction from sucking and biting. Freud proposed that:

Conscious

Preconscious

Unconscious

□ Superego

▨ Ego

▨ Id

Figure 30.1 The relationship between Freud's structure of personality and three levels of consciousness

> ### GLOSSARY
>
> **Fixation** In Freud's theory, the halting of development at a particular stage resulting from a failure to deal with the challenges of that stage.
>
> **Psychosexual stages** In Freud's theory, the stages that children pass through on their way to emotional maturity. At each stage, satisfaction is gained as the libido is directed towards a particular part of the body.

- The oral stage can be subdivided into the passive, receptive, sucking subphase of the earlier months and the later active, aggressive, biting subphase.
- Fixation may be caused either by the overindulgence or by the frustration of a child's oral needs. A child whose oral needs are not satisfied or are overindulged will exhibit the characteristics of this stage in later life. Fixation may express itself in addictions such as smoking, gluttony or alcoholism; nailbiting; the excessive use of sarcasm.

Anal stage (second year of life)

This stage focuses on pleasurable sensations experienced in the mucous membranes of the rectum. The child gains satisfaction from expelling and withholding faeces and is now in a position to exercise some control over these bodily functions. He or she can either please the parents by being 'clean' or can thwart them by making a mess. Thus the pleasurable sensations associated with 'letting go' or 'holding on' become associated with behaviour that has social implications. A significant event in the child's life is the parents' efforts to impose toilet training. Fixation at the anal stage, perhaps resulting from parent–child conflict over toilet training, may give rise to a personality who is exceedingly preoccupied with cleanliness and orderliness and who is mean, obstinate and obsessive in adulthood.

Phallic stage (3 to 6)

Now libidinal energy centres on the genitals and feelings become overtly sexual. Describing first the sequence of events for the male child, Freud defined important issues arising from the **Oedipus complex**. The boy's fantasies include wishes for sexual intimacy with his mother. He envies his father's intimate relationship with his mother and fears punishment in the form of castration for his forbidden wishes. The Oedipus complex is resolved when the child identifies with his father in order to appease him and to become like him in as many ways as possible.

Freud's account of the progress of female children through the phallic stage is less clear-cut and he proposed various explanations for the girl's eventual identification with her mother. Possibly the most widely reported, the **Electra complex**, is that the girl, believing herself to be already castrated, since she does not possess a penis, suffers penis envy. This leads her to seek a strong love attachment to her father, the possessor of a penis, and finally to identify with her mother in order to become like her. The satisfactory resolution of the Oedipus/Electra complex results in the child identifying with the same-sexed parent. Two important consequences stem from this identification:

- The child adopts the **gender-role** which will be assumed through life.
- The child adopts the parents' moral standards, attitudes and prohibitions, together with the moral norms of the society they reflect. Thus, the **superego** is born and the values and beliefs of a culture are passed on from one generation to the next.

If, through insensitive handling by adults, the child does not satisfactorily overcome the Oedipus/Electra complex, problems lie ahead. Psychoanalysts believe that fixation at the phallic stage lies behind most adult neuroses.

Latency period (6 to puberty)

This is a period of relative calm following the turmoil of the phallic stage. During this time, the libido is submerged and does not centre upon any bodily area. It is a time of ego development, particularly in relation to social and intellectual skills.

Genital stage (puberty)

Hormonal changes now stimulate the reemergence of the libido. There is renewed interest in sexual pleasure and all previous sexual drives associated with particular regions of the body come together in an integrated set of adult sexual attitudes and feelings.

Box 30.2 discusses some studies of Freudian ideas.

Evaluation of Freudian theory

Eysenck and Wilson (1973) have raised objections to psychoanalytic theory on a number of counts:

GLOSSARY

Oedipus/Electra complex The major conflict of the phallic stage where the child seeks a strong love attachment to the parent of the opposite sex. Satisfactory resolution of the complex results in the child identifying with the parent.

Box 30.2   Studies of Freud's theories

Freud's work has generated an immense amount of research both into aspects of the theory of psycho-analysis and into the effectiveness of psychoanalysis as a therapy (studies of the latter are discussed in Chapter 33). Detailed reviews of experimental investigations have been carried out by Kline (1981a) and Fisher and Greenberg (1977). Below is a selection of empirical studies which have attempted to test aspects of the theory.

The oral personality

As noted earlier, fixation may be caused either by the overindulgence or by the frustration of a child's oral needs.

Fisher and Greenberg (1977) see the oral personality as being preoccupied with issues of giving and taking, concerns about independence and dependence, ex-tremes of optimism and pessimism, unusual ambivalence, impatience and the continued use of the oral channel for gratification.

A number of studies have examined whether these traits do tend to exist together in a single cluster or whether two clusters exist reflecting the oral passive (sucking) and oral aggressive (biting) subphases. Kline and Storey (1977) reviewed these investigations and found the strongest support for the oral personality in Gold-man-Eisler's (1948) studies where traits such as pessi-mism, passivity, aloofness, oral verbal aggression and autonomy were found to cluster together as were their opposites. However, Goldman-Eisler provided evidence only of face validity for the scales used. Lazare et al. (1966) provided similar results using Goldman-Eisler's items in a questionnaire. In their own study, Kline and Storey (1977) found that characteristics associated with the first 'optimistic' subphase of the oral stage (including dependency, fluency, sociability and relaxation) tended to cluster together as did characteristics (including inde-pendence, verbal aggression, envy, coldness and hostility, malice, ambition and impatience) of the second 'pessi-mistic' subphase.

A second series of investigations examined the relationship between feeding practices and later beha-viour. For example, Yarrow (1973) found a significant correlation between the time spent feeding and later thumb-sucking, those children with the shortest feeding times being the most persistent thumb-suckers. Though some support is claimed for the effects of fixation in the oral stage, an alternative explanation might be that children whose greater need for sucking, for whatever reason, led them to feed more quickly, later sought to satisfy the need through thumb-sucking.

The anal personality

As we have seen, Freud proposed that anal fixation is linked to the child's conflicts with the parents during potty training. The struggle which results either from overharsh potty training or from exceptionally intense pleasure associated with the anal period can later reveal itself in the character traits of orderliness, rigidity, obstinacy and a dislike of waste. The kind of personality in which these traits are combined is known as the anal or obsessive-compulsive personality. Three major reviews of research evidence (Kline, 1972; Fisher and Greenberg, 1977; Pollack, 1979) concluded that these traits do tend to cluster together in the anally oriented personality. However, Hill (1976) identified major methodological weaknesses in six of the studies considered by Kline to be sound ones. Howarth (1982) recognized that there does appear to be a personality type characterized by the orderly, pedantic, self-controlled and controlling indivi-dual who runs the bureaucracy of most nations who might be described as an anally oriented personality. Fonagy (1981; Fonagy and Higgitt, 1984) points out that no evidence exists which suggests that this type of personality received toilet training that was different from that of less obsessive-compulsive types.

Defence mechanisms

Many researchers have attempted to demonstrate the effects of repression ('motivated forgetting') in the laboratory, often by causing an individual to experience anxiety in relation to a particular kind of material or activity and then looking to see if the rate of forgetting increased. Holmes (1974) in a review of such studies found no conclusive evidence of repression. However, Wilkinson and Cargill (1955) claimed that stories with an Oedipal theme were remembered less well than those that were neutral. Levinger and Clark (1961) showed that when asked to remember association words they had produced in response to a number of emotional and neutral stimulus words, participants recalled significantly less of the emotional associations. Kline (1972) claimed that these findings provide clear evidence of repression operating in memory. However, using Levinger and Clark's stimulus words, Parkin et al. (1982) found that if participants delayed recall for one week, emotional associations were *better* recalled than were neutral ones. They concluded that these findings support the known relationship between arousal levels and memory and offer no support for Freud's theory of repression. However, an objection to this study and others like it is that the stimuli used may be too trivial and artificial to activate the deep emotional responses described by Freud.

- Freud's use of a limited sample composed mainly of adults who were suffering some psychological disturbance prevents generalization of his theory to all human beings.
- His use of the clinical case study method was criticized. Accounts of his sessions with patients were not written up until some time later and may have been inaccurate and selective.
- Freud used no quantitative data or statistical analysis in support of his theories.
- Most of the processes described by Freud, for example instinctual drives and defence mechanisms, cannot be directly observed, and inferences drawn about human behaviour are often open to alternative explanations. This makes the generation of precise and testable hypotheses difficult. Not only can the theory not be supported, it cannot be refuted – a serious violation of the scientific method according to Popper (1959).
- Freudian theory is unable to predict an individual's development. It can be used only to explain something after an event.

Criticisms have also been made of Freud's over-emphasis on the role of biological factors in personality development. His insistence that the goal of all behaviour is to satisfy biological needs was not shared by other psychodynamic theorists such as Jung, Adler and Erikson. Whilst recognizing the importance of biological factors, these theorists subscribed also to the social nature of human beings.

Kline (1984), whilst agreeing that some aspects of the theory, for example instinctual drives, cannot easily be tested and should be abandoned, maintained that other aspects can generate testable hypotheses which conform to the demands of the scientific method. Those hypotheses which can be tested should be restated in a refutable form and then subjected to an objective, empirical examination. Kline believes that psychoanalytic theory offers a coherent account of human behaviour in all its complexity and he pleads for bold and original thinking in future attempts to investigate Freudian concepts.

The final comment should perhaps draw attention to the profound effect that Freud's theory has had on psychological thinking and on disciplines such as history, art and English literature.

it seems madness to jettison a set of ideas as stimulating as Freud's because they do not con-

form to a conventionalized methodology at present in favour in psychology. What is required is a scientific psychology that combines theoretical rigour with the rich comprehensiveness of psychoanalysis. (Kline, 1984, p. 157)

? SELF-ASSESSMENT QUESTIONS

1. Briefly explain the nature and function of the three major parts of the personality proposed by Freud: id, ego and superego.
2. What did Freud mean by 'defence mechanisms'? Briefly describe two of them.
3. Explain the concept of 'fixation' in relation to the development of the personality.
4. Comment on the findings of some studies which have investigated:
   (a) the oral personality
   (b) defence mechanisms.
5. Critically evaluate Freud's psychoanalytic theory.
6. Make a judgment about the value of projective techniques in assessing aspects of personality (see Box 30.3).

Person-centred approaches to personality

In the introduction to Part 7, a distinction was made between **idiographic** and **nomothetic theories** of personality. The nomothetic approach, you will recall, emphasizes the similarities between people and it is exemplified by the theories of Eysenck and Cattell discussed in Chapter 29. Idiographic – or person-centred – approaches focus on the uniqueness of individuals and take the view that the essence of personality can only be captured by a detailed study of individual lives and experiences (see Malim et al.,

---

GLOSSARY

Idiographic theories A belief that human beings are unique and can only be understood through the use of techniques, such as ipsative tests or case studies, which are designed to reflect that uniqueness.

Nomothetic theories Based on the idea that there are laws of behaviour which are applied to everyone and can be used to compare people with each other.

Box 30.3   Assessment of personality in relation to psychoanalytic concepts

Freud did not develop an assessment technique to coincide with his theory in the way that, for example, Cattell developed the 16PF (see Chapter 29). However, during the time that psychoanalysis was developing, some complex, subjective methods of assessment known as projective tests were popularized. Projective tests have been loosely defined as ambiguous stimuli to which participants are required to respond. One example – the **Rorschach Test** – requires respondents to describe ten symmetrical shapes which resemble ink blots. The Rorschach Test is described more fully in Box 4.5 in Chapter 4. It is assumed that the individual 'will project much of his own personality, his conflicts and his motivations into his response' (Marx, 1976) to a test stimulus. Participants are not aware of the purposes of the test, so may disclose things about themselves that they would normally be unwilling to reveal. In psychoanalytic terms, this happens by avoiding normal defence mechanisms and gaining access to preconscious or unconscious matter. The tester's task is to interpret these signs. Whilst projective techniques are most likely to be used by psychodynamically oriented psychologists in a clinical setting, other psychologists have used them from a nonpsychodynamic perspective: for example, McClelland et al. (1953) used a test known as the Thematic Apperception Test (TAT) in their work on achievement-motivation.

Criticisms of projective tests

The main objections to projective tests have been summarized by Vernon (1964) as follows:

- There is no adequate theory or evidence to support claims that the tests tap the participant's deeper layers of personality.
- Reliability of projective test scoring on different occasions by the same scorer is not high.
- Studies of the validity of projective tests are poor; the more rigorous the validity studies, the lower are the validity coefficients that emerge.
- Test results have been shown to be affected by such factors as the mood of the participant or the tester, the attitude of the participant or the tester and the race of the tester.

Fonagy and Higgitt (1984) point out that though the tests are still quite widely used in the United States (Wade and Baker, 1977), they no longer form part of the training of British clinical psychologists who seem to have been influenced by critical assessments of the technique (Eysenck, 1959).

The case for projective tests

Many psychologists propose that, despite their shortcomings, the use of projective tests provide valuable 'clinical hunches' which can be followed up using more reliable and valid devices. Kline (1983) argued that there are two points that should be raised in defence of projective tests, the second of which clearly supports their continued use.

First, the usual method of assessing the validity of projective tests is for the responses of the participants to be rated blind: that is, with the rater having no knowledge of the participant. Kline suggests that this is nonsense. The interpretation of projective tests must be undertaken in the context of the participant's life in the same way as the psychoanalyst interprets dreams. In the light of this it might be assumed that demonstrations of invalidity are not so severe as they first appear.

Secondly, the basic objection to projective tests relates to the unreliability of scoring and interpretation. This could be overcome if a method were developed for reliable scoring and analysis. Kline argues that such an objective method has been developed for the Rorschach and used successfully by Holley (1973), namely G analysis. G analysis has been used with tests other than the Rorschach by Vegelius (1976) and Hampson and Kline (1977). In Kline's view, G analysis does allow projective tests to be used in the quantitative study of personality.

Although Freudian ideas have inspired the development of projective techniques, other devices have been used to explore psychoanalytic concepts: for example, standard personality inventories such as the **Myers–Briggs Type Indicator** (Briggs and Myers, 1962). Many elements of Carl Jung's version of psychoanalytic theory (see the Introduction to Part 1) form the basis of the Myers–Briggs test which is widely used in business, commerce and industry and the armed forces for career counselling, team building and assessments for promotion and management potential.

1992, for a detailed consideration of the idiographic/ nomothetic dichotomy). In this section, the work of three theorists will be discussed as examples of an idiographic approach to personality: Gordon Allport, Carl Rogers and George Kelly.

- The approach of Gordon Allport, as has already been noted, was not 'purely' idiographic in that, whilst greatly emphasizing the individuality and uniqueness of each personality, he also recognized the existence of some common traits that all people share to varying degrees.
- Carl Rogers was a leading figure in humanistic psychology, a major force in psychology which gathered momentum towards the middle of the twentieth century. Humanistic psychology (see Chapter 1), with its emphasis on studying the unique and subjective experiences of individual people, provided an important balance to the two major approaches which dominated psychology during the first part of the century: behaviourism, which views human personality as being 'shaped' by the effects of the environment and psychoanalysis (discussed in this chapter) which emphasizes the effects on the human personality of an unconscious mind (see Chapter 1 for a discussion of the major approaches in psychology).
- The third idiographic theorist, George Kelly, sought to understand human personality by examining individuals' own interpretations of themselves and their social world. He used the term personal constructs to denote the dimensions people use in their attempts to interpret the people and events in their lives.

Allport's trait approach

In 1937, Allport published a theory of personality. It was a reaction against previous theories which had been based on the study of abnormal personality and those which had been derived from the study of children or animals. He believed that the study of personality should emphasize the experience of unique, normal human adults and should aim to describe the psychological structures that determine the individual's characteristic ways of thinking and behaving. Some of the main points of Allport's theory are outlined below.

Personality traits

According to Allport, traits have a very real existence. He saw them as mental structures which form a part of each person's personality and which result in that person behaving and thinking in a generally consistent manner. For example, a person who possesses the trait of 'friendliness' would tend to behave in a generally sociable way in a number of different situations, such as mixing with work colleagues or meeting a stranger.

Since Allport valued a common-sense view of human personality, be began his search for personality traits by searching through an English dictionary. He found nearly 18,000 adjectives, for example 'lazy' and 'cheerful', which are used to describe personality (Allport and Odbert, 1936). Personality traits, he believed, can take one of three forms within the individual:

- **Cardinal traits.** These are the most important traits, which have a great influence on an individual's personality. In a few cases, a person's behaviour may be totally dominated by a single trait; for example, extreme meanness or selfishness. Allport believed that personalities like this are relatively rare; most people do not have one single, dominant trait.
- **Central traits.** These are less general traits, though Allport believed that they represent the basic dispositions which characterize an individual's usual ways of dealing with life. For example, one person's central traits might be honesty, liveliness, friendliness and conscientiousness.
- **Secondary dispositions.** These are less influential and consistent traits. They represent a person's specific preferences and attitudes in particular situations.

The whole person

Though Allport's study of personality traits emphasized individual aspects of people, he strongly believed that the study of personality should not lose sight of the whole, unique person. He considered that attempting to measure isolated facets of personality by using rating scales was misguided. Thus Allport's theory aims to provide a detailed and total description of individuals, rather than comparing isolated elements of their personalities with those of other people.

Personality assessment

Allport proposed that people's traits could be identified in various different ways – by direct observation of their behaviour in a range of situations, by interviews to discover their views and goals and by using evidence from letters, diaries and other documents. He urged the study of individuals through detailed and long-term case studies. A famous example of one of his own case studies centred on the personality of a young woman called Jenny. Allport and his assistants identified the central traits of Jenny's personality by analysing her letters to a friend written over many years (Allport, 1965). This study epitomizes the idiographic approach.

Evaluation of Allport

Allport is generally regarded as having made a major contribution to the study of personality. His concern with the uniqueness of individuals and the need to study the whole person has provided an important balance to nomothetic approaches with their emphasis on similarities between people, usually with no consideration of individuality.

Conversely, nomothetic theorists have criticized Allport's rejection of scientific methods of studying personality. Allport believed that the scientific method, with its emphasis on establishing general laws and principles, was not the best route to knowledge about humans. The only meaningful approach, he believed, is to view the world from each individual's unique perspective.

Kirby and Radford (1976) argue that Allport is misguided in that he confused the study of individual differences with the art of biography, which is a descriptive science. Whilst biography makes a valuable contribution to the study of individuals, it does not by itself provide an adequate way of understanding human nature in general. They further comment that if an individual existed who was truly unique, that person would not be recognizable as human, since people are recognizably human because of their similarities.

Carl Rogers: 'self' theory

Rogers's personality theory (see also Chapter 1) originated from his work in the fields of counselling and psychotherapy. In contrast to psychoanalysis, there is no attempt to examine the hidden meanings of people's behaviour or to look for causes in their childhood. The focus is on the here and now and individuals are regarded as the best experts on themselves. How individuals perceive events in their lives determines their reactions to them (Rogers, 1951).

The self

Central to Rogers's theory is the concept of the self (or self-concept), the individual's view, acquired through life experiences, of all the perceptions, feelings, values and attitudes that define 'I' or 'me'. This **perceived self** influences both the individual's perception of the world and his or her own behaviour. The other aspect of self, according to Rogers, is the **ideal self**, one's perception of how one should or would like to be. For example, a woman might perceive herself as successful and respected in her career but with certain shortcomings as a wife and mother (which might or might not be true). Her ideal self might demand that she be equally successful in both these spheres of her life. Good psychological health exists where the perceived self and the ideal self are reasonably compatible. It is when there is a serious mismatch (Rogers refers to this as incongruence) between the two or between the self and the feedback received from the external world that psychological problems arise. In a study of 250 people who were assessed separately on neuroticism and congruence or genuineness (closeness to inner emo-

---

GLOSSARY

Perceived self Rogers's term for the individual's own view of what he or she is like, arrived at through life experiences and through feedback from other people.

Ideal self Rogers's term for one's perceptions of how one should or would like to be.

tional experiences) Tausch (1978) found that individuals with high degrees of incongruence were the most likely to display neurotic symptoms. (Rogers's ideas in relation to the self are also considered in Chapter 24.)

Self-actualization

All people, Rogers believed, are born with the **actualizing tendency**, a motive which drives us to grow and develop into mature and healthy human beings who will realize their full capacities. This actualizing tendency can manifest itself at different levels. At the lowest level it involves basic desires for physical requirements such as food, water and comfort. At a higher level are the needs for self-fulfilment in terms of independence, experience and creativity. This motivation for self-actualization serves as a criterion by which the individual judges all experiences. An event is evaluated as good or bad dependent upon whether it leads to self-actualization.

Positive regard from others

Rogers (1959) assumes that there exists in all people a need for positive regard, which develops as the awareness of the self emerges. Positive regard is seen as respect, acceptance and love from the important people in an individual's life. It can be clearly seen in the young child's need for approval and love from the parents. Sometimes parents' approval is conditional, that is, dependent on the child behaving in the way they would wish, or they may accept the child unconditionally. However, the person needs positive regard not only from others but from himself or herself. Where a person experiences unconditional positive regard, positive self-regard will also be unconditional. Rogers believes that this situation provides the individual with genuine psychological adjustment. However, most people do not achieve this. Love and approval from others is often conditional on the individual behaving in ways that are acceptable: for example, the child who strives to learn a musical instrument in order to please the parents. Thus the individual develops what Rogers refers to as 'conditions of worth', those ways of behaving which will earn positive regard from significant others. This may involve the individual suppressing spontaneous feelings and actions and behaving in ways which are intended to please others. Rogers believes that many psychological disorders arise from attempts to

live our lives by other people's principles rather than our own.

Rogers's client-centred therapy (see Chapter 33) aims to offer the client unconditional positive regard in a warm, accepting atmosphere in order that insight may be gained into disturbing problems and possible solutions explored.

Box 30.4 describes the Q-sort technique, which has been used by Rogers to assess changes in a client's perception of self.

Evaluation of Rogers's theory

Rogers's theory, along with those of other humanistic theorists, has served the valuable purpose of encouraging psychologists to consider the subjective experience of the individual and appreciate the importance of self-regard in human functioning. His approach has had its greatest impact in the fields of psychotherapy and counselling and has provided a welcome alternative to psychoanalytic and learning theory approaches to therapy (see Chapter 33).

As a theory of personality, Rogers's approach has a number of shortcomings, which include the following:

■ It has been suggested that his reliance on self-report is misguided, since people are rarely fully aware of the truth about themselves and in addition may be influenced by the expectations of the investigator.

■ His concepts of self and the actualizing tendency are not sufficiently well-defined to be adequately measured and tested. However, Rogers has made available tape-recordings of his therapy sessions in order that other psychologists may investigate his ideas. Some empirical studies have been carried out using the Personal Orientation Inventory (Shostrum et al., 1976) which claims to be a measure of self-actualization.

Kelly's personal construct theory (PCT)

Kelly (1955) believed that in dealing with the world, people act like scientists. Scientists, he claimed, begin by putting forward theories and hypotheses about what

---

GLOSSARY

Actualizing tendency Rogers's term for a motive that exists in everyone to develop into mature fulfilled human beings.

Box 30.4   The Q-sort technique

This is a technique originally developed by Stephenson (1953) for describing the personality. It was later used by Rogers for examining the self-concept and as an assessment instrument to study changes in the client's perceptions of self during the course of therapy. A full description of the Q-sort technique has been produced by Block (1961/78).

Typically, the procedure for using the Q-sort is as follows:

■ The participant is given a large number of cards, each one containing a descriptive statement such as 'I am likeable', 'I am an impulsive person' or 'I am satisfied with myself'. These are sorted into nine piles with those that are least characteristic of the person in pile one and those most characteristic in pile nine with the remainder being distributed in the intervening piles.

■ The participant is instructed to sort the cards with the majority of them falling in the middle of the continuum and with relatively few falling at either extreme. Thus a rough normal distribution is formed. This makes the results easier to deal with statistically and also controls 'response sets' such as the tendency to stick to average ratings or extreme ratings.

■ In Rogers's procedure, once a profile has been obtained of the participant's perception of 'self', the cards will usually be resorted with the aim being to provide a profile of the 'ideal self'. The two sorts can then be correlated in order to register the degree of similarity or discrepancy between 'self' and 'ideal self'. A low correlation indicates a large discrepancy, implying maladjustment and low self-esteem.

The Q-sort is a flexible technique which can be used to assess individuals' perceptions of a number of different aspects of their lives. It is fully in line with Rogers's belief that people are themselves the best judges of their own feelings and attitudes. However, there is some evidence that individuals may respond in ways which they feel are socially acceptable or in line with the expectations of the investigator.

Studies which have attempted to assess the validity of Q-sort techniques have been equivocal. Truax et al. (1968) found the results of Q-sorts to be in agreement with other psychological measures of adjustment and change in delinquents and neurotics. However, Garfield et al. (1971) found little agreement between eight different measures of outcome in therapy, one of which was the Q-sort. No firm evidence exists in support of the reliability of the Q-sort.

---

the world is like and then proceed to test them out through research. Thus, Kelly considered each person formulates hypotheses or predictions about the world, tests them and, when necessary, revises them in the light of the 'experimental' (interactions with others and with the environment) results. The unique view of the world formed by each individual becomes that individual's idiosyncratic framework which is used to govern his or her behaviour and to interpret further experiences and events. Thus, Kelly maintained, people interpret or construe the world rather than observing it directly.

At any given time, the particular hypotheses an individual holds about the world are called **personal constructs**.

Personal constructs

To understand the individual, Kelly believed, one must know something about that person's personal con-

structs. In turn, understanding the person's personal constructs involves finding out also about his or her behaviour. For example, one cannot know what a woman truly means when she says 'I am in love' without looking at some examples of her behaviour.

Kelly viewed personal constructs as pairs of opposing dimensions which individuals use to describe and make sense of the people and events around them. For example, one person may tend to see others as being either friendly or reserved, either warm or cold; another individual may typically use the constructs of intelligent or dull, honest or dishonest. Kelly believed that an individual's personality was

> **GLOSSARY**
>
> **Personal construct** A term used by George Kelly to describe an individual's unique perceptions, or 'constructs', through which he or she makes sense of the world.

made up of the construct system used to construe (make sense of) the people and events in that individual's life.

Kelly devised a method of gaining access to an individual's constructs known as the role construct repertory grid, usually known simply as the **repertory grid** (see Box 30.5).

Criticisms of personal construct theory (PCT)

■ PCT is seen by many as an imaginative and comprehensive theory which emphasizes the cognitive aspects of human personality. However, it has been criticized because of its failure to allow for other aspects of human functioning. For example, Bruner (1956) argues that the theory

---

Box 30.5   The repertory grid

Kelly mainly used the repertory grid to discover how individuals construe (make sense of) the world in terms of the other people in their lives. However, the technique can also be used to explore other aspects of the person's life such as 'subjects studied at school' in the case of a child, or for adults, 'occupations'.

The diagram illustrates an extract from a repertory grid which has been arrived at to determine the way a fictitious individual, referred to here as James, construes the most important people (significant others) in his life. The procedure would be as follows.

The roles played by these significant others, for example, mother, father, sister, are listed across the top of the grid. James would be asked to fill in the actual names of the people who play these roles in his life. These are known as the elements of the grid.

The purpose of the grid is to find the main constructs James uses to interpret and understand the behaviour of the elements (that is, the named people in his life). These are listed in the right-hand column of the grid. To arrive at these, James would be asked to consider the similarities and differences between the elements. These would be considered in threes; for example, typically he would be asked to state how two of them are alike and the third is different.

If James thought of his mother and father as being alike in that they are both understanding and his sister being different in that she is unsympathetic, the construct to emerge would be understanding–unsympathetic. The constructs are said to be expressed in a bipolar way (showing opposite extremes) with the 'similar' pole placed first. By the time James had worked through all

Elements					Constructs
Mother	Father	Sister	Girl-friend	College tutor	
✓	✓	✕	✓	✕	Understanding – Unsympathetic
					Gentle – Aggressive
					Warm – Cold
					Inteligent – Unintelligent

An extract from a fictitious repertory grid

the people in the grid, he would have revealed his own idiosyncratic framework showing the particular constructs he uses to understand the actions of the people in his life. This procedure would be repeated many times until all the possible constructs had been revealed.

James would then be asked to go through the grid rating each of the people named against all the constructs arrived at. For example, he would consider whether number 4 (girlfriend) was understanding or unsympathetic, and so on. (A tick would indicate the first of the poles and a cross the second.)

When a repertory grid has been completed, it will contain a large amount of information about the individual's ways of viewing the world. This can be extremely helpful in the treatment of mental disorder (see Chapter 33), where the ability to make changes in personal constructs is seen as crucial to the individual's well-being.

The repertory grid is also a very helpful technique which can be used to assist individuals to explore their own true feelings about a problem or dilemma.

does not deal adequately with the possible effect of strong emotions such as love or anger on an individual's construct system.

■ Thomas (1978) argues that it is difficult to think about PCT in isolation from the repertory grid techniques devised by Kelly and his colleagues. The very act of eliciting constructs from individuals imposes limits on their thought processes which constrains the kind of data that are collected. Thus, the theory could be seen as self-validating in the sense that so long as Kelly's techniques are used, no evidence against the theory could be revealed.

Idiographic approaches: some conclusions

Idiographic approaches to personality emphasize the uniqueness of the individual. Therefore they represent an important balance to nomothetic approaches in that they could be said to have brought the person back into psychology. However, if the aim of personality theories is to predict human behaviour, idiographic approaches would allow predictions to be made for only one person at a time. In 1962, Allport and Holt debated the relative virtues of idiographic and nomothetic approaches. Holt argued that only nomothetic approaches satisfy the rigorous scientific methods demanded if psychology is to be considered a science. Allport's response was that idiographic and nomothetic approaches must work together since neither is adequate on its own: idiographic approaches give too isolated a picture of someone while nomothetic ones are too general.

Lamiell (1981) proposes that **idiothetics** provides a compromise. This is an approach which attempts to capture the best of both worlds. As Pervin (1983) says: 'there is an effort to bring the person back into personality research without, however, relinquishing the goal of systematic, general principles of psychological functioning' (p. 268).

❓ SELF-ASSESSMENT QUESTIONS

1. Outline Allport's view of the nature of personality traits. Refer to cardinal traits and central traits.
2. Outline and evaluate Rogers's 'self theory'.
3. Evaluate the use of the Q-sort technique as an assessment of personality.
4. What does Kelly mean by 'personal constructs'? How are they important to an understanding of an individual's personality?
5. What do you believe is the main contribution made by idiographic theories to our understanding of human personality?

Exercise 30.1

See if you can find a friend who will allow you to draw up a repertory grid designed to explore how he or she views some important aspect of their life, either significant people or perhaps possible occupational choices, subject to be studied at college, and so on. You would need to assure your friend that you would treat the resulting information in confidence.

If you are considering people, follow the procedure described in Box 30.5. Suppose you are looking at, say, possible occupations, you would need to get your friend to list a number of different occupations that interest him or her across the top of the grid (elements); otherwise, the procedure would be the same.

When you and your friend have completed the repertory grid, talk through the findings. Does the information it has thrown up provide a good view of your friend's ways of viewing (constructs about) a range of possible occupations? Did your friend find it helpful in clarifying which one is the most attractive and achievable? You could also try out the development of a repertory grid for something like 'which car to choose' or 'where to go on holiday'.

GLOSSARY

Repertory grid A technique used by George Kelly to identify an individual's personal constructs, usually in terms of their relationships with other people in their lives.

Idiothetics An approach which aims to compromise between the two extremes of nomothetic and idiographic approaches by focusing on the uniqueness of the individual, without losing sight of the general principles of human behaviour.

Chapter summary

- Psychodynamic theories of personality include those of Freud as well as Jung, Adler, Anna Freud and Melanie Klein. Central to these theories is the existence of an unconscious mind, and instincts which motivate and regulate human behaviour, particularly eros and thanatos. The source of these instincts is psychic energy, particularly libido, or sexual drive.

- The personality is structured into the id, which operates on the pleasure principle and is the most primitive part of the personality, the ego which operates on the reality principle and which develops as infants adapt to the outside world, and the superego which emerges in early childhood and represents the child's framework of what is right and wrong. The superego has two components, ego ideal and conscience.

- The three elements of personality are in continual conflict which may show itself in dreams or in neurotic symptoms. Defence mechanisms have developed by which individuals may protect themselves from anxiety and guilt.

- The mind operates on three levels: conscious, preconscious and unconscious. This last is the deepest and the most inaccessible except through psychoanalysis and dream interpretation.

- The personality develops in stages, each of which focuses upon a particular centre of libidinal energy. Fixation at any stage may result in personality manifestations These commence with the oral stage where the focus is on the mouth. The oral stage may be divided into passive–receptive and active–aggressive substages and roughly covers the first year of life.

- The anal stage focuses on the rectum. Pleasurable sensations may be obtained by exercising control over the functions of the rectum, retention or expulsion of faeces. Fixations may result in personalities which are excessively orderly, or mean, obstinate and obsessive. This covers the second year of life.

- The phallic stage focuses on the genitals. Important issues centre on the Oedipus complex, focusing on desire for intimacy with the opposite-sex parent. Satisfactory resolution results in identification with the same-sex parent, providing a permanent gender role

as well as the adoption of the parents' moral standards, attitudes and prohibitions.

- During the latency period the libido is submerged and time is given for the ego to develop before the genital stage when the emergence of hormonal changes at puberty renew focus on libido, resulting in adult sexual attitudes and feelings.

- Criticisms of Freud's theory rest upon his very limited sample of mainly disturbed people, his use of clinical case study method, lack of quantitative data and the impossibility of directly observing the instinctual drives and mechanisms he outlines.

- Idiographic theories of personality include those of Allport, Rogers and Kelly. Allport's trait approach was based upon cardinal traits, central traits and secondary dispositions. His study of personality emphasized the experience of unique normal human adults. Traits could be identified by observation, by interviews and by written evidence. He rejected scientific methods for the study of personality, a subject of criticism by nomothetic theorists.

- Rogers's personality theory originated with his counselling and therapeutic work. Central to his theory is 'self', the individual's view of himself or herself. together with the concept of the 'ideal self'. An individual's perception of 'self' and of 'ideal self' determines psychological health. There needs to be a reasonable match between these elements. People have an actualizing tendency, which motivates them to grow up into mature and healthy human beings. This tendency is used as a criterion by which individuals judge their experiences. Individuals also have a need for positive regard from others which needs to be unconditional and also from himself or herself.

- Kelly believed that people act like scientists, hypothesizing what the world is like and then testing these hypotheses. These hypotheses are 'personal constructs', pairs of opposing dimensions by means of which a person makes sense of the world. Kelly attempted to gain access to these constructs by means of a repertory grid.

- Idiographic theories provide a welcome balance against the more quantitative and norm-based approaches of type and trait theorists.

Further reading

Freud, S. (1933/65). *New Introductory Lectures on Psychoanalysis* (J. Strachey, ed. and trans.). New York: Norton. A translation of Freud's theories presented in a very readable form.

Rogers, C. (1969). *Freedom to Learn*. Colombus, OH: Merrill. A general overview of Rogers's views in which he discusses his ideas of personal growth in the context of education.

CHAPTER 31

Atypical development

Learning difficulties   745
▓ Genetic conditions   746
▓ Infectious diseases   747
▓ Environmental hazards   747

Physical and sensory impairment   748
▓ Deafness   748
▓ Blindness   749
▓ Dyslexia   749

Emotional disturbances and behavioural difficulties   751
▓ Autism   752
▓ Attention-deficit hyperactivity disorder (ADHD)   756
▓ Other childhood conditions   758
▓ The family and the atypical child   759

Objectives

By the end of this chapter, you should be able to:

▓ Reach an understanding of theories and research relating to causes and problems associated with learning difficulties;

▓ Describe and make some assessment of research carried out into the psychological effects of physical and sensory impairment and dyslexia;

▓ Appreciate the problems of coping with physical and sensory impairment;

▓ Discuss theories and research in relation to the causes and effects of emotional and behavioural difficulties in childhood and adolescence, including attention-deficit hyperactivity disorder, autism, depressive and feeding disorders;

▓ Discuss evidence which suggests that sufferers from autism appear to have a 'theory of mind' deficiency.

Normal processes of development are genetically preprogrammed, and subject to social and emotional influences, as described in Chapters 19-23. Occasionally development does not follow the usual pattern; this results in what is termed **atypical development**, or development which is not typical of the human species. However, it must be stressed at the outset that while some facets of the child's development may be atypical, there is much within each of them that is 'normal'. They are subject to the same joys and fears as any child, they may just react differently.

Atypical development may occur at various times or for a number of reasons; causes include:

▓ **Genetic structure** (for example, Down's syndrome, where chromosome abnormalities produce developmental differences);

▓ **Pre-natal damage**. Damage while the foetus is in the uterus (e.g., foetal alcohol syndrome);

▓ **Birth process problems**, such as anoxia (lack of oxygen), which may result in generalized brain dysfunction;

- **Biochemical abnormalities**, which may become progressively worse if not treated (e.g., phenylketonuria);
- **Adverse social and emotional environments** during childhood, such as deprivation or abuse;
- **Other**, as yet undetermined causes, which result in developmental problems such as dyslexia, hyperactivity, generalized learning difficulties.

These and other forms of atypical development will be described and discussed in this chapter. Problems arising from these causes may be roughly grouped under three headings:

- Learning difficulties,
- The psychological effects of physical and sensory impairment,
- Emotional disturbances and behavioural difficulties.

Learning difficulties

It was extremely difficult to find a title for this section without causing offence to someone. Terminology for learning difficulties tends to change periodically as stigma become attached to current terms. Historically, those who were judged to be below normal were classified as either 'idiots' or 'imbeciles', often with scant attention to testing for real potential. When these terms became unacceptable to society, the terms 'subnormal' and 'severely subnormal' were substituted. These, too, became unacceptable, and the term 'mentally handicapped' was used, which did not seem to imply the same stigma; recently there has been a move to use the term 'people with learning difficulties', 'people with special needs' or sometimes 'challenging behaviour'. How accurate these descriptive terms are of all forms of learning difficulty, is debatable. What is needed is more acceptance, by the population at large, that humans are not all the same in their intellectual and functional capacities, otherwise the stigma will reattach itself in time to whatever term is used.

Perhaps some parallels could be drawn here, from the field of physical handicaps. Is the term 'cerebral palsied' preferable to 'spastic'? You may think so; sufferers may not. The cerebral palsied Christopher Nolan (in *Under the Eye of the Clock*) refers to himself simply as a 'cripple'). An American professor once said 'we have done terrible things to the American Indians,

Box 31.1   Levels of learning difficulties

Four levels of learning difficulties are categorized by both the International Classification of Diseases (ICD) and the Diagnostic and Statistical Manual of Mental Disorder (DSM) (these are systems for classifying mental disorders and they are discussed fully in Chapter 32). The categories are:

- mild learning difficulties (IQ of 50 to 70),
- moderate learning difficulties (IQ of 35 to 49),
- severe learning difficulties (IQ of 20 to 34) and
- profound learning difficulties (IQ below 20).

Those with profound learning difficulties often exhibit physiological malfunctions as well. Childhood mortality rate is high in this category. Readers are reminded of the discussion in Chapters 4 and 21 on controversies surrounding the use of IQ tests and in particular the dangers of using them to label people. The American Association on Mental Deficiency suggests that the criterion of IQ scores should only be applied after adaptive functioning is assessed. In other words, the way in which the individual adapts and functions in the real world is of greater importance than a scored IQ test.

the least terrible of which is to call them American Indians!' He was commenting on the move to stop the usage of this terminology. The same seems to apply to those who have learning difficulties. As they are all individuals, they may not wish to use the terminology chosen for them.

In Great Britain all children have a right to education, whether disabled or not, until the age of 18. After that, there is no guarantee of training, employment or any further education, yet development is lifelong for all individuals, and necessarily protracted for disabled individuals. They may well be among those who would benefit from having no ceiling to educational age. It is not unknown for adults with

GLOSSARY

Atypical development Development which is not typical of a particular species and does not follow the usual pattern.

Learning difficulties A term often used to describe the characteristics of learning impairment. It includes many kinds of problem, some genetically related, some biochemical.

learning difficulties to start to learn to read at the age of 30-plus.

Learning difficulty does not describe a total syndrome; it includes many types of problem. Some are genetically related, some biochemical, all can be made worse by poor social conditions or alleviated by good management. Some examples are given here, but there is not space to cover every category. The following descriptions are subcategorized into what is currently believed to be the three main causes of learning difficulty: genetic conditions, infectious diseases and environmental hazards.

Genetic conditions

Down's syndrome

Probably the most easily recognizable and best-known form of learning difficulty, the syndrome covers a wide range of ability levels. Physically, individuals are recognizable by being short, usually stout, with a round face and heavy-lidded, usually slanting, eyes (this is why **Down's syndrome** people were called 'mongols' at one time, because their typical appearance was thought to be like that of the Mongoloid race. Some have a large tongue which may protrude, and this also relates to an increased flow of saliva. Finger joints may well be shorter than most people's. Internally many individuals with Down's syndrome suffer from respiratory and heart complaints, especially as they get older. Longevity is not expected; 40 years is about the average life expectancy, though many Down's sufferers live considerably longer than this.

Children with learning difficulties help each other to learn

Sufferers have a chromosome abnormality (the mechanisms of genetics are more fully discussed in the Introduction to Part 4). Most people have 46 chromosomes, 23 from each parent. Down's sufferers have 47, three of Chromosome 21 instead of two, hence the term Trisomy 21. In some, all the body cells are affected; in others, only some of the cells. It is difficult to ascertain whether this corresponds directly to the degree of impaired mental functioning, as Down's sufferers are extremely susceptible to influences in their social environment, and may also be limited by their own level of physical health. Nearly all have a good comprehension of speech, but production of speech varies, and is not assisted by a large tongue.

Development The development of children suffering from Down's syndrome proceeds along usual pathways, but is far more protracted than in nonsufferers, although some reach relatively high levels of functioning, both socially and cognitively. Studies into false belief and theory of mind (described in Chapter 22) all tend to demonstrate that the majority of children with Down's syndrome do not develop a theory of mind in the way that their 'normal' counterparts do. This was demonstrated in a comparison study by Baron-Cohen et al. (1985), which is described later in this chapter, in the section on autism.

Probable causes Why Down's syndrome occurs is still not fully established; statistically it seems most commonly to affect babies of older mothers (over 35 years of age). It was at one time suggested that the origins could be a virus infection of the maternal grandmother during her pregnancy; a women's eggs remain in a suspended state of division from the foetal stage, until they begin to mature after puberty. Alternatively, an explanation could be that the longer the eggs are stored, the greater the chance of damage; this would explain why more Down's syndrome babies are born to mothers over 35. In 1973 women over 35 accounted for only 13 per cent of all pregnancies, but bore more than 50 per cent of the infants with Down's syndrome. Men after puberty

---

GLOSSARY

Down's syndrome A form of mental and physical impairment caused by chromosome abnormalities.

form new sperm cells daily, yet research (Magenis et al., 1977) indicated that in as many as 25 per cent of Down's syndrome cases, the fathers' sperm carried the extra chromosome. And again, advanced parental age is implicated. Down's syndrome can be detected in the early stages of pregnancy by sampling the cells of the amniotic fluid which surrounds the foetus (amniocentesis). A blood test has recently been devised, which will be much simpler and cheaper (and can therefore be offered to all pregnant women, not just those over 35). It obviates the slight risk of unintentional abortion, which is present with the amniocentesis test. If a Down's syndrome baby is detected, in Great Britain, the mother has the right to choose an abortion if she wishes to.

Phenylketonuria (PKU)

Phenylketonuria (PKU) is a relatively rare disease (about one in 14,000 live births), although it is estimated that one person in 70 carries the recessive gene responsible. When a pair of defective recessive genes misdirect the formation of an enzyme, metabolic processes are disrupted. The infant, who is born with normal intellectual capabilities, suffers from a deficiency of the enzyme phenylananine, and its derivative, phenylpruvic acid, builds up in the body. Myelination of the axons in the nervous system is prevented and the brain is affected, especially the neurons of the frontal lobes. This results in profound learning difficulties, though outward physical signs are not obvious. Fortunately this biochemical abnormality is detectable easily in the blood test given routinely to the baby a few days old. If the test is positive, the child can be given a special diet, until six or seven years of age, when brain formation is relatively complete. In this way, damage to the central nervous system is minimized.

Infectious diseases

Before birth

An infectious disease of the expectant mother can affect the foetus in utero; the first three months of foetal development is especially important to development of a healthy brain and nervous system. Diseases such as rubella (German measles), syphilis (a venereal disease, contracted through sexual intercourse with an infected person) and herpes simplex (the same virus which causes cold sores, but can cause more serious problems in other parts of the body), can all cause mental as well as physical abnormalities.

After birth

Some infectious diseases in the young child can affect the child's developing brain, causing learning difficulties; for example, meningitis (inflammation of the meninges, one of the layers of membranes covering and protecting the brain) can cause mild or severe disability or even death. This is likely to be less serious in the child over six years old, as the brain is largely developed by this age. In some young children, a severe attack of measles has been known to result in learning difficulties; for this reason, vaccination against measles was introduced, and incidence of the disease is now relatively rare.

Environmental hazards

In the uterus

In the prenatal environment, the greatest hazard comes from substances taken by the mother. For example:

- **Alcohol**. Foetal alcohol syndrome (FAS) can result from the mother taking alcohol during the first three months of pregnancy. Infants with FAS typically have a small head, flat nose and deep upper lip, small stature and a degree of learning difficulty, usually related to the amount of alcohol consumed.
- **Smoking**. It has also been recently suggested that smoking affects the mental development of the foetus; this applies to passive smoking as well, and expectant fathers as well as expectant mothers are now urged to give up smoking.
- **Drugs**. Drugs taken during pregnancy (prescribed or otherwise) are necessarily transmitted to the foetus; everyone knows of the horrendous physical after-effects of the drug thalidomide, administered to pregnant women for morning sickness. Not all drugs taken by women are

---

GLOSSARY

Phenylketonuria (PKU) A disease caused by a pair of defective recessive genes which leads to the disruption of metabolic processes. It is treatable, but if left untreated, can lead to mental impairment.

recorded and related to mental abnormalities, but undoubtedly many could cause major or minor problems. Heroin, of course, produces babies who are already addicted.

During early childhood

Damage to the developing brain and nervous system can have permanent effects. Causes include the following.

Pollutants   Children can be damaged by pollutants in the environment, such as mercury, which can be transmitted through affected fish. Lead poisoning, through chewing or sucking items painted with a lead-based paint, or in the past, lead soldiers, can cause kidney and brain damage. Lead-based paint production is now prohibited, but the paint may still be in existence in old houses or on old furniture. Lead soldiers are now mainly collectors' items. Lead piping for water supplies is not used nowadays, but may still exist in old buildings.

Accidents   Accidents involving head injuries to young children can cause permanent brain damage. Attempts to minimize this have been made by legislation for the wearing of seat belts, or use of child seats in cars. Falls or blows to the head can also produce brain damage.

Birth injury   Physical damage or anoxia (lack of oxygen) during the birth process can result in a degree of learning difficulty. Prolonged labour can cause anoxia, as can the placenta or umbilical cord becoming damaged during or before the birth process. Vitamin K injections are routinely given to neonates, in order to minimize bleeding from tiny blood vessels in the brain, as this causes learning difficulties. However, it has been suggested that these injections may be related to a rise in childhood cancers, and possibly Vitamin K by mouth would be an acceptable compromise.

SELF-ASSESSMENT QUESTIONS

1. What do you understand by 'atypical development'? What are some of the causes?
2. What are the problems in trying to find acceptable terminology to describe a person who has learning difficulties?
3. Explain what is meant by 'Down's syndrome'. Discuss some of the possible causes.
4. Discuss some infectious diseases that appear during childhood and their likely causes.

Physical and sensory impairment

While some physical and sensory handicaps are in themselves usually recognized easily, the psychological problems and adaptive processes which apply to the individual are not always recognized as being different from those encountered by unaffected individuals. For example, we all recognize that a blind person cannot see, and we extend sympathy for that. Few of us also realize how much we use the sense of sight in balancing; blind people compensate for this by using other processes, but may well not be so confident in their balance as people who are not blind.

This section considers the psychological effects of sensory impairment such as deafness and blindness. It also examines some research into learning disorders such as difficulty learning to read or write or do arithmetic. The term 'dyslexia' is often used in connection with such learning disorders and increasingly there is an assumption that they arise from some kind of neurophysiological dysfunction or damage.

Deafness

Because communication plays such a central role in human society, the deaf child can suffer disadvantages which most of us do not immediately recognize. The majority of deaf children (almost 90 per cent) are born to hearing parents, and therefore live in an environment dominated by spoken language. Studies have shown that most profoundly deaf children are deficient in spoken and written language (Schlesinger and Meadow, 1972), but that the children of deaf parents do as well or better than the children of hearing parents, when in fact you might expect them to fare worse. The explanation offered is that the deaf parents are using sign language between each other and with the child; therefore the child is learning a language at the appropriate time in development, whereas the deaf child in a hearing family has no communication with them unless the parents learn sign language while the child is a baby. If the child is taught only oral language,

A deaf child communicates through sign language

the child has more difficulty developing speech or reading skills than children who are taught a combination of lipreading, sign language and oral language (Moores, 1985).

Children who are deaf, and have deaf parents who use sign language, appear to develop a sense of themselves (self-concept) at the same age as hearing children. They begin to use the sign for 'I' at the age when hearing children use the word 'I', at about 18 or 20 months (Petitto, 1988).

Support for deaf children

Many children with hearing loss can use a hearing aid; these are often now fitted in infancy, which is bound to help normalize the child's early development. A recent advance in assisting hearing-impaired children is the use of cochlear implants, which are more effective than external hearing aids in some forms of deafness. This also has the advantage of assisting speech intelligibility in these children, because if you can hear some speech, you are more likely to reproduce the sounds than if you are having your speech shaped by reinforcement.

Osberger et al. (1994) examined the speech intelligibility of 18 deaf children who had been using cochlear implants for an average of three years. Nine of the children used only oral communication methods, while the other nine used oral, lipreading and sign language. The intelligibility scores (number of words correctly understood by the listener) for the oral communication group was significantly higher than the scores of the children who had been using a mixture of communication methods. Possibly when this group of children had found certain words difficult to pronounce, they would resort to signing, instead of trying to perfect their pronunciation.

Blindness

Blindness may seem a greater affliction than deafness to most of us but, in terms of development, it may be less of a problem. Blind children are still able to communicate verbally, learn to read using Braille, and initiate and maintain social communications through language.

Fraiberg (1977), in a series of studies, found that blind babies commenced smiling at about the same age as others (about three to five weeks). However, one month later, when sighted babies begin to smile more at the sight of their parents, blind babies smile less, presumably because the stimulus to smile is absent.

Mutual gazing between parent and baby is an important part of the bonding process, which is of course not possible where the baby is blind. This, together with the fact that the baby's facial expression is usually bland, may give the parent the feeling that the child does not want to interact, and the parent may feel rejected. This has the effect of lessening the parent's approaches to interaction.

Fraiberg found that this situation could be remedied if the parent were assured that this was normal in blind babies, and was taught to 'read' other signals from the baby. For example, the baby's face may not change at the sound of the parent's voice, but the hands may wave or the body wriggle. These movements can become just as reassuring and reinforcing to the parents of a blind baby as smiles are to the parents of sighted babies. If secure attachments are fostered in this way, it may prevent behaviour such as rocking, head-banging or other repetitive actions which are sometimes shown by blind babies, presumably in an effort to provide comfort and stimulation.

Dyslexia

Dyslexia has been defined as an unexpected failure to learn to read. However, it is a relatively imprecise term which may cover a range of learning problems

> **GLOSSARY**
>
> **Dyslexia** Literally defined as 'nonreading', it is an imprecise term which covers a range of learning problems connected with learning to read, write and spell.

concerned with learning to read, write and spell and in some cases, do arithmetic. Often the child writes letters backwards, or includes all the correct letters in a word, but puts them in the wrong order (see Figure 31.1). This can cause great frustration. Apart from this failure to learn to read, the child usually develops normally. Intelligence is usually normal, other areas of learning proceed at a normal pace and there is no recognizable brain damage which causes loss of functions in other areas of development.

The incidence of dyslexia in the school population has been estimated at around 5 per cent, which means that one or two children in each intake starting school will turn out to be dyslexic (Nicolson, 1996).

Initially the problem was regarded simply as 'slow development' in that particular area of learning. Indeed, dyslexia was regarded by some psychologists as a convenient label proposed by some, largely middle-class, parents to describe their children's inability to develop appropriate reading and writing skills. However, most Western countries now acknowledge and provide support for dyslexia. Pressure from parents and extensive media coverage have resulted in increasing attempts to better understand the problem and to find ways of diagnosing and treating it.

Why does dyslexia occur?

Between 1930 and 1970, researchers looked for evidence of a specific visual deficit in dyslexic children. Hulme (1981) reviewed these early studies and concluded that when methodological and sampling errors were accounted for, little evidence remained to show that dyslexia was due to visual problems. Subsequently, studies turned to investigate phonological awareness – awareness of the individual sounds of words – and some appeared to show links between dyslexia and the production of phonological errors. Recent studies (Siegel, 1993; Stanovich, 1993) have shown that children are likely to have either one or both of the following problems:

■ lack of **phonemic awareness**,
■ a lack of knowledge of the grammar and structure of language.

Findings such as these have been helpful to our understanding of dyslexia. However, they do not tell us why children might have such problems with language in the first place.

Support programmes, particularly those which involve training in individual sounds, have been shown to help children with dyslexia.

One current viewpoint on possible causes of dyslexia is that of Farnham-Diggory (1992), who

---

GLOSSARY

Phonemic awareness An awareness of the individual sounds contained in words.

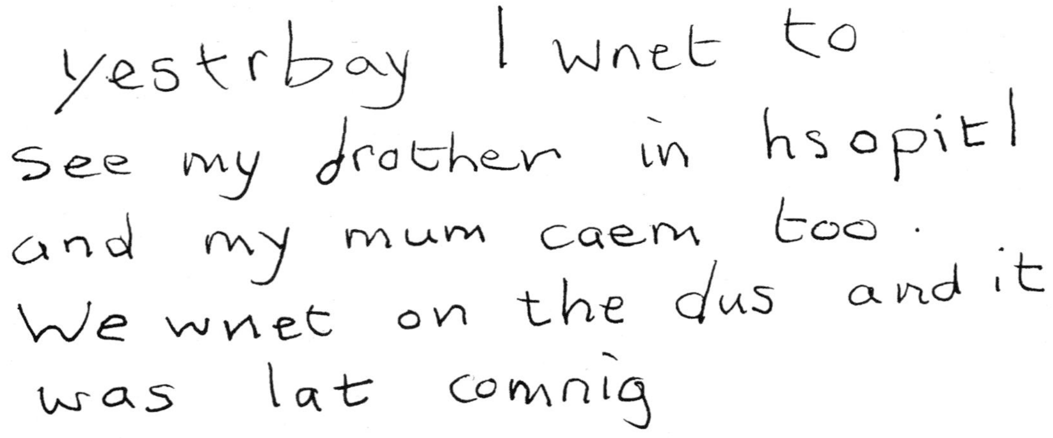

Figure 31.1 Sample of writing:

> yestrbay I wnet to
> see my drother in hsopitl
> and my mum caem too.
> We wnet on the dus and it
> was lat comnig

Figure 31.1 Sample of writing showing some errors that might be made by a child suffering from dyslexia. Note how some of the letters are the wrong way (e.g. 'b' instead of 'd') and how letters in some words are written in the wrong order (e.g. 'wnet' instead of 'went')

suggests that a number of small abnormalities develop in the brain during the prenatal period. The brain tries to compensate for these by forming new connections (remember, the brain is still developing its cells and 'wiring' at this stage); these new connections may slightly rearrange normal information-processing procedures, which subsequently make the specific tasks of reading and spelling difficult.

Screening and diagnosis of dyslexia

Summarizing the events at a symposium on the screening and diagnosis of dyslexia at the London Conference of the British Psychological Society in 1995, Nicolson (1996) said:

> For over 25 years dyslexia has remained the 'enfant terrible' of the psychology world, sparking controversies ranging from the disproved but enduring 'middle class myth', to IQ and dyslexia, dyslexia and genius and dyslexia and crime . . .
> (Nicholson, 1996, p. 81)

The symposium involved a number of papers which provided an overview of current methods for the diagnosis and screening of dyslexia. One paper presented evidence from over 250 children who had been assessed using the Differential Ability Scales at the Dyslexia Institute at Staines in Middlesex. It was suggested that dyslexia may take different forms, since three subgroups of children were identified:

- Typical groups of children with particular verbal/phonological difficulties,
- A group of children who had specific spatial difficulties,
- A smaller group of children who had particular difficulties with some aspects of verbal reasoning.

Two newly developed screening instruments were described:

- **Cognitive Profiling System (CoPS)**. A computerized form of assessment comprising ten subtests which are administered to children in reception classes. The CoPS provides a profile of cognitive skills and attempts to identify those children who are likely to exhibit symptoms of dyslexia during their time at school.
- **Dyslexia Early Screening Tests**. A series of 30-minute tests which can be administered at school

by a teacher. Like the CoPS, the tests yield a profile of cognitive abilities as well as providing an 'at risk' index for dyslexia.

❓ SELF-ASSESSMENT QUESTIONS

1. Briefly discuss some of the problems which might be faced by children who suffer from a sensory impairment, such as deafness or blindness.
2. What are the reasons why a deaf child whose parents are also deaf might develop communication skills more easily than a deaf child with hearing parents?
3. What do you understand by 'dyslexia'? What uncertainties are associated with the definition of dyslexia?
4. What are some of the problems likely to be exhibited by children who are dyslexic?

Emotional disturbances and behavioural difficulties

Emotional disturbances often occur when children *internalize* their problems. This may result in anxiety, depression, eating disorders or other emotional problems.

Behavioural difficulties are often due to children *externalizing* their difficulties; there are a number of ways in which this might happen. Achenbach (1982) suggests two main categories of behavioural problems:

- **Aggressive** (sometimes called 'challenging') **behaviours**, such as arguing, fighting, temper tantrums and disruptiveness,
- **Delinquent behaviours**, such as stealing, pyromania (setting fires), truancy, use of alcohol and drugs.

Hinshaw et al. (1993) suggest that these two patterns of behaviour are largely dependent on age as well as underlying causes. Aggression may well appear early in childhood, and if not handled well by parents, may continue into adolescence and adulthood. Farrington (1991) found strong correlations (0.7) between aggression in childhood and adulthood. Delinquent behaviours, Hinshaw suggested, may not begin until adolescence and may be milder and transitory.

Apart from these, other emotional and behavioural difficulties appear in specific syndromes such as autism, attention-deficit hyperactivity disorder and a range of other childhood disorders, described below. They may have specific physiological or other causes, but as these have not yet been conclusively demonstrated, they may still currently be regarded as conduct disorders.

Autism

Autism is included in this section because a sufferer manifestly displays behavioural difficulties. Autism was initially thought to result from faulty attachment between parent and child. However, this theory is not favoured nowadays and many studies indicate that autism is due to neurological problems, although exactly what these are has not yet been identified.

Autism begins before the age of two and a half years, affects four times more boys than girls (about 5 children in 10,000 are affected), and is distributed throughout all socioeconomic, racial and ethnic groups.

Autism and intelligence

Many children with learning difficulties are readily identifiable on sight (e.g. Down's syndrome) but most autistic children have no identifiably physical abnormalities. This led people to believe that autistic children were all of normal or even superior intelligence, especially as a few show exceptional abilities in a specific direction such as music, for example (see p. 494).

Recent research suggests that 80 per cent of diagnosed autistic children score below 70 on IQ tests. However, the scoring pattern for these children is not uniformly low; some score average or above average on tests such as visual-spatial tests and most score below average on items associated with language (DeMyer, 1975; Rutter and Lockyer, 1967). The validity of using IQ tests on autistic children has been questioned, as it is difficult to hold their attention long enough to indicate what is required of them. They are also unlikely to have had the same cultural or social experiences as other children.

Definitions and indicators of autism

Autism was originally described as a syndrome by Kanner in 1943. He described an 'extreme autistic aloneness', an inability to relate to other people, severe limitations of language and an obsessive desire that everything in the environment remain the same. In addition Rutter in 1966 noted ritualistic and compulsive activities.

Those autistic children who learn to speak seldom use speech effectively; the most common form used is echolalic speech – repeating back to someone what they have just said. Words are produced but without, apparently, much comprehension, and without the effect of communication, which to other children is the whole point of speech.

Baron-Cohen et al. (1996, unpublished) have suggested that there are two particular developmental deficits which can be regarded as early indicators of autism:

■ Lack of joint attention by the age of 18 months. Joint attention, which occurs in normal babies between 9 and 14 months, refers to the communication which occurs between a child and adult when they are focusing on something together.

■ Lack of 'pretend play' by the age of 18 months. Pretend play usually occurs in normal children between the age of 14 and 18 months.

Some autistic adults can work in undemanding environments but most shut themselves in their own self-imposed prisons, living out a solitary life within their families or institutions.

Autism was not accepted into official categorization until the publication of DSM III in 1980. Until then, children with autism had frequently been diagnosed as 'childhood schizophrenics', as their symptoms fitted with those of adult schizophrenics. However, it is not that they have withdrawn from the world, like sufferers from schizophrenia, but have simply never entered it.

DSM criteria for the diagnosis of autism include:

■ onset before 30 months of age (although the diagnosis is often not confirmed until the child is school age);

■ lack of responsiveness to other people;

■ language deficits or abnormal speech patterns.

GLOSSARY

Autism A disorder, thought to arise from neurological problems, which is characterized mainly by uninterest in social contact and interaction.

Box 31.2   Asperger's syndrome

Asperger's syndrome is regarded as a mild variant of autism, where sufferers display many autistic characteristics, but speech is either normal or advanced for the child's chronological age.

A recent study by Klin et al. (1995) compared 21 youngsters identified as suffering from Asperger's syndrome, with 19 diagnosed with higher functioning autism. The groups were matched for age and overall IQ. They were found to differ significantly on skills such as fine motor skills, visual-spatial perception, visual memory and verbal memory, which would seem to indicate that differences run deeper than simply a difference in language skills.

One theory of the causes of Asperger's syndrome is that it is due to malfunctioning of the right cerebral hemisphere. This was supported by McKelvey et al. (1995), who compared CT, MRI and PET scans (see the Introduction to Part 2) of three teenagers with Asperger's syndrome. All three showed atrophy of the right hemisphere and abnormalities of the cerebellum. The left hemisphere did not show any apparent abnormalities. This may also be related to the fact that speech is usually located in the left hemisphere, and speech is normal in sufferers of Asperger's syndrome.

A mild variant of autism is **Asperger's syndrome**, which is described in Box 31.2.

Autism and theory of mind

As we have seen, a characteristic feature of autistic children is a complete disinterest in social contact and interaction; they often play alone and if they do interact, they do so in a rigid stereotyped way as though they were dealing with objects rather than people.

Numerous studies have shown that autistic children appear to be seriously lacking in what Baron-Cohen (1997) terms **'mindreading'** skills or **theory of mind** capabilities, and it has been argued that this 'mindblindness' is the cause of the serious deficit they have in social relationships. Theory of mind relates to the capacity to understand the mental states of other people – to appreciate what other people are thinking and feeling. You will recall that the development of a child's theory of mind was discussed in Chapter 22.

. . . children with autism perform worse on tests of ascribing almost the full range of mental states (intentions, knowledge, pretence, deception, imagination and so on). It is as if they suffer from a specific form of 'mindblindness'.

(Baron-Cohen, 1997, p. 32)

In 1985, Baron-Cohen et al. carried out what has become a classic study into the possible relationship between 'mindblindness' and autism. This study is described in Box 31.3.

It does seem that theory of mind appears to be lacking or seriously deficient in autistic children, relative to other children. However, this deficiency does not apply to all such children. Baron-Cohen et al.'s (1985) study showed that 4 out of the 20 autistic children correctly solved the false belief task. Also, Baron-Cohen (1997) points out that some sufferers from autism do seem to develop degrees of mindreading, though this often occurs later than it should.

How might mindblindness arise?

Baron-Cohen suggests that there is as yet no conclusive answer to the question of how mindblindness arises. However, there are a number of lines of enquiry which researchers are pursuing:

■ **Genetic abnormality** Since there is a strong likelihood that autism itself is heritable, it is possible that there is a genetic base to 'mindblindness'.

■ **Neural abnormality**. It is possible that in normal children there are genetic mechanisms that build neural mechanisms for understanding the world in mentalistic ways. In autism, therefore, an abnormality might be present both at the genetic level and at the neural level. At present, there is no conclusive evidence that one part of the brain is abnormal in all cases of autism.

Box 31.3   Autism and 'mindblindness'

Barón-Cohen et al. (1985) carried out a study with the following groups:

- 20 autistic children aged 6–16 years. Their mental age was around 5 years as measured by a standard verbal IQ test and about 9 years using a nonverbal IQ test. For comparison, 2 other groups were used:
- 27 normal children between 3 and 5 years,
- 14 Down's syndrome children aged 16–17 years, whose IQ ratings were slightly below those of the autistic children. This group was used to act as a control for learning difficulties which did not relate to autism.

The researchers used a modified version of the Sally–Anne 'false belief' task originally used by Wimmer and Perner (1983). See Figure 31.2 (on following page) for a diagrammatic illustration of the task.

In this task, there are two dolls, Sally and Anne (see picture 1). As the child watches, the experimenter causes Sally to put a marble into her basket (picture 2). Sally then leaves (picture 3) and Anne moves the marble into her own basket (picture 4). Sally then returns (picture 5). At this point, the experimenter asks the child three questions:

- 'Where is the marble really?' (reality question),
- 'Where was the marble in the beginning?' (memory question),
- 'Where will Sally look for her marble?' (belief question).

The results were quite striking.

- All the children answered the memory question and the reality question correctly on both trials. This indicated that they had understood what was happening and had remembered it.
- Almost all the normal and Down's syndrome children answered the belief question correctly; this was as expected, particularly for the normal children, since research has shown that children of this age can usually solve a 'false belief' task. However, all but four of the autistic children answered incorrectly. When they were asked 'Where will Sally look for her marble?' they pointed to where the marble really was.

The researchers claimed that these findings supported the view that theory of mind appears to be lacking or seriously impaired in autistic children. Specifically, it was argued that autistic children are unable to appreciate the mental states of other people or assign beliefs to them.

Some criticisms have been made of the procedures used in this experiment:

- De Gelder (1987) pointed out that it is known that autistic children have difficulty with pretend play. Therefore, using dolls to represent real people might cause them some difficulties. However, Leslie and Frith (1987) repeated the study using real children and obtained similar findings.
- Another criticism related to the possibility that the three groups of children may not have been well matched for language ability (Boucher, 1989).

Despite these criticisms, Baron-Cohen et al.'s study has been replicated and the findings supported by many other researchers.

- **Other neurocognitive abnormality**. It is possible that mindblindness arises from a dysfunction in some other neurocognitive function which is important for mindreading to develop.

All of these options are currently the subject of research.

Treatments for autism

A number of treatments have been used to treat some aspects of autism. These include the following:

Behaviour modification   Operant conditioning techniques and modelling (a description of these can be found in Chapter 33) have been used successfully to modify unacceptable behaviours, but these changes do not always generalize from one situation to another. There needs to be consistency between the reward programme used in both the child's school and home.

Holding therapy   Based on the theory that autism was due to faulty attachment between mother and child, this was introduced in the United States. The

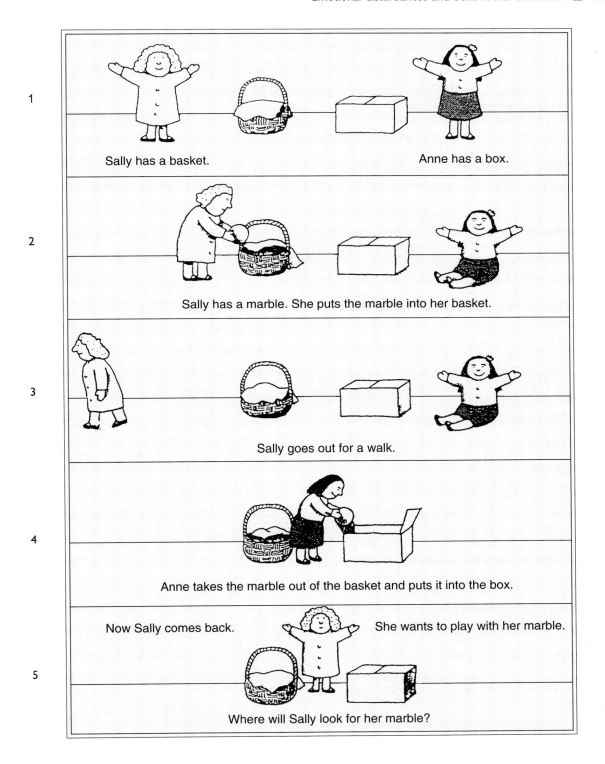

1 Sally has a basket. Anne has a box.

2 Sally has a marble. She puts the marble into her basket.

3 Sally goes out for a walk.

4 Anne takes the marble out of the basket and puts it into the box.

5 Now Sally comes back. She wants to play with her marble.

Where will Sally look for her marble?

Figure 31.2 The Sally–Anne task (from Frith, 1989)

mother holds the child close, resisting attempts to struggle away. Doing this repeatedly is thought to strengthen the bond and reduce isolation. This theory implied blame to the parents, and now that autism is thought to be a neurological rather than behavioural problem, the technique is little used.

Music therapy A number of children and adults with autism are very musical or extremely fond of music. Music therapy is thought to reduce disruptive behaviour and break down isolation.

Drug treatment The drug fenfluramine has been used to reduce serotonin levels, which may lessen some of the aloofness and stereotyped ritualized behaviour.

Attention-deficit hyperactivity disorder (ADHD)

Many children go through a period of hyperactivity during development, when they cannot seem to sit or stand still, they cannot settle to one activity and display the concentration of a butterfly, flitting from flower to flower. These symptoms are sometimes accompanied by aggression, which *may* be another symptom, or may have developed due to parents' or teachers' negative attitudes to the child's hyperactivity.

Episodes of hyperactivity may be a passing phase, which could be due to some emotional upheaval in the child's life, or changes and pressures in the social environment. In some children, these episodes have been related to sensitivity to certain kinds of foods or additives, such as artificial colouring or preservatives. Other children may exhibit hyperactivity as an allergic response to specific foods.

When these symptoms persist, it may be that the child is suffering from a condition known as **attention-deficit hyperactivity disorder (ADHD)**.

What is ADHD?

At the current state of knowledge, ADHD is not easy to define precisely. The term originated in the USA to refer to children and young people whose behaviour appears to be impulsive, overactive and/or inattentive to an extent which is not appropriate for their developmental age and which severely impairs their social and educational progress.

The term ADHD is now used internationally. However, it is not a 'fixed' and clearly defined concept, but is changing and evolving as research findings become available and our understanding of it is increased. Some psychologists go as far as suggesting that ADHD is not really a disorder at all, but a convenient way of labelling and discriminating against children whose behaviour antagonizes the adults in their lives. There are many theoretical and practical questions that still need to be answered.

Diagnosis of ADHD is often done on the basis of six main criteria:

- inattention (to a degree inappropriate for the child's age);
- impulsivity;
- hyperactivity;
- onset before the age of seven;
- duration of at least six months;
- not due to other causes such as severe or profound learning difficulties, schizophrenia or other diagnosable disorder.

It has been estimated that between 3 and 5 per cent of school-age children are diagnosed with ADHD. However, it is possible that some children who are simply hyperactive, easily distracted, or even highly gifted, are being wrongly diagnosed. Considerably more boys than girls are referred for treatment. Some researchers have made links between ADHD in childhood and later delinquency.

Peak age for referral is between the ages of eight and ten years. In a one-to-one situation the symptoms may be absent, but worsen in a situation that requires self-application, such as in the classroom.

Educational and social problems Clearly, having ADHD has serious implications for a child's progress in school. While children so diagnosed are not generally below average intelligence, their behavioural problems, for example inattention and the tendency to be easily distracted from a task, usually result in poor performance for their age. Effective

---

GLOSSARY

Attention-deficit hyperactivity disorder (ADHD) A childhood disorder characterized by excessive activity and an inability to concentrate on a task; sometimes accompanied by aggression.

social interactions can also be a problem for the child with ADHD.

Family problems Parents of a child with ADHD themselves often experience psychological problems. Apart from the stress of attempting to cope with a child who is experiencing difficulties, parents often blame themselves or each other for the apparent problem behaviour and this can lead to considerable family strife.

Coping with ADHD

There is no firm agreement on how best to treat a child with ADHD.

Drug treatment Use of the drug Ritalin can increase attentiveness and decrease activity in children with ADHD. A recent study in the United States by Alto and Frankenberger (1995) examined the long-term effects of Ritalin on cognitive ability and academic achievement. Seventeen children aged seven to eight who had been diagnosed with ADHD were given the drug and matched on the basis of gender, verbal IQ scores and family structure with controls who did not receive the drug. The ADHD group's scores on cognitive ability and academic achievement were lower both before and after receiving the drug, even after matching for verbal abilities; however, after receiving the drug, their rate of learning was similar to the control group on

Effective social interactions can be a problem for the child with ADHD

reading, word analysis, listening, vocabulary and overall achievement.

Parent training Training parents to cope with and manage ADHD is crucial (McBurnett et al., 1993). Parents are trained to supervise their children's medication effectively and to develop and strictly follow a consistent pattern in monitoring and guiding their children's daily routine: for example, keeping to regular times for household tasks, homework and bedtime. Parents are also encouraged to be vigilant in anticipating and deflecting a child's potential problem behaviour and to give copious praise for good behaviour.

The situation in the United Kingdom

In September 1996, a report was published by a working party set up by the British Psychological Society to look at ADHD. Some of the main points of the report appear below.

Causes and answers Viewing ADHD as a single, unitary condition is controversial and there are no simple or single causes or answers. For example, the reference in the title to 'attention deficit' does not imply that there is a *simple* deficiency in the psychological function of attention. Research findings show that attention is affected by a number of different factors in particular situations. The inability to sustain effort over time in order to meet the demands of a task may be influenced by a combination of biological, neurological, psychological and environmental factors.

Assessment Everyday signs of overactivity, impulsivity and inattention do not necessarily justify a child being diagnosed as suffering from ADHD and, before this is done, there should be a thorough investigation of alternative reasons. Assessment of ADHD should be careful and comprehensive and should include data on developmental, medical and family histories. A consideration of the child's unique characteristics and the factors that influence them is more important than the diagnostic classification. The assessment is most helpful when the child is involved in the process as an active partner.

Intervention Effective parenting and teaching strategies arising from research findings, since they take account of individual differences, are likely to be beneficial for all children, not just those suffering from ADHD. However, many studies which have looked at the effectiveness of methods of behavioural management and parent support have been criticized for sampling errors and the use of laboratory or clinical situations rather than naturalistic settings. The BPS report does not recommend or refute the use of psychostimulant drugs, but aims to provide information about the large range of factors which must be involved in tailoring strategies to meet individual needs.

Effective practice The mental health needs of children and young people are best recognized and met through the coordinated efforts of health, education and social services. The development of joint strategies and multidisciplinary networks are likely to be particularly important in responding to the needs identified under the heading ADHD.

Other childhood conditions

Abused children

Although this is a comparatively recent field of study, findings seem to indicate that children who have suffered sexual or physical abuse are likely to show atypical patterns of development. As expected, both forms of abuse are likely to result in emotional problems, demonstrated by either aggression or internalizing behaviour, or both. As yet, few studies have given reliable information as to other effects of sexual abuse, but physical abuse is thought to give rise to cognitive and physiological differences from normal children.

A recent study by Carrey et al. (1996) in Canada, compared the pulse rates and galvanic skin response (GSR) (see the Introduction to Part 2) of matched groups of abused and nonabused children. The abused children showed lower changes in pulse rate and lower GSR responses; in other words their physiological responses which are usually correlated with emotions were 'flattened' or reduced. The same two groups were also given the Wechsler Intelligence Test for Children, the Junior Eysenck Personality Test, and the Quick Neurological Screening Test. Abused children showed higher scores on the Introversion scale, lower scores on Verbal scales and full IQ scores, but no significant differences on the Neurological

Screening. This would seem to support the suggestion that physical abuse delays cognitive development and inhibits physiological responsiveness to the environment. The latter may also suggest a preliminary reason why those who are abused as children sometimes go on to become abusers themselves; if emotional responses are lowered, so may the perception of emotions such as love and pity.

Depressive disorders

Until comparatively recently it was not thought that children suffered from depression. Recent studies have shown that this is more common a problem than was thought, especially among adolescents. Large-scale studies by Achenbach and Edelbrock (1981) and Rutter et al. (1981) found that 10 per cent of preadolescents and 40 per cent of adolescents were described by parents or teachers as appearing miserable or depressed. If depressive episodes last six months or longer, and are accompanied by other symptoms which typify depression, then the individuals are regarded as being clinically depressed or suffering from depressive disorder. Studies suggest that these numbers run at between 3 and 8 per cent for child and adolescent populations (Petersen et al., 1993). Bernstein (1991) found that 50 per cent of adolescent school refusers were depressed; Kolvin et al. (1984) put the figure at 45 per cent. There seems to be an overlap between depression, anxiety and conduct disorders in a number of clinical samples which have been analysed.

This is one problem area where boys do not outnumber girls: the ratio is approximately equal, although in teenage years, girls are beginning to predominate. A number of researchers indicate that the children of depressed parents are more likely to become depressed; whether this is genetically or environmentally influenced has not been clearly demonstrated. Early developmental studies have demonstrated that children of depressed mothers are insecurely attached (see Chapter 19); the depressed mothers tend to be nonresponsive, which promotes a feeling of helpless resignation, which has been identified in many depressed adults.

Tourette's syndrome

Named after the French physician who first described it, this syndrome involves not only a tic (an involuntary movement) but is often accompanied by spitting or shouting brief phrases or words, frequently rude or swearwords. The cause has not been positively identified, but tics may be exacerbated by stress and disappear during sleep.

Tourette's syndrome has been shown to have genetic links through either the mother or the father. Lichter et al. (1995) studied 25 children (average age 10.7 years) where the syndrome had been transmitted via the mother (matrilineal transmission) and 25 children where transmission was through the father (paternal transmission). They found that paternal transmission was associated with increased vocal tic frequency, an early onset of vocal tics relative to motor tics, and predominant ADHD behaviours, including motor restlessness. Matrilineal transmission was characterized by greater motor tic complexity and frequent rituals.

Feeding disorders

Mild eating disorders are extremely common in childhood. Children sometimes are faddy and refuse food, mainly from the primary care-giver. Diagnosis of a full-blown feeding disorder is made only if food refusal is beyond the normal range of behaviour or if the child loses or fails to gain weight over a trial period. There may be repeated regurgitation without nausea. This syndrome was identified and treated in a child as young as nine months (Lang and Melamed, 1969). (See Chapter 33.)

The family and the atypical child

Every pregnant woman hopes to give birth to the 'perfect' baby. When a baby is born who is less than perfect, the family's immediate reaction is that of grief, often linked with components of denial, anger and depression. Frequently there are feelings of guilt: 'Is this due to something I did, or did not do?' Occasionally the child is rejected by the family and will have to be taken into care. Sometimes the child is rejected by one parent only; this is likely to cause disharmony in a family which is due to encounter more than normal levels of stress and disruption.

Once the initial problem is accepted, the family makes day-to-day adaptations to fit with the child's needs and demands. With problems such as autism, which are not recognized at birth, and are often not firmly diagnosed for some years, there is sometimes a feeling of relief when a diagnosis is made. As one mother said, 'At least now when he has a temper tantrum in the supermarket, I can say, I am sorry, my son is autistic, rather than having to keep apologizing for what was interpreted as bad behaviour and bad management.'

Frequently one parent becomes the primary care-giver. This is usually the mother; the father seems to withdraw from care of that child, although the other children may still retain his attention (Bristol et al., 1988). Where family relationships were poor before the birth of a handicapped child, discord is likely to increase, but having a handicapped child does not appear to be the cause of marital break-up where relationships were previously good. With good management, other siblings are usually very accepting of an atypical child.

SELF-ASSESSMENT QUESTIONS

1. Briefly describe some of the criteria and early indicators of autism.
2. Explain why researchers believe that autistic children may lack a theory of mind ('mindreading' skills). Briefly describe a relevant study.
3. Outline some of the possible reasons why some children suffer from mindblindness.
4. What do you understand by attention-deficit hyperactivity disorder (ADHD)? Why is it controversial to think of ADHD as one simple disorder?
5. Outline some of the recommendations made in the recent BPS Working Party report on ADHD.

GLOSSARY

Tourette's syndrome A condition which involves a tic (involuntary movement) which is often accompanied by spitting or shouting.

Chapter summary

The terminology used in relationship to learning difficulties has changed periodically as stigma becomes attached to it. Development is lifelong, but for those with learning difficulties there is no right to education and/or training beyond 18.

Some learning difficulties are the result of genetic abnormality. Down's syndrome is a genetic abnormality resulting from an extra chromosome. Sufferers generally have learning difficulties, though some reach a relatively high level of functioning. Statistically it is most common among children of older mothers (over 35 years). Various causes have been attested but none has been proved. Amniocentesis during pregnancy may detect Down's syndrome before birth and the mother has the right to choose an abortion if she wishes when the defect is identified. More recently cheaper and safer blood tests have been developed.

Phenylketonuria is another genetic disorder which may cause learning difficulties. A deficiency of phenylananine causes profound impairment unless detected at a very early stage and a special diet introduced and maintained until six or seven years of age.

Infectious diseases such as rubella, venereal disease or herpes simplex in expectant mothers may cause mental abnormalities in children; infectious diseases such as meningitis and measles can cause learning difficulties when they occur before the age of about six or seven years after which time the brain is largely developed.

Environmental hazards may also be a cause of impairment. Before birth, foetal alcohol syndrome (FAS), smoking and drugs may also cause problems and in early childhood pollutants such as mercury or lead poisoning may cause permanent damage to the brain and nervous system.

Permanent brain damage may also result from accidental injury such as falls or blows to the head and also from perinatal anoxia. This results from the brain being starved of oxygen during labour.

Sensory impairments such as deafness, blindness or dyslexia may have a profound effect upon normal development. Because communication plays a central role in development, deafness in particular may cause severe difficulties, including deficiencies in written and spoken language. Deaf children of deaf parents frequently fare better than those born to hearing parents, as sign language may already be used in the family. Hearing aids and cochlear implants may mitigate some of the problems.

Blindness is not so likely as deafness to be the cause of impaired development, as blind children can still communicate verbally and learn to read through the use of Braille. There may be some difficulty with the bonding and attachment process through the lack of mutual gazing.

Dyslexia has been defined as the unexpected failure to learn to read and may involve a range of learning problems including reading, writing, spelling and in some cases arithmetic. Causes of dyslexia are not entirely clear and studies have included investigations into visual deficit and phonological awareness. Support programmes have been found to help children suffering from dyslexia. Three subgroups of dyslexics have been identified: those with verbal/ phonological problems, those with spatial problems and those with difficulties with some aspect of verbal reasoning.

Among emotional and behavioural difficulties are autism and attention-deficit hyperactivity disorder. Autistic children have no overt signs of physical abnormality and generally have low measured IQ, though the use of IQ tests may not be appropriate with autistic children. Autistic children have an inability to relate to those around them, seldom use speech effectively, often using echolalic speech, lack joint attention and pretend play. They also have serious lack of 'mindreading skills'. This has been termed 'mindblindness'. Treatments for autism include behaviour modification, holding therapy, music therapy and drug treatment.

Attention deficit hyperactivity disorder (ADHD) involves the persistence of hyperactivity beyond passing phases in development. Six main criteria have been established for this disorder: inattention, impulsivity, hyperactivity, onset before age seven, duration of at least six months and no other identifiable cause. It has serious implications for educational progress and social development and can cause family problems. The drug Ritalin has been used with some benefit as have programmes of training for parents in coping with ADHD children.

Abused children are also likely to show atypical patterns of development. Their physiological responses (for instance, pulse rate and GSR) tended to be flattened or reduced. They show higher Introversion scores on Junior Eysenck Personality Inventories as well as lower Verbal and full IQ scores. This lowering of emotional responses may account for the fact that abused children frequently go on to become abusers.

Depressive disorders account for between 3 and 8 per cent of the child and adolescent population. There seems to be an overlap between depression, anxiety and conduct disorders and up to 50 per cent of adolescent school refusers have been found to be depressed.

Tourette's syndrome involves a tic as well as spitting and shouting phrases or words, frequently swearwords. There have been found to be genetic links through either the mother or the father. Maternal and paternal transmission have been found to be associated by slightly different symptoms: paternal transmission was associated with vocal tics, ADHD symptoms and restlessness; maternal transmission was characterized by a greater motor tic and ritual complexities.

Feeding disorders are common in childhood, but where it goes beyond the normal range of behaviour a child may lose or fail to gain weight and there is need for identification of the problem and treatment.

Atypical development may affect the family. There may be grief, anger and depression. One parent frequently withdraws from care-giving in these circumstances and family discord is more likely to occur.

Further reading

Bee, H. (1990). *The Developing Child*, 7th edn. New York: HarperCollins. Chapter 15 looks at atypical development, considering a range of problems which include learning difficulties, learning disorders, depression and sensory impairment. There is an interesting subsection on problem behaviours among children in Kenya and Thailand.

Harrington, R. (1993). *Depressive Disorder in Childhood and Adolescence*. Chichester: Wiley. A 'hands on', clinical view of depression in young people, including precipitating factors, construct measurement and treatment.

Kerr, A. and McClelland, H. (eds) (1991). *Concepts of Mental Disorder*. London: Gaskell. A range of views from different contributors on a number of different disorders.

CHAPTER 32

The classification, diagnosis and causes of mental disorder

Normality and abnormality   762
- Defining abnormality   763
- Normality   764
- Evaluation of views of normality/ abnormality   766
- The concept of mental illness and the medical model   767

Diagnosis and classification of mental disorders   770
- Classifications of mental disorders   770
- Problems of diagnosis   772

- What can be concluded about diagnosis and classification?   775

Categories and descriptions of mental disorders   776
- Categories of mental disorders   776
- Descriptions of mental disorders   776

Possible causes of mental disorders   783
- Genetic causes   784
- Environmental causes   784
- Neurochemical and neurological causes   786

Objectives

By the end of this chapter you should be able to:

- Discuss the concepts of normality and abnormality;

- Consider whether abnormality should be viewed as mental illness and evaluate alternative views;

- Understand the structure and outline of the two main diagnostic systems in use in Western societies, the ICD and DSM;

- Consider evidence regarding problems of diagnosis, such as those relating to validity, reliability and labelling;

- Be familiar with descriptions of a variety of mental disorders, including their aetiology and prognosis;

- Discuss the genetic, environmental and neurochemical contributions to causes of mental disorder.

Normality and abnormality

This chapter examines whether normality and abnormality should be regarded along a continuum, merging imperceptibly at some undefined point. If this is the case, where does behaviour become 'abnormal' and be deemed to need changing? Each individual tends to regard himself or herself as the norm, so what ruling is acceptable? There is no dividing line separating 'normal' people from 'abnormal' people; the most normal occasionally exhibit abnormal behaviours, just as the most abnormal patients exhibit recognizably normal behaviours and reactions. In addition, normal behaviour in one set of circumstances would not be regarded as normal in other circumstances; behaviour suitable at a party would be regarded as unsuitable at a funeral.

Psychopathology can be defined as the scientific study of mental disorders. The immediate problem this poses is what constitutes a mental disorder and whether this should be regarded as a 'mental illness'. This point is discussed more fully later in this chapter, but it needs to be noted here that the term covers a wide range of conditions, from brief transient episodes to lifelong incapacitation.

Approximately one in ten men and one in seven women will be treated for mental disorder during their lifetime; for the majority these are brief periods, possibly of depression or a delusional state.

Overt behaviours which are unacceptable may be the external symptoms of abnormality which are brought to the notice of psychiatrists and clinical psychologists.

Psychiatrists are doctors who specialize in mental illnesses and attempt to unravel and 'cure' the underlying causes of these behaviours, often through the use of drugs and other physiological methods.

Clinical psychologists are psychologists (holding a first degree in psychology) who have postgraduate training in the use of therapies and the administration and analysis of tests of mental functions: personality tests, cognitive tests, projective tests and other diagnostic tools. In the clinical situation, they also design programmes using a wide range of therapies, to assist both inpatients and outpatients who have mental problems and are seeking to change their thought processes and behaviours.

Treatments and therapies are discussed in Chapter 33.

Defining abnormality

There is no general agreement on how abnormal behaviour may be distinguished from normal behaviour, but one or more of the following criteria are usually applied.

Statistical abnormality

One kind of population distribution, the normal curve (see Chapter 35) suggests that the majority of people are close to the average on any particular characteristic – for example, IQ (see Figure 32.1): that is, very few people fall at either extreme. Behaviour which occurs

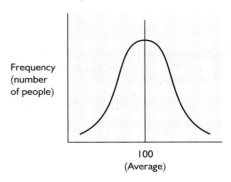

Figure 32.1 The normal curve of distribution in relation to IQ among adults

frequently is viewed as normal, therefore by definition, behaviour which occurs infrequently must be abnormal. By implication, extremely intelligent people are as likely to be defined as abnormal as extremely unintelligent people. Similarly, the statistical frequency of an Einstein or a Hitler would be the same although society may not regard them as being equally preferable. Clearly the desirability of a behaviour is not allowed for in this definition and it is insufficient on its own (Mackay, 1975).

Social abnormality

The criteria for social norms vary from society to society. What is considered acceptable or desirable behaviour in one society may be considered undesirable or abnormal in a different culture. For example: some African tribes revere their members who claim to hear voices; in Western society this may well be viewed as a symptom of schizophrenia or other mental abnormality. Also behaviour within any one society is temporally based, it can only be judged by reference to any one period of time. For example, in Great Britain 70 years ago, bathing machines were used, yet nowadays no one is surprised at 'topless' beaches. On the other hand, fifth-century temples in mid-Asian countries are decorated with partially clad figures,

---

GLOSSARY

Psychiatrist A medical doctor who specializes in the study and treatment of mental disorders.

Clinical psychologist A professional who has a degree in psychology and a postgraduate qualification in the understanding and psychological treatment of mental disorder.

whereas nowadays it is considered an insult to go to a temple scantily clad – even some of the statues have been draped to preserve propriety! In order to be universally acceptable, a definition of abnormality must include more than social compliance.

Maladaptiveness of behaviour

Another suggested definition investigates how an individual's behaviour affects people's lives, or their social group. Some deviant behaviours interfere with the individual's lifestyle: for example, a man so fearful of crowds he cannot ride to work on a bus or a woman so afraid of contamination she cannot hug and kiss her own children. The quality of life for such people is severely impaired, whereas some behaviours are harmful to society. The paranoid who guns down innocent people in the street, or the assassin who believes his action will right wrongs, or even the person who has uncontrollable verbal outbursts and intimidates all around him, are exhibiting abnormal behaviour detrimental to other members of society.

Personal distress

Symptoms of mental disorders often include feeling miserable, anxious or depressed, insomnia, lack of appetite, many aches and pains, feelings of panic or agitation. These all cause the individual some distress, although in many cases other people are unaware of their suffering. Occasionally an individual's depression is deep enough for attempted suicide, while family or friends had no idea of these depths of despair. However, personal distress is not an infallible indicator of mental abnormality; the psychopath who continually offends against society may do so without any feelings of personal distress, but such behaviour can only be viewed as abnormal. Some psychopaths and schizophrenics feel no personal distress, except when society imposes treatment upon them (Cleckley, 1976). (Explanations of what is meant by the terms 'psychopath' and 'schizophrenic' can be found on pp. 778 and 782.)

Legal definition of abnormality

Let us say immediately, this does not have direct influence on the psychological concept, but as abnormal people also live in the real world, the legal definition is obviously relevant. The term 'insane' is used in law, but not by psychiatrists or psychologists for diagnostic purposes; the word implies a clear dividing line. In Great Britain the law is governed by the case of McNaghten, 1843: 'to establish a defence of insanity, it must be clearly proved that, at the time of committing the act, the party accused was labouring under such a defect of reason, from disease of mind, as not to know the nature and quality of the act he was doing; or if he did know it, that he did not know he was doing what was wrong.' This relates to criminal proceedings.

Lack of responsibility for one's actions is also invoked to protect individuals with diminished responsibility, so that others may not take advantage of them by, for example, convincing them to sign away money or property.

In addition to the above discussions of how abnormality might be defined in general terms, the five major approaches in psychology have their own assumptions and criteria relating to what might constitute psychologically abnormal behaviour. These views are briefly discussed in Box 32.1.

Normality

Having realized the difficulties inherent in defining abnormality, it is obviously no less difficult to define normality; both are relative concepts, rather than hard and fast rulings. However, certain characteristics, which are present in the majority of people who are regarded as normal, have been suggested (Jahoda, 1958; Mackay, 1975; Maslow, 1968).

■ **Efficient self-perception**. Most individuals have a realistic awareness of their own capabilities and limitations, feelings, motivations and emotions. As a rule, a normal person does not make false attributions or blame extraterrestrial forces, for 'making me behave like this'.

GLOSSARY

Insane A legal term used to describe a person who is not of sound mind and is unable to distinguish between right and wrong.

Box 32.1 Models or paradigms of abnormality

Different investigators use different models (or paradigms) for conceptualizing abnormal behaviours, how they develop and how best to treat them. The major paradigms reflect the five major approaches to psychology; these are: the physiological (or medical) model, the psychoanalytic model, the learning theory (behaviourist) model, the cognitive model and the humanistic model. The theoretical basis of each is outlined here, the treatments and therapies based on each approach can be found in Chapter 33. (A detailed discussion of the major approaches to psychology is included in Chapter 1.)

The psychoanalytic model
Based on the work of Sigmund Freud, psychoanalytic theorists believe that many of our motivations are unconscious. Conflicts between the three facets of the personality, id, ego and superego, produce defence mechanisms and anxieties which may be maladaptive (see Chapter 30 for a full description of Freud's theory). Post-Freudian theorists may have different perspectives, but all hold that abnormality is rooted in conflicts which need to be brought to the surface, examined and rectified or reconciled.

The physiological or medical model
This model views abnormality as an illness which can be treated by physical methods, such as the use of drugs, to effect control or cure. Diagnosis is carried out in a prescribed, routine manner and the most suitable treatment is prescribed, often in conjunction with nonphysical therapies. Whether abnormality should be viewed as 'mental illness' is a current discussion point, which is explored at greater depth later in this chapter.

The learning theory model
Classical conditioning, discovered by Pavlov (1849-1936), and operant conditioning, the work of B.F. Skinner, form the basis of this theoretical model. Classical conditioning (see Chapter 6) looks at the involuntary responses made by individuals, which can be related to previous learning. For example, Pavlov's dogs learned to salivate when a buzzer was sounded because it was sounded at the same time as food was presented. They later salivated at the sound of the buzzer only – the food was absent. However, the paired association had been made and the involuntary response had been 'programmed in'. Classical conditioning theorists would suggest that people's inappropriate responses to stimuli may arise because in the learning situation the responses were appropriate, but subsequently one of the stimuli was absent. This may account for the formation of the irrational fears of phobics.

Operant conditioning (see Chapter 6) looks at voluntary responses, which are repeated because they are rewarded or reinforced. Skinner's original experiments examined the situations whereby a rat would press a bar in order to obtain food pellets, or a pigeon would peck at coloured lights for food; neither is the 'natural' action of the animal to obtain food, but both soon learned what action brought the desired end-result. In the real-life human situation, reward or reinforcement is usually appropriate to the action made to obtain it; if a child looks to a parent for love, he or she expects love, not food or punishment. If the parental response is not as expected, the child learns a faulty response pattern; that pattern may be the one produced by the child later on, which is then considered an abnormal behaviour, because it is inappropriate.

The cognitive model
The cognitive theorist looks beyond the stimulus–response associations of the learning theorist and recognizes that learning does not occur in a vacuum. New information will be perceived, assimilated, judged and rationalized by the individual in the context of existing knowledge and ideas. Faults in rationalization and conception, or irrational beliefs already held, may produce subsequent abnormal behaviours. In order to change these behaviours, cognitive restructuring (reorganizing thought patterns) may be necessary.

The humanistic model
(also discussed in Chapter 30)
This is really a loose group of theories whose connecting point is that they all study individuals in the context of each one's unique experiences of the world. The individual is seen as striving for self-actualization, seeking to achieve his or her full potential as an individual, once the basic needs have been satisfied. Rogers suggests that everyone has a need for positive self-regard, which is prompted by the positive unconditional regard for others. Personality problems arise when individuals concern themselves too much with other people's evaluations of them. Central to the humanistic model is the idea that there may be a mismatch between the perceived self and the ideal self.

All the above paradigms or models view abnormality from their particular theoretical position. However, in order to assess any one problem, it may be necessary to view it from more than one standpoint. No one model offers a sufficient answer for all the problems of abnormality which may arise.

■ **Realistic self-esteem and acceptance**. It is normal for people to realize their own value as individuals and in relation to family, friends and workmates, rather than feeling 'useless', 'worthless', or, conversely, exhibiting megalomania: 'I am better than everyone at everything'. Knowledge of oneself as an individual can be put into the perspective of one's environment, together with the realization that one is fulfilling one's role in society. However, this is often undermined by periods of unemployment, where work is seen as an intrinsic part of the person's role, and thereby 'self'.

■ **Voluntary control over behaviour**. It is accepted that everyone acts impulsively on occasions – life would be dull and predictable without impulse – but when the occasion demands, normal people can exert self-control. Sometimes, for example during natural disasters, it is amazing to see how controlled some individuals' actions are, in extremely adverse circumstances. On the other hand, people who feel that they have no control over their actions, or think that they are being controlled by forces outside themselves, are regarded as being in need of help. A frequent observation made by those suffering from depression is that they feel 'powerless' to assist themselves, or indeed to do anything.

■ **A true perception of the world**. Usually people know what is going on in the world around them, they are aware of other people's actions and intentions, and are interested in happenings outside themselves. To someone with abnormal perceptions, the only area of interest may be their internalized world; the external world seems to have no relevance to them or, conversely, seems only to wish to punish them.

■ **Sustaining relationships and giving affection**. Sensitivity and the ability to recognize the feelings of others is a necessary prerequisite to sustaining relationships. The ability to give affection is normal, not just constantly seeking love, affection and reassurance, but being able to reciprocate with a real depth of feeling.

■ **Self-direction and productivity**. The majority of people try to organize their lives to some sort of design, in order that they experience a fulfilling lifestyle: a career, family, possessions, hobbies. However, even minor depressions can create feelings of aimlessness, tiredness and lethargy. If one assumes that mental disorder restricts an individual's activity, it is then surprising to regard the productivity and energy of Van Gogh, Munch, Dali, Dylan Thomas and many others who were recognized as suffering from mental disorders as well as being in possession of genius. The courses of mental disorders are not always the same; in some, periods of normality interweave with periods of abnormality, giving rise to pockets of energy and productivity.

Evaluation of views of normality/abnormality

No single definition of abnormality given here is sufficient alone: statistical frequency, social norms, maladaptiveness of behaviour and personal distress must all be taken into consideration when defining and describing abnormal behaviour. Different approaches to psychology attribute different reasons for the development of abnormality. In addition, it should be recognized that there is the potential for abnormal behaviour within everyone and most people will manifest abnormal behaviour at some time in their lives, whether prompted by external circumstances such as a highly stressful environment, or by internal changes. Even less satisfactory is the legal definition of abnormality, where a person is declared insane largely on the basis of a perceived inability to judge between right and wrong or exert control over his or her behaviour. Remember that the term 'insane' is a legal one and is not used in psychiatry.

With regard to the characteristics suggested as belonging to 'normal' people, it is likely that the vast majority of people would admit to falling short of at least one of these, at some time in their lives. Perhaps the easiest route to adopt is to suggest that, as humans, we like to be able to predict the behaviour of others with reasonable accuracy. If we cannot, if it does not seem commensurate with the circumstances as we perceive them, we are concerned and worried at what we perceive as abnormal behaviour. This still leaves open the question of whether it is the actor or the observer who has an abnormal perception. If a person's behaviour seems to be what the majority of people would expect in that particular set of circumstances, it is accepted as normal behaviour.

Box 32.2 Responsibility

It has been argued that society is absolving abnormal behaviour by referring to abnormality as mental illness, thereby removing the responsibility for those actions from the individual; it also removes the responsibility for the cure from the individual ('I am ill, Doctor, please cure me'). On the other hand, it could be argued that some physical illnesses attach blame to the individual: AIDS or venereal diseases have – rightly or wrongly – moral implications, and some stigma also attaches to leprosy or cancer sufferers, for example, who report that they are treated with aversion.

Deviant or ill?

Society today has an ambivalent attitude towards abnormality: whilst recognizing that individuals may be 'victims' of their internal or external environment, it also expects them to take a degree of responsibility for their behaviour in certain circumstances. These are not always well-defined. Is it more humane to label someone mentally ill, rather than deviant or morally defective, as Blaney (1975) suggests? Is it better to be 'mad' than 'bad'? This question has a bearing on the way the person is treated.

Prison or hospital?

Certainly treatment has progressed since the days of torturing the patient to exorcise the devils within; the question now posed is whether, in the last resort, abnormal behaviour should be treated by imprisonment or confinement in a mental hospital? Szasz (1973) suggests that when criminals are imprisoned, they believe it is because society will not tolerate their behaviour; they are still responsible. This may not be strictly true; a number of them regard their circumstances as being responsible for promoting their behaviour (for example, 'poverty made me steal') therefore their attitudes may not be very different from the attitudes of those in mental hospitals labelled 'mentally ill'.

Free to leave

It must be remembered that among those patients who are cared for in a mental hospital (many are now cared for in the community) very few in Great Britain are locked up or detained under any section of the Mental Health Act. Most are free to leave whenever they want provided they understand they are free to go. Many do understand this, and may not want to leave because they feel their behaviour is in some way abnormal; they want to be 'cured'. Undoubtedly there are others who do not understand that they are free to leave, or feel that they are pressured into remaining as voluntary patients, for fear that, if they leave, they will be brought back with a detention order. Szasz argues that there are no 'voluntary' patients; he suggests that people are coerced into psychiatric hospitals on threat of being certified if they do not cooperate voluntarily.

The concept of mental illness and the medical model

A number of psychiatrists, among them Thomas Szasz and R. D. Laing, maintain that abnormality should not be called 'mental illness'. This misnomer, they suggest, implies an illness such as measles or cancer, which is totally out of the control of the individual, thereby removing any responsibility of self-control from him or her. If there is a demonstrable physical reason for the abnormality, it should be called an illness, not a mental illness.

Evidence from signs and symptoms

Physical illnesses are diagnosed from patients' symptoms (pains or problems reported by the patient or others who have connection with him or her) and these can be confirmed by signs such as the outcome of X-rays, blood tests, scans, and so on. Psychiatrists diagnosing mental illness rely a great deal on **symptoms**, reports from the patient or relatives; these may not necessarily be reliable. Signs such as psychological tests may be open to more than one interpretation and therefore are not conclusive.

> GLOSSARY
>
> **Signs** Indicators of an illness based on the outcome of such things as X-rays, physical examination, psychological tests, observation of the patient's behaviour, etc.
>
> **Symptoms** A patient's description of pains, thoughts, feelings or perceptions of problems.

Supporting observations from trained staff are not wholly reliable, as shown by Rosenhan's two experiments (described on p. 774). The lack of agreement on diagnosis by psychiatrists is well known, as demonstrated by Fransella (1975) and Shapiro and Shapiro (1982) (see Problems of diagnosis on p. 772).

The **medical model** of abnormality implies that people who suffer from mental illness are not responsible for their behaviour. The issue of responsibility is discussed in Box 32.2.

Moral not medical context

Heather (1976) suggests that abnormality should be viewed in a moral rather than a medical context. He instances neurosis and personality disorders particularly as lacking evidence of organic causes. Therefore, he argues, these should be treated as moral or behavioural disorders, or alternatively, not disorders of the individual at all, but disorders of a sick society. This echoes Laing's (1965) view of schizophrenia, as a 'sane response to an insane world'. Heather also points out the cultural and temporal differences in defining abnormality, both within a society and between different societies; for example, the diagnosis of schizophrenia is ten times more frequently made in the United States of America than in Great Britain.

The antipsychiatry movement

The **antipsychiatry movement** was started in the 1950s by psychiatrists such as Laing, Cooper and Esterson, who rejected the 'disease' model of mental illness. Laing, while initially recognizing schizophrenia as a cluster of symptoms and behaviours (1964), later suggested that the people labelled as schizophrenic simply needed time to voyage within their 'inner space' and work out their problems for themselves. Offering the patient treatment interferes with this natural healing process (1967). Laing put forward the view in the 1960s that society is far more disturbed by the behaviour of schizophrenics than are the individuals themselves. They perceive their own behaviour to be rational, under what they believe are their circumstances.

A safe environment Laing proposed and inaugurated 'safe houses' for schizophrenics, where they could live without pressures, thereby, he said, removing the need for abnormal behaviours. It must

also be remembered that, at that time, the currently fashionable theory of schizophrenia was the 'family theory': this theory suggested that the family, usually led by the mother (denoted the schizophrenogenic mother), picked on one member of the family, and by constant carping and bullying, turned them into a schizophrenic. Family therapy is offered today where problems are not seen as located solely within one individual; however, this rarely applies where the diagnosis is that of schizophrenia. In the same way, Laing's 'safe houses' may have been the forerunner of the community homes and hostels being set up today (see Chapter 33).

Organic not mental illness Thomas Szasz, in his book *The Myth of Mental Illness* (1967), puts forward the seemingly irrefutable argument that if the 'mind' does not exist, how can it be ill? This book was written during a period when overt behaviour was seen as of paramount importance, and any mental conflict preceding the behaviour could be discounted. Possibly Szasz may have been unwittingly instrumental in the resurgence of the concept of 'mind'. Psychologists today are readier to admit to 'mind' being of importance. As Clare (1980) argues, the idea of a mind without a body is untenable in science, therefore so must be the concept of a body without a mind, the two are inextricably linked.

Szasz argues forcibly that if a so-called 'mental illness' has a demonstrable physical cause, such as deterioration of the brain or nervous system, hormonal or chemical imbalance, then the patient has an illness, not a mental illness, which should be treated medically not mentally. If the 'illness' has no physical origin, then it is not an illness, but a 'problem of living' and should be called such. The patient should be helped, if he or she so chooses, to adapt problematic behaviour to reach a compromise with society. People should be made to realize that they are responsible for their own behaviour.

GLOSSARY

Medical model The assumption that mental disorders are illnesses and treatable through medical means, for example the prescribing of drugs or surgery.

The antipsychiatry movement A movement started in the 1950s by psychiatrists such as Laing and Cooper, in opposition to the medical model of mental disorder.

Tolerance of unusual behaviour Szasz lays blame at society's door for being too rigid in its expectations of people's behaviour. We are not all identical, he argues, therefore it is unreasonable to expect everyone to behave identically in any given situation. Society should be more tolerant of unusual behaviours: people are being treated as mentally ill when they are just different from others. (Those who try to live with someone diagnosed as schizophrenic or manic depressive may disagree, but Szasz would say they are only serving their own ends.)

Labelling Szasz says that society desperately needs to predict behaviour; if it cannot, if people do strange, unpredictable things, then they are labelled 'mad' or 'mentally ill'. This labelling process is a kind of symbolic capture, which precedes the physical capture of hospitalization, drugs or other treatment. Before the advent of asylums in the nineteenth century, Szasz points out, there was no segregation of the 'mentally ill': society was more tolerant and these people mixed with everyone else. Except, one might argue in return, for 'witches' who were burned at the stake, or those who simply could not cope and died of starvation or exposure. The parallel might be drawn that more physical illnesses are identified and treated today, whereas in the past their sufferers would have died without diagnosis or treatment.

Points of view One major difference between Laing and Szasz is that while Laing denied the existence of a disease called schizophrenia, he still offered suggestions for its management; whereas Szasz denied that schizophrenia exists, and argued that it is simply a label set up by society to describe behaviours with which society itself cannot cope.

Bailey (1979) agrees with Szasz on two major points:

- Organically based mental illnesses are not mental but physical illnesses, which manifest mental symptoms.
- Functional mental illnesses (those without physical or organic causes) are not illnesses, but disorders of psychosocial or interpersonal functioning; the mental symptoms which are manifest should help to decide the type of therapy the patient needs. Bailey sees the need for patients to adapt their behaviour to the more recognizable norm, rather than for society to become more tolerant.

Evaluation of the medical model and the antipsychiatry movement

It has been questioned whether mental problems can be assessed and verified in the same way as physical diseases, also whether the acceptance that these problems are an 'illness' absolves the individual from any responsibility for those problems.

The ideas of Szasz and Laing may seem both forward-looking and retrograde at the same time. To expect society today to simply tolerate what are regarded as abnormal behaviours is idealistic; large cities such as London or New York are currently trying to prevent displays of abnormal behaviour such as 'living on the streets'. Populations have now become too overcrowded and too sophisticated to accept aberrant behaviours. Families of those with mental disorders would be put under intolerable pressures trying to continue their lives in the ordinary manner, whilst one of their members was perceived as suffering.

The value of Laing's and Szasz's contributions must not be underestimated; they have made society – and psychiatrists – question anew whether each patient needs to be confined, and for how long. As mentioned previously, the development of community homes, family therapy, moral therapy and facets of other treatments, may well have been influenced by their ideas.

In addition, the separation of illnesses with an organic cause from those with no apparent organic causes, may help to determine treatments. Whether their sufferers are regarded as ill or mentally ill would probably be immaterial to those sufferers, were it not for the stigma of 'labelling' (see the next section).

SELF-ASSESSMENT QUESTIONS

1. What major criteria are applied when attempting to define abnormality, and what are the limitations of each?
2. Briefly describe and contrast two theoretical models of abnormality.
3. How would you describe a normal person? Are there problems with your description?
4. Why does the diagnosis of mental disorder, unlike physical illness, rely more on evidence from symptoms than from signs?
5. Discuss whether the concept of mental illness should relate to morality and responsibility for one's own actions.

6. Discuss Szasz's views of the medical model of abnormality.

Diagnosis and classification of mental disorders

Classifications of mental disorders

Stressful or traumatic events in a person's life sometimes result in abnormal behaviours which may be acute and transitory; other forms of abnormality may be chronic, lifelong or degenerative. Each individual is unique and no two people necessarily follow the same identical pattern, just as no two people share identical environments, life experiences and genetic inheritance.

However, cognitive psychology has demonstrated that human beings find it advantageous to use classification as a method of grouping things, a useful reduction to lengthy descriptions (Bruner, 1966a); if a person is described as 'an African' or 'a European' a mental image is immediately formed, which may be wrong in some respects but gives us a broad outline. In the same way, classification of the many areas of abnormal behaviour attempts to give a broad picture.

Diagnosis of abnormality was, historically, a judgmental affair, which is outside the scope of this book to examine. Kraepelin (1913) made the earliest formal attempts at classification. The necessity for standardization of description and classification of illnesses worldwide was recognized and extended to include abnormal behaviours, the purpose being that a diagnostic label would communicate information quickly and concisely about an individual. For example, the diagnosis of 'schizophrenic' conveys a great deal of immediate information to an informed observer.

Accordingly, the World Health Organization's publication, the International Classification of Diseases (ICD), incorporated mental illnesses. ICD was initially developed from the findings of researchers and clinicians in 40 countries. The tenth edition of this (ICD 10) is currently in use.

In the United States a more extensive diagnostic document has been developed by the American Psychiatric Association: The Diagnostic and Statistical Manual of Mental Disorder (DSM), the fourth edition of which (DSM IV) was published in 1994.

There is a good agreement between these two systems; they are seen as complementary, and both are widely used.

Neurosis and psychosis

Historically, mental illness fell into two major categories, psychosis and neurosis.

■ **Psychosis** was described as involving the whole of the personality; an individual's whole life and behaviours are bound up with his or her problem. There is loss of touch with reality; everyday behaviours such as maintaining social relationships or cleanliness may be totally discarded. Usually the term psychosis was used for long-standing problems, of some severity, such as schizophrenia.

■ **Neurosis** was thought not to affect the whole personality, as the individual was said not to entirely lose touch with reality. Frequently the individual realized that he or she was not functioning normally and could recognize and discuss the threads of their pre-illness behaviours as being the desirable state to which they wished to return.

Currently, both ICD 10 and DSM IV have discontinued the usage of these major divisions; the band was so broad that sweeping generalizations such as 'loss of insight' became meaningless. Categories are now narrower-banded and more specific. One might also suggest that the use of modern psychoactive drugs (see Chapter 33) have changed the outlook on psychosis. A brief discussion of these two diagnostic documents follows. You may also wish to refer to the table of classifications of disorders (Figure 32.3) in conjunction with the following discussion.

> **GLOSSARY**
>
> **Psychosis** A relatively vague term to describe mental disorder which involves the whole of the personality and where an individual loses touch with reality. A term no longer used in ICD 10.
>
> **Neurosis** A relatively vague term generally used to describe anxiety-based disorders such as phobias and obsessive-compulsive behaviour, where the patient retains contact with reality.

ICD 10

One major difference between the organization of the ICD 9 and the ICD 10 is that the latter does not use psychosis and neurosis as major classifications, although the terms 'neurotic' and 'psychotic' are both still used in conjunction with specific categories: for example, 'Neurotic, stress related and somatoform disorders' and 'Acute and transient psychotic disorders'.

Diagnosticians using the ICD 10 identify symptoms which indicate one of the ten major group categories (called two-factor categories), then further investigations are made to refine the diagnosis to a specific category (called three-factor categories), for which diagnostic guidelines are provided by ICD 10; these are necessarily flexible.

Problems of terminology are addressed by ICD 10, including the question of using the term 'mental illness'. In order to avoid implications inherent in that term, the word 'disorder' rather than 'illness' is used throughout. Although this is not an exact term, it implies the existence of a set of symptoms which cause distress and interfere with the functioning of the individual.

The terms 'psychogenic' and 'psychosomatic' are not used in ICD 10, due to their differential meanings and interpretations in different psychiatric conditions and different countries.

DSM IV

Only one level of categories is given in the DSM IV: these are, in the main, similar to the ICD 10 two-factor categories, plus a few of the three-factor categories, although learning difficulties are not given a separate category, but are included as a subcategory of developmental disorders of childhood. The disorders described and listed are similar in both diagnostic manuals, but DSM IV prescribes how the diagnosis should proceed.

Multiaxial system Investigations using DSM IV are organized along five axes. Axes 1 to 3 have to be explored by the psychiatrist for each patient, while Axes 4 and 5 are optional and can be used if the psychiatrist judges them to be relevant.

This multiaxial system requires the diagnostician to utilize a broad range of information:

- Axis 1 examines what type of problem the individual is currently presenting. For example, are there symptoms of schizophrenia or substance use disorder?
- Axis 2 discovers whether the patient has any known previous problems, such as a long-standing history of personality disorder.
- Axis 3 enquires whether there are any physical disorders or enduring conditions, for example diabetes or a recent heart attack, which may or may not be relevant to the current problem, but should be noted.
- Axis 4 examines the severity of psychosocial stressors experienced by the individual, and rates them on a 1 to 6 scale, for example whether there have been any deaths in the family, or marital break-up.
- Axis 5 makes a global assessment of the individual's psychological, social and occupational functioning, both currently and the highest level attained during the past year for comparison. Scores range from 90 (a wide range of interests, general satisfaction with life, no more than everyday problems or concerns) down to 1, where the individual is seen to be in danger of hurting the self or others, or has a persistent inability to maintain personal hygiene, or has shown a serious suicidal attempt.

See Figure 32.2 for an example of the way in which DSM IV can be used.

Figure 32.2 Fictitious example of DSM IV multiaxial diagnosis

Client	A.N. Other
Axis 1:	Psychoactive substance use disorder (heroin addition)
Axis 2:	Antisocial personality
Axis 3:	HIV positive
Axis 4:	Psychosocial stressors: death of several close friends recently
Axis 5:	Current level of functioning, 25; highest level in past year, 41

Structured interviews

In addition to using one of these classification systems, the psychiatrist may well use a structured interview technique where standardized questions are asked of the patient, in order to arrive at an informed, objective decision as regards classification. There will be consultation with the clinical psychologist, who has given the patient standardized psychological tests in order to decide diagnosis and optimum treatment. It may be necessary to run a neurological investigation to establish whether there is an organic basis to the problem.

Box 32.3 distinguishes the concept of 'learning difficulties' from that of 'mental illness'. Some of the ways in which mental abnormality is diagnosed are described in Box 32.4.

Problems of diagnosis

The main problems associated with diagnoses are:

- **Reliability**. Would the diagnosis always remain the same, even if conducted by another diagnostician?
- **Validity**. Does this cluster of symptoms really represent a named diagnosis? Does this classification category have real-life representation?
- **Labelling**. What is going to be the outcome of assigning an individual to a category – is that person effectively 'labelled' for life?

Let us look at these problems in more detail.

Reliability

Does the diagnosis remain the same throughout the patient's illness? If the patient is seen by more than one psychiatrist, are their diagnoses the same? Ullman and Krasner (1975) found reliability to be better for the major categories of disorders, but disturbingly low for other categories.

> **GLOSSARY**
>
> **Reliability** In relation to the diagnosis of mental disorder, this term generally relates to the question of whether psychiatrists are consistent with each other in reaching a diagnosis.
>
> **Validity** In relation to the diagnosis of mental disorder, this term addresses the issue of whether a cluster of symptoms really do represent a named disorder.

Box 32.3   Two broad categories of mental disorder

Although the term 'mental illness' is not used in ICD 10, there still remains inherent the division between 'learning difficulties' (referred to as 'mental handicap' in ICD 10) and 'mental illness', largely because, in Great Britain at least, care specializations fall into one of these two categories. Changes of terminology take a long time to filter through to the real-life situation.

Learning difficulties is not the same as learning difficulties, although both can be alleviated or exacerbated by social and environmental conditions.

Mental handicap is a condition usually present from birth, representing a failure of pre- or postnatal development of intellectual capacity, due to a variety of causes, either genetic, or unfavourable interuterine circumstances, birth trauma or subsequent early damage. Disabilities range from slight learning difficulties to failure of development of the foetal brain. You will recall that learning difficulties were discussed at greater length in Chapter 31.

However, there are 'grey' areas between determining whether some individuals have learning difficulties or are mentally ill; there is still some dispute as to whether autism, for example, should be regarded as a form of learning difficulties or a developmental disorder. In addition, there is nothing to prevent a mental illness being superimposed on those with learning difficulties.

The concept of mental illness, which will also be discussed at much greater length in the next section, presents the idea that individuals can become imbalanced at some time in their lives, and that this illness is diagnosable, treatable and possibly curable. There are, however, some, Laing for example, who argue that abnormal behaviours may be due to abnormal social circumstances, and changes in these will produce a change in the individual, thereby proving how inaccurate is the term 'mental illness' (as was discussed in the previous section).

Box 32.4 Diagnostic tools

This term is used for the various techniques used by the diagnostician, psychiatrist or psychologist, in trying to determine the cause and thereby the classification for abnormalities.

Clinical interview

This is not just a 'cosy chat' with the clinician, but rapport is established with the client, in order to draw out problem areas. Clinicians of humanistic or psychodynamic orientation may work from the premise that clients do not know what is troubling them, and they have to endeavour to find out. Not only answers to questions are recorded, but the client's emotional accompaniment to those answers. In fact, if emotion predominates, they may not reply in words. In this way the clinician's notes would vary qualitatively from a survey interviewer's, who would simply tick 'No reply'.

The need for empathy in the clinical setting is of great importance; situational factors, such as age, sex and appearance of the interviewer may exert strong influence on the client's replies to probing personal questions.

Structured interviews respond to the need to collect standardized information: an example is SADS, the Schedule for Affective Disorders and Schizophrenia. Reliability of diagnosis using SADS is impressive, according to Endicott and Spitzer (1978).

Psychological tests

These fall into three major categories: projective tests, intelligence tests (both discussed in Chapter 4) self-report personality inventories (described and discussed in Chapter 29). A self-report personality inventory which is widely used in clinical settings to help diagnose and guide the treatment of mental disorder is the Minnesota Multiphasic Personality Inventory (MMPI). The MMPI has ten clinical scales, each of which aims to identify a particular clinical group (such as schizophrenia or paranoid personality). The MMPI has recently undergone major revision and is now called MMPI-2.

Physiological tests

A number of physiological techniques may be used in the diagnosis of mental disorder. These include X-ray, scanning techniques such as PET scans, CAT scans and MRI scans which give computerized pictures of the brain, EEG, which measures the electrical activity of the brain. All of these techniques were described in the Introduction to Part 2.

Behavioural observation

It is difficult to observe most behaviour as it actually takes place. The family situation or setting preceding the actual abnormal behaviour may be as important as a description of the isolated behaviour. Many therapists contrive situations in their consulting rooms in order to observe behaviours; this of course invokes the phenomenon of reactivity of behaviour – behaviour which changes simply because it is observed.

The reliability of behavioural assessment depends heavily on the diagnostician's categorizations. Interobserver reliability may be improved through training (Paul, 1966), but this does not necessarily relate to observations made in another institution, let alone across the Atlantic. Bernstein and Nietzel (1980) found that the random observing of observers increased their reliability.

The validity of whether the observed behaviours relate to the client's problem, should be established; if a clinician assumes that frequent lateness for clinic appointments is an indication of hostility, is he or she justified in making such an assertion? Also, is the observed behaviour typical of that individual's behaviour when not being observed? Zeigob et al. (1975) found that mothers acted more positively towards their children when they knew they were being observed than when they were observed surreptitiously.

The situation may influence the observed behaviour; Mischel (1968) argued that situation is more important in determining behaviour than internal factors. (See Chapter 29.)

Observer expectations can also influence observations (as demonstrated by Rosenthal, 1966, where outcomes were found to be as the observer had been led to believe they would be; see Chapters 3 and 34).

Self-monitoring

The self-monitoring of behaviour can be undertaken by clients, although this is not always reliable (Nelson, 1977) as clients are not always motivated to be honest; they may not wish to attribute faults to themselves. Careful questioning about reported behaviour may indicate the point at which intervention should be made, in order to change behaviour. For example, if attention is paid promptly by a client's family to a reasonable request, unreasonable or confrontational behaviour may be averted.

Issues of reliability arose in the classic study by Rosenhan (1973), described in Box 32.5.

Cooper et al. (1972) suggested that ten times as many people are diagnosed as schizophrenic by American psychiatrists as British ones, out of a proportional number presenting.

Fransella (1975) advised that diagnostic categories are not mutually exclusive and may therefore show overlap; on the other hand, different schizophrenics, for example, may exhibit no symptoms in common.

Beck et al. (1962) reported that he and three other psychiatrists diagnosed 153 patients; each patient was seen by two psychiatrists. All four diagnosticians had agreed on the current diagnostic manual, but not on the techniques to be used for gathering information. Overall agreement on diagnosis was only 54 per cent. When these cases were reexamined, Ward et al. (1962) suggested reasons for the low rate of agreement.

■ Inadequacies of the diagnostic system, with unclear criteria, or major categories which were not specific enough, accounted for 62.5 per cent of disagreements.
■ Inconsistencies in information presented by the patient.
■ Inconsistencies in techniques used by the diagnostician: for example, differences in interviewer techniques.

Shapiro and Shapiro (1982) claimed that a severely anxious patient with delusions may be classified as either neurotic or psychotic, depending on the view taken of the intensity of the problem.

Validity

Validity looks at whether a test, a diagnosis, or a situation really is what it says it is. In the context of diagnosis for example, does the descriptive term 'broken leg' adequately and truly describe what the patient is suffering from? In the field of mental disorders, the answer may not always be so self-evident. If reliability is a prerequisite of validity, there have already been shown some doubts. In addition, Heather (1976) states that very few 'causes' of mental illness are known, and there is only a 50 per cent chance of predicting treatment once diagnosis has been made.

■ Bannister et al. (1964) suggested that factors other than diagnosis seem to dictate what treatments are used.

Box 32.5 On being sane in insane places (Rosenhan, 1973)

Rosenhan (1973) carried out what is now regarded as a classic study. Eight 'normal' people requested appointments, at various psychiatric hospitals in the USA; the only symptoms they presented were that they claimed to hear voices saying single words, such as 'hollow' or 'thud'. They were all admitted as patients, subsequently exhibiting no false or aberrant behaviours, although their normal behaviours were sometimes misinterpreted by the staff; for example, one who took notes of his treatment in hospital was identified as having a compulsion to write. None of the psychiatric staff reported any suspicions that these were anything other than genuine patients. Eventually all were discharged, with the diagnosis of 'schizophrenia in remission'; confinement varied from 9 to 52 days.

In a second experiment, a teaching hospital was told of the previous experiment and warned that some pseudopatients might apply for admission, over a three-week period. During that time, 193 patients were admitted; the staff were confident that 41 of these were not genuine patients, and various others were suspected. In fact, they were all genuine patients.

■ Mackay (1975) asserted that because the notion of 'mental illness' is such a vague one, the diagnostic process cannot be a valid one; the choice of treatments is likely to be haphazard.
■ Clare (1980) suggested that the diagnosis of physical illnesses is not as clear-cut or reliable as generally believed: criticism should be directed at those diagnosing, not the diagnostic process.
■ This supports the view of Falek and Moser (1975), where doctors' diagnoses of illnesses such as tonsillitis, or angina, without the support of a definitive laboratory test, showed no greater agreement than psychiatrists' diagnoses of schizophrenia.

Labelling

Once a diagnosis has been made, it is entered in the patient's records and that diagnosis may become synonymous with that individual – they are effectively 'labelled'. There may be a number of consequences to this:

- The person's family and friends may come to regard him or her differently because of the label, and the label may replace the individual.
- Even when the patients are finally discharged, they are not rid of their label; others still remember them by it and it is still on their medical records, which are allegedly confidential, but confidential to how many? In these days of computerization, who knows?
- Laing (1967) suggested that the patient is labelled by a diagnosis in order that he or she may be institutionalized and dehumanized; the label is the 'symbolic capture' of the individual.
- Scheff (1966) suggested that the disorder is a learned social role; the labelled individual acts according to the stereotype. This became known as 'labelling theory'. However, there is little evidence to support this theory. Given that the behaviours shown by schizophrenics, for example, are so disparate and wide-ranging, there is no one stereotype to follow.

Gove's (1970) study showed that there is little conclusive evidence of the social stigma allegedly attached to mental illness, although others have challenged this.

The differing views of normality and abnormality held by different cultures, was investigated by Murphy (1976), who found that both Eskimos and the Yoruba tribe differentiate between their 'shamans' (those who have visions) and their 'crazy people', who exhibit behaviours such as talking to oneself, refusing to speak, delusional beliefs and strange behaviours. Both cultures have different words in their languages for 'shaman' and 'crazy person'.

There are arguments for and against labelling. On the one hand there is the diagnostic convenience of a category, recognizable to other professionals who may encounter the individual. On the other hand there is the suggestion that the person may choose to 'act the part' of the label, or be stigmatized by its attachment, by family, loss of job or friends, or decline in social status.

See also a discussion of the concepts of reliability, validity and labelling in Chapters 3 and 34.

What can be concluded about diagnosis and classification?

The fact that many surveys have shown medical diagnosis to be unreliable is not a valid argument for ceasing to diagnose; the same applies to psychiatric diagnosis.

Spitzer (1976) gave a spirited rebuttal of Rosenhan's studies. The diagnosis 'schizophrenia in remission' is rarely used with genuine patients, therefore the diagnoses were a function of the pseudopatients' behaviours, and therefore should not reflect badly on the psychiatric hospital. He defended the hospital procedures and suggested that any problems with diagnosis lay with individual psychiatrists. He also criticized Rosenhan for his use of the terms 'sane' and 'insane' which, as he said, are legal terms and not used by psychiatrists in hospitals. However, many other psychiatrists and psychologists assert that 'schizophrenia in remission' remains a common diagnosis.

Fonagy and Higgitt (1984) suggested that instead of using diagnostic categories to describe specific 'diseases', terms such as 'anxiety' and 'schizophrenia' should be used descriptively, to make testable hypotheses about mental disorders. If this suggestion were adopted, it might reduce the problem of labelling.

❓ SELF-ASSESSMENT QUESTIONS

1. What are the two major classificatory systems used by Western society? What professional bodies have drawn up these documents?
2. How does diagnosis proceed, using each of these two classificatory systems?
3. Distinguish between 'mental illness' and 'learning difficulties'.
4. Discuss the range of techniques which may be used by clinicians in diagnosing mental disorder.
5. Briefly discuss the findings of studies which have examined reliability and validity in relation to the diagnosis of mental disorder.
6. What are the problems associated with categorization or 'labelling' of mental disorder?

Categories and descriptions of mental disorders

Categories of mental disorders

As discussed previously, major diagnostic categories of mental disorders are set out in ICD 10 and DSM IV, two widely used and complementary classification systems. Although the diagnostic categories are not identical in the two diagnostic systems, they are very similar, and for the purposes of this book are treated in conjunction with each other. In both, specific mental disorders are grouped with others that have similar symptoms or origins, to form major categories which are then given a comprehensive title.

Figure 32.3 lists ten major categories; under each of these are listed a number of specific disorders assigned to each. These are not exhaustive lists but examples, some of which may already sound familiar to those of you who are interested. (A description of some of these disorders is given below.)

Descriptions of mental disorders

This section describes various mental disorders. Included are examples of disorders from each of the main categories named in Figure 32.3. Their **aetiology** (causes), symptoms and prognosis (prediction of the course of the disorder) are outlined wherever possible, unless previously dealt with elsewhere in this book.

Category 1: Organic mental disorders

Organic mental disorders are due to physical deterioration of the brain or degeneration of the nervous system. Specific disorders in this category include the following.

Parkinson's disease Dopamine-producing cells in the brain no longer function effectively. Tremor and a shuffling gait are typical symptoms. In many patients, this can be treated effectively with a drug called L-dopa, but careful monitoring is necessary to prevent overdose. The L-dopa is a synthetic form of dopamine which replaces this necessary neurotransmitter and restores activity to the dopamine circuit. An overdose of L-dopa may produce hallucinations or other symptoms reminiscent of schizophrenia (see the dopamine theory, later in this chapter).

Alzheimer's disease This disorder was first identified in 1860 by the German neurologist Alois Alzheimer. It has been identified in people in their forties and fifties, as well as the elderly, and is classified as a presenile dementia. It usually commences with difficulties of concentration, absent-mindedness and irritability. Mental faculties decline and there is a deterioration in personality and social behaviour. In Alzheimer's, primary degeneration of neurons (brain cells) occurs. (Information on neurons and nervous transmission is contained in Box 32.8.) Cells in the cortex atrophy to such a degree that ventricles in the brain may become larger and sulci (the folds in the cortex) may widen. Hyman et al. (1984) found that cell degeneration particularly affects the hippocampus (a structure in the brain important for laying down memories).

Many potential causes of Alzheimer's disease have been indicated, but none actually proven as yet. It is difficult to establish which of the observed changes is cause, and which effect. The prognosis is poor, with deterioration occurring over 10–12 years. Current research into the cause of Alzheimer's disease is looking into a possible genetic component.

Treatment of Alzheimer's is primarily to reassure the person and provide care and comfort. In the early stages, individuals are better in their own homes, with family and familiar surroundings. 'Reminder notes' (e.g. turn off the cooker, lock the front door) can provide the necessary prompts. Later symptoms may include paranoid delusions, aggression and other behaviours with which the family cannot cope. Institutionalization is not a decision to be taken lightly and counselling is an excellent form of support for the individual and his or her relatives (Zarit, 1980). Practical and moral support for families caring for an Alzheimer's sufferer at home is currently recognized as being of importance, although funds are not always available to provide all the help needed.

Dementia in HIV Human immunodeficiency virus (HIV) is a viral infection which destroys the body's

---

> **GLOSSARY**
>
> **Aetiology** The factors that cause or contribute to the development of a particular medical disorder.
>
> **Organic mental disorders** Disorders which arise from physical deterioration of the brain or degeneration of the nervous system.

Figure 32.3 Specific mental disorders in major categories

1. **Organic mental disorder**
   - Various dementias, e.g. HIV, vascular
   - Alzheimer's disease
   - Disorders due to brain damage or disease
   - Organic amnesias
2. **Psychoactive substance-use disorders**
   - Intoxication, dependence, abuse and withdrawal of substances, e.g. alcohol, opioids, stimulants, cannabis, sedatives, cocaine, tobacco, solvents, hallucinogens
   - With or without complications (e.g. coma, convulsions)
3. **Schizophrenia and delusional disorders**
   - Schizophrenia, e.g. simple, hebephrenic, paranoid, catatonic
   - Persistent delusional disorder
   - Acute and transient psychotic disorders
   - Schizophrenia affective disorders
4. **Mood (affective) disorders**
   - Mania
   - Bipolar affective disorder
   - Single depressive episode
   - Recurrent depressive
   - Other mood (affective) disorders
5. **Neurotic and stress-related disorders**
   - Phobias
   - Anxiety disorders, e.g. panic attacks
   - Obsessive-compulsive disorder
   - Severe stress, e.g. post-traumatic stress syndrome
   - Dissociative disorders, e.g. fugue, amnesia, multiple personality
   - Somatoform disorders, e.g. hypochondria
6. **Behavioural disorders associated with physical disturbances**
   - Eating disorders, e.g. anorexia, bulimia
   - Nonorganic sleep disorders, e.g. insomnia, sleepwalking, nightmares
   - Sexual dysfunction (nonorganic)
   - Puerperal disorders, e.g. puerperal psychosis, postnatal depression
   - Abuse of nondependence substances, e.g. laxatives, vitamins, steroids
7. **Adult personality disorders**
   - Specific personality disorders, e.g. paranoid, schizoid, dissocial
   - Personality changes after catastrophe
   - Habit and impulse disorders, e.g. gambling, pyromania
   - Psychosexual disorders
8. **Learning difficulties**
   - Mild, moderate. Severe or profound categories
9. **Disorders of psychological development**
   - Specific language and speech disorders
   - Specific scholastic disorders, e.g. dyslexia
   - Pervasive disorders, e.g. autism
10. **Childhood and adolescence disorders**
    - Hyperkinetic disorder
    - Conduct disorder
    - Emotional disorders, e.g. phobic anxiety, separation anxiety
    - Social functioning disorders, e.g. elective mutism
    - Tic disorders, e.g. Tourette's syndrome
    - Other, e.g. stuttering, enuresis, feeding disorder

immune responses. It also produces mental disorders, initially causing slowness, forgetfulness, poor concentration and difficulties with problem solving and reading. Apathy and social withdrawal are common; less frequent are seizures or psychoses. It is possible that a degree at least of the apathy and social withdrawal are due to the individual's perception of his or her state of health, as well as physiological deterioration. Counselling is always offered to AIDS sufferers, to try to combat despondency, as well as help with day-to-day problems.

Nurnberg et al. (1984) found that patients exhibited problems with concentration and memory months before AIDS-related illnesses appeared.

Disorders due to brain damage or disease Brain damage can be caused by tumours, infections (such as meningitis), accident or trauma, and physical damage can be located and related to loss of function in the individual. Infections which are cured and tumours which are benign or removed rarely leave residual psychological problems.

Clinical studies in this area have provided much evidence for localization of functions in the brain. Unlike other parts of the body, the brain does not regenerate, and as a rule, if functions are lost, they will not be regained. Notable exceptions to this rule are young children, under five or six years of age, where the brain is still plastic and substitute connections can still be forged.

Patients who are comatose after an accident, sometimes for months, may show a complete recovery of functions, even if this is gradual; the younger the patient, the more complete the recovery.

A concussion (a brief loss of consciousness), or a contusion (bruising of neural tissue, when the brain shifts and compresses against the skullbone, through forceful impact, possibly resulting in coma) are unlikely to cause a change in personality, whereas a laceration (where brain tissue is pierced or torn) is likely to result in personality change. The best-known case was that of Phineas Gage (late nineteenth century) who was working on excavation for the railroad, when a three-and-a-half-foot tamping iron was blasted right through his left cheek and out of the top of his skull. He recovered, with no resultant sensory or motor deficits, but his personality had changed so radically his employers would not give him his job back. (One wonders if he wanted it back!)

Alcohol also causes brain damage. Sufferers of Wernicke's disease have damage to the pons, cerebellum and mamillary bodies, and exhibit drowsiness, confusion and unsteady gait. Those suffering from Korsakoff's psychosis have a similar pattern of damage and behaviour, but in addition exhibit lesions in the thalamus and anterograde amnesia (loss of memory for events following an illness or trauma), often confabulating ('inventing' memories) in order to fill gaps in their memories.

produces a physiological withdrawal state, which may range from anxiety, through convulsions, to delirium, for example delirium tremens experienced by alcoholics, where vivid hallucinations combine with confusion and tremor.

The opioids such as heroin have a similar chemical 'shape' to some of the brain's own chemicals, the endorphins. These appear to have a calming, pain-reducing effect on the individual in the normal situation. When opioids are used the endorphins are underproduced. During withdrawal from heroin

A painting by a patient in a mental institution. Feelings of tension and persecution are fairly evident

Category 2: Psychoactive substance-use disorder

Dependence syndrome is a cluster of physiological, behavioural and cognitive phenomena in which the use of a substance takes on a much higher priority than any other behaviours previously enjoyed by the individual. Tolerance occurs, thereby necessitating more frequent or higher doses of the substance. Persistence with the substance may have physiological consequences (for example, alcohol causing liver damage) or social consequences (for example, loss of a job through drug-related impaired performance or depressive mood-states). Deprivation of the substance

the painful effect is enhanced through the underproduction of the natural calming chemicals. Withdrawal from substance use is best undertaken under medical supervision.

Category 3: Schizophrenia and delusional disorders

Schizophrenia Whether this is one disorder or many, is still a point for discussion, as is the

---

GLOSSARY

Dependence syndrome A condition in which the use of a substance such as drugs or alcohol takes on a much higher priority than any other aspects of the individual's behaviour.

possibility that the origins of schizophrenia may be organic. If so, it should therefore be regarded as an organic disorder.

Kraepelin first presented his description of dementia praecox (schizophrenia) in 1898, as follows: an early onset, progressive intellectual deterioration, hallucinations, delusions, negativisim (doing the opposite of what is required), attentional difficulties, emotional dysfunction and stereotyped behaviour. Not all schizophrenic patients will show all of these symptoms; in fact no two cases are identical (for examples of symptoms, see Box 32.6). DSM IV determines for the diagnostician how many areas of disturbance should be present, from thought, perception, attention, motor functions, affect or emotion, and life function; however, there is no essential symptom which determines classification. ICD 10 does not prescribe what exactly should be included in the diagnosis; this may partially account for the difference in frequency of diagnosing schizophrenia between the United States and Great Britain.

Duration of the disorder must be taken into account in order to distinguish true schizophrenia from brief psychotic episodes (reactive psychoses) or other schizophrenic disorders. Cooper et al. (1972) showed that many patients with a DSM II diagnosis of schizophrenia were actually suffering from brief psychotic episodes, as duration of the problem was not a factor for consideration at that time. Brief psychotic episodes are now diagnosed as personality disorders.

Endicott et al. (1982) found that diagnoses of schizophrenia varied according to the diagnostic system used.

Schneider (1959) identified what he called 'first rank symptoms' which he said are central to defining schizophrenia; these include particular forms of hallucinations and delusions. The layperson's idea of a 'split personality' is incorrect, this is more descriptive of multiple personality (see Category 5) than schizophrenia.

Four subtypes of schizophrenia are identified in ICD 10. At one time it was thought that these were sequential

---

GLOSSARY

Schizophrenia A condition in which the individual experiences a split from reality in the form of, for example, delusions or hallucinations. It takes many different forms and may be one disorder or a number of different ones.

Box 32.6 Examples of symptoms of schizophrenia

Perception and thought disorders in schizophrenia

1. **Schizophrenic slip:** an apparently lucid flow of conversation from the person, but 'slipping' from topic to topic, concept to concept, with no apparent logical relationship.
2. **Clang associations:** the use of words, without regard for their meanings, because they sound similar 'He's a pig like a swig in the dig'.
3. **Literal interpretations:** of proverbs for example: schizophrenic people may literally go looking for 'the light at the end of the tunnel', or commence a discussion about how quick is 'a flash'.
4. **Lack of insight:** sufferers rarely have an ideas why their behaviours are unacceptable, and frequently cannot understand why they should be hospitalized.
5. **Delusions:** holding beliefs that the rest of society would disagree with. Common delusions are **delusions of grandeur:** 'I am God/Napoleon/the Queen' or of **persecution** (paranoia), where individuals believe others are planning to kill or harm them in some way.
6. **Hallucinations,** most often auditory, are experienced by many schizophrenic people. The 'voices' they hear are often saying derogatory or threatening things.
7. **Thought control:** individuals feel that thoughts are no longer their own. They are controlled by others' they may believe that thoughts are transmitted to them by radio waves. The delusion may be so strong that sufferers are convinced there are wires attached to their heads, or radio antennae. They may blame radio or television for this control, and avoid it. Sometimes the insertion is of feelings or sensations rather than words or thoughts.

Other typical symptoms

Affective symptoms: the mood of the individual may either be said to be 'flat' – stimuli fail to elicit an appropriate emotional response – or they may exhibit **inappropriate affect**, for example laughing at sad news, or becoming extremely angry at a simple, uncontroversial question.
Motor symptoms: bizarre motor movements, e.g. waving the hands without cause or complete immobility or purposeless rushing up and down.

and the disease would progress from one 'stage' to another. This is not now thought to be true. There is less tendency nowadays to regard it necessary to classify people into one of these subcategories. The following are the categories which have been identified.

Simple schizophrenia appears during late adolescence. Symptoms include increasing apathy, decline in academic or work performance and gradual social withdrawal. The sufferer may be regarded by others as idle, or a drifter. Diagnosis depends on establishing the gradual progression and worsening of these symptoms. Hallucinations and delusions are not usually manifest.

Hebephrenic schizophrenia (called 'disorganized' in DSM IV) is characterized by hallucinations and delusions which are profuse and less directed than those of the paranoid schizophrenic. Behaviour is changeable, even violent at times, mannerisms are adopted and discarded, as are behavioural rituals. Appearance and personal hygiene may be forgotten. Disorders of thought, perception and attention are prevalent (see Box 32.6). Onset is usually during the early twenties.

Catatonic schizophrenia is typically represented by motor disturbances which tend to fall into extremes. At one extreme, the sufferer is completely immobile for long periods of time, often 'posed' in odd positions, seeming oblivious to all around, yet may later relate details of what has happened during that time. At the other extreme, in the excited state, the individual may run or walk up and down, shouting or talking with great agitation. Between these two extreme states are other distinctive motor disturbances: hand- or finger-waving or strange, jerky movements.

Paranoid schizophrenia is characterized by delusions. These may be grandiose, where individuals are full of their own self-importance or power, sometimes convinced that they are a well-known historical figure such as Napoleon or Jesus Christ, and everyone else is conspiring to keep them prisoner. Alternatively they may suffer delusions of persecution: everyone is talking about them, snippets of conversation in the street are about them, radio and TV programmes refer to them, there are plots to kill them. Sufferers of paranoid schizophrenia are frequently argumentative, agitated and sometimes violent, but they are more alert and verbal than those in other subcategories and their thought processes, although deluded, are not as fragmented.

A discussion of the views of Szasz and Laing, who take differing views on the existence or treatment of schizophrenia, has been included earlier in the chapter.

Category 4: Mood (affective) disorders

Mania The manic person exhibits high activity, elation, is full of grandiose plans, buys things he or she cannot really afford, talks volubly, taking the whole population into his or her confidence.

Reactive depression or single depressive episodes The sufferer feels in a sad, depressed mood, no longer enjoys usual activities, has disturbed sleep patterns or sleeps a great deal, poor appetite and loss of energy and drive. This type of depression differs from recurrent depressive disorder in that this form is usually triggered by an external event, for example a death, but the sadness or mood disturbance exceeds the bounds of a normal reaction. Many people become depressed for short periods of time (one might almost say it would be abnormal not to do so) and recover with no treatment at all. Times of hormonal changes, such as adolescence and menopause, sometimes produce emotional changes which may include depressive episodes.

Recurrent depressive disorder This has no immediately recognizable cause. The patient has recurring bouts of depression; some may be triggered by seemingly minor external events, others not. The result is deeply sad, depressed mood, poor appetite, disturbed sleep patterns, loss of energy, loss of pleasure in any activities, difficulties in concentration or decision making, recurrent thoughts of suicide or death.

Manic depression Manic depression or bipolar affective disorder is where the two extreme states, mania and depression, alternate in the same individual. It is very difficult to treat; if the depressive state is lifted too high for example, by drug treatment, then the person may swing into the manic phase; if the manic state is 'damped down' too much, then the person may slip into depression. These are known as bipolar swings.

Category 5: Neurotic and stress-related disorders

Phobia This is an irrational fear of an object or situation. Some of the most common phobias are arachnophobia (fear of spiders), agoraphobia (fear of public spaces or fear of leaving one's own safe haven) and social phobia (where an individual cannot cope with meeting new people: this is often confused with agoraphobia, as in both cases the affected individual may refuse to go out). Fear of snakes is another common phobia, also claustrophobia (fear of confined spaces), and acrophobia (fear of heights).

Phobias are common but most people can keep them under control and simply practise avoidance. If you are afraid of snakes and live in the city you have no real problem; if you are afraid of heights, don't become a steeplejack!

Agras et al. (1969) found that fewer than 1 per cent of people with phobias required treatment for their phobias; treatment may be necessary when the individuals have to organize their own lives around their phobias. Sufferers usually realize their fears are irrational.

Phobias are thought by learning theorists to originate through faulty learning; either through classical conditioning, by contiguous association, the fear object being present at the same time as a real fear or punishment, or through operant conditioning, by reinforcement of the individual's fear of the object, usually in childhood (as discussed in the learning theory model outlined earlier). Freud and other psychodynamic theorists suggest that phobias are a defence against the anxiety that is produced by repressed id impulses (discussed in Chapter 30).

Obsessive-compulsive disorder Obsessions are recurring thoughts and ideas which dominate a person's consciousness, without his or her active volition. A compulsion is a need to perform a

This women may suffer from arachnophobia – an irrational fear of spiders

stereotyped action or movement, to ward off the feared situation. Anxiety and tension are produced if the individual tries to resist the compulsion.

Somatoform disorder This is classified as conversion type of hysterical neurosis in DSM IV. It is where the individual's actual problem is changed into an acceptable problem. The classical case, described by Freud, is that of Anna O, the woman who could not admit to her resentment at having to look after her invalid father, and therefore developed a 'paralysed' arm, although there was no physical problem present.

Multiple personality In ICD 10 this is classified as a dissociative type of hysterical neurosis and in DSM IV, a dissociative disorder. The person with multiple personality disorder has two or more distinct personalities at the same time, either of which may take over without bidding. Sometimes these personalities are unaware of each other; at other times there is a central personality who is aware of some or all of the others. One of the most interesting was that of Sybil, who had six different personalities (Rheta Schrieber, 1973). Cases are few and far between. Autonomic responses, such as heart-rate, blood pressure and galvanic skin response, have been taken and found to differ for each personality.

Psychoanalytic theory views multiple personality as repression of infantile sexual wishes; Bliss (1980) believes it becomes established in childhood through self-hypnosis. Learning theorists regard it as avoidance responses, to avoid punishment or protect the individual from highly stressful events. Selective memory loss could be accounted for by state-dependent learning (if you learn something when you are happy you are more likely to remember it when you are happy). Because of the rarity of dissociative disorders, they are among the least understood and researched clinical syndromes, relying for data only on clinical case studies.

Post-traumatic stress disorder A delayed and/or protracted response to a stressful event or situation, such as being a witness or a participant in an earthquake or other natural disaster, serious accident, war, witnessing the violent death of others, being a victim of rape, torture or other crime. Symptoms include repeated re-living of the trauma ('flashbacks'), emotional blunting, detachment from other people, fear and avoidance of cues associated with the original trauma. Anxiety and depression are commonly associated with post-traumatic stress disorder.

Paton (1990) looked for these symptoms in two classes of people who helped after the earthquake in Armenia: trained firefighters and volunteers with little or no experience of disasters. The volunteers displayed a lower level of post-traumatic stress on all symptoms. Paton suggests this may be due to higher expectations in the professionals to be able to give help and save lives, and their disappointment at being unable to do so.

Recently these same symptoms have been identified in some individuals who have not been involved in a major catastrophe. Severe reprimands at work, for example, have triggered the same level of anxiety, flashbacks and avoidance responses usually associated with catastrophes (Scott and Stradling, 1992, unpublished).

Category 6: Behavioural disorders associated with physical disturbances

Anorexia nervosa   Three principal symptoms are: serious weight loss, an intense fear of becoming obese, and refusal to eat sufficiently to gain or maintain body weight. The problem is usually first manifest during adolescence and is 20 times more common in girls than boys. The girl fails to menstruate regularly; this and the loss of weight has prompted theorists to suggest that the girl is showing an unwillingness to grow up. Family conflict has also been suggested as a cause; the conflict is deflected on to the sufferer's 'disease'. Learning theorists suggest the young woman is trying to emulate the slim models so valued by society. Psychoanalytic theorists who equate food with sexuality, suggest that refusal of food is really a rejection of sexuality.

The person with anorexia is usually of above average IQ, a perfectionist, well-behaved and conscientious, and frequently comes from a family of high-achievers.

Some sufferers have to be hospitalized and fed intravenously; a percentage die. Behaviour therapies include regimes of isolation followed by company at mealtimes. If the patient eats a meal, rewards follow, such as company of nurses, access to TV, radio or music. Family therapy includes 'the family lunch', where mother and father are asked to unite to persuade the sufferer to eat (Minuchin et al., 1975), the idea being that, if conflict has promoted anorexia, perceived unity will solve the problem.

Bulimia   This has now been recognized as a separate disorder from anorexia nervosa. The person with bulimia seldom reduces weight, never to life-threatening dimensions, as does the anorexic, but does have an equal fear of obesity. Life is a series of 'binges' followed by vomiting; they often feel disgust and helplessness while binging, they are aware their eating patterns are abnormal and go to great lengths to hide them. The continual vomiting has physiological consequences such as intestinal damage and nutritional deficiencies. Various therapies and anti-depressant drugs have been tried with bulimics, with varying claimed successes. No really effective treatment has been found.

(Anorexia nervosa and bulimia are also discussed in Chapter 9.)

Puerperal disorders   Postnatal depression is an abnormal reaction to what is usually considered a happy event: the birth of a baby. The mother feels unable to cope, and in very severe cases may commit suicide or infanticide. Causes are likely to be biochemical or social. Puerperal disorders are recognized at two levels, mild (postnatal depression) and severe (puerperal psychosis). Commencing within six weeks of the birth of the baby, the mother is depressed and cannot relate to her new infant. In severe cases she ignores the infant or threatens to harm it or herself. Because of the danger of suicide or infanticide, prompt treatment is necessary. If anti-depressant drug treatment is ineffective, electroconvulsive therapy may be used (see Chapter 33). Mother and baby are kept together as much as possible, in special 'mother and baby' units, while treatment is undertaken.

Category 7: Adult personality disorders

Explanations based on the trait approach to personality, described in Chapter 29, suggest that these disorders have long-term, inflexible and maladaptive patterns of behaviour. The individual does not lose contact with reality and behaviours are integrated into the person's lifestyle, making treatment difficult. A number of personality disorders are described below.

Antisocial personality   This is also known as **psychopathic (sociopathic) personality**. The disorder has usually revealed itself by the age of 15, through truancy, vandalism or delinquency. In adulthood, the individual may be indifferent to holding a job, keeping within the law, acting in a caring or responsible manner to partners or relatives. Many psychopaths do hold down ordinary jobs, but extend their immorality to the work situation. Frequently they are clever enough to avoid being caught.

Cleckley (1976), suggests that characteristics of the psychopath may include: considerable charm, absence of anxiety, irrational thoughts or other 'neurotic' symptoms, lack of remorse or guilt, while exhibiting unreliability, untruthfulness and insincerity, pathological egocentrism, leading to incapacity for real love and attachment and inability to see oneself as others do (therefore lack of insight).

Hare (1980) lists lack of empathy and lack of concern for others as characteristics typical of psychopaths. Robins (1966) suggests that some psychopaths come from families where discipline is inconsistent or absent and are usually referred to guidance clinics during childhood, for a range of antisocial behaviours. Retrospective studies (studies which look back at a person's past after they have been identified as belonging to a group or category) unfortunately lack comparable control groups, either of peers who were also referred to clinics but did not become psychopaths, or psychopaths who have not been identified by the law during adulthood, and are therefore not included in research data.

The schizoid personality The typical sufferer is aloof, with few friends, and is indifferent to praise and criticism. Individuals may have recurrent illusions and 'magical thinking' (believing themselves to have telepathic powers, for example). Spitzer et al. (1979) suggest that the disorder may be a mild form of schizophrenia. It may be related by virtue of a genetic predisposition to schizophrenia.

The narcissistic personality The sufferer has an extreme sense of self-importance, requires constant attention from others, fantasizes about great successes and exaggerates modest ones, and is likely to exploit others.

The paranoid personality Sufferers are suspicious of people, expect to be mistreated and assume others are discussing them. They are argumentative, overly sensitive and tend to blame others even when at fault themselves. Their extreme jealousy, especially of sexual partners, makes it difficult to maintain close relationships.

Category 8: Learning difficulties

This category is fully discussed in Chapter 31.

Category 9: Disorders of psychological development

A range of disorders can be included under this heading, including autism, dyslexia and attention-deficit hyperactivity. Each of these conditions is discussed in Chapter 31.

Category 10: Childhood and adolescent disorders

This category comprises a seemingly unrelated group of disorders, mostly with unidentified causes. Their common factor is that they are all first observed during childhood. Two disorders, Tourette's syndrome and feeding disorders are briefly described in Chapter 31.

? SELF-ASSESSMENT QUESTIONS

1. Explain what is meant by organic mental disorders. Briefly describe some examples.
2. Briefly outline some of the characteristics of substance use disorder.
3. What is meant by 'multiple personality disorder'?
4. Describe some of the typical behaviours associated with schizophrenia. Why is it difficult to make a diagnosis of schizophrenia?
5. What is the difference between single depressive episodes and recurrent depressive disorder?

Possible causes of mental disorders

If a skier falls and breaks a leg, the doctor can identify the cause of the break: a fall while skiing. Prevention could be suggested, such as make sure you do not fall, or alternatively do not ski at all. Not all physical illnesses have such a direct, uncomplicated cause-and-

GLOSSARY

Psychopathic (sociopathic) personality A disorder in which the individual does not lose touch with reality but habitually behaves in ways which endanger the well-being of others.

INSANITY **IS** HEREDITARY — YOU GET IT
FROM YOUR CHILDREN.

effect pattern; causes of mental disorders are usually even less easily identifiable.

Discussed in three subsections below are three major areas of research relating to causes of mental disorder: genetic, environmental and neurochemical/neurological. These areas are not mutually exclusive, they interact and overlap. Some possible causes of mental impairment were examined in Chapter 31.

Genetic causes

There may well be a **genetic predisposition** for some mental illnesses, as there is for some physical illnesses such as diabetes, but the disease may not be manifest until prompted by some precipitating event, such as a virus infection. (The mechanisms of genetics are discussed in the Introduction to Part 4.)

Likewise with mental disorders, for example a woman may have a genetic predisposition to depression, but a precipitating event such as the birth of a baby happens before the recognizable clinical syndrome of postnatal depression is manifest.

There may be links between genes and mental disorders which have not yet been identified. It has been suggested that Alzheimer's disease (see p. 776) may well begin with a chromosomal abnormality.

Twin studies and family studies have shown that there seem to be strong genetic links in some types of mental disorder. Box 32.7 outlines some research findings.

Environmental causes

As shown in Box 32.7, even when there seems to be a genetic predisposition to mental disorders, such as depression or schizophrenia, environmental influences also appear to play a part. As a simple example, if genetics alone were involved in the transmission and occurrence of mental disorder, the monozygotic twin studies should show 100 per cent concordance. As this is not so, environmental or other influences must be intervening. Various environmental theories have been put forward to account for mental disorders; some are discussed below.

Family theory

Family theory was one of the earlier theories of the cause of schizophrenia. The family is said to treat one of its members in such a bizarre manner that he or she is forced into irrational thought processes and strange behaviours and becomes schizophrenic. At one time the mother was thought to play a major role and the term 'schizophrenogenic mother' was coined to describe the mother who promoted this situation. This has been replaced by the term '**schizophrenogenic family**'. The view that schizophrenia arises from disturbed family interactions received considerable support from Laing (1961). However, although there may be disordered communications and double bind situations arising in some families with a schizophrenic member, research does not offer support for family theory. (An example of a double bind situation is where a parent may not show affection or want a child to be responsive, yet accuses the child of not caring if he or she does not show

GLOSSARY

Genetic predisposition An indicator in an individual's chromosomal/genetic makeup that there is a likelihood of a particular trait developing: for example, schizophrenia.

Schizophrenogenic family A family which is characterized by high levels of conflict and poor communication, creating an atmosphere which may promote the development of schizophrenia.

Box 32.7   Twin and family studies of mental disorder

Allen (1976) looked at the incidence of depression among twins. In monozygotic twins or identical twins (from one egg-cell) when one twin was diagnosed with depression, 40 per cent of their partners also suffered from depression, in other words there was a 40 per cent concordance. In dizygotic or fraternal twins (from two egg-cells) the concordance dropped to 11 per cent, which is a considerable drop, indicating that where twins share identical genes (monozygotic) the concordance is much higher than where twins share only 50 per cent of their genes (dizygotic).

No exact chromosomal defect has as yet been identified as responsible for depression. Research was carried out among the Amish community in the USA, who only marry within their own community and therefore present a restricted gene pool. There Egeland et al. (1987) identified a genetic marker on chromosome 11 as being implicated in manic depression.

However, other studies have identified various different chromosomes as being implicated in depression, so the true situation may not be 'a defective chromosome'. In fact there may be many types of depression, all of which may have different genetic origins, or some may have no genetic links.

In the same way it may be wrong to regard schizophrenia, for example, as one homogeneous disorder; it may be a group of disorders with separate origins.

Gottesman and Shields (1982) studied twins, where schizophrenia had developed, and found a 45 per cent concordance rate among monozygotic twins and 14 per cent concordance among dizygotic twins.

Kety et al. (1968, 1975) points out that the incidence of schizophrenia in the general population is 1 per cent, but if one or both parents are schizophrenic, 40 per cent of the offspring are also diagnosed as schizophrenic if living with one or more of the parents. However, this concordance rate drops dramatically to 3 per cent,

according to Kety, if the offspring have been adopted. This would indicate a strong environmental influence mediating the genetic component.

An indication of the risks of being affected with schizophrenia for the different kinds of relatives of a person suffering from schizophrenia is shown below. These data were pooled from about 40 studies carried out in Western Europe between 1920 and 1987 by Irving Gottesman (1991), a leading researcher in schizophrenia. The data are arranged according to the degree of genetic relatedness. As can be seen, extent of the risk increases as the degree of relatedness becomes closer.

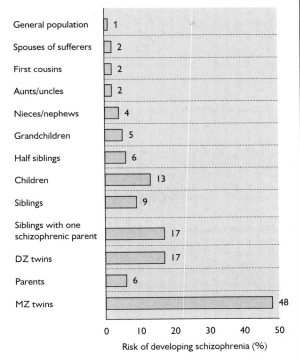

The genetic risk of developing schizophrenia (after Gottesman, 1991)

affection.) The importance of the family's attitudes to a schizophrenic member is highlighted by Brown et al.'s (1966) study, which showed that family attitudes towards expressing support and emotion have a profound effect on whether a schizophrenic relapses and returns to hospital.

Sociogenic hypothesis

Sociogenic hypothesis suggests that schizophrenia is prevalent in lower socioeconomic groups. Hollingshead and Redlich (1958) carried out a ten-year study in Connecticut, USA, and found that schizophrenia rates were twice as high in the lowest socioeconomic group as in the next group. Kohn (1968) reports that this is supported by studies in Denmark, Norway and England. Interpreted in causal terms, being in the lowest social class may in itself cause schizophrenia, due to simply being a member of this social class. One would urge caution in using this interpretation; there may be other factors, such as infections, eating and drinking habits, and even diagnostic problems as discussed in the last chapter, which may be clouding the issue. There is also the possibility that schizophrenic patients may not have started in the lowest socioeconomic group, but have drifted downwards as a result of their schizophrenia (see below).

Social drift theory

Social drift theory suggests that individuals who are schizophrenic are unable to sustain social status and drift downwards to the lowest socioeconomic group. This theory can be examined by comparing the parents' occupations and socioeconomic status with that of the person with schizophrenia. Goldberg and Morrison (1963) did this and found evidence of social drift, but Hollingshead and Redlich (1958) did not, and supported the sociogenic theory, as did Kohn and other researchers.

Sociocultural factors

The influence of cultural factors may be indicated in societies where there is more than one subculture and where diagnostic processes and classification are the same for both. In a study in the former Yugoslavia, researchers found that the incidence of schizophrenia in the Istrian peninsula was twice that of Croatia; each region is occupied by a separate subculture.

Reactive depression

Some types of reactive depression may be thought to have a solely environmental cause, in that they are a reaction to an event in the individual's environment: for example, a death in the family. However, not everyone who loses a close family member suffers from clinical depression which goes beyond the bounds of the normal grief suffered by others. There must be extra factors involved in reactive depression, either genetic, biological or further environmental factors.

Neurochemical and neurological causes

Neurochemicals are biochemicals which are located in the brain (see Box 32.8 for a brief description of nervous transmission, which is described more fully in Chapter 8). Neurotransmitters are chemicals held in the synapse which are released in order to make the next neuron in that circuit fire. This is the way information is passed on through the nervous system. If too much of a neurotransmitter is present (or too little of the enzyme which deactivates it) then the neuron will fire too frequently and misinformation will be passed on.

The dopamine theory

In some schizophrenics too much of the neurotransmitter dopamine is present; this may account for hallucinations and strange motor movements produced, for the dopamine circuit is involved in perception and motor control. Of course, excess dopamine production could be the result of schizophrenia, rather than the cause; research into the dopamine theory is not entirely conclusive as yet.

Phenothiazine drugs block the action of dopamine, thereby lessening schizophrenic symptoms. However, Haracz (1982) found that this applies only to one subgroup of schizophrenics, suggesting that not all produce excess dopamine. This would serve to reinforce the view that schizophrenics are not all suffering from the same disorder.

Mood disorders

Investigations have shown that low levels of the neurotransmitters serotonin and norepinephrine seem to be implicated in depression. Drugs which have been found to alleviate depression are those which are known to raise the levels of serotonin and norepinephrine in the brains of animals (see Chapter 8).

GLOSSARY

Sociogenic hypothesis A term used to describe the possibility that low socioeconomic status makes the development of schizophrenia more likely.

Social drift theory A proposal that individuals who develop schizophrenia may have drifted into the lowest socioeconomic group as a result of their schizophrenia.

Dopamine theory A proposal that the symptoms of schizophrenia are directly caused by an excess of dopamine in the brain.

Box 32.8 The brain and nervous transmission

Q. **How are messages passed around the body?**
A. Messages are passed around the body via a series of **axons** (or nerves) which are linked to **neurons** (or nerve-cell bodies). Transmission of messages along axons within both the brain and the body is an **electrochemical process**; different molecules along the axons are positively and negatively charged. These 'change places' during stimulation and cause a ripple effect of electrical activity along the axon.

Q. **What goes on in the brain?**
A. The **brain** decodes the incoming messages sent along incoming axons, decides what action is to be taken, and sends out messages along other axons to **effectors** such as muscles. Some areas of the brain have been found to have specific functions, but the exact mode of functioning of the brain as a whole is still a mystery to us. This is essentially a simplified explanation; if you are interested in knowing more, there is further reading at the end of Chapter 8.

Q. **Are neurons joined together?**
A. Not directly. There is a minute gap between the axon of one neuron and the **dendrites** (tentacle-like outgrowths of the neuron) of the next cell body. This gap is called the **synaptic cleft**, and messages are passed across this by the chemical action of **neurotransmitters**.

Q. **What is a neurotransmitter?**
A. A chemical contained in a **synapse** (a bulb or button at the end of an axon), which is released on excitation to take up its position on the receptor sites in the dendrites of the next neuron in the chain.
  The action of neurotransmitters can be either **excitatory** (stimulating) or **inhibitory** (damping). When neurotransmitters have transmitted their chemical message and stimulated the neuron to fire, or inhibited it from firing, they are **deactivated**, usually broken down by an **enzyme**, or taken up again into the system. Absence of adequate neurotransmitter substances means that the neuron will not be stimulated enough for the message to be passed on. Too much neurotransmitter means that the neuron will be over-stimulated. Absence of the enzyme means that the neurotransmitter will not be broken down and will continually stimulate the neuron.

Neurological findings

Neurological investigations of the brains of schizophrenics, using CAT or PET scans (see the Introduction to Part 2), show that the ventricles are enlarged, suggesting deterioration or atrophy of brain tissue. Rieder et al. (1983) also found enlarged ventricles in the brains of other psychotic patients, besides schizophrenics.

SELF-ASSESSMENT QUESTIONS

1. What evidence is offered from genetic studies as to the causes of mental disorders?
2. What part might a person's environment play in the course of mental disorder?
3. What are the findings of neurological and neurochemical research into mental disorders?

Chapter summary

■ There is no general agreement on a definition of abnormality, which may be statistical, social, maladaptive or a matter of personal distress. Legally, abnormality involves not knowing right from wrong and/or lack of responsibility for one's actions.

■ Paradigms of abnormality include psychoanalytic, physiological/medical, learning theory, cognitive and humanistic models. Normality is no easier to define but may include efficient self-perception, realistic self-esteem, voluntary control over behaviour, a true perception of the world and the ability to sustain relationships, to give affection and to organize and sustain a fulfilling lifestyle.

■ Some psychiatrists, including Szasz and Laing, maintain that equating abnormality with mental illness removes responsibility from the individual for self-control. Society also has an ambivalent attitude towards abnormality and it has been suggested that it should be viewed in a moral rather a medical context. Laing and others have rejected medical models for mental illness, advocating safe environments for schizophrenics where they could live without pressures. It was suggested that illness was organic rather than mental.

■ Szasz argues that society is too intolerant of behaviour which does not match its expectations. People may be treated as mentally ill when they are just different from others. It is suggested that mental illness is either organic, physical illness exhibiting mental symptoms or disorders of psychosocial or interpersonal functioning.

■ Mental disorder has fallen historically into two categories, psychosis and neurosis. While psychosis involves the whole personality and sufferers lose touch with reality, neurosis does not affect the whole personality and the individual does not lose touch with reality. The International Classification of Diseases (ICD) published by the World Health Organization is now in its tenth edition, while in the United States the American Psychiatric Association has developed the Diagnostic and Statistical Manual of Mental Disorder, the fourth editon of which was published in 1994 (DSMIV).

■ DSMIV uses a multiaxial system of classification, using five main axes of information: current problem, previous problem(s), physical disorders, the severity of psychosocial stressors and finally a global assessment of an individual's functioning.

■ Mental disorder has been put into two broad categories: learning difficulties and mental illness. For diagnosis a clinician may use clinical interviews, psychological and physiological tests, behavioural observation and self-monitoring. Problems with diagnosis include problems of reliability, validity and labelling. Many surveys have shown medical diagnosis to be unreliable but this does not mean that diagnosis should be discontinued. This applies equally to psychiatric diagnosis.

■ Organic mental disorders are due to deterioration of the brain or degeneration of the nervous system. These include Parkinson's disease, which is caused by

a malfunction of the neurotransmission system; Alzheimer's disease, which is classified as presenile dementia, resulting from degeneration of the brain cells; dementia associated with human immunodeficiency virus (HIV) and disorders resulting from brain damage or disease such as meningitis, accident or trauma, or tumours.

■ Alcoholism may cause brain damage which includes Wernicke's disease and Korsakoff's psychosis. The former is associated with damage to the pons, cerebellum and mamillary bodies and the latter additionally causing damage to the thalamus. Anterograde amnesia may result, in addition to the drowsiness, confusion and unsteady gait characteristic of Wernicke's disease.

■ Drug abuse results in a number of physiological, behavioural and cognitive phenomena. Increasing tolerance necessitates more frequent or higher doses of the drug while deprivation of the drug is associated with withdrawal symptoms, which can be severe.

■ Schizophrenia may also be regarded as an organic disorder of which there are four subtypes, simple schizoprenia, hebephrenic schizophrenia, catatonic schizophrenia and paranoid schizophrenia, each of which is characterized by its own symptoms.

■ Mood-related disorders include mania, single or recurrent depressive episodes and manic depression. Mania is characterized by high elation and activity, depression by loss of energy, lack of enjoyment of usual activities and poor drive. Manic depression involves alternation of mania and depression.

■ Neurotic and stress-related disorders include phobias, obsessive-compulsive disorders, somatoform disorders and multiple personality (dissociative disorder). In addition post-traumatic stress disorder, a response to, for instance, an accident or natural disaster, may be classified as a neurotic/stress-related disorder.

■ Behavioural disorders can include eating disorders such as anorexia nervosa or bulimia, and puerperal disorders such as postnatal depression which may be mild or severe. In extreme cases mothers may threaten to harm either themselves or their infants.

■ Personality disorders include dissocial personality (psychopathic or sociopathic personality), schizoid personality, narcissistic personality and paranoid personalities.

- Other disorders include learning difficulties or retardation, and developmental difficulties including autism, dyslexia and ADHD, already discussed elsewhere.

- Causes of mental disorders may be genetic, environmental or neurochemical/neurological. Individuals may have a genetic predisposition to mental disorder: depression, for instance. It is suggested that Alzheimer's disease and schizophrenia may have genetic bases. Environmental causes suggested include family theory, sociogenic hypothesis, social drift theory or sociocultural factors. Some types of reactive depression are thought to have solely environmental causes.

- Neurochemical causes include malfunction of neurotransmitters such as dopamine, serotonin and norepinephrine. These may be implicated in schizophrenia and in depression.

Further reading

Blakemore, C. (1988). *The Mind Machine*. London: BBC Books. A readable and informative book. Each chapter deals with one specific area of mental disorder.

Davison, G. and Neale, J. (1994). *Abnormal Psychology*, 6th edn. New York: Wiley. A very good, in-depth approach to all aspects of abnormality, including description, diagnosis and treatments.

Laing, R.D. (1965). *The Divided Self*. Harmondsworth: Penguin. A readable (though not always credible) account of schizophrenia from a view that opposes the medical model.

Sacks, O. (1985). *The Man Who Mistook His Wife for a Hat*. London: Picador. Each chapter is a case description relating to a particular form of mental problem. A readable and often entertaining book.

CHAPTER 33

Treatments and therapies

Somatic treatments   791
- Drug therapy   791
- Psychosurgery   793
- Electroconvulsive therapy (ECT)   793

Behavioural therapies   795
- Behaviour therapy based on classical conditioning   795
- Behaviour modification based on operant conditioning   797
- Biofeedback   798
- Modelling   799
- Evaluation of behavioural therapies   799

Cognitive-behavioural therapies   800
- Beck's cognitive-behaviour therapy   800
- Rational emotive therapy   800
- Personal construct theory   800
- Evaluation of cognitive-behavioural therapies   801

Psychoanalytic therapies   801
- Classical psychoanalysis   801
- Ego analysis   802
- Play therapy   802
- Evaluation of psychoanalytic therapies   802

Humanistic-existential therapies   803
- Rogers's client-centred therapy   803
- Gestalt therapy   804
- Transactional analysis   804
- Evaluation of humanistic-existential therapies   804

Treatment effectiveness and patient care   804
- Concept of cure   805
- Comparing therapies   805
- Conclusions on treatment effectiveness   806
- Institutionalization or care in the community?   807

Objectives

By the end of this chapter you should be able to:

- Differentiate between various forms of treatment available for mental disorders;

- Relate those treatments to the various models or approaches to psychology from which they are derived;

- Discuss research that indicates which treatment may be beneficial for a specific form of mental disorder;

- Discuss the concept of 'cure' in relation to mental disorders;

- Consider different forms of accommodation available to patients and clients who are undergoing treatment for mental disorders.

There are five major areas into which treatments are divided; these relate to the theories or assumptions of the five main approaches to psychology, as briefly described in the models or paradigms discussed in Chapter 32.

The psychoanalytic model utilizes insight therapies,

where clients are encouraged to examine their past in order to gain insight into their current problem (see pp. 801–2). Many of the theorists who are referred to as humanistic psychologists may have started from a psychoanalytical perspective (for example, Rogers), but now believe that their therapies are best concentrated on the here-and-now situation, rather than looking to the client's past (see the section on humanistic-existential therapies).

The medical model suggests that somatic (physical) treatments are appropriate in order to put right physical maladjustment of the body. This would then automatically be followed by a commensurate adjustment by the mind; these treatments are described in the first section of the chapter.

The learning theory model forms the basis of treatments used by the behaviourists (see the second section of this chapter), who aim to correct problem behaviours instilled through faulty learning, by teaching appropriate behaviours. This is also a basic assumption for the derivation of treatments applied by the cognitive theorists, who also aim to change the faulty thinking which they believe is the precursor of maladaptive behaviours. Methods of doing this vary according to their theoretical persuasion. Cognitive treatments also involve the client's active use of cognitive processes, such as reasoning, in order to change resultant behaviour. A few of these are discussed in the section on cognitive-behavioural therapies.

The final part of this chapter looks at some studies of treatment effectiveness, and also the suitability of different forms of accommodation currently offered to people suffering from mental disorders.

Somatic treatments

Somatic treatments are physical treatments designed to redress a balance in the individual's physical body (soma), in order that psychological functioning will be affected and normalized. This is based on the premise that there is a mind–body relationship (Clare, 1980) and that an imbalance or malfunction of the body, especially the brain, may be the cause or the result of mental disorder. This has already been discussed in Chapter 32 with regard to schizophrenia, for example. This section looks at somatic treatments for mental disorders.

Drug therapy

There are five main groups of drugs used in psychiatry:

- Minor tranquillizers,
- Major tranquillizers (antipsychotic),
- Stimulants,
- Antidepressants,
- Antibipolar drugs.

Each of these five categories is described below (a summary of the five categories is also contained in Figure 8.11 in Part 2).

As with all drugs, care must be taken in their administration. Clinicians must be sure of the capabilities of a patient before sending them home with a bottle of tablets saying, 'Take one three times a day for two weeks, then come back and see me'. Many drugs are addictive, promoting psychological or physiological dependence and therefore must be used under close supervision for short periods of time only.

Minor tranquillizers

As the name suggests, these are used to reduce anxiety in patients who are not deeply disturbed. They are also used for patients who suffer depression where anxiety is also a feature (mainly reactive or exogenous depression, those classified as suffering from single depressive episode syndrome, as described in Chapter 32).

These drugs are usually prescribed by general practitioners, and began to be widely used in the 1950s to replace barbiturates, which had been found to be addictive. However, it was later discovered that the minor tranquillizers also produced psychological and physiological dependence; therefore they are now prescribed less frequently and monitored more carefully than in the 1960s.

Many people who take benzodiazepines complain of drowsiness and lethargy; for this reason and also because of the problem of addiction, long-term usage is not recommended. Noyes et al. (1984) found that these drugs produce greater improvement in patients with

---

GLOSSARY

Somatic treatments Physical treatments designed to restore a balance in the body (soma) in order to improve psychological functioning.

panic disorders or anxious depression, than patients given a placebo. (A placebo is a form of treatment which, unknown to the patient, is not expected to have any effect upon the problem. This is a truer method of comparison than nontreatment of the control group, who would not be expecting to get any better without treatment – as previously shown, expectation is a powerful force in humans. Here the placebo would be a pill or capsule with no active chemical constituents. Of course, one should question the ethics of treatment by placebo; all patients should expect to receive the optimum available treatment for their problem.)

Major tranquillizers

These drugs (also called neuroleptics, or antipsychotic drugs) are used mainly to reduce extreme anxiety in acute psychotic episodes. They are also used for schizophrenics as they appear to reduce the level of delusions and hallucinations as well as anxiety. This was discovered initially by accident; a French surgeon, Laborit, in the 1950s, noted that the drug he gave his patients to reduce surgical shock also made them less anxious about their impending operations. The drug was refined to enhance its anxiety-reducing properties and shortly afterwards Charpentier produced a new phenothiazine derivative called chlorpromazine, which proved very effective in calming schizophrenics. It appears to block impulse transmission in the dopaminergic pathways to the brain.

A study of various treatments available to schizophrenics, carried out by May (1968), found phenothiazines or phenothiazines plus psychotherapy, to be the two equally most effective therapies available, rather than ECT (discussed later), psychotherapy alone or Milieu therapy (a therapy based on the idea of a therapeutic community where patients are kept busy for 85 per cent of their waking hours, given responsibilities and expected to participate in community decisions). The same pattern of results was found in a five-year follow-up (May et al., 1976).

Phenothiazines cannot be regarded as a cure for schizophrenia; patients need to be kept on a maintenance dose in order to prevent relapses. Vaughn and Leff (1976) showed that schizophrenics discharged without drugs were much more likely to relapse and needed to return to hospitalization. Side-effects of phenothiazines can be unpleasant, ranging from dryness of the mouth and blurred vision to tremors closely resembling Parkinson's disease (an organic

disease linked with inadequate dopamine in the brain). These motor effects stem from dysfunction of the nerve tracts descending from the brain to spinal motor neurons.

Stimulants

Amphetamine and piperidyl derivatives are currently prescribed for hyperactive children. It may sound strange to give stimulants to children who are already hyperactive. However, the drug seems to give direction to the activity by increasing concentration. Optimum performance seems to occur when combined with behaviour therapy (Gittleman-Klein et al., 1976).

Side-effects include changes in appearance, for example sunken cheeks, dark circles under the eyes (Mattes and Gittleman, 1983) and in large doses may even interfere with learning and performance on cognitive tasks (Sprague and Sleator, 1977). The drugs may be prescribed in the short term to counteract lethargy and increase alertness and confidence; they are of course open to abuse.

Antidepressants

The tricyclics and MAO (monoamine oxidase) inhibitors are subcategories of antidepressants which produce therapeutic effects by facilitating neural transmission. The tricyclic drugs were found to be more effective in relieving endogenous depression (Stern et al., 1980).

Klerman (1975) found MAO inhibitors to be less effective than tricyclics in relieving depression, but they are still prescribed for patients who do not respond to tricyclics. Care needs to be taken as side-effects of MAO inhibitors can be severe; toxicity can cause damage to liver, brain and cardiovascular system; they also interact with other drugs and foods high in tyramine (for example, broad beans, cheese, chicken liver, yeast extracts) and can cause death. Both MAO inhibitors and tricyclics have been used successfully to treat obsessive-compulsive disorder (Insell et al., 1983), bulimia (Walsh et al., 1984) and panic attacks (Zitrin et al., 1983).

GLOSSARY

Placebo A form of 'mock' treatment, for example an inactive substance such as a sugar pill, which, unknown to the patient, is not expected to have a direct effect upon a disorder.

More recently a new category of drugs, the anxiolytics, has been introduced to alleviate anxiety and depression (for a review see Nutt, 1990). Some of these are the serotonin-specific reuptake inhibitors (SSRI): Prozac, for example. In the brain, these drugs interfere with the reabsorption of serotonin after it has reached the receptor sites; consequently its action is prolonged, and the effect of the serotonin is enhanced. There are claimed to be fewer side-effects with SSRIs than with other antidepressants, probably because of its mode of action.

Antibipolar drugs

These are used to treat people suffering bipolar disorder (manic depression). As discussed previously, the difficulty in treating manic depressive patients arises because overtreatment of either phase can 'tip' the patient's balance into the other phase, or pole. Treatment with lithium carbonate (inorganic salts) seems to iron out the problem of these bipolar swings, although Shopsin et al. (1975) found no difference in effectiveness between neuroleptics and lithium carbonate. However, lithium carbonate also acts as a prophylactic – it forestalls subsequent episodes of mania or depression (Prien et al., 1984). The drug requires the careful monitoring of blood levels, as an overdose can prove fatal.

Psychosurgery

Pioneered by Moniz, in the late 1930s, early psychosurgery was a crude affair. Incisions were made either through the side of the skull or through the orbital region (eye socket) into the frontal lobes, where rotation of surgical instruments destroyed a considerable amount of brain tissue. The rationale was that the frontal lobes controlled the thought processes and emotional expression, therefore if the tracts connecting these to the thalamus and hypothalamus (subcortical brain structures) were severed, irrational, emotional thoughts and behaviours would be lessened.

Exaggerated claims of success for the treatment of schizophrenia, depression, personality and anxiety disorders were made, which were not borne out by later studies of outcome. Robbin (1958, 1959) found that lobotomy produced a slightly higher discharge rate, but these patients were later readmitted. Barahal (1958) did five- to ten-year follow-up studies on lobotomy patients and found that most suffered undesirable side-effects such as listlessness, stupor, seizures and even

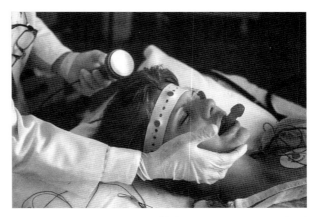

A patient being prepared for ECT. There are important ethical and practical issues associated with its use

death. Also, lobotomized patients often lost something special – their own unique personality. For example, some became child-like or unresponsive to the opinions of others.

Adverse publicity and the advent of use of phenothiazines in the 1950s lowered the rate of lobotomies performed. Currently, surgical techniques are precise and refined, so that very small areas of brain tissue are destroyed. Patients are selected carefully, when other treatments have been ineffective for their severe, long-lasting problems. Higher rates of success have been shown with obsessive compulsive disorder, severe depression and anxiety; the technique is rarely if ever used for schizophrenia.

Electroconvulsive therapy (ECT)

The introduction of electroconvulsive therapy (ECT) replaced insulin therapy – a treatment whereby nondiabetics were injected with insulin to produce coma, and then 'brought round' with intravenous dextrose. Sakel (1938) reported that patients thus treated were less confused and the treatment reduced psychotic symptoms. About the same time, it was

---

GLOSSARY

Psychosurgery The removal of small amounts of brain tissue in specific locations in order to reduce abnormal behaviours such as severe obsessions or (controversially) extreme aggression.

Electroconvulsive therapy (ECT) The delivery of a brief electric current to the head in order to alleviate disorders such as depression.

observed (mistakenly) that schizophrenia patients did not suffer from epilepsy, therefore if they could be given epileptic seizures, it might 'cure' their schizophrenia. Cerletti first used the technique in 1938, in Rome, of administering an electric current to the skull to induce a grand mal seizure to a schizophrenic patient. Nowadays, patients are given a sedative and muscle relaxant, which lessens the possibility of broken bones during seizures.

A course of six to ten treatments is spread over three to four weeks. Often patients show an improvement after only one or two treatments. Currently, unilateral ECT is used, inducing seizure in only one brain hemisphere; this has the effect of causing less confusion and memory loss to the patient than previously experienced in bilateral ECT, but has been shown to be equally therapeutic (Inglis, 1969; Abrams, 1975).

ECT is now used primarily for profoundly depressed patients, who have failed to respond to drug treatment, especially if there is any threat or risk of suicide. It appears to be extremely successful in a number of cases, although the way in which it works is not understood; it does not prevent future episodes of depression. It is not used for schizophrenia as drug therapy is usually more effective.

Box 33.1 examines some of the practical and ethical issues arising from the use of somatic treatments.

? SELF-ASSESSMENT QUESTIONS

1. What do you understand by 'somatic treatments'?
2. What are the major categories of drugs used in psychiatry? Briefly describe some of their effects on behaviour.
3. Briefly discuss some of the practical and ethical problems that arise when somatic treatments are used.

Box 33.1   Somatic treatments – ethical and practical issues

Somatic treatments aim to alter abnormal functioning by intervening directly in the body's processes. Drugs act at the biochemical level, usually by action at the synapse, either reducing or enhancing the action of the neurotransmitter. Psychosurgery changes behaviour by severing brain tissue and physically lessening transmission routes, although whether these changes are for the better or worse, is a point for discussion. The action of ECT, causing brain seizures to reduce depression, is not understood, but may possibly cause a temporary change in neurochemical levels.

Drug therapy is by far the most popular treatment and that which is always tried first. ECT is used selectively and only after drug treatment has been shown to be ineffective. Criticisms of ECT treatment include the following:

- The problems of side-effects, such as confusion and memory-loss.
- We do not know how ECT works, or even (some might argue) if it does work at all; perhaps patients' abnormal behaviours are simply 'damped down' by the trauma of the treatment.
- Ethical questions have been raised as to whether it is permissible to give patients electric shocks, given that it is not known for certain how or even if the treatment provides a 'cure'. Objections have been raised on these grounds by MIND (the National Association for Mental Health) and PROMPT (Protect the Rights of Mental Patients) and similar organizations in the United States.

Protagonists (e.g. Klerman, 1972, 1988) maintain that ECT is the most effective treatment for depression and should therefore be continued. The alternative of drug therapy may provide after-effects which are just as unpleasant.

Psychosurgery is practised rarely, because of the uncertainty of success or side-effects in individual cases and because of the irreversibility of the procedure. There is an on-going and heated controversy about the ethics, usefulness and the side-effects of psychosurgery.

Patients are within their rights to refuse any form of treatment with which they do not agree and ask that an alternative form of treatment be made available. Whether they always understand their rights, given that they are in a disturbed frame of mind, is another matter. The psychiatrist may regard alternative treatments requested to be inappropriate; if that treatment is refused, is the clinician then in the wrong for refusing treatment? The areas of consent and ethics need careful clarification if the best interests of the patient are to be served.

Behavioural therapies

Behavioural therapies are based largely on the theories of operant or classical conditioning, which are briefly described in Chapter 32 and fully discussed in Chapter 6. The premise is that all behaviour is learned; faulty learning is the cause of abnormal behaviour, therefore the individual has to learn the correct or acceptable behaviour.

The first part of this section deals with therapies based on classical conditioning (where involuntary associations and responses are made by the individual); these are usually referred to as **behaviour therapies**. Those based on operant conditioning (described in the latter part of this section) are called **behaviour modification** or sometimes operant conditioning techniques, in order to distinguish them from techniques based on classical conditioning (Walker, 1984). Behaviour modification involves the use of voluntary responses. Finally, the section briefly considers modelling, a technique which is based on the principles of social learning theory (see Chapter 6).

Behaviour therapy based on classical conditioning

This theory suggests that a response is learned and repeated through contiguous association (a chance association in time or place). Pavlov's dogs salivated when a buzzer sounded, because initially the buzzer had sounded when their food was presented. Why do you like a particular name? Is it because the first time you heard it, it was paired with a person you liked? Classical conditioning suggests that a great deal of human learning occurs in this way, not all of it quite so innocuous as this example. Treatments which aim to replace a disadvantageous response pattern with a more appropriate response include: systematic desensitization, aversion therapy, covert sensitization, implosion and flooding. These are described below.

Systematic desensitization

Patients are taught to relax and then shown pictures of their feared object or problem, to desensitize them, or reduce their unfavourable response patterns. These stimuli systematically commence with less threatening and proceed to more threatening representations of the real object. Phobias are often treated successfully in this way. Exposure to the feared object or situation (rather than avoidance, which is usually practised by sufferers) shows the patient that there is no real reason for their anxiety. Between therapy sessions they are given 'homework' and asked to put themselves into what are to them progressively threatening situations. Paul (1966) found systematic desensitization more effective for phobics than insight therapy or attention plus a placebo pill.

Aversion therapy

This is used mainly for addictions or unwanted behaviours. The aim is to attach negative feelings to stimuli which are considered inappropriately attractive. For example, if an emetic is paired with alcohol, the next alcoholic drink becomes less attractive. Electric shocks have been used as the 'pairing' but the ethical questions posed by these discourage their use (see Box 33.2). The effects of aversion therapy may

---

Box 33.2   Aversion therapy to save a life

Lang and Melamed (1969) report the case of a nine-month-old baby, who exhibited **vomiting** and **chronic rumination** (regurgitating food and re-chewing it). Tests had been run, and no physiological problem was revealed. The child was suffering from malnutrition, and was being fed by tube directly into the stomach.

Aversion therapy treatment consisted of one-second shocks delivered to the baby's calf each time he showed signs of vomiting. The baby quickly learned that the way to avoid shocks was by not vomiting. After just two sessions shock was rarely required.

Throughout three weeks of observation and treatment the child steadily gained weight and was able to be discharged from hospital. Five months later he was regarded as completely normal, both physically and psychologically. Aversion therapy had undoubtedly saved his life, although the ethical question of cure through pain remains.

GLOSSARY

Behavioural therapies Treatments for mental disorder which draw on the principles of classical conditioning (behaviour therapy) and operant conditioning (behaviour modification).

be short-lived and, when used, it is often accompanied by other positive techniques.

Covert sensitization

This is similar to aversion therapy but clients are asked to imagine both their attractive stimuli and accompanying negative states, such as electric shocks or vomiting. This reduces the ethical question of unpleasant stimulus pairings.

Implosion therapy and flooding

Used mainly for the treatment of phobias, the essence of both these therapies is to expose the client at the outset to a most fearful situation. The premise is 'fighting fear with fear'. Once the client has been exposed to the most horrific situation he or she can possibly imagine, the object or situation is feared no longer. The therapist encourages the high arousal levels of the situation for up to an hour at a time.

In implosion therapy the therapist also elaborates the situation by constructing stories and outrageous scenarios, as, when linked to psychodynamic theory, the phobia is seen to represent repressed sexual or aggressive id impulses. For example, the spider phobic

I'M USING FLOODING THERAPY FOR HER SPIDER PHOBIA.

may be asked to imagine a giant spider who devours their eyes, crawls into the eye sockets and eats its way into the brain! Implosion therapy takes place in the client's imagination, whereas flooding takes place *in vivo* (a real-life situation). For example, Wolpe (1958) took a patient with a fear of cars for a four-hour car journey. The girl became hysterical as her anxiety levels rose, but eventually became calm and by the end of the journey her fears had disappeared. Extinction of the client's fear responses occur because the usual route of escape or avoidance is blocked by the therapist. Other therapists (e.g. Emmelkamp and Wessels, 1975) found flooding to be more effective than implosion.

Ethical considerations in the use of behaviour therapy are considered in Box 33.3.

Box 33.3 Ethical considerations in the use of behaviour therapy

Systematic desensitization seems a relatively benign technique; it is difficult to realize that flooding, implosion and aversion therapy stem from the same theoretical position. There are serious questions about the ethics of using these methods, especially if they are no more effective than less traumatic methods. Supporters of flooding and implosion therapy claim its effectiveness (Marks, 1981; Barratt, 1969). It is quick and therefore less costly for the client than other protracted therapies. However, the cost to the client may not only be in monetary terms, and some therapists suggest these techniques should be used only when other means fail.

Aversion therapy is not often used nowadays for alcohol-related problems, as pairings have to be repeated in order to be effective, and other methods are more successful. There are ethical controversies about whether therapists should hurt people with electric shocks, even when those people have requested that treatment; they may be requesting punishment rather than treatment. At one time this treatment was used for homosexuals, pairing electric shocks with photographs of attractive men. The effectiveness of this treatment was never satisfactorily proven and the practice has now ceased for ethical reasons. Some investigations have failed to show any superiority of aversion therapy over placebo treatment (Diament and Wilson, 1975).

Behaviour modification based on operant conditioning

Behaviour modification is based on the premise that actions which are rewarded (or reinforced) are more likely to be repeated. Actions or behaviours involved are voluntary behaviours, because the reinforcement is recognized by the individual as relating to that action over which they have control.

Behaviour modification aims to instil appropriate behaviour through the reinforcement of desired or more acceptable actions. This is best achieved in situations where the therapist is in control, as reinforcement must be consistent and unwavering (Wilson and O'Leary, 1980). A range of childhood problems are dealt with by operant techniques: for example, bedwetting, thumb sucking, hyperactivity, poor school performance, extreme social withdrawal. Children are under the control of adults, and therefore susceptible to operant conditioning. It generally produces better rates of improvement than other therapies (Franks, 1984; Ross, 1981). This technique has also been extended, with success, to autistic and mentally retarded children, to improve social skills (Williams et al., 1975) and table manners (Plummer et al., 1977). Lovaas (1973) found that gains achieved in therapy with autistic children were only maintained when their parents continued to reinforce the behaviour.

Reinforcers include praise, attention and some tangible rewards such as special food, sweets or toys. These are primary reinforcers, which the child has instant access to, and can use immediately. Non-reinforcers include ignoring the child when inappropriate behaviours are displayed. (Getting cross with the child, shouting or smacking involve giving the child attention and could therefore be construed as reinforcement of undesirable behaviours.) A fictitious example of how the programme might be used is contained in Box 33.4.

Token economy

Token economy is a natural progression from operant conditioning and uses the idea of secondary reinforcement, where the rewards are not to be used instantly, but take the form of tokens which have to be saved and exchanged later for a reward of the individual's choice. One method used is to give the individual tokens as desirable behaviours occur. These can be saved and exchanged for whatever the person wants; in hospitals,

Box 33.4 Behaviour modification programmes

Jenny is a teenage hostel resident with learning difficulties. She is not yet able to feed herself at meal times, and staff have devised a reinforcement programme to encourage Jenny to eat with a spoon. The reinforcement they decided upon was redcurrant jelly, as Jenny is very fond of this. Each time Jenny performs the correct steps in her programme, she is reinforced with a small teaspoonful of jelly. Task must be broken down into a sequence of steps.

Task breakdown

1. Picks up spoon, right way up.
2. Scoops food from dish on to spoon.
3. Raises spoon to mouth.
4. Tips food into mouth.
5. Returns empty spoon to dish.
6. Retains grip on spoon.
7. Repeats above sequence till food is eaten.

Exercise

Now, can you devise a task breakdown to teach Jenny to clean her teeth? Of course, redcurrant jelly would not be an appropriate reinforcement in this situation, but Jenny does enjoy catching sight of herself in the mirror.

they are exchangeable at the hospital shop for sweets, cigarettes or other items; on the ward they may be exchanged for special privileges such as extra TV viewing time. This technique is generally used with adults, or older children, who can make the association between the immediate, nonusable reinforcer and the later reinforcement.

Paul and Lentz (1977) compared three hospital wards of long-term institutionalized patients. One ward used token economy; one used milieu therapy (where residents are kept busy 85 per cent of their waking hours, and expected to contribute to the

> **GLOSSARY**
>
> **Token economy** A version of behaviour modification where reinforcements are not given in the form of an immediate reward but in the form of tokens which can be exchanged later for a reward of the individual's choice.

common good of their 'community'); the third ward used routine hospital management. Patients were checked monthly over four and a half years of hospitalization and 18 months follow-up. Both token economy and milieu therapy groups reduced symptomatic behaviour more than the routine group. More token economy patients were discharged to community placements, and were better at remaining in their placements than members of the other two groups. However, other social learning methods were used in conjunction with tokens, which were regarded as an excellent method of gaining the severely regressed patients' attention.

Problems of both token economy systems and behaviour modification are similar:

■ Reinforcement must be kept the same by all people who have dealings with the individual.
■ Improved behaviours may not be generalized to the 'real world' situation. The latter, of course, is a criticism of most types of therapy. Behaviour modification seems to cope with this better than most, as indicated by the Paul and Lentz study quoted above.
■ Insight theorists, such as psychoanalysts, suggest that the problem underlying the abnormal behaviours has not been resolved, even when the overt behaviour has been changed; consequently other abnormal behaviours may arise in their place; this is called symptom substitution. Reinforcers must always be appropriate to each individual; these must be carefully chosen, as what is reinforcement to one person may be anathema to another.

Biofeedback

The technique of **biofeedback**, which draws on the principles of both classical and operant conditioning, is discussed in Box 33.5.

Box 33.5 Biofeedback

This technique draws on the principles of both classical and operant conditioning. Individuals are trained to control bodily processes such as heart rate and blood pressure, which are normally under autonomic control rather than voluntary control. Typically, patients are connected to a machine which gives a continuous reading of heart rate and blood pressure. They are trained to relax and are asked to try consciously to reduce one or both. When the readout falls to a given target level, a bell or tone sounds. The patient aims to maintain that level. The reinforcement (as in operant conditioning) for hypertensive patients, in doing this, is the knowledge that they are helping to improve their own health.

Biofeedback techniques developed from studies using rats. Miller and DiCara (1967) showed that animals paralysed by the use of a curare could control their breathing rate and other autonomic functions if given a reward in the form of direct electrical brain stimulation. This was a particularly interesting finding because up to then it had been believed that autonomic functions could only be affected through the process of classical conditioning and that operant conditioning applied only to voluntary behaviour.

Initial results were encouraging, but biofeedback has not been established as a standard treatment for raised blood pressure (Shapiro and Surwit, 1979). Blanchard et al. (1979) believed that relaxation training is more effective. Added to which, it might be necessary for individuals to change their life-styles, in order effectively to lower blood pressure in the 'real world' situation, rather than use biofeedback and assume that a 'cure' has been effective.

Various forms of epilepsy have been treated by biofeedback: patients are trained to increase cortical activity in the sensorimotor cortex. However, improvement was not sustained when training sessions lapsed (Sterman, 1973).

Neuromuscular disorders, such as cerebral palsy, paralysis following stroke or poliomyelitis, have been treated by biofeedback (Basmajian, 1977). Patients are informed by biofeedback of the firing of single muscle cells, and trained to reactivate these. Neural pathways which are disordered are normally under voluntary control and should therefore be ideal for retraining by biofeedback techniques. In damaged tissue, signs of muscle movement are faint and need amplification; this therefore acts both as a reinforcement and as a prompt for further effort.

Modelling

This is based on experimental work in social learning (see Chapter 6), such as that of Bandura (1965), and has been very effective in a clinical setting to treat phobias (Bandura et al., 1969). The technique involves allowing patients to watch both filmed and live models dealing with their phobic object. This results in a reduction in anxiety displayed by individuals when they came face-to-face with their feared object. An approach to health psychology, pioneered by Melamed et al. (1975), utilizes **modelling** to reduce children's fears of dental work or surgery.

Lazarus (1971) used therapist-demonstration to enable clients to rehearse difficult interpersonal behaviours; the therapist demonstrates for the client how to handle a difficult situation, which the client then practises in the therapy session. This approach is now frequently used in many areas of counselling and the technique is used with success in assertiveness training.

Evaluation of behavioural therapies

As has already been noted, many studies have offered testimony to the general success of behavioural therapies. It could be argued that such techniques improve the quality of life for many individuals who suffer from such problems as phobias, obsessive-compulsive disorders and poor personal and social skills. Marks (1981) concluded that behavioural therapies were the preferred choice for the treatment of about 25 per cent of nonpsychotic complaints. However, there have been a number of criticisms.

▨ The focus of behavioural therapies is on the 'here and now'. Overt behaviours are taken to be indicative of the patient's problem and these are to be corrected by therapy. The client's actual behaviour is taken to be the essence of his or her problem. Such therapies are criticized on the grounds that they only change overt behaviour and do not root out underlying causes. Therefore the patient's problem may still exist, and symptom substitution may occur (another maladaptive behaviour may be substituted).

▨ Biofeedback has its applications in behavioural medicine, but its usefulness and applications are more limited than were originally thought. Again, biofeedback could be 'curing' the overt behaviour but not the underlying cause.

▨ In a hospital situation, it has been suggested that improved interaction with staff, due to the introduction of behavioural programmes, is the real reinforcer that has brought about improvement in behaviour patterns (Fonagy and Higgitt, 1984).

▨ Behavioural therapies have been criticized on ethical grounds, in that they aim to remove unacceptable behaviours and substitute acceptable behaviours; decisions on acceptability rest with the therapist. Do therapists have the right to make decisions which affect other people's lives? In the real-world situation, the therapist should discuss with adult patients what their goals are and work towards those; in the case of a child, consultation would be with the child and the parent or guardian.

▨ 'Behaviour modification appears to offer a technology by which we can help people, but we cannot dominate them. Long may that state of affairs continue' (Baddeley, 1990).

⍰ SELF-ASSESSMENT QUESTIONS

1. Briefly describe the theoretical bases of behavioural therapies, such as classical and operant conditioning.
2. Describe a technique based on classical conditioning.
3. Describe a technique based on operant conditioning.
4. What are the strengths and weaknesses of behavioural therapies?

GLOSSARY

Biofeedback techniques Techniques which draw on the theoretical bases of both classical and operant conditioning. Patients are trained to control bodily processes such as heart rate and blood pressure, which are under autonomic control.

Modelling As a form of therapy, a technique which is an application of social learning theory and is used to treat disorders such as phobias. Patients watch a filmed or live model dealing with their phobic object or situation and this reduces anxiety when they are later exposed to the situation themselves.

Cognitive-behavioural therapies

Martin Seligman (1974) put forward his theory of **learned helplessness** as an explanation for depression. If an animal is given electric shocks from which it cannot escape, no matter which area of its environment it runs to, then that animal will lie down and passively accept the shocks. Learned helplessness theory views the depressed adult as having learned the helplessness of their own situation; depressed people often express negative views of themselves, the world around them and the future.

Cognitive restructuring theorists aim not only to change the behaviour of clients, but to change the negative outlook which the client has learned over time. They assist clients to change their perceptions, to use reasoning and through changed thought-processes to alter their behaviour. Descriptions of some of the main types of **cognitive-behavioural therapies** follow.

Beck's cognitive-behaviour therapy

Beck holds that mental disorders, particularly depression, are caused by the client's negative thought patterns which have been learned over years, possibly due initially to early failures or negative events in life, such as death of a close relative. Overgeneralization takes place, and everything is seen as a 'failure'.

Beck's therapy aims to change both cognitive and behavioural levels. Tasks are broken down into small steps, so that clients can see they are achieving something positive. Therapist and client work together to uncover what Beck calls 'automatic thoughts' – for example, a boy tells his father he failed his exam or did not make the football team; unbidden, the father thinks, 'What a lousy father I am'. The therapist helps to restructure the idea that the father is responsible for his son's failures – does it really make him a bad father? What other proof can he offer that he is a bad father?

Rush et al. (1977) compared two groups of depressed patients, one group given psychoactive drugs used for depression, the other 20 sessions of Beck's therapy. After the 12-week period of treatment, 79 per cent of the cognitive therapy group were much improved compared to 20 per cent of the drug group. The cognitive therapy group were also less depressed at follow-up.

Rational emotive therapy

Albert Ellis (1984) believes that people cause themselves emotional turmoil by repeating internalized sentences to themselves; a depressed person may continually internalize 'How worthless I am!' Ellis suggests that the therapist should concentrate on uncovering and restructuring those sentences, rather than looking at historical causes or overt behaviour, as self-statements can mediate emotional arousal. Clients are persuaded to substitute an internal dialogue to ease their problems, thus viewing their relationship to the world in a more rational light.

The views of Beck and Ellis may seem somewhat similar, but their techniques differ in several ways. Beck requires cooperative interaction between client and therapist, to uncover the problem; Ellis believes that forceful interventions may be necessary to disrupt well-learned maladaptive patterns, and will use confrontational methods early in therapy. Where Beck would enquire what made his client think he was a bad father, Ellis would say, 'So what if you are a bad father? Is it logical to be depressed about it? You do not have to be competent at everything. You have other areas of competence.' Ellis has no compunction about calling his client's thoughts 'irrational' and is more directive than Beck.

Personal construct therapy

Based on Kelly's personal construct theory (1955) (described in Chapters 24 and 30), the therapy aims to uncover the client's way of construing (interpreting) the world, and to change any false notions, in order to assist the client in 'functioning' more effectively (Fransella, 1984). Again, there is an interactive relationship between client and therapist. Kelly's repertory grid (see Box 30.5) is used to measure the client's construct system and to monitor the therapeutic process. Kelly's therapy differs in many respects from that of Beck or Ellis, but still aims to uncover the client's cognitive processes which give a

---

> **GLOSSARY**
>
> **Learned helplessness** Seligman's term for a state of apathy or helplessness which may result when an animal or human is unable to escape from a traumatic situation.
>
> **Cognitive-behavioural therapies** A group of therapies which make the assumption that faulty thinking can lead to mental disorder and maladaptive behaviour. Cognitive restructuring, relearning more positive ways of thinking, can lead to changes in behaviour.

personal construct on the world, and may serve to explain and change resultant behaviours.

Evaluation of cognitive-behavioural therapies

The cognitive-behavioural therapies, while not exploring the client's past, examine covert behaviour and internalized thoughts and aim to change those to rational, self-accepting statements. In doing so, the resultant behaviours will change too, and the client's problems will be resolved.

While the techniques of cognitive-behavioural therapists are similar to those of the behaviourists, they pay attention to what their clients perceive the world to be; situations are not regarded as uniform for everyone, so in that way the cognitive-behaviourists are approaching the platform of the humanists. However, as Wessler (1986) states, cognitive restructuring (attempts to change people's thought processes) is only a means to an end, that end being permanent changes in emotions and behaviour.

Cognitive therapies have been criticized on ethical grounds; the client's problem behaviours or thoughts are being changed to those which the therapist sees as acceptable; who is to say that they are correct?

❓ SELF-ASSESSMENT QUESTIONS

1. How do cognitive-behavioural therapies differ from behaviour therapies?
2. Describe an example of a cognitive restructuring therapy.
3. Discuss the strengths and weaknesses of cognitive-behavioural therapies.

Psychoanalytic therapies

Psychoanalytic therapy is based on Freud's psychoanalytic theory (see Chapter 30). Conflicts between the id and ego result in anxiety, which the individual tries to resolve by using defence mechanisms such as the following:

■ repression (pushing unwanted thoughts or memories back into the unconscious mind),
■ regression (going back to an earlier stage in one's life),

■ projection (projecting inadmissible feeling on to others).

The unconscious mind being the keeper of the individual's secret fears and wishes, the therapist aims to uncover these and bring them forward into the conscious mind. This must be done nondirectively, or the therapist could be suggesting his or her own wishes, which would then be used by the client, instead of drawing on the contents of the unconscious. The aim is to provide the client with insight into problems, to gain self-knowledge and understanding.

As discussed in Chapter 30, the purpose of psychoanalysis is to uncover problems, fears and motivations which have been forced into the unconscious mind. When these are consciously recognized they can be dealt with by the client. Freud believed that all psychological problems are rooted in the unconscious. There are many variations and therapies based on Freud's theory; here we shall look at just a few.

Classical psychoanalysis

In classical psychoanalysis the patient lies on a couch, with the therapist sitting out of sight so that the therapist remains anonymous and does not inhibit communication. In this way, the client will not be intimidated or influenced at all by the therapist, even by his or her body language, and relaxation (encouraged by lying on the couch) promotes a free flow of ideas, thoughts and feelings from the client. The client is free to talk about whatever comes to mind, no matter how disjointed or irrelevant it seems. This process is called **free association**. Gradually the client's associations will lead to uncovering of unconscious material. The client may occasionally encounter 'blocks', where he or she will stop talking, or change direction, or even get off the couch and walk over to the window. These 'blocks', Freud said, are important; they may indicate resistances – a point of repression.

GLOSSARY

Psychoanalytic therapy Treatment for mental disorder based on the psychoanalytic theory of Freud. The root of many neurotic problems is seen as lying in the repressed contents of the unconscious mind.

Free association A psychoanalytic technique where the client is encouraged to talk about whatever comes to mind, no matter how inappropriate it may seem.

Freud's consulting room

Dreams are regarded as important to analysis, as Freud assumed that during sleep the ego defences are lowered, allowing repressed wants and desires to come forward. They may also represent **wish fulfilment**, not directly expressing what the individual desires, but disguised in symbolic form within the dream. This is why analysis has to be undertaken by a trained professional.

At some time during therapy sessions, **transference** occurs, when the client transfers emotions on to the therapist which were held previously for significant others in the client's life. This transference is used in interpretation, explaining to the client what he or she has revealed, but specific advice on what to do next is not given; the person is encouraged to find his or her own solution.

Drake and Sederer (1986) suggest that intensive, intrusive therapies such as psychoanalysis can have a negative effect on schizophrenics, necessitating longer periods of hospitalization. They suggest this may be due to emotional overstimulation, which would concur with the findings of studies of schizophrenics from highly emotional families, discussed in Chapter 32.

Ego analysis

Theorists such as Karen Horney, Anna Freud and Erik Erikson emphasize the strength of the ego in the individual (as well as the id) and suggest that ego strength is why people take such an active role in trying to control their environment. Therapists seek to assist their clients in recognizing their ego functions (a set of conscious aims and capabilities, which can control both the id and the environment) and to select the optimum ways of changing themselves in order to interact with their environment to their best advantage.

Play therapy

Play therapy is the application of psychoanalytic therapy to children, who cannot – or will not – verbalize their problems. It was pioneered in the 1930s by Melanie Klein, a practising psychoanalyst (see Chapter 1).

In play therapy, the child acts out problems in a safe environment, the playroom, while the therapist observes, never criticizing or stopping the child from any form of play, however bizarre it may seem. From these observations, the therapist tries to determine the root of the child's problems.

Apart from this analytical process, the child has the opportunity to work through problems, to wreak vengeance on a doll, rather than a sibling or parent, to explore, seek solace and resolve emotional difficulties for himself or herself. Opportunities are given for the child to regress to earlier developmental stages and work through childhood experiences again, to a more satisfactory conclusion.

One version of play therapy is admirably described by Axline, in her book *Dibs: In Search of Self* (1964).

Evaluation of psychoanalytic therapies

The basic assumption of all psychoanalytic therapies is that the clients are not aware of what motivates their actions; it is rooted in the unconscious. Childhood fears and repressions are explored so that they may be rationalized by the adult ego state; an understanding of the root of the problem is the start of the cure.

There are problems of validation associated with psychoanalytical theory, as discussed in Chapter 30. There are further problems associated with evaluating

---

GLOSSARY

Wish fulfilment The expression, often through dreams, of a need or desire disguised in a symbolic form.

Transference During the course of psychoanalysis, the client transfers to the therapist emotions previously directed towards significant others: for example, the parents.

Play therapy Therapy which draws on the principles of psychoanalysis and uses play situations to treat children who are suffering emotional problems.

psychoanalytic therapies. How can internal id–ego conflicts be measured accurately? Who measures improvement – the client, by self-report, or the therapist, by other methods? (For a more detailed discussion of these ideas, see pp. 804–8.)

SELF-ASSESSMENT QUESTIONS

1. What are the fundamental principles and beliefs in psychoanalytic therapy?
2. How does ego analysis differ from classical psychoanalysis?
3. What are some criticisms of psychoanalytic therapies?

Humanistic-existential therapies

Humanistic therapies are a loosely-banded group of therapies with features in common; they are insight-oriented, like psychoanalytic therapies, believing that problems can best be dealt with by increasing the individual's awareness of needs and motivations. However, there is a far greater belief in the individual's freedom of choice; clients are assisted to find their own choice of action and the courage to use it. While the past may be acknowledged, therapies are rooted in the present. Humanistic psychologists also believe in the uniqueness of the individual, that no two cases can ever be identical, because everyone has their own unique combination of circumstances, characteristics and experiences; this is called phenomenology.

Rogers's client-centred therapy

See Chapters 1, 24 and 30 for descriptions of aspects of Rogers's theory of **client-centred therapy**. Emphasis is placed on the free will of the individual. However, Rogers suggests that freedom of choice is a gift which requires courage to use.

The therapist assists the client through accurate empathic understanding, seeing the world through the client's eyes and understanding feelings from the client's phenomenological viewpoint. The genuineness of the therapist is essential; Rogers suggests that if a therapist cannot wholly relate to a client, he or she should agree with the client to see a different therapist. The therapist, through honest self-disclosure, provides a model for the client.

Carl Rogers's therapy is essentially nondirective: the client must be encouraged, supported in a 'safe' environment, to find solutions and choose actions for himself or herself. The client must be given unconditional positive regard, in order to facilitate getting to know the self and learning to deal more effectively with problems, as learning is inhibited if the client feels that the approval of others must be constantly sought.

The possible mismatch between the 'perceived self' and the 'ideal self' can be monitored during therapy by use of the Q-sort technique, described in Chapter 30.

Rogers assumes that self-actualization is the principal human motivation, and that people by nature are innately good. Both of these precepts have been questioned.

Encounter groups

A spin-off from the T-groups started by Rogers, where participants (rather than clients) are encouraged by a facilitator to break down barriers and talk about and act out their emotions and problems. The free interaction and responses by others give new perspectives and promote self-actualization.

In an encounter group, participants are encouraged to talk about and act out their emotions and problems

---

GLOSSARY

Humanistic therapies Therapies where there is a belief that individuals can be helped to gain insight into their own problems and move towards a solution and realize their potential as human beings.

Client-centred therapy Rogers's approach where clients (not 'patients') are encouraged to set their own goals and take control over the process of therapy.

Some writers (for example, Rogers, 1970) suggest that **encounter groups** are effective in facilitating positive change; others suggest that they can actually precipitate psychological disturbances (Lieberman et al., 1973).

Gestalt therapy

Gestalt therapy was founded by Fritz Perls, who, like Rogers, believed that people have an innate goodness which is seeking to express itself. The therapy assumes that the individual brings his or her own wants and needs to any situation. The therapist focuses on the here-and-now, rather than the client's past.

Various techniques are employed, such as the 'empty chair', where clients are encouraged to talk to whoever they see in the chair. Perls believes that the unresolved traumas of the past affect new relationships, but that these should be acted out in the present. Clients are coerced, if necessary, into an awareness of what is happening, and urged to take direct action. The aim is to help people to become 'whole' by acknowledging all facets of themselves.

Transactional analysis

Eric Berne (1968) sees personality as consisting of three ego states: parent, adult and child. In **transactional analysis** these states are identified in role play, when the client and the therapist act out personal transactions or interactions with others. Each person is capable of communicating using either their child, adult or parent state. If this state is not recognized by the partner, underlying misunderstandings occur (because, of course, we do not only communicate in words). Berne identified a number of ways in which individuals use these strategies and interactions destructively; once understood, they can be changed and utilized to give greater control over the individual's life.

Evaluation of humanistic-existential therapies

Rogers was largely instrumental in encouraging evaluative studies of insight therapies, but there are methodological difficulties in doing so, as controlled research into this area is somewhat difficult. Rogers used a technique called 'Q-sort' (see Chapter 30) devised by Stephenson (1953), which aims to aid the client to make an objective assessment about self-perceptions, whether there is a mismatch between the 'perceived self' and the 'ideal self' (what I think I am and what I think I should be). This technique can be used in order to measure improvement during and after therapy. However, there are doubts as to how objective any form of self-assessment can be.

It was suggested that the warmth and personality of the therapist actually effected the 'cure', rather than any specific technique used. Parloff et al. (1978) found that a positive outcome is not necessarily related to the therapist's genuineness and empathy, as had been previously believed.

Many group therapies derived from humanistic therapies not only save on the therapist's time, but clients can learn from one another's opinions; also if a therapist draws a conclusion about you, you can reject this, but if several people in your group come to the same conclusion, it is not so easily rejected.

? SELF-ASSESSMENT QUESTIONS

1. What factors are common to all humanistic therapies?
2. Describe Rogers's therapy. How does this differ from any one of the other therapies?
3. Discuss the strengths and weaknesses of humanistic therapies.

Treatment effectiveness and patient care

'So, which is the best treatment to effect a cure?' the lay reader might ask. Treatment of mental disorders is not

---

GLOSSARY

Encounter group A humanistic therapy where a small group of people are encouraged by a facilitator to talk about and act out their emotions and problems.

Gestalt therapy A humanistic therapy where people are encouraged to become 'whole' by identifying and acknowledging all facets of themselves.

Transactional analysis A therapeutic process where individuals are encouraged to acknowledge three aspects of their personality: parent, adult, child, and to role-play interactions with other people using these three personality states.

that clear-cut; for example, one might state categorically that penicillin is the best treatment for a throat infection and a plaster cast for a broken leg; it is obviously useless to reverse the two treatments. The same therapy is sometimes effective and sometimes ineffective for seemingly the same mental disorder, because no two cases are identical.

Concept of cure

The other problem posed by the above question is the idea of 'cure'. How does one determine that a client is 'cured' of a mental disorder? As mentioned earlier, does the patient decide he or she is cured? Does the therapist decide? Should an independent therapist be called in to make an assessment? If so, should the second therapist be of the same theoretical persuasion as the first? A number of points are important.

What counts as a cure?

First one has to decide what constitutes a cure. Behaviourists would say removal of the aberrant behaviour, removal of the symptom, is seen as a cure for the disorder. If the social phobic can now mix in society, if the snake phobic no longer runs away screaming on seeing a snake, then the behaviourist counts them as cured. Overt behaviour can be seen and measured. But for how long does this constitute a cure – for life?

Symptom substitution

If the patient reenters treatment a year or two later, with symptoms which could be related to their earlier problem, this could be called symptom substitution. It could be argued that they were not really cured initially, but their problems simply driven underground, merely to resurface at the next troubled period in life. Beech et al. (1972) report that symptom substitution is relatively uncommon.

Can cure be evaluated objectively?

Psychoanalytic therapies aim to find the underlying problem, and in recognizing this, the patient will resolve the problem. It is exceedingly difficult to be certain this has occurred. It is impossible to measure id–ego conflicts, even if we are willing to accept that these do in fact occur. Projective tests, for example the Rorschach (see Chapter 4), which aim to measure

internal conflicts are, of course, open to the charge of being scored subjectively. Many of the insight therapies are dependent upon the client–therapist relationship, so can an objective view of 'cure' be reached? Rogers himself suggests that insight therapy is not suitable for patients with severe mental disorders, who have no insight. Somatic treatments, like behaviour therapies, tend to use symptom removal, or changes in overt behaviour, as signs of a 'cure'.

Hello/goodbye and spontaneous remission

One confounding variable in evaluation of any research is the 'hello/goodbye' effect. When patients or clients first commence treatment, they tend to exaggerate their problems and unhappiness to show their need for treatment. At the end of therapy, they may exaggerate their feelings of well-being, in order to show the therapist their appreciation, or to convince themselves they had not wasted time and money. In addition is the phenomenon of spontaneous remission; Bergin and Lambert (1978) reported that between 30 and 60 per cent of patients 'get better' without treatment. Schizophrenia, particularly, is said to fall into the 'rule of thirds'. One third get better on their own, one third get better with treatment, the final third will never show improvement. Patients or clients who are in therapy, but would have exhibited spontaneous remission, are therefore included in statistics showing the number of patients discharged or 'cured'.

Comparing therapies

A number of studies have been conducted comparing behavioural therapies with insight-type therapies,

---

GLOSSARY

Symptom substitution The replacement of one symptom with another which may be related to an earlier problem that was not resolved.

Insight therapies Therapies such as psychoanalysis, where a successful outcome is seen as being closely linked to the client gaining an understanding of, or insight into, his or her own problems.

'Hello/goodbye' effect A term which describes the patient or client's exaggeration of symptoms at the beginning and end of a course of therapy.

Spontaneous remission The improvement of a disorder without any treatment having been given.

such as psychoanalysis and humanistic therapies. Little difference in effectiveness was reported by researchers (Sloane et al., 1975). This may be because specific therapies are usually selected for specific disorders, thereby gaining the optimum chance of success. For example, modelling and systematic desensitization are frequently successful for phobics, whereas psychoanalytic therapies are not; the latter are more useful in problems that require self-understanding. Behaviour therapies and cognitive behaviour therapies are more useful in helping to change a specific aspect of one's behaviour.

None of the therapies are successful alone in treating schizophrenia or manic depression; however, used in conjunction with drugs they help very effectively with problems of day-to-day living.

Box 33.6 contains descriptions of a number of **outcome-research studies** – studies which aim to investigate the effectiveness of various therapeutic treatments.

Conclusions on treatment effectiveness

It is still a matter for discussion how 'cure' is defined in mental disorders. If the aim of therapy is to make the client more comfortable with himself or herself, then the client can give self-ratings; if the aim is to make society comfortable with the client, other criteria must be used.

No one therapy has proved superior for all mental disorders; therapy must be chosen that seems to be the

A warm supportive relationship is important to the success of psychotherapy

---

Box 33.6 Outcome-research studies – do therapies work?

Eysenck (1952) reviewed five studies of the effectiveness of psychoanalysis and 19 studies of eclectic therapies (mixed therapies, such as behaviour modification plus other treatments). He concluded that only 44 per cent of the psychoanalysis patients showed improvement compared to 64 per cent of the eclectic treatment groups. However, Bergin (1971) rereviewed these studies and found that if different criteria were used for 'improvement', the psychoanalysis success rate was raised to 83 per cent. As was noted earlier, it all depends on how one defines 'cure'.

Smith and Glass (1977) reviewed 400 studies of a variety of therapies, and found that any therapy produced a more favourable outcome than no therapy at all.

Smith et al. (1980) did a meta-analysis (a statistical procedure for aggregating and averaging the results of a large number of studies) of 475 studies, each of which compared a therapy group with an untreated control group. They concluded that the average patient receiving any therapy showed greater improvement on outcome measures than 80 per cent of the untreated controls. One can only assume that patients in compared groups were equally matched. One of the methodological problems of meta-analysis is that different researchers use a variety of criteria.

Shapiro and Shapiro (1983) suggest that outcome studies may all show similar results, not only because appropriate therapies are selected for particular client groups, but also that all therapies have two important factors in common: the warm and supportive relationship between therapist and client, and the expectation that things will improve.

'best fit' with the client's problem. In addition, if the client–therapist relationship is seen to be of paramount importance to success, these two individuals must have a 'mutual respect and understanding' (Rogers, 1951).

GLOSSARY

Outcome-research studies Research carried out to examine the effectiveness of psychotherapy.

Institutionalization or care in the community?

Whether patients should remain at home (if they have a home) or enter an institution or hospital for treatment, is an important subject for discussion. Until comparatively recently institutionalization was seen as the obvious choice for most mental disorders, including learning difficulties. It was seen as 'best' – but best for whom, the patient, the patient's family, society? Nowadays there is a strong move to desinstitutionalize or provide care in the community for those experiencing mental disorder. In particular, an attempt is made to keep patients in their own homes. This subsection aims to examine briefly some of the factors involved in these decisions.

Homecare

The majority of patients with mental illnesses or learning difficulties live at home. Some need to be hospitalized for a short time, to receive specific treatments or to give carers a rest, but the aim is to return people to their own homes as soon as possible, to resume their atmosphere of normality. However, this is not always possible: if people have disrupted their family ties to such an extent that reparation would only cause greater problems, or if the problem was precipitated by the family in the first place, then other plans have to be made.

Asylum

The word **asylum** means refuge. Early asylums of the Middle Ages were more like a prison than a refuge, with inmates left in chains. Early treatments, such as tranquillizing chairs or cribs, designed to restrain the patient physically and restrict sensory input, were used in the absence of any drug treatments, in order to calm the person's rages. In fact, cold bath treatment was used until the beginning of the twentieth century. By 1792, Philippe Pinel, in France, had pioneered the removal of chains and the provision of more humanitarian surroundings. From this model, more humanitarian housing and treatment were provided. In looking back at the asylums of the Middle Ages, one has to remember that housing for the vast majority of the population of that time would be deemed unacceptable today.

Institutions

Victorian times saw the building of large institutions for the mentally ill and mentally retarded. Initially both were housed together, but gradually differentiation occurred, after diagnosis and classification were introduced.

The old institutions housed hundreds of patients, usually well away from towns and cities so that they would not offend the sensitivities of 'normal' people. The effect was that the 'norm' of accepted behaviour for each of these institutions was defined by the inmates of each institution. This set a ceiling which many could have exceeded, had they been aware it was desirable or even possible. Many institutions acted as whole communities and were self-supporting in many ways, growing their own food, with the help of the patients. In this way, one might argue, there was good as well as bad in the old institutions. There was also always companionship, even if it could not be called 'friendship', there was always someone else there.

Care in the community

New treatment methods, for example control of long-term disorders with drug therapy, meant that many patients were confined to institutions when they could have been living outside in the community. Unless they had friends or family willing to assist in their rehabilitation, this was not possible. Gradually the idea of sheltered accommodation or community care homes was pioneered, and patients began to be moved out of the big, old institutions into smaller, 'family group' homes or sheltered housing. Sometimes these are run entirely by a group of expatients, often with resident or daytime care assistants.

Problems with care in the community This move, of course, is not without its problems. Although everyone agrees that people should not be made to live in institutions when they could live in houses, there is frequently controversy about where these should be sited (subject to the 'not in my backyard' syndrome).

GLOSSARY
Asylum A term used to describe an institution for the care and treatment of people with mental disorders. Literally means 'refuge'.

Some people released from mental institutions are unable to look after themselves

Ignorance on the part of the general public about what constitutes mental disorder provides fuel for opposition. Until people realize that these individuals are not going to steal from them, harm or frighten their children or lower the tone of the neighbourhood, then prejudice will persist. Much public relations work still needs to be done.

Preparation work also needs to be done with the patients themselves. Providing a house and taking previously institutionalized patients straight from hospital to the house, is not the way to success. Education or reeducation on matters such as shopping, cooking, cleaning and maintaining personal hygiene has to be undertaken. Behavioural therapy may be necessary, to make the quantum leap from acceptable institutional behaviour to acceptable behaviour in the outside world. Facilities such as day centres, sheltered workshops or jobs need to be provided, to avoid the cases of the 'bed and breakfast' expatient, who aimlessly wanders the streets all day until allowed back into the accommodation in the evening. Some psychologists believe that a proportion of homeless people to be found in 'cardboard cities' are individuals who have suffered mental disorder and have been released into the community but are unable, for financial or other reasons, to care for themselves adequately.

Moving patients into the community, health authorities are now realizing, is not the cheap option it first appeared. If homes in the community are to benefit patients, then many factors must be considered and many self-help facilities provided, otherwise we shall simply resurrect the 'revolving door' – patients having to return to hospital for further treatment.

Whether patients are treated at home or as inpatients depends partly on the severity of their problem, partly on the treatment recommended and partly upon whether they have family support. The movement towards care in the community for those suffering from mental disorders is a welcome step, provided it is not regarded solely as a cheap alternative to hospitalization. The careful provision of small-group homes and adequate day-care may well prove just as expensive as the old institutions, but provide increased self-esteem and individualization required by expatients, which is after all the object of the exercise. Sales of the old institutions can be expected to offset some capital costs. Careful monitoring is necessary in this freer situation to ensure that those who need care are not denied it, or counted as outside certain boundaries.

There will always be the need for inpatient accommodation, for acute problems and those who may need temporary removal from their usual place of habitation.

❓ SELF-ASSESSMENT QUESTIONS

1. What are the problems of deciding whether a patient is cured of a mental disorder?
2. Why is it difficult to make a direct comparison of treatment effectiveness?
3. Which treatments have been found to be most effective for which disorders?
4. What forms of accommodation are available today for people suffering from mental disorders?
5. What are the advantages and problems of caring in the community for those who suffer from a mental disorder?

Chapter summary

- Treatment and therapies for mental disorders are related to the five major approaches to psychology. These include the psychoanalytic model, the humanistic perspective, treatments based upon learning theories or cognitive theories as well as those which have a physiological basis.

- Somatic treatments aim to treat imbalances in the individual's physical soma, in order to normalize psychological functioning. These may include drug therapy, psychosurgery or electroconvulsive treatments. Drugs used include tranquillizers, minor tranquillizers to reduce anxiety and major tranquillizers such as chlorpromazine and other drugs based on phenothiazine which are used to treat schizophrenics.

- Stimulants, such as amphetamine, are prescribed for the treatment of hyperactive children. Antidepressants such as tricyclics and monoamine oxidase (MAO) may be used to treat endogenous depression. Lithium carbonate may help to iron out the mood swings of manic depressives.

- Psychosurgery, especially lobotomies, are now much less used than earlier, but with careful selection of patients good success rates have been achieved with sufferers from obsessive compulsive disorder, severe depression and anxiety.

- Electroconvulsive therapy (ECT) is now used primarily for profoundly depressed patients who have failed to respond to drug treatment, and has been successful in a number of cases.

- A number of practical and ethical issues arise from the use of somatic treatments. An ongoing and heated debate centres particularly on the use of ECT and psychosurgery.

- Behavioural therapies based upon classical conditioning include systematic desensitization used to treat phobias, aversion therapy used for the treatment of addictions and other unwanted behaviour and implosion therapy or 'flooding', also used to treat phobias. Behavioural therapies based upon operant conditioning include behaviour modification, and token economies, as used in long-stay hospitals. Modelling based upon social learning theory has been effective in treating phobias in a clinical setting.

- Biofeedback is a particular technique which allows greater control over bodily processes normally under autonomic control. It has been used for the treatment of high blood pressure, some forms of epilepsy and some neuromuscular disorders such as cerebral palsy, stroke or poliomyelitis.

- Therapies based upon altering cognitions include Beck's cognitive-behaviour therapy which has been successfully used to treat depression, rational emotive therapy used for the same purpose and Kelly's personal construct therapy.

- Therapies based upon psychoanalytic theories aim to resolve id–ego conflicts and provide clients with insight into their problems. Free association and dream analysis are aimed at uncovering the unconscious mind. Ego analysis is used to help clients realize the strength of their ego functions and so change themselves. Melanie Klein developed play therapy to apply psychoanalytic principles to the treatment of children. This has been successfully used by Axline among others.

- Therapies based upon humanistic psychology place emphasis on the free will of the individual and are nondirective. These include Rogers's client-centred therapy, encounter groups, Gestalt therapy, and transactional analysis. Encounter groups centre on free interaction to promote self-actualization, Gestalt therapy focuses on the 'here and now' rather than on the past, and transactional analysis postulates three ego states: adult, parent and child. Therapy is aimed at helping clients to recognize the ego state they are using in transactions with others.

- Assessment of the effectiveness of treatments centre on the concept of 'cure'. While behaviourists concentrate on the removal of symptoms, psychoanalytic therapies aim to find the underlying problem. The 'hello/goodbye' effect may confound the evaluation of any treatment. Problems are exaggerated at the commencement of treatment, feelings of well-being are exaggerated at the end of treatment.

- A current debate centres around the best location for treatment of mental disorder. The overall aim has been to return patients home as soon as possible so that they can be as normal as possible. Institutions in the past have been more like prisons or places of safety, keeping those with mental disorders apart from the community. More recently there have been policies of deinstitutionalization. Sheltered accommodation or community care homes have replaced big mental institutions. Problems with these policies include the siting of such 'homes', preparation and educational work with the patients and the difficulty of bridging the gap between acceptable institutional behaviour and behaviour acceptable in the community.

Further reading

Axline, V. (1964). *Dibs: In Search of Self*. Harmondsworth: Penguin. A case study of a very disturbed child who was helped back to mental health through play therapy. The book offers strong support for psychoanalytic therapy.

Beck, A. and Emery, G. (1985). *Anxiety Disorders and Phobias: A Cognitive Perspective*. New York: Basic Books. A description of Beck's theory and therapy to change thought processes, thereby enabling the reduction of anxiety and treatment of phobias.

Davison, G. and Neale, J. (1994). *Abnormal Psychology*, 6th edn. New York: Wiley. A very good, in-depth approach to all aspects of abnormality, including description, diagnosis and treatments.

Nutt, D.J. (1990) The Pharmacology of Human Anxiety, *Pharamacological Therapies*, *47*, 223–266.

Rogers, C. (1961). *On Becoming a Person*. Boston, MA: Houghton Mifflin. Rogers's own description of his beliefs, theory and therapy. The book also offers insights into the man himself.

PART 8

Research methods and statistics

This part of the book provides two things. It gives the reader an overview of the methods used in psychological research, together with an assessment of the advantages and disadvantages inherent in each. This will include some definition of the terms used and an account of the ways in which those who use experimental methods, in particular, have attempted to limit the disadvantages while retaining the advantages of control and objectivity. Secondly, it provides practical help for students in setting up psychological research projects, carrying them through, analysing and reporting the results. There is detail of the use of statistical procedures, both descriptive and inferential, and step-by-step guides to the use of statistical tests of significance.

Contents

INTRODUCTION
Research methodology   813
- Populations   813
- Errors, systematic and random   815
- Theories and hypotheses   816

CHAPTER 34
Some methods used in psychological research   820
- Experiment   820
- Experimental design and the control of variables   825
- Nonexperimental methods   829
- Correlational designs   837
- Some further considerations in research   839

CHAPTER 35
Presenting the results   845
- The use of statistics   845
- Descriptive statistics   847

- Statistical inference and significance   857
- Correlation   864
- Choosing an appropriate test   869

CHAPTER 36
Statistical tests   872
- Nonparametric tests   872
- Parametric tests   881

CHAPTER 37
Interpretation and presentation of research   888
- Interpretation and background to research   888
- Writing research reports   891

CHAPTER 38
Some projects   897
- Experimental projects   897
- Observational studies   899
- Correlational studies   902

Research methodology

As you work through this part of the book, you will be meeting a whole range of ideas which will be strange to you and which sometimes use words in a sense which is not the ordinary one. For this reason, we shall start by highlighting a number of ideas which you will meet later, to ensure that you become familiar with them from the outset.

Populations

Statisticians use the term **population**, not to indicate a collection of people living in a particular place (as we might refer to the population of, say, Australia), but to the group from which a sample is drawn. They may not, indeed, be people at all. They may be fish or even nuts and bolts! A manufacturer might be producing a certain kind of nut. This particular sort of nut would then be the 'population' from which the manufacturer might draw a sample every so often to test for strength or for some other property. A population might consist of numbers relating to a particular group which shares some common characteristics. The definition of population used by statisticians is as follows: 'Any group of numbers, finite or infinite, which refer to real or hypothetical events' (Clegg, 1982, p. 51).

Any numbers which have a common characteristic are included in this. It could be polar bears kept in zoos in Russia or 11+ test results from a group of children in Aberdeen: that is, just a set of scores. Populations can be small or large, the stars in the universe or National Lottery jackpot winners for example. There is further reference to populations in Chapter 35, in relation to statistical tests.

Representative samples

Samples are useful in that they allow researchers to examine the characteristics of the population with which they are concerned without going to the lengths of a detailed examination of the whole of it. Part of a statistician's skill lies in finding samples that are representative of the population from which they are drawn, so that generalizations can be made to the rest of it. It would not be much use just testing the last 30 nuts produced on a Friday afternoon. 'Representative' implies that the sample accurately reflects the composition of the population from which it is drawn; it has the same characteristics (apart from its size) in the same proportion. If the sample is truly representative, you will be able to generalize your results to the whole population.

There are various ways in which this **representative sample** can be approached. Although it is hard, if not impossible, to guarantee a representative sample, it is possible to reduce the chance of bias.

Random samples

This term has a very particular meaning to statisticians. Every member of the population needs to have an equal chance of being represented. Supposing that you were concerned with a population of schoolchildren (perhaps to test their retention of what they had been taught); every child in the population needs to have an equal chance of being picked for testing.

GLOSSARY

Population The group from which a sample is drawn. For statistical purposes this is likely to be some numerical aspect of what is under investigation.

Sample A smaller group drawn from a population.

Representative sample A sample which accurately reflects characteristics of the population from which it is drawn.

How to obtain a random sample

Returning to the problems inherent in obtaining a **random sample** of people for psychological research, you first need to define the population accurately. Suppose, for example, you choose to define your population as 'Londoners'; do you mean all those who live in London, all those who were born there, or perhaps all those who make their living there? In any of these cases, you would need to devise a way in which you could select a sample in which each and every member of the population had an equal chance of being selected. It could be very difficult. If you chose to use a telephone directory: you run up against the problem that not everyone has a telephone, so that you would get a random sample of London telephone subscribers rather than of 'Londoners'. You might think of using the electoral roll, but then you would exclude all those under the age of 18, all foreigners and anyone who for some reason or another had not registered to vote. Your random sample would then be from a population of electors in London, not Londoners.

The answer lies in the careful definition of the population. If you define your population as children attending St George's School (wherever that might be) it is a comparatively simple matter to obtain a list of all those children, write each name on a slip of paper, put the slips into a tombola and draw out however many you needed – bingo! a random sample. Alternatively, you could assign a number to each child on the list and then consult a table of random numbers (there is one included in Appendix 3 of this book). It is a simple matter to obtain your sample. Just open the table, close your eyes and use a pin to light upon a number. That number represents an individual member of your population. You can go on doing this until you have enough for your sample. Suppose, however, that you were trying to compare the performance in some respect of girls and boys in St George's School. Then you have in effect two populations, one of girls and one of boys, and you would have to go about producing your two samples from the two populations in the same way as has been described. You could, of course, get a computer to generate random numbers, in much the same way as ERNIE does for Premium Bond draws, or use the kind of tombola used in the draws for the National Lottery. A random sample has a good chance of being representative of the population from which it is drawn so that you can generalize your findings from observations you have made of the sample and reasonably suggest that they might be true of the whole population. At the very least, the method by which your sample is chosen is free from bias.

So, here is the procedure:

1. Define the population.
2. Establish a list of all the members of that population.
3. Assign a number to each member.
4. Generate random numbers up to the size of the sample(s) you require.
5. Apply the numbers to your list, and you have your sample(s).

Exercise 81.1

You want to compare the lifestyles of pensioners in Brighton and Biarritz.

1. What are your populations?
2. How could you go about drawing up random samples from these populations?

Suggested answers can be found at the end of this introduction (p. 819).

Quota samples

An alternative way to obtain a representative sample is to use a **quota sample**. This is frequently used in surveys. You select characteristics which you consider important as far as your study is concerned. You then systematically choose individuals who possess these characteristics in the same proportions as the population as a whole. You might decide that the important characteristics you needed to consider are sex, age and socioeconomic status. Your sample would need to include individuals who display these characteristics in equal proportion to those evident in the whole population. You could proceed as follows:

GLOSSARY

Random sample A sample which is drawn from a population in such a way that every member of that population has an equal chance of being included.

Quota sample A sample which is drawn from a population in the following way. Characteristics important to the researcher are identified. Individuals who possess these characteristics are selected proportionately to the whole population.

For instance, you reckon that the proportion of males and females in the population is 50:50, so that your sample would need to include 50 per cent males and 50 per cent females.

As far as age is concerned, you could establish broad categories, say, under 20, 20 to 50 and over 50. A preliminary survey might have shown that the proportions of the three age groups in the population were 20 per cent, 40 per cent and 60 per cent respectively. Your sample would include people from each of these age ranges in the same proportions.

As far as socioeconomic status is concerned, you could operate similarly, using a scale of social classes, based upon occupation. Again, a preliminary survey would show you what the proportions of each class were in the population. Your sample would be made up in the same proportions.

In this way, you can claim the sample to be representative, at least as far as the selected characteristics are concerned.

Stratified sampling

Stratified sampling requires a fairly detailed knowledge of the population you are studying, to establish strata or subgroups within the population. Within a school, these subgroups might include year groups, males and females, or perhaps sets or streams. From these population subgroups, you can proceed systematically to draw random samples of the kind described above in the same proportions as occur in the parent population.

Cluster sampling

Cluster sampling is based on the existence of natural groups. It might be families, or houses on an estate, or children in a class. The natural groups are numbered, and a random sample is drawn from these numbers. It might work like this. Within all the primary schools in a particular county, the reception classes are identified and numbered. Suppose there are 45 classes in all, and you wanted a sample of 300 individual children. Assuming roughly 30 children to a class, you would need to draw 10 classes randomly from your 45. Once this was done, you might identify and study in detail particular subgroups, perhaps children under five on entry compared with those over five. This provides you with a representative sample of a large population in a fairly economical way. Unfortunately, there are also risks involved. If one of the clusters chosen happens to be unrepresentative in some way, you have introduced some systematic error.

The aim is always to obtain a sample or samples which are fully representative of the population from which they are drawn. However, this may not always be possible. An opportunity sample is sometimes used, which simply employs those individuals who are available at the time the study is done. It has to be remembered, though, that opportunity samples may not be representative. There must be caution in the way in which such studies are interpreted. Generalization from such results can be risky. Project 5 among the projects at the end of this book (Chapter 38) employs an opportunity sample of people who happen to be passing a particular set of traffic lights at a particular time. Opportunity samples are commonly used by students as they are the easiest to obtain and they do have value in providing a preliminary indication of results, but you need to be aware of their limitations regarding generalization.

Errors, systematic and random

As we are fallible humans, living in a less than perfect world, there is always the chance that error may occur. One of the purposes of the use of statistics is to allow for this random error. You are never going to be able to

---

GLOSSARY

Stratified sampling Random samples are drawn from each stratum or subgroup within a population proportionately to the whole population to form a stratified sample representative of the parent population.

Cluster sampling A means of obtaining a representative sample of a population which is based upon identifying natural groupings within a population. A random sample is drawn from each of these natural groupings and put together to form a cluster sample.

Opportunity sample Samples drawn from a population on the basis of their easy availability rather than because they are representative. Caution needs to be observed in drawing general conclusions from such samples.

Random error Those chance variations or biases which will inevitably occur when any group of individuals are investigated, which cannot be allowed for in the design of a study. Statistical techniques are employed to mitigate the effects of random error.

eliminate it. **Systematic error**, on the other hand, needs to be guarded against and avoided at all costs. This happens where poor research design has allowed a bias to occur which consistently favours one condition in an investigation rather than another. It could be due to sampling error (as above) or perhaps to order effects (the order in which testing is carried out) or to some other foreseeable and preventable source of bias. Chapter 34 will address some of the ways in which sources of systematic error may be brought under control.

Theories and hypotheses

Someone who is engaged in research will from time to time formulate a **theory**. This amounts to the researcher's own interpretation of what the findings of the research carried out thus far seem to show. It is often fairly general in its nature and not in a form in which it can readily be tested. Essentially, it presents an overall picture of where the research seems to be leading. Let us take an example.

In researching the nature of memory, Peterson and Peterson (1959) came to the conclusion that when something was memorized, there was what they termed a memory trace within the brain. This trace gradually decayed over time, and this led to forgetting. They had found that after short intervals of time (for example three to six seconds), recall was generally quite good, but after about 18 seconds much of what had been encountered had been forgotten. They put forward their trace-decay theory: that is, their explanation of what they had found. Later alternative explanations included an interference theory of forgetting, which suggested that other material was interfering with what had to be recalled. Either of these theories represented an explanation of what had been found thus far and provided a basis for further research to test which theory best explained what had been observed.

A theory is not, as it stands, testable. It is too imprecise. In order to test it, it needs to be transposed into the form of a **hypothesis**: that is, a prediction of outcomes in specific circumstances. To do this, each bit of the theory needs to be carefully defined and operationalized. That is to say, it needs to be put into a form which can be tested by experiment, observation or some other form of investigation, such as a correlational study or a survey.

Operationalizing a theory – an example

Supposing we start with a theory that time during which you are doing nothing is perceived as being longer than time which is fully occupied. That in its present form is not testable, but it can be converted into a hypothesis by operationalizing it. You start by identifying precisely what is meant by 'doing nothing'. It might be sitting at an empty table with both mind and body entirely unoccupied. In contrast to this, 'occupied time' might be defined as time spent with a pair of compasses and a sheet of paper, constructing as many designs as possible. It does not much matter what the occupation is, as long as it is defined and clearly something which can be put into practice. It will probably not embrace all the theory. In this instance, 'occupation' might be defined as mental occupation or physical occupation, so that the theory might be operationalized in two ways. Then the researcher will need to tackle the idea of 'perception of time'. This might involve an estimate of time spent. The hypothesis might then be stated as a prediction in some such terms as these: people who sit at an empty table with both mind and body entirely unoccupied will overestimate the time that elapses; while if they are actively engaged creating designs on a sheet of paper with a pair of compasses, they will underestimate it.

Exercise 81.2

Take the following theory and operationalize it as a hypothesis. 'Watching violence on TV results in an increase in aggression.' Define your terms carefully and make a prediction based upon the theoretical idea above.

Suggested answers can be found at the end of this introduction (p. 819).

GLOSSARY

Systematic error Bias affecting one condition systematically more than another. It can be eliminated by careful controls in the design of research. Sampling errors and order effects are examples of systematic error.

Theory An interpretation of the findings of research formulated in a fairly general way. It is not easily tested as it stands but needs to be reformulated as a hypothesis.

Hypothesis A prediction of the outcome of a test of a fairly specific set of circumstances.

Null and alternative hypotheses

A **null hypothesis** (H_o) amounts to a prediction that any difference or similarity found could have been the result of chance variability (perhaps errors in measurement, sampling, the variability of human beings or some other random error), rather than to the real phenomenon you are trying to observe and measure. Retention of the null hypothesis implies that your data indicate that the samples you are looking at are just different samples from the same population, and that the variations you are observing are the result of your sampling and not of any difference between the populations: you just happen to have observed chance variations within the same population. The more observations you take, the less the effect of chance is going to be. For instance, in the example quoted above, retention of the null hypothesis would mean that what you have been observing were just samples from a single population of people, rather than from two populations, one of unoccupied people, the other of occupied people. In other words, your results could have occurred by chance alone.

The **alternative hypothesis** (H_a) accepts that your observations have convinced you that you are observing a real phenomenon and that differences or similarities are not just due to chance. You are, in effect, not looking at two samples from one population but samples from two different populations. There are three ways of reaching this conclusion:

■ Go on making a sufficient number of observations and measurements to convince yourself that there is no reasonable doubt that what you were observing was a real phenomenon.

■ Maybe the differences you have observed are large enough to convince you of this straight away, but this is not usually the case.

■ You may not have the resources to make sufficient observations and measurements to ensure that chance can be ruled out. Therefore, you work out the statistical probability that the observations you are making are due to chance, that you are in fact just looking at two samples of one population.

Let us take an example. Suppose you are theoretically interested in the notion that only children do better in school than those who come from large families. You find samples of each of the populations in question (of children from large families and of only children), ensuring that they are representative. You then test the school performance of each sample. The null hypothesis assumes that what you are looking at are just two samples from a single population of children. The alternative hypothesis is that this is not the case. There are indeed two samples from two different populations, one of only children with better school performance, the other of children from large families who have inferior school performance. What a statistical test of inference will enable you to do is to assess the probability that the predictions of the null hypothesis are true: that there is no difference or similarity between the samples except that which is due to chance. It is up to you then to retain or to reject the null hypothesis on the basis of that probability.

Exercise 81.3

Now take the hypothesis you arrived at in the earlier Exercise 81.2 and express it in two ways:

(a) As a null hypothesis;
(b) As an alternative hypothesis.

Suggested answers may be found at the end of this introduction (p. 819).

One tail or two tails?

A hypothesis may be said to be **one-tailed** or **two-tailed**. This has nothing to do with physiology. It proposes that something is better or worse, quicker or slower, simpler or less simple and so on. A one-tailed hypothesis is directional; a two-tailed hypothesis is

GLOSSARY

Null hypothesis A prediction that there will be no difference (or similarity in the case of a correlational design) between the results obtained of a test under two (or more) conditions except that which might be expected by chance alone. Or to put it in another way, that the two samples will be found to be no more different than if they had been drawn from a single population.

Alternative hypothesis A prediction that the effects on outcomes found after tests of two or more samples will be sufficiently different (or similar in the case of a correlational study) that the researcher can be confident that they did not occur by chance alone. Or to put it in another way, the samples were drawn from more than one population.

nondirectional. For example, if you predict that drinking coffee will improve your learning scores that is directional. Whereas if you predict just that there will be an effect on learning scores from drinking coffee that is nondirectional.

Exercise 81.4

Express your hypothesis (from Exercise 81.2) in two ways:

(a) As a one-tailed hypothesis;
(b) As a two-tailed hypothesis.

Suggested answers may be found at the end of this introduction (p. 819).

Significance and confidence levels

The term **significance** is used in connection with the acceptance of the alternative hypothesis. If you have become convinced of the reality of the phenomenon you are observing by any of the three means described above, then the difference (or the similarity in the case of correlational studies) is described as being significant. You have confidence that what you are observing is not just a chance occurrence. There has to be a point at which you can have this confidence. If, as is most likely, you have worked out the statistical probability of what you are observing occurring by chance, you need to establish a confidence level. Your statistical test (these are described in detail in Chapters 35 and 36) will show the probability (p) that your results could have been due to chance as a percentage (most often, equal to or less than 5 per cent or equal to or less than 1 per cent probability). This is also expressed as a decimal fraction ($p \leqslant 0.05$ or $p \leqslant 0.01$). Which

confidence level you choose is up to you, the researcher, but there are implications.

Type I and type II errors

Whichever choice you make, there is a risk of error. These can be what are termed **type I** or **type II errors**.

A type I error occurs when you reject the null hypothesis and accept the alternative hypothesis ($H\alpha$) when there is no real difference (or similarity). A type II error is the converse of this. You have retained the null hypothesis and concluded that there is no real effect observed, when in fact there is a real difference (or similarity).

Type I and type II errors are fully discussed in Chapter 35.

> **GLOSSARY**
>
> **One-tailed hypothesis** A hypothesis which is directional – one which specifies which way the differences or relationship between results of tests of the samples in a study will go.
>
> **Two-tailed hypothesis** A hypothesis which is nondirectional – one which does not specify the way any differences or relationship found in the results of a test will go.
>
> **Significance** Refers to the confidence a researcher has that the results he or she has obtained did not occur through chance. This is usually gained by conducting a statistical test of significance.
>
> **Type I error** An error which is the result of rejecting the null hypothesis when there is in reality no real difference (or similarity) between the conditions in the experiment (or correlational study).
>
> **Type II error** An error which is the result of retaining the null hypothesis when in reality there is a real difference (or similarity) between the conditions in an experiment (or correlational study).

Suggested answers for the exercises in the Introduction

Exercise 81.1

1. All the pensioners (men and women over 60 or 65) in either Biarritz or Brighton.
2. You could approach the Social Security departments in each town, obtain names of all pensioners resident in the towns, put them in a tombola and draw out samples of appropriate size.

Exercise 81.2

A sample of individuals who regularly (more than three times in a week) watch TV programmes which contain violent incidents (Sample A) will display in their behaviour a greater number of aggressive incidents of behaviour (defined as incidents, either verbal or physical, intended to cause harm or injury to other people) than a similar sample of individuals who do not view TV programmes containing violent incidents (Sample B).

Exercise 81.3

1. There will be no difference in the number of aggressive incidents, as defined in Exercise 81.2, in Sample A than in Sample B except for that which may be accounted for through chance.
2. An alternative hypothesis might read: 'Sample A will display a greater number of aggressive incidents of behaviour than Sample B'.

Exercise 81.4

1. A one-tailed hypothesis would read the same as in the suggested answer to Exercise 81.3 (2).
2. A two-tailed hypothesis might read as follows: 'Sample A will display a different number of incidents of aggressive behaviour than Sample B'. It will not specify whether the difference will be greater or less.

CHAPTER 34

Some methods used in psychological research

Experiment   820
- Settings for experiments   821
- Strengths and weaknesses of experimentation   822

Experimental design and the control of variables   825
- Experimental design   826
- Control of variables   827

Nonexperimental methods   829
- Observation   829
- Survey method   832
- Case study method   833
- Interview techniques   834

Ethogenics   835
- Archival research   835
- Role play and simulation   836

Correlational designs   837
- Some examples of correlation in psychological research   837
- Strengths and weaknesses of correlation   838

Some further considerations in research   839
- Reliability   839
- Validity   840
- Standardization   841
- Expression of scores   842

Objectives

By the end of this chapter you should be able to:

- List and describe some examples of methods commonly used in psychological research, including experiment, observation, survey and case study methods;

- Make an evaluation of the strengths and weaknesses of each method;

- Identify the kinds of research problems for which it is appropriate to use each method.

Experiment

The term **experiment** is frequently used (often wrongly) to refer to a wide range of research procedures. It is necessary at an early stage to make quite clear what the term relates to. In an experiment, the researcher deliberately isolates and manipulates one variable (referred to as the **independent variable** [IV]) in order to observe and measure the effect of this manipulation upon another variable (the **dependent variable** [DV]). There will almost inevitably be other

> **GLOSSARY**
>
> **Experiment** A procedure where a researcher deliberately isolates and manipulates one or more variables (the independent variable) in order to be able to measure the effect of this manipulation on another variable (the dependent variable). All other variables should be controlled.
>
> **Independent variable** A variable in an experiment which is manipulated in order that the researcher can measure the result of such manipulation.

factors which will interfere to cloud the link between IV and DV. These are referred to as **extraneous variables** and they must be carefully controlled by the experimenter. An example set out in Box 34.1 will make this clearer.

Settings for experiments

Experimentation may be conducted in different settings, in a laboratory, in the field or in a natural setting. To illustrate this, some examples follow.

Laboratory experiment

Box 34.2 describes a **laboratory experiment**.

Field experiment

An alternative is a **field experiment** such as is described in Box 34.3.

Natural or quasi-experiment

Another alternative is a **natural experiment**, sometimes referred to as a **quasi-experiment** Here the

setting is a natural one for the participants in the experiment, but instead of the researchers deliberately manipulating the independent variable, changes in the IV occur naturally. It could be argued that it is not an experiment at all because the experimenter does not manipulate the IV. However, the experimenter does take account, in the design of the study, of changes

---

GLOSSARY

Dependent variable The variable in an experiment which a researcher measures to test the result of manipulation of one or more other variables.

Extraneous variables Those variables in an experiment which may cloud or distort the link between independent and dependent variables and which a researcher will endeavour to control so as to mitigate this distortion.

Laboratory experiment An experiment which is conducted in a controlled and artificial situation.

Field experiment An experiment which is conducted in a natural environment (in the 'field').

Natural-experiment Another term used to describe a quasi-experiment. There is no deliberate manipulation of the independent variable but account is taken of naturally occurring changes.

Box 34.1 An example of variables in an experiment

A researcher has noticed that many young people have music on when they are studying. The suggestion has been made that this might have an adverse effect on their learning. In order to set up an experiment to examine the effect of background music upon learning, some definitions need to be established. The IV (the presence or absence of music) needs to be carefully defined. It might be pop, classical or jazz music, for example. It might be loud or quiet. It might be delivered through headphones or by means of a speaker. Similarly, the DV (learning) needs careful definition. It might be the recall of key facts from what has been studied. Extraneous variables needing to be controlled might include:

- The effect of wearing headphones;
- How used the participants are to listening to music;
- The physical conditions of the experiment: lighting, heating, seating;
- The age, sex and academic ability of the participants and so on.

This girl listens to music as she studies. Is her learning affected by the music?

which occur naturally. In this sense, it could be said that the experimenter is deliberately building changes in the independent variable into the experimental design. Namikas and Wehmer (1978) were studying aggression within litters of mice. Male mice which were reared in litters in which they had solely female siblings were more aggressive than those whose litters contained both males and females. Here the independent variable was the composition of the litter. It could vary naturally from one composed entirely of males to one which was entirely female. The dependent variable was the amount of aggressive behaviour

---

Box 34.2 A laboratory experiment on imprinting

Hess (1959) conducted a series of experiments to study the phenomenon of imprinting in ducklings. This is the natural process whereby the young of certain species form an attachment to the first moving thing they see shortly after hatching. This has a clear survival value in the wild.

The ducklings were hatched in an incubator in the laboratory. The first moving thing the newly hatched ducklings saw was a plastic model of a mallard duck on a revolving turntable. In the relatively controlled conditions of the laboratory, this was comparatively easy to bring about. The animals became imprinted on the plastic model and followed it on its travels round the turntable. In this way, Hess was able to identify the timing of the critical periods after hatching, when exposure to the model was most likely to result in imprinting. He could accurately control the time when the ducklings were exposed to their 'mother' and observe imprinting as it occurred. In this experiment, the independent variable was the time between hatching and exposure to the plastic model; the dependent variable was the imprinting of the ducklings on their 'mother'. Extraneous variables which needed to be controlled included any other moving thing which might come within sight of the ducklings, the speed of the revolving turntable and the lighting in the laboratory.

You might consider in the light of what has been said in Chapter 5 about ethics in research whether this experiment breaches the ethical guidelines.

Box 34.3 A field experiment in animal behaviour

Tinbergen and Perdeck (1950) conducted a field experiment in the same area of study, animal behaviour. While Hess's study was conducted in a laboratory, Tinbergen and Perdeck's study was in the 'real world'. Herring gulls nest on the ground or on cliffs near the sea. The parent birds forage at sea or on local rubbish heaps and bring back food to the chicks in their nest. On their return to the nest, they stand near one of the chicks and point their beaks to the ground. The chick then pecks the parent's beak, and food is regurgitated for the chick to feed on.

It was comparatively easy for Tinbergen and his colleague to investigate what kind of stimulus (short of the natural one) would produce the pecking response in the chicks. A number of stimuli were tried: three-dimensional 'mock-ups' of a gull's head, cardboard cut-outs and even a thin red rod. What appeared to be crucial was the presence of a red spot on the parent's beak. Anything red (the thin red rod, for example) produced the desired pecking response. An otherwise totally lifelike mock-up without a red spot produced no response at all. If there was no red spot, the chicks did not peck, the parent bird would not regurgitate and the chicks would starve.

This was an experiment. The researchers were deliberately manipulating the IV (the stimulus presented to the chick) in order to observe the pecking response (the DV). The setting, though, was the bird's own nest, a field environment.

---

observed. The IV varied naturally rather than by deliberate manipulation.

Strengths and weaknesses of experimentation

Strengths of experimentation

The strengths of experimentation include the following:

Control Isolating one or more variables and then manipulating their values to see the effect this has upon another variable makes possible a high degree of control. The experimenter aims to eliminate extraneous variables to concentrate entirely upon the effect that changes in the IV have upon the DV. This can never be totally possible, but control is likely to be greater than in other research methods. Laboratory experiments are likely to be better controlled than field or natural experiments. The experimenter's control over such things as when and where the study should take place, the number and character of the participants and how they should be deployed, is also better.

Cause and effect The systematic manipulation of the IV in order to observe the effect of that manipulation on the DV makes it possible to establish a link between cause and effect.

Objectivity As Popper (1972) has said, it is unrealistic to claim that any observation is totally objective. The experimenter's values, interests, expectations and prejudice will always intrude. Nevertheless, objectivity is a primary aim of scientific study, and it is more nearly realizable with experimentation than with other methods.

Replicability An experimenter can describe in detail exactly what has been done, and this makes replication easier than in some other methods of study. Replication is very important, in that where a study is repeated and similar results obtained, there can be greater confidence in the validity of the theory being tested.

Weaknesses of experimentation

The weaknesses of experimentation include:

Dehumanization Heather (1976) has claimed that experimentation on human beings treats them rather like machines; it 'depersonalizes' and 'dehumanizes' them. The use of the word 'subject' is indicative of the attitude taken towards them, and this has consequently now been replaced by the term 'participant' in most cases. (This is the term we have employed throughout this book.) They are regarded as something passive and inert, propelled into action only by the use of some force upon them, either external or internal. Human beings continue to be regarded by psychologists as some kind of helpless clockwork puppet, jerked into life only when something happens to it (Heather, 1976).

Separation from reality The controlled and contrived situation of the laboratory experiment is divorced from real life. Claxton (1980) spelled out this divorce.

> Much of psychology does not deal with whole people but with a very special and bizarre – almost Frankensteinian – preparation, which consists of a brain attached to two eyes, two ears, and two index fingers. This preparation is only to be found inside small gloomy cubicles, outside which red lights burn to warn ordinary people away . . . It does not feel hungry or tired or inquisitive; it does not think extraneous thoughts or try to understand what is going on. It is, in short, a computer, made in the image of the larger electronic organism that sends it stimuli and records its responses.
>
> (Claxton, 1980, p. 18)

The impression given that real people behave in the way in which experimental participants behave may be misleading. For example, no one in real life would be asked to look at a series of lines drawn on a card, compare them with a test line and say which one matches most closely. And yet this was what Asch (1952), in a classic experiment, asked participants to do. This divorce from reality results in what is termed a lack of ecological validity. Validity is discussed fully later in this chapter.

The participant's perception How the experiment and the part that participants are asked to play in it are perceived can make a vital difference to the behaviour of participants. They will carefully weigh up the situation and react accordingly.

Demand characteristics Orne (1962) used the term **demand characteristics** to describe what happens. The participant responds to cues within the experimental situation such as:

GLOSSARY

Demand characteristics Subtle cues, such as the behaviour of the researcher, which participants pick up in a research setting, and which cause them to behave in ways they believe are expected of them.

- The physical set-up of the experiment,
- The experimenter's behaviour,
- Any clue that might alert the participant to the hypothesis being tested.

Orne and Evans (1965) attempted to explore these effects. A majority of participants (15 out of 18) behaved in ways which were quite alien to them. They were prepared, for example, to pick up a snake which they had been told was poisonous, plunge their hands into a fuming container of what they were told was nitric acid to retrieve a coin and even to throw the 'acid' into the experimenter's face. Outside the experimental situation, they would have been unlikely to do any of these things and, what is more, they suspected no deception. Tedeschi et al. (1985) have described this as a 'pact of ignorance'. Thinking that they have caught on to the experimenter's hypothesis, they go along with it, either to save face or so as not to upset the experiment. Whatever the reason, the behaviour of participants may be abnormal and gives a distorted picture of how they would ordinarily behave.

Compromise of objectivity Objectivity may be compromised by any of the following factors:

- **The biosocial or physical characteristics of the experimenters**. The age, sex, race or appearance of the experimenters, for example, may affect the way in which participants react to them.
- **Experimenter's social skill.** The experimenter's social skills in dealing with participants are also important factors. They will cooperate more readily with an experimenter who is helpful and friendly than with one who is not.

The influence of the participants It has been a recurrent criticism of psychological research that participants tend predominantly to be white, male American undergraduates. This reflects the ease with which this group can be persuaded to take part. This has been shown to be the case most particularly in social psychology. Tedeschi et al. (1985) showed in a survey of research between 1969 and 1979 that 70 per cent of social psychological research projects used college students as participants. Another relevant characteristic of participants in psychological experiments is that they tend to be volunteers. Ora (1965) has found that volunteers are not typical of the population at large. They tend to be more easily

influenced, moody, anxious for approval, aggressive and neurotic than are nonvolunteers. Because they are not typical it is less easy to generalize from them to the whole population.

Participants' roles in the research situation Weber and Cook (1972) have identified four distinct roles which participants adopt in the research situation:

- **The 'faithful' participant.** This participant tries to react to the situation as naturally as possible, either deliberately or out of disinterest.
- **The cooperative participant.** This participant tries to find out the hypothesis being tested in order to help support it.
- **The negativistic participant.** This participant has the objective of trying to find out the hypothesis to ensure that it is not supported.
- **The apprehensive participant.** This participant believes that the experimenter is out to find out some hidden truth about him or her. Every effort will be made to avoid negative evaluation.

The expectations of the experimenter A further cause of distortion can be the expectations which the experimenter has about the outcome of the experiment. Theory and previous research provide the basis for the hypothesis which is being tested, which is a prediction of the outcome. There is a built-in motive to encourage this to be fulfilled. An experiment conducted by Rosenthal (1966) illustrates this. There is detail of this in Box 34.4.

Sampling bias Where generalization needs to be made to a wider group, the sample used has to be typical of that wider group. This has already been discussed in the introduction to this part. Where college students are used as participants, they are seen as bright young adults anxious to volunteer, sometimes in return for much-needed payment. Ora's research mentioned above has shown such volunteers to be atypical. Additionally, students are likely to be atypical in that they have a narrower age and intellectual range than nonstudents. While this **sampling bias** may be acceptable if the intention of the experimenter is to generalize only to other student volunteers, it is not acceptable to widen this generalization to those who do not share these characteristics.

Box 34.4 An experiment to demonstrate the importance of experimenter expectations

Student experimenters were asked to observe rats running through mazes and report their findings. One group was told that their rats were a very bright strain, a second group that their rats were dull. The rats were in fact no different from each other. The results showed that the 'bright' rats had performed much better than the 'dull' ones. Rosenthal discovered three problems relating to the influences exerted by the experimenter:

- Expectations of the experimenter about what it is predicted will be found may be a source of bias.
- Good results at the outset of an experiment may produce expectations in the experimenter which are then transmitted to the participants.
- The interpretation which the researcher puts upon the data will tend to be that which backs up the theory being tested.

Statistical inference Use is frequently made of **statistical inference** (see Chapter 35) to enable experimenters to have confidence that their results can be generalized. This makes use of statistical probability. There is nothing at all wrong in this, providing that those who read their work are aware what the use of statistical inference implies. Later chapters will deal in detail with this. At this point, it is sufficient to illustrate the limitations imposed by statistical inference. It has become customary to employ a criterion of 5 per cent significance as this provides a balance between the likelihood of a type I or a type II error (see Introduction, page 818, and Chapter 35); that is to say, if the statistics show that there is a five in a hundred chance or less that the results obtained could have been due to chance alone, that is held to provide sufficient confidence for the researcher to say that the effect observed is a real one and not the result of chance. However, there still remains a 5 per cent probability that there is no real effect at all, that the results are in fact due to chance. Hence the need for replication, the repeating of an experiment. When we deal with the writing up of experimental reports (Chapter 37), it will be evident

that one of the main reasons for the care taken in reporting is to facilitate replication.

In relation to the remarks above there is further discussion of these issues in Chapter 3.

? SELF-ASSESSMENT QUESTIONS

1. Define an 'experiment'. Define and list its key features.
2. Give a brief definition of 'independent variable' and 'dependent variable'.
3. Describe three different experimental designs.
4. Comment briefly on the strengths and weaknesses of the experimental method.

Experimental design and the control of variables

So far in this chapter, we have examined experimentation and have seen that control of variables is central to it. In this section, we shall attempt to explain some of the ways in which variables can be controlled in the planning and design stage of a study. In this way, the observations and measurements we make will be more likely to reflect what we are trying to study rather than some extraneous factor which had not been taken into account, that is to say, some systematic error.

Failure to control these extraneous factors adequately may result in biased results. That is to say, it becomes unclear how much of the difference observed is the result of the conditions being studied, how much is due to (psychological) effects and how much is due to the influence of extraneous variables.

To take an example, supposing you were conducting an experiment involving the learning of verbal material under two different conditions, say, in total silence or with background music playing. If all the most

GLOSSARY

Sampling bias That bias which arises from faults in the assembling of samples from the population(s) which are being investigated.

Statistical inference Inferences which are made as a result of statistical analysis of data collected from research. This can include inference from statistical tests of significance.

intelligent participants operated in one condition and the least intelligent in the other, differences found in learning might well be due not to the conditions in which the learning was taking place, but to the intelligence of the participants. The effect of the independent variable (music or silence) on the dependent variable (learning success) has been confounded by a variable with which the experiment is not concerned. There are various experimental designs which may be used to achieve effective control.

Experimental design

Experimental design concerns the decisions which are taken when an experiment is set up. It is principally concerned with the ways in which samples are selected and allocated to conditions within an experiment. The term 'condition' relates to the independent variable (IV). This is the variable which an experimenter deliberately manipulates in order to examine the effect of this manipulation on a dependent variable (DV). There a number of designs between which a researcher may choose.

Related/repeated measures design

Related measures design is where there is a clear relationship between the samples used in one condition and the other (or others). This is sometimes referred to as repeated measures as it most often involves using the same participants in two or more conditions. As with most aspects of design, there are advantages and disadvantages with a related measures design. The advantages include:

- **Convenience.** You do not need to recruit as many participants, because you are using the same sample twice (or more).
- **Absence of bias arising from individual differences between people**. The same individuals are being tested under each condition.

However, there are **disadvantages**:

- **Order effects**. These include the effects of fatigue or boredom on participants and also practice effects, all of which may occur because participants are performing in more than one condition and may be sources of bias.

- **Learning and memorization**. There will clearly be some circumstances in which related measures cannot be used at all. An example might be where participants are asked to memorize something under one condition and then under another. The first memorization will be bound to interfere with the second. Even where the material to be memorized is different under each condition there is a likelihood of bias. You are introducing yet another source of systematic error – differences in the material memorized.

Independent measures design

An **independent measures design** involves using different participants for each condition. The advantages and disadvantages of this are the converse of related measures designs. The **advantages** include:

- **Order effects, practice and learning**. These are not problems, because participants are different under each condition.
- **Economy.** The same materials may be used under each condition.

The **disadvantages** include:

- **Cost and inconvenience.** You have to recruit more participants because each participant is used under only one condition.
- **Individual differences**. Humans (or animals) are infinitely variable and there may well be differences between the people you recruit which could sytematically affect one condition and confound your results.

GLOSSARY

Condition A term which refers to the manipulation of the independent variable. A particular change in the characteristics of the independent variable is referred to as an experimental condition.

Related (repeated) measures design An experimental design where there is a relationship between the participant tested under one condition and another (others). Most commonly the same participants are tested under each condition (repeated measures).

Independent measures design An experimental design where there is no relationship between participants tested under each condition.

Matched participants design

Matched participants design involves identifying what you think are the important differences between individuals which may influence the results of your study. These might include intelligence or ability, gender, age, socioeconomic status or some other factor specific to the study you are doing. Then, against every participant recruited for one condition, another, who has been matched for the characteristics you have identified, is recruited for the other condition. Once pairings have been made, participants are allocated randomly to conditions. This is classified for the purpose of statistical analysis as a related measures design because there is a relationship between participants tested under each condition. They have been matched against each other. Again, there are advantages and disadvantages. The advantage of this is that, while it allows you to use a separate set of participants for each condition, you are overcoming the problem of individual differences (at least in so far as the characteristics you have identified are concerned).

The disadvantages include:

- The time and expense involved in pretesting for the characteristics which you have decided to match;
- The difficulty of actually matching people accurately;
- Besides this, there is always the chance that you failed to identify an individual difference which was in fact a source of systematic error.

Single participant design

You may occasionally choose to select just one participant and test him or her a large number of times under different conditions. For instance, you might test an individual's reaction time to an audible stimulus and compare it with his or her reaction time to a visible one. The logic of this is that the participant is a 'source of a population of potential reaction times from which an experimenter can obtain two samples of responses under the headings "visual" and "auditory"' (Radford and Govier, 1980, p. 56). The scores do not come in pairs and cannot be regarded as related to each other. Clearly, the possibility of generalization from this kind of study is very limited, but it can be useful as a preliminary to a larger study. For the purpose of statistical analysis, a single participant design is treated as though it were an independent measures design.

Control of variables

Order effect

The sequence or order in which events occur in an experiment can bias the results which are obtained. This is most likely to happen when we have opted for a related (repeated) measures design: that is, where the same group of participants are tested under each condition. The experience which participants have when taking part in an investigation is bound to have an effect on them. Suppose that an experiment involves performing a particular task a number of times. The consequences are likely to be that:

- Participants get bored or tired performing the same task over and over again. Their responses are unlikely to be as speedy or as accurate on the hundredth as on the first presentation.
- They also learn how to perform the task better as they go along.

In either case (that of fatigue or boredom, or that of learning), the results are likely to be biased.

Counterbalancing In order to get over this bias, the experimenter may counterbalance the order in which the material is presented. Instead of doing all the tests in Condition A first and then the tests in Condition B, both tests would be divided in half and presented in

---

this order – ABBA. This should cut out any bias which might result from putting one or the other consistently first.

Randomization An alternative strategy to avoid this kind of bias is called **randomization**. If it were thought that the time of day when the tests were done might have an effect upon the results, then tests under each condition would need to be randomly allocated across all times of the day. It might be done like this. Suppose there are 30 participants, each doing both tests, and the tests go on from 9 am until 5 pm and last an hour. The names of the participants are put on slips and into a 'hat'. The time slots are also put on slips and into a second 'hat'. Each name is drawn randomly and put together with a time slot also randomly drawn (rather like the draw for the FA Cup). Alternatively, a table of random numbers could be used. In this way, it is chance which determines the order in which the tests are done.

Expectations

We have seen in an earlier part of this chapter that expectations, both of participants and of researchers, can have an effect upon the results obtained. As a result, bias may occur as a result of what are termed demand characteristics. Researchers need to make allowance for this at the planning stage. This might involve using single or double blind techniques.

Single blind In a **single blind design**, the effect of participants' expectations is kept in check by their being unaware, as they complete the tests that make up the research, what the true purpose of the research is. Of course, they could and should be told all about it afterwards. But while the tests are proceeding, they cannot (consciously or unconsciously) influence the results by their expectations of what they feel the 'right' results should be.

Double blind Similarly, the expectations of researchers may be a source of bias. A **double blind** technique may be used to control this. In this, neither the persons administering the tests nor the participants are aware of the real purpose of the study and are only carrying out instructions. An illustration will make this clearer. Morris and Beck (1974) used a double blind technique in the experiment which is detailed in Box 34.5.

Box 34.5 Morris and Beck's study using a double blind technique

In an attempt to test the effectiveness of ECT (electroconvulsive therapy) used in the treatment of depression, simulated ECT was used. Procedures were undertaken exactly as in a genuine treatment session, except that for some participants no current was used. The doctors who administered the trials were unaware which patients were receiving genuine and which simulated ECT. Patients also were only informed afterwards. Morris and Beck (1974) have reported 146 such double blind studies of ECT and of other drug treatments involving the use of substances to simulate drugs. In no case was the simulated treatment found to be more effective than the genuine treatment.

There is an issue of ethical concern here. Is it ethical to give 'real' treatment to some participants and not others?

Standardized instructions

The instructions which are given to participants can make a great deal of difference. **Standardized instructions** need to be carefully prepared beforehand so as to ensure that bias does not result from some participants having instructions worded slightly differently from those of others.

GLOSSARY

Randomization An alternative to counterbalancing used to mitigate order, practice and fatigue effects. The conditions are randomly presented. It is useful when there are several conditions or when the effects of several alternative extraneous variables need to be taken into account.

Single blind technique An experimental design where participants remain unaware of the true aims of the experiment in which they are participating, thus mitigating the effects of demand characteristics.

Double blind technique An experimental design where neither the participants nor the individual administering any tests is aware of the true aims of the experiment. The purpose is to mitigate the effects of the experimenter's expectations on the test results.

Standardized instructions Instructions to be given to participants which are standardized at the design stage of an experiment to avoid bias which might arise from different instructions being given to some participants as compared to others.

Individual differences

It needs to be borne in mind that psychological research is concerned with people and that they are infinitely variable. When a researcher uses an independent measures design, that is to say, when different individuals are tested under each condition, the possibility of bias arises from individual differences, particularly in such things as intelligence, personality and socioeconomic status. There are two main ways of mitigating the bias resulting from individual differences:

■ Using a matched participants design, as described earlier. Individuals are pretested for factors which the researchers think are relevant and are then allocated to the conditions in the experiment so that each member of one sample is matched against a member of the other sample. This is not easy to do except with identical twins.
■ Where there are a large number of participants, the problem of individual differences can be met by randomly allocating participants to each condition. This method is effective only where there is a large enough number of participants (25 or more).

SELF-ASSESSMENT QUESTIONS

1. What are meant by 'order effects'? How can you mitigate the bias which results from order effects?
2. How is it possible to minimize the bias that results from expectations of (a) researchers and (b) participants?
3. What precautions should be taken to ensure that bias does not result from the way in which the participants are briefed?
4. What are meant by 'single blind' and 'double blind' techniques? In what ways can they mitigate bias in experimentation?
5. List some ways in which the use of experimentation makes possible a high degree of control over extraneous variables.

Nonexperimental methods

There will be occasions on which it will not be feasible to intervene in an experimental way to manipulate the independent variable. Alternatives include observation, survey, case study, interview, ethogenic research, archival methods and simulation.

Observation

Observation provides first stage data by which hypotheses may be formed. These hypotheses may then be tested experimentally. Clearly, some control is lost and it is no longer possible to infer cause in the same way as in an experiment, but there may be ethical and practical considerations which make experimentation impossible. Ethical issues have been explored in greater detail in Chapter 5.

Suffice it to say at this point that ethical considerations might make it difficult, for example, to experiment with a baby's feeding regime. It might prove neither practicable nor ethical to experiment on the effect of teacher attitudes on pupil progress. The attitudes which teachers adopt do not easily lend themselves to manipulation. In such instances, observation of what occurs naturally is likely to be more appropriate. We shall examine three types of observation: controlled observation, naturalistic observation and participant observation.

Controlled observation

Controlled observation has much in common with experimentation, as well as some of its advantages and disadvantages. It is likely to be carried out in a laboratory in carefully controlled conditions. The main difference will be that there is no manipulation of the variables. The observer simply observes and measures what is there in the situation. Box 34.6 provides detail of two examples:

Naturalistic observation

An alternative to controlled observation is **naturalistic observation**. Participants are not brought into a

---

GLOSSARY

Observation Method of study in which there is no manipulation of variables as in an experiment, but only careful observation and measurement of phenomena under study.

Controlled observation Observation carried out in carefully controlled conditions, usually in a laboratory setting.

Box 34.6   Two examples of controlled observation

Research has been carried out into the effects on behaviour of circadian rhythms. These are naturally occurring cycles of changes in the human body which affect temperature, blood pressure and urine volume, as well as liver, kidney and endocrine gland activity, on a daily cycle. Activity was often found to be three to five times higher during the day than during the night (Luce, 1971). Without manipulating any of these patterns of activity, but by closely observing a large number of individuals, researchers were able to reach some interesting conclusions. One of the projects to be found at the end of this book deals with the effects of circadian rhythms on performance on a vigilance task.

In sleep laboratories, participants are allowed to sleep naturally but with electrodes attached to points on their scalps to measure the electrical activity in the brain by means of an electroencephalogram (EEG). Observations are made in very closely controlled conditions (Hartmann, 1973).

Both of these areas of research have been discussed in Part 2 of this book.

Box 34.7   An example of naturalistic observation

Kathy Sylva and her colleagues used naturalistic observation in their study of children's play, carried out in a playgroup in Oxfordshire (Sylva et al., 1980). The design of her study was no less rigorously scientific than an experimental design would have been. Decisions had to be made on what categories of behaviour to observe, at what time intervals data should be recorded, what the important features of the natural setting were and how to minimize the effects on the children's behaviour of being observed.

controlled environment, but their spontaneous behaviour is studied in natural surroundings. While this overcomes some of the distortions resulting from an artificial environment, there is some loss of control. This may or may not be a serious matter. Box 34.7 shows an example of naturalistic observation.

Participant observation

A variant on the above is where the researcher actually becomes a part of the group which is being observed. This is designed to minimize the effects on the participants' behaviour of being observed. To illustrate participant observation Box 34.8 provides two examples.

Strengths and weaknesses of observation

Some **strengths** of the observation method are:

Less dehumanization   There is less chance of the dehumanization and distortion of which Heather

speaks (see p. 823), as many observational studies are carried out in the field, although this is by no means always the case. Controlled observation is a case in point.

Less reductionism   Studies of this kind are likely to be more holistic and less reductionist than is often the case with experimental methods. Studies tend to deal with the total situation in which the participants find themselves, rather than with small elements of that situation taken in isolation.

Provision of initial hypotheses   The great strength of observational studies lies in their ability to provide initial hypotheses on which to base more searching examinations. This forms the basis of the **hypothetico-deductive process** which forms the core of the scientific approach to knowledge. This process starts with a theory, perhaps gathered from initial observation, from which an operational hypothesis is

---

> **GLOSSARY**
>
> **Naturalistic observation** Observation of spontaneous behaviour carried out in the natural surroundings of the participants.
>
> **Participant observation** Observation in which the researchers become a part of the group which is being observed.
>
> **Hypothetico-deductive process** A cyclical process used in research where a theory is refined to produce a hypothesis (or hypotheses) and then tested. The results of the test provide the basis for modification of the theory and further testing.

Box 34.8   Two examples of participant observation

A classic study of social relationships in a secondary school was carried out by Hargreaves (1967). He was able to observe and report on the attitudes and behaviour of boys and staff at the school by becoming a member of staff for a year.

Another example was that of Whyte (1955), who became a member of an Italian gang in Boston, Massachusetts. He took part in all the activities of the gang, including gambling and shady political deals. There are clearly ethical implications here from the point of view of both the deceit involved and also the ethical rightness of engaging in criminal activity to obtain data.

deduced, which can be tested and the results of the test used to modify the theory to provide further hypotheses, and so on. This has been discussed in Chapter 3 under the heading of 'Psychology and science'.

Some of the **weaknesses** of the experimental method, mentioned above, apply also to observation:

Artificiality Laboratory-based observation can be just as artificial as experimentation. Behaviour is equally likely to be distorted. Masters and Johnson (1966) set up a laboratory to study human sexual behaviour by means of controlled observation. It would be hard to show that the sexual behaviour of participants remained unaffected by their being in a laboratory, observed by research workers.

Expectancy So long as the participants are aware that they are being studied, expectancy effects and demand characteristics may equally be in evidence. By careful design, however, it is possible to minimize the participants' awareness of being observed and the consequent changes in behaviour which this brings about.

Sampling bias It becomes even more important to ensure that samples observed are typical of the population to which it is intended to generalize the study. This is, however, not always easy to achieve.

Additionally, there are weaknesses which do not apply to experimentation:

Cause and effect Causality is harder to imply in observational studies. Without manipulating variables, it is harder to pinpoint the cause of effects that are observed. For instance, in Hargreaves's study mentioned in Box 34.8, he observed that lower streams in the school had poorer attitudes towards school, lower attainment and worse behaviour than did higher streams. However, it is hard to attribute this definitively to streaming rather than to a number of other possible causes: socioeconomic conditions or intelligence, for example.

Observer bias Especially in cases where the structuring of the observations has not been sufficiently careful, there is a danger of observer bias. The flexibility of a less well-structured design can lead to subjectivity in what is observed. Even in cases where there has been more careful attention to structuring, the structure itself has been the result of conscious decisions taken by the researcher. It is hard to be certain that value judgments have not entered into the taking of these decisions; in fact, it is almost inevitable that they will. This is not necessarily going to be detrimental, but it does need to be borne in mind when evaluating research. An example of observer bias is described in Box 34.9.

Box 34.9   Observer bias in Malinowski's research

An example of this kind of bias can be seen in the research of the Polish anthropologist Malinowski (1927). While he was claiming to be a participant observer among the Trobriand islanders, he still continued to live in a separate hut and to regard the islanders as inferior to himself. His 'participant observation' was therefore not truly participant. His theoretical position also was not objective. He started from a Freudian position, examining the extent to which the islanders exhibited aspects of Freudian belief, such as Oedipal conflict. To have been truly unbiased, he would have needed to put his theoretical beliefs to one side, at least until after he had made his observations. The very fact that he was looking for particular kinds of behaviour made it much more likely that he would find them.

Interobserver reliability Where there is more than one observer, interobserver reliability can be a problem. Care needs to be taken with the instructions that observers are given to ensure that observations are carried out in precisely the same way by all.

Survey method

Another alternative is to use **survey methods**. Typically, the researcher will assemble a large number of questions to be posed to a representative sample of the relevant population. The questionnaire may be a highly structured one with fixed alternative responses, or more open-ended with respondents able to express themselves more freely. The analysis of the responses is clearly more difficult in the latter case, while in the former there is more scope for the surveyor's own biases to intrude.

An example of the survey method is Rutter's *Fifteen Thousand Hours* (Rutter et al., 1979), details of which are in Box 34.10.

Strengths and weaknesses of surveys

Some of the **strengths** of survey methods are:

Economy A major strength of use of surveys is that of economy. A great deal of ground can be covered

---

Box 34.10 An example of survey method, Rutter's *Fifteen Thousand Hours*

The aim was to see how schools differed in academic attainment, attendance and delinquency. The researchers chose 12 schools within a radius of six miles in the Inner London Education Authority area. Survey methods were combined with structured interviews (which might be regarded as oral surveys) and some observation of events in the classroom. Explanatory variables considered included the status and sex composition of the schools' pupils, size and space, age of buildings, the number of sites on which a particular school worked, staffing, class size and school organization and the particular ambience of the schools. It was a very well-conducted piece of research, but it clearly depended upon a number of value judgments made by the researchers on what variables were likely to prove important.

---

and responses gained from a large sample comparatively easily. Rutter's study covered 12 schools in Inner London. A large number of factors were examined and the scope of the outcomes was also wide. The researchers were able to obtain data on attendance, pupil behaviour and academic results.

Provision of initial hypothesis As with observations, surveys may suggest further areas of research for detailed study by other methods.

Some of the **weaknesses** of the survey method are:

Data analysis There is always the danger that decisions on what to investigate will be determined not so much by what is important as by what is easy to analyse.

Memory failure People are frequently questioned in surveys about their past behaviour or practices. It may be difficult for them to be accurate.

Distortions However carefully interviews and questionnaires are structured, there is always the likelihood that people will not respond truthfully. There are several reasons for this, the most important being that:

- They are simply not sufficiently interested to think carefully about their answers;
- Where responses are made anonymously, there will be a tendency to answer in a way which shows the respondent up in the best light;
- The wording of written questions or the use of nonverbal cues in oral questions, tone of voice and so on by interviewers may influence responses;
- There may be several interviewers, each with his or her own set of biases.

Design difficulties There are problems both with closely structured and with open-ended questionnaires. Where the questionnaire is highly structured,

---

GLOSSARY

Survey method A method of research where a large number of participants, forming a representative sample of the population, is questioned, either orally through interview or through written questionnaires.

the preconceptions of the compiler will show through and might force respondents to answer in a way which does not entirely reflect their views. On the other hand, where the survey is more open-ended, this may bring problems of subjectivity in the way in which responses are interpreted.

Response and behaviour mismatches Responses to questions about behaviour, both verbal and written, may not reflect what people actually do. What they do may vary considerably from what they say they do.

Case study method

The methods we have so far examined have been examples of **nomothetic research**. They depend upon the scientific observation of a number of participants and attempt to arrive at principles of behaviour which apply to all of them and which may be generalized to a wider population. The alternative view to take is that human beings are essentially unique individuals and it is this uniqueness, more than what is common among them, which is worthy of study. This is the **idiographic research** approach to the study of behaviour. This has been discussed in Chapters 3 and 4.

Case study is different from experiment, observation and survey in two major respects:

- ■ **Idiographic nature**. It is essentially idiographic in that it involves making a detailed study of single individuals or instances of something: a family, for example.
- ■ **Qualitative data**. It tends to depend more upon **qualitative analysis** rather than **quantitative analysis**; that is to say, upon a verbal description of participants more than upon numerical analysis of features of their behaviour. While numerical measurement of characteristics is not excluded, the emphasis is upon description more than upon measurement.

Case study methods have been fairly extensively used in psychology. Among the most well-known users of the method was Freud. Freud and other psychoanalysts employed case study in their compilation of detailed case histories of the patients they treated. Freud's theories and methods have been fully discussed in Chapter 30. It was from these case histories that their theories of personality were

Box 34.11   An example of case study: Freud's study of 'Little Hans'

Hans was the son of one of Freud's friends, a doctor interested in Freud's work. He developed a phobia of horses and was especially terrified of being bitten by one of them. Freud's interpretation was that in Hans's unconscious mind he harboured incestuous desires for his mother but was afraid that his father would find out and castrate him as a punishment. On a conscious level, he expressed his anxiety in the form of a fear of horses, which symbolized his father, and of biting, which symbolized castration. This explanation was backed up by detailed evidence. Hans particularly feared white horses with blinkers and black round the mouth. His father had a black moustache and sometimes wore glasses. Furthermore, Hans's father sometimes played 'horses' with his son, always as the horse with Hans as the rider. All these data were carefully collected to support Freud's explanation of the phobia. More generally also, the data provided support for the general thesis that boys in the so-called phallic stage suffered from Oedipal conflict (so-called after Oedipus, a figure in Greek mythology). This was characterized by the boy's sexual attraction to his mother and fear of his father's vengeance.

derived. The case of Little Hans illustrates this. This is described in Box 34.11.

GLOSSARY

Nomothetic research Research which attempts to arrive at principles of behaviour which may be applied to a larger group of people or perhaps generalized to a whole population, by making comparisons with norms of behaviour.

Idiographic research Research which concentrates upon detailed study of an individual or individuals as opposed to groups.

Case study Research where a single individual or a small number of individuals are examined individually and in detail and their behaviour analysed.

Qualitative analysis Method of dealing with research data which depends more upon description than upon numerical measurement.

Quantitative analysis Methods of dealing with research data which depends wholly or in large measure upon numerical analysis.

Strengths and weaknesses of case study

Some **strengths** of the case study method are:

Detailed study   Case study allows detailed study of all aspects of an individual case rather than just being concerned with a few measurable characteristics. There is a greater chance that insights might be gained into the nature of behaviour, which might well be missed in other methods of study.

Description and qualitative data   Case study is based more upon description and upon qualitative data, than upon measurement. It is therefore less likely to ignore those facets of behaviour which cannot easily be measured.

Some **weaknesses** of the case study method are:

Generalization   Because case study method deals with only one, or possibly a very few, individuals studied in great depth, it is not as easy to generalize findings to other people. The results of a study of one individual are really only valid in the case of that individual. Great caution should be exercised in generalizing to others.

Subjectivity   Because they are based upon the analysis of qualitative rather than quantitative data, interpretation is in the hands of researchers alone. They also are responsible for deciding what to include in their descriptions and what to leave out. This makes it very easy for the researcher to leave out what does not support his or her theory. For instance, Freud was the sole analyst, observer and interpreter of what he observed in his patients. It was open to him to interpret what he observed in a way which would support his ideas about Oedipal conflict at this particular stage in a boy's development.

Interview techniques

Interviews used in psychological research may vary from those which are tightly scripted and used in conjunction with other survey methods (as in Rutter's study, mentioned above) to free discussion between interviewer and interviewee. Massarik (1981) listed six types of interview:

■ **The hostile interview.** In this case, the two parties have different goals. It might, for instance, be a

police interrogation in which the suspect is trying to limit the amount of information which is elicited, while the interrogator is trying to gain as much information as possible.

■ **The survey interview.** This might be, for example, the kind of interview which ensues when you are stopped on the street by a market researcher. There is little personal involvement on either side. This very lack of personal involvement leads to objectivity.

■ **The rapport interview.** This might be, for example, the kind of interview which takes place when a prospective student applies for a place at college. The goals and boundaries are fairly well defined, and the format is usually laid down beforehand (at least in framework). However, within these limits there is a high degree of interaction, and the interviewer will attempt to establish a rapport with the interviewee. Both are cooperating to reach a single goal (perhaps the right choice of course for the prospective student).

■ **The asymmetrical trust interview.** In this kind of interview, there is one party who is more trustful than the other. Very frequently, this is a matter of superior knowledge and skill. In a doctor–patient interview, the patient is likely to have a high level of trust in the doctor, which may or may not be matched by the doctor's trust in the patient.

■ **The depth interview.** In this kind of interview, common in psychological research, the intention of the interviewer is to establish the greatest possible trust and rapport with the interviewee in order to explore views and motivations in some depth.

■ **The phenomenological interview.** There are few boundaries or limitations in this kind of interview. It often amounts to an open-ended discussion and depends upon trust and caring.

Box 34.12 provides some examples of interviews in use.

Interviews are frequently employed in conjunction with other methods and suffer many of the same

---

GLOSSARY

Interview Research methods based upon face-to-face oral interviews with participants.

Box 34.12 Two examples of interview methods

Lynch (1960) was exploring the 'cognitive maps' which individuals held of their cities, that is to say, the representation they held of them in their minds. Participants were asked to describe a journey from one part of the city to another. Lynch found that individuals paid special attention to distinctive features and that these were not the same in each case. There were also blank areas of the town which they were not able to describe at all. This approach would be described under Massarik's categorization as 'rapport interviewing'.

Kadushin (1976) was interested in parents who had adopted older children (older than five years). He interviewed the parents of 91 such families and derived, from transcripts of the interviews, measures of parental satisfaction. In a large number of cases (between 82 and 87 per cent), there was a high level of satisfaction. Children had developed close relationships with their adoptive parents and showed little sign of the earlier abuse they had suffered. This would be described under Massarik's categorization as 'depth interviewing'.

strengths and weaknesses as survey techniques. A great deal of information may be obtained comparatively easily, although it is much more expensive in terms of staffing. There is also the problem of data analysis, especially in those kinds of interview which are most open-ended. There always has to be a compromise between the maximization of the information gained and the ease with which it may be analysed.

Ethogenics

Harré (1979) suggested that small units of human behaviour, particular acts or actions, were inappropriate as the focus for the study of social behaviour, and that researchers should take episodes rather than individual acts or actions as the unit of study. People, he argued, experience life as a series of episodes, rather like scenes in a play. He also proposed that it was likely to be more meaningful to study people's own accounts of their experiences rather than just looking at their behaviour from outside. This was termed account analysis and was not entirely new. In fact, it goes back

to the importance placed upon introspection in the early days of psychology. But what Harré suggested was that it should be used as a valid technique for investigation rather than a last resort when there was no other method available. For example, Marsh et al. (1978), studying the behaviour of football crowds, used ethogenic methods to discover that deindividuation (the loss of individuality when people become members of a large crowd) was much less than had been thought. A further example of ethogenic methods in use is discourse analysis, the study of the way in which people express themselves in order to obtain insights into, for example, social assumptions. It may reveal racist assumptions, for example, which may not be revealed equally well by looking at acts or actions. There is also a discussion on qualitative methods in Chapter 3 in the context of alternatives to a strictly scientific approach to psychology.

Archival research

In such research, the records and data used, government documents, for instance, or newspaper reports, were not originally produced for the purposes of the study itself. Research reports themselves are often used for archival research. Maccoby and Jacklin (1974) conducted quite large-scale archival research into sex difference in behaviour. More than 2000 studies were reviewed and conclusions were reached that there were few behavioural differences between males and females. Details of this study may be found in Chapter 22.

A technique increasingly being adopted in recent years is that of reanalysing the published statistical results from studies in order to identify trends which are not apparent from simple literature reviews. This meta-analysis, as it has been called, enabled Cooper (1979) to take another look at the studies Maccoby and Jacklin reviewed with special attention to the statistics

---

GLOSSARY

Ethogenics Research which attempts to take episodes rather than individual actions as a focus for study.

Discourse analysis A study of the way in which people express themselves in order to gain insights into social assumptions.

Archival research Research where the researcher attempts to delve into records not produced originally for the purpose of research, such as government documents or news reports.

involved and to conclude that in studies concerning group pressure women tend to conform more than men. Eagly and Wood (1991) have argued that meta-analysis of some of these studies produced strong support for social role theory to explain differences in the behaviour of men and women. There is a definition of meta-analysis in Chapter 22.

Strength and weakness of archival research

Some of the **strengths** of archival research are:

Scope of research Archival research greatly enlarges the scope of research. Records sometimes extend over centuries and across cultures and comparisons can be made which might not otherwise be possible. Hebb (1949) reanalysed, for example, 65 cases collected together by Von Senden of people who had regained their sight after periods of blindness. These cases dated from 1700 to 1928. While the detail contained in some of the earlier studies might well have been suspect, the range of material available is hugely increased.

Demand characteristics and experimenter effects There is no problem with either of these

effects. Because archival material has been, by definition, collected for some other purpose, the researchers are not directly involved with the participants and so they cannot influence the findings.

The main **weakness** of archival research is that it is sometimes a difficult and time-consuming process to locate the archives which are needed.

Role play and simulation

Social psychologists in particular are often interested in areas where it is difficult or impossible to conduct research directly. You cannot go into a courtroom, for instance, to observe the deliberations of a jury. In such circumstances simulation provides a possible alternative. Box 34.13 shows a piece of research involving simulation.

Strengths and weaknesses of role play and simulation

Some **strengths** of role play and simulation are:

Range The principal advantage of simulation and role play is that it allows study of areas which might

---

Box 34.13   An example of the use of simulation in research

Kramer et al. (1990) were interested in the effects of pretrial publicity upon the deliberations of a jury. Participants viewed a videotaped trial of someone accused of armed robbery and then were asked to deliberate as though they were the jury. There were several conditions:

Factual publicity condition
Some of the participants were exposed to pretrial publicity about the facts of the case, that the defendant had an extensive criminal record, for instance.

Emotional publicity condition
A second group learned that the defendant was also a suspect in a 'hit and run' motoring case where a little girl had been killed.

Innocuous publicity condition
Yet another group of the participants were exposed to innocuous pretrial publicity.

Judge's instructions
Some received special instructions from the trial judge to disregard anything which was not evidence presented at the trial itself, specifically reports on television and in the newspapers.

Timing of publicity
Some of the participants got their information immediately before seeing the video, others two weeks before.

Results of the study
The emotional publicity group were found to be much more likely to convict than the innocuous publicity group. The factual publicity group were only found to be more likely to convict if they had the publicity immediately before the video. The judges's instruction had no effect. There may be ethical considerations involved in this study. Perhaps you should refer back to the discussion on ethical questions in Chapter 5 and make up your own mind where this study stands.

otherwise be inaccessible. Appropriate experimental controls can be incorporated into the simulation.

Participant involvement Participants also have a greater degree of involvement than in a more typical experimenter/participant study.

Weaknesses of role play and simulation are:

Lack of reality There is doubt expressed in some quarters as to whether the participants in simulations really would behave the same in a real situation as they do in the simulation. Do they do only what they *think* they would do in the real situation rather than what they would actually do?

Ethical considerations There can be ethical problems too. Zimbardo's well-known prison simulation (Haney et al., 1973) (described in more detail in Chapter 28) put participants into the role of prisoners or warders and this had to be discontinued after six days because of the distress that was being caused.

 SELF-ASSESSMENT QUESTIONS

1. What are the major respects in which observation differs from experimentation?
2. What is meant by (a) 'controlled observation' and (b) 'participant observation'?
3. List some of the strengths and weaknesses of observational methods.
4. List the weaknesses of survey methods.
5. Identify some of the strengths of case study methods.
6. List six types of interview. Which of these are the most open-ended, which the most structured? Identify their usefulness in psychological investigation.
7. What are some of the advantages of archival research?
8. In what ways may role play and simulation be used in psychological research? Why can it sometimes be controversial?

Correlational designs

It is appropriate to discuss **correlation** at this point. It is not a method of study in the same way that experimentation or observation are, but rather a statistical technique. It is widely used to measure the extent to which two variables are related to one another. For instance, a researcher may be interested in whether there is any truth in the suggestion that those who are gifted musically are also likely to be good at mathematics. Or whether those who are creative are also intelligent. Correlation can indicate the degree of relationship which exists in a group of people between one aspect of their behaviour and another.

In practice, correlation operates like this. A researcher sets out to discover whether there is any relationship between one aspect of behaviour and another. For instance, it might be useful to find out whether tests of intelligence and of creative ability were in fact measuring the same thing. A group of participants might be tested, using tests of both intelligence and creativity. A test of correlation would indicate the degree to which the two sets of measurements were related. What is being measured is the degree to which the two sets of measurements vary in harmony with each other. The statistic that results from the analysis is known as a coefficient of covariance or a **correlation coefficient**

Further detail about the ways in which correlation may be expressed and the ways in which correlation coefficients are calculated can be found in Chapters 35 and 36.

Some examples of correlation in psychological research

Box 34.14 gives two examples of the use of correlation.

As will be fully explained in Chapter 35, a negative correlation indicates that there is an inverse relationship between the two measurements (in this case, the smaller the community, the greater likelihood of people being helpful to strangers). The strength of this relationship is indicated by the correlation coefficient.

GLOSSARY

Correlation A technique aimed at discovering the extent to which two variables are related

Correlation coefficient A measurement of the correlation between two variables, expressed as a decimal fraction between zero and 1 with zero representing no relationship and 1 representing a perfect match. The coefficient may be positive or negative.

Box 34.14 Two examples of the use of correlation in psychological research

Hill et al. (1976) set out to test the extent to which people were attracted to those like themselves. They measured the ages, educational attainment, attractiveness and attitudes of 200 couples who were going out together but who had not yet made any formal commitment to one another. On each of these measures, correlations were carried out between the couples. Those who remained together to get engaged or married tended to be more alike on these measures than did those whose relationships ended within the next year.

Rushton (1978) set out to explore whether people living in small towns were likely to be more helpful than those in big cities. Questions such as 'Do you have change for the telephone?' or 'Can you tell me the time?' were asked of individuals in a variety of locations, both small and large. The degree of helpfulness was correlated with the size of the location. People in suburbs or small towns were found to be more likely to be helpful than those in big cities. There was a negative correlation between the size of the location and the helpfulness of the people.

ble (with some caution) to predict the probable value of one variable if we know the value of the other. For example, supposing that a high negative correlation was found between the hours spent watching TV and the grades attained by students in the end-of-term exams, you could predict that a compulsive TV viewer would probably not achieve high grades. It is important to note that this does not imply that TV watching causes low grades. There could easily be a third variable affecting both – lack of interest in the subject, perhaps. If you have a perfect relationship (that is, a correlation of $+1$ or -1), you can make your predictions with absolute certainty. But this does not often happen. With imperfect relationships, this certainty becomes a probability. This probability is related to (a) the number of pairs of scores, and (b) the size of the correlation coefficient.

Assessing the independence of concepts It is valuable to use correlation to assess whether or not the ideas we are examining are distinct and separate, or whether they are simply facets of the same thing. For example, Witkin et al. (1962) developed the concept of field dependence or independence, that is, the ability to analyse a problem distinctly from its context. This is fully discussed in Chapter 29. Field independence was, he claimed, a human characteristic quite separate and distinct from intelligence. In support of this claim, he reported correlational analyses of children's scores on tests of field independence and intelligence test scores taken from the Wechsler Intelligence Scale for Children (WISC). The low correlations which he found showed that there was no significant relationship between the two measures; they were not measuring the same thing. Other researchers, however, have found high correlations between these two measures, indicating that they were measuring at least some of the same characteristics.

A zero coefficient shows that there is no relationship at all, a correlation of 1 (either $+$ or $-$) that there is a perfect match. Values between these extremes are expressed as decimal fractions.

Strengths and weaknesses of correlation

Strengths

Some strengths of correlation are:

Detecting relationships Correlation is valuable in that it is possible to identify the direction and strength of a relationship between two (or more) variables. It allows an investigator to measure relationships between variables without manipulating or controlling them.

Making predictions If we know that there is a high correlation between two variables, it becomes possi-

Weaknesses

Some weaknesses of correlation are:

Correlation and cause As has already been indicated, it is very important to stress that correlation does not imply cause. There may be several variables which are interrelated, and it is difficult to know whether the two chosen for comparison are related by cause and effect. In Hill et al.'s study, mentioned above, similarity to one another is only one of the things which might have affected the durability and success of relationships. The amount of time the couples were able to spend together could equally well have been a factor.

Extrapolation It is often tempting to extrapolate from the findings of a correlational study. We must keep within the limits of the data that have been collected. For example, suppose it has been found that there is a strong relationship (a high positive correlation) between the length of time spent on homework and success in examinations, and the length of time spent on homework varied between half an hour and three hours, while the measure of success varied between one and six GCSE passes. It would be quite erroneous to suggest that if children spent five hours a night on homework, they would be likely to get ten GCSE passes.

❓ SELF-ASSESSMENT QUESTIONS

1. Explain how correlation can help us to assess whether a concept (intelligence, for example) is separate and distinct from another (say, creative ability).
2. Why is it not possible to infer cause from correlation?
3. Explain how the use of correlational techniques may help us to be able to predict behaviour.

Some further considerations in research

Important factors included in this section include reliability, validity and standardization.

Reliability

It is very important that any test which is used in a piece of research should be reliable. That is to say, it should not be like an elastic tape measure, measuring differently depending on how hard you pull it. Every time a test is used, researchers need to be certain that the measures obtained accurately reflect real phenom-

ena. This consistency in measurement may be of several kinds.

Internal consistency

A test needs to be consistent in content. If some parts of a test produce markedly different results from others as a measure of the same phenomenon, then the test is flawed. Accordingly, it is common practice to employ a split-half test of reliability. The scores obtained from a sizeable sample of people are divided into two. Scores from odd-numbered items are correlated against scores obtained from even-numbered items. You would expect, with a reliable test, a correlation of +0.8 or +0.9 with a large sample. You can easily see that dividing a test in this way is preferable to comparing, say, the first half and the second half of the test. Boredom, fatigue and learning are likely to confound your results. Besides, it is often the case that a test will start with easier items and become progressively more difficult.

Consistency over time

It is important that a test measures the same every time it is applied. It will be of no use if results vary wildly each time the test is used even though the participants are very similar. To check this reliability over time, a test–retest technique can be used. A sample of participants is tested twice using the same test, with perhaps a month's interval between tests. Results from the two tests are correlated, and it would be expected that a good test would yield a very high correlation (perhaps +0.8 or +0.9).

Sometimes this kind of test–retest is not really feasible. Too much learning might occur when the test is done the first time, and this would bias the results. In such cases, a different but parallel form of the test might

---

GLOSSARY

Reliability A measurement of either the internal or the external consistency of a test. This may be consistency over time, consistency within the test itself or consistency between testers.

Validity A measurement of the extent to which a test is measuring what it claims to measure.

Standardization The calibration of data obtained from tests according to norms to ensure that any comparisons made are fair.

be used on each occasion. Eysenck and Eysenck (1964) produced two parallel forms of their Personality Inventory for this reason.

Intertester reliability

Yet another question of reliability occurs when more than one researcher is involved in the testing of participants in a study. It is clearly necessary for the way in which the test is carried out to be precisely the same whichever researcher is carrying out the test. There is a need for very explicit instructions and the establishment in advance of clear criteria for judgments which are made. An obvious case for intertester reliability occurs when public examinations are conducted and there are a number of examiners. Before the examining commences, there is a coordination meeting at which the criteria for the award of marks are clearly established. Then, as the marking progresses, samples are withdrawn for scrutiny by the Chief Examiner to ensure that intertest reliability is maintained. It is also possible to correlate the results of one tester's work against that of another to ensure that there is harmony between them. In a well-conducted test, there should be a very high correlation between testers.

Validity

A second issue rests on whether the test a researcher employs actually measures what it is claimed that it measures. This is the issue of validity. There has been some controversy about whether examiners should award marks for English, spelling and punctuation in subjects other than English. It is evident that if they do, they are no longer just testing history, geography or whatever, they are testing English spelling and grammar as well. The examinations' validity as tests of history or geography will have been compromised.

The type of validity which needs to be tested depends upon what the test is for. The following are frequently assessed.

Face validity

A test needs to look as though it tests what it says it tests. An aptitude test for secretaries which involved their speed in climbing ladders would not have good **face validity** but, of course, it would as a test for firefighters.

Predictive validity

A test can be used to predict what might occur in the future. For example, it might be possible to construct an aptitude test for driving. This should assess the likelihood of success before a course of driving instruction. The test's **predictive validity** depends upon how well the results from it correlate with success in the subsequent driving test. A test which has been validated in this way can then be used to make an assessment of how good the course of instruction is. If the test is known to be valid and if many people who have been assessed as having a high aptitude for driving then go on to fail the driving test, the driving instructor could perhaps do better.

Content validity

Content validity relates to testing those skills necessary for good performance. A test of agility might have good content validity in a test for ballet dancers, for instance, while a mental arithmetic test would not.

Concurrent validity

Concurrent validity is perhaps the most useful kind of validity. When there already exists a well-established test for some characteristic, the results of a test produced ostensibly for the same thing ought to correlate highly with it, if it is to be considered to be valid. A correlation of $+0.8$ or $+0.9$ might be expected between the two measures with a large sample. To take an example of this, when $11+$ 'intelligence' tests were widely used, their concurrent validity was frequently assessed by making comparisons between results on

---

GLOSSARY

Face validity The extent to which a test appears to be measuring what it claims to measure.

Predictive validity The extent to which a test is capable of predicting future outcomes. A test of aptitude for typing is valid if it accurately predicts future typing ability.

Content validity The extent to which those skills which are measured by a test are relevant to the overall ability which the test claims to measure.

Concurrent validity The extent to which a test's outcomes match the outcomes of other measures of the same thing.

these tests and on school achievement tests in English and mathematics, the assumption being that intelligent children would be likely to do well in both.

Construct validity

Construct validity relates to the accuracy with which a test measures the psychological construct which it is set up to measure. When there is not total agreement between testmakers about the definition of the psychological construct to be measured, construct validity becomes very difficult to achieve. There have been many tests of creative ability constructed, for example, without any very clear consensus on what creativity amounts to. One way of assessing the construct validity of a test is to match it with other manifestations of the construct in question. People who are generally acknowledged to be 'creative' ought to do well on a creativity test if that is to be seen as having construct validity.

Ecological validity

Ecological validity relates to the extent to which the context in which something is being investigated relates to what is found in the 'real world'. For example, there has been a great deal of research into memory which consists of participants attempting to memorize lists of words. This has nothing whatever to say to us about remembering when Aunt Jane's birthday is; it may have little ecological validity. Neisser (1982) had this to say:

> You need only tell a friend, not himself a psychologist, that you study memory. Given a little encouragement, your friend will describe all sorts of interesting phenomena; the limitations of his memory for early childhood, his inability to remember appointments, his aunt who could recite poems from memory by the hour, the regrettable decline in his ability to remember names, how well he could find his way round his home town after thirty years' absence, the difference between his memory and someone else's. Our research has almost nothing to say about any of these topics.
>
> (Neisser 1982)

What Neisser was saying was that memory research, as then conducted, had poor ecological validity.

Experimental validity

This can be closely related to the above. **External experimental validity** relates to the extent to which the experimental situation represents situations that occur in everyday life. Excessive reliance upon students as participants, for example, distorts the validity of experimentation by removing it from the ambit of the 'person in the street'. Sears (1986) has claimed that this has a distorting influence on the understanding of human behaviour. Researchers need to study different people in different situations if they are to understand the full range of human experience. **Internal experimental validity** relates to such things as demand characteristics (discussed earlier) or **evaluation apprehension** (the way in which the very fact that an individual is being observed or tested alters his or her behaviour). Both internal and external experimental validity need to be considered. When they are lacking, the investigation is likely to be compromised.

Standardization

In order to make fair comparisons between sets of data, you need to compare like with like. When a measuring instrument is calibrated, norms are established as criteria for measurement. A thermometer is calibrated so that the point at which water freezes is zero on the centigrade scale and the point at which it boils is 100 degrees. Similarly, with psychological or scholastic tests, some objective criterion needs to be established. If a child comes home from school, boasting that he got 70 per cent in his maths test, it means very little until norms

---

GLOSSARY

Construct validity The extent to which a test measures the psychological construct which it claims to measure. For example, the extent to which intelligence tests actually measure intelligence.

Ecological validity An assessment of the extent to which a test or an experiment is relevant to what happens in the 'real world'.

External experimental validity Similar to ecological validity. It relates to how close the experimental situation is to real life or to what is typical.

Internal experimental validity The extent to which results of an investigation are free from bias from such things as demand characteristics or evaluation apprehension.

Evaluation apprehension A change in the behaviour of a participant in an experiment or other test which arises from being aware of being tested.

have been established. It may have been a very easy test on which the average mark was 95 per cent. On the other hand, it might have been a test where the average mark was 35 per cent, so that 70 is exceptionally good. Without some standardization, you just do not know. To obtain a norm, a criterion against which to measure any particular score on a test, it is necessary to test a large representative sample of the group for which the test is intended. The hope is to obtain a **normal distribution** of scores, a symmetrical distribution in which the largest number of scores cluster round the **mean** (the arithmetical average). This is also known as a Gaussian curve. The characteristics of this normal distribution are known, so that comparisons can easily be made whenever the test is used. For example, it is known that 68.26 per cent of all the scores in such a distribution fall within one standard deviation of the mean and that 95.44 per cent fall within two standard deviations of the mean (a **standard deviation** is a measurement of how widely dispersed the scores are; it will be fully discussed in Chapter 35). It is therefore possible to make an esti-mate of how likely it is for any particular score to occur.

An example might make this clearer. If a repre-sentative sample against which comparisons are to be made has a mean score of 50 per cent and a standard deviation of 10, then the score of 70 per cent is two standard deviations above the mean, and a score of 30 per cent is two standard deviations below the mean. Two standard deviations from the mean include 95.44 of the scores; what is left amounts to 4.56 per cent, and that is divided between the highest scores and the lowest, between both ends of the curve. We are only interested in the top end (that is, the top 2.28 per cent). As our score of 70 per cent falls two standard deviations above the mean, the chance of a score as high or higher than this happening is 2.28 per cent.

Expression of scores

Z scores

It is possible to express any score as a number of standard deviations above or below the mean. A mean score of 50 would be zero, one of 55 would be +0.5 and one of 45 would be −0.5 (one standard deviation, remember, is 10, half a standard deviation [0.5] is 5). These are known as z scores. It is possible to work out the probability (*p*) that any particular z score has of occurring; a table of the probability of z scores is included in an appendix at the end of this book.

Standard scores

It may be inconvenient to express scores as plus or minus decimal fractions, which is what z scores must inevitably be, so they are frequently converted into something easier and more meaningful. One of the most commonly found **standard scores** is a **quotient**. Quotients assume a mean of 100 and a standard deviation of 15, and are the normal means of expressing intelligence scores. To convert a z score into a quotient, start with the mean (100) and add or subtract 15 times the z score (the formula is $100 \pm 15 \cdot z$).

⁇ SELF-ASSESSMENT QUESTIONS

1. What is meant by 'reliability' and 'validity' in relation to psychological testing? How can you ensure that a test is reliable and valid?
2. What do you mean when you say that an investigation is likely to yield 'ecologically valid' data?
3. Why is it necessary to standardize scores? Explain what is meant by 'z scores' and 'quotients'.

GLOSSARY

Normal distribution (sometimes referred to as a Gaussian curve). A frequency distribution where the mean, median and the mode are the same. This results in a 'bell shaped' curve, found when a large number of measurements are taken of naturally occurring phenomena. It has important character-istics used in inferential statistics.

Mean The arithmetical average of a set of scores, arrived at by totalling the scores and dividing by the number of them.

Standard deviation A measure of the spread of a set of scores. The difference between each score and the mean is computed and squared. These squared differences are totalled and divided by the number of scores. The square root is then taken of the result.

z score A test score expressed as a decimal fraction of the standard deviation above or below the mean of a set of scores. For example, where the mean is 50 and the standard deviation 10 a score of 45 would be represented by a z score of −0.5.

Standard scores Scores which result from standardization of test results. They are usually related to the mean and standard deviation of the scores. Examples include z scores and quotients.

Quotient A standard score which assumes a mean of 100 and a standard deviation of 15.

Chapter summary

■ Experimentation involves the deliberate manipulation of an independent variable in order to measure its effect upon the dependent variable. The strengths of experimentation include control, the assessment of causality, objectivity and replicability. Weaknesses include dehumanization of participants, poor ecological validity and demand characteristics.

■ Experimental design may be varied to ensure that variables are properly controlled. Related measures designs imply a clear relationship between samples used in each condition. This will often be the use of the same participants in each condition (repeated measures). While related measures designs obviate the need for additional control of individual differences between participants, there is danger of bias from order effects and from learning and practice. In some cases it may not be possible to use a related measures design.

■ Alternatively, researchers may choose an independent measures design where there is no relationship between participants in each condition. While these designs do not cause problems of learning, practice or order effects, there may be bias resulting from individual differences. A matched participants design may obviate the bias resulting from individual differences. Characteristics are chosen relevant to the particular study and participants are chosen for each condition, matched for these characteristics. The disadvantages of doing this rest upon the trouble and expense involved.

■ Single or double blind techniques may be employed in order to mitigate some of the effects of expectations, on the part of both experimenters and participants. Further sources of bias may arise from the instructions given to participants. Care needs to be taken to ensure that they are carefully prepared beforehand and presented to participants in precisely the same form.

■ Observational methods are an alternative to experimentation. Participants are observed without any attempt to manipulate variables. Observation may be controlled or naturalistic. Participant observation is another variant where researchers become part of the group which is being observed. There is less chance of the kind of distortion and dehumanization which can occur with experimentation. Observation is less reductionist and more holistic in its nature and can provide initial hypotheses on which to base further studies.

■ There is still a great risk of artificiality, especially in laboratory-based observation. Bias may result from expectancy or demand characteristics. It is even more important than in experimentation to ensure typicality of samples. It may not be possible to generalize the study unless the samples are representative. It is harder to establish cause and effect in an observational study where variables are not manipulated. Observer bias is also an issue. Poor structuring may lead to subjectivity, more careful structuring may result in value judgments being made which need to be taken into account when evaluating research. Interobserver reliability is an issue where enough care has not been taken to ensure consistency of methodology.

■ Survey methods may take a number of forms. A large number of questions are put to a representative sample of the target population, by means of questionnaires or interviews. There may be fixed and structured alternative responses or more open-ended ones. The great strength of survey is that it allows a great deal of ground to be covered economically. Weaknesses include the difficulty of data analysis. Where a survey is highly structured this may limit the usefulness of responses, but where it is less tightly structured there may be subjectivity in interpretation and analysis.

■ Case study methods are essentially idiographic and depend upon qualitative as well as quantitative analysis. There is some weakness in that it is harder to generalize from a case study, and there is likely to be greater subjectivity than with other methods. The strength is that it is holistic. Insights may be gained which might well be missed with other methods.

■ Interviews are frequently used in conjunction with other techniques, especially survey or case study, and may take a variety of forms. Massarik has listed six types of interview: hostile interview or interrogation, survey interview, rapport interview, asymmetrical trust interview, depth interview and phenomenological interview. Interviews have many of the same strengths and weaknesses as surveys and case study techniques.

Ethogenic research involves studying episodes rather than individual acts or actions. Account or discourse analysis studies the way in which individuals express themselves in their accounts of episodes and may prove insights into, for example, social assumptions.

Archival research and meta-analysis involve the reanalysis of data produced for other studies. This greatly enlarges the scope for research. Records may extend over many years and across cultures. Because of the time scale that may be involved there is risk of distortion and it is a very time-consuming process.

Correlational techniques are employed frequently to find relationships between variables. They can be useful in making predictions about future behaviour and in assessing the independence of concepts. There are two main weaknesses: the inability to assess causality by means of correlation and the temptation to extrapolate from the findings of a correlational study.

Reliability and validity are very important considerations in all types of psychological research. Reliability concerns the consistency of measurement both internally and over time while validity concerns the degree to which tests measure what they purport to measure. Standardization allows researchers to make fair comparisons between measures by, as it were, calibrating scales of measurement so that they are comparable.

Further reading

Clegg, F. (1982). *Simple Statistics*. Cambridge: Cambridge University Press. Contains necessary further reading on some of the basic concepts in statistics and the use of quantitative methods.

Coolican, H. (1994). *Research Methods and Statistics in Psychology*, 2nd edn. London: Hodder & Stoughton. This is a good general guide to the use of statistics in psychology and to research methods employed.

CHAPTER 35

Presenting the results

The use of statistics   845
▦ Levels of measurement   846

Descriptive statistics   847
▦ Measures of central tendency   848
▦ Table of raw scores   848
▦ Ranked scores   849
▦ Frequency tables   849
▦ Bar charts and pie charts   849
▦ Frequency distributions   852
▦ Measures of dispersion   854

Statistical inference and significance   857
▦ Inferential statistics   857
▦ Probability   858
▦ Tests of significance   860

Correlation   864
▦ Ways of expressing correlation   864
▦ Correlation coefficients and significance   866

Choosing an appropriate test   869
▦ Degrees of freedom   869

Objectives

By the end of this chapter you should be able to:

▦ Appreciate the value of effective descriptive and inferential statistics when presenting the results of a study;

▦ Produce a variety of descriptive statistics designed to describe and summarize data;

▦ Understand the purposes of inferential statistics in relation to the use of probability and testing for significance;

▦ Understand the principles underlying correlational analyses;

▦ Choose appropriate significance tests to analyse data drawn from your own practical investigations.

There are many different ways of presenting and interpreting the data from a psychological investigation. All of them involve the use of statistics, and this chapter is about helping to make you familiar with a range of statistical techniques that can be used to describe and analyse data.

The use of statistics

Many students of psychology approach statistics with a fair amount of fear and misgiving. Therefore, this chapter is also about helping you to realize the following:

▦ Statistics are a very useful tool which can help you to describe and make sense of the data you collect in your practical work.

▦ It is not necessary for you to be a mathematical genius in order to use a wide range of statistical procedures. The basic techniques for displaying your data are straightforward and easily used –

most of them you will already have encountered at school and in everyday life.

■ Statistics that are used to analyse and assess your data do not involve complicated mathematical procedures or committing long, involved formulas to memory. The tests are available in textbooks such as this one and can be applied in much the same way as if you were following a recipe to make a cake.

There are two main kinds of statistics:

■ Descriptive statistics are used to describe or summarize your data: for example, producing a bar chart or calculating an average such as the mean.

■ Inferential statistics are used to help us to draw conclusions – make inferences – about the data collected in a study.

The following sections will deal with descriptive and inferential statistics respectively.

Before looking in more detail at these two types of statistics, it is important to know something about different kinds of data or levels of measurement.

Levels of measurement

There are several ways of measuring what is observed in an investigation. At the simplest level, you can just count the number of events that occur (**nominal data**); you may wish to record the rank order of things (**ordinal data**) or measure more precisely using various different instruments, such as a ruler or clock (**interval/ ratio data**). Let us examine these in more detail.

Nominal data

Where you wish to categorize something and then to count the number of times something falls into this category, you will be using nominal data. For example, a researcher observing the incidence of aggression in children will probably identify clearly what is meant by an incident of aggression and then go on to count how many of such events occur within a particular space of time and in the particular conditions which are being investigated. This is known as nominal, categorical or frequency measurement.

Where you use numbers (or other identifying features such as letters) simply as labels, this is also considered to be nominal data. Examples of this are the

numbers on a footballer's shirt or those used to identify a train or bus.

Ordinal data

At a slightly more sophisticated level, it is possible to rank events which are observed in order – first, second, third, and so on. This is ordinal measurement. Without accurately measuring the times taken by a group of runners to complete a course, it is still possible to put them in order – 1st, 2nd . . . 54th. This form of measurement tells you something about the participants in the race beyond merely counting them, but at the same time it gives no indication of the differences between them. The runner who finished first may have finished in 59 minutes, the second in 60 minutes and the third in 70 minutes, but with their performance measured in this way (ordinally) no account is taken of these variations. So the amount of information conveyed, while more than with the nominal scale, is still less than with an interval or ratio scale of measurement.

Interval or ratio data

To use the same example, if the organizers of the race timed in minutes how long each of the competitors took to complete the course, they would be employing a ratio scale of measurement. There is a defined difference in the performance of the runners. Each unit of measurement (a minute) is the same in terms of

---

GLOSSARY

Descriptive statistics Those statistics whose purpose is to summarize or describe data. These may include measures of central tendency or dispersion or illustrative figures such as bar charts, histograms and graphs.

Nominal data Sometimes referred to as frequency or categorical data, this is a level of measurement which involves simple counting of events which occur.

Ordinal data Data which involve the ranking of events in order as well as counting them.

Interval data Data in which there is an equal interval of difference between measures. For example, if you measured the length of a path in metres, 4 metres represent exactly double the distance represented by 2 metres and 6 metres half as much distance again.

Ratio data Data which besides the equal intervals of measurement of interval data incorporates a true zero point.

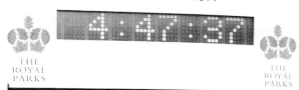

Ordinal measurement may be illustrated by the order in which runners complete a race

Some distinctions between levels of measurement

Hierarchies Levels of measurement are hierarchical. That is to say, each level includes those below it. Ratio measurement includes all the characteristics of interval measurement and adds a fixed zero point. Interval scores include information about order and add to this measurement of the intervals between ranks. Ordinal measurement includes information about numbers in each category and adds to this a rank order. The lowest of the scales of measurement, nominal, simply counts events.

Conversion You can always convert scales of measurement downwards. An interval scale of measurement can easily be converted to ordinal by ranking scores, but some information is lost. If there is doubt about the accuracy of your measurement, it might be advisable to downgrade the level of measurement in this way. If you establish categories for the runners in the race, say those who finish in the first hour, in the first hour and a half and in the first two hours, then you might have 1 finisher in the first category, 17 in the second and 35 in the third. This is nominal measurement and again there has been some information lost.

what it represents as is every other one. The difference between runner 2's and runner 3's performance (1 minute) is ten times as great as that between runners 1 and 2 (10 minutes).

There is one important difference between interval and ratio scales. Ratio data involve a true zero point, whereas zero on an interval scale is purely arbitrary. With measurements such as that of time in seconds or distance in feet, 0 means no time or no distance, since these are ratio scales with clearly defined points of measurement. It is quite in order to say that a measurement of four feet is twice as long as one of two feet. However, this is not the case with an interval scale. A commonly used example of interval scales is temperature as measured by the Celsius and Fahrenheit scales. Zero on both these scales does not mean 'no temperature'. Only the Kelvin scale has a true zero and can therefore be classed as a ratio scale.

Despite this difference between them, it is important to note that for statistical purposes, interval and ratio data are treated in exactly the same way.

Descriptive statistics

Remember that descriptive statistics aim to describe or summarize the data you may have collected in a practical exercise. If descriptive statistics are used well, they will present your results clearly and in a way that can be readily understood by a reader. Figure 35.1 lists the range of descriptive statistics which will be discussed in this section.

It might be helpful to start with a brief note on some of the symbols that you are likely to meet:

$\sum$	Add together
N	The number of items/scores
D	Difference
X	Score

For example:

$$\frac{\sum X}{N}$$

means add the scores together and divide by the number of scores.

Figure 35.1 Kinds of descriptive statistics

Tables	Measures	Graphics
Frequency tables	Central tendency (mean, median, mode)	Bar charts
Tables of raw scores	Dispersion (range, standard deviation)	Histograms
Tables of summary scores	Correlation coefficients	Pie charts
Frequency distribution tables		Scattergrams
Table of ranked scores		Frequency polygons

Measures of central tendency

It is often useful to have one single measure – a typical or representative score – that will summarize a set of scores. There are three key measures of central tendency (or averages) as follows.

Mean

The **mean**, or arithmetic average, is arrived at by adding together all the scores and dividing the result by the number of scores, for example:

$$9 + 7 + 8 + 5 + 6 = 35 \quad \text{Mean} = \frac{35}{5} = 7$$

The formula for the mean is $\dfrac{\sum X}{N}$

Median

The **median** is a value that has as many scores above it as below. It can be found by listing the scores in order of size and identifying the middle one; for example:

$$2\ 3\ 3\ 5\ 7\ 9\ 13 \quad \text{or} \quad 2\ 3\ 4\ 5\ 6\ 8\ 11\ 14$$
$$\text{Median} = 5 \qquad\qquad \text{Median} = 5.5$$

Note: Where there is an even number of scores, an average is taken of the two middle scores (5 and 6 in the second example).

Mode

The **mode** is the most frequently occurring value. It is useful to gain a general impression of the average where there is a large set of numbers; for example:

$$5\ 4\ 5\ 9\ 8\ 5\ 7\ 5\ 8\ 6\ 3\ 4\ 5 \quad \text{Mode} = 5$$

Which measure should I use?

The mean is the preferred average because:

■ It makes use of all the scores and the total.
■ It can be used in other, more advanced, mathematical analyses such as calculating a standard deviation (see Box 35.2).

The mean is useful where scores are fairly evenly distributed about the central value. However, if there are a few very atypical scores, the mean might give a misleading picture of the typical value. Therefore, the median or mode should be used in these cases.

Exercise 35.1

Work out the mean and the median of the following sets of scores. Then decide which measure is the more representative of the set.

(a) 76 77 78 78 79 80

(b) 1 3 76 77 78 78 79 80

Answers on p. 858.

Table of raw scores

A table of **raw scores** involves simply listing the scores drawn from a practical exercise. Imagine you are carrying out an experiment to test out a new memorizing aid you have devised. A way of doing this might be:

First, draw a sample of people who are as representative as possible of the population in which you are interested, say college students aged 17–19 (see the introduction to this part for a discussion of populations and samples).

It would be sensible to compare the performance of a group who made use of the memory aid (the experimental group) with a group who had used a conventional memorizing technique. Therefore, the participants could be randomly allocated to two conditions, A and B. In Condition A, participants would be given a memorizing task, for example a list of 20 nonsense syllables, and would use the new memory aid. In Condition B, the participants would be given the same memorizing task but would be asked to use a conventional technique.

The dependent variable would be the results of the memorizing task – the number of correct syllables recalled; the independent variable would be the use or nonuse of the special memorizing technique. Of course, you would need to carefully control as many extraneous variables as possible (see Chapter 34).

The data you collect might look something like that in Figure 35.2. This kind of table lists each individual

Figure 35.2 Table of raw scores showing number of nonsense syllables correctly recalled

Condition A (with memory aid)			Condition B (without memory aid)		
Participant	Raw scores	Ranked scores	Participant	Raw scores	Ranked scores
1	15	40	21	5	1
2	11	19	22	12	25.5
3	12	25.5	23	13	32.5
4	13	32.5	24	10	13.5
5	10	13.5	25	7	3
6	14	37.5	26	9	8
7	12	25.5	27	10	13.5
8	13	32.5	28	12	25.5
9	9	8	29	8	4.5
10	11	19	30	6	2
11	13	32.5	31	10	13.5
12	14	37.5	32	9	8
13	12	25.5	33	14	37.5
14	12	25.5	34	8	4.5
15	10	13.5	35	11	19
16	11	19	36	9	8
17	13	32.5	37	11	19
18	9	8	38	13	32.5
19	12	25.5	39	10	13.5
20	14	37.5	40	12	24.5

participant's raw score. Note that the labelling of the table is as important as its contents.

Ranked scores

You might also wish to show the relationship between the scores by indicating who scored highest, lowest, and so on. If so, columns can be added in which you indicate **ranked scores** as in Figure 35.2. You will see from Figure 35.2 that participant 1 recalled the greatest number of syllables and participant 21 the least (see Box 35.1 for a description of how to rank data).

Frequency tables

Another kind of table might simply illustrate the number of times a particular event occurred. This would be a table of frequencies. An example might be a table to show how many females scored at a particular level compared with the number of males. If in the data in Figure 35.2, we assume that participants 1–10 and 21–30 are females and the rest males, a table of frequencies to indicate the number of males and females scoring more than 10 would be as in Figure 35.3.

Bar charts and pie charts

Both of these can be used to give an instant graphical representation of the results of a study.

Figure 35.4(a) represents a summary of the data from the memory experiment previously described, in the form of a **bar chart**. You would first need to work out the

---

GLOSSARY

Mean The arithmetical average of a set of scores, arrived at by finding the sum of the scores and dividing that by the number of scores.

Median The middle score in a set of scores which have been ranked. Where there is an odd number of scores there will be an equal number of scores above and below the median; where there is an even number of scores, the median is represented by the mean of the two scores closest to the middle point.

Mode A measure of central tendency representing the most frequently occurring score(s).

Raw scores Scores which are listed as they are drawn from a practical exercise without analysis.

Ranked scores Scores which have been arranged in a rank order.

Box 35.1   Procedure for ranking data

If you have to rank a set of scores, it is helpful to do this on a spare sheet of paper.

1. Place all the scores in order of size with the smallest first. For example:

    3, 5, 6, 7, 8, 10, 12, 15

2. Below each score, place the rank, giving the lowest score rank 1, the next lowest rank 2 and so on. For example:

Score	3	5	6	7	8	10	12	15
Rank score	1	2	3	4	5	6	7	8

3. Suppose you have data for which some of the scores are the same. For example:

    7, 9, 9, 12, 14, 15, 15, 15, 18, 20

    In this case, the scores which are the same, known as tied scores, must share a rank. For example:

Score	7	9	9	12	14	15	15	15	18	20
Rank score	1	2.5	2.5	4	5	7	7	7	9	10

Note: the two 9s would take up ranks 2 and 3. Therefore, the allocated rank is calculated by adding together 2 and 3 and then dividing by 2: $2 + 3 = 5$, divided by $2 = 2.5$. This procedure always applies where you have an *equal* number of tied scores – add together the ranks that would be taken up and then divide by the number of ranks.

The three 15s would take up ranks 6, 7 and 8. Therefore, the allocated rank is 7, the middle one. (Note that the next highest number, 18, then receives the rank 9.)

This procedure applies whenever you have an *unequal* number of tied scores. Look to see which ranks would be taken up by the scores and then allocate the middle one to your tied scores.

Note: Some of the statistical tests described in Chapter 36 require you to rank the data before the test is applied. To do this, you would use the above procedure.

Figure 35.3 Frequency table showing number of males and females scoring higher than 10 in a memorizing task

	Condition A (with the aid)	Condition B (without the aid)
Males	8	5
Females	8	3

mean of the scores for each condition. Note that the dependent variable (syllables recalled) goes on the vertical axis; the horizontal axis represents the independent variable (with or without the aid); the bars represent the mean scores for each of the two conditions.

You could of course also represent the mean scores for males and females separately in the two conditions; it would look like Figure 35.4(b).

The data in Figure 35.3 could be displayed in the form of a **pie chart** (so called because of its shape), as in Figure 35.5(a).

Note that where you are comparing scores drawn from two different conditions as in Figure 35.5(a), a pie chart would not give such an immediate and clear picture as would a bar chart. A pie chart is perhaps more useful for giving a general picture of the proportions of something such as sales of particular commodities. An illustration of this in relation to a fictitious manufacturing company can be seen in Figure 35.5(b). Each section represents a proportion of the total sales and gives only a general picture. More precise information could be given by inserting the actual sales figures into each portion of the pie.

GLOSSARY

Bar chart A means of illustrating scores which involves assigning a vertical bar to each score or group of scores occurring in a particular condition in a study, proportional to the scores themselves. Conventionally the independent variables are represented on the horizontal line; the dependent variables on the vertical bars.

Pie chart A means of illustrating proportions of scores (or of sales or any other commodity) involving dividing a circular 'pie' into proportionate segments.

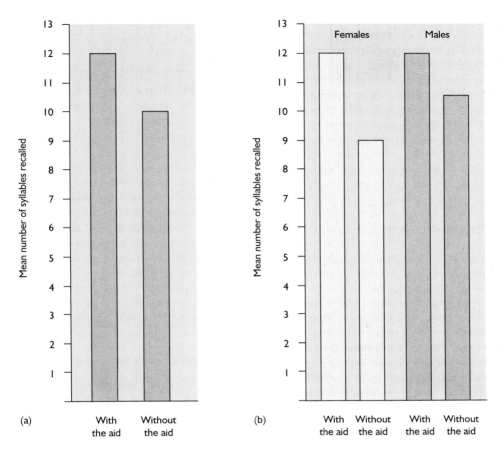

Figure 35.4 (a) Bar chart showing mean number of nonsense syllables correctly recalled; (b) bar chart with mean scores for males and females shown separately

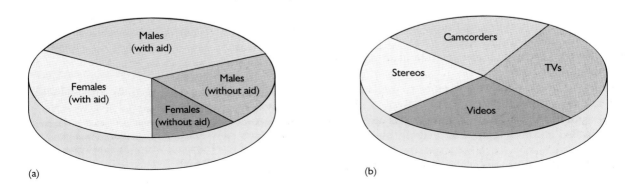

Figure 35.5 Two examples of pie charts: (a) number of males and females scoring higher than 10; (b) proportion of total sales of consumer durables

Frequency distributions

It is often useful to arrange a set of scores in order and indicate the number of times each score occurs. This would be a frequency distribution table. Where there is a large set of numbers, it is a more economical and meaningful way of representing the data. It also has the advantage that it can be represented pictorially in the form of a histogram or frequency polygon (see the next subsection).

As an illustration, if we take the raw data from the memory experiment as shown in Figure 35.2, we can organize it into a **frequency distribution** as follows:

■ Arrange the scores in order from lowest to highest.
■ Indicate how many times each score occurs (the frequency).

Figure 35.6 shows the data from Figure 35.2 reorganized in the form of a frequency distribution. It is helpful to indicate the number of scores, N, at the foot of each column. N is also, of course, the sum of the frequencies. Note that this way of organizing the data includes all the information given in the table of raw scores but more clearly and succinctly. By looking at Figure 35.6, we can get a much clearer picture of the relationship between the two sets of scores.

Histograms

A **histogram** is a graphical form of frequency distribution (see Figure 35.7). To convert the data from Figure 35.6 into two histograms, we would do the following:

1. Draw vertical and horizontal axes.
2. Mark the vertical axes with numbers to represent the frequency of the scores.
3. Mark the horizontal axes in sections to represent the scores.
4. Draw 'boxes' above each score to indicate the number of times it occurs.
5. Ensure that all parts of the histograms are clearly labelled and that there is an overall title.

It is now possible to see at a glance that the scores in Condition A tend to be higher than those in Condition B. It is also obvious that the scores are more 'spread out' in Condition B. Note that in a histogram, it is possible to spot the mode at a glance.

Figure 35.6 Frequency distribution table containing data from Figure 35.2: frequency of scores (nonsense syllables correctly recalled)

Condition A (with the aid)		Condition B (without the aid)	
Score	Frequency	Score	Frequency
		5	1
		6	1
		7	1
		8	2
9	2	9	3
10	2	10	4
11	3	11	2
12	5	12	3
13	4	13	2
14	3	14	1
15	1		
	$N = 20$		$N = 20$

Grouped frequency distribution

In a study which generates a very wide range of frequencies it is usual to classify the data into classes or intervals, for example scores 1–5, 6–10, 11–15, and so on. This would then become a grouped frequency distribution. This can, of course, also be represented as a histogram.

Frequency polygons

Another way of pictorially representing the data from a frequency distribution would be in the form of a **frequency polygon**. Here the 'bars' of the histogram are replaced by dots and the height of each dot represents the frequency of occurrence of each score. This is

---

GLOSSARY

Frequency distribution The tabulation of scores by the frequency with which each occurs.

Histogram A frequency distribution, presented in graphical form. Boxes above each score represent frequencies. The frequency of scores is on the vertical axis; the values of the scores are on the horizontal axis.

Frequency polygon A means of representing a frequency distribution graphically, similar to a histogram. The frequency of each score is represented by a dot. The dots are joined to form a polygon.

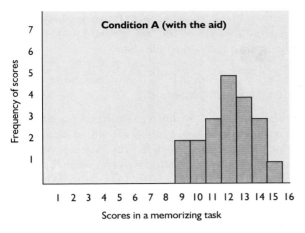

Figure 35.7 Two histograms illustrating the data from Figure 35.6

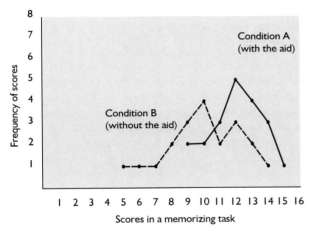

Figure 35.8 Frequency polygon of the scores from Conditions A and B in the memory experiment

illustrated in Figure 35.8, again using the data drawn from Figure 35.6.

Frequency polygons are especially useful where we want to compare two or more sets of data, since we can plot them on the same pair of axes.

Normal distribution

The **normal distribution** (see also the introduction to this Part) is a special kind of frequency distribution which is often arrived at where a large set of measures is collected and then organized into a histogram. For example, suppose we recorded the IQ scores of 500 people randomly drawn from the population and then

organized the scores into a frequency distribution; the resulting histogram would look something like the one in Figure 35.9. (Note that there are so many 'bars' that the end product appears as a smooth line.)

This is a very well-known 'bell-shaped' distribution, which often occurs where a large number of measurements are taken of naturally occurring phenomena: for example, people's heights, weights, foot sizes and many other things.

Characteristics of the normal distribution are:

▨ The mean, median and mode all occur at the same point (the highest point of the curve).
▨ It is symmetrical on either side of the central point of the horizontal axis – the pattern of scores is exactly the same above the mean as it is below.
▨ A large number of scores fall relatively close to the mean on either side. As the distance from the mean increases, the scores become fewer.

The normal curve of distribution can only occur when the data are continuous: that is, at interval or ratio level, rather than separate or discrete, as in frequency data.

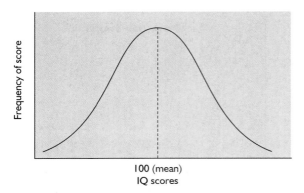

Figure 35.9 A normal distribution showing the frequency of IQ scores in a sample of 500 people

Skewed distributions Sometimes, a set of scores will yield a distribution that is skewed rather than normally distributed. (You may have found this in your own group experiments where you are dealing with a biased rather than a random sample of participants.) In a **skewed distribution**, the mean, median and mode will fall at different points. There are two main kinds of skewed distribution, as indicated in Figure 35.10.

Notice the position of the mean, median and mode in each distribution: the mode is obviously the highest point, where the majority of scores are; the mean is furthest away from the mode; and the median falls between the two.

In a positive skew, the mean is misleadingly high – 'pulled up' by a few extremely high scores; in a negative skew, the mean is relatively low – 'pulled down' by a few very low scores.

A skewed distribution often occurs when a small number of measurements are made or where the measurements are taken from a biased sample drawn from a normally distributed population. It might occur also in a distribution plotted from a set of scores drawn

from a test which was very easy (too many high scores, therefore a negative skew) or very hard (too many low scores, therefore a positive skew).

Measures of dispersion

We have seen that the mean, median and mode are used to summarize sets of numbers by indicating a score which is representative of the set. However, this does not give all the information we need when describing and comparing sets of scores. In order to give a more complete picture, we need to know also how spread out – dispersed – the scores are.

There are a number of measures of **dispersion**, but we shall examine just three: the variation ratio, the range and the standard deviation.

Variation ratio

The **variation ratio** is used in conjunction with the mode (the most frequently occurring value). It allows us to make a judgment about how representative a measure of central tendency the mode is for a particular set of numbers. We can do this by assessing what proportion of the numbers is not 'modal'.

Consider the following set of numbers:

2, 4, 6, 7, 7, 7, 8, 8, 9, 10, 12   Mode = 7

Three numbers (7) are 'modal' and eight are not.

The variation ratio is found by calculating what proportion of the total scores the 'nonmodal' scores constitute. To do this, we divide the number of 'nonmodal' scores (8) by the total number of scores (11):

8 divided by 11 = 0.727

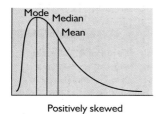

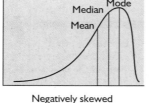

Positively skewed   Negatively skewed

Figure 35.10 Skewed distributions

> **GLOSSARY**
>
> **Skewed distribution** A distribution which is not 'normal'. It may be positively skewed, where the scores are misleadingly low, or negatively skewed, where the scores are abnormally high.
>
> **Dispersion** The spread of scores.
>
> **Variation ratio** A measure of dispersion obtained by assessing the proportion of scores which are not modal. It is useful in assessing how representative a measure of central tendency the mode of a particular set of scores is.

We can now state that 0.727 of our scores are not modal. This implies, of course, that 0.273 are modal. We could represent these figures as percentages by multiplying them by 100. In this case, we could then say that 72.7 per cent of the scores are not accounted for by the mode. This suggests that the mode is not very representative of this particular set of numbers.

Range

The **range** indicates the difference between the lowest score and the highest; for example:

(a) 5 23 33 6 32 27   Mean = 21   Range = 28
(b) 21 19 22 18 25 21   Mean = 21   Range = 7

Note that the means of these two sets of scores are the same, but the dispersions, as indicated by the range, are very different.

As with the mean, the range gives a good description only if the scores are fairly bunched together. If there are one or two extreme scores, as in set (a) above, use of the range can be misleading.

A more powerful measure of dispersion, which reflects how spread out the scores are about the mean, is known as the standard deviation.

Standard deviation

The **standard deviation** indicates the average of the distances of all the scores around the mean. Box 35.2 shows one method of calculating it.

The larger the standard deviation of a set of scores, the more spread out they are relative to the mean. Figure 35.11 illustrates two distributions, one with a large and one with a small standard deviation.

GLOSSARY

Range A measure of dispersion represented by the difference between the lowest and the highest scores.

Standard deviation A measure of dispersion which assesses the average distance of all the scores around the mean.

Box 35.2   Calculating the standard deviation (SD)

Example: Calculating the SD of the numbers 12, 10, 8, 4, 18, 8.

1. First calculate the mean of the scores (10).
2. Subtract the mean from the value of each score, ignoring the signs. This will give you the deviations (2, 0, 2, 6, 8, 2).
3. Square each deviation (4, 0, 4, 36, 64, 4).
4. Add together all the squared deviations. This will give you the sum of squares (112).
5. Count the number of scores (6).
6. Divide the sum of squares in step 4 by the value in step 5. This is the **variance** (22.4).
7. Take the square root of the variance found in step 6. This is the standard deviation (4.73).

Note: The formula for the standard deviation is

$$\sqrt{\frac{\sum (X - \bar{X})^2}{N}}$$

where X = individual score

$\bar{X}$ = mean of scores
N = number of scores

However, where we are calculating the SD of a *sample* of scores in order to estimate the variability within the larger *population* from which it is drawn, using the above formula gives a slight underestimation of the variability. Therefore, in practice, the following formula is usually used when dealing with a sample:

$$\sqrt{\frac{\sum (X - \bar{X})^2}{N - 1}}$$

The standard deviation is expressed in terms of the scores you are analysing; for example, if a standardized IQ test were administered to the general population, it would usually yield a mean of 100 and a standard deviation of 15 (IQ points). It has useful mathematical properties that can be used in more complicated analyses. Many inferential statistical tests involve comparing the means and standard deviations of two or more sets of scores.

The standard deviation and the normal distribution There is a very interesting and useful relationship between the standard deviation and the curve of normal distribution. If we have a set of scores which approximates to a normal distribution, a knowledge

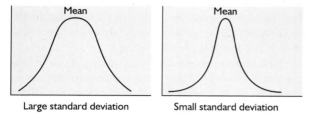

Large standard deviation　　Small standard deviation

Figure 35.11 Graphs illustrating large and small standard deviations

of the mean and standard deviation of the scores would enable us to draw the distribution.

A very important property of the normal distribution is that it always has the same proportion of scores falling between particular points of the distribution. As illustrated in Figure 35.12, 68.26 per cent of all scores fall between one standard deviation below the mean (−1SD) and one standard deviation above the mean (+1SD); 95.44 per cent of all scores fall between two standard deviations below the mean (−2SD) and two standard deviations above the mean (+2SD). Also, because we know the normal curve of distribution is symmetrical, we know that 50 per cent of all the scores fall below the mean and 50 per cent above the mean.

Let us examine how this can be helpful. Imagine that we know from population statistics that the mean height of the Martian population is 92 inches and that the standard deviation is 6 (inches). A normal distribution drawn from a random sample of heights in the Martian population would look like Figure 35.13.

Remember that the curve represents a histogram, so that there are numbers of scores (heights of Martian people) in any part of the distribution in proportion to the area occupied.

It follows from the information in Figure 35.13 that:

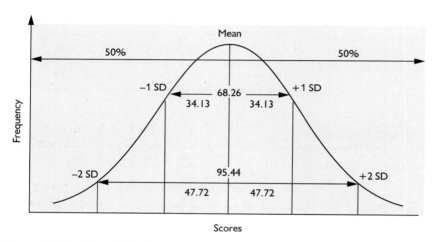

Figure 35.12 Normal distribution

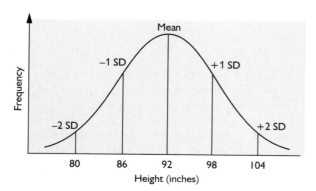

Figure 35.13 Normal distribution showing the heights of the Martian population

- 50 per cent of the Martian population would have heights below the mean and 50 per cent above.
- 68.26 per cent (34.13 per cent below the mean and 34.13 per cent above the mean) of the Martian population would have heights between 86 inches (−1SD) and 98 inches (+1SD).
- 95.44 per cent (47.72 per cent below the mean and 47.72 per cent above the mean) of the Martian population would have heights between 80 inches and 104 inches.

Now try Exercises 35.2 and 35.3.

Exercise 35.2

Suppose you take a random sample of 200 Martians. It is possible to calculate how many are likely to have heights below 98 inches as follows:

■ 100 Martians (50%) fall below 92 inches (the mean).
■ 68 Martians (34.13%) fall between 92 inches and 98 inches.

Therefore:

■ 168 Martians (50% + 34.13% = 84.13%) in our sample are likely to have heights below 98 inches.

See if you can calculate how many Martians in the sample are likely to have heights below 86 inches. Consult Figures 35.12 and 35.13 to check your calculations. The answer is on p. 858.

Exercise 35.3

A maths test is given to 200 children. The mean of the resulting scores is 60 and the standard deviation is 8. Using Figure 35.13 as a guide draw the distribution. See if you can calculate:

(a) How many children scored between 52 and 68.
(b) How many children scored below 52.
(c) How many children scored above 68.

Note: You are being asked 'How many children?' not 'What proportion?'
      The answers are on p. 858.

z *scores*

z scores have already been described in Chapter 34.

It is possible to express any score as a number of standard deviations above or below the mean. For example, if you have a set of scores with a mean of 50 and a standard deviation of 10, the mean score (50) would be zero, one of 55 would be +0.5 and one of 45 would be −0.5. (One standard deviation is 10, therefore half a standard deviation [0.5 of SD] is 5.) These are known as z scores. They are commonly employed

where it is necessary to compare performances on a range of different tests. Because the tests are likely to have different means and standard deviations, it would not make sense to compare results directly, so they are converted to z scores. This can only be done, however, when the scores are normally distributed.

It is possible to work out the probability (p) of any particular z score occurring. A table of the probability of z scores is included at the end of this book (Appendix 3, Table A.2). The figures in the table identify the proportions of scores falling between the mean and any z score.

❓ SELF-ASSESSMENT QUESTIONS

1. Briefly explain the purpose of descriptive statistics. Give two examples.
2. What is meant by the term 'measures of central tendency'? Explain which is the preferred one and in what circumstances it might be misleading to use it.
3. Briefly explain the terms 'frequency distribution', 'histogram' and 'frequency polygon'.
4. In what circumstances would you expect to obtain a normal distribution? What are its characteristics?
5. Draw a rough diagram of a negatively skewed distribution. In what circumstances would you expect it to occur?
6. Explain what is meant by 'standard deviation'. What is its relationship to a normal distribution?

Statistical inference and significance

Inferential statistics

In the first part of this chapter, we dealt fully with a range of descriptive statistics, which you will recall are used to describe and summarize data. We also indicated that there is another category of statistics which is useful when analysing and drawing conclu-

> GLOSSARY
>
> **z score** A means of standardizing scores which involves expressing each score as so many standard deviations above or below the mean. It is possible to assess the probability of any particular z score occurring.

Answers to Exercise 35.1

(a) mean = 78   median = 78

Since the two values are the same and the scores are fairly bunched together, one would use the mean as the preferred average.

(b) mean = 59   median = 77.5

Because there are two very atypical scores, the mean of 59 is not exactly representative of the set. Therefore, it would make sense to use the median as a typical score.

Answer to Exercise 35.2

31 Martians are likely to have heights below 86 inches (50 per cent – 34.13 per cent = 15.87 per cent)

Answers to Exercise 35.3

(a) 136 children (68 per cent)
(b) 32 children (16 per cent)
(c) 32 children (16 per cent)

sions about the results of a study. These are known as **inferential statistics**. Before considering inferential statistics in detail, it is important to look again at the concept of population (see introduction to this part) in relation to statistical testing.

Populations and statistical tests

You will remember from the section on populations and samples in the introduction to this part of the book, that when carrying out research, the term **population** refers to the entire parent group – of humans, animals or even things – from which a sample is selected for testing. It implies that we are dealing with a group that shares some common characteristic. Examples of populations are children under five years old, females living in England, people over six feet tall, sheep in Australia, sufferers from autism, dolphins in captivity, apples grown in Worcestershire, and so on. In statistics, the term population relates to some kind of numerical aspect of the group in which we are interested. It might be IQ scores of people in England and Wales, heights of people living in Ireland or aggression ratings in children.

If we wished to carry out an experiment into, for example, two different ways of teaching mathematics to five-year-olds, we would not of course be able to test the whole population, but would test samples drawn from the population The samples would form two groups, each being taught by a different method, before being assessed. In assessing the results, we would be asking the question 'Is one set of numbers substantially different from the other?' If, after applying an appropriate statistical test, we decided that the two sets of numbers were significantly different, we would then conclude that they had in fact been drawn from two different populations. If, on the other hand, we found no significant difference between the two sets of numbers, we would conclude that they were drawn from the same population. The differences between them represented no more than the differences expected if we drew two samples from a single population. This is a very important idea in statistical testing. (The concept of significance will be discussed later.)

Probability

Inferential statistics make use of the concept of **probability** to determine the likelihood that the results – either a difference between two sets of scores or a correlation – might have occurred by chance.

Consider, for example, the data from our memory experiment described earlier in this chapter. The results, as shown in the frequency distribution and histogram illustrated in Figures 35.6 and 35.7, indicate that there appears to be a difference between the number of nonsense syllables recalled by the experimental group and the number recalled by the control group. Overall, the experimental group appear to have recalled more syllables; the mean score for this group is certainly higher. Can we be sure, however, that this

---

GLOSSARY

Inferential statistics Statistical procedures which allow a researcher to infer from the data the probability that two or more samples are drawn from the same or different populations.

Population The group from which a sample is drawn. For statistical purposes this is likely to be some numerical aspect of what is under investigation.

Probability The likelihood of an event (or events) occurring. Most often used in relation to the likelihood of a particular set of data having occurred by chance alone.

difference has been brought about by the independent variable – the memory aid – thus allowing us to accept the alternative hypothesis? It is possible that it has simply occurred by chance and that we are looking at two samples drawn from the same population. Applying a statistical test will help us to decide whether or not the difference is sufficient to give us the confidence to discount this chance. If we decide we do have the confidence, we would reject the null hypothesis and accept the alternative/experimental hypothesis. If, after applying a statistical test, we decide that the probability of a chance result is small enough to be discounted, we would say that we had obtained a significant result. Before considering this term further, let us look a little more closely at the concept of probability.

As you may already know, probability is to do with how likely it is that a particular situation, event or pattern of numbers occurs by chance. This is something we consider quite often in everyday life. For example, how often have you heard the phrase 'There is a fifty/fifty chance that . . . (something will happen)' or 'There is a million to one chance of it happening'. Put another way, 'fifty/fifty' means that there is an equal chance of something happening or not happening; 'million to one' means that it is a million times more likely that one thing will happen rather than another.

Expressing probability

There are three main ways of expressing probability:

■ As a ratio.
1 in 100, 2 to 1, 1 in 20 (or 1:100, 2:1, 1:20) are examples.

■ As a percentage.
100 per cent probability of something happening means that it is certain to happen.
0 per cent probability means that it is certain not to happen.
5 per cent probability means there is a 5 in 100 (or 1 in 20) chance that it will happen, and so on.

■ As a decimal fraction between 0 and 1.
i.e. p (probability) = 0 0.1 0.2 0.3 0.4 0.5 0.6 0.7 0.8 0.9 1

p = 0, 0.1, 0.2, 0.3, 0.4, 0.5, 0.6, 0.7, 0.8, 0.9, 1

| Certain not | Definitely |
| to happen | will happen |

Note that a probability of 1 is the same as a probability of 100 per cent, so that a 5 in 100 probability may be expressed as follows:

5 in 100 or 5 per cent or 0.05. (This is usually written as $p = 0.05$.)
Thus:
0.5 probability ($p = 0.5$) means that the chance of something happening is 50 per cent, 1 in 2 or 50:50 (an example of this would be the probability of throwing a head or a tail if you tossed a normal coin);
$p = 0.1$ means that there is a 10 per cent or 1 in 10 probability;
$p = 0.05$ means that there is a 5 per cent or 1 in 20 probability;
$p = 0.01$ means that there is a 1 per cent or 1 in 100 probability.

When the results of experimental and other research work are analysed, the levels of probability most commonly employed are $p \leqslant 0.05$ or $p \leqslant 0.01$ (where $\leqslant$ means 'equal to or less than').

Figure 35.14 gives some examples of probabilities expressed as ratios, percentages and decimals.

Assessing probability

In analysing the results of studies, we are constantly asking the question 'What is the probability that this difference/relationship occurred by chance?' Statistical tests such as the Sign, Mann–Whitney and Wilcoxon tests and others described in the next chapter will allow us to estimate this probability. If the probability is small, we can have confidence that the difference (or relationship) is not due to chance. But what do we mean by 'small' – how small? By convention, researchers commonly decide upon 5 per cent or less probability ($p \leqslant 0.05$) as the point at which they will have enough confidence in their results to reject the null hypothesis. This is known as the 5 per cent level of **significance**. It indicates that

> **GLOSSARY**
>
> **Significance** Refers to the confidence a researcher has that the results he or she has obtained did not occur through chance. This is usually gained by conducting a statistical test of significance to assess the probability that the results occurred by chance.

Figure 35.14 Probabilities expressed as ratios, percentages and decimals

Event	Likelihood	Decimal	Percentage	Ratio
That you are alive	Certain	1.00	100	100:100
A tossed coin coming up tails	One in two	0.5	50	50:100
That a dice will come up with a 4	One in six	0.167	$0.16\frac{2}{3}$	$16\frac{2}{3}$:100
(Used when analysing research results)	One in 20	0.05	5	5:100
	One in 100	0.01	1	1:100
That you will walk on Mars next week	Impossible	0.00	0	0:100

there is an equal, or less than, 5 per cent probability that you are just observing two samples from the same population rather than from two different populations, one influenced by the independent variable and one not. In such a case, we would say that we had obtained a significant result.

Tests of significance

Level of significance, then, refers to the level of probability that the results obtained from a study are likely to have occurred by chance. After carrying out a study, we would prepare appropriate descriptive statistics and study them carefully. In some rare cases, this is sufficient to indicate that the results allow us to have confidence that the difference or relationship we were exploring actually exists. However, in the majority of cases, the results are not so clear-cut, and it is necessary to apply an inferential statistical test known as a test of significance before we can be confident enough to reject the null hypothesis and decide to accept the alternative hypothesis. We conclude that the independent variable has had a real effect on the dependent variable.

Two general kinds of tests of significance covered in this book are as follows:

■ **Tests of difference**, which, as the name suggests, enable you to test the significance of a difference between two or more sets of data (see Figure 35.23 for a summary and Chapter 36 for details of how to calculate some tests of difference).
■ **Tests of correlation**, which allow you to examine

the degree of *relationship* between two variables (see later in this chapter for an explanation of the principles of correlational analyses and Chapter 36 for details of how to calculate two tests of correlation).

Box 35.3 shows an example of how inferential statistics might be used.

Although $p \leqslant 0.05$ is the level of significance most commonly adopted by scientists, there may be occasions when you wish to choose a different level of significance. For example, if you wish to have even more confidence in your results you might adopt the more stringent $p \leqslant 0.01$ level. Significance at this level tells us that there is a one in a hundred or less probability that the results occurred by chance. The level chosen would depend upon how crucial might be the correctness of our findings. For example, if we were carrying out research in which a significant result might overturn a well-established theory, we might wish to have the confidence of the $p \leqslant 0.01$ level of significance or even the more stringent $p \leqslant 0.001$ level (one in a thousand or less probability that the results occurred by chance) before we decided to accept our experimental hypothesis.

Box 35.4 shows a summary of the procedure you should follow if you carry out an experiment and wish to calculate the significance of your findings.

Whatever level of significance is chosen, it should be remembered that we are dealing with probabilities rather than certainties. This means that there may be occasions on which our conclusions are wrong – a result that was claimed to be significant was not due to the effect of the independent variable, or a non-

Box 35.3 An example of inferential statistics in use

Let us explore how we might use one test of difference in a hypothetical experiment. Suppose Mrs Chancer, a primary school teacher, believes that playing a word game such as Scrabble will help children's spelling. She decides to test this by first giving a spelling test to all the children in her class.

Her experimental hypothesis is that after playing Scrabble daily for two weeks, spelling performance will be better.

The null hypothesis is that any difference observed will be the result purely of chance factors – spelling performance is not in fact improved.

After two weeks of the children playing Scrabble every day, Mrs Chancer gives them another spelling test.

The results look like this:

Child	Number of correct spellings	
	Test 1 (Before playing Scrabble)	Test 2 (After playing Scrabble)
1	45	56
2	10	22
3	50	75
4	44	45
5	17	35
6	58	60
7	36	45
8	39	43
9	55	50
10	20	39
11	45	60
12	48	72
Means	38.92	50.17

Do you think there is a difference in the two sets of scores? Has the Scrabble made a difference? The mean scores do indicate that there is a marked difference between the two sets of scores. One way of answering these questions would be to apply a test of significance.

Accordingly, Mrs Chancer decides that a Sign test is appropriate. (This is described in detail in the next chapter.) She settles on a 5 per cent ($p \leqslant 0.05$) significance level as her level of confidence. The Sign test is one of a number of tests which will examine whether or not there is a significant difference between two sets of scores – remember that 'significant' in this context means 'unlikely to have occurred by chance'.

The stages Mrs Chancer goes through are these:

- She formulates a null and an alternative hypothesis.
- She decides upon an acceptable significance level.
- She administers the two tests to the children.
- She computes a Sign test in order to estimate the probability that the results occurred by chance.

Look at Chapter 36 and you will see the procedure for calculating a Sign test, along with the calculations for Mrs Chancer's 'Scrabble' experiment. The statistics arrived at are $X = 1$ and $N = 12$. Note that it is possible to assess whether or not this answer is significant by comparing it with the special table of critical values drawn up for the Sign test (see Appendix 3, Table A.5). Each statistical test has its own table of critical values (probabilities, calculated by statisticians, of the null hypothesis being true under different circumstances). For the Sign test, our value must not exceed the table value for us to accept that a result is significant. Note that for some other significance tests, our value must be equal to or better than the table value. When Mrs Chancer consults the table of critical values, the figures tell her that she has a significant result at the 0.05 level. (The probability that the result occurred by chance is equal to or less than 1 in 20.)

On the basis of the Sign test result, she decides to reject the null hypothesis and to accept her experimental hypothesis that playing Scrabble for two weeks did improve children's spelling performance. She is able to say that playing Scrabble for two weeks *significantly* improved the children's spelling.

---

significant result did in fact indicate a real effect of the independent on the dependent variable. Such mistakes are known respectively as type I and type II errors (see also the introduction to this part of the book).

Type I and type II errors

A **type I error** occurs when you reject the null hypothesis and accept the alternative hypothesis when in fact there was no real difference (or similarity). The observed difference was just the difference between

Box 35.4 Procedure used to find statistical significance

1. Formulate hypotheses and design study;
2. Decide on an acceptable significance level (usually $p \leqslant 0.05$);
3. Collect data;
4. Choose an appropriate statistical test (see later in this chapter);
5. Calculate the relevant statistic;
6. Consult the table of critical values;
7. Decide whether the result is significant and whether or not you will reject the null hypothesis and accept the alternative hypothesis.

two samples from a single population. This is most likely to occur when you have chosen a less stringent significance level such as $p \leqslant 0.05$. You have said that you will accept that there are indeed two different populations because the probability of this not being the case is equal to or less than five in a hundred.

A **type II error** is the converse of this. You have accepted the null hypothesis and concluded that there is no real effect observed when in fact there was a significant difference (or similarity). This will be more likely to occur if you adopt a very strict significance level, perhaps 1 per cent ($p \leqslant 0.01$). You have in effect said that you will not accept that your samples come from two different populations unless the probability is equal to or less than one in a hundred that they have come from just one population.

Which statistical test should I choose?

It is suggested that you refer to Figure 35.23 at the end of this chapter as you consider this question.

Which test you choose in order to analyse your data will depend upon two initial factors. The first is whether the data you have collected are independent or related. This will depend upon the kind of research design you are using: related measures, independent measures or matched pairs (see Chapter 34). Some tests, for example the Sign test and related *t*-test, are only suitable for use with related measures designs; others, for example chi-squared (χ^2) and independent *t*-test, are used only where you have an independent measures design. Note that a matched pairs design is

treated as though it is a related measures design. Note also that there are special tests, for example Spearman's rho (ρ) and Pearson's product moment, which deal with correlational analyses. All these tests and some others are explained fully in the next chapter.

The second factor is the level of measurement of your data: nominal, ordinal, interval or ratio (see pp. 846–7). These levels of measurement lead to two different kinds of statistical test. Nominal and ordinal lead to nonparametric tests, while with interval and ratio level data, parametric tests can be considered. Let us consider these two kinds of tests in turn.

Nonparametric tests

The main feature of **nonparametric tests** is that they work only on nominal or ranked (ordinal) data. Indeed, they were devised specifically to deal with data which do not have the sophisticated mathematical properties of interval or ratio data. Nonparametric tests are relatively free of restrictions in their use, in contrast to the more powerful and sophisticated parametric tests. Remember that you can always convert your interval or ratio scores to nominal or ordinal, but not the other way round.

Parametric tests

Parametric tests work on the basis that a number of assumptions have been made about the nature of the data being analysed:

- The data analysed are at the interval or ratio level of measurement.
- The data from the two (or more) conditions are drawn from a population of scores which is

GLOSSARY

Type I (type II) errors Errors which occur when a researcher rejects the null hypothesis when there is in fact no difference (or relationship) between sets of scores except that due to chance (type I error) or retains the null hypothesis when there is in fact a difference (relationship) (type II error).

Nonparametric test A test of significance which does not depend for its validity upon assumptions such as normally distributed populations, homogeneity of variance and interval or ratio levels of measurement.

Parametric test A significance test which depends for its validity upon assumptions concerning the populations from which data are obtained: namely, normal distribution, homogeneity of variance and interval or ratio measures.

normally distributed. Parametric tests should not be used where it is obvious from the data collected that the distribution is skewed.

■ The two (or more) sets of data being analysed are drawn from populations of scores which have similar variances. This concept is referred to as **homogeneity of variance**.

As far as the second and third assumptions are concerned, you may be thinking 'How will I know whether my data are suitable?' There is no simple answer to this question. It is also important to remember that it is the population of scores from which the sample is drawn that is at issue, rather than the scores themselves. However, the following guidelines may be followed in order to arrive at a decision.

Normally distributed? To decide whether your scores indicate a normal distribution, there are two stages.

■ First, you would give them the 'eyeball test': that is, scrutinize them carefully in order to make an initial judgment about whether the population they are drawn from is normally distributed.

■ You may then wish to make a more precise assessment by drawing up a frequency distribution of the scores or applying a chi-squared test of 'goodness of fit' (see Chapter 36). This will allow you to make an assumption about the population from which the scores are drawn. In practice, at this stage in your statistical career, it is probably sufficient to examine the scores carefully and make a judgment.

Homogeneity of variance To decide whether your sets of scores support the assumption of homogeneity of variance (see above) is relatively straightforward and again there are two stages.

■ First, give your data the 'eyeball test'. If there seems to be a similar amount of spread in each set, that may be sufficient.

■ To be more precise, the variance is a measure of how 'spread out' the scores are and, as explained earlier, it is directly related to the standard deviation (it is the standard deviation squared). Therefore, you might then compare the standard deviations of the sets of scores. If one set of scores has a very small standard deviation and the other a very large one, the criterion of homogeneity of

variance is clearly very unlikely to have been met.

But how similar do the variances of the sets of scores have to be? A technique known as an *F*-test or variance – ratio test (see Appendix 3, Table A.9) will show whether there is a significant difference in the sample variances. This will allow a judgment to be made about the population from which the scores are drawn. However, this may, again, in practice not be necessary. Examining the sets of scores and comparing their standard deviations should be sufficient.

To summarize, then, strictly, unless your data support the three assumptions explained above, a parametric test should not be used; you should convert your data to ordinal or nominal form and use an appropriate nonparametric test. In practice, the last two assumptions (normality and homogeneity of variance) are sometimes ignored. This happens in particular with the two *t*-tests. They are said to be robust and will give a reasonably accurate result even where the parametric assumptions are not fully met.

The power of a test Before leaving this discussion of parametric tests, here is a brief explanation of what is meant by 'more powerful', a term which is often used in connection with these tests. This means that the tests are more sensitive than nonparametric tests and are more likely to give an accurate assessment of significance for the following reason. Because the tests work on interval or ratio data, they have more information available to them than tests which make use only of nominal or ordinal data. They take account of the actual scores, rather than simply, say, the rank order of the scores. Therefore, a more confident decision can be made about whether to accept or reject the null hypothesis than can be made after using a nonparametric test.

Caution Finally, a word of caution. Any test which is used on unsuitable data drawn from a poorly designed study is unlikely to give a satisfactory result. Using unsatisfactory data or the wrong statistical technique may lead to your accepting the

---

GLOSSARY

Homogeneity of variance States that the variances (or 'spread') of two (or more) sets of scores are not significantly different. (The variance is the SD squared.)

experimental hypothesis falsely – a type I error – or failing to detect a real effect which is actually there – a type II error.

 SELF-ASSESSMENT QUESTIONS

1. Explain what is meant by the term 'inferential statistics'. Refer to the concepts of 'probability' and 'population'.
2. Express the following in words: $p \leqslant 0.05$; $p \leqslant 0.01$; $p \leqslant 0.10$.
3. What do you understand by 'significance level'? Outline the steps you would take if you carried out an experiment and then wished to assess the significance of your data.
4. What are the assumptions of a parametric test of significance?
5. Outline two factors that will influence your choice of a test which is suitable for analysing the results of an experiment.

Correlation

The use of the statistical technique of correlation has been discussed in Chapter 34. It is recommended that you reread the section on 'Correlational designs' on p. 837 before proceeding to examine correlation further.

Remember that correlation is a statistical technique which allows us to examine the degree of relationship between two variables. An example might be the relationship between the amount of violent TV viewed by a sample of primary school children and the level of aggression they display in the school playground. To investigate this, it would be necessary first to define (a) what should be categorized as 'violent TV', and (b) what behaviour exhibited by the children would be categorized as 'aggressive' and how each would be measured. It should then be possible to collect pairs of scores for each child and to carry out a correlational analysis.

Ways of expressing correlation

Scattergrams

One way to express correlation is graphically, by means of a **scattergram**. Pairs of measurements (for example,

'violent TV' and 'aggression' as previously described) are plotted on a graph, and the pattern which the plots make indicates the relationship between the two measures. Additionally, a **correlation coefficient** can be worked out to express the relationship in figures. The maximum value of a correlation coefficient is 1, and it can be positive or negative; the minimum is 0. Chapter 36 contains a full explanation of the techniques involved in calculating a correlation coefficient.

In terms of interpreting scattergrams and correlation coefficients, it is helpful to note the following. If there is a perfect positive correlation between the two sets of measurements, the coefficient will be $+1$. For example, the number of gallons of petrol you put in your car will exactly match the cost in pounds. The more petrol you buy, the more it will cost. The scattergram will look something like Figure 35.15.

If there is a perfect negative relationship between two sets of measurements, the correlation coefficient will be -1. (Note that -1 does not mean 'no relationship'.)

Suppose you filled your car at the beginning of a journey and then at intervals along the way measured the amount of petrol left in the car as well as the distance you had travelled; there would be a perfect negative correlation. The more miles you have travelled, the less petrol you will have in the car. The scattergram would look something like Figure 35.16.

Suppose that you wanted to test a hypothesis that there was a relationship between people's head circumference and their intelligence (as measured by a standard intelligence test); you would probably find that there was no relationship at all. The correlation coefficient would be zero, and a scattergram would show plots randomly scattered across the graph as in Figure 35.17.

> **GLOSSARY**
>
> **Scattergram** A means of plotting graphically the relationship between two variables. Pairs of variables are represented one on the horizontal axis, the other on the vertical axis. Plots are made where the values of each of the pairs of variables intersect and the resulting pattern indicates the relationship between the two variables.
>
> **Correlation coefficient** The relationship between two variables expressed as a decimal fraction. A perfect match is expressed as 1; no relationship is expressed as 0. The relationship may be positive or negative.

Gallons purchased	Cost in £
I	2
2	4
3	6
4	8
5	I0
6	I2
7	I4

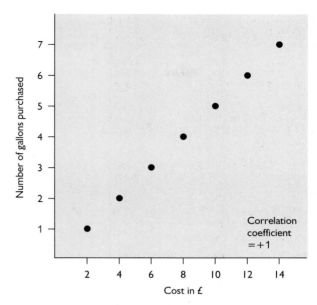

Figure 35.15   Scattergram showing a perfect positive correlation

Miles travelled	Gallons left
20	5
40	4
60	3
80	2
I00	I
I20	0

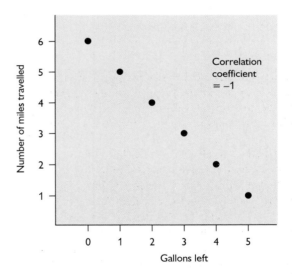

Figure 35.16   Scattergram showing a perfect negative correlation

In practice, in psychological research there are likely to be few perfect correlations, either positive or negative. Imperfect positive or negative correlations are expressed by decimal fractions. If you measured the number of hours devoted to study by a group of psychology students and matched this with the marks gained at the end of the year, you would probably get a positive correlation, but not a perfect one. There may be other factors likely to affect your results. You might get a correlation coefficient of, say, $+0.6$. A scattergram would look something like Figure 35.18.

On the other hand, if you measured the hours spent in the pub by the group and matched this with end-of-year marks, the result would probably be a negative correlation, albeit an imperfect one. There would again be other factors at work. You might obtain a correlation coefficient of -0.4, which, expressed on a scattergram, would look something like Figure 35.19.

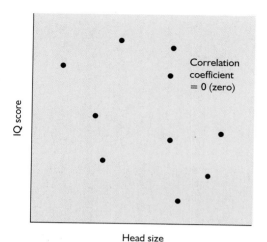

Figure 35.17 Scattergram showing zero correlation coefficient

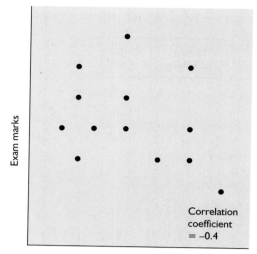

Figure 35.19 Scattergram showing imperfect negative correlation

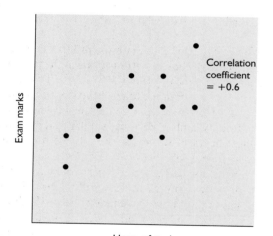

Figure 35.18 Scattergram showing imperfect positive correlation

Exercise 35.4

Draw scattergrams for the following pairs of sets of scores. What do the scattergrams tell you about the degree of relationship between variable A and variable B?

(a) Variables		(b) Variables		(c) Variables	
A	B	A	B	A	B
5	5	11	5	10	2
8	8	9	7	8	1
3	3	7	4	7	3
4	4	5	9	5	4
11	11	6	2	2	10
6	6	4	5	4	6
2	2	8	10	7	5
7	7	5	7	3	9

Answers on p. 868.

When you use the technique of correlation, it is important that you always first draw up a scattergram from the data you have collected. This will allow you to examine the kind of relationship that has emerged and spot nonlinear trends (trends which do not follow a straight line – see below) before you calculate a correlation coefficient.

Correlation coefficients and significance

There are a number of tests which can be used to calculate a correlation coefficient. Two of these – Spearman's rank order correlation (which is nonparametric) and Pearson's product moment (which is parametric) – are described in Chapter 36. Remember that a correlation coefficient always varies between 0 and 1, and it can be positive or negative.

The correlation coefficient is considered to be a descriptive statistic, the size of which indicates the degree of relationship between two variables. However, it can also be tested for significance in the way that the statistic from a test of difference can. In correlation, what is being examined is the probability that the relationship (rather than the difference) between two variables, for example viewing TV violence and aggression in children, occurred by chance. If this probability is 0.05 or less, we have a significant correlation and can infer that there is a relationship between TV violence and aggression. Bear in mind, though, that we could *not* infer that viewing TV violence *caused* aggression. (See the problem of cause and effect in Chapter 34.)

Limitations of tests of correlation

There are a number of kinds of relationship which may not be accurately detected by the Spearman's or Pearson's tests; these are outlined below.

Curvilinear relationships Suppose you obtained data which, when plotted on a scattergram, produced a pattern like one of those in Figure 35.20. These are **nonlinear relationships** (forming a curved rather than a straight line) and would be described as **curvilinear relationships**.

Spearman's rho (ρ) can be used without problems on scores which indicate curvilinear relationships, such as those in Figure 35.20. However, Pearson's test would not give a meaningful correlation coefficient and therefore should not be used.

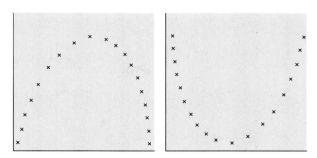

Figure 35.21 Arched and U-shaped relationships, not suitable for either Spearman's or Pearson's tests

Arched or U-shaped relationships Another kind of curvilinear relationship which might be obtained can be seen in Figure 35.21. In both of these, the 'line' starts to change direction, resulting in an arched or U-shaped pattern.

Where your scores produce an arched or U-shaped relationship, the data are too complex for either the Spearman's or the Pearson's test to deal with. Therefore, neither of these tests should be used.

Outliers Another data pattern which needs to be treated with caution when calculating a correlation coefficient involves outliers. An **outlier** is a pair of scores which is extreme and not typical of the rest of the data. Figure 35.22 gives an example of a scattergram which indicates a fairly strong linear relationship apart from the position of one pair of scores – the outlier.

One or more outliers can have a very misleading effect on the interpretation of a correlation coefficient. A decision would have to be made about whether the outlier should be excluded from the analysis (you might be accused of misrepresenting your data) or included (you may fail to detect an otherwise strong relationship, therefore committing a type II error). One

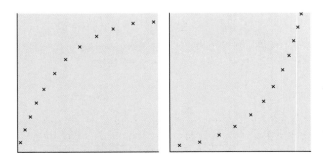

Figure 35.20 Curvilinear relationships, not suitable for Pearson's product moment test

---

GLOSSARY

Nonlinear relationships A relationship between two variables that, when plotted on a scattergram, does not follow a straight line.

Curvilinear relationship A relationship between two variables where a plotted scattergram will describe a curve rather than a straight line.

Outliers Plots on a scattergram which represent values of the variables which are not typical of the data as a whole.

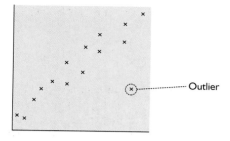

Figure 35.22 An outlier relative to a linear relationship

factor which may help you to decide is the size of your sample. With a large set of scores, an outlier would not exert as great an influence on the correlation coefficient as it would with a small sample. You might therefore decide to include it. However, if you do decide to exclude the outlier from your analysis, it is important that you state this clearly in your report.

Correlation and hypotheses

In a correlational study, the null hypothesis would predict that there is no relationship between the two variables under examination. The alternative hypothesis could be either one-tailed or two-tailed (see introduction to this part). A one-tailed hypothesis would predict either that there would be a positive relationship or that there would be a negative relationship; a two-tailed hypothesis would predict that there was a relationship, but would not indicate its direction.

? SELF-ASSESSMENT QUESTIONS

1. What is the purpose of the statistical technique of correlation?
2. What is a scattergram? Why is it important to draw up a scattergram when you are assessing the degree of correlation between two sets of data?
3. Explain the term 'correlation coefficient'.
4. What do you understand by the 'problem of cause and effect'?
5. Explain how a one-tailed hypothesis might differ from a two-tailed hypothesis in a study which involved a correlational analysis.

Answers to Exercise 35.4

Drawing scattergrams

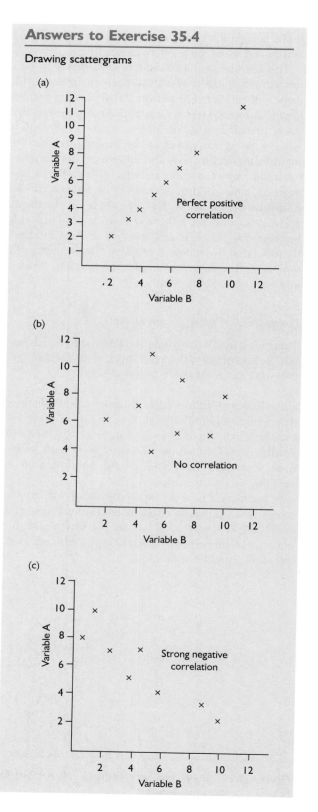

Choosing an appropriate test

You are now in a position to choose an appropriate test in order to analyse the data from an investigation. Ask yourself the following questions; the information in Figure 35.23 will help you to make a decision.

■ Do you require a test of difference (A) or a test of correlation (B)?
■ If you require a test of difference, is your experimental design repeated measures, matched pairs or independent measures?
■ Are your data at the nominal, ordinal or interval/ratio level?
■ Do your data appear to satisfy the assumptions of a parametric test? If the answer is 'Yes', choose an

appropriate parametric test; if 'No', select a nonparametric test.

Degrees of freedom

When you use the tests of significance set out in Chapter 36, you will find that some of them (for example, chi-squared and the two t-tests) require you to calculate a figure that represents the degrees of freedom. Degrees of freedom relate to the total number of values that have to be known, when the total is known, before any missing one can be filled in. An example may make this clearer.

Suppose you have £500, which you have decided to give to four different charities. Once you have decided on the amount you are giving to the first three charities

Figure 35.23 Tests of significance

(A) **Tests of difference**			
Kind of design		Type of data	
	Nominal	Ordinal	Interval/ratio
Repeated measures	Sign test	Wilcoxon signed ranks	Related t-tests
Matched pairs	Sign test	Wilcoxon signed ranks	Related t-tests
Independent measures	Chi-squared (χ^2)	Mann–Whitney U test	Independent t-test
	Nonparametric		Parametric

(B) **Tests of correlation**			
	Nominal	Ordinal	Interval/ratio
	No test, but χ^2 can be used (although it is a test of association)	Spearman's rank order test (r_s)	Pearson's product moment
	Nonparametric		Parametric

– say £150, £150 and £100 – the amount you will give to the fourth charity – £100 – is fixed, given that the total sum you are donating is £500. In this example, there are four values; three of them are free to vary and the fourth is fixed. Therefore we would say that there were three degrees of freedom (3 df).

Here is another example. If I told you that the sum of six numbers was 25 and that five of the numbers were 3, 5, 2, 8 and 4, you would quickly deduce that the missing number was 3. In this case, there are five degrees of freedom (5 df) – five of the six numbers are free to vary.

In a statistical test, the degrees of freedom always relate to the number of scores or categories that are free to vary, given that the total number is known. You will find that when it is necessary to work out degrees of freedom, clear instructions are given.

Chapter summary

■ Descriptive statistics are used to describe or to summarize your data. This can include the provision of graphical illustrations, such as bar charts, the production of tables, and the summarizing of data by means of averages and measures of dispersion.

■ Levels of measurement include nominal, ordinal interval or ratio data which are hierarchical and may be converted downwards but not upwards. Where there is doubt about the accuracy of your measurement it is as well to downgrade the level of measurement, interval to ordinal or ordinal to nominal measurement.

■ Measures of central tendency include mean, median and mode. There is a link to levels of measurement, with the mean linked to interval and ratio measurement, the median to ordinal and the mode to nominal measurement, but they are not exclusive. The mean is the preferred average as it provides the greatest amount of information and is the most versatile.

■ Raw scores are the measurements taken before any analysis has been done. A table of raw scores lists participants and their scores on the test(s) you have conducted. In constructing a table of raw scores it is important to label carefully. It is comparatively simple to rank the scores at this stage. This involves placing the scores in order. Where there are two or more participants with the same score the ranks are averaged.

■ Frequency tables can be drawn up to show the frequency of any score or range of scores. Bar charts or pie charts are convenient ways of displaying the scores. This allows readers to see at a glance the results of your study. Frequency distribution tables are also useful as a means of displaying results, and these may be displayed graphically as a histogram or a frequency polygon.

■ A normal distribution is a particular frequency distribution which forms a typical bell-shaped curve. This often occurs when a large number of measurements are taken of naturally occurring phenomena. It is important because of its special properties. Amongst other things the mean, median and mode coincide. Sometimes a set of scores will yield a distribution which is not 'normal'. It may be positively or negatively skewed.

■ It is also useful to measure the dispersion of the scores and this may be done by means of the variation ratio, the range and the standard deviation. The standard deviation is the most often used and it measures the average distance of all the scores around the mean. This gives a good indication of the spread of the scores. A fixed proportion of the scores will fall between the mean and one, two and three standard deviations above or below the mean, providing that the distribution is 'normal'.

■ This proportion is important because it helps us to calculate the probability of a score occurring. By this means we can assess the likelihood that the scores we obtained were acquired just by chance.

■ Statistical tests of significance are used to allow us to have confidence that the differences between sets of scores we have obtained or the relationship between them, in the case of correlation, are large enough not to have been likely to occur by chance alone.

■ Statistical tests fall into two groups, parametric and nonparametric, the former based upon the assumptions of a normal distribution, interval scores and a similar level of spread of scores, the latter used with ordinal or with nominal levels of measurement.

CHAPTER 36

Statistical tests

Nonparametric tests   872
- The Sign test   872
- The Wilcoxon signed ranks test   872
- Mann–Whitney U-test   873
- Chi-squared test of association   873

- Spearman's rank order test of correlation   874

Parametric tests   874
- Student's *t*-test   874
- Pearson's product moment correlation   876

Objectives

By the end of this chapter you should be able to:

- Understand how to calculate a number of inferential statistical tests;

- Apply them to appropriate data drawn from your own investigations.

Nonparametric tests

Remember that nonparametric tests work on nominal or ordinal data.

The Sign test

The Sign test can be used on data of nominal level. It uses pairs of scores from a related/repeated measures (or matched pairs) design.

Rationale

It compares the number of differences between two conditions which are in one direction with the number in the other direction. This is assessed against what might be expected to occur by chance.

Data from a hypothetical study

Mrs Chancer, a primary school teacher, hypothesizes that playing Scrabble will help children's spelling.

After first giving the children a spelling test, she organizes them to play Scrabble every day for two weeks. She then gives the children another spelling test to see if there is an improvement. In Figure 36.1 on p. 877, an improvement is indicated by a + sign and no improvement by a – sign.

The Sign test procedure for the data in Figure 36.1 is shown on p. 877.

The Wilcoxon signed ranks test

This is used only on data of at least ordinal level. It uses pairs of scores from a related/repeated measures (or matched pairs) design.

Rationale

Like the Sign test, it examines the direction of differences between participants' scores in each condition. However, it is more sensitive since it also takes account of the relative size of the differences by examining their rank order. If the null hypothesis were true, we would expect the ranks to be randomly distributed between the two conditions. However, if the majority of lower ranks were in one condition, we would suspect that the alternative hypothesis were true, that there was a real difference between the two conditions.

Data from a hypothetical study

A group of students were tested to discover how taken in they were by the Müller-Lyer illusion. The researchers hypothesized that there would be a difference between their performance in Condition A, where the Müller-Lyer figure was placed vertically, and Condition B, where the Müller-Lyer figure was placed horizontally. The data are presented in Figure 36.2 on p. 878. The procedure for the test is shown on p. 878.

Mann–Whitney U-test

This works only on data of at least ordinal level. It uses scores from an independent measures design.

Rationale

The test works on ranked data and compares the relative ranks in one condition with those in the other condition. Under the null hypothesis, we should expect to find the ranks randomly distributed between the two conditions. If, however, most of the ranks in one condition were higher than most of the ranks in the other condition it would seem likely that we would find a real difference between the two sets of ranks: that would imply that they were drawn from different populations.

Data for a hypothetical study using the Mann–Whitney U-test

A researcher sets out to compare the number of truancies occurring in two schools. Local concern has been expressed about one of them in particular. It was hypothesized that there would be a difference between the schools in terms of the number of truancies. The data collected are the number of truancies occurring in the two schools over a 12-week period. Note that the Robin School did not keep records for the last two weeks. Since this is an independent measures design it

is not necessary to have the same number of scores in each condition. The data are presented in Figure 36.3 on p. 879, and the procedure for the test is shown on pp. 879–80.

Chi-squared (χ^2) test of association

This works on nominal (frequency) data. It uses frequency data drawn from an independent measures design. Note that, strictly speaking, the expected frequency in any cell should not fall below 5.

Rationale

Chi squared differs from the other tests considered in that it does not work on individual scores but on frequencies – the number of times an event occurs. (These are nominal data; see p. 846.) For example, the number of absentees each day for a week in a school, goals scored in the Premier League last season, passes in the Psychology 'A' level examination this year.

What the test does is to examine the frequencies observed in a study, for example the number of people in different occupations who vote for various political parties, and compares these to the proportions in each category which might be expected to occur by chance. The research hypothesis might predict that people in some occupations would be more likely to vote Conservative and others more likely to vote Labour or Liberal Democrat; the null hypothesis would state that there would be no difference between the different occupational groups. The expected frequency represents what would be expected to occur under the null hypothesis.

Data from a hypothetical study

The psychology results in two colleges produced the distributions of A, B and C grades shown in Figure 36.4 on p. 880. The null hypothesis states that there is no difference between the colleges in terms of the proportions of students obtaining the different grades. The procedure for the test is shown on pp. 880–1.

Note that when we are interpreting the results of a chi-squared analysis only a very careful inspection of the original data will tell us where the most substantial discrepancies lie. If we look at the data in Figure 36.4 we can see that College X had a higher proportion of A and B grades than College Y, but College Y had a higher proportion of C grade passes.

The chi-squared result alone cannot allow us to say that one college is better than the other. There may be other factors responsible for the variation in grades between the two. For example, College X might have a higher proportion of more mature and highly motivated students.

Chi-squared test for goodness of fit

A special use of χ^2 involves comparing data drawn from just one variable to see how far it matches a particular theoretical distribution. In such a case, it is known as χ^2 test of 'goodness of fit'. For example, suppose we wished to investigate the music preferences among members of a local youth club to find out whether there is a bias towards certain types of music. Each member is given just one choice (Figure 36.5, p. 882). The procedure is shown on p. 882.

Chi-squared for 'goodness of fit' and the normal distribution

When we discussed the assumptions for parametric tests (Chapter 35, pp. 862–3) we said that the data for both samples should come from a population whose distribution approximates to normal. You will remember that with a normal distribution there is a fixed proportion of scores between the mean and one, two or three standard deviations from the mean. The chi-squared test for 'goodness of fit' can be used to test whether a large sample of scores varies significantly from a normal distribution. The table of z scores set out in Appendix 3, Table A.2 (p. 913), shows the proportion of scores that fall within various points on the distribution.

Spearman's rank order test of correlation

Spearman's rank order test can be used on related pairs of scores at ordinal level or above.

Rationale

Spearman's rho test of correlation describes the relationship (not the difference) between two variables. The formula for the Spearman's rank order test is as follows:

$$r_S = 1 - \frac{6(\sum d^2)}{N(N^2 - 1)}$$

where d is the difference between pairs of ranks and N is the number of pairs of ranks.

Data from a hypothetical study

The data shown in Figure 36.6 on p. 883 give the scores of a group of students on a standard IQ test and on a measure of cognitive style (CS). It is hypothesized that there will be correlation between the two sets of scores. This will be two-tailed because there is no prediction made as to whether the relationship will be positive or negative. The procedure for the test is shown on p. 883.

Parametric tests

A parametric test rests upon three assumptions (see Chapter 35, pp. 862–3):

- That there are interval or ratio scores.
- That there is homogeneity of variance. That is to say, the spread of the scores needs to be approximately similar. Variance has been discussed on p. 855.
- That the distribution of both populations is approximately 'normal'. Normal distributions have been discussed on p. 853.

Student's t-test

Rationale

The rationale for the t-tests for both related and independent samples involve the concept of the standard error of the mean of the two samples being tested. This rests on the idea that if you were to take a number of random samples from a population, there would be some variation between them. The spread of these variations can be measured statistically in much the same way that the standard deviation from the

---

| GLOSSARY |

Homogeneity of variance Assumption for the use of parametric statistical tests. The populations from which samples are drawn are assumed to have similar dispersion.

Standard error of the mean The fluctuation which might occur in the means from a series of samples drawn from a given population. As the samples become larger so the standard error of the means will become smaller (the means will be closer to the population mean).

mean is measured. Theoretically, the difference between the means of two random samples will be zero, not allowing for random variation. What the *t*-tests do is to test whether the difference in means observed is greater than that which might be accounted for by random variation. The *t*-ratio is defined as the observed difference minus the expected difference (zero), divided by the standard error of the difference between the means.

There are two *t*-tests in use, one for related (repeated) measures and the other for independent measures.

Related t-test

The formula for the *t*-test for related (repeated) measures is as follows:

$$t = \frac{\sum D}{\sqrt{\dfrac{N.\sum (D^2) - (\sum D)^2}{N - 1}}} \qquad \text{df } N - 1$$

where D is the difference between pairs of scores and N is the number of pairs of scores. There are several terms used to describe the kind of data for which this test is appropriate. These include:

- *t*-test for related samples,
- *t*-test for repeated samples (i.e. where the same sample is tested under two conditions),
- *t*-test for paired samples,
- *t*-test for matched samples.

The important point is that the data are paired; this could be done by testing the same sample of partici-pants under different conditions and pairing the data obtained from each participant under one condition with that obtained under the other. Or it might be that the samples are 'matched' (see Chapter 34, p. 827) for characteristics considered important to the study.

Example

In the card-sorting task similar to that described in Chapter 38 (p. 898) participants have been asked to sort a pack of playing cards into two piles (black and red) and again into suits (hearts, diamonds, clubs and spades). The time taken (in seconds) for each

procedure is taken, and a *t*-test is used to determine whether the difference in time taken is significant. The prediction is that it will take longer where there are four choices (for suits) than for two (colours). The results are shown in Figure 36.7 on p. 884.

A *t*-test for paired samples is carried out on the results to determine whether there is any significant difference in the time taken to sort into two and into four piles. Because the prediction is that it will take longer to sort into four piles, this is a one-tailed hypothesis. It is decided to reject the null hypothesis if the probability of a chance result is equal to or less than 5 per cent ($p \leqslant 0.05$). The procedure for the test is as shown on p. 884.

The t-test for independent (unrelated) samples

Where the samples are independent and cannot be paired, a *t*-test for independent samples is used. Bear in mind the assumptions for parametric tests. A useful strategy in this as in other parametric tests such as Pearson's product moment correlation is to start by listing the scores in columns and alongside them their squares (that is, the scores multiplied by themselves). Then write down the sum of each column and the number of scores in each group. The formula for an unrelated *t*-test is as follows:

$$t = \frac{\bar{X}_A - \bar{X}_B}{\sqrt{\dfrac{\left\{ \sum X_A^2 - \dfrac{(\sum X_A)^2}{n_A} \right\} + \left\{ \sum X_B^2 - \dfrac{(\sum X_B)^2}{n_B} \right\}}{N - 2}} \times \dfrac{N}{n_A \cdot n_B}}$$

$$\text{df } N - 2$$

where $\bar{X}_A$ is the mean for sample A, $\bar{X}_B$ is the mean for sample B, n_A is the number of scores in sample A, and n_B is the number of scores in sample B. X represents scores in either group. N represents the total number of scores.

Example

In a similar-card sorting task one group of participants (group A) were asked to sort into two piles (black and red), the other group (group B) were asked to sort into four piles (hearts, diamonds, clubs and spades). The hypothesis (two-tailed) was that there would be a difference in the time taken to sort into two and into four piles. The time taken in seconds by each group are shown in Figure 36.8 on p. 885. The procedure for the test is shown on p. 885.

Pearson's product moment correlation

The Pearson's correlation coefficient is a parametric measure of correlation which reflects the linear relationship between two variables.

Rationale and assumptions

Because it is a parametric measure the same assumptions apply as for a parametric test of difference (for instance, the two t-tests). These are:

■ Interval or ratio level measurement,
■ An approximation of a normal distribution of both samples,
■ Homogeneity of variance (that is, both populations should have similar spread).

Because it is an index of the linear relationship between two variables it can only be used when there is a linear (straight-line) relationship between the variables, that is to say that both variables must vary consistently together along all their values.

This limitation excludes its use where there is a curvilinear relationship between the two variables (see Chapter 35, p. 867). Because of this limitation, you need to draw a scattergram to represent the data (see p. 864) to ensure the relationship is linear before proceeding.

The two variables must be capable of being paired in some way. This will usually be because they come from the same source.

The formula for the product moment correlation (r) is as follows:

$$r = \frac{\sum XY - \frac{(\sum X \sum Y)}{N}}{\sqrt{\left[\sum X^2 - \frac{(\sum X)^2}{N}\right]\left[\sum Y^2 - \frac{(\sum Y)^2}{N}\right]}}$$

where X and Y are the scores in each of the two samples and N is the number of pairs of scores.

As with the other parametric tests described earlier (the related and independent t-tests) it is a useful strategy to list the data and alongside them their squares, and in this case their product.

Mrs Chancer had a suspicion that there was a relationship between 'highly strung children' and absenteeism from school. She had a local educational psychologist measure her pupils' neuroticism, using an Eysenck Junior Personality Inventory (JPI). She also measured the number of half days each pupil had been away the previous term. The results are in Figure 36.9 on p. 886. The absence scores are the X variable here and the JPI scores are the Y variable. Because she is predicting a positive relationship between the two variables this is a one-tailed hypothesis (that JPI and absenteeism are positively related).

The computation will proceed as shown on p. 886.

Figure 36.1 Data for Sign test: spelling test scores before and after playing Scrabble

Participant number	Test 1 (before Scrabble)	Test 2 (after Scrabble)	Sign of difference
1	45	56	+
2	10	22	+
3	50	75	+
4	44	45	+
5	17	35	+
6	58	60	+
7	36	45	+
8	39	43	+
9	55	50	−
10	20	39	+
11	45	60	+
12	48	72	+

Procedure for Sign test	Calculations on the data in Figure 36.1
1. Inspect the difference between each pair of scores. After disregarding pairs of scores that do not differ from each other, count the number of pairs of scores. This number is N.	$N = 12$
2. Where the score in Condition A (after Scrabble) is the larger, put a plus (+) sign in the last column. Where the score in Condition B (before Scrabble) is the larger, put a minus (−) sign in the last column.	See sign of difference column.
3. Count the number of times the less frequent sign occurs. Call this X.	The less frequent sign is (−) $X = 1$
4. Consult the table of critical values (Table A.5, p. 916). The values given relate to a two-tailed test. For a one-tailed test, the significance levels should be halved.	Since Mrs Chancer's hypothesis predicted that the children's spelling would improve, we shall use a one-tailed test. Note for for a one-tailed test significance levels are halved.
5. Find the relevant line of critical values relative to the value of N.	Consult the horizontal line next to $N = 12$.
6. Compare the value of X with the critical values. Since X must be equal to or less than the table value, find the highest level of significance for which X is still the same or smaller.	Our value of X is 1. The critical value for $p \leqslant 0.05$ is 2, so we know that the result is significant. However, the critical value for $p \leqslant 0.025$ is 2, and the critical values under $p \leqslant 0.01$ and $p \leqslant 0.005$ are both 1. Our value of X still does not exceed this. Therefore we shall take the critical value for the lowest significance level as our result. NB: We have halved the significance values, as it is a one-tailed test.
7. Make a statement of significance and decide whether or not to reject the null hypothesis in favour of the alternative hypothesis.	Our difference in results is significant at 0.005, $p \leqslant 0.005$ (one-tailed). We therefore accept the alternative hypothesis that playing Scrabble did improve the children's spelling

Note that unless we used a representative sample of primary school children, we could not generalize our findings to the whole population of primary school children.

Figure 36.2 Data for Wilcoxon signed ranks test: perception of the Müller-Lyer illusion in horizontal and vertical positions

1 Student	2 Condition A (Horizontal) (mm)	3 Condition B (Vertical) (mm)	4 Difference (A−B) (mm)	5 Rank of difference
1	15	17	−2	3.5
2	20	16	4	6.5
3	8	14	6	9
4	12	14	−2	3.5
5	23	16	7	10
6	11	19	−8	11
7	13	16	3	5
8	5	5	0	–
9	7	6	1	1.5
10	9	5	4	6.5
11	14	9	5	8
12	7	8	−1	1.5

Procedure for Wilcoxon signed ranks test	**Calculations on the data in Figure 36.2**
1. Ignore the scores of any student who scored the same in both conditions.	Omit the results for student 8.
2. Calculate the difference between each score in Condition A and its equivalent in Condition B. Remember to subtract in the same direction each time.	See column 4 in Figure 36.2 (A − B).
3. Rank the differences, ignoring the sign of the difference (this converts the data to ordinal level). Give the smallest difference the rank of 1.	See column 5 of Figure 36.2. See also procedure for ranking data on p. 850.
4. Add together the ranks for the positive and negative signs separately. Call whichever is lower T.	Add together the ranks for students with minus signs, 1, 4, 6 and 12 (i.e. 3.5 + 3.5 + 11 + 1.5). This gives a value of 19.5; and for those with plus signs, 2, 3, 5, 7, 9, 10 and 11 (6.5 + 9 + 10 + 5 + 1.5 + 6.5 + 8. = 46.5). T is therefore 19.5.
5. Consult the table of critical values (Appendix 3, Table A.6 on p. 917). Decide whether to take account of one-tailed or two-tailed values.	Since there was no prediction of the *direction* of difference between Condition A and Condition B take account of two-tailed values.
6. Find the relevant line relative to the value of N. N is the number of pairs of scores after ignoring those with zero difference.	The relevant line is N = 11. Student 8 was disregarded.
7. Find the lowest critical value that T does not exceed. If T is larger than all the critical values the result is not significant.	T is 19.5 and larger than all the table values. Therefore it is not significant.
8. Make a statement of significance and decide whether or not to reject the null hypothesis.	Since our result is not significant we must retain the null hypothesis and reject the alternative hypothesis. We must conclude that the orientation of the Müller-Lyer illusion has no effect on students' perception of it.

Figure 36.3 Data for Mann–Whitney test: numbers of truancies from two schools

1 Robin School	2 Ranks	3 Wren School	4 Ranks
10	12	6	2.5
9	10	11	15
12	17	8	8
14	19	7	5
15	20	8	8
17	22	11	15
16	21	7	5
13	18	5	1
10	12	8	8
11	15	6	2.5
		7	5
		10	12

Procedure for Mann–Whitney test

Calculations and comments on the data in Figure 36.3

1. Rank all the scores as if they were one group. Give the smallest score rank 1. (See Box 35.1 for help with ranking.) This converts the data to ordinal level.

See columns 2 and 4 in Figure 36.3.

2. Add up all the ranks for the smaller group. If the groups are the same size use either one. Call this R.

The Robin School has the smaller number of scores. The sum of the ranks for the Robin School is 166, so $R = 166$.

3. Calculate U_1 and U_2 from the following formulas:

$$U_1 = N_S \cdot N_L + \frac{N_S(N_S + 1)}{2} - R$$

$$U_2 = N_S \cdot N_L - U_1$$

where
N_S = the number of scores (ranks) in the smaller sample.
N_L = the number of scores (ranks) in the larger sample.
R = the sum of ranks in the smaller group (or either if they are the same).
Note: Appendix 1 on pp. 907–8 contains some help with tackling formulas.

$$U_1 = 10 \times 12 + \frac{10(10 + 1)}{2} - 166$$
$$= 120 + \frac{110}{2} - 166$$
$$= 120 + 55 - 166$$
$$= 9$$
$$U_2 = 10 \times 12 - 9$$
$$= 120 - 9$$
$$= 111$$

4. Choose the smaller of U_1 and U_2 and call it U.

$U = 9$.

5. Consult the table of critical values of U (Appendix 3, Table A.7, p. 918) and decide whether to take account of one-tailed or two-tailed values on the basis of your hypothesis.

The prediction was that there would be a difference between the Robin School and the Wren School in incidents of truancy, but there was no prediction about the *direction* of the difference. You therefore take account of two-tailed values.

6. Where your two values of N_S and N_L meet, you will find the critical value which must not be exceeded for a two-tailed test. If you have previously decided on a significance level of 0.05 look at this level first; then if your value of U is less, check the table value at the 0.01 level to see if U is still smaller.

$N_S = 10$, $N_L = 12$. Where these two meet shows a critical value of 29 at 0.05 level of significance. As our value of U is 9 this is smaller than the table value so we know it is significant at 0.05 level. Checking the critical value at 0.01 level we find that it is 21 so it is significant at $p \leqslant 0.01$ level.

7. Make a statement of significance and decide whether or not to reject the null hypothesis in favour of the alternative hypothesis.

Our result is significant at 1 per cent level $p \leqslant 0.01$ (two-tailed). We can therefore accept the alternative hypothesis that Robin School has a significantly larger number of truancies than Wren School.

Figure 36.4   Data for chi-squared test: psychology grades in two colleges

	A	B	C	Row totals
College X	6 (a)	42 (b)	15 (c)	63
College Y	8 (d)	42 (e)	46 (f)	96
Column totals	14	84	61	159
				Grand total

Procedure for chi-squared test

Calculations on the data in Figure 36.4

1. Draw up a table such as the one in Figure 36.4. The raw data in the table are known as the frequency observed (F_O). Each box is known as a cell and is given a letter (a), (b), (c) etc. to identify them.

Place the data in a box table and give each cell a letter (a), (b), (c), (d), (e) and (f) to identify it.

2. Obtain row totals, column totals and a grand total.

Insert row totals, column totals and a grand total.

3. Calculate expected frequencies (F_E) for each cell as follows:

$$\frac{\text{Row total} \times \text{column total}}{\text{grand total}}$$

The expected frequencies relate to the passes expected at each grade if there were no difference between the colleges except that due to chance.

Calculate F_E for each cell as follows:

Cell (a) $F_E = \dfrac{63 \times 14}{159} = 5.55$

Cell (b) $F_E = \dfrac{63 \times 84}{159} = 33.28$

Cell (c) $F_E = \dfrac{63 \times 61}{159} = 24.17$

Cell (d) $F_E = \dfrac{94 \times 14}{159} = 8.45$

Cell (e) $F_E = \dfrac{96 \times 84}{159} = 50.72$

Cell (f) $F_E = \dfrac{96 \times 61}{159} = 36.83$

4. Work out degrees of freedom by calculating as follows: (number of rows -1) multiplied by (number of columns -1). In a simple 2×2 chi-squared test the degrees of freedom are always 1.

Work out degrees of freedom (df)
df $= (2-1) \times (3-1) = 2$

5. Apply the formula for chi squared which is as follows:

$$\chi^2 = \sum \frac{|F_O - F_E|^2}{F_E}$$

Note: $|F_O - F_E|^2$ means deduct the smaller frequency from the larger one, ignoring positive or negative signs before squaring and dividing by F_E.

Apply the formula for chi squared as in the table below

Cell	F_O	F_E	$|F_O - F_E|$	$|F_O - F_E|^2$	$\dfrac{|F_O - F_E|^2}{F_E}$
(a)	6	5.55	0.45	0.20	0.04
(b)	42	33.28	8.72	76.04	2.28
(c)	15	24.17	−9.17	84.09	3.48
(d)	8	8.45	−0.45	0.20	0.02
(e)	42	50.72	−8.72	76.04	1.50
(f)	46	36.83	9.17	84.08	2.28
Total					9.60

Total the numbers in the final column to arrive at chi squared (χ^2).

$\chi^2 = 9.60$

6. Consult the table of critical values for chi squared (Appendix 3, Table A.4, p. 915). Use degrees of freedom (df) and table values of chi squared to find critical values.

  Take the highest table value which is lower than the calculated value of chi squared. If chi squared were lower than all the critical values it would not be significant, and we must accept the null hypothesis.

Since no prediction was made that one college would have a better performance than the other use values for a two-tailed test. Look at the line by 2 df. Our calculated value of χ^2 is 9.60, higher than the critical values for 0.05, 0.02 and 0.01. It is, however, not higher than the critical value for 0.001. Our result is therefore significant at 0.01 level.

7. Make a statement of significance. Decide whether to accept or reject the null hypothesis.

Our result is significant at the 1 per cent level ($p \leqslant 0.01$) with 2 df (two-tailed). We can therefore reject the null hypothesis and conclude that there is a significant association between exam grades obtained and the college the students attend.

Note that when interpreting the results of a χ^2 analysis, only a very careful inspection of the original data will tell us where the most substantial discrepancies lie. Looking at the data in Figure 36.4, College X had a higher proportions of A and B grade passes than did College Y, while College Y had a higher proportion of C grade passes.

Note also that the χ^2 result alone cannot allow us to say that one college is 'better' than other factors responsible for the variation in grades between the two. For example, College X might have a higher proportion of mature, highly motivated students.

Figure 36.5 Sample data for chi-squared test of goodness of fit: music preferences among youth club members

	Classical	Rock	Pop	Dance	Folk	Total
Number of times each style was chosen	12	32	32	23	21	120

Procedure for chi-squared test of goodness of fit	Calculation on the data in Figure 36.5
1. List the frequency of preferences for each type of music, as above. Find the total.	Frequency of preferences as table above. Total = 120
2. The expected number of choices for each kind of music if there were no real preference can be worked out as follows: F_E = Total number of observations divided by number of styles of music.	$$F_E = \frac{120}{5} = 24$$ That is, 24 members would choose each style of music
3. Calculate degrees of freedom (df). df = number of alternatives − 1	df = 5 − 1 = 4
4. Apply the following formula for χ^2 $$\chi^2 = \sum \frac{|F_O - F_E|^2}{F_E}$$	Calculations appear in the following table:

Style of music	F_O	F_E	$|F_O - F_E|$	$|F_O - F_E|^2$	$\dfrac{|F_O - F_E|^2}{F_E}$
Classical	12	24	12	144	6
Rock	32	24	8	64	2.67
Pop	32	24	8	64	2.67
Dance	23	24	1	1	0.04
Folk	21	24	3	9	0.38
					$\chi^2 = 11.75$

Consult the table of critical values for χ^2 (Appendix 3, Table A.4, p. 915) using the values for a two-tailed test. With a df of 4 the highest critical value which our value of χ^2 exceeds is 9.49 (this is at the 0.05 level). Therefore the result is significant at the 5 per cent level ($p \leqslant 0.05$). Our conclusion is that the distribution we have found does not fit that which would have occurred by chance. Youth club members have a significant preference for rock or pop music.

Figure 36.6 Data for Spearman's rank order test of correlation: scores from an IQ test and a measure of cognitive style

1 Student	2 IQ	3 CS	4 IQ rank	5 CS rank	6 Difference	7 d_2
1	100	96	2	10	8	64
2	110	75	4	1	3	9
3	95	93	1	9	8	64
4	105	90	3	8	5	25
5	120	85	7	5	2	4
6	125	80	9	3	6	36
7	118	84	6	4	2	4
8	130	78	10	2	8	64
9	115	86	5	6	1	1
10	123	89	8	7	1	1
						$\sum d^2 = 272$

Procedure for Spearman's rank order test of correlation	Calculations on the data in Figure 36.6
1. Rank the scores on variable X (IQ scores) taking the lowest as 1.	See column 4.
2. Rank the scores on variable Y (cognitive style) as before.	See column 5.
3. Subtract rank Y from rank X for each student. There is no need to indicate whether the difference is positive or negative.	See column 6; differences between ranks.
4. Square each difference.	See column 7; squared differences between ranks (d^2).
5. Add up the squared differences (d^2).	$\sum d^2 = 272$: total of squared differences.
6. Insert $\sum d^2$ into the following formula: $$r_S = 1 - \frac{6(\sum d^2)}{N(N^2 - 1)}$$ where N = number of pairs of scores (ranks) d is the difference between pairs of ranks.	$$1 - \frac{6 \times 272}{10(10^2 - 1)}$$ $$= 1 - \frac{1632}{990}$$ $$r_S = 1 - 1.648$$ $$= -0.648$$
7. Consult the table of critical values for Spearman's rank order test (Appendix 3, Table A.8, p. 919).	Take account of levels of significance for a two-tailed test.
8. Find the relevant line relative to the value of N.	$N = 10$.
9. Find the lowest critical value which r_S equals or exceeds. Take no account of signs.	$r_S = -0.648$ which is the same as the table value at the 5 per cent level $(p \leqslant 0.05)$. Therefore it is significant at this level.
10. Make a statement of significance and decide whether or not to reject the null hypothesis.	Since there is a significant negative correlation between IQ and cognitive style as measured by these particular tests a high IQ tends to be matched to a low CS score. We therefore reject the null hypothesis.

Figure 36.7 Data for a related *t*-test: comparison of time taken to sort cards into two and into four piles

Participant	Colours	Suits	Difference, D	D^2
A	64	68	+4	16
B	82	96	+14	196
C	59	57	+2	4
D	82	75	−7	49
E	74	65	−9	81
F	90	95	+5	25
G	65	65	0	0
H	71	78	+7	49
I	87	80	−7	49
J	75	75	0	0
N = 10			$\sum D = +9$	$\sum D^2 = 469$

Procedure for related t-test	Calculations on the data in Figure 36.7
Stage 1: Find $\sum D$ by totalling positive and negative differences separately and subtracting negatives from positives. Note: As this is a one-tailed hypothesis, if the $\sum D$ had been negative we should have had to retain the null hypothesis at this stage, as the results were in the opposite direction from those predicted.	$+4+14+2+5+7=32-7-7-9 = -23$: $\sum D = 9$
Stage 2: Find the sum of the squared differences, $\sum (D)^2$. The easiest way to do this is to form a parallel column as above. Then multiply by N.	$469 \times 10 = 4690$
Stage 3: Square the sum of the differences $(\sum D)^2$	$9^2 = 81$
Stage 4: Subtract the result of stage 3 from the result of stage 2.	$4690 - 81 = 4609$
Stage 5: Find $N - 1$	$10 - 1 = 9$
Stage 6: Divide the result of stage 4 by the result of stage 5.	4609 divided by $9 = 512.11$
Stage 7: Find the square root of the result of stage 6	$\sqrt{512.11} = 22.62$
Stage 8: Divide the result of stage 1 by the result of stage 7 to find t. Degrees of freedom $(N - 1)$	9 divided by $22.62 = 0.39 = t$ df $= 9$, $t = 0.39$
Stage 9: Consult Table A.3 in Appendix 3 (p. 914) to find the critical value of t at the $p \leqslant 0.05$ level (one-tailed).	Critical value is 1.883. As the value of t is less than this critical value, we can conclude that there is not a significant difference. It does not take significantly longer to sort cards into four piles than into two.

Note: If a two-tailed hypothesis had been decided upon (i.e. that there was a difference in the time taken without predicting the direction of that difference) then the critical value of *t* would have been 2.262. The difference would still not have been significant.

Figure 36.8 Data for an independent t-test: a comparison of times taken to sort cards into two and into four piles

Group A (two piles)	Scores squared, X_A^2	Group B (four piles)	Scores squared, X_B^2
65	4225	68	4624
59	3481	60	3600
76	5776	65	4225
84	7056	75	5625
50	2500	78	6084
54	2916	57	3249
62	3844	54	2916
56	3136	96	9216
55	3025	70	4900
65	4225		
$n_A = 10$ $\bar{X}_A = 62.6$ $\sum X_A = 626$	$\sum X_A^2 = 40\,184$	$n_B = 9$ $\bar{X}_B = 69.2$ $\sum X_B = 623$	$\sum X_B^2 = 44\,439$

Procedure for independent t-test	Calculations on the data in Figure 36.8
Stage 1: Subtract the smaller mean ($\bar{X}_A$) from the larger mean ($\bar{X}_B$).	$69.2 - 62.6 = 6.6$
Stage 2: In the first bracket, square $\sum X_A$ and divided by n_A.	$626^2 = 391\,876$ divided by $10 = 39\,187.6$
Stage 3: Subtract the result of stage 2 from $\sum X_A^2$.	$40\,184 - 39\,187.6 = 966.4$
Stage 4: In the second bracket, square $\sum X_B$ and divide by n_B.	$623^2 = 388\,129$ divided by $9 = 43\,125.44$
Stage 5: Subtract the result of stage 4 from $\sum X_B^2$.	$44\,439 - 43\,125.44 = 1313.56$
Stage 6: Add the results of stages 3 and 5.	$966.4 + 1313.56 = 2279.96$
Stage 7: Subtract 2 from the sum of n_A and n_B.	$(10 + 9) - 2 = 17$
Stage 8: Divide the result of stage 6 by the result of stage 7.	2279.96 divided by $17 = 134.115$
Stage 9: Divide N by the product $n_A \times n_B$.	19 divided by $10 \times 9 = 0.211$
Stage 10: Multiply the result of stage 8 by the result of stage 9.	$134.115 \times 0.211 = 28.298$
Stage 11: Find the square root of the result of stage 10.	$\sqrt{28.298} = 5.32$
Stage 12: Divide the result of stage 1 by the result of stage 12.	6.6 divided by $5.32 = 1.241 = t$
Stage 13: Find degrees of freedom $(n_A + n_B) - 2$.	$10 + 9 - 2 = 17$
Stage 14: Consult table of critical values of t at 5 per cent ($p \leqslant 0.05$) for the appropriate degrees of freedom.	Because the value of t in this case (1.241) is less than the critical value (2.11), the null hypothesis must be retained. We conclude that there is no significant difference between the times taken to sort into two and into four piles.

Figure 36.9 Data for Pearson's product moment test: nervous disposition and absence from school

Absence, X	X²	XY	EPI, Y	Y²
10	100	60	6	36
12	144	96	8	64
16	256	224	14	196
7	49	63	9	81
8	64	80	10	100
10	100	70	7	49
14	196	84	6	36
20	400	240	12	144
11	121	165	15	225
$\sum X = 108$	$\sum X^2 = 1430$	$\sum XY = 1082$	$\sum Y = 87$	$\sum Y^2 = 931$

Procedure for Pearson's product moment test	Calculations on data in Figure 36.9
Stage 1: Multiply $\sum X$ by $\sum Y$ and divide by N.	$108 \times 87 = 9396 \div 9 = 1044$
Stage 2: Subtract result of stage 1 from $\sum XY$.	$1082 - 1044 = 38$
Stage 3: In the first bracket below the line square $\sum X$ and divide by N.	$108^2 = 11\,664$ divided by $9 = 1296$
Stage 4: Subtract result of stage 3 from $\sum X^2$.	$1430 - 1296 = 134$
Stage 5: In the second bracket square $\sum Y$ and divide by N.	$87^2 = 7569$ divided by $9 = 841$
Stage 6: Subtract the result of stage 5 from $\sum Y^2$.	$931 - 841 = 90$
Stage 7: Multiply the result of stage 4 by the result of stage 6.	$134 \times 90 = 12\,060$
Stage 8: Find the square root of the result of stage 7.	$\sqrt{12\,060} = 109.82$
Stage 9: Divide the result of stage 2 by the result of stage 8.	38 divided by $109.82 = 0.346 = r$

Correlation coefficient $r = 0.346$. To ascertain whether this correlation is significant consult Table A.10 in Appendix 3 (p. 922). Critical values for a one-tailed test ($N - 2$ degrees of freedom $= 7$) are 0.582 at the $p \leqslant 0.05$ level or 0.798 at $p \leqslant 0.01$ level. This is therefore not a significant correlation. We must conclude that there is no significant relationship between neuroticism as measured by Eysenck's junior personality inventory and rates of absence from school.

Some exercises on statistical tests

Exercise 36.1

A group of ten students were asked whether they found it more productive to work in the morning or the afternoon. The answers they gave were as follows:

Archibald	morning
Rachel	afternoon
Seth	morning
Rebecca	morning
Hilda	morning
John	afternoon
Jacob	morning
Gertrude	morning
Jemima	morning
Michael	afternoon

Use a Sign test to assess whether there was a significant preference for one or the other. You can count the morning preference as +, the afternoon as −. The answer is on p. 889.

Exercise 36.2

The students in Exercise 36.1 were given three hours to complete an assignment on a Thursday afternoon. Then the following morning they completed a second three-hour assignment. The work they had done was assessed and ranked, the best pieces of work getting rank 1, the worst rank 10. The results were as follows:

	Morning	Afternoon
Archibald	7	6
Rachel	6	5
Seth	5	2
Rebecca	8	7
Hilda	9	8
John	3	4
Jacob	2	1
Gertrude	10	9
Jemima	4	3
Michael	2	10

Use a Wilcoxon signed ranks test to find out whether there was a significantly better performance by the students in the morning or the afternoon. The answer is on p. 889.

Exercise 36.3

It was suggested that the gender of the students in Exercises 36.1 and 36.2 might have a bearing on their performance in assignments. They were given an assignment to complete which was to last three hours. A further eight students (four boys and four girls) joined the original ten and their marks on the assignment were as follows:

Boys	Mark	Girls	Mark
Archibald	17	Rachel	12
Seth	12	Rebecca	6
John	18	Hilda	8
Jacob	15	Jemima	14
Michael	10	Gertrude	11
Richard	9	Emma	12
Robert	17	Jane	7
Charles	8	Mary	17
Malcolm	15		

Conduct a Mann–Whitney test on these results to see whether there is any significant difference between the boys and the girls. The prediction is that there will be a difference, but there is no prediction in which direction it would go. The answer is on p. 889.

Exercise 36.4

Use the χ^2 table to check the significance of the following χ^2 values (all two-tailed). What is the probability that each value was due to chance factors?

(a) $\chi^2 = 16.54$; df = 8
(b) $\chi^2 = 32.61$; df = 12
(c) $\chi^2 = 4.24$; df = 3

The answers are on p. 889.

Exercise 36.5

You want to find out whether there is a significant relationship between the ages of students and their performance in a test. Below is a list of dates of birth and the order in which the students came in the final test.

Name	Date of birth	Order
Gertrude	30.6.80	14
Jane	12.9.79	6
Mary	13.4.80	17
Archibald	23.12.79	8
Seth	14.1.80	13
John	2.3.79	2
Jacob	21.7.79	1
Michael	31.8.80	15
Richard	6.12.80	16
Robert	15.6.79	3
Charles	12.5.78	5
Malcolm	13.2.79	4
Rachel	24.4.80	12
Rebecca	3.11.79	10
Hilda	25.3.80	9
Jemima	21.1.79	7
Emma	21.2.80	11

Carry out a Spearman's rank order correlation test on the above data. The answer is on p. 889.

Exercise 36.6

The marks for groups of students in a test in February are compared with those obtained in July to see whether they have made a significant improvement. Their marks are as follows:

Names	February mark	July mark
Archibald	73	81
Rachel	56	74
Seth	43	50
John	34	67
Jemima	67	65
Gertrude	32	43
Jacob	81	78
Emma	45	47
Jane	65	71
Mary	60	63

Do a related t-test on the above marks to test whether the improvement in their marks is significant. The answer is on p. 889.

Chapter summary

- Nonparametric statistical tests are those designed to work on nominal and ordinal data. These include the Sign test, which uses scores from a related/repeated measures design. It compares the number of differences which are in one direction with the number which are in the other direction. This is assessed against what might be expected by chance.

- The Wilcoxon signed ranks test is also designed to work where there is a related measures design. It examines the direction of the differences between scores in each condition similarly to the Sign test but also takes account of the relative size of the differences by means of their rank order.

- The Mann–Whitney U-test is based upon ranked data, comparing the relative ranks in one condition with those in the other. Under the null hypothesis the ranks would be randomly distributed between the two conditions.

- Chi squared is a test of association which works on frequencies. It compares the frequency which might be expected under the null hypothesis with the frequencies observed. It may also be used as a test of 'goodness of fit'.

- Spearman's rank order correlation is a test of correlation which is based upon the differences between the ranks of two sets of paired scores.

- Parametric tests rest on the assumption that there are interval or ratio scores, that the distribution of populations is approximately 'normal' and that there is homogeneity of variance. Student's t-tests have been worked out for related and also for independent measures which are based upon the comparison of the standard error of the means of two samples.

■ Pearson's product moment test for correlation is dependent on the assumptions for parametric tests.

It is designed to measure the linear relationship between two variables which can be paired in some way. It can only be used where the relationship is linear.

Further reading

Clegg, F. (1982). *Simple Statistics*. Cambridge: Cambridge University Press. A fairly comprehensive course book for statistics, covering most areas in a light-hearted manner with cartoon illustrations.

Siegel, S. (1956). *Non-parametric Statistics for the Behavioural Sciences*. New York: McGraw-Hill. An advanced text for those who wish to pursue nonparametric statistical techniques further. It includes trend tests and tests for more than two samples.

Coolican, H. (1994). *Research Methods and Statistics in Psychology*, 2nd edn. London: Hodder & Stoughton. A very sound basic text for statistics for use in psychology.

Answers to Exercises

Exercise 36.1 $X = 3$, $N = 10$ not significant

Exercise 36.2 $T = 9$, $p \leqslant 0.1$ (10 per cent) not significant

Exercise 36.3 $U = 21.5$, $N_S = 7$, $N_L = 8$ not significant

Exercise 36.4

  (a) $p \leqslant 0.05$ (5 per cent)

  (b) $p \leqslant 0.01$ (1 per cent)

  (c) p is greater than 0.05

Exercise 36.5 $r_S = 0.8505$ significant, $p \leqslant 0.01$

Exercise 36.6 $t = 2.466$ with 9 df. Significant at the 5 per cent level (two-tailed) $p \leqslant 0.05$.

CHAPTER 37

Interpretation and presentation of research

Interpretation and background to research 890
- The hypothetico-deductive model 891
- Interpretation of results and design of study 891

Analysis of data and interpretation 892

Writing research reports 893
- Why write a report? 893
- Preparing your first report 894

Objectives

By the end of this chapter you should be able to:

- Interpret your results in the light of the background to the research and the way the research has been designed;

- Produce a research report which accurately reflects your work.

Interpretation and background to research

The results you have obtained are meaningless unless they are related to the problem currently being researched and to the previous work done in this area. An example might make this clearer. You will need to make some analysis of the way in which your results fit what others have done.

Suppose that you are looking at the Stroop phenomenon (Stroop, 1935). This suggests that when two sets of information being received by the brain are incompatible with each other, there is difficulty in dealing with them. For example, when people are presented with words which are names of colours, in print which is a different colour from that which the colour name represents, they will then find it harder to deal with mentally. La Berge (1975) predicted that when printed words are presented to us, automatic reading routines are triggered which will conflict with the task of colour naming if the names of the colours are incompatible with the colour of the print. You have presented the participants in your study with two sets of words: the first, colour names printed in the colours they represent (Condition A): the second, names printed in colours incompatible with what they represent (Condition B). Participants are asked to name the colours in which the words are printed and are timed to see how long they take to do this. The findings show that participants take significantly (that is, beyond chance level) longer to respond under Condition B. You can then claim that this supports the contention of Stroop and La Berge that participants are having greater difficulty dealing with incompatible information.

This example is a fairly simple one, and the link between the time taken to respond and the difficulty of processing the information presented is straightforward, but this may not always be the case. You will, however, always need to take account in your interpretation of what has been found by others and of the theoretical proposition which underlies it – in this case that a human's brain has difficulty in dealing with incompatible information.

The hypothetico-deductive model

Scientific research is based upon the hypothetico-deductive method. This has already been referred to in Chapter 3. A researcher starts with a theoretical proposition. This is then transformed into an operational or testable form by creating a hypothesis. This hypothesis carefully defines any vagueness in the theoretical proposition, replacing abstract ideas with something more concrete. In the above example, the idea of 'incompatibility of information' becomes colour names which do not match the print colours, and 'difficulty' becomes taking longer to respond. There are limitations involved in this process of redefinition and there may be inaccuracies, but the hypothesis thus formed can be tested in a way in which the theoretical proposition cannot. This is the next stage in the process – to test the hypothesis. Then it is necessary to translate the results of this testing in terms of the theory and if necessary modify it. The newly modified theory is then translated into operational terms in a new hypothesis to be tested, and so on ad infinitum. Figure 3.1 in Chapter 3 shows the way in which scientific research is carried out.

What has been done by others is important at each stage. There may have been a theory formulated (for example by Stroop). Hypotheses may have been tested which may or may not embody the same definition in operational terms as that which you propose to test. Remember that theoretical propositions inevitably contain vaguenesses, which may be defined in more than one way.

Interpretation of results and design of study

As you design your study, you must take various decisions, some of which have been highlighted in the introduction to this part of the book. It might be useful to refer back to them. They include the following.

Participants

You have to decide how many participants should be involved and who they should be. We have already seen that the number of participants may affect the confidence you can have that your results are not just due to chance effects. Other factors too, such as typicality (is your sample typical of the population as a whole?), can be important. Such things as age, sex or educational and socioeconomic background may be important. Populations and samples have been discussed in the introduction.

Design of studies

There are a number of choices available to you; these have been fully discussed in the introduction and in Chapters 3 and 34, and each has its implications for the interpretation of your results. When you design a study, it is a balancing act. Each decision you take opens up particular chances of bias. Let us examine some of them.

Method You may decide upon an experimental design rather than one of the other options, such as observation, survey or case study. Your gain in control and in your ability to infer cause is offset by artificiality and the possibility of lack of ecological validity (see Chapter 34).

Design Within experimentation, there are a number of choices. Related (repeated) measures designs free you from the bias that results from individual differences but open up possibilities of bias from order, learning, fatigue and practice effects. Independent measure designs do not suffer from order effects but open up chances of bias from individual differences. In your interpretation of results, you need to be aware of these factors and look for ways in which strategies have been adopted to minimize bias – counterbalancing or randomization, for example, to counter order effects, a large and representative sample to offset the effect of individual differences, together with random allocation to the conditions. Matched subject designs perhaps have the best of both these worlds, but you need to be certain that you have matched for the right characteristics. True

---

GLOSSARY

Hypothetico-deductive method The technique used in most scientific research. It involves commencing with a theory which is then refined to a testable hypothesis, tested by experimentation or other forms of research and finally modified in the light of the research findings.

matching is a very difficult thing to do. Perhaps identical twins are the only truly matched pairs.

Experimenter or participant bias

Bias may also result from experimenter effects or from demand characteristics, as has been seen in the introduction. You need to be aware of this and look for strategies adopted to avoid these sources of bias – single blind or double blind techniques, perhaps.

Correlational designs

You may have chosen a correlational design. In your interpretation of the results of your study, you need to bear in mind that you cannot infer cause from a correlational study. Also the relationship you have found may not be consistent throughout the range of values. The relationship may be a curvilinear one.

Surveys, case studies and other techniques

Choosing a survey, an observation or a case study rather than an experiment also has implications for interpretation. You have perhaps gained in ecological validity and your study is less artificial, but it is not as easy to infer cause. You have also, however, sacrificed some control, and your interpretation needs to take into account the variables which may have influenced your results. Similarly, the choice of interview techniques or archival study brings with it its own constraints in terms of interpretation.

Analysis of data and interpretation

Other factors which may have a bearing on the interpretation of the results of a study include the way in which you have analysed the data obtained. These factors include:

- The samples of the population you have tested.
- The level of measurement you are using.
- The kind of statistical test you use and the confidence level you choose.

All these things have been discussed in some detail elsewhere in this book, but it is worthwhile at this point refreshing your memory and highlighting the ways in which they may affect interpretation.

Population and samples

It is necessary to define clearly the **population** from which you have drawn your **samples** so that you are able to state clearly in your interpretation of the data how far you may legitimately generalize your findings.

Generalizability The term **generalizability** refers to how justified you may be in applying the results of your study to people other than those whom you have actually tested. If you have defined your population carefully and taken a representative sample of that population for testing, then you can reasonably say that your results are generalizable to all the members of that population. What you cannot legitimately do is to say that because you have tested samples of a population of boys and girls at St George's School and discovered that girls do significantly less well in mathematics, but significantly better in English, this is true of all pupils in all secondary schools. Unless a representative sample is used of the entire population, it is not legitimate to generalize beyond the population from which you have taken a sample, although I am afraid that you will find it is frequently done. You can refer back to the introduction for a fuller discussion of populations and samples.

Levels of measurement

The issue of **levels of measurement** relates to the information you collect in your data. Levels of measurement are fully discussed in Chapter 35. It is sufficient at this point to say that the precision you can obtain using interval measurement is greater than that obtained with ordinal or nominal measurement. This

---

GLOSSARY

Population The group from which a sample is drawn. This may be people, but may equally consist of numbers finite or infinite which refer to real or hypothetical events.

Sample Smaller group drawn from a population.

Generalizability The extent to which the results of a study may be applied to a wider group than the sample(s) used.

Level of measurement The kind of measurement used in the study. Interval or ratio measurement have greater precision and contain more information than ordinal measurement which in turn contains more information than nominal measurement.

issue of precision in measurement has two effects upon your interpretation of the data obtained:

Direct effect There is the direct effect upon interpretation resulting from increased accuracy and precision. For example, without using any measurement at all, you might observe that girls learn to talk more quickly than boys. Using nominal measurement, you might begin to quantify this observation, taking a fixed point (say their third birthday) and a criterion for talking and counting in a representative sample, the number of boys and girls reaching that criterion. Using ordinal measurement, you might assess your sample of boys and girls for talking ability and put them in a rank order. Finally, you could use interval measurement and devise a test of talking ability yielding talking 'scores'. As the sophistication of measurement increases, so does precision.

Indirect effect There is an indirect effect upon interpretation which results from the use of statistical tests appropriate to the level of measurement used and the 'power' of those tests accurately to assess the probability that the result obtained was a chance one rather than the effect of the independent variable upon the dependent variable.

Confidence levels and statistical tests

Your interpretation of results will also depend upon the statistical test performed and the **level of significance** found. This amounts to the **level of confidence** you have that the results found are not due to the vagaries of chance but to the effect of the independent variable upon the dependent variable. Clearly, a 1 per cent significance level ($p \leqslant 0.01$) would give you great confidence in affirming that what has been found is a real psychological phenomenon, while a 5 per cent significance level ($p \leqslant 0.05$), although it is perfectly satisfactory, does not give you quite that confidence. If, on the other hand, you have retained the null hypothesis, your results could have been due to chance alone. It is worthwhile saying at this point that if you do retain the null hypothesis and do not find significant results, you have not wasted your time. A larger sample or greater accuracy and precision in measurement might still disclose a real effect. A nonsignificant result is also important in its own right. You are not dealing with certainties or with proof. All

that you can legitimately say is that your findings support or do not support a theoretical idea.

❓ SELF-ASSESSMENT QUESTIONS

1. What choices have you regarding the design of your study? List some factors that might help you make your choice.
2. How far is it legitimate to generalize your results?
3. What is the relationship between the results of the research you may be carrying out and that which others have done?
4. List the main elements of the hypothetico-deductive process of scientific research.

Writing research reports

The final, and very important, stage in carrying out research is the writing of a report. This should be done as quickly as possible after the practical has been carried out and the data interpreted. As many researchers can testify, delaying the writing of the report only results in the whole project 'going cold'. By that is meant that your motivation may become less than it was, and essential details about why certain steps were carried out may be forgotten.

Why write a report?

There are two important reasons for writing a clear and explicit report.

Communication with other researchers

By carefully recording and interpreting your study, you are communicating to other researchers precisely what was done and why. It should be clear, therefore, how your findings add to the store of knowledge and theory already in existence.

> **GLOSSARY**
>
> **Confidence/significance level** The degree to which a researcher can be confident that a result obtained has not been obtained by chance alone. This may be assessed by conducting a statistical test of significance to assess the probability that the results occurred by chance.

Replication

It should be possible for readers to replicate your study: that is, to carry it out again in exactly the way that you did. As has been noted elsewhere, replicability is a very important aspect of the scientific method. Your report is likely to be judged by whether a reader could replicate your study just from the information in your report.

Preparing your first report

Producing an accurate and informative report is not easy, and it is worth spending a little time preparing for it before you start writing. This is particularly important when you are writing a report for the first time. There are a number of ways you can do this:

■ Look at some psychology journals, such as the *British Journal of Psychology*. Read one or two of the reports published, noting particularly their structure and the language used.
■ Read carefully any guidelines on report writing that have been provided by a tutor or which you may have received from an examining board. It is a good idea to keep these guidelines handy during the writing of your first few reports.
■ Try to get hold of some copies of past student reports. There are usually some in schools and colleges that have not been collected by previous students. Ask your tutor.

What kind of language is used?

There are a number of points to bear in mind here:

■ First, remember that much of the report will be written in the past tense. You are describing what has been done, how and why. This seems obvious, but it can be easy to forget in the early stages of report writing.
■ Write in simple, clear, concise sentences, using 'businesslike' language. The purpose of a report is to convey information and ideas. It is not the same as an essay, so there is no need to include long and elaborate descriptive passages. Also, it is rarely necessary to use highly technical language.
■ As far as possible, use impersonal language: for example, 'The participants were shown the stimulus card' rather than 'I showed the stimulus card to the participants', or 'It seems likely that . . .' rather than 'I believe that . . .'.

■ Use nonsexist language, for example he or she rather than he, unless of course the participants are all of the same sex.
■ Do not include names of participants, and avoid anything by which they might easily be identified. Use initials, perhaps, or simply 'participant A' or 'participant B'.

How is a report structured?

There is no single correct way of structuring a report. There is, however, a generally agreed format, which tends to reflect the process of research itself. The main headings are listed below:

TITLE
ABSTRACT (SUMMARY)
INTRODUCTION
METHOD
    Design
    Participants
    Materials/apparatus
    Procedure
RESULTS
    Description
    Treatment of results
DISCUSSION
CONCLUSIONS
REFERENCES
APPENDICES

Each of these sections will be dealt with separately.

Title

This should briefly indicate the essential nature of the study and the topic under investigation. For example 'The experimental study of "Scrabble" as an aid to children's spelling' or 'A survey of gender-related attitudes towards children's play'. It is not adequate to use a title such as 'The Scrabble Experiment'.

Abstract (summary)

An **abstract** is a very brief (usually not more than 150 words) thumbnail sketch of the investigation. It should be possible for the reader to tell enough from the abstract to decide whether the report is relevant and interesting enough to read in detail. Aim to include (very briefly):

- The aim and background idea of the investigation: for example, 'to investigate the effects of a memory aid on a recognition task'.
- An indication of the method and/or design used: for example, 'an independent measures design was used'.
- A description of the participants: for example, 'adult students studying "A" level'.
- A description of the experimental, or other, task: for example, 'participants in the experimental group were shown eight ambiguous pictures'.
- A summary of the results: for example, 'a significant positive correlation was found between ratings of self-esteem and "A" level results'.
- A conclusion: for example, 'findings appear to support Craik and Lockhart's "levels of processing" theory'.

Remember that the above points should be expressed as concisely as possible. Long abstracts are unlikely to gain full marks.

Introduction

This has two main functions. First it should set your study in context relative to other relevant psychological theory and research. Secondly, it should be structured in such a way that a hypothesis or research question emerges from your discussion of background theory and research.

A general strategy for this section might be as follows:

- Briefly describe the general area of research to which your study relates.
- Narrow this down to the specific theory or topic relevant to your study; it might, for example, be Craik and Lockhart's 'levels of processing' theory. This should include a brief review and a critical discussion of three or four of the relevant studies.
- Make it clear how your study is relevant to the theory and research described. This should lead naturally into a clear statement of the aims of the study.
- The aims should clearly explain what the study hopes to achieve; for example, it might be

critically to assess the 'levels of processing' approach to memory by replicating one of Craik and Lockhart's studies and assessing the outcome. A full and clear statement of aims is very important. This is particularly so in more qualitative research, for example a case study, where you might not employ a specific hypothesis.

- Finally, if appropriate (always, in reporting an experiment), clearly state the null and alternative hypotheses (see the introduction to this part of the book). This should be done in very precisely defined terms. For example, in an experiment to investigate the Stroop phenomenon, 'In a card-sorting task, participants will be influenced by the Stroop phenomenon' is too vague. A better hypothesis would be 'In a colour card-sorting task, there will be a difference in the time taken by participants to sort cards where the ink colour conflicts with the colour name than where no conflict occurs (two-tailed)'.

Method

This section should give the reader sufficient information to be able to carry out the study in exactly the way that you have done, that is to replicate the study. It usually has four subsections, as follows.

Design This should give a very brief indication of the general framework of the study: for example, what method was used – experiment, survey, correlational study, and so on. If it is an experiment:

- Say whether it was a related or independent measures design.
- Briefly describe the conditions of the experiment in relation to the independent variable: how many participants were there in each condition? How many trials did they perform?
- Refer to key controls used; for example, how were participants allocated to the two conditions? Was counterbalancing employed?

GLOSSARY

Abstract A brief summary of research, usually included at the beginning of the report. It should include aims, methods used, a summary of results and conclusions drawn.

There is no need to give details here of how the study was carried out. This will come later in the 'Procedure' subsection.

Participants (subjects) Here, a brief description should be given of all participants who took part in the study. Relevant details usually include the total number, age range and sex. Other information may be relevant; for example, occupation, socioeconomic background, educational level, and so on. It is particularly important to state how participants were selected – do they form a representative sample of the population from which they are drawn, or are they an 'opportunity' sample? Particularly important too is whether or not participants were naive, that is to say whether or not they were people with some knowledge or experience of psychological theory or of the particular theory under study.

Materials/apparatus All materials or equipment used should be described. With questionnaires or paper and pencil tests, details of the source should be given, for example, 'Concealed Shapes Test (Bloggs, 1967)', and where possible a copy placed in an appendix. Be careful to state when you have done this: for example, 'Appendix A includes a drawing of the apparatus used'. With specialist equipment, it might be helpful to include a diagram or actual examples of test materials. In some cases, a description should be included of how the materials were prepared.

Procedure Details should be given here of precisely what was done in the investigation. Nothing should be left out. Remember it should be possible for a reader to replicate your study. This might include:

■ Exactly what the participants were required to do, and in what order.
■ Standardized instructions given to the participants.
■ Any controls not referred to in the 'Design' section.
■ How the performance of the participants was measured, and how the results were recorded.

Note that this should be written as a clear statement in the past tense of what was done, not as a set of instructions, such as you might have received on a lab sheet.

Results

If you have quantitative – that is, numerical – data, there are two subsections here:

Descriptive statistics Raw data should not be presented here but should be placed in an appendix and specifically referred to. This section should contain a summary of the data, usually in the form of measures of central tendency and dispersion (see Chapter 35). Bar charts, histograms or other graphical representations might also be included. Each table or chart should be clearly labelled and should have a title explaining its contents.

Treatment of results If you have statistically analysed your results, give details of how this was done: that is, what test of significance was used. Justify your use of the test using the guidelines in Chapter 35.

Clearly state the result of the analysis, making sure you give details of the statistic arrived at, the appropriate critical value, value of N or df, whether a one- or two-tailed test was used, whether the result is significant, and if so at what level. A typical statement might be:

The result of the related t-test was

$t = 3.45$, with 9 df
$p \leqslant 0.01$, two-tailed

State whether the null hypothesis was retained or rejected.

If you wish to include calculations, these should not appear in the results section but in an appendix, specifically referred to.

Qualitative data You may have data which are not quantitative. These **qualitative data** may include introspections (what the participants say they feel about the study as they are taking part in it). These should be summarized and, if necessary, conclusions

---

GLOSSARY

Qualitative data Data in a research report which is not based upon measurement, but upon impressions formed and reactions made to the research procedures. It might include introspections from participants and observations of reactions of participants.

drawn from them. There are also many valid studies where there is no quantitative measurement or statistical analysis. For example, in Project 3 in Chapter 38 your data mainly consists of a transcript of a tape-recording made as you conduct your observation. Your results will consist of a detailed analysis of this (the transcript itself will be in an appendix with excerpts in the main body of the report to illustrate the points you are making). In addition, you may have counted incidents of the techniques under study, and these can be displayed as a table. It is appropriate to comment upon your observations in a qualitative way too. It does not invalidate your work if you have no statistics or statistical test.

Discussion

This section has four main purposes:

- To discuss and expand upon the findings presented in the results section. This should be done in such a way as to draw conclusions about the hypothesis or research question stated in the introduction.
- To discuss the findings of your study in the light of the background literature assessed in the Introduction. To comment, also, upon any differences and similarities between your findings and those in the literature.
- To identify the limitations of the study and modifications that might be appropriate.
- To suggest the direction future research might take in the light of your findings.

A suggested sequence for the discussion is as follows:

- Restate the results, but in the terms of your hypothesis and, if your data are quantitative, without the mathematical precision and detailed analysis of the results section. For example: 'Participants did take significantly longer to sort colour cards where the ink colour conflicted with the colour name, compared with where no conflict existed.'
- Comment on whether the results found were as expected and whether they confirmed the findings from other research. If not, try to suggest possible reasons for the discrepancy.

- Consider whether your findings clarify or enlarge upon a contemporary theory or extend the knowledge of a particular topic.
- Indicate whether or not the sample used allows you to generalize your findings to the population investigated. This will depend upon the extent to which the sample was representative, bearing in mind that few samples used in psychological studies are truly representative.
- Evaluate the methods used in your study, pointing out how it could be improved in the future. Draw attention to any flaws, remembering of course not to be too 'nit-picking' about relatively minor shortcomings.
- Discuss some of the implications of your study for future research.

The main guiding principle for the discussion is to keep it relevant. Do not be tempted to discuss new theory or research that has not been covered in the introduction and which is not directly relevant to your study.

Conclusions

This should be a brief restatement of the statistical findings of the study along with a comment on the extent to which they support or refute the relevant theory or research.

References

You will need to identify the sources for both the studies you have quoted and any books and reference material you have used.

In the text, identify the main author and the date of publication: for example, 'Johnson et al. (1994)'. Note that one or two authors will be referred to individually in the text, more than two as above (et al.).

At the end of your report, you must list all books or journal articles referred to in the body of the report.

In the **References** section, give full details by listing alphabetically all works you have referred to; for example:

GLOSSARY

References A list of sources placed at the end of a research report or other academic work to indicate from where the material referred to has been taken.

Johnson, E., Jones T. and Shipman, S. (1994). *Psychology Review*. London: Stamford Press.

Journal articles are referenced similarly, but you will put the title of the article in full, together with the journal name, volume number and page number; for example:

Zeaman, D. and House, B.J. (1951). The growth and decay of reactive inhibition as measured by alternation behaviour. *Journal of Experimental Psychology, 41,* 177–201.

Sometimes an article is quoted from a book of edited articles. In this case it is referenced as for the following:

Spielberger, C.D., O'Neill, H.F. and Hansen, D.N. (1972). Anxiety, drive theory and computer assisted learning. In B.A. Maher (Ed.), *Progress in Experimental Personality Research*. London: Academic Press.

You should underline book titles and journal names or put them in italics.

Appendices

This section will contain items such as raw data, calculations, questionnaires or copies of any other items referred to in the main body of the report. Different items can be put in separate appendices – Appendix 1, Appendix 2, and so on. Refer to them in the main body of the report where appropriate.

? SELF-ASSESSMENT QUESTIONS

1. Outline some of the key decisions to be taken when designing an investigation.
2. What factors are important when interpreting the results?
3. Why is it important to write a clear and explicit report of your investigation?
4. Outline some of the characteristics of a good report.

Chapter summary

- It is very important that a piece of research should be presented in a way that makes its aims and background very clear. In relation to the background there need to be links to the theories and previous research done in the area you are working in. The interpretation of research will depend upon how it fits in with previous work. A great deal of research in psychology takes the form of a continuous process of formulating and testing hypotheses and then modifying the theories on which the hypothesis is based, creating new hypotheses and testing these.

- The design of the study you have done will affect your interpretation of it. Your choice of participants, the design you have chosen, the controls you have in place will effect your interpretation. The population

you are concerned with and the sample(s) you have drawn from it are important with respect to generalization of results. Levels of measurement may determine the precision with which you can interpret your findings. Analysis and statistical procedures may or may not be appropriate and this too is important.

- While there is no one way of writing research reports there are conventions to be observed. Reports need to be clear and explicit to communicate your findings to other researchers and enable them to replicate. The main headings in a report should include title, abstract, introduction, method, results and discussion. Conclusions, references and appendices also have their place.

Further reading

Robson, C. (1973). *Experiment Design and Statistics in Psychology*. Harmondsworth: Penguin. This book is quite old now, but it contains an excellent chapter (9) on carrying out and writing up experiments.

CHAPTER 38

Some projects

The purpose of this chapter is to provide outlines of possible projects which students or teachers may like to use. It will give you the chance to put into practice some of the things which you will have read about in the previous chapters. The projects are divided into three sections; the first contains experiments, the second, observational studies, and the third, correlational studies. It is of course assumed that before you embark upon any project you will have studied and read about the phenomena you are researching.

Experimental projects

Project 1: The Stroop phenomenon

Stroop (1935) suggested that where the format in which material is presented and the content of the information presented (for example, between the colour of the print used to print colour names and the names themselves) are incompatible, there will be greater difficulty in dealing with them than when the format and the content are compatible (the **Stroop phenomenon**). La Berge (1975) suggested that our automatic reading routines are triggered when words (such as colour names) are presented, and this may interfere with the task of colour naming when there is a conflict between what is read and the information coming in from, say, the colour of the print. The aim of this experiment is to test these suggestions.

Preparation

Hypothesis Devise a hypothesis which can be tested (H_o and H_a). In particular, define what you mean by incompatible information. Define also the form in which the colour naming will be done.

Design Decide upon the experimental design. Are you going to need to counterbalance or randomize the presentation of your material? Do you need to allocate participants randomly to the two conditions? What about other controls: standardized instructions for participants, for example?

Participants Decide upon your participants.

Materials Assemble materials and equipment. You will need a means of printing words in a variety of colours, some compatible with the colour names, some not. You will need a stopwatch to time the responses of your participants.

There may be some difficulty in timing the very short intervals between presenting the words and the participants' response. Decide how you can get over this. One way might be to present the words not one at a time, but in groups or lists, say a group of ten words. Time the responses to the whole list. Is an oral response going to be better than a written one? Are there likely to be problems standardizing colour names? A list of nonsense words (of varying lengths) printed in various colours might help to test La Berge's suggestion of the automatization of reading as well as lists where the colours and content are compatible and where they are incompatible. There is unlikely to be interference with colour naming if the words do not mean anything.

> **GLOSSARY**
>
> **Stroop phenomenon** A situation where there is incompatibility between the content of material presented to an individual and the form in which it is presented, which increases the difficulty of making a response to it: for example, where the colour of the print is at odds with the information presented by that print.

Analysis techniques Decide on how results will be described and presented. What descriptive statistics will you use? What graphical representation of your results is likely to make them clearer? How will you analyse the results? What level of measurement are you using and what will be an appropriate statistical test to use?

Go ahead Assemble your participants and carry out the experiment.

Project 2: Choice response time

This experiment aims to explore Hick's Law (Hick, 1952) on **choice response time**, which sets out the relationship between the number of choices available and the time taken by the brain to choose between them. It has all sorts of practical implications. For example, there are implications for motorists approaching road junctions. It is as well for road planners to keep in mind the time needed to choose between the alternative routes. Hick has suggested that the time needed to make the appropriate choice (response time, RT) will be proportional to the amount of information needed to decide between them. The unit of information used is the bit or binary unit. Where two alternatives are equally probable, one bit of information is needed to decide between them. With four possible choices two bits are needed: one to choose between two pairs of alternatives, and one to choose between the two you have initially chosen. With eight choices, you will need three bits: one to choose which four of the eight alternatives, a second to pick two of the remaining four and a third to choose between the last

two. It is not unlike a football cup competition. Say there are 32 teams competing. The first round whittles that down to 16 (one bit). The second round (one bit) gets the number down to eight, the third round reduces the number of teams to four (one bit). The semifinals reduce these four to two (one bit) and the finals choose between these last two (one bit). So we have five bits of information in all. This amounts to logarithms to the base 2: 32 is 2^5 ($2 \times 2 \times 2 \times 2 \times 2$), 16 is 2^4, 8 is 2^3, 4 is 2^2 and 2 is 2^1. Figure 38.1 shows logarithms to the base 2 for numbers between 1 and 99.

The way in which we suggest you set up various choices is to set participants the task of sorting playing cards. Colours (black and red) give you two choices, suits (♥, ♦, ♣ and ♠) will give you four choices, and numbers (excluding J, Q, K, but including A as 1) give you ten choices. You will need to measure the time taken to complete a sort of the cards.

Preparation

Hypothesis Devise hypotheses (H_o and H_a). You will need to predict what the relationship will be between the number of choices and the time taken. If Hick's Law holds, then participants should take 3.32 times as long to sort into ten piles (choices) as two.

GLOSSARY

Choice response time Time taken by an individual to choose to respond in one way or another to options offered. The more choices available there are at any one time the longer it takes to make the choice.

Figure 38.1 Logarithms to base 2 for numbers between 1 and 99

n	0	1	2	3	4	5	6	7	8	9
0	–	0.00	1.00	1.59	2.00	2.23	2.59	2.81	3.00	3.17
1	3.32	3.46	3.59	3.70	3.81	3.91	4.00	4.09	4.17	4.25
2	4.32	4.39	4.46	4.52	4.59	4.64	4.70	4.76	4.81	4.86
3	4.91	4.95	5.00	5.04	5.09	5.13	5.17	5.21	5.25	5.29
4	5.32	5.36	5.39	5.43	5.46	5.49	5.52	5.55	5.58	5.61
5	5.64	5.67	5.70	5.73	5.75	5.78	5.81	5.83	5.86	5.88
6	5.91	5.93	5.95	5.98	6.00	6.02	6.04	6.07	6.09	6.11
7	6.13	6.15	6.17	6.19	6.21	6.23	6.25	6.27	6.29	6.30
8	6.32	6.34	6.36	6.38	6.39	6.41	6.43	6.44	6.46	6.48
9	6.49	6.51	6.52	6.54	6.55	6.57	6.58	6.60	6.61	6.63

Design Decide on your experimental design. There are clearly going to be several conditions. There is a whole range you could devise beside the three mentioned above, 13, for example, for numbers including court cards. Are you going to employ a related measures design or an independent measures design? How do you intend to control for the effects of boredom, fatigue and learning/practice if you go for a related measures design? Instructions are going to be important to ensure that each sort is carried out in precisely the same way. Is it going to be possible to control the effects of different physical movements between, say, sorting into 13 piles and into two? Can you time just the movements without the mental sorting process? Then subtract these times from those which include sorting? How many sorts should be carried out under each condition?

Participants Decide upon your participants, recruit them and give them their instructions. Instructions should, of course, be standardized, and will clearly depend upon the decisions you make in the design stage.

Materials Assemble materials and equipment. Packs of cards will need to be as similar as possible and shuffled in exactly the same way. Stopwatches will be needed to time each sort as well as some sort of pro forma on which to record your measurements.

Analysis techniques Analysis of your results will clearly involve finding mean times for each condition, having first subtracted movement times. What statistical test is appropriate here? You have more than two conditions and either related or independent measures (whichever you have decided on). You are also interested in the proportionate differences in time taken. Perhaps there is a means to assess whether these proportions are significantly at odds with those which Hick proposed. Again, what kind of significance test can you employ?

Go ahead Finally, assemble your participants and carry out your experiment.

Summary

To sum up, Figure 38.2 is a flowchart showing the stages in the planning of your experiments.

Observational studies
Project 3: Interactive techniques

Schaffer (1977) suggested that there are specific techniques which a mother employs when interacting with an infant. These are outlined in his book *Mothering*. Briefly, the techniques include the following:

- **Phasing**. This describes the way in which the mother watches for an opportunity to slot in to the child's behaviour something she wishes the child to do. Newson and Newson (1976) have illustrated this process, describing how a mother gets an infant to follow a ring dangling in front of his eyes.
- **Adaptive techniques**. This relates to the way in which a mother adapts her behaviour to that of the infant. She does not behave at all as she would if she were interacting with an adult. Movements are slower, gestures are more emphatic, expressions are exaggerated and her speech is more intermittent and simpler. There is a great deal of repetition. Stern (1977) has shown how the stimulation which a mother provides for an infant is not haphazard, but a highly structured activity.
- **Facilitative techniques**. These relate to the way in which a mother makes it easier for the infant to initiate interactions. She may spend time clearing away things which are not immediately in focus, putting things next to each other so that the child

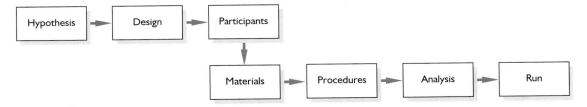

Figure 38.2 Flowchart of decisions to be taken in planning a project

will use them together or making them easier for the child to deal with, perhaps turning something round so that it is more easily grasped. Rather than overtly teaching their children, mothers spend time on what White and Watts (1973) describe as 'low keyed facilitative techniques' aimed at encouraging the child's activity, making suggestions, helping with difficulties, supplying materials, participating in what he or she is doing or lavishing praise and admiration on the efforts the child is making.

■ **Elaborative techniques.** This relates to the way in which a mother first allows a child to show where his or her interest lies and then elaborates upon that interest. If a child shows interest in a toy, the mother will fetch it, if it is out of reach, label it verbally, point out some of its features and demonstrate what it can do, adding a verbal dimension to the child's visual experience and allowing the child to associate sight and sound to acquire another addition to his or her vocabulary.

■ **Initiating techniques.** There are times when the mother takes the initiative, but even here her behaviour is very closely linked to that of the child. Timing is important. The mother ensures that she first catches the child's attention and then directs it to the object she wants the child to become interested in. Then she will check that the child's attention is indeed following where she is pointing.

■ **Control techniques.** These arise out of the need for the mother to be more assertive occasionally. Even here, this is a two-way process, not the arbitrary imposition of control upon the child. There is checking to make sure that the child has understood, that it is appropriate to the child's ability to follow, there are nonverbal gestures to provide the child with help in doing what the mother wants him or her to do, and these are delivered only when the mother is sure that the child's attention is on her.

The aim of this observation is to study the extent to which these techniques which Schaffer has outlined in relation to infants and their interactions with their mothers are used by other adults in their interactions with older children. The basis will be a close observation, accompanied by a tape-recording of the interactions between an adult (perhaps a father or a friend) and an older child between five and eight years old (the important thing is that the older child should be old enough to be able to use language fluently) while the child is performing some manipulative task (this could be anything from baking a cake to assembling Lego or Meccano).

Preparation

Hypothesis Make a clear statement of your aims. You will need to show that the techniques noted by Schaffer will be seen also in interactions by an adult with an older child. Remember that establishing a hypothesis involves operationalizing the ideas you have formulated. The kinds of behaviour you will classify under the heading of each of the techniques Schaffer lists will need to be clearly identified in relation to an older child and another adult. You will need to specify the kind of interaction you are concerned with and the time limits.

Design You will be concerned with your plan of campaign. How will you ensure that the piece of behaviour you record and observe is representative? How will you make sure that both adult and child behave in a natural way? How will you set up the study? What instructions will be given to the participants?

Participants Factors to consider will include the age of the child and the ease with which he or she is likely to interact with the adult, how familiar the adult is with the child, and what you propose the manipulative task should be. Bear in mind the ethical considerations outlined in Chapter 5: for example, informed consent.

Materials Make sure that everything the participants will need for the task is easily available. Set up the tape-recorder and test it. Prepare yourself for observation. Among other things you will need a checklist of points to look for, derived from Schaffer's techniques.

Analysis techniques You have already identified criteria by which you can judge which of the interactions you have observed fall under which category. Replay the tape and write a full transcript. Annotate this with your observations. This will go into your report as raw data in an appendix. From the transcript count incidents of each of Schaffer's techniques. Draw up a frequency table. A bar chart will display clearly whether your findings support the hypothesis or not. You have only one participant so that formal significance testing is not possible. Remember the limitations that this will place upon the generalizability of your study.

Go ahead Run your observation.

Project 4: Piaget's concept of conservation

Piaget (see Chapter 20) developed the idea that children between the ages of about 7 and 11 gradually become increasingly able to conserve. This implies that they are increasingly able to understand that while the overall appearance of objects and materials in relation to features such as volume, number, mass and area may change, the objects themselves remain unchanged; their nature is 'conserved'. For example, a ball of Plasticine contains the same amount of Plasticine when it is rolled out into a sausage shape. Piaget has suggested that below the age of about seven, children will be unable to 'conserve'. It is suggested you could use the services of members of a primary school or a playgroup to investigate three aspects of conservation: conservation of substance (as in the Plasticine example above), **conservation of volume** (liquid poured from a tall beaker into a shallow bowl still retains the same volume) and conservation of number (a row of ten beads remains the same even when spread out to double its length). Later researchers have reported (see Donaldson, 1978) that children achieve conservation earlier than Piaget had suggested and that this might have been because Piaget's experiments tended to be on the adult's terms rather than the child's. When an important adult such as the experimenter spread out the beads, there must have been some real change, whereas when a 'naughty teddy' 'messed them up' this was not the case, as McGarrigle found (reported in Donaldson's book).

The aim of this observation is to test differences in 'conservation' between three- to four-year-olds and children of six to seven.

Preparation

Permission and hypothesis Approach the head-teacher of a primary school and/or a playgroup and outline what you intend to do. Ask permission to use participants of the appropriate ages from his or her school. Obtain permission also from the parents of children participating. Take careful note of ethical considerations which need to be borne in mind (Chapter 5). Establish your hypothesis. Do you predict that you will find what Piaget found or that the younger children will be able to conserve? What is your null hypothesis going to be?

Design What is the design of your observation going to be? What controls will you need to have in place? Is it going to matter what order you test your participants in? What instructions will you give them?

Participants You will need a sample of children of each age. How will you ensure that it is representative, at the least, of children in that school or playgroup? You will clearly need the headteacher's and the class teacher's help in this.

Materials Assemble the equipment you will need: different shaped liquid containers, Plasticine and beads or counters. Tables and chairs will also be needed and perhaps a tape-recorder to record the children's responses. Again you will need to rely upon the good offices of the head and the class teacher.

Analysis techniques How will you analyse your results? What level of measurement are you going to be able to use? Is each child going to be marked down as conserving or not conserving, on each test? Is it going to be useful to include qualitative data in the form of some written account of how the children performed and introspections (how the children themselves said they felt about it)? How will you display your data? What tables, bar charts or graphs are appropriate to use? What about a test of significance? What level of data have you got?

Go ahead Now do your tests.

GLOSSARY
Conservation of volume An understanding that the volume of material remains constant even when the appearance changes.

Project 5: A natural experiment on gender differences

There has been considerable research into the behaviour of men and women. Chapter 22 has highlighted ways in which the behaviour of men and women differs as a result of socialization. According to some researchers, among men, the norm is to take risks, while among women there is a greater tendency towards caution. This may manifest itself in the way in which people drive motor vehicles. When they come to traffic lights at amber, men may tend to take the risk of crossing, while women may be more likely to stop. Similarly, after stopping at lights, men may be more likely to move on the red and amber, while women may wait for green.

This is in the nature of a field study. Participants will be motorists coming to a particular set of lights where observers will record behaviour. The aim will be to test whether risk taking in terms of 'amber gambling' is gender specific.

Preparation

Hypothesis   Establish and formulate a hypothesis, or perhaps two hypotheses, one concerned with stopping at the amber light, the other concerned with moving forward while the lights are still red and amber without waiting for the green. The null hypothesis will assume no distinction between men and women except for the vagaries of sampling error. The alternative hypothesis will predict that there is a difference in the way in which men and women behave when faced with traffic lights. This is a two-tailed hypothesis.

Design   Identify the design of your study. Clearly this will be an independent measures design and the measurement will be nominal (categorical/frequency data). There will clearly be two categories of participant. The categories of conformity or risk taking might be more. This is a decision you will need to take. What do you classify as risk taking? 'Creeping' forward while the lights are still red, moving on the red and amber and waiting might each be categories. Similarly, with stopping at red, there might be more than one classification.

Participants   Your sample of participants will to some extent select themselves. Your decision will be

to select the set of lights which you intend to observe. Should you choose an intersection or perhaps a 'pelican' crossing? Bear in mind that you need to find one where the sample is as representative as you can reasonably find. This will affect the extent to which you are going to be able to generalize.

Standardization   If you have more than one observer it is important to establish interobserver reliability (see Chapter 34). Instructions and procedures should be carefully standardized.

Materials   Your equipment is likely to be minimal. It is as well to have preprinted charts on which you can tally the participants. The conventional method of working is to tally them in fives (JHT, JHT, JHT, II = 17). If you have set criteria involving the time after the lights have changed to amber, you might also need a stopwatch (for example, you might count as amber gambling anyone crossing the lights more than two seconds after the lights change to amber). These criteria need to be clearly set beforehand.

Analysis techniques   This is a frequency-based study so that your analysis should include a frequency table and/or a bar chart. Consult Chapter 35 to ascertain what will be an appropriate test for the significance of your findings. It is an independent measures design using nominal data.

Go ahead   Now run your observation.

Correlational studies

Project 6: Fin angles and the Müller-Lyer illusion

Gregory (1968) has suggested that there is a relationship between the angles of the arrowheads on the Müller-Lyer illusion and the extent of the perceived illusion. This project sets out to test his suggestion. In this classical illusion, it has been demonstrated that a line attached to outward facing arrowheads will appear longer than an identical line attached to inward facing arrowheads. See Figure 13.12.

Preparation

Hypothesis   The design of the study is correlational. The angles of the arrowheads in the Müller-Lyer figure will vary at 10° intervals between 10° and 90°, making a total of nine different arrowhead angles on both the outward facing and inward facing arrowheads. The prediction will be that there will be a relationship (that is, a positive corrrelation) between the angle of the arrowheads and the amount of the perceived illusion. This in turn supports Gregory's contention concerning the explanation for this illusion: that is, that it relates to experience of the use of constancy and distance cues. The observer is encouraged to perceive the line between outward facing arrowheads as being more distant (analogous to looking at the inside corner of a room opposite to the observer) than the line between the inward facing arrowheads. Gregory draws the analogy between that and the outside corner of a building. (There is a more complete account of this theory in Chapter 13 of this book.)

Design Each participant will be shown ten versions of the illusion with arrowheads at angles varying between 10° and 90°. The number of times each angle of arrowhead will be shown to a participant, the order in which they will be presented and the instructions given will need to be carefully considered so as to avoid **systematic error** resulting from order or experimenter effects (see the introduction to this part). The independent variable, then, is the arrowhead angle. The important point to make in your instruction to participants is how the arrowheads should be presented, horizontally or vertically, sliding to the left or to the right. You should consider counterbalancing or randomizing the way in which the arrowheads are presented. The dependent variable is the amount of illusion perceived. This may be measured in the following way.

The arrowheads are presented on a movable slide (see Appendix 2), and the participant is invited to adjust this slide until the lines between the arrowheads appear to be equal. The lines are then measured, and the difference between them is taken to be the amount of the perceived illusion. It might be important that participants are naive, that is to say that they know nothing of the theory they are testing. In this case, you would be using a single blind study.

Participants Recruit participants who are naive, preferably nonpsychologists, as this will minimize participant effects. Each participant will operate

independently. There might in effect be just one participant.

Materials Equipment is important. The materials and method of construction are detailed in Appendix 2. You will need a separate slide for each angle.

Analysis techniques You will correlate two sets of data: (a) fin angle, and (b) amount of perceived illusion. Decide at the planning stage what technique you will adopt to obtain the correlation coefficient and how you will display your results, and the effect this might have on your choice of statistical test.

It is possible that you may end up with a curvilinear relationship. There may be a different amount of illusion perceived at extreme angles (1°, 20° and 8°, 90°). Think about how you might display this.

Go ahead Now run your study.

This project might equally well be run as an experiment testing whether there is a difference between the amount of illusion perceived between, say, 30° and 60° angles or horizontal and vertical presentation.

Project 7: Circadian rhythms

This study aims to examine the relationship between circadian rhythms and performance on a vigilance task. **Circadian rhythms** are variations throughout the 24-hour daily cycle of various physiological functions and characteristics, such as body temperature, metabolism, digestion, food intake, and so on. Horne and Osterberg (1977) have suggested that there are 'morning types' whose performance will be best in the early part of the day, and 'evening types' who are likely to perform better later in the day. There appears to be a correlation between measures of circadian activity (body temperature, for example) and performance on a

---

GLOSSARY

Systematic/constant error Bias which can be eliminated by careful controls in the design of research. Sampling errors and order effects are examples of systematic/constant error.

Circadian constant rhythms Daily cyclical changes in physiological state which affect arousal level.

vigilance task such as watching for an event which happens at infrequent intervals.

Preparation

Hypothesis   You are predicting that there will be a relationship between individuals' temperature at various times of the day (or night) and a specified vigilance task. This might take the form of reaction to a visual stimulus.

Design   You will need to plan the times in the day when you will test temperature as well as visual reaction time. Obviously, the more measurements you are able to make, the more conclusive your conclusions are likely to be. Each correlation will be for a particular individual but, to come to a meaningful conclusion, you will need to use several participants to demonstrate that while there is a correlation between temperature and reaction time, the peaks and troughs will vary between individuals. Controls you will need to think about will include standardizing procedures, methods of measurement and instructions to participants as well as coresearchers.

Participants   You will need to employ a number of participants independently of one another. The interest will be greater if they are not a homogeneous group. You need to have younger people as well as older ones, males as well as females, and individuals from different backgrounds. It might be that the differences between individuals are cultural rather than constitutional. People from a farming background, for example, become accustomed to rising early. There might be greater likelihood that they are 'morning types'.

Materials   You will need a thermometer. Modern instruments are very quick and easy to use. It will need to be accurate because the variations in temperature for healthy people are going to be quite small. As far as the measurement of reaction time is concerned, Piéron's technique (Piéron, 1928), reported also by Woodworth and Schlosberg (1954), is an interesting one based upon gravity. The experimenter holds a metre ruler with his or her thumb vertically against a smooth wall with its lower end against an index mark on the wall at about eye level. The participant's hand is poised over this mark ready to arrest its fall with his or her thumb. The experimenter says 'ready' and suddenly releases the ruler. As the participants see the experimenter's thumb move, they jab their own thumb down against the ruler. The distance the ruler has fallen is then read off the ruler scale at the index mark. This can be converted into an accurate measure of reaction time using the following formula:

$$T = \sqrt{\frac{2S}{G}}$$

where T is the reaction time, S is the fall in cms and G is the acceleration due to gravity (980 cm/sec). Figure 38.3 gives some falls and reaction times.

A quick and easy way to deal with this is to construct a graph with the fall in cms on the base and the time in milliseconds on the vertical axis. Yet another possibility is to construct a reaction time ruler. This might prove a valuable addition to the equipment of a psychology room and is described in Appendix 2.

Analysis techniques   Your analysis in this case will involve computing the correlation coefficient between the reaction time as measured and the time of day for a particular individual. Comparisons may be made between individuals. To avoid bias from order effects, you will need to randomize times of testing over a number of days.

Go ahead   Now run your study.

Figure 38.3   Reaction time, *T*, in seconds and fall, *S*, in cm

T	0.09	0.11	0.12	0.14	0.16	0.17	0.18	0.19	0.20	0.21	0.22	0.23	0.24
S	4	6	8	10	12	14	16	18	20	22	24	26	28

Appendix I

Some basic mathematical rules

Symbols

Some symbols you may meet:

x is used for scores (any scores)

$\sum$ is used to indicate that what follows is to be added together

M is commonly accepted as a symbol for the mean of all the scores, m for the mean of a single sample. The mean is also indicated by a line over a term so that $\overline{X}$ is the mean of the scores

N is used for the number of scores altogether, n for the number in one sample

D implies difference or deviation

p is used for probability (of an event occurring by chance alone)

< means less than

> means greater than

⩽ means equal to or less than

f means frequency

SD means standard deviation

χ^2 is the symbol for chi squared

r is used for a correlation coefficient

Where an estimate has been made of a population statistic from a sample, Greek characters are employed so that:

▪ σ is used for an estimate of the standard deviation of a population made from a sample of it

▪ μ is used for an estimate of a population mean from a sample of it.

Computation

The order in which terms are dealt with in a formula is important:

▪ Brackets ( ) or [ ] indicate that what is contained in them has to be computed first.

▪ Where a symbol is placed over another it means that the upper number has to be divided by the lower so that for example:

$$\frac{\sum x}{N}$$

means that the scores have to be added together and divided by the number of them. It is as though there were brackets around top and bottom terms.

▪ When the brackets have been dealt with, then one term over another is computed and finally division, multiplication, addition and subtraction in that order.

The mnemonic BODMAS has been devised to help you remember the order you have to deal with things (i.e. Brackets Over Division Multiplication Addition Subtraction).

A useful strategy to be adopted for several common computations (t-tests or Pearson's product moment correlation for instance) is to start by listing the scores in columns and alongside them their squares (i.e. the scores multiplied by themselves) and writing down the sum of each column. Supposing that you have two samples, you can list them as follows (these are fictitious examples):

Sample A		Sample B	
X_A	X_A^2	X_B	X_B^2
12	144	14	196
16	256	23	529
19	361	10	100
23	529	10	100
17	289	18	324
25	625	12	144
12	144	30	900
16	256		

$\sum X_A = 140$ $\sum X_A^2 = 2604$ $\sum X_B = 117$ $\sum X_B^2 = 2293$

$n_A = 8$ $n_B = 7$

$N = 15$

m_A (or $\overline{X}_A$) = 17.5 m_B (or $\overline{X}_B$) = 16.7

Faced with a very complex formula, for a *t*-test for independent samples, for example:

$$t = \frac{\bar{X}_A - \bar{X}_B}{\sqrt{\dfrac{\left\{\sum X_A^2 - \dfrac{\left(\sum X_A\right)^2}{n_A}\right\} + \left\{\sum X_B^2 - \dfrac{\left(\sum X_B\right)^2}{n_B}\right\}}{N - 2} \times \dfrac{N}{n_A \cdot n_B}}}$$

You can now work like this:

1. Find the mean of sample A and that of sample B. Subtract mean of B from mean of A. (17.5 − 16.7 = 0.8.) This deals with the terms above the line.
2. Tackle the brackets below the line first. Find the sum of the squared scores in sample A $\left(\sum X_A^2\right)$ (2604). Then take the sum of the scores in sample A (140) and square them $\left(\sum X_B\right)^2$ ($140^2 = 19\,600$) and divide by the number of scores in the A sample (n_A) ($19\,600 \div 8 = 2450$). Subtract this from $\left(\sum X_A^2\right)$ ($2604 − 2450 = 154$). That has dealt with the first large bracket.
3. Do the same for the second large bracket (sample B). You get the following: $117^2 (= 13\,689) \div 7 = 1955.57$. Subtracting this from $\left(\sum X_B^2\right)$ (2293) you get 337.43.
4. Add the results of step 2 and step 3 together (154 + 337.43 = 491.43).
5. Divide by the total number of scores in both samples together (N) less 2 $(N − 2)$ ($491.43 \div 13 = 37.8$).
6. Multiply the number of scores in the A sample by the number in the B sample $(n_A \cdot n_B)$ ($7 \times 8 = 56$).
7. Divide N (the total number of scores in both samples) by the result of step 6 ($15 \div 56 = 0.27$).
8. Multiply the result of step 5 (37.8) by the result of step 7 (0.27). ($37.8 \times 0.27 = 10.2$.)
9. Find the square root of this (the result of step 8) ($\sqrt{10.2} = 3.19$).

10. Take the result of step 1 and divide by the result of step 9 and the answer is *t*. ($0.8 \div 3.19 = 0.25$.) You can then consult the tables to see whether your figure of 0.25 reaches the critical level for the significance level you have chosen.

Calculators

A calculator is clearly a very valuable asset in statistical computation. Ideally you should acquire a scientific calculator with a statistical mode. Used in this mode it is possible to enter data and obtain immediate values for the following:

n, the number of scores
X, the mean
SD, the standard deviation from the mean
σ, the standard deviation from the mean of a population, estimated from a sample of it
$\sum X$, the sum of the scores
$\sum X^2$, the sum of the squares of the scores.

Exercise AI

Use the following formulas to work out the mean and the standard deviation of the following data:

56, 17, 34, 45, 37, 47, 29, 34

$$m = \frac{\sum x}{n} \qquad SD = \sqrt{\frac{\sum(\bar{X} - x)^2}{n}} \qquad \sigma = \sqrt{\frac{\sum(\bar{X} - x)^2}{n - 1}}$$

The answers are at the end of Appendix 2 (p. 910).

Appendix 2

Do-it-yourself psychology equipment

(adapted from *Handbook for GCE Psychology* (Brody et al. 1983)).

Müller-Lyer illusion slides

You will need:

- sheets of card (2, 12 × 25cm sheets for each slide)
- ruler
- protractor
- pencil
- felt-tipped pen
- Stanley knife (or similar craft knife)
- gum or glue.

Procedure

1. Rule a light pencil line along the centre of the cards.
2. 2.5 cm from the edges of the cards draw light pencil lines parallel to it. On one card score lightly along these lines, on the other cut off the strips (see Figure A.1). Fold along the scored lines.

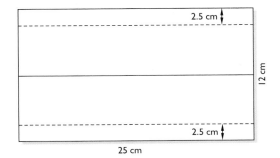

2.5 cm

12 cm

2.5 cm

25 cm

Figure A.1

3. Glue one card to the other to form a sleeve.
4. On the outside of the sleeve, draw a line with felt-tipped pen along the centre pencil line to one edge (the right-hand one is best) about 150 mm long.
5. Using a protractor, mark an angle (10°, 20°, 30° . . . 90° (you will need a separate card for each

angle) and draw a line 20 mm long on either side of the centre line to form an arrowhead. Draw another arrowhead with the same angle where the centre line meets the edge of the sleeve as in Figure A.2.

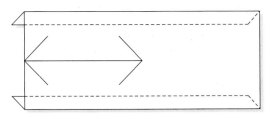

Figure A.2

6. On another card mark a light pencil centre line and two parallel lines 2.9 cm on either side of the centre. Remove the two marked side strips.
7. Rule with felt pen from the left-hand edge to a point 20 mm from the right-hand edge and with a protractor mark and draw an arrowhead pointing towards the left-hand edge at the same angle as on the sleeve. This forms the slide which should slide freely within the sleeve, showing a continuous centre line as in Figure A.3. Figure A.4 shows the completed Müller-Lyer apparatus.

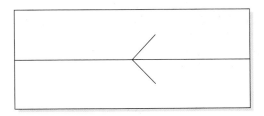

Figure A.3

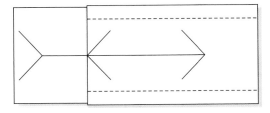

Figure A.4   Completed Müller-Lyer apparatus

Reaction time ruler

You will need:

- strip of wood 2.5 cm × 1 m × 6 mm thick
- strip of paper to cover wood
- glue
- clear Fablon (sticky-backed plastic)

Procedure

Work out for each cm of fall (S) the value of T in milliseconds:

$$T = \sqrt{\frac{2S}{G}}$$

where T is the reaction time, S is the fall in cm and G is the acceleration due to gravity (980 cm/sec). Figure A.5 gives some falls and reaction times.

Construct your scale marked in milliseconds. Print this on to the strip of paper and glue it on to the wood. Finally, cover in clear Fablon to prevent deterioration. In addition to the correlation described in Project 7 there are other uses for a means of measuring reaction times; for instance:

- A comparison of reaction to an audible as opposed to a visual stimulus (in this case the experimenter could blindfold participants and employ a clicker as the ruler is released).
- A study of the latency of reaction time; that is, the effect on reaction time of the interval between the experimenter saying 'ready' and releasing the ruler. This has implications for starting races in athletics.
- A study of vigilance decrement. See Chapter 12 for a discussion of vigilance decrement: that is, the deterioration in reaction times to stimuli, presented at infrequent intervals. Again this has practical implications (does a driver react as quickly after a long uneventful journey on a quiet road as on a busy street?).

Mirror drawing box

This is a valuable piece of equipment for a wide variety of experiments involving learning. You will need:

- self-adhesive mirror tile 30 cm square
- plywood 80 × 65 cm approximately
- wood-strengthening pieces, quarter round 12 mm
- strong wood glue
- matt black blackboard paint

Procedure

Cut out of the plywood the following:

- 1 square 30 × 30 cm to back the mirror
- 1 piece 30 × 32.5 cm for the base
- 1 piece 30 × 22.5 cm for the top
- 2 side pieces 32.5 × 23.75 cm with one corner removed (see Figure A.5).

Glue together and paint with matt black blackboard paint. The completed box is shown in Figure A.6.

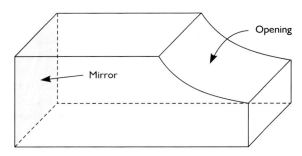

Figure A.6   Completed mirror drawing box

Answers to Exercise A.1

$m = 37.375$
$SD = 11.987$ $\sigma = 11.213$

Figure A.5   Some falls, S, in cm and reaction times, T, in milliseconds

T	90	110	120	140	160	170	180	190	200	210	220	230	240
S	4	6	8	10	12	14	16	18	20	22	24	26	28

Appendix 3

Statistical tables

Table A.1 A table of random numbers

01 61 16 96 94	50 78 13 69 36	37 68 53 37 31	71 26 35 03 71
46 68 05 14 82	90 78 50 05 62	77 79 13 57 44	59 60 10 39 66
00 57 25 60 59	46 72 60 18 77	55 66 12 62 11	08 99 55 64 57
24 98 65 63 21	47 21 61 88 32	27 80 30 21 60	10 92 35 36 12
28 10 99 00 27	12 73 37 99 12	49 99 57 94 82	96 88 57 17 91
07 10 63 76 35	87 03 04 79 88	08 13 13 85 51	55 34 57 72 69
92 38 70 96 92	52 06 79 79 45	82 63 18 27 44	69 66 92 19 09
99 53 93 61 28	52 70 05 48 34	56 65 05 61 86	90 92 10 70 80
93 86 52 77 65	15 33 59 05 28	22 87 26 07 47	86 96 98 29 06
18 46 23 34 27	85 13 99 24 44	49 18 09 79 49	74 16 32 23 02
24 53 63 94 09	41 10 76 47 91	44 04 95 49 66	39 60 04 59 81
22 06 34 72 52	82 21 15 65 20	33 29 94 71 11	15 91 29 12 03
07 16 39 33 66	98 56 10 56 79	77 21 30 27 12	90 49 22 23 62
29 70 83 63 51	99 74 20 52 36	87 09 41 15 09	98 60 16 03 03
57 90 12 02 07	23 47 37 17 31	54 08 01 88 63	39 41 88 92 10
33 35 72 67 47	77 34 55 45 70	08 18 27 38 90	16 95 86 70 75
49 41 31 06 70	42 38 06 45 18	64 84 73 31 65	52 53 37 97 15
65 19 69 02 83	60 75 86 90 68	24 64 19 35 51	56 61 87 39 12
92 09 84 38 76	22 00 27 69 85	29 81 94 78 70	21 94 47 90 12
98 77 87 68 07	91 51 67 62 44	40 98 05 93 78	23 32 65 41 18
00 41 86 79 79	68 47 22 00 20	35 55 31 51 51	00 83 63 22 55
57 99 99 90 37	36 63 32 08 58	37 40 13 68 97	87 64 81 07 83
12 59 52 57 02	22 07 90 47 03	28 14 11 30 79	20 69 22 40 98
31 51 10 96 46	92 06 88 07 77	56 11 50 81 69	40 23 72 51 39
96 11 83 44 80	34 68 35 48 77	33 42 40 90 60	73 96 53 97 86
85 47 04 66 08	34 72 57 59 13	82 43 80 46 15	38 26 61 70 04
72 82 32 99 90	63 95 73 76 63	89 73 44 99 05	48 67 26 43 18
91 36 74 43 53	30 82 13 54 00	78 45 63 98 35	55 03 36 67 68
77 53 84 46 47	31 91 18 95 58	24 16 74 11 53	44 10 13 85 57
37 27 47 39 19	84 83 70 07 48	53 21 40 06 71	95 06 79 88 54
44 91 13 32 97	75 31 62 66 54	84 80 32 75 77	56 08 25 70 29
37 30 28 59 85	53 56 68 53 40	01 74 39 59 73	30 19 99 85 48
75 20 80 27 77	78 91 69 46 00	08 43 18 73 68	67 69 61 34 25
65 95 79 42 94	93 62 40 89 96	43 56 47 71 66	46 76 29 67 02
05 02 03 24 17	47 97 81 56 51	92 34 86 01 82	55 51 33 12 91

Table A.1 A table of random numbers (continued)

```
94 21 78 55 09    72 76 45 16 94    29 95 81 83 83    79 88 01 97 30
34 41 92 45 71    09 23 70 70 07    12 38 92 79 43    14 85 11 47 23
53 14 36 59 25    54 47 33 70 15    59 24 48 40 35    50 03 42 99 36
88 59 53 11 52    66 25 69 07 04    48 68 64 71 06    61 65 70 22 12
65 28 04 67 53    95 79 88 37 31    50 41 06 94 76    81 83 17 16 33

73 43 07 34 48    44 26 87 93 29    77 09 61 67 84    06 69 44 77 75
48 62 11 90 60    68 12 93 64 28    46 24 79 16 76    14 60 25 51 01
28 97 85 58 99    67 22 52 76 23    24 70 36 54 54    59 28 61 71 96
02 63 45 52 38    67 63 47 54 75    83 24 78 43 20    92 63 13 47 48
76 96 59 38 72    86 57 45 71 46    44 67 76 14 55    44 88 01 62 12

77 45 85 50 51    74 13 39 35 22    30 53 36 02 95    49 34 88 73 61
29 18 94 51 23    76 51 94 84 86    79 93 96 38 63    08 58 25 58 94
72 65 71 08 86    79 57 95 13 91    97 48 72 66 48    09 71 17 24 89
89 37 20 70 01    77 31 61 95 46    26 97 05 73 51    53 33 18 72 87
81 30 15 39 14    48 38 75 93 29    06 87 37 78 48    45 56 00 84 47

83 71 46 30 49    89 17 95 88 29    02 39 56 03 46    97 74 06 56 17
70 52 85 01 50    01 84 02 78 43    10 62 98 19 41    18 83 99 47 99
25 27 99 41 28    07 41 08 34 66    19 42 74 39 91    41 96 53 78 72
63 61 62 42 29    39 68 95 10 96    09 24 23 00 62    56 12 80 73 16
68 96 83 23 56    32 84 60 15 31    44 73 67 34 77    91 15 79 74 58

87 83 07 55 07    76 58 30 83 64    87 29 25 58 84    86 50 60 00 25
49 52 83 51 14    47 56 91 29 34    05 87 31 06 95    12 45 57 09 09
80 62 80 03 42    10 80 21 38 84    90 56 35 03 09    43 12 74 49 14
86 97 37 44 22    00 95 01 31 76    17 16 29 56 63    38 78 94 49 81
85 39 52 85 13    07 28 37 07 61    11 16 36 27 03    78 86 72 04 95

97 05 31 03 61    20 26 36 31 62    68 69 86 95 44    84 95 48 46 45
75 89 11 47 11    31 56 34 19 09    79 57 92 36 59    14 93 87 81 40
09 18 94 06 19    98 40 07 17 81    22 45 44 84 11    24 62 20 42 31
84 08 31 55 58    24 33 45 77 58    80 45 67 93 82    75 70 16 08 24
79 26 88 86 30    01 31 60 10 39    53 58 47 70 93    85 81 56 39 38
```

Table A.2 Table of z scores and probabilities

The following table shows the proportion of the whole 'normal distribution' between the mean and a particular standard (z) score. To find the probability of that score occurring subtract the proportion from 0.5000. For instance, the probability of a z score of 2.000 (two standard deviations from the mean) is 0.5000 − 0.4772 = 0.228.

				Second decimal place						
z	0	1	2	3	4	5	6	7	8	9
0.0	.0000	.0040	.0080	.0120	.0160	.0199	.0239	.0279	.0319	.0359
0.1	.0398	.0438	.0478	.0517	.0557	.0596	.0636	.0675	.0714	.0754
0.2	.0793	.0832	.0871	.0910	.0948	.0987	.1026	.1064	.1103	.1141
0.3	.1179	.1217	.1255	.1293	.1331	.1368	.1406	.1443	.1480	.1517
0.4	.1554	.1591	.1628	.1664	.1700	.1736	.1772	.1808	.1844	.1879
0.5	.1915	.1950	.1985	.2019	.2054	.2088	.2123	.2157	.2190	.2224
0.6	.2258	.2291	.2324	.2357	.2389	.2422	.2454	.2486	.2518	.2549
0.7	.2580	.2612	.2642	.2673	.2704	.2734	.2764	.2794	.2823	.2852
0.8	.2881	.2910	.2939	.2967	.2996	.3023	.3051	.3078	.3106	.3133
0.9	.3159	.3186	.3212	.3238	.3264	.3289	.3315	.3340	.3365	.3389
1.0	.3413	.3438	.3461	.3485	.3508	.3531	.3554	.3577	.3599	.3621
1.1	.3643	.3665	.3686	.3708	.3729	.3749	.3770	.3790	.3810	.3830
1.2	.3849	.3869	.3888	.3907	.3925	.3944	.3962	.3980	.3997	.4015
1.3	.4032	.4049	.4066	.4082	.4099	.4115	.4131	.4147	.4162	.4177
1.4	.4192	.4207	.4222	.4236	.4251	.4265	.4279	.4292	.4306	.4319
1.5	.4332	.4345	.4357	.4370	.4382	.4394	.4406	.4418	.4429	.4441
1.6	.4452	.4463	.4474	.4484	.4495	.4505	.4515	.4525	.4535	.4545
1.7	.4554	.4564	.4573	.4582	.4591	.4599	.4608	.4616	.4625	.4633
1.8	.4641	.4649	.4656	.4664	.4671	.4678	.4686	.4693	.4699	.4706
1.9	.4713	.4719	.4726	.4732	.4738	.4744	.4750	.4756	.4761	.4767
2.0	.4772	.4778	.4783	.4788	.4793	.4798	.4803	.4808	.4812	.4817
2.1	.4821	.4826	.4830	.4834	.4838	.4842	.4846	.4850	.4854	.4857
2.2	.4861	.4864	.4868	.4871	.4875	.4878	.4881	.4884	.4887	.4890
2.3	.4893	.4896	.4898	.4901	.4904	.4906	.4909	.4911	.4913	.4916
2.4	.4918	.4920	.4922	.4925	.4927	.4929	.4931	.4932	.4934	.4936
2.5	.4938	.4940	.4941	.4943	.4945	.4946	.4948	.4949	.4951	.4952
2.6	.4953	.4955	.4956	.4957	.4959	.4960	.4961	.4962	.4963	.4964
2.7	.4965	.4966	.4967	.4968	.4969	.4970	.4971	.4972	.4973	.4974
2.8	.4974	.4975	.4976	.4977	.4977	.4978	.4979	.4979	.4980	.4981
2.9	.4981	.4982	.4982	.4983	.4984	.4984	.4985	.4985	.4986	.4986
3.0	.4987	.4987	.4987	.4988	.4988	.4989	.4989	.4989	.4990	.4990
3.1	.4990	.4991	.4991	.4991	.4992	.4992	.4992	.4992	.4993	.4993
3.2	.4993	.4993	.4994	.4994	.4994	.4994	.4994	.4995	.4995	.4995
3.3	.4995	.4995	.4995	.4996	.4996	.4996	.4996	.4996	.4996	.4997
3.4	.4997	.4997	.4997	.4997	.4997	.4997	.4997	.4997	.4997	.4998
3.5	.4998	.4998	.4998	.4998	.4998	.4998	.4998	.4998	.4998	.4998
3.6	.4998	.4998	.4999	.4999	.4999	.4999	.4999	.4999	.4999	.4999
3.7	.4999	.4999	.4999	.4999	.4999	.4999	.4999	.4999	.4999	.4999
3.8	.4999	.4999	.4999	.4999	.4999	.4999	.4999	.4999	.4999	.4999
3.9	.5000	.5000	.5000	.5000	.5000	.5000	.5000	.5000	.5000	.5000

Table A.3 Table of critical values of t

The results are significant at a particular level if the observed value of *t* is greater than the table value. This table gives values for a *two-tailed* test. For a *one-tailed* test, the significance levels are halved.

Degrees of freedom	Significance level, *p*				
	0.1	0.05	0.02	0.01	0.001
1	6.31	12.71	31.82	63.657	636.62
2	2.92	4.30	6.96	9.92	31.60
3	2.35	3.18	4.54	5.84	12.92
4	2.13	2.78	3.75	4.60	8.61
5	2.01	2.57	3.36	4.03	6.87
6	1.94	2.45	3.14	3.707	5.96
7	1.89	2.36	2.99	3.499	5.41
8	1.86	2.31	2.90	3.35	5.04
9	1.83	2.26	2.82	3.25	4.78
10	1.81	2.23	2.76	3.169	4.59
11	1.80	2.20	2.72	3.106	4.44
12	1.78	2.18	2.68	3.05	4.32
13	1.77	2.16	2.65	3.01	4.22
14	1.76	2.14	2.62	2.977	4.14
15	1.75	2.13	2.60	2.947	4.07
16	1.75	2.12	2.58	2.92	4.01
17	1.74	2.11	2.57	2.898	3.96
18	1.73	2.10	2.55	2.878	3.92
19	1.73	2.09	2.54	2.86	3.88
20	1.72	2.09	2.53	2.84	3.85
21	1.72	2.08	2.52	2.83	3.82
22	1.72	2.07	2.51	2.819	3.79
23	1.71	2.07	2.50	2.807	3.77
24	1.71	2.06	2.49	2.797	3.74
25	1.71	2.06	2.48	2.787	3.72
26	1.71	2.06	2.48	2.779	3.71
27	1.70	2.05	2.47	2.77	3.69
28	1.70	2.05	2.47	2.76	3.67
29	1.70	2.04	2.46	2.756	3.66
30	1.70	2.04	2.46	2.75	3.65
40	1.68	2.02	2.42	2.70	3.55
60	1.67	2.00	2.39	2.66	3.46
120	1.66	1.98	2.36	2.617	3.37
∞	1.64	1.96	2.33	2.576	3.29

Table A.4 Table of critical values of chi squared

The results are significant at a particular level if the observed value of χ^2 is greater than the table value. These are the values for a *two-tailed* test. For a *one-tailed* test, the significance levels are halved.

Degrees of freedom	Significance level, p			
	0.05	0.02	0.01	0.001
1	3.84	5.41	6.63	10.83
2	5.99	7.82	9.21	13.81
3	7.81	9.84	11.34	16.27
4	9.49	11.67	13.28	18.47
5	11.07	13.39	15.09	20.51
6	12.59	15.03	16.81	22.46
7	14.07	16.62	18.47	24.32
8	15.51	18.17	20.09	26.12
9	16.92	19.68	21.67	27.88
10	18.31	21.16	23.21	29.59
11	19.67	22.62	24.72	31.26
12	21.03	24.05	26.22	32.91
13	22.36	25.47	27.69	34.53
14	23.68	26.87	29.14	36.12
15	24.99	28.26	30.58	37.67
16	26.23	29.63	32.00	39.25
17	27.59	30.99	33.41	40.79
18	28.87	32.35	34.80	42.31
19	30.14	33.69	36.19	43.82
20	31.41	35.02	37.57	45.31
21	32.67	36.34	38.93	46.78
22	33.92	37.66	40.29	48.27
23	35.17	38.97	41.64	49.73
24	36.41	40.27	42.98	51.18
25	37.65	41.57	44.31	52.62
26	38.88	42.86	45.64	54.05
27	40.11	44.14	46.96	55.48
28	41.34	45.42	48.28	56.89
29	42.56	46.69	49.59	58.30
30	43.77	47.96	50.89	59.70
32	46.19	50.49	53.49	62.49
34	48.60	52.99	56.06	65.25
36	50.99	55.49	58.62	67.98
38	53.38	57.97	61.16	70.70
40	55.76	60.44	63.69	73.40
42	58.12	62.89	66.21	76.08
44	60.48	65.34	68.71	78.75
46	62.83	67.77	71.20	81.40
48	65.17	70.12	73.68	84.04
50	67.50	72.61	76.15	86.66

Table A.5 Table of critical values of X for the Sign test

Results are significant if the observed value of X is equal to or less than the table value. N represents the total number of signs. Note that any zeros are not included in N. This table gives values for a *two-tailed* test. For a *one-tailed* test, the significance levels are halved.

N	Significance level, p 0.1	0.05	0.02	0.01	N	Significance level, p 0.1	0.05	0.02	0.01
5	0				30	10	9	8	7
6	0	0			31	10	9	8	7
7	0	0	0		32	10	9	8	8
8	1	0	0	0	33	11	10	9	8
9	1	1	0	0	34	11	10	9	9
10	1	1	0	0	35	12	11	10	9
11	2	1	1	0	36	12	11	10	9
12	2	2	1	1	37	13	12	10	10
13	3	2	1	1	38	13	12	11	10
14	3	2	2	1	39	13	12	11	11
15	3	3	2	2	40	14	13	12	11
16	4	3	2	2	41	14	13	12	11
17	4	4	3	2	42	15	14	13	12
18	5	4	3	3	43	15	14	13	12
19	5	4	4	3	44	16	15	13	13
20	5	5	4	3	45	16	15	14	13
21	6	5	4	4	46	16	15	14	13
22	6	5	5	4	47	17	16	15	14
23	7	6	5	4	48	17	16	15	14
24	7	6	5	5	49	18	17	15	15
25	7	7	6	5					
26	8	7	6	6					
27	8	7	7	6					
28	9	8	7	6					
29	9	8	7	7					

Table A.6 Table of critical values of *T* for the Wilcoxon test

Results are significant at a particular level if the observed value of *T* is smaller than the table value. This table gives values for a *two-tailed* test. For a *one-tailed* test, the significance levels are halved.

	Significance level, p			
N	0.100	0.050	0.020	0.010
5	0			
6	2	0		
7	3	2	0	
8	5	3	1	0
9	8	5	3	1
10	10	8	5	3
11	13	10	7	5
12	17	13	9	7
13	21	17	12	9
14	25	21	15	12
15	30	25	19	15
16	35	29	23	19
17	41	34	27	23
18	47	40	32	27
19	53	46	37	32
20	60	52	43	37
21	67	58	49	42
22	75	65	55	48
23	83	73	62	54
24	91	81	69	61
25	100	89	76	68
26	110	98	84	75
27	119	107	92	83
28	130	116	101	91
29	140	126	110	100
30	151	137	120	109

Table A.7 Table of critical values of U or U_1 for the Mann–Whitney test

For each value of N_S and N_L there are two numbers. The top one is the value of U which must not be exceeded for significance at the 0.005 level for a *one-tailed* test (0.01 for a *two-tailed* test); the lower one gives the value for the 0.025 level for a *one-tailed* test (0.05 for a *two-tailed* test).

N_S	1	2	3	4	5	6	7	8	9	10	11	12	13	14	15	16	17	18	19	20
N_L																				
2	–	–	–	–	–	–	–	–	–	–	–	–	–	–	–	–	–	–	0	0
	–	–	–	–	–	–	–	0	0	0	0	1	1	1	1	1	2	2	2	2
3	–	–	–	–	–	–	–	–	0	0	0	1	1	1	2	2	2	2	3	3
	–	–	–	–	0	1	1	2	2	3	3	4	4	5	5	6	6	7	7	8
4	–	–	–	–	–	0	0	1	1	2	2	3	3	4	5	5	6	6	7	8
	–	–	–	0	1	2	3	4	4	5	6	7	8	9	10	11	11	12	13	14
5	–	–	–	–	0	1	1	2	3	4	5	6	7	7	8	9	10	11	12	13
	–	–	0	1	2	3	5	6	7	8	9	11	12	13	14	15	17	18	19	20
6	–	–	–	0	1	2	3	4	5	6	7	8	10	11	12	13	15	16	17	18
	–	–	1	2	3	5	6	8	10	11	13	14	16	17	19	21	22	24	25	27
7	–	–	–	0	1	3	4	6	7	9	10	12	13	15	16	18	19	21	22	24
	–	–	1	3	5	6	8	10	12	14	16	18	20	22	24	26	28	30	32	34
8	–	–	–	1	2	4	6	7	9	11	13	15	17	18	20	22	24	26	28	30
	–	0	2	4	6	8	10	13	15	17	19	22	24	26	29	31	34	36	38	41
9	–	–	0	1	3	5	7	9	11	13	16	18	20	22	24	27	29	31	33	36
	–	0	2	4	7	10	12	15	17	20	23	26	28	31	34	37	39	42	45	48
10	–	–	0	2	4	6	9	11	13	16	18	21	24	26	29	31	34	37	39	42
	–	0	3	5	8	11	14	17	20	23	26	29	33	36	39	42	45	48	52	55
11	–	–	0	2	5	7	10	13	16	18	21	24	27	30	33	36	39	42	45	48
	–	0	3	6	9	13	16	19	23	26	30	33	37	40	44	47	51	55	58	62
12	–	–	1	3	6	9	12	15	18	21	24	27	31	34	37	41	44	47	51	54
	–	1	4	7	11	14	18	22	26	29	33	37	41	45	49	53	57	61	65	69
13	–	–	1	3	7	10	13	17	20	24	27	31	34	38	42	45	49	53	57	60
	–	1	4	8	12	16	20	24	28	33	37	41	45	50	54	59	63	67	72	76
14	–	–	1	4	7	11	15	18	22	26	30	34	38	42	46	50	54	58	63	67
	–	1	5	9	13	17	22	26	31	36	40	45	50	55	59	64	69	74	78	83
15	–	–	2	5	8	12	16	20	24	29	33	37	42	46	51	55	60	64	69	73
	–	1	5	10	14	19	24	29	34	39	44	49	54	59	64	70	75	80	85	90
16	–	–	2	5	9	13	18	22	27	31	36	41	45	50	55	60	65	70	74	79
	–	1	6	11	15	21	26	31	37	42	47	53	59	64	70	75	81	86	92	98
17	–	–	2	6	10	15	19	24	29	34	39	44	49	54	60	65	70	75	81	86
	–	2	6	11	17	22	28	34	39	45	51	57	63	69	75	81	87	93	99	105
18	–	–	2	6	11	16	21	26	31	37	42	47	53	58	64	70	75	81	87	92
	–	2	7	12	18	24	30	36	42	48	55	61	67	74	80	86	93	99	106	112
19	–	0	3	7	12	17	22	28	33	39	45	51	57	63	69	74	81	87	93	99
	–	2	7	13	19	25	32	38	45	52	58	65	72	78	85	92	99	106	113	119
20	–	0	3	8	13	18	24	30	36	42	48	54	60	67	73	79	86	92	99	105
	–	2	8	14	20	27	34	41	48	55	62	69	76	83	90	98	105	112	119	127

Table A.8 Table of critical values of r_S for the Spearman's rank order correlation

N is the number of paired scores. r_S must be equal to or greater than the table value to be significant.

| | Level of significance for a one-tailed test | | | |
	0.05	0.025	0.01	0.005
	Level of significance for a two-tailed test			
N	0.10	0.05	0.02	0.01
5	0.900	1.000	1.000	–
6	0.829	0.886	0.943	1.000
7	0.714	0.786	0.893	0.929
8	0.643	0.738	0.833	0.881
9	0.600	0.683	0.783	0.833
10	0.564	0.648	0.746	0.794
12	0.506	0.591	0.712	0.777
14	0.456	0.544	0.645	0.715
16	0.425	0.506	0.601	0.665
18	0.399	0.475	0.564	0.625
20	0.377	0.450	0.534	0.591
22	0.359	0.428	0.508	0.562
24	0.343	0.409	0.485	0.537
26	0.329	0.392	0.465	0.515
28	0.317	0.377	0.448	0.496
30	0.306	0.364	0.432	0.478

Where N is greater than 30 the significance of r_S can be tested by using the following formula:

$$t = r_S \sqrt{\frac{N-2}{1-r_S^2}} \qquad \text{df } N - 2$$

The significance of t can then be checked by using Table A.3 on p. 912.

Table A.9   Table of critical values of *F*

Results are significant at the 5 per cent level if the observed value of *F* is greater than the table value. To test homogeneity of variance, divide the variance of one population by that of the other. The result is *F*. There is homogeneity of variance if *F* is not significant.

		Degrees of freedom for the larger variance						
		1	2	3	4	5	6	7
Degrees of freedom for the smaller variance	1	648	800	864	900	922	937	948
	2	38.50	39.00	39.17	39.24	39.30	39.33	39.35
	3	17.44	16.04	15.44	15.10	14.89	14.74	14.62
	4	12.22	10.65	9.98	9.60	9.36	9.20	9.07
	5	10.01	8.43	7.76	7.39	7.15	6.98	6.85
	6	8.81	7.26	6.60	6.23	5.99	5.82	5.70
	7	8.07	6.54	5.89	5.52	5.29	5.12	4.99
	8	7.57	6.06	5.42	5.05	4.82	4.66	4.53
	9	7.21	5.71	5.08	4.72	4.48	4.32	4.20
	10	6.94	5.46	4.83	4.47	4.24	4.07	3.95
	11	6.72	5.26	4.63	4.28	4.04	3.88	3.76
	12	6.55	5.10	4.47	4.12	3.89	3.73	3.61
	13	6.41	4.97	4.35	4.00	3.77	3.60	3.48
	14	6.30	4.86	4.24	3.89	3.66	3.50	3.38
	15	6.20	4.76	4.15	3.80	3.58	3.41	3.29
	16	6.12	4.69	4.08	3.73	3.50	3.34	3.22
	17	6.04	4.62	4.01	3.66	3.44	3.28	3.16
	18	5.98	4.56	3.95	3.61	3.38	3.22	3.10
	19	5.92	4.51	3.90	3.56	3.33	3.17	3.05
	20	5.87	4.46	3.86	3.51	3.29	3.13	3.01
	21	5.83	4.42	3.82	3.48	3.25	3.09	2.97
	22	5.79	4.38	3.78	3.44	3.22	3.05	2.93
	23	5.75	4.35	3.75	3.40	3.18	3.02	2.90
	24	5.72	4.32	3.72	3.38	3.15	2.99	2.87

		Degrees of freedom for the larger variance						
		8	9	10	12	15	20	24
	1	957	963	969	977	985	993	997
	2	39.37	39.39	39.40	39.42	39.43	39.45	39.4
	3	14.54	14.47	14.42	14.34	14.25	14.17	14.1
	4	8.98	8.90	8.84	8.75	8.66	8.56	8.51
	5	6.76	6.68	6.62	6.52	6.43	6.33	6.28
	6	5.60	5.52	5.46	5.37	5.27	5.17	5.12
	7	4.90	4.82	4.76	4.67	4.57	4.47	4.42
	8	4.43	4.36	4.30	4.20	4.10	3.99	3.95
	9	4.10	4.03	3.96	3.87	3.77	3.67	3.61
Degrees of freedom for the smaller variance	10	3.85	3.78	3.72	3.62	3.52	3.42	3.37
	11	3.66	3.59	3.52	3.43	3.33	3.23	3.17
	12	3.51	3.44	3.37	3.28	3.18	3.07	3.02
	13	3.39	3.31	3.25	3.15	3.05	2.95	2.89
	14	3.29	3.21	3.15	3.05	2.95	2.84	2.79
	15	3.20	3.12	3.06	2.96	2.86	2.76	2.70
	16	3.12	3.05	2.99	2.89	2.79	2.68	2.63
	17	3.06	2.99	2.92	2.82	2.72	2.62	2.56
	18	3.01	2.93	2.87	2.77	2.67	2.58	2.50
	19	2.96	2.81	2.82	2.72	2.62	2.53	2.45
	20	2.91	2.84	2.77	2.68	2.57	2.46	2.41
	21	2.87	2.80	2.73	2.64	2.53	2.42	2.37
	22	2.84	2.76	2.70	2.61	2.50	2.39	2.33
	23	2.81	2.73	2.67	2.57	2.47	2.36	2.30
	24	2.78	2.70	2.64	2.54	2.44	2.33	2.27

Table A.10 Table of critical values of *r* for the Pearson product moment correlation

Results are significant at a particular level if the correlation *r* is equal to or greater than the table value. *N* is the number of pairs of scores.

	Level of significance for a one-tailed test			
	0.05	0.025	0.005	0.0005
	Level of significance for a two-tailed test			
$N-2$	0.10	0.05	0.01	0.001
2	0.9000	0.9500	0.9900	0.9999
3	0.805	0.878	0.9587	0.9911
4	0.729	0.811	0.9172	0.9741
5	0.669	0.754	0.875	0.9509
6	0.621	0.707	0.834	0.9241
7	0.582	0.666	0.798	0.898
8	0.549	0.632	0.765	0.872
9	0.521	0.602	0.735	0.847
10	0.497	0.576	0.708	0.823
11	0.476	0.553	0.684	0.801
12	0.457	0.532	0.661	0.780
13	0.441	0.514	0.641	0.760
14	0.426	0.497	0.623	0.742
15	0.412	0.482	0.606	0.725
16	0.400	0.468	0.590	0.708
17	0.389	0.456	0.575	0.693
18	0.378	0.444	0.561	0.679
19	0.369	0.433	0.549	0.665
20	0.360	0.423	0.537	0.652
25	0.323	0.381	0.487	0.597
30	0.296	0.349	0.449	0.554
35	0.275	0.325	0.418	0.519
40	0.257	0.304	0.393	0.490
45	0.243	0.288	0.372	0.465
50	0.231	0.273	0.354	0.443
60	0.211	0.250	0.325	0.408
70	0.195	0.232	0.302	0.380
80	0.183	0.217	0.283	0.357
90	0.173	0.205	0.267	0.338
100	0.164	0.195	0.254	0.321

Glossary

16PF A rating scale devised by Cattell to assess the structure of personality based on 16 factors.

Ablation Removal of parts of the brain by surgery or by burning out with electrodes in order to observe modifications in an animal's behaviour.

Absent-mindedness Slips of memory relating to things that need to be done.

Absolute refractory period The one or two milliseconds following the firing of a neuron during which the axon cannot fire again.

Absolute stability Whether participants in a study maintain the same score on a test of a characteristic such as personality from one occasion to another.

Absolute threshold That intensity of a stimulus which is the minimum that can be perceived 50 per cent of the time.

Abstract A brief summary of research, usually included at the beginning of the report. It should include aims, methods used, a summary of results and conclusions drawn.

Accommodation A monocular cue to the perception of depth. The lenses of the eyes change shape to focus upon objects at different distances. There is a kinaesthetic sense of this change.

Accommodation A process described by Piaget where schemata are modified to fit a new situation.

Acquiescence response set A tendency in attitude measurement scales for respondents to agree with all items indiscriminately.

Activity theory Suggests that individuals adjust satisfactorily to old age if they remain active and productive.

Actor In social psychology studies, the individual who initiates a piece of behaviour.

Actor–observer effect An explanation of 'fundamental attribution bias' which claims that observers place more emphasis on disposition, actors upon the situation.

Actualizing tendency Rogers's term for a motive that exists in everyone to develop into mature, fulfilled human beings. Similar to Maslow's notion of self-actualization.

Adaptation (1) Fitness of genes to survive in the environment in which they find themselves, thus ensuring individuals reach maturity and reproduce. (2) Piaget's key concept relating to the way in which individuals adjust their behaviour to cope with the environment.

Adaptive behaviour Behaviour which is well-adjusted to the individual's environment and therefore is likely to aid survival.

Adolescence Generally defined as the period of development from the onset of puberty up to adulthood.

Adolescent subculture A term used by Coleman (Coleman et al., 1961) to describe the existence among adolescents of a culture that was separate to the adult culture and which tended to orient young people towards their peers and alienate them from adults.

Advertising Promoting products, services, information or ideas via the mass media with a view to increasing sales.

Aetiology The factors that cause or contribute to the development of a particular medical disorder.

Affectionless psychopathy A syndrome proposed by Bowlby to describe an inability to feel affection for others or to form social relationships.

Ageism Discrimination and prejudice on the basis of age.

Aggregations Impermanent relationships between animals which do not last longer than the immediate cause of their coming together: for instance, for a common food source.

Allele Term used for each member of a pair of genes.

Alpha rhythms Fairly regular brain waves recorded by EEG, characteristic of a relaxed state of wakefulness.

Alternative hypothesis A prediction that the effects on outcomes found after tests of two or more samples will be sufficiently different (or similar in the case of a correlational study) that the researcher can be confident that they did not occur by chance alone. Or to put it in another way, the samples were drawn from more than one population.

Altruism Helping behaviour or self-sacrifice without any apparent benefit to the individual behaving altruistically.

Ambient optical array A component of Gibson's perceptual theory consisting of all the light rays which converge on an individual's retina in a particular position. When this position changes the array will change.

Analogies Elements of an earlier problem are used to to make the solution of a current problem easier.

Analysis by synthesis Neisser's perceptual model where information is extracted from the environment through the senses to correct and update impressions of what the environment might be like.

Androcentric Explaining gender differences from a male standpoint.

Androgens Male sex hormones.

Androgynous Used to describe individuals who possess both masculine and feminine characteristics and whose behaviour does not conform rigidly to that for either males or females.

Anisogamy The fact that males and females do not make an equal contribution to parenthood; the male contributing only sperm, the female contributing also some store of food in the ovum.

Anorexia nervosa An eating disorder mainly affecting adolescents. The individual, fearing obesity, refuses to eat or eats only small amounts, resulting in extreme weight loss.

Anthropomorphism The attributing to animals of human characteristics for which there is no real evidence.

Antiextrapolationists In relation to animal research, a group who believe that it is not reasonable or desirable to apply the findings from animal studies to humans.

Antipsychiatry movement, the A movement started in the 1950s by psychiatrists such as Laing and Cooper, in opposition to the medical model of mental disorder.

Antivivisectionist movement A movement that is opposed to the use of live animals in experiments.

Applied research Research that primarily aims to answer a question which has practical importance.

Approach–approach conflict The conflict which arises when an individual has to decide between two alternatives that are equally attractive.

Archetypes Universal symbols, described by Jung, which repeatedly occur in the religions, art, fables and legends of many different cultures: for example, 'God', 'the wise old man', 'the fairy godmother'.

Archival research Research where the researcher attempts to delve into records not produced originally for the purpose of research, such as government documents or news reports.

Arousal The state of alertness of an individual, which is indicated by the level of activity in the cerebral cortex.

Articulatory loop An element in Baddelely's working memory model that allows for rehearsal of material heard.

Artificial intelligence Involves attempts to program computers to mimic the operation of the human brain.

Asperger's syndrome A condition which is regarded as a mild variant of autism, where sufferers display many autistic characteristics, but speech is normal or advanced for the child's chronological age.

Assimilation The process described by Piaget, where children attempt to fit knowledge of the world around into their existing understanding and experience.

Associationism A movement that emphasized the idea that learning results from the forming of associations between stimuli and events in the environment.

Associationist An approach to explanations of psychological phenomena which emphasize links in the brain between stimuli. Ebbinghaus's memory research is an example.

Associative learning Learning to associate one stimulus with another or with particular consequences.

Assortative mating Suggests that a successful union between two individuals is most likely when the two partners have similarities in characteristics or in behaviour. This is a concept borrowed from ethology.

Asylum A term used to describe an institution for the care and treatment of people with mental disorders. Literally means 'refuge'.

Atomism A belief that to understand a phenomenon, it is best to break it down and study its constituent parts.

Attachment The bond of affection which forms between a child and specific caregivers. The strongest attachments occur from the age of about eight months onwards.

Attention-deficit hyperactivity disorder (ADHD) A childhood disorder characterized by excessive activity and an inability to concentrate on a task; sometimes accompanied by aggression.

Attenuation A mechanism proposed by Treisman, whereby an unattended message is reduced, but may still be attended to if it reaches a threshold of intensity.

Attributes Elements of stimuli before us which are abstracted to enable us to form concepts.

Atypical development Development which is not typical of a particular species and does not follow the usual pattern.

Augmentation principle Where costs are involved for the actor, the action is attributed more to the actor's disposition than it would otherwise be.

Autism A rare developmental disorder which is usually detected in early childhood. The sufferer often exhibits severe limitations in language and an inability to relate to other people.

Autistic thinking Thinking which has no rational purpose. The brain manipulates information available to it for no discernible purpose. Daydreaming is an example.

Autobiographical memory Memory for details of a person's own life events.

Automatic processing Parallel processing of easy or familar tasks.

Autonomic nervous system (ANS) A branch of the PNS which carries messages between the CNS and the body's internal organs and some glands. The ANS is subdivided into the sympathetic and parasympathetic divisions.

Autonomism A notion that same-level explanations are preferable to lower-level ones. For example, humanistic psychologists tend to focus on a person's perceptions but ignore possible biological and physiological influences.

Autonomous reality (moral relativism) Piaget's second stage of moral reasoning which begins to develop around seven. Judgments of moral issues are based on intentions as well as consequences.

Avoidance–avoidance conflict The conflict which arises when an individual is forced to make a decision by weighing up the advantages and disadvantages of an undesirable situation.

Axon The thin, tube-like part of a neuron (nerve cell) which extends out from the nerve cell body.

Babbling The syllable-like sounds produced by a baby from about six months on.

Baby Talk Register (BTR) The simplified form of speech used by adults when talking to children (formerly known as motherese).

Balance In social psychology, relates to the notion that maintenance of a relationship depends upon a balance being maintained between the positive or negative feelings partners in a relationship have towards things and people.

Balance theory Heider's suggestion that there needs to be balance between three elements: a person's behaviour, a second person's behaviour and relevant attitudes.

Bar chart A means of illustrating scores which involves assigning a vertical bar to each score or group of scores occurring in a particular condition in a study, proportional to the scores themselves. Conventionally the independent variables are represented on the horizontal line; the dependent variables on the vertical bars.

Behaviour shaping In operant conditioning, the process involved in the learning of new behaviour by successively reinforcing behaviour which approximates to the desired reponse.

Behavioural ecology Attempts made to understand how animals' ecology (the context in which they live) interacts with their behaviour.

Behavioural therapies Therapeutic techniques that are based on the principles of either classical or operant conditioning.

Behaviourism A revolutionary school of psychology, founded by John Watson, where the focus was the study of observable behaviour to the exclusion of internal mental processes.

Beholder's share The contribution which an individual's personal value system and so on makes to his or her perceptions. The sense that what each person makes of the world is different.

Belief congruence The use of acceptance by others of a person's beliefs to strengthen and validate them.

Bereavement The condition or state of loss, usually brought about by the death of someone close.

Binocular cues to depth Cues to the perception of depth which depend upon the use of both eyes.

Biofeedback techniques Techniques which draw on the theoretical bases of both classical and operant conditioning. Patients are trained to control bodily processes such as heart rate and blood pressure, which are under autonomic control.

Biological reductionism Proposes that behaviour can be best understood through the study of less complex animals.

Biopsychology (physiological psychology) An area of psychology which studies relationships between physiological and psychological make-up and the interactive influence of one on the other.

Bipolar cells Cells located in the retina which pass information from rods and cones to the ganglion cells.

Bogus pipeline technique The technique adopted by Cialdini and others of connecting respondents to attitude tests to what appeared to be a lie detector so that they would believe there was no point in answering other than truthfully.

Bottom-up processing Cognitive processing which deals first with details of an operation and then takes account of context.

Brainwashing Techniques of persuasion which involve the total recasting of an individual's mind-set.

Branching programme A form of programmed learning which provides a variety of routes through the material, depending on the learner's ability, interest and level of understanding.

Bulimia nervosa An eating disorder where the individual fears obesity and consequently 'binges' on certain foods and then induces vomiting or uses laxatives.

Bystander calculus model Embodies Piliavin's suggestion that it is distressing to see someone suffer, which causes arousal. The decision as to whether or not to help amounts to a cost–benefit analysis as to whether the relief of distress is worth the costs involved..

Cardinal traits Allport's term for those personality traits which are most dominant and consistent in a person's personality: for example, extreme kindness and/or generosity.

Case study Research where a single individual or a small number of individuals are examined individually and in detail and their behaviour analysed.

Caste Among animals castes represent complex social relationships which are characterized by discrete functions or roles and sometimes by anatomical differences as well. They tend to be permanent and unchangeable.

Categorical self Lewis and Brooks-Gunn's term to describe the awareness of oneself in terms of categories such as age, gender, attractiveness, ability, and so on.

Catharsis Freud's notion of a 'cleansing' of emotional fears and anxieties, in order to overcome problems associated with them.

Causal schemata Mental representations, based upon experience, of the way in which two or more causes interact to explain an individual's action.

Central executive An element of Baddeley's working model of memory which envisages a control facility to direct information to one or other of the elements in his model.

Central filtering Selection of which stimuli to respond to which takes place in the brain rather than in the senses.

Central nervous system (CNS) The brain and the spinal cord.

Central traits Those personality traits which are not so dominant as cardinal traits, but which Allport saw as representing an individual's usual way of approaching life.

Centration A characteristic of the thinking of young children, where the child may focus upon one feature of the environment, while ignoring others, however relevant.

Choice response time Time taken by an individual to choose to respond in one way or another to options offered. The more choices available there are at any one time the longer it takes to make the choice.

Chromosomes Tightly linked strings of DNA molecules, carried in every cell in the body and inherited in pairs from each parent. Genes are carried on chromosomes.

Ciliary muscles Muscles in the eye which alter the shape of the lens to accommodate to different depths of focus.

Circadian rhythms Daily cyclical changes in physiological state which effect arousal level.

Classical conditioning The process through which a reflex response becomes associated with a stimulus which would not naturally activate that behaviour.

Classification The ability to group objects together in terms of common attributes.

Client-centred therapy Rogers's approach where clients (not 'patients') are encouraged to set their own goals and take control over the process of therapy.

Clinical interview A method used by Piaget to study children in an informal setting, by asking them questions and setting them tasks.

Clinical method of study in physiological psychology, examination of individuals who have suffered accidental damage to the brain in order to understand the effects on physical and psychological functioning.

Clinical psychologist Someone who has successfully completed a first degree in psychology followed by postgraduate training in the assessment and treatment of mental disorder.

Clinical settings Settings (such as hospitals or private practices) where people are receiving treatment for a physical or psychological condition.

Cluster sampling A means of obtaining a representative sample of a population which is based upon identifying natural groupings within a population. A random sample is drawn from each of these natural groupings and put together to form a cluster sample.

Cochlea A snail-shaped structure within the ear that contains auditory sense receptors.

Cocktail party phenomenon A phenomenon described by Cherry where an individual may still attend to a message relevant to him or her while focused on another message in a crowded room.

Cognitive appraisal A process through which we assess the possible effect of a situation on our state of well-being, before responding to it.

Cognitive approach An approach that is concerned with thinking and related mental processes, such as perception, memory, problem solving and language.

Cognitive dissonance A sense of tension brought about by holding beliefs that conflict with one another. Sometimes arises from a mismatch of established attitudes and behaviour.

Cognitive map A hypothetical structure which represents a mental 'picture' of a location or learning situation.

Cognitive processes All the processes involved in thinking and knowing, including perceiving, interpreting, reasoning, remembering, using language.

Cognitive science An interdisciplinary area of research, which studies the use of computers to simulate human thought processes and related phenomena.

Cognitive style This relates to the manner in which people think, remember, perceive and generally process information.

Cognitive/neoassociationistic model of behaviour A model of behaviour which links stimuli of various kinds to emotional feelings and thence to action.

Cognitive-behavioural therapies A group of therapies which make the assumption that faulty thinking can lead to mental disorder and maladaptive behaviour. Cognitive restructuring, re-learning more positive ways of thinking, can lead to changes in behaviour.

Cognitive-developmental approach An approach to the study of development derived initially from Piaget's theory of cognitive development.

Coherence In relation to problem solving, when the elements of the problem and the method of its solution do not fit it will prove hard to solve the problem.

Cohort-sequential design A research design which combines features of cross-sectional design with those of longitudinal design by studying samples of different ages and then comparing them over a period of time.

Commons dilemma The appropriation of resources by an individual or a group, which might be to the detriment of others if other individuals or groups did likewise.

Comparative ethologists Those who study behaviour in animals in the same way as other characteristics.

Complementarity of roles Relates to the idea that two individuals are most likely to form a satisfactory relationship if the role one partner adopts within the relationship complements that of the other partner.

Compliance Acceding to a request made by another person.

Computer simulation The use of computers to replicate and understand human thought processes.

Computerized scanning Techniques which use computers to obtain 'pictures' of the brain in order to study its functioning.

Concurrent validity The extent to which a test's outcomes match the outcomes of other measures of the same thing.

Condition In an experiment, a term that refers to the manipulation of the independent variable. A particular change in the characteristics of the independent variable is referred to as an experimental condition.

Conditioned response (CR) In classical conditioning, a response to a formerly neutral stimulus which because of repeated pairing with a conditioned stimulus produces a conditioned response.

Cones Colour-sensitive photoreceptors in the retina, responsible for vision in bright light.

Confidence/significance level The degree to which a researcher can be confident that a result obtained has not been obtained by chance alone. This may be assessed by conducting a statis-tical test of significance to assess the probability that the results occurred by chance.

Conformity The tendency for members of a group, to behave in a similar way to other members of the group.

Conscience That part of the superego which is concerned with preventing immoral impulses from entering the conscious mind.

Consciousness In general, this refers to a state of awareness of external and internal events experienced by an individual, though a range of more specific definitions have been proposed by different theorists.

Conservation The understanding that objects remain the same in relation to some fundamental characteristic such as number, mass or volume, even though there are changes in shape or arrangement.

Conservative focusing A strategy for concept formation described by Bruner and his colleagues. It involves focusing on one attribute at a time to test it and eventually test all the attributes.

Consideration structure (of leadership) Structure of leadership concerned with morale and group cohesiveness and with relationships with the group members.

Consonant–vowel–consonant trigrams (CVCs) Nonsense syllables, consisting of a consonant followed by a vowel followed by a consonant, used by Ebbinghaus in his research into memory.

Construct validity The extent to which a test measures the psychological construct which it claims to measure. For example, the extent to which intelligence tests actually measure intelligence.

Constructionism A belief that human experience is a construction of reality: individuals shape their own experiences by the way they respond to their ennvironments.

'Constructivist standpoint' Hare-Mustin and Maracek's term to describe the view that men and women are different only because of the social reality we have created about them.

Constructivist An approach to the explanation of psychological phenomena which emphasizes the construction of meaning from stimuli. Bartlett's approach to the study of memory is an example.

Content validity The extent to which those skills which are measured by a test are relevant to the overall ability which the test claims to measure.

Contiguity The need to give reinforcement at or very soon after the presentation of a stimulus or response.

Contingency model A model of leadership devised by Fiedler in which situation and leadership style interact.

Contingent responding The response made by a caregiver following an action instigated by the baby – an 'answer' to, for example, the baby's smile.

Continuity The proposition that humans and animals are one creation differing only in the stage of evolution each has reached.

Continuous reinforcement In operant conditioning, a schedule in which a reinforcer is given to every instance of the desired behaviour.

Control The rigorous design of an investigation to eliminate as far as possible all sources of bias.

Controlled observation Observation carried out in carefully controlled conditions, usually in a laboratory setting.

Controlled processing Serial processing of difficult or unfamiliar tasks.

Conventional morality Kohlberg's second level of moral reasoning, where children's values are influenced by society's rules and norms.

Convergence A binocular cue to depth from the feeling of the movement of the eyeballs moving inwards as you focus upon something nearer.

Core sleep Horne's (1988) term for the first four hours of sleep which he believes are necessary for rest, relaxation and restitution of the brain. The remaining hours (optional sleep) are not essential.

Correlation coefficient A statistic that describes the degree of relationship between two variables: for example, the IQs of children compared with the IQs of their mothers. A perfect match is expressed as 1; no relationship is expressed as 0. The relationship may be positive or negative.

Correspondence In relation to problem solving, when there is a problem to be solved there needs to be a close match between our internal representation of the problem and the elements involved.

Counterbalancing A technique designed to mitigate the effects of the order in which tests are applied in an experiment. The tests to be carried out are divided into two under each of two conditions A and B. They are then conducted in the order ABBA.

Critical life events Events or phases in life – for example, marriage, parenting, unemployment – which induce stress and cause some psychological adjustment to take place.

Critical period Period after hatching when Lorenz claimed imprinting had to occur, about 24 hours.

Cross-cultural studies Studies in which similarities and differences between different cultures are examined.

Crossover The splitting off and shuffling of portions of chromosomes before meiosis, thus increasing the possible number of gametes.

Cross-sectional design A research design which involves groups of individuals who vary on a particular dimension, often age, being compared at the same point in time.

Crystallized intelligence The social manifestation of 'fluid intelligence', which develops in response to experience of the environment.

Cult A group of people who are devoted to a particular system of worship or who pay homage to a particular person or thing.

Culture A system of meanings and customs, relating to such things as values, attitudes, laws, protocols, kinds of dwellings, and so on, shared by some identifiable group.

Culture bound Implies that the content of, for example, an IQ test contains material that is suitable only for members of a particular culture.

Curvilinear relationship A relationship between two variables where a plotted scattergram will describe a curve rather than a straight line.

Cutaneous senses Receptors located mainly in the skin which give information about touch, temperature and pain.

Cyclical theory of perception Neisser's perceptual theory which suggests a continuous process of analysis and synthesis.

Dark adaptation The process whereby the eyes adjust from bright to dim lighting.

Debriefing The investigator's discussing with the participants, following a study, the nature of the research, the findings, and any other matters that are needed to ensure the participants' well-being.

Deep processing Processing of material to be memorized which involves a semantic or meaning element and is therefore more durable.

Defence mechanisms Unconscious strategies, often involving the distortion of reality, used by people to protect themselves from painful anxiety or guilt. Defence mechanisms include repression, denial, projection, displacement and regression.

Dehumanization The effect of anonymity in relation to the victims of violence so that they are no longer regarded as humans.

Deindividuation A feeling of anonymity which results in individuals not taking responsibility for their behaviour.

Demand characteristics The tendency of participants in research to pick up cues and to behave in ways which they believe to be expected of them.

Dependence syndrome A condition in which the use of a substance such as drugs or alcohol takes on a much higher priority than any other aspects of the individual's behaviour.

Dependent variable The variable in an experiment which a researcher measures to test the result of manipulation of one or more other variables.

Deprivation The loss of something; in attachment theory, it relates to the loss of an attachment figure.

Depth perception The perception of the world in three dimensions even though the mechanisms of sensation are two-dimensional.

Descriptive statistics Those statistics whose purpose is to summarize or describe data. These may include measures of central tendency or dispersion or illustrative figures such as bar charts, histograms and graphs.

Determinism A belief that all human behaviour is caused by forces, internal or external, over which one has no control.

Deterministic Emphasizing early experience as determining behaviour patterns.

Development All the physical and psychological changes that take place between birth and old age.

Dichotic listening Listening to messages presented separately to each ear.

Direct perception Gibson's theory of perception which suggests that the senses provide all the information needed for individuals to interact with the environment.

Discontinuity The belief that humans and animals are separate creations. This has been based upon a literal interpretation of the Bible.

Discourse analysis A study of the way in which people express themselves; used to gain insights into social assumptions.

Discrimination In classical conditioning, selectively responding to the CS but not to stimuli which are similar to the CS.

Discriminatory power The ability of a psychological test to separate individuals' performance from one another.

Disengagement theory A theory which suggests that during late adulthood the gradual detachment of an individual from work and social activities will lead to psychological well-being.

Disinhibition A reduction in those forces which restrain people from behaving in an aggressive manner.

Dispersion The spread of scores.

Displacement activity Apparently irrelevant behaviour, interposed into normal behaviour (courtship, for instance, or threat displays) resulting from conflict or stress.

Displacement The ability of language to convey information about things which are not present in time or place.

Dizygotic (DZ) twins 'Fraternal' twins, who have developed from two separately fertilized ova and are no more alike genetically than any two children of the same parents.

Dogmatism, theory of Personality characteristics described by Rokeach involving rigidity of thinking.

Dominant gene A gene that causes an individual to display the characteristics it determines when either allele possesses it.

Door-in-the face Process where compliance with a request follows refusal to comply with a larger request.

Dopamine theory A proposal that the symptoms of schizophrenia are directly caused by an excess of dopamine in the brain.

Double blind technique An experimental design where neither the participants nor the individual administering any tests is aware of the true aims of the experiment. The purpose is to mitigate the effects of the experimenter's expectations on the test results.

Down's syndrome A form of mental and physical impairment caused by chromosome abnormalities.

Dream, the Levinson's term for the significant vision an individual develops early in life in relation to, for example, career or sporting goals for the future.

Dyslexia Literally defined as 'nonreading', it is an imprecise term which covers a range of learning problems connected with learning to read, write and spell.

Echoic memory An immediate memory store for the auditory sense modality. It prolongs auditory stimuli so that they can be processed for the short-term store.

Ecocognitivism The study of mental operations taking into account the 'real life' context in which they occur.

Ecological approach An approach which deals with 'real life' rather than laboratory settings.

Ecological validity A situation where findings (from research) are meaningful in the real world.

Ecology Differences in physical characteristics and behaviour which are related to where individuals are living, the sources of their food and the predators which have to be avoided.

Ecology of development The study of development in the context of the environmental conditions a person experiences or is affected by, directly or indirectly.

Economic defendability In relation to territory occupied by an animal, the balance between the value of the resources within a territory against the energy necessary to defend it.

Ego In Freud's theory, that part of the personality that operates on the 'reality principle': that is, controlling the id's demands until an appropriate time or place. It aims to strike a balance between the demands of the id and of the superego.

Ego ideal That part of the superego which is concerned with the sort of 'good' behaviour that parents would approve of.

Ego identity Erikson's term to describe the sense of self, a secure feeling of who and what one is.

Egocentric speech Internal language used as an aid to thinking. Vygotsky's notion of inner speech. However, in young children and in adults under stress this egocentric language is often expressed.

Egocentrism The inability to see an object or situation from anything but one's own point of view.

Elaborated code of language Code of language used, according to Bernstein, by middle-class children. It employs a large vocabulary, has complex and flexible grammar and syntax and is suited for the expression of abstract ideas.

Elaborated play A term used by Sylva to describe the kind of play which challenges and stimulates and is most likely to enhance a child's cognitive development.

Elaborative rehearsal Deeper rehearsal involving meaning.

Electrical stimulation of the brain (ESB) Placing an electrode in certain parts of the brain in order to stimulate neurons by means of a mild electrical shock. In this way, it is possible to observe the effects of such stimulation on behaviour.

Electroconvulsive therapy (ECT) The delivery of a brief electric current to the head in order to alleviate disorders such as depression.

Electroencephalogram (EEG) A means of measuring electrical activity in the brain by means of electrodes attached to the scalp.

Electro-oculogram A process similar to an EEG but which gives a visual record of eye movements.

Eliciting of responses In relation to animal behaviour, responses may be elicited from another animal.

Emergent norm theory Emergence of norms of behaviour in crowd situations where people involved have nothing obvious in common except the purposes for which the crowd has come together.

Emics The study of a culture from the inside, often with the collaboration of members of the studied culture.

Emotion-focused coping A form of coping with stress which involves attempts to reduce the negative emotions which often accompany stress (Lazarus and Folkman, 1984).

Empathy/altruism hypothesis The hypothesis put forward by Batson that empathy with someone who is in trouble may provide a genuine motivation for helping.

Empiricism An approach that advocates the collection of information through rather than by faith or hearsay.

Enactive representation According to Bruner, the simplest way in which a child gains information about the world, by physical manipulation of the environment.

Encephalization The extent to which a species has evolved a brain of large size.

Encoding specificity principle Recollection of material is easier if the context in which attempts to recall are similar to the context in which memorization took place.

Encounter group A humanistic therapy where a small group of people are encouraged by a facilitator to talk about and act out their emotions and problems.

Endocrine system A system of glands which produce hormones and release them into the bloodstream. The system interacts with the nervous system in influencing many kinds of behaviour, for example 'fight or flight'.

Endogenous factors Factors internal to the individual which may determine arousal level.

Episodic memory The storage of information about events and the relationships between them.

Equilibration (1) A process which acts to ensure that accommodation is consolidated via assimilation and that a balance is maintained between the two. (2) Piaget's term for the process by which we come to terms with experiences in the environment.

Equity theory Stresses the importance of perceived fairness in a relationship regarding the benefits which each partner receives and the costs each incurs.

Ethnic cleansing The removal of a particular cultural group from a geographical area.

Ethnocentric Viewing cultural, racial or gender differences from a particular ethnic standpoint.

Ethnocentrism The process by which our own group is placed at the centre of our consciousness and other groups are sidelined.

Ethogenics Research which attempts to take episodes rather than individual acts or actions as a focus for study.

Ethology The study of behaviour in the natural environment.

Etics To study a culture from the outside using criteria common to the 'home' and the studied culture.

Eugenics An attempt to improve the human race by improving inherited qualities.

Eurocentric Heavily influenced by cultural values that are part of American and European life.

Eusociality Beneficial characteristics among social insects, involving cooperation, division of labour in reproduction and an overlap between generations for life support.

Evaluation apprehension A change in the behaviour of a participant in an experiment or other situation which arises from being aware of being tested.

Evoked cortical response (ECR) The brain's response to a stimulus measured by means of electroencephalogram recordings.

Evolutionarily stable strategies (ESS) Strategies, described by Maynard-Smith, adopted by aggressors and opponents which have the best chance of enhancing life expectancy and reproductive capacity in each.

Excitation-transfer model of aggression Zillman's theory which suggests that aggression occurs as a result of transfer of arousal from one context to another.

Executive processes A category of cognitive skills, which includes metacognition, and involves organizing and planning strategies.

Exemplar A representation of a category of people personified in an image of a particular person in that category.

Existential self A term used by Lewis and Brooks-Gunn to describe the basic awareness of being separate and distinct from others.

Exogenous factors Factors external to the individual which may effect arousal level.

Expectancy-value technique A method of attitude measurement devised by Fishbein and Ajzen, incorporating a value rating scale with more conventional Likert-type statements of attitude.

Experiment A method of investigation in which one or more variables (the independent variable) are manipulated in order to examine their effect on behaviour (the dependent variable), All other variables are controlled.

Experimental reductionism Reduces behaviour to models that show its components and the relationships between them (for example, stimulus–response connections) and can be tested by experimentation.

Exploration Activities where children investigate objects and events or aspects of their own physical ability.

External experimental validity Similar to ecological validity. It relates to how close the experimental situation is to real life or to what is typical.

External speech An aspect of language, described by Vygotsky, as a means of communicating thoughts to others.

Extinction In classical conditioning, the halting of the CR when the CS is repeatedly presented but is not paired with the UCS.

Extraneous variables Those variables in an experiment which may cloud or distort the link between independent and dependent variables and which a researcher will endeavour to control so as to mitigate this distortion.

Extraversion One of the dimensions of personality identified by Eysenck; it is characterized by a number of traits, such as sociability and impulsiveness.

Eysenck Personality Inventory (EPI) A rating scale devised by Eysenck to measure extraversion–introversion and neuroticism–stability.

Eysenck Personality Questionnaire (EPQ) A rating scale devised by Eysenck which measures extraversion, neuroticism and psychoticism.

Face validity The extent to which a test appears to be measuring what it claims to measure.

Face-ism The emphasis placed in men upon depicting their faces while the emphasis in women is on the upper body. An aspect of sexism.

Facial feedback hypothesis A proposal that we recognize emotions through feedback from the facial muscles: for example, smiling will promote feelings of happiness.

Factoid A fact that did not exist until it was created by the media.

Factor analysis A complex statistical technique which is used to find the common factors underlying the scores from a number of different measures (for example, intelligence or personality tests).

False belief task A task set up to discover whether a child possesses a theory of mind. The task requires the child to understand that another person may entertain a belief that is not actually true.

Falsifiability The ability to show, when using the scientific method, that a theory may be false, rather than simply producing data to support it.

Feature analysing Theory of pattern recognition which hypothesizes features of objects stored in memory and scanned for recognition. An object is recognized when sufficient features are matched.

Fertility motivation People's motives for having or not having children.

Field dependence A cognitive style. A field-dependent individual finds it difficult to concentrate on an object, problem or situation while ignoring distracting features of the surrounding context.

Field experiment An experiment which is conducted in a natural environment (in the 'field').

Field independence A cognitive style. A field-independent individual views the world analytically and is able to concentrate on an object, problem or situation without being distracted by its context.

Figural identity Ability to name or identify an object, which Hebb claimed had to be learned.

Figural unity Ability to detect a figure or an object, which Hebb claimed was innate.

Figure–ground An organizing principle of perception suggested by Gestalt psychologists involving the distinction between figures and the background in which they are set.

Fitness Successful adaptation to the environment so that an individual reaches maturity and reproduces, thus passing on its genes.

Five-factor approach to personality An approach which presents a compromise between Eysenck and Cattell and proposes that five factors (the 'Big Five') form the basis of personality structure.

Fixation In Freud's theory, the halting of development at a particular stage resulting from a failure to deal with the challenges of that stage.

Fixed action patterns (FAPs) Species-specific behaviour patterns, genetically programmed and triggered by a stimulus or set of stimuli.

Flocks (of birds)/schools (of fish) More temporary and less stable relationships between animals than societies, but which may last for several months.

Fluid intelligence Basic reasoning ability, which is not much influenced by environmental experience.

Focal attention The process of attending to particular aspects of the environment while other aspects are ignored.

Focus gambling A strategy for concept formation described by Bruner and his colleagues. It involves dealing with two or more attributes at once and varying them to test the response.

Focused attention Where each item in an array is focused upon one at a time and processed.

Foot-in-the-door Process whereby compliance with a small request makes compliance with a larger or less desirable one more likely.

Fraser Darling effect Phenomenon noted by Darling where the grouping of individduals of a species together stimulates sexual activity and therefore reproduction.

Free association A psychoanalytic technique where the client is encouraged to talk about whatever comes to mind, no matter how inappropriate it may seem.

Free will An ability to exercise control over one's behaviour and to make choices.

Frequency distribution The tabulation of scores by the frequency with which each occurs.

Frequency polygon A means of representing a frequency distribution graphically, similar to a histogram. The frequency of each score is represented by a dot. The dots are joined to form a polygon.

Frustration/aggression hypothesis The suggestion made by Dollard that aggression is linked to frustration in reaching a goal.

Functional set A fixation of mind relating to the functions of the various elements of a problem.

Functionalism A school of psychology that drew on Darwin's theory of evolution and which was concerned with the purposes of mental processes.

Fundamental attribution bias A pervasive tendency to explain behaviour in terms of disposition.

Gamete Single unpaired chromosomes formed by meiosis.

Ganglion cells In the retina, groups of nerve cells that collect information from the bipolar cells and pass it to the brain via the optic nerve.

Gardner's theory of multiple intelligences Gardner's theory that there exist seven distinct intelligences, which are independent of each other, but which interact and work together whenever the need arises.

Gender Usually used to refer to psychological/cultural aspects of males and females.

Gender constancy A child's understanding that gender is a consistent and stable characteristic despite changes in appearance, dress or activity.

Gender identity Perception of oneself as masculine or feminine.

Gender role (sex role) Behaviour, attitudes and activities that are considered by a particular society to be appropriate for males and females.

Gender stereotype (sex stereotype) Excessively rigid beliefs about what males and females are like and how they should behave.

Gendercentric Viewing the development of males and females as taking different routes.

Gene The carrier of heredity factors, situated on the chromosomes and represented as a DNA sequence.

Gene–culture coevolution The coming together of genetic evolution culture to allow the human species to develop more rapidly than other species.

General adaptation syndrome (GAS) Selye's (1956) three-stage model which describes the body's physiological responses to stress.

Generalizability The extent to which the results of a study may be applied to a wider group than the sample(s) used.

Generalization In classical conditioning, the process whereby a conditioned response is produced to a stimulus similar to the conditioned stimulus.

Generativity versus stagnation According to Erikson, the most significant psychosocial crisis of middle age. An individual becomes concerned with

contributing to and guiding the next generation (generativity). If this does not occur, the individual experiences a sense of impoverishment or stagnation.

Genetic predisposition An indicator in an individual's chromosomal/genetic makeup that there is a likelihood of a particular trait developing: for example, schizophrenia.

Genotype All the inherited characteristics present in an individual's chromosomes.

Gerontology The scientific study of the elderly and the ageing process.

Gestalt psychology School of psychology that opposed behaviourism and proposed that behaviour should be studied as a whole.

Gestalt therapy A humanistic therapy where people are encouraged to become 'whole' by identifying and acknowledging all facets of themselves.

Global focusing strategy A strategy adopted in Levine's concept formation trials by many intelligent adults which involves keeping track of as many hypotheses as possible at the same time.

Glucostatic theory The proposal that feelings of hunger arise when blood glucose falls below a certain set point.

Good form (Prägnanz) Relates to a tendency (described by Gestalt psychologists) for the brain to seek order out of chaos through isomorphism.

Granfalloon A technique used in persuasive communications to give a product a 'personality' so that buying it gives the consumer a sense of belonging to a special group.

Great Ape Project A project supported by biologists, philosophers and writers, the aim of which is to give the great apes (gorillas, chimpanzees and orang-utans) the same moral rights (including protection under the law) as humans.

Grief A person's response to bereavement, which involves psychological suffering.

Group polarization A tendency for members of a group to take more extreme attitudes and/or decisions than individual members would.

Groupthink A term used for the situation where a group places unanimity of decision ahead of the search for a realistic solution to a problem.

Growth trends White's term for the general developmental characteristics which have been observed during young adulthood.

Habituation Learning to ignore a stimulus which is presented continuously, for example the ticking of a clock or the sound of traffic noise.

Habituation technique A technique developed by Maurer and Barrera to assess neonate perception based upon the length of time the infants fixated on an object before becoming bored with it and looking away.

'Hardy' personality A term used to describe individuals who appear to cope well with stress and to resist illness.

Harem polygyny A mating system where a male has several females to mate with at the same time.

Hassles Daily problems which may cause stress, for example, arguments with partner, waiting in traffic jams, worrying about weight problems.

Headstart An educational enrichment programme designed in the USA to provide enhanced learning experiences for deprived preschool children.

Hedonistic reasoning Eisenberg's term for the preschool child's tendency to consider the implications of moral issues in relation to themselves rather than others.

'Hello/goodbye' effect A term which describes the patient or client's exaggeration of symptoms at the beginning and end of a course of therapy.

Hermaphroditism A condition where a child is born with functioning sexual organs of both sexes.

Heterogeneous summation The additive effect of more than one sign stimulus which provokes a much stronger response than one sign stimulus only in animals.

Heteronomous morality (moral realism) Piaget's first stage of moral realism, where children comply strictly with rules and base judgments about moral issues on consequences rather than intent.

Heterosexism Viewing heterosexist behaviour as normal and homosexuality as deviant.

Heuristic strategies 'Rule of thumb' strategies employed to solve problems based upon what amounts to a 'hunch'.

'Hidden observer' In hypnosis, Hilgard's term for a part of the participant's mind which becomes dissociated from the hypnotized part, and is able to observe what is happening.

Histogram A frequency distribution, presented in graphical form. Boxes above each score represent frequencies. The frequency of scores is on the vertical axis; the values of the scores are on the horizontal axis.

Homeostasis The process by which the body maintains a balanced state through the regulation of, for example, blood pressure, temperature, heart rate, chemical balance, digestion, respiration.

Homogeneity of variance Assumption for the use of parametric statistical tests. The populations from which samples are drawn are assumed to have similar dispersion.

Honeybee dance Dance described by von Frisch by means of which a foraging bee indicates to others in the hive the direction and distance of a food source.

Hospice An establishment which provides a homelike and emotionally supportive setting for terminally ill people.

Hostile attributional bias The tendency for an individual to attribute hostile intent to other people's actions.

Humanistic therapies Therapies where there is a belief that individuals can be helped to gain insight into their own problems and move towards a solution and realize their potential as human beings.

Humanistic/phenomenological approach Concerned with an individual's own subjective perceptions and feelings about their experiences.

Hypnosis Either the inducing of an altered state of consciousness where an individual can be induced by another person to perform involuntary actions (state theory) or a situation where a participant voluntarily complies with suggestions from a hypnotist (nonstate theory).

Hypothesis A testable statement, drawn from a theory, and usually written in the form of a prediction of an expected relationship between two or more variables.

Hypothetico-deductive process A cyclical process used in research where a theory is refined to produce a hypothesis (or hypotheses) and then tested. The results of the test provide the basis for modification of the theory and further testing.

Iconic memory (visual information store (VIS)) An immediate memory store which has the effect of prolonging the stimulus so that it can be processed for the short-term memory.

Iconic representation According to Bruner, a kind of thinking which is based on the use of mental images.

Iconic representation According to Bruner, a nonverbal means of obtaining information by picturing the environment mentally.

Id Freud's term for that part of the personality that is biologically determined. It operates on the 'pleasure principle': that is, seeking pleasure and avoiding pain.

Ideal self Rogers's term for one's perceptions of how one should or would like to be.

Identification The process through which someone adopts the feelings, attitudes and behaviour of another person (or group) and becomes like them.

Idiographic research Research which concentrates upon detailed study of an individual or individuals as opposed to groups.

Idiographic theories A belief that human beings are unique and can be understood only through the use of techniques, such as ipsative tests or case studies, that are designed to reflect that uniqueness.

Idiothetics An approach which aims to compromise between the two extremes of nomothetic and idiographic approaches by focusing on the uniqueness of the individual, without losing sight of the general principles of human behaviour.

Imagery The process of forming mental images of things or events you need to remember. Material to be remembered may have high or low imagery value.

Implicit personality theory Unstated beliefs or assumptions about what characteristics (of people) tend to go together.

Imprinting A form of learning observed in some animals soon after birth, which results in attachment to a parent. They will follow the first moving thing they see shortly after hatching.

Inclusive fitness The sum of an individual's fitness (adaptation to the environment) together with the effect of his/her behaviour on relatives carrying some of his/her genes.

Incus A bony structure in the ear (ossicle) which is struck by the malleus as the tympanic membrane vibrates.

Independent measures design An experimental design where there is no relationship between participants tested under each condition.

Independent variable A variable in an experiment which is manipulated in order that the researcher can measure the result of such manipulation.

Inferential statistics Statistical procedures which allow a researcher to infer from the data the probability that two or more samples are drawn from the same or different populations.

Information-processing approach An approach which considers the human brain to be analogous to a computer and aims to understand how people interpret, store, retrieve and evaluate information.

Informational influence The influence that results from the provision of information that reduces ambiguity.

Informed consent In relation to research studies, ensuring that the participants are informed as fully as possible by the investigator about the purpose and design of the research, before the research proceeds.

Infradian rhythms Body rhythms which promote functions that occur less often than once a day, for example the menstrual cycle in females, or hibernation in some animals.

In-groups/out-groups The group to which an individual belongs is an in-group: out-groups are all the rest.

Initiating structure (of leadership) A structure of leadership where the prime concern is the identification of group goals and the achievement of them.

Inner speech An aspect of language, described by Vygotsky, as a monitor and controller of thinking.

Inoculation In relation to persuasion, the technique of presenting a weakened form of the message to allow people to form counter-arguments.

Insane A legal term used to describe a person who is not of sound mind and is unable to distinguish between right and wrong.

Insight learning Learning in which the learner perceives relationships in a problem suddenly without any obvious trial and error activities.

Insight therapies Therapies such as psychoanalysis, where a successful outcome is seen as being closely linked to the client gaining an understanding of, or insight into, his or her own problems.

Instinctive behaviour Species-specific behaviour which is not controlled by conscious decision-making processes and which has a genetic basis.

Integrity versus despair According to Erikson, the most significant crisis to be overcome in late adulthood. If people feel content and accepting of their lives, integrity is achieved; despair results if it is felt that life has been without real meaning.

Intelligence quotient (IQ) Originally defined in terms of a ratio of a child's mental age and chronological age. IQ is now computed by comparing a child's test performance with that of other children of the same chronological age.

Interactionism (1) As an alternative to reductionism, the study of behaviour by considering a range of different perspectives and methods of study. (2) In relation to personality theory, the view that an individual's personality is influenced by an interaction between internal characteristics (traits) and features of situations in which they operate.

Interactive dualism A theory proposed by Descartes, in which human functioning is seen as an interaction between two independent substances: mind and body.

Interchangeability The two-way nature of language where each party to a communication may send and receive information.

Internal experimental validity The extent to which results of an investigation are free from bias from such things as demand characteristics or evaluation apprehension.

Internal working models A concept proposed by Bowlby to describe representations in children's minds of the kind of relationships they have with parents and other key individuals.

Internalization The process through which standards, beliefs and values become part of one's own motive system.

Interval data Data in which there is an equal interval of difference between measures. For example, if you measured the length of a path in metres, 4 metres represent exactly double the distance represented by 2 metres and 6 metres half as much distance again.

Interview Research methods based upon face-to-face oral interviews with participants.

Intimacy According to Erikson, a critical psychosocial achievement, characterized by the feeling of love and commitment to another person.

Intracultural differences Differences which exist within a culture.

Intrapsychic Attributing behaviour to internal factors.

Introspection The systematic observation by an individual of his or her own mental processes.

Introversion One of the dimensions of personality identified by Eysenck; it is characterized by traits such as reserve, cautiousness and a reluctance to socialize.

Invariant functions Piaget's term for the cognitive processes which do not change with maturity: for example, assimilation and accommodation.

Ipsative tests Tests (for example, projective tests) that are not based on pre-established norms, but which require an individual to reveal his or her personality by responding to ambiguous stimuli or through self-assessment.

Isolation According to Erikson, a feeling that one is disconnected from others in the absence of a true intimate relationship.

Isomorphism A term used by Gestalt psychologists for the tendency of brain fields to adopt good form. They have envisaged electrical fields within the brain which determine patterns of perception and thought.

Joint attention The term used to describe the communication that occurs through the understanding of gestures between a child and adult when they are focusing on something together.

Just noticeable difference (jnd) That change in intensity of a stimulus which can be detected by an individual 50 per cent of the time.

Just world hypothesis The hypothesis that whatever happens to an individual is related to what that individual deserves.

Kin selection Support and help offered by kin to kin within a species in order to increase the chances of the survival of the kin and so of the genes which they share.

Kinaesthesia The process which describes the feedback from sensations in the muscles and joints which provides information about body positions and movement.

Kinaesthetic sense The sensation of the movement of muscles (for example, of the muscles of the eyeball in convergence).

Laboratory experiment An experiment which is conducted in a controlled and artificial situation.

Language acquisition device (LAD) Chomsky's term for an inborn brain mechanism which 'programmes' a child to be able to learn language.

Language Acquisition Support System (LASS) Bruner's term to describe the process of nonverbal communication which occurs between an infant and adult and which encourages the development of the child's language.

Law of effect Thorndike's proposal that behaviour that has positive effects, for example, reward, is likely to be repeated, whereas that which has negative or no effects is not.

Law of mass action The proposal by Lashley that the cortex functions as a whole rather than as separate areas and the effects of damage would depend upon the amount damaged.

Law of Prägnanz (good form) A Gestalt principle of perceptual organization that psychological organization will always be as 'good' as the prevailing conditions allow.

Learned helplessness Seligman's term for a state of apathy or helplessness which may result when an animal or human is unable to escape from a traumatic situation.

Learning difficulties A term used to describe the characteristics of individuals who have a disability that affects their mental functioning. It includes many kinds of problem, some genetically related, some biochemical.

Learning set A hypothetical structure involving memory, representing the learning of a principle which underlies a problem.

Learning theory approach An approach to the study of development based upon behaviourist learning theory and social learning theory.

Learning Relatively permanent changes in behaviour that occur as a result of experience.

Lek A form of territorial organization found in some species of birds and also in a few mammal species. Males form a tight group and display together. This conglomeration of males acts as a lure for females, who come to choose a mate.

Level of measurement The kind of measurement used in the study. Interval or ratio measurement have greater precision and contain more information than ordinal measurement, which in turn provides more information than nominal measurement.

Libido A form of psychic energy that Freud regarded as sexual in nature, compelling people to act in ways likely to reproduce the species.

Lifespan development Development which occurs throughout life, from birth to old age.

Likert scale A method of attitude measurement involving the construction of a number of attitude statements with which respondents are asked to agree or disagree.

Linear programme A form of programmed learning where subject matter is arranged in very small steps, known as frames, which are presented in a logical sequence and require the learner to make a response. The response is reinforced through immediate feedback.

Linguistic relativity The suggestion, made by Whorf, that the language an individual uses influences the way in which he or she thinks.

Linguistic universals Features which are common to all languages: for example, the use of nouns and verbs.

Lloyd Morgan's Canon A principle proposed by Lloyd Morgan that animal behaviour should not be interpreted as arising from higher mental processes if it can be interpreted in terms of simpler mechanisms.

Localization of brain function An assumption that specific areas of the brain control particular psychological functions, such as language.

Localization of sound The ability of the auditory system to detect the location of particular sounds.

Locus of control (internal or external) Rotter's differentiation between those who see their behaviour dictated by forces outside themselves (external locus of control) or whose behaviour is the result of internal factors, such as disposition or ability (internal locus of control.

Logotherapy A theoretical framework and therapy developed by Frankl, which emphasizes the need for individuals to discover their own meaning in life in order to grow and develop psychologically.

Longitudinal design A research design which involves a single group of individuals being studied over a period of time.

Long-term memory Memory for events and experiences stored on a long-term basis (for instance, recognition of someone you have not met for a long time).

Loudness The amplitude of sound waves.

Lure A technique where an enticing offer, found to be unavailable, is used to ensure acceptance of a less favourable offer.

Machine reductionism Uses computer simulations to help explain behaviour such as problem solving, perception, intelligence.

'Magic age' view, the The view that possession of a theory of mind is linked to a child's cognitive development and does not occur in a child under four years of age.

Maintenance rehearsal Shallow rehearsal involving no more than simple repetition.

Malleus A bony structure (ossicle) in the ear which strikes the incus as the tympanic membrane vibrates.

Mastery play The first of Piaget's stages of play activity (sensorimotor), where a child of up to about two years spends time exploring and manipulating objects through sight and touch.

Matched participants design An experimental design where samples to be tested are carefully matched for characteristics considered to be important for the particular experiment. Once matchings have been made the pairs

are allocated randomly, one to each condition. It is treated for statistical purposes as a related measures design.

Maternal deprivation hypothesis Bowlby's theory that very young children should not be deprived of contact with a mother during a particularly sensitive period when the primary attachment relationship is forming.

Maturation The biological process of development through which any organism passes to become adult. It does not imply learning.

Mean The arithmetical average of a set of scores, arrived at by totalling the scores and dividing by the number of them.

Means–ends analysis A problem is broken down into small elements. In each a goal is identified and problems in reaching that goal systematically worked out.

Medial preoptic area An area of the brain just below the hypothalamus, which has been shown to be implicated in male sexual behaviour.

Median The middle score in a set of scores which have been ranked. Where there is an odd number of scores there will be an equal number of scores above and below the median; where there is an even number of scores, the median is represented by the mean of the two scores closest to the middle point.

Mediation The use of a link between what you need to remember and something already established in memory.

Mediators In cognitive psychology, the internal, mental events that occur between a stimulus and the behaviour that results.

Medical model The assumption that mental disorders are illnesses and treatable through medical means, for example the prescribing of drugs or surgery.

Meiosis Process whereby single unpaired cells divide twice to provide four cells each with a full complement of chromosomes.

Memory span The amount of material that can be stored in the short-term memory at any one time.

Mental age A concept which describes a child's performance on an IQ test. If a child of seven performs at the same level as children of eight, then he or she can be said to have a mental age of eight.

Mere exposure effect Zajonc's contention that the amount of a person's exposure to an attitude object will have an effect upon his or her attitude to it.

Meta-analysis A statistical technique which is used to aggregate and analyse the results of a number of independent

studies in relation to a particular hypothesis.

Metabolism The chemical processes within the body which cause food and other substances to be formed into body material.

Metacognition An individual's awareness of his or her own thought processes: for example, remembering or understanding something.

Metacommunication So far as animals are concerned, communication which is designed to qualify or modify other signals. Forequarters are sometimes lowered by carnivores in apparently aggressive play to show that it is not 'for real'.

Metarepresentation The ability to think about and understand one's own thoughts.

Method of loci A mnemonic technique or memory aid that involves visualizing material to be remembered in particular locations.

Midlife crisis The term used to describe the time during middle age when people become conscious of, and often depressed about, their life situation.

Minimax principle The notion that an individual will strive to minimize costs and maximize benefits in a relationship.

Mitosis The process of copying genetic material in each cell and transferring a copy into each new cell.

Mode A measure of central tendency representing the most frequently occurring score(s).

Model A hypothetical, testable proposition about the way some aspect of psychological functioning operates.

Modelling As a form of therapy, a technique which is an application of social learning theory and is used to treat disorders such as phobias. Patients watch a filmed or live model dealing with their phobic object or situation and this reduces anxiety when they are later exposed to the situation themselves.

Modes of representation In Bruner's theory, the different ways in which children internally represent the environment to themselves as their thought processes develop.

Monocular cues to depth Cues to the perception of depth which depend on one eye only.

Monogamy The union of one male and one female of a species to rear at least one brood exclusively.

Monotropy A theory proposed by Bowlby that an infant forms a strong attachment to just one caregiver, usually the mother.

Monozygotic (MZ) twins 'Identical' twins who have developed from a single fertilized ovum and are thought to be genetically identical.

Mood congruence Involves the matching of the affective content of what has to be memorized to the mood you are in when you memorize it.

'Moral absolutism' The holding of an extreme view. For example, in relation to animal research, either that all animal research should be banned or that there should be no restrictions at all.

Moral development The process through which children adopt and internalize the rules and standards of behaviour that are expected in the society they are growing up in.

Moral orientations Gilligan's term for two distinct styles of responding to moral issues: justice and care. Boys are more likely to operate from an orientation of justice, while girls are more likely to operate from an orientation of caring.

'Moral relativism' A compromise view. For example, in relation to animal research, that after weighing up various arguments, some research is permissible and some is not.

Morphemes The smallest unit of language to have a grammatical purpose.

'M-space' A term used by information-processing theorists to describe working memory (roughly equivalent to short-term memory).

Multitrait theories Theories which aim to identify the range of traits that are central to personality and which convey a picture of the whole personality.

Mutation Imperfect copying of genetic material at mitosis, resulting in variations in characteristics.

Mutual reciprocity Schaffer's (1977) term for the reciprocal patterns of interaction which occur between an infant and caregiver.

Natural quasi-experiment Another term used to describe a quasi-experiment. There is no deliberate manipulation of the independent variable but account is taken of naturally occurring changes.

Natural selection The process, proposed by Darwin, through which those organisms best suited to their environment survived and reproduced – the 'survival of the fittest'.

Naturalistic observation Observation of spontaneous behaviour carried out in the natural surroundings of the participants.

Need complementarity A relationship between two partners is more likely to be sustained if the needs of each are complementary to those of the other.

Needs-oriented reasoning Eisenberg's term for the kind of reasoning about moral issues that develops as children grow older. They consider the needs of other people at the expense of their own needs.

Negative reinforcement In operant conditioning, the process whereby a response is made more likely because of the removal or avoidance of something unpleasant (a negative reinforcer). This is not the same as punishment.

Negative-state relief model The model which suggests that people learn in childhood that it is gratifying to help.

Nest sites A form of territorial organization used particularly by pied fly-catchers, based upon the establishment of the best sites in which to set up nests. Males establish sites ahead of the arrival of the females who are attracted by their success in doing this.

Neuromodulators Chemicals that act in conjunction with neurotransmitters, moderating their activity.

Neurons Nerve cells in the nervous system made up of a cell body (soma) from which extend dendrites and the axon. They are of three main types: sensory, connector and motor neurons.

Neuroscience Attempts to find neurological explanations for mental processes.

Neurosis A relatively vague term generally used to describe anxiety-based disorders such as phobias and obsessive-compulsive behaviour, where the patient retains contact with reality.

Neuroticism One of the dimensions of personality identified by Eysenck. Neurotic individuals tend to be more prone to worry and anxiety and are often touchy and irritable.

Neurotransmitter A chemical that is released by one neuron and then crosses the synaptic gap to be received by special receptor sites on the dendrites of the next neuron in the chain.

'New paradigm' research A style of research that uses qualitative methods in the collection and analysis of data: for example, case study or role play.

Nocturnal Active by night rather than by day.

Nominal data Sometimes referred to as frequency or categorical data, this is a level of measurement which involves simple counting of events which occur.

Nomothetic research Research which attempts to arrive at principles of behaviour which may be applied to a larger group of people or perhaps generalized to a whole population, by making comparisons with norms of behaviour.

Nomothetic theories Based on the idea that there are laws of behaviour that are applied to everyone and can be used to compare people with each other.

Nonlinear relationship A relationship between two variables that, when plotted on a scattergram, does not follow a straight line.

Nonparametric test A test of significance which does not depend for its validity upon assumptions such as normally distributed populations, homogeneity of variance and interval or ratio levels of measurement.

Norm of reaction The upper and lower limits of genetic potential within which an individual will develop.

Normal distribution (Sometimes referred to as a Gaussian curve), a frequency distribution where the mean, median and the mode are the same. This results in a 'bell-shaped' curve, found when a large number of measurements are taken of naturally occurring phenomena. It has important characteristics used in inferential statistics.

Normative influence Influence to change behaviour as a result of pressure to conform to the behaviour of other members of a group.

NREM (nonrapid eye movement) sleep A deeper level of sleep in which the cortex of the brain is less active (slow wave sleep).

Null hypothesis A prediction that there will be no difference (or relationship in the case of a correlational design) between the results obtained of a test under two or (more) conditions except that which might be expected by chance alone. Or to put it in another way, that the two samples will be found to be no more different than if they had been drawn from a single population.

Object permanence The belief that objects continue to exist even when they are not visible.

Observation Method of study in which there is no manipulation of variables as in an experiment, but only careful observation and measurement of phenomena under study.

Observational learning (modelling) Learning by imitating the behaviour of a model.

Observer The individual who observes someone doing something and draws inferences from that action.

Oedipus/Electra complex The major conflict of the phallic stage where the child seeks a strong love attachment to the parent of the opposite sex. Satisfactory resolution of the complex results in the child identifying with the parent.

Oestrogen A female sex hormone.

Olfaction The sense of smell.

One-tailed hypothesis A hypothesis which is directional – one which specifies which way the differences or relationship between results of tests of the samples in a study will go.

Ontogenetic adaptation Changes in behaviour occurring within the lifetime of an individual of a species which are advantageous to its survival.

Operant (or instrumental) conditioning The conditioning of voluntary behaviour through the use of reinforcement and punishment.

Operation Piaget's term for a more advanced mental structure that allows an individual to perform a mental action in reverse.

Operational definition A definition that sets out exactly what a particular term means so that it can be measured and quantified.

Operational set A fixation of mind relating to strategies to be employed in solving a problem.

Opponent process theory The proposal that perception of red–green stimuli is a separate and opposing process to the perception of yellow–blue stimuli.

Opportunity sample Samples drawn from a population on the basis of their easy availability rather than because they are representative. Caution needs to be observed in drawing general conclusions from such samples.

Optic chiasma The point at which the optic nerve from each eye meets.

Ordinal data Data which involve the ranking of events in order as well as counting them.

Organic mental disorders Disorders which arise from physical deterioration of the brain or degeneration of the nervous system.

Orientation In relation to animal behaviour, orientation may represent the responses of an animal to the basic environmental situation. For instance, a fish rests with its head upstream.

Outcome-research studies Research carried out to examine the effectiveness of psychotherapy.

Outliers Plots on a scattergram which represent values of the variables which are not typical of the data as a whole.

Pair bond An attachment between a male and a female of a species which may be either permanent or temporary.

Paradigm A common, global theory that carries a set of assumptions about what should be studied and how.

Parallel evolution Similar behavioural or physical evolutionary changes in different species resulting from dissimilar causes.

Parallel processing Attempting to attend to more than one processing operation at the same time.

Parametric test A significance test which depends for its validity upon assumptions concerning the populations from which data are obtained: namely, normal distribution, homogeneity of variance and interval or ratio measures.

Parasympathetic division of the ANS Restores and conserves the body's resources: for example, after a period of activity or threat.

Parsimony When applied to research, an economical explanation that does not go beyond the available data.

Partial reinforcement In operant conditioning, a schedule in which a reinforcer is given only after some responses.

Partial report technique A method devised by Sperling to measure iconic memory. Participants had to report only a designated part of the array before them.

Participant observation Observation in which the researchers become a part of the group which is being observed.

Pavlovian inhibition theory Theory, based upon classical conditioning, developed by Mackworth and used to explain performance decrement.

Peer tutoring A learning situation where a child (the tutee) is tutored through the learning of a task by another child (the tutor) who is slightly more proficient at the task than the first child.

Perceived self Rogers's term for the individual's own view of what he or she is like, arrived at through life experiences and through feedback from other people.

Perception The psychological process whereby the brain makes sense of information coming through the senses.

Perceptual constancy The way in which objects are perceived and recognized as unchanging even though information from the senses changes.

Perceptual defence A predisposition not to perceive something because of unpleasant emotional overtones.

Perceptual hypothesis Gregory's suggestion that data from the senses results in a hypothesis being set up which is then tested through experience.

Performance decrement The amount of worsening of performance on a vigilance task relative to the duration of a task.

Peripheral attention Other aspects of the environment that are not currently the object of focal attention

Peripheral filtering Limitations in the sensitivity of the senses so that an animal may select those stimuli to which it must respond and pass over other stimuli.

Peripheral nervous system (PNS) The spinal and cranial nerves radiating from the CNS to the rest of the body. The PNS is subdivided into the somatic nervous system (SNS) and the autonomic nervous system (ANS).

Persistent vegetative state (PVS) A term used to describe an individual who, following a head injury, anoxia or other trauma, exists in a coma-like state, showing no visible signs of consciousness.

Personal construct A term used by George Kelly to describe an individual's unique perceptions, or 'constructs', through which he or she makes sense of the world.

Perspective taking The ability to understand a problem or situation from someone else's point of view.

Persuasion The act of inducing other people to believe something or perform a particular act.

Pertinence A model of attention proposed by Deutsch and Deutsch where messages are screened for their relevance to the individual just before the output stage.

Phenotype Characteristics, behavioural and physical, inherited by an individual which are openly displayed by that individual.

Phenylketonuria (PKU) A disease caused by a pair of defective recessive genes which leads to the disruption of metabolic processes. It is treatable, but if left untreated, can lead to mental impairment.

Pheromones Chemicals released through sweat, urine or the excretions of specialized glands. In animals they are primary signals for attracting mates. Their importance in humans is uncertain.

Phi phenomenon The perception of movement which results from presenting two separate objects (or lights) in quick succession.

Phonemes The basic sounds that are combined to form words.

Phonemic awareness An awareness of the individual sounds contained in words.

Photoreceptors Light-sensitive receptor cells in the retina of the eye.

Phylogenetic adaptation The adaptation of a species over a period of time by a process of natural selection.

Phylogenetic scale The point to which a particular species has evolved is represented by its position on the phylogenetic scale.

Physiological psychologists Those who study the links between psychological behaviour and physiological make-up.

Physiological reductionism Explanations of behaviour are given in terms of the functions of the nervous system or biochemical processes.

Pie chart A means of illustrating proportions of scores (or of sales or any other commodity) involving dividing a circular 'pie' into proportionate segments.

Pinna External part of the ear.

Pitch The frequency of sound waves.

Pituitary gland The 'master gland', so called because it releases hormones which direct the activity of many other glands.

Placebo A form of 'mock' treatment, for example an inactive substance such as a sugar pill, which, unknown to the patient, is not expected to have a direct effect upon a disorder.

Plasticity The ability of the brain when damage occurs (usually only in young children) to take over the functions of damaged areas.

Play therapy Therapy which draws on the principles of psychoanalysis and uses play situations to treat children who are suffering emotional problems.

Play with rules The third of Piaget's stages of play activity (concrete and formal operations) where the child begins to play increasingly complex games with rules.

Polyandry The mating of one female with several males.

Polygamy Any form of multiple mating, which includes both polyandry and polygyny.

Polygyny threshold model A model of mating behaviour, described by Verner and Wilson, in which the need for the male to care for the brood is related to the desirability for the male to establish several broods and so pass on his genes to more offspring.

Polygyny The mating of one male with several females.

Population The group from which a sample is drawn. For statistical purposes this is likely to be some numerical aspect of what is under investigation.

Positive reinforcement In operant conditioning, the process whereby a response is made more likely by being

following by a desirable stimulus (a positive reinforcer).

Postconventional morality (principled) Kohlberg's final level of moral reasoning, where values are dominated by principles of equality, justice and individual rights.

Postdecisional dissonance Dissonance which arises after a person has made a decision. It may be reduced by enhancing the positive aspects of the decision taken.

Post-Freudians Psychodynamic theorists who subscribe to many of Freud's original ideas, but who have modified aspects of psychoanalytic theory and practice.

Post-traumatic stress disorder A pattern of symptoms which often occur after a traumatic event such as witnessing or being involved in a serious accident or being the victim of a violent crime.

Prägnanz Gestalt principle that the brain attempts to perceive objects in the 'best', most meaningful, way.

Pragmatics In relation to language, how it is used in different social contexts.

Preattentive processing Where a whole array is scanned and processed at once.

Precocial young Offspring of a species which are able to move around and fend for themselves very early in life. These include pheasants, swans and ducks.

Preconscious Part of the mind which contains thoughts and memories which may not be conscious at a given time but which are accessible to us.

Preconventional morality The first level of moral reasoning proposed by Kohlberg. Rules are kept so that punishment is avoided and judgments are dominated by what is favourable to oneself.

Predictive validity The extent to which a test is capable of predicting future outcomes. A test of aptitude for typing is valid if it accurately predicts future typing ability.

Preference technique Technique used by Fantz to assess neonate perception based upon the preference an infant has for one stimulus over another.

Prelinguistic knowledge The ability of young children to communicate and understand the language of others before they are capable of using language themselves.

Primary cues (to depth perception) Those cues (such as convergence and accommodation) which depend upon physiological processes of vision.

Priming The process by which emotional feelings (e.g. anger or sympathy)

make thoughts about aggressive (or prosocial) behaviour more accessible.

Principle of antithesis Darwin's description of the opposed postures adopted by members of the same species signifying threat or appeasement. A threat posture by one individual may trigger an appeasement posture from another.

Privation The lack of something which had never been experienced; in attachment theory, the lack of opportunity to form an attachment bond.

Proactive interference Situation in which previously learned material interferes with the ability to memorize new material.

Probability The likelihood of an event (or events) occurring. Most often used in relation to the likelihood of a particular set of data having occurred by chance alone.

Problem isomorphs Sets of problems with the same structures and solutions but with different details and contexts.

Problem space Consists of all the possible solutions of which a problem solver is aware.

Problem-focused coping An attempt to reduce a stressful situation by trying to understand better its causes and to find possible courses of action.

Processing strategies Explanations for perceived illusions which lay emphasis on the way in which information is processed in the brain.

Productivity The ability of a language user to generate an infinite number of novel utterances.

Progesterone A female sex hormone.

Programmed learning A method of instruction based on the principles of operant conditioning. Individuals work through organized learning material at their own pace and receive feedback on their progress at regular intervals.

Project Headstart A programme in the USA which aims to provide enriched learning experiences for preschool children from deprived backgrounds.

Projective techniques Tests that contain ambiguous stimuli to which individuals will respond by 'projecting' their own meaning. Responses are interpeted and can lead to an assessment of an individual's personality.

Promiscuity Polygamous relationships where there is no pair bond.

Propaganda The communication of a point of view with the aim of persuading people to adopt this view as their own.

Prosocial behaviour Behaviour that is concerned with helping, kindness and generosity towards others.

Prosopagnosis A state in which an individual cannot recognize faces, usually because of brain damage.

Prospective memory Memory for events scheduled to occur in the future.

Prototype models Theory of pattern recognition which hypothesizes 'prototypes' of objects stored in the memory which are compared with objects encountered.

Prototype A fairly fuzzy image we make of people or objects whom we identify as belonging to a particular category.

Psychiatrist A medical doctor who specializes in the study and treatment of mental disorders.

Psychiatry Study and practice dealing with mental and nervous disorders, usually carried out by medical doctors who specialize in mental illness.

Psychoactive drugs Drugs which may alter mood or thought processes.

Psychoanalysis as a therapy A treatment, originally used by Freud, which uses techniques designed to explore the unconscious mind.

Psychoanalytic theory Sigmund Freud's theory of personality, which relied on the study of the unconscious mind.

Psychoanalytic therapy Treatment for mental disorder based on the psychoanalytic theory of Freud. The root of many neurotic problems is seen as lying in the repressed contents of the unconscious mind.

Psychodynamic approach An approach that draws on Freud's psychoanalytic theory and which focuses on the role of motivation and past experiences in the development of personality.

Psychoimmunology The study of mental states and their effect on health.

Psychopathic (sociopathic) personality A disorder in which the individual does not lose touch with reality but habitually behaves in ways which endanger the well-being of others.

Psychopathology The scientific study of mental disorder.

Psychosexual stages In Freud's theory, the stages that children pass through on their way to emotional maturity. At each stage, satisfaction is gained as the libido is directed towards a particular part of the body.

Psychosis A relatively vague term to describe mental disorder which involves the whole of the personality and where an individual loses touch with reality. A term no longer used in ICD 10.

Psychosocial stages Erikson's term for the stages of personality development through which an individual passes during life.

Psychosurgery The removal of small amounts of brain tissue in specific locations in order to reduce abnormal behaviours such as severe obsessions or (controversially) extreme aggression.

Psychotherapy Treatments for mental disorder which use psychological methods, such as behavioural therapies or psychoanalysis, rather than medical methods, such as the prescribing of drugs.

Psywar The psychology of war.

Puberty The period of time during which the reproductive processes mature and secondary sex characteristics develop.

Pumps Stimuli which act over a long period to alter receptivity to stimuli and arousal levels in an animal. They may be hormonal or behavioural.

Punishment The delivery of an undesirable stimulus following a response. Punishment weakens the response and makes it less likely to recur.

Pure research Research carried out primarily for its own sake, to increase knowledge and understanding.

Qualitative analysis Method of dealing with research data which depends more upon description than upon numerical measurement.

Qualitative data Data in a research report which is not based upon measurement, but upon impressions formed and reactions made to the research procedures. It might include introspections from participants and observations of reactions of participants.

Qualitative research Research that involves collecting nonnumerical data.

Quantitative analysis Methods of dealing with research data which depends wholly or in large measure upon numerical analysis.

Quantitative research An approach that involves measurement and analyses in a numerical form.

Quasi-experiment A natural experiment where the independent variable is not manipulated deliberately by an experimenter but where naturally occurring changes are used and are built into the design of the experiment.

Quota sample A sample which is drawn from a population in the following way. Characteristics important to the researcher are identified. Individuals who possess these characteristics are selected proportionately to the whole population.

Quotient A standard score which assumes a mean of 100 and a standard deviation of 15.

Random error Those chance variations or biases which will inevitably occur when any group of individuals are investigated, which cannot be allowed for in the design of a study.

Random sample A sample which is drawn from a population in such a way that every member of that population has an equal chance of being included.

Randomization An alternative to counterbalancing used to mitigate order, practice and fatigue effects. The conditions are randomly presented. It is useful when there are several conditions or when the effects of several alternative extraneous variables need to be taken into account.

Range A measure of dispersion represented by the difference between the lowest and the highest scores.

Ranked scores Scores which have been arranged in a rank order.

Ratio data Data which besides the equal intervals of measurement of interval data incorporates a true zero point.

Rational thinking Logical and rational thought direct towards a purpose.

Raw scores Scores which are listed as they are drawn from a practical exercise without analysis.

Reactance In relation to persuasion, the technique of letting people know that they are being persuaded so that they can react against it.

Receiver operating characteristic Characteristic of individual participants related to their truthfulness and accuracy in reporting what they see.

Recessive gene A gene which displays the characteristics it determines only when both of a pair of alleles possess it.

Reciprocal altruism An apparently altruistic act performed in the expectation that at some time in the future someone else will do the same for oneself.

Reciprocity Relates to the idea that feelings we have for others depend to an extent on the feelings which they express for us.

Recognition of objects The process by which the information received from the senses is interpreted so that objects are recognized.

Recovery Movement A term used to describe a number of approaches and therapies that share similar, humanistically oriented, assumptions. It is illustrated by the '12 steps' approach of Alcoholics Anonymous.

Reductionism A belief that all psychological phenomena can be explained by investigating them at a simpler, more basic, level.

References A list of sources placed at the end of a research report or other academic work to indicate from where the material referred to has been taken.

Refutability The possibility of being able to show that something is unlikely to be true.

Reification The process whereby theoretical concepts may be perceived by people as real entities.

Reinforcement The process whereby a reinforcer increases the likelihood of a response.

Reinforcement/affect theory An application of learning theory to attractions between people. It suggests that we like people who reward us and dislike those who punish us.

Reinforcer In operant conditioning, a stimulus following a response, which makes that response more likely to recur.

Related (repeated) measures design An experimental design where there is a relationship between the participant tested under one condition and another (others). Most commonly the same participants are tested under each condition (repeated measures).

Relative deprivation Feelings of deprivation which are related to external factors such as expectations or perceptions of what others may have.

Relative refractory period A very short period after a neuron has fired during which the threshold of response is increased.

Relative stability Whether the rank order of participants' scores on a characteristic such as personality remain the same relative to each other over a period of time.

Releasers Term used by Lorenz for those stimuli in the environment (sounds, scents and colours) which have evolved to elicit responses in animals.

Reliability (1) In relation to psychometric tests, that the items within them should be consistent with each other and that the test should give consistent results over time. (2) In relation to the diagnosis of mental disorder, this term generally relates to the question of whether psychiatrists are consistent with each other in reaching a diagnosis.

REM (rapid eye movement) sleep Periods of sleep during which the eyes move rapidly and dreaming usually occurs. During REM sleep, motor neurons are inhibited and the limbs are effectively paralysed.

Repertory grid A technique used by George Kelly to identify an individual's personal constructs, usually in terms of their relationships with other people in their lives.

Repisodic memory Term used by Neisser for inaccurate memorization of events, either events which never happened or events similar to schemata already developed.

Replicability The possibility of something being repeated in exactly the same way.

Representative sample A sample which accurately reflects characteristics of the population from which it is drawn.

Response (R) Behaviour that occurs as a reaction to a stimulus and which can be measured.

Restricted code of language Code of language used, according to Bernstein, by working-class children. It is syntactically crude, grammatically simple, restricted in vocabulary and context bound.

Reticular formation Collection of nerve fibres at the base of the brain which moderate arousal levels in relation to incoming sensory stimulation.

Retina A layer of light-sensitive cells at the back of the eye which receives light waves and converts them to electrical pulses for transmission to the brain.

Retinal disparity A binocular cue to the perception of depth. Each eye has a slightly different view of an object providing a cue as to how far the object is away from an observer.

Retroactive interference Interference with earlier memory caused by subsequent learning.

Retrograde amnesia Inability to recall events before a head injury or other trauma while short-term memory remains intact.

Retrospective memory Memory for events in the past.

Reversibility The ability to mentally reverse thought processes and arrive back at the original starting point.

Risky shift phenomenon A term used for the tendency for groups to take risky decisions; coined before it was realized that polarization might result in more conservative decisions.

Ritualization Behavioural responses which have no specific function except to serve as a signal.

Ritualized aggression A stereo-typical display of aggression, serving to communicate a message, but stopping short of actual injury.

Rods Photoreceptors in the retina, sensitive to dim lighting, but not sensitive to colour.

Role A part or parts played by an individual which involve obligations towards and expectations from another individual (the role partner).

Role differentiation The emergence in a group of particular roles assigned or adopted by individual members of the group.

Role diffusion Erikson's term to describe the sense of confusion about the self that is often experienced by adolescents who have failed to achieve a secure ego identity.

Rule set A fixation of mind relating to the parameters or rules within which a problem must be solved.

Salience Feature of particular attributes which makes them prominent so as to attract immediate attention.

Sample A smaller group drawn from a population.

Sampling bias That bias which arises from faults in the assembling of samples from the population(s) which are being investigated.

Scaffolding The supportive framework provided by caregivers and within which a child can learn and develop.

Scattergram A means of plotting graphically the relationship between two variables. Pairs of variables are represented one on the horizontal axis, the other on the vertical axis. Plots are made where the values of each of the pairs of variables intersect and the resulting pattern indicates the relationship between the two variables.

Scene analysis A computer simulation model of pattern recognition. An example is Biederman's recognition by components model.

Schedules of reinforcement In operant conditioning, the varying conditions that determine when a response will be followed by a reinforcer.

Schema Piaget's term for an individual's internal representation, a kind of cognitive plan, of some specific physical or mental ability: for example, grasping an object or understanding how to do multiplication.

Schemata Social cognation cognitive processes and structures that influence and are influenced by social behaviour.

Schematic (aschematic) Relates to the extent to which self-schemata concerning certain characteristics (e.g. masculinity/femininity) have been developed. A schematic person has well-developed self-schemata; an aschematic person does not.

Schizophrenia A condition in which the individual experiences a split from reality in the form of, for example, delusions or hallucinations. It takes many different forms and may be one disorder or a number of different ones.

Schizophrenogenic family A family which is characterized by high levels of conflict and poor communication, creating an atmosphere which may promote the development of schizophrenia.

Schools of psychology Groupings of psychologists who shared common beliefs about human functioning and subscribed to similar methods of study.

Script A framework or structure in the mind formed through experience, relating to behaviour in a particular set of circumstances and brought into play when those circumstances recur.

Secondary cues (to depth perception) Those cues which are in the visual field rather than in the physiological processes of vision.

Secondary dispositions Allport's term for a person's usual ways of behaving in particular situations.

Secondary reinforcer In operant conditioning, a stimulus which becomes reinforcing because of its association with primary reinforcers such as food or water, which have direct biological significance.

Selective exposure In cases of postdecisional dissonance a person may reduce dissonance by seeking out evidence which supports the decision taken.

Self-affirmation The response to a threat to a person's self-concept as a result of cognitive dissonance, involving enhancing some aspect of the self-concept.

Self-categorization The process described by Abrams and Hogg by which people identify with a group in order to maintain and enhance their self-concept.

Self-concept A general sense of who and what one is, including feelings of self-worth.

Self-esteem That part of the self which is concerned with how we evaluate ourselves as people.

Self-evaluation The process through which an individual makes a judgment about his or her own attitudes and behaviour.

Self-schemata Schemata which relate to an individual's concept of self.

Self-socialization In relation to gender role, the process whereby as children develop they become increasingly aware of behaviour associated with both

sexes and structure their own behaviour appropriately.

Semantic differential A method of measuring the affective component of attitudes devised by Osgood.

Semantic memory The storage of information about permanent items of knowledge, usually involving language.

Semantics The meaning of words.

Senescence The period of life when the degenerative processes of ageing set in.

Sensation The stimulation of a sense organ such as the eye or the ear which is necessary for perception to occur.

Sensitive period Period after hatching (birth) during which imprinting or other forms of attachment are most likely to occur. A modification of Lorenz's critical period.

Sentiency Capability of 'sensing', feeling and having consciousness.

Separation anxiety The protest or distress exhibited by a child from about the age of eight months when separated from an attachment figure.

Serial polygyny A mating system where a male mates with several females, one at a time.

Serial processing Completing one processing operation before commencing another.

Seriation The ability to arrange things in order.

Set The predisposition of an individual towards certain cognitions. It manifests itself in perception and also in thinking.

Set point theory In relation to motivation for eating, the proposal that people will eat to maintain their optimum body weight.

Sex The term used to denote biological/genital aspects of being male or female.

Sexual bimaturism The maturation of males and females of a particular species at different ages.

Sexual dimorphism Differences in size and/or coloration between males and females of a species.

Shallow processing Processing of material to be memorized at a structural rather than a semantic level (with reference to its sound or appearance).

Short-term memory Memory for material required only on a short-term basis (for instance, memory of a telephone number retained long enough to dial it).

Sign stimuli Signals to which an animal must respond. For instance, a male stickleback is programmed genetically to respond to the swollen underbelly of a female.

Signal detection theory A theory which aims to assess the degree to which an

individual participant will report what he or she sees accurately and truthfully.

Significance Refers to the confidence a researcher has that the results he or she has obtained did not occur through chance. This is usually gained by conducting a statistical test of significance to assess the probability that the results occurred by chance.

Signs Indicators of an illness based on the outcome of such things as X-rays, physical examination, psychological tests, observation of the patient's behaviour, etc.

Simultaneous scanning A strategy used in problem-solving; similar to successive scanning but all the attributes are altered at once when there is a negative response.

Single blind technique An experimental technique where participants remain unaware of the true aims of the experiment in which they are participating, thus mitigating the effects of demand characteristics.

Single participant design An experimental design where there is just one participant tested under two or more conditions. For statistical purposes it is treated as an independent measures design.

Single-trait theories of personality Theories which focus on one aspect of the personality, rather than attempting to convey a picture of the whole personality.

Situational specificity In relation to personality, the view that people's characteristics are not necessarily fixed and may vary depending on the situation in which they find themselves.

Situationism In relation to personality theory, the view of Mischel and others that characteristics within people (traits) are less important than the situations in which they find themselves.

Size constancy scaling A perceptual process in which knowledge of the size of objects may modify the apparent retinal size of them at different distances. An object at a distance may thus appear larger than its retinal size.

Skewed distribution A frequency distribution that is not 'normal'. It may be positively skewed, where the scores are misleadingly low, or negatively skewed, where the scores are abnormally high.

'Slice of life' school An approach that encourages the study of large sections of behaviour in order to obtain a more complete understanding.

Social attachment A bond of affection directed by a child towards a specific individual.

Social cognition Cognitive processes and structures that influence and are influenced by social behaviour and also the way social situations may influence out thinking.

Social dominance hierarchy Pecking orders which are found among some animals (flocks of hens, for instance, or among red deer herds). There is a dominant animal, to whom the others defer, a second who is able to displace all but the first and then a third and so on.

Social drift theory A proposal that individuals who develop schizophrenia may have drifted into the lowest socio-economic group as a result of their schizophrenia.

Social ethology Attempts made to understand animal behaviour in the context of their social environment.

Social exchange Relates to the theory put forward by Clark that people assess the benefits received from a relationship and balance that against the costs involved, and also against the costs and benefits of alternatives.

Social identity The groups to which we belong represent part of our self-concept. This is social identity and it contributes to self-esteem.

Social learning theory A theory derived from traditional learning theory. It emphasizes the role of observational learning in development and that behaviour is mediated by cognitive variables.

Social loafing The tendency to offload responsibilities onto others.

Social Readjustment Rating Scale (SRRS) A scale developed by Holmes and Rahe (1967) to measure the levels of stress associated with particular life events.

Social referencing The process of gauging another person's emotional response to an ambiguous or uncomfortable situation before responding oneself.

Social representation The construction and transmission to its members by an in-group of its own interpretations of objects, people and events.

Social smiling The voluntary smiles that an infant starts to produce around four to six weeks old, usually prompted by an overture from an adult.

Social stereotype theory Reflection of the whole range of information we possess about a group of people, encapsulating our impression of their characteristics.

Socialization The process by which people learn the ways of a given society or social group, so that they can function within it.

Socially sensitive research Studies in which there are potential social consequences for the participants or the class of individuals represented by the research.

Societies Stable relationships where animals or humans live together in the same group for prolonged periods.

Sociobiology A term coined by Edward Wilson to refer to attempts to explain social behaviour in terms of evolutionary factors.

Socioemotional leadership A style of leadership which places emphasis upon the relationships between the members of a group.

Sociogenic hypothesis A term used to describe the possibility that low socio-economic status makes the development of schizophrenia more likely.

Sociological view of adolescence This approach takes the view that 'storm and stress' during adolescence is caused mainly by external factors such as socialization, role changes, peer pressure, environmental and social changes, and the mass media.

Soft determinism A term used by William James to describe a compromise between free will and determinism. Behaviour is determined by the environment, but there is an element of freedom where people's actions are in line with their wishes.

Somatic nervous system (SNS) A branch of the peripheral nervous system (PNS) which receives sensory information from the external world and carries messages to and from the muscles controlling the skeleton.

Somatic treatments Physical treatments designed to restore a balance in the body (soma) in order to improve psychological functioning.

Sound waves Molecules of air which temporarily change air pressure in the ear and which are recognized by the auditory system as sound.

'Speciesism' Discrimination and exploitation based upon differences between species.

Species-specific behaviour Instinctive behaviour which is found only in a particular species.

'Split brain' patients People who have undergone commisurotomy, an operation that severs the corpus collusum, so that the two hemispheres of the brain are no longer connected.

Spontaneous recovery In classical conditioning, the reappearance of the conditioned response (CR) when the conditioned stimulus (CS) is presented some time after extinction has occurred.

Spontaneous remission The improvement of a disorder without any treatment having been given.

Spreading activation model A model of storage in long-term memory. Items to be remembered are seen as stored in clusters. The strength and distance of interconnecting links between clusters determines speed of access to recalled material.

Standard deviation A measure of dispersion which assesses the average distance of all the scores around the mean.

Standard error of the mean The fluctuation which might occur in the means from a series of samples drawn from a given population. As the samples become larger so the standard error of the means will become smaller (the means will be closer to the population mean).

Standard scores Scores which result from standardization of test results. They are usually related to the mean and standard deviation of the scores. Examples include z scores and quotients.

Standardization In relation to psychometric tests, the process of 'trying out' the test on a representative sample of the population for whom it is intended, and establishing norms (average scores).

Standardized instructions Instructions to be given to participants which are standardized at the design stage of an experiment to avoid bias which might arise from different instructions being given to some participants as compared to others.

Stapes A bony structure (ossicle) in the ear which transmits vibrations from the incus to the oval window.

State-dependent memory Suggests that we are more likely to remember information if we recall it in the same state in which it was learned in the first place.

Statistical inference Inferences which are made as a result of statistical analysis of data collected from research. This can include inference from statistical tests of significance.

Stimulus (S) A situation, event, object or other factor which may influence behaviour.

Stimulus–response (S-R) psychology An approach concerned with studying the stimuli that elicit behavioural responses and the rewards and punishments that may influence these responses.

Strange Situation, the A procedure developed and used by Ainsworth for observing and assessing the attachment behaviour babies display towards their mothers.

Stranger anxiety (wariness) The wariness or distress which a child displays from about eight months of age when faced with a strange adult.

Stratified sampling Random samples are drawn from each stratum or subgroup within a population proportionately to the whole population to form a stratified sample representative of the parent population.

Stress An unpleasant psychological or physiological state produced in response to a stressor.

Stress management A term used to describe a number of psychological techniques which are used to help people to reduce stress: for example, time-management, relaxation, biofeedback, cognitive restructuring (changing the way one thinks about the situation).

Stressor The situation, individual or object which can cause a state of stress in a person.

Stroop phenomenon A situation where there is incompatibility between the content of material presented to an individual and the form in which it is presented, which increases the difficulty of making a response to it: for example, where the colour of the print is at odds with the information presented by that print.

Structural effects Explanations for illusions which emphasize optical features in the eye and neural effects in eye and brain.

Structuralism A school of psychology, founded by Wundt, which focused on the scientific study of conscious experience.

Subvocal speech The view of thinking taken by Watson and other behaviourists that thought was speech which was not vocalized.

Successive scanning A strategy for concept formation described by Bruner and his colleagues. It involves starting with a hypothesis and testing responses to all items which are relevant to that hypothesis. When there is a negative response the hypothesis is changed, one attribute at a time.

Superego In Freud's theory, the moral aspect of the personality made up of the ego-ideal (a sense of what is right and proper) and the conscience (a sense of what is wrong and unacceptable).

Supranormal stimuli Exaggerated stimuli which are more effective than normal stimuli in eliciting a response.

Survey method A method of research where a large number of participants, forming a representative sample of the population, is questioned, either orally through interview or through written questionnaires.

Symbolic play The second of Piaget's stages of play activity (preoperational) where a child begins to use fantasy in play and uses objects to stand for something different.

Symbolic racism A deep-seated form of racism, developed as a result of upbringing, expressed in socially acceptable ways.

Symbolic representation According to Bruner, thinking which involves the representation of the world through symbols such as language or number.

Sympathetic division of the automatic nervous system (ANS) Mobilizes the body's resources when there is a need to be active, for example in threatening situations.

Symptom substitution The replacement of one symptom with another which may be related to an earlier problem that was not resolved.

Symptoms A patient's description of pains, thoughts, feelings or perceptions of problems.

Synapse The small gap (referred to as the synaptic cleft) which exists between the axon of one neuron and the dendrites of the next.

Syntax The grammatical rules that determine how words are combined in sentences.

Systematic desensitization A technique used in behaviour therapy to eliminate phobias by gradually introducing the object of the phobia whilst pairing it with something pleasant.

Systematic error Bias affecting one condition systematically more than another. It can be eliminated by careful controls in the design of research.

Task-oriented leadership A style of leadership, described by Bales, where the leader is more concerned with the attainment of group goals than with relationships between members of the group.

Temperament Basic behavioural characteristics: for example, sociability, responsiveness, distractibility, which are widely believed to be innate: that is, inborn and not resulting from environmental influences.

Template matching Theory of pattern recognition which hypothesizes templates stored in memory against which images may be matched.

Test of significance A test used to assess the level of probability that data obtained occurred by chance.

Theoretical approach Basic assumptions made about the nature of human beings and the theories and research methods needed to study them.

Theory A general system for explaining the underlying principles of a phenomenon.

Theory of mind ('mindreading' skills) A capacity to appreciate what other people are thinking and feeling, which is thought to develop at around the age of three.

Theory of parental investment Trivers' account of the relationship between the investment a parent makes towards the upbringing of offspring and reproductive success.

Threat/appeasement postures Postures adopted by animals to indicate either a threat to another animal or an appeasement response to that threat.

Threshold of sensation The minimum stimulation of a sense organ that can be detected by the individual.

Timbre The nature of sound: that is, the degree of mixing of pure sound frequencies.

Token economy A version of behaviour modification where reinforcements are given not in the form of an immediate reward but in the form of tokens, which can be exchanged later for a reward of the individual's choice.

Tokenism The token acknowledgment of sexism or racism by means of a trivial gesture so that more meaningful steps may be written off as unnecessary.

Top-down processing Cognitive processing which takes account, first, of the holistic context of an operation, then deals with the detail of it.

Tourette's syndrome A condition that involves a tic (involuntary movement), which is often accompanied by spitting or shouting.

Traditional transmission A characteristic of language that it is possible to transfer the skills involved from one generation to the next.

'Traditional' view of adolescence Adolescence is seen as a time when stress and turmoil are inevitable. This view is prevalent among psychoanalytic theorists, who see internal factors such as the intensity of inner drives and sexual feelings as a causal factor.

Trait A term used to describe stable and enduring personality characteristics such as 'liveliness' or 'aggressiveness'.

Transactional analysis A therapeutic process where individuals are encouraged to acknowledge three aspects of their personality: parent, adult, child, and to role-play interactions with other people using these three personality states.

Transactive memory Relates to the situation in a close relationship where two partners in a relationship may jointly has greater memory than either have individually.

Transference During the course of psychoanalysis, the client transfers to the therapist emotions previously directed towards significant others: for example, the parents.

Triarchic theory of intelligence Sternberg's theory which sees intelligence as governed by three systems: componential, contextual, experiential.

Trichromatic theory In relation to the visual system, the proposal by Helmholtz (1885) that there are three types of cone, each being sensitive to light of a particular wavelength, red, green or blue.

Trigger Behaviour which produces an immediate and specific response. For instance, a pregnant female animal licking and grooming her nipples thereby encourages mammary gland growth.

Two-factor theory of emotion Schachter's theory which proposes that both physiological processes and cognitive appraisal are implicated in the experience of emotions.

Two-tailed hypothesis A hypothesis which is nondirectional – one which does not specify the way any differences or relationship found in the results of a test will go.

Tympanic membrane Known as the ear drum, a structure in the ear which vibrates with sound waves and transmits them to ossicles behind it.

Type In relation to personality, a term used to classify people into an 'all or none' category, for example 'extravert'.

Type A personality A pattern of personality characteristics, for example competitiveness, impatience, time-urgency, aggressiveness, which have been linked in the USA with the incidence of heart disease.

Type I error An error which is the result of rejecting the null hypothesis when there is in reality no real difference (or similarity) between the conditions in the experiment (or correlational study).

Type II error An error which is the result of retaining the null hypothesis when in reality there is a real difference (or similarity) between the conditions in an experiment (or correlational study).

Ultimate attribution bias In-group members attribute desirable behaviours to their own internal disposition; outgroups' desirable behaviour is attributed to external circumstances.

Ultradian rhythms Body rhythms which promote functions which occur more than once a day: for example, the hunger cycle.

Unconditional positive regard Relates to Rogers's contention that individuals need the esteem of others without conditions attached.

Unconscious mind A 'hidden' part of the mind harbouring repressed memories that may influence the conscious mind.

Uplifts The more positive things which may give us a good 'feel' to the day, for example getting on well with one's children, receiving an unexpected gift, completing a task.

Vacuum activity Fixed action patterns (FAPs) that occur even when there is no trigger stimulus.

Validity (1) In relation to psychometric tests, that they are testing what they claim to be testing: for example, 'intelligence' or 'personality'. (2) In relation to the diagnosis of mental disorder, this term addresses the issue of whether a cluster of symptoms really do represent a named disorder.

Variant cognitive structures Piaget's term for cognitive structures such as schemas and operations which change as a child grows older.

Variation ratio A measure of dispersion obtained by assessing the proportion of scores which are not modal. It is useful in assessing how representative the mode of a particular set of scores is as a measure of central tendency.

Ventromedial hypothalamus An area of the brain which contains receptors for female hormones and which is implicated in female sexual behaviour.

Vicarious Experiencing something as though it were happening to oneself.

Visual acuity The ability to see the details of a stimulus.

Visual cliff Apparatus devised by Gibson and Walk to test the extent to which babies and small animals are able to perceive depth.

Visuospatial scratchpad An element in Baddeley's model of working memory that allows for visual and spatial rehearsal.

Weber's law A law which governs the relationship between jnd (just noticeable difference) and the background intensity of a stimulus against which a change occurs. The difference in intensity divided by the background intensity is equal to a constant (K) which is different for each sense modality.

Wish fulfilment The expression, often through dreams, of a need or desire disguised in a symbolic form.

Working hypothesis A hypothesis relating to a concept in Levine's studies. Responses would be based upon this. Feedback might either support it or not. While there remained support for it the hypothesis need not be altered.

Working memory model Baddeley's memory model which included a primary acoustic store, an articulatory loop and a visuospatial scratchpad.

Yerkes–Dodson Law A law which relates performance on any of a variety of tasks to arousal level. This is a curvilinear relationship with optimum performance occurring at intermediate arousal levels.

z score A test score expressed as a decimal fraction of the standard deviation above or below the mean of a set of scores. For example, where the mean is 50 and the standard deviation 10 a score of 45 would be represented by a z score of −0.5.

Zone of proximal development (ZPD) Vygotsky's term to describe the area between a child's actual developmental level and the potential level which could be achieved with the help of adults or more experienced peers.

Zygote The union of a single germ cell from the mother (ovum) with a single germ cell from the father (sperm).

Bibliography

Abdalla, I.A. (1991). Social support and gender responses to job stress in Arab culture. *Journal of Social Behaviour and Personality, 6* (7), 273–88.

Abelson, R.P. (1981). Psychological status of the script concept. *American Psychologist, 36,* 715–29.

Abrams, D. and Hogg, M. (1990a). *Social Identity Theory: Constructive and Critical Advances.* London: Harvester Wheatsheaf.

Abrams, D. and Hogg, M. (1990b). Social identification, self categorisation and social influence. *European Review of Social Psychology, 1,* 195–228.

Abrams, R. (1975). What's new in convulsive therapy? In S. Arieti and G. Chrzanowski (eds), *New Dimensions in Psychiatry.* New York: Wiley.

Achenbach, T.M. (1982). *Developmental Psychopathology,* 2nd edn. New York: Wiley.

Achenbach, T.M. and Edelbrock, C.S. (1981). Behavioural problems and competencies reported by parents of normal and disturbed children aged 4 through 16. *Monographs of the Society for Research in Child Development, 46* (1), 188.

Adams, A. (1992). *Bullying at Work.* London: Virago Press.

Adams, D.B. (1986). Ventomedial tegmental lesions abolish offense without disturbing predation or defense. *Physiology and Behavior, 38,* 165–8.

Adams, G.R., Gullotta, T.P. and Markstrom-Adams, C. (1994). *Adolescent Life Experiences,* 3rd edn. Pacific Grove, CA: Brooks/Cole.

Adams, J. (1965). Inequity in social exchange. In L. Berkowitz (ed.), *Advances in Experimental Social Psychology,* vol. 2. New York: Academic Press.

Aderman, D. and Berkowitz, L. (1983). Self concern and the unwillingness to be helpful. *Social Psychology Quarterly, 46,* 293–301.

Adler, N. T. (1974). The behavioural control of reproductive behaviour. In W. Montague (ed.), *Reproductive Behaviour.* New York: Plenum Publishing Company.

Adorno, T.W., Frenkel-Brunswik, E., Levinson, D. and Sanford, N. (1950). *The Authoritarian Personality,* New York: Harper.

Agras, S., Sylvester, D. and Oliveau, D. (1969). The epidemiology of common fears and phobias. unpublished manuscript.

Ainsworth, M.D.S. (1967). *Infancy in Uganda: Infant Care and the Growth of Love.* Baltimore, MD: Johns Hopkins University Press.

Ainsworth, M.D.S. (1969). Object relations, dependency and attachment: a theoretical review of the infant–mother relationship. *Child Development, 40,* 969–1025.

Ainsworth, M.D.S. (1973). The development of infant–mother attachment. In B.M. Caldwell and H.N. Riccuiti (eds), *Review of Child Development Research,* vol. 3. Chicago: University of Chicago Press.

Ainsworth, M.D.S. (1989). Attachments beyond infancy. *American Psychologist, 44,* 709–16.

Ainsworth, M.D.S., Blehar, M.C., Waters, E. and Wall, S. (1978). *Patterns of Attachment: A Psychological Study of the Strange Situation.* Hillsdale, NJ: Erlbaum.

Ajzen, I. (1988). *Attitudes, Personality and Behaviour.* Milton Keynes: Open University Press.

Ajzen, I. (1989). Attitude structure and behaviour. In A.R. Pratkanis, S.J. Breckler and A.G. Greenwald (eds), *Attitude Structure and Function.* Hillsdale, NJ: Erlbaum.

Ajzen, I. and Fishbein, M. (1980). *Understanding Attitudes and Predicting Social Behaviour.* Englewood Cliffs, NJ: Prentice-Hall.

Alatalo, R.V., Lundberg, A. and Glynn, C. (1986). Female pied flycatchers choose territory quality not male characteristics. *Nature (London), 323,* 152–3.

Albert, D.J., Petrovic, D.M. and Walsh, M.L. (1989). Competitive experience activates testosterone-dependent social aggression towards unfamiliar males. *Physiology and Behavior, 45,* 225–8.

Allee, W.C. (1938). *The Social Life of Animals.* New York: Norton.

Allen, M.G. (1976). Twin studies of affective illness. *Archives of General Psychiatry, 33,* 1476–8.

Allport, D.A. (1955). *Becoming.* New Haven, CT: Yale University Press.

Allport, D.A, Antonis, B. and Reynolds, P. (1972). On the division of attention: a disproof of the single channel hypothesis. *Quarterly Journal of Experimental Psychology, 24,* 225–35.

Allport, G.W. (1935). Attitudes. In C.M. Murchison (ed.), *Handbook of Social Psychology.* Worcester, MA: Clark University Press.

Allport, G.W. (1937). *Personality: A Psychological Interpretation.* New York: Holt, Rinehart & Winston.

Allport, G.W. (1954). *The Nature of Prejudice.* Reading, MA: Addison-Wesley.

Allport, G.W. (1958). *The Nature of Prejudice,* 2nd edn. Garden City, NY: Anchor.

Allport, G.W. (1962). The general and unique in psychological science. *Journal of Personality, 30,* 405–21.

Allport, G.W. (1965). *Letters from Jenny.* New York: Harcourt Brace & World.

Allport, G.W. and Odbert, H.S. (1936). Trait names: a psycho-lexical study. *Psychological Monographs: General and Applied, 47* (whole no. 211).

Altman, I. and Chemers, M. (1980). *Culture and Environment.* Monterey, CA: Brookes-Cole.

Altmann, S.A. (1962). The social behavior of anthropoid primates: analysis of recent concepts. In E.L. Bliss (ed.), *Roots of Behavior.* New York: Harper & Brothers.

Alto, J.L. and Frankenberger, W. (1995). Effects of methylphenidate on academic achievement from first to second grade. *International Journal of Disability, Development and Education, 42* (3), 259–73.

Amato, P.R. (1983). Helping behaviour in urban and rural environments: field studies based on taxonomic organisation of helping episodes. *Journal of Personality and Social Psychology, 45,* 571–86.

American Psychiatric Association (1987). *Diagnostic and Statistical Manual of Mental Disorders*, 3rd edn revised. Washington, DC: American Psychiatric Association.

Amira, A. (1990). Family care in Greece. In A. Jamieson and R. Illsely (eds), *Contrasting European Policies for the Care of Older People*, Aldershot: Avebury.

Anand, B.K. and Brobeck, J.R. (1951). Hypothalamic control of food intake in rats and cats. *Yale Journal of Biology and Medicine, 24*, 123–40.

Anastasi, A. (1958). In R.M. Lerner (1986), *Concepts and Theories in Human Development*, 2nd edn. New York: Random House.

Anderson, C.A. (1989). Temperature and aggression: ubiquitous effects of heat on occurrence of human violence. *Psychological Bulletin, 106*, 74–96.

Anderson, C.A. and Anderson, D.C. (1984). Ambient temperature and violent crime: Tests of linear and curvilinear hypotheses. *Journal of Personality and Social Psychology, 46*, 91–7.

Anderson, C.A. and Sechler, E.S. (1986). Effects of explanation and counter-explanation on the development and use of social theories. *Journal of Personality and Social Psychology, 50*, 24–34.

Anderson, L.P. (1991). Acculturative stress: a theory of relevance to black Americans. *Clinical Psychology Review, 11*, 685–702.

Anderson, N.H. (1971). Integration theory and attitude change. *Psychological Review, 78*, 171–206.

Anderson, N.H. (1980). Integration theory applied to cognitive responses and attitudes. In R.E. Petty, T.M. Ostrom and T.C. Brock (eds), *Cognitive Responses in Persuasion*. New York: Erlbaum.

Andreeva, G. (1984). Cognitive processes in developing groups. In L.H. Strickland (ed.), *Directions in Soviet Social Psychology*. New York: Springer Verlag.

Andrew, R.J. (1985). The temporal structure of memory formation. *Perspectives in Ethology, 6*, 219–59.

Andrew, R.J. (ed.) (1991). *Neural and Behavioural Plasticity: The Use of the Domestic Chick as a Model*. Oxford: Oxford University Press.

Animals (Scientific Procedures) Act 1986. London: HMSO.

Antonucci, T.C. and Levitt, M.J. (1984). Early prediction of attachment security: a multivariate account. *Infant Behaviour and Development, 7*, 1–18.

Archer, D., Iritani, B., Kimes, B.B. and Barrios, M. (1983). Face-ism: five studies of sex differences in facial prominence. *Journal of Personality and Social Psychology, 45*, 725–35.

Archer, J. (1989). Childhood gender roles: structure and development. *The Psychologist: Bulletin of the British Psychological Society, 9*, 367–70.

Archer, J. and Lloyd, B. (1985). *Sex and Gender*. Cambridge: Cambridge University Press.

Argyle, M. and Henderson, M. (1985). The rules of friendship. *Journal of Social and Personal Relationships, 1*, 211–37.

Artmann, H., Grau, H., Adelman, M. and Schleiffer, R. (1985). Reversible and non-reversible enlargement of cerebrospinal fluid spaces in anorexia nervosa. *Neuroradiology, 27*, 103–12.

Asch, S.E. (1951). Effects of group pressure upon the modification and distortion of judgements. In H. Guetzkow (ed.), *Social Psychology*, 3rd edn, pp. 174–82. New York: Holt, Rinehart & Winston.

Asch, S.E. (1952). *Social Psychology*. Englewood Cliffs, NJ: Prentice-Hall.

Astington, J.W. (1994). *The Child's Discovery of the Mind*. London: Fontana.

Astington, J.W., Harris, P.L. and Olson, D.R. (1988). *Developing Theories of Mind*. Cambridge: Cambridge University Press.

Aston-Jones, G. and Bloom, F.E. (1981). Activity of norepinephrine-containing locus coeruleus neurons in behaving rats anticipates fluctuations in the sleep–waking cycle. *Journal of Neuroscience, 1*, 876–86.

Atchley, R.C. (1977). *The Social Forces in Later Life*, 2nd edn. Belmont, CA: Wadsworth.

Atchley, R.C. (1991). *Social Forces and Aging: an Introduction to Social Gerontology*, 6th edn. Belmont, CA: Wadsworth.

Atkinson, J.W. and Feather, N.T. (1966). *A Theory of Achievement Motivation*. New York: Wiley.

Atkinson, R.C. and Raugh, M.R. (1975). An application of the mnemonic keyword method to the learning of a Russian vocabulary. *Journal of Experimental Psychology: Human Learning and Memory, 104*, 126–33.

Atkinson, R.C. and Shiffrin, R.M. (1968). Human memory: a proposed system and its control processes. In K.W. Spence and J.T. Spence (eds), *The Psychology of Learning and Motivation: Advances in Research and Theory*, vol. 2. New York: Academic Press.

Atkinson, R.L., Atkinson, R.C., Smith, E.E. and Bem, D.J. (1993). *Introduction to Psychology*, 11th edn. Orlando, FL: Harcourt Brace Jovanovich.

Averill, J.R. (1983). Studies on anger and aggression: implications for theories of emotion. *American Psychologist, 38*, 1145–60.

Averill, J.R. and Boothroyd, P. (1977). On falling in love in conformance with the romantic ideal. *Motivation and Emotion, 1*, 235–47.

Ax, A.F. (1953). The physiological differentiation of fear and anger in humans. *Psychosomatic Medicine, 15*, 433–42.

Axline, V. (1964). *Dibs: In Search of Self*. Harmondsworth: Penguin.

Azrin, N.H., Hutchinson, R.R. and Hake, D.F. (1966). Attack, avoidance and escape reactions to aversive shock. *Journal of Experimental Analysis of Behaviour, 9*, 191–204.

Bachman, C. and Mummer, N. (1980). Male arrangement of female choice in hamadryas baboons. *Behavioural Ecological Sociobiology, 6*, 315–21.

Bachy, V. (1976). Danish permissiveness revisited. *Journal of Communication, 26*, 40–5.

Baddeley, A. (1990). *Human Memory*. Hove, East Sussex: Lawrence Erlbaum Associates Ltd.

Baddeley, A.D. (1978). *The Psychology of Memory*. New York: Basic Books.

Baddeley, A.D. (1981). Reading and working memory. *Bulletin of the British Psychological Society, 35*, 414–17.

Baddeley, A.D. (1984). The fractionation of human memory. *Psychological Medicine, 14*, 259–64.

Baddeley, A.D. and Hitch, G. (1974). Working memory. In G.H. Bower (ed.), *Psychology of Learning and Motivation*, vol. 8. London: Academic Press.

Baddeley, A.D. and Lewis, V.J. (1981). The inner active processes in reading: the inner voice, the inner ear and the inner eye. In A.M. Lesgold and C.A. Perfetti (eds), *Interactive Processes in Reading*. Hillsdale, NJ: Lawrence Erlbaum.

Baerends, G.P. (1957). The ethological concept releasing mechanism illustrated by a study of the stimuli eliciting egg-retrieving in the herring gull. *Anatomical Record, 128*, 518–19.

Baerends, G.P. (1959). The value of the concept releasing mechanism. *Proceedings of the XVth International Congress of Zoology*, London.

Bahr, S. (1973). Effects of power and division of labor in the family. In L. Hoffman and G. Nye (eds), *Working Mothers*. San Francisco: Jossey-Bass.

Bailey, C.L. (1979). Mental illness – a logical misrepresentation. *Nursing Times*, May, 761–2.

Bales, R.F. (1950). *Interaction Process Analysis: A Method for the Study of Small Groups*. Cambridge, MA: Addison-Wesley.

Baltes, P.B., Reece, H.W. and Lippsitt, L.P. (1980). Life-span developmental psychology. *Annual Review of Psychology, 31*, 65–110.

Bandura, A. (1965). Influence of model's reinforcement contingencies on the acquisition of imitative responses. *Journal of Personality and Social Psychology, 1*, 589–95.

Bandura, A. (1969). *Principles of Behaviour Modification*. London: Holt, Rinehart & Winston.

Bandura, A. (1971). Analysis of social modeling processes. In A. Bandura (ed.), *Psychological Modeling*. Chicago: Aldine Atherton.

Bandura, A. (1973). *Aggression: A Social-Learning Analysis*. Englewood Cliffs, NJ: Prentice-Hall.

Bandura, A. (1977). *Social Learning Theory*, 2nd edn. Englewood Cliffs, NJ: Prentice-Hall.

Bandura, A. and MacDonald, F.J. (1963). Influence of social reinforcement and the behaviour of models in shaping children's moral judgements. *Journal of Abnormal and Social Psychology, 67*, 274–81.

Bandura, A., Blanchard, E.B. and Ritter, B. (1969). Relative efficacy of desensitization and modelling approaches for inducing behavioural, affective and attitudinal changes. *Journal of Personality and Social Psychology, 13*, 173–99.

Bannister, D. and Agnew, J. (1977). The child's construing of self. In A.W. Landfield (ed.), *Nebraska Symposium on Motivation 1976*. Lincoln, NE: University of Nebraska Press.

Bannister, D., Salmon, P. and Lieberman, D. (1964). Diagnosis–treatment relationships in psychiatry: a statistical analysis. *British Journal of Psychiatry, 110*, 726–32.

Barahal, H. (1958). 1000 prefrontal lobotomies: five to ten year follow-up study. *Psychiatric Quarterly, 32*, 653–78.

Barclay, C.R. (1986). Schematization of autobiographical memory. In D.C. Rubin (ed.), *Autobiographical Memory*. New York: Cambridge University Press.

Barlow, H.B. (1961). The coding of sensory messages. In W.H. Thorpe and O.L. Zangwill (eds), *Current Problems in Animal Behaviour*. Cambridge: Cambridge University Press.

Barnett, S.A. (1963). *A Study in Behaviour*. London: Methuen.

Baron, R.A. (1971). Reducing the influence of an aggressive model: the restraining effects of discrepant modelling cues. *Journal of Personality and Social Psychology, 20*, 240–5.

Baron, R.A. (1974). Aggression as a function of a victim's pain cues, the level of prior arousal and exposure to an aggressive model. *Journal of Personality and Social Psychology, 29*, 117–24.

Baron, R.A. (1977). *Human Aggression*. New York: Plenum.

Baron, R.A. (1989). Personality and organisational conflict: the type A behaviour problem and self-monitoring. *Organisational Behaviour and Human Decision Processes, 44*, 281–97.

Baron, R.A. and Ball, R.L. (1974). The aggression inhibiting influence of nonhostile humour. *Journal of Experimental Social Psychology, 10*, 23–33.

Baron, R.A. and Ransberger, V.M. (1978). Ambient temperature and the occurrence of collective violence: the 'long hot summer' revisited. *Journal of Personality and Social Psychology, 36*, 351–60.

Baron-Cohen, S. (1997). The child with autism: first lessons in mindreading. *Psychology Review, 3* (3), 30–3.

Baron-Cohen, S., Leslie, A.M. and Frith, U. (1985). Does the autistic child have a theory of mind? *Cognition, 21*, 37–46.

Barratt, C.L. (1969). Systematic desensitisation versus implosive therapy. *Journal of Abnormal Psychology, 74*, 587–92.

Barrera, M. and Maurer, D. (1981). Perception of facial expressions by the three-month-old. *Child Development, 52*, 203–6.

Barrett, P.T. and Kline, P. (1982). The itemetric properties of the Eysenck personality questionnaire: a reply to Helmes. *Personality and Individual Differences, 3*, 73–80.

Bar-Tal, D. (1976). *Prosocial Behaviour: Theory and Research*. Washington, DC: Hemisphere Press.

Bartlett, F.C. (1932). *Remembering: A Study in Experimental and Social Psychology*. Cambridge: Cambridge University Press.

Baruch, G., Barnett, R. and Rivers, C. (1983). *Lifeprints*. New York: McGraw-Hill.

Basmajian, J.V. (1977). Learned control of single motor units. In G.E Schartz and J. Beatty (eds), *Biofeedback: Theory and Research*. New York: Academic Press.

Bateman, A.J. (1948). Intra-sexual selection in drosophila. *Heredity, 2* (3), 349–68.

Bateson, P. (1986). When to experiment on animals. *New Scientist, 109* (1496), 30–2.

Bateson, P. (1991). Assessment of pain in animals. *Animal Behaviour, 42*, 827–39.

Bateson, P. (1992). Do animals feel pain? *New Scientist, 134* (1818), 30–3.

Bateson, P.P.G. (1964). Effect of similarity between rearing and testing conditions on chicks' following and avoidance responses. *Journal of Comparative and Physiological Psychology, 57*, 100–3.

Batson, C.D. (1987). Prosocial motivation: is it ever truly altruistic? *Advances in Experimental Social Psychology, 20*, 65–122.

Batson, C.D. (1990). How social an animal? The human capacity for caring. *American Psychologist, 45*, 36–46.

Batson, C.D. and Oleson, K.C. (1991). Current status of the empathy–altruism hypothesis. *Review of Personality and Social Psychology, 45*, 706–18.

Batson, C.D., O'Quin, K., Fultz, J., Vanderplas, M. and Isen, A.M. (1983). Influence of self-reported distress and empathy on egoistic versus altruistic motivation to help. *Journal of Personality and Social Psychology, 45*, 706–18.

Batteau, D.W. and Markey, P.R. (1968). *Man/dolphin communication. Final Report on contract N00123/67-1103*. 15 December 1966, US Naval Ordnance Test Station, China Lake, CA.

Baumeister, R.F., Chesner, S.P., Senders, P.S. and Tice, D.M. (1988). Who's in charge here? Group leaders do lend help in emergencies. *Personality and Social Psychology Bulletin, 14*, 17–22.

Baumrind, D. (1964). Some thoughts on the ethics of research: after reading Milgram's study of obedience. *American Psychologist, 19*, 421–3.

Bayley, N. (1969). *Bayley Scales of Infant Development*. New York: Psychological Corporation.

Bayley, N. (1970). Development of mental abilities. In P.H. Mussen (ed.), *Carmichael's Manual of Child Psychology*, vol. 1, 3rd edn, pp. 163–209. New York: Wiley.

Baylis, G.C., Rolls, E.T. and Leonard, C.M. (1985). Selectivity between faces in the responses of a population of neurons in the cortex in the superior temporal sulcus of the monkey. *Brain Research, 342*, 91–102.

Beaumont, J.G. (1988). *Understanding Neuropsychology*. Oxford: Blackwell.

Beck, A. and Emery, G. (1985). *Anxiety Disorders and Phobias: A Cognitive Perspective*. New York: Basic Books.

Beck, A.T., Ward, C., Mendelson, M., Mock, J. and Erbaugh, J. (1962). Reliability of psychiatric diagnosis: II. A study of consistency of clinical judgements and ratings. *American Journal of Psychiatry, 119*, 351–7.

Bee, H. (1989). *The Developing Child*, 6th edn. New York: Harper & Row.

Bee, H. (1995). *The Developing Child*, 7th edn. New York: HarperCollins.

Beech, H.R., Watts, F. and Poole, D. (1972). Classical conditioning of sexual deviation: a preliminary note. *Behaviour Therapy, 2*, 233–9.

Beehr, T.A. and Newman, J.E. (1978). Job stress, employee health, and organizational effectiveness: a facet analysis model, and literature review. *Personnel Psychology, 31*, 665–99.

Bellezza, F.S. (1983). The spatial arrangement mnemonic. *Journal of Educational Psychology, 75*, 830–7.

Bellezza, F.S. (1986). A mnemonic based on arranging words in visual patterns. *Journal of Educational Psychology, 78*, 217–24.

Bellisle, F., Lucas, F., Amrani, R. and Le Magnen, J. (1984). Deprivation, palatability and the micro-structure of meals in human subjects. *Appetite, 5*, 85–94.

Belsky, J. and Rovine, M. (1987). Temperament and attachment security in the Strange Situation: a rapprochement. *Child Development, 58*, 787–95.

Belsky, J. and Rovine, M. (1988). Nonmaternal care in the first year of life and the security of infant–parent attachment. *Child Development, 58*, 787–95.

Belsky, J. and Steinberg, L.D. (1978). The effects of day care: a critical review. *Child Development, 49*, 929–49.

Bem, D.J. (1967). Self-perception: an alternative interpretation of cognitive dissonance. *Psychological Review, 74*, 183–200.

Bem, D.J. (1972). Self perception theory. In L. Berkowitz (ed.), *Advances in Experimental Social Psychology*, vol. 6. New York: Academic Press.

Bem, D.J. (1983). Constructing a theory of the triple typology: some (second) thoughts on nomothetic and idiographic approaches to personality. *Journal of Personality, 51*, 566–77.

Bem, D.J. and Allen, A. (1974). On predicting some of the people some of the time: the search for cross-situational consistencies in behaviour. *Psychological Review, 81*, 506–20.

Bem, S. (1974). The measurement of psychological andogyny. *Journal of Consulting and Clinical Psychology, 42*, 155–62.

Bem, S. (1993). *The Lenses of Gender: Transforming the Debate on Sexual Inequality*. New Haven, CT: Yale University Press.

Bem, S.L. (1983). Gender schema theory and its implications for child development: raising gender aschematic children in a gender-schematic society. *Signs: Journal of Women in Culture and Society, 8*, 598–616.

Benedek, T. (1959). Parenthood as a developmental phase. *American Psychoanalytic Association Journal, 7*, 389–417.

Bengston, V.L., Rosenthal, C. and Burton, L. (1990). Families and aging: diversity and heterogeneity. In R.H. Binstock and L.K. George (eds), *Ageing and the Social Sciences*, 3rd edn. San Diego: Academic Press.

Bennett, N. and Dunne, E. (1989). Implementing cooperative groupwork in classrooms. Paper presented at EARLI conference, Madrid.

Bergen, D.J. and Williams, J.E. (1991). Sex stereotypes in the USA revisited. *Sex Roles, 24*, 413–23.

Berger, J., Rosenholz, S.J. and Zelditch, M. Jr (1980). Status organizing process. *Annual Review of Sociology, 6*, 479–508.

Bergin, A. (1971). The evaluation of therapeutic outcomes. In S.L. Garfield and A. Bergin (eds), *Handbook of Psychotherapy and Behaviour Change: An Empirical Analysis*. New York: Wiley.

Bergin, A. and Lambert, M. (1978). The evaluation of therapeutic outcomes. In S.L. Garfield and A. Bergin (eds), *Handbook of Psychotherapy and Be-haviour Change: An Empirical Analysis*, 2nd edn. New York: Wiley.

Berkowitz, L. (1962). *Aggression: A Social Psychological Analysis*. New York: McGraw-Hill.

Berkowitz, L. (1965). Some aspects of observed aggression. *Journal of Personality and Social Psychology, 2*, 359–69.

Berkowitz, L. (1972). Frustrations, comparisons, and other sources of emotion arousal as contributors to social unrest. *Journal of Social Issues, 28*, 77–91.

Berkowitz, L. (1983a). Aversively stimulated aggression. *American Psychologist, 38*, 1135–44.

Berkowitz, L. (1983b). Experience of anger as a parallel process in the display of impulsive 'angry' aggression. In R.G. Geen and E. Donnerstein (eds), *Aggression: Theoretical and Empirical Reviews*. New York: Academic Press.

Berkowitz, L. (1989). Frustration–aggression hypothesis: examination and reformulation. *Psychological Bulletin, 106*, 59–73.

Berkowitz, L. and Alioto, J.T. (1973). The meaning of an observed event as a determinant of its aggressive consequences. *Journal of Personality and Social Psychology, 28*, 206–17.

Berndt, T.J. (1982). The features and effects of friendships in early adolescence. *Child Development, 53*, 1447–60.

Berndt, T.J. (1992). Friendship and friends' influence in adolescence. *Current Directions in Psychological Science, 1*, 156–9.

Berne, E. (1968). *Games People Play*. Harmondsworth: Penguin.

Bernstein, B. (1961). Social structure, language and learning. *Educational Research*, June.

Bernstein, D. and Nietzel, M. (1980). *Introduction to Clinical Psychology*. New York: McGraw-Hill.

Bernstein, G.A. (1991). Comorbidity and severity of anxiety and depressive disorders in a clinic population. *Journal of the American Academy of Child Psychiatry, 30*, 43–50.

Berry, D.S. (1990). The perceiver as naive scientist or the scientist as naive perceiver? An ecological view of social knowledge acquisition. *Contemporary Social Psychology, 14*, 145–53.

Berscheid, E. (1985). Interpersonal attraction. In G. Lindzey and E. Aronson (eds), *Handbook of Social*

Psychology, 3rd edn, vol. 2. New York: Random House.

Berscheid, E. and Walster, E. (1978). *Interpersonal Attraction*, 2nd edn. Reading, MA: Addison-Wesley.

Besson, J.M., Guilbaud, G., Abdelmoumene, M. and Chaouch, A. (1982). Physiologie de la nociception. *Journal of Physiology (Paris)*, 78, 7–107.

Betancourt, H. and Lopez, S.R. (1993). The study of culture, ethnicity and race in American psychology. *American Psychologist*, 48, 629–37.

Bettelheim, B. and Janowitz, M. (1950). *Dynamics of Prejudice: A Psychological and Sociological Study of Veterans*. New York: Harper.

Bharati, A. (1986). The self in Hindu thought and action. In A.J. Marsella, G. Devos and F.L.K. Hsu (eds), *Culture and Self: Asian and Western Perspectives*. London: Tavistock Publications.

Biederman, I. (1987). Recognition by components: a theory of human image understanding. *Psychological Review*, 94, 115–17.

Binet, A. and Simon, T. (1905). Methodes nouvelles pour le diagnostic du niveau intellectuel des anormaux. *L'Annee Psychologique*, 11, 191–244.

Birch, A. (1997). *Developmental Psychology: from Infancy to Adulthood*, 2nd edn. Basingstoke: Macmillan.

Bitterman, M.E. and Kniffin, C.W. (1953). Manifest anxiety and perceptual defense. *Journal of Abnormal and Social Psychology*, 48, 248–52.

Blais, M.R., Sabourin, S., Boucher, C. and Vallerand, R.J. (1990). Toward a motivational model of couple happiness. *Journal of Personality and Social Psychology*, 59, 1021–31.

Blake, R.R. and Mouton, J.S. (1961). Reactions to intergroup competition under win/lose conditions. *Management Science*, 7, 420–35.

Blakemore, C. (1988). *The Mind Machine*. London: BBC Books.

Blakemore, C. and Cooper, C.R. (1970). The development of the brain depends on the visual environment. *Nature*, 228, 477–8.

Blanchard, E.B., Miller, S.T., Abet, G., Haynes, M. and Wicker, R. (1979). Evaluation of biofeedback in the treatment of borderline essential hypertension. *Journal of Applied Behaviour Analysis*, 12, 99–109.

Blanchard, R., Fukunaga, K. and Blanchard, C.B. (1976). Environmental control of defensive reactions to a cat. *Bulletin of Psychonomic Society*, 8, 179–81.

Blaney, P. (1975). Implications of the medical model and its alternatives. *American Journal of Psychiatry*, 132, 911–14.

Blaney, P.H. (1986). Affect and memory: a review. *Psychological Bulletin*, 99, 229–46.

Bliss, E.L. (1980). Multiple personalities: a report of 14 cases with implications for schizophrenia and hysteria. *Archives of General Psychiatry*, 37, 1388–97.

Block, J. (1961/78). *The Q-sort Method in Personality Assessment and Psychiatric Research*. Palo Alto: Consulting Psychologists Press.

Block, J. (1971). *Lives Through Time*. Berkeley, CA: Bancroft Books.

Block, J. (1981). Some enduring and consequential structures of personality. In A.I. Rabin, J. Aronoff, A.M. Barclay and R.A. Zucker (eds), *Further Explorations in Personality*. New York: Wiley.

Bloom, L. (1970). *Language Development: Form and Function in Emerging Grammars*. Cambridge, MA: MIT Press.

Bodmer, W.F. (1972). Race and IQ: the genetic background. In K. Richardson and D. Spears (eds), *Race, Culture and Intelligence*. Harmondsworth: Penguin.

Bogardus, E.S. (1925). Measuring social distance. *Journal of Applied Sociology*, 9, 299–308.

Bohannon, P. (1985a). *All the Happy Families: Exploring the Varieties of Family Life*. New York: McGraw-Hill.

Bohannon, P. (1985b). The six stations of divorce. In L. Cargan (ed.), *Marriage and Family: Coping with Change*. Belmont, CA: Wadsworth.

Booth, A. (1977). Wife's employment and husband stress: a replication and refutation. *Journal of Marriage and the Family*, 39, 645–50.

Booth, T. (1975). *Growing Up in Society*. London: Methuen.

Borden, R.J. (1975). Witnessed aggression: influence of an observer's sex and values on aggressive responding. *Journal of Personality and Social Psychology*, 31, 567–73.

Bornstein, M.H. and Lamb, M.E. (1988). *Developmental Psychology: An Advanced Textbook*, 2nd edn. Hillsdale, NJ: Erlbaum.

Bosse, R. (1991). How stressful is retirement? Findings from the Normative Aging Study. *Journal of Gerontology: Psychological Sciences*, 46 (1), 9–14.

Bouchard, T.J. and McGue, M. (1981). Familial studies of intelligence: a review. *Science*, 22, 1055–9.

Boucher, J. (1989). The theory of mind hypothesis of autism: explanation, evidence and assessment. *British Journal of Disorders of Communication*, 24, 181–98.

Bousfield, W.A. (1953). The occurrence of clustering in the recall of randomly arranged associates. *Journal of General Psychology*, 49, 229–40.

Bower, G.H. (1970). Analysis of a mnemonic device. *American Scientist*, 58, 496–510.

Bower, G.H. (1972). Mental imagery and associative learning. In L. Gregg (ed.), *Cognition in Learning and Memory*. New York: Wiley.

Bower, G.H., Clark, M.C., Lesgold, A.M. and Winzenz, D. (1969). Hierarchical retrieval schemes in recall of categorized word lists. *Journal of Verbal Learning and Verbal Behaviour*, 8, 323–43.

Bower, T.G.R. (1965). Stimulus variables determining space perception in infants. *Science*, 149, 88–9.

Bower, T.G.R. (1981). Cognitive development. In M. Roberts and J. Tamburrini (eds), *Child Development 0–5*. Edinburgh: Holmes McDougall.

Bower, T.G.R., Broughton, J.M. and Moore, M.K. (1970). Infant responses to approaching objects: an indicator of responses to distal variables. *Perception and Psychophysics*, 9, 193–6.

Bowers, K.S. (1973). Situationism in psychology: an analysis and critique. *Psychological Review*, 80, 307–36.

Bowlby, J. (1944). Forty-four juvenile thieves: their characters and home life. *International Journal of Psycho-Analysis*, 25, 19–52 and 107–27.

Bowlby, J. (1951). *Maternal Care and Mental Health*. Geneva: World Health Organization.

Bowlby, J. (1969). *Attachment and Loss*, vol. 1, *Attachment*. New York: Basic Books.

Bowlby, J. (1973). *Attachment and Loss*, vol. 2, *Separation: Anxiety and Anger*. New York: Basic Books.

Bowlby, J. (1980). *Attachment and Loss*, vol. 3, *Loss*. New York: Basic Books.

Bowlby, J. (1988). *A Secure Base: Clinical Applications of Attachment Theory*. London: Tavistock/Routledge.

Bowlby, J. (1988). *A Secure Base: Parent–Child Attachment and Healthy Human Development*. New York: Basic Books.

Braine, M. (1963). On learning the grammatical order of words. *Psychological Review, 70*, 115–20.

Braine, M.D.S. (1963). The ontogeny of English phrase structure. *Language, 39*, 1–14.

Brake, M. (1985). *Comparative Youth Subcultures*. London: Routledge & Kegan Paul.

Brala, P.M. and Hagen, R.L. (1983). Effects of sweetness perception and calorific value of a preload on short term intake. *Physiology and Behaviour, 30*, 1–9.

Breckler, S.J. and Wiggins, E.C. (1989a). On defining attitude and attitude theory: once more with feeling. In A.R. Pratkanis, S.J. Breckler and A.G. Greenwald (eds), *Attitude Structure and Function*. Hillsdale, NJ: Erlbaum.

Breckler, S.J. and Wiggins, E.C. (1989b). Affect versus evaluation in the structure of attitudes. *Journal of Experimental Social Psychology, 25*, 253–71.

Breckler, S.J., Pratkanis, A.R. and McCann, C.D. (1991). The representation of self in multi-dimensional cognitive space. *British Journal of Social Psychology, 30*, 97–112.

Brehm, J.W. (1992). *A Theory of Psychological Reactance*. New York: Academic Press.

Brehm, S.S. (1988). Passionate love. In R.J. Sternberg and M.L. Barnes (eds), *The Psychology of Love*. New Haven, CT: Yale University Press.

Breland, K. and Breland, M. (1961). The misbehaviour of organisms. *American Psychologist, 16*, 681–4.

Bremner, J.G. (1988). *Infancy*. Oxford: Blackwell.

Bretherton, I. (1992). The origins of attachment theory: John Bowlby and Mary Ainsworth. *Developmental Psychology, 28*, 759–75.

Brewer, M.B. (1988). A dual process model of impression formation. In T.K. Srull and R.S. Wyer (eds), *Advances in Social Cognition: A Dual Process Model of Impression Formation*, vol. 1. Hillsdale, NJ: Erlbaum.

Brewer, M.B. and Kramer, R.M. (1985). The psychology of intergroup attitudes and behaviour. *Annual Review of Psychology, 36*, 219–43.

Brewer, M.B. and Kramer, R.M. (1986). Choice behaviour in social dilemmas: the effects of social identity, group size and decision framing. *Journal of Personality and Social Psychology, 50*, 543–9.

Brewer, M.B. and Schneider, S. (1990). Social identity and social dilemmas: a double edged sword. In D. Abrams and M. Hogg (eds), *Social Identity Theory: Constructive and Critical Advances*. London: Harvester Wheatsheaf.

Brewer, M.B., Dull, V. and Lui, L. (1981). Perceptions of the elderly: stereotypes as prototypes. *Journal of Personality and Social Psychology, 41*, 656–70.

Briggs, K.C. and Myers, I.B. (1962). *The Myers–Briggs Type Indicator (Manual)*. Princeton, NJ: ETS.

Brigham, J.C. (1971). Ethnic stereotypes. *Psychological Bulletin, 76*, 15–38.

Bristol, M.M., Gallagher, J.J. and Schopler, E. (1988). Mothers and fathers of young developmentally disabled and nondisabled boys: adaptation and spousal support. *Developmental Psychology, 24*, 441–51.

British Psychological Society (1985). A code of conduct for psychologists. *Bulletin of the BPS, 38*, 41–3.

British Psychological Society (1990). *Ethical Principles for Conducting Research with Human Participants*. Leicester: The British Psychological Society.

Broadbent, D.E. (1958). *Perception and Communication*. Oxford: Pergamon.

Broadbent, D.E. (1977). Levels, hierarchies and the locus of control. *Quarterly Journal of Experimental Psychology, 29*, 181–201.

Broberg, D.J. and Bernstein, I.L. (1989). Cephalic insulin release in anorexic women. *Physiology and Behaviour, 45*, 871–4.

Brody, E.M. (1990). *Women in the Middle: Their Parent Care Years*. New York: Springer.

Brody, R., Sanders, P., Jones, L. and Hayes, N. (1983). *Handbook for GCE Psychology Teachers*. Leicester: Association for the Teaching of Psychology.

Brodzinsky, D., Gormly, A. and Amron, S. (1986). *Lifespan Human Development*, 3rd edn. New York: HRW International Editions.

Bromley, D.B. (1988). *Human Ageing*, 3rd edn. Harmondsworth: Penguin.

Bronfenbrenner, U. (1979). *The Ecology of Human Development*. Cambridge, MA: Harvard University Press.

Broverman, I.K., Vogel, S.R., Broverman, D.M, Clarkson, F.E. and Rosencrantz, P.S. (1972). Sex role stereotypes: a current appraisal. *Journal of Social Issues, 28*, 59–78.

Brown, A.L. and Palincsar, A.S. (1989). Guided, cooperative learning and individual knowledge acquisition. In L.B. Resnick (ed.), *Knowing, Learning and Instruction*. Hillsdale, NJ: Erlbaum.

Brown, C.R. (1986). Cliff swallow colonies as information centres. *Science, 234*, 83–5.

Brown, G.D.A. (1990). Cognitive science and its relation to psychology. *The Psychologist*, August, 339–43.

Brown, G.W. and Harris, T. (1978). *Social Analysis of Depression*. London: Tavistock.

Brown, G.W., Bone, M., Dalison, B. and Wing, J.K. (1966). *Schizophrenia and Social Care*. London: Oxford University Press.

Brown, G.W., Harris, T.O. and Peto, J. (1973). Life events and psychiatric disorders. Part 2. Nature of causal link. *Psychological Medicine*.

Brown, J.C. (1964). Observations of the elephant shrews (*Macroscelidae*) of equatorial Africa. *Proceedings of the Zoological Society of London, 143* (1), 103–19.

Brown, J.L. (1969). The buffer effect and productivity in tit populations. *American Nature, 103*, 347–54.

Brown, P. and Elliot, R. (1965). Control of aggression in a nursery school class. *Journal of Experimental Child Psychology, 2*, 103–7.

Brown, P. and Levinson, S. (1987). *Politeness: Some Universals in Language Use*. Cambridge: Cambridge University Press.

Brown, R. (1965). *Social Psychology*. New York: Free Press.

Brown, R. (1973). *The First Language: The Early Stages*. London: Allen & Unwin.

Brown, R. (1986). *Social Psychology*, 2nd edn. New York: Free Press.

Brown, R. and Bellugi, U. (1964). Three processes in the child's acquisition of syntax. In E.H. Lenneberg (ed.), *New Directions in the Study of Language*. Cambridge, MA: MIT Press.

Brown, R. and Kulik, J. (1977). Flashbulb memories. *Cognition, 5*, 73–99.

Browne, J.A. and Howarth, E. (1977). A comprehensive factor analysis of personality questionnaire items: a test of twenty putative factor hypotheses. *Multivariate Behavioural Research, 12*, 399–427.

Browne, K. (1989). The naturalistic context of family violence and child abuse. In J. Archer and K. Browne (eds), *Human Aggression: Naturalistic Approaches*. London: Routledge.

Brownmiller, S. (1984). *Femininity*. New York: Linden Press.

Bruce, V. and Green, P.R. (1990). *Visual Perception: Physiology, Psychology* and Ecology, 2nd edn. London: Erlbaum.

Bruner, J.S. (1956). You are your constructs. Contemporary Psychology, 1, 355–6.

Bruner, J.S. (1966a). Towards a Theory of Instruction. Cambridge, MA: Harvard University Press.

Bruner, J.S. (1966b). On cognitive growth. In J.S. Bruner, R.R. Olver and P.M. Greenfield (eds), Studies in Cognitive Growth. New York: Wiley.

Bruner, J.S. (1983). Child's Talk. New York: Norton.

Bruner, J.S. (1986). Actual Minds: Possible Worlds. Cambridge, MA: Harvard University Press.

Bruner, J.S. and Kenney, H. (1966). The Development of the Concepts of Order and Proportion in Children. New York: Wiley.

Bruner, J.S. and Minturn, A.L. (1955). Perceptual identification and perceptual organisation. Journal of General Psychology, 53, 21–8.

Bruner, J.S. and Postman, L. (1949). On the perception of incongruity: a paradigm. Journal of Personality, 18, 206–23.

Bruner, J.S., Goodnow, J.J. and Austin, G.A. (1956). A Study of Thinking. New York: Wiley.

Bruner, J.S., Jolly, A. and Sylva, K. (1976). Play: Its Role in Development and Evolution. Harmondsworth: Penguin.

Brunner, E.J., Marmot, M.G., White, I.R., O'Brien, J.R., Etherington, M.D., Slavin, B.M., Kearney, E.M. and Smith, G.D. (1993). Gender and employment grade differences in blood cholesterol, apolipoproteins and haemostatic factors in the Whitehall II study. Atherosclerosis, 102 (2), 195–207.

Brunswik, E. (1956). Perception and Representative Design of Psychological Experiments. Los Angeles: University of California Press.

Bruyer, R., Laterre, C. and Seron, X. (1983). A case of prosopagnosia with some preserved covert remembrance of familiar faces. Brain and Cognition, 2, 257–84.

Bryan, J.H. and Test, M.A. (1967). Models and helping: naturalistic studies in aiding behaviour. Journal of Personality and Social Psychology, 6, 400–7.

Bryant, B., Harris, M. and Newton, D. (1980). Children and Minders. London: Grant McIntyre.

Bryant, P. (1974). Perception and Understanding in Young Children. London: Methuen.

Bryant, P.E. and Colman, A.M. (eds) (1995). Developmental Psychology. Harlow: Longman.

Bull, B.L. and Wittrock, M.C. (1973). Imagery in the learning of verbal definitions. British Journal of Educational Psychology, 43, 289–93.

Burger, J.M. (1986). Increasing compliance by improving the deal: the that's-not-all technique. Journal of Personality and Social Psychology, 51, 277–83.

Burks, B.S. (1928). The relative influence of nature and nurture upon mental development: a comparative study of foster parent–foster child resemblance and true parent–true child resemblance. Yearbook of the National Society for the Study of Education, 27, 219–316.

Burt, C. (1955). The evidence for the concept of intelligence. British Journal of Educational Psychology, 25, 158–77.

Burt, C. (1966). The genetic determination of intelligence: a study of monozygotic twins reared together and apart. British Journal of Psychology, 57, 137–53.

Bushman, B.J. (1984). Perceived symbols of authority and their influence on compliance. Journal of Applied Social Psychology, 14, 501–8.

Bushman, B.J. (1988). The effects of apparel on compliance: a field experiment with a female authority figure. Personality and Social Psychology Bulletin, 14, 559–67.

Bushman, B.J. and Geen, R.G. (1990). Role of cognitive–emotional mediators and individual differences in the effects of media violence. Journal of Personality and Social Psychology, 58, 156–63.

Buss, A.H. (1961). The Psychology of Aggression. New York: Wiley.

Buss, A.H. (1967). Instrumentality of aggression, feedback and frustration as determinants of physical aggression. Journal of Personality and Social Psychology, 3, 153–62.

Buss, A.H. (1971). Aggression pays. In J.L. Singer (ed.), The Control of Aggression and Violence. New York: Academic Press.

Buss, D.M. (1984). Toward a psychology of the person–environment (PE) correlation: the role of spouse selection. Journal of Personality and Social Psychology, 47, 361–77.

Buss, D.M. and Barnes, M. (1986). Preferences in human mate selection. Journal of Personality and Social Psychology, 50, 559–70.

Bussey, K. and Bandura, A. (1984). Influence of gender constancy and social power on sex-linked modelling. Journal of Personality and Social Psychology, 47, 1292–302.

Bussey, K. and Bandura, A. (1992). Self-regulatory mechanisms governing gender-development. Child Development, 63, 1236–50.

Bustard, H.J.R. (1970). The role of behaviour in the natural regulation of numbers in the gekkonid lizard (Gehyra variegate). Ecology, 51 (4), 724–8.

Butterworth, G. (1987). Some benefits of egocentrism. In J.S. Bruner and H. Haste (eds), Making Sense. London: Methuen.

Buzan, T. (1974). Use Your Head. London: BBC Publications.

Byrne, D. (1971). The Attraction Paradigm. New York: Academic Press.

Byrne, D. and Clore, G.L. (1970). A reinforcement model of evaluative responses. Personality: An International Journal, 1, 103–28.

Byrne, D., Clore, G.L. and Smeaton, G. (1986). The attraction hypothesis: do similar attitudes affect anything? Journal of Personality and Social Psychology, 51, 1167–70.

Caciappo, J.T. and Petty, R.E. (1980). Sex differences in influencability: toward specifying the underlying process. Personality and Social Psychology Bulletin, 6, 651–6.

Calhoun, J. (1962). Population density and social pathology. Scientific American, 206, 139–48.

Calvert, S.L. and Huston, A.C. (1987). Television and gender schemata. In L.S. Liben and M.L. Signorella (eds), Children's Gender Schemata. San Francisco: Jossey-Bass.

Campbell, D.T., Tesser, A. and Fairey, P.J. (1986). Conformity and attention to the stimulus: some temporal and contextual dynamics. Journal of Personality and Social Psychology, 51, 315–24.

Campbell, N., Mackeown, W., Thomas, B. and Troscianko, T. (1995). Automatic interpretation of outdoor scenes. Paper for British Machine Vision Conference.

Campfield, L.A., Brandon, P. and Smith, F.J. (1985). On-line continuous measurement of blood glucose and meal pattern in free-feeding rats: the role of glucose in meal imitation. Brain Research Bulletin, 14, 605–17.

Campos, J.J., Barrett, K.C., Lambe, M.E., Goldsmith, H.H. and Sternberg, C. (1983). Socioemotional development.

In M.M. Haith and J.J. Campos (eds), *Handbook of Child Psychology*, vol. 2: *Infancy and Developmental Psychobiology*, 4th edn. New York: Wiley.

Cannon, W.B. (1927). The James–Lange theory of emotions: a critical examination and an alternative. *American Journal of Psychology*, 39, 106–24.

Cannon, W.B. and Washburn, A.L. (1912). An explanation of hunger. *American Journal of Psychology*, 29, 441–54.

Caraco, T., Martindale, S. and Pulliam, H.R. (1980). Flocking advantages and disadvantages. *Nature*, 285, 400–1.

Carl, E.A. (1971). Population control in arctic ground squirrels *Ecology*, 52 (3), 395–413.

Carlson, M. and Miller, N. (1987). Explanation of the relation between negative mood and helping. *Psychological Bulletin*, 102, 91–108.

Carlson, N.R. (1991). *Physiology of Behaviour*. Boston, MA: Allyn & Bacon.

Carlson, V., Cicchetti, D., Barnett, D. and Braunwald, K. (1989). Disorganized/disoriented attachment relationships in maltreated infants. *Developmental Psychology*, 25, 525–31.

Carr, W.J., Martrano, R.D. and Kramer, L. (1970). Response of mice to odours associated with stress. *Journal of Comparative and Physiological Psychology*, 71 (2), 223–8.

Carrey, N.J., Butter, H.J., Persinger, M.A. and Bialik, R.J. (1996). Physiological and cognitive correlates of child abuse. *Journal of the American Academy of Child and Adolescent Psychiatry*, 34 (8), 1067–75.

Carrick, R., Csordas, S.E., Ingham, S.E. and Ingham, K.K. (1962). Studies on the Southern elephant seal (*Mirounga leonina*) – III and IV. *Wildlife Research*, Canberra, Australia.

Carroll, J.B. (ed.) (1956). *Language, Thought and Reality: Selected Writings of Benjamin Lee Whorf*. New York: MIT Press and Wiley.

Carroll, J.B. and Casagrande, J.B. (1958). The function of language classifications in behaviour. In E.E. Maccoby, T.M. Newcombe and E.L. Hartley (eds), *Readings in Social Psychology*. New York: Holt, Rinehart & Winston.

Cartwright, D. (1968). The nature of group cohesiveness. In D. Cartwright and A. Zander (eds), *Group Dynamics: Research and Theory*, 3rd edn. London: Tavistock.

Carver, C.S. and Glass, D.C. (1978). Coronary-prone behaviour pattern and interpersonal aggression. *Journal of Personality and Social Psychology*, 36, 361–6.

Carver, C.S. and Scheier, M.F. (1981). *Attention and Self-Regulation: A Control Theory Approach to Human Behaviour*. New York: Springer Verlag.

Carver, R.P. (1990). Intelligence and reading ability in grades 2–12. *Intelligence*, 14, 449–55.

Case, R. (1978). Intellectual development from birth to adulthood: a neo-Piagetian interpretation. In R. Siegler (ed.), *Children's Thinking: What Develops?* Hillsdale, NJ: Erlbaum.

Case, R. (1985). *Intellectual Development: Birth to Adulthood*. New York: Academic Press.

Cash, T.F., Kehr, J.A., Polyson, J. and Freeman, V. (1977). Role of physical attractiveness in peer attribution of psychological disturbance. *Journal of Consulting and Clinical Psychology*, 45, 987–93.

Catchpole, C., Leisler, B. and Winkler, H. (1985). The evolution of polygyny in the great reed warbler (*Acrocephalus arundinaceus*): a possible case of deception. *Behavioural Ecological Sociobiology*, 16, 285–91.

Cattell, R.B. (1947). Confirmation and clarification of primary personality factors. *Psychometrika*, 12, 197–220.

Cattell, R.B. (1965). *The Scientific Analysis of Personality*. Harmondsworth, Penguin.

Cattell, R.B. (1973). *Personality and Mood by Questionnaire*. San Francisco: Jossey-Bass.

Cattell, R.B. (1995). The fallacy of the five factors in the personality sphere. *The Psychologist*, 8 (5), 207–8.

Cattell, R.B. and Kline, P. (1977). *The Scientific Analysis of Personality and Motivation*. New York: Academic Press.

Cattell, R.B., Eber, H.W. and Tatsnoka, M. (1970). *Handbook for Sixteen Personality Factor Questionnaire*. Champaign, IL: Institute for Personality and Ability Testing.

Cavanagh, P. (1963). The autotutor and classroom instructions. *Occupational Psychology*, 37, 44–9.

Cazden, C. (1965). Environmental assistance to the child's acquisition of grammar. Unpublished doctoral dissertation, Harvard University.

Chaplin, W.F. and Goldberg, L.R. (1984). A failure to replicate the Bem and Allen study of individual differences in cross-situational consistency. *Journal of Personality and Social Psychology*, 47, 1074–90.

Chaplin, W.F., John, O.P. and Goldberg, L.R. (1988). Conceptions of states and traits: dimensional attributes with ideals as prototypes. *Journal of Personality and Social Psychology*, 54, 541–57.

Chemers, M.M. (1983). Leadership theory and research: a systems/process integration. In P.B. Paulus (ed.), *Basic Group Processes*. New York: Springer Verlag.

Chemers, M.M. (1987). Leadership processes: intrapersonal, interpersonal and societal influences. *Review of Personality and Social Psychology*, 8, 252–77.

Cheney, D.L. (1983). Extrafamiliar alliances among vervet monkeys. In R.A. Hinde (ed.), *Primate Social Relationships*. Oxford: Blackwell Scientific Publications.

Cherry, E.C. (1953). Some experiments on the recognition of speech with one or two ears. *Journal of the Acoustical Society of America*, 25, 975–9.

Chickering, A.W. (1976). The double-bind of field dependence/independence in program alternatives for educational development. In S. Messick (ed.), *Individuality in Learning*. San Francisco: Jossey-Bass.

Child, I.L. (1968). Personality in culture. In E.F. Borgatta and W.W. Lambert (eds), *Handbook of Personality Theory and Research*. Chicago: Rand McNally.

Chomsky, N. (1968a). *Language and Mind*. New York: Harcourt Brace.

Chomsky, N.A. (1968b). Language in the mind. In Cashdan, A. et al. (eds), *Language in Education: A Source Book*, prepared by the Language and Learning Course Team at the Open University. London: Routledge & Kegan Paul.

Chomsky, N. (1972). *Language and Mind*, enlarged edn. New York: Harcourt Brace Jovanovich.

Christie, J.F. (1986). Training of symbolic play. In P.K. Smith (ed.), *Children's Play: Research, Development and Practical Applications*. London: Gordon & Breach.

Cialdini, R.B. (1985). *Influence: Science and Practice*. Glenview, IL: Scott-Foresman.

Cialdini, R.B., Baumann, D.J. and Kenrick, D.T. (1981). Insights from sadness: a three step model of the development of altruism as hedonism. *Developmental Review*, 1, 207–23.

Cialdini, R.B., Cacioppo, J.T., Basset, R. and Miller, J.A. (1978). Low-ball procedure for producing compliance: commitment then cost. *Journal of Personality and Social Psychology, 36,* 463–76.

Cialdini, R.B., Darby, B.L and Vincent, J.E. (1973). Transgression and altruism: a case for hedonism. *Journal of Experimental Social Psychology, 9,* 502–16.

Cialdini, R.B., Schaller, M., Houlihan, D., Arps, K., Fultz, J. and Beaman, A.L. (1987). Empathy based helping: is it selflessly or selfishly motivated? *Journal of Personality and Social Psychology, 52,* 749–58.

Cialdini, R.B., Vincent, J.E., Lewis, S.K., Catalan, J., Wheeler, D. and Darby, B.L. (1975). A reciprocal concessions procedure for inducing compliance: door-in-the-face technique. *Journal of Personality and Social Psychology, 21,* 206–15.

Clare, A. (1980). *Psychiatry in Dissent.* London: Tavistock.

Clark, A.M. and Clark, D.B. (1976). *Early Experience: Myth and Evidence.* London: Open Books.

Clark, H.H. and Malt, B.C. (1984). Psychological constraints on language: a commentary on Bresnan and Kaplan and on Givon. In W. Kintsch, J.R. Miller and P.G. Polson (eds), *Methods and Tactics in Cognitive Science.* Hillsdale, NJ: Erlbaum.

Clark, M.S. (1984). Record keeping in two types of relationship. *Journal of Personality and Social Psychology, 51,* 333–8.

Clark, M.S. and Mills, J. (1979). Interpersonal attraction in exchange and communal relationships. *Journal of Personality and Social Psychology, 37,* 12–24.

Clark, N.K. and Stephenson, G.M. (1989). Group remembering. In P.B. Paulus (ed.), *Psychology of Group Influence,* 2nd edn. Hillsdale, NJ: Erlbaum.

Clarke-Stewart, A. (1989). Infant day care. Maligned or malignant? *American Psychologist, 44,* 266–73.

Clausen, J.A. (1975). The social meaning of differential physical and sexual maturation. In S.E. Dragastin and G.H. Elder, Jr (eds), *Adolescence in the Life Cycle.* New York: Halsted.

Claxton, G. (1980). Cognitive psychology: a suitable case for treatment? In G. Claxton (ed.), *Cognitive Psychology: New Directions.* London: Routledge & Kegan Paul.

Clayton, P.J., Halikes, H.A. and Maurice, W.L. (1971). Bereavement of the widowed. *Diseases of the Nervous System, 32,* 594–604.

Clayton, V. and Birren, J.E. (1980). Age and wisdom across the lifespan: theoretical perspectives. In P.B. Baltes and O.G. Brim, Jr (eds), *Lifespan Development and Behaviour,* vol. 1. New York: Academic Press.

Cleckley, J. (1976). *The Mask of Sanity,* 5th edn. St Louis, MO: Mosby.

Clegg, F. (1982). *Simple Statistics.* Cambridge: Cambridge University Press.

Cloninger, C.R. (1987). Neurogenetic adaptive mechanisms in alcoholism. *Science, 236,* 410–16.

Clore, G.L. (1976). Interpersonal attraction, an overview. In J.W. Thibaut, J.T. Spence and R.C. Carson (eds), *Contemporary Topics in Social Psychology.* Morristown, NJ: General Learning Press.

Clore, G.L. and Byrne, D. (1974). A reinforcement–affect model of attraction. In T.L. Huston (ed.), *Foundations of Interpersonal Attraction.* New York: Academic Press.

Clore, G.L. and Kerber, K.W. (1978). Toward an affective theory of attraction and trait attribution. Unpublished manuscript, University of Illinois, Champaign.

Clugston, G.A. and Garlick, P.J. (1982). The response of protein and energy metabolism to food intake in lean and obese man. *Human Nutrition: Clinical Nutrition, 36C,* 57–70.

Clutton-Brock, T.H. and Albon, S.D. (1989). *Red Deer in the Highlands.* Oxford: Professional Books.

Clutton-Brock, T.H., Guinness, F.E. and Albon, S.D. (1982). *Red Deer: The Behaviour and Ecology of Two Sexes.* Chicago: Chicago University Press.

Coates, B., Pusser, H.E. and Goodman, I. (1976). The influence of *Sesame Street* and *Mister Rogers Neighbourhood* on children's prosocial behaviour in preschool. *Child Development, 47,* 138–44.

Cochrane, R. (1974). Crime and personality: theory and evidence. *Bulletin of the British Psychological Society, 27,* 19–22.

Cohen, C. (1987). Nuclear language. *Bulletin of the Atomic Scientist,* June, 17–24.

Cohen, D. (1987). *The Development of Play.* London: Croom Helm.

Cohen, G. (1975). Cerebral apartheid: a fanciful notion? *New Behaviour, 18,* 458–61.

Cohen, L.J. and Campos, J.J. (1974). Father, mother and stranger as elicitors of attachment behaviour in infancy. *Developmental Psychology, 10,* 146–54.

Cohen, S. and Williamson, G.M. (1991). Stress and infectious disease in humans. *Psychological Bulletin, 109,* 5–24.

Cohen, S., Tyrell, D.A.J. and Smith, A.P. (1991). Psychological stress and susceptibility to the common cold. *The New England Journal of Medicine, 325,* 606–12.

Coile, C. and Miller, N.E. (1984). How radical animal activists try to mislead humane people. *American Psychologist, 39,* 700–1.

Coke, J.S., Batson, C.D. and McDavis, K. (1978). Empathic mediation of helping: a two-stage model. *Journal of Personality and Social Psychology, 36,* 752–66.

Cole, M. and Scribner, S. (1974). *Culture and Thought.* New York: Wiley.

Coleman, J.C. (1995). Adolescence. In P.E. Bryant and A.M. Colman (eds), *Developmental Psychology.* London: Longman.

Coleman, J.C. and Hendry, B. (1990). *The Nature of Adolescence,* 2nd edn. London and New York: Routledge.

Coleman, J.S. with Johnston, J.W.C. and Johanasson, K. (1961). *The Adolescent Society: The Social Life of the Teenager and its Impact on Education.* New York: Free Press.

Collins, A.M and Loftus, E.F. (1975). Spreading-activation theory of semantic memory. *Psychological Review, 82,* 407–28.

Collins, A.M. and Quillian, M.R. (1969). Retrieval time from semantic memory. *Journal of Verbal Learning and Verbal Behaviour, 8,* 240–8.

Colombo, J. (1993). *Infant Cognition: Predicting later Intellectual Functioning.* Newbury Park, CA: Sage.

Colvin, J. (1983). Description of siting and peer relationships among immature male rhesus monkeys. In R.A. Hinde (ed.), *Primate Social Relationships.* Oxford: Blackwell Scientific Publications.

Condon, W.D. and Sander, W. (1974). Neonate movement is synchronized with adult speech; interactional participation in language acquisition. *Science, 183,* 99–101.

Condry, J. (1977). Enemies of exploration: self-initiated versus other-initiated learning. *Journal of Personality and Social Psychology, 35,* 459–77.

Conger, J.J. (1977). *Adolescence and Youth.* New York: Harper & Row.

Conger, J.J. and Miller, W.C. (1966). *Personality, Social Class and Delinquency*. New York: Wiley.

Conger, J.J. and Petersen, A. (1984). *Adolescence and Youth: Psychological Development in a Changing World*, 3rd edn. Harper & Row.

Connolly, J.A. and Doyle, A.B. (1984). Relation of social fantasy play to social competence in preschoolers. *Developmental Psychology, 20*, 797–806.

Conrad, C. (1964). Acoustic confusion in immediate memory. *British Journal of Psychology, 55*, 75–84.

Cook, S.W. and Pelfrey, M. (1985). Reactions to being helped in cooperating inter-racial groups. *Journal of Personality and Social Psychology, 49*, 1231–45.

Cooley, C.H. (1902). *Human Nature and the Social Order*. New York: Scribner.

Coolican, H. (1994). *Research Methods and Statistics in Psychology*, 2nd edn. London: Hodder & Stoughton.

Cooper, H.M. (1979). Statistically combining independent studies: a meta-analysis of sex differences in conformity research. *Journal of Personality and Social Psychology, 11*, 131–46.

Cooper, H.M. (1990). Meta-analysis and integrative research review. *Review of Personality and Social Psychology, 11*, 142–63.

Cooper, J. and Fazio, R.H. (1984). A new look at dissonance theory. In L. Berkowitz (ed.), *Advances in Experimental Social Psychology*, vol. 17. New York: Academic Press.

Cooper, J.E., Kendall, R., Gurland, B., Sharple, L., Copeland, J. and Simon, R. (1972). *Psychiatric Diagnosis in New York and London*. Maudsley Monograph no. 20. London: Oxford University Press.

Coopersmith, S. (1968). Studies in self-esteem. *Scientific American, 218*, 96–106.

Coren, S. and Girgus, J.S. (1978). *Seeing is Deceiving: The Psychology of Visual Illusions*. Hillsdale, NJ: Lawrence Erlbaum.

Costa, P.T. and McCrae, R.R. (1993). Bullish on personality psychology. *The Psychologist: Bulletin of the British Psychological Society, 6* (7), 302–3.

Cowan, N. (1984). On short and long auditory stores. *Psychological Bulletin, 90*, 218–44.

Cowie, H. and Ruddock, J. (1988). *Learning Together, Working Together*. London: BP Publications.

Cowie, H. and Ruddock, J. (1990). Learning from one another: the challenge. In H.C. Foot, J. Morgan and R.H. Shute (eds), *Children Helping Children*. Chichester: Wiley.

Cowie, H. and Ruddock, J. (1991). *Cooperative Group Work in the Multi-Ethnic Classroom*. London: BP Publications.

Cox, M.J., Owen, M.T., Lewis, J.M. and Henderson, K.V. (1989). Marriage, adult adjustment and early parenting. *Child Development, 60*, 1015–24.

Cox, O.C. (1948). *Caste, Class and Race*. New York: Doubleday.

Cox, T. (1978). *Stress*. Basingstoke: Macmillan.

Cox, T. and Mackay, C.J. (1976). A psychological model of occupational stress. Paper presented to the Medical Research Council meeting Mental Health in Industry, November, London.

Craik, F.I.M. and Lockhart, R.S. (1972). Levels of processing: a framework for memory research. *Journal of Verbal Learning and Verbal Behaviour, 11*, 671–84.

Craik, F.I.M. and Lockhart, R.S. (1986). CHARM is not enough: comments on Eich's model of cued recall. *Psychological Review, 93*, 360–4.

Craik, F.I.M. and Tulving, E. (1975). Depth of processing and the retention of words in episodic memory. *Journal of Experimental Psychology: General, 104*, 268–94.

Crick, F. and Mitchison, G. (1983). The function of dream sleep. *Nature, 304*, 111–14.

Crocker, J., Fiske, S.T. and Taylor, S.E. (1984). Schematic bases of belief change. In J.R. Eiser (ed.), *Attitudinal Judgement*. New York: Springer Verlag.

Crockett, L.J. and Petersen, A.C. (1987). Pubertal status and psychosocial development: findings from the early adolescent study. In R.M. Lerner and T.T. Foch (eds), *Biological and Psychosocial Interactions in Early Adolescence: A Life-span Perspective*. Hillsdale: Erlbaum.

Cronbach, L.J. and Snow, R.E. (1977). *Aptitudes and Instructional Methods: A Handbook for Research on Interactions*. New York: Irvinton.

Crook, J.H. (1965). The adaptive significance of avian social organisations. *Symposium of the Zoological Society of London, 14*, 181–218.

Crook, J.H. (1970). Social organisation and the environment: aspects of contemporary social ethology. *Animal Behaviour, 18*, 197–209.

Crook, J.H. (1973). The nature and function of territorial aggression. In M.F.A. Montagu (ed.), *Man and Aggression*, 2nd edn. New York: Oxford University Press.

Crosby, J.F. and Jose, N.L. (1983). Death: family adjustment to loss. In C.R. Figley and H.I. McCubbin (eds), *Stress and the Family*. New York: Brunner/Mazel.

Crowder, R.G. (1982). Decay of auditory memory in vowel discrimination. *Journal of Experimental Psychology: Learning Memory and Cognition, 8*, 153–62.

Crutchfield, R.S. (1954). A new technique for measuring individual differences in conformity to group judgement. *Proceedings of the Invitational Conference on Testing Problems*, pp. 69–74.

Cumming, E. and Henry, W. (1961). *Growing Old: A Process of Disengagement*. New York: Basic Books.

Cunningham, M.R. (1981). Sociobiology as a supplementary paradigm for social psychological research. *Review of Personality and Social Psychology, 2*, 69–106.

Cunningham, M.R. (1986). Measuring the physical in physical attraction: quasi-experiments on the sociobiology of female beauty. *Journal of Personality and Social Psychology, 50*, 925–35.

Cuthill, I. (1991). Field experiments in animal behaviour: methods and ethics. *Animal Behaviour, 42* (6), 1006–14.

Cutrona, C.E. (1986). Behavioural manifestations of social support: a microanalytic investigation, *Journal of Personality and Social Psychology, 51*, 201–8.

D'Ydewalle, G., Delhaye, P. and Goessens, L. (1985). Structural, semantic and self-referencing processing of pictorial advertisements. *Human Learning, 4*, 29–38.

Dagan, D. and Volman, S. (1982). Sensory basis for wind direction in first instar cockroaches. *Periplaneta Americana and Journal of Comparative Physiology, 147*, 471–8.

Dane, B., Walcott, C. and Drury, W.H. (1959). The form and duration of the display actions of the goldeneye. *Behaviour, 14*, 265–81.

Dane, F.C. and Harshaw, R. (1991). Similarity–attraction versus dissimilarity–repulsion: the establishment wins again. Paper presented at the South Eastern Psychological Association, New Orleans, March.

Darling, F.F. (1935). *A Herd of Red Deer.* London: Oxford University Press.

Darling, F.F. (1938). *Bird Flocks and the Breeding Cycle: A Contribution to Avian Sociality.* Cambridge: Cambridge University Press.

Darlington, R.B. (1986). Long-term effects of preschool programs. In U. Neisser (ed.), *The School Achievement of Minority Children.* Hillsdale, NJ: Erlbaum.

Darwin, C. (1859). *The Origin of Species.* London: Collins.

Darwin, C. (1872). *Expressions of Emotion in Man and Animals.* London: John Murray.

Darwin, C.J., Turvey, M.J. and Crowder, R.G. (1972). An auditory analogue of the Sperling partial report procedure: Evidence for brief auditory storage. *Cognitive Psychology, 3,* 255–67.

Davidson, J.E. and Sternberg, R.J. (1984). The role of insight in intellectual giftedness. *Gifted Child Quarterly, 28,* 58–64.

Davies, G. (1992). Teaching ethical issues: some examples from research with human participants. *Psychology Teaching New Series,* No. 1, 11–19.

Davies, J.C. (1969). The J-curve of rising and declining satisfaction as a cause of some great revolutions and a contained rebellion. In H.D. Graham and T.R. Gurr (eds), *The History of Violence in America: Historical and Comparative Perspectives.* New York, Praeger.

Davies, M.H. (1980). Measuring individual differences in empathy. *JSAS Catalogue of Selected Documents in Psychology, 10,* 85.

Davies, N.B. (1989). Sexual conflict and the polygyny threshold. *Animal Behaviour, 38,* 226–34.

Davies, N.B. and Brooke, M. de L. (1989). An experimental study of co-evolution between the cuckoo and its hosts. *Journal of Animal Ecology, 58,* 225–36.

Davies, R. (1987). Section in R.L. Gregory (ed.), *The Oxford Companion to the Mind.* Oxford: Oxford University Press.

Davis, D.M. (1990). Portrayals of women in primetime network television: some demographic characteristics. *Sex Roles, 23,* 325–32.

Davis, J.H. (1973). Group decision and social interaction: a theory of social decision schemes. *Psychological Review, 80,* 97–125.

Davis, K. (1947). Final note on a case of extreme isolation. *American Journal of Sociology, 52,* 432–7.

Davison, G. and Neale, J. (1994). *Abnormal Psychology,* 6th edn. New York: Wiley.

Dawkins, R. (1976). *The Selfish Gene.* Oxford: Oxford University Press.

Day, R.H. (1980). Visual illusions. In M.A. Jeeves (ed.), *Psychology Survey No. 3.* London: Allen & Unwin.

De Castro, J.M. and de Castro, E.S. (1989). Spontaneous meal patterns of humans: influence of the presence of other people. *American Journal of Clinical Nutrition, 50,* 237–47.

De Gelder, B. (1987). On not having a theory of mind. *Cognition, 27,* 285–90.

De Jong, W. (1979). An examination of self-perception and the foot-in-the-door effect. *Journal of Personality and Social Psychology, 37,* 2221–39.

De Villiers, P.A. and De Villiers, J. (1979). *Early Language.* London: Fontana.

Deag, J.M. (1977). Aggression and submission in monkey societies. *Animal Behaviour, 25,* 465–77.

Deaux, K. (1985). Sex and gender. *Annual Review of Psychology, 36,* 49–81.

Deaux, K. and Emswiller, T. (1974). Explanations of successful performance on sex-linked tasks: what is skill for the male is luck for the female. *Journal of Personality and Social Psychology, 29,* 80–5.

Deaux, K. and Lewis, L. (1983). Components of gender stereotypes. *Psychological Documents, 13,* 25 (Ms. No. 2583).

Deaux, K., Dane, F.C. and Wrightsman, L.S. (1993). *Social Psychology in the 90's,* 6th edn. Pacific Grove, CA: Brookes-Cole.

Deci, E.L. and Ryan, R.M. (1985). *Intrinsic Motivation and Self-determination in Human Behaviour.* New York: Plenum.

DeLoache, J.S. and Brown, A.L. (1987). Differences in the memory-based searching of delayed and normally developing young children. *Intelligence, 11,* 277–89.

DeLongis, A., Coyne, J.C., Dakof, G., Folkman, S. and Lazarus, R.S. (1982). Relationship of daily hassles, uplifts and major life events to health status. *Health Psychology, 1* (2), 119–36.

Dembroski, T.M. and MacDougall, J.M. (1978). Stress effects and affiliation preferences among subjects possessing the Type A coronary-prone behaviour pattern. *Journal of Personality and Social Psychology, 36,* 23–33.

Dement, W. (1960). The effect of dream deprivation. *Science, 131,* 1705–7.

Dement, W. (1972). *Some Must Watch While Some Must Sleep.* Stanford, CA: Stanford Alumni Association.

Dement, W. and Kleitman, N. (1957). The relation of eye-movements during sleep to dream activity: an objective method for the study of dreaming. *Journal of Experimental Psychology, 53* (5), 339–46.

DeMyer, M. (1975). The nature of the neuropsychological disability of autistic children. *Journal of Autism and Childhood Schizophrenia, 5,* 109–27.

Den Heyer, K. and Barrett, B. (1971). Selected loss of visual and verbal information in short term memory by means of visual and verbal interpolated tasks. *Psychonomic Science, 25,* 100–2.

Dennett, D.C. (1978). Beliefs about beliefs. *Behavioural and Brain Sciences, 1,* 568–70.

Der, G.H. Jr (1980). *Family Structure and Socialization.* New York: Arno Press.

Deregowski, J.B. (1968). Difficulties in pictorial depth perception in Africa. *British Journal of Psychology, 59,* 195–204.

Deregowski, J.B. (1972a). Pictorial perception and culture. In *Psychology in Progress: Readings from Scientific American,* pp. 327–32.

Deregowski, J.B. (1972b). Reproduction of orientation of Koh type figures: a cross-cultural study. *British Journal of Psychology, 63,* 283–96.

Derlega, V.J., Lewis, R.J., Harrison, S., Winstead, B.A. and Costanza, R. (1989). Gender differences in the initiation and attribution of tactile intimacy. *Journal of Non-Verbal Behaviour, 13,* 83–96.

Deutsch, M. (1958). Trust and suspicion. *Journal of Conflict Resolution, 2,* 265–79.

Deutsch, M. (1975). Equity, equality and need: what determines which value will be used as a basis of distributive justice? *Journal of Social Issues, 31,* 137–49.

Deutsch, M. and Gerard, H.B. (1955). A study of normative and informational social influences upon individual judgement. *Journal of Abnormal and Social Psychology, 51,* 629–36.

DeValois, R.L. and DeValois, K.K. (1988). *Spatial Vision.* New York: Oxford University Press.

DeValois, R.L. and Jacobs, G.H. (1984). Neural mechanisms of colour vision. In I. Dorian-Smith (ed.), *Handbook of*

Physiology, vol. 3. Bethesda, MD: American Physiological Society.

Devine, P.G. (1989). Stereotypes and prejudice: their automatic and controlled components. *Journal of Personality and Social Psychology*, 56, 5–18.

Devos, G. (1985). Dimensions of the self in Japanese culture. In A.J. Marsella et al. (eds), *Culture and Self: Asian and Western Perspectives*. London: Tavistock Publications.

Diab, L.N. (1970). A study of intragroup and intergroup relations among experimentally produced small groups. *Genetic Psychology Monographs*, 82, 49–82.

Diament, C. and Wilson, G.T. (1975). An experimental investigation of the effects of covert sensitisation in an analogue eating situation. *Behaviour Therapy*, 6, 499–509.

Diener, E. (1976). Effects of prior destructive behaviour, anonymity, and group presence on deindividuation and aggression. *Journal of Personality and Social Psychology*, 33, 497–507.

Diener, E. (1980). Deindividuation: the absence of self-awareness and self-regulation in group members. In P.B. Paulus (ed.), *Psychology of Group Influence*. Hillsdale, NJ: Erlbaum.

Digman, J.M. and Inouye, J. (1986). Further specification of the five robust factors of personality. *Journal of Personality and Social Psychology*, 50, 116–23.

Dinnerstein, D. (1976). *The Mermaid and the Minotaur: Sexual Arrangements and Human Malaise*. New York: Harper & Row.

Dion, K.K. (1972). Physical attractiveness and evaluation of children's transgressions. *Journal of Personality and Social Psychology*, 24, 285–90.

Dion, K.L., Berscheid, E. and Walster, E. (1972). What is beautiful is good. *Journal of Personality and Social Psychology*, 24, 285–90.

Dipboye, R.L., Arvey, R.D. and Terpstra, D.E. (1977). Sex and physical attractiveness of raters and applicants as determinants of resumé evaluations. *Journal of Applied Psychology*, 61, 288–94.

Dittes, J.E. (1959). Attractiveness of group as a function of self-esteem and acceptance by group. *Journal of Abnormal and Social Psychology*, 53, 100–7.

Dittes, J.E. and Kelley, H.H. (1956). Affects of different conditions of acceptance upon conformity to group norms. *Journal of Abnormal and Social Psychology*, 53, 100–7.

Dodd, B. (1972). Effects of social and vocal stimulation on infant babbling. *Developmental Psychology*, 7, 80–3.

Dodge, K.A. and Crick, N.R. (1990). Social information processing bases of aggressive behavior in children. *Personality and Social Psychology Bulletin*, 16, 8–22.

Dohrenwend, B., Krasnoff, L., Askenasy, A. and Dohrenwend, D. (1978). Exemplification of a method for scaling life events. *Journal of Health and Social Behaviour*, 19, 205–29.

Dollard, J., Doob, L.W., Miller, N.E., Mowrer, O.H. and Sears, R.R. (1993). *Frustration and Aggression*. New Haven, CT: Yale University Press.

Dominowski, R.L. (1974). How do people discover concepts? In R.L. Solso (ed.), *Theories in Cognitive Psychology: The Loyola Symposium*. Hillsdale, NJ: Erlbaum.

Dominowski, R.L. (1977). Reasoning. *InterAmerican Journal of Psychology*, 11, 68–70.

Donaldson, M. (1978). *Children's Minds*. London: Fontana.

Donnerstein, E. (1982). Erotica and human aggression. In R.G. Geen and E. Donnerstein (eds), *Aggression: Theoretical and Empirical Reviews*. New York: Academic Press.

Donnerstein, E., Donnerstein, M. and Evans, R. (1975). Erotic stimuli and aggression: facilitation or inhibition. *Journal of Personality and Social Psychology*, 34, 237–44.

Donnerstein, M. and Wilson, D.W. (1976). The effects of noise and perceived control upon ongoing and subsequent aggressive behaviour. *Journal of Personality and Social Psychology*, 34, 774–81.

Doob, A.N. and Gross, A.E. (1968). Status of frustrator as an inhibitor of horn honking responses. *Journal of Social Psychology*, 76, 213–18.

Drake, R.D. and Sederer, L.I. (1986). The adverse effects of intensive treatment of chronic schizophrenia. *Comprehensive Psychiatry*, 27, 313–26.

Dreiser, T. (1929). *A Gallery of Women*. New York: Boni and Liveright.

Duberman, L. (1973). Step-kin relationships. *Journal of Marriage and the Family*, 35, 283–92.

DuBois, R. (1950). *Neighbours in Action*. New York: Harper.

Duck, J.M. (1990). Children's ideals: the role of real-life versus media figures. *Australian Journal of Psychology*, 42, 19–29.

Duck, S. (1988). *Relating to Others*. Milton Keynes: Open University Press.

Duck, S. (1992). *Human Relationships*, 2nd edn. London: Sage.

Duck, S. (1995). Repelling the study of attraction. *The Psychologist*, 8, 60–3.

Dunn, J. (1984). *Sisters and Brothers*. London: Fontana.

Dunn, J. and Brown, J. (1994). Affect expression in the family, children's understanding of emotions and their interactions with others. *Merrill-Palmer Quarterly*, 40, 120–37.

Dunn, J. and Kendrick, C. (1982). *Siblings: Love, Envy and Understanding*. Oxford: Basil Blackwell.

Dunphy, D.C. (1963). The social structure of urban adolescent peer groups. *Sociometry*, 26, 230–46.

Durkin, K. (1985). *Television, Sex Roles and Children: A Developmental Social Psychological Account*. Milton Keynes and Philadelphia: Open University Press.

Durkin, K. (1995). *Developmental Social Psychology: From Infancy to Old Age*. Oxford: Blackwell.

Dusek, J.B. and Flaherty, J.F. (1981). The development of the self-concept during the adolescent years. *Monographs of the Society for Research in Child Development*, 46 (Serial No. 191).

Eagly, A.H. (1987). *Sex Differences in Social Behaviour: A Social-role Interpretation*. Hillsdale, NJ: Erlbaum.

Eagly, A.H. and Carli, L.L. (1981). Sex of researchers and sex typed communications as determinants of sex differences in influenceability: a meta analysis of social influence studies. *Psychological Bulletin*, 90, 1–20.

Eagly, A.H. and Crowley, M. (1986). Gender and helping behaviour: a meta-analytic review of the social psychological literature. *Psychological Bulletin*, 100, 283–308.

Eagly, A.H. and Steffen, V.J. (1986). Gender and aggressive behaviour: a metaanalytic review of the social psychological literature. *Psychological Bulletin*, 100, 309–30.

Eagly, A.H. and Wood, W. (1991). Explaining sex differences in social behaviour: a meta-analytic perspective. *Personality and Social Psychology Bulletin*, 17, 306–15.

Eames, D., Shorrocks, D. and Tomlinson, P. (1990). Naughty animals or naughty experimenters? Conservation accidents revisited with video-stimulated commentary. *British Journal of Developmental Psychology*, 8, 25–37.

Eaton, W.O. and Enns, L.R. (1986). Sex differences in human motor activity level. *Psychological Bulletin, 100*, 19–28.

Ebbinghaus, H. (1885). *Memory: A Contribution to Experimental Psychology*, trans. H.A Ruger and C.F. Bussenius (1913). New York: New York Teachers' College, Columbia University.

Eccles-Parsons, J. (1983). Expectancies, values and academic behaviors. In J.T. Spence (ed.), *Achievement and Achievement Motives*. San Francisco: Freeman.

Edmunds, G. and Kendrick, D.C. (1980). *The Measurement of Human Aggressiveness*. Chichester: Ellis Horwood.

Edwards, C.P. (1986). Cross-cultural research on Kohlberg's stages: the basis for consensus. In D. Wagner and H. Stevenson (eds), *Cultural Perspectives in Child Development*. San Francisco, CA: W.H. Freeman.

Egeland, J.A., Gerhard, D., Pauls, D., Sussex, J., Kidd, K., Allen, C., Hostetter, A. and Housman, D. (1987). Bipolar affective disorders linked to DNA markers on chromosome 11. *Nature, 325*, 783–7.

Eisenberg, N. (1986). *Altruistic Emotion, Cognition and Behaviour*. Hillsdale, NJ: Erlbaum.

Eisenberg, N. and Mussen, P.H. (1989). *The Roots of Prosocial Behaviour in Children*. New York: Cambridge University Press.

Eisenberg, N., Shell, R., Pasternak, J., Lennon, R., Beller, R. and Mathy, R.M. (1987). Prosocial development in middle childhood: a longitudinal study. *Developmental Psychology, 23*, 712–18.

Eiser, J.R. (1986). *Social Psychology: Attitudes, Cognition and Social Behaviour*. Cambridge: Cambridge University Press.

Ekman, P. (1982). *Emotion in the Human Face*, 2nd edn. New York: Cambridge University Press.

Ekman, P., Friesen, W.V., O'Sullivan, M., Chan, A., Diacoyanni-Tarlatzis, I., Heider, K., Krause, R., Lecompte, W.A., Pitcairn, T., Riccibitti, P.E., Scherer, K., Tomita, M. and Tzvaras, A. (1987). Universals and cultural differences in the judgements of facial expressions of emotion. *Journal of Personality and Social Psychology, 53*, 712–17.

Elgar, M. (1986). House sparrows establish foraging flocks by giving chirrup calls if the resources are divisible. *Animal Behaviour, 34*, 169–74.

Elgar, M. (1989). Predator vigilance and group size among mammals and birds: a critical review of the evidence. *Biological Review, 64*, 1–34.

Elias, C.S. and Perfetti, C.A. (1973). Encoding task and recognition memory: The importance of semantic coding. *Journal of Experimental Psychology, 99*, 151–7.

Elliott, C., Murray, D.J. and Pearson, L.S. (1983). *The British Ability Scales*, rev. edn. Windsor: Nelson-NFER.

Ellis, A. (1984). Rational-emotive therapy. In R.J. Corsini (ed.), *Current Psychotherapies*, 3rd edn. Itasca, IL: Peacock Press.

Emde, R.N. and Harmon, R.J. (1972). Endogenous and exogenous smiling systems in early infancy. *Journal of the American Academy of Child Psychiatry, 11*, 177–200.

Emlen, S. and Oring, L.W. (1977). Ecology, sexual selection and the evolution of mating systems. *Science, 197*, 215–23.

Emmelkamp, P. and Wessels, H. (1975). Flooding in imagination versus flooding in vivo: a comparison with agoraphobics. *Behaviour Research and Therapy, 13*, 7–15.

Empson, J. (1989). *Sleep and Dreaming*. London: Faber & Faber.

Endicott, J. and Spitzer, R.L. (1978). A diagnostic interview: the schedule for affective disorders and schizophrenia. *Archives of General Psychiatry, 35*, 837–44.

Endicott, J., Nea, J., Fleiss, J., Cohen, J., Williams, J.B. and Simon, R. (1982). Diagnostic criteria for schizophrenia: reliability and agreement between systems. *Archives of General Psychiatry, 39*, 884–9.

Entine, A.D. (1976). Midlife counselling: prognosis and potential. *The Personnel and Guidance Journal, 55* (3), 112–14.

Erber, J. (1981). Neural correlates of learning in the honey bee. *Trends in Neurosciences, 4*, 270–3.

Ericsson, K.A. and Simon, H.A. (1980). Verbal reports as data. *Psychological Review, 87*, 215–51.

Erikson, E.H. (1963). *Childhood and Society*. New York: Norton.

Erikson, E.H. (1968). *Identity: Youth and Crisis*. New York: Norton.

Erikson, E.H. (1970). Reflections on the dissent of contemporary youth. *International Journal of Psychoanalysis, 51*, 11–22.

Erikson, E.H. (1980). *Identity and the Life Cycle*. New York: Norton.

Eron, L.D. (1980). Prescription for the reduction of aggression. *American Psychologist, 35*, 244–52.

Eron, L.D. (1982). Parent–child interaction, television violence and aggression of children. *American Psychologist, 37*, 197–211.

Erwin, P. (1993). *Friendship and Peer Relations in Children*. Chichester: Wiley.

Esch, H., Esch, I. and Kerr, W.E. (1965). Sound: an element common to communication of stingless bees and dances of honey bees. *Science, 149*, 320–1.

Escher, M. (1960). Heaven and hell. In M.L. Teuber, Sources of ambiguity in the prints of Mauritz Escher, *Scientific American*, July 1974.

Estes, W.K. (1944). An experimental study of punishment. *Psychology Monographs, 57*, No. 263.

Estes, W.K. (1970). *Learning Theory and Mental Development*. New York: Academic Press.

Etcoff, N.L. (1985). The neuropsychology of emotional expression. In G. Goldstein and R. Tarter (eds), *Advances in Clinical Neuropsychology*, vol. 3. New York: Plenum Press.

Evans, J. St B.T. (1983). *Thinking and Reasoning: Psychological Approaches*. London: Routledge & Kegan Paul.

Ewart, P.H. (1930). A study of the effect of inverted retinal stimulation upon spatially co-ordinated behaviour. *Genetic Psychology Monographs, 7*, 177–366.

Exner, J. (1986). *The Rorschach: a Comprehensive System*, 2nd edn, vol. 1. New York: Wiley.

Eysenck, H.J. (1947). *Dimensions of Personality*. London: Routledge & Kegan Paul.

Eysenck, H.J. (1952). The effects of psychotherapy: an evaluation. *Journal of Consulting Psychology, 16*, 319–24.

Eysenck, H.J. (1959). The Rorschach Test. In O.K. Buros (ed.), *The Fifth Mental Measurement Year Book*. NJ: Gryphon Press.

Eysenck, H.J. (1964). *Crime and Personality*. London: Routledge & Kegan Paul.

Eysenck, H.J. and Eysenck, M.W. (1985). *Personality and Individual Differences: A Natural Science Approach*. New York: Plenum Press.

Eysenck, H.J. and Eysenck, S.B.G. (1964). *Manual of the Eysenck Personality Inventory*. London: ULP.

Eysenck, H.J. and Eysenck, S.B.G. (1969). *Personality Structure and*

Measurement. London: Routledge & Kegan Paul.

Eysenck, H.J. and Eysenck, S.B.G. (1975). *Manual for the Eysenck Personality Questionnaire*. London: Hodder & Stoughton.

Eysenck, H.J. and Eysenck, S.B.G. (1976). *Psychoticism as a Dimension of Personality*. London: Hodder & Stoughton.

Eysenck, H.J. and Wilson, G.D. (1973). *Experimental Studies of Freudian Theories*. London: Methuen.

Eysenck, M.W. (1978). Verbal remembering. In B.M. Foss (ed.), *Psychological Survey No. 1*. London: Allen & Unwin.

Eysenck, M.W. (1982). *Attention and Arousal: Cognition and Performance*. Berlin: Springer Verlag.

Eysenck, M.W. (1984). *A Handbook of Cognitive Psychology*. Brighton: Psychology Press.

Eysenck, M.W. (1994) *Perspectives in Psychology*. Hove: Lawrence Erlbaum Associates.

Eysenck, S.B.G. and Eysenck, H.J. (1970). Crime and personality: an empirical study of the three-factor theory. *British Journal of Criminology*, *10*, 225–39.

Fagot, B.I. (1978). The influence of sex of child on parental reactions to toddler children. *Child Development*, *49*, 459–65.

Fairbairn, S. and Fairbairn, G. (eds) (1987). *Psychology, Ethics and Change*. London: Routledge & Kegan Paul.

Fajardo, D.M. (1985). Author race, essay quality and reverse discrimination. *Journal of Applied Social Psychology*, *15*, 255–68.

Falbo, T. and Polit, D.F. (1986). Quantitative review of the only child literature: research evidence and theory development. *Psychological Bulletin*, *100*, 176–89.

Falek, A. and Moser, H.M. (1975). Classification in schizophrenia. *Archives of General Psychiatry*, *32*, 59–67.

Fantz, R.L. (1961). The origin of form perception. *Scientific American*, *204* (5), 66–72.

Faraday, A. (1973). *Dream Power*. London: Pan.

Farnham-Diggory, S. (1992). *The Learning-Disabled Child*. Cambridge, MA: Harvard University Press.

Farr, R.M. and Moscovici, S. (eds) (1984). *Social Representations*. Cambridge: Cambridge University Press.

Farrell, P. and Rosenberg, S.D. (1981). *Men at Midlife*. Boston, MA: Auburn House.

Farrington, D.P. (1991). Childhood aggression and adult violence: early precursors and later life outcomes. In D.J. Pepler and H.J. Rubin (eds), *The Development and Treatment of Childhood Aggression*, pp. 5–30. Hillsdale, NJ: Erlbaum.

Farrington, D.P., Biron, L. and Le Blanc, M. (1982). Personality and delinquency in London and Montreal. In J.C. Gunn and D.P. Farrington (eds), *Advances in Forensic Psychiatry and Psychology*. Chichester: Wiley.

Farthing, G.W. (1992). *The Psychology of Consciousness*. Englewood Cliffs, NJ: Prentice-Hall.

Fava, M., Copeland, B.M., Schweiger, U. and Herzog, M.D. (1989). Neurochemical abnormalities of anorexia nervosa and bulimia nervosa. *American Journal of Psychiatry*, *146*, 963–71.

Fazio, R.H. (1986). How do attitudes guide behaviour? In R.M. Sorrentino and E.T. Higgins (eds), *Handbook of Motivation and Cognition*. New York: Guilford Press.

Fazio, R.H. (1989). On the power and functionality of attitudes: the role of attitude accessibility. In A.R. Pratkanis, S.J. Breckler and A.G. Greenwald (eds), *Attitude Structure and Function*. Hillsdale, NJ: Erlbaum.

Fazio, R.H., Sanbonmatsu, D.M., Powell, M.C. and Kardes, F.R. (1986). On the automatic activation of attitudes. *Journal of Personality and Social Psychology*, *50*, 229–38.

Fazio, R.H., Zanna, M.P. and Cooper, J. (1977). Dissonance and self perception: an integrative view of each theory's proper domain of application. *Journal of Experimental Social Psychology*, *13*, 464–79.

Feeney, J.A., Noller, P. and Hanrahan, M. (1994). Assessing adult attachment. In M.B. Sperling and W.H. Brown (eds), *Attachment in Adults: Clinical and Developmental Perspectives*. New York: Guilford Press.

Feldman, S.S. and Elliott, G. (1990). *At the Threshold: The Developing Adolescent*. London: Harvard University Press.

Ferris, C. and Branston, P. (1994). Quality of life in the elderly: a contribution to its understanding, *Australian Journal of Ageing*, *13*, 120–3.

Feshbach, S., Stiles, W.B. and Bitter, E. (1967). The reinforcing effect of witnessing aggression. *Journal of Experimental Research in Personality*, *2*, 133–9.

Festinger, L. (1950). Informal social communication. *Psychological Review*, *57*, 271–82.

Festinger, L. (1957). *A Theory of Cognitive Dissonance*. Stanford, CA: Stanford University Press.

Festinger, L. and Carlsmith, J.M. (1959). Cognitive consequences of forced compliance. *Journal of Abnormal and Social Psychology*, *58*, 203–10.

Festinger, L., Pepitone, A. and Newcombe, T. (1952). Some consequences of deindividuation in a group. *Journal of Abnormal and Social Psychology*, *47*, 382–9.

Festinger, L., Schachter, S. and Back, K. (1950). *Social Pressures on Informal Groups: A Study of Human Factors in Housing*. New York: Harper & Row.

Fiedler, F.E. (1964). A contingency model of leadership effectiveness. In L. Berkowitz (ed.), *Advances in Experimental Social Psychology*. New York: Academic Press.

Fiedler, F.E. (1967). *A Theory of Leadership Effectiveness*. New York: McGraw-Hill.

Fischer, C.S. (1963). Sharing in preschool children as a function of the amount and type of reinforcement. *Genetic Psychology Monographs*, *68*, 215–45.

Fishbein, M. and Ajzen, I. (1974). Attitudes towards objects as predictors of single and multiple behaviour criteria. *Psychological Review*, *81*, 59–74.

Fishbein, M. and Ajzen, I. (1975). *Belief, Attitude, Intention and Behaviour: An Introduction to Theory and Research*. Reading, MA: Addison-Wesley.

Fisher, D.L. (1984). Central capacity limits in consistent mapping, visual search tasks: Four channels or more? *Cognitive Psychology*, *16*, 449–84.

Fisher, R.J. (1990). *The Social Psychology of Intergroup and International Conflict Resolution*. New York: Springer Verlag.

Fisher, S. and Greenberg, R. (1977). *The Scientific Credibility of Freud's Theories and Therapy*. Brighton: Harvester Press.

Fiske, A.D. and Schneider, W. (1984). Memory as a function of attention, level of processing and automatization. *Journal of Experimental Psychology: Learning, Memory and Cognition*, *10*, 181–7.

Fiske, S.T. and Taylor, S.E. (1984). *Social Cognition*. Reading, MA: Addison-Wesley.

Floody, O.R. (1983). Hormones and aggression in female mammals. In B.B. Savare (ed.), *Hormones and Aggression*. New York: Plenum Press.

Fogel, A. (1993). *Developing Through Relationships: Origins of Communication, Self and Culture*. New York: Harvester Wheatsheaf.

Fonagy, P. (1981). Experimental research in psychoanalytic theory. In F. Fransella (ed.), *Personality*. London: Methuen.

Fonagy, P. and Higgitt, A. (1984). *Personality Theory and Clinical Practice*. London: Methuen.

Fontana, D. (1988). *Psychology for Teachers*, 2nd edn. Leicester/Basingstoke: British Psychological Society/Macmillan.

Foot, H.C., Morgan, M.J. and Shute, R.H. (1990). *Children Helping Children*. Chichester: John Wiley.

Forsyth, D.R. (1983). *An Introduction to Group Dynamics*. Pacific Grove, CA: Brookes-Cole.

Fouts, R.S. (1972). The use of guidance in teaching sign language to a chimpanzee. *Journal of Comparative Physiological Psychology*, 80, 515–22.

Fowler, C.A., Wolford, G., Slade, R. and Tissinary, L. (1981). Lexical access without awareness. *Journal of Experimental Psychology: General*, 13, 281–90.

Fox, N. (1977). Attachment of Kibbutz infants to mother and metapalet. *Child Development*, 48, 1228–39.

Fraiberg, S. (1977). *Insights from the Blind*. New York: Meridian Books.

Frank, B.M. and Noble, J.P. (1984). Field independence–dependence and cognitive restructuring. *Journal of Personality and Social Psychology*, 47, 1129–35.

Frankenhauser, M. (1983). The sympathetic-adrenal and pituitary adrenal response to challenge: comparison between the sexes. In T.M. Dembroski, T.H. Schmidt and G. Blumchen (eds), *Behavioral Bases of Coronary Heart Disease*. Basel: S. Karger.

Frankenhauser, M., Lundberg, U. and Chesney, M. (1991). *Women, Work and Health: Stress and Opportunities*. New York: Plenum.

Franks, C.M. (1956). Conditioning and personality: a study of normal and neurotic subjects. *Journal of Abnormal Social Psychology*, 52, 143–50.

Franks, C.M. (1957). Personality factors and the rate of conditioning. *British Journal of Psychology*, 48, 119–26.

Franks, C.M. (1984). Behaviour therapy with children and adolescents. In G.T. Wilson, C.M. Franks, K.D. Brownell and P.C. Kendall, *Annual Review of Behaviour Therapy: Theory and Practice*, vol. 9. New York: Guilford.

Franks, J.J. and Bransford, J.D. (1971). Abstraction of visual patterns. *Journal of Experimental Psychology*, 90, 65–74.

Fransella, F. (1975). *Need to Change?* London: Methuen.

Fransella, F. (1984). Personal construct therapy. In W. Dryden (ed.), *Individual Therapy in Britain*. London: Harper & Row.

Franz, C.E., McClelland, D.C. and Weinberger, T. (1991). Childhood antecedents of conventional social accomplishment in midlife adults: a 36 year prospective study. *Journal of Personality and Social Psychology*, 60, 586–95.

Fraser, A.F. and Broom, D.M. (1990). *Farm Animal Behaviour and Welfare*. London: Baillière Tindall.

Fraser, C. (1981). The social psychology of unemployment. In M. Jeeves (ed.), *Psychology Survey No. 3*. London: Allen & Unwin.

Fraser, E.D. (1959). *Home Environment and the School*. London: University of London Press.

Freedman, J.L. and Fraser, S.C. (1966). Compliance without pressure: the foot-in-the-door technique. *Journal of Personality and Social Psychology*, 4, 195–202.

Freeman, D. (1983). *Margaret Mead and Samoa: The Making and Unmaking of an Anthropological Myth*. Cambridge, MA: Harvard University Press.

French, J.R.P. Jr and Raven, B.H. (1959). The bases of social power. In D. Cartwright (ed.), *Studies in Social Power*. Ann Arbor, MI: University of Michigan Press.

French, J.R.P., Caplan, R.D. and Van Harrison, R. (1982). *The Mechanisms of Job Stress and Strain*. New York: Wiley.

Freud, A. (1936). *The Ego and the Mechanisms of Defence*. London: Chatto & Windus.

Freud, A. (1958). Adolescence. In R.S. Eisler, A. Freud, H. Hartman and M. Kris (eds), *Psychoanalytic Study of the Child*, vol. 13. New York: International Universities Press.

Freud, A. and Dann, S. (1951). An experiment in group upbringing. *The Psychoanalytic Study of the Child*, 6, 127–68.

Freud, S. (1921). Group psychology and the analysis of the ego. In J. Strachey (ed.), *Standard Edition of the Complete Psychological Works*, vol. 18. London: Hogarth Press.

Freud, S. (1923). The ego and the id. In J. Strachey (ed.), *Standard Edition of the Complete Psychological Works of Sigmund Freud*, vol. 19. London: Hogarth Press.

Freud, S. (1933). *New Introductory Lectures on Psychoanalysis* (J. Strachey, ed. and trans.). New York: Norton.

Freud, S. (1938). *The Basic Writings of Sigmund Freud*. New York: Modern Library.

Freud, S. (1976). *The Interpretation of Dreams*. Harmondsworth: Pelican Freud Library (Original work published 1900).

Frey, K.S. and Ruble, D.N. (1987). What children say about classroom performance: sex and grade differences in perceived competence. *Child Development*, 58, 1066–78.

Frey, K.S. and Ruble, D.N. (1992). Gender constancy and the 'cost' of sex-typed behaviour: a test of the conflict hypothesis. *Developmental Psychology*, 28, 714–21.

Fried, I., Mateer, C., Ojemann, G., Wohns, R. and Fedio, P. (1982). Organisation of visuospatial functions in human cortex. *Brain*, 105, 349–71.

Friedman, M. and Rosenman, R.H. (1974). *Type A Behaviour and Your Heart*. New York: Knopf.

Frisch, K. von (1967). *The Dance Language and Orientation of Bees*. Cambridge, MA: The Belknap Press of Harvard University.

Fry, C. (1985). Culture, behaving and aging in a comparative perspective. In J.E. Birren and K.W. Schaie (eds), *Handbook of the Psychology of Aging*, 2nd edn. New York: Van Nostrand.

Furnham, A. (1981). Personality and activity preference. *British Journal of Social Psychology*, 20, 57–68.

Furnham, A. (1982). Psychoticism, social desirability and situation selection. *Personality and Individual Differences*, 3, 43–51.

Furnham, A. and Bitar, N. (1993). The stereotyped portrayal of men and women in British television advertisements. *Sex Roles*, 29, 297–310.

Gaebelein, J.W. (1973). Third party instigation of aggression: an experimental approach. *Journal of Personality and Social Psychology, 27, 389–95.

Gaertner, S.L and Dovidio, J.F. (1977). The subtlety of white racism, arousal and helping behaviour. Journal of Personality and Social Psychology, 35, 691–707.

Gaertner, S.L. and McLaughlin, J.P. (1983). Racial stereotypes; associations and ascriptions of positive and negative characteristics. Social Psychology Quarterly, 46, 23–40.

Gale, A. (1981). EEG studies of extraversion–introversion: what's the next step. In H.B. Gibson (ed.), Hans Eysenck: The Man and his Work. London: Peter Owen.

Gallie, D. and Vogler, C. (1994). Labour market deprivation, welfare and collectivism. In D. Gallie, C. Marsh and C. Vogler (eds), Social Change and the Experience of Unemployment. Oxford: Oxford University Press.

Gallie, D., Marsh, C. and Vogler, C. (eds) (1994). Social Change and the Experience of Unemployment. Oxford: Oxford University Press.

Galton, F. (1869). Heredity Genius: An Inquiry into its Laws and Consequences, 2nd edn, reprinted 1978. London: Julian Friedmann.

Ganster, D.C. (1986). Type A behaviour and occupational stress. Journal of Organizational Behaviour Management, 8 (2), 61–84.

Gardner, H. (1982). Developmental Psychology. Boston: Little, Brown & Co.

Gardner, H. (1983). Frames of Mind: The Theory of Multiple Intelligences. London: Heinemann.

Gardner, H. and Feldman, D. (1985). Project Spectrum. Annual Report submitted to the Spencer Foundation. Unpublished.

Gardner, R.A. and Gardner, B.T. (1969). Teaching sign language to a chimpanzee. Science, 165, 664–72.

Gardner, R.W., Jackson, D.N. and Messick, S.J. (1960). Personality organisation in cognitive controls and intellectual abilities. Psychological Issues, 2 (Monograph 8).

Garfield, S.L., Praner, R.A. and Bergin, A.E. (1971). Evaluation of outcome in psychotherapy. Journal of Consulting and Clinical Psychology, 37, 307–13.

Garner, W.R. (1979). Letter discrimination and identification. In A.D. Pick (ed.), Perception and its Development: A Tribute to Eleanor J. Gibson. Hillsdale, NJ: Lawrence Erlbaum.

Garvey, C. (1977). Play. London: Fontana/Open Books.

Geen, R.G. (1968). Effects of frustration, attack and prior training upon aggressive behaviour. Journal of Personality and Social Psychology, 9, 316–21.

Geen, R.G. and Donnerstein, E. (eds) (1983). Aggression: Theoretical and Empirical Reviews. New York: Academic Press.

Geen, R.G. and Stonner, D. (1971). Effects of aggressiveness habit-strength on behaviour in the presence of aggression-related stimuli. Journal of Personality and Social Psychology, 17, 149–53.

Geist, V. (1971). Mountain Sheep: A Study in Behaviour and Evolution. Chicago: University of Chicago Press.

Gellerman, L.W. (1933). Form discrimination in chimpanzees and two-year-old children: I Form (triangularity) per se. Journal of Genetic Psychology, 42, 3–27.

Gelman, R. and Shatz, M. (1977). Appropriate speech adjustments: the operation of conversational constraints on talk to two-year-olds. In M. Lewis and L.A. Rosenblum (eds), Interaction, Conversation and the Development of Language. New York: Wiley.

Gentry, W.D. (1970). Effects of frustration and attack and prior aggressive training on overt aggression and vascular processes. Journal of Personality and Social Psychology, 16, 718–25.

George, J.M. (1991). State or trait: effects of positive mood and prosocial behaviors at work. Journal of Applied Psychology, 76, 299–307.

Gerbner, G., Gross, L., Morgan, M. and Signorielli, N. (1986). Living with television: the dynamics of the cultivation process. In J. Bryant and D. Zillman (eds), Perspectives on Media Effects. Hillsdale, NJ: Erlbaum.

Gershuny, J. (1994). The psychological consequences of unemployment: an assessment of the Jahoda thesis. In D. Gallie, C. Marsh and C. Vogler (eds), (1994). Social Change and the Experience of Unemployment. Oxford: Oxford University Press.

Gibbons, F.X. (1990). Self attention and behaviour: a review and a theoretical update. Advances in Experimental Social Psychology, 23, 249–303.

Gibson, E.J. (1969). Principles of Perceptual Learning and Development. New York: Prentice-Hall.

Gibson, E.J. and Walk, R.D. (1960). The visual cliff. In Psychology in Progress,

Readings from Scientific American, pp. 51–8. San Francisco: Freeman.

Gibson, J.J. (1972). A theory of direct visual perception. In J.R. Royce and W.W. Rozeboom (eds), The Psychology of Knowing. London: Gordon & Breach.

Gibson, J.J. (1986). The Ecological Approach to Visual Perception. Hillsdale, NJ: Lawrence Erlbaum.

Gibson, R.M. and Bradbury, J.W. (1985). Sexual selection in lekking sage grouse: phenotypic correlates of male mating success. Behavioural Ecological Sociobiology, 18, 117–23.

Gilbert, D.T. (1989). Thinking lightly about others: automatic components of the social inference process. In J.S. Uleman and J.S. Bargh (eds), Unintended Thought. New York: Guilford Press.

Gilchrist, J.C. and Nesberg, L.S. (1952). Need and perceptual change in need-related objects. Journal of Experimental Psychology, 44, 369.

Gill, F.B. and Wolf, L.L. (1975). Economics of feeding territoriality in the golden winged sunbird. Ecology, 56, 333–45.

Gilligan, C. (1977). In a different voice: women's conception of the self and of morality. Harvard Educational Review, 47, 481–517.

Gilligan, C. (1982). In a Different Voice: Psychological Theory and Women's Development. Cambridge, MA: Harvard University Press.

Gittleman-Klein, R., Klein, D., Abikoff, H., Katz, S., Gloisten, A. and Kates, W. (1976). Relative efficacy of methylphenidate and behaviour modification in hyperkinetic children: an interim report. Journal of Abnormal Child Psychology, 4, 361–79.

Glassman, W.E. (1995). Approaches to Psychology, 2nd edn. Buckingham: Open University Press.

Goffman, E. (1967). Interaction Ritual: Essays on Face-to-face Behaviour. Garden City, NY: Doubleday.

Goldberg, E. and Morrison, S. (1963). Schizophrenia and social class. British Journal of Psychiatry, 109, 785–802.

Goldberg, L.R. (1993). The structure of phenotypic personality traits. American Psychologist, 48 (2), 26–33.

Goldberg, P. (1968). Are some women prejudiced against women? Trans-Action, 5, 28–33.

Goldfarb, W. (1943). The effects of early institutional care on adolescent personality. Journal of Experimental Education, 12, 106–29.

Goldman, R.J. and Goldman, J.D.G. (1981). How children view old people and ageing: a developmental study of children in four countries. *Australian Journal of Psychology, 3*, 405–18.

Goldman-Eisler, F. (1948). Breast feeding and character formation. *Journal of Personality, 17*, 83–103.

Goleman, D. (1995). *Emotional Intelligence*. London: Bloomsbury.

Gombrich, E.H. (1960). *Art and Illusion*. Oxford: Phaidon Press.

Goodall, J. (1978). Chimp killings: is it the man in them?, *Science News, 113*, 276.

Goodall, J. van Lawick (1968). The behaviour of free living chimpanzees in the Gombe Stream Reserve. *Animal Behaviour Monograph, 1*, 161–311.

Goodall, J. van Lawick (1974). *In the Shadow of Man*. London: Fontana.

Gopnik, A. and Astington, J.W. (1988). Children's understanding of representational change and its relation to the understanding of false belief and the appearance–reality distinction. *Child Development, 59*, 26–37.

Gopnik, A. and Astington, J.W. (1991). Theoretical explanations of children's understanding of the mind. *British Journal of Developmental Psychology, 9*, 77–31.

Gottesman, I. (1991). *Schizophrenia Genesis: The Origins of Madness*. New York: Freeman.

Gottesman, I. and Shields, J. (1982). *Schizophrenia: The Epigenetic Puzzle*. New York: Cambridge University Press.

Göttmark, F. and Andersson, M. (1984). Colonial breeding reduces nest predation in the common gull. *Animal Behaviour, 32*, 323–33.

Gould, J.L., Dyer, F.C. and Towne, W.F. (1985). Recent progress in understanding the honey bee dance language. *Fortschritte der Zoologie, 31*, 141–61.

Gould, S.J. (1981). *The Mismeasure of Man*. London: Penguin.

Gouzoules, S. and Gouzoules, H. (1987). Kinship. In B.B. Smuts, D.L. Cheney, R.M. Seyfarth, R.W. Wrangham and T.T. Struhsacker (eds), *Primate Studies*. Chicago: University of Chicago Press.

Gove, W.R. (1970). Societal reaction as an explanation of mental illness: an evaluation. *American Sociological Review, 35*, 873–84.

Gramza, A.F. (1967). Responses of brooding night hawks to a disturbance stimulus. *Auk, 84* (1), 72–86.

Granberg, D. (1987). Candidate preference, membership group and estimates of voting behaviour. *Social Cognition, 5*, 323–5.

Gray, D.R. and Wedderburn, A.A. (1960). Grouping strategies with simultaneous stimuli. *Quarterly Journal of Experimental Psychology, 12*, 180–4.

Gray, J. (1991). On the morality of speciesism. *Bulletin of the British Psychological Society, 4*, (5), 196–8.

Gray, J.A. (1987). The ethics and politics of animal experimentation. In H. Beloff and A.M. Colman (eds), *Psychological Survey No. 6*. Leicester: The British Psychological Society.

Gray, J.S. and Thompson, A.H. (1953). The ethnic prejudices of white and Negro college students. *Journal of Abnormal and Social Psychology, 48*, 311–13.

Green, D.M. and Swets, J.A. (1966). *Signal Detection in Theory and Psychophysics*. New York: Wiley.

Greene, E., Flynn, M.S and Loftus, E.F. (1982). Inducing resistance of misleading information. *Journal of Verbal Learning and Verbal Behaviour, 21*, 207–19.

Greeno, J.G. (1974). Process of understanding problem solving. In N.J. Castellan Jr, D.B. Pisoni and D.R. Potts (eds), *Cognitive Theory*, vol. 2. Hillsdale, NJ: Erlbaum.

Gregory, R.L. and Wallace, J. (1963). *Recovery from Early Blindness*. Cambridge: Heffer.

Gregory, R.L. (1968a). On how so little information controls so much behaviour. In C.H. Waddington (ed.), *Towards a Theoretical Biology*. Edinburgh: Churchill-Livingstone.

Gregory, R.L. (1968b). Visual illusions. In *Psychology in Progress: Readings from Scientific American*. San Francisco: Freeman.

Gregory, R.L. (1970). *The Intelligent Eye*. London: Weidenfeld & Nicolson.

Gregory, R.L. (1972a). Cognitive contours. *Nature, 238*, 51–2.

Gregory, R.L. (1972b). Visual illusions. In B.M. Foss (ed.), *New Horizons in Psychology*. Harmondsworth: Penguin.

Gregory, R.L. (1996). *Eye and Brain*, 4th edn. London: Weidenfeld & Nicolson.

Griffin, D.R. (1958). *Listening in the Dark*. New Haven, CT: Yale University Press.

Griffin, D.R. (1984). *Animal Thinking*. Cambridge, MA: Harvard University Press.

Groninger, L.D. (1971). Mnemonic imagery and forgetting. *Psychonomic Science, 23*, 161–3.

Gross, R. (1995). *Themes, Issues and Debates in Psychology*. London: Hodder & Stoughton.

Grossman, K.E., Grossman, K., Huber, F. and Wartner, U. (1981). German children's behaviour towards their mothers at 12 months and their fathers at 18 months in Ainsworth's strange situation. *International Journal of Behavioural Development, 4*, 157–81.

Gruber, E.R. and Kersten, H. (1995). *The Original Jesus: The Buddhist Sources of Christianity*. Shaftesbury: Element.

Gruen, A. (1957). A critique and re-evaluation of Witkin's perception and perception–personality work. *Journal of General Psychology, 56*, 73–93.

Grusec, J.E. and Redler, E. (1980). Attribution, reinforcement and altruism. *Developmental Psychology, 16*, 525–34.

Grusec, J.E. and Skubisky, S.L. (1970). Model nurturance, demand characteristics of the modeling experiment, and altruism. *Journal of Personality and Social Psychology, 14*, 352–59.

Grusec, J.E., Kuczynski, L., Rushton, J.P. and Simutis, Z.M. (1978). Modelling, direct instruction, and attributions: effects on altruism. *Developmental Psychology, 14*, 51–7.

Guimond, S. and Dubé-Sinard, L. (1983). Relative deprivation theory and the Québec Nationalist Movement; the cognitive–emotion distinction and the personal–group deprivation issue. *Journal of Personality and Social Psychology, 44*, 526–35.

Guiton, P. (1959). Socialisation and imprinting in brown leghorn chicks. *Animal Behaviour, 16*, 261–94.

Haan, N., Millsap, R. and Hartka, E. (1986). As time goes by: change and stability in personality over 50 years. *Psychology and Aging, 1*, 220–32.

Haartman, L. von (1969). Nest site and the evolution of polygyny in European passerine birds. *Ornis Fennica, 46* (1), 1–12.

Haas, F.J. and Fleming, G.J. (1946). Personnel practices and wartime changes. *Annals of the American Academy of Political and Social Psychology, 244*, 48–56.

Haber, R.N. (1983a). The impending demise of the icon: a critique of the concept of iconic storage in visual information processing. *Behavioural and Brain Sciences, 6*, 1–11.

Haber, R.N. (1983b). The icon is really dead. *Behavioural and Brain Sciences*, 6, 43–55.

Haber, R.N. (1985). An icon can have no worth in the real world: comments on Loftus, Johnson and Shinamura's 'How much is an icon worth?'. *Journal of Experimental Psychology: Human Perception and Performance*, 11, 374–8.

Haider, M., Spong, P. and Linsley, D. (1964). Attention, vigilance, and evoked cortical potential in humans. *Science*, 145, 180–2.

Hall, C.S. and Lindzey, G. (1978). *Theories of Personality*, 3rd edn. New York: Wiley.

Hall, K.R.L. (1960). Social vigilance behaviour of the chacma baboon (*Papio ursinus*). *Behaviour*, 16, 261–94.

Halpin, A.W. (1966). *Theory and Research in Administration*. New York: Macmillan.

Hamilton, W.D. (1964). The genetical evolution of social behaviour, I and II. *Journal of Theoretical Biology*, 7, 1–52.

Hamilton, W.D. (1971a). Selfish and spiteful behaviour in an evolutionary model. *Nature (London)*, 228 (5277), 1218–20.

Hamilton, W.D. (1971b). Geometry for the selfish herd. *Journal of Theoretical Biology*, 31, 295–311.

Hampson, S. (1988). *The Construction of Personality: An Introduction*, 2nd edn. London: Routledge.

Hampson, S. and Kline, P. (1977). Personality dimensions differentiating certain groups of abnormal offenders from non-offenders. *British Journal of Criminology*, 17, 310–31.

Hampson, S.E. (1988). *The Construction of Personality: An Introduction*, 2nd edn. London: Routledge.

Haney, C., Banks, C. and Zimbardo, P. (1973). Interpersonal dynamics in a simulated prison. *International Journal of Criminolgy and Penology*, 1, 69–97.

Haracz, J. (1982). The dopamine hypothesis: an overview of studies with schizophrenic patients. *Schizophrenia Bulletin*, 8, 438–69.

Hardin, G. (1968). The tragedy of the commons. *Science*, 162, 1243–8.

Hardy, G.R. and Legge, D.L (1968). Cross modal induction changes in sensory thresholds. *Quarterly Journal of Experimental Psychology*, 20, 20–9.

Hare, R.D. (1980). A research scale for the assessment of psychopathy in criminal populations. *Personality and Individual Differences*, 1, 111–19.

Hare-Mustin, R.T. and Maracek, J. (1990). *Making a Difference: Psychology and the Construction of Gender*. New Haven, CT: Yale University Press.

Hargreaves, D.H. (1967). *Social Relations in a Secondary School*. London: Routledge & Kegan Paul.

Harlow, H. (1958). The Nature of Love. *American Psychologist*, 13, 637–85.

Harlow, H. and Harlow, M. (1969). Effects of various mother–innant relationships on rhesus monkey behaviours. In B.M. Foss (ed.), *Determinants of Infant Behaviour*, vol. 4. London: Methuen.

Harlow, H.F., Harlow, M.K. and Meyer, D.R. (1950). Learning motivated by a manipulation drive. *Journal of Experimental Psychology*, 40, 228–34.

Harré, R. (1979). *Social Being*. Oxford: Basil Blackwell.

Harrington, R. (1993). *Depressive Disorder in Childhood and Adolescence*. Chichester: Wiley.

Harris, J.E. (1984). Remembering to do things: a forgotten topic. In J.E. Harris and P.E. Morris (eds), *Everyday Memory, Actions and Absent-mindedness*. London: Academic Press.

Harris, M.B. (1974). Mediators between frustration and aggression in a field experiment. *Journal of Experimental Social Psychology*, 10, 561–71.

Harris, P.L. (1983). Infant cognition. In P. Mussen (ed.), *Handbook of Child Psychology*, vol. II. New York: Wiley.

Harris, P.L., Johnson, C.N., Hutton, D., Andrews, G. and Cooke, T. (1989). Young children's theory of mind and emotion. *Cognition and Emotion*, 3, 379–400.

Harter, S. (1982). *The Perceived Competence Scale for Children*. University of Denver.

Harter, S. (1987). The determinants and mediational role of global self-worth in children. In N. Eisenberg (ed.), *Contemporary Topics in Developmental Psychology*. New York: Wiley.

Hartline, H.K. (1938). What the frog's eye tells the frog's brain. *American Journal of Physiology*, 121, 400–6.

Hartmann, E.L. (1973). *The Functions of Sleep*. Newhaven, CT: Yale University Press.

Hartshorne, H. and May, M.A. (1928). *Studies in the Nature of Character*, vol. 1: *Studies in Deceit*. New York: Macmillan.

Hartup, W.W. (1983). Peer relations. In E.M. Hetherington (ed.), *Handbook of Child Psychology*, vol. IV: *Socialisa-*tion, *Personality and Social Development*. New York: Wiley.

Harwood, R.L. and Miller, J.G. (1991). Perceptions of attachment behavior: a comparison of Anglo and Puerto Rican mothers. *Merrill-Palmer Quarterly*, 37, 583–99.

Hatfield, E. (1987). Love. In R.J. Corsini (ed.), *Concise Encyclopaedia of Psychology*. New York: Wiley.

Hatfield, E. and Walster, G.W. (1981). *A New Look at Love*. Reading, MA: Addison-Wesley.

Hawkins, L.H. and Armstong-Esther, C.A. (1978). Circadian rhythms and night-shift working in nurses. *Nursing Times*, 4 May, 49–52.

Hayes, C. (1951). *The Ape in Our House*. New York: Harper & Row.

Hayes, K.J. and Hayes, C. (1952). Imitation in a home raised chimpanzee. *Journal of Comparative and Physiological Psychology*, 45, 450–9.

Hayes, N. (1986). The magic of sociobiology. *Psychology Teaching*, part 2, 2–16.

Hayes, N. (1993). *Principles of Social Psychology*. Hove: Lawrence Erlbaum Associates.

Hays, R.B. (1985). A longitudinal study of friendship development. *Journal of Personality and Social Psychology*, 48, 909–24.

Hays, R.B. and Oxley, D. (1986). Social network development and functioning during a life transition. *Journal of Personality and Social Psychology*, 50, 305–13.

Hazan, C. and Shaver, P. (1987). Romantic love conceptualized as an attachment process. *Journal of Personality and Social Psychology*, 52, 511–24.

Hazan, C. and Shaver, P. (1990). Love and work: an attachment-theoretical perspective. *Journal of Personality and Social Psychology*, 59, 270–80.

Hearnshaw, L.S. (1987). *The Shaping of Modern Psychology*. London: Routledge & Kegan Paul.

Heather, N. (1976). *Radical Perspectives in Psychology*. London: Methuen.

Hebb, D.O. (1949). *The Organisation of Behaviour*. New York: Wiley.

Hebb, D.O. (1958). *A Textbook of Psychology*. Philadelphia: P. Saunders.

Heider, F. (1946). Attitudes and cognitive organization. *Journal of Psychology*, 21, 107–12.

Heider, F. (1958). *The Psychology of Interpersonal Relations*. New York: Wiley.

Heider, F. and Simmel, M. (1944). The experimental study of apparent behaviour. *American Journal of Psychology,* 57, 243–59.

Heiligenberg, W. and Kramer, U. (1972). Aggressiveness as a function of external stimulation. *Journal of Comparative Physiology,* 77, 332–40.

Heim, A. (1970). *Intelligence and Personality – Their Assessment and Relationship.* Harmondsworth: Penguin.

Heinicke, C.H. and Guthrie, D. (1992). Stability and change in husband–wife adaptation and the development of the positive parent–child relationship. *Infant Behaviour and Development,* 15, 109–27.

Hering, E. (1878). *Outlines of a Theory of the Light Sense* (translation). Cambridge, MA: Harvard University Press.

Herman, L., Richards, D.G. and Wolz, J.P. (1984). Comprehension of sentences by bottle-nosed dolphins. *Cognition,* 16, 129–219.

Herman, L.M. (ed.) (1980). *Cetacean Behavior: Mechanisms and Functions.* New York: Wiley Inter-Science.

Herman, R. (1984). The genetic relationship between identical twins. *Early Child Development,* 16, 265–75.

Herriot, P. (1970). *An Introduction to the Psychology of Language.* London: Methuen.

Hersh, S. (1970). *My Lai: A Report on the Massacre and its Aftermath.* New York: Vintage Books.

Hess, E.H. (1959). Imprinting. *Science,* 130, 133–41.

Hess, E.H. (1962). Ethology. In R. Brown, E. Galanter, E.H. Hess and G. Mandler (eds), *New Directions in Psychology.* New York: Holt.

Hess, E.H. (1972). Imprinting in a natural laboratory. In *Psychology in Progress: Readings from Scientific American.* San Francisco: W.H. Freeman.

Hess, R.D. and Shipman, V. (1965). Early experience and the socialization of cognitive modes in children. *Child Development,* 36, 860–86.

Hetherington, A.W. and Ransom, S.W. (1942). Hypothalamic lesions and adiposity in the rat. *Anatomical Record,* 78, 149–72.

Hick, W.F. (1952). On the rate of gain of information. *Quarterly Journal of Experimental Psychology,* 4, 11.

Higgins, E.T. (1987). Self discrepancy: a theory relating self and affect. *Psychological Review,* 94, 319–40.

Hilgard, E. (1979). *Personality and Hypnosis: A Study of Imaginative Involvement,* 2nd edn. Chicago: University of Chicago Press.

Hilgard, E.R. (1977). *Divided Consciousness: Multiple Controls in Human Thought and Action.* New York: Wiley.

Hilgard, E.R. and Atkinson, R. (1979). *Introduction to Psychology,* 7th edn. Harcourt Brace Jovanovitch.

Hill, A.B. (1976). Methodological problems in the use of factor analysis: a critical review of the experimental evidence for the anal character. *British Journal of Medical Psychology,* 49, 145–59.

Hill, C.T., Rubin, Z. and Peplau, L.A. (1976). Break-ups before marriage: the end of 103 affairs. *Journal of Social Issues,* 32 (1), 147–68.

Hill, P. (1993). Recent advances in selected areas of adolescent development. *Journal of Child Psychology and Psychiatry,* 34, 69–90.

Hill, R. (1945). Campus values in mate selection. *Journal of Home Economics,* 37, 554–78.

Hill, T., Lewicki, P., Czyzewska, M. and Boss, A. (1989). Self perpetuating development of encoding biases in person perception. *Journal of Personality and Social Psychology,* 57, 373–87.

Hinde, R.A. (1966). *Animal Behaviour.* London: McGraw-Hill.

Hinde, R.A. (1987). *Individuals, Relationships and Culture: Links between Ethology and the Social Sciences.* Cambridge: Cambridge University Press.

Hinde, R.A. and Rowell, T.E. (1962). Communication by postures and facial expressions in the rhesus monkey (*Macaca mulatta*). *Proceedings of the Zoological Society of London,* 138, 1–21.

Hines, M. (1982). Prenatal gonadal hormones and sex differences in human behaviour. *Psychological Bulletin,* 92, 56–80.

Hinshaw, S.P., Lahey, B.B. and Hart, E.L. (1993). Issues of taxonomy and co-morbidity in the development of conduct disorders. *Development and Psychopathology,* 5, 31–49.

Hirshberg, N. (1978). A correct treatment of traits. In H. London (ed.), *Personality: A New Look at Metatheories.* New York: Macmillan.

Hitler, A. (1962). *Mein Kampf.* Boston: Houghton Mifflin (originally published in 1925).

Hobson, J.A. and McCarley, R.W. (1977). The brain as a dream state generator: an activation–synthesis hypothesis of the dream process. *American Journal of Psychiatry,* 134, 1335–48.

Hobson, R.P. (1990). On acquiring knowledge about people and the capacity to pretend: response to Leslie (1987). *Psychological Review,* 97, 114–21.

Hockett, C.F. (1959). Animal languages and human language. *Human Biology,* 31, 32–9.

Hockett, C.F. (1960). The origin of speech. *Scientific American,* 203, 8–96.

Hodges, J. and Tizard, B. (1989). IQ and behavioural adjustment of ex-institutional adolescents; and social and family relationships of ex-institutional adolescents. *Journal of Child Psychology and Psychiatry,* 30, 53–75; 77–98.

Hoffman, M.L. (1978). Empathy, its development and prosocial implications. In C.B. Keasey (ed.), *Nebraska Symposium on Motivation,* vol 25. Lincoln, NE: University of Nebraska Press.

Hoffman, M.L. (1979). Identification and imitation in children. *ERIC Reports,* ED 175 537.

Hoffman, M.L. (1984). Moral development. In M.H. Bornstein and M.H. Lamb (eds), *Developmental Psychology: An Advanced Textbook.* Hillsdale, NJ: Erlbaum.

Hofling, K.C., Brontzman, E., Dalrymple, S., Graves, N. and Pierce, C.M. (1966). An experimental study in the nurse/physician relationship. *Journal of Mental and Nervous Disorders,* 43, 171–8.

Hogg, M.A. (1992). *The Social Psychology of Group Cohesiveness: From Attraction to Social Identity.* London: Harvester Wheatsheaf.

Hogg, M.A. and Vaughan, G.M. (1995). *Social Psychology: an Introduction.* Hemel Hempstead: Prentice-Hall/Harvester Wheatsheaf.

Hohmann, G.W. (1962). Some effects of spinal cord lesions on experienced emotional feelings. *Psychophysiology,* 3, 143–56.

Holley, J.W. (1973). Rorschach analysis. In P. Kline (ed.), *New Approaches in Psychological Measurement.* Chichester: Wiley.

Hollingshead, A.B. and Redlich, F.C. (1958). *Social Class and Mental Illness: A Community Study.* New York: Wiley.

Holmes, D.S. (1974). Investigations of repression: differential recall of material experimentally or naturally associated with ego threat. *Psychological Bulletin,* 81, 632–53.

Holmes, J.G. (1989). Trust and the appraisal process in close relationships. In W.H. Jones and D. Perlman (eds), *Advances in Personal Relationships*, vol.2. Greenwich, CT: JAI Press.

Holmes, T.H. and Masuda, M. (1974). Life changes and illness susceptability. In B.S. Dohrenwend and B.P. Dohrenwend (eds), *Stressful Life Events: Their Nature and Effects*. New York: Wiley.

Holmes, T.H. and Rahe, R.H. (1967). The Social Readjustment Rating Scale. *Journal of Psychosomatic Research*, 11, 213–8.

Holmes, W.G. and Sherman, P.W. (1982). The ontogeny of kin recognition in two species of ground squirrels. *American Zoologist*, 22, 491–597.

Holstein, C.B. (1976). Irreversible, stepwise sequence in the development of moral judgment: a longitudinal study of males and females. *Child Development*, 47, 51–61.

Holt, R. (1962). Individuality and generalisation in the psychology of personality. *Journal of Personality*, 30, 377–404.

Homans, G.C. (1958). Social behaviour and exchange. *American Journal of Sociology*, 63, 597–646.

Homans, G.C. (1961). *Social Behavior: Its Elementary Forms*, New York: Harcourt Brace & World.

Homans, G.C. (1974). *Social Behaviour: Its Elementary Forms*, rev. ed. New York: Harcourt Brace Jovanovich.

Honzik, M.P. (1986). The role of the family in the development of mental abilities: a 50-year study. In N. Datan, A.L. Greene and H.W. Reese (eds), *Life-span Developmental Psychology: Intergenerational Relations*. Hillsdale, NJ: Erlbaum.

Hoogland, W.G. and Sherman, P.W. (1976). Advantages and disadvantages of bank swallow coloniality. *Ecological Monograph*, 46, 33–58.

Hooker, T. and Hooker, B. I. (1969). Duetting. In R.A. Hinde (ed.), *Bird Vocalizations: Their Relations to Current Problems in Biology and Psychology: Essays presented to W. H. Thorpe*. Cambridge: Cambridge University Press.

Hopfield, J.J. (1984). Neural networks and physical systems with emergent collective computational properties. *Proceedings of the National Academy of Science of the USA*, 81, 3088–92.

Horn, G. (1985). *Memory, Imprinting and the Brain*. Oxford: Clarendon Press.

Horn, G. (1990). Neural bases of recognition memory investigated through an analysis of imprinting. *Philosophical Transactions of the Royal Society of London, Series B*, 329, 133–42.

Horn, J.L. and Donaldson, G. (1980). Cognitive development in adulthood. In O.G. Brim Jr and J. Kagan (eds), *Constancy and Change in Human Development*. Cambridge, MA: Harvard University Press.

Horn, J.M., Loehlin, J.L. and Willerman, L. (1979). Intellectual resemblance among adoptive and biological relatives: the Texas adoption project. *Behaviour Genetics*, 9, 177–207.

Horne, J. (1988). *Why We Sleep: The Functions of Sleep in Humans and Other Mammals*. Oxford: Oxford University Press.

Horne, J.A. and Osterberg, O. (1977). Individual differences in human circadian rhythms. *Biological Psychology*, 5, 179–90.

Hornstein, G.A. (1970). The influence of social models on helping. In J. Macaulay and L. Berkowitz (eds), *Altruism and Helping Behaviour*. New York: Academic Press.

Horowitz, F.D. (1987). *Exploring Developmental Theories: Toward a Structural/Behavioural Model of Development*. Hillsdale, NJ: Erlbaum.

Horowitz, F.D. (1990). Developmental models of individual differences. In J. Colombo and J. Fagen (eds), *Individual Differences in Infancy: Reliability, Stability, Prediction*, pp. 3–18. Hillsdale, NJ: Erlbaum.

Hovland, C.I. and Sherif, M. (1952). Judgmental phenomena and scales of attitude measurement: item displacement in Thurstone Scales. *Journal of Abnormal and Social Psychology*, 47, 822–32.

Howarth, E. (1982). Factor analytical examination of Kline's scales for psychoanalytic concepts. *Personality and Individual Differences*, 3, 89–92.

Howes, D.H. and Solomon, R.L (1951). Visual duration threshold as a function of word probability. *Journal of Experimental Psychology*, 41, 401–10.

Howitt, D. and Owusu-Bempah, J. (1994). *The Racism of Psychology*. London: Harvester Wheatsheaf.

Hsu, F.L.K. (1985). The self in cross-cultural perspective. In Marsella A.J. et al. (eds), *Culture and Self: Asian and Western Perspectives*. London: Tavistock Publications.

Hubel, D.H. (1977). Functional architecture of macaque monkey visual cortex. *Proceedings of the Royal Society of London, Series B*, 198, 1–59.

Hubel, D.H. (1982). Exploration of the primary visual cortex, 1955–78. *Nature*, 299, 515–24.

Hubel, D.H. and Wiesel, T.N. (1962). Receptive fields in the striate cortex of young visually inexperienced kittens. *Journal of Neurophysiology*, 26, 994.

Hubel, D.H. and Wiesel, T.N. (1965). Receptive fields of single neurons in two non-striate visual areas, 18 and 19 of the cat. *Journal of Neurophysiology*, 28, 229–89.

Hubel, D.H. and Wiesel, T.N. (1979). Brain mechanisms of vision. *Scientific American*, 241, 130–44.

Hudson, J.W. and Henze, L.F. (1969). Campus values in mate selection: a replication. *Journal of Marriage and the Family*, 31, 772–5.

Hudson, W. (1960). Pictorial depth perception in subcultural groups in Africa. *Journal of Social Psychology*, 52, 183–208.

Huesmann, L.R., Eron, L.D., Lefkowitz, M.M. and Walder, L.O. (1984). Stability of aggression over time and generations. *Developmental Psychology*, 20, 1120–34.

Hughes, J., Smith, T.W., Kosterlitz, H.W., Fothergill, L.A., Morgan, B.A. and Moris, H.R. (1975). Identification of two related pentapeptides from the brain with potent opiate agonist activity, *Nature*, 258, 577–9.

Hughes, M. (1975). Egocentrism in preschool children. Unpublished doctoral dissertation, Edinburgh University.

Hull, C. (1943). *Principles of Behaviour*. New York: Appleton-Century-Crofts.

Humphrey, N.K. (1976). The social function of intellect. In P.P.G. Bateson and R.A. Hinde (eds), *Growing Points in Ethology*. Cambridge: Cambridge University Press.

Hunter, E.J. (1979). Combat casualties who remain at home. Paper presented at Western Regional Conference of the Interuniversity Seminar Technology in Combat. Navy Postgraduate School, Monterey, CA.

Hunter, J.E. and Schmidt, F.L. (1976). Critical analysis of statistical and ethical implications of various definitions of test bias. *Psychological Bulletin*, 85, 675–6.

Hurvich, L.M. (1981). *Colour Vision*. Sunderland, MA: Sinauer Associates.

Huston, A.C. (1983). Sex-typing. In P.H. Mussen (ed.), *Carmichael's Manual of Child Psychology*, 4th edn. New York: Wiley.

Huston, A.C. (1985). The development of sex-typing: themes from recent research. *Developmental Review, 5,* 1–17.

Hutt, C. (1966). Exploration and play in children. *Symposia of the Zoological Society of London, 18,* 61–81.

Hutt, C. and Bhavnani, R. (1972). Predictions from play. *Nature, 237,* 171–2.

Huxley, J.S. (1914). The courtship habits of the great crested grebe (*Podiceps cristatus*). *Proceedings of the Zoological Society, London, 1914* (2): 491–562.

Hyman, B.T., Van Hoesen, G., Damasio, A. and Barnes, C.L. (1984). Alzheimer's disease: cell-specific pathology isolates the hippocampal formation. *Science, 225,* 1168–70.

Inglis, J. (1969). Electrode placement and the effect of ECT on mood and memory in depression. *Canadian Psychiatric Association Journal, 14,* 463–71.

Insell, T., Murphy, D., Cohen, R., Alterman, I., Itts, C. and Linnoila, M. (1983). Obsessive compulsive disorders. A double-blind trial of clomipramine and clorgyline. *Archives of General Psychiatry, 40,* 605–12.

Insko, C.A., Smith, R.H., Alicke, M.D., Wade, J. and Taylor, S. (1985) Conformity and group size: the concern with being right and the concern with being liked. *Personality and Social Science Bulletin, 11,* 41–50.

Irvine, S.H. (1966). Towards a rationale for testing attainments and abilities in Africa. *British Journal of Educational Psychology, 36,* 24–32.

Isen, A.M. (1987). Positive affect, cognitive processes and social behaviour: the warm glow of success. *Journal of Personality and Social Psychology, 15,* 294–301.

Iyengar, S. and Kinder, D.R. (1987). *News That Matters.* Chicago: University of Chicago Press.

Jackson, B. and Jackson, S. (1979). *Childminder: A Study in Action Research.* London: Routledge & Kegan Paul.

Jackson, L.A. (1992). *Physical Appearance and Gender: Sociobiological and Sociocultural Perspectives.* Albany, NY: State University of New York Press.

Jackson, S.E., Schwab, R.L. and Schuler, R.S. (1986). Toward an understanding of the burnout phenomenon. *Journal of Applied Psychology, 71,* 630–40.

Jahoda, G. (1966). Geometric illusions and environment: a study in Ghana. *British Journal of Psychology, 57,* 193–9.

Jahoda, G. (1983). European lag in the development of an economic concept: a study in Zimbabwe. *British Journal of Developmental Psychology, 1,* 113–20.

Jahoda, M. (1958). *Current Concepts of Positive Mental Health.* New York: Basic Books.

Jahoda, M. (1982). *Employment and Unemployment: A Social-Psychological Analysis.* Cambridge: Cambridge University Press.

James, W. (1890). *Principles of Psychology.* New York: Holt.

Jamieson, A. (1990). Informal care in Europe. In A. Jamieson and R. Illsley (eds), *Contrasting European Policies for the Care of Older People.* Aldershot: Avebury.

Janis, I.L. (1982). *Groupthink: Psychological Studies of Policy Decisions and Fiascos,* 2nd edn. Boston, MA: Houghton Mifflin).

Janis, I.L. and Mann, L. (1977). *Decision Making.* New York: Free Press.

Jarman, P.J. (1974). The social organisation of the antelope in relation to ecology. *Behaviour, 48,* 215–55.

Jarvis, P.A. and Creasey, G.L. (1991). Parental stress, coping and attachment in families with an 18-month-old infant. *Infant Behaviour and Development, 14,* 383–95.

Jason, L.A., Rose, T., Ferrari, J.R. and Barone, R. (1984). Personal versus impersonal methods of recruiting blood donors. *Journal of Social Psychology, 123,* 139–40.

Jellison, J.M. and Green, J. (1981). A self representation approach to the fundamental attribution error: the nom of internality. *Journal of Personality and Social Psychology, 40,* 643–9.

Jemmott, J. and Locke, S. (1984). Psychosocial factors, immunologic mediation and human susceptibility to infectious diseases: how much do we know? *Psychological Bulletin, 95,* 78–108.

Jemmott, J.B. III, Borysenko, M., McClelland, D.C., Chapman, R., Meyer, D. and Benson, H. (1985). Academic stress, power motivation and decrease in salivary secretory immunoglobulin: a secretation rate. *Lancet, 1,* 1400–2.

Jennett, B. (1993). Vegetative survival: the medical facts and ethical dilemmas. *Neuropsychological Rehabilitation, 3* (2), 99–108.

Jennett, B. and Plum, F. (1972). Persistent vegetative state after brain damage: a syndrome in search of a name. *Lancet, i,* 734–7.

Jensen, A.R. (1969). How much can we boost IQ and scholastic achievement? *Harvard Educational Review, 39,* 1–123.

Jerison, H.J. (1985). Animal intelligence and encephalization. *Philosophical Transactions of the Royal Society of London, Series B, 308,* 21–35.

Jermier, J.M., Gaines, J. and McIntosh, NJ. (1989). Reactions to physically dangerous work: a conceptual and empirical analysis. *Journal of Organizational Behaviour, 10,* 15–33.

Johnson, D.W. and Johnson, F.P. (1987). *Joining Together: Group Theory and Group Skills,* 3rd edn. Englewood Cliffs, NJ: Prentice-Hall.

Johnson, J. and Ettema, J.S. (1982). *Positive Images: Breaking Stereotypes with Children's Television.* Beverly Hills and London: Sage.

Johnson, J.E., Erschler, J. and Lawton, J.T. (1982). Intellective correlates of preschoolers' spontaneous play. *Journal of Genetic Psychology, 106,* 115–22.

Johnson, J.H. and Sarason, I. G. (1978). Life stress, depression and anxiety: internal/external control as a moderator variable. *Journal of Psychosomatic Research, 22* (3), 205–8.

Johnson, M.K. and Hasher, L. (1987). Human learning and memory. *Annual Review of Psychology, 38,* 631–68.

Johnston, W.A. and Heinz, S.P. (1978). Flexibility and capacity demands of attention. *Journal of Experimental Psychology: General, 107,* 420–35.

Johnston, W.A. and Wilson, J. (1980). Perceptual processing of non-targets in an attention task. *Memory and Cognition, 8,* 372–7.

Jolicoeur, P. and Landau, M.J. (1984). Effects of orientation on the identification of simple visual patterns. *Canadian Journal of Psychology, 38,* 80–93.

Jolly, A. (1966). *Lemur Behaviour.* Chicago: Chicago University Press.

Jones, E.E. and Davis, K.E. (1965). From acts to disposition: the attribution process in person perception. In L. Berkowitz (ed.), *Advances in Experimental Social Psychology.* New York: Academic Press.

Jones, E.E. and Harris, V.A. (1967). The attribution of attitudes. *Journal of Experimental Social Psychology, 3,* 1–24.

Jones, E.E. and McGillis, D. (1976). Correspondent inferences and the attribution cube: a comparative reappraisal. In J.H. Harvey, W.J. Ickes and R.F. Kidd (eds), *New Directions in Attribution Research*, vol. 1. Hillsdale, NJ: Erlbaum.

Jones, E.E. and Nisbett, R.E. (1972). The actor and the observer: divergent perceptions of the causes of behaviour. In E.E. Jones, D.E. Kanouse, H.H. Kelley, R.E. Nisbett, S. Valins and B. Weiner (eds), *Attribution: Perceiving Causes of Behaviour*. Morristown, NJ: General Learning Press.

Jones, E.E. and Sigall, H. (1971). The bogus pipeline: a new paradigm for measuring affect and attitude. *Psychological Bulletin*, 76, 349–64.

Jones, E.E., Davis, K.E. and Gergen, K.J. (1961). Role playing variations and their informational value for person perception. *Journal of Abnormal and Social Psychology*, 63, 302–10.

Jones, S. (1993). *The Language of the Genes*. London: Harper Collins Flamingo.

Jorgensen, B.W and Cervone, J.C. (1978). Affect enhancement in the pseudo-recognition task. *Personality and Social Psychology Bulletin*, 4, 285–88.

Josephson, W.L. (1987). Television violence and children's aggression. Testing and priming, social script and disinhibition predictions. *Journal of Personality and Social Psychology*, 53, 882–90.

Joule, R.V, Goullioux, F. and Weber, F. (1989). The lure: a new compliance technique. *Journal of Social Psychology*, 129, 741–49.

Judd, C.M. and Park, B. (1988). Outgroup homogeneity: judgements of variability at the individual and group levels. *Journal of Personality and Social Psychology*, 54, 778–88.

Jung, C.G. (1923). *Psychological Types*. London: Routledge & Kegan Paul.

Kacelnik, A. (1984). Central place foraging in starlings (*Sturnus vulgaris*). *Journal of Animal Ecology*, 53, 283–99.

Kadushin, A. (1976). Adopting older children: a summary of its implications. In A.M. Clarke and A.D.B. Clarke (eds), *Early Experience: Myth and Evidence*. London: Open Books.

Kagan, A. and Levi, L. (1975). Health and environment – psychosocial stimuli: a review. In L. Levi (ed.), *Society, Stress and Disease*, vol. 2. New York: Oxford University Press.

Kagan, J. (1989). *Unstable Ideas: Temperament, Cognition and Self* Cambridge, MA: Harvard University Press.

Kahn, A., O'Leary, V.E., Krulewitz, J.E. and Lamm, H. (1980). Equity and equality: male and female means to a just end. *Basic and Applied Social Psychology*, 1, 173–97.

Kahn, S., Zimmerman, G., Csikszentmihaly, M. and Getzels, J.W. (1985). Relations between identity in young adulthood and intimacy at midlife. *Journal of Personality and Social Psychology*, 49, 1316–22.

Kahneman, D. (1973). *Attention and Effort*. Englewood Cliffs, NJ: Prentice-Hall.

Kail, R. and Park, Y. (1992). Global developmental change in processing time. *Merrill Palmer Quarterly*, 38, 525–41.

Kail, R. and Pellegrino, J.W. (1985). *Human Intelligence: Perspectives and Prospects*. New York: Freeman.

Kales, A. and Kales, J.D. (1974). Sleep disorders. *New England Journal of Medicine*, 290, 487–99.

Kamin, L.J. (1977). *The Science and Politics of IQ*. Harmondsworth: Penguin.

Kandel, D.B. (1978). Similarity in real-life adolescent pairs. *Journal of Personality and Social Psychology*, 36, 306–12.

Kanner, L. (1943). Autistic disturbances of affective contact. *Nervous Child*, 2, 217–50.

Kaplan, M.F. (1987). The influence process in group decision making. *Review of Personality and Social Psychology*, 8, 189–212.

Kaplan, M.F. and Miller, C.E. (1987). Group decision making and normative versus informational influence: effects of type of issue and assigned decision rule. *Journal of Personality and Social Psychology*, 53, 306–13.

Kaplan, R.M. and Saccuzzo, D.P. (1989). *Psychological testing: Principles, Applications and Issues*, 2nd edn. California: Brooks Cole.

Karuza, J. Jr and Brickman, P. (1978). Preference for similar and dissimilar others as a function of status. Paper presented at meeting of Mid-Western Psychological Association, Chicago, May.

Katz, D. and Kahn, R.L. (1976). *The Social Psychology of Organisations*. New York: Wiley.

Katz, R. and Wykes, T. (1985). The psychological difference between temporally predictable and unpredictable stressful events: evidence for information control theories. *Journal of Personality and Social Psychology*, 48, 781–90.

Kavanagh, R.E. (1974). *Facing Death*. Baltimore: Penguin.

Kaye, K. (1984). *The Mental and Social Life of Babies*. London: Methuen.

Kaye, K. and Brazelton, T.B. (1971). Mother–infant interaction in the organisation of sucking. Paper delivered to Society for Research into Child Development, Minneapolis.

Kaye, K. and Marcus, J. (1978). Imitation over a series of trials without feedback: age six months. *Infant Behaviour and Development*, 1, 141–55.

Kaye, K. and Marcus, J. (1981). Infant imitation: the sensorimotor agenda. *Developmental Psychology*, 17, 258–65.

Keating, D.P. (1980). Thinking processes in adolescence. In J. Adelson (ed.), *Handbook of Adolescent Psychology*. New York: Wiley.

Keesey, R.E. and Powley, T.L. (1975). Hypothalamic regulation of body weight. *American Scientist*, 63, 558–65.

Keith, J. (1990). Age in social and cultural context: anthropological perspectives. In R.H. Binstock and L.K. George (eds), *Aging and the Social Sciences*, 3rd edn. San Diego: Academic Press.

Kelley, H.H. (1967). Attribution theory in social psychology. *Nebraska Symposium on Motivation*, 15, 192–240.

Kelley, H.H. (1973). The process of causal attribution. *American Psychologist*, 28, 107–28.

Kelley, H.H. and Thibaut, J.W. (1978). *Interpersonal Relations: A Theory of Interdependence*. New York: Wiley Interscience.

Kelley, H.H., Berscheid, E., Christensen, A., Harvey, J.H., Huston, T.L., Levinger, G., McClintock, E., Peplau, L.A. and Peterson, D.R. (1983). *Close Relationships*. New York: Freeman.

Kellogg, W.N. and Kellogg, L.A. (1933). *The Ape and the Child*. New York: McGraw-Hill.

Kelly, G.A. (1955). *The Psychology of Personal Constructs*. New York: Norton.

Kelly, J.B. (1982). Divorce: the adult perspective. In B. Wolman (ed.), *Handbook of Developmental Psychology*. Englewood Cliffs, NJ: Prentice-Hall.

Kelvin, P. and Jarrett, J.E. (1985). *Unemployment: Its Social Psychological Effects*. Cambridge: Cambridge University Press.

Kendrick, D.C. (1981). Neuroticism and extraversion as explanatory concepts in clinical psychology. In H.B. Gibson (ed.), *Hans Eysenck, the Man and his Work*. London: Peter Owen.

Kenrick, D.T. and Stringfield, D.O. (1980). Personality traits and the eye of the beholder: crossing some traditional philosophical boundaries in the search for consistency in all of the people. *Psychological Review, 87*, 88–104.

Kerckhoff, A.C. and Davis, K.E. (1962). Value consensus and need complementarity in mate selection. *American Sociological Review, 27*, 295–303.

Kerr, A. and McClelland, H. (eds) (1991). *Concepts of Mental Disorder*. London: Gaskell.

Kety, S.S., Rosenthal, D., Wender, P. and Schulsinger, F. (1968). The types and prevalence of mental illness in the biological and adoptive families of adopted schizophrenics. In D. Rosenthal and S.S. Kety (eds), *The Transmission of Schizophrenia*. Elmsford, NY: Pergamon.

Kety, S.S., Rosenthal, D., Wender, P., Schulsinger, F. and Jacobson, B. (1975). Mental illness in the biological and adoptive families of adopted individuals who have become schizophrenic: a preliminary report based on psychiatric interviews. In R.R. Fieve, D. Rosenthal and H. Brill (eds), *Genetic Research in Psychiatry*. Baltimore, MD: Johns Hopkins University Press.

Kihlstrom, J.F. (1984). Conscious, subconscious, unconscious: a cognitive view. In K.S. Bowers and D. Meichenbaum (eds), *The Unconscious: Reconsidered*. New York: Wiley.

Kihlstrom, J.F. (1985). Hypnosis. *Annual Review of Psychology, 36*, 385–418.

Kilham, W. and Mann, L. (1974). Level of destructive obedience as a function of transmitter and executant roles in Milgram's obedience paradigm. *Journal of Personality and Social Psychology, 29*, 696–702.

Kiminyo, D.M. (1977). A cross-cultural study of the development of mass, weight, and volume among Kamba children. In P.R. Dasen (ed.), *Piagetian Psychology*. New York: Gardner Press.

Kinder, D.R. and Sears, R.R. (1981). Prejudice and politics: symbolic racism versus racial threats to the good life. *Journal of Personality and Social Psychology, 40*, 414–31.

Kirby, R. and Radford, J. (1976). *Individual Differences*. London: Methuen.

Kirkpatrick, L.A. and Shaver, P.R. (1988). Fear and affiliation reconsidered from a stress and coping perspective: the importance of cognitive clarity and fear reduction. *Journal of Social and Clinical Psychology, 7*, 214–33.

Kitzinger, C. and Coyle, A. (1995). Lesbian and gay couples: speaking of difference. *The Psychologist, 8*, 64–9.

Kleitman, N. (1927). Studies on the physiology of sleep. *American Journal of Physiology, 84*, 386–95.

Klerman, G. (1972). Drug therapy of clinical depression. *Journal of Psychiatric Research, 9*, 253–270.

Klerman, G. (1975). Drug therapy of clinical depressions – current status and implications for research on neuropharmacology of the affective disorders. In D. Klein and R. Gittleman-Klein (eds), *Progress in Psychiatric Drug Treatment*. New York: Bruner/Mazel.

Klerman, G. (1988). Depression and related disorders of mood (affective disorders). In A.M. Nicholi Jnr (ed.), *The New Harvard Guide to Psychiatry*. Cambridge, MA: Harvard University Press.

Klin, A., Volkmar, F.R., Sparrow, S.S. and Cicchetti, D.V. (1995). Validity and neuropsychological characterisation of Asperger's syndrome: convergence with non-verbal learning disabilities syndrome. *Journal of Child Psychology and Psychiatry, 36* (7), 1127–40.

Kline, P. (1972). *Fact and Fantasy in Freudian Theory*. London: Methuen.

Kline, P. (1981a). *Fact and Fantasy in Freudian Theory*, 2nd edn. London: Methuen.

Kline, P. (1981b). Recent research into the factor analysis of personality. In F. Fransella, (ed.), *Personality*. London: Methuen.

Kline, P. (1983). *Personality: Measurement and Theory*. London: Hutchinson.

Kline, P. (1984). *Psychology and Freudian Theory: An Introduction*. London: Methuen.

Kline, P. and Storey, R. (1977). A factor analytical study of the oral character. *British Journal of Social and Clinical Psychology, 16*, 317–28.

Klinnert, M.D. (1984). The regulation of infant behaviour by maternal facial expression. *Infant Behaviour and Development, 7*, 447–65.

Knox, R.E. and Inkster, J.A. (1968). Post decisional dissonance at post time. *Journal of Personality and Social Psychology, 8*, 319–23.

Kobasa, S.C. (1979). Stressful life events, personality and health: an enquiry into hardiness. *Journal of Personality and Social Psychology, 37*, 1–11.

Kobasa, S.C., Maddi, S.R. and Kahn, S. (1982). Hardiness and health: a prospective study. *Journal of Personality and Social Psychology, 42*, 168–77.

Koestler, A. (1970). *The Ghost in the Machine*. London: Pan Books.

Koffa, K. (1935). *Principles of Gestalt Psychology*. New York.

Kohlberg, L. (1966). A cognitive-developmental analysis of children's sex-role concepts and attitudes. In E.E. Maccoby (ed.), *The Development of Sex Differences*. Stanford, CA: Stanford University Press.

Kohlberg, L. (1969). The cognitive-developmental approach. In D.A. Goslin (ed.), *Handbook of Socialisation Theory and Research*. Chicago: Rand McNally.

Kohlberg, L. (1976). Moral stages and moralisation. In T. Linkons (ed.), *Moral Development and Behaviour*. New York: Holt, Rinehart & Winston CBS College Publishing.

Kohlberg, L. and Elfenbein, D. (1975). The development of moral judgments concerning capital punishment. *American Journal of Orthopsychiatry, 54*, 614–40.

Kohler, I. (1964). The formation and transformation of the visual world. *Psychological Issues, 3*, 28–46 and 366–79.

Köhler, W. (1927). *The Mentality of Apes*, 2nd edn. London: Kegan Paul.

Kohn, M.L. (1968). Social class and schizophrenia: a critical review. In D. Rosenthal and S.S. Kety (eds), *The Transmission of Schizophrenia*. Elmsford, NY: Pergamon.

Kolvin, I., Berney, T.P. and Bhate, S. (1984). Classification and diagnosis of depression in school phobia. *British Journal of Psychiatry, 145*, 347–57.

Konečni, V.J. (1975). Annoyance type and duration of post-annoyance activity and aggression: the 'cathartic' effect. *Journal of Experimental Psychology, General, 104*, 76–102.

Konishi, M. (1965). The role of auditory feedback on the control of vocalisation in the white-crowned sparrow. *Zeitschrift f?r Tierpsychologie, 22*, 770–83.

Kotelchuk, M. (1976). The infant's relationship to the father: experimental evidence. In M.E. Lamb (ed.), *The Role of the Father in Child Development*. New York: Wiley.

Kraepelin, E. (1913). *Psychiatry*, 8th edn. Leipzig: Thieme.

Kramer, G.P., Kerr, N.L. and Carroll, J.S. (1990). Pre-trial publicity, judicial remedies and jury bias. *Law and Human Behaviour*, 14, 409–39.

Kramer, R.M. and Brewer, M.B. (1984). Effects of identity on resource use in a simulated commons dilemma. *Journal of Personality and Social Psychology*, 46, 1044–57.

Kramer, R.M. and Brewer, M.B. (1986). Social group identity and the emergence of cooperation in resource conservation dilemmas. In H. Wilke, D. Messick and C. Rutte (eds), *Psychology of Decisions and Conflict*, vol. 3. Frankfurt: Verlag Peter Lang.

Krebs, D.L. and Miller, D.T. (1985). Altruism and aggression. In G. Lindsey and E. Aronson (eds), *Handbook of Social Psychology*, 3rd edn, vol. 2. New York: Random House.

Krebs, J.R. and Davies, N.D. (1987). *An Introduction to Behavioural Ecology*, 2nd edn. Oxford: Blackwell.

Kronhausen, E. and Kronhausen, P. (1964). *Pornography and the Law*, rev. edn. New York: Ballantine.

Kruijt, J.P. (1964). Ontogeny of social behaviour in Burmese red jungle fowl (*Gallus gallus spadiceus*). *Behaviour*, 12, 1–201.

Kruuk, H. (1972). *The Spotted Hyena*. Chicago: Chicago University Press.

Kübler-Ross, E. (1969). *On Death and Dying*. New York: Macmillan.

Kuhn, H.H. (1960). Self attitudes by age, sex and professional training. *Social Quarterly*, 1, 39–55.

Kuhn, T.S. (1962). *The Structure of Scientific Revolutions*. Chicago, IL: University of Chicago Press.

Kummer, H. (1968). Two variations in the social organisation of baboons. In P. Jay (ed.), *Primates: Studies in Adaptation and Variability*. New York and London: Holt Rinehart & Winston.

Kutchinski, B. (1973). The effect of easy availability of pornography on incidence of sex crimes: the Danish experience. *Journal of Social Issues*, 29 (3), 163–81.

Kutnik, P. (1986). The relationship of moral judgement and moral action: Kohlberg's theory, criticism and revision. In S. Modgil and C. Modgil (eds), *Lawrence Kohlberg: Consensus and Controversy*. Philadelphia: Falmer Press.

La Berge, D. (1975). Acquisition of automatic processing in perceptual and associative learning. In P.M.A. Rabbitt and S. Dormic (eds), *Attention and Performance*, vol. 5. London: Academic Press.

La France, M. and Mayo, C. (1976). Racial differences in gaze behaviour during conversations: two systematic observational studies. *Journal of Personality and Social Psychology*, 33, 547–52.

La Pière, R.T. (1934). Attitudes versus actions. *Social Forces*, 13, 230–7.

Labov, W. (1970). *Language in the Inner City*. Philadelphia: University of Pennsylvania Press.

Lader, M. (1975). *The Psychophysiology of Mental Illness*. London: Routledge & Kegan Paul.

Laing, R. (1967). *The Politics of Experience and the Bird of Paradise*. Harmondsworth: Penguin.

Laing, R.D. (1964). Is schizophrenia a disease? *International Journal of Social Psychiatry*, 10, 184–93.

Laing, R.D. (1965). *The Divided Self*. Harmondsworth: Penguin.

Laird, J.D. (1974). Self-attribution of emotion: the effects of facial expression on the quality of emotional experience. *Journal of Personality and Social Psychology*, 29, 475–86.

Lamb, M.E. (1977). The development of mother–infant and father–infant attachments in the second year of life. *Developmental Psychology*, 13, 637–48.

Lamb, M.E. (1987). Introduction: the emergent American father. In M.E. Lamb (ed.), *The Father's Role: Cross-cultural Perspectives*. Hillsdale, NJ: Erlbaum.

Lamb, M.E. and Sutton-Smith, B. (1982). *Sibling Relationships: Their Nature and Significance Across the Lifespan*. Hillsdale, NJ: Erlbaum.

Lamb, M.E., Thompson, R.A., Gardner, W.P., Charnov, E.L. and Estes, D. (1984). Security of infantile attachment as assessed in the 'strange situation': its study and biological interpretation. *Behavioural and Brain Sciences*, 7, 127–71.

Lamiell, J.T. (1981). Toward an idiothetic psychology of personality. *American Psychologist*, 36 (3), 276–89.

Lamm, H. and Kayser, E. (1978). The allocation of monetary gain and loss following dyadic performance: the weight given effort and ability under conditions of high and low intradyadic attraction. *European Journal of Social Psychology*, 8, 275–78.

Landy, D. and Sigall, H. (1974). Beauty is talent: task evaluation as a function of the performers physical attractiveness. *Journal of Personality and Social Psychology*, 29, 299–304.

Lang, P.J. and Melamed, B.G. (1969). Case report: avoidance conditioning therapy of an infant with chronic ruminative vomiting. *Journal of Abnormal Psychology*, 74, 1–8.

Langer, E.J. (1978). Rethinking the role of thought in social interaction. In J.H. Harvey, W.J. Ickes and R.F. Kidd (eds), *New Directions in Attitude Research*, vol. 2. Hillsdale, NJ: Erlbaum.

Langer, J. (1975). Interactional aspects of cognitive organisation. *Cognition*, 3, 9–28.

Langlois, J.H. and Downs, A.C. (1980). Mothers, fathers and peers as socialisation agents of sex-typed play behaviours in young children. *Child Development*, 51, 1237–47.

Langston, J.W., Ballard, P., Tetrud, J. and Irwin, I. (1983). Chronic parkinsonism in humans due to a product of meperidine-analog synthesis. *Science*, 219, 979–80.

Lanyon, R.I. (1984). Personality assessment. *Annual Review of Psychology*, 35, 667–701.

Latané, B. and Darley, J.M. (1970). *The Unresponsive Bystander: Why Doesn't He Help?* New York: Appleton-Century-Crofts.

Latané, B. and Darley, J.M. (1976). Help in a crisis: bystander response in an emergency. In J.W. Thibaut and J.T. Spence (eds), *Contemporary Topics in Social Psychology*. Morristown, NJ: General Learning Press.

Lazare, A., Klerman, G.I. and Armor, D.J. (1966). Oral, obsessive and hysterical personality patterns: an investigation of psychoanalytic concepts by means of factor analysis. *Archives of General Psychiatry*, 14, 624–30.

Lazarus, A.A. (1971). *Behavior Therapy and Beyond*. New York: McGraw-Hill.

Lazarus, J. (1979). The early warning function of flocking in birds: an experimental study with captive quelea. *Animal Behaviour*, 27, 855–65.

Lazarus, R.S. (1966). *Psychological Stress and the Coping Process*. New York: McGraw-Hill.

Lazarus, R.S. (1976). *Patterns of Adjustment*. New York: McGraw-Hill.

Lazarus, R.S. and Folkman, S. (1984). *Stress, Appraisal and Coping*. New York: Springer.

Lazarus, R.S., Kanner, A.D. and Folkman, S. (1980). Emotions: a cognitive-phenomenological analysis. In R. Plutchik and H. Kellerman (eds),

Emotion: Theory, Research and Experience, vol. 1. New York: Academic Press.

Le Boeuf, B. J. (1974). Male–male competition and reproductive success in elephant seals. *American Zoologist*, *14*, 163–76.

Lea, S.E.G. (1984). *Instinct, Environment and Behaviour*. London: Methuen.

Leahy, A.M. (1935). Nature–nurture and intelligence. *Genetic Psychology Monograph*, *17*, 235–308.

Leavitt, H.J. (1951). Some effects of certain communication patterns on group performance. *Journal of Abnormal and Social Psychology*, *46*, 38–50.

LeBon, G. (1908). *The Crowd: A Study of the Popular Mind*. London: Unwin (first published 1896 by Ernest Benn).

Lee, V.E., Brooks-Gunn, J. and Schnur, E. (1988). Does Headstart work? A 1-year follow-up comparison of disadvantaged children attending Headstart, no preschool, and other preschool programmes. *Developmental Psychology*, *24*, 210–22.

Lenneberg, E.H. (1967). *Biological Foundations of Language*. New York: Wiley.

Lerner, M.J. (1966). The unjust consequences of the need to believe in a just world. Paper presented at meeting of the American Psychological Association, New York.

Lerner, M.J. (1977). The justice motive: some hypotheses as to its origins and forms. *Journal of Personality*, *45*, 1–52.

Lerner, M.J. and Miller, D.T (1978). Just-world research and the attribution process: looking back and ahead. *Psychological Bulletin*, *85*, 1030–51

Leslie, A.M. (1987). Pretense and representation: the origins of theory of mind. *Psychological Review*, *94*, 412–26.

Leslie, A.M. and Frith, U. (1987). Metarepresentation and autism: how not to lose one's marbles. *Cognition*, *27*, 291–4.

Lesnik-Oberstein, M. and Cohen, L. (1984). Cognitive style, sensation seeking and assortative mating. *Journal of Personality and Social Psychology*, *46*, 112–7.

Leventhal, H. (1970). Findings and theory in the study of fear communication. In L. Berkowitz (ed.), *Advances in Experimental Social Psychology*, vol. 5. New York: Academic Press

Levine, M.A. (1975). *A Cognitive Theory of Learning*. Hillsdale, NJ: Lawrence Erlbaum.

Levinger, G. and Clark, J. (1961). Emotional factors in the forgetting of word associations. *Journal of Abnormal and Social Psychology*, *62*, 99–105.

Levinson, D.J. (1978). *The Seasons of a Man's Life*. New York: Ballantyne.

Levinson, D.J. (1986). A conception of adult development. *American Psychologist*, *41*, 3–13.

Levitt, E. and Klassen, A. (1974). Public attitudes towards homosexuality: Part of the 1970 national survey by the Institute for Sex Research. *Journal of Homosexuality*, *1*, 29–43.

Levitt, M.J. (1991). Attachment and close relationships: a lifespan perspective. In J.L. Gewirtz and W.M. Kurtines (eds), *Intersections with Attachment*. Hillsdale, NJ: Erlbaum.

Levy, D.J. (1989) Relations among aspects of children's environments, gender schematisation, gender role knowledge and flexibility. *Sex Roles*, *21*, 803–24.

Lewis, C. and Osborne, A. (1990). Three-year-olds' problems with false belief: conceptual deficit or linguistic artefact? *Child Development*, *61*, 1514–9.

Lewis, C.C. (1981). How adolescents approach decisions: changes over grades seven to twelve and policy implications. *Child Development*, *52*, 538–44.

Lewis, M. (1990). Social knowledge and social development. *Merrill-Palmer Quarterly*, *36*, 93–116.

Lewis, M. and Brooks-Gunn, J. (1975). Infants' reaction to people. In M. Lewis and L. Rosenblum (eds), *The Origins of Fear*. New York: Wiley.

Lewis, M. and Brooks-Gunn, J. (1979). *Social Cognition and the Acquisition of Self*. New York: Plenum Press.

Lewis, M., Feiring, C., McGuffoy, C. and Jaskir, J. (1984). Predicting psychopathology in six-year-olds from early social relations. *Child Development*, *55*, 123–36.

Lewis, S.N.C. and Cooper, C.L. (1988). The transition to parenthood in dual-earner couples. *Psychological Medicine*, *18*, 477–86.

Ley, R.G. and Bryden, M.P. (1982). A dissociation of right and left hemispheric effects for recognising emotional tone and verbal content. *Brain and Cognition*, *1*, 3–9.

Leyens, J.-P., Camino, L., Parke, R.D. and Berkowitz, L. (1975). Effects of movie violence on aggression in a field setting and as a function of group dominance and cohesion. *Journal of*

Personality and Social Psychology, *32*, 346–60.

Leyens, J.-P., Herman, G. and Dunand, M. (1982). The influence of an audience on reactions to filmed violence. *European Journal of Social Psychology*, *12*, 131–42.

Leyhausen, P. (1956). Verhaltenstudien an Katzen. *Zeitschrift für Tierpsychologie*, Supplement 2, vi, 120 pp.

Liben, L.S. and Signorella, M.L. (1993). Gender schematic processing in children: the role of initial interpretation of stimuli. *Developmental Psychology*, *29*, 141–9.

Lichter, D.G., Jackson, L. and Schachter, M. (1995). Clinical evidence of genomic imprinting in Tourette's syndrome. *Neurology*, *45* (5), 924–8.

Liebart, R.M. and Schwartzberg, N.S. (1977). Effects of mass media. In M.R. Rosenweig and L.W. Porter (eds), *Annual Review of Psychology*, vol. 28. Palo Alto, CA: Annual Reviews.

Liebart, R.M. and Schwartzberg, N.S. (1977). Effects of mass media. In M.R. Rosenzweig and L.W. Porter (eds), *Annual Review of Psychology*, *28*. Palo Alto, CA: Annual Reviews.

Lieberman, M.A., Yalom, J.D. and Miles, M.B. (1973). *Encounter Groups: First Facts*. New York: Basic Books.

Liebert, R.M. and Sprafkin J. (1988). *The Early Window: Effects of Television on Children and Youth*, 3rd edn. New York: Pergamon Press.

Likert, R. (1932). A technique for the measurement of attitudes. *Archives of Psychology*, *22* (140), 44–53.

Lilly, J.C. (1977). *The Deep Self*. New York: Simon & Schuster.

Lindsay, P.H. and Norman, D.A (1972). *Human Information Processing: An Introduction to Psychology*. New York: Academic Press.

Linssen, H. and Hagendoorn, L. (1994). Social and geographical factors in the explanation of European nationality stereotypes. *British Journal of Social Psychology*, *23*, 165–82.

Linton, H.B. (1955). Dependence on external influence: correlates in perception, attitudes and judgement. *Journal of Abnormal and Social Psychology*, *51*, 502–7.

Linton, M. (1982). Transformations of memory in everyday life. In U. Neisser (ed.), *Memory Observed: Remembering in Natural Contexts*. San Francisco: Freeman.

Linton, M. (1986). Ways of searching and the contents of memory. In D.C. Rubin (ed.), *Autobiographical Mem-*

ory. New York: Cambridge University Press.

Linville, P.W. (1987). Self complexity as a cognitive buffer against stress-related depression and illness. *Journal of Personality and Social Psychology*, *23*, 165–82.

Lipetz, M.E., Cohen, I.H., Dworin, J. and Rogers, L. (1970). Need complementarity, marital stability and marital satisfaction. In T.L. Huston (ed.), *Personality and Social Behaviour*. New York: Academic Press.

Lippitt, R. and White, R. (1943). The social climate of children's groups. In R.G. Barker, J. Kounin and H. Wright (eds), *Child Behaviour and Development*. New York: McGraw-Hill.

Lippman, W. (1922). *Public Opinion*. New York: Harcourt Brace and World.

Litton, I. and Potter, J. (1985). Social representations in the ordinary explanations of a riot. *European Journal of Social Psychology*, *15*, 371–88.

Livingstone, M.S. and Hubel, D.H. (1987). Psychophysical evidence for separate channels for the perception of form, colour, movement and depth. *Journal of Neuroscience*, *7*, 3416–68.

Lloyd, B.B. and Duveen, G. (1992). *Gender Identities and Education: The Impact of Starting School*. Hemel Hempstead: Harvester Wheatsheaf.

Lloyd, B. and Duveen, G. (1993). The development of social representations. In C. Pratt and A.F. Garton (eds), *Systems of Representation in Children: Development and Use*. Chichester: Wiley.

Lock, A. (1980). *The Guided Reinvention of Language*. London: Academic Press.

Loftus, E. and Hoffman, H. (1989). Misinformation and memory: the creation of new memories. *Journal of Experimental Psychology: General*, *118*, 100–4.

Loftus, E.F. (1979). *Eyewitness Testimony*. Cambridge, MA: Harvard University Press.

Loftus, E.F. and Fathi, D.C (1985). Retrieving multiple autobiographical memories. *Social Cognition*, *3*, 280–95.

Loftus, E.F. and Palmer, J.C. (1974). Reconstruction of automobile destruction: an example of the interaction between language and memory. *Journal of Verbal Learning and Verbal Memory*, *13*, 585–9.

Loftus, E.F., Johnson, C.A. and Shinamura, A.P. (1985). How much is an icon worth? *Journal of Experimental Psychology: Human Perception and Performance*, *11*, 1–13.

Loftus, E.F., Miller, D.G. and Burns, H.J. (1978). Semantic integration of verbal information into visual memory. *Journal of Experimental Psychology: Human Learning and Memory*, *4*, 19–31.

London, H. and Exner, J.E. (eds) (1978). *Dimensions of Personality*. New York: Wiley.

Long, J. and Porter, K.L. (1984). Multiple roles of midlife women: a case for new direction in theory, research and policy. In G. Baruch and J. Brooks-Gunn (eds), *Women in Midlife*. New York: Plenum Press.

Lore, R.K. and Schultz, L.A. (1993). Control of human aggression: a comparative perspective. *American Psychologist*, *48*, 16–25.

Lorenz, K.Z. (1937). The companion in the bird's world. In W. Sluckin (ed.), *Imprinting and Early Learning*. London: Methuen.

Lorenz, K.Z. (1950). The comparative method in studying innate behaviours. *Symposium of the Experimental Biological Society*, 221–68.

Lorenz, K.Z. (1952). *King Solomon's Ring*. London: Methuen.

Lorenz, K.Z. (1958). The evolution of behaviour. *Scientific American*, *199* (6), 67–78.

Lorenz, K.Z. (1966). *On Aggression*. London: Methuen.

Lorenz, K.Z. and Tinbergen, N. (1970). Taxis and behaviour patterns in egg-rolling by the greylag goose. In K. Lorenz, *Studies in Human and Animal Behaviour*. London: Methuen.

Louis-Sylvestre, J. and Le Magnen, J. (1980). A fall in blood-glucose levels precedes meal onset in free-feeding rats. *Neuroscience and Biobehavioural Reviews*, *4*, 13–16.

Lovelace, E.A. and Southall, S.D. (1983). Memory for words in prose and their location on the page. *Memory and Cognition*, *11*, 429–34.

Lowenthal, M.F, Thurber, M. and Chiriboga, D. (1975). *Four Stages of Life: A Comparative Study of Women and Men Facing Transitions*. San Francisco: Jossey-Bass.

Luce, G.G. (1971). *Body Time: Physiological Rhythms and Social Stress*. New York: Pantheon.

Luchins, A.S. (1942). Mechanisation in problem solving. *Psychological Monographs*, *54* (6).

Lumsden, C.J. and Wilson, E.O. (1983). *Promethean Fire*. Cambridge, MA: Harvard University Press.

Luria, A.R. and Yudovich, F.I. (1956). *Speech and the Development of Mental Processes in the Child*. London: Staples Press (new edn. 1971 Penguin).

Lynch, K. (1960). *The Image of the City*. Cambridge, MA: MIT Press.

Lyons, N.P. (1983). Two perspectives: on self, relationships and morality. *Harvard Educational Review*, *53*, 125–57.

Lysak, H., Rule, B.G. and Dobbs, A.R. (1989). Conceptions of aggression: prototype or defining features. *Personality and Social Psychology Bulletin*, *15*, 233–43.

Maccoby, E.E. and Jacklin, C.N. (1974). *The Psychology of Sex Differences*. Stanford, CA: Stanford University Press.

Macdonald, D.W. (1986). A meerkat volunteers for guard duty so its comrades can live in peace. *Smithsonian*, April 1985, 55–84.

MacFarlane, A. (1975). Olfaction in the development of social preferences in the human neonate. In Porter, R. and O'Connor, M. (eds), *Parent–Infant Interaction*. Amsterdam: Elsevier.

Mackay, D. (1975). *Clinical Psychology – Theory and Therapy*. London: Methuen.

Mackay, D. (1987). Divided brains – divided minds? In C. Blakemore and S. Greenfield (eds), *Mindwaves*. Oxford: Blackwell.

Mackenzie, B. (1984). Explaining the race difference in IQ: the logic, the methodology and the evaluation. *American Journal of Psychologist*, *39*, 1214–33.

Mackintosh, N.J. (1983). General principles of learning. In T. R. Halliday and P.J.B. Slater (eds), *Animal Behaviour*, vol. 3: *Genes, Development and Learning*, pp. 149–77. Oxford: Blackwell Scientific.

Mackintosh, N.J., Wilson, B. and Boakes, R.A. (1985). Differences in mechanisms of intelligence among vertebrates. *Philosophical Transactions of the Royal Society of London, Series B*, *308*, 53–65.

Mackworth, N.H. (1950). Researches on the measurement of human performance. *Medical Research Council Special Report*, No. 268. London: HMSO.

Macphail, E. (1985). Vertebrate intelligence: the null hypothesis. *Philosophical Transactions of the Royal Society of London, Series B*, *308*, 37–51.

Macphail, E.M. (1987). The comparative psychology of intelligence. *Behavioural Brain Science*, 10, 645–95.

Maddox, G.L. (1964). Disengagement theory: a critical evaluation. *The Gerontologist*, 4, 80–3.

Magenis, R., Overton, K., Chamberlin, J., Brady, T. and Lovrein, E. (1977). Paternal origin of the extra chromosome in Down's syndrome. *Human Genetics*, 37, 7–16.

Magnus, D.B.E. (1958). Experimentelle Untersuchungen zur Bionomie und Ethologie des Kaisermantels (*Argynnis paphia.*). I. Über optische Auslöser Anfliegreaktionen und ihrer Bedeutung für das Sichfinden der Geschlechter. *Zeitschrift für Tierpsychologie*, 15, 307–426.

Main, M. (ed.) (In press). *A Typology of Human Attachment Organisation Assessed in Discourse, Drawings and Interviews.* Cambridge: Cambridge University Press.

Main, M. and Cassidy, J. (1988). Categories of response to reunion with the parent at age 6: predictable from attachment classifications and stable over a 1-month period. *Developmental Psychology*, 24, 415–26.

Main, M. and Solomon, J. (1986). Discovery of a disorganised disoriented attachment pattern. In T.B. Brazelton and M.W. Yogman (eds), *Affective Development in Infancy.* Norwood, NJ: Ablex.

Main, M. and Weston, D.R. (1982). Avoidance of the attachment figure in infancy: descriptions and interpretations. In C.M. Parkes and J. Stevenson-Hinde (eds), *The Place of Attachment in Human Behaviour.* London: Tavistock.

Main, M., Kaplan, K. and Cassidy, J. (1985). Security in infancy, childhood and adulthood: a move to the level of representation. In I. Bretherton and E. Waters (eds), *Growing Points of Attachment Theory and Research*, Monographs of the Society for Research in Child Development, 50 (1-2), no. 209.

Major, B. and Adams, J.B. (1983). Role of gender. Interpersonal orientation and self-presentation in distributive justice behaviour. *Journal of Personality and Social Psychology*, 45, 598–608.

Major, B. and Deaux, K. (1982). Individual differences in justice behaviour. In J. Greenberg and R.L. Cohen (eds), *Equity and Justice in Social Behaviour.* New York: Academic Press.

Malamuth, N.M. and Donnerstein, E. (1982). The effects of aggressive pornographic mass media stimuli. In L. Berkowitz (ed.) *Advances in Experimental Social Psychology*, Vol. 15. New York: Academic Press.

Malamuth, N.M. and Donnerstein, E. (1984). *Pornography and Social Aggression.* New York: Academic Press.

Malim, T. (1994). *Cognitive Processes.* Basingstoke: Macmillan.

Malim, T., Birch, A. and Wadeley, A. (1992). *Perspectives in Psychology.* Basingstoke: Macmillan.

Malinowski, B. (1927). *Sex and Repression in Savage Society.* New York: Harcourt Brace Jovanovich.

Mandler, G. (1982). *Mind and Emotion.* New York: Norton.

Mann, L., Newton, J.W. and Innes, J.M. (1982). A test between deindividuation and emergent norm theories of crowd aggression. *Journal of Personality and Social Psychology*, 42, 260–72.

Mann, R.D. (1959). A review of the relationship between personality and performance in small groups. *Psychological Bulletin*, 56, 241–70.

Manning, M. and Dawkins, M.S. (1992). *Animal Behaviour*, 4th edn. Cambridge: Cambridge University Press.

Mantell, D.M. (1971). The potential for violence in Germany. *Journal of Social Issues*, 27, 101–12.

Marcia, J.E. (1966). Development and validation of ego-identity status. *Journal of Personality and Social Psychology*, 3, 551–8.

Marcia, J.E. (1980). Identity in adolescence. In J. Adelson (ed.), *Handbook of Adolescent Psychology*, pp. 159–187. New York: Wiley.

Markman, E.M., Cox, B. and Machida, S. (1981). The standard object sorting task as a measure of conceptual organisation. *Developmental Psychology*, 17, 115–17.

Marks, G. and Miller, N. (1988). Perceptions of attitude similarity: effect of anchored versus unanchored positions. *Personality and Social Psychology Bulletin*, 14, 92–102.

Marks, I.M. (1981). Review of behavioral psychotherapy: obsessive–compulsive disorders. *American Journal of Psychiatry*, 138, 584–92.

Markus, H. (1977). Self schemata and processing information about the self. *Journal of Personality and Social Psychology*, 35, 63–78.

Markus, H., Crane, M., Bernstein, S. and Siladi, M. (1982). Self schemas and gender. *Journal of Personality and Social Psychology*, 42, 38–50.

Marler, P. and Tamura, M. (1964). Culturally transmitted patterns of vocal behaviour in sparrow. *Science (New York)*, 146, 1483–6.

Marsden, D. (1975). *Workless* (2nd edn, 1982). London: Croom Helm.

Marsh, H.W., Craven, R.G. and Debus, R. (1991). Self-concepts of young children 5 to 8 years of age: measurement and multidimensional structure. *Journal of Educational Psychology*, 83, 377–92.

Marsh, P., Rosser E. and Harré, R. (1978). *Rules of Disorder*. Milton Keynes: Open University Press.

Marshall, G.O. and Zimbardo, P.G. (1979). Affective consequences of inadequately explained physiological arousal. *Journal of Personality and Social Psychology*, 37, 970–88.

Marsland, D. (1987). *Education and Youth.* London: Falmer.

Martin, C.L. (1991). The role of cognition in understanding gender effects. *Advances in Child Development and Behaviour*, 23, 113–49.

Martin, C.L. and Halverson, C.F. Jr (1981). A schematic processing model of sex typing and stereotyping in children. *Child Development*, 52, 1119–34.

Martin, C.L. and Halverson, C.F. Jr (1987). The roles of cognition in sex role acquisition. In D.B. Carter (ed.), *Current Conceptions of Sex Roles and Sex Typing: Theory and Research.* New York: Praeger.

Martin, G.M. and Lett, B.T. (1985). Formation of associations of colored and flavoured food with induced sickness in five main species. *Behavioural and Neural Biology*, 43, 223–37.

Martinez, D.R. and Klinghammer, K. (1970). The behaviour of the whale (*Orcinus orca*): a review of the literature. *Zeitschrift für Tierpsychologie*, 27 (7), 828–39.

Marx, M.H. (1976). *Introduction to Psychology: Problems, Procedures and Principles.* New York and London: Macmillan.

Maschwitz, U. (1964). Gefahrenalarmstoffe und Gefahrealarmierung bei sozialen Hymenopteren, *Zeitschrift für Vergleichende Psychologie*, 47 (6), 596–655.

Maschwitz, U. (1966). Alarm substances and alarm behaviour in social insects. *Vitamins and Hormones*, 24, 267–90.

Maslach, C. (1979). Negative emotional biasing of unexplained arousal. *Journal of Personality and Social Psychology*, 37, 571–77.

Maslach, C. and Jackson, S.E. (1981). The measurement of experienced burnout. *Journal of Occupational Behaviour, 2,* 99–113.

Maslow, A.H. (1968). *Towards a Psychology of Being.* New York: Van Nostrand Reinhold.

Maslow, A. (1970). *Motivation and Personality.* New York: Harper & Row.

Massarik, F. (1981). The interviewing process re-examined. In P. Reason and J. Rowan (eds), *Human Enquiry: A Source Book of New Paradigm Research.* Chichester: John Wiley.

Masserman, J.H. (1950). Experimental neuroses. *Scientific American, 182* (3), 38–43.

Masters, W.H. and Johnson, V.E. (1966). *Human Sexual Response.* Boston, MA: Little Brown.

Masterson, J.F. (1967). *The Psychiatric Dilemma of Adolescence.* Boston, MA: Little, Brown.

Matlin, M. (1992). *Feminist Perspectives in Therapy.* New York: Wiley.

Matlin, M.W. (1989). *Cognition,* 2nd edn. Fort Worth, TX: Holt, Rinehart & Winston.

Matlin, M.W. (1993). *The Psychology of Women,* 2nd edn. Fort Worth, TX: Harcourt Brace Jovanovich.

Mattes, J. and Gittleman, R. (1983). Growth of hyperactive children on maintenance regimen of methylphenidate. *Archives of General Psychiatry, 40,* 317–21.

Matthews, K.A. (1982). Psychological perspectives on the Type A behaviour pattern. *Psychological Bulletin, 9,* 293–323.

Matthews, T. (1988). The association of Type A behaviour with cardiovascular disease: update and critical review. In B. Kent Houston and G.R. Snyder (eds), *Type A Behaviour Pattern: Research, Theory and Intervention.* New York: Wiley.

Maurer, D. (1983). The scanning of compound figures by young infants. *Journal of Experimental Child Psychology, 35,* 437–48.

Maurer, D. and Barrera, M. (1981). Infants' perceptions of natural and distorted arrangements of a distorted face. *Child Development, 52,* 196–202.

Maxwell, G.M. and Coeburgh, B. (1986). Patterns of loneliness in a New Zealand population. *Community Mental Health in New Zealand, 2,* 48–61.

May, P. (1968). *Treatment of Schizophrenia: A Comparative Study of Five Treatment Methods.* New York: Science House.

May, P., Tuma, A.H., Yale, C., Potepan, P. and Dixon, W.J. (1976). Schizophrenia: a follow-up study of results of treatment II. Hospital stay over two to five years. *Psychiatry, 33,* 481–6.

Mayall, B. and Petrie, P. (1977). *Minder, Mother and Child.* Windsor: NFER.

Mayall, B. and Petrie, P. (1983). *Childminding and Day Nurseries: What Kind of Care?* London: Heinemann Educational Books.

Maynard-Smith, J. (1976). Evolution and the theory of games. *American Scientist, 64,* 41–5.

Maynard-Smith, J. (1982). *Evolution and Theory of Games.* Cambridge: Cambridge University Press.

Maynard-Smith, J. and Riechart, S.E. (1984). A conflicting-tendency model of spider agonistic behaviour: hybridpure population line comparison. *Animal Behaviour, 32,* 564.

Mbiti, J.S. (1970). *African Religions and Philosophy.* New York: Doubleday.

McBurnett, K., Harris, S.M., Swanson, J.M. and Piffner, L.J. (1993). Neuropsychological and psychophysiological differentiation of inattention/overactivity and aggression/defiance symptom groups. *Journal of Clinical Child Psychology, 22* (2), 165–71.

McCauley, C. (1989). The nature of social influence in groupthink: compliance and internalization. *Journal of Personality and Social Psychology, 57,* 250–60.

McClelland, D.C., Atkinson, J.W., Clark, R.A. and Lowell, E.L. (l953). *The Achievement Motive.* New York: Appleton-Century-Croft.

McClelland, J.L. and Rumelhart, D.E. (1981). An interactive activation model of context effects in letter perception. Part I: An account of basic findings. *Psychological Review, 88,* 375–407.

McClelland, K. (1982). An exploration of the functions of friends and best friends. Unpublished doctoral dissertation, Rutjers University, NJ.

McClintock, C.G. and McNeel, S.P. (1966). Reward level and game playing behaviour. *Journal of Conflict Resolution, 10,* 98–102.

McCord, R.R. and Wakefield, J.A. Jr (1981). Arithmetic achievement as a function of introversion–extraversion and teacher presented reward and punishment. *Personality and Individual Differences, 2,* 142–52.

McCrae, R.R. and Costa, P.T. (1985). Updating Norman's 'adequate taxonomy': intelligence and personality dimensions in natural language and in questionnaires. *Journal of Personality and Social Psychology, 49,* 710–21.

McCrae, R.R. and Costa, P.T. Jnr (1987). Validation of the five-factor model of personality across instruments and observers. *Journal of Personality and Social Psychology, 52,* 81–90.

McDougall, W. (1920). *The Group Mind.* London: Cambridge University Press.

McFarland, D.J. (1971). *Feedback Mechanisms in Animal Behaviour.* New York: Academic Press.

McGaugh, J.L. (1989). Involvement of hormonal and neuromodulatory systems in the regulation of memory storage. *Annual Review Neuroscience, 12,* 255–87.

McGeoch, J.A. and Macdonald, W.T. (1931). Meaningful relations and retroactive inhibition. *American Journal of Psychology, 43,* 579–88.

McGinnies, E. (1949). Emotionality and perceptual defence. *Psychological Review, 56,* 244–51.

McGinnis, R. (1959). Campus values in mate selection: a repeat study. *Social Forces, 36,* 283–91.

McGrath, J.E. (1984). *Group Interaction and Performance.* Englewood Cliffs, NJ: Prentice-Hall.

McGrew, W.C., Tutin, C.E.G. and Baldwin, P.J. (1979). Chimpanzees, tools and termites: cross-cultural comparisons of Senegal, Tanzania and Rio Muni. *Man, 14,* 185–215.

McGuire, W.J. (1964). Inducing resistance to persuasion: some contemporary approaches. In L. Berkowitz (ed.), *Advances in Experimental Social Psychology,* vol. 1. New York: Academic Press.

McGuire, W.J. (1989). The structure of individual attitudes and attitude systems. In A.R. Pratkanis, S.J. Brerckler and A.G. Greenwald (eds), *Attitude Structure and Function.* Hillsdale, NJ: Erlbaum.

McKellar, P. (1972). *Imagination and Thinking: A Psychological Analysis.* New York: Cohen & West (1st edn 1957).

McKelvey, R., Lambert, R., Mottron, L. and Shevell, M. (1995). Right hemisphere dysfunction in Asperger's syndrome. *Journal of Child Neurology, 10* (4), 310–14.

McKoon, G., Ratcliffe, R. and Dell, G.S. (1986). A critical evaluation of the semantic–episodic distinction. *Journal of Experimental Psychology:*

Learning, Memory and Cognition, 12, 295–306.

McNeill, D. (1966a). Developmental linguistics. In F. Smith and G. Miller (eds), *The Genesis of Language.* Cambridge, MA: MIT Press.

McNeill, D. (1966b). The creation of language. In R.C. Oldfield and J.C. Marshall (eds), *Language.* Harmondsworth: Penguin.

McNeill, D. (1970). *The Acquisition of Language.* New York: Harper & Row.

Meacham, J.A. and Singer, J. (1977). Incentive in prospective remembering. *Journal of Psychology, 97,* 191–7.

Mead, G.H. (1934). *Mind, Self and Society.* Chicago: University of Chicago Press.

Mead, M. (1935). *Sex and Temperament in Three Primitive Societies.* New York: Morrow.

Mead, M. (1939). *From the South Seas: Studies of Adolescence and Sex in Primitive Societies.* New York: Morrow.

Meadows, S. (1986). *Understanding Child Development.* London: Routledge.

Meadows, S. (1995). Cognitive development. In P.E. Bryant and A.M. Colman (eds), *Developmental Psychology.* Harlow: Longman.

Meddis, R. (1983). The evolution of sleep. In A. Mayes (ed.), *Sleep Mechanisms and Functions.* London: Van Nostrand Reinhold.

Mehler, J., Bertoncini, J., Barnière, M. and Jassik-Gerschenfeld, D. (1978). Infant recognition of mother's voice. *Perception, 7,* 491–7.

Meijer, J.H. and Reitveld, W.J. (1989). Neurophysiology of the suprachiasmatic circadian pacemaker in rodents. *Physiological Reviews, 69,* 671–707.

Meilman, P.W. (1979). Cross-sectional age changes in ego identity status during adolescence. *Developmental Psychology, 15,* 230–1.

Melamed, B., Hawes, R., Heiby, E. and Glick, J. (1975). Use of filmed modelling to reduce uncooperative behaviour of children during dental treatment. *Journal of Dental Research, 54,* 797–801.

Melhuish, E.C. (1990). Research on day care for young children in the United Kingdom. In E.C. Melhuish and P. Moss (eds), *Day Care for Young Children: International Perspectives.* London: Routledge.

Meltzoff, A.D. and Gopnik, A. (1993). The role of imitation in understanding persons and developing a theory of mind. In S. Baron-Cohen, T. Tager-Flusberg and D.J. Cohen (eds), *Understanding Other Minds: Perspectives from Autism.* Oxford: Oxford University Press.

Meltzoff, A.N. (1985). Cognitive foundations and social functions of imitation and intermodal representation in infancy. In J. Mehler and R. Fox (eds), *Neonate Cognition: Beyond the Booming, Buzzing Confusion.* Hillsdale, NJ: Erlbaum.

Meltzoff, A.N. and Moore, N.K. (1977). Imitation of facial and manual gestures by human neonates. *Science, 198,* 75–8.

Messick, S. and Associates (1976). *Individuality in Learning.* San Francisco, Jossey-Bass.

Metts, S. (1989). An exploratory investigation of deception in close relationships. *Journal of Social and Personal Relationships, 6,* 159–79.

Michelsen, A. (1989). Ein mechanisches Modell der tanzenden Honigbiene. *Biologie in unserer Zeit, 19* (4), 121–6.

Michelsen, A., Andersen, B.B., Kirchner, W.H. and Lindauer, M. (1989). Honey bees can be recruited by a mechanical model of a dancing bee. *Naturwissenschaften, 76,* 277–80.

Middlebrook, P.N. (1980). *Social Psychology and Modern Life,* 2nd edn. New York: Knopf.

Midlarsky, E. and Midlarsky, M. (1973). Some determinants of aiding under experimentally induced stress. *Journal of Personality, 1,* 305–27.

Midlarsky, M. and Midlarsky, E. (1976). Status inconsistency, aggressive attitude and helping behaviour. *Journal of Personality, 44,* 371–91.

Mikula, G. (1980). On the role of justice in allocation decisions. In G. Mikula (ed.), *Justice and Social Interaction.* New York: Springer Verlag/ Bern: Hans Huber.

Milardo, R.M., Johnson, M.P. and Huston, T.L. (1983). Developing close relationships changing patterns of interaction between pair members and social networks. *Journal of Personality and Social Psychology, 44,* 964–76.

Miles, I. (1983). *Unemployment: Cause and Cure.* Oxford: Martin Robertson.

Miles, L.E., Raynan, D.M. and Wilson, M.A. (1977). Blind man living in normal society has circadian rhythm of 24.9 hours. *Science, 198,* 421–3.

Milgram, S. (1963). The behavioural study of obedience. *Journal of Abnormal and Social Psychology, 67,* 371–8.

Milgram, S. (1965). Some conditions of obedience and disobedience to authority. *Human Relations, 18,* 57–76.

Milgram, S. (1970). The experience of living in cities. *Science, 167,* 1461–8.

Milgram, S. (1974). *Obedience to Authority.* New York: Harper & Row.

Milgram, S. (1977). A psychological map of New York City. In S. Milgram (ed.), *The Individual in a Social World.* Reading MA: Addison-Wesley.

Milgram, S. (1992). *The Individual in a Social World: Essays and Experiments,* 2nd edn. Reading, MA: Addison-Wesley.

Milinski, M. and Heller, R. (1978). Influence of a predator on the optimal foraging behaviour of sticklebacks (*Gasterosteus aculeatus*). *Nature (London), 275,* 642–4.

Miller, A.G. (1986). *The Obedience Experiments: A Case Study of Controversy in Social Science.* New York: Praeger.

Miller, A.G. and Lawson, T. (1989). The effect of an information option on the fundamental attribution error. *Personality and Social Psychology Bulletin, 15,* 194–204.

Miller, G.A. (1956). The magical number seven plus or minus two: some limits on our capacity for processing information. *Psychological Review, 63,* 81–97.

Miller, G.A., Galanter, E. and Pibram, K.H (1960). *Plans and the Structure of Behaviour.* New York: Holt, Rinehart & Winston.

Miller, J.G. (1984). Culture and the development of everyday social explanation. *Journal of Personality and Social Psychology, 46,* 961–78.

Miller, N. and DiCara, L. (1967). Instrumental learning of heart rate changes in curarised rats, shaping and specificity to discriminating stimulus. *Journal of Comparative and Physiological Psychology, 63,* 12–19.

Miller, N.E. and Dollard, J.C. (1941). *Social Learning and Imitation.* New Haven, CT: Yale University Press.

Mills, J. and Clark, M.S. (1982). Exchange and communal relationships. *Review of Personality and Social Psychology, 3,* 121–44.

Minuchin, S., Baker, L., Rosman, B., Liebman, R., Milman, L. and Todd, T. (1975). A conceptual model of psychosomatic illness in children: family organisation and family therapy. *Archives of General Psychiatry, 32,* 1031–38.

Mischel, W. (1968). *Personality and Assessment*. New York: Wiley.

Mischel, W. (1981). *Introduction to Personality*, 3rd edn. New York: Holt, Rinehart & Winston.

Mishkin, M. and Appenzeller, T. (1987). The anatomy of memory. *Scientific American*, 256 (6), 62–71.

Mitchell, G.D. (1964). Paternalistic behaviour in primates. *Psychological Bulletin*, 71, 399–417.

Mitchell, P. (1992). *The Psychology of Childhood*. London: Falmer Press.

Mitchell, P. and Lacohee, H. (1991). Children's early understanding of false belief. *Cognition*, 39, 207–27.

Miyake, K., Chen, S.J. and Campos, J.J. (1985). Infant temperament, mother's mode of interaction and attachment in Japan: an interim report. In I. Bretherton and E. Waters (eds), *Growing Points of Attachment Theory and Research*, Monographs of the Society for Research in Child Development, 50, 276–97.

Money, J. and Erhardt, A.A. (1972). *Man and Woman; Boy and Girl*. Baltimore: Johns Hopkins University Press.

Moniz, E. (1936). *Tentatives operatoires dans le traitement des certaines psychoses*. Paris: Masson.

Moore, B.R. (1973). The role of directed Pavlovian reactions in simple instrumental learning in the pigeon. In R.A. Hinde and J. Stevenson-Hinde (eds), *Constraints on Learning*, pp. 159–88. London: Academic Press.

Moores, D.F. (1985). Early intervention programmes for hearing-impaired children: a longitudinal assessment. In K.E. Nelson (ed.), *Children's language*, vol. 5, pp. 159–196. Hillsdale, NJ: Erlbaum.

Moos, R.H. (1969). Sources of variance in responses to questionnaires and behaviour. *Journal of Abnormal Psychology*, 74, 405–12.

Moran, J.J. and Joniak, A.F. (1979). Effect of language on preference for response to a moral dilemma. *Developmental Psychology*, 15, 337–8.

Moray, N. (1959). Attention in dichotic listening: affective cues and the influence of instructions. *Quarterly Journal of Experimental Psychology*, 11, 56–60.

Morris, C.D., Bransford, J.D. and Franks, J.J (1977). Levels of processing versus transfer appropriate processing. *Journal of Verbal Learning and Verbal Behaviour*, 16, 519–33.

Morris, D. (1959). The comparative ethology of grassfinches and mannikins. *Proceedings of the Zoological Society of London*, 131, 389–439.

Morris, D. (1977). *Manwatching*. St Albans: Panther.

Morris, D. (1982). *Manwatching*. London: Triad/Granada.

Morris, J.B and Beck, A.T. (1974). The efficacy of anti-depressant drugs: a review of the research (1958–72). *Archives of General Psychiatry*, 30, 667–78.

Morris, P.E. (1978). Sense and nonsense in traditional mnemonics. In M.M. Gruneberg, P.E. Morris and R.N. Sykes (eds), *Practical Aspects of Memory*. London: Academic Press.

Moscovici, S. (1988). Notes towards a description of social representation. *European Journal of Social Psychology*, 18, 211–50

Moscovitch, M. and Craik, F.I.M. (1976). Depth of processing, retrieval cues and uniqueness of encoding as factors in recall. *Journal of Verbal Learning and Verbal Behaviour*, 15, 477–58.

Moss, P. (1987). *A Review of Childminding Research*. University of London: Thomas Coram Research Unit.

Mullen, B., Salas, E. and Driskell, J.E. (1989). Salience, motivation and artifact as contributions to the relation between participation rate and leadership. *Journal of Experimental Social Psychology*, 25, 545–59.

Murphy, J. (1976). Psychiatric labelling in cross-cultural perspective. *Science*, 191, 1019–28.

Myerscough, R. and Taylor, S.P. (1985). The effects of marijuana on human physical aggression. *Journal of Personality and Social Psychology*, 49, 1541–6.

Naatanen, R. (1986). Neurophysiological basis of the echoic memory as suggested by event related potentials and magnetoencephalogram. In F. Klix and H. Hagendorf (eds), *Human Memory and Cognitive Capabilities*. Amsterdam: Elsevier.

Namikas, J. and Wehmer, F. (1978). Gender composition of the litter affects the behaviour of male mice. *Behavioural Biology*, 23, 219–24.

National Academy of Sciences, Institutes of Medicine (1984). *Bereavement, Reaction, Consequences and Care*. Washington, DC.

Necker, L.A. (1832). Observations of some remarkable phenomena, seen in Switzerland: and an optical phenomenon which occurs on viewing of a crystal or geometrical solid. *Philosophical Magazine*, I, 329.

Neimark, E.D. (1975). Intellectual development during adolescence. In F.D. Horowitz (ed.), *Review of Child Development Research*, vol. 4. Chicago: University of Chicago Press.

Neisser, U. (1967). *Cognitive Psychology*. New York: Appleton.

Neisser, U. (1976). *Cognition and Reality*. San Francisco, CA: W.H. Freeman.

Neisser, U. (1981). John Dean's memory: a case study. *Cognition*, 9, 1–22

Neisser, U. (1982). *Memory Observed*. San Francisco, CA: W.H. Freeman.

Nelson, B. (1980). *Sea Birds: Their Biology and Ecology*. London: Hamlyn.

Nelson, K., Carskaddon, G. and Bonvillian, J.D. (1973). Syntax acquisition: impact of experimental variation in adult verbal interaction with the child. *Child Development*, 44, 497–504.

Nelson, R.O. (1977). Assessment and therapeutic functions of self-monitoring. In M. Hersen, R. Eisler and P.M. Miller (eds), *Progress in Behavior Modification*. New York: Academic Press.

Nelson, T.O. and Vining, S.K. (1978). Effect of semantic versus structural processing on long term retention. *Journal of Experimental Psychology: Human Learning and Memory*, 4, 198–209.

Neugarten, B.L. (1973). Personality change in late life: a developmental perspective. In C. Eisdorfter and M.P. Lawton (eds), *Psychology of Adult Development and Aging*. Washington, DC: American Psychological Association.

Neugarten, B.L. (1977). Personality and aging. In J.E. Birren and K.W. Shaie (eds), *Handbook of the Psychology of Aging*. New York: Van Nostrand Reinhold.

Newcombe, T.M. (1961). *The Acquaintance Process*. New York: Holt Rinehart & Winston.

Newell, A. and Simon, H.A. (1972). *Human Problem Solving*. Englewood Cliffs, NJ: Prentice-Hall.

Newman, H.H., Freeman, F.N. and Holzinger, K. (1937). *Twins: a Study of Heredity and Environment*. Chicago: University of Chicago Press.

Newman, P.R. and Newman, M.M. (1988). Parenthood and adult development. In R. Palkovitz and M.B. Sussman (eds), *Transitions in Parenthood*. New York: Haworth.

Newson, J. (1979). Intentional behaviour in the young infant. In D.

Schaffer and J. Dunn (eds), *The First Year of Life*. Chichester: Wiley.

Newson, J. and Newson, E. (1976). On the social origins of symbolic functioning. In V.P. Varma and P. Williams (eds), *Rager, Psychology and Education*. London: Hodder & Stoughton.

Ng, S.H. (1990). Androgenic coding of man and his memory by language users. *Journal of Experimental Social Psychology*, *26*, 455–64.

Nicolson, R. (1966). Screening and diagnosis of SpLD/dyslexia. *The Psychologist: Bulletin of the British Psychological Society*, *9*, (2), 81.

Nisbett, R.E and Ross, L. (1980). *Human Inferences: Strategies and Shortcomings in Social Judgement*. Englewood Cliffs, NJ: Prentice-Hall.

Nisbett, R.E. and Wilson, T.D. (1977). Telling more than we can know: verbal reports on mental processes. *Psychological Review*, *84*, 231–59.

Noble, G.K. (1936). Courtship and sexual selection of the flicker (*Colaptes auratus luteus*). *Auk*, *53*, 269–82.

Nobles, W.W. (1976). Extended self: rethinking the so-called negro self concept. In R.L. Jones (ed.), *Black Psychology*. New York: Harper & Row.

Norman, D.A. (1968). Towards a theory of memory and attention. *Psychological Review*, *75*, 522–36.

Norman, D.A. (1969). Memory while shadowing. *Quarterly Journal of Experimental Psychology*, *21*, 85–93.

Norman, D.A. (1976). *Memory and Attention: An Introduction to Human Information Processing*, 2nd edn. New York: Wiley.

Norman, D.A. (1993). Twelve issues for cognitive science. In A.M. Aitkenhead and J.M. Slack (eds), *Issues in Cognitive Modelling*. London: Lawrence Erlbaum/OU.

Norman, W.T. (1963). Toward an adequate taxonomy of personality attributes: replicated factor structure in peer nomination personality ratings. *Journal of Abnormal Social Psychology*, *66*, 574–88.

Novak, D. and Lerner, M.J. (1968). Rejection as a consequence of perceived similarity. *Journal of Personality and Social Psychology*, *9*, 147–52.

Novak, M.A. and Harlow, H.F. (1975). Social recovery of monkeys isolated for the first years of life. I: Rehabilitation and therapy. *Developmental Psychology*, *11*, 453–65.

Noyes, R., Anderson, D., Clancy, J., Crowe, R.R., Slyman, D.J., Ghoneim, M. and Hinrichs, J.V. (1984). Diazepam and propanol in panic disorder and agoraphobia. *Archives of General Psychiatry*, *41*, 287–92.

Numan, M. (1974). Medial preoptic area and maternal behaviour in the female rat. *Journal of Comparative and Physiological Psychology*, *87*, 746–59.

Nurnberg, H., Prudic, J., Fiori, M. and Freedman, E. (1984). Psychopathology complicating acquired immune deficiency syndrome (AIDS). *American Journal of Psychiatry*, *141*, 95–6.

Nutt, D.J. (1990). The pharmacology of human anxiety. *Pharmacological Therapies*, *47*, 223–66.

Nyiti, R.M. (1976). The development of conservation in the Meru children of Tanzania. *Child Development*, *47*, 1622–9.

Offer, D. (1969). *The Psychological World of the Teenager: A Study of Normal Adolescence*. New York: Basic Books.

Olds, J. and Milner, P. (1954). Positive reinforcement produced by electrical stimulation of septal area and other regions of rat brain. *Journal of Comparative Physiological Psychology*, *47*, 419–27.

Olton, D.S. (1979). Mazes, maps and memory. *American Psychologist*, *34*, 583–96.

Olweus, D. (1977). A critical analysis of the 'modern' interactionist position. In D. Magnusson and N.S. Endler (eds), *Personality at the Crossroads: Current Issues in Interactional Psychology*. Hillsdale, NJ: Lawrence Erlbaum.

Olweus, D. (1989). Bully/victim problems among schoolchildren: basic facts and effects of a school based intervention program. In K. Rubin and D. Pepler (eds), *The Development and Treatment of Childhood Aggression*. Hillsdale, NJ: Erlbaum.

Ora, J.P. (1965). Characteristics of the volunteer for psychological investigation. Office of Naval Research Contract 2149 (03), Technical Report 27.

Orians, G. (1969). On the evolution of mating systems in birds and mammals. *American Nature*, *103*, 589–603.

Orne, M.T. and Evans, F.J. (1965). Social control in the psychological experiment: anti social behaviour and hypnosis. *Journal of Personality and Social Psychology*, *51*, 189–200.

Ornstein, R. (1986). *The Psychology of Consciousness*, 2nd edn. Harmondsworth: Penguin.

Osberger, M.J., Robbins, A.M., Todd, S.L. and Riley, A.I. (1994). Speech intelligibility in children with cochlear implants. *Volta Review*, *96* (5), 169–180.

Osborn, A.F. (1957). *Applied Imagination*, rev. edn. New York: Scribners.

Osgood, C.E., Suci, G.J. and Tannenbaum, P.H. (1957). *The Measurement of Meaning*. Urbana, IL: University of Illinois Press.

Oswald, I. (1980). Sleep as a restorative process: human clues. *Progress in Brain Research*, *53*, 279–88.

Packer, C. (1986). The ecology of sociality in fends. In D.I. Rubenstein and R.W. Wrangham (eds), *Ecological Aspects of Social Evolution*. Princeton, NJ: Princeton University Press.

Paivio, A. (1968). A factor-analytic study of word attributes and verbal learning. *Journal of Verbal Learning and Verbal Behaviour*, *7*, 41–9.

Palmarek, D.L. and Rule, B.G. (1979). Effects of ambient temperature and insult on motivation to retaliate. *Motivation and Emotion*, *3*, 83–92.

Palmere, M., Benton, S.L., Glover, J.A. and Ronning, R. (1983). Elaboration and the recall of main ideas in prose. *Journal of Educational Psychology*, *75*, 898–907.

Parke, R.D. and O'Leary, S. (1976). Father—mother–infant interaction in the newborn period: some findings, some observations and some unresolved issues. In K. Reigel and J. Meacham (eds), *The Developing Individual in a Changing World*, vol. 2: *Social and Environmental Issues*. The Hague: Moulton.

Parke, R.D. and Suomi, S.J. (1980). Adult male–infant relationships: human and non-human evidence. In K. Immelman, g. Barlow, M. Main and L. Petrinovitch (eds), *Behavioral Development: The Bielefeld Interdisciplinary Project*. New York: Cambridge University Press.

Parkes, C.M. (1972). *Bereavement: Studies of Grief in Adult Life*. Harmondsworth: Penguin.

Parkes, C.M., Stevenson-Hinde, J. and Marris, P. (eds) (1991). *Attachment Across the Life Cycle*. London: Tavistock/Routledge.

Parkin, A.J., Lewinsohn, J. and Folkard, S. (1982). The influence of emotion on immediate and delayed retention: Levinger and Clark reconsidered. *British Journal of Psychology*, *73*, 389–93.

Parloff, M., Waskow, I. and Wolfe, B. (1978). Research of therapist variables in relation to process and outcome. In S.L. Garfield and A.E. Bergin (eds), *Handbook of Psychotherapy and*

Behavior Change: An Empirical Analysis, 2nd edn. New York: Wiley.

Parten, M.B. (1932). Social participation among preschool children. *Journal of Abnormal and Social Psychology, 27*, 243–69.

Paton, D. (1990). Assessing the impact of disasters on helpers. *Counselling Psychology Quarterly, 3*, 149–52.

Patten, B.M. (1972). The ancient art of memory. *CMD, 39*, 547–54.

Patterson, F.G. (1978). The gestures of a gorilla: language acquisition in another pongid. *Brain and Language, 5*, 72–97.

Patterson, F.G. (1979). Conversation with a gorilla. *National Geographic, 154* (4), 438–65.

Patton, G. (1989). The course of anorexia nervosa. *British Medical Journal, 299*, 139–40.

Paul, G. (1966). *Insight Versus Desensitization in Psychotherapy*. Stanford, CA: Stanford University Press.

Paul, G.L. and Lentz, R. (1977). *Psychosocial Treatment of Chronic Mental Patients: Milieu Versus Social Learning Programs*. Cambridge, MA: Harvard University Press.

Paulus, P.B., Dzindolet, M.T., Poletes, G. and Camacho, L.M. (1993). Perception of performance in group brainstorming: the illusion of group productivity. *Personality and Social Science Bulletin, 19*, 78–89.

Pavlov, I. (1927). *Conditioned Reflexes* (trans. G.V. Anrep). London: Oxford University Press.

Payne, R.S. and McVay, S. (1971). Songs of humpback whales. *Science, 173*, 585–97.

Peck, D. and Whitlow, D. (1975). *Approaches to Personality Theory*. London: Methuen.

Peck, R. (1968). Psychological development in the second half of life. In B.L. Neugarten (ed.), *Midlife and Aging*. Chicago: University of Chicago Press.

Peek, F.W. (1971). Seasonal change in the breeding behaviour of the male red winged blackbird (*Agelaus phoeniceus*). *Wilson Bulletin, 83* (4), 393–5.

Pepperberg, I.M. (1983). Cognition in the African grey parrot: preliminary evidence for auditory/vocal comprehension of the class concept. *Animal Learning Behaviou*r, 11, 179–85.

Pepperberg, I.M. (1987). Interspecies communication: a tool for assessing capabilities in the African grey parrot (*Psittacus erithracus*). In G. Greenberg and E. Tobach (eds), *Language Cognition and Consciousness: Integrative Levels*. Hillsdale, NJ: Erlbaum.

Pepperberg, I.M. (1990a). Conceptual abilities of some non-primate species with an emphasis on an Africa grey parrot. In S.T. Parker and K. Gibson (eds), *Language and Intelligence in Monkeys and Apes: Comparative Development Perspectives*. Cambridge: Cambridge University Press.

Pepperberg, I.M. (1990b). Some cognitive capacities of an African grey parrot (*Psittacus erithracus*). *Advances in the Study of Behaviour, 19*, 357–409.

Perdue, C.W., Dovidio, J.F., Gurtman, M.B. and Tyler, R.B. (1990). Us and them: social categorisation and the process of intergroup bias. *Journal of Personality and Social Psychology, 59*, 475–86.

Perner, J. (1991). *Understanding the Representational Mind*. Cambridge, MA: Bradford Books/MIT Press.

Perner, J., Leekam, S.R. and Wimmer, H. (1987). Three-year-olds' difficulty with false beliefs: the case for a conceptual deficit. *British Journal of Developmental Psychology, 5*, 125–37.

Perry, D.G., Perry, L., Bussey K, English, D. and Arnold, G. (1980). Processes of attribution and children's self punishment following misbehaviour. *Child Development, 51*, 545–51.

Pert, C.B., Snowman, A.M. and Snyder, S.H. (1974). Localisation of opiate receptor binding in presynaptic membranes of rat brain. *Brain Research, 70*, 184–8.

Pervin, L.A. (1983). The stasis and flow of behavior: toward a theory of goals. In M.M. Page (ed.), *Personality: Current Theory and Research, 1982 Nebraska Symposium on Motivation*, vol. 30, pp. 1–53. Lincoln, NE: University of Nebraska Press.

Pervin, L.A. and Lewis, M. (eds) (1978). *Perspectives in Interactional Psychology*. New York: Plenum Press.

Petersen, A.C., Compas, B.E., Brooks-Gunn, J., Stemmler, M., Ey, S. and Grant, K.E. (1993). Depression in adolescence. *American Psychologist, 48*, 155–168.

Peterson, L.R. and Peterson, M. (1959). Short term retention of individual verbal items. *Journal of Experimental Psychology, 58*, 193–8.

Petitto, L.A. (1988). Language in the prelinguistic child. In F.S. Kessell (ed.), *The Development of Language and Language Researchers: Essays in Honour of Roger Brown*, pp. 187–222. Hillsdale, NJ: Erlbaum.

Pettigrew, T.F. (1958). Personality and socio-cultural factors in intergroup relations; a cross national comparison. *Journal of Conflict Resolution, 2*, 29–42.

Pettigrew, T.F. (1979). The ultimate attribution error: extending Allport's cognitive analysis of prejudice. *Personality and Social Psychology Bulletin, 5*, 461–76.

Pettigrew, T.F. (1987). *Modern Racism: American Black–White Relations in the 1960s*. Cambridge, MA: Harvard University Press.

Pettigrew, T.F., Allport, D.A. and Barnett, K.O. (1958). Binocular resolution and perception of race in South Africa. *British Journal of Psychology, 49*, 265–78.

Piaget, J. (1952). *Origins of Intelligence in Children* (trans. M. Cook). New York: International Universities Press.

Piaget, J. (1968). *Six Psychological Studies*. London: University of London Press.

Piaget, J. and Inhelder, B. (1956). *The Child's Conception of Space*. London: Routledge & Kegan Paul.

Piéron, H. (1928). Technique de laboratoire et appareils. *American Psychologist, 27*, 234ff.

Piliavin, J.A., Dovidio, J.F., Gaertner, S.L. and Clark, R.D. III (1981). *Emergency Intervention*. New York: Academic Press.

Pillemer, D.B. (1984). Flashbulb memories of the assassination attempt on President Reagan. *Cognition, 16*, 63–80.

Pillemer, D.B., Rhinehart, E.D. and White, S.H. (1986). Memories of life transitions: the first year in college. *Human Learning, 5*, 109–23.

Pilleri, G. (1979). The blind Indus dolphin. *Endeavours, 3*, 48–56.

Pinker, S. (1984). Visual cognition: an introduction. *Cognition, 18*, 1–63.

Plato, *Republic*, Book X (trans. A.D. Lindsay, 1935). London: Dent Everyman's Library.

Plummer, S., Beer, D. and LeBlanc, J. (1977). Functional consideration in the use of time-out and an effective alternative. *Journal of Applied Behaviour Analysis, 10*, 689–706.

Plutchik, R. (1980). A general psychoevolutionary theory of emotion. In R. Plutchik and H. Kellerman (eds), *Emotion: Theory, Research and Experience*, vol. 1. New York: Academic Press.

Plutchik, R. (1994). *The Psychology and Biology of Emotion*. London: Harper Collins.

Polis, G.E. (1981). The evolution and dynamics of intra-specific predation.

In R.F. Johnson, P.W. Frank and C.D. Michener (eds), *Annual Review of Systematics*, vol. 2. Palo Alto, California: Annual Reviews.

Pollack, J.M. (1979). Obsessive–compulsive personality: a review. *Psychological Bulletin*, 86, 225–41.

Pomazal, R.J. and Clore, G.L. (1973). Helping on the highway: the effects of dependency and sex. *Journal of Applied Social Psychology*, 3, 150–64.

Pomerantz, J.R. (1981). Perceptual organisation in information processing. In M. Kubovy and J.R. Pomerantz (eds), *Perceptual Organisation*. Hillsdale, NJ: Lawrence Erlbaum.

Popper, K. (1959). *The Logic of Scientific Discovery*. London: Hutchinson.

Popper, K. (1972). *Conjectures and Refutations: The Growth of Scientific Knowledge*, 4th edn. London: Routledge & Kegan Paul.

Postman, L., Bruner, J.S and. McGinnies, K. (1948). Personal values as selective factors in perception. *Journal of Abnormal and Social Psychology*, 43, 142–54.

Powell, G.V.N. (1974). Experimental analysis of the social value of flocking by starlings (*Asturnus vulgaris*) in relation to predation and foraging. *Animal Behaviour*, 22, 501–5.

Pratkanis, A. and Aronson, E. (1991) *The Age of Propaganda: Everyday Uses and Abuses of Persuasion*. New York: Freeman.

Pratkanis, A.R. and Greenwald, A.G. (1989). A sociocognitive model of attitude structure and function. In L. Berkowitz (ed.), *Advances in Experimental Social Psychology*, vol. 22. New York: Academic Press.

Pratt, M.W. and Norris, J.E. (1994). *The Social Psychology of Aging*. Oxford: Blackwell.

Pratt, M.W., Golding, G. and Kerig, P. (1987). Lifespan differences in adult thinking about hypothetical and personal moral issues: reflection or regression? *International Journal of Behavioural Development*, 10, 359–75.

Premack, A. J. and Premack, D. (1972). Teaching language to an ape. *Scientific American*, 227 (4), 92–9.

Premack, D. and Woodruff, G. (1978). Does the chimpanzee have a theory of mind? *Behavioural Brain Science*, 1, 515–26.

Presland, P. and Antill, J.K. (1987). Household division of labour: the impact of hours worked in paid employment. *Australian Journal of Psychology*, 39, 273–91.

Pressey, S.L. (1926). A simple apparatus which gives tests and scores – and teaches. *School and Society*, 23, 373–76.

Prien, R., Kupfer, D., Mansky, P., Small, J., Tuason, V., Voss, C. and Johnson, W. (1984). Drug therapy in the prevention of recurrences in unipolar and bipolar affective disorders. *Archives of General Psychiatry*, 41, 1096–104.

Przybyla, D.P.J. (1985). The facilitating effects of exposure to erotica on male prosocial behaviour. PhD Thesis, State University of New York in Albany, NY.

Pulliam, H.R. (1976). The principle of optimal behaviour and the theory of communities. In P.H. Klopfer and P.P.G. Bateson (eds), *Perspectives in Ethology*, pp. 311–32. New York: Plenum Press.

Quinlan, D.M. and Blatt, S.J. (1973). Field articulation and performance under stress: differential prediction in surgical and psychiatric nursing training. *Journal of Consulting and Clinical Psychology*, 39, 517.

Radford, J. and Govier, E. (1980). *A Textbook of Psychology*. London: Sheldon Press.

Radford, J. and Govier, E. (eds) (1991). *A Textbook of Psychology*, 2nd edn. London: Routledge.

Radin, N., Oyresman, D. and Benn, R. (1991). Grandfathers, teen mothers and children under two. In P.K. Smith (ed.), *The Psychology of Grandparenthood: An International Perspective*. London: Routledge.

Rahe, R.H. and Arthur, R.J. (1977). Life change patterns surrounding illness experience. In A. Monat and R.S. Lazarus (eds), *Stress and Coping*. New York: Columbia University Press.

Ramey, C.T. (1992). High-risk children and IQ: altering intergenerational patterns. *Intelligence*, 16, 239–56.

Ramey, C.T. (1993). A rejoinder to Spitz's critique of the Abecedarian experiment. *Intelligence*, 17, 25–30.

Ramirez, A., Bryant, J. and Zillman, D. (1982). Effects of erotica on retaliatory behavior as a function of level of prior provocation. *Journal of Personality and Social Psychology*, 43, 971–78.

Ransford, H.E. (1968). Isolation, powerlessness and violence: a study of attitudes and participation in the Watts riot. *American Journal of Sociology*, 73, 581–91.

Ransom, R.L., Sutch, R. and Williams, S.H. (1991). Retirement: past and present. In A.H. Munnell (ed.), *Retirement and Public Policy: Proceedings of the Second Conference on the National Academy of Social Insurance*. Dubuque, IA: Kendall/Hunt.

Raphael, B. (1985) *The Anatomy of Bereavement: A Handbook for the Caring Professions*. London: Hutchinson.

Ratcliffe, R. and McKoon, G. (1978). Priming in item recognition: evidence for the propositional structure of sentences. *Journal of Verbal Learning and Verbal Behaviour*, 17, 403–17.

Raven, B.H. (1965). Social influence and power. In I.D. Steiner and M. Fishbein (eds), *Current Studies in Social Psychology*. New York: Holt, Rinehart & Winston.

Reason, S.J. (1984). Absent-mindednss and cognitive control. In J.E. Harris and P.E. Morris (eds), *Everyday Memory, Actions and Absent-Mindedness*. London: Academic Press.

Reibstein, J. and Richards, M. (1992). *Sexual Arrangements: Marriage and Affairs*. London: Heinemann.

Reichard, S., Livson, F. and Peterson, P.G. (1962). *Aging and Personality*. New York: Wiley.

Reicher, S.D. (1982). The determination of collective behaviour. In H. Tajfel (ed.), *Social Identity and Intergroup Relations*. Cambridge: Cambridge University Press.

Reicher, S.D. (1984). Social influence in the crowd: attitudinal and behavioural effects of deindividuation in conditions of high and low in-group salience. *British Journal of Social Psychology 23*, 341–50.

Reicher, S.D. (1987). Crowd behaviour in social action. In J.C. Turner, M.A. Hogg, P.J. Oakes, S.D. Reicher and M.S. Wetherall (eds), *Rediscovering the Social Group: A Self-Categorisation Theory*. Oxford: Blackwell.

Reiss, I.L. (1980). *Family Systems in America*, 3rd edn. New York: Holt, Rinehart & Winston.

Rempel, J.K., Holmes, J.G. and Zanna, M.P. (1985). Trust in close relationships. *Journal of Personality and Social Psychology*, 49, 95–112.

Rest, J.R. (1983). Morality. In J. Flavell and E. Markman (eds), *Cognitive Development* in P. Mussen (General Editor). *Carmichael's Manual of Child Psychology* (4d edn). New York: Wiley.

Rheingold, H.L. and Eckerman, C.O. (1973). Fear of the stranger: a critical examination. In H.W. Reese (ed.), *Advances in Child Development and Behaviour*, vol. 8. New York: Academic Press.

Rheta Schreiber, F. (1973). *Sybil*. Harmondsworth: Penguin.

Rhodes, N. and Wood, W. (1992). Self-esteem and intelligence affecting influenceability: the mediating role of message reception. *Psychological Bulletin*, *111*, 156–71.

Richards, G. (1996). *Putting Psychology in its Place: An Introduction from a Critical Historical Perspective*. London: Routledge.

Richards, H.C., Bear, G.G., Stewart, A.L. and Norman, A.D. (1992). Moral reasoning and classroom conduct: evidence of a curvilinear relationship. *Merrill-Palmer Quarterly*, *38*, 176–90.

Rieder, R., Mann, L., Weinerger, D., Kammen, D. van and Post, R. (1983). Computer tomographic scans in patients with schizophrenia, schizoaffective and bipolar affective disorder. *Archives of General Psychiatry*, *40*, 735–9.

Riesen, A.H. (1950). Arrested vision. *Scientific American*, July.

Robbin, A. (1958). A controlled study of the effects of leucotomy. *Journal of Neurology, Neurosurgery and Psychiatry*, *21*, 262–9.

Robbin, A. (1959). The value of leucotomy in relation to diagnosis. *Journal of Neurology, Neurosurgery and Psychiatry*, *22*, 132–6.

Roberts, D.F. and Maccoby, N. (1985). Effects of mass communication. In G. Lindsey and E. Aronson (eds), *Handbook of Social Psychology*, 3rd edn, vol. 2. New York, Random House.

Roberts, P. and Newton, P.M. (1987). Levinsonian studies of women's adult development. *Psychology and Aging*, *2*, 154–63.

Robins, L.N. (1966). *Deviant Children Grown Up*. Baltimore, MD: Williams and Wilkins.

Robinson, W.P. (1981). Language development in young children. In D. Fontana (ed.), *Psychology for Teachers*. Basingstoke: Macmillan/BPS.

Robson, C. (1973). *Experiment Design and Statistics in Psychology*. Harmondsworth: Penguin.

Rodin, J., Schank, D. and Striegel-Moore, R. (1989). Psychological features of obesity. *Medical Clinics of North America*, *73*, 47–66.

Rogers, C.R. (1951). *Client-centered Therapy*. London: Constable.

Rogers, C.R. (1959). A theory of therapy, personality and interpersonal relationships as developed in the client-centred framework. In S. Koch (ed.), *Psychology: A Study of a Science: Formations of the Person in the Social Context*, vol. 3. New York: McGraw-Hill.

Rogers, C.R. (1961). *On Becoming a Person: A Therapist's View of Psychotherapy*. London: Constable.

Rogers, C.R. (1969). *Freedom to Learn*. Colombo, OH: Merrill.

Rogers, C.R. (1970). *Encounter Groups*. Harmondsworth: Penguin.

Rogers, T.B., Kuiper, N.A. and Kirker, W.S. (1977). Self-reference and the encoding of personal information. *Journal of Personality and Social Psychology*, *35*, 677–88.

Rohwer, S. and Rohwer, F.C. (1978). Status signalling in Harris sparrows: experimental deceptions achieved. *Animal Behaviour*, *26*, 1012–22.

Rokeach, M. (1948). Generalized mental rigidity as a factor in ethnocentrism. *Journal of Abnormal and Social Psychology*, *43*, 259–78.

Rokeach, M. (1960). *The Open and Closed Mind*. New York: Basic Books.

Rolls, E.T., Baylis, G.C., Hasselmo, M.E. and Nalwa, V. (1989). The effect of learning on the face selective responses of neurons in the cortex in the superior temporal sulculus of monkeys. *Experimental Brain Research*, *76*, 153–64.

Romzek, B.S. and Dubnick, M.J. (1987). Accountability in the public sector: Lessons from the *Challenger* tragedy. *Public Administration Review*, *47*, 227–38.

Rose, S. (1976). *The Conscious Brain*. Harmondsworth: Penguin.

Rose, S., Kamin, L.J. and Lewontin, R.C. (1990). *Our Genes: Biology Ideology and Human Nature*. Harmondsworth: Penguin.

Rosenberg, M. (1985). Identity: summary. In G.K. Brookings and W.R. Allen (eds), *Beginnings: The Social and Affective Development of Black Children*, pp. 231–6. Hillsdale, NJ: Erlbaum.

Rosenberg, S. and Jones, R.A. (1972). A method for investigating a person's implicit theory of personality: Theodore Dreiser's view of people. *Journal of Personality and Social Psychology*, *22*, 372–86.

Rosenberg, S. and Sedlak, A. (1972). Structural representations of implicit personality theory. *Advances in Experimental Social Psychology*, *6*, 235–97.

Rosenfeld, D., Greenberg, J., Folger, R. and Borys, R. (1982). Effect of an encounter with a black panhandler on subsequent helping for blacks: tokenism or conforming to a negative stereotype. *Personality and Social Psychology Bulletin*, *8*, 664–71.

Rosenhan, D. (1973). On being sane in insane places. *Science*, *179*, 250–58.

Rosenhan, D.L., Salovey, P. and Hargis, K. (1981). The joys of helping: focus of attention mediates the impact of positive affect on altruism. *Journal of Personality and Social Psychology*, *40*, 899–905.

Rosenthal, R. (1966). *Experimenter Effects in Behavioural Research*. New York: Appleton-Century-Croft.

Ross, A.O. (1981). *Psychological Disorders of Childhood: A Behavioral Approach to Theory, Research and Practice*, 2nd edn. New York: McGraw-Hill.

Ross, L. (1977). The intuitive psychologist and his shortcomings. In L. Berkowitz (ed.), *Advances in Experimental Social Psychology*, vol. 10. New York: Academic Press.

Ross, L., Greene, D. and House, P. (1977). The 'false consensus' effect: an egocentric bias in social perception and attribution processes. *Journal of Experimental Social Psychology*, *13*, 279–301.

Rotter, J.B. (1954). *Social Learning and Clinical Psychology*. Englewood Cliffs, NJ: Prentice-Hall.

Rotter, J.B. (1966). Generalised expectancies for internal versus external control of reinforcement *Psychological Monographs*, *30* (1), 1–26.

Rotton, J. and Frey, J. (1985). Air pollution, weather and violent crimes: concomitant time series analysis of archival data. *Journal of Personality and Social Psychology*, *49*, 1207–20.

Rovee-Collier, C. (1993). The capacity for long-term memory in infancy. *Current Directions in Psychological Science*, *2*, 130–35.

Rowell, T. (1974). The concept of social dominance. *Behavioural Biology*, *2*, 131–54.

Rowell, T.E., Hinde, R.A. and Spencer-Booth, Y. (1964). 'Aunt'; infant interaction in captive rhesus monkeys. *Animal Behaviour*, *12*, 219–26.

Rowland, W.J. (1989). Mate choice and the supernormality effect in female sticklebacks (*Gasterosteus aculeatus*). *Behavioural Ecological Sociobiology*, *24*, 433–8.

Rubin, D.C. and Kozin, M. (1984). Vivid memories. *Cognition*, *16*, 81–95.

Rubin, D.C. and Olson, M.J. (1980). Recall of semantic domains. *Memory and Cognition*, *8*, 354–66.

Rubin, D.C., Groth E. and Goldsmith, D.J. (1984). Olfactory cuing of autobiographical memory. *American Journal of Psychology*, *97*, 493–507.

Rubin, J.S., Provenzano, F.J. and Luria, Z. (1974). The eye of the beholder: parents' view on sex of newborns. *American Journal of Orthopsychiatry*, *5*, 353–63.

Rubin, Z. (1973). *Liking and Loving: An Invitation to Social Psychology.* New York: Holt Rinehart & Winston.

Ruble, D.N. (1987). The acquisition of self-knowledge: a self-socialization perspective. In N. Eisenberg (ed.), *Contemporary Topics in Developmental Psychology.* New York: Wiley.

Ruble, D.N. (1988). Sex-role development. In M.H. Bornstein and M.E. Lamb (eds), *Developmental Psychology: an Advanced Textbook.* Hillsdale, NJ: Erlbaum.

Ruble, D.N. and Nakamura, C.Y. (1972). Task orientation versus social orientation in young children and their attention to relevant stimuli. *Child Development*, *43*, 471–80.

Ruble, D.N., Balaban, T. and Cooper, J. (1981). Gender constancy and the effects of sex-typed television toy commercials. *Child Development*, *52*, 667–73.

Rule, B.G. and Leger, G.J. (1976). Pain cues and differing functions of aggression. *Canadian Journal of Behavioural Science*, *8*, 213–22.

Rule, B.G. and Percival, E. (1971). Effects of frustration and attack on physical aggression. *Journal of Experimental Research in Personality*, *5*, 111–8.

Runciman, W.G. (1966). *Relative Deprivation and Social Justice.* London, Routledge & Kegan Paul.

Rush, A., Beck, A., Kovacs, M. and Hollon, S. (1977). Comparative efficacy of cognitive therapy and pharmacotherapy in the treatment of depressed outpatients. *Cognitive Therapy and Research*, *1*, 17–39.

Rushton, J.P. (1978). Urban density and altruism, helping strangers in a Canadian city, suburb and small town. *Psychological Reports*, *33*, 987–90.

Rushton, J.P. and Chrisjohn, R.D. (1981). Extraversion, neuroticism, psychoticism and self-reported deliquency: evidence from eight separate samples. *Personality and Individual Differences*, *2*, 11–20.

Rushton, J.P., Fulker, D.W., Neale, M.C., Nias, D.K.B. and Eysenck, H.J. (1986). Altruism and aggression: the heritability of individual differences. *Journal of Personality and Social Psychology*, *50*, 1192–8.

Russek, M. (1971). Hepatic receptors and the neurophysiological mechanisms controlling feeding behaviour. In S. Ehrenpreis (ed.), *Neurosciences Research*, vol. 4. New York: Academic Press.

Rutter, M. (1966). Prognosis: psychotic children adolescence and early adult life. In J.K. Wing (ed.), *Childhood Autism: Clinical, Educational, and Social Aspects.* Elmsford, NY: Pergamon.

Rutter, M. (1972). *Maternal Deprivation Re-assessed.* Harmondsworth: Penguin.

Rutter, M. (1980). *Changing Youth in a Changing Society: Patterns of Adolescent Disorder.* Cambridge, MA: Harvard University Press.

Rutter, M. (1981). *Maternal Deprivation Reassessed*, 2nd edn. Harmondsworth: Penguin.

Rutter, M. and Lockyer, L. (1967). A five to fifteen year follow-up of infantile psychosis: I. Description of sample. *British Journal of Psychiatry*, *113*, 1169–82.

Rutter, M. and Rutter, M. (1993). *Developing Minds: Challenge and Continuity across the Lifespan.* Harmondsworth: Penguin.

Rutter, M., Maughan, B., Mortimore, P. and Ouston, J. (1979). *Fifteen Thousand Hours.* London: Open Books.

Rutter, M., Tizard, J. and Whitmore, K. (1981). *Education, Health and Behaviour.* Huntington, NY: Krieger.

Rutter, M., Tizard, J. and Whitmore, K. (eds) (1970). *Education Health and Behaviour.* London: Longman.

Ryan, C.M.E. (1982). Mechanisms of individual recognition in birds. Unpublished MPhil dissertation, University of Exeter.

Ryff, C.D. and Heinke, S.G. (1983). Subjective organisation of personality in adulthood and ageing. *Journal of Personality and Social Psychology*, *44*, 807–16.

Saayman, G.S. (1971). Aggressive behaviour in free-ranging chacma baboons (*Papio ursinus*). *Journal of Behavioural Science*, *1*, 77–83.

Sachs, B. and Meisel, R. (1988). The physiology of male sexual behaviour. In E. Knobil and J. Neill (eds), *The Physiology of Reproduction.* New York: Raven Press.

Sacks, O. (1985). *The Man who Mistook His Wife for a Hat.* London: Picador.

Sagi, A. and Lewkowicz, K.S. (1987). A cross-cultural evaluation of attachment research. In L.W.C. Tavecchio and M.H. van Ijzendoorn (eds), *Attachment in Social Networks: contributions to the Bowlby–Ainsworth attachment theory.* Amsterdam: North-Holland.

Sakel, M. (1938). The pharmacological shock treatment of schizophrenia. *Nervous and Mental Diseases Monograph*, *62*.

Salmon, P. and Claire, H. (1984). *Classroom Collaboration.* London: Routledge & Kegan Paul.

Samuels, C.A. and Ewy, R. (1985). Aesthetic perception of faces during infancy. *British Journal of Developmental Psychology*, *3*, 221–8.

Sapir, E. (1947). *Selected Writings in Language, Culture and Personality.* Los Angeles: University of California Press.

Savage-Rumbaugh, E.S., Pate, J.L., Lawson, J., Smith, T. and Rosenbaum, S. (1983). Can a chimpanzee make a statement? *Journal of Experimental Psychology: General*, *112*, 457–92.

Saville, P. and Blinkhorn, S. (1976). *Undergraduate Personality by Factored Scales.* Windsor: National Foundation for Educational Research.

Scarr, S. and McCartney, K. (1983). How people make their own environments: a theory of genotype–environmental effects. *Child Development*, *54*, 24–35.

Scarr, S. and Weinberg, R.A. (1977). Intellectual similarities within families of both adopted and biological children. *Intelligence*, *1*, 170–91.

Scarr-Salapatek, S. (1971). Social class and IQ. *Science*, *174*, 28–36.

Schachter, F.F. (1982). Sibling identification and split-parent identification: a family trend. In M. Lamb and B. Sutton-Smith (eds), *Sibling Relationships.* Hillsdale, NJ: Erlbaum.

Schachter, S. (1959). *The Psychology of Affiliation.* Stanford, CA: Stanford University Press.

Schachter, S. (1964). The interaction of cognitive and physiological determinants of emotional state. In L. Berkowitz (ed.), *Advances in Experimental Social Psychology*, vol. 1. New York: Academic Press.

Schachter, S. and Singer, J.E. (1962). Cognitive, social and physiological determinants of the emotional state. *Psychological Review*, 69, 379–99.

Schaffer, H.R. (1977). *Mothering*. London: Fontana.

Schaffer, H.R. and Emerson, P.E. (1964). Patterns of response to physical contact in early human development. *Journal of Child Psychology and Psychiatry*, 5, 13.

Schaie, K.W. (1983; 1990). The Seattle Longitudinal Study: a twenty-one year exploration of psychometric intelligence in adulthood. In K. W. Schaie (ed.), *Longitudinal Studies of Adult Psychological Development*. New York: Guilford.

Schaller, M. and Cialdini, R.B. (1988). The economics of empathetic helping: support for a mood management motive. *Journal of Experimental Social Psychology*, 24, 163–81.

Schank, R.C. and Abelson, R.P. (1977). *Scripts, Plans, Goals and Understanding: An Enquiry into Human Knowledge Structures*. Hillsdale, NJ: Erlbaum.

Schatz, M. (1994). *A Toddler's Life: Becoming a Person*. New York: Oxford University Press.

Scheerer, M. (1963). Problem solving. *Scientific American*, April.

Scheff, T.J. (1966). *Being Mentally Ill: A Sociological Theory*. Chicago: Aldine.

Schelderup-Ebbe, T. (1935). Social behaviour of birds. In C. Murchison (ed.), *Handbook of Social Psychology*. Worcester, MA: Clark University Press.

Scher, S.J. and Cooper, J. (1988). Motivational basis of dissonance: the singular tale of consequences. *Journal of Personality and Social Psychology*, 56, 899–906.

Scher, S.J. and Cooper, J. (1989). Motivational basis of dissonance: the singular role of behavioural consequences. *Journal of Personality and Social Psychology*, 56, 899–906.

Schiff, M., Dyne, M., Dumaret, A., Stewart, J., Tomkiewicz, S. and Fenigold, J. (1978). Intellectual status of working-class children adopted early into upper-middle class families. *Science*, 200, 1503–4.

Schiffman, H.R. (1976). *Sensation and Perception: An Integrated Approach*. New York: Wiley.

Schiller, P.H. (1957). Manipulative patterns in the chimpanzee. In P.H. Schiller (ed.), *Instinctive Behaviour*. London: Methuen.

Schleidt, W.M., Schleidt, M. and Magg, M. (1960). Störung der Mutter-Kind-Beziehung bei Truthühnein durch Gehöverlust. *Behaviour*, 16, 254–60.

Schleifer, S.J., Keller, S.E., McKegney, F.P. and Stein, M. (1979). The influence of stress and other psychosocial factors on human immunity. Paper presented at the 36th Annual Meeting of the Psychosomatic Society, Dallas, March.

Schlesinger, H.S. and Meadow, K.P. (1972). *Sound and Sign*. Berkeley: University of California Press.

Schmid-Hempel, P., Kacelnik, A. and Houston, A. I. (1985). Honeybees maximise efficiency by not filling their crop. *Behaviour Ecology and Sociobiology*, 17, 61–66.

Schmidt, D.F. and Boland, S.M. (1986). Structure of perceptions of older adults: evidence for multiple stereotypes. *Psychology and Aging*, 11, 255–60.

Schneider, K. (1959). Primary and secondary symptoms in schizophrenia. In S.R. Hirsch and M. Shepherd, M. (eds) (1974), *Themes and Variations in European Psychiatry*. New York: John Wright.

Schneider, W. and Shiffrin, R.M. (1977). Controlled and automatic information processing: I: Detection search and attention. *Psychological Review*, 84, 1–66.

Schoener, T.W. and Schoener, A. (1971). Structural habitats of West Indian anolis lizards. I: Lowland Jamaica. *Breviora*, pp. 368ff.

Schroeder, D.A., Dovidio, J.F., Sibicky, M.E., Matthews, L.L. and Allen, J.L. (1988). Empathic concern and helping behaviour: egoism or altruism? *Journal of Experimental Social Psychology*, 24, 333–53.

Schultz, D.A. (1972). *The Changing Family: Its Function and Future*. Englewood Cliffs, NJ: Prentice-Hall.

Schulz, D. (1987). *A History of Modern Psychology*, 4th edn. New York: Academic Press.

Schulz, N.R., Kaye, D.B. and Hoyer, W.J. (1980). Intelligence and spontaneous flexibility in adulthood and old age. *Intelligence*, 4, 219–31.

Schulz, R. (1978). *The Psychology of Death, Dying and Bereavement*. New York: Addison-Wesley.

Schwartz, B. (1989). *Psychology of Learning and Behaviour*, 3rd edn. New York: Norton.

Schwartz, S.H. (1971). Modes of representation and problem solving: well-evolved is half solved. *Journal of Experimental Psychology*, 91, 347–50.

Schwartz, S.H. (1977). Normative influences on altruism. In L. Berkowitz (ed.), *Advances in Experimental Social Psychology*, vol. 10. New York: Academic Press.

Schwartz, S.H. and David, T.B. (1976). Responsibility and helping in an emergency: effects of blame, ability and denial of responsibility. *Sociometry*, 39, 406–15.

Scodel, A., Minas, J.S., Ratoosh, P. and Lipetz, M. (1959). Some descriptive aspects of two person non-zero sum games I. *Journal of Conflict Resolution*, 3, 114–9.

Scott, M.J. and Stradling, S.G. (1992). Post-traumatic stress disorder without the trauma. Unpublished manuscript.

Sears, D.O. (1986). College sophomores in the laboratory: influences of a narrow base on social psychology's view of human nature. *Journal of Personality and Social Psychology*, 51, 515–30.

Seeley, T. (1985). *Honeybee Ecology*. Princeton, NJ: Princeton University Press.

Segall, M.H., Campbell, D.T. and Herskovitz, M.J. (1966). *The Influence of Culture on Visual Perception*. New York: Bobbs-Merrill.

Selander, R.K. (1972). Sexual selection and dimorphism in birds. In B. Campbell (ed.), *Sexual Selection and the Descent of Man 1871–1971*. Chicago: Aldine.

Selfridge, O.G. (1959). Pandemonium: a paradigm for learning. In *Symposium on the Mechanisation of Thought Processes*. London: HMSO.

Seligman, M. (1974). Depression and learned helplessness. In R.J. Friedman and M.M. Katz (eds), *The Psychology of Depression: Contemporary Theory and Research*. Washington, DC: Winston-Wiley.

Seligman, M.E.P. (1975). *Helplessness: On Depression, Development and Death*. San Francisco: W.H. Freeman.

Selman, R.L. (1976). Social cognitive understanding: a guide to educational and clinical practice. In T. Likona (ed.), *Moral Development and Behaviour: Theory, research and social issues*. New York: Holt, Rinehart & Winston.

Selye, H. (1956). *The Stress of Life*. New York: McGraw-Hill.

Serpell, R. (1970). *Culture's Influence on Behaviour*. London: Methuen.

Shackleton, V. and Fletcher, C. (1984). *Individual Differences: Theories and Applications*. London: Methuen.

Shaffer, L.H. (1975). Multiple attention in continuous verbal tasks. In P.M. Rabbitt and S. Dornic (eds), *Attention and Performance*, vol. 5. London: Academic Press.

Shanab, M.E. and Kahya, K.A. (1977). A behavioural study of obedience in children. *Journal of Personality and Social Psychology*, 35, 530–6.

Shapiro, D. and Surwit, R.S. (1979). Biofeedback. In O.F. Pommerleau and J.P. Brady (eds), *Behavioural Medicine: Theory and Practice*. Baltimore, MD: Williams & Wilkins.

Shapiro, D.A. and Shapiro, D. (1982). Meta-analysis of comparative therapy outcome studies: a replication and refinement. *Psychological Bulletin*, 92, 581–604, 665.

Shapiro, D.A. and Shapiro, D. (1983). Comparative therapy outcome research: methodological implications of meta-analysis. *Journal of Consulting and Clinical Psychology*, 51, 42–53.

Shapiro, P.N. and Penrod, S.D. (1986). Meta-analysis of facial identification studies. *Psychological Bulletin*, 100, 139–56.

Shaver, P. and Hazan, C. (1987). Being lonely, falling in love: perspectives from attachment theory. *Journal of Social Behaviour and Personality*, 2, 105–24.

Shaver, P. and Hazan, C. (1988). A biased overview of the study of love. *Journal of Social and Personal Relationships*, 5, 473–501.

Shaw, M.E. (1964). Communication networks. In L. Berkowitz (ed.), *Advances in Experimental Social Psychology*, vol. I. New York: Academic Press.

Shaw, M.E. (1978). Communication networks fourteen years later. In L. Berkowitz (ed.), *Group Processes*. New York: Academic Press.

Shayer, M. and Wylam, H. (1978). The distribution of Piagetian stages of thinking in British, middle and secondary school children: II. *British Journal of Educational Psychology*, 48, 62–70.

Sheehan, P.W. (1983). Age trends and correlates of children's television viewing. *Australian Journal of Psychology*, 35, 417–211.

Sheehy, G. (1976). *Passages: Predictable Crises of Adult Life*. New York: E.P. Dutton.

Sheldon, W. (1942). *The Varieties of Temperament: A Psychology of Constitutional Differences*. New York: Harper.

Shepherd, G.M. (1988). *Neurobiology*. Oxford: Oxford University Press.

Sherif, M. (1936). *The Psychology of Social Norms*. New York: Harper.

Sherif, M. (1951). A preliminary experimental study of inter-group relations. In J.J. Rohrer and M. Sherif (eds), *Social Psychology at the Crossroads*. New York, Harper & Row.

Sherif, M. (1966). *Group Conflict and Cooperation*. Boston, MA: Houghton Mifflin.

Sherif, M. (ed.) (1962). *Intergroup Relations and Leadership*. New York: Wiley.

Sherif, M., Harvey, O.J, White, B.J., Hood, W.R. and Sherif, C.W. (1961). *Intergroup Conflict and Cooperation: The Robbers Cave Experiment*. Norman, OK: The University of Oklahoma Book Exchange.

Shettel-Neuber, J., Bryson, J.B. and Young, L.E. (1978). Physical attractiveness of the 'other person' and jealousy. *Personality and Social Psychology Bulletin*, 4, 612–15.

Shields, J. (1962). *Monozygotic Twins Brought up Apart and Brought up Together*. Oxford: Oxford University Press.

Shields, J. (1976). Heredity and environment. In H.J. Eysenck and G.D. Wilson (eds), *A Textbook of Human Psychology*. Baltimore, MD: University Park Press.

Shiffrin, R.M. and Schneider, W. (1977). Controlled and automatic human information processing: II: Perceptual learning, automatic attending and a general theory. *Psychological Review*, 84, 127–90.

Shiffrin, R.M. and Schneider, W. (1984). Automatic and controlled processing revisited. *Psychological Review*, 91, 269–76.

Shimizu, N., Oomura, Y., Novin, D., Grijalva, C. and Cooper, P.H. (1983). Functional correlations between lateral hypothalamic glucose-sensitive neurons and hepatic portal glucose-sensitive units in rats. *Brain Research*, 265, 49–54.

Shopsin, B., Gershon, S., Thompson, H. and Collins, P. (1975). Psychoactive drugs in mania. *Archives of General Psychiatry*, 32, 34–42.

Shostrum, E.L., Knapp, R.R. and Knapp, L. (1976). Validation of the personal orientation dimensions. An inventory for the dimensions of actualising. *Educational and Psychological Measurement*, 36 (2), 491–4.

Shuey, A.M. (1966). *The Testing of Negro Intelligence*, 3rd edn. New York: Social Science Press.

Shuntich, R.J. and Taylor, S. P. (1972). The effects of alcohol on human aggression. *Journal of Experimental Research in Personality*, 6, 34–8.

Siegel, L.S. (1993). Phonological processing deficits as the basis of a reading disability. *Developmental Review*, 13, 246–257.

Siegler, R.S. (1981). Developmental sequences within and between concepts. *Monographs of the Society for Research in Child Development, 46* (2, Serial No. 189).

Sigall, H. and Ostrove, N. (1975). Beautiful but dangerous: effects of offender attractiveness and the nature of the crime on juristic judgement. *Journal of Personality and Social Psychology*, 31, 410–14.

Silva, M.L. (1990). Mate selection criteria. Unpublished manuscript, Mercer University, Macon, GA.

Simmons, R.G., Blyth, D.A. and McKinney, K.L. (1983). The social and psychological effects of puberty on white females. In J. Brooks-Gunn and A.C. Petersen (eds), *Girls at Puberty: Biological and Psychological Perspectives*. New York: Plenum Press.

Simon, B. (1971). *Intelligence, Psychology and Education – A Marxist Critique*. London: Lawrence and Wishart.

Simon, H.A. and Hayes, J.R. (1972). Understanding complex task instructions. In D. Klahr (ed.), *Cognition and Instruction*. Hillsdale, NJ: Erlbaum.

Simpson, J.A., Campbell, B. and Berscheid E. (1986). The association between romantic love and marriage: Kephart (1967) twice re-visited. *Personality and Social Psychology Bulletin*, 12, 363–72.

Sinclair-de-Zwart, H. (1969). Developmental psycholinguistics. In *Studies in Cognitive Development*. Oxford: Oxford University Press.

Skeels, H.M. (1966). Adult status of children with contrasting early life experiences. *Monographs of the Society for Research in Child Development*, 31 (whole no. 3).

Skinner, B.F. (1938). *The Behaviour of Organisms*. New York: Appleton-Century-Crofts.

Skinner, B.F. (1953). *Science and Human Behaviour*. New York: Macmillan.

Skinner, B.F. (1957). *Verbal Behaviour*. New York: Appleton-Century-Crofts.

Skinner, B.F. (1971). *Beyond Freedom and Dignity*. London: Jonathan Cape.

Skinner, B.F. (1974). *About Behaviourism*. London: Jonathan Cape.

Slavin, R.E. (1987). Developmental and motivational perspectives on cooperative learning: a reconciliation. *Child Development*, *58*, 1161–7.

Sloane, R., Staples, F., Cristol, A., Yorkston, N. and Whipple, K. (1975). *Psychoanalysis Versus Behavior Therapy*. Cambridge, MA: Harvard University Press.

Sluckin, A. (1981). *Growing Up in the Playground*. London: Routledge & Kegan Paul.

Sluckin, A. (1981). *Growing Up in the Playground: The Social Development of Children*. London: Routledge & Kegan Paul.

Sluckin, W. (1965). *Imprinting and Early Experiences*. London: Methuen.

Smart, L.S. (1992). The marital helping relationship following pregnancy loss and infant death. *Journal of Family Issues*, *13* (1), 81–98.

Smilansky, S. (1968). *The Effects of Sociodramatic Play on Disadvantaged Preschool Children*. New York: Wiley.

Smith, C. and Lloyd, B. (1978). Maternal behaviour and perceived sex of infant: revisited. *Child Development*, *49*, 1263–5.

Smith, F.T. (1943). An experiment in modifying attitudes towards the Negro. Teachers College Contributions to Education No. 887.

Smith, M.L. and Glass, G.V. (1977). Meta-analysis of psychotherapeutic outcome studies. *American Psychologist*, *32*, 752–60.

Smith, M.L., Glass, G.V. and Miller, B.L. (1980). *The Benefits of Psychotherapy*. Baltimore, MD: Johns Hopkins University Press.

Smith, P.K. (ed.) (1986). *Children's Play: Research, Developments and Practical Applications*. London: Gordon & Breach.

Smith, P.K. and Cowie, H. (1991). *Understanding Children's Development*, 2nd edn. Oxford: Blackwell.

Smith, P.K., Dalgleish, M. and Herzmark, G. (1981). A comparison of the effects of fantasy play tutoring and skills tutoring in nursery classes. *International Journal of Behavioural Development*, *4*, 421–41.

Smith, S.M., Brown, H.O., Toman, J.E.P. and Goodman, L.S. (1947). Lack of cerebral effects of D-turbocurarine. *Anaesthesiology*, *8*, 1–14.

Smith, S.M., Glenberg, A. and Bjork, R.A. (1978). Environmental context and human memory. *Memory and Cognition*, *6*, 342–53.

Snarey, J.R. (1985). Cross-cultural universality of social–moral development: a critical review of Kohlbergian research. *Psychological Bulletin*, *97*, 202–32.

Snow, C. (1977). The development of conversation between mothers and babies. *Journal of Child Language, 4*. [pages?]

Sorensen, R. (1973). *Adolescent Sexuality in Contemporary American Society*. Ithaca, NY: Cornell University Press.

Spears, R. and Manstead, A.S.R. (1990). Consensus estimation in the social context. *European Review of Social Psychology*, *1*, 81–109.

Speicher, B. (1994). Family patterns of moral judgement during adolescence and early adulthood. *Developmental Psychology*, *30*, 624–32.

Speisman, J.C., Lazarus, R.S., Mordkoff, A.M. and Davidson, L.A. (1964). The experimental reduction of stress based on ego defence theory. *Journal of Abnormal and Social Psychology*, *68*, 397–8.

Spence, J.T., Helmreich, R.L. and Stapp, J. (1974). The personal attributes questionnaire: a measure of sex role stereotypes and masculinity–femininity. *JSAS Catalog of Selected Documents in Psychology*, *4*, 127.

Spence, J.T., Helmreich, R.L. and Stapp, J. (1975). Ratings of self and peers on sex role attributes and their relation to self-esteem and concepts of masculinity and femininity. *Journal of Personality and Social Psychology*, *32*, 29–39.

Spencer, H. (1851). *Social Statics*. London: Williams & Norgale.

Spencer, H. (1884). *Man versus the State: Essays Reprinted, from Contemporary Review Feb–Jul 1884*. Harmondsworth: Penguin.

Sperling, G. (1960). The information available in brief presentations. *Psychological Monographs*, *74*, 1–29.

Sperry, R.W. (1968). Hemisphere deconnection and unity in conscious awareness. *American Psychologist*, *23*, 723–33.

Spitz, R.A. (1965). *The First Year of Life*. New York: International Universities Press.

Spitzer, R., Endicott, J. and Gibbon, M. (1979). Crossing the border into borderline personality and borderline schizophrenia. *Archives of General Psychiatry*, *36*, 17–24.

Spitzer, R.L. (1976). More on pseudoscience and the case for psychiatric diagnosis. *Archives of General Psychiatry*, *33*, 459–70.

Spoehr, K.T. and Lehmkuhler, S.W. (1982). *Visual Information Processing*. San Francisco: W.F Freeman.

Sprague, R. and Sleator, E. (1977). Methylphenidate in hyperkinetic children. Differences in dose effects on learning and social behaviour. *Science*, *198*, 1274–76.

Sprecher, S. (1986). The relation between inequity and emotions in close relationships. *Social Psychology Quarterly*, *49*, 309–21.

Squire, L.R. (1986). Mechanisms of memory. *Science*, *232*, 1612–19.

Sroufe, L.A. and Fleeson, J. (1986). Attachment and the construction of friendships. In W.W. Hartup and Z. Rubin (eds), *Relationships and Development*. Hillsdale, NJ: Erlbaum.

Stacey, B. and Pike, R. (1970). Apparent size, apparent depth, and the Müller-Lyer illusion. *Perception and Psychophysics*, *7*, 125–8.

Stanovich, K.E. (1993). A model for studies of reading disability. *Developmental Review*, *13*, 225–45.

Steele, C.M. (1988). The psychology of self affirmation: sustaining the integrity of the self. *Advances in Experimental Social Psychology*, *21*, 261–302.

Steiner, I.D. (1972). *Group Processes and Productivity*. New York: Academic Press.

Steiner, I.D. (1976). Task performing groups. In J.W. Thibaut and J.T. Spence (eds), *Contemporary Topics in Social Psychology*. Morristown, NJ: General Learning Press.

Stephan, W.G. and Rosenfeld, D. (1978). Effects of desegregation on racial attitudes. *Journal of Personality and Social Psychology*, *36*, 795–804.

Stephan, W.G. and Stephan, C.W. (1984). The role of ignorance in intergroup relations. In N. Miller and M.B. Brewer (eds), *Groups in Contact: The Psychology of Desegregation*. New York: Academic Press.

Stephenson, W.U. (1953). *The Study of Behaviour*. Chicago: University of Chicago Press.

Sterman, H.B. (1973). Neurophysiological and clinical studies of sensorimotor EEG feedback training: some effects on epilepsy. *Seminars in Psychiatry*, *5*, 507–25.

Stern, D.N. (1977). The infant's stimulus world during social interaction. In H.R. Schaffer (ed.), *Studies in*

Mother–Infant Interaction. London: Fontana.

Stern, S., Rush, J. and Mendels, J. (1980). Toward a rational pharmacotherapy of depression. *American Journal of Psychiatry, 137*, 545–52.

Sternberg, R.J. (1984). What should intelligence tests test? Implications of a triarchic theory of intelligence for intelligence testing. *Educational Researcher, 13* (1), 5–15.

Sternberg, R.J. (1985). *Beyond IQ: A Triarchic Theory of Human Intelligence.* Cambridge University Press.

Sternberg, R.J. (1986). A triangular theory of love. *Psychological Review, 93*, 119–35.

Sternberg, R.J. (1988). *The Triarchic Mind: A New Theory of Human Intelligence.* New York: Viking.

Sternberg, R.J. (1990). *Metaphors of Mind: Conceptions of the Nature of Intelligence.* Cambridge: Cambridge University Press.

Sternberg, R.J. (in press). *Sternberg Triarchic Abilities Test.* San Antonia, TX: The Psychological Corporation.

Stewart, J.E. (1980). Defendants' attractiveness as a factor in the outcome of criminal trials: an observational study. *Journal of Applied Social Psychology, 10*, 348–61.

Stewart, R.A. (1980). Habitability and behavioural issues of space flight. *Small Group Behaviour, 19*, 431–55.

Stogdill, R. (1974). *Handbook of Leadership.* New York: Free Press.

Stoller, R.J. (1976). Sexual excitement. *Archives of General Psychiatry, 33*, 899–909.

Stoner, J.A.F. (1961). A comparison of individual and group decisions including risk. Master's Thesis, Massachusetts Institute of Technology.

Storms, M.D. (1973). Videotape and attribution process: reversing actors' and observers' points of view. *Journal of Personality and Social Psychology, 27*, 165–75.

Storms, M.D. and Nisbett, R.E. (1970). Insomnia and the attribution process. *Journal of Personality and Social Psychology, 2*, 319–28.

Stratton, G.M. (1897). Vision without inversion of the retinal image. *Psychological Review, 4*, 341–60 and 463–81.

Streib, G.F. and Schneider, C. (1971). *Retirement in American Society.* Ithaca, NY: Cornell University Press.

Stroebe, M.S. and Stroebe, W. (1983). *Bereavement and Health.* New York: Cambridge University Press.

Stroebe, W., Lenkert, A. and Jonas, K. (1988). Familiarity may breed contempt: the impact of student exchange on national stereotypes and attitudes. In W. Stroebe, A. Kruglanski, D. Bar-Tal and M. Hewstone (eds), *The Social Psychology of Intergroup Conflict: Theory, Research and Applications.* New York: Springer Verlag.

Stroh, C.M. (1971). *Vigilance – The Problem of Sustained Attention.* Oxford: Pergamon.

Stroop, J.R (1935). Studies of interference in serial verbal reactions. *Journal of Experimental Psychology, 18*, 643–62.

Strube, M.J., Turner, C.W., Cerro, D., Stevens, J. and Hinchey, F. (1984). Interpersonal aggression and Type A coronary-prone behaviour pattern: a theoretical distinction and practical implications. *Journal of Personality and Social Psychology, 47*, 839–47.

Stunkard, A.J., Sorensen, T.I.A., Harris, C., Teasdale, T.W., Chakraborty, R., Schull, W.J. and Schulsinger, F. (1986). An adoption study of human obesity. *New England Journal of Medicine, 314*, 193–8.

Sugarman, L. (1990). *Lifespan Development.* London and New York: Routledge.

Sugden, D., Vanacek, J., Klein, D., Thomas, T. and Anderson, W. (1985). Activation of protein kinase C potentiates isoprenaline-inclued cyclic AMP accumulation in rat pinealocytes, *Nature, 314*, 359–62.

Sumner, W.G. (1906). *Folkways.* Boston, MA: Ginn.

Svaetichin, G. (1956). Spectral response curves from single cones. *Acta Physiologica Scandinavica, 39* (Suppl. 134), 17–46.

Svare, B. and Gandelman, R. (1976). Postpartum aggression in mice: the influence of suckling stimulation. *Hormones and Behaviour, 7*, 407–16.

Sweller, J. and Levine, M. (1982). Effects of global specificity on means-end analysis and learning. *Journal of Experimental Psychology: Learning Memory and Cognition, 8*, 463–74.

Swim, J., Borgida E. and Maruyama, G. (1989). Joan McKay versus John McKay: do gender stereotypes bias evaluation? *Psychological Bulletin, 105*, 4-09-29.

Sylva, K.D., Roy, D. and Painter, M. (1980). *Childwatching at Playgroup and Nursery School.* London: Grant McIntyre.

Symonds, M. (1975). Victims of violence: psychological effects and after-effects. *American Journal of Psychology, 35*, 19–26.

Szasz, T. (1967). *The Myth of Mental Illness.* London: Paladin.

Tajfel, H. (1978). Intergroup behaviour. II: Group perspectives. In H. Tajfel and C. Fraser (eds), *Intergroup Behaviour.* Oxford: Blackwell.

Tajfel, H. (1982). Social psychology of intergroup relations. *Annual Review of Social Psychology, 33*, 1–39.

Tajfel, H. and Turner, J.C. (1986). The social identity theory of intergroup behaviour. In S. Worchel and W.G. Austin (eds), *Psychology of Intergroup Relations*, 2nd edn. Chicago: Nelson-Hall.

Takahashi, K. (1986). Examining the Strange Situation procedure with Japanese mothers and 12-month old infants. *Developmental Psychology, 22*, 265–70.

Takahashi, K. (1990). Are the key assumptions of the Strange situation procedure universal? A view from Japanese research. *Human Development, 33*, 23–30.

Tanabe, T., Iino, M., Ooshima, Y. and Tagaki, S.F. (1974). An olfactory area in the prefrontal lobe. *Brain Research, 80*, 127–30.

Tausch, R. (1978). Facilitative dimensions in interpersonal relations: verifying the theoretical assumptions of Carl Rogers in school, family, education, client-centred therapy. *College Student Journal, 12*, 3.

Taylor, A., Sluckin, W., Davies, D.R., Reason, J.T., Thomson, R. and Colman, A.M. (1982). *Introducing Psychology.* Harmondsworth: Penguin.

Taylor, S.E. (1982). Social cognition and health. *Personality and Social Psychology Bulletin, 8*, 549–62.

Taylor, S.P. (1986). The regulation of aggressive behaviour. In R.J Blanchard and D.C. Blanchard (eds), *Advances in the Study of Aggression*, Orlando, FL: Academic Press.

Taylor, S.P. and Gammon, C.B. (1975). Effects of type and dose of alcohol on human physical aggression. *Journal of Personality and Social Psychology, 34*, 938–41.

Taylor, S.P., Gammon, C.B. and Capasso, D.R. (1976). Aggression as a function of the interaction of frustration and physical attack. *Journal of Social Psychology, 84*, 261–7.

Teachman, J.D., Call, V.A. and Carver, K.P. (1994). Marital status and the duration of joblessness among white men. *Journal of Marriage and the Family, 56*, 415–28.

Tedeschi, J.T., Lindskold, S. and Rosenfeld, P. (1985). *Introduction to Social Psychology*. New York: West.

Terman, L.M. (1921). In symposium: intelligence and its measurement. *Journal of Educational Psychology*, 12, 127–33.

Terrace, H.S. (1979). How Nim Chimpsky changed my mind. *Psychology Today*, 13, 65–76.

Terrace, H.S., Pettito, L.A., Sanders, D.J. and Bever, T.G. (1979). On the grammatical capacities in apes. In *Children's Language*, vol. II. New York: Gardner Press.

Tesch, S.A. (1983). Review of friendship development across the life span. *Human Development*, 26, 266–76.

Tesser, A. and Paulhus, D.L. (1976). Toward a casual model of love. *Journal of Personality and Social Psychology*, 34, 1095–105.

Tesser, A. Gatewood, R. and Driver, M. (1968). Some determinants of gratitude. *Journal of Personality and Social Psychology*, 9, 233–6.

Thibaut, J.W. and Kelley, H.H. (1959). *The Social Psychology of Groups*, New York: Wiley.

Thibaut, J.W. and Kelley, H.H. (1978). *Interpersonal: A Theory of Interdependence*. New York: Wiley.

Thomas, L. (1978). A personal construct approach to learning in education, training and therapy. In F. Fransella (ed.), *Personal Construct Psychology*. London: Academic Press.

Thomas, R.M. (1992). *Comparing Theories of Child Development*, 3rd edn. Belmont, CA: Wadsworth.

Thompson, C.P. (1982). Memory for unique personal events: the room mate study. *Memory and Cognition*, 10, 324–32.

Thompson, C.P. (1985). Memory for unique personal events: effects of pleasantness. *Motivation and Emotion*, 9, 277–89.

Thompson, C.P., Skowronski, J.J. and Lee, D.J. (1987). Reconstructing the date of a personal event. Paper presented at the Second International Conference on Practical Aspects of Memory, Swansea.

Thompson, R.A. and Lamb, M.E. (1983). Continuity and change in socioemotional development during the second year. In R. Emde and R. Harmon (eds), *Emotions in Early Development*. New York: Academic Press.

Thorndike, E.L. (1913). *Educational Psychology*. New York: Columbia University Press.

Thorpe, W.H. (1963). *Learning and Instinct in Animals*, 2nd edn. London: Methuen.

Thurstone, L.L. (1938). Primary mental abilities. *Psychometric Monograph*, 1.

Tinbergen, N. (1951). *The Study of Instinct*. Oxford: Oxford University Press.

Tinbergen, N. (1959). Comparative studies of the behaviour of gulls (*Laridae*): a progress report. *Behavior*, 15, 1–70.

Tinsley, B.J. and Parke, R.D. (1984). Grandparents as support and socialization agents. In M. Lewis. (ed.), *Beyond the Dyad*. New York: Plenum.

Tizard, B. and Hodges, J. (1978). The effect of early institutional rearing on the development of eight-year old children. *Journal of Child Psychology and Psychiatry*, 12, 99–118.

Tobias, P. (1974). IQ and the nature–nurture controversy. *Journal of Behavioural Science*, 2, 24.

Todt, D. (1975). Social learning of vocal patterns and models of their applications in grey parrots. *Zeitschrift für Tierpsychologie*, 39, 178–88.

Tolman, E.C. (1948). Cognitive maps in rats and men. *Psychological Review*, 55, 189–208.

Tousignant, J.P., Hall, D. and Loftus, E.F. (1986). Discrepancy detection and vulnerability to misleading post-event information. *Memory and Cognition*, 14, 329–38.

Tout, K. (1989). *Aging in Developing Countries*. Oxford: Oxford University Press.

Townsend, P. (1957). *The Family Life of Old People*. London: Routledge & Kegan Paul.

Treisman, A.M. (1960). Contextual cues in dichotic listening. *Quarterly Journal of Experimental Psychology*, 12, 242–8.

Treisman, A.M. (1964a). Verbal cues, language and meaning in selective attention. *American Journal of Psychology*, 77, 206–9.

Treisman, A.M. (1964b). Monitoring and storage of irrelevant messages in selective attention. *Journal of Verbal Learning and Verbal Behaviour*, 3, 449–59.

Treisman, A.M. and Geffen, G. (1967). Selective attention: Perception or response? *Quarterly Journal of Experimental Psychology*, 19, 1–18.

Treisman, A.M. and Gelade, G. (1980). A feature integration theory of attention. *Cognitive Psychology*, 12, 96–136.

Treisman, A.M. and Riley, J.G.A. (1969). Is selective attention selective perception or selective response? A further test. *Journal of Experimental Psychology*, 79, 27–34.

Trevarthen, C. (1974a). Conversations with a one-month-old. *New Scientist*, 62, 230–5.

Trevarthen, C. (1974b). Conversations with a two-month-old. *New Scientist*, 62, 320–3.

Trevarthen, C. (1975). Early attempts at speech. In R. Lewin (ed.), *Child Alive*. London: Temple Smith.

Triandis, H.C. (1971). *Attitudes and Attitude Change*. New York: Wiley.

Triandis, H.C. and Vassiliou, V. (1967). Frequency of contact and stereotyping. *Journal of Personality and Social Psychology*, 7, 316–38.

Trites, R.L. (ed.) (1979). *Hyperactivity in Children: Etiology, Measurement and Treatment Implications*. Baltimore, MD: University Park Press.

Trivers, R.L. (1971). The evolution of reciprocal altruism. *Quarterly Review of Biology*, 46 (4), 35–57.

Trivers, R.L. (1972). Parental investment and sexual selection. In B. Campbell (ed.), *Sexual Selection and the Descent of Man 1871–1971*. Chicago: Aldine.

Trivers, R.L. (1974). Parent offspring conflict. *American Zoologist*, 14, 249–69.

Troll, L.E. (1982). *Continuations: Adult Development and Aging*. Monterey, CA: Brooks/Cole.

Truax, C.B., Schuldt, W.J. and Wargo, D.G. (1968). Self-ideal concept congruence and improvement in group psychotherapy. *Journal of Consulting and Clinical Psychology*, 32, 47–53.

Tulving, E. (1962). Subjective organisation in free recall of unrelated words. *Psychological Review*, 69, 344–54.

Tulving, E. (1972). Episodic and semantic memory. In E. Tulving and W. Donaldson (eds), *Organisation of Memory*. London: Academic Press.

Tulving, E. (1983). *Elements of Episodic Memory*. New York: Oxford University Press.

Tupes, E.C. and Christal, R.E. (1961). Recurrent personality factors based on trait ratings. USAF ASD Technical Report, no. 61-97.

Turnbull, C. (1961). *The Forest People: A Study of Pygmies of the Congo*. New York: Simon & Schuster.

Turner, C.W and Berkowitz, L. (1972). Identification with film aggressor (covert role taking) and reactions to film violence. *Journal of Personality and Social Psychology, 21*, 256–64.

Turner, J.S. and Helms, D.R. (1995). *Lifespan Development*, 5th edn. Orlando, FL: Harcourt Brace College Publishers.

Turner, M.E., Pratkanis, A.R., Probasco, P. and Leve, C. (1992). Threat, cohesion and group effectiveness: testing a social identity maintenance perspective on groupthink. *Journal of Personality and Social Psychology, 63*, 781–96.

Turner, P.J. (1993). Attachment to mother and behaviour with adults in preschool. *British Journal of Developmental Psychology, 11*, 75–89.

Turner, R.H. (1974). Collective behaviour. In R.E.L. Faris (ed.), *Handbook of Modern Sociology*. Chicago, IL: Rand McNally.

Tyerman, A. and Spencer, C. (1983). A critical test of Sherif's Robbers Cave experiments: intergroup competition and cooperation between well-acquainted individuals. *Small Group Behaviour, 14*, 515–31.

Tyler, S.W., Hertl, P.T., McCallum, M.C. and Ellis, H.C. (1979). Cognitive effort and memory. *Journal of Experimental Psychology: Human Learning and Memory, 5b*, 607–17.

Ullman, L. and Krasner, L. (1975). *A Psychological Approach to Abnormal Behavior*, 2nd edn. Englewood Cliffs, NJ: Prentice-Hall.

Ullman, S. (1984). Visual routines. *Cognition, 18*, 97–159.

Underwood, G. (1974). Moray vs the rest: the effects of extended shadowing practice. *Quarterly Journal of Experimental Psychology, 26*, 368–72.

Unger, R. and Crawford, M. (1992). *Women and Gender: A Feminist Psychology*. New York: McGraw-Hill.

US Riot Commission (1968). *Report of the National Advisory Commission on Civil Disorders*. New York: Bantam Press.

Vagg, P.R. and Hammond, S.B. (1976). The number and kind of invariant personality Q factors: a partial replication of Eysenck and Eysenck. *British Journal of Social and Clinical Psychology, 15*, 121–30.

Vaillant, G.E. (1977). *Adaptation to Life: How the Best and Brightest Came of Age*. Boston, MA: Little, Brown.

Valentine, E.R. (1982). *Conceptual Issues in Psychology*. London: George Allen & Unwin.

Valentine, E.R. (1992). *Conceptual Issues in Psychology*, 2nd edn. London: Routledge.

Valins, S. (1966). Cognitive effects of false heart-rate feedback. *Journal of Personality and Social Psychology, 4*, 400–8.

Van de Pompe, G. and de Heus, P. (1993). Work stress, social support and strains among male and female managers. *Anxiety, Stress and Coping: An International Journal, 6* (3), 215–29.

van der Heijden, A.H.C. (1981). *Short Term Visual Information Forgetting*. London: Routledge & Kegan Paul.

van Ijzendoorn, M.H. and Kroonenberg, P.M. (1988). Cross-cultural patterns of attachment: a meta-analysis of the Strange Situation. *Child Development, 59*, 147–56.

van Knippenberg, A. and Ellemers, N. (1990). Social identity and intergroup differentiation processes. *European Review of Social Psychology, 1*, 137–69.

Vaughn, C. and Leff, J. (1976). The influence of family and social factors on the course of psychiatric illness. A comparison of schizophrenic and depressed neurotic patients. *British Journal of Psychiatry, 129*, 125–37.

Vegelius, J. (1976). On various G index generalisations and their applicability within the clinical domain. *Acta Univ. Uppsaliensis*.

Verner, J. (1965). Breeding biology of the long-billed marsh wren. *Condor, 67* (1), 6–30.

Verner, J. and Wilson, M.F. (1966). The influence of habitats on mating systems of N. American passerine birds. *Ecology, 47*, 143–7.

Vernon, M.D. (1970). *Perception through Experience*. London: Methuen.

Vernon, P.A. (ed.) (1987). *Speed of Information Processing and Intelligence*. Norwood, NJ: Ablex.

Vernon, P.A. and Mori, M. (1992). Intelligence, reaction times and peripheral nerve conduction velocity. *Intelligence, 16*, 273–88.

Vernon, P.E. (1964). *Personality Assessment*. London: Methuen.

Vernon, P.E. (1969). *Intelligence and Cultural Environment*. London: Methuen.

Vernon, P.E. (1972). The distinctiveness of field dependence. *Journal of Personality, 40*, 366–91.

Veroff, J. and Feld, S. (1970). *Marriage and Work in America: A Study of Motives and Roles*. New York: Van Nostrand Reinhold.

Vestergaard, K. (1980). The regulation of dust bathing and other patterns in the laying hen: a Lorenzian approach. In R. Moss (ed.), *The Laying Hen and its Environment*. The Hague: Martinus Nijhoff.

Vincent, C.E. (1964). Socialisation data in research on young marrieds. *Acta Sociologica*, August.

Vines, G. (1981). Wolves in dog's clothing. *New Scientist, 91*, 648–52.

Voissem, N.H. and Sistrunk, F. (1971). Communication schedules and cooperative game behaviour. *Journal of Personality and Social Psychology, 19*, 160–7.

Vom Saal, F.S. and Bronson, F. (1980). Sexual characteristics of adult females correlates with their blood testosterone levels during development in mice. *Science (New York), 208*, 597–9.

Von Bekesy, G. (1960). *Experiments in Hearing*. New York: McGraw-Hill.

Von Helmholtz, H.L.F. (1885). *Sensations of Tone*. London: Longmans.

Von Wright, J.M, Anderson, K. and Stenman, U. (1975). Generalisation of conditioned GSRs in dichotic listening. In P.M.A. Rabbitt and S. Dornic (eds), *Attention and Performance*, vol. 5. London: Academic Press.

Vygotsky, L.S. (1962). *Thought and Language*. Cambridge, MA: MIT Press.

Vygotsky, L.S. (1967). Play and the role of mental development in the child. *Soviet Psychology, 5*, 6–18.

Vygotsky, L.S. (1978). *Mind in Society* (ed. M. Cole, V. John-Steiner, S. Scribner and E. Souberman). Cambridge, MA: Harvard University Press.

Waal, F. van der (1989). *Chimpanzee Politics*. Baltimore, MD: Johns Hopkins University Press.

Waddington, D., Jones, K. and Critcher, C. (1987). Flashpoints of public disorder. In G. Gaskell and R. Benewick (eds), *The Crowd in Contemporary Britain*. London: Sage.

Wade, N.J. and Swanston, M. (1991). *Visual Perception*. London: Routledge.

Wade, T.C. and Baker, T.B. (1977). Opinions and use of psychological tests. *American Psychologist, 32*, 874–82.

Wagstaff, G.F. (1981). *Hypnosis, Compliance and Belief*. Brighton: Harvester.

Walker, I. and Mann, L. (1987). Unemployment, relative deprivation and social protest. *Personality and Social Psychology Bulletin, 13*, 275–83.

Walker, L.J., de Vries, B. and Trevethan, S.D. (1987). Moral stages and moral orientations in real-life and hypothetical dilemmas. *Child Development, 58*, 842–858.

Walker, S. (1984). *Learning Theory and Behaviour Modification.* London: Methuen.

Walsh, B., Stewart, J., Roose, S., Gladis, M. and Glassman, A. (1984). Treatment of bulimia with phenelzine. *Archives of General Psychiatry, 41,* 1105–9.

Walster E., Walster, G.W. and Berscheid E. (1978). *Equity: Theory and Research.* Boston, MA: Allyn and Bacon.

Walters, R.H. and Brown, M. (1963). Studies of reinforcement of aggression III: Transfer of responses to an interpersonal situation. *Child Development, 34,* 536–71.

Wapner, S. (1976). Process and context in the conception of cognitive style. In S. Messick and Associates, *Individuality in Learning.* San Francisco: Jossey-Bass.

Warburton, F.W. (1951). The ability of the Gurkha recruit. *British Journal of Psychology, 42,* 123–33.

Ward, C., Beck, A.T., Mendelson, M., Mock, J. and Erbaugh, J. (1962). The psychiatric nomenclature: reasons for diagnostic disagreement. *Archives of General Psychiatry, 7,* 198–205.

Warr, P.B. and Jackson, P. (1985). Factors influencing the psychological impact of prolonged unemployment and of re-employment. *Psychological Medicine, 15,* 795–807.

Warren, J.M. (1965). Primate learning in comparative perspective. In A.M. Schrier, H.F. Harlow and F. Stollnitz (eds), *Behaviour of Non-human Primates,* vol. 1, pp. 249–81. New York: Academic Press.

Wartner, U.G., Grossman, K., Fremmer-Bombik, E. and Suess, G. (1994). Attachment patterns at age six in South Germany: predictability from infancy and implications for preschool behaviour. *Child Development, 65,* 1014–27.

Waters, E. (1978). The reliability and stability of individual differences in infant–mother attachment. *Child Development, 49,* 483–94.

Watson, J.B. (1913). Psychology as a behaviourist views it. *Psychological Review, 20,* 158–77.

Weaver, D.B. (1974). An inter-cultural test of empiricist vs physiological explanations for cross-cultural differences in geometric illusion susceptibility using two illusions in Ghana. Unpublished doctoral dissertation, North Western University, Evanston, IL.

Webb, E.J., Campbell, D.T., Schwartz, R.D. and Sechrest, L. (1969). *Unobtrusive Measures: Non-reactive Research in Social Sciences.* Chicago: Rand-McNally.

Webb, W.B. (1982). Some theories about sleep and their clinical implications. *Psychiatric Annals, 11,* 415–22.

Weber, S.J and Cook, T.D. (1972) Subject effects in laboratory research: an examination of subject roles, demand characteristics and valid inference. *Psychological Bulletin, 77,* 273–95.

Wegner, D.M. (1986). Transactive memory: a contemporary analysis of the group mind. In B. Mullen and G.R. Goethals (eds), *Theories of Group Behaviour.* New York: Springer Verlag.

Wegner, D.M., Erber, R. and Raymond, P. (1991). Transactive memory in close relationships. *Journal of Personality and Social Psychology, 61,* 923–9.

Weiner, B. (1975) 'Spontaneous' causal thinking. *Psychological Bulletin, 97,* 74–84.

Weiner, B. (1979). A theory of motivation for some classroom experiences. *Journal of Educational Psychology, 71,* 3–25.

Weiner, B. (1985). An attributional theory of achievement motivation and emotion, *Psychological Review, 92,* 548–73.

Weiner, B. (1986). *An Attributional Theory of Motivation and Emotion.* New York: Springer Verlag.

Weiner, M.J. and Wright, F.E. (1973). The effects of undergoing arbitrary discrimination upon subsequent attitudes toward a minority group. *Journal of Applied Social Psychology, 3,* 94–102.

Weisberg, R.W. and Alba, J.W. (1981). An examination of the alleged role of 'fixation' in the solution of several 'insight' problems. *Journal of Experimental Psychology: General, 110,* 169–92.

Weiskrantz, L. (1986). *Blindsight: A Case Study and its Implications.* Oxford: Oxford University Press.

Wells, C.G. (1985). *Language Development in the Preschool Years.* Cambridge: Cambridge University Press.

Wells, M.J. (1962). *Brain and Behaviour in Cephalopods.* London: Heinemann Educational.

Wells, P.H. and Wenner, A.M. (1973). Do honey bees have a language? *Nature (London), 4,* 28–38.

Werner, E. (1991). Grandparent–grandchild relationships amongst US ethnic groups. In P.K. Smith (ed.), *The Psychology of Grandparenthood: An International Perspective.* London: Routledge.

Werner, E.E. (1986). A longitudinal study of perinatal risk. In D.C. Farran and J.C. McKinney (eds), *Risk in Intellectual and Psychosocial Development,* pp. 3–28. Orlando, FL: Academic Press.

Werner, E.E., Gilliam, J.F., Hall, D.J. and Mittlebach, G.E. (1983). An experimental test of the effects of predation risk on habitat use in fish. *Ecology, 64,* 1540–8.

Wessler, R.L. (1986). Conceptualising cognitions in the cognitive–behavioural therapies. In W. Dryden and W. Golden (eds), *Cognitive Behavioural Approaches to Psychotherapy.* London: Harper & Row.

Westcott, M.R. (1982b). On being free and feeling free. Paper presented to the 20th International Congress of Applied Psychology, Edinburgh.

Wheeler, L., Reis, H. and Neslek, J. (1983). Loneliness, social interaction and sex roles. *Journal of Personality and Social Psychology, 45,* 943–53.

White, B.L and Watts, J.C. (1973). *Experience and Environment.* New York: Prentice-Hall.

White, J.W. and Gruber, K.J. (1982). Instigative aggression as a function of past experience and target characteristics. *Journal of Personality and Social Psychology, 42,* 1069–75.

White, R. (1975). *Lives in Progress,* 3rd edn. New York: Holt, Rinehart & Winston.

Whyte, W.F. (1955). *Street Corner Society: The Social Structure of an Italian Slum.* Chicago: Chicago University Press.

Wilcox, J. and Webster, E. (1980). Early discourse behaviour: an analysis of children's responses to listener feedback. *Child Development, 51,* 1120–5.

Wilder, D.A. (1977). Perception of groups, size of opposition and social influence. *Journal of Experimental Social Psychology, 13,* 253–68.

Wilder, D.A. (1986). Social categorization: implications for creation and reduction of intergroup bias. In L. Berkowitz (ed.), *Advances in Experimental Social Psychology,* vol. 19. New York: Academic Press.

Wilke, H. and Lanzetta, J.T. (1970). The obligation to help: the effects of the amount of prior help on subsequent helping behaviour. *Journal of Experimental Social Psychology, 6,* 488–93.

Wilkinson, F.R. and Cargill, D.W. (1955). Repression elicited by story material based on the Oedipus complex. *Journal of Social Psychology*, *42*, 209–14.

Wilkinson, G.S. (1984). Reciprocal food sharing in the vampire bat. *Nature (London)*, *308*, 181–4.

Wilkinson, P.F. and Shank, C.C. (1977). Rutting-fight mortality among musk oxen on Banks Island, Northwest territories, Canada. *Animal Behaviour*, *24*, 756–8.

Wilkinson, R.T., Morlock, H.C and Williams, H.L. (1966). Evoked cortical response during vigilance. *Psychonomic Science*, *4*, 221–2.

Williams, J.D., Dudley, H.K. and Overall, J.E. (1972). Validity of the 16PF and the MMPI in a mental hospital setting. *Journal of Abnormal Psychology*, *80*, 261–70.

Williams, J.E. and Best, D.L. (1990). *Measuring Sex Stereotypes: A Multination Study*. Newbury Park, CA: Sage.

Williams, J.G. and Solano, C.H. (1983). The social reality of feeling lonely: friendship and reciprocation. *Personality and Social Psychology Bulletin*, *2*, 237–42.

Williams, L., Martin, G., McDonald, S., Hardy, L. and Lambert, L. Snr (1975). Effects of a backscratch contingency of reinforcement for table serving on social interaction with severely retarded girls. *Behaviour Therapy*, *6*, 220–29.

Wilson, E.O. (1965). Chemical communication in social insects. *Science*, *149*, 1064–7.

Wilson, E.O. (1971). *The Insect Societies*. Cambridge, MA: Belknap Press of Harvard University.

Wilson, E.O. (1975). *Sociobiology: The New Synthesis*. Cambridge, MA: Belknap Press of Harvard University.

Wilson, E.O. (1978). *On Human Nature*. Cambridge, MA: Belknap Press of Harvard University.

Wilson, E.O. (1992). *The Diversity of Life*. Cambridge, MA: Harvard University Press.

Wilson, E.O. and Regnier, F.E. (1971). The evolution of the alarm defense system in Formicine ants. *American Naturalist*, *105* (943) 279–89.

Wilson, G.T. and O'Leary, K.D. (1980). *Principles of Behavior Therapy*. Englewood Cliffs, NJ: Prentice-Hall.

Wilz, K.J. (1970). Causal and functional analysis of dorsal pricking and nest activity in the courtship of the three spined stickleback (*Agasterosteus aculeatus*). *Animal Behaviour*, *18*, 115–24.

Wimmer, H. and Perner, J. (1983). Beliefs about beliefs: representations and constraining function of wrong beliefs in young children's understanding of deception. *Cognition*, *13*, 103–28.

Winch, R.F., Ktsanes, I. and Ktsanes, V. (1954). The theory of complementary needs in mate selection. *American Sociological Review*, *19*, 241–9.

Wiseman, R. (1975). Crisis theory and the process of divorce. *Social Casework*, *56*, 205–12.

Wiseman, S. (1964). *Education and Environment*. Manchester: Manchester University Press.

Wispé, L.G. (1972). Positive forms of social behaviour: an overview. *Journal of Social Issues*, *28*, 1–19.

Witkin, H.A. (1949). The nature and importance of individual differences in perception. *Journal of Personality*, *18*, 145–70.

Witkin, H.A. (1950). Individual differences in ease of perception of embedded figures. *Journal of Personality*, *19*, 1–15.

Witkin, H.A. (1976). Cognitive style in academic performance and in teacher–student relations. In S. Messick and Associates, *Individuality in Learning*. San Francisco: Jossey-Bass.

Witkin, H.A. (1977). Role of the field dependent and field independent cognitive style in academic evolution: a longitudinal study. *Journal of Educational Psychology*, *69* (3), 197–211.

Witkin, H.A., Goodenough, D.R., Karp, S.A., Dyke, R.B. and Faterson, H.F. (1962). *Psychological Differentiation*. New York, Wiley.

Wolfgang, A.P. (1988). Job stress in the health professionals: a study of physicians, nurses and pharmacists. *Behavioral Medicine*, *14*, 43–7.

Wollen, K.A., Weber, A. and Lowry, D.H. (1972). Bizarreness versus interaction of mental images as determinants of learning. *Cognitive Psychology*, *2*, 518–23.

Wolpe, J. (1958). *Psychotherapy for Reciprocal Inhibition*. Stanford, CA: Stanford University Press.

Wood, D.J. (1988). *How Children Think and Learn*. Oxford: Blackwell.

Wood, D.J., Bruner, J.S. and Ross, G. (1976). The role of tutoring in problem-solving. *Journal of Child Psychology and Psychiatry*, *117*, 89–100.

Wood, F., Taylor, B., Penny, R. and Stump, D. (1980). Regional cerebral bloodflow response to recognition memory versus semantic classification tasks. *Brain and Language*, *9*, 113–22.

Woodworth, R.S. and Schlosberg, H. (1954). *Experimental Psychology*. London: Methuen.

Worchel, S., Andreoli, V.A. and Folger, R. (1977). Intergroup cooperation and intergroup attraction: the effect of previous interaction and outcome of combined effort. *Journal of Experimental Social Psychology*, *13*, 131–40.

World Health Organisation (1988). *International Classification of Diseases*, 10th rev. Geneva: WHO.

Worthington, A. (1969). Paired comparison scaling of brightness judgments: a method for the measurement of perceptual defence. *British Journal of Psychology*, *60* (3), 363–8.

Wortman, C.B. and Silver, R.C. (1990). Successful mastery of bereavement and widowhood: a life-course perspective. In P.B. Baltes and M.M. Baltes (eds), *Successful Aging: Perspectives from the Behavioral Sciences*. New York: Cambridge University Press.

Wright, E.O., Shire, K., Hwang, S.L., Dolan, M. and Baxter, J. (1992). The non-effects of class in the gender division of labor in the home: a comparative study of Sweden and the United States. *Gender and Society*, *6*, 252–82.

Yamamoto, T., Yuyama, N. and Kawamura, Y. (1981). Central processing of taste perception. in Y. Katsuki, R. Norgren and M. Sato (eds), *Brain Mechanisms of Sensation*. New York: Wiley.

Yarrow, L. (1973). The relationship between nutritive sucking experiences in infancy and non-nutritive sucking in childhood. In H.J. Eysenck and G.D. Wilson (eds), *The Experimental Study of Freudian Theories*. London: Methuen.

Yarrow, L.J. (1964). Separation from parents during early childhood. In M.L. Hoffman and L.W. Hoffman (eds), *Review of Child Development Research*, vol. 1. New York: Russell Sage Foundation.

Yerkes, R.M. and Dodson, J.D. (1908). The relation of strength of stimulus to rapidity of habit formation. *Journal of Comparative Neurology and Psychology*, *18*, 459–82.

Yonas, A. (1981). Infants' responses to optical information for collision. In J.R. Alberts and M.R. Peterson (eds), *Development of Perception: Psychobiological Perspectives*, vol. 2. New York: Academic Press.

Youngblade, L.M. and Belsky, J. (1992). Parent–child antecedents of 5-year-olds close friendships: a longitudinal study. *Developmental Psychology, 28,* 700–13.

Youniss, J. (1994). Children's friendships and peer culture: implications for theories of network and support. In F. Nestemann and K. Hurrelmann (eds), *Social Networks and Social Support in Childhood and Adolescence.* Berlin: de Gruyter.

Zajonc, R.B. (1968). Attitudinal effects of mere exposure. *Journal of Personality and Social Psychology, 9,* 1–27.

Zarit, S. (1980). *Aging and Mental Disorders: Psychological Approaches to Assessment and Treatment.* New York: Free Press.

Zeigob, L., Arnold, S. and Forehand, R. (1975). An examination of observer effects in patient–child interactions. *Child Development, 46,* 509–12.

Zigler, E. and Berman, W. (1983). Discerning the future of early childhood intervention. *American Psychologist, 38,* 894–906.

Zillman, D. (1979). *Hostility and Aggression.* Hillsdale, NJ: Erlbaum.

Zillman, D. (1988). Cognition excitation interdependencies in aggressive behaviour. *Aggressive Behaviour, 14,* 51–64.

Zillman, D. and Bryant, J. (1982). Pornography, sexual callousness and the trivialization of rape. *Journal of Communication, 32* (4), 10–21.

Zillman, D. and Cantor, J.R. (1976). Effect of timing of information about mitigating circumstances on emotional responses to provocation and retaliatory behaviour. *Journal of Experimental Social Psychology, 12,* 38–55.

Zillman, D., Bryant, J., Cantor, J.R. and Day, K.D. (1975). Irrelevance of mitigating circumstances in retaliatory behaviour at high levels of excitation. *Journal of Research in Personality, 9,* 282–293.

Zimbardo, P.G. (1970). The human choice: individuation, reason and order versus deindividuation, impulse and chaos. In W.J. Arnold and D. Levine (eds), *Nebraska Symposium on Motivation, 1969.* Lincoln, NE: University of Nebraska Press.

Zimbardo, P.G. (1979). *Psychology and Life,* 10th edn. Glenview, IL: Scott Foresman.

Zimbardo, P.G. and Leippe, M.R. (1991). *The Psychology of Attitude Change and Social Influence.* New York: McGraw-Hill.

Zimbardo, P.G., Banks, W.C., Craig, H. and Jaffe, D. (1973). A pirandellian prison: the mind is a formidable jailer. *New York Times Magazine,* 8 April, 38–60.

Zitrin, C., Klein, D., Woerner, M. and Ross, D. (1983). Treatment of phobias 1. Comparison of imipramine hydrochloride and placebo. *Archives of General Psychiatry, 40,* 125–38.

Zuckerman, M., Lazzaro, M.M. and Waldgeir, D. (1979). Undermining effects of the foot-in-the-door technique with exstrinsic rewards. *Journal of Applied Social Psychology, 9,* 292–6.

Index

16PF   715, 716

a priori method   60
Abelson, R.P.   574
ablation   17
abnormality   707–8, 762 ff
  cognitive model of   765
  criteria   764
  defining   763
  diagnosis of   776
  legal definition   764
  medical model of   767–70
  models or paradigms of   765
Abrams, D.   591, 663, 679
Abrams, R.   794
absent-mindedness   305
absolute refractory period   166–7
absolute stability   553
absolute threshold   257
abstract, of report   894
abused children   758
accommodation   264, 317, 461
  of the eye   154
account analysis   835
Achenbach, T.M.   751, 758
acoustic coding   295
acquiescence response set   659
ACTH   360
activity theory   560
actor–observer effect   582–3, 584–5
actualizing tendency   28, 738
acuity, visual   152
Adams, A.   221, 539
Adams, J.   601
adaptation   342–3, 461, 495
adaptive behaviour   106, 624
addiction   44, 195
Aderman, D.   645
ADHD   *see* attention-deficit
  hyperactivity disorder
Adler, A.   11, 18
Adler, N.T.   373
adolescence   525, 535–43
  and cognitive growth   541–42
  and female identity   538
  identity   537–39
  late and early maturation   536–7
  peer relationships   542–43
  physical changes   536
  sociological view of   539
  theories of   539–40, 541
  traditional view of   539
adoption studies   497–8
Adorno, T.W.   627, 669

adrenocorticotrophic hormone
  (ACTH)   181, 360
Adult Attachment Interview   444
adulthood   543–64
  early   546, 547–52
  late   557–64
  middle   552–6
advertising   79–86
  and attention   244
aetiology   776
affectionless psychopathy   446
affiliation   594 ff
  patterns of   595
ageism   665
aggregation   396
aggression   55, 402 ff, 623 ff, 751
  alcohol and drugs   630
  biological explanations of   403, 623
  biosocial explanations of   403, 624
  cognitive/neoassociationist model
    of   630
  control of   634
  environmental factors in   403, 628
  ethologically based theories of   623
  excitation/transfer theory of   624
  factors influencing   626
  female   406
  frustration/aggression hypothesis
    for   624
  irritable   404
  physiological factors   403
  pornography and   634
  psychoanalytic theories of   623
  ritualized   698
  social learning explanations of   627
  sociobiology and   624
Agras, S.   781
AI   *see* artificial intelligence
Ainsworth, M.D.S.   430, 439–42, 606
Ajzen, I.   649, 650, 651, 652
Akeakamai   388–9
alarm responses   376
Alatalo, R.V.   400–1
Albert, D.J.   403
Alcoholics Anonymous (AA)   31
Alexander, B.K.   44
Allee, W.C.   397
allele   342
Allen, M.G.   785
Allport, G.W.   243, 247, 252, 648–9,
  662, 666, 668, 673, 736–7
  trait approach   736
alpha rhythms   255
alternative hypothesis   817
Altman, I.   573

Altman, S.A.   377
Alto, J.L.   757
altruism   413, 636
  reciprocal   414, 636
Alzheimer's disease   776
Amato, P.R.   644
ambient optical array   270
American Sign Language (ASL)   384–5
Amira, A.   558
amygdala   173
anal stage   732, 733
analogies   328
analysis
  by synthesis   271
  qualitative   833, 896
  quantitative   833
Anand, B.K.   188
Anastasi, A.   51, 55, 57, 500
Anderson, C.A.   580, 628, 629
Anderson, L.P.   230
Anderson, N.H.   650
Andreeva, G.   621
Andrew, R.J.   368–9
androcentric bias   74
androgens   194
androgynous behaviour   587
androgyny   514
animals
  behaviour   337 ff
  communication   372
  sensory world of   373
  study   340
  teaching human language to   382
  thinking   365 ff
anisogamy   409
anorexia nervosa   191, 782
ANS   *see* autonomic nervous system
anthropomorphism   365
antibipolar drugs   793
anti-depressants   792
antiextrapolationists   114
anti-psychiatry movement   768
antithesis, principle of   361
antivivisectionist movement   112
Antonucci, T.C.   440
anxiety   219
appeasement   361
appendices, use in reports   898
applied research   35
approach–approach conflict   221
Archer, D.   664
Archer, J.   512, 523
archetypes   11
archival research   835
Argyle, M.   602, 603

Aristotle 3, 12
arousal 252, 255, 373
arousal level theory of vigilance 255
arousal theory 193, 201
articulatory loop 299–300
artificial intelligence (AI) 241
Artmann, H. 192
Asch, S. 105, 678, 823
ASL see American Sign Language
Asperger's syndrome 753
assimilation 317, 461, 452
associationism 7, 289
associative learning 125, 126–31
assortative mating 607
Astington, J.W. 367, 530
Aston-Jones, G. 211
asylum 807
Atchley, R.C. 561
Atkinson, J.W. 722
Atkinson, R.C. 25, 291, 309
Atkinson, R.L. 187
Atkinson–Shiffrin model of
     memory 25
atomism 9
attachment 412, 430, 436–48, 605
   after infancy 443–4, 552
   cross-cultural variations 439–42,
      443
   criticisms of the construct 442
   and internal working models 444–5
   security of 439
   theory 605
attention 244 ff
   focal 204
   focused 251, 252
   joint 484
   pertinence model of 249
   resource-based model of 252
   selective 244, 246, 248
   sustained 253
attention-deficit hyperactivity disorder
   (ADHD) 756
attenuation 247
attitude measurement 659–61
   expectancy-value technique of 661
attitudes 648 ff
   balance theory of 654–5
   and behaviour 650
   Bogardus's social distance scale 660
   cognitive development of 654
   formation of 653
   functions of 649
   Likert scales 659
   measurement of 659–61
   Osgood's semantic differential 660
   sociocognitive model of 650
   theories of 651–2
   Thurstone's scale 659
attraction 594 ff
   law of 596
   theories of 598
attributes 319
attribution 581 ff
   bias in 584

covariation model of 582–3
   process 637
attributional theory 201
atypical development 707, 744 ff
   emotional disturbances and
      behavioural difficulties 751–8
   learning difficulties 745–6
   physical and sensory
      impairment 748–51
auditory listening task 253
augmentation principle 583
aunting 413
authoritarian personality 669–70
authority, method of 60
autism 531–2, 752–6
   definitions of 752
   and intelligence 752
   and 'mindblindness' 754
autistic thinking 317
autobiographical memory 303
automatic processing 251
autonomic nervous system (ANS) 165,
      178–79, 713
autonomism 45
autonomous morality 506
Averill, J.R. 201, 604
aversion therapy 23, 107, 795
avoidance–avoidance conflict 222
awareness 204
   phonemic 750
Ax, A.F. 199, 200
Axline, V. 802
axons 152, 165, 166
Ayllon, T. 107
Azrin, N.H. 625

babbling 478–9
babies' behaviour 433
Baby Talk Register (BTR) 480, 482, 483
Bachman, C. 408
Bachy, V. 634
Baddeley, A.D. 290, 296, 299, 300, 799
Baerends, G.P. 374
Bahr, S. 549
Bailey, C.L. 769
balance theory 598, 654
Bales, R.F. 688, 689, 691
Baltes, P.B. 421
Bandura, A. 138–9, 391, 405, 506, 507,
      572, 625, 626–7, 637, 654, 798
Bannister, D. 526, 774
bar charts 849, 850
Barahal, H. 793
Barday, C.R. 305
Barlow, H.B. 375
Barnett, S.A. 132
Baron, R.A. 70, 625, 627, 628, 629,
      634, 635
Baron-Cohen, S. 752, 753, 754
Barratt, C.L. 796
Barrera, M. 279
Barrett, P.T. 712
Bar-Tal, D. 643
Bartlett, F. 241, 289

Baruch, G. 553
Basmajian, J.V. 798
BAT see body adjustment test
Bateman, A.J. 409
Bateson, P. 117, 119, 438
Batson, C.D. 639–40
Batteau, D.W. 387
Baumeister, R.F. 643
Baumrind, D. 686
Bayley, N. 489, 498
Baylis, G.C. 197
Beaumont, J.G. 171, 172, 212
Beck, A.T. 774, 800
Beck's cognitive behaviour
      therapy 800
Bee, H. 424, 467, 495
Beech, H.R. 805
Beehr, T.A. 228
behaviour
   adaptive 106
   androgynous 587
   animal 339 ff
   babies' 433
   eusocial 398
   helping 636–7
   instinctive 353
   modelling 637
   modification 23, 106, 116, 130, 135,
      797
   observation 773
   parental 433
   prosocial 511
   risk-taking 355
   shaping 23, 128
   social 502 ff
   social, of animals 395 ff
   species-specific 353
   tests 364
   therapy 23, 106, 795
behavioural ecology 345
behavioural therapies 22, 106–8, 135,
      795
behaviourism 8, 9, 49, 65
behaviourist (learning theory)
      approach 21
   evaluation of 24
   practical applications of 22
behaviourist model of thinking 318
beholder's share 271
belief congruence theory 670
belief, false 529
Bellezza, F.S. 309
Bellisle, F. 189
Belsky, J 54, 441, 449
Bem, D.J. 588, 656, 721
Bem, S. 514, 522
Bem's self-perception theory 588
Benedek, T. 551–2
Bengston, V.L. 549
Bennett, N. 473
bereavement 412, 563, 564
Bergen, D.J. 514
Berger, J. 693
Bergin, A.E. 21, 805, 806

Berkeley, G. 47
Berkowitz, L. 619, 625, 630, 631, 632, 635
Berndt, T.J. 542, 543
Berne, E. 804
Bernstein, B. 332
Bernstein, G.A. 758, 773
Berry, D.S. 576
Berry, J.W. 67
Berscheid, E. 595, 609, 610
Besson, J.M. 162
Betancourt, H. 424
betrothal 410
Bettelheim, B. 669, 686
Bharati, A. 590
bias
    culture 68–71
    gender 71, 72–6
    hostile attributional 628
    race 71–2, 75–6
    test 95–6
    tester 94–5
    ultimate attribution 618
Bible (Book of Genesis) 340
Biederman, I. 268
bimaturism 411
    sexual 411
Binet, A. 488
binocular cues, to depth perception 262
biofeedback 23, 179, 233, 798
    techniques 135, 798
biological reductionism 43
biopsychology 145 ff
    clinical study of 146
    experimental study of 148
    scientific inference 148
biorhythms 208
biosocial approach, to gender 518
bipolar cells 152
Birch, A. 239, 318, 645
birds, flock of 396–7
Bitterman, M.C. 273
Blais, M.R. 608
Blake, R.R 621
Blakemore, C. 113, 155, 281
Blanchard, E.B. 194, 450, 798
Blaney, P. 767
Blaney, P.H. 310
Bless, H. 83
blindness 749
blindsight 151
blindspot 152–3
Bliss, E.L. 781
Block, J. 544, 739
Bloom, K. 483
Bobo doll experiments 138
Bodmer, W.F. 499
body
    internal environment 145
    rhythms 208
body adjustment test (BAT) 723
Bogardus, E.S. 660
Bogardus's scale 660

Bohannon, P. 550
Booth, A. 549
Booth, T. 544
Borden, R.J. 629
Bornstein, M.H. 429
Bosse, R. 562
bottom-up processing 242, 268
Bouchard, T.J. 496
Boucher, J. 754
Bousfield, W.A. 297
Bower, G.H. 297, 308, 309
Bower, T.G.R 279, 280, 282, 465
Bowers, K.S. 720
Bowlby, J. 109, 340, 356, 430, 436–8, 444, 445, 446–8, 563, 605
BPS see British Psychological Society
Bradshaw, J. 31
brain 169
    areas of 169
    damage 777
    electrical stimulation of the (ESB) 17
    functions of 169
    lateralization of 170
    'split-brain' patients 171
    structure 169
brain functions, localization of 16
Braine, M.D.S. 384
brainstem 171
brainwashing 85
Brake, M. 540, 541
Brala, P.M. 190
branching programme 136
Breckler, S.J. 587, 650
Brehm, S.S. 596, 608
Breland, K. 132
Bremner, J.G. 432
Bretherton, I. 443
Brewer, M.B. 577, 615, 623, 665
Briggs, K.C. 735
Brigham, J.C. 671
brightness constancy 265
Brislin, R. 68
Bristol, M.M. 759
British Psychological Society (BPS) 38, 102, 117, 427, 751
Broadbent, D.E. 25, 113, 243, 245, 246, 252
Broberg, D.J. 192
Broca, P. 12, 16, 170
Brody, E.M. 644
Brodzinsky, D. 551
Bronfenbrenner, U. 422, 423, 442
Broverman, I.K 663
Brown, A.L. 473
Brown, C.R. 397
Brown, G.D.A. 241
Brown, G.W. 611, 785
Brown, J.C. 379
Brown, J.L. 400
Brown, P. 634, 683
Brown, R. 304, 383, 479, 480, 483, 670
Browne, J.A. 716
Browne, K. 439

Brownmiller, S. 514
Brown–Peterson technique 294
Bruner, J.S. 26, 272, 320, 321, 453, 460, 468, 470–1, 472, 483, 484, 740, 770
Brunner, E.J. 224
Brunswik, E. 271
Brunswik's model 271
Bruyer, R. 197
Bryan, J.H. 637
Bryant, P. 450, 465
BTR see Baby Talk Register
buffer, sensory 246
Bulhan, H.A. 70
bulimia nervosa 190, 192, 782
Bull, B.L. 309
bullying 221
Burger, J.M. 682
Burks, B.S. 497
Burt, C. 488, 493, 496, 497
Bushman, B.J. 633, 685
Buss, D.M. 606, 607, 625
Bussey, K. 522, 523
Bustard, H.J.R. 412
Butterworth, G. 469, 484
Byrne, D. 596, 598
Byrne's law of atraction 596
bystander calculus model of prosocial behaviour 640
bystander intervention 644

Cacioppo, J.T. 83, 680
Calhoun, J. 403, 406
Calvert, S.L. 520
Campbell, D.T. 680
Campbell, N. 168
Campfield, L.A. 189
Campos, J.J. 441
Cannon, W.B. 187, 188, 198, 199
Cannon–Bard theory 199
Caraco, T. 403
cardinal traits 736
care
    in the community 807–8
    instinct and 412
    paternal 413
Carl, E.A. 376
Carlson, M. 645
Carlson, V. 441
Carr, W.J. 376
Carrey, N.J. 758
Carrick, R. 411
Carroll, J.B. 331
Cartwright, D. 694
Carver, C.S. 627, 697
Carver, R.P. 490
Case, R. 474, 476
case study method 833
Cash, T.F. 597
caste 398
    nutrition and 398–9
CAT (or CT) scan 147
Catchpole, C. 402
categorical self 525

catharsis 452, 635
cathexis 728
Cattell, R. 93, 710, 715, 716, 717, 718
Cattell's theory 715
causal schemata 584
Cavanagh, P. 137
Cazden, C. 480, 482
cells
    bipolar 152
    ganglion 152
central executive 300
central filtering, of signals 375
central nervous system (CNS) 164, 169
    brain 169
    spinal cord 173
central tendency, measures of 848
central traits 736
centration 462
cerebellum 173
Chaiken, S. 83
Chaplin, W.F. 577, 721
Chemers, M.M. 690
chemical signals 378
Cheney, D.L. 408
Cherry, C. 245, 246
chi squared (c²), test of
        association 873
    table of critical values 915
    test of goodness of fit 874
Chickering, A.W. 724
Child, D. 705
childminding 448–9, 450
children's play 451
choice response time 900
Chomsky, N. 239, 388, 482–4
Christie, J.F. 455
chromosomes 341, 746
Cialdini, R.B. 639, 640, 645, 661, 681, 682
ciliary muscles 154, 264
circadian rhythms 208, 252, 256, 905
Clare, A. 768, 774, 791
Clark, A.M. 448
Clark, H.H. 383
Clark, M.S. 599–600
Clark, N.K. 694
Clarke-Stewart, A. 450
classical conditioning 8, 21, 126–28, 254, 653, 765, 795
    in humans 127
classical psychoanalysis 801
classification 464
Clausen, J.A. 536
Claxton, G. 823
Clayton, P.J. 563
Clayton, V. 559
Cleckley, J. 764, 783
Clegg, F. 813
client-centred therapy 29, 588, 738, 803
clinical interview 460, 773
clinical method of study 146
clinical psychologists 37, 708, 763, 772

clinical psychology 37
clinical settings 106
cliques 543
clock test 253
Cloninger, C.R. 195
Clore, G.L. 596, 597, 672
closure 9, 269
Clugston, G.A. 214
cluster sampling 815
Clutton-Brock, T.H. 405, 407
CNS see central nervous system
Coates, B. 637
cochlea 157
Cochrane, R. 715
cocktail party phenomenon 245, 246
coding, acoustic 295
coefficient of relationship 838
coevolution 346–8
cognition 237
    social 573
cognitive appraisal 199, 200
cognitive approach 24
    evaluation 27
cognitive approaches to therapy 799–800
cognitive development 459–486
    see also Bruner; Piaget; Vygotsky; information-processing
cognitive dissonance 86, 654
cognitive maps 131–2, 133
cognitive model of abnormality 765
cognitive processes 239, 459
cognitive psychology 25, 36, 239, 241
    models in 25
cognitive science 13, 27, 241
cognitive styles 722
cognitive/neoassociationistic model 630
cognitive-behavioural therapies 799–801
cognitive-developmental approach 427, 502–4
    to moral development 506–12
    to gender 519–23
    evaluation 523
Cohen, C. 630
Cohen, G. 44, 172
Cohen, L.J. 439
Cohen, S. 226
coherence, in problem solving 323–4
cohort research designs 425
cohort sequential design 425
Coile, D.C. 113
Coke, J.S. 639
Cole, M. 284
Coleman, J.S. 536, 540, 541, 542
collective unconscious 11
Collins, A.M. 297–8
Colman, A.M. 96
Colombo, J. 489
colour constancy 265
colour vision 153
    opponent process theory 154
    trichromatic theory 153

colour-opponent cells 154
Colvin, J. 408
coma 205
commons dilemma 622
communication
    animal 372 ff
    modes of 377
    networks 692
    tactile 377
community, care in the 807–8
comparative ethology 345
comparative psychology 36, 339–40
complementarity
    of need 596
    of rules 609
compliance 677 ff
components, recognition by 268
computer simulation 474
computerized scans 146–8
    CAT (or CT) 146–7
    MRI 146–7
    PET 146–7
concealed shapes test (CST) 723
concept formation 319 ff
conclusions, presentation of 897
concrete operations 464
concurrent validity 840
condition (independent variable) 826
conditioned response 126
conditioned stimulus 126
conditioning 8
    biological limits 130
    classical 8, 21, 126–28, 131, 254, 653, 765, 795
    operant 21, 128–30, 765, 796
Condon, W.D. 412
Condry, J. 589
cones 152
confidence level and statistical tests 893
conflict
    approach–approach 221
    avoidance–avoidance 222
    and cooperation 614
    and display 361
conformity 677 ff
confounding of variables 826
Conger, J.J. 510, 538
Connolly, J.A. 455
Conrad, C. 295
conscience 505
conscious or unconscious processing 251
conscious thought 317
consciousness 203
    altered states of 205–8
    levels of 204
conservation 463, 464, 466—7
    of volume 333, 903
consideration structure (of leadership) 689
consistency of personality 718–22
consonant–vowel–consonant trigrams (CVCs) 289

constancy
   perceptual 264
   shape 264
   size, 264, 282
construct validity 841
constructionism 53
constructivism 73, 289
content validity 840
context, in perception 276
contiguity 130, 132
contingency model 690
contingent responding 431
continuity 340
continuous reinforcement 129
control 61
   experimental 825 ff
   locus of 589
controlled observation 440, 829
controlled processing 251
conventional morality 507
convergence 262
Cook, S.W. 672
Cooley, C.H. 524
Cooper, H.M. 656, 657, 658, 835
Cooper, J.E. 774, 779
cooperative group work 473
Coopersmith, S. 228, 526, 527, 590
coping with stress 231–33
core sleep 215
Coren, S. 277–8
corpus callosum 173
correlation 837, 864 ff
   coefficient 496, 837, 864, 866
correspondence, in problem
      solving 324
correspondent inference theory 581–2
cortex 169–71
Costa, P.T. 718
counselling psychology 37
counterbalancing 827
Cousins, N. 17
covariation model of attribution 582–3
covert sensitization 796
Cowan, N. 294
Cowie, H. 473
Cox, M.J. 551
Cox, O.C. 667
Cox, T. 227
Craik, F.I.M. 26, 290, 300–2
Crawford, M. 75
Crick, F. 216
critical life events 543
critical period 356, 438, 446, 448
Crocker, J. 573
Crockett, L.J. 536
Cronbach, L.J. 720
Crook, J.H. 345, 401, 623
Crosby, J.F. 564
cross-cultural studies 278, 284
crossover 342
cross-sectional research designs 425,
   426
crowd influence 696 ff
Crowder, R.G. 293

Crutchfield, R.S. 680
crystallized intelligence 92
CST see concealed shapes test
cues, sensory 274
cults 84–6
cultural evolution 353
cultural influences 424, 425, 439,
   441–2, 443
cultural psychology 68–70
cultural set 274
culture 68, 346, 424
   and self 590
culture boundedness 67
Cumming, E. 560
Cunningham, M.R. 597, 624
cure 805–6
curvilinear relationships 867
Curzon, L. 137
cutaneous senses 160, 161
Cuthill, I. 115
Cutrona, C.E. 594
cyclical theory, of perception 271

Dagan, D. 352
Dane, F.C. 358, 596
dark adaptation 153
Darling, F. 397, 407
Darlington, R.B. 498
Darwin, C. 7, 195, 340, 341, 344
Darwin, C.J. 293
Darwinism, social 344
Davidson, J.E. 495
Davies, J.C. 619
Davies, M.H. 634
Davies, N.B 362, 402
Davies, R. 219
Davis, D.M. 520
Davis, J.H. 693
Davis, K. 429
Dawkins, M. 120
Dawkins, R. 345, 418
day care 449–50
Day, R.H. 276
De Castro, J.M. 189
De Fries, J.C. 56
De Gelder, B. 754
De Jong, W. 681
deafness 748–9
Deag, J.M. 408
death 562
Deaux, K. 577, 595, 663, 664, 689
debriefing 102
deception 684
Deci, E.L. 589
deep processing 301
defence
   mechanisms 232, 730
   perceptual 273
degrees of freedom 869–70
dehumanization 630, 823
deindividuation 630, 696
Deloache, J.S. 476
DeLongis, A. 223
demand characteristics 64, 823

Dembroski, T.M. 627
Dement, W. 212, 213
dementia 776
DeMyer, M. 752
Den Heyer, K. 295
Dennott, D.C. 367
dependence syndrome 778
dependent variable 62
depression 758, 780–6
deprivation 445 ff
   relative 619
   studies, of perception 278, 281
depth perception 262–3, 279
Deregowski, J.B. 285–6
Derlega, V.J. 603
Descartes, R. 12
descriptive statistics 847 ff
desensitization, systematic 795
determinism 45, 47–50, 61
   biological 47, 48
   environmental 47, 49
   soft 46, 48
deterministic bias 74
Deutsch, J.A. 25, 249
Deutsch, M. 602, 622, 679
DeValois, R.L. 154
development 422
   atypical 707, 744 ff
   cognitive 459
   cultural influences on 424
   ecology of 422
   female 539, 54
   human 419 ff
   influences on 421
   moral 504
developmental psychology 36, 419,
   425
Devine, P.G. 662, 663, 664
Devos, G. 590
Dewey, J. 7
Diab, L.N. 621
Diagnostic and Statistical Manual of
   Mental Disorder (DSM) 708, 770,
   771
diagnostic tools 773
Diament, C. 796
dichotic listening 245
dictionary unit 248
Diener, E. 697
difference thresholds 258
diffusion of responsibility 644
Digman, J.M. 718
dimorphism, sexual 356
Dinnerstein, D. 551
Dion, K.L. 597
Dipboye, R.L 597
direct perception, theory of 270
discontinuity 340
discourse analysis 67, 835
discovery learning 468
discrimination 126, 572, 662 ff
discriminatory power 94
discussion of results 897
diseases, infectious 747

disengagement theory 559–60
disinhibition 629
disorder
   depressive 758
   social 698
   sociopathic 782
dispersion, measures of 848, 854
displacement 386
   activity 359
dissonance
   cognitive 86
   post-decisional 658
distinctiveness 302
distortion studies of perception 278, 283
Dittes, J.E. 597
divorce 549–50
dizygotic (DZ) twins 496
DNA fingerprinting 410
Dodd, B. 481
Dodge, K.A. 628
dogmatism 670
Dollard, J. 624
domain specificity 526–8
dominance
   and sex 408
   social 407 ff
dominant genes 342
Dominowski, R.L. 323
Donaldson, M. 466, 903
Donnerstein, E. 628, 634
door-in-the-face 681
dopamine theory 786
double blind technique 828
Down's syndrome 746
dream analysis 12, 729, 802
dream, the 546
dreaming 212, 215–17
   theories of 215–17
Dreiser, T. 579
drug therapy 791–3
drug-induced states 208
drugs 208
   antibipolar 793
   effects on mood and behaviour 177, 208
   performance decrement and 256
   psychoactive 108, 177, 791
DSM see Diagnostic and Statistical Manual of Mental Disorder
dualism, interactive 3
Duberman, L. 549
DuBois, R.D. 674
Duck, J.M. 518
Duck, S. 611
Dunn, J. 434, 510
Dunphy, D.C. 543
Durkin, K. 503, 510, 512, 520, 539, 547, 553, 558, 560, 633
Dusek, J.B. 540
D'Ydewalle, G. 302
dyslexia 749

Eagly, A.H. 515, 627, 644, 681, 836

Eames, D. 467
early adulthood 547–52
early experience 449
eating
   disorders 190
   motivation for 188–90
Eaton, W.O. 514
Ebbinghaus, H. 8, 12, 241, 289
Eccles-Parsons, J. 519
echoic memory 293
echolalia 388
ecocognitivism 241
ecological approach 241, 270, 291
ecological validity 27, 64, 115, 303, 596, 841
ecology 345
   behavioural 345
   of development 422
economic defendability 400
ECR see evoked cortical response
ECT see electroconvulsive therapy
Edmunds, G. 715
educational psychology 37
Edwards, C.P. 509
EEG see electroencephalogram
EFT see embedded figures test
Egeland, J.A. 785
ego 11, 728–9, 802
   ideal 605
ego identity 537
egocentric speech 334
egocentrism 462, 463, 465, 466, 530
Eisenberg, N. 505, 511–2, 638, 646
Eisenberg's model of prosocial reasoning 511
Ekman, P. 196, 671
elaborated code of language 332
elaborated play 454
elaboration, in memory 302
elaborative rehearsal 301
Elder, G.H. 538
elderly, stereotypes of the 558
Electra complex 732
electrical stimulation of the brain (ESB) 17
electroconvulsive therapy (ECT) 108, 793, 828
electroencephalogram (EEG) 146, 210, 254, 255
electro-oculogram 212
Elgar, M. 355, 397
Elias, C.S. 301
eliciting of responses 373
Elliott, C. 489
Ellis, A. 800
embedded figures test (EFT) 273, 723
Emde, R.N. 430
emergent norm theory 697
emic 70
Emlen, S. 401
Emmelkamp, P. 796
Emmert's Law 265
emotion 195 ff
   facial feedback hypothesis 196

perception and 273
physiological aspects 197
recognition of 196
theories of 198
emotional disturbances 751
emotion-focused coping 231
empathy 639
empathy/altruism hypothesis 639
empiricism 3, 51, 61
empiricists, British 3
   Locke, J. 3
   Hobbes, T. 3
Empson, J. 211
enactive representation 333
encephalization 363
encoding specificity principle 310
encounter groups 803
Endicott, J. 773, 779
endocrine system 180–84
endogenous factors 256
Entine, A.D. 555
environmental factors in aggression 403, 628
environmental hazards, pre- and post-natal 747, 748
epilepsy 208
episodic memory 295–6
equilibration 317, 462
equity theory 601
Erber, J. 369
Ericsson, K.A. 323
Erikson, E. 18, 20, 74, 222, 453, 506, 544–5, 525, 537, 551, 554, 559, 802
Eron, L.D. 633
Eros 728
error 815 ff
   random 815
   systematic 816, 905
   type I 818, 861
   type II 818, 862
Erwin, P. 528
ESB see electrical stimulation of the brain
Esch, H. 366, 381
Estes, W.K. 129
Etcoff, N.L. 197
ethics 101–21
   BPS guidelines 102–4
   in clinical settings 106–8
   in developmental psychology 426–7
   in physiological psychology 149
   and persuasion 89
   in psychometric testing 95–8
   in research with animals 112–20
   in research with humans 102–5
   and socially sensitive research 108–12
ethnic cleansing 72
ethnocentrism 74, 616
ethogenics 835
ethology 24, 130, 340, 345, 437, 438, 623
   comparative 345
   social 345

etic 70
eugenics 72
Eurocentrism 67
eusocial behaviour 398
evaluation apprehension 694, 841
Evans, J. St B. 240
evoked cortical response (ECR) 241,
    256, 293
evolution 342
    cultural 353
    parallel 352
evolutionarily stable strategies
    (ESS) 361
Ewart, P.H. 283, 284
exchange relationship 599 ff
excitation/transfer theory 624, 625
executive processes 476
exemplar 577
existential self 525
exogenous factors 256
exosystem 423
expectancy-value technique of attitude
    measurement 661
expectations 823 ff, 828
    of experimenter 824
    of participants 823–4
experience, early 449
experiment 61, 63, 820 ff
    field 821
    laboratory 821
    natural or quasi- 821
    social psychology of the 62, 64–5
experimental control 825 ff
experimental design 825
experimental method 148
Experimental Psychology Society 117
experimental reductionism 43
experimenter effects 64, 824
exploration, in play 454
exposure, selective 657, 659
external experimental validity 841
external speech 333
external/internal locus of control 589
extinction 126
extraneous variables 821
extraversion 711
eyewitness testimony 303, 305–7
Eysenck, H. 20, 710, 711, 712, 715,
    716, 718, 732, 735, 806, 840
Eysenck, M. 116, 249, 270, 271, 275,
    303, 319
Eysenck Personality Inventory
    (EPI) 93, 712
Eysenck Personality Questionnaire
    (EPQ) 712

F test 920
    table of critical values 920
face validity 840
face-ism 664
faces, recognition of 306, 311
facial feedback hypothesis 196
factoid 86
factor analysis 710

Fagot, B.I. 519
Fajardo, D.M. 666
Falbo, T. 435
Falek, A. 774
false belief 529–31
falsifiability 20
family dynamics 435
Fantz, R. 279, 280
Faraday, A. 212
Farnham-Diggory, S. 751
Farr, R.M. 618
Farrell, P. 553
Farrington, D.P. 715, 751
fathers 431, 432–3
Fava, M. 192
Fazio, R.H. 650, 653, 656
feature analysis 267
feature integration 251
Fechner, G. 12, 258
feeding disorders 759
feelings 5
Feeney,, J.A. 552
Feldman, S.S. 538
female development 538, 54
Fernando, S. 95
Ferris, C. 560
fertility motivation 551
Feshbach, S. 625
Festinger, L. 60, 595, 655, 656, 692,
    696
Fiedler, F.E. 690
field dependence–field independence
    (FD-I) 273, 722–3
field experiment 821
field research 821–2
fields of study in psychology 36–7
figural identity 283
figural unity 282
figure–ground 9–10, 269, 277
Fischer, C.J. 637
fish, school of 397, 398
Fishbein, M. 650, 653
Fisher, R.J. 251, 621
Fisher, S. 20, 733
Fiske, S.T. 301, 584
fitness 624
    inclusive 413
five factors approach to personality ('Big
    Five') 717–18
fixation 731, 732
fixed action patterns (FAP) 358, 623
flashbulb memory 304
flock, of birds 396, 397
flooding 796
Floody, O.R. 184
fluid intelligence 92
focal attention 204
focus gambling 320
focused attention 251, 252
Fonagy, P. 733, 735, 775, 799
Fontana, D. 499, 526
food
    availability 355
    scarcity 401

Foot, H.C. 472
football crowds 698
foot-in-the-door technique 681
forensic psychology 37
formal operations 464
Forsyth, D.R. 693
Fouts, R. 386
Fowler, C.A. 615
Fox, N. 439
Foyel, A. 524
Fraiberg, S. 749
Frank, B.M. 724
Frankenhauser, M. 227, 434
Frankl, V. 29–30
Franks, C.M. 714, 797
Franks, J.J. 267
Fransella, F. 768, 774, 800
Franz, C.E. 445
Fraser Darling effect 397
Fraser, A.F. 360
Fraser, C. 555
Fraser, E.D. 498
free association 13, 728, 801
free will 46–7, 50
    and behaviourism 49
    and determinism 45
    and humanistic psychology 50
    and psychoanalysis 48
Freedman, J.L. 681
freedom, degrees of 869–70
Freeman, D. 540
French, J.R.P. Jr 223, 683
frequency
    distributions 852
    measurement 846
    polygons 852
    tables 849
Freud, A. 18, 19, 49, 448, 539, 730
Freud, S. 10–11, 12, 65, 69, 109–10,
    139, 190, 215, 232, 317, 452, 505,
    518, 623, 634, 696, 727–34, 781
Freud's psychoanalytical theory 727
Frey, K.S. 521
Fried, I. 197
Friedman, M. 229, 722
friendship, love and marriage 602
Frisch, K. von 127, 348, 380
Frith, U. 755
frustration/aggression hypothesis 624
Fry, C. 558
functional set 328
functionalism 7
fundamental attribution bias 584
Furnham, A. 113, 520, 714

Gaebelein, J.W. 625
Gaertner, S.L 640, 665
Gale, A. 714
Gallie, D. 555, 556
Galton, F. 496
galvanic skin response (GSR) 225
gamete 342
ganglion cells 152
Ganster, D.C. 230

Gardner, A.R, 723
Gardner, H. 451, 492, 509, 524
Gardner, R.A. 384, 388
Gardner's theory of multiple
 intelligences 492, 499
Garfield, S.L. 739
Garner, W.R. 267
Garnham, A. 42
Garvey, C. 451
Gaussian curve 842
Geen, R.G. 625, 629, 631, 632
Geist, V. 411
Gellerman, E.W. 364
Gelman, R. 480, 482, 484
gender 54, 72, 75, 231, 513–523
 androgyny 514
 biological factors 516–18
 biosocial theory 518
 constancy 519–20, 523
 cognitive-developmental theory 522
 differentiation 515–16
 identity 513, 514
 and the media 520
 role (sex role) 503, 513, 517, 520,
  732
 schematic processing theory 521
 and socialization 518–20
 stereotypes 513–14, 520
gendercentric bias 74
gene–culture coevolution 346, 347
General Adaptation Syndrome
 (GAS) 17, 225
General Problem Solver 26
generalizability 892
generalization 126, 572
generativity versus stagnation 554
genes 51, 341
 dominant 342
 recessive 342
genetic predisposition 784
genetic transmission 343
genetics 341
genital stage 732
genotype 55, 341
Gentry, W.D. 625
George, G.M. 644
Gerbner, G. 88
gerontology 557
Gershuny, J. 556
Gestalt
 laws of perceptual
  organization 269, 270, 318
 model of thinking 318, 329
 psychology 9, 329
 therapy 804
Gibbons, F.X. 585
Gibson, E.J. 267, 280, 281
Gibson, J.J. 270, 275, 276
Gibson, R.M. 400
Gilbert, D.T. 584
Gilchrist, J.C. 272
Gill, F.B. 400
Gilligan, C. 505, 512
Gittleman-Klein, R. 792

Glassman, W.E. 31
global focusing strategy 322
glucose receptors 189
glucostatic theory 189
Goffman, E. 683
Goldberg, L.R. 718, 786
Goldberg, P. 664
Goldfarb, W. 446
Goldman, R.J. 558
Goldman-Eisler, F. 733
Gombrich, E.H. 271
gonadotrophic hormone 180
gonads 182
good form (Prägnanz) 269, 318
Goodall, J. van Lawick 404, 408, 412
Goodall, J. 113, 120
Gopnik, A. 529, 530
Gottesman, I. 785
Göttmark, F. 397
Gould, J.L. 382
Gould, S.J. 418, 493, 710
Gouzoules, S 408
Gove, W.R. 775
Graham, S. 69
Gramza, A.F. 415
Granberg, D. 585
grandparents 435–6
granfalloon 84
Gray, J.A. 117, 247, 248, 673
Great Ape Project 120
Green, D.M. 259
Green, S. 116, 119
Greene, E. 306
Greeno, J.G. 323
Gregory, R.L. 150, 262, 270, 274, 275,
 281, 284
grief 563
Griffin, D.R. 366, 374
Groninger, L.D. 309
Gross, R. 55, 109
Grossman, K.E. 441
group 690 ff
 characteristics of 691
 communication networks 692
 decision making 690 ff
 hunting 398
 living 398
 memory 694
 norms 693
 polarization 695
 risky shift phenomenon 695
 size 691
groups, roles in 692
groupthink 618, 694
growth hormone 180
growth trends 547–8
Gruber, E.R. 590
Gruen, A. 724
Grusec, J.E. 637, 638
GSR see galvanic skin response
Guimond, S. 620
Guiton, P. 356

Haan, N. 553, 554

Haartman, L. von 401, 411
Haber, R.N. 292
habituation technique 279
habituation 125–6, 204
Haider, M. 256
Hall, C.S. 705
Hall, J. 98
Hall, K.R.L. 415
Halpin, A.W. 689
Hamilton, W.D. 396, 397, 414
Hampson, S. 705, 710. 712, 716, 718.
 719, 721, 735
Haney, C. 837
Haracz, J. 786
Hardin, G. 622
hardy personality 230
Hare, R.D. 783
Hare-Mustin, R.T. 73
Hargreaves, D. 831
Harlow, H. 134, 194, 437, 446, 448
Harré, R. 835
Harris, J.E. 306
Harris, M.B. 280, 625
Harris, P.L. 530, 531
Harter, S. 526–8
Hartline, H.K. 154
Hartman, L. von 830
Hartshorne, H. 95, 719
Hartup, W.W. 542
Harwood, R.L. 443
hassles 223
Hatfield, E. 603, 604
Hawkins, L.H. 209
Hayes, K.J. 384
Hayes, N.J. 418, 590
Hays, R.B. 595, 603
Hazan, C. 605–6
Headstart 96, 498
health psychology 37
hearing 155
 anatomy of the ear 156–7
 properties of sound 155–6
Hearnshaw, L.S. 239
Heather, N. 768, 774, 823
Hebb, D.O. 43, 55, 168, 282, 283, 836
Hebb/Vernon model of intelligence 55
hedonistic reasoning 511
Heider, F. 581, 598, 654
Heiligenberg, W. 404
Heim, A. 488, 715
Heinicke, C.H. 551
'hello/goodbye' effect 805
Helmholtz, H.F.L. von 5, 153
helping behaviour 636–7
heredity–environment issue (nature–
 nurture debate) 422, 496–500
Hering, E. 153
heritability 499
Herman, L. 387, 388–9, 390
Herman, R. 497
hermaphroditism 518
Herriot, P. 481, 483
Hersh, S. 630
Hess, E.H. 356–7, 822

Hess, R.D.   332, 624
heterogeneous summation   374
heteronomous morality   506
heterosexism   74
Hetherington, A.W.   188
heuristic strategies   318
Hewstone, M.   70
hibernation theory   215
Hick, W.F.   900
hidden observer   207
hierarchies (social dominance)   407–8
hierarchy of needs   29, 30
Higgins, E.T.   588
Hilgard, E.R.   205, 207
Hill, A.B.   733
Hill, C.T.   607, 608, 838
Hill, P.   538
Hill, R.   606
Hill, T.   577, 578
Hinde, R.A.   377, 418
Hines, M.   517
Hinshaw, S.P.   751
hippocampus   173
Hippocrates   12, 706, 709
Hirshberg, N.   710
histograms   852
Hitler, A.   82, 86, 87, 616, 688
Hobson, J.A.   216
Hobson, R.P.   530
Hockett, C.F.   383, 393
Hofestede, G.   68, 69
Hoffman, M.L   506, 507, 510
Hofling, K.C.   686
Hogg, M.   578, 595, 673, 695
Hohmann, G.W.   198
Holley, J.W.   735
Hollingshead, A.B.   785, 786
Holmes, D.S.   733
Holmes, J.   106
Holmes, J.G.   608
Holmes, T.H.   222, 550
Holmes, W.G.   356, 415
Holstein, C.B.   512
Homans, G.C   572, 601
homecare   807
homeostasis   187–8
homogeneity of variance   863, 874
homosexuals   665
honeybee dance   380–2
Honzik, M.P.   490
Hoogland, W.G   398
Hooker, T.   377
Hopfield, J.J.   217
horizontal–vertical illusion   284
hormones   180–1
Horn, G.   369
Horn, J.L.   557
Horn, J.M.   497
Horne, J.   212, 215
Horne, J.A.   905
Horney, K.   49, 802
Hornstein, G.A.   637
Horowitz, F.D.   422
hospice movement   563

hostile attributional bias   628
Hovland, C.I.   82, 660
Howarth, E.   733
Howes, D.H.   273
Howitt, D.   67, 75, 109
Hsu, F.L.K.   590, 591
Hubel, D.H.   13, 113, 155, 241, 267, 281
Hudson, J.W.   606
Hudson, W.   285–6
Huesmann, L.R   633
Hughes, J.   176
Hughes, M.   466
Hull, C.L.   131
Hulme, C.   750
human development   419 ff
human language, teaching to animals   382
humanistic (phenomenological) approach   28–31, 33, 50, 65, 736, 765
    therapies   803–4
Hume, D.   47
Humphrey, N.K.   399–400
Hunter, E.J.   224
Hunter, J.E.   97
Hurvich, L.M.   154
Huston, A.C.   513, 518, 523
Hutt, C.   454–5
Huxley, J.S.   351
Huxley, T.H.   344
Hyman, B.T.   776
hyperactivity   756
hypnosis   205–7
    theories of   207
hypothalamus   172
hypothesis   62, 816
    alternative   817
    null   817
    one-tailed   817, 818
    two-tailed   817, 818
hypothetico-deductive method   830, 891

ICD   see International Classification of Diseases
iconic memory   291, 293
iconic representation   333, 470
id   11, 728–9
ideal self   29, 737
identification   139
identity, social   615, 663
idiographic approach   705–6, 734, 833
idiographic theories   93, 705
idiothetics   741
illusions
    structural effects and   277
    visual   274 ff
imagery, in memory   308
Imich, A.   98
imitation, in infancy   432
immediate (or sensory) memory   292
immune system   225, 226

impairment, physical and sensory   748–51
implicit personality theory   579
implicit social theory   579, 580
implosion therapy   796
impression formation   576
imprinting   355–7, 411, 438, 446
inclusive fitness   413
independence from parents   415–6
independent measures design   826
independent variable   62, 820
individual differences   36
infant imitation   432
infant tests   489
infectious diseases   747
inference
    scientific   148
    statistical   825
information processing   25, 240, 474–8
    approach   474
    developmental aspects   474–6
    efficiency of   475
    individual differences   476
informational influence   679
informed consent   102
infradian rhythms   209
Inglis, J.   794
in-group   577, 614
initiating structure (of leadership)   689
innate releasing mechanism (IRM)   375, 376
inner speech   333
inoculation   89
insanity   764
insect senses   373
Insell, T.   792
insight   329
    learning   132–34
    therapy   805
Insko, C.A.   680
instinct
    and care   411
    and learning   350
instinctive behaviour   353
instinctual drives   728
Institute of Medical Ethics   119
institutions   807
instructions, standardization of   828
instrumental conditioning   653
    see also operant conditioning
integrity versus despair   559
intelligence   110, 487–501
    A, B, C   55
    artificial (AI)   241
    crystallized   92
    fluid   92
    inherited   496
    and IQ   488–91
    Hebb/Vernon model of   55
    Sternberg's triarchic theory of   492–5
    theories of   492–5
intelligence quotient (IQ)   422, 488–91
    culture and   491

intelligence quotient (IQ) (*cont.*)
    environmental influences on 498–9
    labelling 96
    and race 499
intelligence tests 91–4, 488–91
    predictive ability 490
    problems with the use
        of 94–8 490–1
    reliability of 94, 490
    validity of 94, 490
    standardization 94
interactionism 45
    in relation to personality 720
interactive dualism 3
interchangeability 386
interference effects, in memory 297
interference
    proactive 297
    retroactive 296
intergroup conflict 617
intergroup cooperation 617
internal environment of the body 145
internal experimental validity 841
internal working models 444–5
internal–external locus of control 589,
    722
internalization 505, 506
International Classification of Diseases
        (ICD) 708, 770, 771, 772
interpretation of results 890 ff
    and analysis of data 891
    and background to research 890
    and design of study 890–9
interval level of measurement 846
interval/ratio data 846
intervention, teacher 471
interviews
    clinical 460
    techniques 834
intimacy 550
intracultural differences 442
intrapsychic bias 74
introduction, of report 895
introspection 6, 65, 322
introversion 711
    and vigilance 256
intuition, method of 60
invariant functions 462
IQ see intelligence quotient
Irvine, S.H. 491
Isaacs, W. 116
Isen, A.M. 644
isolation 551
isomorphism 318
Israeli kibbutzim 439
Iyengar, S. 88

Jackson, B. 450
Jackson, L.A. 528, 558
Jackson, S.E. 223
Jahoda, G. 284, 467, 475
Jahoda, M. 555–6, 764
James, W. 7, 12, 46, 204
James–Lange theory 198–9

Jamieson, A. 558
Janis, I.L. 694, 695
Jarman, P.J. 401
Jarvis, P.A. 441
Jason, L.A. 646
J-curve of relative deprivation 619
Jellison, J.M. 584
Jemmott, J. 611
Jemmott, J.B. 226
Jennett, B. 205
Jensen, A.R. 96, 110, 499
Jerison, H.J. 363
Jermier, J.M. 223
Johnson, D.W. 691
Johnson, J.H. 229, 455, 520
Johnson, M.K. 296
Johnston, W.A. 250
joint attention 484
Jolicoeur, P. 266
Jolly, A. 399
Jones, E.E 581, 582, 584, 661
Jones, S. 410
Jorgensen, B.W. 598
Josephson, W.L. 632–3
Joule, R.V. 683
Joyce, W. 87
Judd, C.M. 577
Jung, C. 11, 18, 215, 710
just noticeable difference, in
        sensation 258
just world hypothesis 585

Kacelnik, A. 355
Kadushin, A. 835
Kagan, A. 227
Kagan, J. 510
Kahn, A. 602
Kahn, S. 544
Kahneman, P. 252–3, 256
Kail, R. 475
Kamin, L.J. 497, 499
Kandel, D.B. 596
Kanner, L. 752
Kanzi, the chimpanzee 385–6
Kaplan, M.F. 95, 97, 695, 696
Kaplan, R.M. 97
karma 590
Karuza, J. Jr 596
Katz, D. 693
Katz, R. 224
Kavanagh, R.E. 563
Kaye, K. 340, 431, 432
Kea, the dolphin 388
Keating, D.P. 467
Keesey, R.E. 189
Keith, J. 558
Kelley, H.H. 582, 583, 584, 599, 607,
    608
Kellogg, W.N. 384
Kelly, G. 706, 738–9, 800
Kelly, G.A 580, 671
Kelly, J.B. 550
Kelly's personal construct theory
        (PCT) 738

Kelvin, P. 556
Kendrick, D.C. 714
Kenrick, D.T. 721
Kerckhoff, A.C. 596
Kety, S.S. 785
Kihlstrom, J.F. 204, 205
Kilham, W. 684
Kiminyo, D.M. 467
kin selection 413
kinaesthesia 160, 162
    kinaesthetic receptors 154
    kinaesthetic sense 262
Kinder, D.R. 664
Kirby, R. 737
Kirkpatrick, L.A. 595
Klein, M. 18–19, 453, 802
Kleitman, N. 214
Klerman, G. 792, 794
Klin, A. 753
Kline, P. 20, 91, 92, 94, 97, 98, 716,
    733, 734, 735
Klinnert, M.D. 431
Knox, R.E. 658
Kobasa, S.C. 230
Koestler, A. 46, 114
Koffka, K. 9, 269
Kohlberg, L. 74, 504, 507–10, 511, 512,
    519, 521, 541–2
Köhler, I. 283, 284
Köhler, W. 9, 13, 132–34, 269, 318
Kohn, M.L. 786
Koko, the chimpanzee 385
Kolvin, I. 758
Konecni, Y.J 635
Konishi, M. 348
Korsakoff's syndrome 195
Kotelchuk, M. 433
Kraepelin, E. 770, 779
Kramer, R.M. 623, 836
Krebs, D.L. 354, 624, 636
Kronhausen, F. 634
Kruijt, J.P. 403
Kruuk, H. 398
Ku Klux Klan 630, 697
Kübler-Ross, E 562
Kuhn, H.H. 524
Kuhn, T.S. 66, 345
Kummer, H. 408
Kutchinski, B. 634
Kutnik, P. 510

La Berge, D. 890, 899
La France, M. 671
labelling 96, 769, 772, 774–5
laboratory experiment 821
laboratory work 821
Labov, W. 332
LAD see language acquisition device
Lader, M. 714
Laing, R.D. 767, 768, 769, 775, 784
Laird, J.D. 196
Lamb, M.E. 433, 434, 435, 441, 443
Lamiell, J.T. 741
Lamm, H. 602

Lana, the chimpanzee 385
Landy, D. 597
Lang, P.J. 107, 116, 759, 795
Langer, E.J. 574
Langer, J. 507
Langlois, J.H. 519
Langston, J.W. 175
language
　elaborated code of 332
　human, teaching to animals 382
　restricted code of 332
　thinking and 316
language acquisition 469, 478–84
　sequence of 478–9
　and social interaction 484
　studies of 480–1
　theories of 481–3
language acquisition device
　(LAD) 482, 483
Language Acquisition Support System
　(LASS) 484
Language of the Genes (S. Jones) 410
Lanyon, R.I. 714
LaPiere, R.T 650
Lashley, K. 13
LASS *see* Language Acquisition
　Support System
Latané, B. 642–3, 644
late adulthood 557–63
latency period 732
Law of Effect 8, 128
Law of Mass Action 17, 170
Law of Prägnanz (ggod form) 269
Lazare, A. 733
Lazarus, A.A. 799
Lazarus, J. 397
Lazarus, R.S. 199, 200, 223, 227, 231
Lazarus's cognitive theory 199
Le Boeuf, B.J. 402
Le Bon, G. 696
Lea, S.E.G. 358, 404
leadership 643, 687 ff
　consideration structure of 689
　initiating structure of 689
　task structure and 688
Leahy, A.M. 497
learned helplessness 220, 229, 799
learning 124–39
　associative 125, 126–31
　cognitive 131–34
　definition of 124–5
　habituation 125–6, 204
　insight 132–4
　and instinct 350
　latent 133
　learning sets 134
　observational 137–9
　and performance 138
　sets 134
　simple 125–31
　trial and error 128, 133
learning difficulties 745–6,
learning sets 134

learning theory approach 21, 426,
　481–2
　evaluation 24
least preferred coworker (LPC)
　scale 690
Leavitt, H.J. 692
Lee, V.E. 498
Legge, D. 44
lek 400
Lenneberg, E.H. 483
Lerner, M.J. 585, 638
Lerner, R.M. 52, 55, 57
Leslie, A.M. 530, 754
Lesnik-Oberstein, M. 607
levels
　of confidence 893
　of the environment 52
　of explanation 32, 34
　of measurement 846, 892
　of processing 300–3
　of significance 893
Leventhal, H. 82
Levine, M.A. 322
Levinger, G. 733
Levinson, D.J. 546, 553, 554–5
Levitt, E. 663
Levitt, M.J. 444
Levy, D.J. 520
Levy-Leboyer, C. 110
Lewis, C.C. 531
Lewis, M. 434, 439, 467, 525, 526,
Ley, R.G. 197
Leyens, J.P. 632
Leyhausen, P. 379
Liben, L.S. 521
libido 11, 19, 728, 731, 732
Lichter, D.G. 759
Lieberman, M.A. 804
Liebert, R.M. 631, 632, 646
life events 543
lifespan development 421, 543–4
Likert scales 659
Likert, R. 659
Lilley, J.C. 208
limbic system 170–1, 173
Lindsay, G. 105
Lindsay, P.H. 267
linear programme 136
linguistic relativity hypothesis 331
linguistic universals 482
Linssen, H. 577
Linton, H.B. 724
Linton, M. 303–4
Linville, P.W. 587
Lipetz, M.E 596
Lippitt, R. 688, 689
Lippman, W. 577
listening, dichotic 245
Litton, I. 619
Livingstone, M.S. 155
Lloyd Morgan's canon 365
Lloyd, B.B. 523, 663
localization
　of brain functions 16

　of sound 157
location constancy 265
loci, method of 309
Lock, A. 431
Locke, J. 12, 47, 239
locus
　of cause 588
　of control 228, 589
Loftus, E.F. 26, 292, 304, 306, 307
logotherapy 30
London, H. 722
Long, J. 553
longitudinal research designs 425, 426
long-term memory 292, 368
Lore, R.K. 424
Lorenz, K.Z. 43, 113, 116, 340, 348,
　352, 353, 355, 358, 374–5, 378,
　403–4, 412, 438, 605, 634
loudness 156
Louis-Sylvestre, J. 189
Lovaas, O.I. 23, 797
love 603 ff
Lovelace, E.A. 310, 312
Lowenthal, M.F. 548
Luchins, A.S. 328
Lumsden, C.J. 346, 347, 417
lure 682
Luria, A.R. 334
Lynch, K. 835
Lyons, N.P. 512
Lysak, H. 629

Maccoby, E.E. 514, 515, 519, 627, 724,
　835
Macdonald, D.W. 397, 415
MacFarlane, A. 412,
machine reductionism 43
Mackay, D. 763–4, 774
Mackenzie, B. 499
Mackintosh, N.J. 364
Mackworth, N.H. 239, 253–4
Macphail, E.M. 363
Maddox, G.L. 560
Magenis, R. 747
'magic age' view 530
Magnus, D.B.E. 375
Maier, S.F. 17
Main, M. 440, 442, 444, 445
maintenance rehearsal 301
Major, B. 602
major tranquillizers 792
Malamuth, N.M. 634
Malim, T. 734
Malinowski, B. 832
malleus 157
Mandler, G. 201
Mann, L. 406, 697
Mann, R.D. 688
Manning, A. 363, 364–5, 368
Manning, M. 127
Mann–Whitney U-test 873
　table of critical values 918
Mantell, D.M. 684
maps, cognitive 131–2, 133

Marcia, J. 537, 538
marital rules 549
Marks, G. 585
Marks, I.M. 796, 799
Markus, H. 587
Marler, P. 348–9
marriage 548–9
Marsh, H.W. 526–7
Marsh, P. 698, 835
Marshall, G.O. 605
Marsland, D. 540
Martin, C.L. 521
Martin, G.M. 132
Martinez, D.R. 398
Marx, M.H. 735
Maschwitz, U. 376
Maslach, C. 200, 223, 586
Maslow, A.H. 28, 29, 193, 764
Massarik, F. 834
Masserman, J.H. 360
Masson, J. 106
Masters, W.H. 831
Masterson, J.F. 540
mastery play 452
matched participants design 827
mate selection 409, 606
maternal deprivation
        hypothesis 446–8
mathematical symbols 907
mating, assortative 607
mating systems 401
Matlin, M.W 73, 549
Mattes, J. 792
Matthews, K.A. 627
Matthews, T. 230
maturation 279, 285, 358
Maurer, D. 125, 279
Maxwell, G.M. 610
May, P. 792
Mayall, B. 450
Maynard-Smith, J. 361, 405, 406
Mbiti, J.S. 590
McBurnett, K. 757
McCauley, C. 694
McClelland, D.C. 722, 735
McClelland, J.L. 268
McClintock, C.G. 622
McCord, R.R. 721
McCrae, R.R. 718
McDougall, W. 696
McFarland, D.J. 193
McGarrigle, J. 466
McGaugh, J.L. 369
McGeoch, J.A. 297
McGinnies, E. 273
McGinnis, R. 606
McGrath, J.E. 693
McGrew, W.C. 353
McGuire, W.J. 89, 649
McKellar, P. 317
McKelvey, R. 753
McNeill, D. 389, 481, 483
Meacham, J.A. 305–6
Mead, G.H. 524

Mead, M. 517, 539 540
Meadows, S. 442, 454, 455, 473, 475, 525
mean (average) 842, 848
means–ends analysis 327
measurement
    interval level of 846
    levels of 846, 892
    nominal level of 846
    ordinal level of 846
    ratio level of 846–7
measures
    of central tendency 848
    of dispersion 854
Meddis, R. 214
media 519, 520
medial preoptic area 194
median 848
mediation in memory 312–3
mediators 24
medical model of abnormality 767–9
meditation 207
Mehler, J. 412, 430
Meijer, J.H. 210
Meilman, P.W. 537
meiosis 342
Melamed, B. 799
Melhuish, E.C. 450
Meltzoff, A.N. 432
memory 28 ff
    Atkinson–Shiffrin model of 25
    autobiographical 303
    different kinds of 368
    echoic 293
    elaboration in 302
    episodic 295–6
    flashbulb 304
    iconic 291
    imagery in 308
    immediate (or sensory) 292
    interference effects in 297
    long-term 368
    mediation in 312–3
    models of 290–303
    prospective 305, 306
    real-life 303
    repisodic 305
    semantic 295–6
    semantic categorization in 297
    short-term 294, 368
    state-dependent 310–11
    study of 368
    transactive 694
    working 299
memory organization 297
    spreading activation model of 298
    typicality effect in 298
memory span 294
menstrual cycle 184
mental age 488
mental disorder 708, 762 ff
    classification and diagnosis 770–75
    categories and descriptions 776–83
    diagnostic tools 773

possible causes of 783
    problems of diagnosis 772–75
mental illness 708, 767–9
Mercer, D. 23
mere exposure effect 653
mesosystem 423
Messick, S. 722
meta-analysis 442, 514
metabolism 190
metacognition 475–6
metacommunication 378
metarepresentation 531
method
    of authority 60
    description in reports 895–4
    of intuition 60
    of loci 309
    scientific 61–4
    of tenacity 60
Metts, S. 608
Michelsen, A. 348, 382
microsystem 422
middle adulthood 552–6
Middlebrook, P.N. 630
Midlarsky, E. 643
midlife crisis 552, 553
Mikula, G. 602
Milardo, R.M. 604
Miles, I. 556
Miles, L.E. 210
milestones in socio-emotional
        development 430
Milgram, S. 70, 105, 110, 509, 573, 629, 644, 684, 686
Milinski, M. 355
Miller, A.G. 584, 686
Miller, G.A 294, 311, 318
Miller, J.G. 584
Miller, N. 115, 116, 572, 798
Mills, J. 599
mind
    theory of 528–32, 753
    unconscious 10, 204–5, 728
mind/body problem 4–5, 16
mindblindness 753
mindreading skills see theory of mind
minimax principle 601
minor tranquillizers 791
Minuchin, S. 782
Mischel, W. 706–7, 719, 720, 773
Mishkin, M. 369
Mitchell, G.D. 413
Mitchell, P. 528, 529, 531
mitosis 342
Miyake, K. 441
mnemonic techniques 312–3
mode 848
model/rival training 391, 392
modelling 137, 240
    behaviour 637
    as therapy 799
models 25
    of abnormality 765
    in cognitive psychology) 25

of memory 290–303
in psychology 240
of stress 225
modes of representation 470
Moghaddam, F.M. 68
Money, J. 517, 518
monocular cues, to depth
    perception 262–3
monogamy 410
monotropy 438
monozygotic (MZ) twins 496
mood congruence 310–11
Moores, D.F. 749
Moos, R.H. 72, 728
moral absolutism 116
moral development 504, 505–12
    and gender 512
    social contexts of 510
    stages of 508, 511
moral orientations 511
moral realism 506
moral relativism 116, 117, 506
morality
    conventional 507
    heteronomous 506
    postconventional 507
    preconventional 507
Moran, J.J. 509
Moray, N. 246
morphemes 478
Morris, C.D. 303
Morris, D. 196, 340, 360, 396
Morris, J.B 351, 828
Morris, P.E. 313
Morton, D. 120
Moscovici, S. 618
Moscovitch, M. 302
motion parallax 263
motivation 187–95
    arousal theory 193
    curiosity and exploration 194
    to eat 188–90
    homeostatic 187–8
    nonhomeostatic 193
    in perception 272–3
    psychohydraulic model of 404
    and set 272
motor theory, of thought 318
MRI scan 147
M-space 474
Much, N. 68
Mullen, B. 688
Müller, J. 12
Müller-Lyer illusion 274
multiple intelligences, Gardner's theory
    of 492, 499
multiple personality 781
multitrait approaches to
    personality 710 ff
Murphy, J. 775
muscles, ciliary 264
mutation 342
mutual reciprocity 429
Myers–Briggs Type Indicator 735

Myerscough, R. 630

Naatanen, R. 293
Namikas, J. 405, 822
nativist theory 51, 482, 484
natural experiment 821
natural selection 7
naturalistic observation 460, 829
nature/nurture see heredity/
    environment
Necker cube 276
need
    for achievement (n Ach) 722
    complementarity of 596
    hierarchy of 29, 30
needs-oriented reasoning 511
negative reinforcement 129
negative state relief model 639
Neimark, E.D. 467
Neisser, U. 26, 249, 271, 291, 305–6,
    841
Neisser's cyclical theory of
    perception 271
Nelson, B. 397
Nelson, K. 480, 482, 484
Nelson, R.O. 773
Nelson, T.O. 303
neo-Darwinism 624
neonate studies, of perception 278–81
nervous system 164 ff
nest sites 400
network, social 595
networks
    communication 692
    neural 168
Neugarten, B.L. 553, 560
neural networks 168
neural transmission 166–7, 787
neurochemicals 174
neuromodulators 176
neurons 165
neuroscience 241
neurosis 770
neuroticism 711
neurotransmitter 167, 174, 787
new paradigm research 66
new racism 72
Newcombe, T.M 596
Newell, A. 13, 26, 318, 326, 327
Newman, H.H. 496, 497
Newman, P.R. 552
Newson, J. 430–1
Ng, S.H. 664
Nicolson, 750, 751
Nim Chimpsky, the chimpanzee 386
Nisbett, R.E 323, 582
Noble, G.K. 380
Nobles, W.W. 590
nocturnal activity 209
nominal data 846
nominal level of measurement 846
nomothetic approach 705–6, 734
nomothetic methods 833
nomothetic theories 93

noncommon effects 582
nonhomeostatic motivation 193
nonlinear relationships 867
nonparametric tests 862, 872
nonrapid eye movement sleep
    (NREM) 212
nonsense syllables 8
nonstate theory 207
norm of reaction 55, 500
normal distribution 853, 842
    and standard deviation 855
normality/abnormality 707–8, 762–7
Norman, D.A. 25, 205, 249
Norman, W.T. 717, 718
normative influence 679
norms, social 638
Novak, D. 596
Novak, M.A. 437, 448
Noyes, R. 791
NREM see nonrapid eye movement
    sleep
null hypothesis 817
Numan, M. 194
Nurnberg, H. 777
nutrition, and caste 398–9
Nutt, D.J. 794
Nyiti, R.M. 467

obedience 683 ff
obesity 190
object permanence 462, 465
objects
    recognition of 262
    superimposition of 263
observation 829
    controlled 440, 829
    naturalistic 460, 829
    participant 830
observational learning 137–9
observer 582
obsessive–compulsive disorder 781
occupational (industrial)
    psychology 37
occupational stress 223
Oedipus/Electra complex 505, 518,
    732
oestrogen 194
Offer, D. 540
old racism 72
Olds, J. 13, 173, 194
olfaction (smell) 159–60
Olton, D.S. 132, 133
Olweus, D. 426, 720
one-tailed hypothesis 817, 818
ontogenetic adaptation 350, 354
ontogeny 344, 352
operant (instrumental)
    conditioning 21, 128–30, 131,
    654, 765, 797–8
    in humans 130
operational definition 61–2
operational set 328
operationalizing 816
operations 461

opiates 178
opponent process theory 154
opportunity sample 815
optic chiasma 154
optical array, ambient 270
optimal foraging theory (OFT) 354
optional sleep 215
Ora, J.P. 64, 824
oral stage 731–2
order effects 826, 827
ordinal data 846
ordinal level of measurement 846
organic mental disorders 776
organization 269, 297
  in perception 269
  in memory 297
  social 395
Orians, G. 411
orientation 372
Orne, M.T. 64, 823, 824
Ornstein, R. 172, 217
Osberger, M.J. 749
Osborn, A.F 694
Osgood, C.E 660
Osterberg, O. 905
Oswald, I. 214
outcome-research studies 806
out-group 577, 614
outlier 867
Owusu-Bempah, J. 72

Packer, C. 398
pain 162
pair bond 411
Paivio, A. 308
Palmarek, D.L. 628
Palmer, C. 95
Palmere, M. 302
pancreas 182
pandemonium model 267
paradigm 32, 66, 345, 765
parallel evolution 352
parallel processing 242
parametric tests 862, 874
paranoid personality 783
parasympathetic division of the
    ANS 179, 180
parental behaviour 433
parental care 409–10
parental investment, theory of 409
parental responsiveness 431, 440–1
parental styles 538, 539
parenting 431, 550–52
parent–offspring conflict 415–6
parents, independence from 415–6
Parke, R.D. 433, 519
Parkes, C.M. 412, 445
Parkin, A.J. 733
Parkinson's disease 776
Parloff, M. 804
parsimony 61
Parten, M.B. 452
partial reinforcement 129
partial report technique 292

participant observation 830
participants' perceptions 823
paternal care 413
pathways, visual 151
Paton, D. 782
Patten, B.M. 309
pattern recognition 265 ff
Patterson, F.G. 385, 387
Patton, G. 192
Paul, G.L. 773, 795, 797
Paulus, P.B 694
Pavlov, I. 8, 12, 21, 126–28, 254, 348
Pavlovian inhibition theory, of
    vigilance 254
Payne, R.S 378
PCT see personal construct theory
Pearson's product moment test of
    correlation 876
  table of critical values 922
Peck, D. 717
Peck, R. 554, 559
Peek, F.W. 411
Peele, S. 43, 44
peer tutoring 472–3
Peirce, C.S. 9
Pepperberg, I.M. 364, 389, 391–2, 393
perceived self 29, 737
perception 150, 261 ff
  context in 276
  cyclical theory of 271
  deprivation studies of 278, 281
  depth 262
  distortion studies of 278, 283
  emotion and 273
  motivation in 272–3
  neonate studies of 278–81
  pictorial 285
  theory of 269
perceptual constancy 262, 264
perceptual defence 273
perceptual hypotheses 270
perceptual organization, Gestalt laws
    of 269, 318
Perdue, C.W. 615
performance decrement 253
  drugs and 256
  personality and 254
performance, learning and 138
peripheral attention 204
peripheral filtering, of signals 375
peripheral nervous system (PNS) 164
  autonomic 165
  somatic 165
Perner, J. 529, 531
Perry, D.G. 638
persistent vegetative state (PVS) 205
person schemata 576
personal construct theory (PCT) 580,
    738–41
personal construct therapy 800
Personal Orientation Inventory 32
personality 705 ff
  consistency of 706–7 718–22
  disorders 782

five factors approach to ('Big
    Five') 717–18
  hardy 230
  implicit, theory 579
  issues and assumptions 705–8
  multitrait approaches 710–18
  multiple 781
  paranoid 783
  performance decrement and 254
  psychodynamic theories of 727 ff
  single-trait approaches to 722–5
  tests 93–5, 712, 716, 735, 739
  trait approaches to 706
  Type A 229, 627, 722
  type approaches to 706, 709–10
  Type B 229
perspective taking 503
persuasion 79–90
  communication model 80–3
  ethics and 89–90
  recent models 83
  propaganda and warfare 86–7
  techniques of 80–3, 85
Pert, C.B. 17, 176
pertinence model, of attention 249
Pervin, L.A. 720, 741
PET scan 146–7
Petersen, A.C. 758
Peterson, L.R 294, 816
Petitto, L.A. 749
Pettigrew, T.F 274, 618, 664, 669
Petty, R.E. 83
Pfaffenberger, C. 116
phallic stage 732
phenomenological viewpoint 28
phenotype 341
phenylketonuria (PKU) 747
pheromones 177, 378, 399
phi phenomenon 9
phobias 780–1
phonemes 478
phonemic awareness 750
photoreceptors 152
phylogenetic adaptation 350, 354
phylogenetic scale 356
phylogeny 344, 350
physical and sensory
    impairment 748–51
physical attractiveness 597
physiological approach 15–18, 36
physiological psychology 36, 145
physiological reductionism 42
physiological tests 773
Piaget, J. 13, 27, 69, 239, 318, 331, 333,
    391, 452, 460, 463, 468, 469, 476,
    503, 504, 528, 541
Piaget's theory 460–8, 502, 505, 506–7,
    530
  cross-cultural studies 467
  developmental stages 462–4, 465
  educational implications 468
  evaluation of 464–7
  moral development and 505, 506–7
  play and 452

pictorial perception 285
pie charts 850
Piéron, H. 906
Pike, K.L. 70
Piliavin, J.A. 640
Piliavin's cost/arousal model 641
Pillemer, D.B. 304
Pilleri, G. 214
pineal gland 182
Pinker, S. 266
pinna 157
pitch 156
pituitary gland 180
pituitary hormones 181
PKU see phenylketonuria
placebo 200, 792
planned behaviour, theory of 651–2
planning strategy 327–8
plasticity 173
Plato 3, 266
play 451–6
   characteristics of 451
   elaborated 454
   and exploration 454–5
   with rules 452
   social aspects 452
   studies of 453–5
   symbolic 452
   theorists 452
   therapy 19, 453, 802
   tutoring 455
   value of 455
pleasantness 597
pleasure principle 729
Plummer, S. 797
Plutchik, R. 196
PNS see peripheral nervous system
Poggendorf illusion 278
Polis, G.A. 416
politeness, theory of 683
Pollak, J.M. 733
polyandry 411
polygamy 410
polygyny threshold model 402, 411
polygyny 411
   harem 411
   serial 411
Pomazal, R.J 644
Pomerantz, J.R. 270
Ponzo illusion 275
Popper, K. 20, 62, 734, 823
population 813, 858, 892
pornography and aggression 634
positive regard 738, 803
positive reinforcement 128
post-aggression recess 404
post-break-up loneliness 610–11
postconventional morality 507
post-decisional dissonance 658–9
post-Freudians 18
Postman, L. 273
post-traumatic stress disorder 224, 781–2
Powell, G.V.N. 397

pragmatics 478
Prägnanz 10, 269, 318
Pratkanis, A.R. 80, 83, 87, 89, 650, 651
Pratt, M.W. 444, 559, 560
preattentive processing 251
precocial young 411
preconscious 204, 730
preconscious thought 317
preconventional morality 507
predation 398
predictive validity 840
preference technique 279
prejudice 662 ff
   authoritarian personality and 669–70
   causes of 666–71
   exploitation theory 667
   reduction of 671–4
   scapegoat theory of 669
prelinguistic knowledge 483
Premack, A.J. 385
Premack, D. 367
preoperational stage 462–4
Presland, P. 549
Pressey, S.L. 135
Prien, R. 793
primary acoustic store 300
primary cues, to depth 264
priming 300, 631
prisoner's dilemma 621
privation 447
proactive interference 297
probability 858
problem isomorphs 328
problem solving 323 ff
   coherence in 324
   correspondence in 324
problem space 327
problem-focused coping 231, 232
procedure, description of in reports 896
processes, cognitive 239, 459
processing strategies (and illusions) 277, 278
processing
   automatic 251
   bottom-up 242, 268
   conscious or unconscious 251
   deep 301
   levels of 300–3
   serial 242
   shallow 300–1
   top-down 242, 268
production blocking 694
productivity 387
professional activities of psychologists 37
progesterone 194
programme
   branching 136
   linear 136
programmed learning 135–37
   branching programmes 136
   linear programmes 136

Project Headstart 96, 498
projective tests 91, 93, 735
prolactin 181
Promethean Fire (Lumsden, C.J. and Wilson, E.O.) 346
promiscuity 409
propaganda 79–80, 86–7
prosocial behaviour 511, 636 ff
   bystander calculus model of 640
prosocial reasoning, Eisenberg's model of 511
prosopagnosis 197
prospective memory 305, 306
prototypes 574, 576
proximal development, zone of 453, 469, 472, 473, 504proximity 269
Przybyla, D.J.P 644
psychiatrist 108, 708, 762, 772
psychiatry 108
psychoactive drugs 108, 177, 791
psychoanalysis 10, 48–9, 65, 801–3
   classical 801
   defence mechanisms 232, 730, 733
   dreams 12, 729, 801
   free association 728, 801
   as therapy 13, 801–2
   studies 733
   transference 802
   evaluation 732, 734
psychodynamic approach 18–21, 426, 452–3
   and gender 518
   to moral development 505–6
psychodynamic theories of personality 727 ff
psychohydraulic model of motivation 404
psychoimmunology 17
psychological tests 773
psychologists
   clinical 763
   professional activities of 37
   qualifications 37
psychology 3–5
   clinical 37
   cognitive 25, 36, 240
   comparative 36, 339–40
   counselling 37
   definitions 3
   developmental 36, 421 ff
   educational 37
   fields of study in 36
   forensic 37
   Gestalt 9, 329
   health, sports, community 37
   models in 25
   occupational (industrial) 37
   philosophical origins of 4
   physiological 36, 145
   pre-scientific 3–5
   scientific 5, 59–67
   schools of 5
   social 36, 569 ff
   stimulus–response 21

psychometric testing 37, 91–8
  controversies 94–8
  intelligence 92–3
  ipsative 91
  personality 93–4
  projective techniques 91, 93
psychopathic disorder 782
psychopathic (sociopathic)
      personality 782
psychopathology 708, 763
psychopathy, affectionless 446
psychophysics 257
psychosexual stages 11, 731–2
psychosis 770
psychosocial stages 20, 544, 545
psychosurgery 108, 793
psychotherapy 106, 790 ff
psychoticism 711
psywar 86–7, 90
puberty 535–6
Pulliam, H.R. 403
pumps 3373, 379
punishment 129
  vicarious 138
pupil (eye) 151
pure research 35
PVS see persistent vegetative state

Q-sort technique 32, 739, 803, 804
qualitative analysis 833, 896
qualitative approach 66
qualitative data 896
quantitative analysis 833
quantitative approach 66
quasi-experimental research 822
questionnaires 832
Quinlan, D.M. 724
quota sample 814
quotient 842

race and IQ 499
racism 72, 664–5
  new 72
  old 72
  symbolic 664
radar test 253
Radford, J. 827
Radin, N. 436
Rahe, R.H. 223
Ramey, C.T. 498
Ramirez, A. 634
random error 815
random numbers, table of 911–10
random samples 813–4
randomization 828
range 855
ranked scores 849
Ransford, H.E. 635
Ransom, R.L. 561
Raphael, B. 611
rapid eye movement (REM) 211, 212
Ratcliffe, R. 296
ratio level of measurement 846–7
rational emotive therapy 800

rational thinking 317
Raven, B.H 683
raw scores 848
reactance 89
reaction, norm of 55, 500
realistic conflict theory 620
reality principle 729
real-life memory 303 ff
Reason, S.J. 305
reasoned action, theory of 651
reasoning
  hedonistic 511
  needs-oriented 511
receiver operating characteristics 259
receptors
  glucose 189
  kinaesthetic 154
recessive genes 342
reciprocal altruism 414, 636
reciprocity principle 597, 638
recogition
  by components 268
  of faces 306, 311
  of objects 262
record keeping in relationships 600
Recovery Movement 30–1
reductionism 16, 41–5
  biological 43
  experimental 43
  machine 43
  physiological 16, 42
references, in reports 897
reflex arc 173
refutability 62
Reibstein, J. 548, 551
Reichard, S. 560
Reicher, S.D. 618, 697, 698
reification 95
reinforcement 128–30, 135, 136, 518,
      571
  continuous 129
reinforcement/affect theory 598–9
reinforcer 128, 136
related measures design 826
relationship break-up 607 ff
relationship dissolution model 609,
      611
relationships 594 ff
relative deprivation 619
  J-curve of 619
relative refractory period 167
relative stability 553
releaser 374
reliability 94, 772, 774, 839
REM (rapid eye movement) sleep 211,
      212
Rempel, J.K. 607
repeated measures design see related
      measures design
repertory grid technique 93, 580, 740
repisodic memory 305
replicability 61–2
replication 823, 894
report

introduction of 895
  references in 897
  title of 894
report writing 893 ff
representation
  iconic 333, 470
  modes of 470
  social 618–9
  symbolic 333, 470
representative sample 813
repression 232, 730
research
  applied 36
  archival 835–6
  designs 424
  methods and statistics 811 ff
  new paradigm 66
  pure 35
  quasi-experimental 821
  socially sensitive 108
resource-based model of attention 252
response
  eliciting of 373
  mechanisms 145
  selectivity in 375
responsibility 767
  diffusion of 644
responsiveness, parental 431, 440–1
Rest, J.R. 509, 542
restricted code of language 332
results
  analysis of 897
  discussion of 897
  interpretation of 890 ff
  presentation of 845, 896
reticular activating system 171, 713
reticular formation 171, 373
retina 151
retinal disparity 262
retirement 560–62
retroactive interference 296
retrograde amnesia 368
retrospective memory 305
reversibility 461, 464
revising, for exams 313
RFT see rod and frame test
Rheingold, H.L. 442
Rheta Schreiber, F. 781
Rhodes, N. 83
rhythms
  body 208
  circadian 209, 252, 256, 905
  infradian 209
  sleep 210
Richards, H.C. 510
Rieder, R. 787
Riesen, A.H. 113, 281
risk-taking behaviour 355
risky shift 695
ritualization 351
ritualized aggression 698
Robbers' Cave experiment 617
Robbin, A. 793
Roberts, D.F. 646